Dreamweaver® 8 Bible

Dreamweaver® 8 Bible

Joseph W. Lowery

WILEY

Wiley Publishing, Inc.

Dreamweaver® 8 Bible

Published by
Wiley Publishing, Inc.
10475 Crosspoint Boulevard
Indianapolis, IN 46256
www.wiley.com

Copyright © 2006 by Wiley Publishing, Inc., Indianapolis, Indiana

Published simultaneously in Canada

ISBN-13: 978-0-471-76312-3
ISBN-10: 0-471-76312-8

Manufactured in the United States of America

10 9 8 7 6 5 4 3 2

1B/SW/QR/QW/IN

For general information on our other products and services or to obtain technical support, please contact our Customer Care Department within the U.S. at (800) 762-2974, outside the U.S. at (317) 572-3993 or fax (317) 572-4002.

Library of Congress Cataloging-in-Publication Data

Lowery, Joseph (Joseph W.)
 Dreamweaver 8 bible / Joseph W. Lowery.
    p. cm.
 Includes index.
 ISBN-13: 978-0-471-76312-3 (paper/cd-rom)
 ISBN-10: 0-471-76312-8 (paper/cd-rom)
 1. Dreamweaver (Computer file) 2. Web sites–Authoring programs. 3. Web site development. 4. Web sites–Design. I. Title.
 TK5105.8885.D74L68538 2006
 006.7'86–dc22

                             2005034343

Wiley also publishes its books in a variety of electronic formats. Some content that appears in print may not be available in electronic books.

About the Author

Joseph Lowery has been writing about computers and new technology since 1981. He is the author of the previous editions of *Dreamweaver Bible* and *Fireworks Bible* as well as the recent publishing of *CSS Hacks and Filters* (all published by Wiley). He is also the author of *Joseph Lowery's Beyond Dreamweaver, Dreamweaver MX 2004 Killer Tips* (with Angela Buraglia), and *Dreamweaver MX 2004 Web Application Recipes* and *Dreamweaver 8 Recipes* (with Eric Ott), all published by New Riders. He has also written books on HTML and using the Internet for business. His books are international bestsellers, having sold more than 400,000 copies worldwide in eleven different languages. Joe is also a consultant and trainer and has presented at Seybold in both Boston and San Francisco, Macromedia conferences in the U.S. and Europe, and at ThunderLizard's Web Design World. He is currently the Director of Marketing for WebAssist, the leading provider of Macromedia extensions.

About the Captivate Designer

One of the innovations in *Dreamweaver 8 Bible* is the inclusion of Captivate simulations on the CD-ROM, one for each of the Dreamweaver Techniques in the book. All of these interactive movies were created by Mark Fletcher.

Mark Fletcher has been in the I.T. industry for 16 years. He began his career as a database administrator and for the last 5 years has been a web developer / trainer for the Virtual Training Company. Mark is involved in developing training courses on Dreamweaver amongst other Macromedia Internet Products. He is a regular contributor to Macromedia's Developer Centre. Mark is also a training partner for the Macromedia extension developer WebAssist.com. Mark was also the technical editor for *CSS Hacks and Filters* by Joseph Lowery (Wiley Publishing). Mark lives on the Northwest coast of the United Kingdom with his wife Vanessa and their two children, Joel and Lucy. Mark can be reached on his personal Web site, http://www.mark-fletcher.co.uk.

Credits

For two men who brought new dimensions of fatherhood into my life,
Gavin Langmuir and Paul Wanner — Cheers!

Contents at a Glance

Contents

Part II: Designing and Crafting Core Pages   153

Chapter 6: Accessing the Code Directly 155

Part III: Adding Advanced Design Features 357

Part V: Including Multimedia Elements 721

Chapter 23: Fireworks Integration. 723

Chapter 24: Inserting Flash and Shockwave Elements 747

Part VI: Enhancing Productivity and Web Site Management   827

Acknowledgments

Dreamweaver continues to grow with each release, and only a team of Web-savvy personnel can describe its capabilities with grace and precision. I'm extremely happy and proud to have had just such a team involved in bringing *Dreamweaver 8 Bible* to life.

Looking for a technical editor *par excellence*? Well, keep looking, 'cause I'm hanging onto mine. Derren Whiteman has made sure the material is on the technical straight-and-narrow with his wide-ranging expertise and adept juggling of multiple operating systems and configurations. Thanks for all your work, Derren; you've really had a significant impact on the book.

Macromedia has been wonderfully supportive of my efforts to bring out the most detailed *Bible* possible. I can only imagine the collective groan that goes up when yet another e-mailed question from me — with a deadline, no less — arrives. Warm thanks and heartfelt appreciation to Jay London, Randy Edmunds, Alain Dumesney, John Albano, and all the other Dreamweaver engineers and techs who allowed me to pick their brains. I'd also like to single out the Dreamweaver Technical Support staff, whose answers to users' queries have been tremendous sources of information. And who's that in the back of the room? Macromedia management — in the form of David Mendels, Beth Davis, Susan Morrow, Jennifer Taylor, and others — has opened many, many doors to me. They should all stand up and take a bow. Finally, I, and the rest of the Dreamweaver community, am beholden to Kevin Lynch and Paul Madar for their vision and hard work in bringing this dream home.

To me, there's no higher compliment than to be told that I know my business. Well, the folks I work with at Wiley sure know their business: Executive Editor Chris Webb and all the additional support staff. I'd like to call out all the hard work and wonderful patience of Maryann Steinhart, who replaced my long-time Bible editor Jodi Jensen. Although I didn't think it possible, Maryann has done a great job filling Jodi's editorial shoes — high praise in my eyes.

One last note of appreciation: To all the people who took a chance with some of their hard-earned money and bought the previous editions of this book. That small sound you hear in the background is me applauding you in thanks for your support. I hope my efforts continue to be worthy.

Introduction

Dreamweaver 8 stands at the center of a complex series of overlapping worlds. In one realm, designers of static Web page are looking to expand their knowledge base into data-driven sites. Over there, you'll find application developers — some savvy in Active Server Pages and ASP.NET, some in ColdFusion, and others in PHP — anxious to develop for the Internet. The spectrum of experience in both camps runs the gamut from eager novice to experienced professional, all of whom benefit from the advanced style capabilities of Cascading Style Sheets (CSS). There's yet another group of prospective Web craftsmen and artists who want to do it all and are looking for a place to start. Dreamweaver 8 is the one program robust enough for them all, and the *Dreamweaver 8 Bible* is your guidebook to all its features and capabilities.

What's in a name? In the case of Macromedia's Dreamweaver, you find one of the most appropriate product names around. Web page design is a blend of art and craft; whether you're a deadline-driven professional or a vision-filled amateur, Dreamweaver provides an intuitive way to make your Web visions a reality. Dreamweaver implies development, and it excels at producing multifaceted Web pages that bring content locked in a data store to the surface.

To use this book, you need only two items: the Dreamweaver software and a desire to make cutting-edge Web pages. (Actually, you don't even need Dreamweaver to begin; the CD-ROM that accompanies this book contains a trial version.) From quick design prototyping to ongoing Web site management, Dreamweaver automates and simplifies much of a Webmaster's workload. Dreamweaver is not only the first Web authoring tool to bring the ease of visual editing to an HTML-code–oriented world, it also brings a point-and-click interface to complex coding whether server-side or client-side. The *Dreamweaver 8 Bible* is designed to help you master every nuance of the program. Are you styling your pages with CSS? Are you building multipage Web applications? Are you creating a straightforward layout with the visual editor? Do you need to extend Dreamweaver's capabilities by building your own custom objects? With Dreamweaver and this book, you can weave your dreams into reality for the entire world to experience.

Who Should Read This Book?

Dreamweaver attracts a wide range of Web developers. Because it's the first Web authoring tool that doesn't rewrite original code, veteran designers are drawn to using Dreamweaver as their first visual editor. Because it also automates complicated effects, beginning Web designers are interested in Dreamweaver's power and performance. *Dreamweaver 8 Bible* addresses the full spectrum of Web professionals, providing basic information on HTML if you're just starting, as well as advanced tips and tricks for seasoned pros. Moreover, this book is a complete reference for everyone working with Dreamweaver on a daily basis.

What Hardware and Software Do You Need?

Dreamweaver 8 Bible includes coverage of Dreamweaver 8. If you don't own a copy of the program, you can use the trial version on this book's CD-ROM. Written to be platform-independent, this book covers both Macintosh and Windows versions of Dreamweaver 8.

Macintosh

Macromedia recommends the following minimum requirements for running Dreamweaver on a Macintosh:

- ✦ Power Mac G3 or higher, 500 MHz
- ✦ Mac OS 10.2.6
- ✦ 128MB of available RAM
- ✦ 275MB of available disk space
- ✦ 256-color monitor capable of 800 x 600 resolution (OS X requires thousands of colors)
- ✦ CD-ROM drive

Windows

Macromedia recommends the following minimum requirements for running Dreamweaver on a Windows system:

- ✦ Intel Pentium III processor, 600MHz or equivalent
- ✦ Windows 2000, XP, or Windows Server 2003
- ✦ 128MB of available RAM
- ✦ 275MB of available disk space
- ✦ 256-color monitor capable of 800 x 600 resolution
- ✦ CD-ROM drive

Note   These are the minimum requirements. As with all graphics-based design tools, more capability is definitely better for using Dreamweaver, especially in terms of memory and processor speed.

How This Book Is Organized

Dreamweaver 8 Bible can take you from raw beginner to full-fledged professional if read cover to cover. However, you're more likely to read each section as needed, taking the necessary information and coming back later. To facilitate this approach, *Dreamweaver 8 Bible* is divided into seven major task-oriented parts. After you're familiar with Dreamweaver, feel free to skip around the book, using it as a reference guide as you increase your own knowledge base.

The early chapters present the basics, and all chapters contain clearly written steps for the tasks you need to perform. In most chapters, you encounter sections labeled Dreamweaver Techniques, completely re-written for this version of the Dreamweaver Bible. *Dreamweaver Techniques* are step-by-step instructions for accomplishing specific Web designer tasks; taken together, the Dreamweaver Techniques constitute an entire how-to course. These step-by-step instructions are self-contained in each chapter, so you're free to explore them in any order you choose. You'll find all the practice files for working on the Techniques on the CD-ROM, both as starting points and as completed files. Naturally, you can also use the Dreamweaver Techniques as stepping stones for your own explorations into Web page creation.

You'll find yet another new addition to the Dreamweaver Bible on the CD-ROM: interactive simulations for each Dreamweaver Technique. Created by master trainer Mark Fletcher with Macromedia Captivate, these simulations give you the opportunity to practice all the steps in each Technique. As my dad used to say, "Get it in your hand and you'll get it in your head."

The accompanying CD-ROM also offers a vast number of additional Dreamweaver server behaviors, objects, commands, and other extensions, in addition to relevant code from the book.

Part I — Laying the Groundwork in Dreamweaver 8

Part I begins with a look at what's new in Dreamweaver 8 — and there's an awful lot to cover. Next up, you'll find an overview of Dreamweaver's philosophy and design. To get the most out of the program, you need to understand the key advantages it offers over other authoring programs and their deficiencies, which Dreamweaver addresses. Part I takes you all the way to setting up your first site.

Part II — Designing and Crafting Core Pages

Although Dreamweaver is partly a visual design tool, its roots derive from the language of the Web: HTML. Part II gives you a solid foundation in the basics of HTML, even if you've never seen code. It also shows you how to get the most out of Dreamweaver's code environment with any language. Chapter 6 describes what you need to know about the overall structure of a Web page, including the all-important `<meta>` tags.

Reflecting the current emphasis in Web design on Cascading Style Sheets, Chapter 7 lays the foundation to CSS. In this chapter, you learn the basics of CSS, as well as how to define and apply styles in Dreamweaver. Following the introduction to CSS, you learn the three fundamentals of static Web pages: text, images, and links. In Chapters 8, 9, and 10, you explore how to completely incorporate these elements.

Part III — Adding Advanced Design Features

After you master the basics, you're ready to learn about some of Dreamweaver's true power tools in Part III. First up is one of the most important constructs of HTML: `<div>` tags, also known in Dreamweaver as layers. Chapter 11 examines this brave new world of pixel-perfect positioning, layers that fly in and then disappear as if by magic, and Web sites that can change their look and feel at the click of a mouse. Chapter 12 offers an in-depth look at the capabilities of Dreamweaver behaviors. These bring a great deal of interactivity to layers specifically and to your Web page in general. Each standard behavior is covered in detail with step-by-step instructions.

Chapter 13 explores the various uses of tables — from a clear presentation of data to organizing entire Web pages. Here you learn how to use Dreamweaver's visual table editing capabilities to resize and reshape your HTML tables quickly. Forms are an essential element in dynamic Web page design, and you learn all about them in Chapter 14. Chapter 15 presents another fundamental HTML option: lists. You study the list in all its forms: numbered lists, bulleted lists, definition lists, nested lists, and more.

Chapter 16 investigates the somewhat complex world of frames. You see how Dreamweaver has greatly simplified the task of building and managing these multifile creations, particularly with the Frame objects. You also learn how to handle more advanced design tasks such as updating multiple frames with just one click. If you want to delve into the 4th dimension in Web design, you' get an opportunity in Chapter 17 with the exploration of timelines.

Part IV — Incorporating Dynamic Data

Chapter 18 begins an in-depth investigation of Dreamweaver's power to create dynamic Web pages by describing how to set up your basic connections and recordsets. Chapter 19 explains how to insert text from a data source onto your Web page and how to format it after it's incorporated. You also see how to relate other Web page elements — such as images, Flash movies, and other media files — to a data source. Chapter 20 continues the exploration by delving into Dreamweaver's powerful Repeat Region server behavior as well as discussing techniques for hiding and showing your data at will.

One of Dreamweaver's most useful features, the Live Data Preview, is examined extensively in Chapter 21. Chapter 22 enters the world of multipage applications and explains how variables and other data can be passed from one page to another.

Part V — Including Multimedia Elements

In recent years, the Web has moved from a relatively static display of text and simple images to a full-blown multimedia circus with streaming video, background music, and interactive animations. Part V contains the power tools for incorporating various media files into your Web site.

Graphics remain the key medium on the Web today, and Macromedia's Fireworks is a top-notch graphics generator. Chapter 23 delves into methods for incorporating Fireworks graphics — with all the requisite rollover and other code intact. Special focus is given to the Dreamweaver-to-Fireworks communication link and how your Web production efforts can benefit from it.

In addition to Dreamweaver, Macromedia is perhaps best known for one other contribution to Web multimedia: Flash. Chapter 24 explores the possibilities offered by incorporating Flash and Shockwave movies into Dreamweaver-designed Web pages and includes everything you need to know about configuring MIME types. You also find step-by-step instructions for building Shockwave inline controls and playing Shockwave movies in frame-based Web pages, as well as how to add Flash Buttons, Flash Text, and the new Flash elements.

Chapter 25 covers digital video in its many forms — downloadable AVI files, streaming RealVideo displays, panoramic QuickTime movies, and the newest, hottest media: Flash video. Chapter 26 focuses on digital audio, with coverage of standard WAV and MIDI sound files as well as the newer streaming audio formats like MP3.

Part VI — Enhancing Productivity and Web Site Management

Although Web page design gets all the glory, Web site management pays the bills. In Part VI, you see how Dreamweaver makes this essential part of any Webmaster's day easier to handle. Chapter 27 starts off with a look at the use of Dreamweaver Templates and how they can speed up production while ensuring a unified look and feel across your Web site. Chapter 28 covers the Library, which can significantly reduce any Webmaster's workload by providing reusable — and updatable — page elements. Chapter 29 describes Dreamweaver's built-in tools for maintaining cross- and backward-browser compatibility.

Until now, individual Web developers have been stymied when attempting to integrate Dreamweaver into a team development environment. File locking was all too easily subverted, allowing team members to inadvertently overwrite revisions. Site reports were limited in scope and output only to HTML, and, worst of all, version control was nonexistent. Dreamweaver 8 tackles all these concerns while laying a foundation for future connectivity.

In Chapter 30, you see how you can tie Dreamweaver into an existing Visual SourceSafe or WebDAV version control system. Other new features covered include custom file view columns and enhanced Design Notes accessibility.

I can't think of any new technology on the Web that has gained widespread acceptance as quickly as XML has. In a nutshell, XML (short for Extensible Markup Language) enables you to create your own custom tags that make the most sense for your business or profession. Although XML doesn't enjoy full browser support as of this writing, it's only a matter of time — and little time at that. Chapter 31 shows you how to apply this fast-approaching technology of tomorrow in Dreamweaver today, with a special section on Dreamweaver 8's new XML/XSLT technology.

Part VII — Extending Dreamweaver

Dreamweaver is a program with immense capabilities for expanding its own power. Chapter 32 explores the brave new world of Dreamweaver extensibility, with complete coverage of using and building commands as well as custom tags, translators, floaters, and C-level Extensions. With its own set of objects and behaviors, Dreamweaver complements HTML's extensibility. Finally, Chapter 33 examines server behaviors, describing every standard one in detail and then exploring the use of the Server Behavior Builder, Dreamweaver's tool for creating custom server behaviors.

Appendix

The appendix describes the contents of the CD-ROM that accompanies this book. Throughout this book, whenever you encounter a reference to files or programs on the CD-ROM, please check this appendix for more information.

Conventions Used in This Book

I use the following conventions throughout this book.

Windows and Macintosh Conventions

Because *Dreamweaver 8 Bible* is a cross-platform book, it gives instructions for both Windows and Macintosh users when keystrokes for a particular task differ. Throughout this book, the Windows keystrokes are given first; the Macintosh are given second in parentheses, as follows:

To undo an action, press Ctrl+Z (Command+Z).

The first action instructs Windows users to press the Ctrl and Z keys in combination, and the second action (in parentheses) instructs Macintosh users to press the Command and Z keys together.

Key Combinations

When you are instructed to press two or more keys simultaneously, each key in the combination is separated by a plus sign. For example:

Ctrl+Alt+T (Command+Option+T)

The preceding tells you to press the three listed keys for your system at the same time. You can also hold down one or more keys and then press the final key. Release all the keys at the same time.

Mouse Instructions

When instructed to *click* an item, move the mouse pointer to the specified item and click the mouse button once. Windows users use the left mouse button unless otherwise instructed. *Double-click* means clicking the mouse button twice in rapid succession.

When instructed to *select* or *choose* an item, you may click it once as previously described. If you are selecting text or multiple objects, click the mouse button once, press Shift, and then move the mouse to a new location and click again. The color of the selected item or items inverts to indicate the selection. To clear the selection, click once anywhere on the Web page.

Menu Commands

When instructed to select a command from a menu, you see the menu and the command separated by an arrow symbol. For example, when instructed to execute the Open command from the File menu, you see the notation File ⇨ Open. Some menus use submenus, in which case you see an arrow for each submenu, as follows: Insert ⇨ Form Object ⇨ Text Field.

Typographical Conventions

I use *italic* type for new terms and for emphasis and **boldface** type for text that you need to type directly from the computer keyboard.

Code

A special typeface indicates HTML or other code, as demonstrated in the following example:

```
<html>
<head>
<title>Untitled Document</title>
</head>
<body bgcolor="#FFFFFF">
</body>
</html>
```

This code font is also used within paragraphs to designate HTML tags, attributes, and values such as `<body>`, `bgcolor`, and `#FFFFFF`. All HTML tags are presented in lowercase, as written by Dreamweaver, although browsers are not generally case-sensitive in terms of HTML.

The code continuation character (⤵) at the end of a code line indicates that the line is too long to fit within the margins of the printed book. You should continue typing the next line of code before pressing the Enter (Return) key.

Navigating This Book

Various signposts and icons are located throughout *Dreamweaver 8 Bible* for your assistance. Each chapter begins with an overview of its information and ends with a quick summary.

Icons appear in the text to indicate important or especially helpful items. Here's a list of the icons and their functions:

Tip   Tips provide you with extra knowledge that separates the novice from the pro.

Note   Notes provide additional or critical information and technical data on the current topic.

New In Dreamweaver   Sections marked with a New in Dreamweaver icon detail an innovation introduced in Dreamweaver 8.

Cross-Reference   Cross-Reference icons indicate places where you can find more information on a particular topic.

Caution   The Caution icon is your warning of a potential problem or pitfall.

On the CD-ROM   The On the CD-ROM icon indicates that the accompanying CD-ROM contains a related file in the given folder. See the appendix for more information about where to locate specific items.

This Book's Web Site

You'll find three bonus elements on this book's Web site, www.wiley.com/go/dreamweaver8bible.

Bonus Chapter 1, "Creating and Using Objects," shows you the tremendous potential of Dreamweaver objects. You'll explore standard Dreamweaver objects, and then learn to create your own objects and take advantage of the extensibility features in Dreamweaver.

Bonus Chapter 2, "Creating a Behavior," examines the basic features pertaining directly to behaviors, and provides a good look at the process of creating a behavior. You also survey the Document Object Model and check out the Dreamweaver API.

The bonus appendix, "Toolbars and Menus," is a good reference document, explaining all of the Insert bar's categories' options and all of the menus' choices (including keyboard short-cuts, when applicable). It's a resource new Dreamweaver users will want to keep handy.

Further Information

You can find more help for specific problems and questions by investigating several Web sites. Macromedia's own Dreamweaver Web site is the best place to start:

www.macromedia.com/software/Dreamweaver/

I heartily recommend that you visit and participate in the official Dreamweaver newsgroup:

news://forums.macromedia.com/macromedia.Dreamweaver

You can also e-mail me at

jlowery@idest.com

I can't promise instantaneous turnaround, but I answer all my mail to the best of my abilities.

Laying the Groundwork in Dreamweaver 8

What's New in Dreamweaver 8

Longevity in software, like in many other things, is a double-edged sword: on one hand, survival is to be congratulated and honored, on the other there's always the question of "What else can you do?" In many ways, Dreamweaver 8 is a return to the core philosophy of fulfilling customer demand while exceeding expectations. Many of the new features are to be greeted with a cry of "Finally!" Others emerge as a delightful technogeek surprise.

I like to think of version 8 as the give-them-what-they-want release. Let's start with the name, shall we? Although Dreamweaver MX and MX 2004 were certainly classy, they weren't immediately informative. Macromedia realized that the simplicity of version numbering was far more valuable than high-end branding and thus Dreamweaver 8, and Studio 8, were born. This back-to-basics attitude carried through with an ongoing commitment to squash as many legacy bugs as possible while putting out the most stable release in recent years. Although bug fixes and performance enhancements are essential, they don't tip the scale for existing or new customers. New features do. New features are the driving force of any upgrade, and this release has them in spades. Dreamweaver 8's enhancements fit the needs of most every Web professional, no matter if their primary focus is as a coder, designer, developer, or just someone who needs to balance on the cutting edge.

Coding Enhancements

Normally new features added to Dreamweaver's coding engine tend to be hidden under the hood. Though coders will notice a great number of changes as they work — like the improved code hinting — one feature jumps off the screen the first time you switch to Code view. The new Coding toolbar, shown in Figure 1-1, brings access to a slew of brand-new technologies to the forefront while promoting a number of existing features up-front and center. One highlight of the Coding toolbar is how it makes the new code collapse implementation even more useful. Not only can any tag or selection be reduced to a single, still available line, but with a single modifier key, coders can inverse their selection to hide everything except the code they want to concentrate on. The Coding toolbar also makes applying comments — to HTML, CSS, JavaScript, XML, and any supported application server — a one-click operation; removing comments is just as easy.

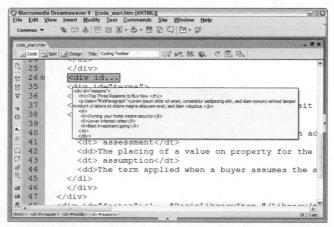

Figure 1-1: Collapse a single tag or any selection with the options found on the new Coding toolbar.

Hand coders will relish the intuitiveness and sophistication of the revamped code completion feature. Previously, Dreamweaver would present the closing tag immediately after you entered the final character of the opening tag, resulting in an instant tag pair, like <p></p>. Like many coders, I found that I ended up cutting and pasting the closing tag way too often. To overcome this workflow impediment, Dreamweaver now waits to insert the closing tag until you signal that you're ready by entering the first two characters of every HTML closing tag, </. The code completion algorithm is smart enough to understand which closing tag is needed and supplies it. This new style of code completion even works with deeply nested code. Best of all, if you prefer the previous code completion techniques — or none at all — it's waiting for your selection in Preferences.

Cross-Reference You see how all the new coding features integrate into Dreamweaver in Chapter 6.

Design Upgrades

Since the first version, design in Dreamweaver has always been a unique experience, unlike that of any other layout tool. Because Dreamweaver was for Web and not printed page authoring, standard options in the designer's toolbox were forgivingly absent.

No more. Dreamweaver 8 introduces a number of design-oriented tools that will be instantly recognized and indispensable. One of these features, guides, allows designers to more easily apply a key tenet of good design: alignment. Both horizontal and vertical guides can be dragged out of the rulers and placed anywhere on the page—just as in other industry-leading graphic programs like Adobe Photoshop or Macromedia Fireworks. You can set your guides to snap to objects like divs or layers and/or your objects to snap to guides. Toggle them in and out of view with a quick keyboard shortcut or a centrally placed toolbar control.

But what use are guides without some means of ensuring that your alignment is pixel-perfect? The complementary new feature, zoom, gives you complete visual feedback throughout the page (see Figure 1-2). Magnify your page to a preset level or use the Zoom tool to select an area of interest. Apply the Fit All setting to see how your page works as a whole—and continue editing it at the same time.

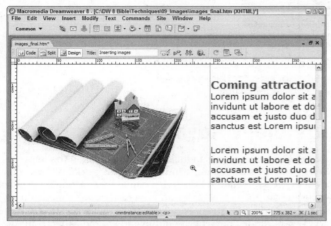

Figure 1-2: Zoom in or out via preset magnification levels or use the Zoom tool.

Dreamweaver's overall view, whether magnified or not, has undergone significant improvement as well, especially regarding CSS rendering. Dreamweaver maintains a striking balance between rendering for the most popular browser and standards-based output. Styled form elements—even the under-used, but enormously powerful ones like the `<fieldset>` tag—are displayed properly. Designers playing further out on the edge with CSS pseudo-elements like `:first-letter` and `:first-line` will be thrilled to see their experimentation rendered clear as a bell.

Best of all, CSS-based layouts—long unusable in Dreamweaver—look great in 8. More and more Web professionals are turning to CSS layouts as their de facto technique. Anyone working in this area will welcome the CSS layout tools now available in Dreamweaver 8. Inserting `<div>` tags—the cornerstone of CSS layouts—is easier than ever with one-click access from the Common category of the Insert bar. Once your `<div>` tags are in place, Dreamweaver provides a range of visualization tools to bring your vision into reality. See how all the `<div>` tags interrelate with a click of the CSS Layout Backgrounds option. Keep your `<div>` tags outlined at design-time for quick selection and manipulation. Turn on the CSS Layout Box Model feature to visually grasp the essential margin, border, padding, and width values of any selected `<div>`, as shown in Figure 1-3. Like many Dreamweaver tools, the CSS visualization commands are a great learning tool as well as a superb design aid.

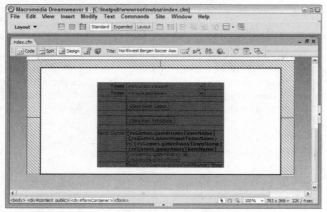

Figure 1-3: The CSS Layout Box Model feature clearly depicts essential aspects of a `<div>` tag used for layout.

Workflow and Technology Advancements

Macromedia recognizes that the CSS revolution is in full force and has taken the improvements in Dreamweaver 8 well beyond the Document window. The CSS workflow has been totally rethought, as is evident in the rejuvenated CSS Styles panel. By splitting style sheet functions into two parts — one an overview of all styles and the other a tight focus on styles impacting on the current selection — the CSS Styles panel becomes much greater than the sum of its parts. The All and Current modes have both unique and shared aspects. In All mode, you can see the full complement of style sheets and styles assigned to a page, whether they're embedded or external. Current mode drills-down to the selected tag and displays all the associated properties; a toggle allows you to see where a selected property originates from or the full cascade of applicable rules. Hover over any rule to see where it's stored and its specificity, an indicator of how the rule is applied.

Both modes share a common Properties pane, which now gives you three different ways to list a rule's properties: by category, alphabetically, and set properties. The final option is an innovation in Dreamweaver 8 that shows just the properties and values that have been previously defined. Even better, the set properties view provides an option for adding more properties directly into the panel (see Figure 1-4).

Mac users finally got to see why so many PC Dreamweaver users were in love with the tabbed interface. Starting with Dreamweaver 8, multiple open documents appear as tabs across the top. As with the PC versions, you can switch between documents with a single click and tell at a glance which files are currently available. This features really ramps up productivity on the Mac.

Speaking of productivity — what was designated as designers' number 1 time-waster? Uploading files via FTP. Previously in Dreamweaver, uploading a site was either considered a moment to kick back and enjoy some enforced down-time or a frustrating, when-will-this-be-over experience. In Dreamweaver 8, FTP (and Secure FTP) transfers have been isolated as an independent process and can run in the background. Designers are free to set their site publishing in motion and return to work whenever they like. A progress bar keeps you up-to-date on what's happening and a log is ready for viewing at any time.

Figure 1-4: No need to reopen a dialog box or external style sheet with the revised CSS Styles panel: just click the Add Property link.

So what will you do with all that free time? Why not master an emerging technology like XML/XSLT? Dreamweaver 8 makes it easy with full support for integrating XML data via XSLT (Extensible Style Sheet Transformation). And when I say full, I mean everyone can use them: both client-side and server-side integrations are included. Application servers (ASP, ColdFusion, PHP, and ASP.NET) can either display a full XSLT page dynamically transformed or an XSLT fragment — like an RSS feed from a blog or other service — within a server-side page. All the necessary code is supplied so you can create repeat regions, conditional regions, and even multiple conditional regions (see Figure 1-5).

Figure 1-5: Integrate XML data converted with XSLT into any type of page, client-side or server-side.

Flash video is not so much emergent as roaring-out-of-the-gate technology—and now it's drag and drop easy in Dreamweaver 8. Choose from progressive download or streaming video formats and Dreamweaver adapts to request the necessary information, including a choice of player skins; you'll even get a chance to customize the message for folks who don't have the necessary player installed. Once you've published your Flash video (.flv) file to the server— standard for progressive download, Flash Media Server for streaming—your video is ready to roll. The integration between the new Flash video format possible in Flash 8 Professional (part of Studio 8) and Dreamweaver 8 is a thing of beauty. Just like Dreamweaver 8.

Figure 1-6: Inserting video on a Web page just got as easy as dropping in a Flash file.

Summary

Improvements in Dreamweaver 8 have been applied across the board with benefits for any type of user.

✦ Web professionals who spend more time in Code view will greatly appreciate the new Coding toolbar and all of its highly accessible features, including code collapse.

✦ Code completion has been revamped to perform more like most coders work.

✦ On the design front, guides and zoom levels make sophisticated, clean, professional-level layouts more possible.

✦ CSS rendering has been kicked up a notch with a greater rendering facility for many types of page constructs, including form elements and CSS pseudo-elements such as :first-letter for drop-cap effects.

✦ CSS layouts have become increasingly important and a series of tools for helping the designer are available in Dreamweaver 8, including CSS Layout Background and CSS Box Model Layout.

✦ All the CSS development and management tools have been consolidated into a single area, the CSS Styles panel. The panel displays both an overview and a close-up look at all the styles applied to the page. New properties for existing styles can be added easily and directly.

✦ Dreamweaver 8 now offers tools for displaying XML data in an XSLT format through client- or server-side pages.

✦ Flash video files can be easily inserted into any Web page in either progressive download or streaming format; Dreamweaver's dialog box adjusts to your choice and presents just the options you'll need.

In the next chapter, you get an overview of Dreamweaver from top to bottom.

✦　　✦　　✦

Introducing Dreamweaver 8

Dreamweaver 8, by Macromedia, is a professional Web site development program for creating static pages and dynamic Web applications. Among its many distinctions, it was the first Web authoring tool capable of addressing multiple server models. This feature makes it equally easy for developers of ASP, ColdFusion, or JavaServer Pages to use it. In its latest incarnation, Dreamweaver has refined the user interface and sharpened its focus. In addition to creating straight HTML pages with enhanced Cascading Style Sheet (CSS) rendering, it is also suitable for coding a wide range of Web formats including JavaScript, XML, and ActionScript — to name a few.

Dreamweaver is truly a tool designed by Web developers for Web developers. Designed from the ground up to work the way professional Web designers do, it speeds site construction and streamlines site maintenance. This chapter describes the philosophical underpinnings of the program and provides a sense of how Dreamweaver blends traditional HTML and other Web languages with cutting-edge server-side techniques and CSS design standards. You also learn some of the advanced features that it offers to help you manage a Web site.

The Dynamic World of Dreamweaver

Dreamweaver is a program very much rooted in the real world. Web applications are developed for a variety of different server models, and Dreamweaver writes code for the most widely used ones. Because the real world is also a changing world, its extensible architecture opens the door for custom or third-party server models as well.

Moreover, Dreamweaver recognizes the real-world problem of incompatible browser commands and addresses that by producing code that is compatible across browsers. It includes browser-specific HTML validation so you can see how your existing or new code works in a particular browser. It even checks your pages automatically upon opening and gives you a full report that you can act on.

Dreamweaver 8 extends the real-world concept to the workplace. Features such as the Assets panel streamline the production and maintenance process on large Web sites. The advanced Design view makes it possible to quickly structure whole pages during the production stage, while maintaining backward compatibility with browsers when the pages are published. Dreamweaver's CSS rendering is top-of-the-line and lets you design with Web standards like no other program. Dreamweaver's Commands capability enables Web designers to automate their most difficult Web creations, and its Server Behavior Builder enables them to easily insert frequently used custom code.

Connecting to the World's Data

Connectivity is more than a buzzword in Dreamweaver; it's an underlying concept. Dreamweaver makes it possible to connect to any data source supported by the most widely used application servers: ASP, ASP.NET, ColdFusion, PHP, JSP, and even XML. Moreover, the actual connection type is quite flexible; developers can opt for a connection that is easier to implement but less robust or one that requires slightly more server-side savvy and offers greater scalability. A special set of features is available for transforming XML data into a browser-ready format using Extensible Stylesheet Transformation (XSLT) technology. Dreamweaver offers a choice of languages for a number of applications servers and a collection of ready-to-use CSS standard designs, as shown in Figure 2-1.

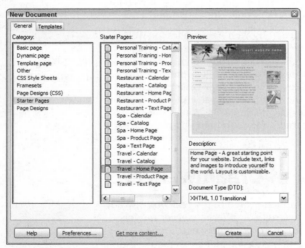

Figure 2-1: Get a jump-start on building your Web pages by choosing a page — and the corresponding tags — from Dreamweaver's extensive collection.

Dreamweaver accesses standard recordsets — subsets of a database — as well as more sophisticated data sources, such as session or application variables and stored procedures. Through their implementation of cookies and server-side code, Web applications designed in Dreamweaver can track visitors or deny them entrance.

You also find support in Dreamweaver for high-end technologies such as Web services, JavaBeans, and ColdFusion components. Dreamweaver enables you to introspect elements of all technologies, enabling coders to quickly grasp the syntax, methods, and functions required.

True Data Representation

One of Dreamweaver's truly innovative features integrates the actual data requested with the Web page — while still in the design phase. Live Data view sends the page-in-process to the application server to depict records from the data source within the page, as shown in Figure 2-2. All elements on the page remain editable; you can even alter the dynamic data's formatting and see those changes instantly applied. Live Data view shortens the work cycle by showing the designer exactly what the user will see. In addition, the page can be viewed under different conditions through the Live Data Settings feature.

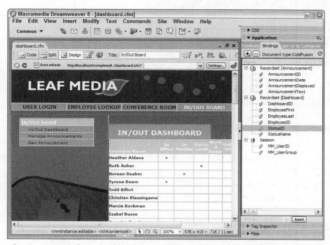

Figure 2-2: When in Live Data view, you can edit the Web page to accommodate the actual data used.

Integrated Visual and Text Editors

In the early days of the World Wide Web, most developers hand-coded their Web pages using simple text editors such as Notepad and SimpleText. The second generation of Web authoring tools brought visual design or WYSIWYG (what you see is what you get) editors to market. What these products furnished in ease of layout, they lacked in completeness of code. Professional Web developers were required to hand-code their Web pages, even with the most sophisticated WYSIWYG editor.

Dreamweaver acknowledges this reality and has integrated a superb visual editor with its browser-like Document view. You can work graphically in Design view, or programmatically in Code view. You even have the option of a split-screen view, which shows Design view and Code view simultaneously, as shown in Figure 2-3. Any change made in the Design view is reflected in the Code view and vice versa. If you prefer to work with a code editor you're more familiar with, Dreamweaver enables you to work with any text editor. Moreover, the program includes two of the best: a full-version of HomeSite for Microsoft Windows developers and a trial version of BBEdit for Macintosh developers. Dreamweaver enables a natural, dynamic flow between the visual and code editors.

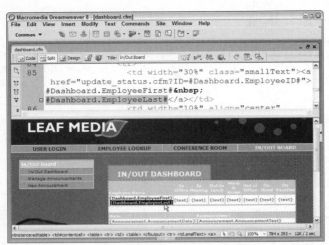

Figure 2-3: Dreamweaver enables you to work with a visual WYSIWYG editor and a code editor simultaneously.

Dreamweaver further tightens the integration between the visual design and the underlying code with the Quick Tag Editor. Web designers frequently adjust the HTML code minutely — changing an attribute here or adding a single tag there. The Quick Tag Editor, which appears as a small pop-up window in the Design view, makes these code tweaks quick and easy.

World-Class Code Editing

Coding is integrally tied to Web page development, and Dreamweaver's coding environment is second-to-none. If you're hand-coding, you'll appreciate the Code Hints (see Figure 2-4), code collapse, and code completion features that Dreamweaver offers. Many of these elements have been encapsulated into a Coding toolbar displayed along the side of Code view. Not only do all these features speed development of HTML pages, but Dreamweaver's underlying Tag Libraries extend their use to the full range of other code formats such as JavaScript, ActionScript, and XML.

Dreamweaver's Code view is easy on the eyes as well with syntax coloring that can be turned off and on at will. To get around the page quickly, use either the standard line-numbering facility or the advanced Code Navigation feature; Code Navigation lists all the functions found on a page and instantly jumps to that code when a function is selected.

Veterans and novices alike find Dreamweaver's Tag Chooser and Tag inspector indispensable. As the name implies, the Tag Chooser enables the coder to select a tag from a full list of tags in the various Web markup languages including HTML, CFML, PHP, ASP, ASP.NET, and more.

The Tag inspector gives a complete overview of all the aspects of a selected tag. Not only do you get to see a full array of all the associated properties — far more than could ever fit in the Property inspector — but you can also modify their values in place. Any applied JavaScript behaviors are also displayed in the Tag inspector. Perhaps the most innovative feature of this inspector is a CSS-related one, which displays any style impacting on a tag with completely modifiable properties and values. Select a CSS style and the Tag inspector becomes the Rule inspector for quick and easy CSS editing.

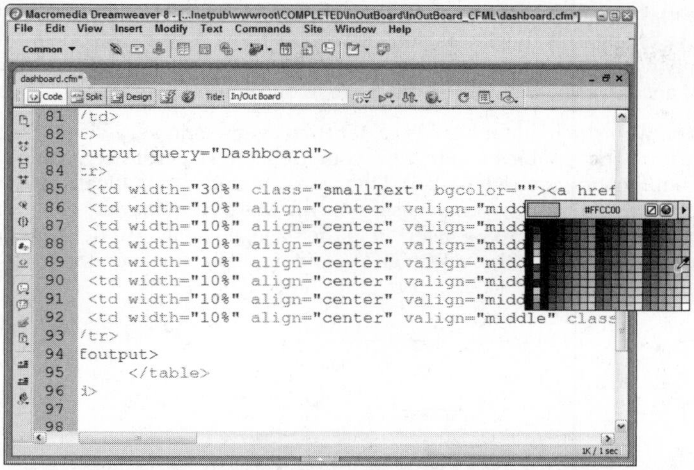

Figure 2-4: Code Hints speed hand-coding by displaying all the attributes available for a specific tag, including color.

Code is far more than just a series of individual tags, of course. Dreamweaver's Snippets panel stores the most commonly used sections of code just a drag and drop away. Dreamweaver comes with hundreds of snippets ready to use — and gives you a way to add your own at any time.

Roundtrip HTML

Most Web authoring programs modify any code that passes through their system — inserting returns, removing indents, adding `<meta>` tags, uppercasing commands, and so forth. Dreamweaver's programmers understand and respect the fact that all Web developers have their own particular coding styles. An underlying concept, Roundtrip HTML, ensures that you can move back and forth between the visual editor and any HTML text editor without your code being rewritten.

Web Site Maintenance Tools

Dreamweaver's creators also understand that creating a site is only a part of the Webmaster's job. Maintaining the Web site can be an ongoing, time-consuming chore. Dreamweaver simplifies the job with a group of site management tools, including a library of repeating elements and a file-locking capability for easy team updates.

New In Dreamweaver

Dreamweaver's built-in FTP transfer engine has undergone a major overhaul. Not only is it faster than ever, but now it fits the designer's workflow even more concisely with the capability to work in the background. Designers are now free to begin a large publishing operation and return to Dreamweaver to continue crafting pages while the FTP transfer is in process. You're free to bring up the log at any time to view the details.

Speed is another essential aspect in Web site maintenance. With Dreamweaver's siteless editing mode, you can make changes as quickly as you can connect to a server. You don't define an entire site if you only want to alter a couple of pages; just set up a server connection. Dreamweaver lets you access, edit, and publish the page in one smooth workflow.

Overall in Dreamweaver, Web site maintenance is easier than ever — and very visual. Take note of the Site Map feature that enables you to view your Web site structure at a glance and to access any file for modification (see Figure 2-5). Links are updated automatically or, if a file moves from one directory to another, are under user control. Moreover, not only can you access a library of repeating elements to be inserted in the page, you can also define templates to control the entire look and feel of a Web site — and modify a single template to update all the pages sitewide.

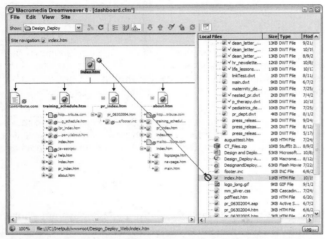

Figure 2-5: The Dreamweaver Site Map isn't just a pretty picture — it's interactive.

Team-Oriented Site Building

Until now, individual Web developers have been stymied when attempting to integrate Dreamweaver into a team-development environment. File-locking was all too easily subverted, enabling revisions to be inadvertently overwritten; site reports were limited in scope and only output to HTML; and, most notable of all, version control was nonexistent. Dreamweaver 8 addresses all these concerns while laying a foundation for future connectivity.

Dreamweaver 8 supports two industry-standard source control systems: Visual SourceSafe (VSS) and WebDAV. Connecting to a Visual SourceSafe server is well integrated into Dreamweaver; simply define the VSS server as your remote site and add the necessary connection information. WebDAV, although perhaps less well known than VSS, offers an equally powerful and more available content-management solution. More importantly, Macromedia has developed the source-control solution as a system architecture, enabling other third-party content-management or version-control developers to use Dreamweaver as their front end.

ColdFusion developers have long enjoyed the benefits of Remote Development Services (RDS) — and now, RDS connectivity has been added to Dreamweaver. Through RDS, teams of developers can work on the same site stored on a remote server. Moreover, you can connect directly to an RDS server without creating a site.

Extensible architecture also underlies Dreamweaver's site reporting facility. Dreamweaver ships with the capability to generate reports on usability issues (such as missing Alt text) or workflow concerns (such as who has what files checked out). Users can also develop custom reports on a project-by-project basis.

The Dreamweaver Interface

When creating a Web page, Webmasters do two things repeatedly: They insert an element — whether text, image, or layer — and then they modify it. Dreamweaver excels at such Web page creation. The Dreamweaver workspace combines a series of windows, panels, and inspectors to make the process as fluid as possible, thereby speeding up the Webmaster's work.

Easy Text Entry

Although much of the World Wide Web's glitz comes from multimedia elements such as images and sound, Web pages are primarily a text-based medium. Dreamweaver recognizes this and makes the text cursor the default tool. To add text, just click in Dreamweaver's main workspace — the Document window — and start typing. As shown in Figure 2-6, the Text Property inspector even enables you to change characteristics of the text, such as the size, font, position, or color by assigning a Cascading Style Sheet (CSS) style. Dreamweaver even helps you along by automatically creating a style if none has been previously assigned.

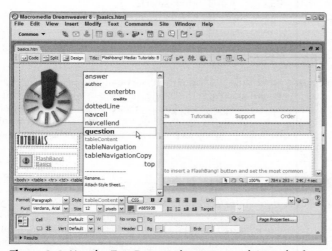

Figure 2-6: Use the Text Property inspector to change the format of the selected text with CSS.

Drag-and-Drop Data Fields

It's one thing to make a connection to a data source; it's quite another to actually insert the dynamic data in the proper place on the Web page. Dreamweaver makes drag and drop easy with the Bindings panel. All the available data sources for a page are displayed in an expandable tree outline in the Bindings panel, as shown in Figure 2-7. You can insert an instance of any dynamic field displayed in the panel onto the page by either dropping it into place or by clicking the Insert button.

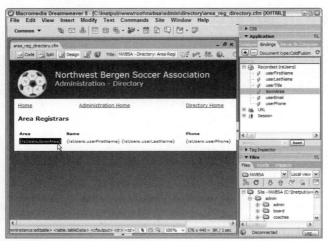

Figure 2-7: Drag any field from the Bindings panel onto a selected placeholder phrase to quickly turn a static page into a dynamic one.

One-Stop Object Modification

You can select Web page elements other than text from the Insert bar. Adding a picture to a Web page is as easy as clicking the Image icon from the Insert bar. Dreamweaver asks you to select the file for the image, and your image appears at your current cursor position. After your graphic is onscreen, selecting it brings up the appropriate Property inspector to enable you to make modifications. The same technique works for all inserted elements — from horizontal rules to Shockwave movies.

Accessing and Managing Resources

One standout addition to Dreamweaver's interface is the Assets panel, shown in Figure 2-8. The Assets panel gathers all the various elements used in an individual site: images, background and text colors, external URLs, included scripts, Flash movies, Shockwave content, and QuickTime media, as well as Dreamweaver templates and library items. Sizeable thumbnails of graphics and media are displayed in the preview pane of the Assets panel — you can even play Flash, Shockwave, and QuickTime elements in preview before dragging them onto the page. Moreover, often-used resources can be listed in a Favorites category, distinguishing them from the rest of the assets found in the site.

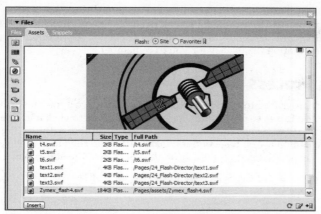

Figure 2-8: You can preview a Flash movie with the Assets panel before placing it on the Dreamweaver page.

Complete Custom Environment

Dreamweaver enables you to customize your workspace to suit yourself. Much of Dreamweaver's power derives from the various windows, panels, and inspectors, all of which are movable. Just drag them wherever you want them onscreen or keep them docked to the side. Want to see your page by itself? You can hide all windows at the touch of a function button; press it again, and your controls are revealed.

Dreamweaver's customization capabilities extend even further. If you find that you are repeatedly inserting something, such as a QuickTime video or WAV sound file, you can add that element to your Insert bar. Dreamweaver even enables you to add a specific element — a Home button, for example — to the Insert bar. In fact, you can add entire categories of objects if you like. Moreover, Dreamweaver 8 exposes the entire menu structure for customization — you can change not only keyboard shortcuts, you can also add custom menus.

Cross-Reference   For more information about customizing your Insert bar, see Chapter 32.

Managing Keyboard Shortcuts

Keyboard shortcuts are great in theory: Just press a key combination to activate an essential feature. Unfortunately, in reality, there are too many essential features, too few single-purpose keys on the keyboard and, most importantly, too few brain cells to retain all the widely varied keyboard combinations that the working designer must master.

Macromedia has taken steps to ease keyboard-shortcut overload across its entire product line, and Dreamweaver's no exception. Dreamweaver offers a Keyboard Shortcut Editor that enables you to both standardize and customize the key combinations used in the program. Choose from a Macromedia standard set — common to Dreamweaver, Fireworks, and Flash — or use a set taken from Dreamweaver MX 2004.

If you're a ColdFusion Studio user switching to Dreamweaver, you'll really appreciate the capability to add keyboard shortcuts to snippets. You can even select a set from an entirely different program such as HomeSite or BBEdit. Best of all, any keyboard shortcut can be personalized to represent a combination that's easy for you to remember.

Simple Selection Process

As with most modern layout programs, to modify anything in Dreamweaver, you must select it first. The usual process to do this is to click an object to highlight it or to click and drag over a block of text to select it. Dreamweaver adds another selection option with the Tag Selector feature. Click anywhere on a Web page under construction and then look at Dreamweaver's status bar. The applicable tags appear on the left side of the status bar.

In the example shown in Figure 2-9, the Tag Selector shows `<mm:editable>` `<div.catalog>` `<table>` `<tr>` `<td>` `<div>` `<p>`.

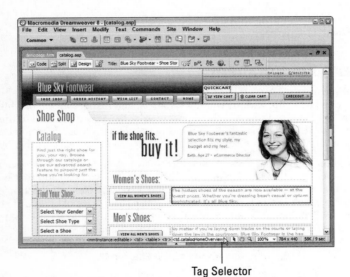

Tag Selector

Figure 2-9: Choosing the `<p>` tag in Dreamweaver's Tag Selector is a quick and easy way to highlight the current paragraph on your Web page.

Click one of these tags, and the corresponding elements are selected on your page, ready for modification. The Tag Selector is a terrific timesaver; throughout this book, I point out how you can use it in various circumstances.

Enhanced Layout Options

Dreamweaver works much more like a desktop publishing program than do many other visual HTML editors. Today's browser capabilities permit images and text to be placed in specific locations on the Web page—a concept known as *absolute positioning*. To enable you to take full advantage of this power, Dreamweaver includes guides, rulers, and grids. Both vertical and horizontal guides are supported. You can specify the type of measurement to be used (inches, pixels, or centimeters), as well as the spacing and appearance of the grid lines. You can even have objects snap to the guides or grid for easy alignment.

New In Dreamweaver The capability to magnify all or any portion of the page is now available, complementing Dreamweaver's other layout tools. Choose from a select set of magnifications from a menu or keyboard shortcut or use the Zoom tool to magnify a desired area. You can also opt to view the full page or hone in on any selected object.

Dreamweaver has always made it easy for designers new to the Web to build nice-looking interactive Web pages without having to know HTML. Dreamweaver's Layout mode is a good example of that focus. Layout mode enables designers to draw tables and cells directly on the screen for positioning content. After they are drawn, you can modify cells by dragging borders or moving the entire cell. You can also include nested tables.

Cross-Reference To find out more about absolute positioning, see Chapter 11; you can learn more about Layout mode in Chapter 13.

Plugin Media Preview

For a browser to display anything beyond standard format graphics, a plugin is generally required. Plugins extend the capability of most browsers to show animations, play music, or even explore 3D worlds. Dreamweaver is one of the first Web authoring tools to enable you to design your Web page with an active plugin playing the extended file; with all other systems, you have to preview your page in a browser to see the active content.

The active content feature in Dreamweaver enables the playback of plugins such as Macromedia Flash, Shockwave, and others. However, this feature extends beyond that. Many Web pages are coded with server-side includes, which traditionally require the page to be viewed through a Web server. Dreamweaver translates much of the server-side information so that the entire page—server-side includes and all—can be viewed in its entirety at design time.

Extended Find and Replace

The Web is a fluid medium. Pages are constantly in flux, and because changes are relatively easy to effect, corrections and additions are the norm. Quite often, a Web designer needs to update or alter an existing page—or series of pages. Dreamweaver's enhanced Find and Replace feature is a real power tool when it comes to making modifications.

Find and Replace works in the Document window, whether in Design view or Code view, as well as in the Code inspector to alter code and regular content. Moreover, changes are applicable to a selected section, the current page, the working site, selected Web pages, or an entire folder of pages, regardless of the number. Complex Find and Replace queries can be stored and retrieved later to further automate your work.

Up-to-Date Code Standards

Most Web pages are created in HyperText Markup Language (HTML). This programming language — really a series of tags that modify a text file — is standardized by an organization known as the World Wide Web Consortium, or W3C (www.w3.org). Each new release of HTML incorporates an enhanced set of commands and features. The majority of browsers in use today recognize the current version, HTML 4. Dreamweaver writes clear, easy-to-follow, real-world, browser-compatible HTML version 4.01 code whenever you insert or modify an element in the visual editor.

If you're working in Extensible HyperText Markup Language (XHTML), Dreamweaver has you covered as well with a number of tools. With one operation, Dreamweaver converts an existing page from HTML to XHTML. When coding from the ground up, you can set any page type — static or dynamic — to be XHTML-compliant.

Additionally, Dreamweaver includes complete Unicode support. Unicode is an encoding standard that enables Web browsers to display characters from almost any language worldwide. Dreamweaver displays Unicode properly at design time and runtime.

Cutting-Edge CSS Support

Browser support for Cascading Style Sheets (CSS) has been steadily growing, and Dreamweaver has greatly enhanced its own support in response. In addition to enhanced rendering in the Design view for advanced CSS effects such as backgrounds and positioning, Dreamweaver has made it far simpler to apply CSS from the ground up.

Editing CSS has undergone a complete makeover in Dreamweaver 8. Now editing a CSS style is just as easy as applying one. The CSS Styles panel (see Figure 2-10) displays all the current styles — both internal and external — with detailed characteristics. Double-click any style to modify it.

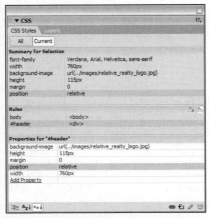

Figure 2-10: The CSS Styles panel is your one-stop shop to create, apply, and modify styles, whether from an embedded or external style sheet.

CSS is well on its way to becoming the standard approach to Web design, and it pervades every aspect of Dreamweaver. CSS styles can now be applied — and created — right from the Property inspector. Dreamweaver properly renders the more advanced CSS properties, such as float and fixed background, so that designers can truly concentrate on the look of a site rather than hassling with code hacks.

Addressing Accessibility

Accessibility is an issue of great concern to many Web developers. Increasingly, many designers labor under a mandate to produce accessible sites, especially in consideration of Section 508 of the Federal Rehabilitation Act. To help designers create accessible pages, Dreamweaver optionally displays additional attributes for key Web page objects such as tables, forms, images, media, and frames. These attributes — like summary for the `<table>` tag — are always available through the Tag inspector when enabled through Dreamweaver's Preferences.

In addition, Dreamweaver is accessible as a tool itself. A number of screen readers, including JAWS for Windows and Window Eyes, are supported. Furthermore, the entire Dreamweaver interface can be navigated without using the mouse.

Straightforward Text and Graphics Support

Text is a basic building block of any Web page, and Dreamweaver makes formatting your text a snap. After you've inserted your text, either by typing it directly or pasting it from another program, you can change its appearance. You can use the generic HTML formats, such as the H1 through H6 headings and their relative sizes, or you can use font families and exact point sizes.

Chapter 8 shows you how to work with text in Dreamweaver.

Additional text support in Dreamweaver enables you to add both numbered and bulleted lists to your Web page. The Text Property inspector provides buttons for both kinds of lists as well as easy alignment control. Some elements, including lists, offer extended options. In Dreamweaver, clicking the Property inspector's Expander arrow opens a section from which you can access additional controls.

Graphics are handled in much the same easy-to-use manner. Select the image or its place-holder to enable the Image Property inspector. From there, you can modify any available attributes, including the image's source, its width or height, and its alignment on the page. Need to touch up your image? Send it to your favorite graphics program with just a click of the Edit button.

You learn all about adding and modifying images in Chapter 9.

Enhanced Table Capabilities

Other features — standard, yet more advanced — are similarly straightforward in Dreamweaver. Tables are a key component in today's Web pages, and Dreamweaver gives you full control over all their functionality. It changes the work of resizing the column or row of a table, previously a dreary hand-coding task, into an easy click-and-drag motion. Likewise, you can delete all the width and height values from a table with the click of a button. The Table Property inspector centralizes many of these options in Dreamweaver.

The nitty-gritty of table editing is often tedious and tricky: Grabbing just the right selection in a tightly formatted table row is meticulous work. Dreamweaver's Expanded mode takes the guesswork out of precise selection by visually exploding the table at design time to make all the elements far more accessible, as shown in Figure 2-11. You can switch between Standard, Layout, and Expanded modes at the click of the mouse.

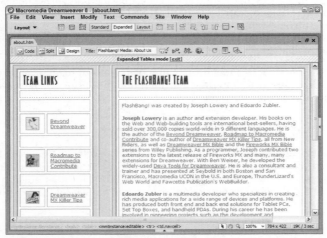

Figure 2-11: By temporarily displaying borders with increased cell padding and cell spacing, Expanded mode makes table editing far easier.

Tables are flexible in Dreamweaver. Font changes can be applied to any number of selected cells, rows, or columns. Standard commands enable you to automatically format or sort a table as well.

Cross-Reference   You can find all you need to know about tables in Chapter 13.

Easy Form Entry

Forms, the basic vehicle for Web page data exchange, are just as easy to implement as tables in Dreamweaver. Switch to the Forms category of the Insert bar and insert any of the available elements: text boxes, radio buttons, checkboxes, and even drop-down or scrolling lists. With the Validate Form behavior, you can easily specify any field as a required field and check to ensure that the requested type of information has been entered.

Click-and-Drag Frame Setup

Frames, which enable separate Web pages to be viewed on a single screen, are often considered one of the most difficult HTML techniques to master. Dreamweaver employs a click-and-drag method for establishing your frame outlines. After you've set up your frame structure, open the Frames panel (see Figure 2-12) to select any frame and modify it with the Property inspector. Dreamweaver writes the necessary code for linking all the HTML files in a frameset, no matter how many Web pages are used. Dreamweaver keeps frame creation simple with the Frames menu on the Insert bar's Layout category.

Frames Panel

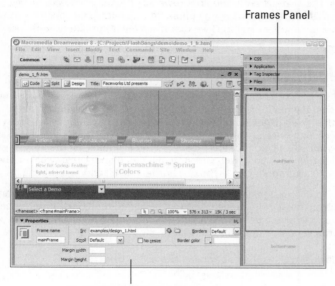

Frame Property Inspector

Figure 2-12: In Dreamweaver, you use the Frames panel to choose which frame you want to modify through the Property inspector.

For more information about creating frame-based Web pages, see Chapter 16.

Multimedia Enhancements

Dreamweaver enables you to drop in any number of multimedia extensions, plugins, applets, or controls. Just click the appropriate button on the Insert bar and modify with the Property inspector. Two multimedia elements, Shockwave movies and Flash files — both from Macromedia — warrant special consideration in Macromedia's Dreamweaver. When you insert either of these objects, Dreamweaver automatically includes the necessary HTML code to ensure the widest browser acceptance, and you can edit all the respective properties.

Dreamweaver fully supports a wide range of multimedia output through custom objects that enable complex images, audio, and presentations to be easily inserted and displayed in Web pages.

Next-Generation Features

Dreamweaver was among the first Web authoring tools to work with the capabilities brought in by the 4.0 generation of browsers. The latest browsers all support variations of Dynamic HTML (DHTML). Moreover, the current generation of browsers adheres to the Cascading Style Sheet (CSS) standards for the most part, with support for absolute and relative positioning. Dreamweaver gives Web developers an interface that translates these advanced possibilities into reality.

Dynamic Style Updates

Dreamweaver completely supports the Cascading Style Sheet (CSS) specification agreed upon by the World Wide Web Consortium. CSS gives Web designers more flexible control over almost every element on their Web pages. Dreamweaver applies CSS capabilities as if they were styles in a word processor. For example, you can make all the <h1> tags blue, italic, and put them in small caps. If your site's color scheme changes, you can make all the <h1> tags red — and you can do this throughout your Web site with one command. Dreamweaver gives you style control over type, background, blocks, boxes, borders, lists, and positioning.

Dreamweaver enables you to change styles online as well as offline. By linking a CSS change to a user-driven event such as moving the mouse, text can be highlighted or de-emphasized, screen areas can light up, and figures can even be animated. Moreover, it can all be done without repeated trips to the server or huge file downloads.

Cross-Reference   Details about using Cascading Style Sheets begin in Chapter 7.

Flash and Fireworks Integration

Dreamweaver 8 has upped the ante for integration with Macromedia's graphics engine, Fireworks. Now, images derived from Fireworks are identified as such, both in the Property inspector and in the Assets panel. Graphics can be optimized to alter the file size, cropping, transparency, or many other aspects right from within Dreamweaver.

Dreamweaver has picked up a couple of tricks from its close association with Fireworks and can now handle basic graphics editing on its own. Use Dreamweaver to crop, resample, brighten, darken, or sharpen any GIF or JPEG image. All the tools are immediately accessible from the Image Property inspector.

If more extensive modification is required, click the Edit button to send the graphic back to Fireworks, if that's your designated graphics editor. More impressively, you can edit sliced images — maintained as a borderless table in HTML — in their entirety. Fireworks even respects (to a degree) HTML alterations such as changes to URLs or conversion of an image slice to a text block. This degree of integration lends an amazing fluidity to the workflow.

New In Dreamweaver   Video on the Web has been a long-standing wish for many designers — a wish that has now come true, thanks to Flash video. Dreamweaver has embraced Flash video whole-heartedly and Web page designers have a clear path for easily inserting instant-on videos in their site. Flash video is available in either a progressive download or streaming format, both of which are fully supported in Dreamweaver.

Flash has yet another format: compiled Flash files. Dreamweaver takes advantage of these new creations by incorporating the first of a series of Flash elements: Image Viewer. The Image Viewer, shown in Figure 2-13, is a Flash movie that enables you to set attributes within Dreamweaver, providing you with a full range of design options and customization.

Figure 2-13: Add JPEGs and set animated transitions to create your own slide show with the Flash element Image Viewer.

You can send Flash movies to be edited directly from within Dreamweaver, just as you can with Fireworks. After you have completed your editing operation in Flash, just click Done, and your revised movie is republished and inserted back into Dreamweaver.

Server-Side Behaviors

The driving forces behind Dreamweaver's Web application creation are its server behaviors. A server behavior is code written in a language understood by the particular server model that is executed on the server. Dreamweaver comes standard with a wide variety of useful server behaviors, ranging from one that replicates records on a page to another that restricts access to a page.

You apply and manage server behaviors from the Server Behaviors panel, shown in Figure 2-14. Unlike the Bindings panel, from which you drag fields onto the page, the main area of the Server Behaviors panel indicates which server behaviors have been inserted into the page. If the server behavior has user-defined parameters, they can be altered by double-clicking the entry in the panel.

XML and XSLT Integration

Extensible Markup Language (XML) has piqued the interest of many Web designers, intranet developers, and corporate users because of its underlying customizable nature. With XML, tags are created to describe the use of the information, rather than its appearance. Another standards-based technology, Extensible Stylesheet Transformation (XSLT) controls the data styling.

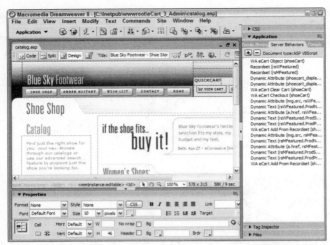

Figure 2-14: Quickly identify the page elements affected by a server behavior by selecting the entry in the Bindings panel.

New In Dreamweaver

Dreamweaver has taken the next step with XML and made it possible for almost any designer to incorporate XML data right into her own Web pages. Through the use of XSLT, Dreamweaver displays XML data from RSS feeds and other sources. Dreamweaver's implementation exposes this technology on both the client-side and server-side, widening its appeal to a range of designers.

Dreamweaver is capable of exporting and importing XML tags, no matter what the tag definition. You can also create, modify, and validate XML files in Dreamweaver. As XML grows in popularity, Dreamweaver is ready to handle the work.

3D Layers

One particular Dynamic HTML feature enables Dreamweaver to be called "the first 3D Web authoring tool." Until Dynamic HTML, Web pages existed on a two-dimensional plane—images and text could only be placed side by side. Dreamweaver supports absolute positioning with CSS—known colloquially as layers—meaning that objects can be placed in front of or behind other objects. Layers can contain text, graphics, links, and controls—you can even nest one layer inside another.

As the prevalence of CSS grows across the Web, more and more designers are applying their absolute positioning properties to <div> tags directly. This process keeps the layout properties (the CSS rules) separate from the content and makes for simpler maintenance. Dreamweaver offers an easy-to-apply <div> tag object, right from the Insert bar's Common category (see Figure 2-15).

Another way to create a layer in Dreamweaver is by clicking the Draw Layer button on the Insert bar. Dreamweaver places the necessary CSS inline with the layer (<div>) tag. After they are created, layers can be positioned anywhere on the page by clicking and dragging the selection handle. As with other Dreamweaver objects, you can modify a layer through the Property inspector.

Insert Div Tag

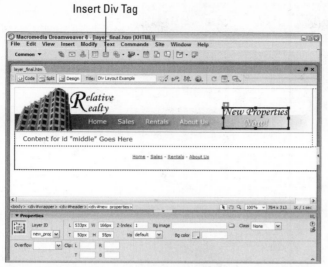

Figure 2-15: Position your content through ⟨div⟩ tags or drawn layers—with Dreamweaver, it's up to you.

Cross-Reference See Chapter 11 for detailed information about using ⟨div⟩ tags and layers in Dreamweaver.

JavaScript Behaviors

Through the development of JavaScript behaviors, Dreamweaver combines the power of JavaScript with the ease of a point-and-click interface. A *behavior* is defined as a combination of an event and an action—whenever your Web page user does something that causes something else to happen, that's a behavior. What makes behaviors extremely useful is that they require no programming whatsoever.

Behaviors are JavaScript-based, and this is significant because JavaScript is supported to varying degrees by existing browsers. Dreamweaver has simplified the task of identifying which JavaScript command works with a particular browser. You simply select the Web page element that you want to use to control the action and open the Behaviors panel. As shown in Figure 2-16, Dreamweaver enables you to pick a JavaScript command that works with all browsers, a subset of browsers, or one browser in particular. Next, you choose from a full list of available actions, such as go to a URL, play a sound, pop up a message, or start an animation. You can also assign multiple actions to an event and even determine when they occur.

Cross-Reference For complete details about working with JavaScript behaviors, see Chapter 12.

Figure 2-16: Dreamweaver offers only the JavaScript commands that work with the browser you specify.

Program Extensibility

One of Dreamweaver's primary strengths is its extensibility. Virtually no two Web sites are alike, either in their design or execution. With such a tremendous variety of results, the more flexible a Web authoring tool, the more useful it is to a larger group of designers. When it was introduced, Dreamweaver broke new ground with objects and behaviors that were easily customizable. Now, Dreamweaver lengthens its lead with custom floaters, commands, translators, and Property inspectors. The basic underpinnings of Dreamweaver can even be extended with C-Level Extensibility options.

Objects and Behaviors

In Dreamweaver parlance, an *object* is a bit of HTML code that represents a specific image or HTML tag, such as a <table> or a <form>. Dreamweaver's objects are completely open to user customization, or even out-and-out creation. For example, if you'd rather import structured data into a table without a border instead of with the standard 1-pixel border, you can easily make that modification to the Insert Tabular Data object file—right from within Dreamweaver—and every subsequent table is similarly inserted. Objects are accessed from the Insert bar as well as through the menus.

Objects are terrific timesaving devices, essentially enabling you to drop in significant blocks of HTML code at the click of a mouse. Likewise, Dreamweaver behaviors enable even novice Web designers to insert complex JavaScript functions designed to propel pages to the cutting edge. Dreamweaver ships with a full array of standard behaviors—but that's only the tip of the behavior iceberg. Because behaviors are also customizable and can be built by anyone with a working knowledge of JavaScript, many Dreamweaver designers have created custom behaviors and made them publicly available.

On the CD-ROM

You can find a large assortment of custom objects, behaviors, and commands on the CD-ROM that accompanies this book.

Server Behavior Builder

Server behaviors are key to Dreamweaver's success as a Web application authoring tool. Although Dreamweaver provides a full palette of server behaviors for handling many of the required tasks, the needs of Web developers are too diverse and numerous. Dreamweaver cannot supply a server behavior for every occasion. Enter Dreamweaver's Server Behavior Builder, shown in Figure 2-17, a terrific tool for creating custom server behaviors.

Figure 2-17: With the Server Behavior Builder, you can create a new behavior from the ground up or modify an existing behavior.

The Server Behavior Builder is engineered to handle a wide range of circumstances. Some server behaviors can be encapsulated in a single line of code repeated verbatim, whereas others require multiple blocks of programming involving several user-supplied parameters — you can construct almost any kind of code with the Server Behavior Builder. After you create the custom server behavior, you can apply and modify it just like any of the standard Dreamweaver server behaviors.

Commands and Floating Panels

Objects and behaviors are great ways to help build the final result of a Web page, but what about automating the work of producing that page? Dreamweaver employs commands to modify the existing page and streamline production. A great example is the Sort Table command, standard with Dreamweaver. If you've ever had to sort a large table by hand — meticulously moving data, one row at a time — you can appreciate the power of this option the first time you use a command to alphabetize or otherwise sort a table

Commands hold a great promise — they are, in effect, more powerful than either objects or behaviors combined. In fact, some of the more complex objects, such as the Rollover Image object, are actually commands. Commands can also extract information sitewide and offer a powerful programmable language within Dreamweaver.

Creating a Dreamweaver command is easy for anyone, thanks to the History panel. Aside from displaying every action you undertake as you build your Web page, the History panel enables you to select any number of those actions and save them as a command. Your new command is instantly available to be called from the menu whenever you need it.

After only a few moments with Dreamweaver, you become accustomed to its use of floating panels. You can even create custom floating panels, perhaps to show existing resources or to provide a whole new interface for modifying an HTML element.

Adjustable Insert Bars

The Insert bar is more than just part of a new look for Dreamweaver. Now, designers can quickly see all the available object categories and switch to them with a single click. More importantly — from an extensibility standpoint — new categories can be developed and integrated into the Dreamweaver workspace on a contextual basis. In other words, if you create a category for SMIL, you can set the preferences so that it displays only when you are working on an SMIL file.

The Insert bar is quite accessible to new users. You can even switch between the different categories being available as drop-down list or as a series of tabs. The ultimate in accessibility, however, has to be the Insert bar's Favorites category. Now you can personalize an entire category and display just those objects you use most frequently.

Custom Tags, Translators, and Property Inspectors

In Dreamweaver, almost every part of the user interface can be customized — including the tags themselves. You can easily add new tags and specify how they should be formatted via the Tag Library Editor; you can even import entire tag sets represented by DTDs. After you've developed your custom third-party tags, you can display and modify their current properties with a custom Property inspector. Moreover, if your custom tags include content not typically shown in Dreamweaver's Document window, you can build a custom translator, enabling the content to be displayed.

Programs such as Dreamweaver are usually built in the programming language called C or C++, which must be compiled before it is used. Generally, the basic functions of a C program are frozen solid; there's no way that you can extend them. This is not the case with Dreamweaver, however, which offers a C-Level Extensibility that permits programmers to create libraries to install new functionality into the program. Translators, for example, normally rely on new C libraries to display content in Dreamweaver that could not be shown otherwise. Companies can use the C-Level Extensibility feature to integrate Dreamweaver into their existing workflow and maximize productivity.

Automation Enhancements

Web site design is the dream job; Web site production is the reality. After a design has been finalized, its execution can become repetitive and burdensome. Dreamweaver offers a number of ways to automate the production work, keeping the look of the Web pages consistent — with minimum work required.

Rapid Application Development with Application Objects

Although it's true that almost every active Web site has one or more unique situations that require some custom coding, it's equally true that the same type of Web application is used repeatedly. It's hard to find an e-commerce–enabled site that doesn't use some variation of the master-detail Web application in which a search returns a list of matches (the master page), each of which links to a page with more information (the detail page). Likewise, every intranet administration application requires the capability to add, edit, and remove records. To speed the development of these types of applications, Dreamweaver includes a series of Application objects, some of which reduce a 20-step operation to a single dialog box, like the one shown in Figure 2-18.

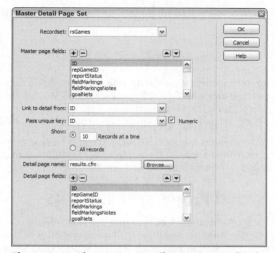

Figure 2-18: The Master Detail Page Set Application object provides rapid development for a common Web application.

Here are some of the Application objects that come standard with Dreamweaver:

✦ Dynamic Table

✦ Master Detail Page Set

✦ Recordset Navigation Bar

✦ Recordset Navigation Status

✦ Record Insertion Form

✦ Record Update Form

Although they vary in complexity, all are guaranteed timesavers. In addition to creating pages as needed, Application objects can also insert dynamic data and apply server behaviors.

Importing Office Documents

Much of the Web's content originates from other sources — in-house documents produced by a word processor or spreadsheet program. Dreamweaver bridges the gap between the offline and online world with a variety of useful import features.

Microsoft Word, perhaps the premier word processor, is great at creating and storing word processing documents but not so accomplished at outputting standard HTML. An HTML file derived from Word is, to put it mildly, bloated with extraneous and repetitive code.

Content from Word can be simply copied and pasted into Dreamweaver. Dreamweaver handles the conversion from Word to HTML, automatically retaining most formatting in clean HTML. The same copy/paste functionality applies to Excel.

For full documents, you can use Dreamweaver's Import Word HTML command. This feature strips out the unnecessary code and even permits you to format the code as you format your other Dreamweaver files. The Import Word HTML command offers a wide range of options for cleaning up the code.

Of course, not all Web content derives from word processing documents — databases and spreadsheets are the other two legs of the modern office software triangle. With the Import Tabular Data command, Dreamweaver offers the capability to incorporate data from any source that can export structured text files. Just save your spreadsheet or database as a comma, tab, or otherwise delimited file and bring it directly into Dreamweaver in the table style of your choice.

Reference Panel

Even the most advanced coder needs a reference when including seldom-used HTML tags or arcane JavaScript functions. Dreamweaver includes built-in references with HTML, JavaScript, and Cascading Style Sheets. Dreamweaver's guide is context-sensitive; highlight a tag or function in Code view and press Shift+F1 to get a breakdown on syntax and browser compatibility.

In addition to the resources already noted, you can use a ColdFusion Markup Language reference from Macromedia. UsableNet has contributed a valuable guide to accessibility issues, and two new guides from Wrox are onboard — one for ASP 3.0 and one for JSP.

History Panel

The repetitiveness of building a Web site is often a matter of entering the same series of commands over and over. You might, for example, need to add a vertical margin of 10 pixels and a horizontal margin of 5 around most, but not all, of the images on a page. Rather than selecting each image and then repeatedly entering these values in the Property inspector, you can now enter the values once and save that action as a command.

You can find the feature that brings this degree of automation to Dreamweaver in the History panel. The History panel shows each step taken by a designer as the page is developed. Although this visual display is great for complex, multilevel undo actions, the capability to save any number of your steps as an instantly available command is truly timesaving.

Site Management Tools

Updating and revising are on-going for nearly every Web site. For this reason, site management tools are as important to a Web authoring program as site creation tools. Dreamweaver delivers on both counts.

Object Libraries

In addition to site management functions that have become traditional, such as FTP publishing, Dreamweaver adds a whole new class of functionality called *libraries*. One of the truisms of Web page development is that if you repeat an element across your site, you're sure to have to change it — on every page. Dreamweaver libraries eliminate that drudgery. You can define almost anything as a Library element: a paragraph of text, an image, a link, a table, a form, a Java applet, an ActiveX control, and so on. Just choose the item and open the Library category of the Assets panel (see Figure 2-19). After you've created the Library entry, you can reuse it throughout your Web site. Each Web site can have its own library, and you can copy entries from one library to another.

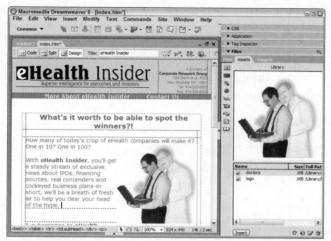

Figure 2-19: Use Dreamweaver's Library feature to simplify the task of updating elements repeated across many Web pages.

Being able to include boilerplate Web elements is one issue; being able to update them across the site simultaneously is quite another! You can easily change a library entry through the Library category of the Assets panel. After the change is complete, Dreamweaver detects the modification and asks if you want to update your site. Imagine updating copyright information across a 400+ page Web site in the wink of an eye, and you start to understand the power of Dreamweaver libraries.

To find out more about making sitewide changes with library items, see Chapter 28.

Super-Charged Templates

The more your Web site grows, the more you find yourself using the same basic format for different pages. Dreamweaver enables the use of Web page templates to standardize the look and feel of a Web site and to cut down on the repetitive work of creating new pages. A Dreamweaver template can hold the basic structure for the page — an image embedded in the background, a navigation bar along the left side, or a set-width table in the center for holding the main text, for example — with as many elements predefined as possible.

Dreamweaver templates are far more than just molds for creating pages, however. Basically, templates work with a series of locked and editable regions. To update an entire site based on a template, all you have to do is alter one or more of the template's locked regions. Naturally, Dreamweaver enables you to save any template that you create in the same folder, so that your own templates, too, are accessible through the Templates category of the Assets panel.

You find more about using and creating templates in Chapter 27.

Dreamweaver templates are much more than just editable and uneditable regions, however. Dreamweaver gives the designer a high degree of control with such features as repeating regions — which, for example, enable a table row to be repeated as many times as needed but constrain the other areas of a table. You're also able to hide and show areas of a page conditionally with optional regions, as shown in Figure 2-20. Dreamweaver's template power extends to nested templates, so that changes can ripple down through a series of locked and editable regions.

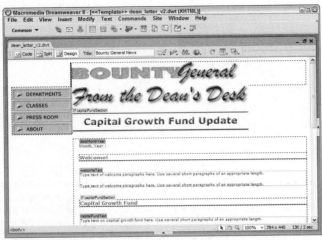

Figure 2-20: This template contains editable, repeating, and optional regions.

Browser Targeting

Browser targeting is another site management innovation from Dreamweaver. One of the major steps in any site development project is to test the Web pages in various browsers to look for inconsistencies and invalid code. Dreamweaver's Browser Targeting function enables you to check your HTML against any existing browser's profile. Dreamweaver includes predefined profiles for several browsers, and you can create a profile for any browser you'd like to check.

Cross-Reference To learn how you can set up your own profile for Browser Targeting, see Chapter 29.

You can also preview your Web page in any number of browsers. Dreamweaver enables you to specify primary and secondary browsers that can display your page at the press of a function key. You can install up to 18 other browsers for previewing your Web page. The entire list of browsers is available through the Preview in Browser command in the File menu.

Converting Web Pages

Although Web site designers may have access to the latest HTML tools and browsers, much of the public uses older, more limited versions of browsers. Dreamweaver gives you the power to build Web pages with the high-end capabilities of fourth-generation browsers — and to convert those pages so that older browsers can also display what you've created. Moreover, you can take previously designed Web pages that use tables and upgrade them to take advantage of the latest HTML features with the Tables to Layers command. Dreamweaver goes a long way toward helping you bridge the gap between browser versions.

Verifying Links

Web sites are ever-evolving entities. Maintaining valid connections and links amid all that diversity is a constant challenge. Dreamweaver includes a built-in Link Checker so you can verify the links on a page, in a directory, or across your entire site. The Link Checker quickly shows you which files have broken links, which files have links to external sites, and which files may have been *orphaned* (so that no other file connects with them).

FTP Publishing

The final step in Web page creation is publishing your page on the Internet. As any Webmaster knows, this final step is one that happens repeatedly as the site is continually updated and maintained. Dreamweaver includes an FTP (File Transfer Protocol) publisher that simplifies the work of posting your site; FTP publishing is now handled as a background process. More importantly, Dreamweaver enables you to synchronize your local and remote sites with one command.

Security is a prime concern among many Webmasters, and many developers have switched to using Secure FTP (SFTP). Dreamweaver lists SFTP among its supported file-transfer flavors.

Not all the files found in your local site need to be uploaded to the remote site. Dreamweaver includes a feature called *cloaking*, which permits the designer to designate folders that should be excluded during synchronization operations.

You can work with sites originating from a local folder, such as one on your own hard drive. Or, in a collaborative team environment, you can work with sites being developed on a remote server. Dreamweaver enables you to set up an unlimited number of sites to include the source and destination directories, FTP usernames, passwords, and more.

The Dreamweaver Files panel, shown in Figure 2-21, is a visual interface in which you can click and drag files or select a number of files and transfer them with the Get and Put buttons. You can even set the preferences so the system automatically disconnects after remaining idle for a user-definable period of time.

Site Map

Web sites can quickly outgrow the stage in which the designer can keep all the linked pages in mind. Dreamweaver includes a visual aid in the Web site management toolbox: the Site Map. With the Site Map, the Web designer can see how the entire Web site is structured. However, you can use the Site Map to do far more.

It can be used to establish the structure of the Web site in addition to viewing it. New pages can be created, and links can be added, modified, or deleted. In fact, the Site Map is so powerful, it becomes a site manager as well.

Figure 2-21: The Files panel enables you to publish your Web site directly from within Dreamweaver to your application server with Put or to retrieve them with Get.

File Check In/Check Out

On larger Web projects, more than one person is usually responsible for creation and daily upkeep of the site. An editor may need to include the latest company press release, or a graphic artist may have to upload a photo of the newest product — all on the same page. To avoid conflicts with overlapping updates, Dreamweaver has devised a system by which Web pages can be marked as checked out and locked to prevent any other corrections until the file is once again checked in.

Dreamweaver places a green checkmark over a file's icon in the Site Files window when you have checked it out and a red checkmark if another member of your team has checked it out. In addition, so you won't have to guess who that team member is, Dreamweaver displays the name of the person next to the filename. You can also keep track of who last checked out a particular Web page (or image) — Dreamweaver keeps an ongoing log listing the file, person, date, and time of the check-out.

Summary

Building any Web site — whether static or dynamic — is half craft and half art, and Dreamweaver is the perfect tool for blending these often dueling disciplines. Dreamweaver's visual editor enables quick and artful page creation, and at the same time, its integrated text editors offer the detail-oriented focus required by programmers. Dreamweaver's key advantages include the following:

✦ Dreamweaver works the way professional Web developers do, with integrated visual and text editors. Dreamweaver won't convert your code when it's used with pre-existing Web pages.

✦ It supports HTML standard commands with easy entry and editing of text, graphics, tables, and multimedia elements.

✦ Dreamweaver provides straightforward yet robust connectivity to data sources and access to the most popular server models.

✦ It makes cutting-edge features, such as Dynamic HTML and Cascading Style Sheets, easy to use.

✦ A super-charged editor features advanced options like code completion and Code Hints.

✦ With Dreamweaver's Live Data view, you can construct your page while viewing the actual data to be displayed in the online application.

✦ Dreamweaver offers you a variety of reusable server behaviors, JavaScript behaviors, object libraries, commands, Application objects, and templates to streamline your Web page creation.

✦ Enhanced templates are possible with optional and conditional regions.

✦ Dreamweaver's wide range of site management tools includes FTP publishing, with a file-locking capability that encourages team creation and maintenance, as well as a built-in Link Checker, cloaking capabilities, and visual Site Map.

In the next chapter, you get an in-depth tour of Dreamweaver's features.

✦　　✦　　✦

Touring Dreamweaver

Dreamweaver's user interface is efficient, powerful, and flexible. By offering a wide variety of customizable tools and controls, Dreamweaver helps you tailor its workspace to your specific preferences and needs so that you can focus on the task of creating your Web site. This chapter provides a detailed overview of the Dreamweaver workspace so you know where all the tools are when you need to use them.

Choosing a Workspace Layout

One of Dreamweaver's greatest strengths is its flexibility. The makers of Dreamweaver realize that not everyone works in the same way, and they have created a product that you can customize to maximize your efficiency. By default, Dreamweaver provides three different workspace layouts and even allows you to customize your own.

New In Dreamweaver

You can access these options by choosing Window ⇨ Workspace Layout and selecting one of the submenu choices: Coder, Designer, or Dual Screen. (Coder and Designer are Windows only.)

The default layout option is referred to as the Designer workspace. This configuration enables you to open several documents within the same window. Here, Dreamweaver's many panels are organized into groups and docked on the right side of the window. The Designer is illustrated in Figure 3-1.

A variation on the Designer workspace is the Coder workspace option. Here, the panels are docked on the left side of the window rather than the right. With this option, when you first open documents, you are presented with the code for the document, rather than a view that reflects what the page will look like when viewed in a browser. Figure 3-2 shows the Coder workspace layout.

Insert bar

Menus

Panels

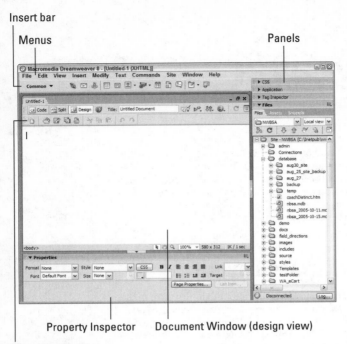

Property Inspector   Document Window (design view)

Document Toolbar

Figure 3-1: Dreamweaver's Designer workspace places docked panel groups on the right.

Cross-Reference You have numerous options for customizing Dreamweaver. Later in this chapter, you learn how to move the panels and toolbars, dock or float the panels, hide, show, or resize panels, and more. Chapter 4 systematically covers many additional customization options, referred to within Dreamweaver as *preferences*.

The third option, Dual Screen, is useful if you have two monitors for the same computer. When invoked, the Dual Screen layout undocks all the major components (Property inspector, panel groups, and Code inspector) so that they can be positioned exactly how you like.

All customized layouts can be saved for later retrieval. Once you've set up the desired layout, you can choose Window ➪ Workspace Layout ➪ Save Current to store your customized environment. When you opt to save your current layout, a dialog box appears for you to name your layout; after confirming your choice by clicking OK, your new layout option is displayed in the Workspace Layout submenu. Select Window ➪ Workspace Layout ➪ Manage to delete or rename your custom layouts.

Tip If you aren't sure which workspace works best for you, don't worry; you aren't committed to your initial choice. You can alter your workspace at any time.

Menus

Panels

Document Toolbar

Insert Bar

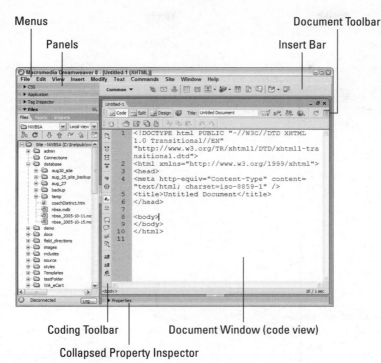

Coding Toolbar

Document Window (code view)

Collapsed Property Inspector

Figure 3-2: The Coder style workspace opens documents in Code view and docks panels on the left.

The workspace for Macintosh users, shown in Figure 3-3, is a variation of the Windows version. In this workspace, each document opens in a separate window, and the tools are grouped into floating panels that can be docked to each other. On a Mac, the Dreamweaver menus appear in place of the standard Finder operating system menus, rather than within the Document window.

As you can see in Figures 3-1, 3-2, and 3-3, all the workspaces comprise the same basic elements even though they are laid out differently on the screen. For the most part, you work with those elements in the same way, regardless of workspace; the only major difference between the workspaces is the location of the tools onscreen. The basic elements of Dreamweaver include the following:

✦ Document window

✦ Toolbars

✦ Insert bar

✦ Property inspector

✦ Panels

✦ Menus

The rest of this chapter takes you on a tour of each of these basic interface elements.

Insert Bar

Menus

Insert Bar Panels

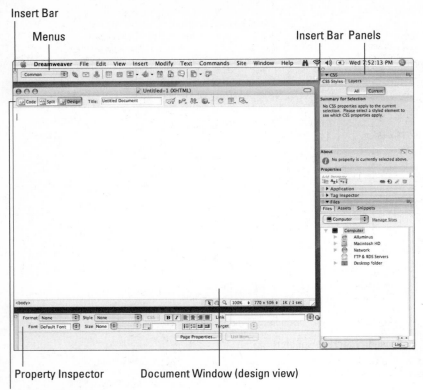

Property Inspector

Document Window (design view)

Document Toolbar

Figure 3-3: The workspace for Macintosh enables users to position panels wherever they would like.

Viewing the Document Window

Dreamweaver's primary work area is the Document window. When you first start Dreamweaver, you see what is essentially an empty canvas surrounded by tool panels and toolbars. This canvas is where you create your Web pages by typing headlines and paragraphs; inserting images and links; and creating tables, forms, and other HTML elements.

You can open more than one document at once in Dreamweaver, and all of your documents are viewed within the same window. On Windows, if the documents are not maximized, you can see more than one document at once using the tile commands on the Window menu. On a Mac, each new document is automatically opened in a tab off of the previous document. If you want to separate documents, Control+click the document tab and choose Move to New Tab. This adds a great deal of flexibility to Mac document windows because you can have multiple documents open in multiple document windows.

If you maximize a document, all the open documents are maximized. Switch between the open documents by clicking the appropriate tab for the document, located near the top of the window. The buttons to minimize, restore, and close a maximized document on Windows are located in the upper-right corner of the Dreamweaver Document window. On a Mac, the buttons to close, minimize, and restore a group of tabbed documents remain in the upper left of the document window. To close one document, click the close widget to the left of the filename on each tab. You can also right-click a document tab and choose Close from the context menu to close the document. Figure 3-4 illustrates maximized documents within the Windows workspace.

Figure 3-4: In the Dreamweaver workspace on Windows, switch between maximized documents using tabs.

If you open more documents than it can show, Dreamweaver displays Next and Previous arrows that enable you to scroll through the tabs.

Switching Views in the Document Window

Typical Web design tasks consist of visually creating a page in Dreamweaver, perhaps tweaking the underlying code to achieve the exact effect you want, and making sure your Web application is performing as expected with Dreamweaver's Live Data view (if you are creating dynamic pages). You can do all these things without ever leaving the Dreamweaver Document window, simply by switching the view of the page you are editing.

Design and Code Views

In Design view, you lay out a page visually. As your Web page begins to take shape, Design view shows you a close representation of how the page looks when viewed through a browser such as Firefox or Internet Explorer. You can even see active elements, such as QuickTime movies or Shockwave and Flash files in your Web page as you're building it. You can switch to Design view with the View ➪ Design menu command or by clicking the Show Design View button on the Document toolbar, described in the section "Accessing the Toolbars" later in this chapter.

As the name suggests, Code view displays the underlying code used to create the document, whether that is HTML, CSS style definitions, or JavaScript — whatever code is used to create the page is visible to you in Code view. If you are working in the Coder style workspace, Code view is the default view; but you can also switch to Code view by choosing the View ➪ Code menu command or by clicking the Show Code View button on the Document toolbar.

Tip   You can choose View ➪ Code and Design to split the Document window, so that both Code view and Design view are visible at the same time. You can also do this by clicking the Show Code and Design Views button on the Document toolbar.

When you switch document views, the switch applies to the currently active open document and to any subsequent documents you open. It does not, however, change the view of other open documents.

Live Data View

If you are creating a Web application that includes dynamic elements from a database, Dreamweaver offers an alternate version of Design view for your page — Live Data view. In Live Data view, Dreamweaver displays your page with data from your data source. Toggle Live Data view on and off by choosing View ➪ Live Data or by clicking the Live Data View button on the Document toolbar (as described later in this chapter). A keyboard shortcut, Ctrl+Shift+R (Command+Shift+R) also enables Live Data view.

Live Data view is one of Dreamweaver's key features. When you're in Live Data view, you can lay out your page — formatting text items, adjusting graphics, and modifying tables — while the actual data from your application is onscreen. The live data that Dreamweaver displays replaces data source placeholders such as {rs.employeeID} with the selected information pulled from the database's designated field, as shown in Figure 3-5.

Live Data view requires that a connection to a testing server, either local or remote, be properly established in the Site Definition dialog box. If Dreamweaver is unable to complete the connection, an error message appears with several possible solutions listed.

Cross-Reference   Live Data view is extremely helpful in building your Web applications. Find out more about how to use this important feature in Chapter 21.

Working with the Status Bar

The status bar is found at the bottom of the Document window. Embedded here are three important tools: the Tag Selector, the Window Size pop-up menu, and the Download Indicator. These helpful status bar tools provide the Web designer with several timesaving utilities.

Tag Selector

The Tag Selector is an excellent example of Dreamweaver's elegant design approach. On the left side of the status bar, you see a listing of the current HTML tags. When you first open a blank page in Dreamweaver, you see only the <body> tag. If you type a line of text and then press Enter (Return), the paragraph tag <p> appears. Your cursor's position in the document determines which tags are displayed in the Tag Selector. The Tag Selector keeps continuous track of where you are in the HTML document by displaying the tags surrounding your current cursor position. This becomes especially important when you are building complex Web pages that use such features as nested tables.

Live Data View

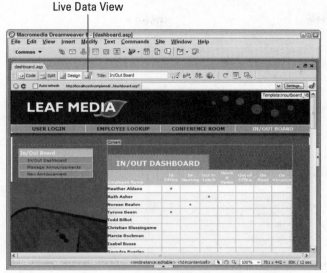

Figure 3-5: Live Data View lets you work on the Web page—altering the format and layout—while working with actual data from your application.

As its name implies, the Tag Selector does more than just indicate a position in a document. Using the Tag Selector, you can quickly choose any of the elements surrounding your current cursor. After an element is selected, you can modify or delete it. If you have the Property inspector (described later in this chapter) onscreen, choosing a different code from the Tag Selector makes the corresponding options available in the Property inspector.

Tip   If you want to quickly clear most of your HTML page, choose the <body> tag in the Tag Selector and press Delete. All graphics, text, and other elements you have inserted through the Document window are erased. Left intact is any HTML code in the <head> section, including your title, <meta> tags, and any preliminary JavaScript. The <body> tag is also left intact.

In a more complex Web page section, such as the one shown in Figure 3-6, the Tag Selector shows a wider variety of HTML tags. As you move your pointer over individual codes in the Tag Selector, they are highlighted; click one, and the code becomes bold. Tags are displayed from left to right in the Tag Selector—starting on the far left with the most inclusive (in this case, the <body> tag) and proceeding to the narrowest selection (here, the italic <h1> tag) on the far right.

As a Web page developer, you're constantly selecting elements in order to modify them. Rather than rely on the click-and-drag method to highlight an area—which often grabs unwanted sections of your code, such as <td> tags—use the Tag Selector to unerringly pick just the code you want. Dreamweaver's Tag Selector is a subtle but extremely useful tool that can speed up your work significantly.

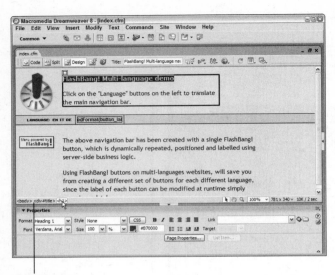

Tag Selector

Figure 3-6: The Tag Selector enables you to highlight just the code you want. Here, selecting the `<h1>` tag chooses only the portion of the text enclosed by that tag.

Right-clicking (Control+clicking) an item in the Tag Selector displays a menu that contains several tag-editing commands. Using this menu in Design view, you can remove the tag or select a `class` or `id` attribute for the tag. From either Design view or Code view, you can also modify the tag by choosing Edit Tag from the context menu.

Select, Hand, and Zoom Tools

With the greater layout flexibility made possible by CSS positioning comes the need for more powerful design tools. The first set of tools on the right side of the Status bar offer Dreamweaver designers a number of options for viewing and interacting with the page at design-time.

New In Dreamweaver With the new Zoom enhancement, Dreamweaver 8 joins the ranks of other page layout programs by offering designers the ability to magnify a page for finer design control. This set of tools — Select, Hand, Zoom, and the Set Magnification pop-up menu — work together. In the typical design session, Dreamweaver is generally in Select mode, which allows the selection and manipulation of any and all page elements. Choose the Hand tool to pan around a page that is larger than the Document window, whether the page is magnified or not.

The Zoom tool works in a multi-faceted fashion similar to graphic applications like Photoshop and Fireworks. Once you've selected the Zoom tool, you can:

✦ Magnify a specific section of the page by clicking on that area; each click increasing the magnification according to the values in the Set Magnification pop-up menu. For example, one click magnifies the area from 100% to 150% and then another goes to 200% magnification and so on. Press Alt (Option) to zoom out of an area.

✦ Drag a rectangle around the area to magnify to view that section at the highest magnification, as shown in Figure 3-7.

Figure 3-7: Get in tight for close-up work with Dreamweaver's Zoom tool.

To zoom in or out by a preset amount, select a value from the Set Magnification pop-up menu. Magnification options range from 6% to 6400% You can also opt to zoom in on a specific selection by choosing Fit Selection, the width of the page by choosing Fit Width, or view the entire page by choosing Fit All. If you prefer to view the page at a specific magnification not found on the Set Magnification pop-up menu, you can enter the value directly in the field and press Tab; there's no need to enter the percent symbol, %.

Tip   If you're zoomed in or out of a page, double-click the Zoom tool to return to 100% magnification.

Keyboard shortcuts are also available for zooming in and out of the page. Press Ctrl+= (Command+=) to zoom in and Ctrl+- (Command+-) to zoom out.

To return to editing, the page — at any magnification level — click the Select tool.

Window Size Pop-up Menu

The universality of the Internet enables virtually any type of computer system from anywhere in the world to access publicly available Web pages. Although this accessibility is a boon to global communication, it forces Web designers to be aware of how their creations look under various circumstances — especially different screen sizes.

The Window Size pop-up menu gives designers a sense of how their pages look on different monitors. Located just right of center on the status bar, the Window Size pop-up menu indicates the screen size of the current Document window, in pixels, in *width* x *height* format. If you resize your Document window, the Window Size indicator updates instantly. This indicator gives you an immediate check on the dimensions of the current page.

The Window Size pop-up menu goes beyond just telling you the size of your screen, however — it also enables you to quickly view your page through a wide variety of monitor sizes. Naturally, your monitor must be capable of displaying the larger screen dimensions in order for you to select them.

To select a different screen size, click once on the expander arrow to the right of the displayed dimensions to bring up a menu listing the standard sizes, as shown in Figure 3-8. Click a size from the menu.

Note   If no sizes are listed in the status bar, you may be in Code view, described later in this chapter. Select View ⇨ Design to gain access to the Window Size pop-up menu. If you can see the menu, but the options are disabled, your Document window is maximized (this happens only in the Dreamweaver integrated workspace for Windows users).

Figure 3-8: You can change your current screen size to any of seven standard sizes — or add your own custom sizes — with the Window Size pop-up menu.

The standard sizes, and their most common uses, are as follows:

✦ 592w

✦ 536 x 196 (640 x 480, Default)

✦ 600 x 300 (640 x 480, Maximized)

✦ 760 x 420 (800 x 600, Maximized)

✦ 795 x 470 (832 x 624, Maximized)

✦ 955 x 600 (1024 x 768, Maximized)

✦ 544 x 378 (MSN TV, formerly WebTV)

The first option, 592w, is the only option that does not change the height as well as the width. Instead, this option uses the current window height and just alters the width.

Tip   You can set up your own custom screen settings by choosing Edit Sizes from the Window Size pop-up menu. This option opens the Status Bar category of the Preferences dialog box. Chapter 4 describes how to modify the pop-up list.

The dimensions offered by the Window Size pop-up menu describe the entire editable area of a page. The Document window has been carefully designed to match specifications set by the primary browsers. Both the left and right margins are the same width as both the Netscape and Microsoft browsers, and the status bar matches the height of the browser's bottom row as well. The height of any given browser environment depends on which toolbars are being used; however, Dreamweaver's menu bar is the same height as the browsers' menu bars.

Tip
If you want to compensate for the other browser user-interface elements, such as the toolbar and the Address bar (collectively called *chrome*), you can decrease the height of your Document window by approximately 72 pixels. Combined, Netscape Navigator's toolbar (44 pixels high) and Address bar (24 pixels high) at 68 pixels are slightly narrower than Internet Explorer's total chrome. Microsoft includes an additional bottom separator that adds 6 pixels to its other elements (toolbar, 42 pixels; and Address bar, 24) for a total of 72 pixels. Of course, with so many browser variables, the best design course is to leave some flexibility in your design.

Download Indicator

So, you've built your Web masterpiece, and you've just finished uploading the HTML, along with the 23 JPEGs, 8 audio files, and 3 Flash movies that make up the page. You open the page over the Internet and — surprise! — it takes five minutes to download. Okay, this example is a tad extreme, but every Web developer knows that opening a page from your hard drive and opening a page over the Internet are two vastly different experiences. Dreamweaver has taken the guesswork out of loading a page from the Web by providing the Download Indicator.

The Download Indicator is located to the right of the Window Size item on the status bar. As illustrated in Figure 3-9, Dreamweaver gives you two values, separated by a slash character:

✦ The cumulative size of the page, including all the associated graphics, plugins, and multimedia files, measured in kilobytes (K)

✦ The time it takes to download at a particular modem connection speed, measured in seconds (sec)

Tip
You can check the download size of any individual graphic by selecting it and looking at the Property inspector — you can find the file size in kilobytes next to the thumbnail image on the left.

The Download Indicator is a handy real-world check. As you build your Web pages, it's a good practice to monitor your file's download size — both in kilobytes and seconds. As a Web designer, you ultimately have to decide what your audience will deem is worth the wait and what will have them reaching for that Stop button. For example, the graphic shown in Figure 3-8 is attractive and, at under 10K, it helps keep the entire page at an acceptable 50K. Remember that all the component parts of a page make up the total file weight shown in the Download Indicator.

Cross-Reference
Not everybody has the same modem connection. If you are working with an intranet or on a broadband site, you can set your connection speed far higher. Likewise, if your site gets a lot of traffic, you can lower the connection speed. Change the anticipated download speed through Dreamweaver's Preferences dialog box, as explained in Chapter 4.

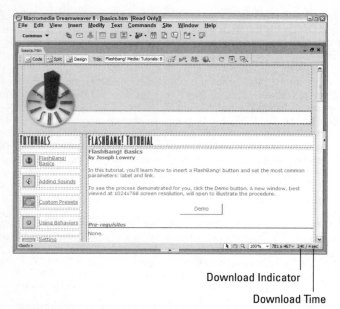

Download Indicator

Download Time

Figure 3-9: Note the Download Indicator whenever you lay out a page with extensive graphics or other large multimedia files.

Accessing the Toolbars

Regardless of the job—whether it's hanging a picture or fixing a faucet—work goes faster when your tools are at your fingertips. The same principle holds true for Web site building: The easier it is to accomplish the most frequently required tasks, the more productive you'll be as a Web designer. Dreamweaver puts a number of repetitive tasks, such as previewing your page in a browser, just a function key away. However, there are far more necessary operations than there are function keys. In an effort to put needed functionality right up front, Dreamweaver incorporates three toolbars—Standard, Document, and Style Rendering— located across the top of the Document window. One other toolbar is available only when you are in Live Data view and another when you're in Code or Split view.

Note   Although the Insert bar is also listed under View ⇨ Toolbars, along with the Standard and Document toolbars, its central role in the Dreamweaver workspace warrants separate coverage. See the section "Selecting from the Insert Bar," later in this chapter.

The Document Toolbar

The Document toolbar gives you quick access to commands that affect the entire document. Like the Standard toolbar, you can hide and show the Document toolbar with a menu command: View ⇨ Toolbars ⇨ Document. One of the Document toolbar's best features is the quick and easy access it offers to changing your Web page's title, as shown in Figure 3-10.

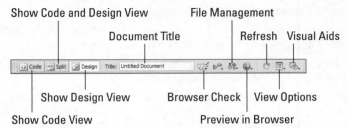

Figure 3-10: The Document toolbar offers easy access to an important element of a Web page, the title.

The first set of buttons in the Document toolbar is dedicated to the various views: Code, Code and Design, and Design. These buttons are mutually exclusive because only one view can be shown at a time. To the right of the first three buttons is one more view-related button: Live Data view. As previously explained, when Live Data view is enabled, Dreamweaver sends your page to the testing server and incorporates the results in an editable format on the screen. When you switch to Live Data view, another toolbar becomes visible; it is described later in this chapter in the section "The Live Data Toolbar."

Next to the Live Data View button is a text field for displaying and altering the title of your document. Dreamweaver, by default, titles every new page *Untitled Document*. Not only is it considered bad form to keep this default title, search engines need a relevant title to properly index a site. To change a page title, enter the new text in the Title field and press Enter (Return) to confirm your modification.

Checking for Browser Errors

With the wide range of browsers in the market today—many with different rendering capabilities—Web designers need to keep a close eye on their page from start to finish. Dreamweaver's browser-checking features are both automatic and on-demand. By default, Dreamweaver checks every page upon opening and displays a different Browser Check icon depending on whether errors are found.

Dreamweaver checks the page against whichever browsers you specify in the Target Browsers dialog box, opened by choosing Settings from the Browser Check menu. You have the option of choosing any or all of six different browsers and specifying the minimum acceptable browser version.

The Browser Check menu offers these options:

✦ **Check Browser Support:** Checks the current page against the browser versions selected in the Settings dialog box.

✦ **Next Error:** Displays the first (or next) problem Dreamweaver found in Split view with the cause of the error marked with a wavy red underline. Mouse over the error to see an explanation of the error in a tooltip; Dreamweaver also lists the browser or browsers in which the error occurs.

✦ **Preview Error:** Displays the prior error, again marked with a red wavy underline.

✦ **Show All Errors:** Opens the Target Browser Check category of the Results panel with a list of all the problems found in the document. Double-click an entry to highlight that error in Split view.

✦ **Auto-Check On Open:** Toggles the automatic checking feature.

✦ **Edit Ignored Error List:** Opens the Exceptions.xml file, which contains the browser check errors you want Dreamweaver to ignore during the checking process.

✦ **Settings:** Opens the Target Browsers dialog box where you specify which browser and browser version you want Dreamweaver to check.

The Auto-Check On Open option is enabled by default. I find that this is especially useful when working with pages inherited from another designer. However, I prefer to disable the automatic check when I'm creating documents from the ground up and run the Check Browser Support option when I'm finished.

For more details about using Dreamweaver's Browser Check features, see Chapter 29.

Managing Files

The File Management button contains Web-publishing–related commands. While maintaining a Web site, you'll often be required to make small alterations such as changing a bit of text or rescaling an image. I prefer to post these changes as quickly as possible to get the work off my virtual desk. The Get and Put options, along with the Check In and Check Out options, found on the Document toolbar under File Management, greatly simplify the process and speed up my work. Note that these commands are only available if you have defined a remote site as part of your site definition.

The File Management button offers these options:

✦ **Turn Off Read Only:** Unlocks the current file for editing. This command is enabled only if the current document is marked as read-only. (On the Macintosh, the Turn Off Read Only option is called Unlock.)

✦ **Get:** Transfers the remote file to the local site.

✦ **Check Out:** Marks the file as checked out and gets the remote file.

✦ **Put:** Transfers the local file to the remote site.

✦ **Check In:** Marks the file as checked in and puts the file to the remote site.

✦ **Undo Check Out:** Replaces the local version of the page with the remote version, effectively undoing any changes made on the local file.

✦ **Design Notes:** Opens the Design Notes dialog box for the current page.

✦ **Locate In Site:** Selects the current page in the file listings of the Site panel. This command is only enabled if the current file has been saved.

Previewing Your File

Although Dreamweaver gives you a good representation of what your page looks like when rendered in a browser, it's not perfect — even with Live Data view. So many variations exist among the different browser programs — not to mention versions — that you absolutely must test your page throughout the development process.

Selecting the Preview in Browser button on the Document toolbar presents a dynamic list of available browsers. All the browsers entered in Preferences appear first, with the primary and secondary browsers leading the list.

The final entry under the toolbar's Preview/Debug in Browser button is Edit Browser List. When invoked, this command opens the Preview in Browser category of Preferences, enabling you to add, remove, or otherwise manage the browsers on your system in relation to Dreamweaver.

Cross-Reference See Chapter 4 for details about working with the Preview in Browser preferences.

Easy Refresh and Viewing Options

The next two items on the Document toolbar are the Refresh button and the View Options button. Use the Refresh button when you've altered code directly in the Code view and you're ready to apply those changes in the Design view; this option is especially useful when the split-screen Code and Design view is in operation.

View Options is a welcome but somewhat schizophrenic button found on the far right of the Document toolbar. The options that it makes available depend on the view mode currently employed. If, for example, you're in Design view and choose View Options, you're given the option to hide various layout aids such as rulers and guides. If, on the other hand, you're in Code view, View Options toggles code-oriented functions such as Word Wrap and Line Numbers. Best of all, if you're in the split-screen Code and Design view, you get both sets of view options! The view options (all of which act as toggles) under Design view are as follows:

- ✦ Head Content
- ✦ Rulers
- ✦ Grid
- ✦ Guides
- ✦ Tracing Image
- ✦ Design View on Top

When in Code view, the View Options are as follows:

- ✦ Word Wrap
- ✦ Line Numbers
- ✦ Highlight Invalid HTML
- ✦ Syntax Coloring
- ✦ Auto Indent

The layout-oriented Visual Aids are only available in Design view. A series of options toggle Web page–focused helper tools on and off. One command, Show/Hide All Visual Aids, displays or conceals all of them at once. The Visual Aids are:

- ✦ Hide All Visual Aids
- ✦ CSS Layout Backgrounds
- ✦ CSS Layout Box Model
- ✦ CSS Layout Outlines
- ✦ Layer Outlines
- ✦ Table Widths
- ✦ Table Borders
- ✦ Frame Borders
- ✦ Image Maps
- ✦ Invisible Elements

The Standard Toolbar

When first enabled, the Standard toolbar appears across the top of the Dreamweaver window, whether you're in Design view or Code view. As shown in Figure 3-11, the Standard toolbar offers some of the most frequently used editing commands, familiar to you from any word processing program.

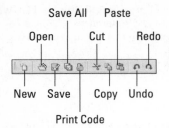

Save All   Paste

Open   Cut   Redo

New   Save   Copy   Undo

Print Code

Figure 3-11: The Standard toolbar contains frequently used editing commands.

The first group of buttons you find on the Standard toolbar includes New, Open, Save, Save All and Print Code. These create a new document, open an existing document, save the current document, save all open documents, and print the code of the current document. The next group of buttons includes Cut, Copy, and Paste. These enable you to place a selected item on the clipboard and then paste it into another location. The final group of buttons on the Standard toolbar includes the all-important Undo and Redo. Undo removes the effects of the last action you performed, and Redo repeats the most recent action or performs an undone action again.

You can toggle the Standard toolbar on and off by choosing View ➪ Toolbars ➪ Standard. In Windows, you can reposition the Standard toolbar by clicking one of the separator bars between the toolbar buttons and then dragging. If you drag the Standard toolbar away from the edge of the window, it becomes a floating toolbar. You can dock the Standard toolbar by dragging it to the top or bottom edge of the window. On a Macintosh, the Standard toolbar cannot be repositioned.

The Style Rendering Toolbar

One of the reasons CSS is increasingly used for layout is its capability to target different media types. While Web designers most frequently do not specify a media type at all—which is the same as using the same for all output devices—savvy designers take the time to optimize their pages for both screen and printer at a minimum.

New In Dreamweaver

In all, the W3C specification recognizes six different media types: Screen, Print, Handheld, Projection, TTY, and TV. Through the Style Rendering toolbar (see Figure 3-12), Dreamweaver allows designers to switch from one type to another, if defined. This feature is extremely helpful for quickly converting a standard screen-based layout to one that is more print-friendly. As Web designers re-style their content to fit other devices, like handhelds, the Style Rendering toolbar becomes indispensable.

The final button on the Style Rendering toolbar toggles the rendering of CSS. This ability is extremely helpful when optimizing your CSS; for example, without CSS layout, you can quickly tell how a screen reader would approach your page and determine if content needs to be repositioned to make it more understandable.

The Coding Toolbar

The Coding toolbar is quite different from the toolbars in a number of ways. First, it's only available in Code view and, second, it's a vertical rather than horizontal toolbar. The Coding toolbar also cannot be repositioned in either Windows or Macintosh. These differences, however, quickly fall by the wayside once coders understand the power inherent in the toolbar.

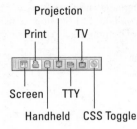

Projection
Print | TV

Screen | TTY
Handheld | CSS Toggle

Figure 3-12: The Style Rendering toolbar not only allows you to quickly switch between CSS media types, but you can also toggle CSS rendering on and off.

New In Dreamweaver

Much of the functionality is unique to the Coding toolbar (see Figure 3-13) although a few commands are replicated from elsewhere in the Dreamweaver interface for ease of use. The very top button, Open Documents, falls into the former category; click the Open Documents button to see a list of all files currently open. What distinguishes this button from other file listings — on the document tabs and under the Window menu — is the listing of the full path to the file rather than just the filename. The first time you have four files from separate folders, all named `index.html`, open at the same time, you'll immediately grasp the value of this feature.

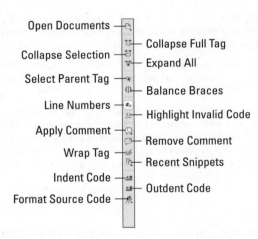

Open Documents
Collapse Selection — Collapse Full Tag
Select Parent Tag — Expand All
Line Numbers — Balance Braces
Apply Comment — Highlight Invalid Code
Wrap Tag — Remove Comment
Indent Code — Recent Snippets
Format Source Code — Outdent Code

Figure 3-13: The Coding toolbar hugs the left edge of Code view, easily accessible to the power coder.

The next group of functions relate to Dreamweaver's Code Collapse functionality. Included in this group are Collapse Full Tag, Collapse Selection, and Expand All. When clicked, Collapse Full Tag expands the current selection to the immediate tag and collapses the code. Press Alt (Option) while clicking either Collapse Full Tag or Collapse Selection to collapse all except the current tag or selection, respectively: a very useful feature when you're trying to focus on one aspect of your code.

The next group of buttons helps coders verify proper code. Select Parent Tag quickly highlights the tag surrounding the current selection while Balance Braces selects code within the matching set of parentheses, braces, or square brackets. Both the Line Numbers and Highlight Invalid Code can also be found in the Visual Aids menu option of the Document toolbar.

Comments are an essential building block of any programming language and Dreamweaver supports a wide range of them. Under the Apply Comments button, you'll find the option to insert HTML, JavaScript, CSS comments, and more. The different types of comments available are:

✦ <!– HTML Comments –>

✦ // CSS or JavaScript single line style comments

✦ /* CSS or JavaScript block style comments */

✦ 'Visual Basic single line style comments

✦ ASP, ASP.NET, JSP, PHP, or ColdFusion style comments, depending on the application server used

Each of the comments options wrap a selection in the chosen comment style; in the case of single line style comments, the comments are placed at the start of each selected line. If no code is highlighted, an empty comment of the desired type is inserted.

Paired with the Apply Comment button is one for deleting them, Remove Comment. The Remove Comment feature uncomments any selected code and will remove multiple comments unless they are nested. In the case of nested comments, only the outer comments are deleted.

Need a quick way to add a parent tag to a selection? Choose Wrap Tag and you can easily enter the desired outer element, along with any desired attributes and values. Press Enter (Return) to confirm your choices and the parent tag code is inserted.

You can wrap content with much more than a single tag through the Recent Snippets button. The Recent Snippets feature lists the 10 most recently used snippets, which can be either wrap or block type.

The final buttons on the Coding toolbar are used for styling your code. The Indent Code and Outdent Code buttons move selected code blocks in or out according to the options set in the Code Format category of Preferences. The final button, Format Source Code, allows you to style either the entire document or a selection of your code according to the Code Format Settings — which, along with another code style option, Tag Libraries — is also available under this menu.

The Live Data Toolbar

Dreamweaver's Live Data view has its own toolbar, shown in Figure 3-14. Enabling the Auto Refresh option forces Dreamweaver to update the data in the page whenever its data format is altered. For example, if you include a date field in your page, you might want to alter the format from something like March 31, 2006 to 31 March, 2006. The Auto Refresh option is particularly helpful when your data is enclosed by a Repeat Region server behavior. Auto Refresh, however, does not apply when you modify the HTML formatting, such as when you make selected text bold or alter its color. To see the HTML format changes applied to all the Live Data, click the Refresh button on the Live Data toolbar.

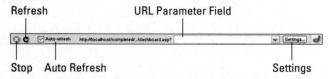

Figure 3-14: Live Data view has its own toolbar.

The Live Data toolbar also includes a field for entering URL parameters. This feature is handy when the dynamic content on your page requires an argument passed from a form or other method. By entering different values in the URL field, you can test your page under a variety of different data conditions.

Selecting from the Insert Bar

The Insert bar holds the items most frequently used — the primary colors, as it were — when designing Web pages. You can select everything from images to ActiveX plugins to HTML comments from the Insert bar. Figure 3-15 illustrates the Insert bar.

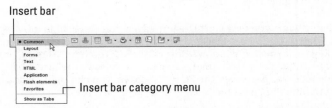

Figure 3-15: Switch categories from the pop-up menu on the Insert bar.

The Insert bar is divided into separate categories of objects: Common, Layout, Forms, Text, HTML, Application, Flash elements, and Favorites. Additional advanced categories are available for various server-side scripting languages: ASP, ASP.NET, CFML Basic, CFML Flow, CFML Advanced, JSP, PHP, and XSLT. These advanced categories are available only when the currently open document is of the relevant file type, as determined by its file extension. Table 3-1 shows the file extensions related to each category.

Table 3-1: File Types for Advanced Categories

Insert Bar Category	Related File Extensions
ASP	.asp
ASP.NET	.aspx, .ascx
CFML Basic	.cfm, .cfc
CFML Flow	.cfm, .cfc
CFML Advanced	.cfm, .cfc
JSP	.jsp
PHP	.php, .php3
XSLT	.xsl

The initial view is of the Common category. Switch from one category to another by selecting the appropriate choice from the category menu (see Figure 3-16).

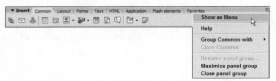

Figure 3-16: You can switch your Insert bar view from menu to tab and back again.

Tip   If you prefer the Insert bar tab view rather than the menu view, choose Show As Tabs from the bottom of the category menu. To switch back, choose Show As Menu from the Insert bar Options menu, as shown in Figure 3-16.

If the Insert bar is not available when you first start Dreamweaver, you can enable it by choosing Window ➪ Insert, View ➪ Toolbars ➪ Insert, or by pressing the keyboard shortcut, Ctrl+F2 (Command+F2). Likewise, choosing Window ➪ Insert, View ➪ Toolbars ➪ Insert, or the shortcut again, closes the Insert bar. On a Macintosh, you can also remove the Insert bar from your screen by clicking its Close button. In the PC workspaces, you can right-click any toolbar and deselect Insert to hide the Insert bar.

To reposition the Insert bar, do one of the following:

✦ In the workspaces on Windows, the Insert bar can be docked at the top or bottom of the Dreamweaver window, or it can be undocked and treated as a floating panel. To move the Insert bar, first switch to Tab view by choosing Show As Tabs from the Insert bar's category menu. Next, move the cursor over the gripper at the upper-left corner of the Insert bar so that the cursor changes to a four-headed arrow; then drag the Insert bar to the desired location. When it is floating, you can also move the Insert bar by clicking the drag bar and dragging, but the Insert bar can only be docked again using the gripper.

✦ On a Macintosh, you can move the Insert bar by clicking the drag bar at the left of the Insert bar and dragging to another location.

Tip   When the Insert bar is floating, you can dock other panels with it by dragging the tab of the panel onto the Insert bar. You can also drag the Insert bar on top of other panels, but only if they are floating. You cannot combine the Insert bar with panels that are already docked to the Dreamweaver window.

The following sections describe each category in the Insert bar.

Common Objects

The most frequently used HTML elements, aside from text, are accessible through the Common category of the Insert bar.

The Insert bar in Dreamweaver uses menu buttons in each category, like the Images and Media menus in the Common category. Menu buttons are identifiable by a small downward-pointing arrow to the right of the button. Numerous objects are contained within each menu group; when you choose an object, that object becomes the default item for the menu. For example, if you choose Image Placeholder from the Images menu group, the icon for that menu item is displayed in the Insert bar. Image Placeholder then becomes the default until another item from the group, such as Image or Fireworks HTML, is chosen. The very first time any menu button is accessed, no default object yet exists, and you must choose an object from the menu group.

The Common category contains three submenus: Images, Media, and Templates. Everything from basic images to the navigation bar is available from the Images group, as shown in Figure 3-17. Dreamweaver facilitates the inclusion of external elements — such as multimedia animations, Java applets, plugins, and ActiveX controls — through the Media group of the Insert bar's Common category. Templates are special Dreamweaver documents that define the layout and visual design of a page. The most common template options are found under the Template menu on the Insert bar's Common category.

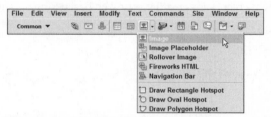

Figure 3-17: Graphic-related objects are grouped under the Images menu in the Common category.

Many of the common objects open a dialog box that enables you to browse for a file or specify parameters. If you prefer to enter all your information (including the necessary filenames) through the Property inspector or in Code view, you can turn off the automatic appearance of the dialog box for some objects when inserted through the Insert bar or the menus. Choose Edit ➪ Preferences and, from the General category, clear the Show Dialog When Inserting Objects option. In the Common category, this option affects the Hyperlink, Email Link, Named Anchor, Insert Table, Image, Image Placeholder, and Flash objects.

Note

Additional Preferences settings, located in the Accessibility category of the Preferences dialog box, also cause dialog boxes to appear when you insert an object using the Insert bar. These accessibility dialog boxes appear even if the Show Dialog When Inserting Objects option is clear.

Layout Objects

You use the Layout category of the Insert bar to work with tables, <div> tags, layers, and frames — objects that enable you to define the layout of your page. Dreamweaver offers you three ways to work with tables. You can use Standard mode (where you define the structure of a table using dialog boxes, menu commands, and the Property inspector); Expanded Table mode (where the table structure is made more obvious for easy modification); and Layout mode (where you create tables and cells by drawing them). Switch between these three mutually exclusive modes by clicking their buttons in the Layout category. The Layout category also contains objects for manipulating table structure, such as those for adding a row or column, as shown in Figure 3-18. The Frames menu button lists a full range of frame layouts.

Figure 3-18: Whether working with `<divs>` or `<table>` tags, the Layout category has what you need.

 Note   Because of the visual nature of tables and layers, many of the objects in the Layout category can be used only in Design view.

Forms Objects

The form is the primary method for implementing HTML interactivity. The Forms category of the Insert bar gives you the basic building blocks for creating your Web-based form, as shown in Figure 3-19.

Figure 3-19: Implementing forms is a key aspect of Web applications.

Text Objects

The text objects represent the most commonly used text formatting HTML tags, such as those needed to emphasize text, change the font face, or create bulleted lists (see Figure 3-20). 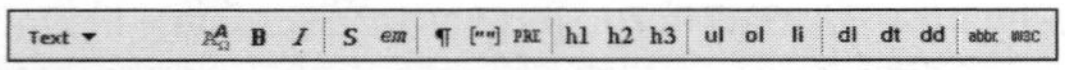

Figure 3-20: Change the format of selected text by choosing a Text object.

The Text objects behave differently, depending on whether you are working in Design view or Code view. If you are working in Code view, Dreamweaver puts you in charge, and simply surrounds whatever text is selected with the appropriate HTML tags. If no text is selected, the tag pair is inserted at the current text insertion point.

In Design view, Dreamweaver also surrounds selected text with the appropriate tag pair. But in some situations, Dreamweaver does more than blindly surround the selected text with the specified HTML tags. The following examples illustrate the additional processing that occurs in Design view:

✦ In Design view the Paragraph, Preformatted Text, Heading 1, Heading 2, and Heading 3 objects are treated as mutually exclusive. If you select text that is formatted as a Heading 1, and then you click the Heading 2 button on the Insert bar, Dreamweaver not only surrounds the selected text with `<h2></h2>` tags, but also removes the `<h1></h1>` tags that were there before. In Code view, Dreamweaver simply adds the `<h2></h2>` tags without automatically removing the `<h1></h1>` tags. This is inappropriate coding and should be avoided.

✦ When you select one or more paragraphs of text in Design view and then click the Unordered List button, Dreamweaver creates a bulleted list by inserting `<ul></ul>` tags around the selected text, as in Code view. But in Design view, Dreamweaver additionally converts each paragraph to a separate item in that list by inserting the appropriate `<li></li>` tags. The same is true for Ordered lists and Definition lists.

In Design view, if no text is selected when you click one of the text formatting buttons in this category, no tags are added until you start typing. This feature helps prevent the inclusion of empty tag pairs within your document.

The Text category contains a single menu button: Characters. Certain special characters — such as the copyright symbol ((c)) — are represented in HTML by codes called *character entities*. Dreamweaver eases the entry of these complex, hard-to-remember codes with the Characters objects. The most commonly used characters are included as separate objects, and another button opens a dialog box with additional special characters from which to choose. The Characters category also contains objects for inserting a line break and a non-breaking space.

HTML

The objects in the HTML category of the Insert bar insert a variety of HTML tags, some of which have visual representation on the page, but most of which work behind the scenes. This category is made up of a single object for inserting the horizontal rule tag, and four menu buttons: Head, Tables, Frames, and Script, as shown in Figure 3-21.

Figure 3-21: Tags in the HTML category help with the overall structure of the page.

General document information — such as the title and any descriptive keywords about the page — are written into the <head> section of an HTML document. The Head menu objects enable Web designers to drop in these bits of code in a handy object format. Although Dreamweaver enables you to see the <head> objects onscreen via the View ⇨ Head Content menu option, you don't have to have the Head Content visible to drop in the objects. Simply click any of the objects, and a dialog box opens, prompting you for the needed information.

Both the Tables and Frames menus are intended to work in Code view, inserting basic HTML tags without parameters or additional structures. For example, the Table Tag object inserts just that and nothing more, whereas the Table object (found on both the Common and Layout categories) inserts the entire table structure with all the requested rows, columns, and cells. The Script menu objects simplify the task of adding custom scripts or server-side includes to your page.

Application Objects

Although the layout of a Web page and the dynamic content that fills it may vary widely, many of the structures underlying basic Web applications remain the same. For example, the same basic code that is used to insert employee records into a Human Resources database may be used to add a new entry into a database that maintains a DVD collection. Dreamweaver removes much of the tedium of scripting common Web applications by supplying objects in the Application category of the Insert bar.

With a single Application object, you can build an entire Web application that displays a list of records, enables you to navigate through them, displays which records are currently onscreen, and links to another page with detailed information from a selected record. Dreamweaver's Application objects can be used separately or together. The Master Detail Page Set object includes two other Application objects: the Recordset Navigation Bar object and the Recordset Navigation Status object.

Application objects, shown in Figure 3-22, are particularly powerful when combined with Dreamweaver's template feature. It's possible, for example, to create a basic Master Detail Page Set with the Application object and then apply a template to give the page a specific look and feel, thereby integrating it into a site. Numerous menu buttons bring almost all of Dreamweaver's server-side power to the Insert bar.

Figure 3-22: Common Web applications, such as the Master Detail Page Set, are created in one action with Dreamweaver's Application objects.

Flash Elements

Flash elements are Flash movies that can be configured in Dreamweaver. After a Flash element is added, its attributes are available in the Tag inspector for personalization. Dreamweaver ships with one Flash element, Image Viewer, which enables designers to easily create slide shows with a variety of animated transitions. Newly added Flash elements — whether from Macromedia or other developers — are also displayed in this category.

Favorites

Because you can choose from an overwhelming number of objects on the Insert bar, the Favorites category is a welcome and productive addition to Dreamweaver. Initially, no objects are displayed in the Favorites category — it's up to you to choose which objects to include. All modification of the Favorites category is handled through the Customize Favorite Objects dialog box (see Figure 3-23), which shows all the available objects on the left and the selected objects on the right. Objects can be grouped through use of a dotted-line separator.

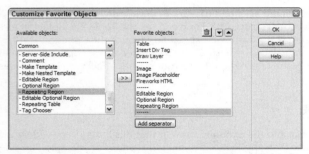

Figure 3-23: Use the Customize Favorite Objects dialog box to personalize your Insert bar for maximum productivity.

To add, remove, or modify objects in the Favorites category, follow these steps:

1. Choose Favorites from the Insert bar menu or tab.

2. Right-click (Control+click) and choose Customize Favorites from the context menu. You can actually perform the same action from any category/tab of the Insert bar to open the Customize Favorite Objects dialog box.

3. In the Customize Favorite Objects dialog, select the category holding the object you want to display in the Favorites category from the drop-down list under Available Objects. The All category displays every available object, sorted by category. If you know what category your object is in, it's quicker to select that category from the list.

4. Choose an object from those listed in the Available Objects area and select the double-arrow button. The selected item moves to the Favorite Objects list.

5. Repeat steps 3 and 4 to declare additional objects as favorites.

6. Change the order in which the objects are displayed by selecting an object and then clicking Up or Down to move the object left or right, respectively.

7. To delete an object from the Favorites list, select it and choose Remove.

8. To group objects together, choose Add Separator to insert a dotted-line divider.

9. When you're finished, click OK.

The objects you've selected, in the order you've specified, appear in the Favorites category. You can modify these objects at any time by re-opening the Customize Favorite Objects dialog.

ASP Objects

If you are creating Active Server Pages, the ASP category of the Insert bar can speed up the development of your code. Only available when the current document is named with an extension of .asp, this category contains the building blocks of an ASP page.

ASP.NET Objects

The ASP.NET category is only available on the Insert bar if the active document has a file extension of .aspx or .ascx. The objects in this category give you quick access to frequently referenced elements of an ASP.NET page.

CFML Objects

The CFML category of the Insert bar gives you access to the most frequently used objects in the ColdFusion toolbox. This category is only available on the Insert bar if the active document has a file extension of .cfm or .cfc. The first is Flow, which inserts ColdFusion markup tags that alter the flow of control through the code. The second is Advanced, which provides numerous advanced functions, such as those which enable you to transfer files and data using a variety of protocols.

Tip　You can find detailed descriptions of the ColdFusion tags in the Reference panel. To view the ColdFusion documentation, select Window ➪ Reference, and then select Macromedia CFML Reference from the Book drop-down list.

JSP Objects

The JSP category on the Insert bar includes objects that aid in adding code specific to JavaServer Pages. This category is only visible when the currently active document has a file extension of .jsp.

Tip   You can get information about JSP tags without leaving Dreamweaver. To view the JSP documentation, choose Window ➪ Reference, and then select Wrox JSP Reference from the Book drop-down list.

PHP Objects

The PHP category of the Insert bar enables you to insert code used in the PHP server-side scripting language. This category is only available if you are working in a document with the extension of .php, .php3, .php4, or .php5.

XSLT Objects

If you're building either an XSLT fragment or full page, you'll have access to the XSLT object category of the Insert bar. This category replicates features available from the Insert ➪ XSLT Objects menu and includes Dynamic Text, Repeat Region, Conditional Region, Multiple Conditional Region, and XSL Comment.

Getting the Most Out of the Property Inspector

Dreamweaver's Property inspector is your primary tool for specifying an object's particulars. What exactly those particulars are — in HTML, they are known as *attributes* — depends on the object itself. The contents of the Property inspector vary depending on which object is selected. For example, click anywhere on a blank Web page, and the Property inspector shows text attributes for format, font name, size, and so on. If you click an image, the Property inspector displays a small thumbnail of the picture, and the image's attributes for height and width, image source, link, and alternative text (see Figure 3-24).

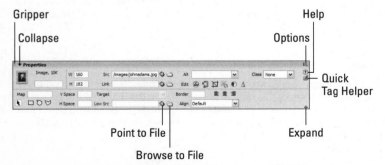

Figure 3-24: The Property inspector takes many forms, depending on which HTML element you select.

Manipulating the Property Inspector

You can enable the Property inspector by choosing Window ➪ Properties or selecting the keyboard shortcut, Ctrl+F3 (Command+F3). As with the Insert bar, the Property inspector can be closed by clicking the Close button (only available if the Property inspector is floating), unchecking Window ➪ Properties, or by choosing the keyboard shortcut again. You can also close the Property inspector by selecting Close Panel Group from the Options menu, which is accessed by clicking the Option button at the right of the Property inspector's title bar. On the PC, you can collapse the Property inspector so that only the title bar is left showing by clicking the Properties name on its window.

You can reposition the Property inspector in one of the following ways:

✦ If the Property inspector is floating, you can click and drag the drag bar that appears along the left edge of the window and move it to a new location. On Windows only, you can also click and drag any open gray area in the floating inspector itself, a difference between it and the Insert bar. This technique is handy for quickly moving the inspector aside, out of your way. When you move the floating inspector near the edge of the screen or near a window border, the Property inspector snaps to the edge of the window or screen.

✦ In the PC workspace, whether the inspector is docked or floating, you can move it by clicking on the gripper and dragging the inspector. In this workspace, the Property inspector can be docked at the top or the bottom of the Dreamweaver window. If you move or resize the Dreamweaver window, the docked Property inspector moves with the window.

The Property inspector initially displays the most typical attributes for a given element. To see additional properties, click the expander arrow in the lower-right corner of the Property inspector. Virtually all the inserted objects have additional parameters that can be modified. Unless you're tight on screen real estate, it's a good idea to keep the Property inspector expanded so you can see all your options.

Tip In addition to using the expander arrow, you can reveal (or hide) the expanded attributes by double-clicking any open gray area of the Property inspector.

Property Inspector Elements

Many of the attributes in the Property inspector are text boxes; just click in any one and enter a value. If a value already appears in the text box, whether a number or a name, double-click it (or click and drag over it) to highlight the information and then enter your new data — the old value is immediately replaced. You can see the effect of your modification by pressing the Tab key to move to the next attribute or by clicking in the Document window.

Using the Quick Tag Editor, you can make small additions to the code without switching to Code view. Located on the right of the Property inspector, just below the Help button, the Quick Tag Editor pops open a small window to display the code for the currently selected tag. You can swiftly change attributes or add special parameters not found in the Property inspector.

For several attributes, the Property inspector also provides drop-down list boxes that offer a limited number of options. To open the drop-down list of available options, click the arrow button to the right of the list box. Then choose an option by highlighting it.

Tip Some options on the Property inspector are a combination drop-down list and text box — you can select from available options or type in your own values. For example, when text is selected, the font name and size are combination list/text boxes.

If you see a folder icon next to a text box, you have the option of browsing for a filename on your local or networked drive or manually inputting a filename. Clicking the folder opens a standard Open File dialog box (called Select File in Dreamweaver); after you've chosen your file and clicked OK (Open or Choose on Macintosh), Dreamweaver inputs the filename and any necessary path information in the correct attribute.

Dreamweaver enables you to quickly select an onscreen file (in either a Document window or the Site panel) as a link, with its Point to File icon, found next to the folder icon. Just click and drag the Point to File icon until it touches the file (or the filename from the Site panel) that you want to reference. The path is automatically written into the Link text box.

Certain objects such as text, layers, and tables enable you to specify a color attribute. The Property inspector alerts you to these options with a small color box next to the text box. You can type in a color's name (such as **blue**) or its six-figure hexadecimal value (such as **#3366FF**), or select the color box. Choosing the color box opens a color picker, shown in Figure 3-25, that displays the colors common to both the Netscape and Microsoft browsers — the so-called *browser-safe colors*. You can go outside of this range by clicking the System Color Picker icon in the upper-right corner of the color picker. Selecting this icon opens a full-range Color dialog box in which you can choose a color visually or enter its red, green, and blue values or its hue, saturation, and luminance values.

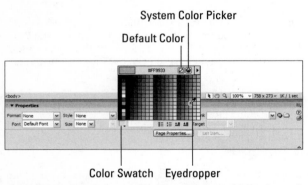

Figure 3-25: Dreamweaver's color picker enables you to choose from a wide selection of colors, from the palette or right off the desktop, with the Eyedropper tool.

The color picker in Dreamweaver is very flexible. Not only can you choose from a series of color swatches, but you can also select any color onscreen with Dreamweaver's Eyedropper tool. The Eyedropper button has two modes: If you select Snap To Web Safe from the color picker's context menu, the Eyedropper snaps the selected color to its nearest Web-safe neighbor; if you deselect Snap To Web Safe, colors are sampled exactly. If you'd like to access the system color picker, the color wheel button opens it for you. You can also use the Default Color tool, which deletes any color choice previously inserted. Finally, you can use the color picker's context menu to change the swatch set shown. By default, the Color Cubes view is shown, but you can also view swatches in a Continuous Tone configuration or in Windows OS, Macintosh OS, or Grayscale colors. Although the Web designer may not use these options frequently, Macromedia standardized the color picker across its product line to make it easier to switch between applications.

Tip   To close the color picker without selecting a color, click in the empty gray area at the top of the color picker.

On the PC, the Property inspector also includes an Options menu. Open this context-sensitive menu by clicking the Options menu icon, located in the upper-right corner of the Property inspector. The commands on this menu vary depending on what type of object has been selected in the Document window. Some basic commands, however, are always available, regardless of what has been selected, such as the following:

✦ **Help:** Opens a Help topic for the current Property inspector

✦ **Rename Panel Group:** Enables you to rename the Property inspector

✦ **Close Panel Group:** Closes the Property inspector

Note   Two additional commands that are typically available for panels, Group Properties With and Maximize Panel Group, are disabled for the Property inspector. You cannot dock the Property inspector with other panels, and you cannot change the height of the Property inspector.

Another aspect of the Property inspector is worth noting. The circled question mark in its upper-right corner is the Help button. Clicking this button invokes online Help and displays specific information about the particular Property inspector you're using.

Customizing Your Workspace with Dockable Panels

Dreamweaver is known for its powerful set of tools: behaviors, layers, and so much more. Dreamweaver presents its tools in a variety of panels, as shown in Figure 3-26. Panels can be combined into the same window; when grouped together in this way, each panel is displayed as a tab within the panel group. The panel groups can be floating or docked to each other. On the PC, the panel groups can also be docked within the Dreamweaver window.

Collapsed Panel Groups

Panels

Figure 3-26: Dreamweaver's many tools reside in panels, which can float anywhere on the screen, or, on the PC, can be docked within the Document window.

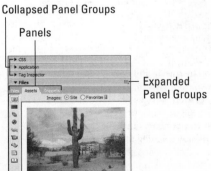

Expanded Panel Groups

Table 3-2 lists each of the panels available in Dreamweaver, along with a description and a cross-reference to chapters in this book that provide more information about the panel. It also lists a keyboard shortcut that you can use to open the panel. If the keyboard shortcut is different between Mac and Windows platforms, the Mac shortcut is listed in parentheses after the Windows shortcut.

Table 3-2: Dreamweaver Panels

Panel	Keyboard Shortcut	Description	Detailed Information
CSS Styles	Shift+F11 (N/A)	Enables you to create external and embedded CSS style sheets.	See Chapter 7
Layers	F2	Enables you to view and change some characteristics of layers.	See Chapter 11
Behaviors	Shift+F4	Enables you to create Dynamic HTML effects.	See Chapter 12
Databases	Ctrl+Shift+F10 (Command+Shift+F10)	Provides a bird's-eye view of all the connections currently defined for your site, enabling you to add new connections, browse tables, views, and stored procedures for each database, and add the necessary server-side include to use that connection.	See chapters in Part IV
Bindings	Ctrl+F10 (Command+F10)	Enables you to create recordsets and datasets and display that information on your page. You can also bind data to tag attributes and form elements and set the formatting for dynamic elements.	See chapters in Part IV
Server Behaviors	Ctrl+F9 (Command+F9)	Gives you access to prewritten server-side scripts that are used in applications. For example, you can use server behaviors to create, update, or delete records.	See Chapter 33
Components	Ctrl+F7 (Command+F7)	Enables you to quickly add new JavaBeans components (if you're using JSP) or Web Services (if you're using JSP or .NET), or ColdFusion components (if you're using ColdFusion). Setting up the JavaBeans or Web Service gives you full introspection to all the pieces of that component.	See Chapter 19
Files	F8	Manages the files in your local, remote, and testing sites.	See Chapter 5

Panel	Keyboard Shortcut	Description	Detailed Information
Assets	F11 (Option+F11)	Gives you access to many components that make up your site, including images, colors, URLs, Flash and Shockwave objects, movies, scripts, templates, and library items.	See the following: Images: Chapter 9 Colors: Chapter 8 URLs: Chapter 10 Flash: Chapter 24 Shockwave: Chapter 24 Movies: Chapter 25 Scripts: Chapter 6 Templates: Chapter 27 Library: Chapter 28
Snippets	Shift+F9 (N/A)	Gives you access to prewritten snippets of code for common scenarios.	See Chapter 6
Tag Inspector	F9 (Option+F9)	Displays a collapsible outline of the tags used on the current page, enabling you to quickly determine if tags are correctly nested, and to view and change tag attributes.	See Chapter 6
Search	F7 to open the Results panel and then choose the Search category	Shows the results of a Find All request.	See Chapter 8
Validation	F7 to open the Results panel and then choose the Validation category	When you validate a document, the results are displayed in this panel.	See Chapter 29
Target Browser Check	F7 to open the Results panel and then choose the Target Browser Check category	Displays results of a target browser check.	See Chapter 29
Link Checker	F7 to open the Results panel and then choose the Link Checker category	Shows the results when you check for broken links within your site.	See Chapter 10
Site Reports	F7 to open the Results panel and then choose the Site Reports category	Displays the output from a variety of site reports.	See Chapter 30
FTP Log	F7 to open the Results panel and then choose the FTP Log category	Lists the results of FTP operations.	See Chapter 5
Server Debug (Windows only)	F7 to open the Results panel and then choose the Server Debug category	Enables you to browse your page directly in Dreamweaver's Design window as if it were a Web browser. This is different from Live Data view because the page is not editable.	See Chapter 33

Continued

Table 3-2 *(continued)*

Panel	Keyboard Shortcut	Description	Detailed Information
Reference	Shift+F1	Presents extensive reference documentation for HTML, CSS, JavaScript, accessibility guidelines, and a variety of server-side scripting languages.	See Chapter 6
History	Shift+F10 (N/A)	Tracks each change you make, enabling you to undo and redo multiple steps at a time.	See Chapter 8
Frames	Shift+F2	Enables you to select and rename frames within a frameset.	See Chapter 16
Code Inspector	F10 (Option+F10)	Provides an alternative to Code view in a floating window.	See Chapter 6
Timelines	Alt+F9 (Option+F9)	Enables you to add and modify time-related Dynamic HTML effects, such as moving items across a page.	See Chapter 17

Hiding and Showing Panels

Because of the large number of panels available in Dreamweaver, your workspace can become cluttered very quickly. To reduce the amount of screen real estate taken up by the individual panels, but still utilize their power, Dreamweaver enables you to group multiple panels in a single window. These groups of related panels are called, not surprisingly, *panel groups*. Whenever one panel is docked with another in a panel group, each panel becomes accessible by clicking its representative tab. Selecting the tab brings the panel to the front.

You can also display individual panels by using the keyboard shortcuts listed in Table 3-2, or by using commands in the Window menu; a separate command opens each panel. Using any of these methods opens the panel or brings it to the top if it is hidden; if the panel is already on top, any of these actions collapses the panel group so that only its title bar is showing.

Tip   One very important keyboard shortcut to remember is the F4 key, which hides all panels. This shortcut immediately clears the screen of everything except the basic Document window—the Insert bar, the Property inspector, all toolbars, and all panels are immediately hidden, enabling you to enter content in your pages without distraction. Pressing F4 again restores all the hidden tools.

On the PC, the panel groups may be docked along the edges of the Dreamweaver window. In this situation, you can collapse all the panel groups to maximize your work area by clicking the button that appears along the border of the panel area, as shown in Figure 3-27. This action collapses only the panel groups docked on one edge of the screen, leaving intact toolbars, floating panels, or even panels docked along a different edge of the window.

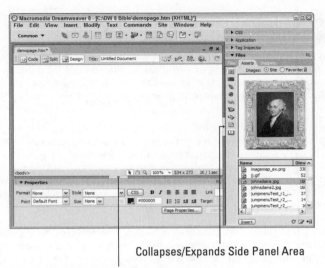

Collapses/Expands Side Panel Area

Collapses/Expands Bottom Panel Area

Figure 3-27: You can collapse all the panel groups along one edge of the screen with the click of a single button.

In any workspace, you can collapse an individual panel group so that just its title bar is showing. To do this, click the panel group name in the title bar, or click the small triangle next to the panel group name.

Tip

To resize any floating panel, click and drag its borders. On the Mac, you can resize only by dragging the resize handle in the bottom-right corner of a window. If the panel groups are docked together, you can drag the border of the panel area to resize all the panel groups in that area.

You can also right-click (Control+click) the title bar of the panel group or click the Options menu on the right of the title bar, and then select Maximize Panel Group from the drop-down list. This action expands the panel to the fullest possible height, but leaves the panel width unchanged.

Finally, if you want to close a panel group entirely so that even its title bar is not visible, click the Options menu located on the right of the title bar in an open panel group, and then select Close Panel Group from the drop-down list. You can also right-click (Control+click) in the title bar and then select Close Panel Group, even if the panel group is collapsed. The next time you open any panel within the group, the entire panel group opens automatically.

Note

The Options menu also gives you access to Help for the currently displayed panel, and may contain additional commands specific to the panel that is open.

Customizing Panel Groups

Dreamweaver comes with related panels already combined into panel groups. However, you're not limited to the predefined panel groups. In fact, the panel groups are completely customizable, giving you optimum control over your workflow. Moving panels from one group to another, creating new groups, and renaming panel groups are straightforward operations. If you want, you can also remove little-used panels from groups and reorder the panels within a group.

To move a panel from one group to another, start by opening the panel you want to move. Next, right-click (Control+click) in the title bar of the panel group, select Group *<panel>* With (in the context menu), and click the name of the panel group where you want the panel to reside. The same command is available from the Options menu, accessed by clicking the icon at the right of an open panel group's title bar. This command removes the current panel from its original panel group, and adds the panel's tab to the right of the existing tabs in the target panel group.

Tip   To reorder panels within a panel group, open the panel, right-click (Control+click) on the title bar of the panel group, select Group *<panel>* With and then click the name of the current panel group. This moves the currently open panel to the right-most position in the group. By repeatedly moving panels within the current group, you can achieve the order you want.

To create a new panel group, open a panel that you want to include in the new group and right-click (Control+click) in the title bar of the current panel group. Then choose Group *<panel>* With ➪ New Panel Group. This creates a new, separate panel group that contains the removed panel. Initially, the name of the new panel group is the same as the panel name, but you can change it, as explained in the following paragraph. You can add other panels to your new panel group, using the method described previously; your new panel group name automatically shows up in the context menu for the panel group. You can also dock the new panel group with others, and on the PC, you can dock the panel group within the Document window.

Note   Some caveats apply when customizing panels. You cannot combine panels with the Insert bar or the Property inspector without undocking the panels first. Also, if you customize your panel groups and then change workspace layouts, your customizations are lost.

Dreamweaver initially assigns a new panel group the same name as the first panel in the group. You can change this name — or the name of one of Dreamweaver's original panel groups — by choosing Rename Panel Group from the Options menu, accessed by clicking the icon at the right of an open panel group's title bar. The same command is available by right-clicking the panel group title bar.

How do you remove a panel from a panel group? First choose the Group *<panel>* With ➪ New Panel Group command on the Options menu to move the panel to its own group. Then close the panel group for the removed panel by right-clicking (Control+clicking) in the title bar and choosing Close Panel Group.

You can move a panel group by clicking the gripper icon in the panel group's title bar (see Figure 3-28) and dragging the window to any location on the screen.

Gripper

Expand/Collapse Arrow   Options

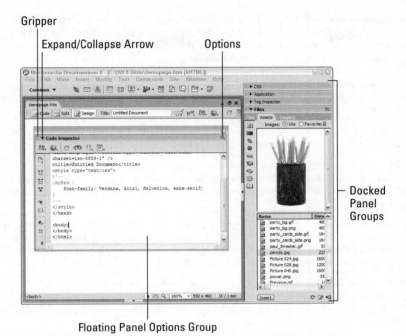

Floating Panel Options Group

Figure 3-28: Use the gripper to dock and undock panel groups.

In the Macintosh workspace, you can dock panel groups to each other and the left and right edges of the screen, but you cannot dock them with the Document window. On the PC, not only can you dock floating panel groups together, you can dock panel groups with the left and right edges of the screen as well as the Document window; when you move or resize the Dreamweaver window, the docked panels move, too. To dock panel groups, drag the window by the gripper over another panel group, or to the edge of the window, until the outline of the window changes to indicate it is in position. When you release the mouse button, the panel group is docked. Although you can move floating panels by dragging the title bar, panels can be docked only when you are dragging with the gripper.

Tip   On the PC, you are not limited to having your panels on one edge of the window. You can dock panels to both the left and right sides of the screen at the same time, although this reduces your work area considerably unless you have a large monitor.

Accessing the Menus

Like many programs, Dreamweaver's menus duplicate most of the features accessible through panels. Certain features, however, are available only through the menus in the Document window or through a corresponding keyboard shortcut. This section offers a reference guide to the menus when you need a particular feature or command. (Note to Windows users: The menus referred to here are those for the Document window and not the Files panel; the menu options particular to the Files panel are covered in Chapter 5.)

Almost every element placed in the Document window has a shortcut menu associated with it. To access a shortcut menu, right-click (Control+click) any area or object. The shortcut menus are context-sensitive and vary according to which object or area is selected. Using the shortcut menus can enhance your productivity tremendously.

Following is a glance at the various Dreamweaver Document window menus. You can find explanations of each command (along with its keyboard shortcuts for Windows and Mac) on this book's Web site.

✦ **File menu** — Contains commands for file handling and overall site management. All import, export, and convert features are also found in this menu.

✦ **Edit menu** — Provides the commands necessary to quickly modify your page — or recover from a devastating accident. Many of the commands (Cut, Copy, and Paste, for example) are standard in other programs; others, such as Paste HTML, are unique to Dreamweaver.

✦ **View menu** — As you build your Web pages, you may find that it's helpful to be able to turn certain features on and off. The View menu centralizes all these commands and switches between Design view and Code view. One of the handiest commands hides all the visual aids with a keyboard shortcut, Ctrl+Shift+I (Command+Shift+I).

✦ **Insert menu** — Contains the same items available through the Insert bar. In fact, if you add additional objects, you can see your objects listed on the Insert menu the next time you start Dreamweaver. All objects selected from the Insert menu are added to the page at the current cursor position.

✦ **Modify menu** — Inserting objects is less than half the battle of creating a Web page. Most Web designers spend most of their time adjusting, experimenting with, and tweaking the various elements. The Modify menu lists all Dreamweaver's commands for altering existing selections.

✦ **Text menu** — The Internet was initially an all-text medium, and despite all the multimedia development, the World Wide Web hasn't traveled far from those beginnings. The Text menu commands cover overall formatting as well as text-oriented functions such as spell checking.

✦ **Commands menu** — Commands are user-definable code capable of affecting almost any tag, attribute, or item on the current page — or even the current site. Commands increase your productivity by automating many of the mundane, repetitive tasks in Web page creation.

Dreamweaver comes with several handy commands, but they are truly just the tip of the iceberg. Commands are written in a combination of HTML and JavaScript and can be created and modified by any capable JavaScript programmer.

The first few items on the Commands menu enable you to create, add, and manage custom commands. The additional items represent standard commands that come with Dreamweaver. If you add custom commands to Dreamweaver, they also appear in this menu.

✦ **Site menu** — Web designers spend a good portion of the day directly interacting with a Web server: putting up new files, getting old ones, and generally maintaining the site. To ease the workflow, Dreamweaver groups site-management commands in their own menu.

✦ **Window menu** — The Window menu manages both program and user-opened windows. Through this menu you can open, close, arrange, bring to the front, or hide all the additional Dreamweaver screens.

Tip

The commands for Dreamweaver's various windows, panels, and inspectors are toggles. Select a command once to open the window; select it again to close it.

✦ **Help menu** — Provides access to Dreamweaver's excellent online Help, as well as special examples and lessons.

Summary

In this chapter, you were introduced to some of the power of Dreamweaver and had a look at its well-designed layout. From the Insert bar to the various customizable panels, Dreamweaver offers you an elegant, flexible workspace for creating next-generation Web sites. Here are some of the key points covered in this chapter:

✦ Windows users can choose from two basic workspace layouts, whereas Macintosh users have the freedom to structure their workspace unencumbered. The same basic tools are available in each layout; the primary difference involves where the panels are located.

✦ The Document window is your main canvas for visually designing your Dreamweaver Web pages. This window includes simple, powerful tools such as the Tag Selector, Zoom, and the Window Size pop-up menu.

✦ Frequently used tools are available on Dreamweaver's various toolbars. The toolbars can be displayed or hidden depending on your personal preferences.

✦ The Insert bar is Dreamweaver's toolbox. Highly customizable, the Insert bar holds the elements you need most often, grouped into useful categories. You can customize one category of the Insert bar, Favorites, and place your own most commonly used objects together.

✦ Dreamweaver's mechanism for assigning details and attributes to an HTML object is the Property inspector. The Property inspector is context-sensitive, and its options vary according to the object selected.

✦ Many of Dreamweaver's tools reside in separate panels, which can be combined into panel groups. Panel groups can be docked or floated, hidden or shown depending on your workflow.

✦ Dreamweaver's full-featured menus offer complete file manipulation, a wide range of insertable objects, the tools to modify them, and extensive online — and on the Web — help. Many menu items can be invoked through keyboard shortcuts.

In the next chapter, you learn how to customize Dreamweaver to work the way you work by establishing your own preferences for the program and its interface.

✦   ✦   ✦

Setting Your Preferences

◆ ◆ ◆ ◆

In This Chapter

Dreamweaver made to order

Customizing Dynamic HTML specs

Extending preferences outside Dreamweaver

Specifying your code formatting

◆ ◆ ◆ ◆

Everyone works differently. Whether you need to conform to a corporate style sheet handed down from the powers that be or you think, "it just looks better that way," Dreamweaver offers you the flexibility to shape your Web page tools and your code output. This chapter describes the options available in Dreamweaver's Preferences and then details how you can instruct Dreamweaver to format source code your way.

Customizing Your Environment

The vast majority of Dreamweaver's settings are controlled through the Preferences dialog box. You can open Preferences by choosing Edit ⇨ Preferences (Dreamweaver ⇨ Preferences) or by using the keyboard shortcut Ctrl+U (Command+U). Within Preferences, you find 20 different subjects listed on the left side of the screen. As you switch from one category to another by selecting a name from the Category list, the options available for that category appear in the main area of the dialog box. Most changes to Preferences take effect immediately after you close the window by clicking the OK button. This chapter covers all the options available in each category; the categories are grouped by function rather than by order of appearance in the Category list.

General Preferences

Dreamweaver's General Preferences, shown in Figure 4-1, cover the program's appearance, user operation, and fundamental file settings. The appearance of the program's interface may seem to be a trivial matter, but Dreamweaver is a program for designers and coders — to whom work environment is extremely important. These user-operation options are based purely on how you, the user, work best. The following sections describe the various options available from this screen.

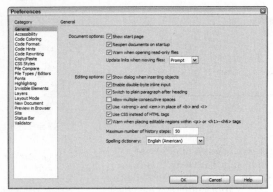

Figure 4-1: Dreamweaver's General Preferences enable you to change your program's appearance and certain overall operations.

Document Options

The first area of the General category, Document Options, determines how you work with HTML and other files.

Tip

In choosing all the preferences, including the General ones, you can work in two ways. If you are a seasoned Web designer, you probably want Dreamweaver to work in your established manner to minimize the learning curve. If you're just starting out as a Web-page creator, work with the default options for a while and then try other options. You should know right away which style works for you.

Show Start Page Option

The Start page is a very helpful innovation that gets you up and running right away in Dreamweaver—whether you're just starting out or in the middle of editing a full site. If you're new to the program, Dreamweaver's start page gives you quick access to tutorials and a tour of the key features. After you've worked with the program for a while, you'll appreciate the immediate access to the more recently opened files and one-click creation of static or dynamic pages. The start page displays when Dreamweaver launches or when no document is currently open.

The Dreamweaver start page is extremely handy, but if it doesn't fit within your workflow, you can disable it. Clear the Show Start Page checkbox and, depending on your other settings and actions, the next time Dreamweaver opens you see either a blank, documentless environment or your previously opened files.

The start page changes from time to time because it includes a Flash movie (located in the lower-right corner) that uses dynamically set parameters to display different information if you're connected to the Internet when running Dreamweaver.

Reopen Documents On Startup Option

In an ideal world, a Web designer works on one page at a time, carefully crafting each and every detail. Well, it's far from an ideal world and often designers are working on several pages simultaneously—and over multiple sessions. If your workflow fits into this real-world model, this option makes your life a little easier.

When I'm working on a Web application, I often have four to six pages (or more) open simultaneously. If I'm continuing my work from one day to the next, the first thing I do is to make sure I've opened all the files that I need. With the Reopen Documents On Startup option selected, Dreamweaver automatically opens any files left unclosed when I last quit the program. If this option is left unselected, you see either the start page or a documentless environment.

Warn When Opening Read-Only Files Option

Read-only files have been locked to prevent accidental overwriting. Optionally, Dreamweaver can warn you when such a file is opened. The warning is actually more than just an alert, however. Dreamweaver provides an option on the warning dialog box to make the file writable, (or check it out if you're using the Check In/Check Out feature). Alternatively, you can just view the file.

Cross-Reference See Chapter 30 for more on the Check In/Check Out feature.

Although Dreamweaver enables you to edit the file either way, if the document is still read-only when you save your changes, the Save As dialog box appears, and you are prompted to store the file under a new name.

Update Links Option

As your site grows in complexity, keeping track of the various links is an increasingly difficult task. Dreamweaver has several enhanced features to help you manage links, and the Update Links When Moving Files option is one of them. Dreamweaver can check each link on a page when a file is moved — whether it is the Web page you're working on or one of the support files, such as an image, that goes on the page. The Update Links option determines how Dreamweaver reacts when it notes an altered link.

By default, the Update Links When Moving Files option is set to Prompt, which causes Dreamweaver to alert you to any link changes and requires you to verify the code alterations by clicking the Update button. To leave the files as they are, click the Don't Update button. You can elect to have Dreamweaver automatically keep your pages up to date by selecting the Always option from the Update Links drop-down list. Finally, you can select the Never option, and Dreamweaver ignores the link changes necessary when you move, rename, or delete a file.

As a general rule, I keep my Update Links option set to Always. It is a very rare circumstance when I intentionally maintain a bad link on my Web page. Likewise, I recommend using the Never option with extreme caution.

New In Dreamweaver If you're wondering how you can alter your workspace arrangement and can't find the Change Workspace button that used to be on the General category of Preferences, don't fret. Dreamweaver has replaced that simple toggle with a more comprehensive toolset called Workspace Layout. With this new facility, Windows users can quickly choose a new panel layout from the default choices (Coder, Designer, and Dual Screen) or create custom ones; Macintosh users have Default and Dual Screen options along with the option for creating custom layouts. Just set up your workspace environment how you'd like it and choose Window ➪ Workspace Layout ➪ Save Current (see Figure 4-2). You can even rename or delete saved custom layouts by selecting Window ➪ Workspace Layout ➪ Manage.

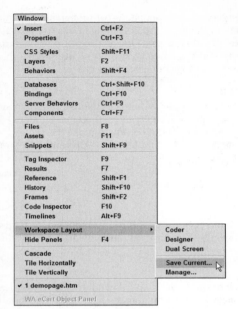

Figure 4-2: Save and recall your favorite workspace layouts through the new Workspace Layouts menu option.

Editing Options

The second main section of the General category of the Preferences consists of numerous checkbox options you can turn on or off. Overall, these options fall into the user-interaction category, reflecting how you like to work. Take the Show Dialog When Inserting Objects option, for example. Some Web creators prefer to enter all their attributes at one time through the Property inspector and would rather not have the dialog boxes appear for every inserted object. Others want to get their file sources in immediately and modify the rest later. Your selection depends on how you want to work. The following sections describe various other options.

Show Dialog When Inserting Objects Option

By default, almost all the objects that Dreamweaver inserts — via either the Insert bar or the Insert menu — open an initial dialog box to gather needed information. In some cases, the dialog box enables you to input a URL or browse for a source file. Turning off the Show Dialog option causes Dreamweaver to insert a default-sized object, or a placeholder, for the object in this circumstance. You must then enter all attributes through the Property inspector.

Tip   To selectively avoid the prompts, leave this option checked, but press Ctrl+click (Option+click) on an object to skip the prompt.

Enable Double-Byte Inline Input Option

Some computer representations of languages, primarily Asian languages, require more raw descriptive power than others. The ideogram for *snow*, for example, is far more complex than a four-letter word. These languages need twice the number of bytes per character and are known as *double-byte languages*. In versions of Dreamweaver before 2, all double-byte characters had to go through a separate text-input window, instead of directly into the Document window.

Dreamweaver now simplifies the page creation process for double-byte languages with the Enable Double-Byte Inline Input option. If selected, this option enables double-byte characters to be entered directly into the Document window. To use the old method of inserting such characters, deselect this option.

Switch To Plain Paragraph After Heading Option

This may seem like a small thing, but this nifty little feature is one of my favorites. If this option is not enabled, pressing Enter (Return) after a heading tag (<h1> or <h2>, for example) causes the next line to maintain the heading style. Check the Switch To Plain Paragraph After Heading option so that the next line is a standard paragraph (<p>) tag.

Use the Switch To Plain Paragraph After Heading option to speed up your workflow. You'll almost always want a heading followed by a plain paragraph. This option gets rid of one more click of the mouse or shortcut key, making your workflow that much faster.

Allow Multiple Consecutive Spaces Option

Some designers prefer adding two spaces after every period, or they like to use multiple spaces to indent paragraphs to maintain a print-type appearance. Without this option selected, this type of spacing requires pressing Ctrl+Shift+Space (Command+Shift+Space) to add a   to the document. Check this option, and Dreamweaver adds the 's for you, without requiring the additional keyboard shortcut.

Tip   This option may seem wonderful at first, but I recommend leaving it unchecked. Having a single space after a sentence is the standard online and is even becoming standard practice in most print applications. (You'll find no double spaces in this little tome.) Enabling this option only encourages bad habits.

Use <strong> and <em> In Place Of <b> and <i> Option

In new HTML and XHTML standards, the <b> and <i> tags are deprecated because they don't imply any structural significance to the text they surround. Many screen readers may even completely ignore the <b> and <i> tags. Check this box to use the more syntactically correct <strong> and <em> tags in their place.

The option to use <strong> and <em> tags enables you to create more descriptive HTML code. Individuals using screen readers benefit, and you make your code more syntactically correct, further separating style from content.

Use CSS Instead Of HTML Tags Option

This one little option is key to many aspects of Dreamweaver's design-time behavior. In an effort to encourage best Web page design practices — which favor Cascading Style Sheet (CSS) over HTML tags — Dreamweaver, by default, now writes CSS styles for page properties, text formatting, and more. However, should you need to work with legacy pages and maintain the code as written, you might find HTML tags to be more suitable, and you should deselect this option.

Warn When Placing Editable Regions Within <p> or <h1>-<h6> Tags

Sometimes Dreamweaver adheres a bit too strictly to the rules for my taste — and this preference addresses one of those times. In Dreamweaver templates, editable regions define areas of the page that can be altered in the pages derived from templates. Most often, designers wrap editable regions around block elements such as headings or paragraphs. However, there are occasions when it is advantageous to make just the content within block tags editable and lock the surrounding tags themselves. I, for example, apply this technique when I want a template-derived page to always start with a single <h1> heading, but know that the heading will always be different. Dreamweaver regards this approach with suspicion because such an editable region will not allow the user to press Enter (Return) and add more block level tags.

New In Dreamweaver

To prevent novices from inadvertently limiting the expansion of content within an editable region, Dreamweaver displays an alert whenever a template is saved that has an editable region within a block element. You can continue the save — and the subsequent updating of template-derived pages — or you can cancel and correct the situation. In previous versions, Dreamweaver displayed this error without recourse, even when the coding it was protesting to was intentional. By disabling this option, you can avoid having to repeatedly dismiss the alert.

If you're new to Dreamweaver and its template technology, I recommend that you enable this option. Doing so will likely save you grief on your initial template-derived pages and prevent you from having to redo the templates. However, once you've worked with templates for a while, I suggest you disable this option; the technique of embedding editable regions within block tags is a common one and not having to acknowledge the alert over and over again, a major time-saver.

Maximum Number Of History Steps Option

Almost every Dreamweaver action, except the mouse click, is listed in the History panel. These steps can be undone by moving the slider on the History panel or choosing Edit ⇨ Undo. A limit exists, however, to the number of steps that can be tracked. By default, the limit is set to 50.

Although 50 history steps are more than enough for most systems, you can alter this number by changing the Maximum Number Of History Steps value. When the maximum number of history steps is exceeded, the oldest actions are wiped from memory and made unrecoverable. The history steps are not discarded when a file is saved.

Spelling Dictionary Option

The Dictionary option enables you to select a spell-checking dictionary from any of those installed. In addition to the standard English-language version, which has 15 options — Danish, Dutch, English (American), English (British), English (Canadian), Finnish, French, German (Classic), German (New Spelling), Italian, Norwegian (Bokml), Portuguese (Brazilian), Portuguese (Iberian), Spanish, and Swedish — additional dictionaries exist online. As of this writing, dictionaries in the following other languages are also available: German, Spanish, Swedish, French, Italian, Brazilian-Portuguese, and Catalan. You can download these dictionaries from Macromedia's Dreamweaver Exchange at www.macromedia.com/support/dreamweaver/documentation/dictionary.html. After a dictionary is downloaded, save the .dat file in the Configuration\Dictionaries folder and restart Dreamweaver.

To select a different dictionary for spell checking, select the Dictionary option button and choose an item from the drop-down list. Dreamweaver also maintains a personal dictionary (although it's not visible on the list) to hold any words you want Dreamweaver to learn during the spell-checking process. So the next time you spell check a technical document, just click Add for each word Dreamweaver catches that you want it to remember. That word is then added to the personal dictionary, and you never have to worry about it again.

Preferences for Invisible Elements

By their nature, all HTML markup tags remain unseen to one degree or another when presented for viewing through the browser. You may want to see certain elements while designing a page, however. For example, adjusting line spacing is a common task, and turning on the visibility of the line break tag <br> can help you understand the layout.

Dreamweaver enables you to control the visibility of 13 different codes, as well as of dynamic data and server-side includes — or rather their symbols, as shown in Figure 4-3. When, for example, a named anchor is inserted, Dreamweaver shows you a small gold shield with an anchor emblem. Not only does this shield indicate the anchor's position, but you can also manipulate the code with cut-and-paste or drag-and-drop techniques. Moreover, clicking a symbol opens the pertinent Property inspector and enables quick changes to the tag's attributes.

Figure 4-3: You can show or hide any or all of the 13 invisible elements listed in the Preferences dialog box and determine the appearance of recordset fields and includes.

Tip   Temporarily hide all invisible elements by deselecting View ➪ Visual Aids ➪ Invisible Elements.

The 13 items controlled through the Invisible Elements panel are as follows:

✦ Named Anchors

✦ Scripts

✦ Comments

✦ Line Breaks

✦ Client-Side Image Maps

✦ Embedded Styles

✦ Hidden Form Fields

✦ Form Delimiter

✦ Anchor Points For Layers

✦ Anchor Points For Aligned Elements

✦ Visual Server Markup Tags (ASP, CFML)

✦ Nonvisual Server Markup Tags (ASP, CFML)

✦ CSS Display: None

Most of the Invisible Elements options display or hide small symbols in Dreamweaver's visual Document window. Several options, however, show an outline or another type of highlight. Turning off Form Delimiter, for example, removes the dashed line that surrounds a form in the Document window.

Tip   You may have noticed that the ColdFusion tags and Active Server Page tags are combined into one symbol, Server Markup tags. Dreamweaver's capability to handle dynamic pages generated by databases makes these invisible elements essential. I generally leave the Nonvisual Server Markup Tags option unchecked, because these icons flag server-side coding in the page and tend to interrupt the flow of the design.

Dreamweaver-developed pages often include references to *dynamic text*. Dynamic text is text that is replaced by an entry from a recordset when the page is processed by the application server. Dreamweaver uses what is called *dot notation* in programming circles to fully display these names, such as {rsMaillist.EmailAddress}, enclosed in curly braces. When designing a page, the field names may be longer than the actual data, and the full dot notation becomes a visual hindrance rather than an aid. In these situations, you may want to use Dreamweaver's alternative dynamic text syntax, an empty pair of curly braces: {}. Enable this option from the Show Dynamic Text As drop-down list on the Invisible Elements panel.

When designing dynamic sites you may often use server-side includes to speed development and updates. Unfortunately, rendering these in the design window can often cause problems if you are conditionally including multiple files. Uncheck the Show Contents Of Included Files option to disable rendering your server-side includes.

Highlighting Preferences

Dreamweaver is extremely extensible — custom functions are better handled, server-side markup is more acceptable, and more third-party tags are supported. Many of these features depend on hidden capabilities that are not noticeable in the final HTML page. The Web designer, however, must take them into account. Dreamweaver employs user-selectable highlighting to mark areas on a Web page under construction.

The Highlighting panel of the Preferences dialog box, shown in Figure 4-4, enables you to choose the highlight color for eight different types of extended objects:

✦ Mouse-Over

✦ Editable Regions

✦ Nested Editable regions

✦ Locked Regions

✦ Library Items

✦ Third-Party Tags

✦ Untranslated Live Data

✦ Translated Live Data

In each case, select the color swatch to open Dreamweaver's color picker and choose a high-light color. Then, use the Eyedropper to pick a color from the Web-safe palette or from the desktop. After you've chosen an appropriate color, be sure to select the related Show check-box so that the highlighting is displayed; all but the highlighting for nested editable regions can be toggled to be shown or hidden.

Note   You can see the Locked Region highlighted in Templates only if you open the Code view; the Display view only highlights Editable Regions. You see the Live Data highlighting only while actually viewing your page in Live Data mode.

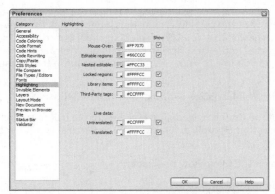

Figure 4-4: Use the Highlighting preferences to control how template regions, library items, and third-party tags appear in the Document window.

Status Bar Preferences

The Status Bar is a handy collection of different tool sets: the Tag Selector, the Select tool, the Hand tool, the Zoom tool, the Set Magnification pop-up menu, the Window Size pop-up menu, and the Connection Speed indicator. The Status Bar category of the Preferences dialog box, shown in Figure 4-5, controls options for two of the tools.

Window Sizes Option

The Window Sizes list at the top of the Status Bar category shows the current options for the Window Size pop-up menu. This list is completely user-editable and enables you to add new window sizes, modify existing dimensions, add descriptions, or delete rarely used measurements.

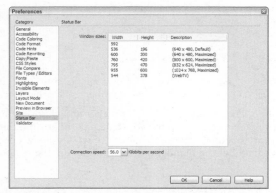

Figure 4-5: Use the Status Bar category to evaluate your real-world download times.

As discussed in Chapter 3, the Window Size pop-up is a Dreamweaver feature that enables you to instantly change your screen size so that you can view and build your page under different monitor conditions. To change any of the current dimensions, simply click the measurement you want to alter and enter a new value. You can also change any description of the existing widths and heights by clicking in the Description column and entering your text. Although you can enter as much text as you like, it's not practical to enter more than about 15 to 20 characters.

To enter a new set of dimensions in the Window Sizes list box, follow these steps:

1. From the Status Bar category of the Preferences dialog box, locate the last entry in the current list. If the last entry is not immediately available, use the vertical scroll bar to move to the end.

2. Click once in the Width column on the line below the last entry.

3. Enter the desired width of the new window size in pixels.

4. Press Tab to move to the Height column.

5. Enter the desired height for the new window size.

6. Press Tab again.

7. Optionally, you can enter short, descriptive text in the Description column, and then press Tab when you're finished.

8. To continue adding new sizes, repeat Steps 2 through 6. Click OK when you finish.

Caution   You don't have to enter the word *pixels* or the abbreviation *px* after your values in the Width and Height columns of the Window Size list box, but you can. If you enter any dimensions under 20, Dreamweaver converts the measurement to its smallest possible window size, 20 pixels.

Connection Speed Option

Dreamweaver understands that not all access speeds are created equal, so the Connection Speed option enables you to check the download time for your page (or the individual images) at a variety of rates. The Connection Speed setting evaluates the download statistics in the status bar. You can choose from seven preset connection speeds, all in kilobits per second: 14.4, 28.8, 33.6, 56, 64, 128, and 1,500. The lower speeds (14.4 through 56) represent various dial-up modem connection rates — if you are building a page for the mass market, you should consider selecting 56. Use the 128 setting if your audience connects through an ISDN line. If you know that everyone will view your page through a direct LAN connection, change the connection speed to 1,500.You are not limited to these preset settings. You can type any desired speed directly into the Connection Speed text box. If you find yourself designing for an audience using DSL or cable modems, change the Connection Speed to 150 or higher.

File Types / Editors Preferences

Refinement is often the name of the game in Web design, and quick access to your favorite modification tools — whether you're modifying code, graphics, or other media — is one of Dreamweaver's key features. The File Types / Editors category, shown in Figure 4-6, is where you specify the program you want Dreamweaver to call for any file type you define.

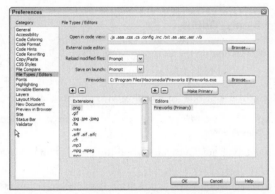

Figure 4-6: Assign your favorite HTML, graphics editors, and more through the newly extended File Types / Editors category of the Preferences dialog box.

Open In Code View Option

It's not just an HTML world — many other code types are commonly found on a Web designer's palette such as XML, XSL, PHP, or Perl. Dreamweaver's internal code is full-featured enough to handle a wide variety of code and, with the Open In Code View option, you can determine which types you'd like it to handle. By default, JavaScript (.js), text (.txt), and Active Server Application (.asa) files are automatically opened in Code view. Dreamweaver attempts to open any other selected file type in Design view.

If you find yourself hand-editing other file types, such as XML files, you can add their extension to the Open in Code View field. Separate extensions with a space, and be sure to begin each one with a period.

External Code Editor Option

Dreamweaver recognizes the importance of your choice of a text editor. Although Dreamweaver ships with two extremely robust code editors — as well as its excellent built-in code editor — you can opt to use any other program. To select your editor, enter the path in the External Code Editor text box or click the Browse button to choose the appropriate executable file.

Two editors, BBEdit for Macintosh and HomeSite for Windows, are integrated with Dreamweaver to varying degrees. Both of the editors can be called from within Dreamweaver, and both have Dreamweaver buttons for returning to the main program — switching between the editor and Dreamweaver automatically updates the page. Like Dreamweaver's internal HTML editor, BBEdit highlights the corresponding code to a selection made in Dreamweaver; this property does not, however, extend to HomeSite. You specify and control your external editor selection with the following options.

Note   HomeSite 5.5+ is included on both the Studio 8 and Dreamweaver 8 CD-ROMs.

Enable BBEdit Integration (Macintosh only) Option

Dreamweaver for Macintosh ships with this option activated. If you prefer to use another editor, deselect this option. Uncheck this box to enable the External Code Editor fields.

Reload Modified Files Option

The drop-down list for this setting offers three options for working with an external editor:

✦ **Prompt:** Detects when files are updated by another program and enables you to decide whether to update them within Dreamweaver.

✦ **Always:** Updates the file in Dreamweaver automatically when the file is changed in an outside program.

✦ **Never:** Assumes that you want to make all updates from within Dreamweaver yourself.

Personally, I prefer to have Dreamweaver always update my files. I find that it saves a couple of mouse clicks — not to mention time.

Save On Launch Option

Any external HTML editor — even the integrated HomeSite or BBEdit — opens and reads a previously saved file. Therefore, if you make any changes in Dreamweaver's visual editor and switch to your editor without saving, the editor shows only the most recently saved version. To control this function, you have three options:

✦ **Prompt:** Determines that unsaved changes have been made and asks you to save the file. If you do not, the external editor reverts to the last saved version.

✦ **Always:** Saves the file automatically before opening it in the external editor.

✦ **Never:** Disregards any changes made since the last save, and the external editor opens the previously saved file.

Here, again, as with Reload Modified Files, I prefer to always save my files when switching back and forth.

Tip If you try to open a file that has never been saved in an external editor, Dreamweaver prompts you to save it regardless of your preference settings. If you opt not to save the file, the external editor is not opened because it has no saved file to display.

Fireworks Option

Dreamweaver enjoys a tight integration with its sister graphics program, Macromedia Fireworks. To empower Dreamweaver with Fireworks capabilities, such as Launch and Edit, Dreamweaver has to know where Fireworks is installed. If you install Studio 8, the path to Fireworks is prefilled for you and shown in this option. If you install Fireworks separately, you'll need to click Browse and locate the Fireworks executable.

Defining Editors for Different File Types

Dreamweaver has the capability to call an editor for any specified type of file at the click of a button. For example, when you import a graphic, you often need to modify its color, size, shape, transparency, or another feature to make it work correctly on the Web page. Rather than starting your graphics program independently, you load the image, make the changes, and resave the image. Dreamweaver enables you to send any selected image directly to your editor. After you've made your modifications and saved the file, the altered image appears automatically in Dreamweaver.

The capability to associate different file types with external editors applies to more than just images in Dreamweaver. You can link one or more editors to any type of media — images, audio, video, even specific kinds of code. The defined external editor is invoked when the file is double-clicked in the Files panel. Because the editors are assigned according to file extension, as opposed to media type, one editor can be assigned to GIF files and another to JPEGs. The selection is completely customizable.

Note If you have the same file type both defined to Open in Code View and set up in the editor list, the file defaults to opening in Code view.

When you double-click a file in the Files panel, that file type's primary editor runs. Dreamweaver offers the capability to define multiple editors for any file extension. You might, for instance, prefer to open certain JPEGs in Fireworks and others in Photoshop. To choose an alternative editor, right-click (Control+click) the filename in the Files panel and select the desired program from the Open With menu option. The Open With option also enables you to browse for a program.

To assign an editor to an existing file type, follow these steps:

1. Select the file type from the Extensions list.

2. Click the Add (+) button above the Editors list. The Add External Editor dialog box opens.

3. Locate the application file of the editor and click Open when you're ready. You can also select a shortcut or alias to the application.

4. If you want to select the editor as the primary editor, click Make Primary while the editor is highlighted.

To add a new file type, click the Add (+) button above the Extensions list and enter the file extension — including the period — in the field displayed at the bottom of the list. For multiple file extensions, separate each extension with a space, as shown here:

```
.doc .dot .rtf
```

Tip   Looking for a good almost-all-purpose media editor? QuickTime Pro makes a great addition to Dreamweaver as the editor for AIFF, AU, WAV, MP3, AVI, MOV, animated GIF files, and others. The Pro Player is wonderful for quick edits and optimization, especially with sound files. It's available from the Apple Web site (`www.apple.com/quicktime`) for both platforms for around $30.

Finally, to remove an editor or a file extension, select it and click the Delete (–) button above the corresponding list. Note that removing a file extension also removes the associated editor.

Cross-Reference   Make sure that your graphics program is adept at handling the three graphic formats used most on the Web: GIFs, JPEGs, and PNG images. Macromedia makes Fireworks, a graphics editor designed specifically for the Web, which integrates seamlessly with Dreamweaver. In fact, it integrates so nicely that this book includes an entire chapter on it, Chapter 23.

Copy/Paste Preferences

Dreamweaver has beefed up its copy and paste prowess when it comes to text. Now, when a copied section of any text document — including those from Microsoft Office — is pasted into Dreamweaver, Dreamweaver automatically converts the formatting to HTML, preserving the full range of original formatting. Moreover, you can even drag entire documents right onto the Dreamweaver Web page — what happens next depends on the settings in the Copy/Paste preferences, shown in Figure 4-7.

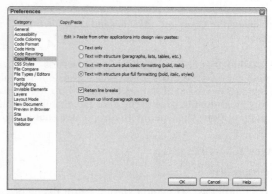

Figure 4-7: The Copy/Paste settings affect any text pasted into Dreamweaver.

New In Dreamweaver   With the Copy/Paste options, you can determine how text from documents outside of Dreamweaver is added to the page. Best of all, this feature works hand-in-glove with the new Paste Special command, which gives you the opportunity to change the setting on a case-by-case basis.

The four main Copy/Paste options are:

✦ **Text Only:** Pastes completely unformatted text; even line breaks or paragraphs are removed.

✦ **Text with Structure:** Pastes unstyled text while retaining structured elements such as lists, paragraphs, line breaks and tables.

✦ **Text with Structure Plus Basic Formatting:** Adds simple formatting, such as bold, italic, and underline, to structured text. If the text is copied from an HTML document, the pasted text retains any HTML text style tags, including `<b>`, `<i>`, `<u>`, `<strong>`, `<em>`, `<abbr>`, and `<acronym>`.

✦ **Text with Structure Plus Full Formatting:** Pasted text keeps all structure and formatting. If the copied text retains inline CSS styles, Dreamweaver pastes them as well.

Two other options are available for modifying your copy/paste preferences. The Retain Line Breaks maintains line breaks in pasted text; if you choose Text Only, this option is disabled. The Clean Up Word Paragraph Spacing option works with the Text with Structure and Text with Structure Plus Basic Formatting choices to remove additional space between paragraphs.

New Document Preferences

Dreamweaver has greatly improved the New Document interface. You can now quickly choose which type of document you want to create, as well as select from built-in page designs and CSS. The New Document dialog appears each time you press Ctrl+N (Command+N) or choose File ⇨ New. Use the New Document preferences (shown in Figure 4-8) to refine how you interact with this New Document dialog box.

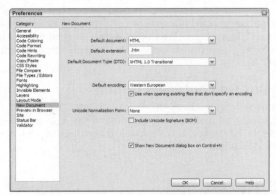

Figure 4-8: Choose your default document extensions, encoding, and HTML version.

Default Document Type Option

This list menu contains all the default document types in the New Document dialog box (File ⇨ New). Choose which document type you want to be the default for quickly creating new documents. If you design ASP applications more often than plain HTML files, just choose ASP VBScript or ASP JavaScript from the list menu. You can also choose templates, XML files, PHP files, and the list goes on.

Default Extension Option

You can define a default extension for each document type in Dreamweaver. This means that if your server requires all ASP files to have the .dan extension and all your ColdFusion pages to have the .joe extension, you can change the extension to fit your needs. Simply enter the desired file extension, with a leading period.

Default Document Type (DTD)

A document type or DTD is a line of code found at the top of an HTML page that lets the browser know how to render the following file. DTDs are also used to validate the page against a chosen set of specifications.

New In Dreamweaver

The Default Document Type (DTD) option allows to select which DTD, if any, you'd like to include by default. This option is originally set to XHTML 1.0 Transitional, a standard now among many Web designers. You can choose from other XHTML and HTML selections. You can always change the DTD by choosing File ➪ Convert and then selecting one of the entries presented in the sub-list.

Encoding Options

The Encoding options determine the character set in which you want your Web page to be displayed. The Default Encoding option for the English version of Dreamweaver is initially set to Western European. Developers of multilanguage sites may find it better to choose Unicode (UTF-8) as the encoding option. New pages use whatever choice you make from the Default Encoding list; however the encoding can be altered in the Page Properties on a per-page basis. When opening existing pages without an encoding, the selected encoding is added if the accompanying option (Use when opening existing files that don't specify an encoding) is checked.

The Unicode Normalization Form list enables you to choose how the Unicode characters are converted to binary format. The Include Unicode Signature option determines whether a byte order mark (BOM) is attached to the file. Neither of these options has any effect unless the Default Encoding is set to Unicode (UTF-8).

Show New Document Dialog Box On Control+N Option

If you consistently use the same document type, uncheck this box to prevent the New Document dialog box from coming up when you press Ctrl+N (Command+N). This can measurably speed up creating new documents. Leave this box checked to see the New Document dialog box every time you create a new document.

Adjusting Advanced Features

Evolution of the Web and its language, HTML, never ends. New features emerge, often from leading browser developers. A developer often introduces a feature similar to those marketed by his competitors but that works in a slightly different way. The HTML standards organization — the World Wide Web Consortium, also known as the W3C — can then endorse one approach or introduce an entirely new method of reaching a similar goal. Eventually, one method usually wins the approval of the marketplace and becomes the accepted coding technique.

To permit the widest range of features, Dreamweaver enables you to designate how your code is written to accommodate the latest Web features: accessibility options, layers, and style sheets. The default preferences for these elements offer the highest degree of cross-browser and backward compatibility. If your Web pages are intended for a more specific audience, such as a Netscape Navigator-only intranet, Dreamweaver enables you to take advantage of a more specific feature set. Furthermore, Dreamweaver also gives you control over its Layout Mode, enabling you to set options globally or on a site-by-site basis.

Accessibility Preferences

Dreamweaver offers much improved support for accessibility options. With the passing of the Section 508 statute (`www.usdoj.gov/crt/508/508home.html`), all government agencies are required to make their sites as accessible as possible (and making your own site accessible isn't such a bad idea). Dreamweaver makes that transition just a little easier for you by allowing you to manage which accessibility options you want to enable by using the accessibility preferences, as shown in Figure 4-9.

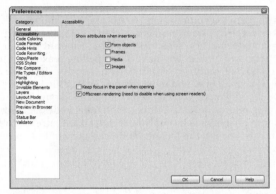

Figure 4-9: Choose the tags where you want additional accessibility options to appear while you are coding.

Show Attributes When Inserting Option

Check the box next to each tag for which you want to view additional accessible options when you insert that object into your page. If you check the box next to Form objects, you get an expanded dialog the next time you insert any form element, such as a text field or checkbox.

Inserting a form element with the accessibility options enabled gives you a much wider range of options, including labels and the capability to set an access key and tab index. The same holds true for frames, media, and images.

Keep Focus in the Panel When Opening Option

When Dreamweaver opens a panel, such as the Files panel or CSS Styles panel, it typically returns focus to the Document window, either in Design view or Code view. If you're using a screen reader, you'd then need to locate and select the opened panel to work in it. Apply the Keep Focus in the Panel when Opening option to maintain selection in the opened panel.

Offscreen Rendering Option (Windows only)

Dreamweaver uses double buffering (drawing into an offscreen bitmap before drawing to the screen) to prevent flickering. Unfortunately, this confuses screen readers, devices that help blind people use applications (such as Dreamweaver). If you're using a screen reader, disable this option.

Layout Mode Preferences

In Layout Mode, a column in a table can be set to automatically match the size of the browser window; if the window is resized, the column is stretched or shrunk accordingly. To maintain the structure of such tables and other complex layout devices, professional designers often include an added row on the top or bottom of the table. This additional row is sized to be 1-pixel high, with the same number of cells as the table itself. Within each cell (except for the resizable cell) is a transparent GIF image, sized to match the cell's dimensions. This image is sometimes called a *shim* — Dreamweaver and other Macromedia applications refer to it as a *spacer*. One of the major functions of the Layout Mode category of Preferences is managing these spacers.

Dreamweaver automatically includes spacers if a column is set to Autostretch and the Autoinsert Spacers When Making Autostretch Tables option is selected, as it is by default (see Figure 4-10). If you decide not to include spacers, select Never. Which should you choose? I find that spacers definitely help; and, unless you have a compelling reason not to use them — such as a corporate edict, I advise you to go with the default option. Because a spacer is an actual graphic image, albeit a small one, you must include such a file in every site. Dreamweaver creates one for you if you like, or you can select an existing one. The option for creating or locating a spacer is offered when an autostretch table is designated. However, if you prefer not to worry about spacers each time you create an autostretch table, you can preselect an existing image to use through the Layout Mode category of Preferences. This option is set on a sitewide basis.

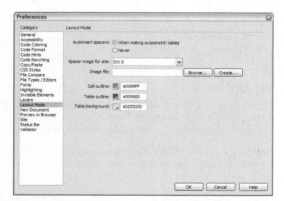

Figure 4-10: Spacers are used to maintain a table's complex layout; you can set which spacer is used on a site-by-site basis through the Layout Mode category of Preferences.

To set a spacer image for a site, follow these steps:

1. In the Layout Mode category of Preferences, choose the site to be affected from the Spacer Image For Site drop-down list.

2. If you do not have a transparent, single-pixel GIF image available, click Create. Dreamweaver opens the Save Spacer Image File As dialog box.

3. Select a location within your site to store the spacer file. If you like, you can also rename the file from `spacer.gif` to something else.

4. If a graphic on your site is using a transparent, single-pixel GIF image, click Browse to locate the graphic. As noted earlier, Fireworks uses such a file, stored as `spacer.gif`. If you have Fireworks-sliced images in your site, I recommend selecting `spacer.gif` as your Dreamweaver spacer to reduce the number of redundant spacer files on the site.

The remaining options found under the Layout Mode category are concerned with the various colors used:

✦ **Cell Outline:** The color of the layout cell when it is selected; the default is bright blue.

✦ **Table Outline:** The color of the outline surrounding the entire table; the outline is initially set to dark green.

✦ **Table Background:** The color of the layout table where no layout cell has been drawn; a light gray is the default background color.

Should your site design make any of the colors unusable — if, for example, your page background is the same light gray as the default table background — you can alter the colors by selecting the color swatch and choosing a new color from the standard color picker.

Layers Preferences

Aside from helping you control the underlying coding method for producing layers, Dreamweaver enables you to define the default layer. This capability is especially useful during a major production effort in which the Web development team must produce hundreds of layers spread over a Web site. Being able to specify in advance the initial size, color, background, and visibility saves numerous steps — each of which would have to be repeated for every layer. Figure 4-11 shows the layout of the Layers category of the Preferences dialog box. The controls accessible through the Layers category are described in the following sections.

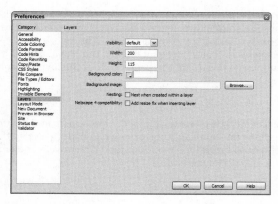

Figure 4-11: In the Layers category of Preferences, you can predetermine the structure of the default Dreamweaver layer.

Visibility Option

Layers can be either visible or hidden when the Web page is first loaded. A layer created using the default visibility option is always displayed initially; however, no specific information is written into the code. Selecting Visible forces Dreamweaver to include a `visibility:visible` line in your layer code. Likewise, if you select Hidden from the Visibility options, the layer is initially hidden.

Use the Inherit option when creating nested layers. Creating one layer inside another makes the outer layer the parent and the inner layer the child. If the parent layer is visible and the child layer is set to `visibility:inherit`, the child is also visible. This option makes it possible to affect the visibility of many layers with one command — hide the parent layer, and all the inheriting child layers disappear as well.

Width and Height Options

When you choose Draw Layer from the Insert bar, you drag out the size and shape of your layer. Choosing Insert ⇨ Layout Objects ⇨ Layer puts a layer of a default size and shape at your current cursor position. The Width and Height options enable you to set these defaults. Select the text boxes and type in your new values. Dreamweaver's default is a layer that is 200 pixels wide and 115 pixels high.

Background Color Option

Layers can have their own background colors independent of the Web page's overall background color (which is set as a `<body>` attribute). You can define the default background color of any inserted layer through either the Insert menu or the Insert bar. For this preference setting, type a color, either by its standard name or as a hexadecimal triplet, directly into the text box. You can also click the color swatch to display the Dreamweaver browser-safe color picker.

Caution   Note that although you can specify a different background color for the layer, you can't alter the layer's default text and link colors (except on a layer-by-layer basis) as you can with a page. If your page and layer background colors are highly contrasting, be sure your text and links are readable in both environments. A similar caveat applies to the use of a layer's background image, as explained in the next section.

Background Image Option

Just as you can pick a specific background color for layers, you can select a different background image for layers. You can type a file source directly into the Background Image text box or select your file from a dialog box by clicking the Browse button. The layer's background image supersedes the layer background color, just as it does in the HTML page. Similarly, just as the page's background image tiles to fill the page, so does the layer's background image.

Nesting Option

The two best options regarding layers seem to be directly opposed: overlapping and nesting layers. You can design layers to appear one on top of another, or you can code layers so that they are within one another. Both techniques are valuable options, and Dreamweaver enables you to decide which one should be the overriding method.

If you are working primarily with nested layers and plan to use the inheritance facility, check the Nest When Created Within A Layer option. If your design entails a number of overlapping but independent layers, make sure this option is turned off. Regardless of your preference, you can reverse it on an individual basis by pressing the Ctrl (Command) key when drawing out your layers.

Netscape 4 Compatibility Option

Netscape 4.x has a particularly annoying problem when displaying Web pages with layers. When the user resizes the browser, all the CSS positioning information is lost — in other words, all your layers lose their exact positioning and typically align themselves on the left. The only solution is to force Netscape to reload the page after the browser has been resized.

When the Netscape 4 Compatibility option is enabled, Dreamweaver automatically includes a small JavaScript routine to handle the resizing problem. The code is inserted in the <head> section of the page when the first layer is added to the page. If additional layers are added, Dreamweaver is smart enough to realize that the workaround code is already included and does not add more unnecessary code.

Many Web designers run into this problem as they begin to explore the possibilities of Dynamic HTML. Although the problem was fixed with the release of Netscape 6, you should enable this option if you are planning to support Netscape 4.x browsers.

CSS Styles Preferences

The CSS Styles category (see Figure 4-12) is entirely devoted to how your code is written. As specified by the W3C, CSS declarations — the specifications of a style — can be written in several ways. One method displays a series of items, separated by semicolons:

```
H1 {
    font-family: Arial, Helvetica, sans-serif;
    font-size: 12pt;
    line-height: 14pt;
    font-weight: bold;
}
```

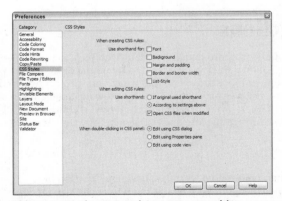

Figure 4-12: The CSS Styles category enables you to code the style sheet sections of your Web pages in a graphics-designer–friendly manner.

Certain properties (such as Font) have their own grouping shorthand, developed to be more readable to designers coming from a traditional print background. A second, shorthand method of rendering the preceding declaration follows:

```
H1 { font: bold 12px/14px Arial, Helvetica, sans-serif; }
```

With the CSS Styles category, you can enable the shorthand method for any or all the five different properties that permit it. Select any of the checkboxes under Use Shorthand For to have Dreamweaver write your style code in this fashion.

The second option on the CSS Styles category determines how Dreamweaver edits styles in previously coded pages. If you want to retain the format of the original page, click Use Shorthand If Original Used Shorthand. If you want Dreamweaver to write new code in the manner that you specify, select Use Shorthand According To Settings Above.

The final option in this group, Open CSS Files When Modified, gives the designer a bit of a safety net when working with external CSS files. When this option, Dreamweaver does indeed open the CSS file when you make a change in any of the CSS rules, whether through the CSS Style definition dialog or the Relevant CSS panel; however, it's important to understand why the CSS file is opened. If the file is not opened, Dreamweaver cannot undo the CSS modification. It's not necessary to switch to the CSS file and undo the changes from that document; Dreamweaver handles the modifications from any page linked to the external CSS file. You must, however, save the CSS file when you're done, confirming the final styles being used. Although it may seem a bit awkward to have an external file open while working on another, I recommend selecting the Open CSS Files When Modified option.

New In Dreamweaver   Dreamweaver gives designers the option to modify CSS styles the way they prefer. The fastest technique for beginning the modification process is to double-click a selector in the CSS Styles panel; what happens next depends on the settings of the final group of options in this preference category. Under the When Double-Clicking in CSS Panel options, there are three options. The first, Edit with CSS Dialog, opens Dreamweaver's standard CSS Definition dialog box. The second, Edit Using Properties Pane, reveals the Properties pane of the CSS Styles panel, if necessary, and puts the focus on the first property's value. The final option, Edit Using Code View, displays the selected rule in Code view whether it is contained in the current document or in an external file.

Making Online Connections

Dreamweaver's visual layout editor offers an approximation of your Web page's appearance in the real world of browsers — offline or online. After you've created the initial draft of your Web page, you should preview it through one or more browsers. And when your project nears completion, you should transfer the files to a server for online, real-time viewing and further testing through a File Transfer Protocol (FTP) program. Dreamweaver gives you control over all these stages of Web-page development through the Site and Preview In Browser categories.

Site Preferences

As your Web site takes shape, you spend more time with the Files panel portion of Dreamweaver. The Site category, shown in Figure 4-13, enables you to customize the look-and-feel of your site, as well as to enter essential connection information. The available Site preferences are described in the following sections.

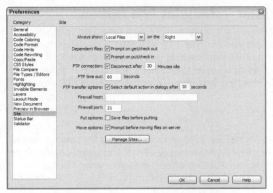

Figure 4-13: Options for Dreamweaver's Files panel are handled through the Site category.

Always Show Local/Remote Files On The Right/Left Option

The full-screen Files panel is divided into two panes: one showing local files and one showing remote files on the server. By default, Dreamweaver puts the local pane on the right and the remote pane on the left. However, Dreamweaver enables you to customize that option. Like many designers, I'm used to using other FTP programs in which the remote files are on the right and the local files on the left; Dreamweaver enables me to work the way I'm used to working.

To switch the layout of your expanded Files panel, switch to full-screen mode and open the Site preferences. Select the file location you want to change to (Local Files or Remote Files) from the Always Show drop-down list or select the panel you want to change to (Right or Left) from the On The drop-down list. Be careful not to switch both options or you end up where you started!

Dependent Files Options

Web pages are seldom just single HTML files. Any graphic — whether it's in the background, part of your main logo, or used on a navigational button — is uploaded as a separate file. The same is true for any additional multimedia add-ons such as audio or video files. If you've enabled File Check In/Check Out when defining your site, Dreamweaver can also track these so-called dependent files.

Enabling the Prompt checkboxes causes Dreamweaver to ask you if you'd like to move the dependent files when you transfer an HTML file. You can opt to show the dialog box for Get/Check Out, Put/Check In, or both.

Tip You're not stuck with your Dependent Files choice. If you turn off the Dependent Files prompt, you can make it appear by pressing the Alt (Option) key while clicking the Get or Put button.

FTP Connection: Disconnect After __ Minutes Idle Option

You can easily forget you're online when you are busy modifying a page. You can set Dreamweaver to automatically disconnect you from an FTP site after a specified interval. The default is 30 minutes; if you want to set a different interval, you can select the FTP Connection value in the Disconnect After text box. Dreamweaver then asks if you want to continue to wait or to disconnect when the time limit is reached, but you can maintain your FTP connection regardless by deselecting this option.

FTP Time Out Option

Client-server communication is prone to glitches. Rather than hanging up your machine while trying to reach a server that is down or slow, Dreamweaver alerts you to an apparent problem after a set period. You can determine the number of seconds you want Dreamweaver to wait by altering the FTP Time Out value. The default is 60 seconds.

FTP Transfer Options: Select Default Action In Dialogs After __ Seconds Option

I often start a large FTP process (like uploading an entire site) and then go for my morning blast of coffee. Unfortunately, this means that I sometimes miss a prompt, such as "Do you want to overwrite this file?" or "Do you want to upload all dependent files?" With earlier versions of Dreamweaver, I'd come back an hour later (I drink a lot of coffee) and nothing would be done. Check this handy option to have Dreamweaver accept the default action for the prompt after a set number of seconds.

This action is enabled by default, but be sure you know what the default values for most dialogs are before checking this box. The default action for uploading files is to include dependent files. If you have out-of-date files on your local machine, the latest awesome logo your graphic designer uploaded last night might be overwritten.

Firewall Host and Firewall Port Options

Dreamweaver enables users to access remote FTP servers outside their network firewalls. A firewall is a security component that protects the internal network from unauthorized outsiders, while enabling Internet access. To enable firewall access, enter the Firewall Host and External Port numbers in the appropriate text boxes; if you do not know these values, contact your network administrator.

If you're having trouble transferring files through the firewall via FTP, make sure the Use Firewall (in Preferences) option is enabled in the Site Definition dialog box. You can find the option on the Testing Server category.

Put Options

Certain site operations, such as putting a file on the remote site, are now available in the Document window. It's common to make an edit to your page and then quickly choose the Site ⇨ Put command — without saving the file first. In this situation, Dreamweaver prompts you with a dialog box to save your changes. However, you can avoid the dialog box and automatically save the file by choosing the Save Files Before Putting option.

Move Options

Every now and then sites need to be restructured. To make sure that all the appropriate dependent files are transferred when an HTML file is moved, select the Prompt Before Moving Files on Server option.

Manage Sites Button

Dreamweaver offers access to your site definitions from the Preferences dialog box. Just click the Manage Sites button to open the Manage Sites dialog box. This option is the same as choosing Manage Sites from the Sites pop-up on the Files panel.

See Chapter 5 to learn how to use the site definitions.

Preview in Browser Preferences

Browser testing is an essential stage of Web page development. Previewing your Web page within the environment of a particular browser gives you a more exact representation of how it looks when viewed online. Because each browser renders the HTML with slight differences, you should preview your work in several browsers. Dreamweaver enables you to select both a primary and secondary browser, which can both be called by pressing a function key. You can name up to 18 additional browsers through the Preview in Browser category shown in Figure 4-14. This list of preferences is also called when you choose File ➪ Preview in Browser ➪ Edit Browser List.

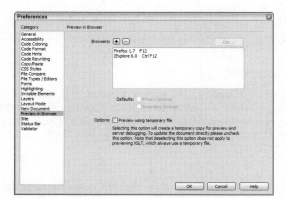

Figure 4-14: The Preview in Browser category lists browsers currently available for preview and enables you to modify the list.

To add a browser to your preview list, follow these steps:

1. Choose Edit ➪ Preferences (Dreamweaver ➪ Preferences) or press the keyboard shortcut Ctrl+U (Command+U).

2. Select the Preview in Browser category.

3. Click the Add (+) button.

4. Enter the path to the browser file in the Path text box or click the Browse button to pick the file from the Select Browser dialog box.

5. After you have selected your browser application, Dreamweaver fills in the Name field. You can alter this name if you want.

6. If you want to designate this browser as your primary or secondary browser, select one of those checkboxes in the Defaults section.

7. Click OK when you're finished.

8. You can continue to add browsers (up to a total of 20) by following steps 3 through 7. Click OK when you're finished.

After you've added a browser to your list, you can modify your selection by following these steps:

1. Open the Preview in Browser category and highlight the browser you want to alter.

2. Click the Edit button to open the Edit Browser dialog box.

3. After you've made your modifications, click OK to close the dialog box.

Tip   You can quickly designate a browser as your primary or secondary previewing choice without going through the Edit screen. From the Preview in Browser category, select the desired browser and check either Primary Browser or Secondary Browser. Note that if you already have a primary or secondary browser defined, this action overrides your previous choice.

You can also easily remove a browser from your preview list. Follow these steps:

1. Open the Preview in Browser category and choose the browser you want to delete from the list.

2. Click the Remove (–) button and click OK.

Dreamweaver can use temporary files for previewing your work in a browser. The temporary files generally have `TMPXXXXX.html`-type names and are automatically deleted when you quit Dreamweaver. With this option selected, Dreamweaver previews the last saved file; if your file has been modified since the last save, Dreamweaver asks if you'd like to save the file. This option is unchecked by default.

Caution   If you have this checkbox selected, and Dreamweaver does not shut down normally, the temporary files are not deleted. Feel free to delete them the next time you launch Dreamweaver.

Customizing Your Code

For all its multimedia flash and visual interactivity, the Web is based on code. The more you code, the more particular about your code you are likely to become. Achieving a consistent look and feel to your code enhances its readability and, thus, your productivity. In Dreamweaver, you can even design the HTML code that underlies a Web page's structure.

Every time you open a new document, the default Web page already has several key elements in place, such as the language in which the page is to be rendered. Dreamweaver also enables you to customize your work environment by selecting default fonts and even the colors of your HTML code.

Fonts Preferences

In the Fonts category, shown in Figure 4-15, you can control the basic language of the fonts as seen by a user's browser and the fonts that you see when programming. The Font Settings section enables you to choose Western-style fonts for Web pages to be rendered in English, one of the Asian languages — Japanese, Traditional Chinese, Simplified Chinese, Thai, or Korean — or another language, such as Arabic, Cyrillic, Greek, Hebrew, or Turkish. If you change the Font Settings in the Page Properties for a document, the font sizes defined in these preferences are used.

Dreamweaver now offers 15 encoding options on Windows and 19 on the Mac. One of the encodings, Unicode, has platform-specific configurations so be sure to examine the options before you make a selection.

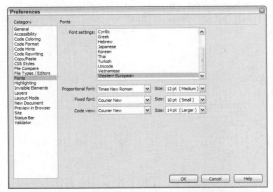

Figure 4-15: Use the Fonts category to set the font encoding for each Web page and the fonts you use when programming.

In the bottom portion of the Fonts category, you can alter the default font and size for three different fonts:

✦ **Proportional Font:** This font option sets the default font used in Dreamweaver's Document window to depict paragraphs, headings, and lists.

✦ **Fixed Font:** In a fixed font, every character is allocated the same width. Dreamweaver uses your chosen fixed font to depict preformatted-styled text.

✦ **Code View:** The Code View font is used by Dreamweaver's built-in text editor. You should probably use a monospaced font such as Courier or Monaco. A monospaced font makes it easy to count characters, which is often necessary when debugging your code.

For all font options, select your font by clicking the list and highlighting your choice of font. Change the font size by selecting the value in the Size text box or by typing in a new number.

Caution Don't be misled into thinking that by changing your Proportional Font preference to Arial or another font, you cause all your Web pages to appear automatically in that typeface. Changing these font preferences affects only the default fonts that you see when developing the Web page; the default font that the user sees is controlled by the user's browser. To ensure that a different font is used, you have to specify it for any selected text through the Text Properties inspector.

Code Hints Preferences

With Code Hints, your work in Code view is much more productive. You can now start typing a tag in Code view, and Dreamweaver shows you a list of available codes. Start typing **<b** and a list appears with <b> highlighted. Type **<bl** and <blockquote> is highlighted. After the tag you want is highlighted, just press Enter (Return) to insert the proper tag. But wait, there's more. The Code Hints also include all the available attributes for each tag, and when you add the closing > symbol, the matching closing tag can be automatically inserted for you. The Code Hints preferences shown in Figure 4-16 determine how Code Hints work for you.

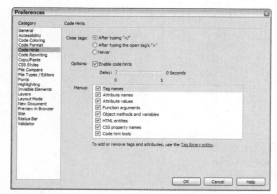

Figure 4-16: Code Hints speed your coding while keeping your entries accurate, whether you're working in HTML or CSS.

Close Tags

Dreamweaver gives you two ways to handle code completion. The first option, After Typing "</" works by inserting the closing tag after you enter the first two characters. This has become my preferred technique because it allows me to enter the opening tag, the enclosed code, and then to close it with just two characters.

If you prefer the legacy method, choose the After Typing the Open Tag's ">" option. With this option selected, after I type <b> into Code view, the corresponding </b> will be added as soon as I type the last > in the bold tag.

Auto Tag Completion is one of my favorite features in Dreamweaver, and it definitely keeps me from forgetting those pesky closing tags. Whichever method fits you best, I recommend you select one of them and speed up your coding.

Options: Enable Code Hints

This checkbox determines whether you get the new Dreamweaver Code Hints. If you have this box enabled, you can set the delay before the Code Hints drop-down menu appears. I leave the delay set to 0 so that Code Hints display as soon as I start typing.

Code Rewriting Preferences

The exception to Dreamweaver's policy of not altering imported code occurs when HTML or other code is incorrectly structured. Dreamweaver automatically fixes tags that are nested in the wrong order or have additional, unnecessary closing tags — unless you tell Dreamweaver otherwise by setting up the Code Rewriting preferences accordingly (see Figure 4-17).

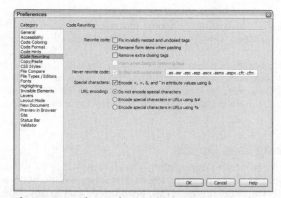

Figure 4-17: The Code Rewriting category can be used to protect nonstandard HTML from being automatically changed by Dreamweaver.

Dreamweaver accommodates many different types of markup languages, not just HTML, through the Never Rewrite Code In Files With Extensions option. Moreover, you can prevent Dreamweaver from encoding special characters, such as spaces, tildes, and ampersands in URLs or attribute values. Dreamweaver is now extremely flexible. The following sections describe each of the options available through the Code Rewriting category.

Fix Invalidly Nested And Unclosed Tags Option

When enabled, this option repairs incorrectly placed tags. For example, if a file contains the following line:

```
<h3><b>Welcome to the Monkey House!</h3></b>
```

Dreamweaver rewrites it as follows:

```
<h3><b>Welcome to the Monkey House!</b></h3>
```

Open that same file with this option turned off, and Dreamweaver highlights the misplaced code in the Document window. Double-clicking the code brings up a window with a brief explanation.

Rename Form Items When Pasting Option

In general, static Web pages require each form element to be uniquely named; with this option selected, you can quickly insert a series of text fields with similar attributes and still be assured that they are individually named. However, with dynamic applications, the names may be supplied dynamically, and you don't want to have that code overwritten. Unchecking this box prevents Dreamweaver from renaming all your form elements.

Remove Extra Closing Tags Option

When you're editing your code by hand, it's fairly easy to miss a closing tag. Dreamweaver cleans up such code if you enable the Remove Extra Closing Tags option. You may, for example, have the following line in a previously edited file:

```
<p>And now back to our show...</p></i>
```

Notice that the closing italic tag, `</i>`, has no matching opening partner. If you open this file in Dreamweaver with the Remove option enabled, Dreamweaver plucks out the offending `</i>`.

Tip   In some circumstances, you want to ensure that your pages remain as originally formatted. If you edit pages in Dreamweaver that have been preprocessed by a server unknown to Dreamweaver (prior to displaying the pages), be sure that you disable both the Fix Invalidly Nested And Unclosed Tags option, where possible, and the Remove Extra Closing Tags option.

Warn When Fixing Or Removing Tags Option

If you're editing a lot of Web pages created on another system, you should enable the Warn When Fixing Or Removing Tags option. If this setting is turned on, Dreamweaver displays a list of changes that have been made to your code in the HTML Corrections dialog box. The changes can be quite extensive when Dreamweaver opens what it regards as a poorly formatted page.

Caution   Remember that after you've enabled these Rewrite Code options, the fixes occur automatically. If this sequence happens to you by mistake, immediately close the file (without saving it!), disable the Code Rewriting preferences options, and reopen the document.

Never Rewrite Code Preferences

Many of the database connectivity programs, such as ColdFusion, use proprietary tags embedded in a regular Web page to communicate with their servers. Dreamweaver enables you to explicitly protect file types identified with a particular file extension.

To enter a new file type in the Never Rewrite Code options, select the In Files With Extensions field. Enter the file extension of the file type, including the period, at the end of the list. Be sure to separate your extensions from the others in the list with a space on either side.

Special Character Encoding Preferences

By encoding special characters such as <, >, &, and " in attribute values, Dreamweaver ensures that the characters are interpreted correctly by the browser. This works well for static pages, but many dynamic pages use the same characters in their server-side code. If you find that your application server is misinterpreting attributes with these characters, disable the Encode <, >, &, and " In Attribute Values Using & option.

URL Encoding Preferences

In addition to the rewriting of proprietary tags, many middleware vendors face another problem when trying to integrate with Dreamweaver. By default, earlier versions of Dreamweaver encoded all URLs so that Unix servers could understand them. The encoding converted all special characters to their decimal equivalents, preceded by a percent sign. Spaces became %20, tildes (~) became %7E, and ampersands were converted to &. Although this is valid for Unix servers, and helps to make the Dreamweaver code more universal, it can cause problems for many other types of application servers.

Dreamweaver gives you the option to disable the URL encoding, if necessary, or choose the type of encoding you prefer for special characters. If you choose to encode them using &#, Dreamweaver uses numeric character entities; this is the default option. Select the Encode Special Characters In URLs Using % option and Dreamweaver uses decimal equivalents.

In general, however, it's best to leave the URL encoding option set to the default unless you find your third-party tags being rewritten destructively.

Code Colors Preferences

HTML code is a combination of the tags that structure the language and the text that provides the content. A Web page designer often has difficulty distinguishing swiftly between the two — and finding the right code to modify. Dreamweaver enables you to set color preferences for the code as it appears in Code view or the Code inspector. You can not only alter colors for the background, default tags, and text and general comments, but also specify certain tags to get certain colors.

Dreamweaver now enables you to specify color coding for individual document types. If you want different code coloring in VBScript documents, HTML, and PHP documents, you can customize the coloring for each individually. The only color on the main dialog box is the default background color. This isn't the page background color, but the Code view background color.

To modify any of the elements for a specific document type, select the document type as illustrated in Figure 4-18, and click Edit Coloring Scheme.

After you click Edit Coloring Scheme, you get the Edit Coloring Scheme For HTML dialog box, which enables you to change every facet of Dreamweaver's color coding, as shown in Figure 4-19.

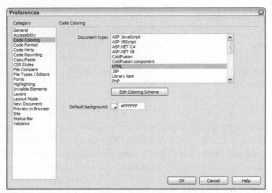

Figure 4-18: Use the Code Coloring category to custom color-code the HTML inspector.

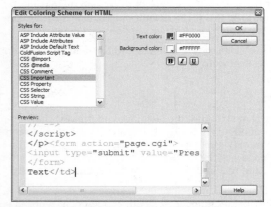

Figure 4-19: The Edit Coloring Scheme dialog box provides a method to completely customize the way you view your raw page code.

The left-hand Styles For box contains every type of tag you could ever want to color. Just select a tag type and then click the color swatch to select one of the 216 colors displayed in the color picker. After the color picker opens, you can also choose the small palette icon to select from the full range of colors available to your system. The color picker also enables you to use the Eyedropper tool to pick a color from the Document window.

As you change colors, you can see a preview of how your code looks in the Preview window.

Code Format Preferences

Dreamweaver includes a fantastic tool for customizing your HTML with the easy-to-use, point-and-click preferences category called Code Format. Most of your HTML code parameters can be controlled through the Code Format category.

In the Code Format category, you can also decide whether to use indentations — and if so, whether to use spaces or tabs and how many of each — or to turn off indents for major elements such as tables and frames. You can also globally control the case of your HTML tags and their attributes. As you can see in Figure 4-20, the Code Format category is full-featured.

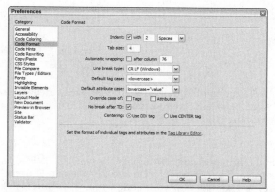

Figure 4-20: The Code Format category enables you to shape your HTML to your own specifications.

To examine the available options in the Code Format category, separate them into four areas: indent control, line control, case control, and centering.

Indent Control Options

Indenting your code generally makes it more readable. Dreamweaver defaults to indenting most HTML tags with two spaces, giving extra indentation grouping to tables and frames. All these parameters can be altered through the Code Format category of the Preferences dialog box.

The first indent option enables indenting, and you can switch from spaces to tabs. To permit indenting, make sure a checkmark is displayed in the Indent checkbox. If you prefer your code to be displayed flush left, turn off the Indent option altogether.

To use tabs instead of the default spaces, select Tabs from the drop-down list. If you anticipate transferring your code to a word-processing program for formatting and printing, you should use tabs; otherwise, stay with the default spaces.

Dreamweaver formats both tables and frames as special indentation groups. Within each of these structural elements, the related tags are indented (or nested) more than the initial two spaces. As you can see in Listing 4-1, each table row (<tr>) is indented within the table tag, and the table data tags (<td>) are nested within the table row.

Listing 4-1: An Indented Code Sample

```
<table border="1" width="75%">
 <tr>
   <td>Row 1, Column 1</td>
   <td>Row 1, Column 2</td>
   <td>Row 1, Column 3</td>
 </tr>
 <tr>
   <td>Row 2, Column 1</td>
   <td>Row 2, Column 2 </td>
   <td>Row 2, Column 3</td>
 </tr>
</table>
```

The other two items in the indent control section of Code Format preferences category are Indent Size and Tab Size. Change the value in Indent Size to establish the size of indents using spaces. To alter the size of tab indents, change the Tab Size value.

Line Control Option

The browser is responsible for ultimately formatting an HTML page for viewing. This formatting includes wrapping text according to each user's screen size and the placement of the paragraph tags (<p>...</p>). Therefore, you control how your code wraps in your HTML editor. You can turn off the automatic wrapping feature or set it for a particular column through the Line Control options of the Code Format category.

To turn off the automatic word-wrapping capability, deselect Automatic Wrapping. When you are trying to debug your code and are looking for specific line numbers and character positions, enable this option. You can also set the specific column after which word wrapping should take effect. Be sure Automatic Wrapping is enabled and then type your new value in the After Column text box.

Tip   If you're using Code view or the Code inspector, selecting the Word Wrap option overrides the Automatic Wrapping setting in the Code Format category.

The Line Break Type setting determines which line break character is appended to each line of the page. Each of the major operating systems employs a different ending character: Macintosh uses a carriage return (CR), Unix uses a line feed (LF), and Windows uses both (CR LF). If you know the operating system for your remote server, choosing the corresponding line break character ensures that the file has the correct appearance when viewed online. Click the drop-down arrow button next to Line Break Type and select your system.

Caution   The operating system for your local development machine may be different from the operating system of your remote server. If so, using the Line Break Type option may cause your HTML to appear incorrect when viewed through a simple text editor (such as Notepad or TextEdit). Dreamweaver's Code view and Code inspector, however, do render the code correctly.

Case Control Options

The case of HTML tags is becoming more and more important. In XHTML, all tags and attribute names must be in lowercase. If you're coding in regular HTML, case is only a personal preference among Web designers. That said, some Webmasters consider case a serious preference and insist that their code be all uppercase, all lowercase, or a combination of uppercase and lowercase. Dreamweaver gives you control over the tags and attributes it creates, as well as over case conversion for files that Dreamweaver imports. The Dreamweaver default for both tags and attributes is lowercase.

Tip   Lowercase tags and attributes are also less fattening, according to the W3C. Files with lowercase tag names and attributes compress better and thus transmit faster.

You can also use Dreamweaver to standardize the letter case in tags of previously saved files. To alter imported files, select the Override Case Of Tags and/or the Override Case Of Attributes options. When enabled, these options enforce your choices made in the Case For Tags and Case For Attributes option boxes in any file Dreamweaver loads. Again, be sure to save your file to keep the changes.

The No Break After TD checkbox ensures that there is no line break after the `<td>` tag in your document. Putting a line break after the `<td>` can create display anomalies in some browsers, such as unwanted space. I recommend leaving this one checked.

Centering

When an object — whether it's an image or text — is centered on a page, HTML tags are placed around the object (or objects) to indicate the alignment. Since the release of HTML 3.2, the `<center>` tag has been deprecated by the W3C in favor of using a `<div>` tag with an `align="center"` attribute. By default, Dreamweaver uses the officially preferred method of `<div align="center">`.

Many Web designers are partial to the older `<center>` tag and prefer to use it to align their objects. Dreamweaver offers a choice with the Centering option in the Code Format category. To use the new method, select the Use DIV Tag option (the default). To switch to the older `<center>` method, select the Use CENTER Tag option. Although use of `<center>` has been officially discouraged, it is so widespread that all browsers continue to support it.

Cross-Reference   Not only can you customize your general code preferences, with Dreamweaver's Tag Library Editor you can modify all the various tags individually — as well as import entire new tag sets. For details on how the Tag Library Editor works, see Chapter 32.

Validator Preferences

Dreamweaver offers the capability to validate against multiple HTML schemes and server-side languages. You can even choose which types of errors you'd like Dreamweaver to warn you about. In Figure 4-21, notice that you can choose just the specs you want to support.

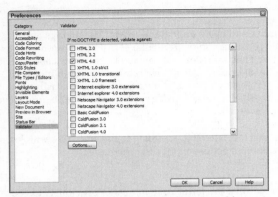

Figure 4-21: The Validator preferences enable you to validate against one or multiple HTML schemes or server-side languages.

The Validate Against list includes the following entries:

✦ HTML 2.0

✦ HTML 3.2

✦ HTML 4.0

✦ XHTML 1.0 Strict

✦ XHTML 1.0 Transitional

✦ XHTML 1.0 Frameset

✦ Internet Explorer 3.0 Extensions

✦ Internet Explorer 4.0 Extensions

✦ Netscape Navigator 3.0 Extensions

✦ Netscape Navigator 4.0 Extensions

✦ Basic ColdFusion

✦ ColdFusion 3.0

✦ ColdFusion 3.1

✦ ColdFusion 4.0

✦ ColdFusion 4.5

✦ ColdFusion 5.0

✦ ColdFusion MX

✦ ColdFusion MX 7

✦ Synchronized Multiple Integration Language 1.0

✦ Wireless Markup Language

✦ JavaServer Page Tags

Clicking Options enables you to choose which types of errors you want Dreamweaver to display and check for. The Display list includes Errors, Warnings, Custom Messages, and Nesting Errors. The Check For list includes Quotes In Text and Entities In Text. All options are checked by default, as shown in Figure 4-22.

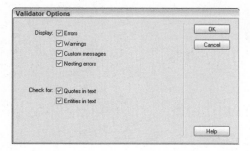

Figure 4-22: The Validator options enable you to choose exactly what you want the validator to check for.

Summary

Creating Web pages, like any design job, is easier when the tools fit your hands. Through Preferences, you can make Dreamweaver work the way you work. When you're examining and setting Dreamweaver's preferences, keep these points in mind:

✦ Dreamweaver enables you to customize your Web page design and HTML coding environment through a series of easy-to-use, point-and-click categories.

✦ Dreamweaver's startup options include a Start Page that brings your recent documents within one-click reach as well as the opportunity to automatically reopen all your documents from your previous session.

✦ You can decide how best to use cutting-edge features, such as layers and style sheets, depending on the degree of cross-browser and backward compatibility you need.

✦ Dreamweaver gives you plenty of elbow room for previewing and testing by providing for 20 selections on your browser list.

✦ Set the level of validation you want to strive for through the Validator preferences.

In the next chapter, you learn how to define a site in Dreamweaver.

✦   ✦   ✦

Setting Up Sites and Servers

Web sites — especially those integrating Web applications — are far more than collections of HTML documents. Every image — from the smallest navigational button to the largest background image — is a separate file that must be uploaded with your HTML page. Moreover, if you use any additional elements, such as an included script, background sound, digital video, or Java applet, these files must be transferred as well. To preview the Web site locally and view it properly on the Internet, you have to organize your material in a specific manner.

In Dreamweaver, the process of creating a site can also involve developing Web applications in a particular server model. Dreamweaver is unique in its capability to author sites for a variety of server models. Although it is possible to mix pages developed for different server models, it's not really practical. Dreamweaver enables you to select one server model for each site.

Dreamweaver gives Web developers who work with existing sites a direct connection to the server. Working in this mode enables you to make quick corrections to a page and transfer files, but many of Dreamweaver's special features require that you establish a local site.

As I describe in this chapter, each time you begin developing a new site, you define several initial parameters, including the chosen server model (provided, of course, you are creating a dynamically driven site, such as a Web application). These steps lay the groundwork for Dreamweaver to properly link your local development site with a remote online site, as well as to link properly to your data sources (again, for dynamically driven sites). This chapter begins with a brief description of approaches to online design, aimed primarily at those who are just starting to create Web sites. The remainder of the chapter is devoted to the mechanics of setting up your site and basic file manipulation. You also learn how to connect directly to servers, without establishing a local site.

Planning Your Site

Planning in Web design, just as in any other design process, is essential. Not only does careful planning cut your development time considerably, but it makes it far easier to achieve a uniform look and feel for your Web site — making it friendlier and easier to use. This section briefly covers some of the basics of Web site design: what to focus on, what options to consider, and what pitfalls to avoid. If you are an established Web site developer who has covered this ground before, feel free to skip this section.

Primary Considerations

Even before you choose the overarching structure for your site (as discussed in the following sections), you need to address the all-important issues of message, audience, and budget.

Deciding What You Want to Say

If I had to pick one overriding concern for Web site design, it would be to answer the following question: What are you trying to say? The clearer you are about your message, the more focused your Web site will be. To this end, I find it useful to try to state the purpose of the Web site in one sentence. "Creating the coolest Web site on the planet" doesn't count. Although it could be regarded as a goal, it's too open-ended to be useful. Here are some examples of clearly stated Web site concepts:

✦ To provide the best small-business resource center focused on Macromedia software

✦ To chronicle the world's first voyage around the world by hot air balloon

✦ To advertise music lessons offered by a collective of keyboard teachers in New York City

Targeting Your Audience

Right behind a site's concept — some would say neck-and-neck with it — is the site's audience. Who are you trying to reach? Quite often, a site's style is heavily influenced by a clear vision of the site's intended audience. Take, for example, Macromedia's monthly Edge newsletter (www.macromedia.com/newsletters/edge/). The Edge is an excellent example of a site that is perfectly pitched toward its target; in this case, the intended audience is composed of professional developers and designers. Hence, the site is snazzy but informative, and it is filled with exciting examples of cutting-edge programming techniques.

In contrast, a site that is devoted to mass-market e-commerce must work with a very different group in mind: shoppers. Everyone at one time or another falls into this category, so I am really talking about a state of mind, rather than a profession. Many shopping sites use a very straightforward page design that is easily maneuverable, comforting in its repetition — where visitors can quickly find what they are looking for and, with as few impediments as possible, buy it.

Determining Your Resources

Unfortunately, Web sites aren't created in a vacuum. Virtually all development work happens under real-world constraints of some kind. A professional Web designer is accustomed to working within a budget. In fact, the term *budget* can apply to several concepts.

First, you have a monetary budget — how much is the client willing to spend? This translates into a combination of development time (for designers and programmers), materials (custom graphics, stock photos, and the like), and ongoing maintenance. You can build a large site with many pages that pulls dynamically from an internal database and requires very little hands-on upkeep. Alternatively, you can construct a small, graphics-intensive site that must be updated by hand weekly. It's entirely possible that both sites end up costing the same.

Second, *budget* also applies to the amount of time you can afford to spend on any given project. The professional Web designer is quick to realize that time is an essential commodity. The resources needed when undertaking a showcase for yourself when you have no deadline are very different from those needed when you sign a contract on June 30 for a job that must be ready to launch on July 4.

The third real-world budgetary item to consider is bandwidth. The Web, with faster Internet connections and an improved infrastructure, is slowly shedding its image as the World Wide Wait. However, many users are still stuck with slow modems, which means that Webmasters must keep a steady eye on a page's weight — how long it takes to download under the most typical modem rates. Of course, you can always decide to include that animated video masterpiece that takes 8minutes to download on a cable modem — you just can't expect everyone to wait to see it.

In conclusion, when you are trying to define your Web page, filter it through these three ideas: message, audience, and the various faces of the budget. The time spent visualizing your Web pages in these terms is time decidedly well spent.

Design Options

Many Web professionals borrow a technique used extensively in developing other mass-marketing forms: *storyboarding*. Storyboarding for the Web entails first diagramming the various pages in your site — much like the more traditional storyboarding in videos or filmmaking — and then detailing connections for the separate pages to form the overall site. How you connect the disparate pages determines how your visitors navigate the completed Web site.

> **Cross-Reference**
> In addition to formulating a Web site design, Web application developers must often be aware of how the data sources used by the site are structured. See Chapter 18 for a discussion of concerns and techniques in developing database layouts.

The following sections describe the basic navigational models. The Web designer should be familiar with them all because each one serves a different purpose, and they can be mixed and matched as needed.

The Linear Approach

Prior to the World Wide Web, most media formats were linear — that is, one image or page followed another in an unalterable sequence. In contrast, the Web and its interactive personality enable the user to jump from topic to topic. Nevertheless, you can still use a linear approach to a Web site and have one page appear after another, like a multimedia book.

The linear navigational model, shown in Figure 5-1, works well for computer-based training applications and other expository scenarios in which you want to tightly control the viewer's experience. Some Web designers use a linear-style entrance or exit from their main site, connected to a multilevel navigational model. With Dynamic HTML, you can achieve the effects of moving through several pages in a single page through layering.

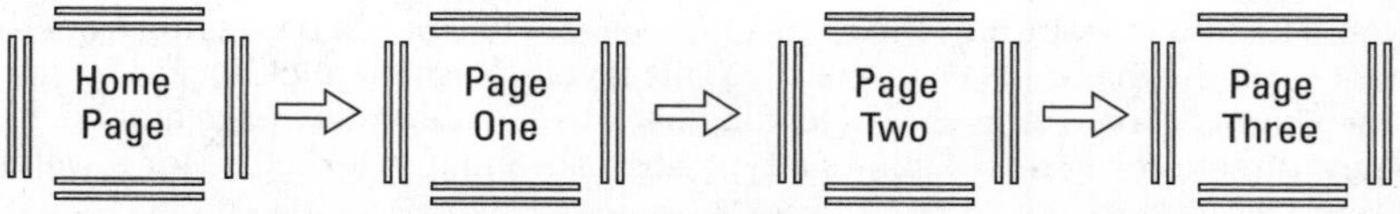

Home Page ⇨ Page One ⇨ Page Two ⇨ Page Three

Figure 5-1: The linear navigational model takes the visitor through a series of Web pages.

Caution

Keep in mind that Web search engines can index the content of every page of your site separately. Each page of your site — not just your home page — becomes a potential independent entrance point. Therefore, make sure every page includes navigation buttons back to your home page, especially if you use a linear navigational model.

The Hierarchical Model

Hierarchical navigational models emerge from top-down designs. These start with one key concept that becomes your home page. From the home page, users branch off to several main pages; if needed, these main pages can, in turn, branch off into many separate pages. Everything flows from the home page; it's very much like a company's organizational chart, with the CEO on top followed by the various company divisions.

The hierarchical Web site, shown in Figure 5-2, is best known for maintaining a visitor's sense of place in the site. Some Web designers even depict the treelike structure as a navigation device and include each branch traveled as a link. This enables visitors to quickly retrace their steps, branch by branch, to investigate different routes.

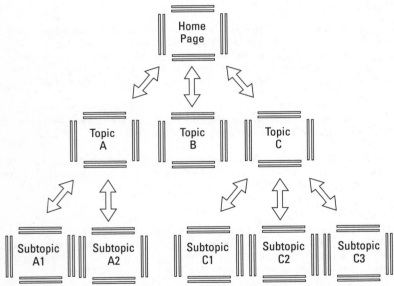

Figure 5-2: A hierarchical Web layout enables the main topics to branch into their own subtopics.

The Spoke-and-Hub Model

Given the Web's flexible hyperlink structure, the spoke-and-hub navigational model works extremely well. The hub is, naturally, the site's home page. The spokes projecting from the center connect to all the major pages in the site. This layout permits quick access to any key page in just two jumps — one jump always leading back to the hub/home page and one jump leading in a new direction. Figure 5-3 shows a typical spoke-and-hub structure for a Web site.

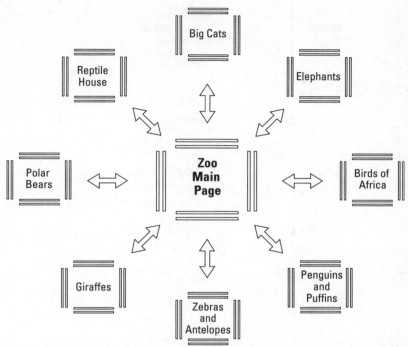

Figure 5-3: This storyboard diagram for a zoo's Web site shows how a spoke-and-hub navigational model might work.

The main drawback to the spoke-and-hub structure is the required return to the home page. Many Web designers get around this limitation by using frames to make the first jump off the hub into a Web page; this way, the navigation bars are always available. This design also enables visitors using nonframes-capable browsers to take a different path.

The Full Web Design

The seemingly least structured approach for a Web site — full Web — takes the most advantage of the Web's hyperlink capabilities. This design enables virtually every page to connect to every other page. The full Web design, shown in Figure 5-4, works well for sites that are explorations of a particular topic because the approach encourages visitors to experience the site according to their own needs, not based on the notions of any one designer. The danger in using full Web for your site design is that a visitor can literally get lost. As an escape hatch, many Web designers include a link to a clickable site map, especially for large-scale sites using this design.

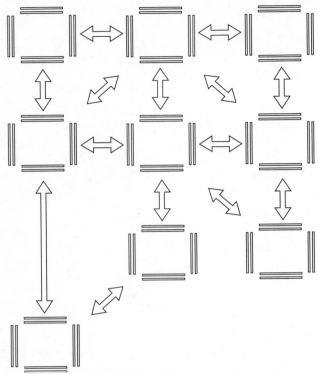

Figure 5-4: In a full Web design, each page can have multiple links to other pages.

Mapping Dynamic Pages for Web Applications

Many, if not most, Web applications require more than one Web page. One variation on a search engine, for example, might use the following:

✦ An entry page containing the form elements (text field, list boxes, and so on) that make up the search criteria

✦ A results page that displays the list of items matching the search criteria; each of the items typically provides a link to a detail page and more information

✦ A detail page (or pages) that provide more information — this page is linked from the results page

✦ An error page, if the initial search criteria do not have any matches

The experienced Web developer maps out the structure for all the anticipated Web applications in the site before beginning the building process. In addition to providing a truer picture of the work involved, mapping the required pages highlights potentially redundant pages — for example, the same error page may be used throughout the site — and pinpoints areas that would benefit from dynamic data application. The Web application map can also serve as a workflow schematic that shows which pages are static HTML and could be built by an HTML designer with little or no coding experience (typically, the entry and error pages); and which pages are dynamic Web pages that require data-aware designers.

Defining a Site

Now that you've decided on a design and mapped your site, you're ready to set it up in Dreamweaver. When you define a site, you are telling Dreamweaver where to store your Web pages locally, where to transfer them to remotely, as well as the style of code in which to write them. Defining a site is an essential first step.

The Site Definition dialog box provides two operational modes: Basic and Advanced. In Basic mode, also known as the Site Definition Wizard, you specify the bare essentials for editing, testing, and sharing your site files. In Advanced mode, you can specify all your site parameters, from the most basic down to the most obscure.

Using the Site Definition Wizard

There are two main paths through the Site Definition Wizard:

✦ One for sites that do not use a server technology — sites that contain no server-side code, just client-side HTML, JavaScript, and so on

✦ One for sites that use a server technology — sites that contain server-side code, such as ColdFusion, ASP, JSP, and so on

To keep things simple, I've written a separate procedure for each of these paths, which I provide in the following sections. Be sure to choose the correct path before you launch into your site definition!

Note

Using the Site Definition Wizard to define a new site is a quick, convenient way to get a site off the ground. In some cases, however, it is not complete. Depending on the site, you might have to use the Advanced tab of the Site Definition dialog box to specify additional site options, such as testing server details, cloaking, and so on.

Defining a Site That Does Not Use a Server Technology

To use the Site Definition Wizard to define a site that *does not* use a server technology (that is, a site that contains no server-side code), perform the following steps:

1. Choose Site ➪ Manage Sites.

2. In the Manage Sites dialog, click New and select Site from the submenu to open the Site Definition dialog box.

3. Click the Basic tab of the Site Definition Wizard if it is not already selected. If a message appears informing you that the root folder you have chosen is the same as another folder, ignore it, and click OK to close the message box.

   In the What Would You Like To Name Your Site? field, type a name to identify your site within Dreamweaver, as shown in Figure 5-5. Choose a descriptive name; spaces are fine, for example, mySite, my_site, My Site, and so on are all acceptable. To keep things simple, I recommend avoiding apostrophes, such as Joe's Site, joe's_site, and so on.

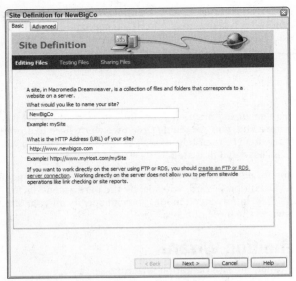

Figure 5-5: Use the Site Definition Wizard to define a new site.

4. If you know it, enter the Web address of your site in the What Is The HTTP Address (URL) Of Your Site? field. Be sure to enter the fully formed URL beginning with `http://`; click Next when you're done.

5. In the second page of the wizard, Editing Files, Part 2, select No to the prompt Do You Want To Work With A Server Technology? Click Next to proceed.

6. In the Editing Files, Part 3 page of the wizard, select the appropriate option for How Do You Want To Work With Your Files During Development? The choices are: Edit Local Copies On My Machine Then Upload To Server When Ready or Edit Directly On Server Using Local Network.

   If you choose Edit Local Copies On My Machine, you must create and/or specify the site's root folder on your local disk in the Where On Your Computer Do You Want To Store Your Files? field.

   If you choose Edit Directly On Server Using Local Network, you must create and/or specify the site's root folder on your network in the Where Are Your Files On The Network? field.

7. Click Next to move to the Sharing Files page of the wizard.

Note   This page of the wizard does not appear if you chose Edit Directly On Server Using Local Network in step 6.

In the How Do You Connect To Your Remote Server? field list box, select the appropriate option: FTP, Local/Network, RDS, SourceSafe Database, or WebDAV. If you do not know which option to choose, or if you want to specify your server connection type later, select None. (For more information on each of these options, turn to Dreamweaver's built-in help.)

Depending on the option you choose, a set of suboptions appears. Respond appropriately to these.

8. Click Next to move to the Sharing Files, Part 2 page of the wizard.

Note

This page of the wizard does not appear if you chose None in step 7 or Edit Directly On Server Using Local Network in step 6.

Select the appropriate option for the prompt Do You Want To Enable Checking In And Checking Out Files? Select Yes to ensure that different people cannot edit the same document at the same time. Select No if this is not a concern.

Caution

The Check In/Check Out system is a version-control system that is only effective if all members of the development team have the setting enabled. When someone has checked out a file, and you attempt to open it, Dreamweaver prompts you that the file is checked out. If someone on the team doesn't have Check In/Check Out enabled, however, he or she doesn't receive such a prompt. That person can open, edit, and upload the file, posing a potential version-control issue. See Chapter 30 to learn more about Dreamweaver's Check In/Check Out feature.

9. Click the Next button to move to the final, Summary page of the wizard. Review your selections; if necessary, use the Back button to change them.

10. When you've confirmed your choices, click Done to create your site. An alert box informs you that Dreamweaver is going to create a site cache, which makes various site operations run faster.

11. In the Files panel, click the Expand/Collapse button to expand to remote/local pane view. In the Local Files pane (on the right, by default), Dreamweaver shows the local root folder for your newly defined site to enable you to view all your local disks/folders/files. In the Remote Site pane (on the left, by default), Dreamweaver shows your remote folders/files (depending on your site definition, you might need to click the Connects To Remote Host button to show the remote folders/files).

Defining a Site That Uses a Server Technology

To use the Site Definition Wizard to define a site that uses a server technology (that is, a site that contains server-side code), perform the following steps:

1. Choose Site ➪ Manage Sites.

2. In the Manage Sites dialog, click New and select Site from the submenu to open the Site Definition dialog box.

3. Click the Basic tab of the Site Definition Wizard if it is not already selected. If a message appears informing you that the root folder you have chosen is the same as another folder, ignore it, and click OK to close the message box.

In the What Would You Like To Name Your Site? field, enter a name to identify your site within Dreamweaver (refer to Figure 5-5). Choose a descriptive name; spaces are fine, for example, mySite, my_site, My Site, and so on are all acceptable. To keep things nice and simple, I recommend avoiding apostrophes, such as Joe's Site, joe's_site, and so on.

4. If you know it, enter the Web address of your site in the What Is The HTTP Address (URL) Of Your Site? field. Be sure to enter the fully formed URL beginning with `http://`; click Next when you're done.

5. Click Next to move to the second page of the wizard, Editing Files, Part 2. Select Yes to the prompt Do You Want To Work With A Server Technology? Specify the server technology in the Which Server Technology? drop-down list: ColdFusion, ASP, PHP, and so on.

   Dreamweaver recognizes if you have ColdFusion installed on your system and notifies you that it is available for use.

6. Click Next to move to the Editing Files, Part 3 page of the wizard. Select the appropriate option for How Do You Want To Work With Your Files During Development? The choices are: Edit And Test Locally; Edit Locally Then Upload To Remote Testing Server; or Edit Directly On Remote Testing Server Using Local Network.

   If you choose either of the first two options, you must create and/or specify the site's root folder on your local disk in the Where On Your Computer Do You Want To Store Your Files? field.

   If you choose Edit Directly On Remote Testing Server Using Local Network, create and/or specify the site's root folder on your network in the Where Are Your Files On The Network? field.

7. Click Next to move to the Testing Files page of the wizard. At this point, the Site Definition Wizard branches off into several different subpaths, depending on the option you chose in step 5.

Note   Your step 7 subpath might consist of one or several wizard pages. The thing to remember: All step 7 subpaths eventually lead to step 8's Summary page.

Describing all possible subpaths would take several pages, and to wade through them would be counterproductive. Fortunately, the options you must choose in each subpath are quite self-explanatory: the absolute URL of your remote site root (`http://hostname/ path/filename`), the method you use to connect to your remote server (such as FTP, Local/Network, or RDS), and so on.

Tip   Remember: If you get confused or stuck, help is but a keypress (F1) or a mouse click (Help button) away.

One option you might not be familiar with is: Do You Want To Enable Checking In And Checking Out Files? Select Yes to ensure that different people cannot edit the same document at the same time. Select No if this is not a concern.

Caution   The Check In/Check Out system is a version-control system that is only effective if all members of the development team have the setting enabled. When someone has checked out a file and you attempt to open it, Dreamweaver prompts you that the file is checked out. If someone on the team doesn't have Check In/Check Out enabled, however, he or she doesn't receive such a prompt. That person can open, edit, and upload the file, posing a potential version-control issue. See Chapter 30 to learn more about Dreamweaver's Check In/Check Out feature.

8. When you have successfully worked through all your step 7 subpaths, the final Summary page of the wizard appears. Review your selections, as listed in the Summary page; if necessary, use the Back button to change them.

9. When all is well, click Done to create your site. An alert box informs you that Dreamweaver is going to create a site cache, which makes various site operations faster. (Note: If the Don't Show Me This Message Again option is selected, this alert box does not appear.) Click OK to have Dreamweaver create your specified site.

10. In the Files panel, click the Expand/Collapse button to expand to remote/local pane view. In the Local Files pane (on the right, by default), Dreamweaver shows the local root folder for your newly defined site to enable you to view all your local disks/folders/files. In the Remote Site pane (on the left, by default), Dreamweaver shows your remote folders/files (depending on your site definition, you might need to click the Connects To Remote Host button to show the remote folders/files).

Setting Up Your Site

In this Technique, you set up a site that is used throughout this book in the other Dreamweaver Techniques. The process is simple, but essential.

1. If you haven't already transferred the Dreamweaver Technique files from the book's CD-ROM to your system, copy the entire folder named Techniques to your computer.

2. Select the main Technique folder and disable the Read-Only status from the CD-ROM.

   ✦ If you're on Windows, right-click the Techniques folder in a file manager and choose Properties; when the Properties dialog box opens, deselect the Read-Only option and click OK. When asked to confirm the attribute changes, make sure that the option to apply changes to this folder, subfolders, and files is selected.

   ✦ If you're in Macintosh, select the transferred folder in Finder and choose File ➪ Get Info. When the Info dialog box opens, deselect the Locked option under the General tab.

3. Choose Site ➪ New Site.

4. In the Advanced tab of the Site Definition dialog box, enter **Techniques** in the Site Name field.

5. Select the folder icon next to the Local Root Folder field.

6. In the Choose Local Root Folder dialog box, locate and select the Techniques folder; click OK when you're done.

   Because this site is used just for demonstration purposes for non-dynamic pages, there's no need to establish a remote or testing site.

7. Click OK to create the site.

In Dreamweaver Techniques found in subsequent chapters, you'll be directed to open a file in the Techniques site just established.

Using Advanced Mode

Advanced mode comprises eight categories of information: Local Info, Remote Info, Testing Server, Cloaking, Design Notes, Site Map Layout, File View Columns, and Contribute. Note that only the first three categories—Local Info, Remote Info, and Testing Server—are essential for site definition. Once I became familiar with the interface, I found Advanced mode to be much easier to navigate than Basic mode.

Cross-Reference

The other categories in the Site Definition dialog box Advanced mode (Cloaking, Design Notes, Site Map Layout, and File View Columns) are helpful for working in a team environment and for working visually with Dreamweaver's Site Map; you can find more information on these features later in this chapter and in Chapter 30.

The three main steps to defining a site in Dreamweaver are

1. Locate the folder to be used for the local development site.

2. Enter the remote site information.

3. If you are creating a Web application, specify the testing server model to be used for the site.

Establishing Local Connections

After your site is on your Web server and fully operational, it consists of many files—server-side pages, plain HTML, graphics, and other media files—that make up the individual Web pages. All these associated files are kept on the server in one folder, which may use one or more subfolders. This main folder is called the *remote site root*. In order for Dreamweaver to properly display your linked pages and embedded images—just as they are displayed online—the program creates a mirror of your remote site on your local development system. This primary mirror folder on your system is known as the *local site root*.

You must establish the local site root at the beginning of a project. This ensures that Dreamweaver duplicates the complete structure of the Web development site when it comes time to publish your pages to the Web. One of Dreamweaver's key site-management features enables you to select just the HTML pages for publication; Dreamweaver then automatically transfers all the associated files, creating any needed folders in the process. The mirror images of your local and remote site roots are critical to Dreamweaver's capability to expedite your workload in this way.

Tip

If you do decide to transfer an existing Web site to a new Dreamweaver local site root, run Dreamweaver's Link Checker after you've consolidated all your files. Choose Site ⇨ Check Links Sitewide or press the keyboard shortcut Ctrl+F8 (Command+F8). The Link Checker informs you of broken links and orphan files.

To set up a local site root folder in Dreamweaver, follow these steps:

1. Choose Site ⇨ Manage Sites.

2. In the Manage Sites dialog, choose New and select Site from the submenu to open the Site Definition dialog box. The Site Definition dialog box opens, as shown in Figure 5-6. If the Advanced tab is not already selected, select it now.

Note   If the root folder you have chosen is the same as another site folder, a prompt appears. If you have intentionally chosen the same folder, it's safe to ignore the warning and click OK to close it. However, using the same folder for multiple sites is not a typical practice, and it should be undertaken only by advanced users.

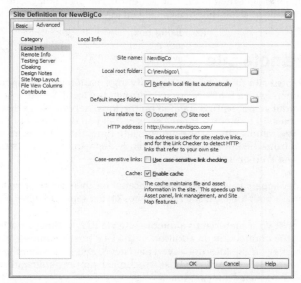

Figure 5-6: Set up your local site root through the Site Definition dialog box.

3. From the Local Info category, type a name for your site in the Site Name text box. This is the name that appears in the Sites drop-down list and the Edit Sites dialog box.

4. Specify the folder to serve as the local site root by either typing the pathname directly into the Local Root Folder text box or clicking the folder icon to open the Choose Local Root Folder dialog box. When you've made your choice there, click the Select button.

5. Leave the Refresh Local File List Automatically option selected. This option ensures that new files are automatically included in the list, and it relieves you from having to select the Refresh command manually.

6. If your site is to have a dedicated images folder, specify it in the Default Images Folder text box. Note that your Default Images Folder can have subfolders.

7. Choose which type of links you'd prefer to use by default: Relative To Site Root or Document Relative. If you're unsure, leave the standard option, Document Relative.

8. Enter the full URL for your site in the HTTP Address text box. When checking links for your Web site, Dreamweaver uses the HTTP address to determine whether absolute links, such as `www.idest.com/dreamweaver/index.htm`, reference external files or files on your site.

9. If you'd like to make sure that your links match files' names, including their case, choose the Use Case-Sensitive Link Checking option.

   This option is most helpful when your site is hosted on a Unix server that relies on case-sensitive filenames.

10. For fastest performance, select the Enable Cache option. Having a site cache enables Dreamweaver to store information that makes certain key site tasks, such as link updates, run faster.

Specifying the Remote Site

In addition to defining the local site root, you must specify information pertaining to the remote site. The remote site may be a folder accessed through the local network or via FTP (File Transfer Protocol). If your remote site is located on the local network — in this arrangement, the remote site is often said to be on a *staging server* — all you do is select or create the particular folder to house the remote site. At the appropriate time, the network administrator or other designated person from the Information Technology department exports the files from the staging server to the Web or intranet server.

Note   Many Dreamweaver developers have a Web server located on their development system, making it possible to have both the local and remote sites on the same machine.

If, on the other hand, you post your material to a remote site via FTP, you need various bits of information to complete the connection. In addition to the FTP host's name — used by Dreamweaver to find the server on the Internet — you also need, at a minimum, the user name and password to log on to the server. The host's technical support staff can provide you with this and any other necessary information.

Caution   Although it's entirely possible to develop your site locally without establishing a remote site root, it's not a recommended practice. Web sites require extensive testing in real-world settings — something that's just not possible with a local development setup. If you don't have the necessary information to establish a remote site root initially, you can still begin development locally; just be sure to transfer your files to your remote site and begin testing as soon as possible.

To enter the remote site information, follow these steps:

1. Continuing in the Site Definition dialog box, select the Remote Info category.

2. From the Access drop-down list, shown in Figure 5-7, choose the Web-server access description that applies to your site (FTP is shown in Figure 5-7):

   • **None:** Choose this option if your site is being developed locally and is not to be uploaded to a Web server at this time.

   • **FTP:** Select this option if you connect to your Web server via File Transfer Protocol (FTP).

   • **Local/Network:** Select this option if you are running a local Web server and want to store your remote site on your local drive, or if your Web server is mounted as a network drive.

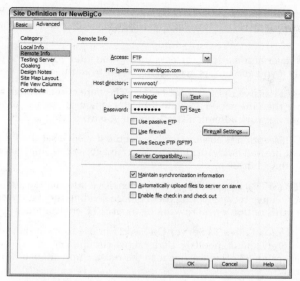

Figure 5-7: Choose whether your remote site is to be accessed via the local network or by FTP in the Remote Info category.

- **RDS:** Choose this option if you are working with a ColdFusion site that has Remote Development Services (RDS) enabled.

- **SourceSafe Database:** Select this option to integrate Dreamweaver's Check In/Check Out system with a running version of Microsoft's Visual SourceSafe.

- **WebDAV:** Choose this option to store your files remotely in a Web-based Distributed Authoring and Versioning (WebDAV) system.

3. If you selected None for access, skip the rest of this procedure and continue with the next section, "Adding Testing Server Details."

4. If you selected FTP for access, complete the following options:

- **FTP Host:** Enter the host name of the FTP connection for your Web server, which is usually in the form `ftp.sitename.com`. Do not include the full URL, such as `ftp://ftp.sitename.com`.

- **Host Directory:** Enter the directory in which publicly accessible documents are stored on the server. Typical host directory names are `www/public/docs/` and `public_html/`. Your remote site root folder is a subfolder of the host directory. If you are unsure of the exact name of the host directory, check with your Web server administrator. Often, the FTP host connects to the correct directory automatically, and you can leave this field blank.

- **Login:** Enter the login name you have been assigned for access to the Web server.

- **Password:** Enter the password necessary for you to gain access to the Web server. Note that many servers are case-sensitive when it comes to logins and passwords!

- **Save:** Dreamweaver automatically selects this option after you enter a password. Deselect it only if you and others access the server from the current system.

- **Use Passive FTP:** Passive FTP establishes the FTP connection through the local software, rather than the server. Certain firewall configurations use passive FTP; check with your network administrator to see if you need it.

- **Use Firewall:** This option is automatically selected if you've set the Preferences with the correct firewall host/port information (to access this information, click the Firewall Settings button).

- **Use Secure FTP (SFTP):** Secure FTP protects sensitive information such as passwords and user names by encrypting them before sending the data over the Internet. Select this option if you're working in an SFTP environment.

- **Automatically Upload Files To Server On Save:** Choose this option to store files locally and remotely simultaneously. Under most circumstances, I do not recommend that this option be selected, because the risk for uploading unfinished work is too great.

- **Enable File Check In And Check Out:** Select this option when working with other designers or contributors on a site.

- **Test:** After you've specified all your FTP parameters, you can click the Test button to verify that Dreamweaver can connect successfully to your Web server.

5. If you're having trouble connecting to your server, click Server Compatibility. A small dialog box opens with two options: Use FTP Performance Optimization and Use Alternative FTP Move Method. The first option is selected by default; deselect it if Dreamweaver cannot connect to your server. Choose the second option if errors occur either when rollbacks are enabled or when moving files on the remote server.

6. If you selected Local/Network for access, enter the name of the remote folder in the Remote Folder text box or click the folder icon to locate the folder. If you want to automatically update the remote file list (recommended), select the Refresh Remote File List Automatically option. You also have the option to automatically upload files to the remote server when saved locally (not recommended) and to enable file check in and check out — a valuable option when working on a site with others.

Adding Testing Server Details

The final primary element for defining sites using the Advanced tab is supplying the server application information. One key aspect of Dreamweaver's power is its capability to create the same application for different server models using different scripting languages. The Live Data Preview — which enables designers to work with data directly from the data source — is another unique Dreamweaver feature. Settings in the Testing Server category of the Site Definition dialog box control both of these features.

To set the Testing Server options, follow these steps:

1. Continuing in the Site Definition dialog box, choose the Testing Server category, as shown in Figure 5-8.

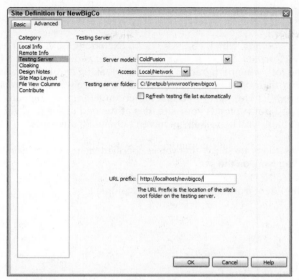

Figure 5-8: Before you can create any dynamic pages in Dreamweaver, you must choose a server model from the Testing Server category.

2. From the Server Model list, choose the application server to be used in this site: ASP JavaScript, ASP VBScript, ASP.NET C#, ASP.NET VB, ColdFusion, JSP, PHP MySQL, or None.

3. To set the way in which you connect with your testing server, choose FTP, Local/Network, or None from the Access list. If you choose None, Live Preview is not available. The options for FTP and Local/Network are the same as those found in the Remote Info category.

Tip   After selecting your options, it's always a good idea to click Test to make sure your connection is solid.

4. In the URL Prefix field, enter the HTTP address for the root folder on the testing server. If you're working locally, your URL Prefix is likely to start with `http://localhost/`.

5. Click OK to close the Site Definition dialog box.

Note   Dreamweaver doesn't save the site definition information until the program exits. If Dreamweaver should *unexpectedly quit* — the politically correct term for *crash* — any changes made to the Site Definition dialog box in the session are lost.

Cloaking Site Folders

Dreamweaver supports *site cloaking*, which enables you to exclude (cloak) specified site folders from operations such as Put, Get, Check In/Out, Synchronize, and so on. (For a full list of cloaked operations, see the following paragraphs.) The site cloaking feature can save you a significant amount of upload/maintenance time. Suppose that you're working on a site that contains several dozen large MP3 files, all stored in a folder named mp3s. You can cloak the mp3s folder, so that when you put (upload) your site files at the end of the day, you don't end up re-putting all those mp3 files, which most likely haven't changed, anyway.

Note   A site's folder-cloaking settings are sticky; after you've specified them, Dreamweaver remembers them whenever you work on the site.

Cloaking excludes cloaked folders from the following operations:

✦ Put, Get

✦ Check In, Check Out

✦ Reports

✦ Select Newer Local, Select Newer Remote

✦ Sitewide commands, such as Check Links Sitewide and Find And Replace Entire Site

✦ Synchronize

✦ Asset panel contents

✦ Template and library updating

Cloaking and uncloaking site folders is a breeze. Follow these steps:

1. In the Files panel, select the desired site from the drop-down list box. Note that this site must have cloaking enabled in the Site Definition dialog box, which is the default site setting. If, however, you need to enable cloaking for a site, choose Site ➪ Cloaking ➪ Enable Cloaking.

2. Select the folder(s) you want to cloak or uncloak.

3. From the Options menu of the Files panel, choose Site ➪ Cloaking ➪ Cloak or Site ➪ Cloaking ➪ Uncloak. Alternatively, you can right-click (Control+click) a selected folder and use the context menu. A red, diagonal line across the selected folders appears or disappears to show that they are cloaked or uncloaked, as shown in Figure 5-9.

   To uncloak all site folders (and files), choose Site ➪ Cloaking ➪ Uncloak All from the Options menu or the pop-up context menu.

Caution   When you uncloak an entire site, you cannot undo it! If you want to recloak folders, you have to do so manually.

Figure 5-9: You can easily cloak or uncloak your site folders.

Managing Site Info

You can change any of the information associated with your local site roots by choosing Site ➪ Manage Sites. Select the site you want to modify from the Manage Sites dialog box and click the Edit button; you see the corresponding information, which you can edit.

After your participation in a project has ended, you can remove the site from your list. In the Edit Sites dialog box, choose the site you want to remove, and click the Remove button. Note that this action removes the site only from Dreamweaver's internal site list; it *does not* actually delete any files or folders from your hard drive.

Tip Before you remove a site, make sure you export the site settings by choosing Export from the Manage Sites dialog box (Site ➪ Manage Sites). The exported file preserves all the connection information and can be imported through the Manage Sites dialog box at a later date.

With the local site root folder established, Dreamweaver can properly manage links regardless of whether the document relative or site root relative format is used.

Cross-Reference You can find a discussion of document relative and site root relative addressing in Chapter 10.

Working Directly with Servers

Web designers work under a variety of conditions. Some designers are tasked with making small modifications to a range of individual Web pages on a variety of sites rather than focusing on the development and maintenance of complete sites. For these types of jobs, it is often unnecessary to define a site in Dreamweaver—all you really need is a connection to the server. After you establish a server connection, you can download files to your local system, make your modifications, and put the altered files back on the server.

If you prefer, Dreamweaver now gives you the option to work without establishing a site. You can create connections via either FTP (File Transfer Protocol) or RDS (Remote Development Services). RDS is a component of the ColdFusion server used for file transfer. After the server connection is created, Dreamweaver lists the available files in the Files panel, just like a standard site. When you open a file, that file and any dependent files are transferred to your local system for editing. If you save the file, Dreamweaver automatically stores the modified file on the server and erases the local copy.

Although convenient for simple modifications, working without a defined site does have its limitations. If you use this technique, none of Dreamweaver's sitewide features are available, including templates, library items, check in/check out, cloaking, and link checking, among others.

Caution   You should exercise extreme care when working directly with server files. In most situations, it is strongly advised that you work with Dreamweaver's defined site structure, particularly if other designers are working on the site. Without some sort of revision control, such as Dreamweaver's Check In/Check Out feature, it is entirely possible that work can be inadvertently lost.

Establishing a Siteless Server Connection

Whether or not you define a site, you create, edit, and remove server connections by using the Manage Sites dialog box. The type of remote access—FTP or RDS—you choose for a server determines how the connection is listed. Connections using FTP are listed with an `ftp://` preface, whereas those using RDS start with `rds://`, as in `rds://myclientserver`.

Caution   Certain sitewide operations, such as link checking, synchronizing sites, and templates, are not available when working directly with a server.

To set up an FTP server connection, follow these steps:

1. Choose Site ➪ Manage Sites.

2. In the Manage Sites dialog box, click New and select FTP & RDS Server from the pop-up menu, as shown in Figure 5-10.

Figure 5-10: The Manage Sites dialog also manages server connections.

Dreamweaver reminds you that although server connections enable you to work directly with files on the server, you cannot carry out sitewide actions.

3. When the Configure Server dialog box opens, enter an appropriate title to identify the connection in the Name field.

4. Make sure FTP is chosen from the Access Type list. Dreamweaver displays different fields according to the Access Type chosen; the FTP fields are shown in Figure 5-11.

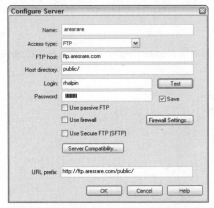

Figure 5-11: The same information used to set up a remote site with FTP is used for an FTP server.

5. Enter the FTP address in the FTP Host field. The FTP Host should be a partial Internet address, such as ftp.idest.com.

6. Enter the site root folder, if any, in the Host Directory field. Depending on the FTP server setup, you may or may not have a host directory. Often such directories have names like www/ or public/.

7. Enter the Login name and Password in the corresponding fields. It's a good idea to verify your connection information at this stage by clicking Test. Dreamweaver lets you know whether the connection is made successfully.

8. Select any of the necessary optional settings:

   • Use Passive FTP

   • Use Firewall

   • Use Secure FTP (SFTP)

9. If you have selected the Use Firewall option, click Firewall Settings and make sure the Firewall Host and Firewall Port settings are correct.

10. Set the Internet address in the URL Prefix field to correspond to the site root.

11. Click OK when you're finished to create the connection.

To set up an RDS connection to a ColdFusion server, follow these steps:

1. Choose Site ➪ Manage Sites.

2. In the Manage Sites dialog box, click New and select FTP & RDS Server from the pop-up menu. Dreamweaver reminds you that although server connections enable you to work directly with files on the server, you cannot carry out sitewide actions; feel free to select the Don't Show Me This Message Again option at any point.

3. Enter an appropriate title for your RDS connection in the Name field of the Configure Server dialog box.

4. Select RDS from the Access Type list.

5. Click Settings to open the Configure RDS Server dialog box, shown in Figure 5-12.

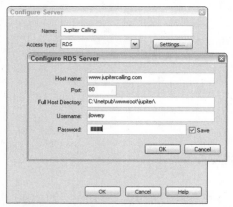

Figure 5-12: Access the Configure RDS Server dialog through the Settings button.

6. In the Configure RDS Server dialog, enter the URL or IP address for the server in the Host Name field.

7. Enter the appropriate Port number; the default Port value is 80.

8. In the Full Host Directory field, enter the path to the site folder on the remote system, for example, `c:\inetput\wwwroot\bigco\`.

9. If necessary, enter the username and password in the appropriate fields. The Username and Password field options may not appear, depending on the settings of the ColdFusion Administrator.

10. Select Save to retain your settings. If you do not select Save, you must re-enter the settings information every time you connect to the server.

11. Click OK to close the Configure RDS Server dialog.

12. Enter the Internet address to the server root in the URL Prefix field.

13. Click OK to close the dialog and create the server connection.

When you're finished defining either an FTP or RDS server, you can continue managing your sites and server connections or click Done to close the Manage Sites dialog. If a server is selected when you close the dialog, Dreamweaver connects to the server and displays the available files in the Files panel.

Accessing Server Files

After being defined, all the servers are listed along with the sites in the Files panel pop-up menu. As noted earlier, the type of server is used as a preface to the defined name. Thus, all the FTP servers are grouped together as are all the RDS servers; servers are listed above the standard site list in the pop-up menu, as shown in Figure 5-13. Choose any server from the list to open a connection and list the files. After the files are listed, you can choose any one just as you would select a file from a defined site, by double-clicking the filename to open the file. Dreamweaver automatically downloads the file and any dependent files, such as images, needed to render the page.

Figure 5-13: All server connections are found above the defined sites in the Files panel pop-up.

Tip   Although there is no Expand/Collapse icon displayed atop the docked Files panel when a server connection is chosen, the full-window option is still available from the Options menu: Expand Files Panel. After the panel is expanded, click the Expand/Collapse icon to return to the condensed panel view.

In addition to sites and server connection, the Files panel also provides access to local and mapped network drives. You find the additional connections at the top of the pop-up list, above the defined sites and servers.

Note   For the files of a mapped network drive to appear, you must be logged in to that drive.

After you finish modifying the page, choose File ➪ Save to put the modified files back on the server.

Creating and Saving New Pages

You've considered message, audience, and budget issues. You've chosen a design. You've set up your site and its address. All the preliminary planning is completed, and now you're ready to really rev up Dreamweaver and begin creating pages. This section covers the basic mechanics of opening and saving Web pages during development.

Starting Dreamweaver

Start Dreamweaver as you would any other program. Double-click the Dreamweaver program icon, or single-click if you are using Internet Explorer's Desktop Integration feature in Windows or if you have Dreamweaver's icon in your Dock on OS X. After the splash screen, Dreamweaver opens with the Start Page, which lists 10 of your previously opened documents and also offers a full range of new document types. Choose HTML from the Start Page to create a new blank page. This page is created from the `Default.html` file found in Dreamweaver's Configuration/DocumentTypes/NewDocuments folder. Of course, you may want to replace the original `Default.html` file with one of your own—perhaps with your copyright information. All your blank pages are then created from the template that you've designed.

Tip   If you do decide to create your own Default template, it's probably a good idea to rename the Dreamweaver Default template—as `Original-Default.html` or something similar— prior to creating your new, personalized Default template.

Building Placeholder Pages

One technique you might find helpful—and especially so with the use of *document-relative addressing* in Dreamweaver Web projects—is what I call *placeholder pages*. These placeholder pages provide an effortless way to include links as you create Web pages.

Suppose, for example, you've just finished laying out most of the text and graphics for your home page and you want to put in some navigation buttons. You drop in your button images and align them just so. All that's missing are the links. If you're using document-relative addressing, the best way to assign a link is to click the Browse for File button in the Property inspector and select your file. But what do you do if you haven't created any other pages yet and there aren't any files to select? That's when you can put placeholder pages to work.

After you've designed the basics of your site and created your local site root, as described previously in this chapter, start with a blank Dreamweaver page. Type a single identifying word on the page and save it in the local site root. Repeat this step for all the Web pages in your plan. When it comes time to make your links, all you have to do is point and click to the appropriate placeholder page. This arrangement also gives you an immediate framework for link testing. When it comes time to work on the next page, just open up the correct placeholder page and start to work.

Another style of working involves using the Files panel as your base of operations, rather than the Document window. It's very easy in Dreamweaver to choose File ➪ New File from the Files panel Options menu several times and create the basic files of your site. You can even create a file and immediately link to it by choosing Site ➪ Link to New File from a selected file icon in the Site map. A dialog box opens, which enables you to specify the filename, the title of the new document, and the text for the link. Moreover, you can create any needed subfolders, such as ones for images or other media by choosing File ➪ New Folder from the Options menu or pop-up context menu.

Opening Existing Files

To open an existing file that belongs to a site you've defined in Dreamweaver, select the site in the Files panel and double-click the file icon. Recently opened files, regardless of their origin, are available through the Start Page or from the File ⇨ Open Recent menu.

To open an existing file that does not belong to a site defined in Dreamweaver — or that was created in a different program — choose File ⇨ Open or Ctrl+O (Command+O), and choose the file from the File Open dialog box.

Tip   You can enable/disable Dreamweaver from automatically repairing HTML syntax errors in your files when it opens them. Choose Edit ⇨ Preferences (Dreamweaver ⇨ Preferences) to open the Preferences dialog box, select the Code Rewriting category and check/uncheck the desired options: Fix Invalidly Nested and Unclosed Tags, Rename Form Items when Pasting, Remove Extra Closing Tags, and so on. To have Dreamweaver report its syntax repairs, select the Warn When Fixing or Removing Tags option.

To add an entry, place your cursor at the end of the line above where you want your new file format to be placed, and press Enter (Return). Type in your file extension(s) in capital letters followed by a colon and then the text description. Save the `Extensions.txt` file and restart Dreamweaver to see your modifications.

Opening a New File

You can work on as many Dreamweaver files as your system memory can sustain. When you choose File ⇨ New or the keyboard shortcut Ctrl+N (Command+N) and select a file type from the New Document dialog box, Dreamweaver opens a new blank file of your specified type. (For more on this, see the section "Creating New Documents" later in this chapter.)

Tip   If you are using the Windows version of Dreamweaver and are working with maximized documents, you can easily switch among open files by clicking their respective tabs at the top of the Document window or by using the Windows menu.

Each time you open a new file, Dreamweaver temporarily names the file `Untitled-n`, where n is the next number in sequence. This naming convention prevents you from accidentally overwriting a new file opened in the same session.

Note   Using the New Document dialog box to create new documents of all types (HTML, JavaScript, ASP, ColdFusion, and so on) is discussed in detail later in this chapter in the section "Creating New Documents."

Saving Your File

Saving your work is very important in any computer-related task, and Dreamweaver is no exception. To initially save the current file, choose File ⇨ Save or use the keyboard shortcut Ctrl+S (Command+S). The Save dialog box opens; you can enter a filename and, if you wish, a different path.

By default, all HTML files are saved with an `.htm` filename extension. Different file formats are saved with different extensions; XML documents, for example, are stored with an `.xml` extension. To save your file with another extension, such as `.shtml` or `.xhtml`, change the Save as Type option to the specific file type and then enter your full filename *with* the extension.

Opening Other Types of Files

Dreamweaver defaults to searching for HTML files with an extension of `.htm`, `.html`, or `.xhtml`. To look for other types of files, click the Files of Type arrow button. Dreamweaver allows several other file types, including server-side includes (`.shtml`, `.shtm`, `.stm`, or `.ssi`), Active server pages (`.asp`), and ColdFusion (`.cfm`, `.cfml`, or `.cfc`). To load a valid HTML file with a different extension, select the All Files option.

If you are working consistently with a different file format, you can add your own extensions and file types to Dreamweaver's Open dialog box. In the Configuration folder, open an editable text file called `Extensions.txt` in Dreamweaver or in your favorite text editor to make any additions. The syntax must follow the format of the standard `Extensions.txt` file:

```
HTM,HTML,SHTM,SHTML,HTA,HTC,XHTML,STM,SSI,JS,AS,ASC,ASR,XML,XSL,XSD,DTD,X
SLT,RSS,RDF,LBI,DWT,ASP,ASA,ASPX,ASCX,ASMX,CONFIG,CS,CSS,CFM,CFML,CFC,TLD,
TXT,PHP,PHP3,PHP4,PHP5,TPL,LASSO,JSP,JSF,VB,VBS,VTM,VTML,INC,JAVA,EDML,
WML:All Documents
HTM,HTML,HTA,HTC,XHTML:HTML Documents
SHTM,SHTML,STM,SSI,INC:Server-Side Includes
JS:JavaScript Documents
XML,DTD,XSD,XSL,XSLT,RSS,RDF:XML Files
LBI:Library Files
DWT:Template Files
CSS:Style Sheets
ASP,ASA:Active Server Pages
ASPX,ASCX,ASMX,CS,VB,CONFIG:Active Server Plus Pages
CFM,CFML,CFC:ColdFusion Templates
AS:ActionScript Files
ASC:ActionScript Communication Files
ASR:ActionScript Remote Files
TXT:Text Files
PHP,PHP3,PHP4,PHP5,TPL:PHP Files
LASSO:Lasso Files
JSP,JST:Java Server Pages
JSF:Fireworks Script
TLD:Tag Library Descriptor Files
JAVA:Java Files
WML:WML Files
EDML:EDML Files
VBS:VBScript Files
VTM,VTML:VTML Files
```

Caution

Although it may seem kind of backward in this day and age of long filenames, it's still a good idea to choose all-lowercase names for your files without spaces or punctuation other than an underscore or hyphen. Otherwise, not all servers read the filename correctly, and you have problems linking your pages.

Saving to Remote Servers

The section "Working Directly with Servers" described how Dreamweaver automatically transfers a modified file to a defined server when you are working in a siteless mode. But do you know that you can also store files on any server?

The capability to save to a remote server comes in handy in a number of situations. If a designer has files to work on locally and the connection information needed for uploading them, he doesn't need to create a local site. All he needs is a connection to the server and the knowledge of where the file should be stored. Because the designer is working without a locally defined site, the file must be saved in a particular location.

To save a file on a remote server, follow these steps:

1. Choose File ⇨ Save to Remote Server. The Save File dialog box, shown in Figure 5-14, appears. Server connections, as well as any site with a remote server, are displayed.

Figure 5-14: Servers must be previously defined in Dreamweaver to be listed in the Save File dialog box.

2. Double-click on the server where you want to store the file. Dreamweaver connects to the server and retrieves a folder and file listing.

3. Navigate to the desired folder and enter a name for your file in the Filename field.

4. Click Save to transfer the file or Cancel to abort.

Dreamweaver transfers the current file as well as any dependent files.

Tip   The Save to Remote Server feature can also be used to move a file from one site to another. Instead of choosing a server connection from the Save File dialog, select a previously defined site. Selecting the site opens the remote server for the selected site.

Closing the File

When you're done working on a file, you can close it by choosing File ➪ Close or by using the keyboard shortcut Ctrl+W (Command+W). If you've made any changes to your file since last saving it, Dreamweaver prompts you to save it. Click Yes to save the file or No to close it without saving your changes.

Note You can easily tell whether a file has been altered since the last save by looking at the title bar. Dreamweaver places an asterisk after the filename in the title bar for modified files. Dreamweaver is even smart enough to properly remove the asterisk should you reverse your changes with the Undo command or the History panel. On OS X you also see that the close widget on the document window appears filled in when the file is unsaved.

Quitting the Program

When you're finished working for the day — or, more often, the late, late night — you can close Dreamweaver by choosing File ➪ Exit (File ➪ Quit) or by using the standard keyboard shortcut Ctrl+Q (Command+Q).

Tip Have to stop work in the middle of a session and want to get back to work ASAP? Leave one or more documents open when you close Dreamweaver and they'll reappear when the program next launches. To enable this feature, choose the Reopen On Startup option from the General category of Preferences.

Creating New Documents

Dreamweaver provides three methods for creating new documents:

✦ Select your preferred document type from the Create New column of the Dreamweaver Start Page.

✦ You can use the New Document dialog box to create a new document of a type that you select from a comprehensive list within the following categories: Basic Page, Dynamic Page, Template Page, Other, CSS Style Sheets, Framesets, Page Designs (CSS), Page Designs, and Page Designs (Accessible). If you work with multiple document types, this is the way to go.

✦ You can create a new document of a default type that you've specified in the Preferences dialog box. If you work mostly with one document type — HTML, ColdFusion, or ASP, for example — this method can prove very convenient.

Using the New Document Dialog Box

To create a new document using the New Document dialog box, follow these steps:

1. Choose File ➪ New to open the New Document dialog box, as shown in Figure 5-15.

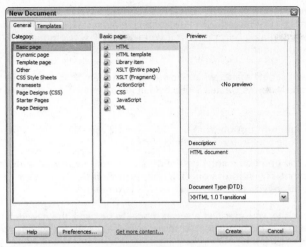

Figure 5-15: Choose the type of new file you want to start with through the New Document dialog box.

2. In the Category list of the General panel, select the category of document that you want to create: Basic Page, Dynamic Page, Template Page, Other, and so on.

3. In the Document Type list, select the specific type of document you want to create: HTML, ColdFusion, JavaScript, and so on.

4. If desired, select a different option from the Document Type (DTD) list. Note that this setting does not stick; you'll need to reset it each time or select a new DTD option in the New Document category of Preferences.

5. Click Create to create a new, blank document of the selected category/type.

If you want to create a new document based on a custom template, use the Templates — rather than the General — panel of the New Document dialog box. For more information on creating/using templates, see Chapter 27.

Creating a New Default Document

If you often create one type of document — HTML or ColdFusion files, for example — you can take advantage of Dreamweaver's default document feature to save yourself some document creation time and trouble. By using the techniques described in this section, you can open a new document of your default type (HTML, ColdFusion, and so on) with one quick keyboard shortcut — in other words, without having to work your way through the New Document dialog box. It's a must for the Dreamweaver power user!

To create a new default document, follow these steps:

1. Choose Edit ➪ Preferences (Dreamweaver ➪ Preferences) to open the Preferences dialog box, and select the New Document category. If the document type you want is not already defined as the Default Document Type, define it now.

Note the Show New Document Dialog On Ctrl+N (Command+N) option. Uncheck this box if you want Ctrl+N (Command+N) to create a new default document without showing the New Document dialog box; check it if you want Ctrl+N (Command+N) to show the New Document dialog box.

Tip   If you are a Windows user, no matter what Show New Document Dialog On Ctrll+N setting you choose, Ctrl+Shift+N always creates a new default document *without* showing the New Document dialog box.

If desired, select a different option from the Document Type (DTD) list. When you're finished, click OK to close the Preferences dialog box.

2. After you perform the preceding step, you're done. To create a new default document, simply press Ctrl+Shift+N (Windows only). If you turned off the Show New Document Dialog On Ctrl+N option, you can also press Ctrl+N (Command+N).

Note   If, when defining your site, you specified a server model to be used, the new default document is the file type that corresponds to that server model — despite the Preferences dialog box setting you have chosen.

Previewing Your Web Pages

When using Dreamweaver or any other Web authoring tool, it's important to frequently check your progress in one or more browsers. Dreamweaver's Document window offers a near-browser view of your Web page, but because of the variations among the different browsers, it's imperative that you preview your page early and often. Dreamweaver offers you easy access to a maximum of 20 browsers — and they're just a function key away.

Note   Don't confuse Dreamweaver's View Live Data mode with the Preview in Browser feature. With View Live Data, Dreamweaver can only show you an approximation of how your page will look on the Web. Not all aspects of your page — such as links and rollovers — are active. You need to preview and test your page in a variety of browsers to see how your page looks and behaves on the Web.

You add a browser to your preview list by choosing File ➪ Preview in Browser ➪ Edit Browser List or by choosing the Preview in Browser category from the Preferences dialog box. Both actions open the Preview in Browser category of the Preferences. The steps for editing your browser list are described in detail in Chapter 4. Here's a brief recap:

1. Choose File ➪ Preview in Browser ➪ Edit Browser List to open the Preview in Browser Preferences category.

2. To add a browser (up to 20), click the Add (+) button and fill out the following fields in the Add Browser dialog box (see Figure 5-16):

   • **Name:** When you choose the browser application, Dreamweaver automatically provides a name for the browser. You can accept this name, or change it by typing a new name in the Name field.

   • **Application:** Type in the path to the browser program or click the Browse button to locate the browser executable (.exe) file.

   • **Primary Browser/Secondary Browser:** If you want, select one of these checkboxes to designate the current browser as such.

Figure 5-16: It's best to leave the Name field blank until you choose the browser executable in the Application field; Dreamweaver automatically fills in the name and removes any previously entered value.

3. After you add a browser to your list, you can easily edit or delete it. Reopen the Preview in Browser Preferences category and highlight the browser you want to modify or delete.

4. To alter your selection, click the Edit button. To delete your selection, click the Remove (–) button.

5. After you finish your modifications, click OK to close the dialog box.

After you add one or more browsers to your list, you can preview the current page in these browsers. Choose File ➪ Preview in Browser ➪ *BrowserName*, where *BrowserName* indicates the particular program. Dreamweaver saves the page to a temporary file, starts the browser, and loads the page.

In order to view any changes you've made to your Web page under construction, you must select the Preview in Browser menu option again (or press one of the function keys for primary/secondary browser previewing, described in the following paragraph). Clicking the Refresh/Reload button in your browser does not load in any modifications. The temporary preview files are deleted when you quit Dreamweaver.

Tip   Dreamweaver saves preview files with a filename like the following: `TMP5c34jymi4q.asp`; a unique name is generated with each preview to ensure that the browser does not load the page from the cache. If Dreamweaver unexpectedly quits, these TMP files are not deleted. Feel free to delete any such TMP files you find in your site; or use them as backups to restore unsaved work should a crash occur.

You can also use keyboard shortcuts to preview two different browsers by pressing a function key. Press F12 (Option+F12) to preview the current Dreamweaver page in your primary browser, and Ctrl+F12 (Command+F12) to preview the same page in your secondary browser. These are the primary and secondary browser settings you establish in the Preview In Browser Preferences panel, explained in Chapter 4.

You can easily reassign your primary and secondary browsers. Go to the Preview in Browser Preferences category, select the desired browser, and select the appropriate checkbox to designate the browser as primary or secondary. In the list of browsers, you see the indicator of F12 (Option+F12) or Ctrl+F12 (Command+F12) appear next to the browser's name.

Tip   In addition to checking your Web page output on a variety of browsers on your system, it's also a good idea to preview the page on other platforms. If you're designing on a Macintosh, try to view your pages on a Windows system, and vice versa. Watch out for some not-so-subtle differences between the two environments in terms of color rendering (colors in Macs tend to be brighter than in PCs) and screen resolution.

Putting Your Pages Online

The final phase of setting up your Dreamweaver site is publishing your pages to the Web. When you begin, this publishing process is up to you. Some Web designers wait until everything is absolutely perfect on the local development site and then upload everything at once. Others like to establish an early connection to the remote site and extend the transfer of files over a longer period of time.

I fall into the latter camp. When I start transferring files at the beginning of the process, I find that I catch my mistakes earlier and avoid having to effect massive changes to the site after everything is up. For example, in developing one large site, I started out using mixed-case filenames, as in ELFhome.html. After publishing some early drafts of a few Web pages, however, I discovered that the host had switched servers; on the new server, filenames had to be entirely lowercase. Had I waited until the last moment to upload everything, I would have been faced with an unexpected and laborious search-and-replace job.

Transferring with FTP

After you've established your local site root — and you've included your remote site's FTP information in the setup — the actual publishing of your files to the Web is a very straightforward process.

New In Dreamweaver Putting and getting files to and from your server, while easy, can be incredibly time-consuming. Dreamweaver frees its users from the drudgery of waiting for files to transfer through its background FTP feature. Uploading and retrieving files is a separate computer process in Dreamweaver, distinct from working in Design and Code view. When you initiate a publishing event, the Background File Activity dialog box with a small progress bar appears, as seen in Figure 5-17. You can dismiss the dialog by clicking Hide; when hidden, file activity can be seen in the bottom of the Files panel. An ongoing log is shown when you click Details, and can be saved when the transfers have been completed by clicking Save Log.

Figure 5-17: Dreamweaver transfers files through a background FTP process so you can continue working while files are being published.

To transfer your local Web pages to an online site, follow these steps:

1. Choose Window ➪ Files or press F8 to open the Files panel, and select the desired site from the Site drop-down list.

2. In the Files panel, click the Connect button. (You may need to connect to the Internet first.) Dreamweaver displays a message box showing the progress of the connection.

3. If you didn't enter a password in the Remote Info category when you defined the site, or if you entered a password but didn't opt to save it, Dreamweaver asks you to type in your password. When the connection is complete, the directory listing of the remote site appears in the Files panel.

4. Click the Expand/Collapse button to expand the Files panel into its two-pane view: Remote pane on the left, Local pane on the right. In the Local pane (green icons), select the folder(s) and file(s) you want to upload—or, to upload the entire site, select the site folder (at the top of the list)—and then click the Put File(s) button, as shown in Figure 5-18.

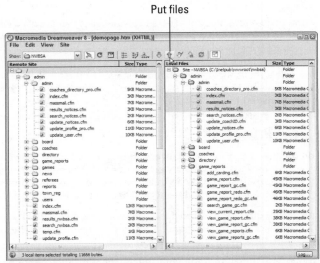

Put files

Figure 5-18: Use the Put File(s) button in the Files panel to transfer files, folders, and entire sites.

5. If Dreamweaver asks if you would like to move the dependent files as well, click Yes to transfer all embedded graphics and other objects, or No if you'd prefer to move these yourself. You can also select the Don't Ask Me Again checkbox to make transfers of dependent files automatic in the future.

6. The Background File Transfer dialog box appears. Click Hide to hide the dialog box and continue working in Dreamweaver; click Details to see the files being transferred.

   If hidden, you can restore the Background File Transfer dialog box by clicking the globe icon at the bottom of the Files panel.

7. After each file has successfully transferred, Dreamweaver places a checkmark next to its icon—provided that File Check In/Out is enabled in the site's Remote Info category.

8. When you finish transferring your files, click the Disconnect button.

9. If you'd like to store the log file, display the Background File Transfer dialog box (if necessary) and click Save Log.

Note   Dreamweaver provides an FTP Log panel that displays all your FTP file transfer activity (Puts, Gets, and so on). This panel is particularly useful for troubleshooting FTP transfer errors. For more information, see the next section, "Using the FTP Log Panel."

Remember that the only files you have to highlight for transfer to the remote site are the HTML files. As noted previously, Dreamweaver automatically transfers any dependent files (if you allow it), which means that you'll never forget to move a GIF again. (Nor will you ever move an unnecessary file, such as an earlier version of an image, by mistake.) Moreover, Dreamweaver automatically creates any subfolders necessary to maintain the site's integrity. These two features combined will save you substantial time and worry.

Caution   Be aware that Dreamweaver does not always know to include files that are used within scripts; you might need to upload these files manually.

Now you have made your site a reality, from the planning stages to the local site root and onto the Web. Congratulations — all that's left is to fill those pages with insightful content, amazing graphics, and wondrous code.

Using the FTP Log Panel

Like all data transfers on the Internet, FTP file transfers sometimes go awry: Servers are busy or down, file/directory permissions are improperly set, passwords are misspelled, and so on. If you run into an FTP transfer problem with your Dreamweaver Put File(s) or Get File(s) command, you can use the FTP Log panel to find out exactly what went wrong.

The FTP Log panel displays all your FTP file-transfer activity. To display the FTP Log panel, first choose Windows ➪ Results or use the keyboard shortcut F7. Then, select the FTP Log category from the Results panel.

FTP logs may seem complex and indecipherable, but the information they contain is invaluable for troubleshooting FTP errors. Figure 5-19, for example, displays the FTP log that results from Putting (uploading) a file to a remote server.

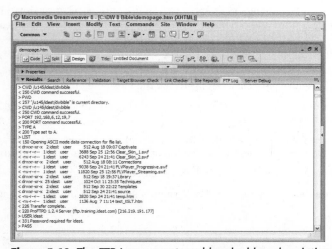

Figure 5-19: The FTP Log generates a blow-by-blow description of actions taken.

Summary

In this chapter, you learned some options for planning your Web site and what you need to do in Dreamweaver to initialize the site. As you plan your site and set up your servers, keep these points in mind:

✦ Put as much time into planning your site as possible. The more clearly conceived the site, the cleaner the execution.

✦ Set up your local site root in Dreamweaver right away. The local site root is essential for Dreamweaver to properly publish your files to the remote site later.

✦ If you are creating a Web application, choose one server model per site and set it when you define your site. This step is needed so that Dreamweaver knows the type of server code to write.

✦ Although necessary for many operations, you don't need to define a site to work with a Web page. If you have the required connection information, you can work directly with files on a server. Opening a file from a directly connected server copies the file to your local system; when you save the file, Dreamweaver automatically puts it back on the server and removes the local version.

✦ Preview early, often, and with various browsers. Dreamweaver gives you quick function-key access to a primary (F12/Option+F12) and secondary (Ctrl+F12/Command+F12) browser. Check your pages frequently in these browsers, and then spend some time checking your pages against other available browsers and browser versions.

✦ Establish an early connection to the Web and use it frequently. You can begin publishing your local site through Dreamweaver's Site window almost immediately.

In the next chapter, you learn how to use Dreamweaver to begin coding your Web pages.

✦   ✦   ✦

Designing and Crafting Core Pages

Accessing the Code Directly

As far as most designers are concerned, in a perfect world, you could lay out a complex Web site with a visual authoring tool and never have to see the HTML and other code, much less modify it. Dreamweaver takes you a long way toward this goal — in fact, you can create many types of Web pages using only Dreamweaver's Design view. As your pages become more complex, however, you may need to tweak your code in one way or another.

Programmers, on the other hand, are happiest working directly with the code. To accomplish their goals efficiently, coders need a responsive, flexible editor capable of handling a wide range of computer languages. Just how much assistance is required is a matter of personal taste: Some code writers want all the help they can get, with features such as syntax coloring, code completion, and Code Hints, among others. Other programmers just want the editor to stay out of their way.

Dreamweaver tries to give coders the best of both worlds by providing a full-featured editor with numerous options. In addition to the features mentioned in the preceding paragraph, Dreamweaver includes full tag libraries in numerous languages: HTML, CFML, ASP.NET, JSP, and PHP, to name a few. Both hand-coders and visual designers can enjoy the benefits of Dreamweaver tools such as the Snippets panel, for adding chunks of code via drag-and-drop, and the Tag Inspector, for displaying all the attributes of a chosen tag — and making them editable as well. This chapter covers all these features and more.

Although the Internet is made up of a plethora of technologies, HTML is still at the heart of a Web page. This chapter gives you a basic understanding of how HTML works and provides you with the specific building blocks to begin creating Web pages. This chapter also gives you your first look at a Dreamweaver innovation: Code view, for altering the code side by side with the visual environment. The other Dreamweaver-specific material in this chapter — which primarily describes how Dreamweaver sets and modifies page properties — is suitable for even the most accomplished Web designers. Armed with these fundamentals, you are ready to begin your exploration of Web-page creation.

The Structure of a Web Page

The simplest explanation of how HTML works derives from the full expansion of its acronym: Hypertext Markup Language. *Hypertext* refers to one of the World Wide Web's main properties — the capability to jump from one page to another, no matter where the pages are located on the Web. *Markup Language* means that a Web page is actually a heavily annotated text file. The basic building blocks of HTML, such as `<strong>` and `<p>`, are known as *markup elements*, or *tags*. The terms *element* and *tag* are used interchangeably.

An HTML page, then, is a set of instructions (the tags) suggesting to your browser how to display the enclosed text and images. The browser knows what kind of page it is handling based on the tag that opens the page, `<html>`, and the tag that closes the page, `</html>`. The great majority of HTML tags come in such pairs, in which the closing tag always has a forward slash before the keyword. Two examples of tag pairs are: `<p>`...`</p>` and `<title>`...`</title>`. A few important tags are represented by a single element: the image tag `<img>`, for example.

The HTML page is divided into two primary sections: the `<head>` and the `<body>`. Information relating to the entire document goes in the `<head>` section: the title, description, keywords, and any language subroutines called from within the `<body>`. The content of the Web page is found in the `<body>` section. All the text, graphics, embedded animations, Java applets, and other elements of the page are found between the opening `<body>` and the closing `</body>` tags.

When you start a new document in Dreamweaver, the basic format is already laid out for you. Listing 6-1 shows the code from a Dreamweaver blank Web page.

Listing 6-1: **The HTML for a New Dreamweaver Page**

```
<!DOCTYPE HTML PUBLIC "-//W3C//DTD HTML 4.01 Transitional//EN">
<html>
<head>
<title>Untitled Document</title>
<meta http-equiv="Content-Type" content="text/html; charset=iso-8859-1">
</head>

<body>

</body>
</html>
```

I cover the opening `<!DOCTYPE>` tag a little later in this chapter in the section "doctype and doctype Switching." First, you should notice how the `<head>`...`</head>` pair is separate from the `<body>`...`</body>` pair and that both are contained within the `<html>`...`</html>` tags.

Notice also that the `<meta>` tag has two additional elements:

```
http-equiv="Content-Type"
```

and

```
content="text/html; charset=iso-8859-1"
```

These types of elements are known as *attributes*. Attributes modify the basic tag and can either be equal to a value or stand-alone. I cover the specifics of the <meta> tag later in this chapter; for now you should focus on just the syntax. Attributes are made up of name/value pairs where the attribute is set to be equal to some value, typically in quotes. Not all tags have attributes, but when they do, the attributes are specific.

One last note about an HTML page: You are free to use carriage returns, spaces, and tabs as needed to make your code more readable. The interpreting browser ignores all but the included tags and text to create your page. I point to some minor, browser-specific differences in interpretation of these elements throughout the book, but generally, you can indent or space your code as you wish.

Cross-Reference The style in which Dreamweaver inserts code is completely customizable. See Chapter 4 for details on changing your code preferences and Chapter 32 to see how you can adjust your tags more specifically with the Tag Library Editor.

Expanding into XHTML

The latest version of HTML is known as XHTML, short for Extensible HTML. XHTML is based on XML and, as such, has a more rigid syntax than HTML. For example, tags that do not enclose content — the so-called *empty tags* — are written differently. In HTML, a line-break tag is

```
<br>
```

whereas in XHTML, the line-break tag is

```
<br />
```

Notice the additional space and the closing slash. Other differences include an opening XML declaration, as well as a specific doctype tag placed before the opening <html> tag. All tags must be in lowercase, and all attribute values must appear in quotes (but not necessarily lowercase) as follows:

```
<table align="RIGHT">
```

Dreamweaver makes it easy to code in XHTML and even to convert existing pages from HTML to XHTML. To work in XHTML from the ground up, set the Document Type (DTD) option to one of the XHTML options available on the New Document category of Preferences (available when you choose Edit ➪ Preferences on Windows or Dreamweaver ➪ Preferences on a Mac). Selecting this option automatically set an identical option on the New Document dialog box (File ➪ New), which you can change on a case-by-case basis, if necessary. After a document has been set as an XHTML file, all the tags are written in the proper style.

To change an HTML page into an XHTML one, choose File ➪ Convert ➪ XHTML. The conversion is automatically applied to the current document; no standard method exists to convert an entire site.

Because Dreamweaver has taken the pain out of using XHTML, the question is: Should you code in XHTML or HTML? As in most situations, it depends. Many larger companies that work extensively in XML require well-formed XHTML pages. Because it is the latest version of the Web's core language — and recommended by the W3C — you'll be perfectly poised for the future. One aspect of the future is the proliferation of Internet devices other than the computer: PDAs, cell phones, and set-top boxes, among others. For these types of devices, XHTML is far more portable than HTML.

However, you should be aware that not all browsers render XHTML pages exactly the same as they do HTML pages. The problems stem largely from older browsers (version 4 and earlier for both Internet Explorer and Netscape). If the audience for your site is heavily dependent on older browsers, you should probably stick with HTML for the time being; on the other hand, if the site's audience is fairly up-to-date and forward-looking, code in XHTML.

doctype and doctype Switching

The very first element of an HTML page — even before the `<html>` tag — is, increasingly, a `doctype` declaration. As the name implies, a `doctype` declaration specifies the language or, more specifically, the DTD (Document Type Definition) in use for the file that follows. To validate their page, many authors include `doctype` statements like the following:

```
<!DOCTYPE HTML PUBLIC "-//W3C//DTD HTML 4.01 Transitional//EN">
```

This `doctype` is inserted by default when Dreamweaver creates a new static HTML page.

Note   The latest — in fact, the last — version of HTML recommended by the W3C is version 4.01. After this version, the W3C recommended the switch to XHTML.

Recent browser versions inspect the `doctype` element in order to determine how the page should be rendered. Engaging in a practice known as `doctype` *switching*, these browsers (Internet Explorer 5.x and Safari 1.x or higher on the Macintosh, Internet Explorer 6 on Windows, and Netscape 6 or higher) work in two modes: strict and regular. When a browser is in strict mode, a page must be well-formed and validate without error to be rendered properly. Strict rendering is more consistent across browsers. The regular mode is far looser and more forgiving in how the page is coded; however, the page is more likely to be rendered differently in the varying browser versions.

You can ensure that your pages are rendered in the regular mode in a number of ways:

✦ Do not include a `doctype` declaration at all.

✦ Use a `doctype` declaration that specifies an HTML version earlier than 4.0.

✦ Use a `doctype` declaration that declares a transitional DTD of HTML 4.01, but does not include a URL to the DTD.

To trigger a browser's strict rendering mode:

✦ Use a `doctype` declaration for XML or XHTML.

✦ Use a `doctype` declaration that declares a strict DTD of HTML 4.01.

✦ Use a `doctype` declaration that declares a transitional DTD of HTML 4.01 that includes a URL to the DTD.

When including a URL to the DTD, the `doctype` looks as follows:

```
<!DOCTYPE HTML PUBLIC "-//W3C//DTD HTML 4.01 Transitional//EN"
"http://www.w3.org/TR/html4/loose.dtd">
```

You have several alternatives in Dreamweaver for including whichever doctype you choose. Hand-coding is a sure but tedious method; the doctype statement is somewhat cumbersome and certainly not easy to remember precisely. You could also alter the standard HTML page by changing the Default.html file found in your Dreamweaver 8\Configuration\DocumentTypes\NewDocuments folder.

Cross-Reference

For more details on altering the default page template, see Chapter 27.

Another approach is to create a custom snippet that enables you to drag the desired code right onto the page on a case-by-case basis. Use of the Snippets panel is covered later in this chapter in the "Adding Code through the Snippets Panel" section.

Which approach you take — strict or regular — depends, as with HTML and XHTML, on your audience. If a significant number of your site's audience uses older browsers, stay with a regular doctype. If the statistics for your site indicate that a high percentage of visitors are using more current browsers, go with a strict doctype. Of course, some clients or managers may mandate that their designers use a specific doctype.

Defining <head> Elements

Information pertaining to the Web page overall is contained in the <head> section of an HTML page. Browsers read the <head> to determine how to render the page — for example, is the page to be displayed using the Western, the Chinese, or some other character set? Search engine spiders also read this section to quickly glean a summary of the page.

When you begin inserting JavaScript (or code from another scripting language such as VBScript) into your Web page, all the subroutines and document-wide declarations go into the <head> area. Dreamweaver uses this format by default when you insert a JavaScript behavior.

Dreamweaver enables you to insert, view, and modify <head> content without opening an HTML editor. Dreamweaver's View Head Content capability enables you to work with <meta> tags and other <head> HTML code as you do with the regular content in the visual editor.

Establishing Page Properties

When you first open a page in Dreamweaver, your default Web page is untitled, with no background image and only a plain, white background. You can change any of these properties and more through Dreamweaver's Page Properties dialog box.

Note

If the Use CSS Instead Of HTML Tags option is enabled in Preferences (the default), the Page Properties attributes are written into an internal style sheet. With the option disabled, attributes entered through the Page Properties dialog box are written into the <body> tag.

As usual, Dreamweaver gives you more than one method for accessing the Page Properties dialog box. You can choose Modify ➪ Page Properties, or you can use the keyboard shortcut Ctrl+J (Command+J).

Tip   Here's another way to open the Page Properties dialog box: Click the Page Properties button of the Text Property inspector.

The Page Properties dialog box, shown in Figure 6-1, gives you easy control over the overall look and feel of the HTML page.

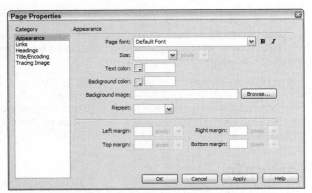

Figure 6-1: Change your Web page's overall appearance through the Page Properties dialog box.

Note   Technically, some of the values you assign through the Page Properties dialog box are applied to the `<body>` tag; because they affect the overall appearance of a page, however, they are covered in this `<head>` section.

The main categories of the Page Properties dialog box are Appearance, Links, Headings, Title/Encoding, and Tracing Image.

Appearance

The Appearance category controls the overall look and feel of the current document. The Appearance options, shown in Figure 6-1, include:

✦ **Page Font:** You can set the font family from the drop-down list or select Edit Font List to make more options available. Fonts can optionally be set to bold and/or italic.

✦ **Size:** You can choose a default size from the list or enter a specific value. Both absolute (9, 10, 12, and so on) and relative (xx-small, medium, larger, and so on) are available. If an absolute value is used, any of the standard measurement systems such as pixels, points, or ems can be chosen.

✦ **Text Color:** Click this color swatch to control the color of default text.

✦ **Background Color:** Click this color swatch to change the background color of the Web page. Select one of the browser-safe colors from the drop-down list, or enter its name or hexadecimal representation (for example, "#FFFFFF") directly into the text field.

✦ **Background Image:** You can determine the graphic displayed in the page background. The filename to the source file can either be entered in the field directly or chosen by clicking the Browse button. If the image is smaller than your content requires, the browser tiles the image to fill out the page; specifying a background image overrides any selection in the Background Color field.

Tip

To gain greater control over your background image, set the parameters through the CSS Rule Definition dialog when defining a CSS rule for the `<body>` tag. Through CSS, you can control the way the image tiles — if at all — as well as its placement.

✦ **Margins:** You can enter values here to change the page margin settings. As with the text size, the various measurement systems are available.

Note

If you set the Preferences to use HTML tags rather than CSS, you enter the margin settings into the `<body>` tag.

Links

Hyperlinks are a critical aspect of any Web page, and the Links category of the Page Properties dialog box sets their initial and interactive appearance. In this category, you find the following options (see Figure 6-2):

✦ **Link Font:** You can set the typeface for links. The default choice is to use the same font as the rest of the page, an option set in the Appearance category. You can also opt to bold or italicize a link.

✦ **Size:** You can set the font size for the link. If you do not enter a value, links are displayed in the same size as the standard font.

✦ **Link Color:** Click this color swatch to modify the color of any text designated as a link, or the border around an image link.

✦ **Visited Links:** Click this color swatch to select the color that linked text changes to after a visitor to your Web page has selected that link and then returned to your page.

✦ **Rollover Links:** Select the color you want to appear when the user's mouse moves over the link.

✦ **Active Links:** Click this color swatch to choose the color to which linked text changes briefly when a user selects the link. The active link flashes very briefly during a normal operation and many designers don't bother specifying this parameter.

✦ **Underline Style:** You can determine how the link uses underlines. Designers have the choice of always underlining the link, never underlining it, displaying the underline only on rollover, or hiding it during rollover.

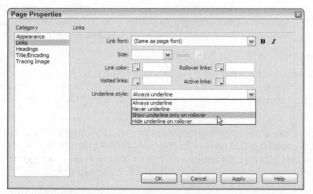

Figure 6-2: Make links as obvious or subtle as you like by changing their font, size, color, and underline style.

Headings

Dreamweaver enables you to control the headings on a page separately from the paragraph text, if you so desire. By default, all headings (tags <h1> through <h6>) share the same font as set for the page, but you can choose a new font from the Heading Font list. Any font chosen here applies to all headings, but sizes and colors for each heading may be set independently, as shown in Figure 6-3.

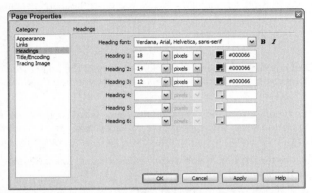

Figure 6-3: Although you can use a different font for your headings in many designs, be careful not to define too many color and size variations.

Tip Again, if you want more control, use the CSS Style Definition dialog to define a style for any heading tag.

Title/Encoding

Fundamental aspects of the Web page are set in the Title/Encoding category. Use the Title field to enter the Web page title; what you enter here appears in the browser's title bar when your page is viewed. Search engine spiders also read the title as one of the important indexing cues.

Tip You can also change the document title in Dreamweaver's Document toolbar. Just enter the information in the Title field and press Enter (Return) to confirm the modification. You see the new title appear in the program's title bar and whenever you preview the page in a browser.

The Encoding options determine the character set in which you want your Web page to be displayed. The default option for the English version of Dreamweaver is Western European. Developers of multilanguage sites may find it better to choose Unicode (UTF-8) as the encoding option.

If Unicode is selected, both the Unicode Normalization Form list and the Include Unicode Signature (BOM) option become available, as shown in Figure 6-4. The Unicode Normalization Form list chooses how the Unicode characters are converted to binary format. The Unicode Signature option determines whether a byte order mark (BOM) is attached to the file.

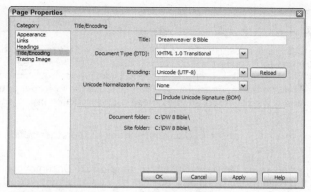

Figure 6-4: Unicode support in Dreamweaver is vital for developing multilanguage Web sites.

The Page Properties dialog box also displays the document folder if the page has been saved and the current site root folder if one has been selected.

Tracing Image

The Tracing Image category enables you to pick a graphic that can be used as a layout guide; the tracing image is displayed only in Dreamweaver. Select the file by clicking the Browse button and locating a GIF, JPG, or PNG file. After you've selected your file, you can set the degree of opaqueness by changing the Transparency slider, shown in Figure 6-5.

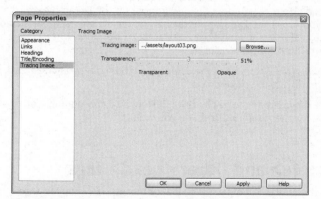

Figure 6-5: The tracing image is only visible at design time.

Cross-Reference The Tracing Image option is a powerful feature for quickly building a Web page based on design comps. For details about this feature and how to use it with Dreamweaver layers, see Chapter 11.

Choosing Colors from an Onscreen Image

One of the features found throughout Dreamweaver, the Eyedropper tool, is especially useful in the Page Properties options. The Eyedropper tool appears whenever you open any of Dreamweaver's color swatches, such as those attached to the Background, Text, and Links colors. You can not only pick a color from the Web-safe palette that appears, but you can also use the Eyedropper to select any color on any page — including system colors such as those found in dialog boxes and menu strips.

To use the Eyedropper tool to choose a color for the background (or any of the other options) from an onscreen image, follow these steps:

1. Insert your image on the page and, using the vertical scroll bar, position the Document window so that the image and the Page Properties dialog box can be viewed simultaneously.

   If your image is too big to fit both it and the Page Properties dialog box on the same screen, temporarily resize your image by dragging its sizing handles. You can restore the original image size when you have finished by clicking the Refresh button on the Image Property inspector.

2. Open the Page Properties dialog box by choosing Modify ➪ Page Properties or using the keyboard shortcut Ctrl+J (Command+J).

3. Drag the Page Properties dialog box to a place where the image can be seen.

4. Select the Background color swatch (or whichever one you want to change). The Dreamweaver color picker opens, and the pointer becomes an eyedropper.

5. Move the Eyedropper tool over the image until you find the correct color. (In Windows, you must hold the mouse button down as you drag the Eyedropper off the Dreamweaver dialog box to the image.) As you move the Eyedropper over an image, its colors are reflected in the color well, and its hex value is shown on the color picker. Click once when you've found the appropriate color. The color picker closes.

6. Repeat steps 4 and 5 to grab other colors from the screen for other color swatches. Click OK when you've finished modifying the page properties.

You don't have to keep the image on your page to get its color. Just insert it temporarily and then delete it after you've used the Eyedropper to grab the shade you want.

Understanding <meta> and Other <head> Tags

Summary information about the content of a page — and a lot more — is conveyed through `<meta>` tags used within the `<head>` section. The `<meta>` tag can be read by the server to create a header file, which makes it easier for indexing software used by search engines to catalog sites. Numerous different types of `<meta>` tags exist, and you can insert them in your document just like other objects.

One `<meta>` tag is included by default in every Dreamweaver page. The Document Encoding option of the Page Properties dialog box determines the character set used by the current Web page and is displayed in the `<head>` section as follows:

```
<meta http-equiv="Content-Type" content="text/html; charset=iso-8859-1">
```

The preceding `<meta>` tag tells the browser that this page is, in fact, an HTML page and that the page should be rendered using the specified character set (the `charset` attribute). The key attribute here is `http-equiv`, which is responsible for generating a server response header.

Cross-Reference

After you've determined your `<meta>` tags for a Web site, the same basic `<meta>` information can go on every Web page. Dreamweaver gives you a way to avoid having to insert the same lines repeatedly: templates. After you've set up the `<head>` elements the way you'd like them, choose File ➪ Save As Template. If you want to add `<meta>` or any other `<head>` tags to an existing template, you can edit the template and then update the affected pages. For more information about templates, turn to Chapter 27.

In Dreamweaver, you can insert a `<meta>` tag or any other tag using the `<head>` tag objects, which you access via the Head menu in the Insert bar's HTML category (see Figure 6-6) or the Insert ➪ HTML ➪ Head Tags menu option. The `<head>` tag objects are described in Table 6-1 and subsequent subsections.

Figure 6-6: Quick access to hidden code is available through the Head menu of Insert bar's HTML category.

Table 6-1: Head Tag Objects

Object	Description
Meta	Inserts information that describes or affects the entire document
Keywords	Includes a series of words used by some search engines to index the current Web page and/or site
Description	Includes a text description of the current Web page and/or site
Refresh	Reloads the current document or loads a new URL within a specified number of seconds
Base	Establishes a reference for all other URLs in the current Web page
Link	Inserts a link to an external document, such as a style sheet

Inserting Tags with the Meta Object

The Meta object is used to insert tags that provide information for the Web server through the `HTTP-equiv` attribute, and to include other overall data that you want in your Web page but not made visible to the casual browser. Some Web pages, for example, have built-in expiration dates after which the content is to be considered outmoded. In Dreamweaver, you can use the Meta object to insert a wide range of descriptive data.

You can access the Meta object in the Head menu in the HTML category of the Insert bar or via the Insert menu by choosing Insert ➪ HTML ➪ Head Tags ➪ Meta. Like all the Head objects, you don't have to have the Head Content visible to insert the Meta object; although you do have to choose View ➪ Head Content if you want to edit the object. To insert a Meta object, follow these steps:

1. Choose Insert ➪ HTML ➪ Head Tags ➪ Meta or select the Meta object from the Head menu in the HTML category of the Insert bar. Your current cursor position is irrelevant. The Meta dialog box opens, as shown in Figure 6-7.

Meta icon

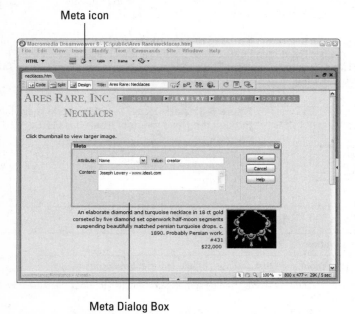

Meta Dialog Box

Figure 6-7: The Meta object enables you to enter a full range of `<meta>` tags in the `<head>` section of your Web page.

2. Choose the attribute: Name or an HTTP equivalent from the Attribute list box. Press Tab.

3. Enter the value for the selected attribute in the Value text box. Press Tab.

4. Enter the value for the content attribute in the Content text box.

5. Click OK when you have finished.

You can add as many Meta objects as you want by repeating steps 1 through 4. To edit an existing Meta object, you must first choose View ➪ Head Content to reveal the `<head>` code, indicated by the various icons. Click the Meta icon and make your changes in the Property inspector.

Aiding Search Engines with the Keywords and Description Objects

Take a closer look at the tags that convey indexing and descriptive information to some search engine spiders. These chores are handled by the Keywords and Description objects. As noted in the sidebar, "Built-In Meta Commands," the Keywords and Description objects output specialized `<meta>` tags.

Both objects are straightforward to use. Choose Insert ⇨ HTML ⇨ Head Tags ⇨ Keywords or Insert ⇨ HTML ⇨ Head Tags ⇨ Description. You can also choose the corresponding objects from the Head menu in the Text category of the Insert bar. After they are selected, these objects open similar dialog boxes with a single entry area, a large text box, as shown in Figure 6-8. Enter the values — whether keywords or a description — in the text box and click OK. You can edit the Keywords and Description objects, like the Meta object, by clicking their icons in the Head area of the Document window, revealed by choosing View ⇨ Head Contents.

Keywords icon

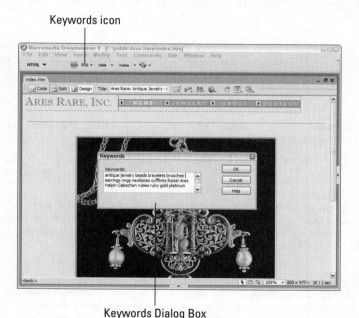

Keywords Dialog Box

Figure 6-8: Entering information through the Keywords object helps search engines correctly index your Web page.

Caution

Although you can enter paragraph returns in your Keywords and Description objects, you have no reason to. Browsers ignore all such formatting when processing your code.

Built-In Meta Commands

Although Dreamweaver presents six different Head objects, `<meta>` tags form the basis of four of them: Meta, Keywords, Description, and Refresh. By specifying different `name` attributes, the purpose of the `<meta>` tags changes. For example, a Keywords object uses the following format:

```
<meta name="keywords" content="dreamweaver, web, authoring,
HTML, DHTML, CSS, Macromedia">
```

whereas a Description object inserts this type of code:

```
<meta name="description" content="This site is devoted to
extensions made possible by Macromedia's Dreamweaver, the
premier Web authoring tool.">
```

It is possible to create all your `<meta>` tags with the Meta object by specifying the `name` attribute and giving it the pertinent value, but it's easier to just use the standard Dreamweaver Head objects.

What you place in the Keywords and Description objects can have a big impact on the accessibility of your Web page. If, for example, you want to categorize your Web page as an homage to the music of the early seventies, you could enter the following in the Content area of the Keywords object:

```
music, 70s, 70's, eagles, ronstadt, bee gees, pop, rock
```

In the preceding case, the content list is composed of words or phrases, separated by commas. Use sentences in the Description object, as follows:

```
The definitive look back to the power pop rock stylings of early 1970s
music, with special sections devoted to the Eagles, Linda Ronstadt, and
the Bee Gees.
```

Keep in mind that the content in the Description should complement and extend both the Keywords and the Web page title. You have more room in both the Description and Keywords objects — actually, an unlimited amount — than in the page title, which should be on the short side in order to fit into the browser's title bar.

Caution   When using `<meta>` tags with the Keywords or Description objects, don't stuff the `<meta>` tags repeatedly with the same word. The search engines are engineered to reject too many instances of the same words, and your description will not get the attention it deserves.

Refreshing the Page and Redirecting Users

The Refresh object forces a browser to reload the current page or to load a new page after a designer-set interval. The Web page visitor usually controls refreshing a page; if, for some reason, the display has become garbled, the user can choose Reload or Refresh from the menu to redraw the screen. Impatient Web surfer that I am, I often stop a page from loading to see what text links are available and then — if I don't see what I need — I hit Reload to bring in the full page. The code inserted by the Refresh object tells the server, not the browser, to reload the page. This can be a powerful tool, but it can lead to trouble if used improperly.

To insert a Refresh object, follow these steps:

1. Choose Insert ⇨ HTML ⇨ Head Tags ⇨ Refresh or select the Insert Refresh object from the Head menu in the Text category of the Insert bar. The Refresh dialog box, shown in Figure 6-9, opens.

Refresh icon

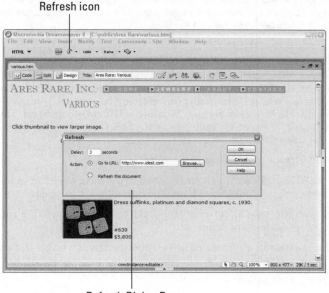

Refresh Dialog Box

Figure 6-9: Use the Refresh object to redirect visitors from an outdated page.

2. Enter the number of seconds you want to wait before the Refresh command takes effect in the Delay text box. The Delay value is calculated from the time the page finishes loading.

3. Select the desired Action:

   • Go To URL

   • Refresh This Document

4. If you selected Go To URL, enter a path to another page in the text box or click the Browse button to select a file.

5. Click OK when you have finished.

The Refresh object is most often used to redirect a visitor to another Web page. The Web is a fluid place, and sites often move from one address to another. Typically, a page at the old address contains the Refresh code that automatically takes the user to the new address. It's good practice to include a link to your new URL on the change-of-address page because not all browsers support the Refresh option. One other tip: Keep the number of seconds to a minimum — there's no point in waiting for something to happen automatically when you could click a link.

Caution   If you elect to choose the Refresh This Document option, use extreme caution, for several reasons. First, you can easily set up an endless loop for your visitors in which the same page is constantly being refreshed. If you are working with a page that updates often, enter a longer Refresh value, such as 300 or 500. You should be sure to include a link to another page to enable users to exit from the continually refreshed page. You should also be aware that many search engines will not index pages using the `<meta>` refresh tag because of widespread abuse by certain industries on the Web.

Changing Bases

Through the Base object, the `<head>` section enables you to exert fundamental control over the basic HTML element: the link. The code inserted by this object specifies the base URL for the current page. If you use relative addressing (covered in Chapter 10), you can switch all your links to another directory — even another Web site — with one command. The Base object takes two attributes: `Href`, which redirects all the other relative links on your page; and `target`, which specifies where the links are rendered.

To insert a Base object in your page, follow these steps:

1. Choose Insert ➪ HTML ➪ Head Tags ➪ Base or select the Base object from the Head menu of the Text category of the Insert bar. The Base dialog box opens.

2. Input the path that you want all other relative links to be based on in the Href text box or click the Browse button to pick the path.

3. If you want, enter a default target for all links without a specific target to be rendered in the Target text box.

4. Click OK when you've finished.

Proper Previewing with Set Mark of the Web

When Microsoft released its Service Pack 2 (SP2) update for Windows XP, it introduced a number of security measures intended to protect users from malicious content. Unfortunately, it also made it harder for Web designers to do their work. Part of the normal workflow of any Dreamweaver designer is previewing the page in the browser. If you attempt to preview your page in an Internet Explorer browser with Windows XP SP2 installed, you'll get a warning concerning active content on the local machine. Although this warning can be simply dismissed, it's a major hassle to do so repeatedly while in the design phase. To Internet Explorer, active content includes JavaScript, Flash, Active X objects, or Java applets.

To lower the designer's stress levels, Dreamweaver engineers included an Insert Mark of the Web command. When Commands ➪ Insert Mark of the Web is selected, this command inserts a bit of code that indicates the page was saved from the Web in an HTML comment, like this:

```
<!-- saved from url=(0014)about:internet -->
```

With the Mark of the Web code in place, Internet Explorer will not display the warning. Once the code is added to the page, it can be removed when it's time to publish by choosing Commands ➪ Remove Mark of the Web.

How does a `<base>` tag affect your page? Suppose you define one link as follows:

```
images/backgnd.gif
```

Normally, the browser looks in the same folder as the current page for a subfolder named images. A different sequence occurs, however, if you set the `<base>` tag to another URL in the following way:

```
<base href="http://www.testsite.com/client-demo01/">
```

With this `<base>` tag, when the same `images/backgnd.gif` link is activated, the browser looks for its file in the following location:

```
http://www.testsite.com/client-demo01/images/backgnd.gif
```

 Caution Because of the all-or-nothing capability of `<base>` tags, many Webmasters use them cautiously, if at all.

Linking to Other Files

The Link object indicates a relationship between the current page and another page or file. Although many other intended uses exist, the `<link>` tag is most commonly used to apply an external Cascading Style Sheet (CSS) to the current page. This code is entered automatically in Dreamweaver when you create a new linked style sheet (as described in Chapter 7), or you can add the attributes yourself with the Link object. The `<link>` tag is also used to include TrueDoc dynamic fonts.

 Tip One other popular use of the `<link>` tag is to create *favicons*. A favicon is a small icon that appears in the Favorites menu of Internet Explorer browsers when you mark a site as a Favorite or bookmarked. To have a favicon appear when a page is bookmarked, create a favicon using one of the tools listed at `www.favicon.com` and upload that image file to your site. Then put a tag like this on your page:

```
<LINK REL="SHORTCUT ICON" HREF="/images/fav.ico">.
```

where `fav.ico` is the name of the icon file, here stored in the images folder at the root of the site.

To insert a Link object, first choose Insert ➪ HTML ➪ Head Tags ➪ Link or select the Insert Link object from the Head group on the HTML category of the Insert bar. This action opens the Link dialog box, shown in Figure 6-10.

Figure 6-10: The Link object is primarily used to include external style sheets.

Next, enter the necessary attributes, as shown in Table 6-2.

Table 6-2: Attributes for the Link Object

Attribute	Description
Href	Path to the file being linked. Use the Browse button to open the Select File dialog box.
ID	Used by scripts to identify this particular object and affect it if need be.
Title	Displayed as a ToolTip by Internet Explorer browsers.
Rel	Keyword that describes the relationship of the linked document to the current page. For example, an external style sheet uses the keyword stylesheet.
Rev	Like Rel, also describes a relationship, but in the reverse. For example, if home.html contained a link tag with a Rel attribute set to intro.html, intro.html could contain a link tag with a Rev attribute set to home.html.

Note   Aside from the style sheet use, little browser support exists for the other link functions. However, the World Wide Web Consortium (W3C) supports an initiative to use the <link> tag to address other media, such as speech synthesis and Braille devices, and it's entirely possible that the Link object will be used for this purpose in the future.

Adding to the <body>

The content of a Web page — the text, images, links, and plugins — is all contained in the <body> section of an HTML document. The great majority of <body> tags can be inserted through Dreamweaver's visual layout interface.

To use the <body> tags efficiently, you need to understand the distinction between logical styles and physical styles used in HTML. An underlying philosophy of HTML is to keep the Web as universally accessible as possible. Web content is intended to be platform- and resolution-independent, but the content itself can be styled by its intent as well. This philosophy is supported by the existence of logical <body> tags (such as <code> and <cite>), with which a block of text can be rendered according to its meaning, and physical style tags for directly italicizing or underlining text. HTML enables you to choose between logical styles, which are relative to the text, or physical styles, which can be regarded as absolute.

Logical Styles

Logical styles are contextual, rather than explicit. Choose a logical style when you want to ensure that the meaning, rather than a specific look, is conveyed. Table 6-3 shows a listing of logical style tags and their most common usage. Tags not supported through Dreamweaver's visual interface are noted.

Table 6-3: HTML Logical Style Tags

Tag	Usage
`<big>`	Increases the size of the selected text relative to the surrounding text. Not currently supported by Dreamweaver.
`<cite>`	Citations, titles, and references; usually shown in italic.
`<code>`	For showing programming code, usually displayed in a monospaced font.
`<dfn>`	Defining instance; used to mark the introduction of a new term.
`<em>`	Emphasis; usually depicted as underlined or italicized text.
`<kbd>`	Keyboard; used to render text to be entered exactly.
`<s>`	Strikethrough text; used for showing text that has been deleted.
`<samp>`	Sample; a sequence of literal characters.
`<small>`	Decreases the size of the selected text relative to the surrounding text; not currently supported by Dreamweaver.
`<strong>`	Strong emphasis; usually rendered as bold text.
`<sub>`	Subscript; the text is shown slightly lowered beneath the baseline.
`<sup>`	Superscript; the text is shown slightly raised above the baseline.
`<tt>`	Teletype; displayed with a monospaced font such as Courier.
`<var>`	Variable; used to distinguish variables from other programming code.

Logical styles are becoming increasingly important now that more browsers accept Cascading Style Sheets. Style sheets make it possible to combine the best elements of both logical and physical styles. With CSS, you can easily make the text within your `<code>` tags blue, and the variables, denoted with the `<var>` tag, green.

Tip
By default, Dreamweaver is now set to use logical styles `<strong>` and `<em>` whenever you click the Bold and Italic buttons on the Property inspector, respectively. Choose Edit ➪ Preferences (Dreamweaver➪Preferences) and, in the General category of the Preferences dialog box, deselect the Use `<strong>` And `<em>` In Place Of `<b>` And `<i>` option if you'd prefer not to use the logical styles.

Physical Styles

HTML picked up the use of physical styles from modern typography and word processing programs. Use a physical style when you want something to be absolutely bold, italic, or underlined (or, as we say in HTML, `<b>`, `<i>`, and `<u>`, respectively). You can apply the bold and the italic tags to selected text through the Property inspector or by choosing Text ➪ Style; the underline style is available only through the Text menu.

With HTML version 3.2, a fourth physical style tag was added: `<font>`. Most browsers recognize the `size` attribute, which enables you to make the selected text larger or smaller, relatively or directly. To change a font size absolutely, select your text and then choose Text ⇨ Size; Dreamweaver inserts the following tag, where *n* is a number from 1 to 7:

```
<font size=n>
```

To make text larger than the default text, select Text ⇨ Size Increase and then choose the value you want. Dreamweaver inserts the following tag:

```
<font size=+n>
```

The plus sign (+) indicates the relative nature of the font. Make text smaller than the default text by choosing Text ⇨ Size Decrease; Dreamweaver inserts this tag:

```
<font size=-n>
```

You can also expressly change the type of font used and its color through the `face` and `color` attributes. Because you can't be sure what fonts are on a user's system, common practice and good form dictate that you should list alternatives for a selected font. For instance, rather than just specifying Palatino — a sans serif font common on PCs but relatively unknown on the Mac — you could insert a tag such as the following:

```
<font face=" Palatino, Times New Roman, Times, sans-serif">
```

 Caution   In the preceding case, if the browser doesn't find the first font, it looks for the second one (and so forth, as specified). Dreamweaver handles the `font face` attribute through its Font List dialog box, which is explained fully in Chapter 8.

Working with Code View and Code Inspector

Although Dreamweaver offers many options for using the visual interface of the Document window, sometimes you just have to tweak the code by hand. Dreamweaver's acceptance by professional coders is due in large part to the easy access to the underlying code. Dreamweaver includes several methods for directly viewing, inputting, and modifying code for your Web page. For large-scale additions and changes, you might consider using an external HTML editor such as BBEdit or Homesite, but for many situations, the built-in Code view and Code inspector are perfectly suited and much faster to use.

Code view is one of the coolest tools in Dreamweaver's code-savvy toolbox. You can either view your code full-screen in the Document window, split-screen with Design view, or in a separate panel, the Code inspector. The underlying engine for all Code views is the same.

You can use either of the following methods to display the full-screen Code view:

✦ Choose View ⇨ Code.

✦ Click the Show Code View button on the toolbar. Code view is displayed, as shown in Figure 6-11.

Figure 6-11: Code view is easily accessible from the Document toolbar.

You can access the split-screen Code and Design view with either of the following methods:

✦ Choose View ➪ Code and Design.

✦ Click the Show Code and Design Views button on the Document toolbar.

To change the relative size of the Code and Design views, drag the splitter bar up or down. In the split-screen Code and Design view, Code view is shown on top of the Design view. You can reverse that order by choosing View ➪ Design View on Top or selecting Design View on Top from the View Options button on the toolbar.

You have two ways to open the Code inspector. You can either choose Window ➪ Code Inspector or use the keyboard shortcut F10. After you open it, the Code inspector (see Figure 6-12) behaves like any other floating panel in Dreamweaver: The Code inspector can be resized, moved, hidden, and, on Windows, docked above or below the Document window or grouped with other panels. When the Code inspector is opened initially, it is automatically selected. If you click in the Document window with the Code inspector open, the inspector dims but still reflects changes made in the document.

In all Code views, Dreamweaver does not update the Design view of the document immediately — whereas changes in Design view are instantly reflected in any open Code view. This delay is enforced to enable the code to be completed before being applied. To apply modifications made in the code, switch to Design view; if Design view is open, click anywhere in it to give it focus. Should Dreamweaver detect any invalid HTML, such as an improperly closed tag, the offending code is flagged with a yellow highlight in both Design and Code views. Select the marked tag to see an explanation and suggestions for correcting the problem in the Property inspector.

Refresh

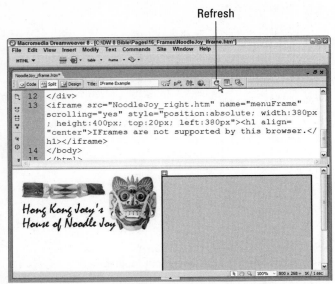

Figure 6-12: To update Design view while still working in the Code view, click the handy Refresh button — either on the Document toolbar or the Property inspector — or press F5.

You can also apply code changes to Design view by saving the document or by clicking the Refresh button on the toolbar or the Property inspector. The Refresh button becomes active only when modifications are made in any Code view. You also have a keyboard and menu alternative: Pressing F5 has the same effect as choosing View ➪ Refresh Design View.

Generally, the Code view and Code inspector act like a regular text editor. Simply click anywhere in the inspector to add or modify code. Double-click a word to select it. Select an entire line by moving your pointer to the left edge of the code — where the pointer becomes a right-pointing arrow — and clicking once. Multiple lines can be selected in this same fashion by dragging the right-pointing arrow. After a section of code is selected, you can drag and drop it into a new location; pressing the Ctrl (Option) key while dragging makes a copy of the selection. You can move from word to word by pressing Ctrl (Command) in combination with any of the arrow keys.

Enabling Code View Options

Some special features in Dreamweaver's code editor simplify the task of writing HTML and other types of code. When in any Code view, some of these features can be toggled on and off by choosing the command either from the View ➪ Code View Options list or under the View Options button on the Document toolbar:

✦ **Word Wrap:** Wraps lines within the boundaries of the Code view window or Code inspector to eliminate the need for horizontal scrolling.

✦ **Line Numbers:** Displays a number for every line in the code; this feature is extremely helpful when used in combination with the JavaScript Debugger, which reports the line number of an error in the code.

✦ **Highlight Invalid HTML:** Toggles the highlighting of invalid tags in Code view when Design view is refreshed. Invalid tags are always highlighted in the Design view.

✦ **Syntax Coloring:** Syntax coloring makes code easier to read. Basic tags and keywords are shown in one color, with text in another color. Three different types of code are given different colors: Reserved Keywords, Other Keywords, and Strings. These colors are set in the Code Color category of Preferences. You can also set a color for an individual tag to further distinguish it if you like.

✦ **Auto Indent:** Auto Indent is another feature intended to improve code readability. With Auto Indent enabled, pressing Enter (Return) at the end of a line causes the new line to start at the same indentation as the preceding line. Press Backspace (Delete) to move the indented line closer to the left margin. The number of characters for each indentation is set in the Code Format category of Preferences.

You can also easily change the indentation — in or out — for selected blocks of code. To further indent a block of code, select it and then press Tab. To decrease the level of indentation for a selected code block, press Shift+Tab. Alternatively, you can choose Edit ⇨ Indent Code or use the keyboard shortcut Ctrl+. (Command+.) to indent a code block. Similarly, you choose Edit ⇨ Outdent Code or use the keyboard shortcut Ctrl+, (Command+,) to outdent it.

Tip   Although the keyboard shortcuts for Indenting and Outdenting code may seem arbitrary at first, they're actually easy to remember. The period and comma used in those shortcuts are on the same key as the left angle bracket (>) and right angle bracket (<) respectively — which indicates the direction of the code shift.

As a further aid to help you find your way through a maze of code, Dreamweaver includes the Balance Braces command. JavaScript is notorious for using parentheses, brackets, and curly braces to structure its code — and it's easy to lose sight of where one enclosing brace begins and its closing mate ends. Dreamweaver highlights the content found within the closest pair of braces to the cursor when you choose Edit ⇨ Balance Braces or use the keyboard shortcut Ctrl+' (Command+'). If you select the command again, the selection expands to the set of surrounding braces. When the selection is not enclosed by parentheses, brackets, or curly braces, Dreamweaver sounds an alert.

Although most Web designers who use the code editor in Dreamweaver prefer to manually enter their code, the power of the Insert bar is still at your disposal for rapid code development. Any element available from the Insert bar can be inserted directly into Code view or the inspector. To use the Insert bar, you must first position your cursor where you would like the code for the object to appear. Then select the element or drag and drop the element from the Insert bar to Code view or the inspector.

Cross-Reference   Keep in mind that Dreamweaver's code editor is highly customizable. You can change the way the lines wrap by using indents for certain tag pairs; you can even control the amount of indentation. All the options are outlined for you in Chapter 4.

Printing Code

Although you may spend the vast majority of your time writing, modifying, and debugging your code onscreen, there are times when you need to see it in hard copy.

Dreamweaver offers the option of printing out your code. Choose File ➪ Print Code to open the standard operating system Print dialog box. You have the option to print all the code or a selection; you cannot, however, print individual pages of your code. Press the keyboard shortcut Ctrl+P (Command+P) to send your code directly to the printer. Although Dreamweaver does not print the syntax coloring, you can print line numbers by enabling them in Code view options.

Using the Coding Toolbar

Much of the special tools and functionality aimed at helping the coder are concentrated in the Coding toolbar. The Coding toolbar, enabled by default, is attached to the left side of Code view. In all, there are 15 different buttons and menu buttons that greatly enhance the coding experience in Dreamweaver.

New In Dreamweaver   The Coding toolbar's functions are a combination of old and new; some of the features have been placed on the Coding toolbar for ease of use while others cannot be found anywhere else in Dreamweaver The very top button, Open Documents, falls into the latter category and brings some much needed access when working with multiple files. Select Open Documents to see a listing of all files currently open. Unlike the tabs or the list in the Windows menu, the Open Documents list shows the full path of each entry, as shown in Figure 6-13; this is an essential distinction for designers who want pages from multiple directories and even multiple sites open at the same time.

Figure 6-13: The Coding toolbar's Open Documents feature displays the full path for all currently available files.

Code Collapse

Code collapse — a new feature in Dreamweaver 8 — is the focus of the next group of buttons in the Coding toolbar. Code collapse allows you to hone in on your work by temporarily condensing specific sections of the code into a single line or, alternately, condensing all but the selection. Hover your cursor over the collapsed element to see the first 10 lines of code in a tooltip (see Figure 6-14).

The three buttons in this group work in concert with your cursor position and selection in Code view:

✦ **Collapse Full Tag:** Expands the current selection or cursor position to the immediately surrounding tag and collapses the code.

✦ **Collapse Selection:** Reduces the current selection to a collapsed single line.

✦ **Expand All:** Extends all condensed portions of code in the current document.

Figure 6-14: Code collapse lets you concentrate on just the code you're working on, while keeping the hidden code accessible via tooltips.

Any code marked as collapsed retains that state after it has been saved, closed, and re-opened. If you press Alt (Option) while clicking either Collapse Full Tag and Collapse Selection, Dreamweaver inverses the normal collapse operation. For example, if your cursor is placed in a `<div>` tag and you press Alt (Option) while clicking Collapse Full Tag, all the code outside of the current `<div>` tag is collapsed.

You can also expand and collapse code outside of the Coding toolbar. Whenever you select any portion of the code, handles appear at the top and bottom of your selection to the left of the code. Click either of the handles to collapse the code; click the single collapsed handle again to expand it. As noted earlier, you can hover over the collapsed code to see the first 10 lines in a tooltip.

Collapsing and Moving Code

In this Technique, you use various features of the Coding toolbar including Dreamweaver's code collapse feature to make it easy to move code from one place on the page to another.

1. In the Techniques site, expand the 06_Code folder and open the `code_start.htm` file.

2. While in Design view, place your cursor in the first heading, Relative Realty Benefits.

3. Switch to Code view.

4. From the Coding toolbar, click Select Parent Tag once to select the `<h1>` tag and then again to select it's parent, `<div id="benefits">`.

5. Click Collapse Full Tag from the Coding toolbar.

   Hover your cursor over the collapsed code to see the hidden code in the tooltip.

6. Place your cursor in the code for the next div, `<div id="reasons">`.

7. Choose Collapse Full Tag again.

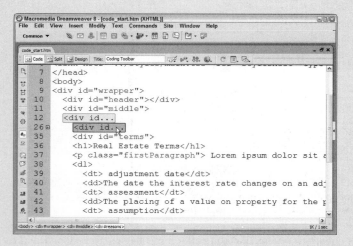

8. Select the code line containing the just-collapsed tag and drag it in front of the first collapse code.

9. From the Coding toolbar, click Expand All.

   The two different sections of the page have now been switched. One last operation will clean up the look of the code.

10. From the bottom of the Coding toolbar, choose Format Source Code ⇨ Apply Source Formatting.

11. Switch to Design view and save your page.

Familiarity with the functions of the Coding toolbar will greatly help your coding productivity.

END

Code Selection and Highlight

Coders will appreciate the ability to quickly select and identify different groups of code with the next series of buttons on the Coding toolbar:

✦ **Select Parent Tag:** Expands the selection from the current cursor position to enclose the surrounding tag.

✦ **Balance Braces:** Selects code within the matching set of parentheses, braces, or square brackets; if the code is nested, click again to select the parentheses, braces, or square brackets.

✦ **Line Numbers:** Toggles the line numbers on the left of Code view.

✦ **Highlight Invalid Code:** Marks broken code with a yellow highlight.

The last two options, Line Numbers and Highlight Invalid Code, are also found in the View Options menu option of the Document toolbar.

Commenting Code

The next two buttons of the Coding toolbar focus on comments. Because Dreamweaver is a Web page editor, you'll find a variety of different types of comments available under the first menu button, Apply Comments:

✦ <!– HTML Comments –>

✦ // CSS or JavaScript single line style comments

✦ /* CSS or JavaScript block style comments */

✦ 'Visual Basic single line style comments

✦ ASP, ASP.NET, JSP, PHP, or ColdFusion style comments, depending on the application server used

Each of the comments options wrap a selection in the chosen comment style; in the case of single line style comments, the comments are placed at the start of each selected line. If no code is highlighted, an empty comment of the desired type is inserted.

The Remove Comment button follows Apply Comment. The Remove Comment feature uncomments any selected code and will remove multiple comments unless they are nested. In the case of nested comments, only the outer comments are deleted.

Other Coding Toolbar Functions

Need a quick way to add a parent tag to a selection? Choose Wrap Tag and you can easily enter the desired outer element, along with any desired attributes and values. Press Enter (Return) to confirm your choices and the parent tag code is inserted.

Note

Although the Wrap Tag function resembles the Quick Tag Editor, you cannot use it to toggle between the three different modes as you can in the Quick Tag Editor.

You can wrap content with much more than a single tag through the Recent Snippets button. A snippet is a block of code that has been stored by Dreamweaver and can be inserted at any point. The Recent Snippets feature lists the 10 most recently used snippets, which can be either wrap or block type. For more information about Snippets, see the "Adding Code through the Snippets Panel" section later in the chapter.

The final buttons on the Coding toolbar are used for styling your code. The Indent Code and Outdent Code buttons move selected code blocks in or out according to the options set in the Code Format category of Preferences. The final button, Format Source Code, allows you to style either the entire document or a selection of your code according to the Code Format Settings — which, along with another code style option, Tag Libraries — is also available under this menu.

Enhancing Code Authoring Productivity

One of the reasons why the Web grew so quickly is that the basic tool for creating Web pages was ubiquitous: Any text editor would do. That's still true, but just as you can cut down any tree with a hand saw, that doesn't make it the right tool — the most efficient tool — for the job. Dreamweaver includes numerous features and options that make it a world-class code editor and not just for HTML. The Tag Library feature makes Dreamweaver a terrific code-editing environment for almost any Web language, including XHTML, XML, ColdFusion, ASP, ASP.NET, JSP, and PHP. Moreover, the database structure underlying the tag libraries means that the libraries can be expanded or modified at any time. New tags, attributes, and even entire languages can be added by hand or imported in a number of methods, including from a DTD schema.

Dreamweaver's tag libraries offer numerous benefits that greatly enhance the coding experience. Chief among these benefits are Code Hints and Tag Completion.

Code Hints and Tag Completion

Writing code is an exact art. If you enter `<blickquote>` instead of `<blockquote>`, neither Dreamweaver nor the browser renders the tag properly. Perhaps an even bigger problem than misspelling tags and attributes is remembering them all. As more and more developers of static Web pages go dynamic, many are finding the sheer amount of information they need is quite daunting. Don't worry, hand-coders, Dreamweaver's Code Hints feature help you avoid those misspellings and prompt your memory — making you more efficient in the process.

The Code Hints tool is a valuable aid to all Web designers, even beginners. It's a quick way to develop a tag as you type it by displaying a pop-up list of tags (as shown in Figure 6-15), attributes and, in some cases, even values for each tag. Best of all, Code Hints work the way you want to work. If you're a touch-typist, your hands never have to leave the keyboard to accept a particular tag or attribute. If you prefer to use the mouse, you can easily double-click to select your entry. If you like, Dreamweaver even completes your code with an ending tag.

The Code Hints that appear are stored in Dreamweaver's Tag Library database and can be modified by choosing Edit ⇨ Tag Libraries. Code Hints are available for Web languages HTML (including XHTML), CFML, ASP.NET, JSP, JRun Custom Library, ASP, PHP, and WML, as well as Dreamweaver templates tags and Sitespring Project Site tags.

Cross-Reference   Code Hints are enabled by default. To disable them or to control the speed with which the pop-up list appears, choose Edit ⇨ Preferences (Dreamweaver ⇨ Preferences) and select the Code Hints category. See Chapter 4 for a detailed explanation of all the options.

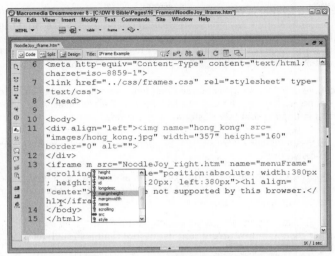

Figure 6-15: Master the use of the Code Hints feature to give your code writing a major productivity boost.

When Code Hints is turned on, follow these steps to use this helpful feature:

1. In Code view, enter the opening tag bracket, <. The Code Hint pop-up list instantly shows all the tags for the document type of the current page.

2. To move down the list, type the first letter of the tag. With each letter that you type, Dreamweaver homes in on the indicated tag.

3. When the proper tag is highlighted, press Enter (Return) and the code is inserted. Alternatively, you can scroll down the list and double-click the desired tag to insert it.

4. To add attributes to the tag, enter a space. The attribute list for the current tag is displayed.

5. As with the tag, type until the desired attribute is highlighted in the list and then press Enter (Return). Attributes are, for the most part, followed by an equals sign and a pair of quotes for the value. The cursor is positioned in between the quotes.

6. Enter the desired value for the attribute.

7. If the attribute can only accept a certain range of values, such as the `align` attribute, the accepted values also appear in the Code Hints pop-up list. If you choose one of the specified values, the cursor moves to the end of the name-value pair after the closing quote.

8. Enter a space to continue adding attributes or enter the closing tag bracket, >.

9. Insert any content to follow the opening tag.

10. When you're ready to add the closing tag, just type the first two characters </ and Dreamweaver adds the rest of the tag.

Dreamweaver's Tag Completion feature is really quite intelligent and can easily handle any number of nested tags. For example, let's say you start with an opening <div> tag and then begin to enter your headings and <p> tags. As you enter the closing characters </ after each tag, Dreamweaver completes the proper tag. If, after all other tags are closed you type in the closing characters, Dreamweaver will finish the final </div> tag automatically.

Cross-Reference   There are actually a couple of different styles of Code Completion and you can choose which one you'd prefer—or none at all—from the Code Hints category of Preferences. All the various options are covered in Chapter 4 in the "Customizing Your Code" section.

In addition to straight text, Dreamweaver offers several types of attribute values, each with its own special type of drop-down list:

✦ **Color:** When a color-related attribute is entered, Dreamweaver displays a color palette and eyedropper cursor for sampling the color. When a color is picked, its corresponding hexadecimal value is entered into the code.

✦ **Font:** For attributes requiring the name of a font, such as the <font> tag's face attribute, Dreamweaver displays the current font list of font families (such as Arial, Helvetica, sans serif), as well as an option to edit that list.

✦ **Style:** Enter the class attribute in almost any tag, and you see a complete list of available CSS styles defined for the current page. Other CSS controls, such as Edit Style Sheet and Attach Style Sheet, are also available.

✦ **File:** Should an attribute require a filename, Dreamweaver opens the standard Select File dialog box to enable you to easily locate a file or choose a data source.

Code Hints aren't just for entering new tags; you can take advantage of their prompting when modifying existing code as well. To add an attribute, place your cursor just before the closing bracket and press the spacebar to trigger the Code Hints pop-up menu. To change an entered value, delete both the value and the surrounding quotes; the pop-up options appear after the opening quote is entered.

Modifying Blocks of Code

If you're a fan of Frank Herbert's *Dune*, you know the phrase "Fear is the mindkiller." You don't have to be a sci-fi aficionado to know that when it comes to coding, mindless repetition is one big time-killer. Quite often, you repeat the same function—like converting all the tags to lowercase—for a section of your code. These types of procedures quickly become tedious, and performing them one at a time is grossly inefficient. For commonly performed operations, Dreamweaver has a far better way.

Dreamweaver's Selection menu is activated whenever a section of code is selected. Twenty-seven varied, but extremely useful, functions are available, as shown in Figure 6-16. All the procedures take effect immediately and require no further dialog box or interaction. Just select the code, choose the operation, and you're done. The Selection functions are especially helpful when cleaning imported code or when converting code to text or vice versa.

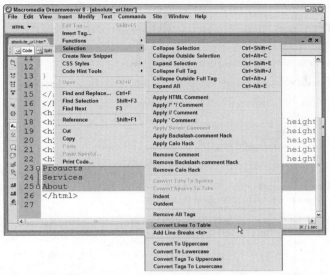

Figure 6-16: Quickly alter the formatting or modify the code itself of any selected code block through the Selection commands.

The Selection menu includes the following:

✦ **Collapse Selection:** Collapses the selected code.

✦ **Collapse Outside Selection:** Collapses all but the selected code.

✦ **Expand Selection:** Expands any collapsed code inside the selection.

✦ **Collapse Full Tag:** Collapses the nearest parent tag.

✦ **Collapse Outside Full Tag:** Collapses all but the nearest parent tag.

✦ **Expand All:** Expands all collapsed code in the document.

✦ **Apply HTML Comment:** Inserts an HTML comment: <!-- -->.

✦ **Apply /* */ Comment:** Inserts a multi-line JavaScript/CSS comment: /* */.

✦ **Apply // Comment:** Inserts a single line JavaScript/CSS comment at the start of a code line: //.

✦ **Apply ' Comment:** Inserts a single line ASP comment at the start of a code line: '.

✦ **Apply Server Comment:** Inserts a comment applicable to the current server model.

✦ **Apply Backslash-Comment Hack:** Adds a CSS hack to hide styles from Internet Explorer for the Mac 4.x.

✦ **Apply Caio Hack:** Adds a CSS hack to hide styles from Netscape 4.x.

✦ **Remove Comment:** Removes any kind of comment in the current selection.

✦ **Remove Backslash-Comment Hack:** Removes a previously applied Backslash-comment hack.

✦ **Remove Caio Hack:** Removes a previously apply Caio hack.

✦ **Convert Tabs To Spaces:** Changes every tab used for indenting to four spaces.

✦ **Convert Spaces To Tabs:** Substitutes a tab for every four spaces.

✦ **Indent:** Indents the code block one tab stop.

✦ **Outdent:** Outdents the selected code one tab stop.

✦ **Remove All Tags:** Strips all tags from a code block, leaving the content.

✦ **Convert Lines To Table:** Places each individual line, separated by a carriage return, into a table row and the entire code selection in a table.

✦ **Add Linebreaks <br>:** Inserts a `<br>` tag at the end of every line; if the page is XHTML-compliant, the `<br/>` tag is used instead.

✦ **Convert To Uppercase:** Changes the selected code block — both tags and content — to uppercase.

✦ **Convert To Lowercase:** Lowercases the selection of code, including all the tags and content.

✦ **Convert Tags To Uppercase:** Uppercases only the tags in the current selection; all code within the tag, including attributes and values, are uppercased.

✦ **Convert Tags To Lowercase:** Changes all the code within tags (again, including attributes and values) to lowercase.

If the results of your Selection operation are not to your liking, press Ctrl+Z (Command+Z) to undo the command.

Inserting Code with the Tag Chooser

If you'd rather point and click than type, Dreamweaver has you covered.

With the Dreamweaver Tag Chooser, you have access to all the standard tags in HTML/XHTML, CFML, ASP.NET, JSP, JRun Custom Library, ASP, PHP, and WML, and the Macromedia-specific tags for Dreamweaver templates and Sitespring Project Sites. Open the Tag Chooser in one of several ways:

✦ Choose Insert ⇨ Tag.

✦ Right-click (Control+click) in Code view and choose Insert Tag from the context menu.

✦ Press the keyboard shortcut Ctrl+E (Command+E).

✦ Position your cursor where you'd like the tag to appear — in either Code or Design view — and select Tag Chooser from the Insert bar's Common category.

✦ Drag the Tag Chooser button from the Insert bar's Common category to the appropriate place in either Code or Design view.

The tags are grouped under their respective languages. Selecting any of the languages from the list on the left displays all the available tags on the right. Most of the languages have a plus sign which, when selected, expands the chosen language and displays various functional groupings of tags, such as Page Composition, Lists, and Tables, as shown in the background of Figure 6-17. Under HTML Tags, you can expand the tag groupings further to see, in some cases, tags separated into additional categories such as General, Browser-Specific, and Deprecated.

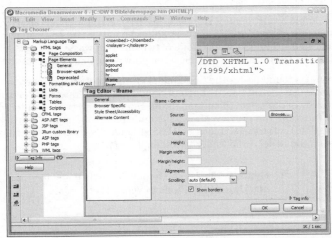

Figure 6-17: When you select your page element from the Tag Chooser (shown in the background), you have a wealth of options in the Tag Editor (foreground).

If you're confused about what a specific tag is for or how it's used, click the Tag Info button. The bottom half of the dialog box converts to a context-sensitive reference panel. Exactly what information is available depends on the tag itself. For most HTML tags, you find a description, examples, and a list of browsers in which the tag is recognized. Much of the information available is also available in the Reference panel (covered later in this chapter); however, not all tags are covered.

When you've chosen a tag and either double-clicked it or selected Insert, the Tag Editor opens. Each tag has its own user interface with full accessibility and CSS options. As shown in Figure 6-17, selecting a category from the list on the left displays the available options on the right.

Note   Custom tags or attributes entered into the Tag Library are not displayed in the Tag Chooser.

After entering all the desired parameters in the Tag Editor, clicking OK inserts the code into the page with the cursor in-between the opening and closing tags (or after the tag if it is empty). The Tag Chooser uses a nonmodal window and remains open until Close is selected.

Caution   Because the Tag Chooser is nonmodal, you may not realize that you have already inserted the desired tag, causing you to select Insert again. Dreamweaver does not prevent you from entering multiple versions of the same tag.

Adding Code through the Snippets Panel

Using the valuable Snippets feature, you can save portions of HTML code for easy recall in other files. It's a lot easier than copying and pasting blocks of code from various files. Tag snippets range from a single tag, such as an HTML comment, to a full navigation layout. Commonly used JavaScript and other language functions and methods are also good candidates to be turned into snippets for later use.

Dreamweaver provides a notable assortment of snippets, but the most important aspect of this feature is that it's extensible. Coders and noncoders alike can easily add any commonly used section of code for later reuse. Snippets work in one of two different ways: A snippet either inserts a solid code block at the cursor point or wraps a selection with before and after code.

By default, the Snippets panel is found under the Code panel group; to open it directly, choose Window ➪ Snippets or use the keyboard shortcut Shift+F9. The Snippets panel, shown in Figure 6-18, shows a preview of the selected snippet. If the snippet itself is not rendered onscreen, like a JavaScript function, the preview shows the code itself; otherwise, you see exactly what the code looks like on the page, minus any CSS stylings. Rearrange your snippets by dragging them within the panel, from folder to folder, if you like.

Figure 6-18: Use the handy Snippets panel to quickly reuse portions of your code.

To insert a snippet, follow these steps:

1. Display the Snippets panel if it's not already open by choosing Window ➪ Snippets.

2. Find the desired snippet by expanding the folder and, if necessary, subfolders.

3. To insert a snippet as a block of code:

   a. Position the cursor where you'd like the code to appear.

   b. Double-click the snippet (or snippet icon) or select the snippet and click Insert.

Alternatively, you can drag the snippet into position in either Code view or Design view.

4. To wrap a snippet around some existing code or page elements:

    a. Select the code or elements.

    b. Double-click the snippet or select the snippet and click Insert.

Again, you can drag the snippet onto the selected code.

Tip   You can quickly hide a section of a page by selecting it and then choosing the Comment, Multiline snippet from the Comments category of the Snippets panel.

Although Dreamweaver's standard code snippets are handy, you don't realize the real value of the Snippets panel until you begin adding your own snippets. To help you manage your snippets, Dreamweaver enables you to create new folders, rename existing ones, or delete ones no longer needed. All this functionality is available through the options menu on the Snippets panel, as well as through the context menu. Snippets, as well as folders, can be renamed, deleted, edited, and, of course, created.

Tip   Before you begin to create your own code snippet, select it first. The Snippets dialog box is modal, and you cannot access other Dreamweaver windows while it is open. The selected code is copied to the Insert Before text field.

To save code as a snippet, follow these steps:

1. Click the New Snippet button on the bottom of the Snippets panel.

2. Enter a name to be displayed in the Snippets panel in the Name field.

3. If you like, you can enter a brief description of the snippet in the Description field.

4. Choose the type of Snippet you're creating: Wrap Selection or Insert Block. The dialog box changes depending on your choice.

5. If you chose Wrap Selection, enter the code to appear prior to the selection in the Insert Before field, and the code to appear after in the Insert After field.

6. If you chose Insert Block, enter the code in the Insert Code field. If you switch from Wrap Selection to Insert Block, Dreamweaver appends the Insert Before field with the contents of the Insert After field.

7. Choose how you would like the snippet to be displayed in the preview area of the Snippets panel, rendered in Design view or as code.

Caution   If you choose the Design preview option for code that does not display in a browser, such as a JavaScript function, it won't be as readable. You still see the code in the preview area, but it does not appear in a monospace font, and all whitespace formatting (such as tabs) appears to be lost.

8. Click OK when you're finished.

You'll remember that when hand-coding, the last 10 used snippets are available directly from the Coding toolbar's Recent Snippets command.

Using the Reference Panel

Pop quiz: What value of a form tag's `enctype` attribute should you use if the user is submitting a file?

    A. `application/x-www-form-urlencoded`

    B. `multipart/form-data`

    C. `multipart/data-form`

Unless you've recently had to include such a form in a Web page, you probably had to pull down that well-worn HTML reference book you keep handy and look up the answer. All code for the Web — including HTML, JavaScript, and Cascading Style Sheets (CSS) — must be precisely written or it is, at best, ignored; at worst, an error is generated whenever the user views the page. Even the savviest of Web designers can't remember the syntax of every tag, attribute, and value in HTML, every function in JavaScript, or every style rule in CSS. A good reference is a necessity in Web design. (By the way, the answer to the pop quiz is B.)

Macromedia has lightened the load on your bookshelf considerably with the addition of the Reference panel, shown in Figure 6-19. With the Reference panel, you can quickly look up any HTML tag and its attributes, as well as JavaScript objects and CSS style rules. Dynamic site builders can rely on references for CFML, ASP, PHP, JSP, XML, and XSLT. In addition, the panel contains a complete reference on Web-related accessibility issues from UsableNet. Not only does the Reference panel offer the proper syntax for any code in question, it also displays the level of browser support available in most situations. Moreover, you don't have to dig through the tag lists to find the information you need — just highlight the tag or object in question and press the keyboard shortcut Shift+F1.

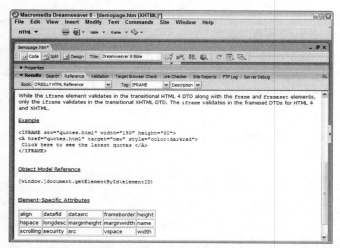

Figure 6-19: To quickly look up a tag, select it in the Tag Selector or in Code view and then press Shift+F1 to open the Reference panel.

You have three different ways to open the Reference panel:

✦ Choose Window ➪ Reference.

✦ Click the Reference button on the toolbar.

✦ Use the Shift+F1 keyboard shortcut.

Tip

To find reference details for the attributes of an HTML tag, a JavaScript object, or a CSS style rule included on a Web page, open Code view and select the code in question prior to choosing Shift+F1 or clicking the Reference button on the toolbar.

To look for information about code not included in the page, follow these steps:

1. Display the Reference panel by choosing Window ➪ Reference or using the keyboard shortcut Shift+F1. The Reference panel appears as a tab in the Results panel.

2. Select the required guide from the Book drop-down list. The standard options are as follows:

   • Macromedia ColdFusion Function Reference

   • Macromedia CFML Reference

   • O'Reilly ASP.NET Reference

   • O'Reilly ASP Reference

   • O'Reilly CSS Reference

   • O'Reilly HTML Reference

   • O'Reilly JavaScript Reference

   • O'Reilly JSP Reference

   • O'Reilly PHP Pocket Reference

   • O'Reilly SQL Language Reference

   • O'Reilly XML Reference

   • O'Reilly XSLT Reference

   • UsableNet Accessibility Reference

3. Choose the primary topic from the Style/Tag/Object drop-down list. The list heading changes depending on which Book is selected.

Tip

You can move quickly to a topic by selecting the drop-down list and then pressing the key for the first letter of the term being sought. Then you can use the down arrow to move through items that start with that letter. For example, if you were looking for information about the JavaScript regular expressions object, you could press **r** and then the down arrow to reach RegExp.

4. If desired, you can select a secondary topic from the second drop-down list. The second list is context-sensitive. For example, if you've chosen an HTML tag, the secondary list displays all the available attributes for that tag. If you've chosen a JavaScript object, the secondary list shows the available properties for that object. The information shown depends, naturally, on the book, topic, and subtopic chosen.

The Reference panel's context menu enables you to switch between three different font sizes: small, medium, and large. This capability is especially useful when working at resolutions higher than 800 x 600. You also have an option to connect directly to O'Reilly Books Online.

Tip   Any code in the Reference panel can be copied by right-clicking (Control-clicking) and choosing Copy. Dreamweaver automatically selects the entire code block with a single click, ready to be copied.

Modifying Code with the Tag Inspector

Since Dreamweaver's beginning, one of my favorite features has been the Property inspector. I really appreciate how it adapts for a selected tag. However, the Property inspector is not without its drawbacks. The feature's main deficiency is key to its design — the Property inspector has only a limited amount of room. To encompass the full range of possible attributes for all the possible tags, Dreamweaver needs a more wide-open solution. Enter the Tag Inspector.

The Tag inspector (Window ➪ Tag Inspector) is a panel that, like the Property inspector, displays the attributes of the selected tag. The Tag inspector, however, presents the attributes and values in the same two-column layout regardless of the selection: attributes on the left and values on the right. Any displayed attribute can be modified through the Tag inspector — simply click into the attribute's value field to make a change. After you've clicked elsewhere or pressed Enter (Return) to move to the next attribute, the attribute/value pair is written into your tag.

Value fields are not just simple text fields, although you can enter the attribute by hand if you want. The value fields change according to the type of attribute. Attributes that can use a predefined value display a pop-up list with all the possible values; for example, click an `<a>` tag and the pop-up value list for the `target` attribute contains `_blank`, `_parent`, `_self`, and `top` (as shown in Figure 6-20). Such pop-up lists are also editable — which means you can enter a value not in the list. Color-type attributes, such as `bgcolor`, offer the Macromedia standard color picker, whereas attributes requiring a filename display both Browse to File (the folder) and Point to File (the crosshairs) icons. All value fields include a lightning bolt icon for inserting dynamic data, such as a field, from a recordset.

Show category view

Show list view

Figure 6-20: Use the Tag inspector to quickly modify any or all attributes of any tag on the page.

You can view the attributes in one of two ways: by category or alphabetically. Two buttons at the top of the panel control the view: Click the one on the left to see a breakdown of attributes by categories (General, Browser Specific, CSS/Accessibility, Language, and Uncategorized). The A-to-Z button on the right lists the attributes alphabetically.

 Tip   Attributes that Dreamweaver is unaware of can be added by entering them into the last row of the Tag Inspector. To remove an existing attribute, select it and then press Backspace (Delete).

Rapid Tag Modification with the Quick Tag Editor

I tend to build Web pages in two phases: Generally, I first lay out my text and images to create the overall design, and then I add details and make alterations to get the page just right. The second phase of Web page design often requires that I make a small adjustment to the HTML code, typically through the Property inspector, but occasionally I need to go right to the source — the code.

Dreamweaver offers a feature for making minor, but essential alterations to the code: the Quick Tag Editor. The Quick Tag Editor is a small pop-up window that appears in the Document window and enables you to edit an existing tag, add a new tag, or wrap the current selection in a tag. One other feature makes the Quick Tag Editor even quicker to use: A handy list of tags or attributes cuts down on typing.

To call up the Quick Tag Editor, use any of the following methods:

✦ Choose Modify ⇨ Quick Tag Editor.

✦ Press the keyboard shortcut Ctrl+T (Command+T).

✦ Click the Quick Tag Editor icon on the Property inspector.

Working with the Hint List

The Quick Tag Editor has a rather nifty feature referred to as the *hint list*. To make it even quicker to use the Quick Tag Editor, a list of tags pops up when you pause in your typing. When you're entering attributes within a tag, a list of appropriate parameters pops up instead of tags. These lists are tied to what, if anything, you've already typed. Suppose, for instance, you've begun to enter **blockquote** and have only gotten as far typing **b** and **l**. When the hint list appears, it scrolls to *blink* — the first tag in the list starting with those two letters. If you continue typing **o**, *blockquote* is selected. All you have to do to insert it into your code is press Enter (Return).

Following are a few other hint list hints:

✦ Scroll to a tag by using the up or down arrow keys.

✦ Double-clicking the selected hint list item also inserts it into the code.

✦ After the hint list is open, press Esc if you decide not to enter the selected tag or attribute.

✦ If an attribute has a set series of values that can be applied (for example, the `<div>` tag's `align` attribute can only be set to left, right, or center), those values are accessible via the hint list.

✦ Control how quickly the hint list appears — or even if it appears at all — by altering the Quick Tag Editor preferences.

The Quick Tag Editor has three modes: Insert HTML, Wrap Tag, and Edit HTML. Although you can get to all three modes from any situation, which mode appears initially depends on the current selection. The Quick Tag Editor's window (see Figure 6-21) appears above the current selection when you use either the menu or keyboard method of opening it, or next to the Property inspector when you click the icon. In either case, you can move the Quick Tag Editor window to a new location onscreen by dragging its title bar.

Figure 6-21: The Quick Tag Editor is great for quickly tweaking your code.

Tip   Regardless of which mode the Quick Tag Editor opens in, you can toggle to the other modes by pressing the keyboard shortcut Ctrl+T (Command+T).

The Quick Tag Editor offers built-in code hinting, just like that found in Code view. See the "Working with the Hint List" sidebar later in this chapter for details about this feature.

Insert HTML Mode

The Insert HTML mode of the Quick Tag Editor is used for adding new tags and code at the current cursor position; it is the initial mode when nothing is selected. The Insert HTML mode starts with a pair of angle brackets enclosing a blinking cursor. You can enter any tag—whether standard HTML or custom XML—and any attribute or content within the new tag. When you're finished, just press Enter (Return) to confirm your addition.

To add new tags to your page using the Quick Tag Editor Insert HTML mode, follow these steps:

1. Position your cursor where you would like the new code to be inserted.

2. Choose Modify ➪ Quick Tag Editor or use the keyboard shortcut Ctrl+T (Command+T) to open the Quick Tag Editor. The Quick Tag Editor opens in Insert HTML mode, as shown in Figure 6-22.

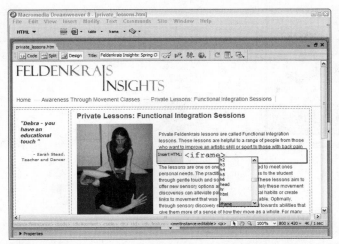

Figure 6-22: Use the Quick Tag Editor's Insert HTML mode to add tags not available through Dreamweaver's visual interface.

3. Enter your HTML or XML code.

Tip

Use the right arrow key to move quickly past the closing angle bracket and add text after your tag.

4. If you pause while typing, the hint list appears, selecting the first tag that matches what you've typed so far. Use the arrow keys to select another tag in the list and press Enter (Return) to select a tag.

5. Press Enter (Return) when you're finished.

The Quick Tag Editor is fairly intelligent and tries to help you write valid HTML. If, for example, you leave off a closing tag, such as `</b>`, the Quick Tag Editor automatically adds it for you.

Wrap Tag Mode

Part of the power and flexibility of HTML is the capability to wrap one tag around other tags and content. To make a phrase appear bold and italic, the code is written as follows:

```
<b><i>On Sale Now!</i></b>
```

Note how the inner `<i>`...`</i>` tag pair is enclosed by the `<b>`...`</b>` pair. The Wrap Tag mode of the Quick Tag Editor surrounds any selection with your entered tag in one easy operation.

Note

The Wrap Tag mode appears initially when you have selected just text (with no surrounding tags) or an incomplete tag (the opening tag and contents, but no closing tag). The Wrap Tag mode is visually similar to the Insert HTML mode, as you can see in Figure 6-23.

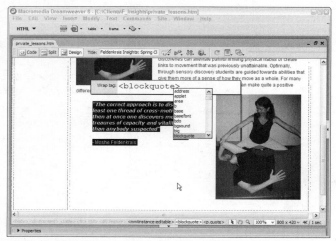

Figure 6-23: Enclose any selection with a tag by using the Quick Tag Editor's Wrap Tag mode.

However, rather than just include exactly what you've entered into the Quick Tag Editor, Wrap Tag mode also inserts a closing tag that corresponds to your entry. For example, you want to apply a tag not available as an object: the subscript, or `<sub>`, tag. After highlighting the text that you want to mark up as subscript (the 2 in the formula H_2O, for example), you open the Quick Tag Editor and enter **sub**. The resulting code looks like the following:

```
H<sub>2</sub>0
```

Caution You can enter only one tag in Wrap Tag mode; if more than one tag is entered, Dreamweaver displays an alert informing you that the tag you've entered appears to be invalid HTML. The Quick Tag Editor is then closed, and the selection is cleared.

To wrap a tag with the Quick Tag Editor, follow these steps:

1. Select the text or tags you want to enclose in another tag.

2. Choose Modify ➪ Quick Tag Editor or use the keyboard shortcut Ctrl+T (Command+T) to open the Quick Tag Editor.

3. If you select a complete tag, the Quick Tag Editor opens in Edit Tag mode; press the keyboard shortcut Ctrl+T (Command+T) to toggle to Wrap Tag mode.

4. Enter the tag you want.

5. If you pause while typing, the hint list appears. It selects the first tag that matches what you've typed so far. Use the arrow keys to select another tag in the list and press Enter (Return) to select a tag from the hint list.

6. Press Enter (Return) to confirm your tag.

   The Quick Tag Editor closes, and Dreamweaver places the tag before your selection and a corresponding closing tag after it.

Edit Tag Mode

If a complete tag—either a single tag, such as `<img>`, or a tag pair, such as `<h1>`...`</h1>`—is selected, the Quick Tag Editor opens in Edit Tag mode. Unlike the other two modes (in which you are presented with just open and closing angle brackets and a flashing cursor), the Edit Tag mode displays the entire selected tag with all its attributes, if any. You can always invoke the Edit Tag mode when you start the Quick Tag Editor by clicking its icon in the Property inspector.

The Edit Tag mode has many uses. It's excellent for adding a parameter not found on Dreamweaver's Property inspector. For example, when you are building a form, some text fields have pre-existing text in them—which you want to clear when the user clicks into the field. To achieve this effect you add a minor bit of JavaScript, a perfect use for the Edit Tag mode. Therefore, you can just select the `<i>` tag from the Tag Selector and then click the Quick Tag Editor icon to open the Quick Tag Editor. The `<imgnput>` tag appears with your current parameters, as shown in Figure 6-24. After you have opened it, tab to the end of the tag and enter this code:

```
onFocus="if(this.value=='Email Required')this.value='';"
```

In this example, `Email Required` is the visible text in the field—the value, which automatically clears when the field is selected.

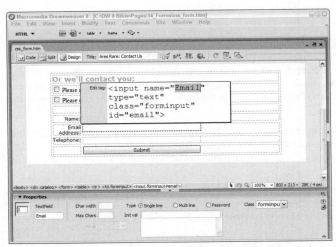

Figure 6-24: In Edit Tag mode, the Quick Tag Editor shows the entire tag, with attributes and their values.

To use the Quick Tag Editor in Insert HTML mode, follow these steps:

1. Select an entire tag by clicking its name in the Tag Selector.

2. Choose Modify ➪ Quick Tag Editor.

3. To change an existing attribute, tab to the current value and enter a new one.

4. To add a new attribute, tab and/or use the arrow keys to position the cursor after an existing attribute or after the tag, and enter the new parameter and value.

Tip

If you don't close the quotation marks for a parameter's value, Dreamweaver does it for you.

5. If you pause briefly while entering a new attribute, the hint list appears with attributes appropriate for the current tag. If you select an attribute from the hint list, press Enter (Return) to accept the parameter.

6. When you've finished editing the tag, press Enter (Return).

In addition to this capability to edit complete tags, Dreamweaver has a couple of navigational commands to help select just the right tag. The Select Parent Tag command—keyboard shortcut Ctrl+[(Command+[)—highlights the tag immediately surrounding the present tag. Going in the other direction, the Select Child Tag—keyboard shortcut Ctrl+] (Command+])—selects the next tag, if any, contained within the current tag. Both commands are available under the Edit menu. Exercising these commands is equivalent to selecting the next tag in the Tag Selector to the left (parent) or right (child).

Caution

Although it works well in Design view, unfortunately the Select Child command does not function in Code view.

Adding Java Applets

Java is a platform-independent programming language developed by Sun Microsystems. Although Java can also be used to write entire applications, its most frequent role is on the Web in the form of an applet. An *applet* is a self-contained program that can be run within a Web page.

Java is a compiled programming language similar to C++. After a Java applet is compiled, it is saved as a class file. Web browsers call Java applets through, aptly enough, the `<applet>` tag. When you insert an applet, you refer to the primary class file much as you call a graphic file for an image tag.

Each Java applet has its own unique set of parameters—and Dreamweaver enables you to enter as many as necessary in the same manner as plugins and ActiveX controls. In fact, the Applet object works almost identically to the Plugin and ActiveX objects.

Caution

Keep two caveats in mind if you're planning to include Java applets in your Web site. First, most (but not all) browsers support some version of Java—the newest release has the most features, but the least support. Second, all the browsers that support Java offer the user the option of disabling it because of security issues. Be sure to use the Alt property to designate an alternative image or some text for display by browsers that do not support Java.

A Java applet can be inserted in a Web page with a bare minimum of parameters: the code source and the dimensions of the object. Java applets derive much of their power from their configurability, and most of these little programs have numerous custom parameters. As with plugins and ActiveX controls, Dreamweaver enables you to specify the basic attributes through the Property inspector and the custom ones via the Parameters dialog box.

To include a Java applet in your Web page, follow these steps:

1. Position the cursor where you want the applet to originate and choose Insert ⇨ Media ⇨ Applet. You can also click the Insert Applet button from the Media group on the Common category of the Insert bar. The Insert Applet dialog box opens.

2. From the Select File dialog box, enter the path to your class file in the File Name text box or click the Browse button to locate the file. An Applet object placeholder appears in the Document window. In the Applet Property inspector (see Figure 6-25), the selected source file appears in the Code text box, and the folder appears in the Base text box.

Applet icon

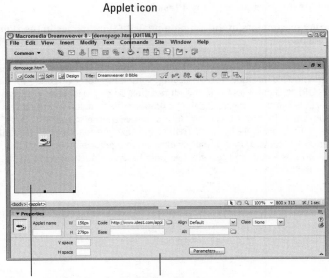

Applet placeholder   Applet Property inspector

Figure 6-25: Use the Insert Applet button to insert a Java Applet object and display the Applet Property inspector.

Note   The path to your Java class files cannot be expressed absolutely; it must be given as an address relative to the Web page that is calling it.

3. Enter the height and width of the Applet object in the H and W text boxes, respectively. You can also resize the Applet object by clicking and dragging any of its three sizing handles.

4. You can enter any of the usual basic attributes, such as a name for the object, as well as values for Align, V, and/or H Space in the appropriate text boxes in the Property inspector.

5. If you want, enter the online directory where the applet code can be found in the Base text box. If none is specified, the document's URL is assumed to be this attribute, known as the *codebase*.

6. To display an alternative image if the Java applet is unable to run (typically, because the user's browser does not support Java or the user has disabled Java), enter the path to the image in the Alt field. You can use the folder icon to locate the image as well. Text may also serve as the alternative content if you don't want to use an image. Any text entered into the Alt field is displayed in the browser as a ToolTip.

7. To enter any custom attributes, click the Parameters button to open the Parameters dialog box.

8. Click the Add (+) button and enter the first parameter. Press Tab to move to the Value column.

9. Enter the value for the parameter, if any. Press Tab.

10. Continue entering parameters in the left column, with their values in the right. Click OK when you've finished.

Tip   Because of the importance of displaying alternative content for users not running Java, Dreamweaver provides a method for displaying something for everyone. To display an image, enter the URL to a graphics file in the Alt text box. To display text as well as an image, you have to do a little hand-coding. First select a graphics file to insert in the Alt text box and then open Code view. In the `<img>` tag found between the `<applet>` tags, add an `alt="your_message"` attribute by hand (where the text you want to display is the value for the `alt` attribute). Now your Java applet displays an image for browsers that are graphics-enabled but not Java-enabled, and text for text-only browsers such as Lynx. In this sample code, I've bolded the additional `alt` attribute.

```
<applet code="animate.class" width=100 ⤴
height=100>
<param name=img1 value="/images/1.jpg">
<param name=img2 value="/images/2.jpg">
<img src="animation.gif" alt="Animate for ⤴
Life!" width=100 height=100>
</applet>
```

Some Java class files have additional graphics files. In most cases, you store both the class files and the graphics files in the same folder.

Adding JavaScript and VBScript

When initially developed by Netscape, JavaScript was called LiveScript. This browser-oriented language did not gain importance until Sun Microsystems joined the development team and the product was renamed JavaScript. Although the rechristening was a stroke of marketing genius, it has caused endless confusion among beginning programmers — JavaScript and Java have almost nothing in common outside of their capability to be incorporated in a Web page. JavaScript is used primarily to add functionality on the client-side of the browser (for tasks such as verifying form data and adding interactivity to interface elements) or to script Netscape's servers on the server-side. Java, on the other hand, is an application-development language that can be used for a wide variety of tasks.

Conversely, VBScript is a full-featured Microsoft product. Both VBScript and JavaScript are scripting languages, which means that you can write the code in any text editor and compile it at runtime. JavaScript enjoys more support than VBScript. JavaScript can be rendered by both Netscape and Microsoft browsers (as well as other browsers such as WebTV, Opera, and

Sun's HotJava), whereas VBScript is read only by Internet Explorer on Windows systems. Both languages have their fans. In Dreamweaver, both types of code are inserted in the Web page in the same manner.

Inserting JavaScript and VBScript

If only mastering JavaScript or VBScript were as easy as inserting the code in Dreamweaver! Simply go to the Script menu on the HTML category of the Insert bar and click the Script button, or choose Insert ➪ HTML ➪ Script Objects ➪ Script and enter your code in the Insert Script dialog box. After you click OK, a Script icon appears in place of your script.

Of course, JavaScript or VBScript instruction is beyond the scope of this book, but every working Web designer must have an understanding of what these languages can do. Both languages refer to and, to varying degrees, manipulate the information on a Web page. Over time, you can expect significant growth in the capabilities of the JavaScript and VBScript disciplines.

 Cross-Reference   Dreamweaver, through the application of its behaviors, goes a long way toward making JavaScript useful for nonprogrammers. To learn more about behaviors, see Chapter 12.

Use the Script Property inspector (see Figure 6-26) to select an external file for your JavaScript or VBScript code. You can also set the language type by opening the Language drop-down list from the Script window and choosing either JavaScript or VBScript. Because different features are available in the various releases of JavaScript, you can also specify JavaScript 1.1 or JavaScript 1.2. Choose a specific version of JavaScript when you initially insert the script — you cannot change the setting from the Script Property inspector. Naturally, you can also make the adjustment in Code view.

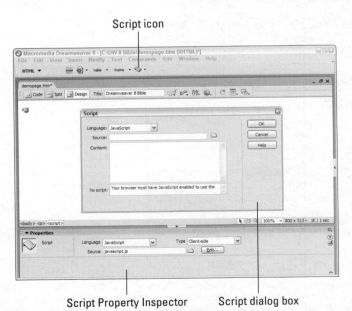

Figure 6-26: The generous Script dialog box provides plenty of room for modifying your JavaScript or VBScript.

When you choose JavaScript or VBScript as your Language type, Dreamweaver writes the code accordingly. Both languages use the `<script>` tag pair, and each is specified in the `language` attribute, as follows:

```
<script language="JavaScript">alert("Look Out!")</script>
```

With Dreamweaver, you are not restricted to inserting code in just the `<body>` section of your Web page. Many JavaScript and VBScript functions must be located in the `<head>` section. To insert this type of script, first choose View ➪ Head Content or, from the Options menu of the toolbar, select Head Content. Next, select the now visible `<head>` window and choose Insert ➪ Invisible Tags ➪ Script, or click the Insert Script object. Enter your script as described earlier in this section and then select the main Document window, or choose View ➪ Head Content again to deselect it.

You can also indicate whether your script is based on the client-side or server-side by choosing the Type option from the Property inspector. If you choose server-side, your script is enclosed in `<server>`...`</server>` tags and is interpreted by the Web server hosting the page.

Editing JavaScript and VBScript

Dreamweaver provides a large editing window for modifying your script code. To open this Script Properties window, select the placeholder icon for the script you want to modify and then click the Edit button on the Script Property inspector. You have the same functionality in the Script Properties window as in the Script Property inspector; namely, you can choose your language or link to an external script file (see Figure 6-27).

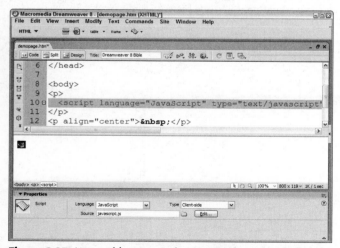

Figure 6-27: Insert either JavaScript or VBScript using the Insert bar's Script object.

Tip   Some older browsers break when loading a JavaScript Web page and display the code written between the `<script>`...`</script>` tag pair. Although Dreamweaver doesn't prevent this problem by default, you can use a trick to prevent this anomaly. In Code view or the Code inspector, insert the opening comment tag (`<!--`) right after the opening `<script>` tag. Then insert the closing comment tag (`-->`), preceded by two forward slashes, right before the closing `</script>`. An example follows:

```
<script language="Javascript">
<!--
[JavaScript code goes here]
//-->
</script>
```

The comment tags effectively tell the older browser to ignore the enclosed content. The two forward slashes in front of the closing comment tag are JavaScript's comment indicator, which tells it to ignore the rest of the line.

Validating Your Page

Syntax — the rules governing the formation of statements in a programming language — is important regardless of which language your pages employ. Earlier browsers tended to be more relaxed about following the syntactical rules of HTML, but as standardization becomes increasingly important, browsers — and businesses — are following suit. Certain languages, such as XML, require the code to be proper or it just won't work. To ensure that a page is correctly written, the page should be validated. The Web offers numerous validation services — most notably the one run by the W3C at `http://validator.w3.org/` — but you don't need to leave Dreamweaver to validate your pages ever again.

With Dreamweaver's Validation feature you can check a single page or an entire site. After it is checked, the resulting errors and warnings, if any, can be stored in an XML file for future output. Any error can be double-clicked to go right to the offending element for immediate correction.

As with other Dreamweaver-style reports, the Validation feature resides in the Results panel, as shown in Figure 6-28. To display the Validation panel, choose Window ➪ Results and click the Validation tab. Controls for the Validation panel are found along the left, and the panel is divided into three sections: *File*, which lists the file being referenced; *Line*, which lists the line number on which the error can be found; and *Description*, which contains a brief overview of the problem.

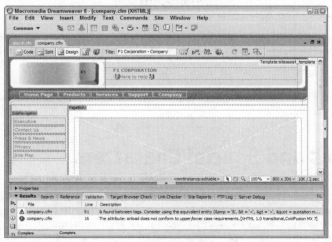

Figure 6-28: You can easily validate your pages from within Dreamweaver using the Validation feature.

Clicking the Validate button—the triangle in the left margin of the Validation tab shown in Figure 6-28—unveils a menu of options:

✦ **Validate Current Document:** Checks the onscreen document against the validation preferences

✦ **Validate Entire Site:** Runs through the entire current site, checking for validation errors

✦ **Validate Selected Files In Site:** Checks files selected in the Site panel

Note If no files are selected in the Files panel and Validate Selected Files In Site is chosen, the entire site is validated. To halt a site validation in process, click the Stop button on the Validation panel.

✦ **Settings:** Displays the Validation category in Preferences

Cross-Reference Part of the power of Dreamweaver's Validation feature comes from its extensive options. To get a full overview of all your options, see Chapter 4.

To validate a page, follow these steps:

1. Make sure the Validation options you want are set in Preferences. If not, click the Validate button and choose Settings.

Caution If you validate CFML (ColdFusion) and HTML in the same document, the Validator won't be able to assess the number sign (#) correctly. Why not? Because, in CFML, # is an error and ## is correct; in HTML, the converse is true: ## is an error and # is correct.

2. Select Validate and then Validate Current Document. Dreamweaver's validation engine goes through the entire page and displays any errors, warnings, and other messages in the Validation panel.

3. To correct an error, double-click the entry. Dreamweaver highlights the offending tag in Code view, where you can make any modifications necessary.

4. Select More Info to see additional details, if available, about the current error.

5. To store the results of the validation as an XML file, select Save Report and enter the name for the file. Dreamweaver, by default, supplies the filename `ResultsReport.xml`.

6. To view a listing of the results in your primary browser, choose Browse Report.

Tip Use Browse Report and then print the file from your browser as a quick way to get a hard copy of the validation results.

Inserting Symbols and Special Characters

When working with Dreamweaver, you're usually entering text directly from your keyboard, one keystroke at a time, with each keystroke representing a letter, number, or other keyboard character. Some situations, however, require special letters that have diacritics or common symbols, such as the copyright symbol, which are outside of the regular, standard character set represented on your keyboard. HTML enables you to insert a full range of such character entities through two systems. The more familiar special characters have been assigned a mnemonic code name to make them easy to remember; these are called *named characters*. Less typical characters must be inserted by entering a numeric code; these are known as *decimal characters*. For the sake of completeness, named characters also have a corresponding decimal character code.

Both named and decimal character codes begin with an ampersand (&) symbol and end with a semicolon (;). For example, the HTML code for an ampersand symbol is

```
&amp;
```

Its decimal character equivalent is

```
&#38;
```

Caution   If, during the browser-testing phase of creating your Web page, you suddenly see an HTML code onscreen rather than a symbol, double-check your HTML. The code could be just a typo; you may have left off the closing semicolon, for instance. If the code is correct and you're using a named character, however, switch to its decimal equivalent. Some of the earlier browser versions are not perfect in rendering named characters.

Named Characters

HTML coding conventions require that certain characters, including the angle brackets that surround tags, be entered as character entities. Table 6-4 lists the most common named characters.

Table 6-4: Common Named Characters

Named Entity	Symbol	Description
&lt;	<	A left angle bracket or the less-than symbol
&gt;	>	A right angle bracket or the greater-than symbol
&amp;	&	An ampersand
&quot;	"	A double quotation mark
	°	A nonbreaking space
&copy;	©	A copyright symbol
&reg;	®	A registered mark
&trade;	™	A trademark symbol, which cannot be previewed in Dreamweaver but is supported in Internet Explorer

Tip   Those characters that you can type directly into Dreamweaver's Document window, including the brackets and the ampersand, are automatically translated into the correct named characters in HTML. Try this when in split-screen Code and Design view. You can also enter a nonbreaking space in Dreamweaver by pressing Ctrl+Shift+spacebar (Command+Shift+spacebar) or by choosing the Nonbreaking Space object.

Decimal Characters and UTF-8 Encoding

To enter almost any character that has a diacritic — such as á, ñ, or â — in Dreamweaver, you must explicitly enter the corresponding decimal character into your HTML page. As mentioned in the preceding section, decimal characters take the form of &#number;, where the number can range from 00 to 255. Not all numbers have matching symbols; the sequence from 14 through 31 is currently unused. The upper range (127 through 159), only partially supported by Internet Explorer and Netscape Navigator, is now deemed invalid by the W3C. In addition, not all fonts have characters for every entity.

Dreamweaver uses UTF-8 encoding for characters higher than 127. UTF-8 is an ASCII-compatible version of Unicode character set. Unicode provides a unique number for every character in every language; however, the raw Unicode number is rendered in 16-bit words, unreadable by browsers — a problem solved by UTF-8.

UTF-8 also uses numbers, but does away with the upper limit of 255. For example, the UTF-8 encoding for the trademark symbol is ™, whereas the no-longer–used number entity is ™. Fortunately, you don't have to remember complex codes — all you have to do is use the Character objects.

Using the Character Objects

Not only is it difficult to remember the various name or number codes for the specific character entities, it's also time-consuming to enter the code by hand. The Dreamweaver engineers recognized this problem and created a series of Character objects, which are found under the Characters menu of the Insert bar's Text category or the Insert ⇨ HTML ⇨ Special Characters submenu.

Ease of use is the guiding principle for the new Character objects. Eleven of the most commonly used symbols, such as © and ®, are instantly available as separate objects. Inserting the single Character objects is a straightforward point-and-click affair. Either drag the desired symbol to a place in the Document window or position your cursor and select the object. The individual Character objects are described in Table 6-5.

Table 6-5: Character Objects

Icon	Name	HTML Code Inserted
BR↵	Line Break	
↧	NonBreaking Space	
❝	Left Quote	“
❞	Right Quote	”
▬	Em-Dash	—
£	Pound	£

Icon	Name	HTML Code Inserted
€	Euro	`&#8364;`
¥	Yen	`&yen;`
©	Copyright	`&copy;`
®	Registered	`&reg;`
TM	Trademark	`&#8482;`

Note
You may notice that the Character objects insert a mix of named and number character entities. Not all browsers recognize the easier-to-identify named entities, so for the widest compatibility, Dreamweaver uses the number codes for a few objects.

The final object in the Characters menu is used for inserting these or any other character entity. The Insert Other Character object displays a large table with symbols for 99 different characters, as shown in Figure 6-29. Simply select the desired symbol, and Dreamweaver inserts the appropriate HTML code at the current cursor position. By the way, the very first character — which appears to be blank — actually inserts the code for a nonbreaking space, also accessible via the keyboard shortcut Ctrl+Shift+spacebar (Command+Shift+spacebar). The nonbreaking space is also available in the Characters menu in the Text category of the Insert bar.

Note
Keep in mind that the user's browser must support the character entity for it to be visible to the user; again, testing is essential. In the case of the Euro symbol, for example, that support is still not widespread. In some instances, where the appearance of a particular character is critical, a graphic may be a better option than a UTF-8 entity.

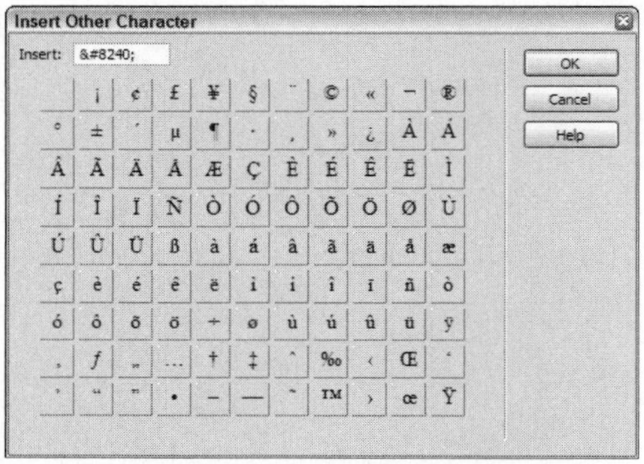

Figure 6-29: Use the Insert Other Character object to insert the character entity code for any of 99 different symbols.

Summary

Creating Web pages with Dreamweaver is a special blend of using visual layout tools and HTML coding. Regardless, you need to understand the basics of HTML so that you have the knowledge and the tools to modify your code when necessary. This chapter covered the following key areas:

✦ An HTML page is divided into two main sections: the `<head>` and the `<body>`. Information pertaining to the entire page is kept in the `<head>` section; all the actual content of the Web page goes in the `<body>` section.

✦ You can change the color and background of your entire page, as well as set its title, through the Page Properties dialog box.

✦ Use `<meta>` tags to summarize your Web page so that search engines can properly catalog it. In Dreamweaver, you can use the View Head Contents feature to easily alter these and other `<head>` tags.

✦ When possible, use logical style tags, such as `<strong>` and `<cite>`, rather than hard-coding your page with physical style tags. Style sheets bring a great deal of control and flexibility to logical style tags.

✦ Java applets can be inserted as Applet objects in a Dreamweaver Web page. Java source files, called *classes*, can be linked to the Applet object through the Property inspector.

✦ Dreamweaver offers a simple method for including both JavaScript and VBScript code in the `<body>` section of your HTML page. Script functions that you want to insert in the `<head>` section can now be added by choosing View ➪ Head Content.

✦ Special extended characters such as symbols and accented letters require the use of HTML character entities, which can either be named (as in `&quot;`) or in decimal format (as in `&#34;`).

In the next chapter, you learn how to work with Cascading Style Sheets — also known as CSS — to style and lay out your Web pages in Dreamweaver.

✦   ✦   ✦

Building Style Sheet Web Pages

All publications, whether on paper or the Web, need a balance of style and content to be effective. Style without content is all flash with no real information. Content with no style is flat and uninteresting, thus losing the substance. Traditionally, HTML has tied style to content wherever possible, preferring logical tags such as <strong> to indicate emphasis to physical tags such as <b> for bold. But although this emphasis on the logical worked for many single documents, its imprecision made achieving style consistency across a broad range of Web pages unrealistic, if not impossible.

The Cascading Style Sheets specification has changed this situation—and much more. As support for Cascading Style Sheets (CSS) grows, more Web designers can alter font faces, type size, spacing, and many other page elements with a single command—and have the effect ripple not only throughout the page, but also throughout a Web site. Moreover, an enhancement of CSS, initially called CSS-P (for positioning), is the foundation for what has become commonly known as *layers*.

Dreamweaver was one of the first Web-authoring tools to make the application of Cascading Style Sheets user-friendly—and in this latest version, Dreamweaver has integrated CSS throughout the program. Through Dreamweaver's intuitive interface, the Web designer can access more than 70 different CSS settings, affecting everything from type specs to multimedia-like transitions. Dreamweaver enables you to work the way you want: Create your complete style sheet first and then link it when you're ready, or make up your styles one-by-one as you build your Web page. Dreamweaver's advanced CSS rendering helps you create the design you visualize every step of the way.

In this chapter, you find out how CSS works and why you need it. As you work through a Dreamweaver Technique to remove underlines from links, you also walk through a typical style sheet session. With that experience under your belt, you're ready for the later sections with detailed information on the current CSS commands—and how to apply those commands to your Web page and site. Also, the section on defining styles helps you understand what's what in the Style Definition dialog box. You learn how you can create external style sheets to establish—and maintain—the look and feel of an entire Web site with a single document. Finally, you see how Dreamweaver's special CSS features, including design time style sheets, make the CSS promise a reality.

Understanding Cascading Style Sheets

The Cascading Style Sheets system significantly increases the design capabilities for a Web site. If you are a designer used to working with desktop publishing tools, you may recognize many familiar features in CSS, including the following:

✦ Commands for specifying and applying font characteristics

✦ Traditional layout measurement systems and terminology

✦ Pinpoint precision for page layout

Cascading Style Sheets are able to apply many features with a simple syntax that is easy to understand. If you're familiar with the concept of using styles in a word processing program, you'll have no trouble grasping style sheets.

Here's how the process works: CSS instructions are given in rules; a style sheet is a collection of these rules. A rule is a statement made up of an HTML or custom style, called a *selector*, and its defined properties and values. For example, a CSS rule that makes the contents of all <h1> tags (the selector) red (#FF0000 in hexadecimal, the value) in color (the property) looks like the following:

```
h1 {
    color: #FF0000;
}
```

A CSS property and its associated value are collectively referred to as a *declaration*.

In the following sections, you see the various characteristics of CSS — grouping, inheritance, and cascading — working together to give style sheets their flexibility and power.

Grouping Properties

A Web designer often needs to change several style properties at once. CSS enables you to group declarations by separating them with semicolons. For example:

```
h1 {
    color:#FF0000;
    font-family:Arial,Helvetica,sans-serif;
    font-size:18pt;
}
```

The Dreamweaver interface provides a wide range of options for styles. If you look at the code, you find that Dreamweaver groups your selections exactly as shown in the preceding example. You can group selectors as well as declarations. Separate grouped selectors with commas rather than semicolons. For example:

```
h1, h2, p, em {
    color:green;
    text-align:left;
}
```

Inheritance of Properties

CSS rules can also be applied to more than one tag through inheritance. The HTML tags enclosed within the CSS selector can inherit most, but not all, CSS declarations. Suppose you set all <p> tags to the color red. Any tags included within a <p>...</p> tag pair then inherit that property and are also colored red.

Inheritance is also at work within HTML tags that involve a parent-child relationship, such as a list. Whether numbered (ordered, <ol>) or bulleted (unordered, <ul>), a list comprises any number of list items, designated by <li> tags. Each list item is considered a child of the parent tag, <ol> or <ul>. Look at the following example:

```
ol {
   color:#FF0000;
}
ul {
   color:#0000FF;
}
```

Using the preceding example, all ordered list items appear in red (#FF0000); all unordered list items appear in blue (#0000FF). One major benefit to this parent-child relationship is that you can change the font for an entire page with one CSS rule. The following statement accomplishes this change:

```
body {
   font-family: Verdana, Arial, Helvetica, sans-serif;
}
```

The change is possible in the previous example because the <body> tag is considered the parent of every HTML element on a page.

Tip   There's one exception to the preceding rule: tables. Netscape browsers (through version 4.75) treat tables differently than the rest of the HTML <body> when it comes to style sheets. To change the font of a table, you specify something like the following:

```
td {
   font-family: Verdana, Arial, Helvetica, sans-serif;
}
```

Because every cell in a table uses the <td> tag, this style sheet declaration affects the entire table.

Cascading Characteristics

The term *cascading* describes the capability of a local style to override a general style. Think of a stream flowing down a mountain; each ledge encountered by the stream has the potential to change its direction. The last ledge determines the final direction of the stream. In the same manner, one CSS rule applying generally to a block of text can be overridden by another rule applied to a more specific part of the same text.

For example, you've defined, using style sheets, all normal paragraphs — <p> tags — as a particular font in a standard color, but you mark one section of the text using a little-used tag such as <samp>. If you make a CSS rule altering both the font and color of the <samp> tag, the section takes on the characteristics of that rule.

The cascading aspect of style sheets also works on a larger scale. One of the key features of CSS is the capability to define external style sheets that can be linked to individual Web pages, acting on their overall look and feel. Indeed, you can use the cascading behavior to fine-tune the overall Web-site style based on a particular page or range of pages. Your company may, for instance, define an external style sheet for the entire company intranet; each division could then build upon that overall model for its individual Web pages. For example, suppose that the company style sheet dictates that all <h2> headings are in Arial and black. One department could output its Web pages with <h2> tags in Arial, but colored red rather than black, whereas another department could make them blue.

Tip   Dreamweaver has a great learning tool built in to help you understand inheritance and cascading: the Relevant CSS tab of the Tag inspector. Select any tag and you can see what CSS rules are being applied to the selection; rules that are applied, but not taking effect because of inheritance or cascading properties are marked with a red strike-through. This feature is explained in greater detail later in this chapter.

Defining New Class and ID Selectors for Extended Design Control

Redefining existing HTML tags is a step in the right direction toward consistent design, but the real power of CSS comes into play when you define custom selectors. One type of custom selector is called a *class*; class selector names always begin with a period. Here's a simple example: To style all copyright notices at the bottom of all pages of a Web site to display in 8-point Helvetica all caps, you could define a tag like this:

```
.cnote {
  font-family:Helvetica, sans-serif;
  font-size:8pt;
  font-transform:uppercase
}
```

If you define this style in an external style sheet and apply it to all 999 pages of your Web site, you have to alter only one line of code (instead of all 999 pages) when the edict comes down from management to make all the copyright notices a touch larger. After a new class has been defined, you can apply it to any range of text, from one word to an entire page.

Classes are typically applied to more than one element on a page. You could, for example, have more than one paragraph styled as a copyright notice in various parts of the page. A custom tag intended to be applied to a single element, such as a <div> tag that contains the footer content, is called an *ID selector*. An ID selector is identified by its beginning pound sign — technically called an octothrope — for example, #footer. If you want the footer content to really stand out, you could style it with white type against a black background with a red border. The CSS rule looks like this:

```
#footer {
    color: #FFFFFF;
    background: #000000;
    border: thin solid #FF0000;
}
```

An ID selector is applied to a tag through the self-named id attribute, minus the pound sign. Thus, the <div> tag that holds the footer content is coded like this:

```
<div id="footer">Footer content goes here</div>
```

Designers use a combination of class and ID selectors — as well as other types of selectors — when laying out the page. It's considered a best practice to avoid using class selectors when the CSS rule is intended to be applied only once on the page; in those situations, an ID selector is the better choice.

Specificity

The specificity of a CSS rule determines which rule takes effect when two or more rules conflict. For example, let's say you have one rule that sets the color of an <h1> tag to dark gray, like this:

```
h1 { color: #333333; }
```

and another rule that sets the color of a class called .alert to bright red:

```
.alert { color: #FF0000; }
```

What would happen when the browser encounters code like this:

```
<h1 class="alert">Attention all shoppers!</h1>
```

As you might suspect, the .alert rule would be applied and the <h1> tag would appear red. The reason this is true is because the .alert selector is more specific than the <h1> tag selector. The W3C CSS specification (no relation) provides a different weight for each kind of selector.

A rule's specificity is noted with four comma-separated values. For example, the specificity for the <h1> rule is

```
0,0,0,1
```

because there is one tag element in the selector. Whereas the specificity for the .alert rule is

```
0,0,1,0
```

because there is one class element in the selector. Any positive value in the second-to-last column outweighs any value in the last column.

The formula for creating specificity is as follows:

```
Total inlines styles, total ID selectors, total class and pseudo-class
selectors, total tag elements
```

Inline styles are the most specific — and the most rarely used these days — so they trump any other type of selector. If two rules have the same specificity and are applied to the same selection, the rule that comes later in the style sheet — because it is physically closer to the code — wins.

How Styles Are Applied

CSS applies style formatting to your page in one of three ways:

✦ Via an external, linked style sheet

✦ Via an embedded styles

✦ Via inline style rules

External Style Sheets

An external style sheet is a file containing the CSS rules; it links one or more Web pages. One benefit of linking to an external style sheet is that you can customize and change the appearance of a Web site quickly and easily from one file.

Two different methods exist for working with an external style sheet: the link method and the import method. Dreamweaver initially defaults to the link method, but you can also choose import if you prefer.

For the link method, a line of code is added outside of the `<style>` tags, as follows:

```
<link href="mainstyle.css" rel="style sheet" type="text/css">
```

The import method writes code within the style tags, as follows:

```
<style type="text/css">
<!--
@import url("newstyles.css");
-->
</style>
```

Comparing the link and the import methods, the link method is better supported among browsers, including Netscape 4.x. Because of Netscape 4.x's lack of standards support in CSS and other issues, however, the link method isn't necessarily your best choice.

Tip   You can take advantage of Netscape 4.x's lack of support for the import method to offset its rather quirky support of CSS in general. Create two style sheets: one to handle Netscape 4.x issues and one for newer browsers, such as Internet Explorer 4.x and up and Netscape 6. Use the link technique to bring in the NS4.x-based style sheet and import for the second style sheet. By writing the code in the following sequence, the second style sheet overrides the same selector rules in the first style sheet and is ignored by Netscape 4.x:

```
<link href="mainstyleNS.css" rel="style sheet" ⤵
type="text/css">
<style type="text/css">
<!--
@import url("mainstyles.css");
-->
</style>
```

Embedded Styles

Embedded styles are those typically written into the actual file at the top of a Web page within a `<style>`...`</style>` tag pair. Placing style sheets within the header tags has become a convention that many designers use, although you can also apply a style sheet anywhere on a page.

The `<style>` tag for a Cascading Style Sheet identifies the type attribute as `text/css`. A sample embedded style listing looks like the following:

```
<style type="text/css">
<!--
p {
  font-family: "Arial, Helvetica, sans-serif";
  color: #000000;
}
.cnote {
  font: 8pt "Arial, Helvetica, sans-serif";
  text-transform: uppercase;
}
h1 {
  font: bold 18pt Arial, Helvetica, sans-serif;
  color: #FF0000;
}
-->
</style>
```

The HTML comment tags `<!--` and `-->` prevent older browsers that can't read style sheets from displaying the CSS rules.

Inline Styles

The final method of applying a style inserts it within HTML tags using the `style` attribute — a technique known as *inline styles*. This method is the most local of all the techniques; that is, it is closest to the tag it is affecting and, therefore, has ultimate control — because of the cascading nature of style sheets as previously discussed.

Caution　As my mother used to say, "Just because you can do something, doesn't mean you should." Generally, inline styles are not used because they exert such a high level of control, and modifying the style must be done on an item-by-item basis, which defeats much of the purpose of CSS.

When you create a layer within Dreamweaver, you notice that the positioning attribute is a Cascading Style Sheet inline within a `<div>` tag like the following:

```
<div id="Layer1" style="position:absolute; visibility:inherit; left:314px;
top:62px; width:194px; height:128px; z-index:1">
</div>
```

For all its apparent complexity, the Cascading Style Sheets system becomes straightforward in Dreamweaver. Often, you won't have to write a single line of code. But even if you don't have to write code, you should understand the CSS fundamentals of grouping, inheritance, and cascading.

Working with the CSS Styles Panel

The CSS Styles panel is Dreamweaver's central point for establishing, modifying, and learning about Cascading Style Sheets. It is, by far, the most complex and sophisticated of any of Dreamweaver's panels and requires a bit of explanation to help you to understand how best to use it. You can open the CSS Styles panel by choosing Window ➪ CSS Styles or use the keyboard shortcut, Shift+F11; the CSS Styles panel is available by default and its title bar can be double-clicked to expose it as well.

The CSS Styles panel can be viewed in two separate ways: All mode and Current mode. In brief, All mode displays the embedded and external CSS styles contained in the current page; it does not display inline styles. Current mode shows every style rule affecting the current selection on the page, regardless of whether the source is defined in an inline, embedded, or external style rule.

Personally, I tend to work in All mode during the initial development of a page and then switch to Current when I need to drill-down into a particular style. Both modes allow for rapid modification of any defined CSS properties and the equally speedy setting of new attributes.

All Mode

Enter All mode by selecting All at the top of the CSS Styles panel. Once selected, you'll note that the panel is divided into two parts, the All Rules pane and the Properties pane. The All Rules pane shows every embedded and external style rule associated with the current page. Select any rule to see its properties and values in the Properties pane (see Figure 7-1).

All Rules pane

All mode   Properties pane

Figure 7-1: Use All modes to see the full list of embedded and external style rules for the current page.

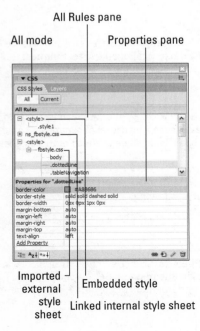

Imported external style sheet

Embedded style

Linked internal style sheet

Dreamweaver's All mode enables you to tell, at a glance, where a custom style is from — whether it's from a linked external style sheet or included in the current document. The CSS Styles panel displays the containing tag `<style>` if the styles are embedded or imported; expand the `<style>` entry to determine if it contains styles or an imported sheet or both. You may recall that the code for importing a style sheet is placed within a `<style>` tag. Linked style sheets are shown with just the filename, as you can see in Figure 7-1.

Note The style rules are presented in the order they appear in the embedded style tag or external style sheet. To adjust the order of the rules, right-click (Control-click) on the style rule you want to move and choose Go To Code from the context menu. Dreamweaver displays the rule in Code view for you to cut and paste into another location.

Select any rule in the All Rules pane to see its properties and values in the Properties pane. By default, only the currently set properties are displayed. There are two other ways to display the properties, Category view and List view. You can choose the way you'd like to see the properties by selecting from one of the buttons on the bottom left of the Properties pane:

✦ **Category View:** Separates the CSS properties and values into the same nine categories found in the CSS Rule Definition dialog: Font, Background, Block, Border, Box, List, Positioning, Extensions and Tables, Content and Quotes. This view is useful when you want to add one or more new properties in a specific category.

✦ **List View:** Shows an alphabetical listing of the properties with the applied ones listed first. Use this view when you know the name of a property but don't want to enter it by hand.

✦ **Show Only Set Properties:** Displays only the currently set properties as well as an option to add a new one. Once you've gained familiarity with CSS properties, you'll find this view the most efficient because it both isolates your current properties and provides a direct route to defining new ones.

For any property displayed, you can modify the current value directly. Details are provided in a later section in this chapter, "Editing and Managing Style Sheets."

Current Mode

As the name implies, Current mode focuses on the current selection (see Figure 7-2); click Current to enter into this mode. Current mode has three separate panes rather than the two of All mode — you can change the height of any by dragging the separating border up or down within the CSS Styles panel.

Choose any entry in the Tag Selector or select any section of the page and the CSS Styles panel under Current mode displays all the properties applicable to that selection, regardless of their origin, in the top section known as the Summary for Selection pane. The next area on the panel is the Rules pane, which either shows information about the property currently selected in the Summary for Selection pane or all the rules affecting the current selection; two buttons on the Rules pane title bar allow you to switch between views. The final area while in Current mode — the Properties pane — works the same way as it does in All mode.

The Summary for Selection pane lists both properties and values; each entry is listed in order of specificity, the property with lowest specificity appearing first. Furthermore, if there are two conflicting properties only the one with the highest specificity is shown. While subtle, these applications of specificity are a valuable debugging and teaching tool.

Summary for Selection pane

Current button

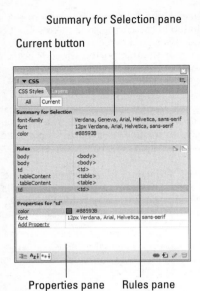

Figure 7-2: Get detailed information and control over the current selection by entering Current mode.

Properties pane   Rules pane

For instance, let's say you're trying to change the line-height of a particular paragraph where the property is declared in two different rules: p and .openingParagraph. If you try to change the line-height for the p rule, you won't see a difference, in either Dreamweaver or your browser. A glance at the Summary for Selection pane while the paragraph in question is selected will show just the property for the .openingParagraph rule.

How do you tell which rule a displayed property is from? Dreamweaver offers a number of methods. Hover your cursor over any property in the Summary for Selection pane and the property's location — both rule and document — appear in a tooltip. The Rules panel provides another alternative. Click any property in the Summary for Selection pane and, if the Rules pane is in the About view, you'll see a brief sentence describing the properties location. When in Rules view, the Rules pane shows a cascade of all of the — you guessed it — rules affecting the current selection; the one containing the property selected in the Summary for Selection pane is highlighted as shown in Figure 7-3. You switch between the About view and the Rules view by clicking the Show Information about Selected Property button and the Show Cascade of Rules for Selected Tag button, respectively, located on the right of the Rules pane title bar.

Tip   Move your cursor over any property in the Rules panel while in Rules view to see the tooltip that notes both the properties location and specificity.

The final pane, Properties, is almost exactly the same in the Current mode as it is in All mode. Again, the Show Only Set Properties option is the default and you can, if desired, switch to either Category or List view by using the buttons at the bottom of the CSS Styles panel.

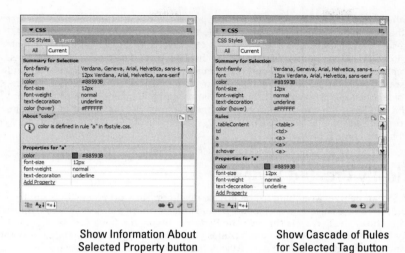

Show Information About
Selected Property button

Show Cascade of Rules
for Selected Tag button

Figure 7-3: Find out where a property is defined through the About view
and see the cascade of rules in the Rules view.

The Properties pane in Current mode differs from the same pane in All mode in one respect.
Both applied and irrelevant properties are displayed. The irrelevant properties are noted with
a strikethrough. If you place your cursor over the property, Dreamweaver explains why the
property is not relevant in a tooltip. The two most common reasons a property is marked as
irrelevant are because it is overridden by another rule or not inherited.

Creating and Applying a Style Sheet in Dreamweaver

Dreamweaver uses three primary tools to implement Cascading Style Sheets: the CSS Styles
panel, the Edit Style Sheet dialog box, and the Style Definition dialog box. You use the CSS
Styles panel to view all the styles available or those that are being applied to the currently
selected HTML tag; the CSS Styles panel also provides a direct link to modifying any property
or for adding properties to any rule. The Edit Style Sheet dialog is useful for managing groups
of styles and style sheets, whereas the Style Definition dialog defines the CSS rules themselves.
With these three interfaces, you can accomplish the following:

> ✦ Link or import all your styles from an external style sheet
>
> ✦ Create new selectors and specify their rules
>
> ✦ Apply styles to selected text or to a particular tag surrounding that text
>
> ✦ Modify any styles you create

Caution The fourth-generation browsers (and above) support many of the attributes from the first draft of the Cascading Style Sheets standard. Unfortunately, neither Netscape Navigator 4.0 nor Microsoft Internet Explorer 4.0 fully supports CSS Level 1. Of the earlier browsers, only Internet Explorer 3.0 supports a limited set of the CSS Level 1 features: font attributes, indents, and color. However, this support is rendered differently in Internet Explorer 3.0 and 4.0. Netscape Navigator 3.0 does not support any of the features of CSS Level 1. On the brighter side, Netscape Navigator 6.2 shows an almost complete compliance of CSS 1 and quite a lot of CSS 2, the current version of Internet Explorer (6.0) is almost as complete, and the current version of Safari, while only at 2.2, supports all of CSS 1, almost all of CSS 2, and even boasts some CSS 3 support.

Automatically Created Styles

The world of CSS can be overwhelming to the novice designer: How do you even begin to master this complex set of rules and concepts? Dreamweaver offers many routes to explore CSS, but perhaps the easiest entry is through the Property inspector. Set a font face, font size, or color on any bit of text and Dreamweaver applies your formatting as a new style, automatically created and stored internally. The new style is then added to the list of available styles, right in the Property inspector.

Not only does Dreamweaver automatically create styles, it does so in an intelligent fashion that prevents duplicate styles. If you choose the same color, font face, or size as an existing style—whether it's an automatically generated style or not—Dreamweaver uses the existing style and, if necessary, deletes the temporary style. Any style created can be modified to add other characteristics or renamed to fit within your naming scheme.

Walk through the following steps to see how Dreamweaver automatically builds styles:

1. Select the text you want to style, either by highlighting it or choosing the tag from the Tag Selector. If you select a portion of text rather than the entire tag, the style is applied to a `<span>` tag surrounding your selection; otherwise, the style is applied to the containing element, like a `<p>` or heading tag.

2. From the Property inspector, select a new typeface for the text by choosing Geneva, Arial, Helvetica, sans serif from the Font list. Dreamweaver creates a new CSS class called `styleN`, where `N` is an incrementing number starting with 1; if this is the first automatically generated style on the page, the style is called `style1`. The style is applied to the tag containing the text and listed both in the CSS Styles panel and the Property inspector Styles list as shown in Figure 7-4.

3. From the Property inspector, choose a color for your text, like blue, from the color picker. Dreamweaver adds this new property to the existing style.

4. Place your cursor in another unstyled paragraph or heading.

5. Choose the same typeface as before from the Font list. Dreamweaver creates a new style, `style2`, to apply this new format. Now there are two autogenerated styles: `style1` and `style2`.

6. Select the same color as previously applied. To avoid creating two styles with the exact same properties, Dreamweaver applies `style1` to the text and deletes `style2`. Now, whenever you want text in this typeface and font, just apply the style rather than change the formatting through the Property inspector.

Auto-created style

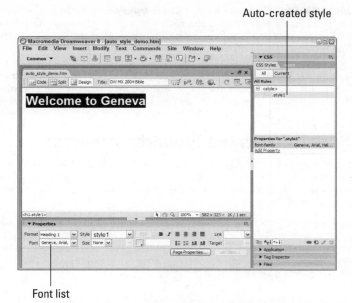

Font list

Figure 7-4: Autogenerated styles are immediately available to apply or modify.

Note

As mentioned earlier, Dreamweaver looks at font, size, and color for its autogenerated styles. In the example, I purposely left size out of the mix to demonstrate that you don't need all three values set to create a style or style match. Any additional formatting set through the Property inspector, such as alignment, is applied with tag attributes (for example, `align`), rather than added to the CSS style.

If certain conditions are met, Dreamweaver may modify the existing style rather than create a new one. These conditions are

✦ A style named style*N* — the Dreamweaver naming convention for automatically created styles — is currently applied.

✦ The style is embedded and not in an external style sheet.

✦ The style is applied only once — to the current selection.

Again, the modifications only apply to the font face, size, and color attributes.

Although the automatically created styles are a good jumping-off place, regard them only as the beginning of your study of CSS. The styles created should be renamed to make them more meaningful; it's far easier to remember how the `.headline` class should be used than `.style1`. Renaming is an option initiated through the CSS Styles panel and carried out interactively with Dreamweaver's Find and Replace dialog.

You should also, where possible, maintain your styles in external style sheets rather than embedding them. You can easily export the autocreated styles by choosing File ➪ Export ➪ Export CSS Styles. After you export the styles, delete the embedded styles and link the external style sheet to the page.

Tip   All autogenerated styles are embedded into the page, except in one circumstance. If you format text in a Dreamweaver template (where all but specified areas of the document are locked) without an unlocked region in the `<head>` area, Dreamweaver places the style in-line.

Applying Styles through the Property Inspector

In addition to automatically creating CSS styles, Dreamweaver also enables you to apply any defined style directly through the Property inspector. The immediate availability of CSS styles is a major boon to productivity and is extremely helpful for designers working in a site fully committed to using Cascading Style Sheets.

To apply a class style from the Property inspector, select a page element and then make your choice from the Style drop-down list as shown in Figure 7-5; to make it simpler for you, a style is previewed in the Style list. If the tag allows an ID to be assigned, all available ID selectors are listed in a similar list. However, unlike class selectors, after an ID selector has been assigned to a tag, Dreamweaver no longer displays it in the ID list.

Figure 7-5: CSS styles are previewed and applied from the Property inspector.

Attaching an External Style Sheet

Now that CSS-enabled browsers dominate, more Web designers are encountering clients with existing external style sheets. To apply the site's design specifications to a new page, all the designer need do is connect the current page to the CSS document. Dreamweaver provides a streamlined method for doing just that.

The Attach Style Sheet button, found on the CSS Styles panel, is a straightforward solution for linking external style sheets to the current document. When Attach Style Sheet is selected, the Attach External Style Sheet dialog box, shown in Figure 7-6, appears. Here, you can choose between the two previously discussed methods for attaching an external style sheet: link or import. You'll also have the option to target your style sheet for a specific media type.

Figure 7-6: Use the Link method for style sheets readable by older browsers (like Netscape 4.x) and the Import for more current browsers.

If you're not sure which style sheet is the appropriate one, you can check it out before applying. Just select the existing style sheet and click Preview. Dreamweaver applies the selected style sheet to the current page. If you choose another style sheet or click Cancel, the sheet is removed.

After you've made your choice, click Browse to locate a previously existing style sheet. When selected, a standard Select File dialog box appears with the *.css filter set. Simply locate the style sheet and select it: Dreamweaver inserts the necessary code into the <head> of your document. If any HTML tags — such as <p> or any of the heading tags — on your page are defined in the style sheet, you see an immediate change in your document.

Tip If you don't have an external style sheet and want to create one, just enter the path and filename in the text field, making sure to use the .css extension. Dreamweaver notes that the file cannot be found and asks if you want to proceed. Click OK, and, when you create your first style, Dreamweaver also creates the CSS file with the requested filename.

The final option on the Attach External Style Sheet dialog box, the Media list, is discussed in the next section.

Choosing a Media Type

One of the most important facets of the Cascading Style Sheet specification is the ability to style a page for a specific *media type*. A media type is a means of communication, such as computer screen, printer, or TTY device. The W3C identifies eight media types: aural, braille, handheld, print, projection, screen, TTY, and TV. If no media type is declared, the style sheet is applied to all devices that render the page. If one is declared, a media attribute is added to the code, like this (addition bolded for emphasis):

```
<link href="Techniques/styles/main.css" rel="style sheet"
type="text/css" media="screen" />
```

The bulk of today's designers do not apply a media type at all. However, an increasing number have started to create different style sheets: one to be viewed on the computer screen and another to be printed. Dreamweaver makes this easy by including a media list on the Attach External Style Sheet dialog box. The list includes the eight media types recognized by the W3C as well as another one from the specification, all. It's considered a best practice to add a media attribute to your page and recommended to use all to cover every media type, screen for computer screen and print for printer.

Tip   If you'd like declare your style sheet for multiple media types, enter the desired types in a comma-separated list through the Media field of the Attach External Style Sheet dialog box.

Rendering Different Styles

Dreamweaver's Style Rendering toolbar complements the development of separate style sheets. After you've defined a style sheet for a specific media type, such as print, you can use the Style Rendering toolbar to select the desired media type and Dreamweaver will render your page as if it were that medium. To display the Style Rendering toolbar (see Figure 7-7), choose View ➪ Toolbars ➪ Style Rendering or right-click (Control-click) any other visible toolbar and choose Style Rendering. Two media types—aural and braille—are not included in the Style Rendering toolbar because their rendition is beyond Dreamweaver's scope.

Figure 7-7: The Style Rendering toolbar quickly changes the media type for Dreamweaver to emulate.

Another option on the Style Rendering toolbar is to disable all CSS rendering altogether. Select the Toggle Rendering Of CSS Displays option on the far right of the toolbar to view the page without CSS; select again to enable CSS rendering. This feature is extremely helpful for both debugging CSS pages and viewing the order in which screen readers will present the page.

Applying, Changing, and Removing a Style

As noted, any HTML tags redefined as CSS styles in an attached style sheet are automatically applied to your document. However, any custom CSS style must be applied on a case-by-case basis. Most Web designers use a combination of HTML and custom CSS styles. Only custom CSS styles appear in the CSS Styles panel in Apply Styles mode.

In Dreamweaver, you can apply a style in four main ways: from the Property inspector, the menus, the Tag Selector, or the CSS Styles panel.

To apply an existing custom style using the Property inspector, follow these steps:

1. To apply the style to a section of the page enclosed by an HTML tag, select the tag from the Tag Selector; if you're applying the style to text, you can also just place your cursor in the text without selecting the containing tag.

   To apply the style to a section that is not enclosed by a single HTML tag, use your mouse to highlight that section in the Document window.

2. Select the custom style from the Styles list in the Property inspector for class styles or from the ID list for ID selectors, if available. Dreamweaver applies the custom style either by setting the `class` or `id` attribute of the selected tag to the custom style. If you select only text and not an enclosing tag, Dreamweaver wraps a `<span>` tag around the selection.

The second approach is to use the menus to apply a style to your pages. Follow these steps:

1. Highlight the text to which you're applying the style, either by using the Tag Selector or by using the mouse.

2. Choose Text ➪ CSS Styles ➪ Your Style. The same dynamic CSS Styles list is maintained in the context menu, accessible through a right-click (Control+click) on the selected text.

The third approach is to use the Tag Selector exclusively. Right-click (Control+click) the selected tag name in the Tag Selector and choose the style from either the Class or ID submenus.

Finally, you can use the CSS Styles panel itself to apply a style:

1. Select the tag or text to which you want to apply your style.

2. In the CSS Styles panel, right-click (Control+click) the style and choose Apply from the context menu.

Note   Dreamweaver supports multiple classes for rendering purposes, but there is no method except hand-coding to apply more than one class to a tag.

Changing Styles

Changing from one applied custom style to another is extremely straightforward in Dreamweaver. Just place your cursor anywhere within the styled text and select a different custom style from the Styles list on the Property inspector. Dreamweaver changes the old style to the new instantly. You get the same results if you switch styles from the Tag Selector or use the menus.

But what if you want to apply a new style to a text range within an existing `<span>` tag? Dreamweaver, by design, avoids nested `<span>` tags. Here's how it works. Suppose that you're working with the following code:

```
<span class="bodyCopy">Developing strategies to survive requires industry
insight and forward thinking in this competitive marketplace.</span>
```

If you apply a custom style called `hype` to the phrases *industry insight* and *forward thinking* by first selecting those phrases and then choosing `hype` from the Styles list, the code looks like this:

```
<span class="bodyCopy">Developing strategies to survive requires
</span><span class="hype">industry insight</span>
<span class="bodyCopy"> and </span><span class="hype">forward
thinking</span><span class="bodyCopy"> in this competitive
marketplace.</span>
```

Dreamweaver wraps each phrase in a distinct `<span>` tag so that nesting is entirely avoided. This behavior enables the style of each phrase to be altered more easily.

Caution   Although the use of the `<span>` tag is unavoidable under some circumstances, you should be careful not to overuse it. It's far better to apply a logical tag that makes sense in the context, such as `<em>` (emphasis) or `<cite>`, and then create a CSS style that formats those tags for the look you want.

Removing Applied Styles

Getting rid of an applied style is just as easy as changing it. Now, just position your cursor anywhere in the stylized text and select None from the Styles list. Dreamweaver also removes the no-longer–needed `class` attribute for all but the `<span>` tag. If you remove the class from a selection marked by `<span>` tags, Dreamweaver deletes the surrounding `<span>` tags.

Note   Be sure your cursor is *positioned within* styled text and *not selecting any*. Selecting None from the Styles list on the Property inspector when just text — not tags — is highlighted forces Dreamweaver to remove the style from the tag and apply it to `<span>` tags on either side of the now unstyled text.

Styles can also be removed through the Tag Selector — just right-click (Control+click) any styled tag on the Tag Selector and choose Set Class ➪ None.

Applying External Style Sheet Styles

In this Technique, you attach an existing style sheet to a page and assign styles to various page elements.

1. In the Technique site, expand the 07_css folder and open `css_start.htm`.

2. If necessary, press Shift+F11 to expose the CSS Styles panel.

3. At the bottom of the CSS Styles panel, click Attach Style Sheet.

4. When the Attach External Style Sheet dialog box opens, click the Browse button.

5. In the Select Style Sheet dialog, browse to the styles folder in the root of the site and select `primary.css`.

6. From the Media list of the Attach External Style Sheet dialog box, choose All; click OK when you're ready.

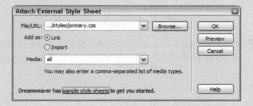

You'll notice that certain parts of the page, like the headings and paragraphs, are automatically styled because the style sheet includes rules for those tags. Now, let's apply some styles to specific page elements.

1. Place your cursor in the first heading, Coming attractions.

2. From the Tag Selector, choose the `<div>` tag to the left of the `<h1>` tag.

3. In the Property inspector, select middle from the Div ID list.

The `#middle` style adds an outside border and increases the padding. Now, add a class to differentiate the first paragraph under each heading.

1. Place your cursor in the first paragraph beneath the initial heading.

2. Right-click the `<p>` tag in the Tag Selector and choose Set Class ⇨ firstParagraph.

3. Repeat the preceding steps 1 and 2 for each of the remaining paragraphs under the different headings.

Finally, apply classes to the images to help the page flow.

1. Select the first image on the page.

2. From the Property inspector's Class list, choose `.imageLeft`.

3. Repeat the preceding steps 1 and 2 for the remaining images, alternating between the `.imageLeft` **and** `.imageRight` **classes.**

4. When you're done, save your page.

The two image-related styles align the image differently and add additional padding to complete the effect.

Defining New Rules

Clicking the New CSS Rule button in the CSS Styles panel brings up a dialog box (see Figure 7-8) where you specify the type of style you're defining. You can opt to create the new styles in an external style sheet, the default, or in the current document. After you've chosen the type of style, select the Define In This Document Only option to create an embedded style. Any style sheets already linked to — or imported into — the current document appear in the drop-down list along with the New Style Sheet File option. If you choose Define In (New Style Sheet File), a standard file dialog box opens for you to name your new CSS file and select its path.

Note   Dreamweaver attempts to help you choose your selector based on your current selection by including the cascade of selectors in the Selectors field with the Advanced option chosen. For example, if your cursor is in an `<em>` tag within a paragraph with a class of `.firstParagraph`, which is within a div named `middle`, which, in turn is inside another div named `wrapper`, the Selector field will be prepopulated with:

```
#wrapper #middle .firstParagraph em
```

If you want to take advantage of this very specific selector, leave the field as is and click OK. If, on the other hand, you want to broaden the selector a bit, remove the outer selectors that appear first in the field. You're also free to clear the entire field and start over.

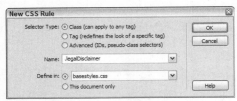

Figure 7-8: The first step in defining a new style is to select a style type and enter a name for the style, if it's a custom one.

The following sections explain the three style types — Class, Tag, and Advanced — in depth.

Class

Making a custom style is the most flexible way to define a style on a page. The first step in creating a custom style is to give it a name; this name is used in the `class` attribute. The name for your class must start with a period and must be alphanumeric without punctuation or special characters. If you do not begin the name of your custom style with a period, Dreamweaver inserts one for you. Here are some typical names you can use:

```
.master
```

```
.pagetitle
```

```
.bodytext
```

Caution   Although you can give your classes names such as *body*, *title*, or any other HTML tag, this approach is not a good idea. Dreamweaver warns you of the conflict if you try this method. You should also be aware that class names are case-sensitive.

Tag

The second radio button in the New Style dialog box is Tag. This type of style provides an excellent tool for making quick, global changes to existing Web pages. Essentially, the Tag style enables you to modify the features of your existing HTML tags. When you select this option, the drop-down list displays over 90 HTML tags in alphabetical order. Select a tag from the drop-down list and click OK. As you become more familiar with HTML, you're free to simply enter the tag into the Tag field.

Advanced

Because of its flexibility, you may find that you use the Advanced option frequently. If you're not defining a class or setting up a tag style, the general rule is to use Advanced. Enter the selector directly in the Advanced field; Dreamweaver allows almost any type of input, whether it recognizes the selector type or not. In addition to ID and descendant selectors (covered later in this chapter), you can also group selectors when applying a single style to multiple tags and/or classes. If, for example, you want to create a style for the `<body>`, `<td>`, and `<th>` tags, you enter the tag names in the Advanced field (without their delimiters) in a comma-separated list like this:

```
body,td,th
```

The Advanced option is also useful for defining *pseudo-classes* and *pseudo-elements*. A pseudo-class represents dynamic states of a tag that may change under user action or over time. Several standard pseudo-classes associated with the `<a>` tag are used to style hypertext links. When you choose Advanced, the drop-down list box contains four customization options, which can all be categorized as pseudo-classes:

✦ `a:link` — Customizes the style of a link that has not been visited recently

✦ `a:visited` — Customizes the style of a link to a page that has been recently visited

✦ `a:hover` — Customizes the style of a link while the user's mouse is over it

> **Note** The `a:hover` pseudo-class is a CSS Level 2 specification and is not supported by Netscape 4.x. Furthermore, `a:active` links are always colored red, regardless of the CSS specifications.

✦ `a:active` — Customizes the style of a link when it is selected by the user

> **Tip** Dreamweaver does not preview pseudo-class styles (except for `a:link`), although they can be previewed through a supported browser.

A pseudo-element, on the other hand, gives you control over contextually defined page elements: For example, `p:first-letter` styles the first letter in every paragraph tag, enabling a drop-cap design. Because of their specific nature, Dreamweaver does not display any pseudo-elements in the Advanced list. You can, however, enter your own — Dreamweaver 8 does a fine job of rendering both the `:first-letter` and `:first-line` pseudo-elements.

> **Note** Dreamweaver does not render the lesser-used pseudo-elements `:before` and `:after` in the Design view. Preview your page in a compatible browser — such as Netscape 6.x or higher or Opera 5.x or higher — to see these in action.

Descendants and Other Advanced Selectors

Dreamweaver also enables you to enter some of the more advanced additions to the CSS selector palette through the Advanced field.

One such selector is the *descendant* selector. Descendant selectors are contextual selectors because they specify one tag within another. A descendant selector, for example, permits you to give paragraphs within a table a different style than paragraphs outside a table. Similarly, text nested within two blockquotes (giving the appearance of being indented two levels) can be given a different color, font, and so on than text in a single blockquote.

Applying CSS Hacks

As any designer beginning to work with CSS knows, not all browsers are created equally. In fact, browsers vary wildly in their CSS support. To achieve cross-browser compatibility with CSS, designers have resorted to using what are referred to as *CSS hacks*. A CSS hack is the use of CSS code in an unintended fashion to make CSS elements unavailable to certain browsers. In other words, a CSS hack acts as a filter. Dreamweaver includes two of the most common hacks that allow you to hide CSS from two of the most problematic browsers: Netscape 4.x and Internet Explorer 5 for Mac. Both hacks are only available from within Code view through the context menu; commands for applying and removing each hack are included.

To hide a CSS rule from Netscape 4.x, use the Ciao hack. In Code view, select the CSS code you want to make sure that Netscape 4.x does not attempt to render and right-click (Control-click). From the context menu that appears, choose Selection ➪ Apply Ciao Hack. Dreamweaver wraps your selection with the following code:

```
/*/*/
/* */
```

The first line starts hiding code from Netscape 4.x and the second line stops the hiding.

You can hide CSS rules from Internet Explorer 5 for Mac in a similar fashion with the Backslash-comment hack. To hide particular rules, select them and then right-click (Control-click) to bring up the context menu. Choose Selection ➪ Apply Backslash-comment hack; Dreamweaver wraps your selection with the following code:

```
/*Start hiding from IE Mac \*/
/*Stop hiding from IE Mac */
```

To remove either of these hacks select the entire code block, including the opening and closing hack lines, and choose Selection ➪ Remove Backslash-comment hack or Selection ➪ Remove Caio.

For example, to style text within nested blockquotes, enter the following in the Advanced field of the New Style dialog box:

```
blockquote blockquote
```

In essence, you are creating a custom style for a set of HTML tags used in your document. This type of CSS selector acts like an HTML tag that has a CSS style applied to it; that is, all page elements fitting the criteria are automatically styled. You can also combine custom styles with redefined HTML styles in a descendant selector.

Other advanced selectors that you can enter in the Advanced field include

✦ **ID:** An id selector is identified by a pound sign (like #footer) that can be assigned to any page element using the same id attribute (for example, <div id="footer">).

✦ **Child:** Selects an element that is a direct child of another element. For example, in a div tag with nested div elements, div > p selects the paragraphs in the outermost div tag only.

✦ **Adjacent-sibling:** Selects an element that immediately follows another. For example, in an unordered list with two list items, li + li selects the second list item, but not the first.

✦ **Universal:** Selects any element. This selector may be used to skip one or more genera-
tions of tags. Use `body * p` to select paragraphs contained within `div` elements that are
children of the `body` tag, for example.

✦ **Attribute:** Selects tags with specified attributes. You can select tags if they either contain the attribute (`p[align]`) or if they contain an attribute set to a specific value
(`p[align="left"]`).

Best of all, these selectors are rendered correctly in Dreamweaver's Design view. As of this
writing, only the most CSS-compliant browsers (such as Firefox, Netscape 6.2 and higher
or Safari) properly render these selectors; but CSS support is gaining ground in each new
browser release.

Note   Dreamweaver warns you if you enter what it considers an invalid selector type; however, you
are given the option to use the selector if you choose.

Editing and Managing Style Sheets

Style sheets, like most elements of a Web page, are almost never set in stone. Designers need
to be able to modify style rules — whether they're embedded or from an external style sheet —
at a moment's notice. Through the CSS Styles panel's Edit Styles mode, Dreamweaver provides
near-immediate access.

CSS Styles Panel

As discussed earlier, the CSS Styles panel in All mode displays all the styles attached to the current page, whether embedded or external. Presented in a collapsible outline (see Figure 7-9),
Dreamweaver shows the styles in the order in which they are defined in the code. The style
list is more than just a pretty display — it's a direct pipeline to editing each style. You can select
any style and click the Edit Style button, and Dreamweaver displays the CSS Rule Definition
dialog box with the current style's settings.

Figure 7-9: Both embedded and external styles are shown in
the Edit Styles mode of the CSS Styles panel.

If you'd prefer to work directly with the CSS code, double-click the style. Dreamweaver goes to the style selected in the editing option of your choice, as defined in the CSS Styles category of the Preferences. You can choose between using the Edit CSS dialog box, the Properties pane, or Code view.

Tip   Modifying or deleting a style in an external style sheet causes that style sheet to open. Dreamweaver does this so that the modification or deletion can be undone. You can force the style sheet not to open by unchecking the Open CSS Files When Modified option in the CSS Styles category of the Preferences; but, if you do, changes to the style sheet cannot be undone.

If you have an external CSS editor such as TopStyle or Style Master defined — and the Use External Editor option selected — double-clicking a style opens the style sheet in that editor. Access the Use External Editor option by right-clicking (Control-clicking) in the CSS Styles panel or by selecting the CSS Styles panel Options menu.

To delete a style, select the style and click the Delete CSS Rule button.

Note   If you're looking for a single reference on CSS hacks, check out *CSS Hacks and Filters* written by this book's author and published by Wiley. For more details, visit www.idest.com/csshacks/.

CSS Styles Panel Properties Pane

Although the CSS Rule Definition dialog is helpful when establishing CSS rules, it's not the most direct route for modifying them. Dreamweaver supplies a much quicker facility for viewing and changing existing styles: the Properties pane of the CSS Styles panel (see Figure 7-10).

Figure 7-10: Insert a new property directly into a rule through the Properties pane's Add Property link.

New In Dreamweaver   To change the value of a property, click into the corresponding field on the right of the CSS Properties tab. Color-based properties, like background-color, include a standard Dreamweaver color picker to simplify your selection; properties requiring a URL offer both Point-to-File and Browse-for-File icons. Those properties that use specific keywords, like display, provide a list of acceptable values. In all cases, the value can also be entered by hand. This is especially useful when working with properties that accept compound values, like border, for which entering the values in proper order (style, color, width) is valid. Hover over a property value to see a code hint. After you've inserted your new value, press Enter (Return) or click anywhere to confirm the change; Dreamweaver immediately renders the results.

To add a new property to an existing rule in the Properties pane, follow these steps:

1. In the Properties pane, click Add New Property.

2. Enter the property in the blank field that appears. Alternatively, you can choose a property from the drop-down list.

3. Press Tab or Enter (Return) to move to the second column.

4. Enter the value for the new property.

Tip   Rather than type out the whole property, you can enter just the first few letters and press Alt+Down arrow (Option+Down arrow). Dreamweaver goes right to the first matching property. Press Enter (Return) after you've found your match to move to the second column to enter the desired value(s).

You can add new properties through the CSS panel in either All or Current modes. All mode works best when you're editing CSS from a top-down perspective. If you'd prefer a bottom-up approach, switch to Current mode and select the tag containing the existing style rather than the style itself.

 Crafting a Print Style Sheet

In this Technique, you attach a print style sheet to a page and change the styles so that the document is more printer-friendly.

1. In the Technique site, expand the 07_css folder and open `print_start.htm`.

2. From the CSS Styles panel, click Attach Style Sheet.

3. When the Attach External Style Sheet dialog box opens, click the Browse button.

4. In the Select Style Sheet dialog, browse to the styles folder in the root of the site and select `print.css`.

5. From the Media list of the Attach External Style Sheet dialog box, choose Print; click OK when you're ready.

To see the changes you'll make take effect, you'll need to switch to print style rendering.

1. Choose View ⇨ Toolbars ⇨ Style Rendering.

2. From the Style Rendering toolbar, click Render Print Media Type, or choose View ⇨ Style Rendering ⇨ Screen Media Type.

3. In the CSS Styles panel, make sure you're in All mode; if not, click All.

Continued

Continued

For your first change to the print style sheet, hide those page elements that are not relevant in print: the header and footer.

1. In the CSS Styles panel, expand the `print.css` entry and select the `#header` style.

2. Click Edit Style at the bottom of the CSS Styles panel.

3. When the CSS Rule Definition dialog box opens, switch to the Block category and, from the Display list, choose None.

4. Repeat steps 1–3, selecting the `#footer` style from the CSS Styles panel instead.

Now, you need to adjust certain styles so they are more suitable for print.

1. In the CSS Styles panel, select the `#wrapper` style

2. From the Properties pane, click in the value column next to the width property and enter **auto**; press Enter (Return) when you're done.

3. In the CSS Styles panel, select the h1 style.

4. From the Properties pane, click in the color swatch next to the color property and select black (#000000) from the pop-up color picker.

5. Select the value next to the font-size property and enter **14pt**; press Enter (Return) to confirm your choice.

6. Repeat steps 3–5, selecting the `p, td, th` style and changing the font-size property to **12pt**.

7. With the `p, td, th` style still selected, click Add Property and enter **line-height**; press Enter (Return) and then enter **18pt**.

The final step is to add a heading that appears only in the print version of the page. To accomplish this, you'll need to hide the content in the screen-oriented style sheet.

1. Place your cursor on the first image on the page and switch to Code view.

2. Press Left-arrow to move the cursor in front of the `<img>` tag and enter the following code `<h1>Relative Realty</h1>`; return to Design view when you're done.

3. Place your cursor in the new `<h1>` tag and, from the Property inspector's Style list, choose `printOnly`.

4. In the Style Rendering toolbar, choose Switch to Render Screen Media Type, or choose View ➪ Style Rendering ➪ Screen Media Type.

   You'll notice that the heading — redundant in screen mode — is also visible here. You can change that by adding a style.

5. In the CSS Styles panel, select the `primary.css` entry and click New CSS Rule.

6. In the New CSS Rule dialog box, switch the Selector Type set to Class and change the Name field to **.printOnly**; click OK when you're ready.

7. Switch to the Block category and, from the Display list, choose None; click OK to confirm the change and close the dialog box.

8. Select File ➪ Save All to store all the changes.

You can easily see the differences by switching between the Screen and Print icons on the Style Rendering toolbar.

Styles and Their Attributes

After you've selected a type and name for a new style or chosen to edit an existing style, the CSS Rule Definition dialog box opens. A Category list from which you select a style category (just as you select a category of preferences in Dreamweaver's Preferences dialog box) is located on the left side of this dialog box.

Dreamweaver offers you eight categories of CSS styles to help you define your style sheet:

✦ Type	✦ Border
✦ Background	✦ List
✦ Block	✦ Positioning
✦ Box	✦ Extensions

You can define styles from one or all categories. The following sections describe each style category and its available settings.

Note   Although CSS rendering has been vastly improved in Dreamweaver 8, not all possible CSS attributes are viewable in the Design view.

Type Options

The Type category specifies the appearance and layout of the typeface for the page in the browser window. The Type category, shown in Figure 7-11, is one of the most widely used and supported categories — it can be rendered in Internet Explorer 3.0 and above and Navigator 4.0 and above.

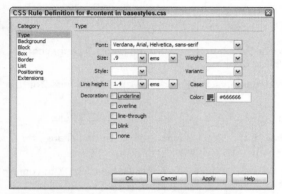

Figure 7-11: The Type Settings category includes some of the best-supported CSS attributes.

Table 7-1 explains the settings available in this category.

Table 7-1: CSS Type Attributes

Type Setting	Description
Font	Specifies the font or a collection of fonts, known as a font *family*. You can edit the font list by selecting Edit Font List from the drop-down list. (This sequence opens the Edit Font List dialog box, as described in Chapter 8.)
Size	Selects a size for the selected font. If you enter a value, you can then select the measurement system in the adjacent text box (the default is pixels). The relative sizes, such as small, medium, and large, are set relative to the parent element. Values can be selected from the drop-down list or entered by hand.
Style	Specifies a normal, oblique, or italic attribute for the font. An oblique font may have been generated in the browser by electronically slanting a normal font.
Line Height	Sets the line height of the line (known as *leading* in traditional layout). Typically, line height is a point or two more than the font size, although you can set the line height to be the same as or smaller than the font size for an overlapping effect.
Decoration	Changes the decoration for text. Options include underline, overline, strike-through, blink, and none. The blink decoration is displayed only in Netscape 4.x and earlier browsers.

Type Setting	Description
Weight	Sets the boldness of the text. You can use the relative settings (light, bold, bolder, and boldest) or apply a numeric value. Normal is around 400; bold is 700.
Variant	Switches between normal and small caps. Small caps is a font style that displays text as uppercase, but the capital letters are a slightly larger size.
Case	Forces a browser to render the text as uppercase, lowercase, or capitalized.
Color	Sets a color for the selected font. Enter a color name or select the color swatch to choose a browser-safe color from the color picker.

Background Options

Since Netscape Navigator 2.0, Web designers have been able to use background images and color. Thanks to CSS Background attributes, designers can now use background images and color with increased control. Whereas traditional HTML background images are restricted to a single image for the entire browser window, CSS backgrounds can be specified for a single paragraph or any other CSS selector. (To set a background for the entire page, apply the style to the <body> tag.) Moreover, instead of an image automatically tiling to fill the browser window, CSS backgrounds can be made to tile horizontally, vertically, or not at all (see Figure 7-12). You can even position the image relative to the selected element.

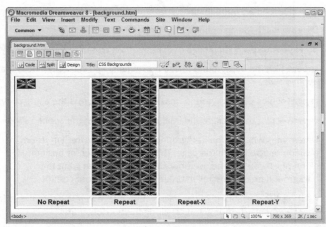

Figure 7-12: You can achieve a number of different tiling effects by using the Repeat attribute of the CSS Background category.

The latest versions of both primary browsers support the CSS Background attributes shown in Figure 7-13 and described in Table 7-2.

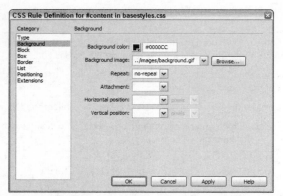

Figure 7-13: The CSS Background options give you a much wider range of control over background images and color.

Table 7-2: CSS Background Attributes

Background Setting	Description
Background Color	Sets the background color for a particular style. Note that this setting enables you to set background colors for individual paragraphs or other elements.
Background Image	Specifies a background image.
Repeat	Determines the tiling options for a graphic:
	no repeat displays the image in the upper-left corner of the applied style.
	repeat tiles the background image horizontally and vertically across the applied style.
	repeat-x tiles the background image horizontally across the applied style.
	repeat-y tiles the background image vertically down the applied style.
Attachment	Determines whether the background image remains fixed in its original position or scrolls with the page. This setting is useful for positioned elements. If you use the overflow attribute, you often want the background image to scroll in order to maintain layout control.
Horizontal Position	Controls the positioning of the background image in relation to the style sheet elements (text or graphics) along the horizontal axis.
Vertical Position	Controls the positioning of the background image in relation to the style sheet elements (text or graphics) along the vertical axis.

Block Options

One of the most common formatting effects in traditional publishing, long absent from Web publishing, is justified text—text that appears as a solid block. Justified text is possible with the Text Align attribute, one of the seven options available in the CSS Block category, as shown in Figure 7-14. Indented paragraphs are also a possibility.

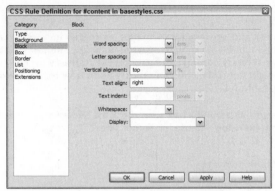

Figure 7-14: The Block options give the Web designer enhanced text control.

Dreamweaver includes an option for setting the Display attribute. As the name implies, the Display attribute determines how an element should be presented. Display accepts a wide-range of values — 18 in all — but only a few are currently supported by even the latest browsers. That said, the supported values — block, inline and, curiously enough, none — are very important indeed. Setting a Display attribute to None effectively hides the element to which the CSS attribute is applied; setting the same attribute to Block or Inline reveals the element. Many collapsible/expandable lists depend on the Display attribute to achieve their effects.

Table 7-3 lists the CSS Block options.

Table 7-3: CSS Block Attributes

Block Setting	Description
Word Spacing	Defines the spacing between words. You can increase or decrease the spacing with positive and negative values, set in ems by default. (In CSS, one *em* is equal to the height of a given font.) If you have a 12 pt. font, to increase the spacing between words to 24 pts., set the Word Spacing value to 2 ems.
Letter Spacing	Defines the spacing between the letters of a word. You can increase or decrease the spacing with positive and negative values, set in ems by default.
Vertical Alignment	Sets the vertical alignment of the style. Choose from baseline, sub, super, top, text-top, middle, bottom, or text-bottom, or add your own value.
Text Align	Sets text alignment (left, right, center, and justified).
Text Indent	Indents the first line of text on a style by the amount specified.
Whitespace	Controls display of spaces and tabs. The normal option causes all whitespace to collapse. The Pre option behaves similarly to the <pre> tag; all whitespace is preserved. The Nowrap option enables text to wrap if a tag is detected.
Display	Determines how a tag is represented. Possible values include none, inline, block, list-item, run-in, compact, marker, table, inline-table, table-row-group, table-header-group, table-footer-group, table-row, table-column-group, table-column, table-cell, and table-caption.

Box Options

The Box attribute defines the placement and settings for elements (primarily images) on a page. Many of the controls (shown in Figure 7-15) emulate spacing behavior similar to that found in `<table>` attributes. If you are already comfortable using HTML tables with cell padding, border colors, and width/height controls, you can quickly learn how to use these Box features, which are described in Table 7-4.

Tip   To have the same padding or margins all around a box area, check the Same For All option. This option allows you to set one value — Top — to use for all four sides.

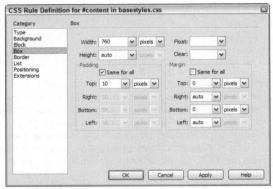

Figure 7-15: The CSS Box attributes define the placement of HTML elements on the Web page.

Table 7-4: CSS Box Attributes

Box Setting	Description
Width	Sets the width of the element.
Height	Defines the height of the element.
Float	Places the element at the left or right page margin. Any text that encounters the element wraps around it.
Clear	Sets the side on which layers cannot be displayed next to the element. If a layer is encountered, the element with the Clear attribute places itself beneath the layer.
Margin	Defines the amount of space between the borders of the element and other elements in the page.
Padding	Sets the amount of space between the element and the border or margin, if no border is specified. You can control the padding for the left, right, top, and bottom independently.

Border Options

With Cascading Style Sheets, you can specify many parameters for borders surrounding text, images, and other elements such as Java applets. In addition to specifying separate colors for any of the four box sides, you can also choose the width of each side's border, as shown in the CSS Border panel (see Figure 7-16). You can use eight different types of border lines, including solid, dashed, inset, and ridge. As with the `Padding` and `Margin` attributes in the Box category, Dreamweaver includes a Same For All option under the `Style`, `Width`, and `Color` attributes to save you the work of having to enter the same value for all four sides. Table 7-5 lists the Border options.

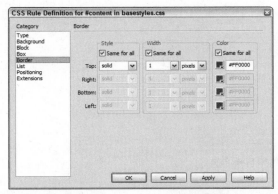

Figure 7-16: Borders are useful to highlight a section of text or a graphic.

Table 7-5: CSS Border Attributes

Border Setting	Description
Style	Sets the style of the border. You can use any of the following border styles: dotted, dashed, solid, double, groove, ridge, inset, and outset.
Width	Determines the width of the border on each side. Choose thin, medium, thick, or enter a number to set a width.
Color	Sets the color of the border on each side.

Tip: CSS Border attributes are especially useful for highlighting paragraphs of text with a surrounding box. Use the Box panel's `Padding` attributes to inset the text from the border.

List Options

CSS gives you greater control over bulleted points. With Cascading Style Sheets, you can now display a specific bulleted point based on a graphic image, or you can choose from the standard built-in bullets, including disc, circle, and square. The CSS List category also enables you to specify the type of ordered list, including decimal, Roman numerals, or A-B-C order. Figure 7-17 shows and Table 7-6 describes the settings for lists.

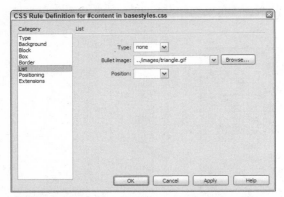

Figure 7-17: Use the CSS List category to specify a graphic to use as a bullet.

Table 7-6: List Category for Styles

List Setting	Description
Type	Selects a built-in bullet type. The options include disc, circle, square, decimal, lowercase Roman, uppercase Roman, lowercase alpha, and uppercase alpha.
Bullet Image	Sets an image to be used as a custom bullet. Enter the path to the image in the text box.
Position	Determines if the list item wraps to an indent (the default) or to the margin.

Positioning Options

For many designers, positioning has increased creativity in page layout design. With positioning, you have exact control over where an element is placed on a page. The positioning attributes are often applied to div tags to create page layouts without resorting to tables. Figure 7-18 shows the various attributes that provide this pinpoint control of your page elements. The options are described in Table 7-7.

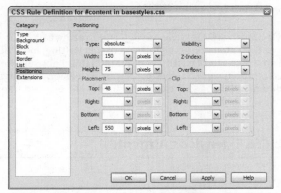

Figure 7-18: Control over the placement of elements on a page frees the Web designer from the restrictions imposed with HTML tables and other old-style formats.

Table 7-7: CSS Positioning Attributes

Positioning Setting	Description
Type	Determines whether an element can be positioned absolutely or relatively on a page. The third option, static, does not enable positioning and renders elements as they would be positioned with regular HTML.
Width	Sets the width of the element.
Height	Sets the height of the element.
Visibility	Determines whether the element is visible, hidden, or inherits the property from its parent.
Z-Index	Sets the apparent depth of a positioned element. Higher values are closer to the top.
Overflow	Specifies how the element is displayed when it's larger than the dimensions of the element. Options include the following: Clip, where the element is partially hidden; None, where the element is displayed and the dimensions are disregarded; and Scroll, which inserts scroll bars to display the overflowing portion of the element.
Placement	Sets the styled element's placement and dimensions with the left and top attributes and the width and height attributes, respectively.
Clip	Sets the visible portion of the element through the top, right, bottom, and left attributes.

Cross-Reference

Dreamweaver layers are built upon the foundation of CSS positioning. For a complete explanation of layers and their attributes, see Chapter 11.

Extensions Options

The specifications for Cascading Style Sheets are rapidly evolving, and Dreamweaver has grouped some cutting-edge features in the Extensions category. As of this writing, most of the Extensions attributes (see Table 7-8) are supported by Internet Explorer 4.0 and above, whereas only the Cursor extension is supported in Netscape Navigator 6.x. The Extensions settings shown in Figure 7-19 affect three different areas: page breaks for printing, the user's cursor, and special effects called *filters*.

Table 7-8: CSS Extensions Attributes

Extensions Setting	Description
Pagebreak	Inserts a point on a page where a printer sees a page break. Currently supported only by Internet Explorer, versions 5.0 and higher.
Cursor	Defines the type of cursor that appears when the user moves the cursor over an element. Currently supported by Internet Explorer, versions 4.0 and higher as well as Netscape 6
Filter	Filters enable you to customize the look and transition of an element without having to use graphic or animation files. Currently supported only by Internet Explorer 4.0 and above.

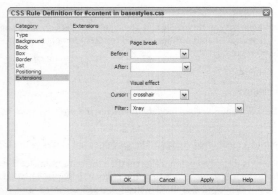

Figure 7-19: The CSS Extensions panel enables some terrific effects, which, unfortunately, are not well supported across the board.

Note   One of the problems with the Web's never-ending evolution of page design is evident when you begin to print the page. The Pagebreak attribute alleviates this problem by enabling the designer to designate a style that forces a page break when printing; the break can occur either before or after the element is attached to the style. This attribute is especially important for print media styles.

The Filter attribute offers 16 different special effects that can be applied to an element. Many of these effects, such as Wave and Xray, are quite stunning. Several effects involve transitions, as well. Table 7-9 details these effects.

Table 7-9: CSS Filters

Filter	Syntax	Description
Alpha	Alpha (Opacity=*opacity*, FinishOpacity=*finishopacity*, Style=*style*, StartX=*startX*, StartY=*startY*, FinishX=*finishX*, FinishY=*finishY*)	Sets the opacity of a specified gradient region. This can have the effect of creating a burst of light in an image.
	Opacity is a value from 0 to 100, where 0 is transparent and 100 is fully opaque.	
	StartX, **StartY**, **FinishX**, and **FinishY** are pixel values indicating where the effect should start and end.	
	Style can be 0 (uniform), 1 (linear), 2 (radial), or 3 (rectangular).	
BlendTrans*	blendTrans (duration=*duration*)	Causes an image to fade in or out over a specified time.
	Duration is a time value for the length of the transition, in the format of **seconds.milliseconds**.	
Blur	blur (Add=*add*, Direction=*direction*, Strength=*strength*)	Emulates motion blur for images.
	Add is any integer other than 0.	
	Direction is any value from 0 to 315 in increments of 45.	
	Strength is any positive integer representing the number of pixels affected.	
Chroma	chroma (Color= *color*)	Makes a specific color in an image transparent.
	Color must be given in hexadecimal form, for example, #rrggbb.	
DropShadow	Dropshadow (Color=*color*, OffX=*offX*, OffY=*offY*, Positive=*positive*)	Creates a drop shadow of the applied element, either image or text, in the specified color.
	Color is a hexadecimal triplet.	
	OffX and *OffY* are pixel offsets for the shadow.	
	Positive is a Boolean switch; use 1 to create shadow for nontransparent pixels and 0 to create shadow for transparent pixels.	

Continued

Table 7-9 *(continued)*

Filter	*Syntax*	*Description*
FlipH	FlipH	Flips an image or text horizontally.
FlipV	FlipV	Flips an image or text vertically.
Glow	Glow (Color=*color*, Strength=*strength*)	
	Adds radiance to an image in the specified color.	
	Color is a hexadecimal triplet.	
	Strength is a value from 0 to 100.	
Gray	Gray	Converts an image in grayscale.
Invert	Invert	Reverses the hue, saturation, and luminance of an image.
Light*	Light	Creates the illusion that an object is illuminated by one or more light sources.
Mask	Mask (Color=*color*)	Sets all the transparent pixels to the specified color and converts the nontransparent pixels to the background color.
	Color is a hexadecimal triplet.	
RevealTrans*	RevealTrans (duration=*duration*, transition=*style*)	Reveals an image using a specified type of transition over a set period of time.
	Duration is a time value that the transition takes, in the format of *seconds.milliseconds*.	
	Style is one of 23 different transitions.	
Shadow	Shadow (Color=*color*, Direction=*direction*)	Creates a gradient shadow in the specified color and direction for images or text.
	Color is a hexadecimal triplet.	
	Direction is any value from 0 to 315 in increments of 45.	
Wave	Wave (Add=*add*, Freq=*freq*, LightStrength=*lightstrength*, Phase=*phase*, Strength=*strength*)	Adds sine wave distortion to the selected image or text.
	Add is a Boolean value, where 1 adds the original object to the filtered object and 0 does not.	
	Freq is an integer specifying the number of waves.	
	LightStrength is a percentage value.	

Filter	Syntax	Description
Wave	*Phase* specifies the angular offset of the wave, in percentage (for example, 0% or 100% = 360 degrees, 25% = 90 degrees). *Strength* is an integer value specifying the intensity of the wave effect.	
Xray	Xray	Converts an image to inverse grayscale for an X-rayed appearance.

* These three transitions require extensive documentation beyond the scope of this book.

Design Time Style Sheets

Cascading Style Sheets give the designer an awesome flexibility with respect to the overall look and feel of a site. In fact, it's entirely possible for sites to be designed with multiple style sheets, each one applicable to a particular condition. With a little JavaScript or server-side coding, different style sheets can be applied according to which browser is being used, the platform employed, even the screen resolution at work. How does Dreamweaver know which style sheet to use? With the design time style sheets feature, of course.

The design time style sheets feature enables you to show a specific style sheet while hiding others as you work. One key use of this command is to utilize a style sheet that is linked from your page dynamically at runtime. Your style sheets, in other words, do not have to be specifically attached to your page for you to be able to use them.

To set up design time style sheets, follow these steps:

1. From the CSS Styles panel Options menu choose Design Time Style Sheets. Alternatively, choose Text ➪ CSS Styles ➪ Design Time. Whichever method you choose, the Design Time Style Sheets dialog box, shown in Figure 7-20, is displayed.

Figure 7-20: Use the Design Time Style Sheet feature to display a variety of style sheets while you're creating the page.

2. To show a specific style sheet, click the Add (+) button above the Show Only At Design Time list area and select an external style sheet from the Select File dialog box.

3. To hide a specific style sheet, click the Add (+) button above the Hide At Design Time list area and select an external style sheet from the Select File dialog box.

4. To delete a listed style sheet from either list, select the entry and click the Remove (–) button above the list.

Caution   The Design Time Style Sheet information is stored in a design note; make sure that you do not unwittingly delete any such design note file.

5. Click OK when you're finished.

Summary

In this chapter, you discovered how you can easily and effectively add and modify Cascading Style Sheets. With CSS, you can now accomplish all the following:

✦ Define external style sheets to control the look and feel of an entire site

✦ Create styles automatically when working with the Text Property inspector

✦ Update and change styles easily with the CSS Styles panel

✦ Easily apply generated styles to an element on a page

✦ Position fonts and elements, such as images, with pinpoint accuracy

✦ Exercise control over the layout, size, and display of fonts on a page

✦ Set up style sheets so that they're visible only at design time

In the next chapter, you learn how to insert and format text in Dreamweaver.

✦   ✦   ✦

Working with Text

If content is king on the Web, then certainly style is queen; together they rule hand in hand. Entering, editing, and formatting text on a Web page is a major part of a Webmaster's job. Dreamweaver gives you the tools to make the task as clear-cut as possible. From headlines to comments, this chapter covers the essentials of working with basic text; inserting and formatting dynamic data is covered in Chapter 19.

At first, Web designers didn't have many options for manipulating text. However, now the majority of browsers understand a number of text-related commands, and the designer can specify the font as well as its color and size. Dreamweaver includes a range of text-manipulation tools. All these topics are covered in this chapter, along with an important discussion of how to manipulate whitespace on the Web page.

Starting with Headings

Text in HTML is primarily composed of headings and paragraphs. Headings separate and introduce major sections of the document, just as a newspaper uses headlines to announce a story and sub-heads to highlight essential details. HTML has six levels of headings; the syntax for the heading tags is ⟨hn⟩, where n is a number from 1 to 6. The largest heading is ⟨h1⟩, and the smallest is ⟨h6⟩.

Note   Although Dreamweaver is capable of outputting several different types of Web pages — ASP, ColdFusion, JSP, and so on — after the page has been executed on the application server, straight HTML is returned to the visitor's browser. So even though you'll find numerous references to HTML pages throughout this chapter, understand that even though the pages may be stored as ASP pages or other types, HTML is the result.

Remember that HTML headings are not linked to any specific point size, unlike type produced in a page layout or word processing program. Headings in a Web document are sized relative to one another, and their final, exact size depends on the browser used. The sample headlines in Figure 8-1 depict the basic headings as rendered through Dreamweaver and as compared to the default paragraph font size. As you can see, some headings are rendered in type smaller than that used for the default paragraph. Headings are usually displayed with a boldface attribute.

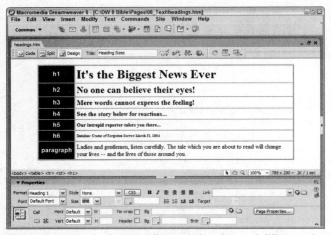

Figure 8-1: Standard HTML allows six headings of different sizes.

Several methods set text as a particular heading size in Dreamweaver. In all cases, you first select the text you want to affect. If you are styling a single line or paragraph as a heading, just position the cursor anywhere in the paragraph to select it. If you want to convert more than one paragraph, click and drag out your selection.

Tip   You can't mix heading levels in a single paragraph. That is, you can't have a word with an `<h1>` heading in the same line with a word styled with an `<h4>` heading. Furthermore, headings belong to a group of HTML text tags called *block elements*. All block elements are rendered with a paragraph return both above and below, which isolates (*blocks*) the text. To work around both of these restrictions, use Cascading Style Sheets, described in Chapter 7, to achieve the effect of varying sizes for words within the same line or for lines of different sizes close to one another.

After the text for the heading is selected, choose your heading level in one of the following ways:

✦ Choose Text ⇨ Paragraph Format and then one of the Headings (1 through 6) from the submenu.

✦ Click the Heading 1, Heading 2, or Heading 3 button from the Text category of the Insert bar.

✦ Make your selection from the Text Property inspector. (If it's not already open, display the Text Property inspector by selecting Window ⇨ Properties.) In the Text Property inspector, open the Format drop-down list (see Figure 8-2) and choose one of the six headings.

Tip   You can also use keyboard shortcuts for assigning headings. Headings 1 through 6 correspond to Ctrl+1 through Ctrl+6 (Command+1 through Command+6). The Paragraph option is rendered with Ctrl+Shift+P (Command+Shift+P); remove all formatting with Ctrl+0 (Command+0).

Figure 8-2: You can convert any paragraph or line into a heading through the Format options in the Text Property inspector.

Headings are often used in a hierarchical fashion, largest to smallest — but you don't have to do it that way. You can have an <h3> line followed by an <h1> paragraph, if that's what your design needs.

Caution
Be careful when using the smallest headings, <h4> to <h6>; they are likely to be difficult to read on any resolution higher than 800 x 600.

Working with Paragraphs

Usually the bulk of text on any Web page is composed of paragraphs. Paragraphs in HTML are denoted by the <p> and </p> pair of tags. When your Web page is processed, the browser formats everything between those two tags as one paragraph and renders it to fit the user's screen, word wrapping as needed at the margins. Any additional line breaks and unnecessary whitespace (beyond one space between words and between sentences) in the HTML code are ignored.

Tip
In the earliest versions of HTML, paragraphs used just the opening <p> tag. Browsers rendered everything after a <p> tag as one paragraph, until they reached another <p> tag. As of HTML 3.2, however, an optional closing </p> tag was added. Because so many Web pages have been created with just the opening paragraph tag, most browsers still recognize the single-tag format, even though the latest versions of the HTML standard require the closing tag. Dreamweaver automatically inserts both the opening and closing tags when you create a paragraph. To be on the safe side in terms of future compatibility, enclose your paragraphs within both opening and closing tags when you do any hand-coding.

Dreamweaver starts a new paragraph every time you press Enter (Return) when composing text in the Document window. If you have the Code view or the Code inspector open when you work, you can see that Dreamweaver inserts the following code with each new paragraph:

```
<p> </p>
```

The code between the tags creates a nonbreaking space that enables the new line to be visible. You won't see the new line if you have just the paragraph tags with nothing in between (neither a character nor a character entity, such as):

```
<p></p>
```

Caution
Some browsers, such as Netscape Navigator 4.x, totally ignore empty <p></p> tags. If you are hand-coding an empty paragraph, be sure to include a nonbreaking space within the paragraph.

When you continue typing, Dreamweaver replaces the nonbreaking space with your input, unless you press Enter (Return) again. Figure 8-3 illustrates two paragraphs with text followed by paragraphs with the nonbreaking space still in place.

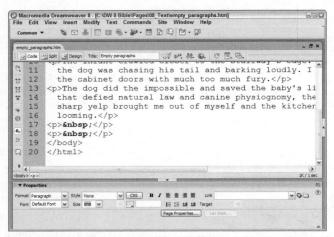

Figure 8-3: Dreamweaver automatically wraps any text inserted into the Document window. If you press Enter (Return) without entering text, Dreamweaver enters paragraph tags surrounding a nonbreaking space.

You can easily change text from most other formats, such as a heading, to paragraph format. First, select the text you want to alter. Then, in the Property inspector, open the Format drop-down list and choose Paragraph. You can also chooseText ➪ Paragraph Format ➪ Paragraph from the menu or use the keyboard shortcut Ctrl+Shift+P (Command+Shift+P).

All paragraphs are initially rendered on the page in the default font at the default size. The user can designate these defaults through the browser preferences, although most people don't bother to alter them. If you want to change the font name or the font size for selected paragraphs explicitly, use the techniques described in the upcoming section "Modifying Text Format" or use Cascading Style Sheets, described in Chapter 7.

> Remember that you can always use the Tag Selector on the status bar to select and highlight any tag surrounding your current cursor position. This method makes it easy to see exactly what a particular tag is affecting.

Editing Paragraphs

By and large, the editing features of Dreamweaver are similar to other modern word processing programs — with one or two Web-oriented twists. Like other programs, Dreamweaver has Cut, Copy, and Paste options, as well as Undo and Redo commands.

The twists come from the relationship between the Design and Code views of the Document window, which give Dreamweaver special functionality for copying and pasting text and code. You learn how that works in the following sections.

Inserting Text

You've already seen how you can position the cursor on the page and directly enter text. In this sense, Dreamweaver acts like a word processing program rather than a page layout program. On a blank page, the cursor starts at the top-left corner of the page. Words automatically wrap to the next line when the text exceeds the right margin. Press Enter (Return) to end the current paragraph and start the next one.

In previous versions of Dreamweaver, when you create a paragraph formatted as a heading and then press Enter (Return), the new paragraph is also formatted as a heading. Now you can control this behavior. If you select Edit ➪ Preferences, click the General category, and then select the Switch To Plain Paragraph After Heading option, pressing Enter (Return) after a heading creates a plain paragraph. By default, this option is enabled.

Cutting, Copying, and Pasting

Text can be moved from one place to another — or from one Web document to another — using the standard cut-and-paste techniques. No surprises here: Before cutting or copying anything, you must select it. Select by clicking the mouse at the beginning of the text you want to cut or copy, drag the highlight to the end of your selection, and then release the mouse button.

Here are some other selection methods:

✦ Double-click a word to select it.

✦ Move the pointer to the left margin of the text until the pointer changes to a right-facing arrow. Click once to highlight a single line. Click and drag down the margin to select a group of lines.

✦ Position the cursor at the beginning of your selection. Hold down the Shift key and then click once at the end of the selection.

✦ Select everything in the body of your document by using Edit ➪ Select All or the keyboard shortcut Ctrl+A (Command+A).

✦ Use the Tag Selector in the status bar to select text or other objects contained within specific tags.

✦ You can also select text by holding down the Shift key and using the right or left arrow key to select one character at a time. If you hold down Ctrl+Shift (Command+Shift), press the right or left arrow key to select one word at a time.

✦ Hold down the Shift key and then press the up or down arrow key to select a line at a time. Pressing Ctrl+Shift (Command+Shift) as you press the up or down arrow key selects a paragraph at a time.

Dreamweaver provides quick access to the most common editing commands, such as Cut, Copy, and Paste, through the Standard toolbar. To enable the toolbar, choose View ➪ Toolbars ➪ Standard.

When you want to move a block of text, first select it and then use Edit ➪ Cut, the Cut button on the Standard toolbar, or the keyboard shortcut Ctrl+X (Command+X). This sequence places the text on your system's clipboard. To paste the text, move the pointer to the new location, click once to place the cursor, and then select Edit ➪ Paste or use the keyboard shortcut Ctrl+V (Command+V). The text is copied from the clipboard to its new location. You can continue pasting this same text from the clipboard until another block of text is copied or cut.

To copy text, the procedure is much the same. Select the text using one of the preceding methods and then use Edit ➪ Copy, the Copy button on the Standard toolbar, or Ctrl+C (Command+C). The selected text is copied to the clipboard, and the original text is left in place. You then position the cursor in a new location and select Edit ➪ Paste (or use the keyboard shortcut).

Using Drag-and-Drop

The other, quicker method for moving or copying text is the drag-and-drop technique. After you've selected your text, release the mouse button and move the cursor over the highlighted area. The cursor changes from an I-beam to an arrow. To move the text, click the selected area with the arrow cursor and drag your mouse to a new location. The arrow cursor now has a box attached to it, indicating that it is carrying something. As you move your cursor, a bar (the insertion point) moves with you, indicating where the text will be positioned. Release the mouse button to drop the text.

You can duplicate text in the same manner by holding down the Ctrl (Option) key as you drag and drop your selected text. When copying this way, the box attached to the cursor is marked with a plus sign (on Macintosh computers, the box is the same size as the text selection, and no plus sign appears).

To completely remove text, select it and then choose Edit ➪ Clear or press Delete. The only way to recover deleted text is to use the Undo feature described later in this section.

Inserting Text from Other Text Applications

The Paste command can also insert text from another program into Dreamweaver. If you cut or copy text from a file in any other program—whether it is a word processor, spreadsheet, or database program—Dreamweaver inserts it at the cursor position. The results of an ordinary Paste operation may be undesirable, however. To more closely control the text inserted into Dreamweaver, use Paste Special.

New In Dreamweaver

Paste Special allows you to choose exactly how you'd like the copied text inserted into your document. Choose from a range of options that give you the flexibility to add straight text, structured text, structured text with simple formatting, or fully formatted text. The options can be preset in the Copy/Paste category of the Preferences and adjusted on a case-by-case basis.

After you've copied text in another application, choose Edit ➪ Paste Special. You're presented with a dialog box with four options:

✦ **Text Only:** Pastes completely unformatted text; even line breaks or paragraphs are removed.

✦ **Text with Structure:** Pastes unstyled text while retaining structured elements such as lists, paragraphs, line breaks, and tables.

✦ **Text with Structure Plus Basic Formatting:** Adds simple formatting, such as bold, italic, and underline, to structured text. If the text is copied from an HTML document, the pasted text retains any HTML text style tags, including `<b>`, `<i>`, `<u>`, `<strong>`, `<em>`, `<abbr>`, and `<acronym>`.

✦ **Text with Structure Plus Full Formatting:** Pasted text keeps all structure and formatting. If the copied text retains inline CSS styles, Dreamweaver pastes them as well.

Two other options are available for modifying your paste output. The Retain Line Breaks option maintains line breaks in pasted text; if you choose Text Only, this option is disabled. The Clean Up Word Paragraph Spacing option works with the Text with Structure and Text with Structure Plus Basic Formatting choices to remove additional space between paragraphs.

If you use the standard Paste command, Dreamweaver can only insert only plain, unformatted text — any bold, italic, or other styling in the original document is not retained in Dreamweaver. Paragraph breaks, however, are retained and reproduced in two different ways. A single paragraph return becomes a line-break (a <br> tag) in Dreamweaver, whereas text separated by two returns is formatted into two HTML paragraphs, using the <p>...</p> tag pair.

Note   If you need to import a great deal of text and want to retain as much formatting as possible, you can use another text application, such as Microsoft Word, to save your text as an HTML file. Then open that file in Dreamweaver with the Import ⇨ Word HTML command.

Copying and Pasting Code

As mentioned earlier in this chapter, Dreamweaver includes a couple of twists to the standard Cut, Copy, and Paste operations. Dreamweaver's Design and Code views enable you to copy and paste both text and code.

Put simply, to copy only text from Dreamweaver to another application, use the Edit ⇨ Copy command in Design view; to copy both text and code, use the Edit ⇨ Copy command in Code view.

Within Dreamweaver itself, content copied from Design view and pasted in Code view using Edit ⇨ Paste appears as plain text without any code. To insert text and code, you'd need to use the Edit ⇨ Paste Special command and select either of the options that include formatting: Text with Structure Plus Basic Formatting or Text with Structure Plus Full Formatting.

Undo, Redo, and the History Panel

The Undo command has to be one of the greatest inventions of the 20th century. Make a mistake? Undo! Want to experiment with two different options? Undo! Change your mind again? Redo! The Undo command reverses your last action, whether you changed a link, added a graphic, or deleted the entire page. The Redo command enables you to reverse your Undo actions.

To use the Undo command, choose Edit ⇨ Undo, select Undo from the Standard toolbar, or press the keyboard shortcut Ctrl+Z (Command+Z); any of these commands undoes a single action at a time. Dreamweaver displays all your previous actions on the History panel, so you can easily see what steps you took. Choose Window ⇨ History to view the History panel. To undo multiple actions, drag the slider in the History panel to the last action you want to keep, or just click in the slider track at that action.

Dreamweaver's implementation of the Undo command enables you to back up as many steps as set in Maximum Number of History Steps, found in the General category of Preferences. The History steps can even undo actions that took place before a document was saved. Note that the History panel has additional features besides multiple applications of the Undo command.

The complement to the Undo command is the Redo command. To reverse an Undo command, choose Edit ➪ Redo, click the Redo button on the Standard toolbar, or press Ctrl+Y (Command+Y). To reverse several Undo commands, drag the slider in the History panel back over the grayed-out steps; alternatively, click once in the slider track at the last of the steps you'd like to redo.

Tip   The best use I've found for the Redo command is in concert with Undo. When I'm trying to decide between two alternatives, such as two different images, I'll replace one choice with another and then use the Undo/Redo combination to go back and forth between them. Because Dreamweaver replaces any selected object with the current object from the clipboard — even if one is a block of text and the other is a layer — you can easily view two separate options with this trick. The History panel enables you to apply this procedure to any number of steps.

A variation of the Redo command is the Repeat command. When your last action was the Undo command, the Edit menu shows the Redo command. But if the last action you performed was not Undo, the Edit menu shows the Repeat command, which allows you to repeat your last action. You can use the same button on the Standard toolbar to Repeat and Redo. In addition, the Repeat command has the same keyboard shortcut as Redo: Ctrl+Y (Command+Y). The Repeat command is useful, for example, when you need to create several links to the same location. To do this, create the first link, and then select the next text you want to link and use the Repeat command to add the next link.

On the CD-ROM   Although the History panel enables you to replay any series of selected steps at the click of a button, you have to click that button every time you want to replay the steps. I developed a custom extension called Repeat History with which you can repeat selected steps any number of times. You'll find Repeat History in the Additional Extensions folder on the CD-ROM.

Entering and Pasting Text

In this Technique, you practice entering headings and pasting text copied from another application into Dreamweaver.

1. In the Techniques site, expand the 08_Text folder and open `text_start.htm`.

2. Highlight and delete the placeholder text, Content for id "middle" Goes Here.

3. Enter the heading: **Neighborhood Watch: East Side**.

4. With your cursor still in the heading, from the Property inspector's Format list, choose h1.

5. Make sure your cursor is at the end of the heading and press Enter (Return).

   A new paragraph is created. Rather than type in a paragraph of text, use Dreamweaver's advanced copy/paste ability to bring in formatted text.

6. In the 08_Text folder, double-click the `neighborhood.rtf` file to open it in your text editor.

7. In your text editor, select all the text and copy it.

8. Back in Dreamweaver, place your cursor on the line below the heading.

9. Choose Edit ➪ Paste Special.

10. In the Paste Special dialog box, choose the Text plus Basic Formatting option; make sure the Clean up Word Paragraph Spacing option is selected and click OK.

Dreamweaver converts the copied text to HTML and inserts it into the page.

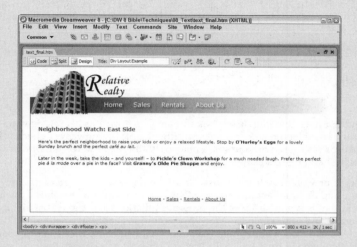

11. Save your page.

The next time you open the Paste Special dialog box, the chosen setting will be remembered.

Checking Your Spelling

A typo can make a significant impression, and not the one you want to make. Not many things are more embarrassing than showing a new Web site to a client and having that client point out a spelling error. Dreamweaver includes an easy-to-use Spell Checker to avoid such awkward moments. Make it a practice to spell check every Web page before it's posted online.

You start the process by choosing Text ➪ Check Spelling or pressing the keyboard shortcut Shift+F7. This sequence opens the Check Spelling dialog box, as shown in Figure 8-4.

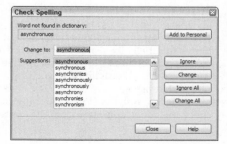

Figure 8-4: Dreamweaver's Spell Checker double-checks your spelling and can find the typos on any Web page.

Spell-Checking in Non-English Languages

A variety of language dictionaries are built into Dreamweaver, so you can check spelling in a number of languages. Dreamweaver can check spelling in the following languages: Danish, Dutch, English (American), English (British), English (Canadian), Finnish, French, German (Classic Spelling), German (New Spelling), Italian, Norwegian, Portuguese (Brazilian), Portuguese (Iberian), Spanish, and Swedish.

Open Preferences (Edit ➪ Preferences on Windows, Dreamweaver ➪ Preferences on a Mac) and, in the General category, expand the Spelling Dictionary list. Choose the new language from the drop-down list, and you're ready to spell correctly in another tongue.

After you've opened the Check Spelling dialog box, Dreamweaver begins searching your text for errors. Unless you have selected a portion of your document, Dreamweaver checks the full document, regardless of where your cursor is placed. When text is selected, Dreamweaver checks the selection first and then asks if you'd like to do the entire document.

Dreamweaver checks your Web page text against two dictionaries: a standard dictionary for your chosen language and a personal dictionary to which you can add words. If the Spell Checker finds any text that is not in either of the program's dictionaries, the text is highlighted in the Document window and appears in the Word Not Found In Dictionary field of the dialog box. A list of suggested corrections appears in the Suggestions list box, with the topmost one highlighted and also displayed in the Change To box. If Dreamweaver cannot find any suggestions, the Change To box is left blank. At this point, you have the following options:

✦ **Add to Personal:** Click this button to include the word in your personal dictionary and prevent Dreamweaver from tagging it as an error in the future.

✦ **Ignore:** Click this button when you want Dreamweaver to leave the currently highlighted word alone and continue searching the text.

✦ **Change:** If you see the correct replacement among the list of suggestions, highlight it and click the Change button. If no suggestion is appropriate, type the correct word into the Change To text field and then click this button.

✦ **Ignore All:** Click this button when you want Dreamweaver to disregard all occurrences of this word in the current document.

✦ **Change All:** Click this button to replace all instances of the current word within the document with the word in the Change To text field.

Using Find and Replace

Dreamweaver's Find and Replace features are both timesaving and lifesaving (well, almost). You can use Find and Replace to cut your input time substantially by searching for abbreviations and expanding them to their full state. You can also find a client's incorrectly spelled name and replace it with the correctly spelled version—that's a lifesaver! However, that's just the tip of the iceberg when it comes to what Find and Replace can really do. The Find and Replace engine should be considered a key power tool for any Web developer. Not only can you search multiple files, but you can also easily check the code separately from the content.

Here's a short list of what the Find and Replace feature makes possible:

✦ Search the Document window to find any type of text.

✦ Search the underlying HTML to find tags, attributes, or text enclosed within tags.

✦ Look for text within specific tags with specific attributes — or look for text that's outside of a specific tag with specific attributes.

✦ Find and replace patterns of text, using wildcard characters called *regular expressions*.

✦ Apply any of the preceding Find and Replace operations to the current document, the current site, any folder, or any group of selected files.

The basic command, Find and Replace, is found with its companion, Find Next, under the Edit menu. You can use both commands in either Dreamweaver's Design or Code view. Although invoked by a single command, the Find feature can be used independently or in conjunction with Replace.

Find and Replace operations can be applied to one or a series of documents. In addition to searching all or part of the current document, you can also apply Find and Replace to all the files in a folder or an entire site. Furthermore, individual files selected in the Files panel are also searchable.

Finding on the Visual Page

The most basic method of using Find and Replace takes place in the Document window. Whenever you need to search for any text that can be seen by the public on your Web page — whether it's to correct spelling or change a name — Dreamweaver makes it fast and simple.

The Find and Replace dialog box, unlike most of Dreamweaver's dialog boxes, is actually a *nonmodal window*. This technical term just means that you can easily move back and forth between your Document window and the Find and Replace dialog box without having to close the dialog box first, as you do with the other Dreamweaver dialog boxes.

Whether you are working with a long, involved document or you just want to look in a particular area, you'll welcome Dreamweaver's new capability to search a selection. Just highlight the text you want to search and, in the Find and Replace dialog box, choose Selected Text from the Find In drop-down list. You can search just selected code, too.

To find some text on your Web page, follow these steps:

1. From the Document window, choose Edit ⇨ Find and Replace or use the keyboard shortcut Ctrl+F (Command+F). If the Search panel is open, you can also click the Find and Replace button (the small green triangle) on the panel.

2. In the Find and Replace dialog box, shown in Figure 8-5, make sure that Text is the selected Search option.

3. In the text field next to the Search option, type the word or phrase you're looking for.

Tip If you select your text *before* launching the Find dialog box, it automatically appears in the Search text field if it contains fewer than 255 characters. Should you select text containing a greater number of characters, Dreamweaver assumes you want to search the selection and keeps the Search field clear.

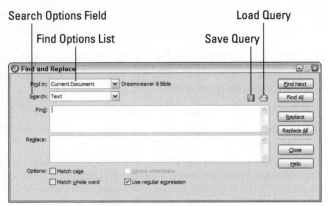

Figure 8-5: The Find and Replace dialog box.

4. Select the appropriate search options, if any:

   - If you want to find an exact replica of the word as you entered it, select the Match Case checkbox; otherwise, Dreamweaver searches for all variations of your text, regardless of case.

   - To force Dreamweaver to disregard any whitespace variations, such as additional spaces, hard spaces, or tabs, select the Ignore Whitespace Differences option. For most situations, it's a good idea to leave this default option enabled.

   - Selecting Use Regular Expressions enables you to work with Dreamweaver's wild-card characters (discussed later in this section). Use Regular Expressions and Ignore Whitespace Differences are mutually exclusive options.

5. Click the Find Next button to begin the search from the cursor's current position.

   - If Dreamweaver finds the selected text, it highlights the text in the Document window.

   - If Dreamweaver doesn't find the text in the remaining portion of the document, it automatically continues the search from the beginning of the document until the entire document has been checked.

   - If Dreamweaver doesn't locate the search term, it displays a message saying the term has not been found.

6. If you want to look for the next occurrence of your selected text, click the Find Next button again.

7. You can enter other text to search or exit the Find dialog box by clicking the Close button.

The text you enter in the Find and Replace dialog box is kept in memory until it's replaced by your next use of the Find feature. After you have executed the Find command once, you can continue to search for your text without redisplaying the Find and Replace dialog box, by selecting Edit ➪ Find Next, or by using the keyboard shortcut F3 (Command+G). If Dreamweaver finds your text, it is highlighted just as it is when the Find and Replace dialog box is open. However, the Edit ➪ Find Next command searches indefinitely through your document; no message displays after it has searched the entire file. The Find Next command gives you a quick way to search through a long document — especially when you put the F3 (Command+G) key to work.

Instead of locating one instance of your text at a time, you can also look for all occurrences of your text at once. To do this, open and set up the Find and Replace dialog as previously described, but choose Find All instead of Find Next. When you choose Find All, Dreamweaver closes the Find and Replace dialog box and opens the Search panel. The Search panel displays each found occurrence on a separate line, as shown in Figure 8-6. A message at the bottom of the Search panel also tells you how many occurrences of your selection, if any, were found. If you want to search for a different term, click the Find and Replace button (the small green triangle) in the Search panel to reopen the Find and Replace dialog box.

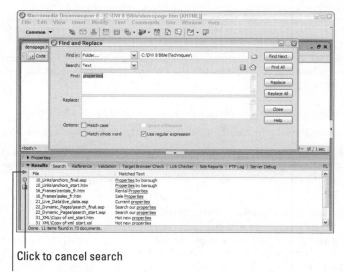

Click to cancel search

Click to reopen file and replace

Figure 8-6: The Search panel displays results of a Find All command.

Tip

To quickly move from one found selection to another in the Document window, double-click an entry in the Search panel. Dreamweaver highlights the selection, scrolling the Document window, if necessary. Note, however, that the results listed in the Search panel may take you to the wrong location if you add or remove content in the document after you perform the search.

If you perform two Find All operations in a row, the Search panel automatically clears the results of the first search and replaces them with the results of the new search. To manually clear the Search panel, right-click (Control+click) and choose Clear Results.

Caution If you edit the document after performing a Find All, the results of the search may no longer be valid. In this situation, double-clicking an item in the Search panel may no longer take you to the correct place in the document. If you have added or removed text in the document after performing a Find All, perform the search again by clicking the Find and Replace button (the small green triangle) in the Search panel to reopen the Find and Replace dialog box. If no text is selected in the Document window before you open the Find and Replace dialog box, the search parameters should automatically be set up; you just click Find All again.

When you replace text in the Document window, it is replaced regardless of its formatting. For example, suppose you have the following paragraph:

> Mary's accusation reminded Jon of studying synchrones in high school. *Synchrones*, he recalled, were graphs in which the lines constantly approached zero, but never made it. "Yeah," he thought, "That's me, all right. I'm one big **synchrone**."

Upon discovering that *synchrone* should actually be *asymptote*, you could use the Find and Replace feature to replace all the plain, italic, and bold versions of the *synchrone* text simultaneously.

Tip It's possible to alter formatting as well — to change all the formatting to bold only, for example — but for that you need to perform your Find and Replace operations on the underlying code, as discussed in the following section.

Follow these steps to use Dreamweaver's Replace feature in the Document window:

1. Choose Edit ➪ Find and Replace or use the keyboard shortcut Ctrl+F (Command+F).

2. In the Find and Replace dialog box, make sure that Text is the selected Search option and then, in the text field next to the Search option, type the word or phrase you're looking for. You can also copy and paste text from the Document window into the Search field.

3. In the Replace With text field, type the substitute text.

Tip Need more room for your Find or Replace entries? The Find and Replace dialog box can be widened by dragging the border as you would a window; Macintosh users should drag the lower-right corner as usual.

4. Click the Find Next button. Dreamweaver begins searching from the current cursor position. If Dreamweaver finds the text, it is highlighted.

5. To replace the highlighted occurrence of the text, click the Replace button. Dreamweaver replaces the found text with the substitute text and then automatically searches for the next occurrence.

6. If you want to replace all instances of the Search text, click the Replace All button. When Dreamweaver has found all the occurrences of your Search text, it displays a message telling how many replacement operations were made.

Caution The Search panel applies to Find operations, but not to Replace operations. When you click Replace All, Dreamweaver does not update the Search panel to list items that have been replaced. Further, if you click Find All and then perform a Replace All, the previous results in the Search panel may no longer correctly reflect the location of the text you just replaced, and changed items in the Search panel are not flagged.

Tip To rerun individual Find and Replace operations, highlight the appropriate step in the History panel (choose Window ➪ History) and click the Replay button. You cannot, however, use the History panel to repeat a Find All operation.

Searching the Code

The power curve ramps up significantly when you start to explore Dreamweaver's Find and Replace capabilities for HTML code. Should your client decide that he wants the company's name to appear in blue, bold, 18-point type throughout the 300-page site, you can accommodate him with a few keystrokes — instead of hours of mind-numbing grunt work.

You can perform three different types of searches that use the HTML in your Web page:

✦ You can search for text anywhere in the HTML code. With this capability, you can look for text within `alt` or any other attribute — and change it.

✦ You can search for text relative to specific tags. Sometimes you need to change just the text contained within the `<b>` tag and leave all other matching text alone.

✦ You can search for specific HTML tags and/or their attributes. Dreamweaver's Find and Replace feature gives you the capability to insert, delete, or modify tags and attributes.

Looking for Text in the Code

Text that appears onscreen is often replicated in various sections of your off-screen HTML code. It's not uncommon, for example, to use the `alt` attribute in an `<img>` tag that repeats the caption under the picture. What happens if you replace the wording using the Find and Replace dialog box with the Search field set to Text? You're still left with the task of tracking down the `alt` attribute and making that change as well. Dreamweaver enables you to act on both content and programming text in one operation — a major savings in time and effort, not to mention aggravation.

Storing and Retrieving Queries

Dreamweaver enables you to develop extremely complex search queries. Rather than forcing you to repeatedly re-enter Find and Replace queries, Dreamweaver enables you to save and load them when needed. Dreamweaver saves the queries with a `.dwr` file extension.

To save a query, select the Diskette icon on the Find and Replace dialog box. The standard Save Query (Save Query To File) dialog box appears for you to enter a filename; the appropriate file extension is appended automatically. To load a previously saved query, click the Folder icon on the Find and Replace dialog box to open the Load Query dialog box. Although only queries with a `.dwr` extension are being saved in the current version, you can still load both `.dwq` and `.dwr` files saved from previous Dreamweaver versions.

Although saving and opening queries is an obvious advantage when working with complex wild-card operations, you can also make it work for you in an everyday situation. If, for example, you have a set series of acronyms or abbreviations that you must convert repeatedly, you can save your simple text queries and use them as needed without having to remember all the details.

To find and replace text in both the content and the code, follow these steps:

1. Choose Edit ⇨ Find and Replace to open the Find and Replace dialog box.

2. Select the parameters of your search from the Find In option: Current Document, Entire Current Local Site, Selected Files In Site, or Folder. If you choose Selected Files In Site, select the files of interest in the Site panel.

3. From the Search drop-down list, select the Source Code option.

4. Enter the text you're searching for in the text field next to the Search option.

5. If you are replacing, enter the new text in the Replace With text field.

6. Select any options desired: Match Case, Ignore Whitespace Differences, or Use Regular Expressions.

7. Choose your Find/Replace option: Find Next, Find All, Replace, or Replace All. If you are in Design view, the Code inspector opens.

8. If Dreamweaver hasn't automatically closed the Find and Replace dialog box (it closes automatically for the Find All and Replace All commands), click Close when you are finished.

Caution As with all Find and Replace operations — especially those in which you decide to Replace All — you need to exercise extreme caution when replacing text throughout your code. If you're unsure about what's going to be affected, choose Find All first and, with Code view or inspector open, step through all the selections. You do this to be positive that no unwanted surprises occur. Should you replace some code in error, you can always undo the operation — but only if the document is open. Replacing text or code in a closed file — as is done when the operation is performed on a folder, the current site, or selected files in the Site panel — is not undoable. Therefore, it is wise to back up your site before performing a Replace All operation.

Using Advanced Text Options in Find and Replace

In Find and Replace operations, the global Replace All isn't appropriate for every situation; sometimes you need a more precise approach. Dreamweaver enables you to fine-tune your searches to pinpoint accuracy. You can look for text within particular tags — and even within particular tags with specific attributes. Moreover, you can find (and replace) text that is outside of particular tags with specific attributes.

Dreamweaver assists you by providing a drop-down list of standard tags. The tags shown depend on the type of document you are viewing, as determined by the filename extension of the open file. For example, although most document types see HTML tags, a document with the .cfm extension would also see ColdFusion tags. You can also search for your own custom tags. In addition, you don't have to try to remember which attributes go with which tag; Dreamweaver supplies you with a context-sensitive list of attributes that changes according to the tag selected.

In addition to using the tag's attributes as a search filter, Dreamweaver can also search within the tag for text or another tag. Most HTML tags are so-called *container tags* that consist of an opening tag and a closing tag, such as <em> and </em>. You can set up a filter to look for text surrounded by a specific tag pair — or text outside of a specific set of tags. For example, if you are searching for the word *big*

```
The big, red boat was a <em>big</em> waste of money.
```

you can build a Find and Replace operation that changes one instance of the word (big, red) but not the other (<em>big</em>) — or vice versa.

To look for text in or out of specific tags and attributes, follow these steps:

1. Choose Edit ➪ Find and Replace to open the Find and Replace dialog box.

2. Select the parameters of your search from the Find In option: Current Document, Current Site, Folder, or Selected Files In Site.

3. From the Search drop-down list, select the Text (Advanced) option. The Add (+) and Remove (−) tag options are made available, as shown in Figure 8-7.

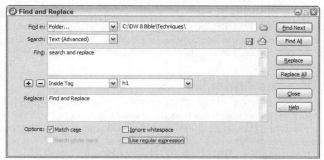

Figure 8-7: The advanced text features of Find and Replace enable you to manipulate text and code simultaneously.

4. Enter the text you're searching for in the text field next to the Search drop-down list.

5. Select either Inside Tag or Not Inside Tag from the drop-down list. Remember that Inside Tag refers to text that is enclosed within a beginning and ending tag pair, such as `<h2></h2>`.

6. Select the tag to include or exclude from the adjacent drop-down list or type your own tag.

7. To add a further restriction on the search, click the Add (+) button. Another line of search options is added to the dialog box.

8. Select the additional search filter. The available options are listed in Table 8-1.

Table 8-1: Search Filters

Filter	Description
With Attribute	Enables you to select any attribute from the adjacent drop-down list. You can set this attribute to be equal to, less than, greater than, or not equal to any given value by choosing from the available drop-down lists.
Without Attribute	Finds text within a particular tag that does not include a specific attribute. Choose the attribute from the adjacent drop-down list.
Containing	Searches the tag for either specified text or another user-selectable tag found within the initial tag pair.
Not Containing	Searches the tag for either text or a tag not found within the initial tag pair.
Inside Tag	Enables you to look for text that is within two (or more) sets of specific tags.
Not Inside Tag	Enables you to look for text that is in one tag, but not in another tag, or vice versa.

9. To continue adding filter conditions, click the Add (+) button and repeat step 8.

10. To remove a filter condition, click the Remove (–) button.

11. If you are replacing text, enter the new text in the Replace With text field.

12. Select any options you want: Match Case, Ignore Whitespace Differences, or Use Regular Expressions.

13. Choose your Find/Replace option: Find Next, Find All, Replace, or Replace All.

Tip

You can continue to add conditions by clicking the Add (+) button. In fact, I was able to add so many conditions that the Find/Replace dialog box began to disappear off the screen (although I wouldn't recommend this in practice). To quickly erase all conditions, change the Search option to Text or Source Code and then change it back to Text (Advanced).

Replacing HTML Tags and Attributes

Imagine a new edict has come down from the HTML gurus of your company: No longer is the `<b>` tag to be used to indicate emphasis; from now on, use only the `<strong>` tag. Oh, and by the way, change all the existing pages — all 3,000+ Web and intranet pages — so that they're compliant. Dreamweaver makes short work out of nightmare situations such as this by giving you the power to search and replace HTML tags and their attributes.

But Dreamweaver doesn't stop there. Not only can you replace one tag with another, you can also perform the following:

✦ Change or delete the tag (with or without its contents).

✦ Set an attribute in the tag to another value.

✦ Remove any or all attributes.

✦ Add text and/or code before or after the starting or the ending tag.

To alter your code using Dreamweaver's Find and Replace feature, follow these steps:

1. As with other Find and Replace operations, choose Edit ➪ Find and Replace to open the dialog box.

2. Select the parameters of your search from the Find In drop-down list: Current Document, Entire Current Local Site, Folder, or Selected Files In Site.

3. From the Search drop-down list, select the Specific Tag option.

   The dialog box changes to include the tag functions.

4. Select the desired tag from the option list next to the Search drop-down list.

Tip

You can either scroll down the list box to find the tag or you can type the first letter of the tag in the box. Dreamweaver scrolls to the group of tags that begin with that letter when the list is visible. To scroll further in the list, type the second and subsequent letters, or use the down or up arrow keys.

5. You can limit the search by specifying an attribute and value or with other conditions, as discussed in detail in the previous section.

Note

If you want to search for just a tag, click the Remove (–) button to eliminate the additional condition.

6. Make a selection from the Action list shown in Figure 8-8.

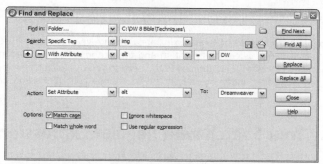

Figure 8-8: The Action list enables you to replace tags or modify them by setting the existing attributes or adding new ones.

The Action list options are listed in Table 8-2.

Table 8-2: Action List Options

Action	Description
Replace Tag & Contents	Substitutes the selected tag and all included content with a text string; the text string can include HTML code
Replace Contents Only	Changes the content between the specified tags to a given text string, which can also include HTML code
Remove Tag & Contents	Deletes the tag and all contents
Strip Tag	Removes the tag but leaves the previously enclosed content
Change Tag	Substitutes one tag for another
Set Attribute	Sets an existing attribute to a new value or inserts a new attribute set to a specific value
Remove Attribute	Deletes a specified attribute
Add Before Start Tag	Inserts a text string (with or without HTML) before the opening tag
Add After End Tag	Inserts a text string (with or without HTML) after the ending tag
Add After Start Tag	Inserts a text string (with or without HTML) after the opening tag
Add Before End Tag	Inserts a text string (with or without HTML) before the end tag

Note

Not all the options listed in the preceding list are available for all tags. Some so-called empty tags, such as <img>, consist of a single tag, not tag pairs. Empty tags have only the Replace Tag and Remove Tag options (instead of Replace Tag & Contents, Replace Contents Only, and Remove Tag & Contents) and the Add Before and Add After options (instead of Add Before Start Tag, Add After Start Tag, Add Before End Tag, and Add After End Tag).

7. Select any options desired: Match Case, Ignore Whitespace Differences, or Use Regular Expressions.

8. Choose your Find/Replace option: Find Next, Find All, Replace, or Replace All.

Tip   You don't have to apply a single action to all the instances Dreamweaver locates if you choose Find All. In the Search panel, select a single item and then choose Replace. Dreamweaver makes the revision and places a green dot next to the item so you can tell it has been altered. If you want, you can then select another item from the list, choose a different action, and select Replace.

Concentrating Your Search with Regular Expressions

As powerful as all the other Find and Replace features are, they are boosted to a higher level of flexibility with the addition of regular expressions. I've referred to regular expressions as being similar to wildcards in other programs, but their capabilities are actually far more extensive.

Regular expressions are best described as a *text pattern matching system*. If you can identify any pattern in your text, you can manipulate it with regular expressions. What kind of pattern? Imagine you have a spreadsheet-like table with lots of numbers, showing both dollars and cents, mixed with explanatory text. With regular expressions, you can match the pattern formed by the dollar sign and the decimal point and reformat the entire table, turning all the figures deep blue with a new font — all in one Find and Replace operation.

Note   If you're into Unix, you recognize regular expressions as being very close to the grep utility — *grep*, by the way, stands for Get Regular Expressions and Print. The Find and Replace feature in BBEdit, available only on a Macintosh, also features a grep-like syntax.

You can apply regular expressions to any of the types of Find and Replace operations previously discussed by just clicking the Use Regular Expressions checkbox. Note that when you select Use Regular Expressions, the Ignore Whitespace Differences option is deselected. This is because the two options are mutually exclusive.

The most basic regular expression is the text itself. If you enable the feature and then enter **th** in the Search text field, Dreamweaver locates every example of *th* in the text and/or source. Although this capability by itself has little use beyond what you can also achieve with standard Find and Replace operations, it's important to remember this functionality as you begin to build your patterns.

Caution   When entering text in the Search field of the Find and Replace dialog box, do not include any extra spaces after your search string. Dreamweaver interprets the spaces as part of your search string, and the search only finds your text when it is followed by a space.

Wildcard Characters

Initially, it's helpful to be able to use what are traditionally known as *wildcards* — characters that match certain different types of characters. The wildcards in regular expressions represent single characters and are described in Table 8-3. In other words, no single regular expression represents all the characters, as the asterisk does when used in PC file searches (such as *.*). However, such a condition can be represented with a slightly more complex regular expression (described later in this section).

Table 8-3: Regular Expression Wildcard Characters

Character	Matches	Example
.	Any single character, including letters, numbers, spaces, punctuation, control characters (like line feed), and so on	**w.c** matches **wac**ky and How **c**ould you? but not watch.
\w	Any single alphanumeric character, including the underscore	**w\wc** matches **wac**ky and **W3C** but not How could you?
\W	Any single non-alphanumeric character	**jboy\Widest.com** matches **jboy@idest.com.**
\d	Any single numeric character 0–9	**y\dk** matches **Y2K.**
\D	Any single nonnumeric character	**\D2\D** matches **Y2K** and **H2O.**
\s	Any single whitespace character, including space, nonbreaking space, tab, form feed, or line feed	**\smedia** matches the **media** but not Macromedia.
\S	Any single non-whitespace character	**\Smedia** matches Macr**omedia** but not the media.
\t	A tab character	Matches any single tab character in the HTML source.
\f	Form feed	Matches any single form-feed character in the HTML source.
		A form feed is a control character used to force a page break when printing. Although unlikely, it is possible for this character to appear in your HTML document if you converted a print document to HTML. Most browsers ignore the form-feed character, but you might want to search for and remove the form feed using the \f regular expression. A form feed is more likely to occur in a text document.
\n	Line feed	Matches any single line-feed character in the HTML source.
\r	Carriage return	Matches any single carriage-return character in the HTML source.

Tip   The backslash character (\) is used to escape special characters so that they can be included in a search. For example, if you want to look for an asterisk, you need to specify it as follows: *. Likewise, when trying to find the backslash character, precede it with another backslash character: \\.

Matching Character Positions and Repeating Characters

With regular expressions, not only can you match the type of character, but you can also match its position in the text. This feature enables you to perform operations on characters at the beginning, end, or middle of the word or line. Regular expressions also enable you to find instances in which a character is repeated an unspecified number of times or a specific number of times. Combined, these features broaden the scope of the patterns that can be found. Table 8-4 details the options available for matching by text placement and character repetition.

Table 8-4: Regular Expression Character Positions and Repeating Characters

Character	Matches	Example
^	If searching text in the current document, this only finds the search string if it immediately follows the cursor. If searching source code or searching text in multiple documents, this regular expression only finds the search string if it beginning document.	If searching text in the current document, **^I** matches the first **I** in *Call me Ishmael.* only if the cursor is positioned after the *a* in the word *Call*. Clicking Find Next would find the second **I** in *Call*, but clicking Next again would not find the **I** in *Ishmael* because the character of the is at the immediately following the cursor is not an **I**. If searching source code, **^<** matches the opening **<** in the *HTML <!DOCTYPE . . . >* statement, assuming the **<** is the first character in the document.
$	End of a document	**d$** matches the final **d** in *Be afraid. Be very afraid* if that is the last character in the document.
\b	A word boundary, such as a space or carriage return.	**\btext** matches ***text****book* but not *SimpleText*.
\B	A nonword boundary inside a word.	**\Btext** matches *Simple**Text*** but not *textbook*.
*	The preceding character zero or more times.	**b*c** matches ***BB****C* and *the* **c***old*. In the first example, both **B**'s and the **C** match because the expression **b*c** causes Dreamweaver to look for any number of **b**'s followed by a **c**. In the second example, only the **c** matches because **b*** means to search for zero or more instances of the **b**.
+	The preceding character one or more times.	**b+c** matches ***BBC*** but not *cold*.
?	The preceding character zero or one time.	**ac?e** matches ***ace*** and ***aerie*** but not *axiomatic*.
{n}	Exactly *n* instances of the preceding character.	**e{2}** matches *r**ee**d* and each pair of two **e**'s in *Ai**ee****ee****ee**!*; but nothing in *Dreamweaver*.
{n,m}	A minimum of *n* and a maximum of *m* instances of the preceding character.	**C{2,4}** matches #***CC****00FF* and #***CCCC****00*, but not the full string #*CCCCCC*. If you searched with the regular expression **C{2,4}**, it would first locate the first four **C**'s in the string #*CCCCCC*. If you clicked Find Next, the search would locate the last two **C**'s in the string because the search is looking for two, three, or four **C**'s in a row.

Matching Character Ranges

Beyond single characters, or repetitions of single characters, regular expressions incorporate the capability of finding or excluding ranges of characters. This feature is particularly useful when you're working with groups of names or titles. Ranges are specified in set brackets. A match is made when any one of the characters within the set brackets, not necessarily all the characters, is found. Descriptions of how to match character ranges with regular expressions can be found in Table 8-5.

Table 8-5: Regular Expression Character Ranges

Character	Matches	Example
[abc]	Any one of the characters a, b, or c	**[lmrt]** matches the individual **l** and **m**'s in *lemmings,* and the **r** and **t** in *roadtrip.*
[^abc]	Any character except a, b, or c	**[^etc]** matches each character in **GIFs,** but not *etc* in the phrase **GIFs** *etc.*
[a-z]	Any character in the range from a to z	**[l-p]** matches **l** and **o** in *lowery,* and **m, n, o,** and **p** in *pointman.*
x|y	Either x or y	**boy|girl** matches both **boy** and **girl.**

Using Grouping with Regular Expressions

All the regular expressions described previously relate to finding a certain string of text within your documents. But after you've located a particular string using regular expressions, how can you use that particular string in the Replace With field? For example, the following list of names:

✦ John Jacob Jingleheimer Schmidt

✦ James T. Kirk

✦ Cara Fishman

can be rearranged so that the last name is first, separated by a comma, like this:

✦ Schmidt, John Jacob Jingleheimer

✦ Kirk, James T.

✦ Fishman, Cara

Dreamweaver enables replacement of regular expressions through grouping expressions. Grouping is perhaps the single most powerful concept in regular expressions. With it, any matched text pattern is easily manipulated. To group a text pattern, enclose it in parentheses in the Find text field. Regular expressions can manage up to nine grouped patterns. In the Replace text field, each grouped pattern is designated by a dollar sign ($) in front of a number (1–9) that indicates the position of the group. For example, enter **$3** in the Replace With box to represent the third grouped pattern in the Find box.

Caution

Remember that the dollar sign is also used after a character or pattern to indicate the last character in a line in a Find expression.

Table 8-6 shows how regular expressions use grouping.

Table 8-6: Regular Expressions Grouping

Character	Matches	Example
(p) (entered in the Find In box)	Any pattern p	**(\b\w*)\.(\w*\b)** matches two patterns, the first before a period and the second, after, such as in a filename with an extension. The backslash before the period escapes it so that it is not interpreted as a regular expression.
$1, $2 . . . $9 (entered in the Replace With box)	The *n*th pattern noted with parentheses	If the Search field contains the pattern **(\b\w*)\.(\w*\b)**, and the Replace With field contains the pattern **$1's extension is ".$2"**, *Chapter09.txt* would be replaced with ***Chapter09's extension is ".txt"***.

Controlling Whitespace

Whitespace refers to any portion of the page that doesn't contain text, images, or other objects. It includes the space between words and the space above and below paragraphs. This section introduces ways to adjust paragraph margins and the spacing between paragraphs.

Indenting Text

In Dreamweaver, you cannot indent text as you do with a word processor. Tabs normally have no effect in HTML. One method to indent a paragraph's first line uses nonbreaking spaces, which can be inserted with the keyboard shortcut Ctrl+Shift+Spacebar (Command+Shift+Spacebar). Nonbreaking spaces are an essential part of any Web designer's palette because they provide single-character spacing — often necessary to nudge an image or other object into alignment. You've already seen the code for a nonbreaking space —   — that Dreamweaver inserts between the <p>...</p> tag pair to make the line visible.

You can optionally configure Dreamweaver to insert nonbreaking spaces in situations where it would normally ignore the spaces that you type. For example, whenever you type more than one space in a row or when you enter a space at the beginning of a paragraph, HTML, and therefore Dreamweaver, ignores the space. However, if you choose Edit ➪ Preferences (Dreamweaver ➪ Preferences) and select the Allow Multiple Consecutive Spaces option in the General category, Dreamweaver inserts nonbreaking spaces automatically as you type. If you find yourself inserting nonbreaking spaces frequently, enabling this option speeds up your work. Use care when enabling this feature, however. If you are used to having extra spaces ignored, you may inadvertently add undesired spaces within your text.

Tip   If you normally create paper documentation, you may be used to adding two spaces between sentences. For online documentation, use only a single space after a period. Adding two spaces not only goes against the norm, it's more work and can increase your file size by inserting all those extra nonbreaking spaces!

Dreamweaver offers other methods for inserting a nonbreaking space. You can enter its character code —   — directly into the HTML code or you can use the Nonbreaking Space button in the Characters menu in the Text category of the Insert bar. You can also style your text as preformatted; this technique is discussed later in this chapter.

Tip Cascading Style Sheets offer another method for indenting the first line of a paragraph. You can set an existing HTML tag, such as <p>, to any indent amount using the Text Indent option found on the Block panel of the Style Sheet dialog box. You can find a full discussion of text indent and other style sheet controls in Chapter 7.

Working with Preformatted Text

Browsers ignore formatting niceties considered irrelevant to page content: tabs, extra line feeds, indents, and added whitespace. You can force browsers to read all the text, including whitespace, exactly as you have entered it by applying the preformatted tag pair <pre>...</pre>. This tag pair directs the browser to keep any additional whitespace encountered within the text. By default, the <pre>...</pre> tag pair also renders its content with a monospacefont such as Courier. For these reasons, the <pre>...</pre> tag pair was used to lay out text in columns in the early days of HTML before tables were widely available.

You can apply the preformatted tag through the Property inspector, the Insert bar, or the menus. Regardless of the technique for inserting preformatted text, it is easiest to work in Code and Design views — applying changes in Code view and seeing the result in Design view. Select the text, or position the cursor where you want the preformatted text to begin; then use one of these methods to insert the <pre>...</pre> tags:

✦ In the Property inspector, open the Format list box and choose Preformatted.

✦ On the Insert bar, choose the Text category and click the Preformatted Text button.

✦ Choose Text ⇨ Paragraph Format ⇨ Preformatted Text.

✦ Choose Insert ⇨ HTML ⇨ Text Objects ⇨ Preformatted Text.

The <pre> tag is a block element format, like the paragraph or the headings tags, rather than a style. This designation as a block element format has two important implications. First, you can't apply the <pre>...</pre> tag pair to part of a line; when you use this tag pair, the entire paragraph is altered. Second, you can apply styles to preformatted text — this enables you to increase the size or alter the font, but at the same time maintain the whitespace feature made possible with the <pre> tag. All text in Figure 8-9 uses the <pre> tag; the column on the left is the standard output with a monospace font; the column on the right uses a different font in a larger size.

The
 Tag

Just like headings, the paragraph tag falls into the class of HTML objects called *block elements*. As such, any text marked with the <p>...</p> tag pair is always rendered with an extra line above and below the text. To have a series of blank lines appear one after the other, use the break tag <br>.

Note In XHTML documents, the break tag is coded as <br />. Dreamweaver inserts the correct tag based on the document type.

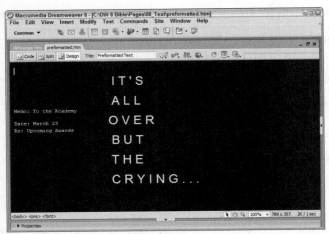

Figure 8-9: Preformatted text gives you full control over the line breaks, tabs, and other whitespace in your Web page.

Break tags are used within block elements, such as headings and paragraphs, to provide a line break where the `<br>` is inserted. Dreamweaver provides two ways to insert a `<br>` tag: Choose the Line Break button from the Characters menu in the Text category of the Insert bar, or use the keyboard shortcut Shift+Enter (Shift+Return).

Figure 8-10 demonstrates the effect of the `<br>` tag. The menu items in Column A on the left are the result of using the `<br>` tag within a paragraph. In Column B on the right, paragraph tags alone are used. The `<h1>` heading is also split at the top with a break tag to avoid the insertion of an unwanted line.

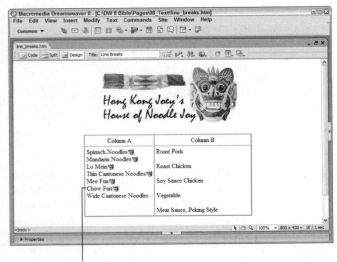

Line Break Symbol

Figure 8-10: Break tags, denoted by shield symbols, wrap your lines without the additional line spacing created by `<p>` tags.

Overcoming Line-Spacing Difficulties

Line spacing is a major issue and a common problem for Web designers. A design often calls for lines to be tightly spaced, but also to be of various sizes. If you use the break tag to separate your lines, you get the tight spacing required, but you won't be able to make each line a different heading size. As far as HTML and your browser are concerned, the text is still one block element, no matter how many line breaks are inserted. If, on the other hand, you make each line a separate paragraph or heading, the line spacing is unattractively *open*.

You can use one of several workarounds for this problem. First, if you're using line breaks, you can alter the size of each line by selecting it and choosing a different font size, either from the Property inspector or the Text ⇨ Size menu.

A second option renders all the text as a graphics object and inserts it as an image. This gives you total control over the font's appearance and line spacing, at the cost of added download time.

For a third possible solution, look at the section on preformatted text in this chapter. Because you can apply styles to a preformatted text block (which can include line breaks and extra white-space), you can alter the size, color, and font of each line, if necessary.

Ultimately, the best solution is to use Cascading Style Sheets (CSS). The majority of browsers now in use support line spacing through CSS; however, if 3.0 browser compatibility is a site requirement, use one of the other methods outlined here.

You can enable Dreamweaver to mark <br> tags with a symbol: a gold shield with the letters BR and the standard Enter/Return symbol. To make the break symbol visible, you must first choose Edit ⇨ Preferences (Dreamweaver ⇨ Preferences) and select the Line Breaks checkbox in the Invisible Elements category. Then show invisible elements by choosing View ⇨ Visual Aids ⇨ Invisible Elements.

Working with Microsoft Office Documents

The ubiquitous nature of Microsoft Office has intricately tied Word and Excel to the Web. Quite often, content stored in documents from these programs must be integrated into a Web page. Putting a meeting agenda drafted in Word or a production schedule laid out in Excel on the Web are just some of the tasks faced — and dreaded — by office personnel every day. Dreamweaver provides a number of methods to ease the transition from offline Office documents to online content. No matter the path you take, you'll have a range of options to paste your content how you want it to appear.

Copying and Pasting Office Content

Dreamweaver automatically converts material copied from Word and Excel into clean HTML. The procedure is truly transparent: Simply copy your content in either Word or Excel using the standard copy or cut commands, switch to Dreamweaver, and paste by choosing Edit ⇨ Paste or using the standard keyboard shortcut Ctrl+V (Command+V). The content is pasted according to the settings chosen in the Copy/Paste category of Preferences. These options are the same found in the Paste Special dialog box covered earlier in this chapter and in the following section, "Importing Office Documents."

Because Dreamweaver is actually converting material from one format to another, you may experience a short delay after pasting. If a great deal of conversion is needed — the more heavily the original content is formatted, the more conversion is required — Dreamweaver displays an alert to let you know that the operation might take some time and gives you the option to cancel.

Importing Office Documents

Existing Word or Excel files can be imported directly into Dreamweaver in a single operation. Dreamweaver automatically converts the content from the Office format to HTML. To begin an import operation, choose File ➪ Import and then either Word Document or Excel Document from the submenu.

The content is pasted according to the option chosen at import time. The available options are selected from a list at the bottom of the Import Word Document (see Figure 8-11) and Import Excel Document dialog boxes and echo those found in the Copy/Paste category of Preferences.

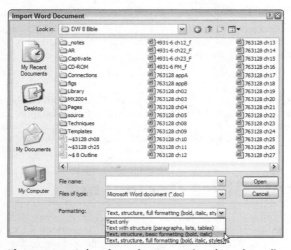

Figure 8-11: Select from the Formatting drop-down list.

✦ **Text Only:** Pastes completely unformatted text; even line breaks or paragraphs are removed.

✦ **Text with Structure:** Pastes unstyled text while retaining structured elements such as lists, paragraphs, line breaks, and tables.

✦ **Text, Structure, Basic Formatting:** Adds simple formatting, such as bold, italic, and underline, to structured text. If the text is copied from an HTML document, the pasted text retains any HTML text style tags, including `<b>`, `<i>`, `<u>`, `<strong>`, `<em>`, `<abbr>`, and `<acronym>`.

✦ **Text, Structure, Full Formatting:** Pasted text keeps all structure and formatting. If the copied text retains inline CSS styles, Dreamweaver pastes them as well.

✦ **Clean up Word Pagagraph Spacing:** Removes additional spaces between copied Word paragraphs; this option is available when either the Text with Structure or Text, Structure, Basic Formatting option is selected.

Excel documents are converted to tables with content formatted according to the options.

Dragging and Dropping Word and Excel Files

Not all Office documents are appropriate for converting to HTML. In some situations, it's best to leave the document in the original format and link to it from the Web page. Intranets — where access to Word or Excel is practically guaranteed and lengthy documents are the norm — are prime candidates for this type of design decision. Dreamweaver offers an easy way to make Office files Web accessible and gives you the option to use it as you see fit.

You've seen how a copy and paste operation from Word and/or Excel is relatively seamless. That's fine for material on the clipboard, but what about entire documents? Dreamweaver permits such Microsoft Office documents to be dragged and dropped right onto the page. What happens next for Windows users depends on the settings in Preferences. In the Office Copy/Paste category, you have two basic options: insert the content (formatted according to the standard options) or create a link to the document. On the Macintosh, a link is always created.

When an Office document is dragged onto the Web page (whether from the Files panel or the desktop), the Insert Document dialog box appears, as shown in Figure 8-12. If you opt to insert the file, Dreamweaver automatically converts the document according to the options selected. When you choose to create a link, a text link to the file is inserted.

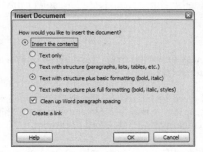

Figure 8-12: Drag and drop Office files wherever you'd like the converted document or link to appear.

Tip   Dreamweaver will remember the option chosen from one import operation to the other; these settings are independent of the choices made in the Copy/Paste category of Preferences.

Importing Word HTML

Microsoft Word has offered an option to save its documents as HTML since the release of Word 97. Unfortunately, Microsoft's version of HTML output is, at best, highly idiosyncratic. Although you could always open a Word HTML file in Dreamweaver, if you ever had to modify the page — which you almost always do — it took so long to find your way through the convoluted code that you were almost better off building the page from scratch. Fortunately, that's no longer the case with Dreamweaver.

Tip   Another reason to import an HTML file exported from Word, rather than just directly opening and editing it in Dreamweaver, is file size. Results vary, but importing a Word HTML document can reduce its size by half, or even more.

The capability to open and clean up Word HTML documents is a key workflow enhancement for Dreamweaver. Dreamweaver can successfully open and clean up files from Microsoft Word 97, Word 98, Word 2000, Word 2002, or Word 2003. You can even apply the current Code Format profile from Preferences so that the HTML is styled to look like native Dreamweaver code.

Naturally, before you can import a Word HTML file, you must create one. To export a document in HTML format in Word 97/98, you choose File ➪ Save as HTML; in Word 2000/2002, the command has changed to File ➪ Save as Web Page. Although the wording change may seem to be a move toward less jargon, it's significant what Word actually exports. Starting with Word 2000 (and all the Office 2000 products), Microsoft heartily embraced the XML standard and uses a combination of standard HTML and custom XML code throughout its exported Web pages. For example, here's the opening tag from a Word 2000 document, saved as a Web page:

```
<html xmlns:o="urn:schemas-microsoft-com:office:office"
xmlns:w="urn:schemas-microsoft-com:office:word"
xmlns:dt="uuid:C2F41010-65B3-11d1-A29F-00AA00C14882"
xmlns="http://www.w3.org/TR/REC-html40">
```

Dreamweaver alters the preceding code to

```
<html>
```

If you accept the defaults, bringing a Word HTML file into Dreamweaver is pretty easy:

1. Choose File ➪ Open. When the Select File dialog box opens, navigate and select the file that you exported from Word.

2. Choose Commands ➪ Clean Up Word HTML.

   Dreamweaver detects whether the HTML file was exported from Word 97/98 or Word 2000 or later and changes the interface options accordingly.

Caution   If Dreamweaver can't determine what version of Word generated the file, an alert appears. Although Dreamweaver still tries to clean up the code, it may not function correctly. The same alert appears if you inadvertently select a standard non-HTML Word document.

3. Select options as desired and click OK to confirm the import operation. Dreamweaver cleans up the code according to the options you've selected; for large documents, you may have to wait a noticeable amount of time for this operation to complete. If the Show Log On Completion option is selected, Dreamweaver informs you of the modifications made.

For most purposes, accepting the defaults is the best way to quickly bring in your Word HTML files. However, because Web designers have a wide range of code requirements, Dreamweaver provides a full set of options for tailoring the Word-to-Dreamweaver transformation to your liking. Two different sets of options exist: one for documents saved from Word 97/98 and one for those saved from Word 2000 or newer. The different sets of options can be seen on the Detailed tab of the Clean Up Word HTML dialog box; the Basic tab is the same for both file types. Table 8-7 details the Basic tab options, the Word 97/98 options, and the Word 2000 or newer options.

Table 8-7: Import Word HTML Options

Option	Description
Basic	
Remove all Word specific markup	Deletes all Word-specific tags, including Word XML, conditional tags, empty paragraphs, and margins in `<style>` tags.
Clean up CSS	Deletes Word-specific CSS code, including inline CSS styles where styles are nested, Microsoft Office (mso) designated styles, non-CSS style declarations, CSS style attributes from tables, and orphaned (unused) style definitions.
Clean up <font> tags	Deletes `<font>` tags that set the default body text to an absolute font size.
Fix invalidly nested tags	Deletes tags surrounding paragraph and block-level tags.
Set background color	Adds a background color to the page. Word normally doesn't supply one. The default added color is white (#ffffff). Colors can be entered as hexadecimal triplets with a leading hash mark or as valid color names, such as `red`.
	Dreamweaver sets the background color by adding the `bgcolor` attribute to the `<body>` tag. If you do not have to support older browsers, you may, instead, wish to assign a background color using Cascading Style Sheets, described in Chapter 7.
Apply source formatting	Formats the imported code according to the guidelines of the current Code Format profile set in Preferences.
Show log on completion	Displays a dialog box that lists all alterations when the process is complete.
Detailed Options for Word 97/98	
Remove Word specific markup	Enables the general clean-up of Word-inserted tags
Word meta and link tags from <head> document	Specifically enables Dreamweaver to remove Word-specific `<meta>` and `<link>` tags from the `<head>` section of a
Clean up <font> tags	Enables the general clean-up of `<font>` tags
Convert size [7-1] to	Specifies which tag, if any, is substituted for a `<font size=n>` tag. Options are
	* `<h1>` through `<h6>`
	* `<font size=1>` through `<font size=7>`
	* Default size
	* Don't change

Continued

Table 8-7 *(continued)*

Option	Description
Detailed Options for Word 2000 or newer	
Remove Word specific markup	Enables the general clean-up of Word-inserted tags
XML from <html> tag	Deletes the Word-generated XML from the `<html>` tag
Word meta and link tags from <head>	Specifically enables Dreamweaver to remove Word-specific `<meta>` and `<link>` tags from the `<head>` section of a document
Word XML markup	Enables the general clean-up of Word-inserted XML tags
<![if...]><![endif]> conditional tags and their contents	Removes all conditional statements
Remove empty paragraphs and margins from styles	Deletes `<p>` tags without a closing `</p>`, empty `<p></p>` pairs, and styles tags including margin attributes — for example, `style='margin-top:0in'`
Clean up CSS	Enables the general clean-up of Word-inserted CSS tags
Remove inline CSS styles when possible	Deletes redundant information in nested styles
Remove any style attribute that starts with "mso"	Eliminates Microsoft Office (mso) specific attributes
Remove any non-CSS style declaration	Deletes nonstandard style declarations
Remove all CSS styles from table rows and cells	Eliminates style information from `<table>`, `<tr>`, and `<td>` tags
Remove all unused style definitions	Deletes any declared styles that are not referenced in the page

Styling Your Text

Initially, the Internet was intended to make scientific data widely accessible. Soon it became apparent that even raw data could benefit from being styled contextually without detracting from the Internet's openness and universality. Over the short history of HTML, text styles have become increasingly important, and the W3C has sought to keep a balance between substance and style.

Dreamweaver enables the Web designer to apply the most popular HTML styles directly through the program's menus and Property inspector. Less prevalent styles can be inserted through the integrated text editors or by hand. All the styling techniques covered in this section can be applied to dynamically inserted text.

Depicting Various Styles

HTML contains two types of style tags that are philosophically different from each other: logical tags and physical tags. The physical tags describe what text looks like; these include tags for bold, italic, and underlined text. HTML's logical styles denote what the text represents (such as code, a citation, or something typed from the keyboard) rather than what the text will actually look like. The eventual displayed appearance of logical styles is up to the viewer's browser.

Logical styles can be described as structural. They are useful when you are working with documents from different sources — reports from different research laboratories around the country, for instance — and you want a certain conformity of style. If you are trying to achieve a particular look using logical styles, you should consider using the Cascading Style Sheets feature instead of, or in addition to, logical styles. You can apply logical style tags and then use Cascading Style Sheets to define how that style will look when viewed in a browser.

Cross-Reference

The styles that can be applied through regular HTML are just the tip of the iceberg compared to the possibilities available using Cascading Style Sheets. For details about using this feature, see Chapter 7.

Whereas logical styles are utilitarian, physical styles such as boldface and italic are decorative or presentational. With the advent of Cascading Style Sheets, use of the physical style tags is no longer the preferred method of styling text. However, physical tags are still supported and are still very widely used. Even with Cascading Style Sheets, both physical and logical styles have their uses in material published on today's Web. In Dreamweaver, logical and physical style tags can be accessed by choosing Text ⇨ Style and selecting from the available style name options. A checkmark appears next to the selected tags. Style tags can be nested (put inside one another), and you can mix logical and physical tags within a word, line, or document. You can have a bold, strikethrough, variable style; or you can have an underlined, cited style. (Both variable and cite are particular logical styles covered later in this section.)

Note

You can also add the most commonly used styles — bold, italic, strong, and emphasis — by clicking the appropriate button in the Text category of the Insert bar.

Figure 8-13 compares how styles are rendered in Dreamweaver, Internet Explorer 6.0, and Mozilla Firefox. Although the various renderings are mostly the same, notice the subtle difference between how the Keyboard style is rendered in Dreamweaver (far left) and in either browser. The various styles may be rendered quite a bit differently in other browsers and other browser versions.

Two of the physical style tags — bold and italic — are controlled by a Preferences setting. Although you can use the <b> and <i> tags to style text, it is considered better practice to use the equivalent logical tags, <strong> and <em>. Dreamweaver enables you to specify which tags to use via the Use <strong> And <em> In Place Of <b> And <i> option in the General category of Preferences. If this option is checked (the default), <strong> and <em> tags are used to code bold or italic text, respectively; if the option is clear, <b> and <i> tags are used.

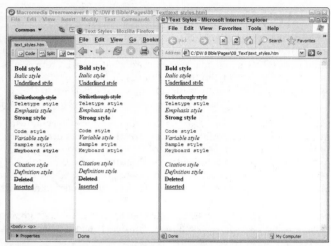

Figure 8-13: In this comparison chart, the various renderings of style tags are from Dreamweaver, Mozilla Firefox, and Internet Explorer 6.0 (from left to right, respectively).

To actually apply bold or italic formatting using either the logical or physical tags, select the text and then click the Bold or Italic button on the Text Property inspector, or use the keyboard shortcuts (Ctrl+B (Command+B) and Ctrl+I (Command+I), respectively). Buttons for bold, italic, strong, and emphasis are also available in the Text category of the Insert bar. If the General Preference setting (discussed previously) is set, then the Bold button on the Insert bar does the same thing as the Strong button, and the Italic button inserts the same code as the Emphasis button.

Caution　One physical style, the underline tag, ⟨u⟩, is available only through the Text ⇨ Style menu. Use this tag with caution. By default, browsers use underlining to designate links; if you style text with an underline, users expect that text to link somewhere. It's good practice to restrict use of underlining to hotspots, and to avoid underlining as a way to highlight text, even for headings.

Both physical and logical style tags are described in Table 8-8.

Table 8-8: Text Style Tags

Style	Tag	Description
Bold	⟨b⟩	Text is rendered with a bold style.
Italic	⟨i⟩	Text is rendered with an italic style.
Underline	⟨u⟩	Text is rendered underlined.
Strikethrough	⟨s⟩	Used primarily in edited documents to depict edited text. Usually rendered with a line through the text.

Style	Tag	Description
Teletype	`<tt>`	Used to represent an old-style typewriter. Rendered in a monospace font such as Courier.
Emphasis	`<em>`	Used to accentuate certain words relative to the surrounding text. Most often rendered in italic.
Strong	`<strong>`	Used to strongly accentuate certain words relative to the surrounding text. Most often rendered in boldface.
Code	`<code>`	Used to depict programming code, usually in a monospace font.
Variable	`<var>`	Used to mark variables in programming code. Most often displayed in italic.
Sample	`<samp>`	Used to display characters in a literal sequence, usually in a monospace font.
Keyboard	`<kbd>`	Used to indicate what the user should input. Often shown in a monospace font, sometimes in boldface.
Citation	`<cite>`	Used to mark citations, references, and titles. Most often displayed in italic.
Definition	`<dfn>`	Used to denote the first, defining instance of a term. Usually displayed in italic.
Deleted	`<del>`	Used to denote deleted text, to aid in document authoring and editing. You can often find these tags in documents imported from Word HTML files that used the Track Changes feature. Although not fully supported in some browser versions, this style is typically depicted as a line through the text.
Inserted	`<ins>`	Used to denote inserted text. Like the Deleted style, this is used during the authoring process to keep track of changes. You can often find these tags in documents imported from Word HTML files that used the Track Changes feature. The style is usually depicted as underlined text.

Using the \<address> Tag

Currently, Dreamweaver does not support one useful style tag: the `<address>` tag. Rendered as italic text by browsers, the `<address>`...`</address>` tag pair often marks the signature and e-mail address of a Web page's creator.

Note

An easy way to do this in Dreamweaver is to use the Quick Tag Editor. Select your text and then press Ctrl+T (Command+T) to automatically enter Wrap Tag mode. If Tag Hints is enabled, all you have to do is start typing **address,** and press Enter (Return) twice to accept the hint and confirm the tag. In Code view and the Code inspector, the `<address>`...`</address>` tag pair is also available as a Code Hint.

If you're applying the `<address>` tag to multiple lines, use `<br>` tags to form line breaks. The following example shows the proper use of the `<address>` tags:

```
<address><p>The President<br>
1600 Pennsylvania Avenue NW<br>
Washington, DC 20500</p></address>
```

This preceding code is shown on a Web browser as follows:

The President

1600 Pennsylvania Avenue NW

Washington, DC 20500

Tip   To remove a standard style, highlight the styled text, choose Text ➪ Style, and select the name of the style you want to remove. The checkmark disappears from the style name. To remove a nonstandard tag such as `<address>`, choose the tag in the Tag Selector and right-click (Control+click) to open the context menu; then select Remove Tag.

Adding Abbreviations and Acronyms

Two other tags worth noting designate abbreviations, `<abbr>...</abbr>`, and acronyms, `<acronym>...</acronym>`. The abbreviation or acronym is enclosed within the tag pair. Both tags include a `title` attribute, which is used to specify the full text of the abbreviation or acronym. The following code shows examples of both tags:

```
<abbr title="Incorporated">Inc.</abbr>
<acronym title="Object-oriented Programming">OOP</acronym>
```

The `<abbr>` and `<acronym>` tags are relatively new and are not yet widely used. These tags are not intended to actually change the visual style of the text in a browser, but instead they enable programs that process the document to clearly identify acronyms and abbreviations. For example, in the future, words marked as abbreviations could allow non-visual browsers to read the expanded word, rather than sounding out the abbreviation. If designated as an abbreviation, the letters *PA* could be read as *Pennsylvania* rather than as the word *pa*. In the future, this tag could also be used to provide alternate text for search engines, spell checkers, and translation programs.

In Dreamweaver, you can insert acronyms or abbreviations by clicking the Acronym or Abbreviation button on the Text category of the Insert bar. You can also choose the appropriate command from the Insert ➪ HTML ➪ Text Objects menu. These commands open a dialog box where you can enter the expanded text for the acronym or abbreviation.

Modifying Text Format

As a Web designer, you easily spend at least as much time adjusting your text as you do getting it into your Web pages. Luckily, Dreamweaver puts most of the tools you need for this task right at your fingertips. Many of the text-formatting options are available through the Text Property inspector or the Tag inspector, whether you're styling your text in CSS or HTML `<font>` tags.

On the Web today, designers have largely moved to using Cascading Style Sheets and away from hard-coding text with `<font>` and other tags. Both 4.0+ versions of the major Web browsers support Cascading Style Sheets to some extent, and Internet Explorer has had some support since version 3.0. Text formatting enjoys the most widespread browser support of all the CSS rules.

Although CSS is now the preferred method of styling text — as well as the rest of the page — you may still encounter `<font>` tags in legacy pages. Dreamweaver allows you to work in both styles: To switch from the default CSS style properties, choose Edit ➪ Preferences (Dreamweaver ➪ Preferences) and, from the General category, deselect the Use CSS Instead Of HTML Tags option. The following section discusses working in both modes.

Cross-Reference   Refer to Chapter 7 if you're new to CSS and looking for a little background on how to create and apply styles.

Adjusting Font Size

Whether you're using CSS or `<font>` tags to format your text, you can alter its size in a variety of ways. Both methods allow you to specify text size in either an absolute or a relative measurement. You can also size any amount of text, from a single character to an entire page, with both techniques.

Sizing with CSS

The best-practice route for setting font size with CSS is to apply an existing style — declared either in an internal or external style sheet — to a tag or selection of text. However, you can also select a value from the Size field of the Property inspector as shown in Figure 8-14. If no style has been previously attached to the selection, Dreamweaver automatically creates an internal style named style*N* where *N* is an incremented number. For example, the first style created in this fashion is named style1 and the second style2, and so on. After the automatically generated style is created, you can apply it to other selections.

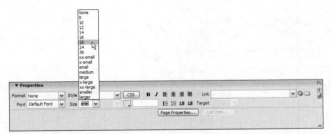

Figure 8-14: If the text size you want is not listed, you can enter it into the Size field.

In CSS, the aptly named `font-size` property controls the size of the text. When declared in a selector, `font-size` is used like this

```
h1 { font-size: 36px; }
```

or like this

```
#mainsidebar { font-size: 1.2em; }
```

or this

```
.legal { font-size: xx-small; }
```

As you can see, the `font-size` value may be a precise value (36px), a percentage (1.2em), or an absolute-size keyword (xx-small). In addition to pixels — abbreviated as px — CSS supports other measurement systems: points (pt), inches (in), centimeters (cm), millimeters (mm), and picas (pc).

Tip

Many designers advocate using pixel measurements as a way to achieve a consistent look and feel across browsers.

CSS provides three different relative-based measurement systems for sizing text: em, ex, and percentage (%). All three assume that a specific font size has been declared for the parent or containing tag; if no specific font size is defined, the default setting of the parent's font size is used for comparison. A font-size of `1em` is equivalent to whatever the containing tag's font-size is; for example, if the containing `<div>` tag has a font-size of 20px, a selector with a font-size set to `1.2em` is rendered as `24px` — because 20 times 1.2 is equal to 24. Percentage measurements work exactly the same way as em measurements; `1.2%` is the same as `1.2em`.

The `ex` measurement, however, is quite different. Short for x-height, the `ex` measurement system is based on the height of a lowercase x in the current font. Character heights vary quite substantially from one font to another: At 72 pixels, an x in Times is about 32px high whereas in Arial, it's almost 40px. Because of the widely varying differences, the `ex` measurement system is rarely used.

There are seven `font-size` keywords, which correspond to the HTML size attribute values 1–7. The two are similar in that both rely on the browser for final size interpretation, and the sizes for both are relative to each other, as shown in Figure 8-15.

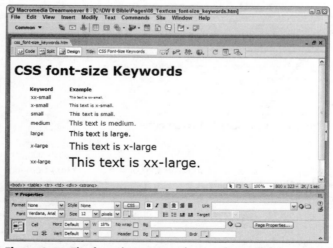

Figure 8-15: The font-size property keywords parallel the `<font>` tag's size attribute values.

CSS specifications include two additional keywords: larger and smaller. These relative-based keywords are obviously intended to be used in relation to the current font size. For example, in a <div> where the font-size value is 10px, any text whose font-size value is larger would be rendered at about 12px, whereas a smaller value would display text at 8px.

In Dreamweaver, the font-size property is set in the Type category of the CSS Rule Definition dialog box or in the Relevant CSS category of the Tag inspector.

Applying <font> Sizes

When you work with <font> tags, the six HTML heading types enable you to assign relative sizes to a line or to an entire paragraph. In addition, HTML gives you a finer degree of control through the size attribute of the font tag. In contrast to publishing or CSS environments, both traditional and desktop, font size is not specified in HTML with points. Rather, the <font> tag enables you to choose one of seven different explicit sizes that the browser can render (absolute sizing), or you can select one relative to the page's basic font. Figure 8-16 shows the default absolute and relative sizes, compared to a more page-designer–friendly point chart (accomplished with Dreamweaver's Cascading Style Sheets features).

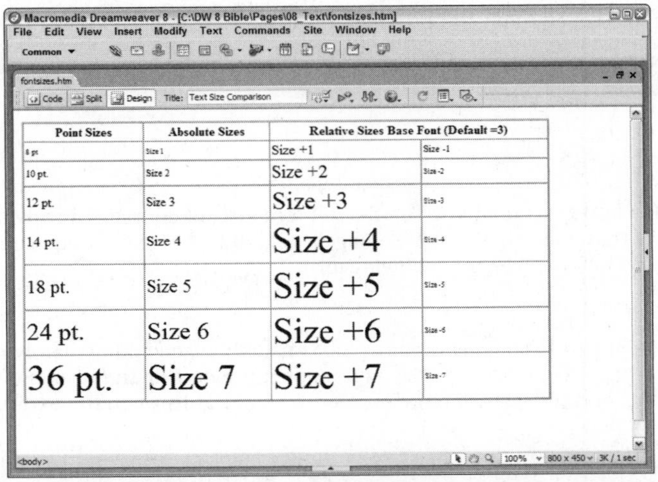

Figure 8-16: This chart shows the relationships between the various font sizes in an HTML browser as compared to real-world point sizes.

Which way should you go — absolute or relative? Some designers think that relative sizing gives them more options. As you can see by the chart in Figure 8-16, browsers are limited to displaying seven different sizes no matter what — unless you're using Cascading Style Sheets. Relative sizing does give you additional flexibility because you can resize all the fonts in an entire Web page with one command. Absolute sizes, however, are more straightforward to use and can be coded in Dreamweaver without any additional HTML programming. Once again, it's the designer's choice.

Absolute Size

You can assign an absolute font size through either the Property inspector or the menus. In both cases, you choose a value, 1 (smallest) through 7 (largest), to which you want to resize your text; you might note that this order is the reverse of the heading sizes, which range from H1 to H6, largest to smallest.

To use the Property inspector to pick an absolute font size, follow these steps:

1. Select your text.

2. In the Property inspector, open the Size drop-down list of options. If the Size drop-down list is not visible on the Text Property inspector, click the Toggle CSS/HTML Mode icon, located to the right of the Format drop-down list.

3. Choose a value from 1 to 7.

To pick an absolute font size from the menu, follow these steps:

1. Select your text.

2. Choose Text ➪ Size and pick a value from 1 to 7, or Default (which is 3).

Note   You can also click the Font Tag Editor button in the Text category of the Insert bar to adjust font size, color, and so on.

Relative Size

To what exactly are relative font sizes relative? The default font size, of course. The advantage of relative font sizes is that you can alter a Web page's default font size with one command, the `<basefont>` tag. The tag takes the following form

```
<basefont size="value">
```

where value is a number from 1 to 7. The `<basefont>` tag is usually placed immediately following the opening `<body>` tag. Dreamweaver does not support previewing the results of altering the `<basefont>` tag, and the tag has to be entered by hand or through the external editor.

You can distinguish a relative font size from an absolute font size by the plus or minus sign that precedes the value. The relative sizes are plus or minus the current `<basefont>` size. Thus, a `<font size="+1">` is normally rendered with a size 4 font because the default `<basefont>` is 3. If you include the following line in your Web page:

```
<basefont size="5">
```

text marked with a `<font size="+1">` is displayed with a size 6 font. Because browsers display only seven different size fonts with a `<basefont size="5">` setting — unless you're using Cascading Style Sheets — any relative size over `<font size="+2">` won't display differently when previewed in a browser.

Caution   If you change the basefont value, some browsers do not correctly handle relative font sizes for text within tables. In this case, you use absolute sizes. Also, Dreamweaver itself does not recognize the `<basefont>` tag; so to accurately see a page that uses relative sizes and the `<basefont>` tag, view it in a browser.

Relative font sizes can also be selected from either the Property inspector or the menus. To use the Property inspector to pick a relative font size, follow these steps:

1. Select your text or position the cursor where you want the new text size to begin.

2. In the Property inspector, open the Size drop-down list of options. If the Size drop-down list is not visible on the Text Property inspector, click the Toggle CSS/HTML Mode icon, located to the right of the Format drop-down list.

3. To increase the size of your text, choose a value from +1 through +7. To decrease the size of your text, choose a value from –1 to –7.

To pick a relative font size from the menus, follow these steps:

1. Select your text or position the cursor where you want the new text size to begin.

2. To increase the size of your text, choose Text ⇨ Size Change and pick a value from +1 to +4. To decrease the size of your text, choose Text ⇨ Size Change and pick a value from –1 to –3. Note that the full range of relative sizes (+1 to +7 and –1 to –7) is not available through the Size Change menu because Dreamweaver assumes the base font value is 3.

Adding Font Color

Unless you assign a color to text on your Web page, the browser uses its own default, typically black. To change the font color for the entire page, choose Modify ⇨ Page Properties and select a new color from the Text Color swatch. If your Preferences are set to use CSS, the style is written into an internal style sheet for `body`, `td`, and `th` selectors; otherwise, the `color` attribute is added to the `<body>` tag.

You can also apply color to individual headings, words, or paragraphs that you have selected in Dreamweaver. As with text size, when working with CSS the best way to set a color for a selected tag or text range is to apply an existing style that includes the desired color. Font color is defined through the Type category of the CSS Rule Definition dialog or the color attribute of the Tag inspector's Relevant CSS category.

Whether working in CSS or `<font>` tags, text color is expressed in either a hexadecimal color number or a color name. The hexadecimal color number is based on the color's red-green-blue value and is written like this:

    #FFFFFF

The preceding represents the color white. You can also use standard color names instead of the hexadecimal color numbers. A sample color code line follows:

    I'm <font color="green">GREEN</font> with envy.

In CSS, the same `color` attribute is used, but written somewhat differently:

    .envy {color:green;}

Again, you have several ways to add color to your text in Dreamweaver. Click the color box in the Property inspector to display the color picker, displaying a limited palette of colors. Clicking the System Color Picker button in the color picker enables you to choose from a full-spectrum Color dialog box.

Tip

If you want to apply the same color that you've already used elsewhere in your site to your text, you can display the Color category on the Assets panel (choose Window ➪ Assets). Just select the text in the Document window, select the color swatch in the Assets panel, and click the Apply button in the Assets panel. Only colors applied via <font> tags are shown in the Assets panel.

If you approach your coloring task via the menus, the Text ➪ Color command takes you immediately to the Color dialog box. To use the Property inspector to color a range of text, follow these steps:

1. Select the text you want to color, or position the cursor where you want the new text color to begin. If you're using CSS, a <span> tag is applied with auto-generated style (style1).

2. From the Property inspector, you can

   - Type a hexadecimal color number directly into the Text Color text field
   - Type a color name directly into the Text Color text field
   - Select the color box to open the color picker

3. If you chose to type a color name or number directly into the Text Color text field, press Tab or click in the Document window to see the color applied.

4. If you clicked the color box, select your color from the palette of colors available. As you move your pointer over the color swatches, Dreamweaver displays the color and the color's hexadecimal number above.

5. For a wider color selection, open the Color dialog box by selecting the System Color Picker icon in the upper-right corner of the color picker.

To access the full-spectrum color picker in Windows, follow these steps:

1. Select your text or position your cursor where you want the new text color to begin.

2. Choose Text ➪ Color to open the Color dialog box, shown in Figure 8-17.

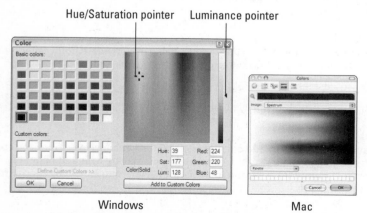

Figure 8-17: Use the Color (Colors) dialog box to choose a color for your font outside of the browser-safe palette.

3. Select one of the 48 preset standard colors from the color swatches on the left of the Color dialog box, or use either of the following methods:

   • Select a color by moving the Hue/Saturation pointer and the Luminance pointer.

   • Enter decimal values directly into either the Red, Green, and Blue boxes or the Hue, Saturation, and Luminance boxes.

4. If you create a custom color, you can add it to your palette by clicking Add To Custom Colors. You can add up to 16 custom colors.

5. Click OK when you are finished.

Caution

When you add a custom color to your palette in Windows, the new color swatch goes into the currently selected swatch or, if no swatch is selected, the next available swatch. Make sure you have selected an empty or replaceable swatch before clicking the Add To Custom Colors button. To clear the custom colors, first set the palette to white by bringing the Luminance slider all the way to the top. Then, click the Add To Custom Colors button until all the color swatch text fields are empty.

Dreamweaver's Color Pickers

Dreamweaver includes a color picker for selecting colors for all manner of HTML elements: text, table cells, and page background. Dreamweaver's color picker — in keeping with the Macromedia common user interface — offers a number of palettes from the context menu from which to choose your colors: Color Cubes, Continuous Tone, Windows OS, Mac OS, and Grayscale. The most common choices for Web designers are Color Cubes and Continuous Tone, both of which display the 216 Web-safe colors common to the Macintosh and Windows palettes.

After you've opened the text color picker by selecting the color box on the Property inspector, the cursor changes shape into an eyedropper. This eyedropper can sample colors from any of the displayed swatches or from any color onscreen. Simply click the color box and drag the eyedropper over any graphic to choose a color.

If you choose a color outside of the safe range, you have no assurances of how the color is rendered on a viewer's browser. Some systems select the closest color in RGB values; some use dithering (positioning two or more colors next to each other to simulate another color) to try to overcome the limitations of the current screen color depth. Therefore, be forewarned: If possible, stick with the browser-safe colors, especially when coloring text. Select the Snap-To-Web–Safe option in the color picker's context menu to automatically convert the colors you choose to the closest browser-safe color.

Mac Users: Bring up the system color picker by clicking the System Color Picker button on the Dreamweaver color picker. The system color picker for Macintosh is far more elaborate than the one available for Windows. The Mac version has several color schemes to use: CMYK (for print-related colors), RGB (for screen-based colors), HTML (for Web-based colors), and Crayon (for kid-like colors). The CMYK, HTML, and RGB systems offer you color swatches and three or four sliders with text-entry boxes; they accept percentage values for RGB and CMYK, and hex values for HTML. Depending on your OS version, one or more of the color systems also have a Snap-To-Web color option for matching your chosen color to the closest browser-safe color. The Hue, Saturation, and Brightness sliders also have color wheels.

To access the full-spectrum color picker in Macintosh systems (see Figure 8-17), follow these steps:

1. Select the text or position your cursor where you want the new text color to begin.

2. Choose Text ⇨ Color to open the Color dialog box.

3. In the Macintosh color picker, the list of available pickers is displayed across the top of the dialog like a toolbar, and each particular interface's options are shown below as they are selected. Choose a color picker, by clicking on its icon in the top toolbar, and create the color you want in the rest of the dialog below.

   The number and type of color pickers vary from system to system, depending on the version of the operating system and whether you've added any third-party color pickers.

4. When you've found the desired color, click OK.

Assigning a Specific Font

Along with size and color, you can also specify the typeface in which you want particular text to be rendered. Because of HTML's unique way of handling fonts, Dreamweaver uses a special method for choosing font names for a range of selected text. Before you learn how to change a typeface in Dreamweaver, you should more fully examine how fonts in HTML work.

About HTML Fonts

Page layout designers can incorporate as many different fonts as available to their own systems. Web layout designers, on the other hand, can use only those fonts on their viewers' systems. If you designate a paragraph to be in Bodoni Bold Condensed, for instance, and put it on the Web, the paragraph is displayed with that font only if that exact font is on the user's system. Otherwise, the browser uses the default system font, which is often Times or Times New Roman.

Fonts are specified with the `<font>` tag, aided by the `face` attribute. Because a designer can never be certain which fonts are on visitors' computers, HTML enables you to offer a number of options to the browser, as follows:

```
<font face="Arial, Helvetica, sans-serif">Swiss Maid Foundry</font>
```

The browser encountering the preceding tag first looks for the Arial font to render the enclosed text. If Arial isn't there, the browser looks for the next font in the list, which in this case is Helvetica. If it fails to find any of the specified fonts listed, the browser uses whichever font has been assigned to the category for the font — sans serif in this case.

Selecting a Font

The process for assigning a font name to a range of text is similar to that of assigning a font size or color. Instead of selecting one font name, however, you're usually selecting one font series. That series could contain three or more fonts as previously explained. Font series are chosen from the Font list in the CSS Rule Definition dialog's Text category, the Property inspector, or through a menu item. Dreamweaver enables you to assign any font on your system — or even any font you can name — to a font series, as covered in the section "Editing the Font List," later in this chapter.

Font Categories

The W3C and some Web browsers recognize five main categories of fonts. Although serif and sans serif are most commonly used, the most recent versions of Internet Explorer and Netscape Navigator support all five generic font categories. In some browsers, the user can control which fonts display for each category.

As illustrated in the following figure, the generic font categories include

✦ **Serif:** These fonts are distinguished by serifs, small cross-strokes that appear at the ends of the main strokes of each character. Serif fonts tend to be slightly easier to read on paper, but more difficult to read when viewed on a screen. You may want to limit use of serif fonts to headings or small blocks of text, unless your document is meant to be printed. Examples of serif fonts include Times New Roman, MS Georgia, and Garamond.

✦ **Sans serif:** These fonts are without serifs, meaning that the letters do not have finishing strokes at the tops and bottoms. Sans serif fonts are easier to read on a screen, and so they are a good choice for large blocks of text within a Web page. Sans serif fonts found on many computers include Arial, Helvetica, and Verdana.

✦ **Monospace:** The distinguishing characteristic of monospace fonts is that all their characters are the same width. These fonts are typically used to depict code samples or in other circumstances that require characters to be precisely aligned. Commonly used monospace fonts include Courier and Courier New.

✦ **Cursive:** These fonts simulate writing in long hand, with strokes joining adjacent letters in a word. Because they can be difficult to read onscreen, you should avoid using large blocks of cursive text. These fonts are more appropriate for page banners or headings, to provide an elegant tone for a Web page. Examples of cursive fonts are Zapf-Chancery and Lucida Handwriting.

✦ **Fantasy:** The characters in these fonts are highly decorative, but still represent letters and numbers (as opposed to pictures or symbols). As with Cursive fonts, you may not want to use these for large blocks of text, but rather employ them to lend emphasis or to set the tone for a page. Examples of Fantasy fonts include Curlz MT, Critter, and Jokerman.

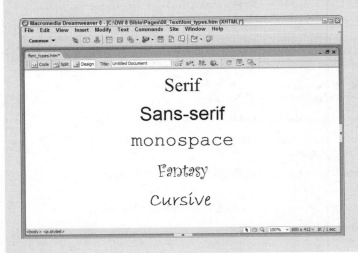

To assign a specific font series to your text, follow these steps:

1. Select the text or position your cursor where you want the new text font to begin.

2. From the Property inspector, open the drop-down list of font names. You can also display the list of fonts by choosing Text ➪ Font from the menu bar.

3. Select a font from the Font List. To return to the system font, choose Default Font from the list.

It's also possible to enter the font name or font series directly in the Property inspector's Font drop-down list box.

Editing the Font List

With the Edit Font List dialog box, Dreamweaver gives you a point-and-click interface for building your font lists. After the Edit Font List dialog box is open, you can delete an existing font series, add a new one, or change the order of the list so your favorite ones are on top. Figure 8-18 shows the sections of the Edit Font List dialog box: the current Font List, the Available Fonts on your system, and the Chosen Fonts. The Chosen Fonts are the individual fonts that you've selected to be incorporated into a font series.

Figure 8-18: Dreamweaver's Edit Font List dialog box gives you considerable control over the fonts that you can add to your Web page.

Follow these steps to construct a new font series and add it to the font list:

1. To open the Edit Font List dialog box, either expand the Font drop-down list in the Property inspector and select Edit Font List, or choose Text ➪ Font ➪ Edit Font List.

2. If the Chosen Fonts box is not empty, clear the Chosen Fonts box by clicking the Add (+) button at the top of the dialog box. You can also scroll down to the bottom of the current Font List and select (Add fonts in list below).

3. Select a font from the Available Fonts list. The font categories, such as sans serif and cursive, appear at the end of the available fonts list.

4. Click the << button to transfer the selected font to the Chosen Fonts list.

5. To remove a font you no longer want or have chosen in error, highlight it in the Chosen Fonts list and click the >> button.

6. Repeat steps 3 through 5 until the Chosen Fonts list contains the alternative fonts you want.

7. If you want to add another, separate font series, repeat steps 2 through 6.

8. Click OK when you are finished adding fonts.

To change the order in which font series are listed in the Font List, follow these steps:

1. In the Edit Font List dialog box, select the font series that you want to move.

2. If you want to move the series higher up the list, click the up arrow button at the top right of the Font List. If you want to move the series lower down the list, click the down arrow button.

To remove a font series from the current Font List, highlight it and click the Remove (–) button at the top-left of the list.

Remember that the fonts must be on your system to make them a part of your font list. To add a font unavailable on your computer, type the name of the font into the text field below the Available Fonts list and press Enter (Return).

Aligning Text

You can easily align text in Dreamweaver, just as you can in a traditional word processing program. HTML supports the alignment of text to the left or right margin, or in the center of the browser window. Another option, called Justify, causes text to be flush against both left and right margins, creating a block-like appearance. The Justify value is supported in browsers 4.0 and later on Windows platforms.

Like a word processing program, Dreamweaver aligns text one paragraph at a time. You can't left-align one word, center the next, and then right-align the third word in the same paragraph.

To align text, use one of several methods: a CSS style, a menu command, the Property inspector, or a keyboard shortcut. When declaring an alignment in CSS, select a value from the Text Align list found in the Block category of the CSS Rule Definition dialog box.

To use the menus, choose Text ⇨ Align and then pick the alignment you prefer (Left, Right, Center, or Justify). Figure 8-19 illustrates the Text Property inspector's Alignment buttons.

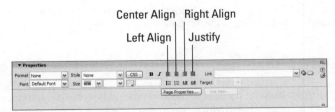

Figure 8-19: The Text Property inspector includes buttons to left align, center, right align, and justify your text.

The alignment keyboard shortcuts are as follows:

✦ **Left:** Ctrl+Alt+Shift+L (Command+Option+Shift+L)

✦ **Center:** Ctrl+Alt+Shift+C (Command+Option+Shift+C)

✦ **Right:** Ctrl+Alt+Shift+R (Command+Option+Shift+R)

✦ **Justify:** Ctrl+Alt+Shift+J (Command+Option+Shift+J)

Indenting Entire Paragraphs

HTML offers a tag that enables you to indent whole paragraphs, such as inset quotations or name-and-address blocks. Not too surprisingly, the tag used is called the `<blockquote>` tag. Dreamweaver gives you instant access to the `<blockquote>` tag through the Indent and Outdent buttons located on the Text Property inspector, as shown in Figure 8-20.

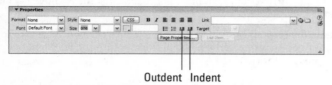

Outdent Indent

Figure 8-20: Indent and adjust the indentation of paragraphs and blocks of text by using the Indent and the Outdent buttons.

To indent one or more paragraphs, select them and click the Indent button in the Property inspector. Paragraphs can be indented multiple times; each time you click the Indent button, another `<blockquote>`...`</blockquote>` tag pair is added. Note that you can't control how much space a single `<blockquote>` indents a paragraph — that characteristic is determined by the browser.

You also have the option of indenting your paragraphs through the menus by choosing Text ➪ Indent. You can also add the `<blockquote>` tag by clicking the Blockquote button in the Text category of the Insert bar.

If you find that you have over-indented, use the Outdent button, also located on the Property inspector. The Outdent button has no effect if your text is already at the left edge. Alternatively, you can choose Text ➪ Outdent.

Tip   You can tell how many `<blockquote>` tags are being used to create a particular look by placing your cursor in the text and looking at the Tag Selector.

Incorporating Dates

With the Web constantly changing, keeping track of when information is updated is important. Dreamweaver includes a command that enables you to insert today's date in your page, in almost any format imaginable. Moreover, you can set the inserted date to be automatically updated every time the page is saved. This means that every time you make a modification to a page and save it, the current date is added.

The Insert Date command uses your system clock to get the current date. In addition, you can elect to add a day name (for example, Thursday) and the time to the basic date information. After the date text is inserted, it can be formatted like any other text — adding color or a specific font type or changing the date's size.

To insert the current date, follow these steps:

    1. Choose Insert ➪ Date or select the Date object from the Common category of the Insert bar. The Insert Date dialog box, shown in Figure 8-21, is displayed.

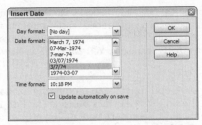

Figure 8-21: Keep track of when a file is updated by using the Date command.

2. If desired, select a Day Format to include in the date from the drop-down list. The options are as follows:

[No Day]	Thu
Thursday,	thu,
Thursday	thu
Thu,	

3. Select the desired date format from the drop-down list. The example formats are as follows:

March 7, 1974	7/03/74
07-Mar-1974	07.03.1974
7-mar-74	07.03.74
03/07/1974	7-03-1974
3/7/74	7 March, 1974
1974-03-07	74-03-07
7/3/74	

Tip
If you are creating Web pages for the global market, consider using the format designated by the 1974-03-07 example. This year-month-day format is an ISO (International Organization for Standardization) standard and is computer-sortable.

4. Select the desired time format, if any, from the drop-down list. The example formats are as follows:

[No Time]

10:18 PM

22:18

5. If you want the date modified to include the current date every time the file is saved, select the Update Automatically On Save option.

6. Click OK when you're finished.

Tip   It's easy to format an inserted date when the Update Automatically On Save option is *not* selected—it's just plain text, and the formatting can be added easily through the Text Property inspector. However, if the date is to be automatically updated, it's inserted as a special Macromedia data type with its own Property inspector. You can style it, however, by applying a CSS style.

If your date object includes the Automatic Update option, you can modify the format. Select the date and, in the Property inspector, click the Edit Date Format button. The Edit Date Format dialog box opens, which is nearly identical to the Insert Date dialog box, except the Update Automatically On Save option is not available.

Commenting Your Code

How do you know when to begin inserting comments into your HTML code? You know the first time you go back to an earlier Web page, look at the code, and say, "What on earth was I thinking?" You should plan ahead and develop the habit of commenting your code now.

Browsers run fine without your comments, but for any continued development — of the Web page or of yourself as a Webmaster — commenting your code is extremely beneficial. Sometimes, as in a corporate setting, Web pages are co-developed by teams of designers and programmers. In this situation, commenting your code may not just be a good idea; it may be required. An HTML comment looks like the following:

```
<!-- Created by Hummer Associates, Inc. -->
```

You're not restricted to any particular line length or number of lines for comments. The text included between the opening of the comment, <!--, and the closing, -->, can span regular paragraphs or HTML code. In fact, one of the most common uses for comments during the testing and debugging phase of page design is to *comment out* sections of code as a means of tracking down an elusive bug.

To insert a comment in Dreamweaver, first place your cursor in either the Document window or the Code inspector where you want the comment to appear. Then click the Comment button in the Common category of the Insert bar. This sequence opens the Comment dialog box, where you can type the desired text; click OK when you've finished. Figure 8-22 shows a completed comment in Design and Code views, with the corresponding Property inspector open.

By default, Dreamweaver inserts a Comment symbol in the Document window. You can hide the Comment symbol by choosing Edit ➪ Preferences (Dreamweaver ➪ Preferences) and then deselecting the Comments checkbox in the Invisible Elements category. You can also hide any displayed Invisibles by choosing View ➪ Visual Aids ➪ Invisible Elements or using the keyboard shortcut, Ctrl+Shift+I (Command+Shift+I).

You can also add a comment using the Snippets panel. To use this method, choose Window ➪ Snippets to open the panel and then expand the Comments folder. In the Document window, position the cursor where you want the comment to go. In the Snippets panel, double-click the type of comment you want to add or select the comment, and click the Insert button. If you are working in Code view, type your comment between the inserted tags. If you are working in Design view, select the Comment symbol; then, in the Comment Property inspector, replace any default text that Dreamweaver may have added with your comment.

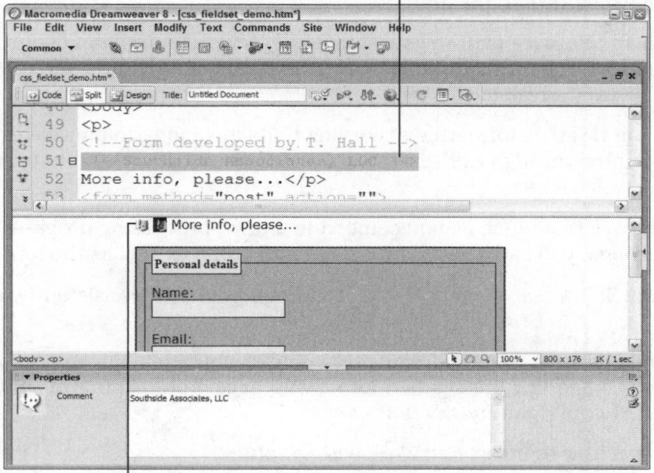

Comment in HTML code

Comment Symbol

Figure 8-22: Comments are extremely useful for inserting into the code information not visible on the rendered Web page.

Tip   The Snippets panel is really good for commenting out a section of code or text already on the page. With your code or text selected, choose the desired comment style and drop it right on your selection. Presto, chango — instant comments!

To edit a comment, double-click the Comment symbol to display the current comment in the Property inspector. A comment can be moved or duplicated by selecting its symbol and then using the Cut, Copy, and Paste commands under the Edit menu. You can also right-click (Control+click) the Comment symbol to display the context menu. Finally, you can click and drag Comment symbols to move the corresponding comment to a new location.

Summary

Learning to manipulate text is an essential design skill for creating Web pages. Dreamweaver gives you all the tools you need to insert and modify the full range of HTML text quickly and easily. As you work with text on your Web pages, keep these points in mind:

✦ HTML headings are available in six different sizes: <h1> through <h6>. Headings are used primarily as headlines and subheads to separate divisions of the Web page.

✦ Blocks of text are formatted with the paragraph tag <p>. Each paragraph is separated from the other paragraphs by a line of whitespace above and below. Use the line break tag, <br>, to make lines appear directly above or below one another.

✦ Dreamweaver offers a full complement of text-editing tools — everything from Cut and Paste to Find and Replace. Dreamweaver's separate Design and Code views make short work of switching between text and code.

✦ Dreamweaver's Find and Replace feature goes a long way toward automating your work on the current page as well as throughout the Web site. Both content and code can be searched in a basic or very advanced fashion.

✦ Where possible, text in HTML is formatted according to its meaning. Dreamweaver applies the styles selected through the Text ➪ Style menu. For most styles, the browser determines what the user views.

✦ You can format Web page text much as you can text in a word processing program. Within certain limitations, you can select a font's size and color, as well as the font face.

✦ Dreamweaver's HTML Styles feature enables you to format your text consistently and quickly.

✦ HTML comments are a useful (and often requisite) vehicle, which remains unseen by the casual viewer, for embedding information into a Web page. Comments can annotate program code or insert copyright information.

In the next chapter, you learn how to insert and work with graphics.

✦   ✦   ✦

Inserting Images

The Internet started as a text-based medium primarily used for sharing data among research scientists and among U.S. military commanders. Today, the Web is as visually appealing as any mass medium. Dreamweaver's power becomes even more apparent as you use its visual layout tools to incorporate background and foreground images into your Web page designs.

Completely baffled by all the various image formats out there? This chapter opens with an overview of the key Web-oriented graphics formats, including PNG. This chapter also covers techniques for incorporating both background and foreground images — and modifying them using the methods available in Dreamweaver. You also learn about animation graphics and how you can use them in your Web pages, plus techniques for creating rollover buttons and navigation bars.

Web Graphic Formats

If you've worked in the computer graphics field, you know that virtually every platform — as well as every paint and graphics program — has its own proprietary file format for images. One of the critical factors driving the Web's rapid, expansive growth is the use of cross-platform graphics. Regardless of the system you use to create your images, these versatile files ensure that the graphics can be viewed by all platforms.

The trade-off for universal acceptance of image files is a restricted field: just two file formats, with a possible third coming into view. Currently, only GIF and JPEG formats are fully supported by browsers. A third alternative, the PNG graphics format, is experiencing a growing acceptance.

You need to understand the uses and limitations of these formats to apply them successfully in Dreamweaver. The following sections look at the fundamentals.

GIF

The Graphics Interchange Format (GIF) was developed by CompuServe in the late 1980s to address the problem of cross-platform compatibility. With GIF viewers available for every system from PC and Macintosh to Amiga and NeXT, the GIF format became a natural choice for an inline (adjacent to text) image graphic. GIFs are bitmapped images, which means that each pixel is given or mapped to a specific color. You can have up to 256 colors for a GIF graphic. These images are generally used for line drawings, images of text, logos, or cartoons — anything that doesn't require thousands of colors for a smooth color blend, such as a photograph. With a proper graphics tool like Macromedia Fireworks, you can reduce the number of colors in a GIF image to a minimum, thereby compressing the file and reducing download time.

The GIF format has two varieties: regular (technically, GIF87a) and an enhanced version known as GIF89a. This improved GIF file brings three important attributes to the format. First, GIF89a supports transparency, whereby one or more colors can be set to automatically match the background color of the page containing the image. This property is necessary for creating nonrectangular-appearing images. Whenever you see a round or irregularly shaped logo or illustration on the Web, a rectangular frame is displayed as the image is loading — this is the actual size and shape of the graphic. The colors surrounding the irregularly shaped central image are set to transparent in a graphics-editing program (such as Macromedia Fireworks or Adobe Photoshop) before the image is saved in GIF89a format.

Note   Most of the latest versions of the popular graphic tools default to using GIF89a, so unless you're working with older, legacy images, you're not too likely to encounter the less flexible GIF87a format.

Although the outer area of a graphic seems to disappear with GIF89a, you won't be able to overlap your Web images using this format without using layers. Figure 9-1 demonstrates this situation. In this figure, the same image is presented twice — one lacks transparency, and one has transparency applied. The image on the left is saved as a standard GIF without transparency, and you can plainly see the shape of the full image. The image on the right was saved with the white background color made transparent, but while the central figure seems to float on the background, its full shape is still there.

Figure 9-1: The same image, saved without GIF transparency (left) and with GIF transparency (right).

The second valuable attribute contributed by GIF89a format is *interlacing*. One of the most common complaints about graphics on the Web is lengthy download times. Interlacing won't speed up your GIF downloads, but it gives your Web page visitors something to view other than a blank screen. A graphic saved with the interlacing feature turned on gives the appearance of developing, like an instant picture, as the file is downloading. Use of this design option is up to you and your clients. Some folks swear by it; others can't abide it.

Animation is the final advantage offered by the GIF89a format. Certain software programs enable you to group your GIF files together into one large page-flipping file. With this capability, you can bring simple animation to your page without additional plugins or helper applications. Unfortunately, the trade-off is that the files get very big, very fast. For more information about animated GIFs in Dreamweaver, see the section "Applying Simple Web Animation" later in this chapter.

JPEG

The JPEG format was developed by the Joint Photographic Experts Group specifically to handle photographic images. JPEGs offer millions of colors at 24 bits of color information available per pixel, as opposed to the GIF format's 256 colors and 8 bits. To make JPEGs usable, the large amount of color information must be compressed, which is accomplished by removing what the compression algorithm considers redundant information.

Note   JPEG files can be named with a file extension of `.jpg`, `.jpeg`, or `.jpe`. However, the most commonly used extension is `.jpg`.

The more compressed your JPEG file, the more degraded the image. When you first save a JPEG image, your graphics program asks you for the desired level of compression. For example, consider the three images shown in Figure 9-2 and compare the effects of JPEG compression ratios and resulting file sizes to the original image itself. Note, however, that results vary depending on the image. As you can probably tell, JPEG does an excellent job of compression so that even a substantial degree of compression has only minimal visible impact. Keep in mind that every graphic has its own reaction to compression.

JPEG - No compression - 26K   JPEG - 50% Compression - 6K   JPEG - 90% Compression - 2K

Figure 9-2: JPEG compression can save your Web visitors significant download time with little loss of image quality.

Tip   With the JPEG image-compression algorithm, the initial elements removed from a compressed image are the least noticeable. Subtle variations in brightness and hue are the first to disappear. When possible, preview your image in your graphics program while adjusting the compression level to observe the changes. With additional compression, the image grows darker and less varied in its color range.

If you use Fireworks as your graphics editor, you can optimize image file size without leaving Dreamweaver. See Chapter 23 to learn more.

With JPEGs, what is compressed for storage must be uncompressed for viewing. When a visitor's browser accesses a JPEG picture on your Web page, the image must first be downloaded to the browser and then uncompressed before it can be viewed. This dual process adds additional time to the Web-browsing process, but it is time well spent for photographic images.

Unlike GIFs, JPEGs have neither transparency nor animation features. A newer strand of JPEG called Progressive JPEG gives you the interlacing option of the GIF format, however. Although not all browsers support the interlacing feature of Progressive JPEG, they render the image regardless.

PNG

The latest entry into the Web graphics arena is the Portable Network Graphics format, or PNG. Combining the best of both worlds, PNG has lossless compression — meaning no pixels are lost when the file is compressed — like GIF, and is capable of rendering millions of colors, like JPEG. Moreover, PNG offers an interlacing scheme that appears much more quickly than either GIF or JPEG, as well as superior transparency support.

One valuable aspect of the PNG format enables the display of PNG pictures to appear more uniform across various computer platforms. Generally, graphics made on a PC look brighter on a Macintosh, and Mac-made images seem darker on a PC. PNG includes gamma correction capabilities that alter the image depending on the computer used by the viewer.

Before the 4.0 versions, the various browsers supported PNG only through plugins. After PNG was endorsed as a new Web graphics format by the W3C, both 4.0 versions of Netscape and Microsoft browsers added native, inline support of the new format for Windows. On Macs, PNG format is supported in Internet Explorer 5.2, Safari 1.0 and above, as well as Netscape 6 and above; Netscape 4.x browsers still require the plugin. Perhaps most important, however, Dreamweaver was among the first Web-authoring tools to offer native PNG support. Inserted PNG images are previewed in the Document window just like GIFs and JPEGs. Browser support for all PNG features is currently not widespread enough to warrant a total switch to the PNG format (image transparency is not fully supported in Internet Explorer for Windows, although it is promised for Internet Explorer 7), but its growing acceptance certainly bears watching.

 Tip

If you're excited about the potential of PNG, check out Macromedia's Fireworks, the first Web graphics tool to use PNG as its native format. Fireworks takes full advantage of PNG's alpha transparency features and enhanced palette.

Excellent resources for more information about the PNG format are the PNG home page at www.libpng.org/pub/png/ and the W3C's PNG page at www.w3.org/Graphics/PNG.

Using Inline Images

An inline image can appear directly next to text — literally in the same line. The capability to render inline images is one of the major innovations in the evolution of the World Wide Web. This section covers all the basics of inserting inline images and modifying their attributes using Dreamweaver.

Inserting Images

You can open and preview any graphic in a GIF, JPEG, or PNG format in Dreamweaver. You have many options for placing a graphic on your Web page:

✦ Position your cursor in the document, and from the Common category of the Insert bar, click the Image button.

✦ Position your cursor in the document, and from the menu bar, choose Insert ➪ Image.

✦ Position your cursor in the document and press Ctrl+Alt+I (Command+Option+I).

✦ Drag the Image button from the Images menu of the Insert bar's Common Category onto your page.

✦ Drag an icon from your file manager (Explorer on Windows or from the Finder or the Desktop on a Mac) or from the Files panel onto your page.

✦ Drag a thumbnail or filename from the Image category of the Assets panel onto your page. This capability is covered in detail in a subsequent section, "Dragging Images from the Assets Panel."

For all methods except those using the Assets panel or the file manager, Dreamweaver opens the Select Image Source dialog box (shown in Figure 9-3) and asks you for the path or address to your image file. Remember that in HTML, all graphics are stored in separate files linked from your Web page.

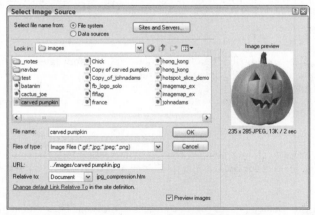

Figure 9-3: In the Select Image Source dialog box, you can keep track of your image's location relative to your current Web page.

Note   Dreamweaver's Select Image Source dialog box includes two main options at the top: Select File Name From File System or From Data Sources. This chapter covers inserting static images from the file system. For information about including dynamic images from data sources, see Chapter 19.

Whether you are choosing from the file system or a data source, the image's address can be a filename, a directory path and filename on your system, a directory path and filename on your remote system, or a full URL to a graphic on a completely separate Web server. The file doesn't need to be immediately available for the code to be inserted into your HTML.

New In Dreamweaver   If you've got an always-on Internet connection such as cable or DSL, Dreamweaver displays images referenced by absolute URLs right in Design view. Dreamweaver automatically reads and includes the width and height dimensions in the generated source code.

From the Select Image Source dialog box, you can browse to your image folder and preview images before you load them. If you are using Mac OS X, the image preview is automatically enabled. On Windows, select the Preview Images option.

In the lower portion of the dialog box, the URL text box displays the format of the address that Dreamweaver inserts into your code. Below the URL text box is the Relative To list box. Use it to declare an image relative to the document you're working on (the default) or relative to the site root. (After you've saved your document, you can see its name displayed beside the Relative To list box.)

When you insert an image, you may also see the Image Tag Accessibility Attributes dialog box, depending on your preference settings. See the section "Adding Image Descriptions" for more information about this dialog box.

Cross-Reference   To take full advantage of Dreamweaver's site management features, you must open a site, establish a local site root, and save the current Web page before beginning to insert images. For more information about how to begin a Dreamweaver project, see Chapter 5.

Relative to Document

After you've saved your Web page and chosen Relative to Document, Dreamweaver displays the address in the URL text box. If the image is located in a folder on the same level as or within your current site root folder, the address is formatted with just a path and filename. For instance, if you're inserting a graphic from the subfolder named Images, Dreamweaver inserts an address like the following:

```
images/logo.jpg
```

If you try to insert an image currently stored outside of the local site root folder, Dreamweaver automatically copies the image file to your Default Images Folder, specified when you first created the site.

Tip   To change the setting for your Default Images Folder, choose Site ➪ Manage Sites; and in the Manage Sites dialog box, select the current site and click Edit. In the Local Info category of the Advanced tab of the Site Definition dialog box, you can specify the Default Images Folder.

If your site does not include a Default Images Folder, you see the prompt window shown in Figure 9-4, asking if you want to copy the image to your local site root folder. If you click Yes, Dreamweaver gives you an opportunity to specify where the image should be saved within the local site. Whenever possible, keep all your images within the local site root folder so that Dreamweaver can handle site management efficiently.

Figure 9-4: Dreamweaver reminds you to keep all your graphics within the local site root folder for easy site management.

If you attempt to drag an out-of-site image file from the Files panel or from your file manager, and you click No to the prompt asking to copy the file to your site, the file is not inserted. If you attempt to insert the file using the Select Image Source dialog box and answer No, the file is inserted with the `src` attribute pointing to the path of the file. In this case, Dreamweaver appends a prefix that tells the browser to look on your local system for the file. For instance, the file listing looks like the following in Windows:

```
file:///C|/Dreamweaver/images/logo.jpg
```

whereas on the Macintosh, the same file is listed as follows:

```
file:///Macintosh HD/Dreamweaver/images/logo.jpg
```

Caution If you upload Web pages with this `file:///C|` (`file:///Macintosh HD`) prefix in place, the links to your images are broken. It is easy to miss this error during your testing. Because your local browser can find the referenced image on your system, even when you are browsing the remote site, the Web page appears perfect. However, anyone else browsing your Web site sees only placeholders for broken links. To avoid this error, always save your images within your local site.

Dreamweaver also appends the `file:///C|` prefix (or `file:///Macintosh HD` in Macintosh) if you haven't yet saved the document in which you are inserting the image. However, when you save the document, Dreamweaver automatically updates the image addresses to be document-relative.

Relative to Site Root

If you select Site Root in the Relative To field of the Select Image Source dialog box, and you are within your site root folder, Dreamweaver appends a leading forward slash to the directory in the path. The addition of this slash enables the browser to correctly read the address. Thus, the same `logo.jpg` file appears in both the URL text box and the HTML code as follows:

```
/images/logo.jpg
```

When you use site-root–relative addressing and you select a file outside of the site root, the image file is automatically copied to your Default Images Folder, if one exists. If your site does not have a Default Images Folder, you get a reminder from Dreamweaver about copying the file into your local site root folder — just as with document-relative addressing.

Making Images Dynamic

Once you're familiar with creating data source connections and establishing recordsets in Dreamweaver, you can display images dynamically. Dreamweaver doesn't actually insert images from a database, but rather inserts the path and filenames of the images—right into the `src` attribute of the `<img>` tag.

The data contained in the field can consist of just a filename, like `logo.gif`, or a path and filename, like `/images/logo.gif`. Under most circumstances, it's better to have just the filename; this structure provides the most flexibility because the path to the file can be prepended by Dreamweaver.

Follow these steps to include an image dynamically:

1. Make sure you have defined a recordset with at least one field consisting of paths to graphics.

2. Position your cursor where you want your dynamic image to appear.

3. From the Common category of the Insert bar, click Image. Alternatively, you can drag the Image button to the proper place on the page. In either case, the Select Image Source dialog box appears.

4. Navigate to any folder within your Local Root directory. Dreamweaver mishandles the insertion of the image from a data source if the dialog attempts to reference an image outside the site.

5. From the Select Image Source dialog box, Windows users should choose the Select File Name From Data Sources option at the top of the page. Macintosh users should click the Data Source button found just above the URL field.

6. If necessary, expand the data source to locate and select the appropriate image field. Dreamweaver places the code for inserting the dynamic image into the URL field.

7. If your image data (the paths to the images) contains spaces, tildes, or other nonstandard characters, the data must be encoded to be read properly by the server. From the Format list, select one of the following:

   Encode—Server.HTMLEncode (ASP JavaScript or Visual Basic)

   Encode—HTMLEncodedFormat (ASP C#)

   Encode—URLEncoded Format (ColdFusion)

   Encode—Response.EncodeURL (JSP)

8. If your data is stored as filenames only, enter any required path in the URL field before the existing code. The path information may be document-relative, site-root–relative, or absolute.

9. Click OK when you're finished.

Cross-Reference   For more details about using dynamic sources for your images, see Chapter 19.

Dragging Images from the Assets Panel

Web designers often work from a collection of images, much as a painter uses a palette of colors. Reusing images builds consistency in the site, making it easier for a visitor to navigate through it. However, trying to remember the differences between two versions of a logo — one named logo03.gif and another named logo03b.gif — used to require inserting them both to find the desired image. Dreamweaver eliminates the visual guesswork and simplifies the reuse of graphics with the Assets panel.

The Images category is key to the Assets panel. Not only does the Assets panel list all the GIF, JPEG, and PNG files found in your site — whether or not they are embedded in a Web page — selecting any graphic from the list instantly displays a thumbnail. Previewing the images makes it easy to select the proper one, and then all you need to do is drag it from the Assets panel onto the page.

Before you can use graphics from the Assets panel, you must inventory the site by choosing the Refresh Site List button, as shown in Figure 9-5. When you click the Refresh button (or choose Refresh Site List from the context menu on the Assets panel), Dreamweaver examines the current site and creates a list of the graphics, including their sizes, file types, and full paths. To see an image, just click its name, and a thumbnail appears in the preview area of the panel.

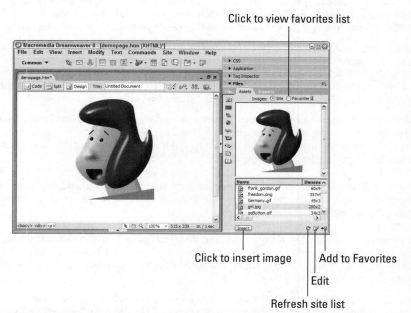

Figure 9-5: Reuse any graphic in your site or from your Favorites collection by dragging it from the Assets panel.

Tip

To increase the size of the thumbnail, make the preview area larger by dragging open the border between the preview and list areas and/or increasing the size of the entire panel. Dreamweaver enlarges the size of the thumbnail while maintaining the width:height ratio, so if you just move the border or resize the panel a little bit, you may not see a significant change. Thumbnails are never displayed larger than their actual size.

You can insert an image from the Assets panel onto your Web page in two ways:

✦ Drag the image or the file listing onto the page.

✦ Place your cursor where you'd like the image to appear. Select the image in the Assets panel and then click the Insert button.

Caution

Do not double-click the image or listing in the Assets panel to insert it onto the page; double-clicking invokes the designated graphics editor, be it Macromedia Fireworks, Adobe Photoshop, or another program, and opens that graphic for editing. From the Document window, Ctrl+double-clicking (Command+double-clicking) accomplishes the same thing.

The Dreamweaver Assets panel is designed to help you work efficiently with sites that contain many images. For example, in large sites, it's often difficult to scroll through all the graphics filenames looking for a particular image. To aid your search, Dreamweaver enables you to sort the Images category by any of the columns displayed in the Assets panel: Name, Size, Type, or Full Path. Clicking the column heading once sorts the assets in an ascending order by that criterion; click the column heading again to sort by that same criterion in a descending order.

You can also use the Favorites list to separately display your most frequently used images, giving you quicker access to them. To add an image to the Favorites list, select the image in the Assets panel, and then click the Add to Favorites button or select Add to Favorites from the Assets panel context menu. To retrieve an image from Favorites, first select the Favorites option at the top of the Assets panel. To switch back to the current site, choose the Site option.

Dreamweaver makes it easy to organize your favorite images by enabling you to create folders in the Favorites list. To create a folder, click the New Favorites Folder button in the Assets panel with the Favorites list displayed. Add images to the folder by dragging the image names in the Favorites list to the folder.

Note

Moving an image to a folder in your Favorites list does not change the physical location of the image file in your site. You can organize your Favorites list however you choose without disrupting the organization of files in your site.

If one or more objects are selected on the page, the inserted image is placed after the selection; Dreamweaver does not permit you to replace a selected image with another from the Assets panel. To change one image into another, double-click the graphic on the page to display the Select Image Source dialog box.

One final point about adding images from the Assets panel: If you reference a graphic from a location outside of the site, Dreamweaver asks that you copy the file from its current location. You must click the Refresh Site Files button to display this new image in the Assets panel.

Tip

When you click the Refresh button, Dreamweaver adds new images (and other assets) to the cache of current assets. If you add assets from outside of Dreamweaver — using, for example, a file manager — you might need to completely reload the Assets panel by Ctrl+clicking (Command+clicking) the Refresh button, or by selecting Recreate Site List from the Assets panel context menu.

Including Images

Dreamweaver offers a number of ways of inserting images. In this Dreamweaver Technique, you get to practice a number of common methods.

1. From the Techniques site, expand the 09_Images folder and open the `images_start` file.

2. Place your cursor in front of the first heading: Coming attractions.

3. From the Insert bar's Common category, choose Images: Image.

4. When the Select File dialog opens, navigate to the images folder in the root of the Techniques site and locate `blueprint.jpg`; click OK when you're ready.

5. In the Property inspector, choose imageLeft from the Style drop-down list.

6. You can also use the Assets panel to insert images from your site. Place your cursor in front of the second heading: Big house, big garage.

7. Choose Window ➪ Assets to bring the Assets panel to the front.

8. Select the Images category, the first icon on the left of the Assets panel.

9. Locate `under_contruction_01.jpg` and click Insert.

10. In the Property inspector, choose imageLeft from the Style drop-down list.

11. You can also simply drag images directly onto the page from the Files panel. In the panel, expand the images folder and drag `under_contruction_02.jpg` to the left of third heading, Room to Grow.

Continued

Continued

12. In the Property inspector, choose imageRight from the Style drop-down list.

Each of the methods demonstrated works well; use the one you're most comfortable with when adding graphics to a page.

Optimizing and Altering Images

It's the rare graphic that integrates into the Web page design unaltered. Digital photographs often need to be cropped and almost always need to be reduced — either in dimensions, file size, or both. Other images may need to be sharpened to achieve an immediate effect or lightened to fit better into the page palette. Dreamweaver provides several pathways to the perfect Web image:

✦ **Image editing within Dreamweaver:** Without even leaving Dreamweaver, you can crop, resample, sharpen, and alter brightness and contrast of any selected GIF or JPG graphic. You don't even have to have a graphics editor such as Fireworks installed. You'll see how shortly.

✦ **Graphic optimization through Fireworks within Dreamweaver:** For more sophisticated image operations — without full-scale editing — choose Optimize in Fireworks. A Fireworks-style dialog box opens within Dreamweaver where you can compare different outcomes before committing to a scaling, resampling, or conversion operation. You'll explore this option a little later in the "Employing the Optimize in Fireworks Command" section.

✦ **Round-trip editing from Dreamweaver to your graphics editor:** For the most complex image modifications, use an external graphics editor such as Adobe Photoshop or Fireworks. Dreamweaver sends files to the editor of your choosing.

The route you take depends on the depth of the modifications required. A key difference among these three different types of operations (one that you'll want to factor into your image-editing decision) is that the tools within Dreamweaver work on the actual graphic exported for Web use. After the page containing the image is saved, changes cannot be reversed. If Fireworks is your graphics editor, both the Optimize and Graphics Editor options can utilize the source files and create the exported file. The main advantage to using source graphics is that you have much greater control and flexibility; many types of changes can be done and undone as many times as needed. The primary disadvantage is that not all Web designers have the option to alter the source graphics.

Regardless of which route you choose, you'll find it's easy to get there. Dreamweaver has centralized access to all of the graphic tools in the most appropriate place — the Image Property inspector (see Figure 9-6).

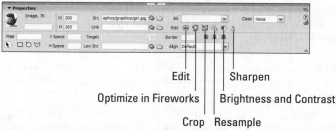

Figure 9-6: Dreamweaver includes a range of image-editing tools right on the Property inspector.

Begin your tour of Dreamweaver image altering options by looking at the built-in tools first.

Cropping Graphics

If you want to show only part of photograph in the real world, you'd use a pair of scissors to crop off what you don't want. With digital graphic tools, no scissors are needed. Images are cropped for two main reasons: to focus attention on a particular area or to reduce file size. Often these reasons work hand-in-glove because a cropped image is always smaller than the original in both physical dimensions and file size.

Dreamweaver's cropping tool is both powerful and easy to use. When you choose to crop a graphic, a shaded border appears within the graphic. The edges of the border can be dragged to determine how the image should be trimmed. The region outside the border is darkened, but you can still the full image so you can be sure a vital part of the graphic is not inadvertently cut.

To crop an image, follow these steps:

1. Select the image you want to crop.

2. In the Property inspector, click the Crop button.

3. Dreamweaver displays an alert to warn you that the cropping operation changes the selected image; click OK to clear the dialog. A shaded border appears within the selected image, as shown in Figure 9-7.

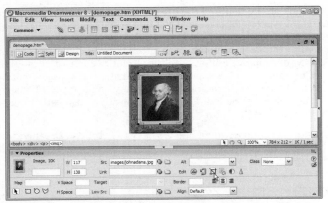

Figure 9-7: A positionable, shaded border appears so that you can crop your images on screen.

4. Drag the selection handles that appear in the middle of each side to crop the image in a single direction; the cursor changes to a two-headed arrow when in the correct position to crop a side.

5. To move the entire cropping area, drag the highlighted rectangle into the desired position; you can move the cropping area when the cursor is shown as a four-headed arrow.

6. To cancel the cropping operation, click anywhere outside the graphic.

7. Complete the crop by double-clicking within the image.

After cropping, you can reverse the effect by choosing Edit ➪ Undo — but only until the page is saved or sent to an external graphics editor.

Resampling after Resizing

Finding the perfect size for an image is often a matter of trial-and-error: It's important that a graphic work together with the entire page layout for maximum effect. Dreamweaver makes it easy to resize an image — just drag the sizing handles to the desired location. (You can find a complete discussion of Dreamweaver's resizing features later in this chapter in the "Adjusting Height and Width" section.) However, resizing an image in Dreamweaver is not the same as rescaling it in a graphics program; Dreamweaver merely draws the image to fit the chosen dimensions, much as a browser would. It doesn't actually re-create the graphic.

To get the cleanest, clearest representation of a resized graphic, you must resample the image. *Resampling* refers to the process of adding or subtracting pixels when the image is resized. If a graphic's dimensions are increased, pixels are formulaically added; make the image small and pixels are removed according to a similar algorithm. Dreamweaver includes a resampling option, which becomes available when an image is resized, either by dragging the sizing handles or changing the values in the Width and Height fields of the Property inspector.

Resampling in Dreamweaver is a one-click affair — no parameters are set. Just choose the resized image and click the Resample button on the Property inspector. As with the other built-in tools, an alert informs you that the graphics file is being changed (unless you've selected the Don't Show Me This Message Again option).

How the image resamples really depends on the image itself and the difference between the original image size and the new size. Sometimes, resampling in either direction results in satisfactory images (see Figure 9-8). Typically, I find that small differences work far better than large ones; if you're making a major change in image size, it's often better to use a dedicated graphics editor such as Fireworks or Photoshop.

Figure 9-8: These three images demonstrate how an image can be resampled after it has been reduced or increased in size.

Affecting Brightness and Contrast

Digital photography has opened the floodgates for posting images on the Web. Unfortunately, not all images look as good as they might. If you want to make the graphic lighter or darker or perhaps use a little more contrast, Dreamweaver has just the tool you need. The Brightness and Contrast command offers independent control over the two interlinked aspects of an image. Best of all, the Brightness/Contrast dialog box offers a Preview option, as shown in Figure 9-9, so that you can see the changes to the image in real-time.

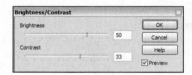

Figure 9-9: Preview the changes when using the Brightness and Contrast control to make sure you're getting the effect you want.

To alter the brightness and/or contrast of an image, follow these steps:

1. Select the image you want to modify.

2. Click the Brightness and Contrast button on the Property inspector. Dreamweaver displays the Brightness/Contrast dialog box.

3. Make sure the Preview box is selected to see the changes applied as you move the controls.

4. Drag the Brightness slider to the left or right; dragging the slider to the left lowers the brightness; dragging it to the right increases brightness. Alternatively, you can enter a value directly in the Brightness field. Acceptable values are from –100 to 100, with 0 being the default.

5. Move the Contrast slider to the right to increase the contrast or to the left to decrease it. Alternatively, you can enter a value between –100 and 100 in the Contrast field.

6. When you're finished, click OK.

Although Brightness and Contrast is most frequently associated with photographic JPG images, it can also be used for GIFs. However, be careful if your GIF has a transparent area; altering the brightness and/or contrast too much could make the transparent area visible.

Sharpening Graphic Lines

In Web applications, fuzzy logic is generally sought after, but fuzzy photos are not. You can clear up blurry images with Dreamweaver's Sharpen command found on the Property inspector.

The Sharpen command examines the edges found within a graphic and programmatically increases the contrast of the related pixels. Flat areas of color are left unaffected. The Sharpen dialog (see Figure 9-10) offers a sliding scale from 0 to 10 where 10 represents the maximum amount of sharpening available in one operation. As with the Brightness/Contrast dialog, you can select the preview option.

Figure 9-10: Bring your images into focus with Dreamweaver's Sharpen feature.

Note If you're using Fireworks and need more sharpening power than Dreamweaver offers, try applying the Unsharp Mask in Fireworks. Despite the name, this filter is terrific for sharpening blurry images and, when applied as a Live Filter from the Property inspector, is totally reversible in a Fireworks native PNG file.

Employing the Optimize in Fireworks Command

Not all images are Web-ready — especially those that are used in other media such as printing. To provide the best online experience, Web graphics must balance appearance and file size. You want your images to look as good as possible at the lowest possible file size because a small file is quicker to download. The process of achieving the balance between the image quality and file size is called *optimizing*. You can optimize your images without leaving Dreamweaver by running the Optimize in Fireworks command.

Tip Even though Fireworks does not open, you need Fireworks installed to run the Optimize in Fireworks feature. If the program is not installed and the command is selected, Dreamweaver gives you the opportunity to download a free trial version of Fireworks.

The Optimize in Fireworks command actually opens a dialog box that originated in Fireworks as the Export Preview dialog. Exporting from Fireworks is a major step and a lot of options are at your fingertips during the process. Here's just a little of what's possible:

✦ Switch formats from GIF to JPEG or vice versa. Other formats include animated GIF and PNG.

✦ Alter the palette depth (the number of colors) or transparency in GIF images.

✦ Change the JPEG compression quality.

✦ Rescale an image by an exact percentage or to a specific width or height.

✦ Crop a figure visually.

✦ Control the frame rate for animated GIF as well as the looping options.

✦ Visually compare up to four different optimized images at the same time (see Figure 9-11).

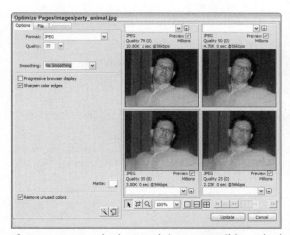

Figure 9-11: Get the best Web image possible at the lowest file size through the Optimize in Fireworks command.

When you first launch Optimize in Fireworks — either by clicking the same-named button on the Property inspector or choosing the command from the Commands menu — Dreamweaver presents a dialog that asks whether you'd like to edit the source PNG file or the current file. When you choose the source file, Dreamweaver automatically re-exports the file and stores the changes when you're done.

Cross-Reference For a full explanation of all that's possible through the Optimize in Fireworks command, see Chapter 23.

Editing Images

Although Dreamweaver includes some tools for cropping, sharpening, and otherwise revising images in your Web pages, it is not a full-featured graphics editor. Certain tasks — such as slicing a larger graphic into sections or adding text to an image — are beyond Dreamweaver's scope. You can, however, set up your graphics editor of choice to work hand-in-hand with Dreamweaver. Specify your primary graphics editor for each type of graphic in the File Types/Editors category of Preferences.

 ## Changing Graphics

Dreamweaver's built-in graphic functions are perfect for low-level quick fixes when an image needs to be cropped or resampled. In this Dreamweaver Technique, you'll get an opportunity to adjust one picture in a number of ways.

1. Open the `images_start.htm` file worked on in the last Dreamweaver Technique.

2. Select the second image on the page, next to the "Big house, big garage" heading.

   As you see, this image has a few problems in the outer part of the picture; with Dreamweaver, you can crop those right out of view.

3. On the Property inspector, click Crop.

4. Dreamweaver alerts you that taking this action will affect the selected image; click OK to continue.

5. Move the cropping handles on the top and left to exclude the white patches; move the cropping handles on the right and bottom to the outer edge of the images.

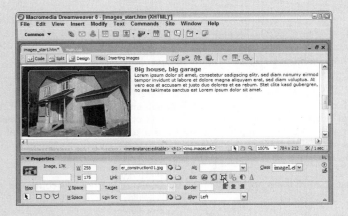

6. When you've moved the cropping handles to the correct position, double-click in the center of the image to confirm your changes.

   The image is still a bit too big; you can use the built-in Rescale tool to make a simple adjustment.

7. Select the image again and drag the lower-right sizing handle inward to reduce the image size; press the Shift key while dragging to constrain the width/height ratio.

8. Stop resizing the image when the Width attribute in the Property inspector is 215 pixels.

While the image appears to be resized, it now needs to be resampled so that it is actually reduced in file size.

9. On the Property inspector, click Resample.

You'll notice that the image file size shown in the Property inspector is reduced from 14K to 10K.

10. Dreamweaver again alerts you that taking this action will affect the selected image; click OK to continue.

11. When you're done, save your page.

Although you will always need to work with a graphics editor like Photoshop or Fireworks for major image modifications, Dreamweaver does a great job on last-minute fixes all by itself.

After you've picked an image editor, clicking the Edit button in the Property inspector opens the application with the current image. After you've made the modifications, just save the file in your image editor and switch back to Dreamweaver. The new, modified graphic has already been included in the Web page. If you change the image size, you can click the Reset Size button on the Image Property inspector to see your changes.

If you are using Macromedia Fireworks as your image editor, here is some good news: Dreamweaver and Fireworks work very closely together, enabling you to create and modify images with round-trip ease. Find out more in Chapter 23.

Modifying Image Attributes

When you insert an image in Dreamweaver, the image tag, `<img>`, is inserted into your HTML code. The `<img>` tag takes several attributes; the most commonly used can be entered through the Property inspector. Code for a basic image looks like the following:

```
<img src="images/myimage.gif" width="172" height="180">
```

Dreamweaver centralizes all its image functions in the Property inspector. The Image Property inspector, shown in Figure 9-12, displays a small thumbnail of the image as well as its file size. Dreamweaver automatically inserts the image filename in the Src text box (as the `src` attribute). To replace a currently selected image with another, click the folder icon next to the Src text box, or double-click the image itself. This sequence opens the Select Image Source dialog box. When you've selected the file, Dreamweaver automatically refreshes the page and corrects the code.

Figure 9-12: The Image Property inspector gives you total control over the HTML code for every image.

If the Image Property inspector is open when you insert your image, you can begin to modify the image attributes immediately.

Naming Your Image

When you first insert a graphic into the page, the Image Property inspector displays a blank text box next to the thumbnail and file size. Fill in this box with a unique name for the image, to be used in JavaScript and other applications.

Adjusting Height and Width

The width and height attributes are important because browsers build Web pages faster when they know the size and shape of the included images. Dreamweaver reads these attributes when the image is first loaded. The width and height values are initially expressed in pixels and are automatically inserted as attributes in the HTML code.

Browsers can dynamically resize an image if its height and width on the page are different from the original image's dimensions. For example, you can load your primary logo on the home page and then use a smaller version of it on subsequent pages by inserting the same image with reduced height and width values. Because you're only loading the image once and the browser is resizing it, download time for your Web page can be significantly reduced.

Note   Resizing an image just means changing its appearance onscreen; the file size stays exactly the same. To reduce a file size for an image, you need to scale it down in a graphics program such as Fireworks or, once you've resized it in Dreamweaver, click Resample in the Property inspector.

To resize an image in Dreamweaver, select the image and type the desired number of pixels in the Property inspector's H (height) and W (width) fields. With Dreamweaver, you can also visually resize your graphics by using the click-and-drag method. A selected image has three sizing handles located on the right, bottom, and lower-right corners of its bounding box. Click any of these handles and drag it out to a new location — when you release the mouse, Dreamweaver resizes the image. To maintain the current height/width aspect ratio, hold down the Shift key after starting to drag the corner sizing handle.

If you alter either the height or the width of an image, Dreamweaver displays the Property inspector values in bold in their respective fields. You can restore an image's default measurements by clicking the H or the W independently — or you can click the Reset Size button to restore both values.

Caution   If you elect to enable your viewer's browser to resize your image on-the-fly using the height/width values you specify, keep in mind that the browser is not a graphics-editing program and that its resizing algorithms are not sophisticated. View your resized images through several browsers to ensure acceptable results.

Using Margins

You can offset images with surrounding whitespace by using the margin attributes. The amount of whitespace around your image can be designated both vertically and horizontally through the vspace and hspace attributes, respectively. These margin values are entered, in pixels, into the V Space and H Space text boxes in the Image Property inspector.

The V Space value adds the same amount of whitespace along the top and bottom of your image; the H Space value increases the whitespace on the left and right sides of the image. These values must be positive; HTML doesn't allow images to overlap text or other images (outside of layers). Unlike in page layout, negative whitespace does not exist.

Note   The hspace and vspace attributes are deprecated in HTML 4.0. This means that, although the attributes are currently still supported, another preferred method achieves the same effect in newer browsers. In most cases, the margins should be implemented using Cascading Style Sheets, described in Chapter 7.

Adding Image Descriptions

It's easy for Web designers to get caught up in the visual design of their Web pages; after all, designers can devote hours to creating a single graphic or to perfectly positioning a graphic on the page relative to other information. Remember, however, that graphics aren't the most effective communication method in every circumstance. Luckily, the <img> tag includes two attributes that enable you to describe your image using plain text: alt and longdesc.

The alt attribute gives you a means to include a short description of a graphic. It is used in many ways:

✦ As a page is loading over the Web, the image is first displayed as an empty rectangle if the <img> tag contains width and height information. Some browsers display the alt description in this rectangle while the image is loading, offering the waiting user a written preview of the forthcoming image.

✦ In many browsers, the alt text displays as a ToolTip when the user's pointer passes over the graphic.

✦ A real benefit of alt text is providing input for browsers that don't graphics. Remember that text-only browsers are still in use, and some users, interested only in content, turn off the graphics to speed up the text display.

✦ The W3C is working toward standards for browsers for the visually impaired, and the alt text can be used to describe the image.

For all these reasons, it's good coding practice to associate an alt description with all your graphics. In Dreamweaver, you can enter this alternative text in the Alt text box of the Image Property inspector.

Tip   If the <img> tag does not contain an alt attribute, some screen readers read the filename when they encounter the image, which slows down how quickly visually impaired users can get to the real information on your page. For images that are purely visual and don't contribute to the meaning of your content, such as bullets or spacer images, include a blank alt attribute. To do this, open the Image Property inspector and select <empty> from the Alt drop-down list.

Currently, the alt attribute is the most valuable tool you have for providing a textual description of your images. However, some images are just too complicated to describe in a few words and are too important to gloss over. For these situations, the latest HTML specification includes the longdesc attribute. Although none of the major browsers currently support this attribute, Dreamweaver is anticipating the future by enabling you to specify a longdesc for your images.

In Dreamweaver, choose Edit Preferences, and in the Accessibility category, select the Images checkbox. When you add a new image to your page, the Image Tag Accessibility Attributes dialog box appears, as shown in Figure 9-13. In the Long Description text box, click the folder icon to navigate to an HTML file that contains a textual description of the image.

Figure 9-13: The Image Tag Accessibility Attributes dialog box appears when you select the Images option in the Accessibility Preferences.

Caution
The Image Tag Accessibility Attributes dialog box is not displayed if you add a new image by dragging it from the Files panel. It does appear, however, if you drag the image from the Assets panel, or use the Insert bar or Insert menu to add the image.

Bordering a Graphic

When you're working with thumbnails (small versions of images) on your Web page, you may need a quick way to distinguish one from another. The border attribute enables you to place a one-color rectangular border around any graphic. To turn on the border, enter the desired width of the border, measured in pixels, in the Border text box located on the lower half of the Image Property inspector. Entering a value of 0 explicitly turns off the border.

Note
A preferred method for adding a border to an image is to use Cascading Style Sheets, described in Chapter 7. Note that Cascading Style Sheets are not supported in older browsers.

One of the most frequent cries for help among beginning Web designers results from the sudden appearance of a bright blue border around an image. Whenever you assign a link to an image, HTML automatically places a border around that image; the color is determined by the Page Properties Link color, where the default is bright blue. Dreamweaver intelligently assigns a 0 to the border attribute whenever you enter a URL in the Link text box. If you've already declared a border value and enter a link, Dreamweaver won't zero-out the border. You can, of course, override the no-border option by entering a value in the Border text box.

Specifying a lowsrc

Another option for loading Web page images, the lowsrc attribute, displays a smaller version of a large graphics file while the larger file is loading. The lowsrc file can be a grayscale version of the original, or a version that is physically smaller or reduced in color or resolution. This option is designed to significantly reduce the file size for quick loading.

Select your lowsrc file by clicking the file icon next to the Low Src text box in the Image Property inspector. The same criteria that apply to inserting your original image also apply to the lowsrc picture.

Tip

One handy lowsrc technique first proportionally scales down a large file in a graphics-processing program. This file becomes your lowsrc file. Because browsers use the final image's height and width information for both the lowsrc and the final image, your visitors immediately see a blocky version of your graphic, which is replaced by the final version when the picture is fully loaded.

Working with Alignment Options

Just like text, images can be aligned to the left, right, or center. In fact, images have much more flexibility than text in terms of alignment. In addition to the same horizontal alignment options, you can align your images vertically in nine different ways. You can even turn a picture into a floating image type, enabling text to wrap around it.

Horizontal Alignment

When you change the horizontal alignment of a line—from left to center or from center to right—the entire paragraph moves. Any inline images that are part of that paragraph also move. Likewise, selecting one of a series of inline images in a row and realigning it horizontally causes all the images in the row to shift.

In Dreamweaver, the horizontal alignment of an inline image is changed in exactly the same way that you realign text—with the alignment buttons found on the Image Property inspector. As with text, buttons exist for left, center, and right. Although these are very conveniently placed on the Image Property inspector, the alignment attribute is actually written to the <p> or other block element enclosing the image.

Note

The align attribute, whether attached to a <p> tag for horizontal alignment, or to an <img> tag for vertical alignment (as described in the following section), is deprecated in HTML 4.0. Instead of using the align attribute, you can use Cascading Style Sheets, described in Chapter 7.

Vertical Alignment

Because you can place text next to an image—and images vary so greatly in size—HTML includes a variety of options for specifying just how image and text line up. As you can see from the chart shown in Figure 9-14, a wide range of possibilities is available.

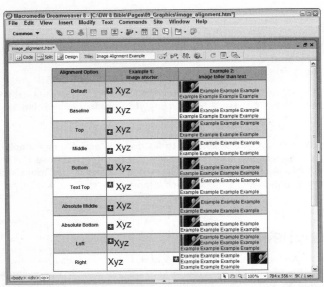

Figure 9-14: You can align text and images in one of nine different ways.

To change the vertical alignment of any graphic in Dreamweaver, open the Align drop-down list in the Image Property inspector and choose one of the options. Dreamweaver writes your choice into the `align` attribute of the `<img>` tag. The various vertical alignment options are listed in Table 9-1, and you can refer back to Figure 9-14 for examples of each type of alignment.

Table 9-1: Vertical Alignment Options

Option	Result
Browser Default	No alignment attribute is included in the `<img>` tag. Most browsers use the baseline as the alignment default.
Baseline	The bottom of the image is aligned with the baseline of the surrounding text.
Top	The top of the image is aligned with the top of the tallest object in the current line.
Middle	The middle of the image is aligned with the baseline of the current line.
Bottom	The bottom of the image is aligned with the baseline of the surrounding text.
Text Top	The top of the image is aligned with the tallest letter or object in the current line.
Absolute Middle	The middle of the image is aligned with the middle of the tallest text or object in the current line.
Absolute Bottom	The bottom of the image is aligned with the descenders (as in y, g, p, and so forth) that fall below the current baseline.
Left	The image is aligned to the left edge of the browser or table cell, and all text in the current line flows around the right side of the image.
Right	The image is aligned to the right edge of the browser or table cell, and all text in the current line flows around the left side of the image.

The last two alignment options, Left and Right, are special cases; details about how to use their features are covered in the following section.

Wrapping Text

Most browsers support wrapping text around an image on a Web page—long a popular design option in conventional publishing. As noted in the preceding section, the Left and Right alignment options turn a picture into a floating image type. This type is so called because the image can move depending on the amount of text and the size of the browser window.

Tip   Using both floating image types (Left and Right) in combination, you can actually position images flush-left and flush-right, with text in the middle. Insert both images side by side and then set the leftmost image to align left and the rightmost one to align right. Insert your text immediately following the second image.

Your text wraps around the image depending on where the floating image is placed (or anchored). If you enable the Anchor Points for Aligned Elements option in the Invisible Elements category of Preferences, Dreamweaver inserts a Floating Image Anchor symbol to mark the floating image's place. Note that the image itself may overlap the anchor, hiding the anchor from view. Figure 9-15 shows two examples of text wrapping: a left-aligned image with text flowing to the right, and a right-aligned image with text flowing to the left.

Floating image anchor

Set image alignment

Figure 9-15: Aligning an image left or right enables text to wrap around your images.

The Floating Image Anchor is not just a static symbol. You can click and drag the anchor to a new location and cause the paragraph to wrap in a different fashion. Be careful, however. If you delete the anchor, you also delete the image it represents.

You can also wrap a portion of the text around your left- or right-aligned picture and then force the remaining text to appear below the floating image. However, Dreamweaver cannot currently insert the HTML code necessary to do this task through the Image Property inspector. You have to force an opening to appear by inserting a break tag, with a special clear attribute, where you want the text to break. This special <br> tag has three forms:

- ✦ <br clear=left> — Causes the line to break and the following text to move down vertically until no floating images are on the left

- ✦ <br clear=right> — Causes the line to break and the following text to move down vertically until no floating images are on the right

- ✦ <br clear=all> — Moves the text following the image down until no floating images are on either the left or the right

A quick way to add the clear attribute is to position your cursor where you want the text to break, and press Shift+Enter. Next, in Code view, right-click the <br> tag and select Edit Tag <br> from the context menu. The Tag Editor dialog box displays; select the appropriate Clear option and click OK.

Adding Background Images

In this chapter, you've learned about working with the surface graphics on a Web page. You can also place an image in the background of an HTML page. This section covers some of the basic techniques for incorporating a background image in your Dreamweaver page.

Add an image to your background either by using Cascading Style Sheets (CSS) or by modifying the Page Properties. The Cascading Style Sheet method is preferred because it gives you additional control over your background image. However, older browser versions do not support Cascading Style Sheets; if you must support browser versions earlier than Internet Explorer 4.0 and Netscape Navigator 4.0, you are limited to changing the Page Properties.

Cross-Reference   If you aren't familiar with Cascading Style Sheets, you may want to read Chapter 7 before trying the following procedure. That chapter gets you started with general CSS concepts and outlines specific options for implementing background images.

To implement a background image using Cascading Style Sheets, follow these steps:

1. Choose Window ➪ CSS Styles.

2. On the CSS Styles panel, click Edit Styles and then click the New CSS Style button.

3. In the New Style dialog box, choose Redefine HTML Tag, and in the Tag drop-down list, select Body. These selections create a background image for the entire document. You can also select a different tag or choose the Make a Custom Style option to assign a background image to a single element on the page, such as a table cell or paragraph.

4. Specify whether you want to save the style definition in an external style sheet or in the current document, and then click OK.

5. In the CSS Style Definition dialog box, select the Background category.

6. In the Background Image field, type the path and filename for the image file, or click Browse to navigate to the file.

7. Designate any other background options, and then click OK.

To specify a background image using the Page Properties, choose Modify ⇨ Page Properties or select Page Properties from the shortcut menu that pops up when you right-click (Control+click) in any open area on the Web page. In the Page Properties dialog box, select a graphic by clicking the Browse button next to the Background Image text box. You can use any file format supported by Dreamweaver — GIF, JPEG, or PNG.

There are two key differences between background images and the foreground inline images discussed in the preceding sections of this chapter. First and most obvious, all other text and graphics on the Web page are superimposed over your chosen background image. This capability can bring extra depth and texture to your work; unfortunately, you have to make sure the foreground text and images work well with the background.

Basically, you want to ascertain that enough contrast exists between foreground and background. You can set the default text and the various link colors using Cascading Style Sheets or through the Page Properties dialog box, shown in Figure 9-16. When trying out a new background pattern, you should set up some dummy text and links. Then click the Apply button on the Page Properties dialog box to test different color combinations.

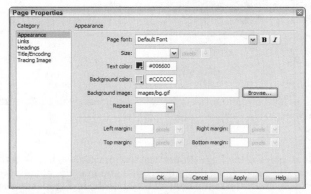

Figure 9-16: If you're using a background image, be sure to check the default colors for text and links to make sure enough contrast exists between background and foreground.

The second distinguishing feature of background images is that the viewing browser completely fills either the browser window or the area behind the content of your Web page; whichever is larger. Suppose you have created a splash page with only a 200 x 200 foreground logo, and you've incorporated an amazing 1,024 x 768 background that took you weeks to compose. No one can see the fruits of your labor in the background — unless he resizes his browser window to 1,024 x 768. On the other hand, if your background image is smaller than either the browser window or what the Web page content needs to display, the browser and Dreamweaver repeat (tile) your image to make up the difference.

Tiling Images

Web designers use the tiling property of background images to create a variety of effects with very low file-size overhead. The columns typically found on one side of Web pages are a good example of tiling. Columns are popular because they enable the designer to place navigational buttons in a visual context. An easy way to create a column that runs the full length of your Web page is to use a long, narrow background image.

In the following figure, the background image is 45 pixels high, 800 pixels wide, and only 6KB in size. When the browser window is set at 640 x 480 or 800 x 600, the image is tiled down the page to create the vertical column effect. You could just as easily create an image 1,000 pixels high by 40 pixels wide to create a horizontal column.

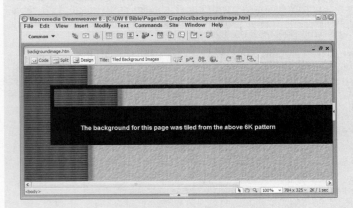

The background for this page was tiled from the above 6K pattern

If you are using Cascading Style Sheets to implement your background image, you can control whether the image tiles horizontally, vertically, in both directions, or not at all.

If you implement the background image using Page Properties, the image always tiles both horizontally and vertically, filling the page as just described. But if you implement your background image using Cascading Style Sheets, you can control whether the image tiles horizontally, vertically, in both directions, or not at all.

Tip   With Cascading Style Sheets, you not only can attach a background image to a page, but you can also attach a background image to an individual element on a page, such as a single paragraph. Cascading Style Sheets also enable you to designate whether the background image should scroll with the foreground text, or if it should remain stationary while the foreground text scrolls over the background. These options are not available with the Page Properties method.

Dividing the Web Page with Horizontal Rules

HTML includes a standard horizontal line that can divide your Web page into specific sections. The horizontal rule tag, <hr>, is a good tool for adding a little diversion to your page without adding download time. You can control the width (either absolutely or relative to the browser window), the height, the alignment, and the shading property of the rule. These horizontal rules appear on a line by themselves; you cannot place text or images on the same line as a horizontal rule.

To insert a horizontal rule in your Web page in Dreamweaver, follow these steps:

1. Place your cursor where you want the horizontal rule to appear.

2. From the Common category of the Insert bar, click the Horizontal Rule button or choose Insert ➪ HTML ➪ Horizontal Rule. Dreamweaver inserts the horizontal rule; and the Property inspector, if visible, shows the attributes that you can change for a horizontal rule (see Figure 9-17).

Figure 9-17: The Horizontal Rule Property inspector controls the width, height, and alignment for these HTML lines.

3. To change the width of the line, enter a value in the Property inspector width (W) text box. You can insert either an absolute width in pixels or a relative value as a percentage of the screen:

   • To set a horizontal rule to an exact width, enter the measurement in pixels in the width (W) text box and press the Tab key. If it is not already showing, select Pixels in the drop-down list.

   • To set a horizontal rule to a width relative to the browser window, enter the percentage amount in the width (W) text box, press the Tab key, and select the percent sign (%) in the drop-down list.

4. To change the height of the horizontal rule, type a pixel measurement in the height (H) text box.

5. To change the alignment from the default (centered), open the Align drop-down list and choose another alignment.

6. To disable the default embossed look for the rule, clear the Shading checkbox.

7. If you intend to reference your horizontal rule in JavaScript or in another application, you can give it a unique name. Type the name in the unlabeled text box located directly to the left of the H text box.

Note The HTML 4.0 standard lists the `align`, `noshade`, `width`, and `size` attributes of the `<hr>` tag as deprecated. However, current browsers still support these attributes.

To modify any inserted horizontal rule, simply click it. (If the Property inspector is not already open, you have to double-click the rule.) As a general practice, size your horizontal rules using the percentage option if you are using them to separate items on a full screen. If you are using the horizontal rules to divide items in a specifically sized table column or cell, use the pixel method.

Tip The Shading property of the horizontal rule is most effective when your page background is a shade of gray. The default shading is black along the top and left, and white along the bottom and right. The center line is generally transparent (although Internet Explorer enables you to assign a color attribute). If you use a different background color or image, be sure to check the appearance of your horizontal rules in that context.

Many designers prefer to create elaborate horizontal rules; in fact, custom rules are an active area of clip art design. These types of horizontal rules are regular graphics and are inserted and modified as such.

Applying Simple Web Animation

Why include a section on animation in a chapter on inline images? On the Web, animations are, for the most part, inline images that move. Outside of the possibilities offered by Dynamic HTML (covered in Part IV), Web animations typically are either animated GIF files or are created with a program such as Flash that requires a plugin. This section takes a brief look at the capabilities and uses of GIF animations.

A GIF animation is a series of still GIF images flipped rapidly to create the illusion of motion. Because animation-creation programs compress all the frames of the animation into one file, a GIF animation is placed on a Web page in the same manner as a still graphic.

In Dreamweaver, click the Image button in the Insert bar or choose Insert ➪ Image and then select the file. Dreamweaver shows the first frame of your animation in the Document window. To play the animation, preview your Web page in a browser.

As you can imagine, GIF animations can quickly grow to be very large. The key to controlling file size is to think small: Keep your images as small as possible with a low bit-depth (number of colors) and use as few frames as possible.

To create your animation, use any graphics program to produce the separate frames. One excellent technique uses an image-processing program such as Adobe Photoshop and progressively applies a filter to the same image over a series of frames. Figure 9-18 shows the individual frames created with Photoshop's Lighting Effects filter. When animated, a spotlight appears to move across the word.

Figure 9-18: The five images shown are frames of an animated GIF image that are compressed into one file using an image-editing program.

You need an animation program to compress the separate frames and build your animated GIF file. Many commercial programs, including Macromedia's Fireworks, can handle GIF animation. QuickTime Pro can turn individual files or any other kind of movie into an animated GIF, too. Most animation programs enable you to control numerous aspects of the animation: the number of times an animation loops, the delay between frames, and how transparency is handled within each frame.

Tip

If you want to use an advanced animation tool but still have full backward compatibility, check out Flash, from Macromedia. Flash is best known for outputting small vector-based animations that require a plugin to view, but it can also save animations as GIFs or AVIs. See Chapter 24 for more information.

Including Banner Ads

Banner ads have become an essential aspect of the World Wide Web; for the Web to remain, for the most part, freely accessible, advertising is needed to support the costs. Banner ads have evolved into the de facto standard. Although numerous variations exist, a banner ad is typically an animated GIF of a particular width and height, within a specified file size.

The Standards and Practices Committee of the Interactive Advertising Bureau (IAB) established a series of standard sizes for banner ads. Although no law dictates that these guidelines have to be followed, the vast majority of commercial sites adhere to the suggested dimensions. The most common banner sizes (in pixels) and their official names are listed in Table 9-2; additional banner guidelines are available at the IAB Web site (www.iab.net).

Table 9-2: IAB Advertising Banner Sizes

Dimensions	Name
468 x 60	Full Banner
234 x 60	Half Banner
125 x 125	Square Button
88 x 31	Micro Bar
120 x 90	Button 1
120 x 60	Button 2
120 x 240	Vertical Banner
160 x 600	Wide Skyscraper
120 x 600	Skyscraper

Acceptable file size for a banner ad is not as clearly specified, but it's just as important. The last thing a hosting site wants is for a large, too-heavy banner to slow down the loading of its page. Most commercial sites have an established maximum file size for any given banner ad size. Generally, banner ads are around 10KB, and no more than 12KB. The lighter your banner ad, the faster it loads and — as a direct result — the more likely Web page visitors stick around to see it.

Note   Major sites often have additional criteria for using rich media in banner ads, such as Flash animations or JavaScript. These may include file size, length of animation, behavior when the ad is clicked, and so on.

Inserting a banner ad on a Web page is very straightforward. As with any other GIF file, animated or not, all you have to do is insert the image and assign the link. As any advertiser can tell you, the link is as important as the image itself, and you should take special care to ensure that it is correct when inserted. Advertising links are often quite complex because they not only link to a specific page, but may also carry information about the referring site. Several companies monitor how many times an ad is selected — the *clickthru rate* — and often a CGI program is used to communicate with these companies and handle the link. Here's a sample URL from CNet's `News.com` site:

`xxxhttp://home.cnet.com/cgi-acc/clickthru.acc ⤸`

`clickid=00001e145ea7d80f00000000&adt=003:10:100&edt=cnet&cat=1:1002:&site=CN`

Obviously, copying and pasting such URLs is highly preferable to entering them by hand.

Advertisements often come from an outside source, so a Web page designer may have to allow space for the ad without incorporating the actual ad. Some Web designers create a plain rectangular image of the appropriate size to serve as a placeholder, until the actual image is ready. In Dreamweaver, placeholder ads can easily be maintained as Library items and placed as needed from the Assets panel, as shown in Figure 9-19.

Cross-
Reference

See Chapter 28 for information on creating and using Dreamweaver Library items.

Figure 9-19: Use the Library to store standard banner ad images
for use as placeholders.

If you'd prefer not to use placeholder graphics as just described, you can instead insert a
plain `<img>` tag — with no `src` parameter. When an `<img>` tag without a `src` attribute is in the
code, Dreamweaver displays a plain rectangle that can be resized to the proper banner ad
dimensions in the Property inspector.

You can insert a placeholder image by clicking the Image Placeholder button on the Insert
bar, or by choosing Insert ➪ Image Objects ➪ Image Placeholder. In the resulting Image
Placeholder dialog box, you can enter an image name, dimensions, color, and alternate text.
When the real graphics file is ready, use the Src text box on the Property inspector to specify
the new file. The image name and alternate text remain unchanged when you assign the new
file, but the dimensions automatically change to match those of the actual image.

Inserting Rollover Images

Rollovers are among the most popular of all Web page effects. A *rollover* (also known as a
mouseover) occurs when the user's pointer passes over an image and the image changes in
some way. It may appear to glow or change color and/or shape. When the pointer moves
away from the graphic, the image returns to its original form. The rollover indicates interactivity, and attempts to engage the user with a little bit of flair.

Rollovers are usually accomplished with a combination of HTML and JavaScript.
Dreamweaver was among the first Web-authoring tools to automate the production of
rollovers through its Swap Image and Swap Image Restore behaviors. Later versions of
Dreamweaver make rollovers even easier with the Rollover Image object. With the Rollover
Image object, you just pick two images to make a rollover.

Cross-Reference

If you use Fireworks as your image-editing tool, refer to Chapter 23 to learn another method for creating rollover images.

Technically speaking, a rollover is accomplished by manipulating an `<img>` tag's `src` attribute. Recall that the `src` attribute is responsible for providing the actual filename of the graphic to be displayed; it is, quite literally, the source of the image. A rollover changes the value of `src` from one image file to another. Swapping the `src` value is analogous to having a picture within a frame and changing the picture while keeping the frame.

Caution

The picture frame analogy is appropriate on one other level: It serves as a reminder of the size barrier inherent in rollovers. A rollover changes only one property of an `<img>` tag, the source—it cannot change any other property, such as height or width. For this reason, both your original image and the image displayed during the rollover should be the same size. If they are not, the alternate image is resized to match the dimensions of the original image.

Dreamweaver's Rollover Image object automatically changes the image back to its original source when the user moves the pointer off the image. Optionally, you can elect to preload the images with the selection of a checkbox. Preloading is a Web page technique that reads the intended file or files into the browser's memory before they are displayed. With preloading, the images appear on demand, without any download delay.

Rollovers are typically used for buttons that, when clicked, open another Web page. In fact, JavaScript requires that an image include a link before it can detect when a user's pointer moves over it. Dreamweaver automatically includes the minimum link necessary: the # link. Although JavaScript recognizes this symbol as indicating a link, no action is taken if the image is clicked by the user; the #, by itself, is an empty link. You can supply whatever link you want in the Rollover Image object.

Tip

Some browsers link to the top of the page when they encounter a # link. If you want to create a rollover image that doesn't link anywhere, change the # to the following:

```
javascript:;
```

You can change this directly in Code view, or in the Link field of the Property inspector for the button.

To include a Rollover Image object in your Web page, follow these steps:

1. Place your cursor where you want the rollover image to appear and choose Insert ➪ Image Objects ➪ Rollover Image, or select Rollover Image from the Images menu on the Insert bar's Common category. You can also drag the Rollover Image button to any existing location on the Web page. Dreamweaver opens the Insert Rollover Image dialog box shown in Figure 9-20.

2. You can enter a unique name for the image in the Image Name text box, or you can use the name automatically generated by Dreamweaver.

3. In the Original Image text box, enter the path and name of the graphic you want displayed when the user's mouse is not over the graphic. You can also click the Browse button to select the file. Press Tab when you're done.

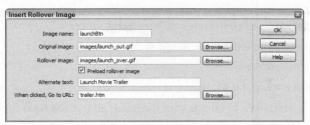

Figure 9-20: The Rollover Image object makes rollover graphics quick and easy.

4. In the Rollover Image text box, enter the path and name of the graphic file you want displayed when the user's pointer is over the image. You can also click the Browse button to select the file.

5. In the Alternate Text field, type a brief description of the graphic button.

6. If desired, specify a link for the image by entering it in the When Clicked, Go To URL text box or by clicking the Browse button to select the file.

7. To enable images to load only when they are required, deselect the Preload Images option. Generally, it is best to leave this option selected (the default) so that the appearance of the rollover is not delayed.

8. Click OK when you're finished.

Tip

Keep in mind that the Rollover Image object inserts both the original image and its alternate, whereas the Swap Image technique is applied to an existing image in the Web page. If you prefer to use the Rollover Image object rather than the Swap Image behavior, nothing prevents you from deleting an existing image from the Web page and inserting it again through the Rollover Image object. Just make sure that you note the path and name of the image before you delete it, so you can find it again.

Adding a Navigation Bar

Rollovers are nice effects, but a single button does not constitute a navigation system for a Web site. Typically, several buttons with a similar look and feel are placed next to one another to form a *navigation bar*. To make touring a site as intuitive as possible, the same navigation bar should appear on each page. You can achieve this effect by placing a copy of the navigation bar on each page, or by creating a frameset with one frame containing the navigation bar. Consistency of design and repetitive use of the navigation bar simplifies getting around a site—even for a first-time user.

Some designers build their navigation bars in a separate graphics program and then import them into Dreamweaver. Macromedia Fireworks, with its capability to export both images and code, makes this a strong option. Other Web designers, however, prefer to build separate rollover images in a graphics program and then assemble all the pieces at the HTML layout stage. Dreamweaver automates such a process with its Navigation Bar object.

The Navigation Bar object incorporates rollovers — and more. A Navigation Bar element can use up to four different images, each reflecting a different user action:

✦ **Up:** The user's pointer is away from the image.

✦ **Over:** The pointer is over the image.

✦ **Down:** The user has clicked the image.

✦ **Over While Down:** The user's pointer is over the image after it has been clicked.

One key difference separates a fully functioning navigation bar from a group of unrelated rollovers. When the Down state is available, if the user clicks one of the buttons, any other Down button is changed to the Up state. The effect is like a series of mutually exclusive radio buttons: You can show only one selected in a group. The Down state is often used to indicate the current selection.

Tip   Although you can use the Navigation Bar object on any type of Web design, it works best in a frameset context, with one frame for navigation and one for content. If you insert a navigation bar with Up, Over, Down, and Over While Down states for each button in the navigation frame, you can target the content frame and gain the full effect of the mutually exclusive Down states.

Before you can use Dreamweaver's Navigation Bar object, you have to create a series of images for each button — one for each state you plan to use, as demonstrated in Figure 9-21. It's completely up to the designer how the buttons appear, but it's important that a consistent look and feel be applied to all the buttons in a navigation bar. For example, if the Over state for Button A reveals a green glow, rolling over Buttons B, C, and D should cause the same glow.

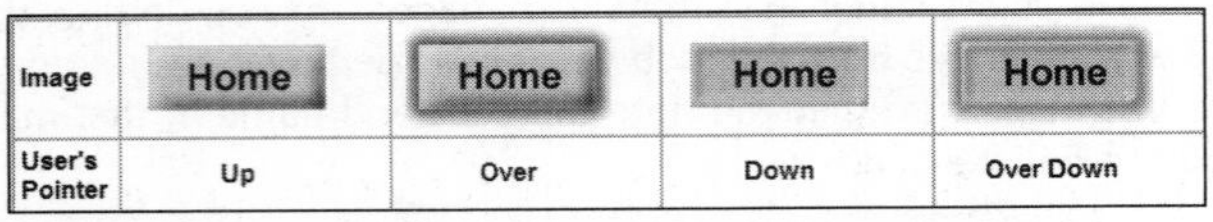

Image	Home	Home	Home	Home
User's Pointer	Up	Over	Down	Over Down

Figure 9-21: Before you invoke the Navigation Bar object, create a series of buttons, using a separate image for each state to be used.

To insert a navigation bar, follow these steps:

1. From the Insert bar, click the Images: Navigation Bar button. The Insert Navigation Bar dialog box appears, as shown in Figure 9-22.

2. Enter a unique name for the first button in the Element Name field and press Tab.

   Be sure to use Tab rather than Enter (Return) when moving from field to field. When Enter (Return) is pressed, Dreamweaver attempts to build the navigation bar. If you have not completed the initial two steps (providing an Element Name and a source for the Up Image), an alert is displayed; otherwise, the navigation bar is built.

3. In the Up Image field, enter a path and filename or browse to a graphic file to use.

Figure 9-22: Add elements one at a time in the Insert Navigation Bar dialog box.

4. Select files for each of the remaining states: Over, Down, and Over While Down. If you don't want to use all four states, just specify the same image more than once. For example, if you don't want a separate Over While Down state, use the same image for Down and Over While Down.

5. If you want, enter a brief description of the button in the Alternate Text field.

6. Enter a URL or browse to a file in the When Clicked, Go To URL field.

Tip

If you do not enter a URL, Dreamweaver inserts a hash mark (#) in the generated code to create a null link for the button. Although the hash mark is supposed to cause a jump to nowhere when the button is clicked, the hash mark actually causes some browsers to jump to the top of the page. Although this is unusual in a navigation bar, if you want to create a button that doesn't link anywhere, consider entering `javascript:;` in the Go To URL field to create a null link that won't cause browsers to jump to the top of the page.

7. If you're using a frameset, select a target for the URL from the drop-down list adjacent to the Browse button.

8. Enable or disable the Preload Images option as desired. For a multistate button to be effective, the reaction has to be immediate, and the images must be preloaded. It is highly recommended that you enable the Preload Images option.

9. If you want the current button to display the Down state first, select the Show "Down Image" Initially option. When this option is chosen, an asterisk appears next to the current button in the Nav Bar Elements list. Generally, you don't want more than one Down state showing at a time.

10. To set the orientation of the navigation bar, select either Horizontally or Vertically from the Insert drop-down list.

11. If you want to contain your images in a table, keep the Use Tables option selected. If you decide not to use tables in a horizontal configuration, images are presented side by side; when you don't use tables in a vertical configuration, Dreamweaver separates every element with line breaks (`<br>` tag).

12. Click the Add (+) button and repeat steps 2 through 9 to add the next element.

13. To reorder the elements in the navigation bar, select an element in the Nav Bar Elements list and use the Up and Down buttons to reposition it in the Elements list.

14. To remove an element, select it and click the Delete (–) button.

Each page can have only one Dreamweaver-built navigation bar. If you try to insert a second, Dreamweaver asks if you'd like to modify the existing series. Clicking OK opens the Modify Navigation Bar dialog box, which is identical to the Insert Navigation Bar dialog box, except you can no longer change the orientation or table settings. You can also alter the inserted navigation bar by choosing Modify ➪ Navigation Bar.

 Cross-Reference If you're looking for even more control over your navigation bar, Dreamweaver also includes the Set Nav Bar Image behavior, which is fully covered in Chapter 12.

Summary

In this chapter, you learned how to include both foreground and background images in Dreamweaver. Understanding how images are handled in HTML is an absolute necessity for the Web designer. As you're inserting images into your Web pages, keep these key points in mind:

✦ Web pages are restricted to using specific graphic formats. Virtually all browsers support GIF and JPEG files. PNG finally seems to be gaining acceptance, but it is not universally viewable without additional plugins. Dreamweaver can preview all three image types.

✦ Images are inserted in the foreground in Dreamweaver through the Image button on the Insert bar or from the Assets panel. After the graphic is inserted, almost all modifications can be handled through the Property inspector.

✦ You can use HTML's background image function to lay a full-frame image or a tiled series of the same image underneath your text and graphics. Tiled images can be employed to create columns and other designs with small files.

✦ Simple graphic editing chores — including cropping and resampling — are available right from Dreamweaver's Property inspector; for finer control, you'll need a graphics editor installed and then you can use either the Optimize in Fireworks or Edit options.

✦ The simplest HTML graphic is the built-in horizontal rule. It is useful for dividing your Web page into separate sections. You can size the horizontal rule either absolutely or relatively.

✦ Animated images can be inserted alongside and in the same manner as still graphics. The individual frames of a GIF animation must be created in a graphics program and then combined in an animation program.

✦ With the Rollover Image object, you can easily insert simple rollovers that use two different images. To build a rollover that uses more than two images, you have to use the Swap Image behavior.

✦ You can add a series of interrelated buttons — complete with four-state rollovers — by using the Navigation Bar object.

In the next chapter, you learn how to use hyperlinks in Dreamweaver.

✦   ✦   ✦

Establishing Web Links

L inks *are* the Web. Everything else about the medium can be replicated in another form, but without links, there would be no World Wide Web. As your Web design work becomes more sophisticated, you'll find additional uses for links: sending mail, connecting to an FTP site — even downloading software.

In this chapter, you learn how Dreamweaver helps you manage various types of links, as well as how to set anchors within documents to get smooth and accurate navigation and establish targets for your links. To give you a full picture of the possibilities, this chapter begins with an overview of Internet addresses, called URLs.

Understanding URLs

URL stands for Uniform Resource Locator. An awkward phrase, it is one that, nonetheless, describes itself well — the URL's function is to provide a standard method for finding anything on the Internet. From Web pages to newsgroups to the smallest graphic on the most esoteric of pages, everything can be referenced through the URL mechanism.

A typical URL for a Web page can have up to six different parts. Each part is separated by some combination of a slash, colon, and hashmark delimiter. When entered as an attribute's value, the entire URL is generally enclosed within quotes to ensure that the address is read as one unit. A generic URL using all the parts looks like the following:

```
scheme://server:port/path/file#anchor
```

Here's an example that uses every section:

```
http://www.idest.com:80/Dreamweaver/index.htm#bible
```

From left to right, the parts are as follows:

✦ `http:` — The URL scheme used to access the resource. A scheme is an agreed-upon mechanism for communication, typically between a client and a server. The scheme to reference Web servers uses the HyperText Transfer Protocol (HTTP). Other schemes and their related protocols are discussed later in this section.

✦ www.idest.com—The name of the server providing the resource. The server can be either a domain name (with or without the www prefix) or an Internet Protocol (IP) address, such as 199.227.52.143.

✦ :80—The port number to be used on the server. Most URLs do not include a port number, which is analogous to a telephone extension number on the server, because most servers use the defaults.

✦ /Dreamweaver—The directory path to the resource. Depending on where the resource (for example, the Web page) is located on the server, the following paths can be specified: no path (indicating that the resource is in the public root of the server), a single folder name, or a number of folders and subfolders.

✦ /index.htm—The filename of the resource. If the filename is omitted, the Web browser looks for a default page, often named index.html or index.htm. The browser reacts differently depending on the type of file. For example, GIFs and JPEGs are displayed by themselves; executable files and archives (Zip, StuffIt, and so on) are downloaded.

✦ #bible—The named anchor in the HTML document. This part is another optional section. The named anchor enables the Web designer to send the viewer to a particular section of an HTML page.

Although http is one of the most prevalent communication schemes used on the Internet, other schemes are also available. Whereas HTTP is used for accessing Web pages, the other schemes are used for such things as transferring files between servers and clients or for sending e-mail. Table 10-1 describes the most common schemes used in URLs.

Table 10-1: Common URL Schemes and Associated Protocols

Scheme Syntax	Protocol	Usage
ftp://	File Transfer Protocol (FTP)	Links to an FTP server that is typically used for uploading and downloading files. The server may be accessed anonymously, or it may require a username and password.
http://	HyperText Transfer Protocol (HTTP)	Used for connecting to a document available on a World Wide Web server.
javascript:	JavaScript	Although it is not part of a true URL, some browsers support a scheme of javascript:, indicating the browser should execute JavaScript code. This provides an easy way to execute JavaScript code when a user clicks a link.
mailto:	Simple Mail Transfer Protocol (SMTP)	Opens an e-mail form with the recipient's address already filled in. These links are useful when embedded in your Web pages to provide visitors with an easy feedback method.
news://	Network News Transfer Protocol (NNTP)	Connects to the specified Usenet newsgroup. Newsgroups are public, theme-oriented message boards on which anyone can post or reply to a message.
telnet://	TELNET	Enables users to log on directly to remote host computers and interact directly with the operating system software.

Part of the richness of today's Web browsers stems from their capability to connect with all the preceding (and additional) services.

Tip The `mailto:` scheme enables you not only to open up a preaddressed e-mail form, but also, with a little extra work, to specify the topic. For example, if Joe Lowery wants to include a link to his e-mail address with the subject heading "Book Feedback," he can insert a link such as the following:

```
mailto:jlowery@idest.com?subject=Book%20Feedback
```

The question mark acts as a delimiter that enables a variable and a value to be passed to the browser; the `%20` is the decimal representation for a space that must be read by various servers. When you're trying to encourage feedback from your Web page visitors, every little bit helps.

Surfing the Web with Hypertext

Often, you assign a link to a word or phrase on your page, an image such as a navigational button, or a section of graphic for an image map (a large graphic in which various parts are links). To test the link, you preview the page in a browser; links are not active in Dreamweaver's Document window.

Designate links in HTML through the anchor tag pair: `<a>` and `</a>`. The anchor tag generally takes one main attribute — the hypertext reference, which is written as follows:

```
href="link name"
```

When you create a link, the anchor pair surrounds the text or object that is being linked. For example, if you link the phrase `Back to Home Page`, it may look like the following:

```
<a href="index.html">Back to Home Page</a>
```

If you attach a link to the image `logo.gif`, your code looks as follows:

```
<a href="home.html"><img src="images/logo.gif"></a>
```

Creating a basic link in Dreamweaver is easy. Simply follow these steps:

1. Select the text, image, or object you want to establish as a link.

2. In the Property inspector, enter the URL in the Link text box as shown in Figure 10-1. You can use one of the following methods to do so:

   • Type the URL directly into the Link text box.

   • Click the Browse for File folder icon to the right of the Link text box to open the Select File dialog box, where you can browse for the file.

   • Click the Point to File icon and drag your mouse to an existing page in the Files panel or anchor on the current page. This feature is explained later in this section.

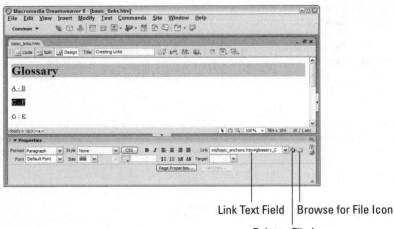

Link Text Field | Browse for File Icon

Point to File Icon

Figure 10-1: You can enter your link directly into the Link text box, click the folder icon to browse for a file, or point to the file directly with the Point to File icon.

You can also create a link by dragging a URL from the Assets panel onto a text or image selection, a procedure covered more fully later in this chapter.

Finally, you can create a link using the Insert menu or Insert bar. Without selecting any text, first choose Insert ➪ Hyperlink, or in the Common category of the Insert bar, click the Hyperlink button. The Hyperlink dialog box opens and you can specify the hotspot text, the URL for the link, and a link target (described later). This method also enables you to specify the following:

✦ **Tab index:** A number specifying the order in which a user can tab through the page. Links with lower numbers are tabbed to first, and links with no tab index defined appear last in the tab order.

✦ **Title field:** A description of the link. In Netscape 6.0 and Internet Explorer 6.0, the text appears as a ToolTip when the user holds the cursor over the link.

✦ **Access key:** A single letter that serves as the keyboard equivalent for the hyperlink. Access keys work only in the most recent browser versions, and they do not work consistently. Pressing the Alt (Option) key plus the access key may just select the link, or it may actually execute the link.

Note   If you don't see the Hyperlink dialog box when you insert a hyperlink, choose Edit ➪ Preferences and, in the Common category, select the Show Dialog When Inserting Objects option.

Regardless of how you create a link in Dreamweaver, a few restrictions exist for specifying URLs. Dreamweaver does not support any letters from the extended character set (also known as High ASCII), such as ¡, à, or ñ. Complete URLs must have fewer than a total of 255 characters. You should be cautious about using spaces in pathnames and, therefore, in URLs. Although most browsers can interpret the address, spaces are changed to a %20 symbol for proper Unix usage. This change can make your URLs difficult to read.

Note   Whitespace in your HTML code usually doesn't have an adverse effect on what is displayed in a browser. However, Netscape browsers are sensitive to whitespace when assigning a link to an image. If you isolate your image tag from the anchor tags as in the following example

```
<a href="index.htm">
<img src="images/Austria.gif" width="34" ⊃
height="24">
</a>
```

some older Netscape browser versions attach a small blue underscore—a tail, really—to your image. Because Dreamweaver automatically codes the anchor tag properly, without any additional whitespace, this odd situation occurs only with hand-coded or previously coded HTML.

Text links are most often rendered with a blue color and underlined. Depending on the background color for your page, you may want to change the color of text links to improve readability. You can specify the document-link color by choosing Modify ➪ Page Properties and selecting the Links color box. In Page Properties, you can also alter the color to which the links change after being selected (the Visited Links color), and the color flashed when the link is clicked (the Active Links color).

Eliminating Underlines from Links

Disabling the underline for the anchor tag, <a>, which is normally associated with hyperlinked text, is one modification commonly included in style sheets.

Caution   Be careful when using this technique. Underlined text is a standard method of indicating a hyperlink on the Web, and some clients or users may find your pages not as intuitive if the underline indicator is no longer visible.

To disable the underline on the anchor tag, follow these steps:

1. Open the CSS Styles panel by choosing Window ➪ CSS Styles. The CSS Styles panel, shown in Figure 10-2, displays existing styles and provides controls for creating and managing styles.

2. In the CSS Styles panel, click the New CSS Rule button. This action opens the New CSS Rule dialog box.

3. Select the Tag option and choose the anchor tag, a, from the drop-down list. Finally, select Define In This Document Only to create an internal CSS style sheet or choose an external style sheet from the drop-down list. Click OK, and the CSS Style Definition dialog box opens.

Tip   You can also select the Advanced option rather than Tag and choose a:link from the drop-down list. You can even employ the a:hover style, which enables text to change color or style on rollover. You must, however, define the four CSS Selector styles in a particular order for them to work correctly. Start by defining the a:link class and then proceed to define a:visited, a:hover, and a:active, in that order. Note that you can preview only the a:link altered styles in Dreamweaver; to see the other styles you need to preview the page in a browser.

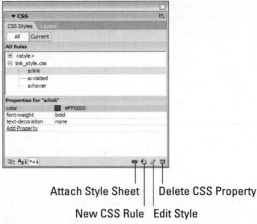

Attach Style Sheet | Delete CSS Property

New CSS Rule   Edit Style

Figure 10-2: The Dreamweaver CSS Styles panel helps
you apply consistent styles to a Web page.

4. In the Style Definition window, make sure that the correct category is displayed by
   selecting Type from the list of categories.

5. In the Decoration section of the Type category, select the None option. You can also
   make any other modifications to the anchor tag style, such as color or font size. Click
   OK when you're finished.

Tip   Many designers, myself included, like to make the link apparent by styling it bold and
putting it in a different color.

The Style Definition window closes, and any style changes instantly take effect on your page.
If you have any previously defined links, the underline disappears from them.

Now, when viewed through a browser, any links that you insert on your page still function as
links — the user's pointer still changes into a pointing hand, and the links are active — but no
underline appears.

One variation on this technique is to make the underline appear only when the mouse rolls
over the link. To accomplish this variation, define a CSS rule for the a:hover selector and set
the Decoration to Underline.

Tip   This technique works for any text used as a link. To eliminate the border around an image
designated as a link, the image's border must be set to 0 in the Property inspector.
Dreamweaver handles this automatically when a graphic is made into a link.

Inserting URLs from the Assets Panel

Internet addresses get more complicated every day. Trying to remember them all correctly
and avoid typos can make the Web designer's job unnecessarily difficult. You can use the
Dreamweaver Assets panel's URLs category to drag-and-drop the trickiest URLs with ease.

The Assets panel lists URLs that are already referenced somewhere within your site. If you want to link to the same URL again, just drag it from the Assets panel.

Tip   To avoid rework, after you have typed a URL for a link in a document, test that link in a browser to be sure it's correct. Then when you assign the same URL to other links using the Assets panel, you can be confident that the link works as expected.

The Assets panel lists only full Internet addresses — whether to files (such as `http://www.idest.com/dreamweaver/`) or to e-mail addresses (such as `mailto:jlowery@idest.com`). Document- or site-relative links are not listed as Assets. To assign a link to a document- or site-relative page, use one of the other linking methods discussed in this chapter, such as pointing to a file.

To assign a URL from the Assets panel, follow these steps:

1. If the Assets panel is not already visible, choose Window ➪ Assets to display it.

2. Click the URLs icon on the side of the Assets panel to display that category, as shown in Figure 10-3.

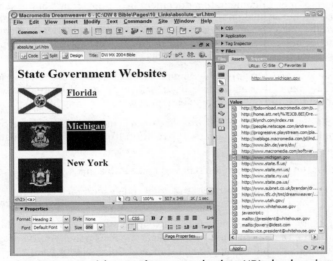

Figure 10-3: Banish typos from your absolute URLs by dragging a link from the Assets panel to any selected text or graphic.

3. If necessary, click the Refresh Site List button on the Assets panel to list the most current links found in the site.

Note   As with other Assets panel categories, you need to click the Refresh Site List button to make available all the possible URLs in a site. Alternatively, you could choose Refresh Site List from the context menu on the panel. Either action causes Dreamweaver to scan all the Web pages within the site and extract all of the complete Internet addresses it finds.

4. In the Document window, select the text or image you want the link assigned to.

5. Drag the desired link from the Assets panel onto the selected text or image; alternatively, highlight the link in the panel and click the Apply button.

If you don't select text or an image before dragging the URL from the Assets panel, a link is still created in your document. In this situation, Dreamweaver uses the URL name as the hotspot.

The Edit button on the Assets panel is unavailable for the URLs category. Links cannot be edited; they can only be applied as shown in the preview area.

Pointing to a File

Dreamweaver provides an alternative method of identifying a link — pointing to it. By using the Point to File icon on the Property inspector, you can quickly fill in the Link text box by dragging your mouse to any existing named anchor or file visible in the Dreamweaver environment. With the Point to File feature, you can avoid browsing through folder after folder as you search for a file you can clearly see onscreen.

You can point to another open document, to a document in another frame in the same window, or to any named anchor visible on the screen. If your desired link is a named anchor located farther down the page, Dreamweaver automatically scrolls to find it. You can even point to a named anchor in another document, and Dreamweaver enters the full syntax correctly. Named anchors are covered in detail later in this chapter.

Perhaps one of the slickest ways to apply the Point to File feature is to use it in tandem with the Files panel. The Files panel lists all the existing files in any given Web site, and when both it and the Document window are onscreen, you can quickly point to any file.

Pointing to a file uses what could be called a *drag-and-release* mouse technique, as opposed to the more ordinary point-and-click or drag-and-drop method. To select a new link using the Point to File icon, follow these steps:

1. Select the text or the graphic that you'd like to make into a link.

2. In the Property inspector, click and hold the Point to File icon located to the right of the Link text box.

3. Holding down the mouse button, drag the mouse until it is over an existing link or named anchor in the Document window or a file in the Files panel. As you drag the mouse, a line extends from the Point to File icon, and the reminder Drag to a file to make a link appears in the Link text box.

4. When you locate the file you want to link to, release the mouse button. The filename with the accompanying path information is written into the Link text box as shown in Figure 10-4.

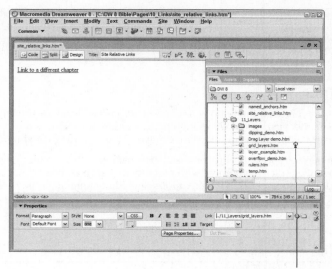

Point to File icon

Figure 10-4: The Point to File icon enables you to quickly insert a link to any onscreen file.

Addressing Types

Three types of URLs are used as links: absolute addresses, document-relative addresses, and site-root–relative addresses. The following list briefly looks at these address types.

✦ Absolute addresses require the full URL, as follows:

```
http://www.macromedia.com/software/dreamweaver/
```

This type of address is most often used for referencing links on another Web server.

✦ Document-relative addresses know the scheme, server, and path aspects of the URL. Include additional path information only if the link is outside the current Web page's folder. Links in the current document's folder can be addressed with their filenames only. To reference an item in a subfolder, just name the folder, enter a forward slash, and then enter the item's filename, as follows:

```
images/background.gif
```

✦ Site-root–relative addresses are indicated with a leading forward slash:

```
/navigation/upndown.html
```

This example links to a file named upndown.html stored in the navigation directory at the current site root. Dreamweaver translates site-relative links to document-relative links when the Preview in Browser feature is used.

Tip You can set your preference for document- or site-root–relative links on a site-by-site basis. Open your Site Definition dialog box by double-clicking the displayed site name in the Files panel drop-down list. In the General category of the Site Definition dialog box, choose the Links Relative To option you'd prefer.

Checking Links

A Webmaster must often perform the tedious but necessary task of verifying the links on all the Web pages in a site. Because of the Web's fluid nature, links can work one day and break the next. Dreamweaver includes powerful link-checking and link-updating capabilities.

Dreamweaver can generate reports for broken links, external links (links to files outside your site), and to orphaned files (files in your site with no links to them). You can check links for an open document, for all documents in a site, or for selected documents in the Files panel.

 Linking to Files

Linking to files properly is an essential task in building Web sites. In this Dreamweaver Technique, you practice linking to other files from text phrases and images.

1. From the Techniques site, expand the 10_Links folder and open the `links_start` file.

2. Select the phrase at the end of the first paragraph of placeholder text, Learn more....

3. In the Property inspector next to the Link field, click Browse for File (the folder icon) to open the Select File dialog box.

4. When the Select File dialog box opens, navigate to the 10_Links folder and choose `split_level_details.htm`; click OK when you're done.

The proper path is entered into the Link field by Dreamweaver. Assigning a link to a graphic is just as easy.

5. Select the image next to the Ranch style 2 bedroom label.

6. From the Property inspector, drag the Point to File icon to the Files panel and hover over the new_properties subfolder within the 10_Links folder.

The new_properties subfolder expands.

7. Select `ranch_style.htm` and release your left mouse button.

8. Repeat steps 5–7, selecting the image next to the Multi-level gardener's delight label and selecting `multi_level.htm` in the new_properties folder.

9. Save your page.

10. Press F12 to test your links in the browser.

It's especially important to let Dreamweaver write your links for you when target files are located in a different folder. Get into the habit of using the Browse for File and Point to File icons and you'll save yourself from linking errors.

To check links in the current document, choose File ➪ Check Page ➪ Check Links, or press Shift+F8. To generate a link report for the entire site, open the Files panel (Window ➪ Files), and, from the Site menu, choose Check Links Sitewide. To report on links for certain files, select the files or folders in the Files panel, right-click (Control+click) and then choose Check Links ➪ Selected Files/Folders. If the Link Checker panel is open, you can also click the Check Links button and then select the scope of your check: current document, entire site, or selected files in the site.

Tip   To stop an in-progress link check, click the Cancel button in the Link Checker panel.

All these methods open the Link Checker panel, displaying the results of the link check. In the Show drop-down list at the top of the Link Checker panel, select the report you want to see: Broken links, External links, or Orphaned Files. The Orphaned Files report is only available if you check the entire site. The broken links report verifies not only clickable hotspots to other HTML files, but also references to graphics and other external files.

You can save the link report by clicking the Save Report button on the Link Checker panel, or by right-clicking (Control+clicking) in the panel and choosing Save Results from the pop-up menu. To clear the Link Checker panel, right-click (Control+click) in the Link Checker panel and choose Clear Results.

Double-clicking an entry in the Link Checker panel opens the document where the error occurred, with the broken link selected. You can quickly correct the link using the Property inspector or by choosing Modify ➪ Change Link. To remove the link but leave the hotspot text, clear the Link field in the Property inspector, or choose Modify ➪ Remove Link. If the same URL is referenced in more than one place in your site, you can change all occurrences of it at once. To do this, choose Site ➪ Change Link Sitewide from the main menus, and enter the URL to be changed and then the new URL. Finally, click OK.

Adding an E-Mail Link

E-mail links are very common on the Web. When a user clicks an e-mail link, it displays a window for sending a new e-mail message (rather than opening a new Web page as a regular link does). The message window is convenient because it is preaddressed to the recipient. All the user has to do is add a subject, enter a message, and click Send.

Dreamweaver includes an object that streamlines the process of adding e-mail links. Just enter the text of the line and the e-mail address, and the link is ready. E-mail links, like other links, do not work when clicked in Dreamweaver. They must be previewed in a browser.

To enter an e-mail link, follow these steps:

1. Position your cursor where you want the e-mail link to appear.

2. From the Common category on the Insert bar, click the Email Link button. The Email Link dialog box, shown in Figure 10-5, appears.

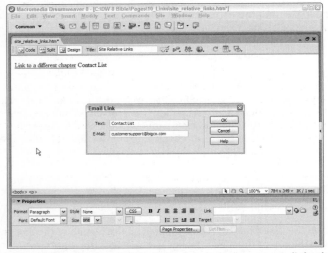

Figure 10-5: The Email Link dialog box helps you create links that make it simple for your Web page visitors to send e-mail messages.

3. Enter the visible text for the link in the Text field.

4. Enter the e-mail address in the E-Mail field.

Caution   The e-mail address must be in the format name@company.com. Dreamweaver does not check to ensure that you've entered the proper format.

5. Click OK when you're finished.

E-mail Warnings

Here's a bit of the frustration that Web designers sometimes face: On some browsers, notably Internet Explorer, users may see a dialog box when the e-mail link is first selected. The dialog box informs them that they are about to send an e-mail message over the Internet. The user has the option not to see these warnings, but there's no way for the Web designer to prevent them from appearing when an e-mail link is used. However, another method of collecting data from users — HTML forms — doesn't require the users to have e-mail software installed on their computer, and it allows users to send information to the server without receiving the warning message. Chapter 14 explains how to create HTML forms.

Note

If you already have the text for the e-mail link in the document, you can use the Property inspector to insert an e-mail link. Just highlight the text and in the Link field of the Property inspector, enter the URL in the following format:

```
mailto:name@company.com
```

Make sure that the URL is a valid e-mail address with the @ sign properly placed.

Navigating with Anchors

Whenever you normally link to an HTML page, through absolute or relative addressing, the browser displays the page from the top. Your Web visitors must scroll to any information rendered below the current screen. One HTML technique, however, links to a specific point anywhere on the page regardless of the display window's contents. This technique uses *named anchors*. A named anchor is simply an HTML anchor tag pair (`<a>`...`</a>`) that includes a `name` attribute. The named anchor serves as a target for links, allowing links to the middle of a page, or wherever the named anchor is located within the document.

Using named anchors is a two-step process. First, you place a named anchor somewhere on your Web page. This placement is coded in HTML as an anchor tag using the `name` attribute, with nothing between the opening and closing tags. In HTML, named anchors look like the following:

```
<a name="bible"></a>
```

The second step includes a link to that named anchor from somewhere else on your Web page. If used, a named anchor is referenced in the final portion of an Internet address, designated by the hash mark (#), as follows:

```
<a href="http://www.idest.com/Dreamweaver/index.htm#bible">
```

You can include any number of named anchors on a page and any number of links to named anchors on the current page or different pages. Named anchors are commonly used with a table of contents or index.

To insert a named anchor, follow these steps:

   1. Place the cursor where you want the named anchor to appear.

2. Choose Insert ➪ Named Anchor. You can also click the Named Anchor button in the Common category of the Insert bar or use the keyboard shortcut Ctrl+Alt+A (Command+Option+A).

3. The Named Anchor dialog box opens. Type the anchor name in the text box.

Named anchors are case-sensitive and must be unique within the page.

When you click OK, Dreamweaver places a named anchor symbol in the current cursor location and opens the Named Anchor Property inspector (shown in Figure 10-6).

In Design view, named anchors are represented by a small yellow icon with — surprise! — an anchor image on it in the page. If you can't see the named anchor symbol, choose View ➪ Visual Aids ➪ Invisible Elements; if the symbol is still not visible, update your Preference settings for the Invisible Elements category.

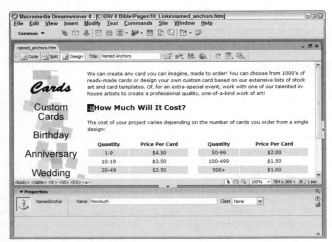

Figure 10-6: The Named Anchor tag enables you to link to specific areas of a Web page.

4. To change an anchor's name, click the named anchor symbol within the page and alter the text in the Property inspector.

As with other invisible symbols, the named anchor symbol can be cut and pasted or moved using the drag-and-drop method.

Moving Within the Same Document

One of the major advantages of using named anchors is the almost instantaneous response viewers receive when they link to named anchors from the same page. The browser just scrolls to the particular place in the document because the entire page is already loaded. For long text documents, this capability is an invaluable timesaver.

After you have placed a named anchor in your document, you can link to the anchor. You can create more than one named anchor in your document before adding links to the anchors. To create a link to a named anchor in the same document, follow these steps:

1. Select the text or image that you want to designate as a link.

2. In the Link text box of the Property inspector, type a hash mark (#) followed by the exact anchor name:

   `#start`

   Remember that anchor names are case-sensitive and must be unique in each document.

Tip   Place the named anchor one line above the heading or image to which you want to link the viewer. Browsers tend to be quite literal. If you place the named anchor on the same line, the browser renders it against the top of the window. Placing your named anchor up one line gives your topic a bit of breathing room in the display.

In Dreamweaver, you can also use the Point to File icon to choose a named anchor link. If your named anchor is in the same document, just drag the Point to File icon to the named anchor symbol. When you release the mouse, the address for the named anchor is inserted into the Link text box. If the named anchor is on the same page, but offscreen, Dreamweaver automatically scrolls the Document window as you drag toward the edge. In Windows, the closer you move to the edge, the faster Dreamweaver scrolls. Dreamweaver returns the screen to your original location, with the new link at the top of the screen after you release the mouse button.

In long documents with a table of contents or index linking to a number of named anchors, it's common practice — and a good idea — to place a link back to the top of the page after every screen or every topic. This technique enables your users to return to the menu quickly and pick another topic without having to manually scroll all the way back.

Using Named Anchors in a Different Page

If your table of contents is on a separate page from the topics of your site, you can use named anchors to send the viewer anywhere on a new page. The technique is the same as already explained for placing named anchors, but with one minor difference when it comes to linking. Instead of placing a hash mark and name to denote the named anchor, you must first include the URL of the linked page.

Suppose you want to call the disclaimer section of a legal page from your table of contents. You could insert something like the following in the Link text box of the Property inspector:

`legal.htm#disclaimer`

This link, when activated, first loads the referenced Web page (`legal.htm`) and then goes directly to the named anchor place (`#disclaimer`). Figure 10-7 shows how you enter this in the Property inspector. Keep in mind that you can use any form of addressing prior to the hash mark and named anchor.

Figure 10-7: You can link to any part of a separate Web page using named anchors.

Inserting Named Anchors

Named anchors are an excellent way to navigate within a page. In this Dreamweaver Technique, you add links and named anchors to a page to allow the user to move about the page more easily. To save time, three of the five named anchors have been done for you.

1. From the Techniques site, expand the 10_Links folder and open the `anchors_start` file.

2. Scroll down the page and place your cursor in front of the Queens heading.

3. Choose Insert ⇨ Named Anchor.

4. When the Named Anchor dialog box appears, enter **queens** in the Anchor Name field.

5. Near the top of the page, select the Queens entry in the list.

6. In the Property inspector's Link field, enter **#queens** and press Tab.

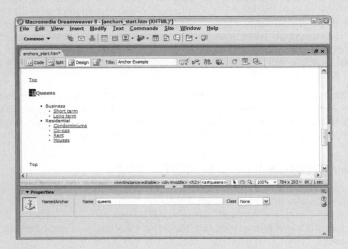

7. Repeat steps 2–6 to create a named anchor named **statenIsland** and link for the Staten Island entry, **#statenIsland**.

   It's good practice on a long page to include a link to the top of the page for every named anchor section. Again, most of the work has been done for you: you'll just need to add anchor links for the last two sections and a named anchor at the top of the page.

8. Scroll to the Queens section and select the word Top at the bottom of that section.

9. In the Property inspector's Link field, enter **#top** and press Tab.

10. Repeat steps 8 and 9 to add a link named **#top** to the word Top following the Staten Island section.

11. The last action is to insert a named anchor named top. Place your cursor at the top of the page and select Insert ⇨ Named Anchor.

12. When the Named Anchor dialog box opens, enter **top**.

13. Save your page and press F12 to test it in a browser.

END

When you test, notice that the page moves up and down with each anchor link selected.

Creating Null Links

One of the more obscure uses for named anchors comes into play when you are trying to use Dreamweaver's JavaScript Behavior feature. Because JavaScript needs to work with a particular type of tag to perform onMouseOver and other events, a useful trick is to create a null link—a link that doesn't actually link to anywhere.

You create a null link by marking some text or an image with a link to #nowhere. You can use any name for the nonexistent named anchor. In fact, you don't even have to use a name—you can just use a hash mark (#) by itself.

There's one problem to note, however: Netscape browsers have a tendency to send the page to the top if a link of this type is used. Many programmers have begun to substitute an empty call to a JavaScript function instead, such as javascript:. Dreamweaver itself now uses javascript:; instead of # when a new behavior is attached to an image.

Targeting Your Links

Thus far, all the links discussed in this chapter have had a similar effect: They open another Web page or section in your browser's window. What if you want to force the browser to open another window and load that new URL in the new window? HTML enables you to specify the target for your links.

Cross-Reference
Targets are most often used in conjunction with frames—that is, you can make a link in one frame open a file in another. For more information about this technique, see Chapter 16.

Targets do more than just display a page in a certain frame. Take a look at one of the HTML predefined targets used in a situation where you want to load another URL into a new window.

To specify a new browser window as the target for a link, follow these steps:

1. Select the text or image you want to designate as your new link.

2. In the Property inspector, enter the URL into the Link text box. After you've entered a link, the target option becomes active.

3. In the Target drop-down list, select _blank, as shown in Figure 10-8. You can also type it in the list box. Either way, Dreamweaver inserts a _blank option in the Target list box. Now, when your link is activated, the browser spawns a new window and loads the referenced link into it. The user has both windows available.

Figure 10-8: With the Target attribute, you can force a user's browser to open a separate window to display a specific link.

The _blank target is most often used when the originating Web page is acting as a jump station and has numerous links available. By keeping the original Web page open, the user can view another site without losing the origin point. You can even use a _blank target with links to named anchors in the same document.

Caution   Some versions of key online services, such as America Online and MSN TV (formerly WebTV), don't enable their built-in browsers to open new windows. Every link that is accessed is displayed in the same browser window.

Three other system-wide targets exist: _top, _parent, and _self. Both _top and _parent are primarily used with framesets: The _top target replaces the outermost frameset, and _parent replaces the frameset containing the current page. These two have the same effect, except in the case of nested framesets. The _self target is the default behavior, and only the current page is replaced.

Summary

Whether they are links for Web site navigation or jumps to other related sites, hypertext links are an essential part of any Web page. Dreamweaver gives you full control over your inserted links. Keep in mind the following points about links:

✦ Through a unique URL, you can access virtually any Web page, graphic, or other item available on the Internet.

✦ The HyperText Transfer Protocol (HTTP) is one of the most common methods of Internet connection, but Web pages can link to other formats, including FTP, e-mail, and newsgroups.

✦ Any of the three basic address formats — absolute, document-relative, or site-root– relative — can be inserted in the Link text box of Dreamweaver's Property inspector to create a link.

✦ Dreamweaver has several quick linking capabilities in the Assets panel and Point to File feature.

✦ Named anchors give you the power to jump to specific parts of any Web page, whether the page is the current one or one that is located on another server.

✦ With the _blank target attribute, you can force a link to open in a new browser window, leaving your original window available to the user.

In the next chapter, you learn how to work with layers and <div> tags in Dreamweaver.

✦   ✦   ✦

Adding Advanced Design Features

Working with Divs and Layers

For many years, page designers have taken for granted the capability to place text and graphics anywhere on a printed page — even enabling graphics, type, and other elements to bleed off a page. This flexibility in design has eluded Web designers until recently. Lack of absolute control over layout has been a high price to pay for the universality of HTML, which makes any Web page viewable by any system, regardless of the computer or the screen resolution.

Lately, however, the integration of positioned layers within the Cascading Style Sheets specification has brought true absolute positioning to the Web. Page designers with a yen for more control welcome the precision offered with Cascading Style Sheets-Positioning (CSS-P). CSS-P styles are typically applied to <div> tags, which are used to separate a page into different areas or divisions. In Dreamweaver jargon, a layer is a <div> tag dragged out with your mouse with the CSS-P styles automatically created and embedded in the page.

Dreamweaver's implementation of <div> tags and layers turns the promise of CSS-P into an intuitive, designer-friendly, layout-compatible reality. As the name implies, layers offer more than pixel-perfect positioning. You can stack one layer on another, hide some layers while showing others, move a layer across the screen, and even move several layers around the screen simultaneously. Layers add an entirely new dimension to the Web designer's palette. Dreamweaver enables you to create page layouts using layers.

This chapter explores every aspect of how layers work in Web pages. With the fundamentals under your belt, you learn how to create, modify, populate, and activate <div> tags and layers on your designs.

Divs and Layers 101

When the World Wide Web first made its debut in 1989, few people were concerned about the aesthetic layout of a page. In fact, because the Web was a descendant of Standard Generalized Markup Language (SGML) — a multiplatform text document and information markup specification — layout was trivialized. Content and the capability to use hypertext to jump from one page to another were emphasized. After the first graphical Web-browser software (Mosaic) was released, it quickly became clear that a page's graphics and layout could enhance a Web site's accessibility and marketability. Content was still king, but design was moving up quickly.

The first attempt at Web page layout was the server-side image map. This item was typically a large graphic (usually too hefty to be downloaded comfortably) with hotspots. Clicking a hotspot sent a message to the server, which returned a link to the browser. The download time for these files was horrendous, and the performance varied from acceptable to awful, depending on the server's load.

The widespread adoption of tables, released with HTML 2.0 and enhanced with HTML 3.2, radically changed layout control. Designers gained the capability to align objects and text — but a lot of graphical eye candy was still left to graphic files strategically located within the tables. The harder designers worked at precisely laying out their Web pages, the more they had to resort to workarounds such as nested tables and 1-pixel-wide GIFs used as spacers. To relieve the woes of Web designers everywhere, the W3C included a feature within the new Cascading Style Sheets specifications that allows for absolute positioning of an element upon a page. Absolute positioning enables an element, such as an image or block of text, to be placed anywhere on the Web page. Browser support for Cascading Style Sheets-Positioning specification began with fourth-generation browsers and has grown steadily ever since.

The addition of the third dimension, depth, truly turned the positioning specs into layers. Now objects can be positioned side by side, and they have a *z-index* property as well. The z-index gets its name from the practice in geometry of describing three-dimensional space with *x, y,* and *z* coordinates; z-index is also called the *stacking order* because objects can be stacked upon one another.

All these attributes, and others such as background color, can be assigned to a CSS style, as shown in the following code:

```
#header {
    position: absolute;
    z-index: 1;
    height: 115px;
    width: 400px;
    left: 100px;
    top: 50px;
    background: #FFCC33;
}
```

The CSS style is then applied to a `<div>` tag to represent an area on the page, like this:

```
<div id="header">Header content goes here.</div>
```

Dreamweaver calls `<div>` tags that are drawn with your mouse *layers*; the CSS style is automatically created and embedded in the page for you. Drawing out the same layer results in the same CSS code, except the selector name is automatically created for you (Layer1, Layer2, and so on) and the code is embedded in the page, like this:

```
<style type="text/css">
<!--
#Layer1 {
    position: absolute;
    z-index: 1;
    height: 115px;
```

```
       width: 400px;
       left: 100px;
       top: 50px;
       background: #FFCC33;
     }
     -->
     </style>
```

The `<div>` code is also added for you, sans content, like this:

```
<div id="Layer1"></div>
```

Although both approaches are valid, many designers prefer to keep the CSS information in the style sheet rather than embedded. As you see in this chapter, Dreamweaver supports both methods fully.

If you don't define a unit of measurement for layer positioning, Dreamweaver defaults to pixels. If you edit out the unit of measurement, the Web browser defaults to pixels.

Note

Netscape developed two additional proprietary tags for using layers in its 4.x browser: `<layer>` and `<ilayer>`. The primary difference between the two tags has to do with positioning: The `<layer>` tag is used for absolute positioning, and the `<ilayer>` tag for relative positioning. These tags are not supported in Navigator 6.0 or later; instead, Netscape's more recent browsers fully support the CSS standard tags, `<div>` and `<span>`.

Positioning Measurement

The positioning of layers is determined by aligning elements on an x-axis and a y-axis. In CSS, the x-axis (defined as *Left* in CSS syntax) begins at the left side of the page, and the y-axis (defined as *Top* in CSS syntax) is measured from the top of the page down. As with many of the other CSS features, you have your choice of measurement systems for Left and Top positioning. All measurements are given in Dreamweaver as a number followed by the abbreviation of the measurement system (without any intervening spaces). The measurement system options are as follows:

Unit	Abbreviation	Measurement
Pixels	Px	Relative to the screen
Points	pt	1 pt = 1/72 in
Inches	in	1 in = 2.54 cm
Centimeters	cm	1 cm = 0.3937 in
Millimeters	mm	1 mm = 0.03937 in
Picas	pc	1 pc = 12 pt
EMS	Em	The height of the element's font
Percentage	%	Relative to the browser window

Placing <div> Tags

As noted earlier, CSS-P information can be defined in a style sheet or inline. Defining the CSS rule in a style sheet (either external or internal) has the benefit of truly separating content from presentation, which, in turn, makes it easier to reshape the content via another style sheet for another medium. A block of text, for example, can be positioned on the right when viewed in a monitor and left when printed out. Moreover, many designers find that centralizing the layout information in a style sheet is a far more effective way to work. Often the same layout is used on multiple pages of a site; with CSS-P rules in an external style sheet, you can modify the layout of all the related pages simply by altering the CSS in the style sheet. To accomplish the same change when the CSS is applied inline would require extensive search-and-replace and the re-uploading of every altered file.

Dreamweaver recognizes the importance of the <div> tag in modern Web site design with the integration of the <div> object. Not only is the insertion of the <div> tag now possible in Design view, but Dreamweaver also provides visual feedback indicating placement and easy modification through the Property and Tag inspectors.

Defining a CSS Rule for a <div> Tag

When using a <div> object, the typical workflow is to first create the required CSS rules. In most cases, the CSS rule uses the ID selector because it is applied to only one <div> tag. It's a good idea to give your CSS rules descriptive names, such as #header, #footer, #mainContent, and #navigation.

Cross-Reference   If you're not familiar with creating CSS style rules, see Chapter 7 for more information.

To create a CSS rule for use with <div> tags, follow these steps:

1. Choose Window ➪ CSS Styles to open the CSS Styles panel.

2. From the CSS Styles panel, click the New CSS Rule button. This action opens the New CSS Rule dialog box.

3. From the New CSS Rule dialog box, set the Type option to Advanced.

4. Enter a name for your new style in the Selector field. It's a good idea to create the style for your <div> tag as an ID. To create an ID, preface the style name with a pound sign, as in #mainContent.

5. If you want to create your style in an external style sheet, use the Browse button to locate an existing style sheet.

6. If you want to add the style to the <head> region of the current document, select Define In This Document Only.

7. Click OK when you're finished to open the CSS Rule Definition dialog.

8. Select the Positioning category.

9. From the Positioning category (see Figure 11-1), enter desired values for the following attributes: Type, Width, Height, Visibility, Z-Index, Overflow, Placement (Top, Right, Bottom, and Left), and Clip settings (Top, Right, Bottom, Left). Overflow and Clip settings are optional.

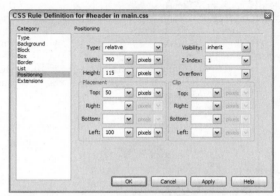

Figure 11-1: Use the Positioning category of the CSS Rule Definition dialog box to set layer attributes in an internal or external style sheet.

The Type attribute offers three options: Absolute, Relative, and Static. An Absolute <div> uses the upper-left corner as the origin for the Left and Top measurements, whereas Relative <div> tags originate from the current location. Use Static when you don't want to place the <div> in a certain position, but you still want to specify a rectangular block. Static <div> types ignore the Left and Top attributes.

10. If appropriate, select other categories and enter any additional style sheet attributes. Click OK when you're finished.

Inserting the <div> Tag

After you have defined your CSS rule, follow these steps to add a <div> tag to the page:

1. Place your cursor where you want the <div> tag to appear. You can also select content on a page you'd like to wrap a <div> tag around.

2. From the Layout category of the Insert bar, click the Insert Div Tag button. Alternatively, you can choose Insert ➪ Layout Objects ➪ Div Tag. Dreamweaver displays the Insert Div Tag dialog box, as shown in Figure 11-2.

3. Choose the CSS rule from either the Class or ID list. Dreamweaver shows only those IDs that have not been previously applied.

Tip If the CSS rule is not available from either of the lists—perhaps because the style sheet is dynamically applied—you can enter the name directly into either the Class or ID field. However, unless Design Time Style Sheets are used to show the styles, the layout won't render properly in Dreamweaver.

Insert Div Tag

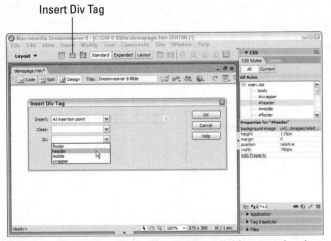

Figure 11-2: Dreamweaver lists all the available CSS rules that can be applied to a new `<div>` tag either as a Class or an ID.

4. Select where you'd like the tag placed from the Insert list. Dreamweaver provides different options depending on the makeup of the page and whether content is already selected. Only tags with assigned IDs are listed, along with the `<body>` tag. Here are the Insert options you can choose from:

- **At Insertion Point:** Inserts the `<div>` tag at the current cursor position. This option is available only if no content is selected.

- **Wrap Around Selection:** Wraps the `<div>` tag around the currently selected content. Available only if a selection was made prior to inserting the `<div>` tag.

- **Before Tag:** Puts the tag before the tag selected in the adjacent field.

- **After Tag:** Inserts the `<div>` tag after the tag selected in the adjacent field.

- **After Start Of Tag:** Places the `<div>` tag immediately following the opening tag in a tag pair, before any content within the tag.

- **Before End Of Tag:** Inserts the tag right before the closing tag in a tag pair, after any content within the tag.

Caution   Be sure *not* to insert the `<div>` tag in the middle of an empty tag. Empty tags, you may remember, are tags that have no corresponding closing tag and enclose no content, such as `<img>`.

5. Click OK when you're finished to insert the tag.

If the `<div>` tag was not wrapped around previously selected content, Dreamweaver adds placeholder text to help identify the tag and its class or ID. As another helpful aid to identification, a red outline appears when your cursor crosses the outer boundary of the `<div>`. This highlight is controlled by the Mouse-Over option found in the Highlighting category of Preferences. The red outline is replaced by a thick blue one when the `<div>` tag is selected, as shown in Figure 11-3.

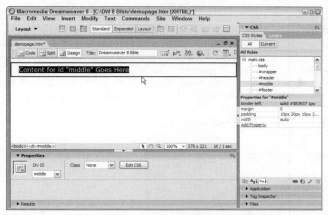

Figure 11-3: A thick, blue outline appears around the div when selected.

Select the `<div>` in Design view and the Property inspector displays all the current attributes. If you make any changes in the Property inspector, such as adding or altering the background color, the change is written into the associated CSS style rule. If the `<div>` tag's position property is set to absolute, the outline is supplemented with positioning and sizing handles. The interaction between object, Property inspector, and style sheet holds true if you drag the selected `<div>` around the page or resize it using the sizing handles; see the following section, "Modifying a Layer," for more details. You can also modify `<div>` tag properties by editing the style rule directly or by altering its properties on the Tag Inspector panel.

Caution If your layout is controlled by an external style sheet that also controls the layout of other pages in your site, be careful when adjusting the properties of a `<div>` tag. When you make changes, Dreamweaver modifies the CSS style rule in the external style sheet, potentially altering the layout of other pages using the same style sheet.

Visualizing <div> Tags

The `<div>` tag is a structural element, not intended to be apparent when viewed through the browser at run-time. Design-time, however, is another matter. Designers often need to be able to see the underlying structure to craft their layouts; they also need to be able to hide the structure at any point so they can see a browser-like view while designing.

New In Dreamweaver Dreamweaver provides a full slate of visualization options for CSS layouts. Each of the options, found under the Visual Aids menu button on the Document toolbar or the View ➪ Visual Aids menu item, can be toggled in and out of view at will. There are three different visualizations that can be used singly or in combination: CSS Layout Backgrounds, CSS Layout Box Model, and CSS Layout Outlines.

The three CSS layout visualization options apply to other page elements in addition to `<div>` tags. Any page element with the CSS declaration of `display:block`, `position:absolute`, or `position:relative` is considered a block layout element and is affected as well. For example, if an `<a>` tag style was set to `display:block`—a common method used when developing CSS navigation buttons—it would be rendered with the visualizations like `<div>` tags.

CSS Layout Backgrounds

In the early stages of laying out a page, it's often helpful to see your basic building blocks clearly depicted. When you invoke the CSS Layout Background options from the Visual Aids menu, Dreamweaver clears any background image or color previously defined in the CSS styles and replaces them with a different solid color for each `<div>` tag. The resulting patchwork shows at a glance how the page is structured (see Figure 11-4). This option is also useful when debugging layouts because it clearly shows which `<div>` tags — if any — overlap.

Figure 11-4: Turn on CSS Layout Backgrounds when first creating your CSS layout or debugging it.

Tip   The colors assigned to each of the `<div>` backgrounds are random and can't be predefined. A new set of colors is used every time you toggle CSS Layout Backgrounds into view.

CSS Layout Box Model

All CSS block elements are rendered in the browser according to the CSS box model. The box model, established by the W3C CSS standards body, determines how much room a block element actually takes up on the page. The amount of space required for a block element, such as a `<div>` tag, is a combination of the declared width, plus the padding, border, and margin settings. For example, say a div tag has the following style declared:

```
#myBox {
   width:200px;
   padding:10px;
   border:5px;
   margin:10px;
}
```

Although nominally, the myBox style appears to be 200 pixels wide, CSS specifications indicate that it will actually take up 250 pixels of space. Here's how the space requirement is figured:

```
200 pixels content area width
 10 pixels padding-left
 10 pixels padding-right
```

```
 5 pixels border-left
 5 pixels border-right
10 pixels margin-left
10 pixels margin-right
250 pixels width total
```

To make it easy for you to design with the box model in mind, Dreamweaver provides the CSS Layout Box Model visual aid. When enabled, any selected `<div>` tag or otherwise affected block element, depicts all the contributing elements: content area (the width), padding, borders, and margins. Both the padding and margins are shown with colored diagonal lines, although in opposing directions, as shown in Figure 11-5.

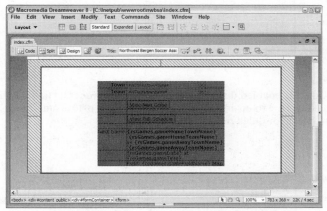

Figure 11-5: The CSS Layout Box Model visual aid reveals the unseen reserved space around layout elements.

Dreamweaver not only reveals how the layout element is constructed visually, you'll also receive a wealth of information from tooltips that appear as you move your cursor around the element. The information in the tooltip varies according to cursor's position:

✦ Hover over the content area to see all the CSS properties, including those related to the box model.

✦ Move your cursor over the padding or margin areas to see their respective values; for example, Margin: 10px.

✦ With the cursor over the border, the tooltip reveals the current values for the margin, border, and padding properties.

I recommend turning on the CSS Layout Box Model feature in the fine-tuning and debugging stages of your Web page development; it's a great tool for understanding exactly why elements on your page are positioned the way they are.

CSS Layout Outlines

CSS Layout Outlines, when enabled, place a border around `<div>` tags and other block layout elements (see Figure 11-6). The outline is a dashed style for inserted `<div>` tags and a solid border for drawn Dreamweaver layers.

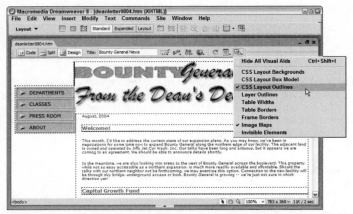

Figure 11-6: Highlight your `<div>` tags at design-time with CSS Layout Outlines.

I tend to keep CSS Layout Outlines enabled during most of my design process; I find having the outlines visible quickly allows me to insert content in just the right places and, more importantly, select the `<div>` tags for quick refinement.

 ## Applying a CSS Layout

In this Technique, you apply previously defined CSS styles to a variety of `<div>` tags to create a basic layout.

1. From the Techniques site, expand the 11_Divs-Layers folder and open `div_start.htm`.

   The first style to apply acts as a container for the entire page; to apply this properly, you'll need to position the cursor properly.

2. Place your cursor in the series of links on the page and click the `<p>` tag in the Tag Selector.

3. From the Insert bar's Layout category, click Insert Div Tag.

4. When the Insert Div Tag dialog box opens, make sure the Insert list is set to Wrap Around Selection.

5. From the ID list, choose Wrapper and click OK.

Next, add the first of three `<div>` tags, the header so that it appears with the `wrapper` `<div>` tag:

1. From the Insert bar's Layout category, click Insert Div Tag.

2. From the Insert list, choose After Start Of Tag and then, when the adjacent list appears, select `<div id="wrapper">`.

3. From the ID list, choose Header and click OK.

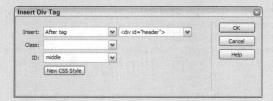

4. Click Delete to remove the selected placeholder text.

Now you're ready to insert the `middle <div>` tag after the `header <div>` tag:

1. From the Insert bar's Layout category, click Insert Div Tag.

2. From the Insert list, choose After Tag and then, when the adjacent list appears, select `<div id="header">`.

3. From the ID list, choose Middle and click OK.

The final `<div>` wraps around navigation links and forms the bottom area, the footer:

1. Place your cursor in the series of links on the page and click the `<p>` tag in the Tag Selector.

2. From the Insert bar's Layout category, click Insert Div Tag.

3. When the Insert Div Tag dialog box opens, make sure the Insert list is set to Wrap Around Selection and, from the ID list, choose Footer; click OK when you're done.

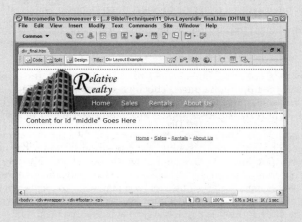

4. Save your page.

Your new CSS-based layout is now ready to be filled out with content.

Creating Layers with Dreamweaver

Dreamweaver enables you to drag out embedded styled <div> tags, also known as *layers*, creatively and precisely—and without coding. You can drag out a layer, placing and sizing it by eye, or choose to do it by the numbers—it's up to you. Moreover, you can combine the methods, quickly eyeballing and roughing out a layer layout and then aligning the edges precisely. For Web design that approaches conventional page layout, Dreamweaver even includes rulers and a grid to which you can snap your layers. Creating layers in Dreamweaver can be handled in one of three ways:

✦ You can drag out a layer after clicking the Draw Layer button on the Insert bar.

✦ You can add a layer in a predetermined size by choosing Insert ⇨ Layout Objects ⇨ Layer.

✦ You can create a layer with mathematical precision through the CSS Styles panel.

The first two methods are quite intuitive and are explained in the following section. The CSS Styles panel method is examined later.

Inserting a Layer Object

When you want to draw out your layer quickly, use the object approach. If you come from a traditional page-designer background and are accustomed to using a program such as QuarkXPress or PageMaker, you're already familiar with drawing out frames or text boxes with the click-and-drag technique. Dreamweaver uses the same method for placing and sizing new layer objects. To draw out a layer as an object, follow these steps:

1. From the Layout category of the Insert bar, click the Draw Layer button. Your pointer becomes a crosshairs cursor. (If you decide not to draw out a layer, you can press Esc at this point or just click once without dragging to abort the process.)

2. Click anywhere in your document to position the layer and drag out a rectangle. Release the mouse button when you have an approximate size and shape that is satisfactory (see Figure 11-7).

After you've dragged out your layer, notice several changes to the screen. First, the layer now has a small box on the outside of the upper-left corner. This box, shown in Figure 11-8, is the Selection handle, which you can use to move an existing layer around the Web page. When you click the selection handle, eight resize handles appear around the perimeter of the layer.

Another subtle but important addition to the screen is the Layer icon. Like the other Invisible Element icons, the Layer icon can be cut, copied, pasted, and repositioned. When you move the Layer icon, however, its corresponding layer does not move—you are actually only moving the code for the layer to a different place in the HTML source. Generally, the location of the actual layer code in the HTML is immaterial—however, you may want to locate your layer source in a specific area to be appropriately placed for accessibility purposes. Dragging and positioning Layer icons one after another is a quick way to achieve this task.

Using the Insert ⇨ Layout Objects ⇨ Layer Command

The second method for creating a layer is to use the menus. Instead of selecting an object from the Insert bar, choose Insert ⇨ Layout Objects ⇨ Layer. Unlike the click-and-drag method, inserting a layer through the menu automatically creates a layer in the upper-left corner; the default size is 200 pixels wide x 115 pixels high.

Layer Icon   Draw Layer   Selected Layer

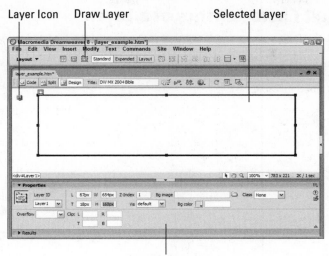

Layer Property Inspector

Figure 11-7: After selecting the Draw Layer object in the Insert bar (Layout category), the pointer becomes crosshairs when you are working on the page. Click and drag to create the layer.

Selection Handle

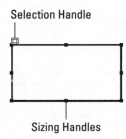

Sizing Handles

Figure 11-8: After a layer is created, you can move it by dragging the selection handle and size it with the resize handles.

Although the layer is by default positioned in the upper-left corner of the Document window, it does not have any coordinates listed in the Property inspector. The position coordinates are added when you drag the layer into a new position. If you repeatedly add new layers through the menus without moving them to new positions, each layer stacks directly on top of the previous one, with no offset.

Caution

It's important to assign a specific position (left and top) to every layer. Otherwise, the browser displays all layers directly on top of one another. To give a layer measurements, after you've inserted it through the menu, be sure to drag the layer, even slightly, or manually type coordinates in the Property inspector.

Setting Default Characteristics of a Layer

You can designate the default size—as well as other features—of the inserted layer with Insert ➪ Layout Objects ➪ Layer. Choose Edit ➪ Preferences (Dreamweaver ➪ Preferences) or use the keyboard shortcut Ctrl+U (Command+U) to open the Preferences dialog box. Select the Layers category. The Layers Preferences category (see Figure 11-9) helps you set the layer attributes described in Table 11-1.

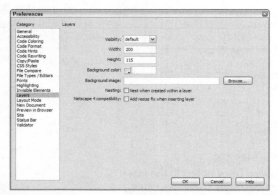

Figure 11-9: If you're building layers to a certain specification, use the Layers Preferences category to designate your options.

Table 11-1: Layers Preferences

Layer Preference	Description
Visibility	Determines the initial state of visibility for a layer. The options are default, inherit, visible, and hidden.
Width	Sets the width of the layer in the measurement system of your choice. The default is 200 pixels.
Height	Sets the height of the layer in the measurement system of your choice. The default is 115 pixels.
Background Color	Sets a color for the layer background. Select the color from the color palette of Web-safe colors.
Background Image	Sets an image for the layer background. In the text box, enter the path to the graphics file or click the Browse button to locate the file.
Nesting	If you want to nest layers when one layer is placed in the other automatically, check the Nest When Created Within A Layer checkbox.
Netscape 4 Compatibility	Select this option to add code for a workaround to a known problem in Navigator 4.x browsers, which causes layers to lose their positioning coordinates when the user resizes the browser window.

Choosing Relative Instead of Absolute Positioning

In many cases, absolute positioning uses the top-left corner of the Web page—the position at which the `<body>` tag begins—as the point of origin for positioning the layers. You can also specify measurements relative to other objects, such as `<divs>`. Dreamweaver offers several methods to accomplish relative positioning.

Using the Relative Attribute

In the first method for handling relative positioning, you select Relative as the Type attribute in the Style Sheet Positioning category. Relative positioning does not force a fixed position; instead, the positioning is guided by the HTML tags around it. For example, you may place a list of some items within a table and set the positioning relative to the table. You can see the effect of this sequence in Figure 11-10. Notice that Dreamweaver does not display sizing handles or a selection handle for relative layers.

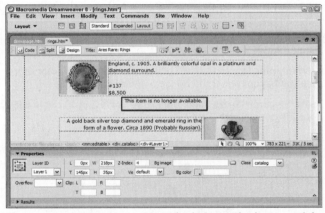

Figure 11-10: Layer1 is positioned relative to the bottom of the table.

Relative attributes can be useful, particularly if you want to place the positioned objects within free-flowing HTML. Free-flowing HTML repositions itself based on the size of the browser. When you're using this technique, remember to place your relative layers within absolutely positioned layers. Otherwise, when the end user resizes the browser, the relative layers position themselves relative to the browser and not to the absolutely positioned layers. This situation can produce messy results—use relative positioning with caution when mixed with absolute layers.

Using Nested Layers

The second technique for positioning layers relatively uses nested layers. After you nest one layer inside another, the inner layer uses the upper-left corner of the outer layer as its orientation point. One approach for created a nested layer is to position your cursor in the outer layer or `<div>` tag and press Alt (Option) after you start to drag out your layer. For more details about nesting layers, refer to the section "Nesting with the Layers Panel," later in this chapter.

Modifying a Layer

Dreamweaver helps you deftly alter layers after you have created them. Because of the complexity of managing layers, Dreamweaver offers a tool in addition to the usual Property inspector: the Layers panel. This tool enables you to select any of the layers on the current page quickly, change layer relationships, modify their visibility, and adjust their stacking order. You can also alter the visibility and stacking order of a selected layer in the Property inspector, along with many other attributes. Before any modifications can be accomplished, however, you have to select the layer.

Selecting a Layer

You can choose from several methods to select a layer for alteration (see Figure 11-11). The selection method you choose generally depends on the complexity of your page layout:

✦ When you have only a few layers that are not overlapping, just click the selection handle of a layer to select it.

✦ When you have layers placed in specific places in the HTML code (for example, a layer embedded in a table using relative positioning), click the Layer icon.

✦ When you have many overlapping layers that are being addressed by one or more JavaScript functions, use the Layers panel to choose a layer by name.

✦ When you're working with invisible layers, click the <div> (or <span>) tag in the Tag Selector to reveal the outline of the layer.

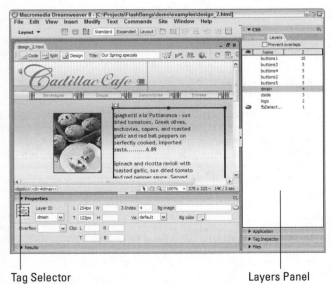

Tag Selector   Layers Panel

Figure 11-11: There are four different methods for selecting a layer to modify.

Resizing a Layer

To resize a layer, position the pointer over one of the eight resize handles surrounding the selected layer. When over the handles, the pointer changes shape to a two- or four-headed arrow. Now click and drag the layer to a new size and shape.

You can also use the arrow keys to resize your layer with more precision. The following keyboard shortcuts change the width and height dimensions while the layer remains anchored by the upper-left corner:

✦ When the layer is selected, press Ctrl+arrow (Command+arrow) to expand or contract the layer by 1 pixel.

✦ Press Ctrl+Shift+arrow (Command+Shift+arrow) to increase or decrease the selected layer by 10 pixels.

Tip You can quickly preview the position of a layer on a Web page without leaving Dreamweaver. Deselecting the View ➪ Visual Aids ➪ Layer Borders option leaves the layer outline displayed only when the layer is selected; otherwise, it is not shown.

Moving a Layer

The easiest way to reposition a layer is to drag the selection handle. If you don't see the handle on a layer, click anywhere in the layer. You can drag the layer anywhere on the screen — or off the bottom or right side of the screen. To move the layer off the left side or top of the screen, enter a negative value in the left and top (L and T) text boxes of the Layer Property inspector.

Tip To hide the layer completely, match the negative value with the width or height of the layer. For example, if your layer is 220 pixels wide and you want to position it offscreen to the left (so that the layer can slide onto the page at the click of a mouse), set the Left position at –220 pixels.

As with resizing layers, you can also use the arrow keys to move the layer more precisely:

✦ Press any arrow key to move the selected layer 1 pixel in any direction.

✦ Use Shift+arrow to move the selected layer by 10 pixels.

Using the Layer Property Inspector

You can modify almost all the CSS-P attributes for your layer right from the Layer Property inspector, shown in Figure 11-12. Certain attributes, such as width, height, and background image and color are self-explanatory or recognizable from other objects. Other layers-only attributes such as visibility and inheritance require further explanation. Table 11-2 describes all the Layer properties, and the following sections discuss the features unique to layers.

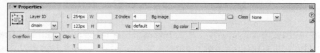

Figure 11-12: The Layer Property inspector makes it easy to move, resize, hide, and manipulate all the visual elements of a layer.

Table 11-2: Layer Property Inspector Options

Layer Attribute	Possible Values	Description
BgColor	Any hexadecimal or valid color name	Background color for the layer.
BgImage	Any valid graphic file	Background image for the layer.
Clip (Top, Bottom, Left, Right)	Any positive integer	Measurements for the displayable region of the layer. If the values are not specified, the entire layer is visible.
H (Height)	Any integer measurement in pixels, centimeters, millimeters, inches, points, percentage, ems, or picas	Vertical measurement of the layer.
L (Left)	Any integer measurement in pixels, centimeters, millimeters, inches, points, percentage, ems, or picas	Distance measured from the origin point on the left.
Name	Any unique name without spaces or special characters	A label for the layer so that it can be addressed by style sheets or JavaScript functions.
Overflow	`visible`, `scroll`, `hidden`, or `auto`	An indication of how text or images larger than the layer should be handled.
T (Top)	Any integer measurement in pixels, centimeters, millimeters, inches, points, percentage, ems, or picas	The distance measured from the origin point on the top.
Tag	`span` or `div`	Type of HTML tag to use for the layer.
Vis (Visibility)	`default`, `inherit`, `visible`, or `hidden`	An indication of whether a layer is displayed. If visibility is set to `inherit`, the layer takes on the characteristic of the parent layer.
W (Width)	Any integer measurement in pixels, centimeters, millimeters, inches, points, percentage, ems, or picas	The horizontal measurement of the layer.
Z-Index	Any integer	Stacking order of the layer relative to other layers on the Web page. Higher numbers are closer to the top.

Inserting a Layer

In this Technique, you add a Dreamweaver layer to a CSS layout. The layer is absolutely positioned within a relatively positioned `<div>` tag so that if the centered layout moves, the layer stays in the proper place.

1. From the 11_Div_Layers folder, open `layer_start.htm`.

2. Place your cursor in the header `<div>`.

3. From the Insert bar's Layout category, click Draw Layer.

4. Begin dragging out a rectangle on the right side of the header div and, while dragging, press and hold Alt (Option). When your rectangle is approximately 150 pixels wide by 50 pixels high, release the mouse and then Alt (Option).

   By pressing Alt (Option) while drawing the layer, Dreamweaver puts the code for the layer at the cursor position, inside the header `<div>`, effectively nesting the layer.

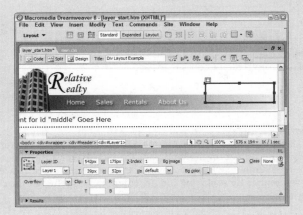

5. With your cursor inside the newly drawn layer, switch to the Insert bar's Common category and click Images: Image.

6. In the Select Image Source dialog box, navigate to the images folder and select `new_properties.jpg`.

   You'll note that the Property inspector shows the images dimensions as 166 x 55 pixels.

7. Select the layer handle and in its Property inspector, change the Width value to **166px** and Height to **55px**.

8. Precisely position the layer by setting the Left value to **533px** and Top to **50px**.

   The last step is to rename the layer and its accompanying style from the generic Layer1 to something more precise.

Continued

Continued

9. In the Property inspector's Name field, enter **new_properties**.

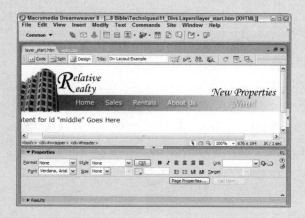

10. Save your page.

If you test your page by previewing in the browser, you'll notice that the absolutely positioned layer stays in the correct place even if the window is resized.

Name

Names are important when working with layers. So you can refer to them properly for both CSS and JavaScript purposes, each layer must have a unique ID attribute, unique among the layers and unique among every other object on the Web page. Dreamweaver automatically names each layer as it is created in sequence: Layer1, Layer2, and so forth. You can enter a name that is easier for you to remember by replacing the provided name in the text box on the far left of the Property inspector.

Caution   Netscape Navigator 4.x is strict about its use of the ID attribute. You must ensure that you give the layer an alphanumeric name that does not use spacing or special characters (such as the underscore or percentage sign). Moreover, make sure your layer name begins with a letter and not a number—in other words, layer9 works, but 9layer can cause problems.

Tag Attribute

The Tag drop-down list contains the HTML tags that can be associated with the layer. By default, the positioned layer has <div> as the tag, but you can also choose <span>. As previously noted, the <div> and <span> tags are endorsed by the World Wide Web Consortium group as part of its CSS standards.

Visibility

Visibility (Vis in the Property inspector) defines whether you can see a layer on a Web page. Four values are available:

✦ **Default:** Enables the browser to set the visibility attribute. Most browsers use the inherit value as their default.

✦ **Inherit:** Sets the visibility to the same value as that of the parent layer, which enables a series of layers to be hidden or made visible by changing only one layer.

✦ **Visible:** Causes the layer and all its contents to be displayed.

✦ **Hidden:** Makes the current layer and all its contents invisible.

Remember the following when you're specifying visibility:

✦ Whether or not you can see a layer, remember that the layer still occupies space on the page and demands some of the page-loading time. Hiding a layer does not affect the layout of the page, and invisible graphics take just as long to download as visible graphics.

✦ When you are defining the visibility of a positioned object or layer, do not use default as the visibility value. A designer does not necessarily know whether the site's end user has set the default visibility to visible or hidden. Designing an effective Web page can be difficult without this knowledge. The common browser default is for visibility to be inherited, if not specifically shown or hidden.

Overflow

Normally, a layer expands to fit the text or graphics inserted into it. You can, however, restrict the size of a layer by changing the height and width values in the Property inspector. What happens when you define a layer to be too small for an image, or when an amount of text depends on the setting of the layer's overflow attribute? CSS layers (the <div> and <span> tags) support four different overflow settings:

<div> versus <span>

The major difference between <div> and <span> is that the <div> is a block-level element, and the <span> is inline.

When you are positioning relatively (the elements are in the normal flow of the document), a <div> always causes the next element to appear on a new line. Block-level elements, such as <h1> and <p>, always create a new line unless the display property is set to inline using CSS.

The reverse is true of <span> tags. The <span> tag is an inline element and displays just like an image or link, without altering the text around it.

Generally <div> tags are used for block level elements that require positioning, and <span> tags are more commonly used to apply inline formatting over positioning.

If you're trying to manipulate layers via JavaScript, note that Netscape 4 does not allow scripting of <span> tags. For this reason alone, if you want to keep Netscape support, it is advisable to use <div> tags over <span> tags for positioned elements.

✦ **Visible (Default):** All the overflowing text or image is displayed, and the height and width settings established for the layer are ignored.

✦ **Hidden:** The portion of the text or graphic that overflows the dimensions is not visible.

✦ **Scroll:** Horizontal and vertical scroll bars are added to the layer regardless of the content size or amount, and regardless of the layer's measurements.

✦ **Auto:** When the content of the layer exceeds the width and/or height values, horizontal and vertical scroll bars appear.

Currently, support for the `overflow` attribute is spotty at best. Dreamweaver doesn't display the result in the Document window; it must be previewed in a browser to be seen. Navigator offers limited support: Only the attribute's `hidden` value works correctly, and just for text. Only Internet Explorer 4.0 or later and Netscape 6 render the `overflow` attribute correctly, as shown in Figure 11-13.

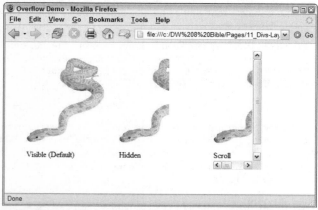

Figure 11-13: When your contents are larger than the dimensions of your layer, you can regulate the results with the `overflow` attribute.

Clipping

If you're familiar with the process of cropping an image, you'll quickly grasp the concept of clipping layers. Just as desktop publishing software hides but doesn't delete the portion of the picture outside the crop marks, layers can mask the area outside the clipping region defined by the Left, Top, Right, and Bottom values in the Clip section of the Layer Property inspector.

All clipping values are measured from the upper-left corner of the layer. You can use any CSS standard measurement system: pixels (the default), inches, centimeters, millimeters, ems, or picas.

The current implementation of CSS supports only rectangular clipping. When you look at the code for a clipped layer, you see the values you inserted in the Layer Property inspector in parentheses following the `clip` attribute, with the `rect` (for rectangular) keyword, as follows:

```
<div id="Layer1" style="position:absolute; left:54px; top:24px; ⟳
width:400px; height:115px; z-index:1; visibility:inherit; ⟳
clip:rect(10px 100px 100px 10px)">
```

A Visual Clipping Technique

In Dreamweaver, you cannot draw the clipping region visually—the values have to be explicitly input in the Clip section of the Layer Property inspector. That said, a trick using a second temporary layer can make it easier to position your clipping. Follow these steps to get accurate clipping values:

1. Insert your original layer and image.

2. Nest a second, temporary layer inside the first, original layer (click the Draw Layer button in the Insert bar and draw out the second layer inside the first).

   If you have your Layer Preferences set so that a layer does not automatically nest when created inside another layer, press the Alt (Option) key while you draw your layer to override the preference.

3. Position the second layer over the area you want to clip. Use the layer's sizing handles to alter the size and shape, if necessary.

4. Note the position and dimensions of the second layer (the Left, Top, Width, and Height values).

5. Delete the second layer.

6. In the Property inspector for the original layer, enter the Clip values as follows:

   - **L:** Enter the Left value for the second layer.
   - **T:** Enter the Top value for the second layer.
   - **R:** Add the second layer's Left value to its Width value.
   - **B:** Add the second layer's Top value to its Height value.

Dreamweaver displays the clipped layer after you enter the final value. The following figure shows the original layer and the temporary layer on the left, and the final clipped version of the original layer on the right.

Generally, you specify values for all four criteria: Left, Top, Right, and Bottom. You can also leave the Left and Top values empty or use the keyword auto—which causes the Left and Top values to be set at the origin point: 0,0. If you leave any of the clipping values blank, the blank attributes are set to auto.

Z-index

One of a layer's most powerful features is its capability to appear above or below other layers. You can change this order, known as the *z-index*, dynamically. Whenever a new layer is added, Dreamweaver automatically increments the z-index—layers with higher z-index values are positioned above layers with lower z-index values. The z-index can be adjusted manually in either the Layer Property inspector or the Layers panel. The z-index must be an integer, either negative or positive.

Tip   Although some Web designers use high values for the z-index, such as 3,000, the z-index is completely relative. The only reason to increase a z-index to an extremely high number is to ensure that a particular layer remains on top.

Certain types of objects—including Java applets, Plugins, and ActiveX controls—ignore the z-index setting when included in a layer and appear as the uppermost layer. However, certain ActiveX controls—most notably Flash—can be made to respect the z-index. If you need HTML content on top of active content, you can always hide the layer containing the ActiveX control when necessary.

Caution   Working with the above and below attributes can be confusing. Notice that they determine which layer is to appear on top of or underneath the current layer, and not which layer the present layer is above or below.

Background Image or Color

Inserting a background image or color with the Layer Property inspector works like changing the background image or color for a table (as explained in Chapter 13). To insert an image, enter the path to the file in the Bg Image text box or select the folder icon to locate the image file on your system or network. If the layer is larger than the image, the image is tiled, just as it would be in the background of a Web page or table.

To give a layer a background color, enter the color name (either in its hexadecimal or nominal form) in the Bg Color text box. You can also select the color box to pick your color from the color palette.

The Layers Panel

Dreamweaver offers another tool to help manage the layers in your Web page: the Layers panel. Although this tool doesn't display as many properties about each element as the Property inspector, the Layers panel gives you a good overview of all the layers on your page. It also provides a quick method of selecting a layer—even when it's offscreen—and enables you to change the z-index and the nesting order.

The Layers panel, shown in Figure 11-14, can be opened either through the Window menu (Window ➪ Layers) or by pressing the keyboard shortcut F2.

Figure 11-14: Use the Layers panel to quickly select — or alter the visibility or relationships of — all the layers on your page.

Modifying Properties with the Layers Panel

The Layers panel lists the visibility, name, and z-index settings for each layer. You can modify all these properties directly through the Layers panel.

The visibility of a particular layer is noted by the eye symbol in the first column of the inspector. Clicking the eye symbol cycles you through three different visibility states:

✦ **Eye closed:** Indicates that the layer is hidden

✦ **Eye open:** Indicates that the layer is visible

✦ **No eye:** Indicates that the visibility attribute is set to the default (which, for both Navigator and Internet Explorer, means inherit)

Tip   To change all your layers to a single state simultaneously, click the eye symbol in the column header. Unlike the individual eyes in front of each layer name, the overall eye toggles between open and shut.

You can also change a layer's name (in the second column of the Layers panel). Just double-click the current layer name in the inspector; the name is highlighted. Type in the new name and press Enter (Return) to complete the change.

You can alter the z-index (stacking order) in the third column in the same manner. Double-click the z-index value; and then type in the new value and press Enter (Return). You can enter any positive or negative integer. If you're working with the Netscape proprietary layer tags, you can also alter the above or below values previously set for the z-index through the Property inspector. Use A for above and B for below.

Tip   To change a layer's z-index interactively, you can drag one layer above or below another in the Layers panel. This action causes all the other layers' z-index values to change accordingly.

Nesting with the Layers Panel

Another task managed by the Layers panel is nesting or unnesting layers. This process is also referred to as *creating parent-child layers*. To nest one layer inside another through the Layers panel, follow these steps:

1. Choose Window ➪ Layers or press F2 to open the Layers panel.

2. Press the Ctrl (Command) key, click the name of the layer to be nested (the child), and drag it on top of the other layer (the parent).

3. When you see a rectangle around the parent layer's name, release the mouse. The child layer is indented underneath the parent layer, and the parent layer has a minus sign (a downward-pointing triangle on the Mac) attached to the front of its name.

4. To hide the child layer from view, click the minus sign (a downward-pointing triangle on the Mac) in front of the parent layer's name. After the child layer is hidden, the minus sign turns into a plus sign (a right-pointing triangle on the Mac).

5. To reveal the child layer, click the plus sign (a right-pointing triangle on the Mac).

6. To undo a nested layer, select the child layer and drag it to a new position in the Layers panel.

Caution

When it comes to nested layers, Netscape Navigator 4.x does not play well with others. When you do decide to use nested layers, test early and often to be sure that pre-Netscape 6 browsers are behaving.

You can use the nesting features of the Layers panel to hide many layers quickly. If the visibility of all child layers is set to the default — with no eye displayed — then by hiding the parent layer, you cause all the child layers to inherit that visibility setting and also disappear from view.

Tip

You can also delete a layer from the Layers panel. Just highlight the layer to be removed and press the Delete key. Dreamweaver also enables you to delete nested layers as a group by selecting the parent layer and pressing Delete. If you want to remove a parent layer but keep all children, the Tag Selector can be used. Select the parent tag, right-click (Control+click), and then choose Remove Tag.

Aligning Layers

With the capability to position layers anywhere on a page comes additional responsibility and potential problems. In anything that involves animation, correct alignment of moving parts is crucial. As you begin to set up your layers, their exact placement and alignment become critical. Dreamweaver includes two tools to simplify layered Web page design: the ruler and the grid.

Rulers and grids are familiar concepts in traditional desktop publishing. Dreamweaver's ruler shows the x-axis and y-axis in pixels, inches, or centimeters along the outer edge of the Document window. The grid crisscrosses the page with lines to support a visual guideline when you're placing objects. You can even enable a snap-to-grid feature to ensure easy, absolute alignment.

Using the Ruler

With traditional Web design, "eyeballing it" was the only option available for Web page layout. The absolute positioning capability of layers remedied this deficiency. Now online designers have a more precise and familiar system of alignment: the ruler. Dreamweaver's ruler can be displayed in several different measurement units and with your choice of origin point.

To toggle the ruler in Dreamweaver, choose View ⇨ Rulers ⇨ Show or use the keyboard shortcut Ctrl+Alt+R (Command+Option+R). Horizontal and vertical rulers appear along the top and the left sides of the Document window, as shown in Figure 11-15. As you move the pointer, a light-gray line indicates the position on both rulers.

Figure 11-15: Use the horizontal and vertical rulers to assist your layer placement and overall Web page layout.

By default, the ruler uses pixels as its measurement system. You can change the default by choosing View ➪ Rulers and selecting either inches or centimeters.

Dreamweaver also enables you to move the ruler origin to a new position. Normally, the upper-left corner of the page acts as the origin point for the ruler. On some occasions, it's helpful to start the measurement at a different location — at the bottom-right edge of an advertisement, for example. To move the origin point, select the intersection of the horizontal and vertical rulers and drag the crosshairs to a new location. When you release the mouse button, both rulers are adjusted to show negative values above and to the right of the new origin point. To return the origin point to its default setting, choose View ➪ Rulers ➪ Reset Origin, or you can simply double-click the intersection of the rulers.

Tip　You can access a ruler context menu by right-clicking (Control+clicking) the ruler itself. The context menu enables you to change the system of measurement, reset the origin point, or hide the rulers.

Working with Guides

With the advent of CSS layouts, Web designers found themselves needing a toolset more traditionally associated with graphic programs: guides. A guide is a single, thin, positionable line used at design-time to align elements on a page. Guides are either horizontal or vertical and stretch from one edge of the browser window to the other.

New In
Dreamweaver　Dreamweaver guides are wonderfully powerful and incorporate standard features found in graphic programs like Photoshop and Fireworks as well as some unique Web-centric options. Guides can be shown or hidden, set precisely, varied in color, snap-to-the-grid and/or objects. You can even have objects snap to guides. Dreamweaver designers will find guides a welcome addition to their working toolbox.

Before you can display a guide, you have to meet two conditions: the View ➪ Guides ➪ Show Guides option must be enabled along with View ➪ Rulers ➪ Show Rulers. The standard method for deploying a guide in Dreamweaver is the same as in those other programs: with rulers displayed, the user drags a guide onto the document (see Figure 11-16). Horizontal guides are dragged from the ruler on the top edge while vertical guides are dragged from the left edge ruler. You can have as many guides on your page as you want.

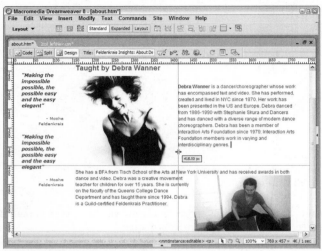

Figure 11-16: Guides work well in a CSS-P layout design environment.

Positioning and Removing Guides

To place a guide on the page, follow these steps:

1. Choose View ➪ Rulers ➪ Show Rulers to toggle the rulers into view.

2. Select View ➪ Guides ➪ Show Guides so that the option is checked.

3. To place a horizontal guide on the page, drag a guide from the ruler at the top of the page.

4. To place a vertical guide on the page, drag a guide from the ruler at the left of the page.

Once positioned, guides can be moved at any time. You can visually position guides by dragging them to a new location on the page; when your cursor is over the guide, you'll see a tooltip with the precise horizontal or vertical coordinate of the guide in pixels from the top or left of the page, respectively.

To remove a single guide, drag it back into the horizontal or vertical ruler. You can remove all guides on the page by selecting View ➪ Guides ➪ Clear Guides. If you just want to hide the guides, choose View ➪ Guides ➪ Show Guides again or use the keyboard shortcut, Ctrl+; (Command+;).

Displaying Guide Measurements

One of the slicker guide features implemented in Dreamweaver is the display of distance measurement. If you have a single horizontal or vertical guide onscreen and press Ctrl (Command), Dreamweaver will show you the distance from the guide to the window's edge in your cursor area. Place your cursor between two guides of the same type (either horizontal or vertical), press Ctrl (Command), and you'll see the distance that separates them, as shown in Figure 11-17.

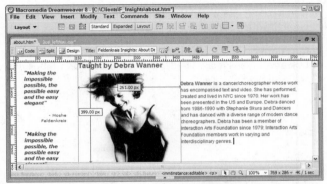

Figure 11-17: Bring up the distance between two guides in pixels by pressing Ctrl on Windows and Command on the Macintosh.

Locking and Snapping Guides

Dreamweaver gives you complete control over guides and positionable page elements. You can lock your guides so that they are not accidentally moved when repositioning elements. You can also snap your elements to your guides or guides to your elements — or both. Here's how it's all done:

✦ Prevent your guides from being moved by choosing View ➪ Guides ➪ Lock Guides or using the keyboard shortcut, Ctrl+Alt+; (Command+Option+;).

✦ Align your layout blocks to existing guides by enabling View ➪ Guides ➪ Snap Guides or using the keyboard shortcut, Ctrl+Shift+; (Command+Shift+;).

✦ Snap guides to the edges of layout blocks by selecting View ➪ Guides ➪ Guides Snap to Elements or using the keyboard shortcut, Ctrl+Shift+/ (Command+Shift+/).

Tip　Guides are retained when you save the page and restored when the page is re-opened.

Precise Guide Placement

Guides can be positioned precisely as well as by dragging. To set a guide's horizontal or vertical placement to a specific value, follow these steps:

1. Double-click the guide you want to move.

2. When the Move Guide dialog box opens, enter the desired position in the Location field.

3. Select the measurement system (pixels, centimeters, inches, or percentages) from the list.

   To use the percentage measurement, enter a value between 0.00 and 100.00; Dreamweaver will reposition the guide according to the width or height of your Document window.

4. Click OK.

Editing Guide Settings

By default, the guides are colored a bright green and the distance indicators a dark blue. If these colors don't contrast enough with your layout to be seen clearly, you can adjust the colors through the Edit Guides dialog box. The Edit Guides dialog box also provides all-in-place access to basic guide controls: Show Guides, Snap To Guides, Lock Guides, Guides Snap To Elements, and Clear All (see Figure 11-18). To access the Edit Guides dialog box, choose View ➪ Guides ➪ Edit Guides.

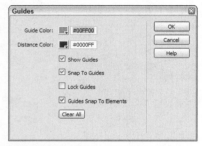

Figure 11-18: Alter the color of your guides for maximum visibility.

Showing the Browser Window Fold

One application in the guide featureset unique to Dreamweaver is especially useful for Web designers. When a browser displays a Web page, the portion initially visible is said to be "above the fold." The concept of a *fold* comes from the world of newspaper journalism where papers are divided into a top and bottom portion by the way they are folded. Dreamweaver can quickly display the fold of a browser window — that is, the viewable area — through guides.

Six of the most common browser window configurations are available through the Guides submenu:

✦ 640 x 480, Default

✦ 640 x 480, Maximized

✦ 800 x 600, Maximized

✦ 832 x 624, Maximized

✦ 1024 x 768, Maximized

✦ WebTV

You'll recognize the dimensions from the Window Size selector on the Status bar. When you select any of these options from the View ➪ Guides menu, Dreamweaver inserts two guides — one horizontal and another vertical — to form the right and bottom edge of the browser window (see Figure 11-19). With these guides onscreen, designers can place their key content so that it will be visible immediately in the chosen screen resolution.

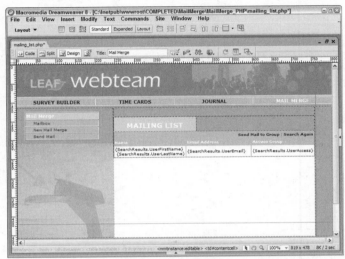

Figure 11-19: Make sure your most important content is above the fold with guides.

Aligning Objects with the Grid

Rulers and guides are generally good for positioning single objects, but a grid is extremely helpful when aligning one object to another. With Dreamweaver's grid facility, you can align elements visually or snap them to the grid. You can set many of the grid's other features, including grid spacing, color, and type.

To turn on the grid, choose View ➪ Grid ➪ Show or press Ctrl+Alt+G (Command+Option+G). By default, the grid is displayed with tan lines set at 50-pixel increments.

The snap-to-grid feature is enabled by choosing View ➪ Grid ➪ Snap To or with the keyboard shortcut Ctrl+Alt+Shift+G (Command+Option+Shift+G). When activated, snap-to-grid causes the upper-left corner of a layer to be placed at the nearest grid intersection when the layer is moved.

Like most of Dreamweaver's tools, you can customize the grid. To alter the grid settings, choose View ➪ Grid ➪ Settings, and the Grid Settings dialog box opens. In the Grid Settings dialog box, shown in Figure 11-20, you can change any of the settings shown in Table 11-3 (just click OK when you've finished adjusting the settings).

Table 11-3: Grid Settings Dialog Box Options

Grid Setting	Description
Color	Change the default color (light blue) by selecting the color box (which brings up color palette) or by typing a new value in the text box.
Show Grid	Show or hide the grid with this checkbox toggle.
Snap To Grid	Toggle the checkbox to enable or disable the snap-to-grid feature.
Spacing	Adjust the distance between grid points by entering a numeric value in the text box.
Spacing Unit of Measure	Select pixels, inches, or centimeters from the Spacing drop-down list.
Display	Choose either solid lines or dots for the gridlines.

Figure 11-20: Dreamweaver's grid feature is extremely handy for aligning a series of objects.

Adding Elements to a Layer

After you have created and initially positioned your layers, you can begin to fill them with content. Inserting objects in a layer is just like inserting objects in a Web page. The same insertion methods are available to you:

✦ Position the cursor inside a layer, choose Insert in the menu bar, and select an object to insert.

✦ With the cursor inside a layer, select any object from the Insert bar. Note that you cannot select the Draw Layer object.

✦ Drag an object from the Insert bar and drop it inside the layer.

A known problem exists with Netscape Navigator 4.x browsers and nested layers — and layers in general — using the <div> tag. Whenever the browser window is resized, the layers lose their left and top position and are displayed along the left edge of the browser window or parent layer. Dreamweaver includes the capability to insert code that serves as a workaround for this problem. With this code in place, if the browser is resized, the page reloads, repositioning the layers. If you want the code to be automatically inserted the first time you add a layer to your page, select the Add Resize Fix When Inserting Layers option found on the Layers category of Preferences. You can also insert it on a case-by-case basis by choosing

Commands ⇨ Add/Remove Netscape Resize Fix. As the name implies, this command also deletes the Netscape Resize Fix code.

Forms and Layers

When you're mixing forms and layers, follow only one rule: Always put the form completely inside the layer. If you place the layer within the form, all form elements after the layer tags are ignored. With the form completely enclosed in the layer, the form can safely be positioned anywhere on the page and all form elements still remain completely active.

Although this rule means that you can't split one form onto separate layers, you can set up multiple forms on multiple layers — and still have them all communicate to one final CGI or other program. This technique uses JavaScript to send the user-input values in the separate forms to hidden fields in the form with the Submit button. Suppose, for example, that you have three separate forms gathering information in three separate layers on a Web page. Call them formA, formB, and formC on layer1, layer2, and layer3, respectively. When the Submit button in formC on layer3 is selected, a JavaScript function is first called by means of an onClick event in the button's <input> tag. The function, in part, looks like the following:

```
function gatherData() {
    document.formC.hidden1.value = document.formA.text1.value
    document.formC.hidden2.value = document.formB.text2.value
}
```

Notice how every value from the various forms is sent to a hidden field in formC, the form with the Submit button. Now, when the form is submitted, all the hidden information gathered from the various forms is submitted along with formC's own information.

Note

The code for this separate-forms approach, as shown in the preceding listing, works in Internet Explorer. Netscape 4.*x*, however, uses a different syntax to address forms in layers. To work properly in Netscape 4.*x*, the code must look like the following:

```
document.layers["layer3"].document.formC. ⊃
hidden1.value=document.layers["layer1"]. ⊃
document.formA.text1.value
```

To make the code cross-browser compatible, you can use an initialization function that allows for the differences, or you can build the code into the onClick function. (For more information about building cross-browser–compatible code, see Chapter 29.)

Creating Your Page Design with Layers

Although the advantage to designing with layers is the greater flexibility it affords, one of the greatest disadvantages of using layers is that they are viewable in only the most recent generation of browsers. Dreamweaver enables you to get the best of both worlds by making it possible for you to use layers to design complex page layouts, and then to transform those layers into tables that can be viewed in earlier browsers. Designing this way has some limitations — you can't, for example, actually layer items on top of one another. Nevertheless, Dreamweaver's capability to convert layers to tables (and tables to layers) enables you to create complex layouts with ease.

Using the Tracing Image

Page-layout artists are often confronted with Web-page designs that have been mocked up in a graphics program. Dreamweaver's Tracing Image function enables you to use such images to guide the precise placement of graphics, text, tables, and forms in your Web page, enabling you to match the original design as closely as possible.

In order to use a Tracing Image, the graphic must be saved in either JPG, GIF, or PNG format. After the Tracing Image has been placed in your page, it is viewable only in Dreamweaver — it will never appear in a browser. A placed Tracing Image hides any background color or background graphic in your Web page. Preview your page in a browser or hide the Tracing Image to view your page without it.

Caution   If you're concerned about your page validating, be sure to remove the Tracing Image after you've completed the page. The Tracing Image uses a number of attributes, like `tracingsrc` and `tracingopacity`, none of which validate, inside the `<body>` tag.

Adding the Tracing Image to Your Page

To add a Tracing Image to your Dreamweaver page, choose View ➪ Tracing Image ➪ Load. This brings up a Select Image Source dialog box that enables you to select the graphic to use as a Tracing Image. Clicking Select brings up the Page Properties dialog box, shown in Figure 11-21, in which you can specify the opacity of the Tracing Image in a range from Transparent (0%) to Opaque (100%). You can change the Tracing Image or its transparency at any point by choosing Modify ➪ Page Properties to bring up the Page Properties dialog box. You can toggle between hiding and showing the Tracing Image by choosing View ➪ Tracing Image ➪ Show. You can also enter the Tracing Image directly in the Page Properties dialog box by entering its path in the Tracing Image text box or by clicking the Browse button to locate the image.

Note   Even though the Browse dialog for the Tracing Image enables you to choose from a data source, the image is not displayed on the page.

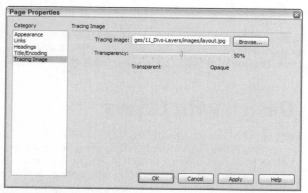

Figure 11-21: Setting the transparency of the Tracing Image to a setting such as 50 percent can help you differentiate between it and the content layers you are positioning.

Moving the Tracing Image

The Tracing Image cannot be selected and moved the same way as other objects on your page. Instead, you must move the Tracing Image using menu commands. You have several options for adjusting the Tracing Image's position to better fit your design. First, you can align the Tracing Image with any object on your page by selecting the object and then choosing View ➪ Tracing Image ➪ Align with Selection. This lines up the upper-left corner of the Tracing Image with the upper-left corner of the bounding box of the object you've selected.

To precisely or visually move the Tracing Image to a specific location, choose View ➪ Tracing Image ➪ Adjust Position. Enter the *x* and *y* coordinates into their respective boxes in the Adjust Tracing Image Position dialog box, as shown in Figure 11-22. For more hands-on positioning, use the arrow keys to nudge the tracing layer up, down, left, or right, one pixel at a time. Holding down the Shift key while pressing the arrow keys moves the Tracing Image in 5-pixel increments. Finally, you can return the Tracing Image to its default location of 9 pixels down from the top and 11 pixels in from the left by choosing View ➪ Tracing Image ➪ Reset Position.

Figure 11-22: Use the Adjust Tracing Image Position dialog box to precisely place your graphic template.

Preventing Overlaps

In order to place layers on your page that can later be converted to a table, the layers must not overlap. Before you begin drawing out your layers, open the Layers panel — either by choosing Window ➪ Layers or by pressing F2 — and put a checkmark in the Prevent Overlaps checkbox at the top of the Layers panel. You can also choose Modify ➪ Arrange ➪ Prevent Layer Overlaps to toggle overlap protection on and off.

Activating Layers with Behaviors

Although absolute positioning is a major reason to use layers, you may have other motives for using this capability. All the properties of a layer — the coordinates, size and shape, depth, visibility, and clipping — can be altered dynamically and interactively. Normally, dynamically resetting a layer's properties entails some fairly daunting JavaScript programming. Now, with one of Dreamweaver's hallmarks — those illustrious behaviors — activating layers is possible for nonprogrammers as well.

Cross-Reference If you want to learn more about behaviors, Chapter 12 describes Dreamweaver's rich behaviors feature.

Behaviors consist of two parts: the event and the action. In Dreamweaver, three standard actions are designed specifically for working with layers:

✦ **Drag Layer:** Enables the user to move the layer and get a response to that movement.

✦ **Set Text of Layer:** Enables the interactive alteration of the content of any layer to include any HTML, not just text.

✦ **Show-Hide Layers:** Controls the visibility of layers, either interactively or through some preprogrammed action on the page.

You can find detailed information about these actions in their respective sections in Chapter 12. The following sections outline how to use these behaviors to activate your layers.

Drag Layer

For the Web designer, positioning a layer is easy: Click the selection handle and drag the layer to a new location. For the readers of your pages, moving a layer is next to impossible — unless you incorporate the Drag Layer action into the page's design.

With the Drag Layer action, you can set up interactive pages in which the user can rearrange elements of the design to achieve an effect or make a selection. The Drag Layer action includes an option that enables your application to execute a JavaScript command if the user drops the layer on a specific target. In the example shown in Figure 11-23, each pair of shoes is in its own layer. When the user drops a pair in the bag, a one-line JavaScript command opens the desired catalog page and order form.

Figure 11-23: On this interactive page, visitors can drop merchandise into the shopping bag; this feature is made possible with the Drag Layer action.

After you've created all your layers, you're ready to attach the behavior. Because Drag Layer initializes the script to make the interaction possible, you should always associate this behavior with the `<body>` tag and the `onLoad` event. Follow these steps to use the Drag Layer action and to designate the settings for the drag operation:

1. Choose the `<body>` tag from the Tag Selector in the status bar.

2. Choose Window ➪ Behaviors or press Shift+F4. The Behaviors panel opens.

3. In the Behaviors panel, click the Add (+) button and make sure that 4.0 and Later Browsers is selected from the Show Events For flyout.

4. Click the Add (+) button and choose Drag Layer from the Add Action drop-down list.

5. In the Drag Layer dialog box, select the layer you want to make available for dragging.

6. To limit the movement of the dragged layer, select Constrained from the Movement drop-down list. Enter the coordinates needed to specify the direction to which you want to limit the movement in the Up, Down, Left, and/or Right text boxes.

7. To establish a location for a target, enter coordinates in the Drop Target: Left and Top text boxes. You can fill these text boxes with the selected layer's present location by clicking the Get Current Position button.

8. You can also set a snap-to area around the target's coordinates. When released in the target's location, the dragged layer snaps to this area. Enter a pixel value in the Snap If Within text box.

9. Click the Advanced tab.

10. Designate the drag handle:

    • To enable the entire layer to act as a drag handle, select Entire Layer from the drop-down menu.

    • If you want to limit the area to be used as a drag handle, select Area Within Layer from the drop-down menu. Enter the Left and Top coordinates as well as the Width and Height dimensions in the appropriate text boxes.

11. If you want to keep the layer in its current depth and not bring it to the front, deselect the checkbox for While Dragging: Bring Layer To The Front. To change the stacking order of the layer when it is released after dragging, select either Leave On Top or Restore Z-index from the drop-down list.

12. To execute a JavaScript command when the layer is dropped on the target, enter the code in the Call JavaScript text box. If you want the script to execute every time the layer is dropped, enter the code in the When Dropped: Call JavaScript text box. If the code should execute only when the layer is dropped on the target, make sure there's a check in the Only If Snapped checkbox.

13. To change the event that triggers the action (the default is onLoad), select an event from the drop-down list in the Events column.

Targeted JavaScript Commands

You can enter the following simple yet useful JavaScript commands in the Snap JavaScript text box of the Drag Layer dialog box:

✦ To display a brief message to the user after the layer is dropped, use the alert() function:

```
alert("You hit the target")
```

✦ To send the user to another Web page when the layer is dropped in the right location, use the JavaScript location object:

```
location = "http://www.yourdomain.com/yourpage.html"
```

The location object can also be used with relative URLs.

Set Text of Layer

You've seen how layers can dynamically move, and change their visibility and their depth — but did you know that you can also change a layer's *content* dynamically? With Dreamweaver, you can do it easily. A standard behavior, Set Text of Layer, enables you to swap the entire contents of one layer for whatever you'd like. You're not limited to exchanging just text, either. Anything you can put into HTML, you can swap — which is pretty much everything!

This behavior is extremely useful for putting up context-sensitive help and other information. Rather than construct a series of layers that you show and hide, a single layer is used, and just the contents change. To use Set Text of Layer, follow these steps:

1. Insert and name your layers as desired.

2. Select the graphic, button, or text link you'd like to act as the trigger for changing the content of the layer.

3. Choose Window ➪ Behaviors or press Shift+F4 to open the Behaviors panel.

4. Choose Set Text ➪ Set Text of Layer from the Add (+) drop-down list. The Set Text of Layer dialog box (shown in Figure 11-24) shows a list of the available layers in the current Web page and provides a space for the new content.

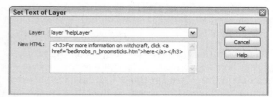

Figure 11-24: Swap out all the contents of a layer using the Set Text of Layer behavior.

5. Select the layer you want to alter from the Layer drop-down list.

6. Enter the text or code in the New HTML text area. You can enter either plain text, which is rendered in the default paragraph style, or any amount of HTML code, including `<img>`, `<table>`, or other tags.

Tip

If you're entering a large amount of HTML, don't bother doing so by hand — Dreamweaver can do it for you. On a blank page, create your HTML content and then select and copy it. Then, in the Set Text of Layer dialog box, paste the code using Ctrl+V (Command+V).

7. Click OK when you're finished.

If you want several layers to change when a single event is triggered, just add more Set Text of Layer behaviors to the same object.

Note

You may need to change the behavior event from its default; to do so, click the down arrow in between the Event and Action columns on the Behaviors panel and choose a new event from the list.

Show-Hide Layers

The capability to implement interactive control of a layer's visibility offers tremendous potential to the Web designer. The Show-Hide Layers action makes this implementation straightforward and simple to set up. With the Show-Hide Layers action, you can simultaneously show one or more layers while hiding as many other layers as necessary. Create your layers and give them a unique name before invoking the Show-Hide Layers action. To use Show-Hide Layers, follow these steps:

1. Select an image, link, or other HTML tag to which to attach the behavior.

2. Choose Window ➪ Behaviors or press Shift+F4 to open the Behaviors panel.

3. Choose Show-Hide Layers from the Add (+) drop-down list. The Show-Hide Layers Dialog (see Figure 11-25) shows a list of the available layers in the open Web page.

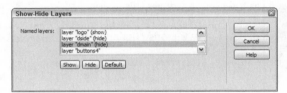

Figure 11-25: With the Show-Hide Layers behavior attached, you can easily program the visibility of all the layers in your Web page.

4. To cause a hidden layer to be revealed when this event is fired, select the layer from the list and click the Show button.

5. To hide a visible layer when this event is fired, select its name from the list and click the Hide button.

6. To restore a layer's default visibility value when this event is fired, select the layer and click the Default button.

7. Click OK when you are finished.

8. If the default event is not suitable, use the drop-down list in the Events column to select a different one.

Creating a Loading Layer

As Web creations become more complex, most designers want their layers to zip onscreen and offscreen or appear and disappear as quickly as possible for the page's viewer. A layer can act only when it has finished loading its content — the text and images. Rather than have the user see each layer loading in, some designers use a loading layer to mask the process until everything is downloaded and ready to go.

A loading layer is fairly easy to create. Dreamweaver supplies all the JavaScript necessary in one behavior, Show-Hide Layers. Keep in mind that because this technique uses layers, it's good only for 4.0 browsers and later.

To create a loading layer, follow these steps:

1. Create all layers with the contents in place and the visibility property set as default.

2. Create the loading layer. (Choose Insert ➪ Layout Objects ➪ Layer or click the Draw Layer button in the Layout category of the Insert bar.)

3. Enter and position whatever contents you want displayed in the loading layer while all the other layers are loading.

4. Open the Layers panel by pressing F2.

5. Turn off the visibility for all layers except the loading layer. In essence, you're hiding every other layer.

6. Select the `<body>` tag from the Tag Selector.

7. Choose Window ➪ Behaviors or press Shift+F4 to open the Behaviors panel.

8. Click the Add (+) action button and choose Show-Hide Layers from the drop-down list.

9. In the Show-Hide Layers dialog box, select the loading layer and click the Hide button.

10. Select all the other layers and set them to Show. Click OK when you are finished.

11. Leave `onLoad` (the default) as the event to trigger this action.

Now, when you test your Web page, you should see only your loading layer until everything else is loaded. Then the loading layer disappears, and all the other layers are made visible.

Summary

Layers are effective placement tools for developing the layout of a page. Anyone used to designing with desktop publishing tools can quickly learn to work with `<div>` tags and layers effectively. Keep these points in mind:

✦ A `<div>` tag can be styled for layout purposes using CSS.

✦ Dreamweaver calls a drawn out `<div>` tag with embedded CSS styling a layer.

✦ Layers are visible only on fourth-generation and later browsers.

✦ Dreamweaver includes a number of visual aids to help you create a `<div>`-based layout.

✦ Layers can be used to place HTML content anywhere on a Web page.

✦ You can stack layers on top of one another. This depth control is referred to as the *stacking order* or the *z-index*.

✦ Layers can be constructed so that the end user can display or hide them interactively, or alter their position, size, and depth dynamically.

✦ Dreamweaver provides guides, rulers, and grids to help with layer placement and alignment.

✦ You can easily activate Layers by using Dreamweaver's built-in JavaScript behaviors.

In the next chapter, you learn how to use Dreamweaver behaviors to enhance the interactivity of your sites.

✦   ✦   ✦

Using Behaviors

Behaviors are truly the power tools of Dreamweaver. With Dreamweaver behaviors, any Web designer can make layers appear and disappear, execute any number of rollovers, and control a Shockwave movie—all without knowing even a snippet of JavaScript. In the hands of an accomplished JavaScript programmer, Dreamweaver behaviors can be customized or created from scratch to automate the most difficult Web effect.

Creating behaviors is one of the more challenging Dreamweaver features to master (you can tackle it in Bonus Chapter 1 on this book's web site). Implementing these gems, however, is a piece of cake. This chapter examines the concepts behind behaviors and the reality of using them. It details the use of all the behaviors included with Dreamweaver, as well as some from notable third-party sources. This chapter also contains tips for managing your ever-increasing library of behaviors.

Here's a guarantee for you: After you get the hang of using Dreamweaver behaviors, your Web pages will never be the same.

Understanding Behaviors, Events, and Actions

A *behavior*, in Macromedia parlance, is the combination of an event and an action. In the electronic age, you push a button (the event) and something (the action) occurs—such as changing the channel on the TV with your remote.

In Dreamweaver, events can be something as interactive as a user's click of a link or as automatic as the loading of a Web page. Behaviors are said to be attached to a specific element on your page, whether it's a text link, an image, or even the <body> tag.

Dreamweaver has simplified the process of working with behaviors by including default events in every object on the Web page. Instead of having to think about both *how* you want to do something and *what* you want to do, you only have to focus on the *what*—the action.

To understand the concept of behaviors and how they are structured, examine the four essential steps for adding a behavior to your Web page:

1. **Pick a tag.** All behaviors are connected to a specific HTML element (tag). You can attach a behavior to everything from the `<body>`, to an `<a>` tag, to the `<textarea>` of a form, and so on.

✦ ✦ ✦ ✦

In This Chapter

Behavior basics

Dreamweaver Technique: Incorporating Behaviors

Adding a behavior's event and action

Dreamweaver Technique: Modifying Behaviors

Looking at the standard behaviors

✦ ✦ ✦ ✦

If a certain behavior is unavailable, it's because the necessary element isn't present on the page.

2. **Choose your target browser.** Different browsers — and the various browser versions — support different events. Dreamweaver enables you to choose either a specific browser, such as Internet Explorer 6, or a browser range, such as version 4 and higher browsers.

3. **Select an action.** Dreamweaver enables only those actions available to the specific elements on your page. You can't, for instance, choose the Show-Hide Layer action until you insert one or more layers. Behaviors guide you to the workable options.

4. **Enter the parameters.** Behaviors get their power from their flexibility. Each action comes with its own dialog box that contains parameters you can use to customize the JavaScript code output. Depending on the action, you can choose source files, set attributes, and enable/disable features. The parameter dialog box can even dynamically update to reflect your current Web page.

Dreamweaver 8 comes with 27 cross-browser–compatible actions, and both Macromedia and third-party developers have made many additional actions available, with even more in the works. Behaviors greatly extend the range of possibilities for the modern Web designer — with no requirement to learn JavaScript programming. All you need to know about attaching behaviors is presented in the following section.

Attaching a Behavior

When you see the code generated by Dreamweaver, you understand why setting up a behavior is also referred to as *attaching* a behavior. As previously noted, Dreamweaver needs a specific HTML tag to assign the behavior (step 1). The anchor tag <a> is often used because, in JavaScript, links can respond to several different events, including onClick. Here's an example:

```
<a href="#" onClick="MM_popupMsg('Thanks for coming!')">Exit Here</a>
```

You're not restricted to one event per tag or even one action per event. Multiple events can be associated with a tag to handle various user actions. For example, you may have an image that does all the following things:

✦ Highlights when the user's pointer moves over the image

✦ Reveals a hidden layer in another area of the page when the user clicks the mouse button on the image

✦ Makes a sound when the user releases the mouse button on the image

✦ Starts a Flash movie when the user's pointer moves away from the image

Likewise, a single event can trigger several actions. Updating multiple frames through a single link used to be difficult — but no more. Dreamweaver makes it easy by enabling you to attach several Go to URL actions to the same event, onClick. In addition, you are not restricted to attaching multiple instances of the same action to a single event. For example, in a site that uses a lot of multimedia, you can tie all the following actions to a single onClick event:

✦ Begin playing an audio file (with the Play Sound action).

✦ Move a layer across the screen (with the Play Timeline action).

✦ Display a second graphic in place of the first (with the Swap Image action).

✦ Show the copyright information for the audio piece in the status bar (with the Set Text of Status Bar action).

You can even determine the order of execution for the actions connected to a single event.

With Dreamweaver behaviors, hours of complex JavaScript coding are reduced to a handful of mouse clicks and a minimum of data entry. All behavior assigning and modification are handled through the Behaviors panel.

Using the Behaviors Panel

The Behaviors panel provides two columns (see Figure 12-1) that neatly sum up the behaviors concept in general: events and actions. After you attach a behavior, the triggering event (onClick, onMouseOver, and so on) is shown on the left, and its associated action — what exactly is triggered — is on the right. A down arrow between the event and action, when clicked, displays other available events for the current browser model. Double-click the action to open its parameter dialog box, where you can modify the action's attributes.

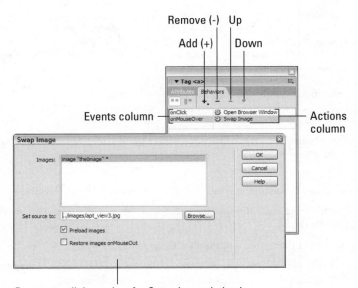

Parameter dialogue box for Swap Image behavior

Figure 12-1: You can handle everything about a behavior through the Behaviors panel.

As usual in Dreamweaver, you have your choice of methods for opening the Behaviors panel:

✦ Choose Window ➪ Behaviors.

✦ Select the Behaviors tab from the Tag Inspector panel, if visible.

✦ Use the keyboard shortcut Shift+F4 (an on/off toggle).

Tip   The Behaviors panel can be closed by toggling it off with Shift+F4 or hidden along with all the other panels by pressing F4.

After you have attached a behavior to a tag and closed the associated action's parameter dialog box, Dreamweaver writes the necessary HTML and JavaScript code into your document. Because it contains functions that must be callable from anywhere in the document, the bulk of the JavaScript code is placed in the `<head>` section of the page; the code that links selected tags to these functions is written in the `<body>` section. A few actions, including Play Sound, place HTML code at the bottom of the `<body>`. However, most of the code — there can be a lot of code to handle all the cross-browser contingencies — is placed between `<script>`...`</script>` tags in the `<head>`.

Adding a Behavior

The procedure for adding (or attaching) a behavior is simple. As noted earlier, you can assign only certain events to particular tags, and these options are further limited by the type of browser used.

Note   Even in the latest browsers, key events such as `onMouseDown`, `onMouseOver`, and `onMouseOut` work only with anchor tags. To circumvent this limitation, Dreamweaver can enclose an element, such as `<img>`, with an anchor tag that links to nowhere — `src="javascript:;"`. Events that use the anchor tag in this fashion appear in parentheses in the drop-down list of events.

To add a behavior to an element in your Web page, follow these steps:

1. Select an object (element) in the Document window.

Tip   If you want to assign a behavior to the entire page, select the `<body>` tag from the Tag Selector (below the Document window).

2. Open the Behaviors panel by choosing Window ➪ Behaviors or by pressing Shift+F4.

3. Click the Add (+) button to reveal the available options, as shown in Figure 12-2. Select one from the drop-down list.

4. Enter the desired values in the action's parameter dialog box.

5. Click OK to close the dialog box when you're finished. Dreamweaver adds a line to the Behaviors panel displaying the attached event and its associated action.

A trigger — whether it's an image or a text link — may have multiple behaviors attached to it. One graphical navigation element can, for instance, perform a Swap Image when the user's mouse moves over it, a Swap Image Restore when the mouse moves away, and, when clicked, show another Web page in an additional, smaller window with the Open Browser Window behavior.

Tip   Dreamweaver includes a Get More Behaviors menu option at the bottom of the Add (+) drop-down list. To use this feature, connect to the Internet and select Get More Behaviors in Dreamweaver. You are whisked away to the Dreamweaver Exchange, a service from Macromedia with a huge selection of extensions of all flavors, including behaviors.

Incorporating Behaviors

In this technique, you add a series of Dreamweaver standard behaviors that display a different image whenever a link is moused over.

1. In the Files panel, switch to the Dreamweaver Bible working site previously created.

2. Go to Techniques\12_Behaviors and open the file `behaviors_start.htm`.

3. Select the text `Living Room` beneath the picture.

4. In the Link field of the Property inspector, enter `javascript:;` to create a link.

5. Choose Windows ➪ Behaviors to open the Behaviors panel.

6. In the Behaviors panel, click Add (+) and select Swap Image.

7. When the Swap Image dialog box opens, set the following parameters:

✦ Select Browse and choose `apt_view1.jpg` from the Techniques/images folder.

✦ Uncheck the Restore image onMouseOut option.

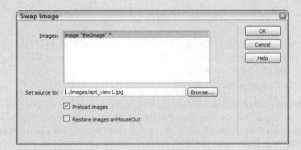

8. Click OK when you're done.

Note that the behavior has been added to the Behaviors panel with the default event, onMouseOver.

9. Select the text `Kitchen North` and repeat steps 4–8, selecting `apt_view2.jpg` as the file to show in the Swap Image behavior dialog.

10. Select the text `Kitchen South` and repeat steps 4–8, selecting `apt_view3.jpg` as the file to show in the Swap Image behavior dialog.

11. Save your page.

When you're done, each of the three links underneath the picture will have its own behavior; test the page in a browser to verify that the images change when your mouse rolls over the different links.

END

Figure 12-2: The Add (+) drop-down list changes according to what's on the current page and which tag is selected.

Managing Events

Every time Dreamweaver attaches a behavior to a tag, it inserts an event for you. The default event that is chosen is based on two criteria: the browser type and the selected tag. The different browsers in use have widely different capabilities, notably when it comes to understanding the various event handlers and associated tags.

For every specification or browser combination in the Show Events For submenu of the Add (+) drop-down list, Dreamweaver has a corresponding file in the Configuration\Behaviors\ Events folder. Each tag listed in each file, such as IE4.0.htm, has at least one event associated with it. The entries look like this:

```
<INPUT TYPE="Text" onBlur="*" onChange="" onFocus="" onSelect="">
```

The default event for each tag is marked with an asterisk; in the preceding example, onBlur is the default event. After you've selected an action and completed its parameter dialog box, the default event appears in the Events column of the Behaviors panel alongside the action in the Actions column.

Tip   If you find yourself changing a particular tag's default event over and over again to some other event, you might want to modify the appropriate Event file to pick your alternative as the default. To do this, open the relevant browser file found in the Dreamweaver 8\Configuration\Behaviors\Events folder, switch to Code view, and move the asterisk to a different event for that particular tag. Resave the file and restart Dreamweaver to try out your new default behavior.

If you don't want to select the default event in a certain instance, you can easily choose another. To do so, click the down arrow next to the displayed event in the Behaviors panel and select the event you want in the drop-down list (see Figure 12-3).

Figure 12-3: You can change the event by selecting a different one from the drop-down list.

The entry selected determines which events are available. By default, 4.0 and Later Browsers is chosen. To change your choice, select Show Events For from the Events list and pick one of the following:

✦ 4.0 and Later Browsers	✦ IE 5.5
✦ HTML 4.01	✦ IE 6.0
✦ IE 4.0	✦ Netscape 4.0
✦ IE 5.0	✦ Netscape 6.0

New In Dreamweaver For the first time in its history, Dreamweaver has based the behavior event options on a specification as well as the various browser implementations. Choose HTML 4.01 if you want to ensure that your event options follow the recommendations of the W3C.

The Dreamweaver 8\Configuration\Behaviors\Events folder contains HTML files corresponding to these eight browser models offered in the Show Events For submenu. You can open these files in Dreamweaver, but Macromedia asks that you not edit them — with one exception. Each file contains the list of tags that have supported *event handlers* (the JavaScript term for events) in that browser. The older the browser, the fewer event handlers are included — unfortunately, this also means that if you want to reach the broadest Internet audience, your event options are limited. In the broadest category, 4.0 and Later Browsers, only 16 different tags can receive any sort of event handler.

Listing 12-1 shows the event-handler definitions for the 4.0 and Later Browsers category.

Listing 12-1: The Event File for 4.0 and Later Browsers

```
<A onClick="*" onDblClick="" onKeyDown="" onKeyPress="" onKeyUp=""
onMouseDown="" onMouseOut="" onMouseOver="" onMouseUp="">

<AREA onClick="" onDblClick="" onMouseOut="" onMouseOver="*">

<BODY onBlur="" onError="" onFocus="" onLoad="*" onResize="" onUnload="">

<FORM onReset="" onSubmit="*">

<FRAMESET onBlur="" onFocus="" onLoad="*" onResize="" onUnload="">

<IMG onAbort="" onError="" onLoad="*">

<INPUT TYPE="Button" onBlur="" onClick="*" onFocus="" onMouseDown=""
       onMouseUp="">

<INPUT TYPE="Checkbox" onBlur="" onClick="*" onFocus="" onMouseDown=""
onMouseUp="">

<INPUT TYPE="File" onBlur="" onChange="*" onFocus="" onKeyDown="" onKeyPress=""
onKeyUp="">

<INPUT TYPE="Password" onBlur="" onChange="*" onFocus="" onKeyDown=""
onKeyPress="" onKeyUp="">

<INPUT TYPE="Radio" onBlur="" onClick="*" onFocus="" onMouseDown=""
onMouseUp="">

<INPUT TYPE="Reset" onBlur="" onClick="*" onFocus="" onMouseDown=""
onMouseUp="">

<INPUT TYPE="Submit" onBlur="" onClick="*" onFocus="" onMouseDown=""
onMouseUp="">

<INPUT TYPE="Text" onBlur="*" onChange="" onFocus="" onKeyDown="" onKeyPress=""
onKeyUp="" onSelect="">

<SELECT onBlur="" onChange="*" onFocus="">

<TEXTAREA onBlur="" onChange="*" onFocus="" onKeyDown="" onKeyPress=""
onKeyUp="" onSelect="">
```

By contrast, the Event file for Internet Explorer 6.0 shows support for every tag under the HTML sun — 94 in all — with almost every tag capable of handling any type of event.

Triggering Custom Functions

Although the standard behaviors can accomplish a great deal — and extensions available from the Macromedia Exchange can do even more — sometimes a developer needs to trigger a custom function. Dreamweaver provides a way to link an event to a function quickly, right in the Behaviors panel. The action column of the Behaviors panel not only displays behaviors applied in the usual manner, but it is also editable. In other words, you can enter your own function call directly into the Behaviors panel, and Dreamweaver writes the code into the tag.

Here's how it works. Suppose you want to trigger a custom JavaScript function called `showTotal()` whenever the user clicks a special graphic:

1. Select the image, and in the Link field of the Property inspector, enter `javascript:;`.

2. In the Behaviors panel, click the Event column and choose an event from the drop-down list. In this case, select `onClick`.

3. Enter the custom function call and any arguments in the Action column. The function might be entered like this: `showTotal('checkout','USD')`, where the two arguments are presented in a comma-separated list, using single quotes.

4. Press Tab to confirm the code entry.

If you check the `<a>` surrounding the image, you find that Dreamweaver has now added the following to the tag: `onClick="showTotal('checkout','USD')"`.

The function call or arguments can include dynamic components; a lightning bolt symbol that opens the Dynamic Data dialog is available from the Action column. Moreover, you can combine your custom function call with other standard behaviors. To remove the code, select the custom entry and click Remove (–), just as you would for a regular behavior.

Note   Although any HTML tag could potentially be used to attach a behavior, the most commonly used by far are the `<body>` tag (for entire-page events such as `onLoad`), the `<img>` tag (used as a button), and the link tag, `<a>`.

To find the default event for a tag, simply select the tag in a document, use Add Actions to attach any valid actions to it, and see what event appears alongside the action in the Behaviors panel. To find the default event for a tag as used by a particular browser, specify the browser in the Show Events For submenu of the Add (+) drop-down list, and proceed as described previously.

Standard Actions

As of this writing, 27 standard actions ship with Dreamweaver 8. Each action operates independently of and is different from the others, although many share common functions. Each action is associated with a different parameter dialog box to enable easy attribute entry.

The following sections describe each of the standard actions: what the action does, what requirements must be met for it to be activated, what options are available, and most important of all, how to use the action. Each action is written to work with all browser versions 4 and above. However, some actions do not work as designed in the older browsers: Netscape

Navigator 3.0, for instance, cannot perform the layer-related behaviors and almost all behaviors are ignored in Internet Explorer 3.0.

Call JavaScript

With Call JavaScript, you can execute any JavaScript function — standard or custom — with a single mouse click or other event. As your JavaScript savvy grows, you'll find yourself using this behavior again and again.

Call JavaScript is straightforward to use; simply type the JavaScript code or the name of the function you want to trigger into the dialog box. If, for example, you want to get some input from a visitor, you can use JavaScript's built-in `prompt()` method like this:

```
result = prompt('Whom shall I say is calling?','')
```

When this code is triggered, a small dialog box appears with your query (here, `'Whom shall I say is calling?'`) and a blank space for an input string. The second argument in the `prompt()` method enables you to include a default answer — to leave it blank, just use an empty string (two single quotes with nothing in between), as shown in the preceding code snippet.

Note   You can use either single or double quotes in your Call JavaScript behavior; Dreamweaver automatically adjusts for whichever you choose. I find it easier to use single quotes because Dreamweaver translates double quotes into character entities; that is, " becomes `&quot;`.

Naturally, you can use Call JavaScript to handle more complex chores as well. To call a specific custom function that is already in the `<head>` section of your page, just enter its name — along with any necessary arguments — in the Call JavaScript dialog box, shown in Figure 12-4.

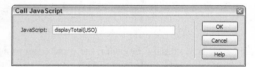

Figure 12-4: Trigger any JavaScript function by attaching a Call JavaScript behavior to an image or text.

To use the Call JavaScript behavior, follow these steps:

1. Select the object to trigger the action.

2. From the Behaviors panel, click the Add (+) button and select Call JavaScript.

3. In the Call JavaScript dialog box, enter your code in the JavaScript text box.

4. Click OK when you're finished.

Change Property

The Change Property action enables you to dynamically alter properties of each of the following tags:

✦ `<div>`

✦ `<form>`

✦ `<img>`

✦ `<layer>`

✦ `<select>`

✦ `<span>`

✦ `<textarea>`

You can also alter the following `<input>` types:

✦ `checkbox`

✦ `password`

✦ `radio`

✦ `text`

The tags, as well as the browser being targeted, determine exactly which properties can be altered. For example, the `<div>` tag and Internet Explorer 4.0 combination enables you to change virtually every style sheet option on-the-fly. The Change Property dialog box (see Figure 12-5) offers a list of the selected tags in the current page.

Figure 12-5: The Change Property dialog box enables you to alter attributes of certain tags dynamically.

Caution   It's important that you name the objects you want to alter so that Dreamweaver can properly identify them. Remember to use unique names that begin with a letter and contain no spaces or special characters.

This behavior is especially useful for changing the properties of forms and form elements. Be sure to name the form if you want to use Change Property in this manner. To use the Change Property action, follow these steps:

1. Select the object to trigger the action.

2. From the Behaviors panel, click the Add (+) button and select Change Property.

3. In the Change Property dialog box, choose the type of object whose property you want to change — FORM, DIV, INPUT/TEXT, and so on — from the Type of Object drop-down list.

4. In the Named Object drop-down list, select the name of the object whose property you want to change.

5. Click the Select radio button. Select the target browser in the small list box on the far right and choose the property to change. If you don't find the property in the drop-down list box, you can type it yourself in the Enter text box.

Note Many properties in the various browsers are read-only and cannot be dynamically altered. Those properties listed in the option list are always dynamic.

6. In the New Value text box, type the property's new value to be inserted when the event is fired.

7. Click OK when you're finished.

Check Browser

Some Web sites are increasingly split into multilevel versions of themselves to gracefully handle the variety of browsers in operation. The Check Browser action acts as a type of browser router, capable of sending browsers to appropriate URLs or just letting them stay on the current page. The Check Browser action is generally assigned to the <body> tag and uses the onLoad event. If the Check Browser behavior is used in this fashion, it's a good idea to keep the basic page accessible to all browsers, even those with JavaScript disabled.

The Check Browser parameter dialog box (see Figure 12-6) is quite flexible and enables you to specify decimal version numbers for the two main browsers. For instance, you may want to let all users of Navigator 4.04 or later stay on the current page and send everyone else to an alternative URL. The URLs can be either relative, such as `dreamweaver/index.htm`, or absolute, such as `http://www.idest.com/dreamweaver/index.htm`.

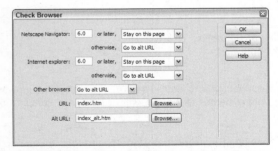

Figure 12-6: The Check Browser action is a great tool for segregating old and new browsers.

To use the Check Browser action, follow these steps:

1. Select the object to trigger the action.

2. From the Behaviors panel, click the Add (+) button and select Check Browser.

3. Use the Check Browser parameter fields to specify the Netscape Navigator and Internet Explorer versions and whether you want the browser to stay on the current page, go to another URL, or proceed to a third alternative URL.

Note   With both major browsers, you can specify the URL that the lower version numbers should visit.

4. Set the same options for all other browsers, such as Opera.

5. Enter the URL and alternative URL options in their respective text boxes; or click the Browse button to locate the files.

6. Click OK when you're finished.

Check Plugin

If certain pages on your Web site require the use of one or more plugins, you can use the Check Plugin action to see if a visitor has the necessary plugin installed. After Check Plugin has examined this, it can route users with the appropriate plugin to one URL and users without it to another URL. You can look for only one plugin at a time, but you can use multiple instances of the Check Plugin action, if needed.

By default, the parameter dialog box for Check Plugin (see Figure 12-7) offers five plugins: Flash, Shockwave, LiveAudio, QuickTime, and Windows Media Player. You can check for any other plugin by entering its name in the Enter text box. Use the name exactly as it appears in bold (without the version number) in Netscape's About Plug-ins area; for example: Nullsoft Winamp Plug-in for Gecko.

Figure 12-7: Running a media-intensive site? Use the Check Plugin action to divert visitors without plugins to alternative pages.

One very unfortunate hitch: Internet Explorer is pretty much crippled with respect to cross-browser plugin detection. In Windows, Internet Explorer can only detect Flash and Shockwave plugins. And on Macintosh platforms, Internet Explorer cannot detect any plugins at all. The best way to handle both browsers is to use both ActiveX controls and plugins.

Tip   If you use a particular plugin regularly, you may also want to modify the Check Plugin.js file found in your Actions folder. Add your new plugin to the PLUGIN_NAMES array (this holds "nice" plugin names as they appear in the parameter dialog box) and PLUGIN_VALUES array (this holds "internal" plugin names, as they appear in Netscape's About Plug-ins) in the initGlobals() function.

To use the Check Plugin action, follow these steps:

1. Select the object to trigger the action.

2. From the Behaviors panel, click the Add (+) button and select Check Plugin.

3. Select a plugin from the drop-down list or type another plugin name in the Enter text box.

Note   The names presented in the drop-down list are abbreviated — more recognizable names — and not the formal names inserted into the code. For example, when you select Shockwave, `Shockwave for Director` is actually input into the code. On the other hand, any plugin name you enter manually into the Enter field is inserted verbatim.

4. If you want to send users who are confirmed to have the plugin to a different page, enter that URL (absolute or relative) in the If Found, Go to URL text box or use the Browse button to locate the file. If you want these users to stay on the current page, leave the text box empty.

5. In the Otherwise, Go to URL text box, enter the URL for users who do not have the required plugin.

6. Should the plugin detection fail — which, as explained earlier, happens regularly in Internet Explorer, whether or not the plugin is actually present — you can keep the user on the initial page. To do so, enable the Always Go to First URL if Detection Is Not Possible option. Otherwise, if the detection fails for any reason, users are sent to the URL listed in the Otherwise field.

7. Click OK when you're finished.

Control Shockwave or Flash

The Control Shockwave or Flash action enables you to command your Shockwave and Flash movies through external controls. With it, you can build your own interface for your Shockwave or Flash movie. This action can be used in conjunction with the `autostart=true` attribute (entered through the Property inspector's parameter dialog box for the Shockwave or Flash file) to enable a replaying of the movie.

You must have a Shockwave or Flash movie inserted in your Web page for the Control Shockwave or Flash action to be available. The parameter dialog box for this action (see Figure 12-8) lists by name all the Shockwave or Flash movies that are found in either an `<embed>` or `<object>` tag. You can set the action to control the movie in one of four ways: Play, Stop, Rewind, or Go to Frame. You can choose only one option each time you attach an action to an event. If you choose the last option, you need to specify the frame number in the text box. Note that specifying a Go to Frame number does not start the movie there; you need to attach a second Control Shockwave or Flash action to the same event to play the file.

Figure 12-8: Build your own interface and then control a Shockwave or Flash movie externally with the Control Shockwave or Flash action.

Tip Be sure to name your Shockwave or Flash movie. Otherwise, the Control Shockwave or Flash action lists both unnamed <embed> and unnamed <object> for each file, and you cannot write to both tags as you can with a named movie.

To use the Control Shockwave or Flash action, follow these steps:

1. Select the object to trigger the action.

2. From the Behaviors panel, click the Add (+) button and select Control Shockwave or Flash.

3. In the Control Shockwave or Flash dialog box, select a movie from the Movie drop-down list.

4. Select a control by clicking its button:

   • **Play:** Begins playing the movie at the current frame location.

   • **Stop:** Stops playing the movie.

   • **Rewind:** Returns the movie to its first frame.

   • **Go to Frame:** Displays a specific frame in the movie. If you choose this option, you must enter a frame number in the text box.

5. Click OK when you're finished.

Drag Layer

The Drag Layer action provides some spectacular — and interactive — effects with little effort on the part of the designer. Drag Layer enables your Web page visitors to move layers — and all that they contain — around the screen with the drag-and-drop technique. With the Drag Layer action, you can easily set up the following capabilities for the user:

✦ Enabling layers to be dragged anywhere on the screen

✦ Restricting the dragging to a particular direction or combination of directions — a horizontal sliding layer can be restricted to left and right movement, for instance

✦ Limiting the drag handle to a portion of the layer such as the upper bar or enabling the whole layer to be used

✦ Providing an alternative clipping method by enabling only a portion of the layer to be dragged

✦ Enabling changing of the layers' stacking order while dragging or on mouse release

✦ Setting a snap-to target area on your Web page for layers that the user releases within a defined radius

✦ Programming a JavaScript command to be executed when the snap-to target is hit or every time the layer is released

Cross-Reference Layers are one of the more powerful features of Dreamweaver. To get the most out of the layer-oriented behaviors, familiarize yourself with layers by examining Chapter 11.

One or more layers must reside in your Web page before the Drag Layer action becomes available for selection from the Add (+) drop-down list. You must attach the action to the <body> — you can, however, attach separate Drag Layer behaviors to different layers to get different layer-dragging effects.

Drag Layer's parameter dialog box (see Figure 12-9) includes a Get Current Position button that puts the left and top coordinates of the selected layer into the Drop Target Left/Top boxes. If you plan on using targeting, make sure to place your layer at the target location *before* attaching the behavior.

Figure 12-9: With the Drag Layer action, you can set up your layers to be repositioned by the user.

To use the Drag Layer action, follow these steps:

1. Make sure that you have one or more layers on your page; then select the <body> tag.

2. From the Behaviors panel, click the Add (+) button and select Drag Layer.

3. If the Basic tab of the parameter dialog box is not selected, select it now.

4. In the Layer drop-down list, select the layer you want to make draggable.

5. To limit the movement of the layer, change the Movement option from Unconstrained to Constrained. Text boxes for Up, Down, Left, and Right appear. Enter pixel values in the text boxes to control the range of motion:

   • To constrain movement vertically, enter positive numbers in the Up and Down text boxes and zeros in the Left and Right text boxes.

   • To constrain movement horizontally, enter positive numbers in the Left and Right text boxes and zeros in the Up and Down text boxes.

   • To enable movement in a rectangular region, enter positive values in all four text boxes.

6. To establish a location for a target for the dragged layer, enter coordinates in the Drop Target: Left and Top text boxes. Click the Get Current Position button to fill these text boxes with the layer's current location.

7. To set a snap-to area around the target coordinates where the layer falls if released in the target location, enter a pixel value in the Snap if Within text box.

8. For additional options, select the Advanced tab of the parameter dialog box.

9. If you want the whole layer to act as a drag handle, select Entire Layer from the Drag Handle drop-down list. If, instead, you want to limit the area to be used as a drag handle, select Area Within Layer from the Drag Handle drop-down list. L(eft), T(op), W(idth), and H(eight) text boxes appear. In the appropriate boxes, enter the left and top coordinates of the drag handle in pixels, as well as the dimensions for the width and height.

10. To control the positioning of the dragged layer, set the following While Dragging options:

   • To keep the layer in its current depth (that is, to avoid bringing it to the front when it is dragged), deselect the checkbox for While Dragging: Bring Layer to the Front.

   • To change the stacking order of the layer when it is released, select the checkbox and pick either Leave on Top or Restore z-index from the drop-down list.

11. To execute a JavaScript command while the layer is being dragged, enter the command or function in the Call JavaScript text box.

12. To execute a JavaScript command when the layer is dropped on the target, enter the code in the When Dropped: Call JavaScript text box. If you want the JavaScript to execute only when the layer is snapped to its target, select the Only if Snapped option. This option requires that a value be entered in the Snap if Within text box in the Basic tab.

13. Click OK when you're finished.

Note

If you — or others on your team — have the requisite JavaScript programming skills, you can gather information output from the Drag Layer behavior to enhance your pages. Dreamweaver declares three variables for each draggable layer: MM_UPDOWN (the y coordinate), MM_LEFT RIGHT (the x coordinate), and MM_SNAPPED (true, if the layer has reached the specified target). Before you can get any of these properties, you must get an object reference for the proper layer. Another function, MM_findObj(layername), handles that chore.

Go to URL

Dreamweaver brings the same power of links — with a lot more flexibility — to any event with the Go to URL action. One of the trickier tasks in using frames on a Web page is updating two or more frames simultaneously with a single button click. The Go to URL action handily streamlines this process for the Web designer. Go to URL can also be used as a preload router that sends the user to another Web page after the onLoad event has finished. The Go ToURL dialog box (see Figure 12-10) displays any existing frames in the current page or frameset. To load multiple URLs at the same time, select the first frame from the Open In list and enter the desired page or location in the URL text box. Next, select the second frame from the list and enter its URL; and so on. If you select a frame to which a URL is already assigned, that address appears in the URL text box.

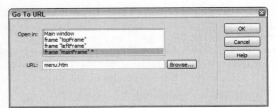

Figure 12-10: You can update two or more frames at the same time with the Go to URL action.

To use the Go to URL action, follow these steps:

1. Select the object to trigger the action.

2. From the Behaviors panel, click the Add (+) button and select Go to URL.

3. From the Go To URL dialog box, select the target for your link from the list in the Open In window.

4. Enter the path of the file to open in the URL text box or click the Browse button to locate a file. An asterisk appears next to the frame name to indicate that a URL has been chosen.

5. To select another target to load a different URL, repeat steps 3 and 4.

6. Click OK when you're finished.

Show Pop-Up Menu and Hide Pop-Up Menu

Navigation is the *raison d'etre* for the Show Pop-Up Menu/Hide Pop-Up Menu behavior duo. These behaviors are used to create a DHTML-style pop-up menu. A user mouses over a navigational link and down pops a custom menu with a set of context-sensitive sublinks. When the user mouses away, the pop-up menu disappears.

Caution Show Pop-Up Menu/Hide Pop-Up Menu is based on code written for Fireworks MX. The JavaScript routines used are not optimal and may cause considerable problems in various browsers, particularly when used with templates. A much better navigation menu system utilizing CSS was introduced in Fireworks 8; unfortunately, these menus can only be edited in Dreamweaver by hand. Where possible, designers would be better served by using the newer CSS-based menus in Fireworks 8 and avoiding implementing new menus with the Dreamweaver behaviors. For more information on the CSS-based menus, see Chapter 23, "Fireworks Integration."

To use the Show Pop-Up Menu and Hide Pop-Up Menu actions to create a pop-up menu, perform these steps:

1. Select the object to trigger the action.

2. From the Behaviors panel, click the Add (+) button and select Show Pop-Up Menu.

3. The Show Pop-Up Menu dialog box that appears comprises four tabs: Contents, Appearance, Advanced, and Position, as shown in Figure 12-11.

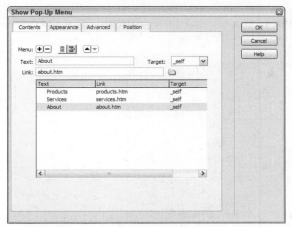

Figure 12-11: Create a DHTML-style pop-up menu using the Show Pop-Up Menu behavior.

4. Use the Contents tab to set the name (Text field), structure (Outdent/Indent Item and Move Item Up/Down buttons), URL (Link field), and target (_blank, _parent, _top, _or _self) of the items to appear in the pop-up menu.

5. Use the Appearance tab to set the orientation of the pop-up menu (Vertical or Horizontal). You can also use it to set various properties of the font used for the menu items and for their Up State and Over State colors.

6. Use the Advanced tab to set various properties of the menu cells, including size, spacing, color, text indent, border width, and delay before the menu appears after the trigger object is moused over.

7. Use the Position tab to set where the menu appears relative to the trigger object.

8. Click OK when you're finished. After you've successfully attached a Show Pop-Up Menu action to an object, Dreamweaver automatically attaches a Hide Pop-Up Menu item to it.

Jump Menu and Jump Menu Go

Although most behaviors insert original code to activate an element of the Web page, several behaviors are included to edit code inserted by a Dreamweaver object. The Jump Menu and Jump Menu Go behaviors both require a previously inserted Jump Menu object before they become active. The Jump Menu behavior is used to edit an existing Jump Menu object, and the Jump Menu Go behavior adds a graphic image as a Go button.

 Cross-Reference   To find out more about the Jump Menu object, see Chapter 14.

To use the Jump Menu behavior to edit an existing Jump Menu object, follow these steps:

1. Select the Jump Menu object previously inserted into the page.

2. In the Behaviors panel, double-click the listed Jump Menu behavior.

3. Make your modifications in the Jump Menu dialog box, as shown in Figure 12-12. You can alter the existing menu item names or their associated URLs, add new menu items, or reorder the list through the Jump Menu dialog box.

Figure 12-12: Use the Jump Menu behavior to modify a previously inserted Jump Menu object.

4. Click OK when you're finished.

To add a button to activate the Jump Menu object, follow these steps:

1. Select the image or form button you'd like to make into a Go button. A Jump Menu object must be on the current page for the Jump Menu Go behavior to be available.

2. From the Behaviors panel, select Jump Menu Go from the Add (+) drop-down list. The Jump Menu Go dialog box, shown in Figure 12-13, is displayed.

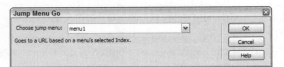

Figure 12-13: Add a graphic or standard button as a Go button with the Jump Menu Go behavior.

3. Select the name of the Jump Menu object you want to activate from the option list.

4. Click OK when you're finished.

Open Browser Window

Want to display your latest design in a borderless, nonresizable browser window that's exactly the size of your image? With the Open Browser Window action, you can open a new browser window and specify its exact size and attributes. You can even set it up to receive JavaScript events.

You can also open a new browser window with a regular link by specifying `target="_blank"`, but you can't control any of the window's attributes with this method. You do get this control with the parameter dialog box of the Open Browser Window action (see Figure 12-14). This dialog enables you to set the window width and height and select whether to display the

Navigation Toolbar, Location Toolbar, Status Bar, Menu Bar, Scrollbars as Needed, and/or Resize Handles. You can also name your new window, a necessary step for advanced JavaScript control.

Figure 12-14: Use the Open Browser Window action to program a pop-up advertisement or remote control.

You have to explicitly select any of the attributes that you want to appear in your new window. Your new browser window contains only the attributes you've checked, plus basic window elements such as a title bar and a Close button.

Caution   Most modern browsers have pop-up blockers that will stop the Open Browser Window from functioning. While there is nothing you, as a page designer, can do to override the pop-up blocker, you might consider adding a note to your page indicating that pop-up windows are in use on your page.

To use the Open Browser Window action, follow these steps:

1. Select the object to trigger the action.

2. From the Behaviors panel, click the Add (+) button and select Open Browser Window.

3. In the URL to Display text box, enter the address of the Web page you want to display in the new window. You can also click the Browse button to locate the file.

4. To specify the window's size, enter the width and height values in the appropriate text boxes. You must enter *both* a width and height measurement, or the new browser window opens to its default size.

5. Check the appropriate Attributes checkboxes to show the desired window features.

6. If you plan on using JavaScript to address or control the window, type a unique name in the Window Name text box. This name cannot contain spaces or special characters. Dreamweaver alerts you if the name you've entered is unacceptable.

7. Click OK when you're finished.

Play Sound

The Play Sound action is used to add external controls to an audio file that normally uses the Netscape LiveAudio plugin or the Windows Media Player. Supported audio file types include WAV, MID, AU, and AIFF files. The Play Sound action — which is generally used to add invisible background music to a page — inserts an `<embed>` tag with the following attributes:

   ✦ `loop=false`

   ✦ `autostart=false`

   ✦ `mastersound`

   ✦ `hidden=true`

   ✦ `width=0`

   ✦ `height=0`

Instead of automatically detecting which sound files have been inserted in the current Web page, Play Sound looks for the sound file to be inserted through the action's dialog box (see Figure 12-15).

Figure 12-15: Give your Web page background music and control it with the Play Sound action.

Note   Dreamweaver can detect if a visitor's browser has the Windows Media Player installed and, if so, it issues the appropriate commands.

To use the Play Sound action, follow these steps:

1. Select the object to trigger the action.

2. From the Behaviors panel, click the Add (+) button and select Play Sound.

3. To play a sound, enter the path to the audio file in the Play Sound text box or click the Browse button to locate the file.

4. Click OK when you're finished.

Popup Message

You can send a quick message to your users with the Popup Message behavior. When triggered, this action opens a JavaScript alert box that displays your specified message. You enter your message in the Message text box on the action's parameter dialog box (see Figure 12-16).

Figure 12-16: Send a message to your users with the Popup Message action.

To use the Popup Message action, follow these steps:

1. Select the object to trigger the action.

2. From the Behaviors panel, click the Add (+) button and select Popup Message.

3. Enter your text in the Message text box.

4. Click OK when you're finished.

Tip

You can include JavaScript functions or references in your text messages by surrounding the JavaScript with curly braces. For example, you can incorporate today's date in a message like this:

```
Welcome to our site on {new Date()}!
```

You could also pull data from a form into your alert-box message, as in this example:

```
Thanks for filling out our survey,
{document.surveyForm.firstname.value}.
```

If you need to display a curly brace in a message, you must precede it with a backslash character, as in \{ or \}.

Preload Images

Designs commonly require a particular image or several images to be displayed immediately when called by an action or a timeline. Because of the nature of HTML, all graphics are separate files that are normally downloaded when needed. To get the snappy response required for certain designs, graphics need to be preloaded or cached so that they are available. The Preload Images action performs this important service. You designate the images you want to cache for later use through the Preload Images parameter dialog box (see Figure 12-17).

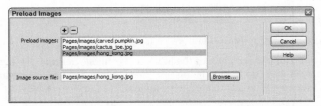

Figure 12-17: Media-rich Web sites respond much faster when images have been cached with the Preload Images action.

Note

You don't need to use the Preload Images action if you're creating rollovers. Both the Rollover object and the Swap Image action enable you to preload images from their dialog boxes.

To use the Preload Images action, follow these steps:

1. Select the object to trigger the action.

2. From the Behaviors panel, click the Add (+) button and select Preload Images.

3. In the Preload Images parameter dialog box, enter the path to the image file in the Image Source File text box, or click the Browse button to locate the file.

4. To add another file, click the Add (+) button and repeat step 3.

Caution

After you've specified your first file to be preloaded, be sure to click the Add (+) button for each successive file you want to add to the list. Otherwise, the highlighted file is replaced by the next entry.

5. To remove a file from the Preload Images list, select it and click the Remove (–) button.

6. Click OK when you're finished.

Set Nav Bar Image

The Set Nav Bar Image action, like the Jump Menu actions, enables you to edit an existing Dreamweaver object, the Navigation Bar object. This object, inserted from the Common panel of the Insert bar, consists of a series of designer-specified images acting as a group of navigational buttons. The Set Nav Bar Image action enables you to modify the current Navigation Bar object by adding, reordering, or deleting images as buttons, as well as by setting up advanced rollover techniques. In fact, you can think of the Set Nav Bar Image action as a super-duper Swap Image behavior.

Cross-Reference

To refresh your memory about the capabilities of the Navigation Bar object, see Chapter 9.

The main aspect that sets a navigation bar apart from any other similar series of rollover images is that the navigation bar elements relate to one another. When you select one element of a navigation bar, by default, all the other elements are swapped to their up state. The Set Nav Bar Image action enables you to modify that default behavior to a rollover in another area or any other image swap desired. You can also use Set Nav Bar Image to include another image button in the navigation bar.

To modify an existing Navigation Bar object, follow these steps:

1. Choose any image in the Navigation Bar object.

2. From the Behaviors panel, double-click any of the Set Nav Bar Image actions displayed for the image. The same Set Nav Bar Image dialog box (see Figure 12-18) opens regardless of whether you select an action associated with the `onClick`, `onMouseOver`, or `onMouseOut` event.

3. Make any desired edits — changing the Up, Over, Down, or Over While Down state images or their respective URLs or targets — from the Basic tab of the dialog box.

4. To change any other images that interact with the current image, select the Advanced tab.

5. From the drop-down list in the Advanced category, choose the state for which you want to trigger changes:

   • Over Image or Over While Down Image

   • Down Image

Figure 12-18: Modify an existing Navigation Bar object through the Set Nav Bar Image action.

6. Select the image you want to change from the Also Set Image list. Dreamweaver lists all the named images on the current page, not just those in the navigation bar.

7. Select the path of the new image to be displayed in the To Image File text field. An asterisk appears after the current image in the list box, signifying that a swap image has been chosen.

8. If you choose Over Image or Over While Down Image as the triggering event, an optional field, If Down, To Image File enables you to specify another graphic to swap for the image of the down-state image.

9. To alter other images with the same triggering event, repeat steps 6 through 8.

Note   Only one Navigation Bar object can exist on a page.

Set Text of Frame

Dreamweaver has grouped together four similar behaviors under the Set Text heading. The first of these, Set Text of Frame, enables you to do much more than change a word or two — you can dynamically rewrite the entire code for any frame. You can even incorporate JavaScript functions or interactive information into the new frame content.

The Set Text of Frame action replaces all the contents of the `<body>` tag of a frame. Dreamweaver supplies a handy Get Current HTML button that enables you to easily keep everything you want to retain and change only a heading or other element. Naturally, you must be within a frameset to use this behavior, and the frames must be named correctly — that is, uniquely without special characters or spaces.

To change the content of a frame dynamically, follow these steps:

1. Select the triggering object.

2. From the Behaviors panel, click the Add (+) button and choose Set Text ⇨ Set Text of Frame. The Set Text of Frame dialog box opens, as shown in Figure 12-19.

Figure 12-19: The Set Text of Frame behavior enables you to interactively update the contents of any frame in the current frameset.

3. Choose the frame you want to alter from the Frame drop-down list.

4. Enter the code for the changing frame in the New HTML text area. Keep in mind that you're changing not just a word or phrase, but all the HTML contained in the `<body>` section of the frame.

Tip   With all four Set Text behaviors, you can include JavaScript code by enclosing it in curly braces: {...}.

5. If you want to keep the majority of the code, click the Get Current HTML button and change only those portions necessary.

6. To maintain the frame's `<body>` attributes, such as the background and text colors, select the Preserve Background Color option. If this option is not selected, the frame's background and text colors are replaced by the default values (a white background and black text).

7. Click OK when you're finished.

Set Text of Layer

The Set Text of Layer behavior is similar to the previously described Set Text of Frame behavior in that it replaces the entire HTML contents of the target. The major difference, of course, is that with one behavior, you're replacing the code of a layer; with the other behavior, you're replacing the code of the frame's `<body>`.

Tip   Unlike Set Text of Frame, Set Text of Layer provides no button for getting the current HTML. Here's a workaround. Before invoking the behavior, select and copy all the elements inside the layer. Because Dreamweaver copies tags, as well as text, in the Document window, you can just paste the clipboard into the New HTML text area. Be careful not to select the layer tag, `<div>`, or the layer's contents — if you do, you are pasting a layer in a layer.

To set the text of a layer dynamically, follow these steps:

1. Make sure that the layer you want to change has been created and named properly.

2. Select the object to trigger the action.

3. From the Behaviors panel, click the Add (+) button and choose Set Text ➪ Set Text of Layer from the option list. The Set Text of Layer dialog box opens, as shown in Figure 12-20.

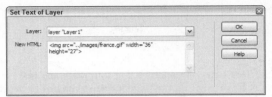

Figure 12-20: Replace all the HTML in a layer with the Set Text of Layer behavior.

4. Select the layer to modify from the Layer drop-down list.

5. Enter the replacement code in the New HTML text area.

6. Click OK when you're finished.

Set Text of Status Bar

Use the Set Text of Status Bar action to display a text message in the browser's status bar based on a user's action, such as moving the pointer over an image. The message stays displayed in the status bar until another message replaces it. System messages, such as URLs, tend to be temporary and visible only when the user's mouse is over a link.

Note At this time, the Set Text of Status Bar doesn't work with the current version of Firefox (1.0.7); it does, however, fail without error.

The only limit to the length of the message is the size of the browser's status bar; you should test your message in various browsers to make sure that it is completely visible.

Tip To display a message only when a user's pointer is over an image or link, use one Set Text of Status Bar action, attached to an onMouseOver event, with your desired status-bar message. Use another Set Text of Status Bar action, attached to an onMouseOut event, that has a null string (" ") as the text.

You enter all text in Message text box of the Set Text of Status Bar parameter dialog box (see Figure 12-21).

Figure 12-21: Use the Set Text of Status Bar action to guide your users with instructions in the browser window's status bar.

To use the Set Text of Status Bar action, follow these steps:

1. Select the object to trigger the action.

2. From the Behaviors panel, click the Add (+) button and select Set Text of Status Bar.

3. Enter your text in the Message text box.

4. Click OK when you're finished.

Set Text of Text Field

Set Text of Text Field, the final Set Text behavior, enables you to update any text or text area field, dynamically. A text field must be present on the page for the behavior to be available. To change the displayed text of a text or text area field, follow these steps:

1. From the Behaviors panel, click the Add (+) button and choose Set Text ⇨ Set Text of Text Field from the Add Action list. The Set Text of Text Field dialog box is displayed, as shown in Figure 12-22.

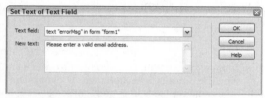

Figure 12-22: Dynamically update text/text area form elements with the Set Text of Text Field behavior.

2. Select the desired text field from the drop-down list.

3. Enter the new text and/or JavaScript in the New Text area.

4. Click OK when you're finished.

Show-Hide Layers

One of the key features of Dynamic HTML layers is their capability to appear and disappear on command. The Show-Hide Layers action gives you easy control over the visibility attribute for all layers in the current Web page. In addition to explicitly showing or hiding layers, this action can also restore layers to the default visibility setting.

The Show-Hide Layers action typically reveals one layer while concealing another; however, you are not restricted to hiding or showing just one layer at a time. The action's parameter dialog box (see Figure 12-23) shows you a list of all the layers in the current Web page from which you can choose as many as you want to show or hide.

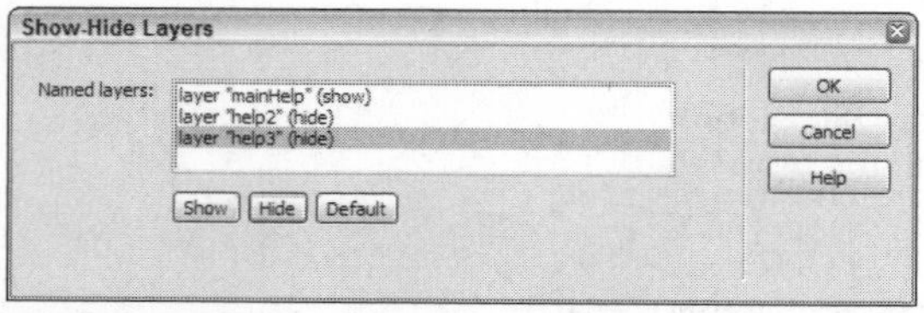

Figure 12-23: The Show-Hide Layers action can make any number of hidden layers visible, hide any number of visible layers, or both.

To use the Show-Hide Layers action, follow these steps:

1. Select the object to trigger the action.

2. From the Behaviors panel, click the Add (+) button and select Show-Hide Layer. The Show-Hide Layers parameter dialog box displays a list of the available layers in the current Web page.

3. To show a hidden layer, select the layer from the Named Layers list and click the Show button.

4. To hide a shown layer, select its name from the list and click the Hide button.

5. To restore a layer's default visibility value, select the layer and click the Default button.

6. Click OK when you're finished.

Swap Image and Swap Image Restore

Button rollovers are one of the most frequently used techniques in Web design today. In a typical button rollover, a user's pointer moves over one image, and the graphic appears to change in some way, seeming to glow or change color. Actually, the onMouseOver event triggers the almost instantaneous swapping of one image for another. Dreamweaver automates this difficult coding task with the Swap Image action and its companion, the Swap Image Restore action.

In recognition of how rollovers commonly work in the real world, Dreamweaver makes it possible to combine Swap Image and Swap Image Restore in one easy operation—as well as to preload all the images. Moreover, you can use a link in one frame to trigger a rollover in another frame without having to tweak the code as you did in earlier Dreamweaver versions.

When the dialog box for the Swap Image action opens (see Figure 12-24), it automatically loads a list of all the image names it finds in the current Web page. You select the image you want to change—which could be the same image to which you are attaching the behavior—and specify the image file you want to replace with the rolled-over image. You can swap more than one image with each Swap Image action. For example, if you want an entire submenu to change when a user rolls over a particular option, you can use a single Swap Image action to switch all the submenu button images.

Figure 12-24: The Swap Image action is used primarily for handling button rollovers.

Note   If the Restore Images onMouseOut option was selected in the Swap Image parameter dialog box, Dreamweaver adds two lines to the Behaviors panel: Swap Image and Swap Image Restore.

If you choose not to enable the Restore Images onMouseOut option, which changes the image back to the original, you attach the Swap Image Restore action to another event. The Swap Image Restore action can be used only after a Swap Image action. No parameter dialog box exists for the Swap Image Restore action—just a dialog box confirming your selection.

Caution   If the swapped-in image has different dimensions than the image it replaces, the swapped-in image is resized to the height and width of the first image.

To use the Swap Image action, follow these steps:

1. Select the object to trigger the action.

2. From the Behaviors panel, click the Add (+) button and select Swap Image.

3. In the Swap Image parameter dialog box, choose an available image from the Images list.

4. In the Set Source To text box, enter the path to the image that you want to swap. You can also click the Browse button to locate the file. An asterisk appears at the end of the selected image name to indicate an alternative image has been selected.

5. To swap additional images using the same event, repeat steps 3 and 4.

6. To preload all images involved in the Swap Image action when the page loads, make sure the Preload Images option is checked.

7. To cause the selected images to revert to their original source when the user mouses away from the selected object, make sure that the Restore Images onMouseOut option is selected.

8. Click OK when you're finished.

Timelines: Play Timeline, Stop Timeline, and Go to Timeline Frame

Any Dynamic HTML animation in Dreamweaver happens with timelines, but a timeline can't do anything without the actions written to control it. The three actions in the timeline set — Play Timeline, Stop Timeline, and Go to Timeline Frame — are all you need to set your Web page in motion.

Before the Timeline actions become available, at least one timeline must be on the current page. All three of these related actions are located in the Timeline submenu. Generally, when you are establishing controls for playing a timeline, you first attach the Go to Timeline Frame action to an event and then attach the Play Timeline action to the same event. By setting a specific frame before you enable the timeline to start, you ensure that the timeline always begins at the same point.

Cross-Reference   For more detailed information on using timelines, see Chapter 17.

The Play Timeline and Stop Timeline actions have only one element on their parameter dialog box: a drop-down list box offering all timelines in the current page.

The Go to Timeline Frame action's parameter dialog box (see Figure 12-25), aside from enabling you to pick a timeline and enter a specific go-to frame, also gives you the option to loop the timeline a set number of times.

Figure 12-25: The Go To Timeline Frame parameter dialog box enables you to choose a go-to frame and designate the number of loops for the timeline.

Tip　If you want the timeline to loop an infinite number of times, leave the Loop text box empty and turn on the Loop option in the Timelines panel.

To use the Go to Timeline Frame action, follow these steps:

1. Select the object to trigger the action.

2. From the Behaviors panel, click the Add (+) button and choose Timeline ⇨ Go to Timeline Frame.

3. In the Go To Timeline Frame parameter dialog box, choose the timeline for which you want to set the start frame.

4. Enter the frame number in the Go to Frame text box.

5. If you want the timeline to loop a set number of times, enter a value in the Loop text box.

6. Click OK when you're done.

To use the Play Timeline action, follow these steps:

1. Select an object to trigger the action and choose Timeline ⇨ Play Timeline from the Add (+) drop-down list in the Behaviors panel.

2. In the Play Timeline parameter dialog box, choose the timeline that you want to play.

3. Click OK when you're done.

To use the Stop Timeline action, follow these steps:

1. Select an object to trigger the action and choose Timeline ⇨ Stop Timeline from the Add (+) drop-down list in the Behaviors panel.

2. In the Stop Timeline parameter dialog box, choose the timeline that you want to stop.

3. Click OK when you're done.

Note　You can also choose All Timelines to stop every timeline on the current Web page from playing.

Validate Form

When you set up a form for user input, you establish each field with a purpose. The name field, the e-mail address field, and the ZIP Code field all have their own requirements for input. Unless you are using a CGI program specifically designed to check the user's input, form fields usually accept input of any type. Even if the CGI program can handle it, this server-side method ties up server time and is relatively slow. The Dreamweaver Validate Form action checks any text field's input and returns the form to the user if any of the entries are unacceptable. You can also use this action to designate any text field as a required field.

Validate Form can be used to check either single or multiple text fields in a form. If you attach a Validate Form action to a single text box, you alert the user to any errors as he is filling out this field. To check multiple form fields, the Validate Form action must be attached to the form's <form> tag.

The Validate Form dialog box (see Figure 12-26) enables you to designate any text field as required, and you can evaluate its contents. You can require the input of a text field to be a number, an e-mail address (for instance, jdoe@anywhere.com), or a number within a range. The number range you specify can include positive whole numbers, negative numbers, or decimals.

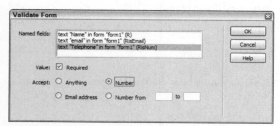

Figure 12-26: The Validate Form action checks your form's entries client-side, without CGI programming.

To use the Validate Form action, follow these steps:

1. Select the form object to trigger the action: a single text field or the <form> tag (use the Tag Selector) for multiple text fields.

2. From the Behaviors panel, click the Add (+) button and select Validate Form.

3. If you are validating an entire form, select a text field from the Named Fields list. If you are validating a single field, the selected form object is chosen for you and appears in the Named Fields list.

4. To make the field required, select the Value: Required checkbox.

5. To set the kind of input expected, select one of the following Accept options:

   • **Anything:** Accepts any input.

   • **Number:** Enables any sort of numeric input. You cannot mix text and numbers, however, as in a telephone number such as (212) 555-1212.

   • **Email Address:** Looks for an e-mail address with the @ sign. (Note that this is not a foolproof e-mail address check, because it validates illegal addresses such as human@somewhere, @somewhere.com, human@somewhere.overtherainbow, and so on.)

- **Number from:** Enables you to enter two numbers, one in each text box, to define the number range.

6. Click OK when you're finished.

Installing, Managing, and Modifying Behaviors

The standard behaviors that come with Dreamweaver are indeed impressive, but they're really just the beginning. Because existing behaviors can be modified and new ones created from scratch, you can continue to add behaviors as you need them.

To install a new Dreamweaver behavior, follow these steps:

1. Locate the behavior, which must be packaged as an MXP extension file; for example: `alignLayer.mxp`, `cleanupPage.mxp`, and so on.

On the CD-ROM

The CD-ROM that comes with this book contains several useful MXP behavior extension files. In addition, you can find a large selection of MXP extension files on the Dreamweaver Exchange site, which you can reach by choosing Help ⇨ Dreamweaver Exchange.

2. To install the extension in Dreamweaver, or in Fireworks or Flash for that matter, either double-click the MXP extension file, or choose Help ⇨ Manage Extensions to open the Extension Manager (as shown in Figure 12-27) and choose File ⇨ Install Extension to select the file. Some extensions remain inaccessible until you've quit and restarted Dreamweaver; in most cases, you will be prompted to do so.

Note

Depending on your browser, you might be given the choice of installing a Dreamweaver Exchange extension file directly from the Exchange site or to save it first to disk and install it from there. If you choose to install the extension file directly from the Exchange site, the Extension Manager handles the installation automatically. If you choose to save the extension file to disk, a good place to save it is the Downloaded Extensions folder within your Dreamweaver 8 folder.

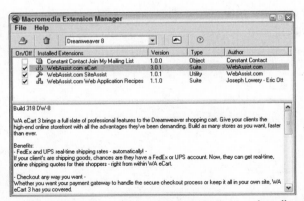

Figure 12-27: You use the Extension Manager to install and remove MXP extension files from Dreamweaver, Fireworks, or Flash.

Altering the Parameters of a Behavior

You can alter any of the attributes for your inserted behaviors at any time. To modify a behavior you have already attached, follow these steps:

1. Open the Behaviors panel.

2. Select the object in the Document window or the tag in the Tag Selector to which your behavior is attached.

3. Double-click the action that you want to alter. The appropriate dialog box opens, with the previously selected parameters.

4. Make any modifications to the existing settings for the action.

5. Click OK when you are finished.

Modifying Behaviors

To further reveal the power of Dreamweaver's standard behaviors, add another series of behaviors to your practice page. In the process, you'll get a chance to adjust attributes of an applied behavior.

1. From the Files panel, re-open the `behaviors_start.htm` file previously worked upon.

2. Place your cursor anywhere in the `Living Room` text.

3. From the Behaviors panel, click Add (+) and select Open Browser Window.

4. In the Open Browser Window dialog, set the following parameters:

   ✦ Click the Browse button and choose `living_room.htm` from the dialog box.

   ✦ In the Window width field, enter `200`.

   ✦ In the Window height field, enter `100`.

   ✦ Select the Resize Handles option.

5. Click OK when you're done.

   A second behavior is added to the link in the Behaviors panel, with the default event of onClick.

6. Save your file and press F12 to preview the page in the browser.

7. Click the `Living Room` link to test the behavior.

8. You'll notice that the window height is too small for the text; you can easily make the adjustment. In Dreamweaver's Behaviors panel, double-click the Open Browser Window event to re-open the dialog box.

9. Change the Window height value to 150; click OK when you're done.

10. To verify that the change is sufficient, test the page in the browser as before.

11. In Dreamweaver, repeat steps 2–5 for the `Kitchen North` link and set the Browser Window behavior to open `kitchen.htm` with a width of 200 pixels and height of 150 pixels.

12. Repeat steps 2–5 for the `Kitchen South` link and again set the Browser Window behavior to open `kitchen.htm` with a width of 200 pixels and height of 150 pixels.

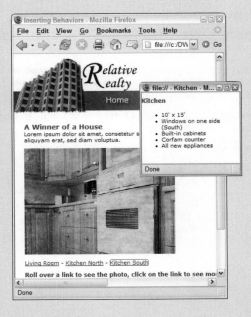

13. Save your page.

Test your page in the browser to verify that all the windows open as expected.

Sequencing Behaviors

When you have more than one action attached to a particular event, the order of the actions is often important. For example, you should generally implement the Go to Timeline Frame action ahead of the Play Timeline action to make sure the timeline is playing from the correct frame. To specify the sequence in which Dreamweaver triggers the actions, reposition them as necessary in the Actions column. To do this, simply select an action and use the up and down arrow buttons (refer to Figure 12-1) to reposition it in the list.

Deleting Behaviors

To remove a behavior from a list of behaviors attached to a particular event, simply highlight the behavior and click the Remove (–) button.

Summary

Dreamweaver behaviors can greatly extend the Web designer's palette of possibilities — even if the Web designer is an accomplished JavaScript programmer. Behaviors simplify and automate the process of incorporating common and not-so-common JavaScript functions. The versatility of the behavior format enables anyone proficient in JavaScript to create custom actions that can be attached to any event. When considering behaviors, keep the following points in mind:

✦ Behaviors are combinations of events and actions.

✦ Behaviors are written in HTML and JavaScript and are completely customizable from within Dreamweaver.

✦ Different browsers support different events. Dreamweaver enables you to select a specific browser or a browser range, such as all 4.0 browsers, on which to base your event choice.

✦ Dreamweaver includes 27 standard actions. Some actions are not available unless a particular object is included on the current page.

In the next chapter, you learn how to work with tables and structured data.

✦   ✦   ✦

Setting Up Tables

Tables bring structure to a Web page, and they are especially important when displaying data for Web applications. Whether it is used to align numbers in a spreadsheet or arrange columns of information on a page, an HTML table brings a bit of order to otherwise free-flowing content. Initially, tables were implemented to present raw data in a more readable format. It wasn't long before Web designers adopted tables as the most capable tool to control page layout. Although the current trend in Web design is to use CSS-based layout rather than table-based, tables remain the perfect method for presenting structured information.

Dreamweaver's implementation of tables reflects this trend in Web page design. Drag-and-drop table sizing, easy organization of rows and columns, and instant table reformatting all help get the job done in the shortest time possible. Table editing features enable you to select and modify anything in a table — from a single cell to multiple columns. Moreover, using Dreamweaver's commands, you can sort static table data in a variety of ways or completely reformat it.

Cross-Reference

This chapter covers everything you need to know to get started creating HTML tables in Dreamweaver. You can also dynamically add data to tables from an external data source using server-side processing. Using dynamic data is covered in Chapter 19.

It should be recognized that some legacy sites and pages continue to use table-based layout. For designers maintaining such sites, Dreamweaver includes a feature that takes table layout to the next level of ease of use and power. With the Layout mode, designers can draw out individual cells with a stroke of the mouse, and Dreamweaver automatically creates a borderless, content-ready table. You can even add nested tables to maintain design integrity. You still need to know the basics of table functionality to get the most out of this tool, but Layout mode offers you a technique for visually structuring your Web page.

Although CSS gives Web designers another route to precise layout control, many Web designers find that a combination of tools is required to get the desired effects and maintain wide browser compatibility. In short, HTML tables are going to be around for a long time.

HTML Table Fundamentals

A table is basically a grid that expands as you add text or images. Tables consist of three main components: rows, columns, and cells. *Rows* extend across a table from left to right, and *columns* run up and down. A *cell* is the area within the intersection of a row and a column; it's where you enter your information. Cells expand to fit whatever they hold. If you have enabled the table border, your browser shows the outline of the entire table and each cell.

In HTML, the structure and all the data of a table are contained between the table tag pair, `<table>` and `</table>`. The `<table>` tag can take numerous attributes, determining a table's width (which can be given in absolute pixel measurement or as a percentage of the screen) as well as the border, alignment on the page, and background color. You can also control the size of the spacing between cells and the amount of padding within cells.

Note You can insert a `<table>`...`</table>` pair directly in your code by choosing Insert ➪ Table Objects ➪ Table or by clicking the Table Tag button in the Tables category of the Insert bar. You must do this in Code view, where you can see the exact location of your cursor before inserting the tag pair.

HTML uses a strict hierarchy when describing a table. You can see this clearly in Listing 13-1, which shows the HTML generated from a simple table in Dreamweaver.

Listing 13-1: Code for an HTML Table

```
<table border="1" width="75%">
  <tr>
    <td> </td>
    <td> </td>
    <td> </td>
  </tr>
  <tr>
    <td> </td>
    <td> </td>
    <td> </td>
  </tr>
  <tr>
    <td> </td>
    <td> </td>
    <td> </td>
  </tr>
</table>
```

Note The ` ` in the table code is HTML for a non-breaking space. Dreamweaver inserts this code in each empty table cell because some browsers collapse the cell without it. Enter any text or image in the cell, and Dreamweaver automatically removes the ` ` code.

Rows

After the opening `<table>` tag comes the first row tag `<tr>`...`</tr>` pair. Within the current row, you can specify attributes for horizontal alignment or vertical alignment. In addition, browsers recognize row color as an added option.

If you are working directly in Code view, you can insert a `<tr>`...`</tr>` pair by choosing Insert ➪ Table Objects ➪ TR or by clicking the Table Row button in the Tables category of the Insert bar. See "Inserting Rows and Columns" later in this chapter for methods of inserting rows in Design view.

Cells

Cells are marked in HTML with the `<td>...</td>` tag pair. No specific code exists for a column; rather, the number of columns is determined by the maximum number of cells within a single table row. For example, in Listing 13-1, notice the three sets of `<td>` tags between each `<tr>` pair. This means the table has three columns.

Note   Most `<tr>` attributes are better set up using CSS; attributes like `bgcolor` were deprecated under HTML 4.0 and XHTML 1.0 specifications and have been removed from XHTML 1.1 entirely.

A cell can span more than one row or column — in these cases, you see a `rowspan=value` or `colspan=value` attribute in the `<td>` tag, as illustrated in Listing 13-2. This code is also for a table with three rows and three columns, but the second cell in the first row spans two columns.

Listing 13-2: HTML Table with Column Spanning

```
<table width="75%"  border="0">
  <tr>
    <td> </td>
    <td colspan="2"> </td>
  </tr>
  <tr>
    <td> </td>
    <td> </td>
    <td> </td>
  </tr>
  <tr>
    <td> </td>
    <td> </td>
    <td> </td>
  </tr>
</table>
```

Cells can also be given horizontal or vertical alignment attributes, which override any similar attributes specified by the table row. When you give a cell a particular width, all the cells in that column are affected. Width can be specified either in an absolute pixel measurement or as a percentage of the overall table.

Note   Again, modern Web designers prefer to use CSS rather than HTML attributes to format and style table cells. Both the `align` and `bgcolor` attributes have been deprecated and recent browsers don't support other attributes such as height.

In Code view, you can insert a `<td>...</td>` pair to define a single table cell by choosing Insert ➪ Table Objects ➪ TD or by clicking the Table Data button in the Tables category of the Insert bar.

Column and Row Headings

HTML uses a special type of cell called a *table header* for column and row headings. Information in these cells is marked with a `<th>` tag and is generally rendered in boldface, centered within the cell.

To insert a `<th>`...`</th>` pair for a table heading cell, choose Insert ⇨ Table Objects ⇨ TH or click the Table Heading button in the Tables category of the Insert bar. See the section "Setting Cell, Column, and Row Properties" later in this chapter for another way to designate table header cells.

Tip   After the initial `<table>` tag, you can place an optional caption for the table. In Dreamweaver, you can enter the `<caption>` tag in the Code view or Code inspector by choosing Insert ⇨ Table Objects ⇨ Caption. From Code view, you can also click the Table Caption button in the Tables category of the Insert bar.

The following example shows how the tag works:

```
<caption valign="bottom">Table of Periodic Elements</caption>
```

Inserting Tables in Dreamweaver

You can control almost all of a table's HTML features through Dreamweaver's point-and-click interface. To insert a table in the current cursor position, use one of the following methods:

✦ Choose Insert ⇨ Table.

✦ Click the Table button in either the Common or Layout category of the Insert bar.

✦ Use the keyboard shortcut: Ctrl+Alt+T (Command+Option+T).

Depending on your preference settings, any one of these methods either immediately inserts a table into your page or opens the Table dialog box. The dialog box is bypassed — and the previous settings used — if the Show Dialog When Inserting Objects option in Preferences is not enabled. The Table dialog box, shown in Figure 13-1, contains the values shown in Table 13-1 when it is first displayed.

Table 13-1: Default Values for the Table Dialog Box

Attribute	Default	Description
Rows	3	Sets the number of horizontal rows.
Columns	3	Sets the number of vertical columns.
Width	200 pixels	Sets the preset width of the table. This can be specified as a percentage of the containing element (screen, layer, or another table) or an absolute pixel size.
Border	1 pixel	Sets the width of the border around each cell and the entire table.
Cell Padding	0	Sets the space between a cell's border and its contents, measured in pixels. A value of 0 indicates no margin space within the cell.

Attribute	Default	Description
Cell Spacing	0	Sets the number of pixels between each cell. A value of 0 indicates no space between cells.
Header	None	Determines whether the top row and/or column is designated as a header cell. In addition to simply creating the header cell with `<th>` tags instead of the usual `<td>`, this attribute adds the `scope` attribute to the cell. The `scope` attribute helps nonvisual browsers interpret and present the structure of the table, by indicating whether the cell is a column heading or a row heading. In visual browsers, text in header rows or columns is typically displayed as bold and centered.
Caption	Blank	Sets a brief description for the table.
Align Caption	default	Enables you to specify whether the table caption appears at the top, bottom, left, or right of the table. Choosing default does not add an `align` attribute to the `<caption>` tag and uses the browser's default alignment instead. Note that the `align` attribute on the `<caption>` tag is deprecated in HTML 4.0. This means that, although the attribute is still currently supported, the preferred method to achieve the same effect in newer browsers is to use CSS.
Summary	Blank	Enables you to add the `summary` attribute to your `<table>` tag. The summary is a verbal description of the table layout, so that people who are having the page read to them (for example, through a nonvisual browser) can understand it. For example, your summary could say, "This table compares the number of students and teachers in each Minnesota secondary school for the years 1997 through 2002. It lists each school in Minnesota, grouped by school district. For each of the years 1997 through 2002, there are columns for the number of students and number of teachers in each school." This is particularly important for complex tables. The text you enter for the summary is not displayed in visual browsers.

If you aren't sure of the number of rows and/or columns you need, put in your best guess — you can add or delete rows or columns later as necessary.

The default table is sized to take up 200 pixels of the browser window. You can alter this percentage by changing the value in the Width text box. The table maintains this proportion as you add text or images, except in the following situations:

✦ When an image is larger than the specified percentage

✦ When the `nowrap` attribute is used for the cell or table row and there is too much text to fit

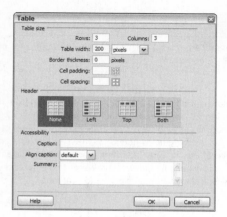

Figure 13-1: The Table dialog box starts out with a default table of three columns and three rows; you can adjust it as needed.

In either case, the percentage set for the table is ignored, and the cell and table expand to accommodate the text or image. (For further information on the `nowrap` attribute, see the "Cell Wrap" section later in this chapter.)

Note   The Table dialog box uses what are called *sticky* settings, displaying your previously used settings the next time you open the dialog box. This handy feature enables you to set the border width to 0, for example, and forget about resetting it each time.

If you prefer to enter the table width as an absolute pixel value, instead of the relative percentage, type the number of pixels in the Width text box and select Pixels in the drop-down list of width options.

With Dreamweaver's Table Widths feature, you can tell at a glance whether your table and cells are set to percentages or pixels — and exactly what these values are. The Table Widths feature is a design-time visual aid that appears above or below (depending on its position in the window) a table when one or more table cells are active. The widths are presented in two lines: the outermost line shows the width of the entire table, and the innermost line displays cell-width measurements.

With the Table Widths feature enabled, tables or cells using percentages actually display two values. The first value shown is the actual percentage; it is followed by a second value in parentheses that indicates the current size in pixels. For example, if a table is set to 75% and placed in a browser window where the interior screen width is 774 pixels, the actual width of the table is 425 pixels. Dreamweaver displays 75% (425), as shown in Figure 13-2. The same figure shows two other tables: one at 100%, which takes up the full width of the browser window, minus any margins. The third table is fixed at 400 pixels — approximately half of an 800 x 600 window.

Although viewing Table Widths definitely helps with certain stages of the design process, it can impede others. To turn off the dimensioning, deselect View ➪ Visual Aids ➪ Table Widths; the same option exists under the View Options menu of the Document toolbar.

Tip   You don't have to declare a width for your table at all. If you delete the value in the Width text box of the Table dialog box, your table starts out as small as possible and only expands to accommodate inserted text or images. However, this can make it difficult to position your cursor inside a cell to enter content — a situation Expanded Tables mode (covered later in this chapter) is intended to alleviate.

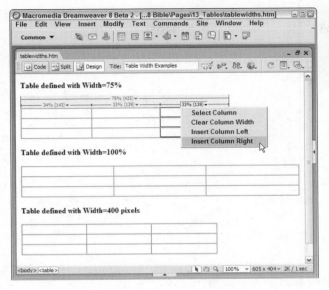

Figure 13-2: In addition to displaying overall table and column widths, the Table Width visual aid provides a quick method for working with columns.

The Table Widths features also offers a number of context menus to make table operations even easier. Click the down arrow next to the table width measurement to select the table, clear all heights and/or widths, make all widths consistent, or hide the table widths. Choose the down arrow over a column to select that column, clear the column width, or insert columns to either side.

Adding a Table to the Page

In this first technique of the chapter, you practice inserting two tables and setting their initial values.

1. In the Files panel, switch to the Dreamweaver Bible working site previously created.

2. Expand the 13_Tables folder and open the file `table_start.htm`.

3. Place your cursor at the end of the first paragraph under the About Us heading and press Enter (Return) to create a new line.

4. From the Insert bar's Common category, click the Table object.

5. When the Insert Table dialog box opens, set the following parameters:

   Rows: **4**

   Columns: **2**

   Table width: **300 pixels**

   Border Thickness: **0**

Continued

Continued

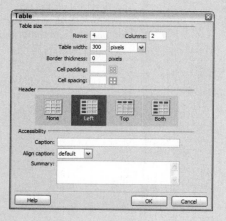

6. Leave both the Cell padding and Cell spacing fields blank.

7. In the Header area, select Left.

8. Leave all the fields in the Accessibility area at their defaults and click OK.

The first table is inserted at the cursor position, ready for data. Now, add a second table near the bottom of the page.

1. Place your cursor at the end of the paragraph under the Our top staff heading and press Enter (Return).

2. Click the Table object on the Insert bar.

3. When the Insert Table dialog box opens, set the following parameters:

Rows: **4**

Columns: **4**

Table width: **75 percent**

Border Thickness: **0**

6. Leave both the Cell padding and Cell spacing fields blank.

7. In the Header area, select Top.

8. Leave all the fields in the Accessibility area at their defaults and click OK.

9. Save your page.

In the next techniques, you continue working with these practice tables, adding content and changing their structure.

END

Modifying Tables

Most modifications to tables start in the Property inspector. Dreamweaver helps you manage the basic table parameters — width, border, and alignment — and provides attributes for other useful but more arcane features of a table. These include converting table width from pixels to percentage of the screen, and vice versa.

Selecting Table Elements

As with text or images, the first step in altering a table (or any of its elements) is selection. Dreamweaver simplifies the selection process, making it easy to change both the properties and the contents of entire tables, selected rows or columns, and even non-adjacent cells. You can change the vertical alignment of a row, for example, with a click or two of the mouse — instead of highlighting and modifying each individual cell.

Note   All the following discussions about table selections pertain only to Standard mode; they are not applicable in Layout mode.

In Dreamweaver, you can select the following elements of a table:

✦ The entire table

✦ A single row

✦ Multiple rows, either adjacent or separate

✦ A single column

✦ Multiple columns, either adjacent or separate

✦ A single cell

✦ Multiple cells, either adjacent or separate

After you select a table element, you can modify its properties.

Selecting in Expanded Tables Mode

It's fairly easy to select table elements when the table is fully expanded — but tables aren't always set to a 100% width. In fact, designers often remove all table width values for their layouts, thus collapsing the table to fit the content. Although this is often necessary, you may have difficulty placing your cursor in the right cell in a collapsed table. You can speed up the selection and design process considerably by temporarily entering into Expanded Tables mode.

To enable Expanded Tables mode, choose View ➪ Table Mode ➪ Expanded Tables Mode or use the keyboard shortcut F6. You can also easily switch between it and the two other Dreamweaver modes (Standard and Layout) by selecting buttons found on the Layout category of the Insert bar. An indicator bar appears on top of the document window when you enter Expanded Tables mode.

Expanded Tables mode makes cell selection easier by temporarily adding a border (if there is none) and increasing the cell padding and spacing. These visual changes effectively make the table view much more apparent and selection far easier. All changes take place only in Dreamweaver's Design view — no code is ever rewritten. While you are in Expanded Tables mode, an outline (red, by default) appears around the table or any cells your cursor moves over. The outline color is controlled by the Mouse-Over option found on the Highlighting category of Preferences. Ctrl+click (Command+click) an outlined cell or table to select it.

Tip   You don't need to be in Expanded Tables mode to see the table outlines. If the Mouse-Over option is enabled, the outlines appear when you're in Standard mode when you hold down the Ctrl (Command) key and move over the table.

Expanded Tables mode is best used on an as-needed basis, and you can quickly toggle between it and Standard mode by pressing F6.

Selecting an Entire Table

Several methods are available for selecting the entire table, whether you're a menu- or mouse-oriented designer. To select the table via a menu, do one of the following:

✦ With the cursor positioned in the tables, choose Modify ➪ Table ➪ Select Table.

✦ With any table row already selected, choose Edit ➪ Select Parent Tag or use the keyboard shortcut, Ctrl+[(Command+[).

✦ Right-click (Control+click) inside a table to display the context menu and choose Table ➪ Select Table.

To select an entire table with the mouse, use one of the following techniques:

✦ Click the bottom or right border of the table. You can also click anywhere along the table border when the pointer becomes a four-sided arrow.

✦ Select the <table> tag in the Tag Selector.

✦ Click immediately to one side of the table and drag the mouse over the table.

The selected table is surrounded by a black border, with sizing handles on the right, bottom, and bottom-right corner (as shown in Figure 13-3), just like a selected graphic.

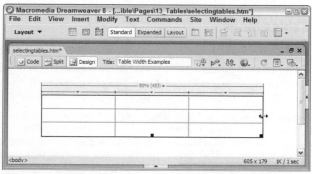

Figure 13-3: A selected table can be identified by the black border outlining the table and the three sizing handles.

Selecting a Row or Column

Altering rows or columns of table text without Dreamweaver is a major, time-consuming chore. Each cell has to be individually selected, and the changes applied. Dreamweaver has an intuitive method for selecting single or multiple columns and rows, comparable — and in some ways, superior — to major word processing programs.

As with entire tables, you have several methods for selecting columns or rows. None of the techniques, however, uses the main menus; row and column selections are handled primarily with the mouse. In fact, you can select an entire row or column with one click.

The one-click method for selecting a single column or row requires that you position your pointer directly above the column or to the left of the row you want to choose. This is similar to the way you select a row or column in a Microsoft Word table. Move the pointer slowly toward the table — when the pointer becomes a single arrow, with the arrowhead pointing down for columns and to the right for rows, click the mouse. All the cells in the selected column or row are bounded with a black border. Any changes now made in the Property inspector, such as a change in font size or color, affect all of the cells in the selected column or row.

You can select multiple, contiguous columns or rows by dragging the single arrow pointer across several columns or rows. To select a number of columns or rows that are not next to one another, press the Ctrl (Command) key while selecting each individual column, using the one-click method.

Tip   If you have trouble positioning the mouse so that the single-arrow pointer appears, you can use two other methods to select columns or rows. In the first method, you click and drag across all the cells in a column or row. The second method uses another keyboard modifier, the Shift key. With this technique, click once in the first cell of the column or row. Then, hold down the Shift key while you click in the final cell of the column or row (on a Mac OSX, you must perform two single-clicks in the final cell). You can also use this technique to select multiple adjacent columns or rows; just click in the last cell of another column or row.

Selecting Cells

Sometimes you need to change an attribute of just a few cells in a table, but not the entire row — or you might need to merge several cells to form one wide column span. In these situations, and many others, you can use Dreamweaver's cell selection capabilities. Like columns and rows, you can select multiple cells, whether they are adjacent or not.

Individual cells are generally selected by dragging the mouse across one or more cell boundaries. To select a single cell, click anywhere in the cell and drag the mouse into another cell. As you pass the border between the two cells, the initial cell is highlighted. If you continue dragging the mouse across another cell boundary, the second cell is selected, and so on. Note that you have to drag the mouse into another cell and not cross the table border onto the page. For example, to highlight the lower-right cell of a table, you drag the mouse up or to the left.

Tip   You can also select a single cell by pressing the Ctrl (Command) key and clicking once in the cell, or you can select the rightmost <td> tag in the Tag Selector.

Extended cell selection in Dreamweaver is handled identically to extended text selection in most word processing programs. To select adjacent cells, click in the first desired cell, press and hold the Shift key, and click in the final desired cell. Dreamweaver selects everything in a rectangular area, using the first cell as the upper-left corner of the rectangle and the last cell as the lower-right corner. You could, for instance, select an entire table by clicking in the upper-left cell and then Shift+clicking the lower-right cell.

Just as the Shift key is used to make adjacent cell selections, the Ctrl (Command) key is used for all non-adjacent cell selections. You can highlight any number of individual cells — whether or not they are next to one another — by pressing the Ctrl (Command) key while you click in each cell.

Tip   If you Ctrl+click (Command+click) a cell that is already selected, that cell is deselected —
regardless of the method you used to select the cell initially.

Editing a Table's Contents

Before you learn how to change a table's attributes, let's look at basic editing techniques.
Editing table text in Dreamweaver is slightly different from editing text outside of tables. When
you begin to enter text into a table cell, the table borders expand to accommodate your new
data, assuming no width has been set. The other cells appear to shrink; but they, too, expand
after you start typing in text or inserting an image. Unless a cell's width is specified, the cell
currently being edited expands or contracts, and the other cells are forced to adjust their
width. Figure 13-4 shows a table (with one row and three columns) in three different states. In
the top table, only the first cell contains text; notice how the other cells have contracted. In
the middle table, text has been entered into the second cell as well, and you can see how the
first cell is now smaller. Finally, in the bottom table, all three cells contain text, and the other
two cells have adjusted their width to compensate for the expanding third cell.

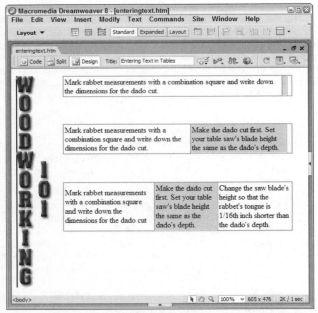

Figure 13-4: As text is entered into a cell, the cell expands and
other cells contract, even if they already contain text.

If you look closely at the bottom table in Figure 13-4, you can see that the text doesn't line up
vertically. That's because the default vertical alignment in Dreamweaver, as in most browsers,
provides for entries to be positioned in the middle of the cell. (Later in this section, you learn
how to adjust the vertical alignment.)

The expandability of table cells is very significant when you are inserting information from a data source because the data is often of varying length. See Chapter 21 for details about how to use Dreamweaver's Live Data view to check your layout.

Moving Through a Table

When you've finished entering your text in the first cell, you can move to the next cell in the row by pressing the Tab key. When you reach the end of a row, pressing Tab takes your cursor to the first cell of the next row. To go backward, cell to cell, press Shift+Tab.

Pressing Tab has a special function when you're in the last cell of a table—it adds a new row, with the same column configuration as the current one.

The Home and End keys take you to the beginning and end, respectively, of the cursor's current line. If a cell's contents are large enough for the text to wrap in the cell, move to the top of the current cell by pressing Ctrl+Home (Command+Home). To get to the bottom of the current cell in such a circumstance, press Ctrl+End (Command+End).

When you're at the beginning or end of the contents in a cell, you can also use the arrow keys to navigate from cell to cell. Use the left and right arrows to move from cell to cell in a row, and the up and down arrows to move from cell to cell in a column. When you come to the end of a row or column, the arrow keys move to the first cell in the next row or column. If you're moving left to right, the cursor goes from the end of one row to the beginning of the next row—and vice versa if you move from right to left. When moving from top to bottom, the cursor goes from the end of one column to the start of the next, and vice versa when moving bottom to top.

To enter a table without using the mouse, position the cursor directly before the table, press Shift+right arrow to select the table, and then press the down arrow key to move into the first cell. To move out of a table without using the mouse, move the cursor to the first or last cell in the table, press Ctrl+A (Command+A) to select the cell, and then press the left arrow if the cursor is in the first table cell, or the right arrow if the cursor is in the last cell. Alternatively, press Ctrl+A (Command+A) twice to select the entire table and then use either the left or right arrow to exit the table.

Cutting, Copying, and Pasting in Tables

In the early days of Web design, woe to you if you should accidentally leave out a cell of information. It was often almost faster to redo the entire table than to make room by meticulously cutting and pasting everything, one cell at a time. Dreamweaver ends that painstaking work forever with its advanced cutting and pasting features. You can copy a range of cells from one table to another and maintain all the attributes (such as color and alignment as well as the content—text or images). You can also copy just the contents and ignore the attributes.

Dreamweaver has one basic restriction to table cut-and-paste operations: Your selected cells must form a rectangle. In other words, although you can select non-adjacent cells, columns, or rows and modify their properties, you can't cut or copy them. Should you try, you get a message from Dreamweaver like the one shown in Figure 13-5; the table above the notification in this figure illustrates an incorrect cell selection.

Inserting Table Content

In this Technique, you begin inserting content into the table so you can see first-hand how table cells react to text and images.

1. From the Files panel, open the previously saved `table_start.htm` file.

2. Enter the following content in the top table:

   Founded   1995

   Headquarters   New York, NY

   Agents   35

   Notice that as you enter content, the width of the table cells changes to accommodate the text; you can refresh the table at any time by clicking outside of it. The entries in the first column are automatically bolded and centered because they are table header or `<th>` tags.

3. Enter the following content in the bottom table, leaving the first column blank:

Leading Agents	Specialty	Contact
Paul Thrasher	Rentals	paul@rrealty.com
Lydia Catch	Houses	lydia@rrealty.com
Frank Gordon	Co-ops	frank@rrealty.com

4. Place your cursor in the blank cell of the first column, second row and choose Image from the Common category of the Insert bar.

5. When the Select Image Source dialog box opens, navigate to the images folder in the root of the Techniques site and select `paul_thrasher.jpg`.

6. Repeat steps 4 and 5 for the next two cells, inserting `lydia_catch.jpg` and `frank_gordon.jpg` respectively.

7. Save your page.

The table grows to compensate for the size of the images. In the next Technique, you adjust the table's properties to achieve a different look and feel.

Copying Attributes and Contents

When you copy or cut a cell using the regular commands, Dreamweaver automatically copies everything — content, formatting, and cell format — in the selected cell. Then, pasting the cell reproduces it — however, you can get different results depending on where the cell (or column or row) is pasted.

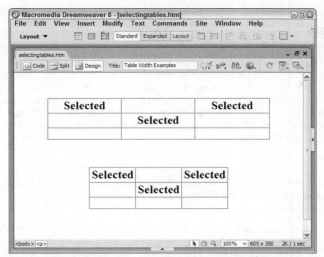

Figure 13-5: Dreamweaver enables you to cut or copy selected cells only when they form a rectangle.

To cut or copy both the contents and the attributes of any cell, row, or column, follow these steps:

1. Select the cells you want to cut or copy. Remember that to cut or copy a range of cells in Dreamweaver, they must form a solid rectangular region.

2. To copy cells, choose Edit ➪ Copy or use the keyboard shortcut, Ctrl+C (Command+C).

3. To cut cells, choose Edit ➪ Cut or use the keyboard shortcut, Ctrl+X (Command+X). If you cut an individual cell, the contents are removed, but the cell remains. If, however, you cut an entire row or column, the cells are removed.

4. Position your cursor to paste the cells in the desired location:

   • To replace a cell with a cell on the clipboard, click anywhere in the cell to be replaced. If you cut or copy multiple cells that do not make up a full column or row, click in the upper-left corner of the cells you want to replace. For example, a range of six cells in a 2 x 3 configuration replaces the same configuration when pasted. Dreamweaver alerts you if you try to paste one configuration of cells into a different cell configuration.

   • To insert a new row with the row on the clipboard, click anywhere in the row immediately below where you'd like the new row to appear.

   • To insert a new column with the column on the clipboard, click anywhere in the column immediately to the right of where you'd like the new column to appear.

   • To replace an existing row or column in a table, select the row or column. If you've cut or copied multiple rows or columns, you must select an equivalent configuration of cells to replace.

- To insert a new table based on the copied or cut cells, click anywhere outside of the table.

5. Paste the copied or cut cells by choosing Edit ➪ Paste or pressing Ctrl+V (Command+V).

Tip   To move a row or column that you've cut from the interior of a table to the exterior (the right or bottom), you have to first expand the number of cells in the table. To do this, first select the table by choosing Modify ➪ Table ➪ Select Table or by using one of the other techniques previously described. Next, in the Table Property inspector, increase the number of rows or columns by altering the values in the Rows or Cols text boxes. Finally, select the newly added rows or columns and choose Edit ➪ Paste.

Copying Contents Only

You often need to move data from one cell to another, while keeping the destination cell's attributes, such as its background color or border, intact. For this, use Dreamweaver's facility for copying just the contents of a cell.

To copy only the contents, select a cell and copy as previously described; then, instead of choosing Edit ➪ Paste, choose Edit ➪ Paste Special or use the keyboard shortcut, Ctrl+Shift+V (Command+Shift+V). Once the Paste Special dialog box opens, choose the Text Only option and click OK. Unlike copying both contents and attributes, as described in the previous section, content-only copying has a couple of limitations:

✦ You can copy the contents only one cell at a time, and you can paste those contents into only one cell at a time.

✦ You can't replace the entire contents of one cell with another and maintain all the text attributes (font, color, and size) of the destination cell in Design view. If you select all the text to be replaced, Dreamweaver also selects the CSS styles or `<font>` tag that holds the attributes and replaces those as well; instead of applying the CSS style to the `<td>` tag, however, it wraps the text in a similarly styled `<span>` tag. The workaround for HTML-formatted text is to select and copy the source text as usual, and then select all but one letter or word in the destination cell, paste the contents, and delete the extra text. With CSS, cut and paste the entire text and then right-click (Control-click) on the `<span>` tag in the Tag Selector and choose Remove Tag.

Working with Table Properties

The `<table>` tag has a large number of attributes, and most of them can be modified through Dreamweaver's Property inspector. As with all objects, you must select the table before it can be altered. Choose Modify ➪ Table ➪ Select Table or use one of the other selection techniques previously described.

After you've selected the table, the Property inspector presents the table properties, as shown in Figure 13-6. If the inspector isn't open, choose Window ➪ Properties.

Figure 13-6: The expanded Table Property inspector gives you control over all the table-wide attributes.

Centering a Table in CSS

The align attribute in the `<table>` tag is deprecated in HTML 4.0, which means a newer, preferred method of achieving the same effect is available. In this case, Cascading Style Sheets (CSS), covered in Chapter 7, provide the preferred method of setting an object's alignment. To center a table using CSS, you need two CSS rules: one for the table itself and one for a `<div>` surrounding the table. If, for example, the `class` of the `div` is `centerDiv`, the CSS rules look like this:

```
.centerDiv {
    text-align: center;
}
.centerDiv table {
    margin-right: auto;
    margin-left: auto;
    text-align: left;
}
```

Without the `text-align: left` attribute in the `.centerDiv table` rule, the text in the table is centered. This approach works in all current browsers, in both strict and regular modes. (To find out more about strict and regular modes, see Chapter 6.)

This CSS code is used later in this chapter in a Dreamweaver Technique.

Setting Alignment

Aligning a table in Dreamweaver goes beyond the expected left, right, and center options. You can also make a table into a free-floating object, around which you can wrap text — to the left or right.

Figure 13-7 illustrates some of the different results you can get from aligning your table.

Because the `<table>` tag is a block element, CSS can be used to float the table on the page to the left or right. Subsequent text wraps around the table to one side or the other. Although Dreamweaver lets you align the table left or right from the Property inspector to achieve a similar effect in older browsers, the `align` attribute in tables has been deprecated.

To align the table without allowing text to wrap, you need to put the table within a `<div>` tag and set the `<div>` tag's align style to `left`, `right`, or `center` values with CSS. Although you may be tempted to use the `<div>` tag's align attribute, that attribute also has been deprecated.

Resizing a Table

The primary sizing control on the Table Property inspector is the W (Width) text box. You can assign a new width for the entire table in either a screen percentage or pixels. Just enter your value in the W text box and then select % or Pixels in the drop-down list of options.

Dreamweaver also provides a quick and intuitive way to resize the overall table width, the column widths, or the row height. Pass your pointer over any of the table's borders, and the pointer becomes a two-headed arrow; this is the resizing pointer. When you see the resizing pointer, you can click and drag any border to new dimensions.

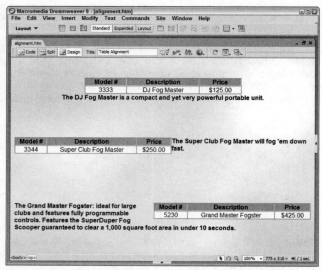

Figure 13-7: Tables can be centered, as well as aligned left or right—with or without text wrapping.

As noted earlier, tables are initially sized according to their contents. After you move a table border in Dreamweaver, however, the new sizes are written directly into the HTML code, and the column width or row height is adjusted—unless the contents cannot fit. If, for example, an inserted image is 115 pixels wide and the cell has a width of only 90 pixels, the cell expands to fit the image. The same is true if you try to fit an extremely long, unbroken text string, such as a complex URL, into a cell that's too narrow to hold it.

Dreamweaver enables you to set the height of a table using the H (Height) text box in much the same way as the Width box. However, the height of a table—whether in pixels or a percentage—is maintained only as long as the contents do not require a larger size. A table's width takes precedence over its height, and a table expands vertically before it expands horizontally.

> **Note**
>
> The height attribute for the `<table>` tag has been removed in HTML 4.0 and higher by the W3C, and its further use is highly discouraged. Although rendered in Dreamweaver, the attribute no longer functions properly in most modern browsers, including Firefox, Safari, and Netscape 6.x.

Changes to the width of a cell or column are shown in the `<td>` tags, as are changes to a row's height and width, using the `width` and `height` attributes, respectively. You can see these changes by selecting the table, cell, column, or row affected and looking at the W and H text box values.

> **Note**
>
> You can also set the height and width using Cascading Style Sheets, described in Chapter 7. If you don't have to support older browsers, using styles is the preferred method of designating these attributes.

For an overall view of what happens when you resize a cell, row, or column, it's best to look at the HTML. Here's the HTML for an empty table, resized:

```
<table border="1" width="70%">
  <tr>
    <td width="21%"> </td>
    <td width="34%"> </td>
    <td width="45%"> </td>
  </tr>
  <tr>
    <td width="21%" height="42"> </td>
    <td width="34%"> </td>
    <td width="45%"> </td>
  </tr>
  <tr>
    <td width="21%" height="42"> </td>
    <td width="34%"> </td>
    <td width="45%"> </td>
  </tr>
</table>
```

Notice how the width for both the cells and the entire table are expressed as percentages. If the table width were initially set at a pixel value, the cell widths would have been, too. The row height values, on the other hand, are shown as an absolute measurement in pixels.

You can switch from percentages to pixels in all the table measurements, and even clear all the values at once, with the click of a button. Several measurement controls appear in the lower-left portion of the expanded Table Property inspector, as shown in Figure 13-8.

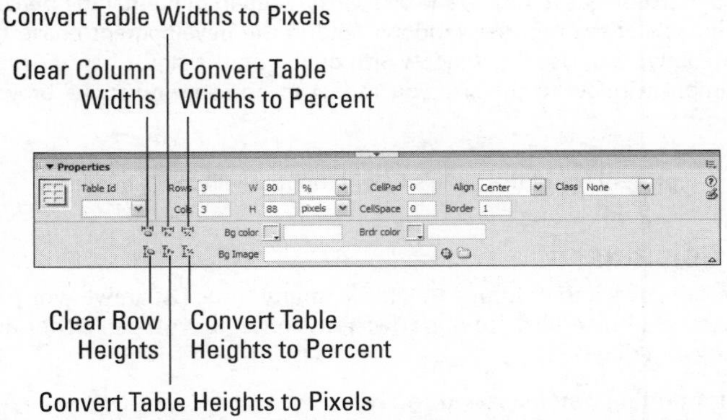

Convert Table Widths to Pixels

Clear Column | Convert Table
Widths | Widths to Percent

Clear Row | Convert Table
Heights | Heights to Percent

Convert Table Heights to Pixels

Figure 13-8: You can make table-wide changes with the control buttons in the Table Property inspector.

Table 13-2 shows the measurement controls provided in the Table Property inspector.

Table 13-2: Table Property Inspector Measurement Controls

Measurement Control Button	*Description*
Clear Column Widths	Deletes all the `width` attributes found in the `<td>` tags
Convert Table Widths to Pixels	Translates the current width of all cells and the entire table from percentages to pixels
Convert Table Widths to Percent	Translates the current width of all cells and the entire table from pixels to percentages
Clear Row Heights	Erases all the `height` attributes in the current table
Convert Table Heights to Pixels	Translates the current height of all cells and the entire table from percentages to pixels
Convert Table Heights to Percent	Translates the current height of all cells and the entire table from pixels to percentages

Note   Selecting Clear Row Heights doesn't affect the table height value.

If you clear both row heights and column widths, the table goes back to its "grow as needed" format and, if empty, shrinks to its smallest possible size.

Caution   When converting width percentages to pixels, and vice versa, keep in mind that the percentages are relative to the size of the browser window—and in the development phase that browser window is Dreamweaver. Use the Window Size option on the status bar to expand Dreamweaver's Document window to the size you expect to be seen in various browser settings.

Note that row height is a percentage of the table's height, not the window's height.

Inserting Rows and Columns

You can change the number of rows and columns in a table at any time. Dreamweaver provides a variety of methods for adding and removing rows and columns; you can either add them directly or by invoking a dialog box.

You have several options for adding a single row directly:

✦ Position the cursor in the last cell of the last row and press Tab to add a new row below the present one.

✦ Choose Modify ⇨ Table ⇨ Insert Row to insert a new row above the current row.

✦ Right-click (Control+click) in the table to open the context menu and choose Table ⇨ Insert Row. Rows added in this way are inserted above the current row.

You have two ways to add a new column to your table directly:

✦ Choose Modify ⇨ Table ⇨ Insert Column to insert a new column to the left of the current column.

✦ Right-click (Control+click) to open the context menu and choose Table ⇨ Insert Column from the context menu. The column is inserted to the left of the current column.

You can add multiple rows and columns in either of the following ways:

✦ Increase the number of rows indicated in the Rows text box of the Table Property inspector. All new rows added in this manner appear below the last table row. Similarly, you can increase the number of columns indicated in the Cols text box of the Table Property inspector. Columns added in this way appear to the right of the last column.

✦ Use the Insert Rows or Columns dialog box.

The Insert Rows or Columns feature enables you to include any number of rows or columns anywhere relative to your current cursor position.

To add multiple columns using the Insert Rows or Columns dialog box, follow these steps:

1. Position the cursor anywhere in the row or column next to where the new row or column will be inserted.

2. Open the Insert Rows or Columns dialog box (shown in Figure 13-9) by choosing Modify ⇨ Table ⇨ Insert Rows or Columns or by choosing Table ⇨ Insert Rows or Columns from the context menu.

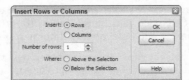

Figure 13-9: Use the Insert Rows or Columns feature to add several columns or rows simultaneously.

3. Select either Rows or Columns.

4. Enter the number of rows or columns you want to insert — you can either type in a value or use the arrows to increase or decrease the number.

5. Select where you want the rows or columns to be inserted.

   • If you have selected the Rows option, you can insert the rows either above or below the selection (the current row).

   • If you have selected the Columns options, you can insert the columns either before or after the current column.

6. Click OK when you're finished.

Deleting Rows and Columns

The easiest way to delete a row or column is to select it and press the Delete key. You can also use the context menu to remove the current column or row by choosing Delete Column or Delete Row, respectively.

Alternatively, you can use the Table Property inspector to delete multiple columns and rows by reducing the numbers in the Cols or Rows text boxes. Columns are deleted from the right side of the table, and rows are removed from the bottom.

Caution Exercise extreme caution when deleting columns or rows. Dreamweaver does not ask for confirmation, and it removes these columns and/or rows whether or not they contain data.

Setting Table Borders and Backgrounds

Borders are the solid outlines of the table itself. A border's width is measured in pixels; the default width is 1 pixel. You can alter this width in the Border field of the Table Property inspector.

To make the border invisible, specify a border of 0 width. You can still resize your table by clicking and dragging the borders, even when the border is set to 0. When the View ➪ Visual Aids ➪ Table Borders option is selected, Dreamweaver displays a thin dashed line to represent the border; this line is not visible when the page is viewed in a browser.

When the border is visible, you can also see each cell outlined. The width of the outline around the cells stays constant, regardless of the border's width. However, you can control the amount of space between each cell with the CellSpace value in the Table Property inspector, covered in the section "Working with Cell Spacing and Cell Padding" later in this chapter.

To change the width of a border in Dreamweaver, select your table and enter a new value in the Border text box. With a wider border, you can see the default shading: The top and left sides are a light shade, and the bottom and right sides are darker, giving the table border a pseudo-3D appearance. Figure 13-10 shows single-cell tables with borders of various widths, contrasting `background` attribute and CSS style usage.

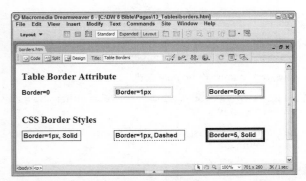

Figure 13-10: Borders are far more flexible when applied with CSS.

In Dreamweaver, you can directly assign colors to the border. To choose a color for the border, select the Brdr color box or enter a color name or hexadecimal color value in the adjacent text box. Again, you get much greater control and standards compliance if you use CSS.

In addition to colored borders, a table can also have a colored background. (By default, the table is initially transparent.) Choose the background color in the Table Property inspector by selecting a color in the Bg color box or entering a color name or hexadecimal color value in the adjacent text box. As you learn later in this chapter, in "Setting Cell, Column, and Row Properties," you can also assign background colors to rows, columns, and individual cells — if used, these specific colors override the background color of the entire table.

Working with Cell Spacing and Cell Padding

HTML gives you two methods to add whitespace in tables. Cell spacing controls the width between each cell, and cell padding controls the margins within each cell. You can set these values independently through the Table Property inspector.

Tip   If no cell spacing or padding value is indicated in the Table Property inspector, most browsers use a default value of 2 pixels for cell spacing and 1 pixel for cell padding. If your Web page design calls for a close arrangement of cells, explicitly change either (or both) the CellSpace or CellPad values to 1 or 0.

To change the amount of whitespace between each cell in a table, enter a new value in the CellSpace text box of the Table Property inspector. If you want to adjust the amount of whitespace between the borders of the cell and the actual cell data, alter the value in the CellPad text box of the Table Property inspector. Figure 13-11 shows an example of tables with wide (10 pixels) cell spacing and cell padding values (the shaded space is the actual cell size).

Figure 13-11: You can add additional whitespace between each cell (cell spacing) or within each cell (cell padding).

Merging and Splitting Cells

You have seen how cells in HTML tables can extend across (span) multiple columns or rows. By default, a cell spans one column or one row. Increasing a cell's span enables you to group any number of topics under one heading. You are effectively merging one cell with another to create a larger cell. Likewise, a cell can be split into multiple rows or columns.

Dreamweaver enables you to combine and divide cells in two different ways. If you're more comfortable with the concept of merging and splitting cells, you can use two handy buttons on the Property inspector. If, on the other hand, you prefer the older method of increasing and decreasing row or column span, you can still access these commands through the main menu and the context menus.

To combine two or more cells, first select the cells you want to merge. Then, from the Property inspector, click the Merge Cells button or press the keyboard shortcut, M. If the Merge button is not available, multiple cells have not been selected.

To divide a cell, follow these steps:

1. Position your cursor in the cell to be split.

2. From the Property inspector, click the Split Cell button or press the keyboard shortcut, Ctrl+Alt+S (Command+Option+S). The Split Cell dialog box (shown in Figure 13-12) appears.

Figure 13-12: Use the Split Cell dialog box to divide cells horizontally or vertically.

3. Select either the Rows or Columns option to indicate whether the cell is to be split horizontally or vertically.

4. Enter the number of rows or columns in the text box or use the arrows to change the value.

5. Click OK when you're finished.

You can achieve the same effect by using the menus. To do so, first position the cursor in the cell to be affected and then choose one of the following commands from the Modify ➪ Table menu:

Command	Description
Increase Row Span	Joins the current cell with the cell below it
Increase Column Span	Joins the current cell with the cell immediately to its right
Decrease Row Span	Separates two or more previously spanned cells from the bottom cell
Decrease Column Span	Separates two or more previously spanned cells from the right edge

Existing text or images are put in the same cell if the cells containing them are joined to span rows or columns. Figure 13-13 shows a table containing both row and column spanning.

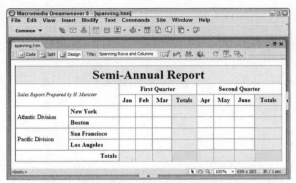

Figure 13-13: This spreadsheet-like report was built using Dreamweaver's row- and column-spanning features.

Tip Show restraint when splitting and merging cells, or your table will be difficult to maintain. When you are building a complex table such as the one in Figure 13-14, it's best to map out your table before you begin constructing it and to complete it prior to entering your data.

Dreamweaver TECHNIQUE ## Adjust Table Properties

In this Technique, you practice aligning tables to achieve two different effects as well as merging cells and clearing column widths.

1. Open the `table_start.htm` file previously worked upon.

2. From the CSS Styles panel, click New CSS Rule.

3. In the New CSS Rule dialog box, choose the Class option and enter **.rightTable** in the Name field; click OK when you're done.

4. Switch to the Box category and, from the Float list, choose Right and then click OK.

5. Select the first table by dragging your mouse across the right border into the table.

6. From the Property inspector's Style list, choose rightTable.

Notice that the table is instantly positioned to the right and the following paragraph flows to the left. Now position the bottom table in the center without wrapping.

1. Select the bottom table.

2. From the Layout category of the Insert bar, choose Insert Div Tag.

The necessary CSS rules (discussed earlier in the "Centering a Table in CSS") are already in the attached CSS style sheet.

Continued

Continued

3. When the Insert Div Tag dialog box opens, leave the Insert list entry set to Wrap Around Selection.

4. Choose centerDiv from the Class list and click OK when you're done.

Dreamweaver creates a surrounding `<div>` tag and centers the table within it.

Your final task is to remove the widths from the lower table columns so that they tightly fit the data.

1. Select the bottom table again, if necessary.

2. From the lower portion of the Property inspector, click Clear Column Widths.

3. Save your page.

The table columns collapse to just the widths needed.

Setting Cell, Column, and Row Properties

In addition to the overall table controls, Dreamweaver helps you set numerous properties for individual cells one at a time, by the column or by the row. When attributes overlap or conflict, such as different background colors for a cell in the same row and column, the more specific target has precedence. The hierarchy, from most general to most specific, is as follows: tables, rows, columns, and cells.

You can call up the specific Property inspector by selecting the cell, row, or column you want to modify. The Cell, Row, and Column Property inspectors each affect similar attributes. The following sections explain how the attributes work, both in general and — if any differences exist — specifically (in regard to the cell, column, or row).

Horizontal Alignment

You can set the Horizontal Alignment attribute, `align`, to specify the default alignment, or left, right, or center alignment, for the contents of a cell, column, or row. This attribute can be overridden by setting the alignment for the individual line or image. Generally, left is the default horizontal alignment for cells.

Vertical Alignment

The HTML `valign` attribute specifies whether the cell's contents are vertically aligned to the cell's top, middle, or bottom, or along the baseline. Typically, browsers align cells vertically in the middle by default. Select the Vertical Alignment option arrow in the Cell, Column, or Row Properties inspector to specify a different alignment.

Top, middle, and bottom vertical alignments work pretty much as you would expect. A baseline vertical alignment displays text near the top of the cell and positions the text — regardless of font size — so that the baselines of all the text in the affected row, column, or cell are the same. Figure 13-14 illustrates how images and text of various sizes are displayed under the different vertical alignment options.

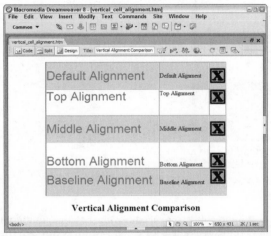

Figure 13-14: You can vertically align text and images in several arrangements in a table cell, row, or column.

Cell Wrap

Normal behavior for any cell is to automatically wrap text or a series of images within the cell's borders. You can turn off this automatic feature by selecting the No Wrap option in the Property inspector for the cell, column, or row.

You might use this option, for example, if you need three images to appear side by side in one cell. In analyzing the results, however, you might find that, on some lower-resolution browsers, the last image wraps to the next line.

Note   A preferred method of preventing the contents of a cell from wrapping is to use Cascading Style Sheets to define a style with the `white-space` attribute set to `nowrap`; the `nowrap` attribute has been deprecated for `<td>` tags.

Table Header Cells

Quite often in tables, a column or row functions as the heading for that section of the table, labeling all the information in that particular section. Dreamweaver has an option for designating these cells: the Header option. Table header cells are usually rendered in boldface and centered in each cell. Figure 13-15 shows an example of a table in which both the first row and first column are marked as table header cells.

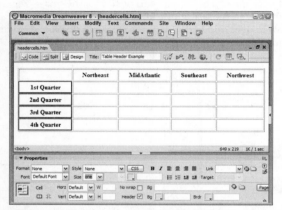

Figure 13-15: Table header cells are a good way to note a category's labels — for a row, column, or both.

Cell Width and Height

The gridlike structure of a table makes it impossible to resize only one cell in a multicolumn table. Therefore, the only way you can enter exact values for a cell's width is through the W text box available in the Column Properties inspector. You can enter values in pixels or as a percentage of the table. The default enables cells to automatically resize with no restrictions outside of the overall dimensions of the table.

Similarly, whenever you change a cell's height, the entire row is altered. If you drag the row to a new height, the value is written into the H text box for all cells in the row. On the other hand, if you specify a single cell's height, the row resizes, but you can see the value only in the cell you've changed. If different cells in the same row are assigned different heights, the row is sized to the tallest height.

Color Elements

Just as you can specify color backgrounds and borders for the overall table, you can do the same for columns, rows, or individual cells. Corresponding color swatches and text boxes are available in the Property inspector for the following:

✦ **Bg (Background Color):** Specifies the color for the selected cell, row, or column. Selecting the color box opens the standard color picker. This tag has been deprecated for all table elements — including `<table>`, `<tr>`, and `<td>` — and it is strongly advised that CSS be used to apply coloring.

✦ **Brdr (Border Color):** Controls the color of the single-pixel border surrounding each cell.

As with all Dreamweaver color pickers, you can use the Eyedropper tool to select a color from the Web-safe palette or from any item on a page. You can also click the Default color button to delete any previously selected color. Finally, click the System Color Picker button to open the Color dialog box and select any available color.

Working with Table Formats

Tables keep data organized and generally make it easier to find information quickly. Large tables with many rows, however, tend to become difficult to read unless they are formatted with alternating rows of color or some other device. Formatting a large table is often an afterthought, and a time-consuming affair as well — unless, of course, you use Dreamweaver's Format Table command.

Caution   The Format Table command uses out-of-fashion `<font>` tags and deprecated `bgcolor` attributes to achieve its effects. To remain standards compliant, use CSS to style the table's rows and columns.

The Format Table command enables you to choose from a variety of preset formats that you can further customize. This versatile command can style the top row, alternating rows in the body of the table, the left column, and the border. It's best to completely build the structure of your table — although you don't have to fill it with data — before formatting it; otherwise, you might have to reformat it when new rows or columns are added.

To apply one of the preset table formats, follow these steps:

1. Position the cursor anywhere within the table to be formatted.

2. Choose Commands ➪ Format Table. The Format Table dialog box (shown in Figure 13-16) opens.

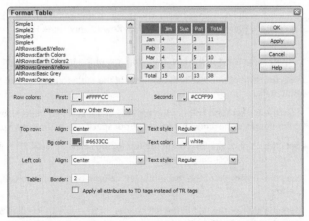

Figure 13-16: Select any one of the preset formats from the Format Table dialog box or customize your own.

3. Select any of the options from the scrolling list box on the left side of the Format Table dialog box. As you select an option, a representation of the table appears to the right, and the attribute values used are displayed below.

4. When you've found a table format that's appropriate, click OK to close the dialog box and the format is applied.

The preset formats are divided into three groups: Simple, AltRows, and DblRows. The Simple formats maintain the same background color for all rows in the body of the table but change the top row and the left column. The AltRows formats alternate the background color of each row in the body of the table; you have eight different color combinations from which to choose. The final category, DblRows, alternates the background color of every two rows in the body of the table.

Although 17 different formats may seem like a lot of options, they are actually just the jumping-off place for what's possible with the Format Table command. After selecting a preset format, you can further customize any of the variables applied to create that format. Remember, you don't have to apply the changes to your selected table to see the effect — you can preview the results directly in the Format Table dialog box. Table 13-3 shows the variable attributes in the Format Table dialog box.

Table 13-3: Variable Attributes from the Format Table Dialog Box

Attribute	Description
Row Colors: First	Enters a color (in color name or hexadecimal format) for the background of the first row in the body of a table. The row colors do not affect the top row of a table unless no top row color is defined.
Row Colors: Second	Enters a color (in color name or hexadecimal format) for the background of the second row in the body of a table. The row colors do not affect the top row of a table.
Row Colors: Alternate	Establishes the pattern for using the specified row colors. Options are <do not alternate>, Every Other Row, Every Two Rows, Every Three Rows, and Every Four Rows.
Top Row: Align	Sets the alignment of the text in the top row of the table to left, right, or center.
Top Row: Text Style	Sets the style of the text in the top row of the table to Regular, Bold, Italic, or Bold Italic.
Top Row: Bg Color	Sets the background color of the top row of the selected table. Use either color names or hexadecimal values. If not specified, the first row color is used.
Top Row: Text Color	Sets the color of the text in the top row of the selected table. Use either color names or hexadecimal values.
Left Col: Align	Sets the alignment of the text in the left column of the table to Left, Right, or Center.
Left Col: Text Style	Sets the style of the text in the left column of the table to Regular, Bold, Italic, or Bold Italic.
Border	Determines the width of the table's border, in pixels.
Options: Apply All Attributes to TD Tags Instead of TR Tags	Specifies attribute changes at the cell level, `<td>`, rather than the default, the row level, `<tr>`

The final option in the Format Table dialog box, Apply All Attributes to TD Tags Instead of TR Tags, should be used in only two situations. First, use it if the selected table is nested inside of another table and you want to override the outer table's `<tr>` format. Second, use it if you anticipate moving cells from one table to another and want to maintain the formatting. Generally, the code produced by selecting this option is bulkier, and it could affect a page's overall download size if the table is sufficiently large.

Caution Currently, you can't save your custom format without editing the `tableFormats.js` JavaScript file in the Commands folder. Otherwise, you need to reenter the selections each time you apply them.

Sorting Tables

Have you ever painstakingly built a table, alphabetizing every last entry by last name and first name, only to have the client call with a list of 13 additional names? "Oh, and could you sort them by ZIP Code instead of last name?" Dreamweaver contains a Table Sort command designed to make short work of such requests. All you do is select your table, and you're ready to do a two-level–deep sort, either alphabetically or numerically.

The Sort Table command can rearrange a table of any size; more importantly, it's HTML-savvy, and gives you the option of keeping the formatting of your table rows. This capability enables you to maintain a table with alternating row colors and still sort the data—something not even the most powerful word processors can handle. The Sort Table command is useful for generating different views of the same data without having to use a database.

The Sort Table command is straightforward to use; just follow these steps:

1. Position the cursor inside the table.

2. Choose Commands ➪ Sort Table. The Sort Table dialog box (shown in Figure 13-17) opens.

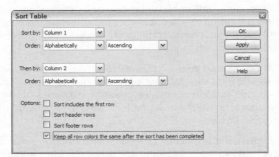

Figure 13-17: Sort your tables numerically or alphabetically with the Sort Table command.

3. Select the primary sort column from the Sort By option list. Dreamweaver automatically lists every column in the selected table in the option list.

4. Set the type of the primary sort by picking either Alphabetically or Numerically from the first Order option list.

5. Select the direction of the sort by selecting either Ascending or Descending from the second Order option list.

6. If you want to add a second level of sorting, repeat steps 3 through 5 in the Then By section.

7. If your selected table does not include a header row, select the Sort Includes the First Row option.

8. If your selected table includes one or more rows coded within <thead>...</thead> or <tfoot>...</tfoot> tags, and you want those rows to be included in the sort, select the appropriate option.

Note   The <thead> and <tfoot> HTML tags designate one or more table rows as forming a table heading or footer. The footer displays at the bottom of the table. It is typically used to duplicate the heading for long tables. These tags are not supported on all browsers.

9. If you have formatted your table with alternating row colors, choose the Keep All Row Colors the Same After the Sort Has Been Completed option.

10. Click OK when you're finished.

Tip   As with any sorting program, if you leave blank cells in the column on which you're basing the sort, those rows appear as a group on top of the table for an ascending sort and at the end for a descending sort. Make sure that all the cells in your sort criteria column are filled correctly.

Importing Tabular Data

In the computer age, there's nothing more frustrating than having information in a digital format and still having to enter it manually — either by typing it in or by cutting and pasting — to get it on the Web. This frustration is multiplied when it comes to table data, whether created in a spreadsheet or database program. You have to transfer numerous small pieces of data, and it all has to be properly related and positioned.

Dreamweaver's Import Table Data command goes a long way toward alleviating the tedium — not to mention the frustration — of dealing with tabular information. The Import Table Data command reads any delimited text file and inserts the information in a series of rows and columns. You can even set most characteristics for the table to be created, including the width, cell padding, cell spacing, and border.

Quite often, the first step in the process of importing table data into Dreamweaver is exporting it from another program. Most spreadsheet and database programs have some capability to output information in a text file. Each bit of data (whether it's from a cell of a spreadsheet or a field of a database) is separated — or *delimited* — from every other bit of data by a special character, typically a tab or comma. In Dreamweaver, you can use the Import Table Data dialog box to choose which delimiter is used, ensuring a clean transfer with no loss of data.

Tip   Although you have many types of delimiters to choose from, you might want to default to exporting tab-delimited files. With a tab-delimited file, you usually don't have to worry if any of your data contains the delimiter—which would throw off the import. However, testing has shown that Dreamweaver correctly handles comma-delimited files with and without quotes, so you can also use that format safely.

To import a tabular data file, follow these steps:

1. Be sure the data you want to import has been saved or exported in the proper format: a delimited text file.

2. Open the Import Tabular Data dialog box, shown in Figure 13-18, in one of the following ways:

   • Choose File ⇨ Import ⇨ Tabular Data.
   • Choose Insert ⇨ Table Objects ⇨ Import Tabular Data.
   • Click the Tabular Data button in the Common category of the Insert bar.

Figure 13-18: Any external data saved in a delimited text file can be brought into Dreamweaver with the Import Tabular Data command.

3. Click the Browse button to find the desired file.

4. Select the delimiter used to separate the fields or cells of data from the Delimiter option list. The options are Tab, Comma, Semicolon, Colon, and Other.

Tip   If you select a file with a .csv extension, the comma delimiter is automatically chosen, although you can change the option if necessary. CSV is short for Comma-Separated Values.

5. If you choose Other from the Delimiter list, a blank field appears to the right of the list. Enter the special character, such as the pipe (|), used as the delimiter in the exported file. Now that the imported file characteristics are set, you can predefine the table into which the information will be imported.

6. If you want to set a particular table width, enter a value in the Set field and select either Pixels or Percent from the option list. If you want the imported file to determine the size of the table, keep the Fit to Data option selected.

7. Enter any Cell Padding or Cell Spacing values desired, in their respective fields. As with standard tables, if you don't enter a value, most browsers interpret Cell Padding as 2 pixels and Cell Spacing as 1 pixel.

8. If you'd like to style the first row, pick Bold, Italic, or Bold Italic from the Format Top Row option list. This option is typically used when the imported file contains a header row.

9. Set the Border field to the desired width, if any. If you don't want a border displayed at all, set the Border field to 0.

10. Click OK when you're finished.

Although the Import Table Data option is under the File menu, it doesn't open a new file — the new table is created at the current cursor position.

Caution   If your data is imported incorrectly, double-check the delimiter used (by opening the file in a text editor). If Dreamweaver is expecting a comma delimiter and your file uses tabs, data is not formatted properly.

Designing with Layout Mode

As mentioned at the beginning of this chapter, some Web designers regard tables as one of their primary layout tools. This is because, except for CSS layers, tables are the only way you can even get close to positioning your page elements the way you want them to appear. Granted, it takes a lot of work to do this with raw tables, but designers are a persistent group — and now that persistence has paid off in a big way.

Caution   Designers are strongly advised to use CSS rather than Layout mode to create new layout designs. As this point in the Web's development, Layout mode should be used only to work on legacy sites where CSS layouts are not an option.

When you're in Layout mode, you draw out separate areas to hold your content, and Dreamweaver automatically converts these areas to cells and tables. The layout cells are very pliable and can easily be moved about the page, resized, and reshaped. Moreover, Layout mode gives you professional design power with options to stretch tables to fit the browser window and to size columns precisely.

Although they share the same underlying HTML structure, tables and cells created in Layout mode differ from those created in Standard mode in several ways:

✦ Borders are set to 0, meaning they are turned off.

✦ Cell padding and cell spacing are also set to 0 to enable content to appear directly side-by-side.

✦ Layout tables optionally include an extra row, whose columns hold a 1-pixel–high, transparent GIF image called a *spacer*.

✦ Columns in a layout table are either set to a fixed pixel width or designed to automatically stretch to the full width of the page.

In addition to these physical differences, Layout mode has a different look as well. Each layout table is marked with a tab, and the column width is identified either at the top or bottom of each column (as shown in Figure 13-19). Where the column width is displayed depends on the table's placement in the Document window.

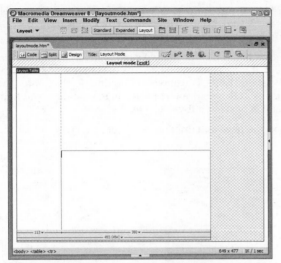

Figure 13-19: In Layout mode, tables and columns are immediately identifiable and extremely flexible.

Dreamweaver puts the access to Layout and Standard modes on the Insert bar. To switch modes, click Standard to go to the traditional mode; click Layout to return to Layout mode. If the Insert bar is not open, you can also switch to Layout mode by choosing View ➪ Table View ➪ Layout Mode or by using the keyboard shortcut, Ctrl+F6 (Command+F6). To switch to Standard mode, you can also choose View ➪ Table View ➪ Standard Mode or use the keyboard shortcut Shift+Ctrl+F6 (Shift+Command+F6).

Note   Don't fret about your existing pages: They'll show up just fine in Layout mode. In fact, looking at a well-designed legacy page in Layout mode helps you understand the layout of professionally designed pages by clearly showing table structure and nested tables.

One caveat applies when changing from Standard to Layout mode: Standard table cells without content — those that are either totally empty or contain only a non-breaking space — must be explicitly created in Layout mode before text, graphics, or other content can be added.

Drawing Cells and Tables

Although you can use Layout mode to modify the structure of existing pages, this view is best when designing Web pages from the ground up. The Draw Layout Cell and Draw Table commands enable you to quickly lay out the basic structure of your page by defining the key document areas. For example, with just four mouse moves in Layout mode, you can design a page with sections for a logo, a navigation bar, a copyright notice, and a primary content area. Now you are ready to fill out the design with graphics, text, and other assets. Here's how it works:

1. On a blank page, click the Layout mode button in the Layout category of the Insert bar. When you first enter Layout mode, Dreamweaver displays a Help screen to explain how

the feature works. After you're comfortable working in Layout mode, feel free to select the Don't Show Me This Message Again option to prevent further appearances of the dialog box.

2. Click the Draw Layout Cell button in the Layout category of the Insert bar. The cursor changes to a plus sign. Although it may seem backward, it's best to initially use Draw Layout Cell, rather than Draw Layout Table. Dreamweaver automatically creates the HTML table necessary to hold any cells you draw, resulting in fewer tables and tighter code. The Draw Table command is best used to make a nested table.

3. Move your cursor anywhere on the page and drag out a layout cell. Figure 13-20 shows an example.

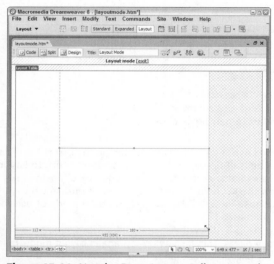

Figure 13-20: Use the Draw Layout Cell command to define the basic page structure in Layout mode.

Dreamweaver creates a table around the cell; the cell is drawn in the current background color with the surrounding table shown in an alternate color. The outline of a layout cell is highlighted in red when the mouse moves over it and turns blue when selected; likewise, a Layout table's outline is green. All these colors can be user-defined in Preferences.

Tip   If you're within 8 pixels of the edge of the Document window or another layout cell, the border of the new layout cell snaps to that edge. Press the Alt (Option) key while drawing a layout cell to temporarily disable snapping.

4. Repeat step 3 until your layout is complete. Dreamweaver drops out of Draw Layout Cell mode after your first cell is created; to create several layout cells in a row, press Ctrl (Command) while dragging.

The first cell you draw is in the current background color with the surrounding table shown in an alternate color. Cells in the alternate color represent areas of the page where you can draw more cells, but they do not necessarily represent part of the actual table structure. Think of these cells as a Layout mode visual aid, which suggests where additional cells may be added. If you switch to Standard mode, you see that the table in Figure 13-21 actually consists of three cells and doesn't extend to the right side of the page as shown in Layout mode. Figure 13-21 shows the same table in Standard mode.

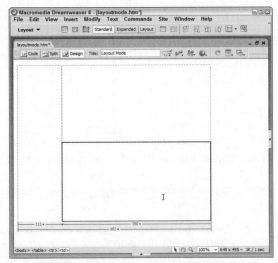

Figure 13-21: Standard mode shows only the actually defined table cells.

As indicated earlier, the Draw Table command is best suited for creating nested tables. Just as its name implies, a table is nested when it is placed within an existing table. Nested tables are useful when a design requires that a number of elements — for example, a picture and a related caption — remain stationary in relation to one another, while text on the page flows according to the size of the browser window.

To create a nested table in Layout mode, follow these steps:

1. Click the Layout button in the Layout category of the Insert bar.

2. Click the Draw Layout Table button, also in the Layout category of the Insert bar.

3. When the cursor is over an area of the table unoccupied by a layout cell, the cursor changes to a plus sign, and a layout table can be dragged out. (When not over a valid area, the cursor is shown as a slashed circle — the universal sign for *not allowed*.) The new layout table is inserted, as shown in Figure 13-22.

4. As with the Draw Layout Cell command, the Draw Layout Table command defaults to dragging one table at a time. To draw several tables in a row, press Ctrl (Command) while dragging out a layout table.

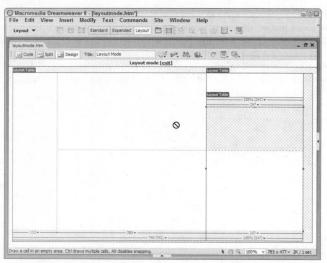

Figure 13-22: Nested tables are easily added with the Draw Layout Table command.

5. To divide the nested layout table into multiple areas, click the Draw Layout Cell button to drag out new cells.

Note

To convert a nested table to rows and columns in the outer table, click a column heading in the nested table and select Remove Nesting from the drop-down list, as shown in Figure 13-23.

Although Layout mode is an excellent method for quickly structuring a page, you should be aware of some limitations:

✦ Layout tables and cells can only be drawn in the area of the Document window that does not have any code associated with it. In other words, you need to draw layout cells and tables below the apparent end of the document. The result is that the new table code is placed right before the closing body tag.

✦ Two objects are disabled while in Layout mode: the standard Table object and the Layer object. To add either of these objects to the page, return to Standard mode.

✦ Layout cells and tables cannot be copied, cut, or pasted. These operations are available in Standard mode, however.

It's worthwhile to note that Layout mode works exceedingly well with Dreamweaver's Grid feature. With the grid showing (View ➪ Grid ➪ Show Grid) and Snap to Grid enabled (View ➪ Grid ➪ Snap to Grid), laying out cells and tables precisely is quite literally a snap. With Dreamweaver's Layout mode, complex but useful designs, like the one shown in Figure 13-24, are within easy reach.

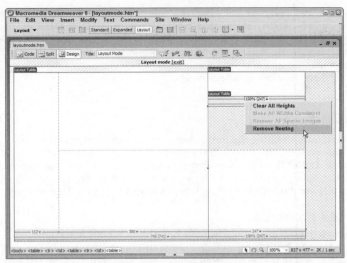

Figure 13-23: Choose the Remove Nesting command to integrate a nested table into the parent table.

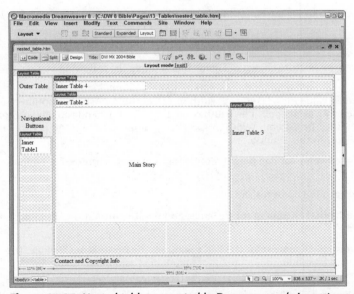

Figure 13-24: Nested tables — created in Dreamweaver's Layout mode — offer the Web designer tighter command of Web page elements.

Caution   Under certain circumstances, Dreamweaver mistakenly creates empty table cells — cells without a non-breaking space — which can break a table's structure in some browsers. This occurs most frequently when the table is resized by dragging the border of a layout table. You can avoid this problem by resizing the table via the Property inspector. If you do encounter any empty cells, be sure to enter a non-breaking space in the `<td>` tag by hand in the code or explicitly draw out a cell in Layout mode.

Modifying Layouts

Layout mode not only facilitates creating the initial design for a page, it also makes the inevitable modifications more straightforward. You can position cells within a layout table much like layers on a page. Unlike layers, however, cells cannot overlap. Resizing layout cells and tables is also simpler. Unlike Standard mode, in which any table or cell border is draggable, in Layout mode, cells and tables have sizing handles — much like a selected image.

Changing Layout Cell Properties

For you to easily manipulate layout and cells, the cells have to be readily selectable. Dreamweaver handles that chore with colorful flair. Pass your cursor over any layout cell; when you pass the border of a cell, it changes from blue to red. Click once on the red highlighting, and the cell is selected. A selected cell is notable by the eight sizing handles placed on its perimeter. After a cell is selected, the Property inspector displays its available attributes.

Tip   To select a cell without moving the cursor over the border, Ctrl+click (Command+click) anywhere in the cell.

The Layout Cell Property inspector (shown in Figure 13-25) offers the following key attributes:

✦ **Width:** Enter a pixel value for a Fixed cell width or select the Autostretch option to enable the cell to grow as needed. The width of each cell is shown on top of each column in Layout mode. The Column Width property is an important one and is explained in greater detail later in this section.

✦ **Height:** Enter a pixel value for cell height. Percentages are not permitted in Layout mode.

✦ **Bg:** Choose a background color for the cell.

✦ **Horz:** Select a horizontal alignment for the cell's content; the options are Default, Left, Center, and Right.

✦ **Vert:** Choose a vertical alignment for the cell's content; the options are Default, Top, Middle, Bottom, and Baseline.

✦ **No Wrap:** When enabled, this option prevents content — text and images — from wrapping to the next line, which, if the column is in Autostretch mode, may alter the width of the cell.

✦ **Class:** Sets the selected cell to a defined CSS class.

Figure 13-25: Although similar to the standard Cell Property inspector, the Layout Cell Property inspector offers a different set of options.

Note Not all the attributes of a table cell are available through the Layout Cell Property inspector. To add a background image, specify a border color, designate the cell as a header cell, or split the cell, switch to Standard mode.

To reshape or resize a layout cell, drag any one of the sizing handles on the border of the cell into the unused area of a table. Likewise, you can drag a cell into any open table area—that is, any area of the table unoccupied by another cell—by holding down the Ctrl key (Command key) as you click and drag.

Tip To maintain the width-height ratio of a cell, press Shift while resizing.

Changing Layout Table Properties

Tables may be similarly selected and resized. Layout tables are selected by clicking the title bar marking the table, or by Ctrl+clicking (Command+clicking) inside an open area within the table or on the table border. If the layout table is nested within another table, it can even be dragged to a new location within the outer table. Non-nested tables cannot be dragged to a new location on the page, however.

After a layout table is selected, the attributes in the Layout Table Property inspector become available, as shown in Figure 13-26:

✦ **Width:** Enter a pixel value for a Fixed table width or select the Autostretch option to allow the table to grow as needed.

✦ **Height:** Enter a pixel value for table height. Percentages are not permitted in Layout mode.

✦ **Bg:** Choose a background color for the table.

✦ **CellPad:** This controls the amount of space between the content and the cell border throughout the table. The default value is 0.

✦ **CellSpace:** This controls the amount of space between cells throughout the table. The default value is 0.

✦ **Class:** Sets the selected table to a defined CSS class.

✦ **Clear Row Heights:** This button removes any set height values for all rows and reduces the table to existing content.

Caution When used with nested tables, Dreamweaver doesn't redraw the cell border to match the table border; to correct this, drag the bottom cell border to match that of the table.

✦ **Make Cell Widths Consistent:** This button changes the width of all cells to the size of their respective content. If a cell is stretched beyond its original, fixed size by an image or some text, the column header of the layout cell shows the fixed size next to the actual size in parentheses. Clicking the Make Cell Widths Consistent button adjusts the fixed size to match the actual size.

✦ **Remove All Spacers:** Clicking this button deletes all single-pixel images used, to ensure browser compatibility for layout tables and their corresponding rows. Spacers are discussed in the section "Altering Column Widths," later in this chapter.

✦ **Remove Nesting:** This button converts a nested table to rows and cells of the outer table. This feature is available only in Layout mode, and it provides a quick way of removing nested tables from a page.

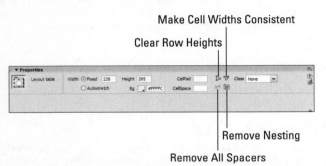

Figure 13-26: The Layout Table Property inspector includes important options for converting nested tables and sizing cells to fit existing content.

Altering Column Widths

The table elements in Layout mode borrow a couple of pages from the professional Web designer's manual. For example, any column can easily be converted from a fixed width to a flexible width — in Dreamweaver this is known as *autostretch*. When a table uses the autostretch option, one column has a flexible width, and all other columns are of fixed width.

You can alter the width of a fixed-width column in a number of ways:

✦ Visually select the cell and drag a sizing handle to a new position.

✦ For pixel-precise width, use the Layout Cell Property inspector and enter the size in the Width field. If the cell is currently in Autostretch mode, select the Fixed Width option to enable the value field.

✦ To convert an Autostretch column to its current onscreen pixel width, choose Make Column Fixed Width from the column header menu (accessed by clicking the down triangle in the center of the column width header), as shown in Figure 13-27.

✦ Insert content wider than the set width and choose Make Cell Widths Consistent from the Layout Table Property inspector.

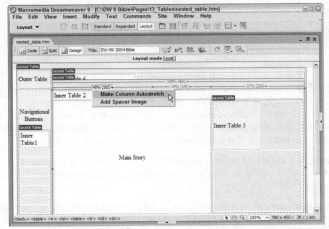

Figure 13-27: You can switch between fixed width and autostretch by using the column header menu.

To make a fixed-width column automatically stretch, choose Make Column Autostretch from the column header menu. Only one column can be made to autostretch. When you set a column to autostretch, Dreamweaver automatically converts any previously defined autostretch column to a fixed width.

When the autostretch option is chosen for a layout table, Dreamweaver inserts a spacer (a single-pixel, transparent GIF) in a new row along the bottom of the table. The spacer is sized to match the width of each of the fixed-width columns. Only the autostretch column does not have a spacer image.

If you've ever painstakingly created a complex table only to find that it looks great in one browser but collapses into an unidentifiable mess in another, you're going to love spacers. Web site designers have long used spacer images as a way to ensure a table's stability. Because no browser collapses a column smaller than the size of the largest image it contains, spacers retain a table's design under any circumstances.

Dreamweaver gives you several options when working with spacers:

✦ You can have Dreamweaver create a spacer for you.

✦ You can use an existing image as a spacer.

✦ You can opt to never include spacers.

The first time autostretch is applied as an option in a table, Dreamweaver displays the Choose Spacer Image dialog box, which enables you to create or locate a spacer image. If you choose to create a new spacer, you select a location in the current site in which to store it. Generally, you would save such a file in an images, assets, or media folder.

That image is then automatically inserted whenever an autostretch table or cell is created. One reason for using an existing image rather than a new one is if you work with sliced tables from Fireworks. Fireworks creates a single-pixel GIF image titled spacer.gif. The choice of a spacer image is a site-wide preference that can be viewed or changed by selecting the Layout mode category of Dreamweaver Preferences. Although it is not recommended practice, you can even disable spacers entirely in the Layout mode category of Preferences.

Summary

Tables are extremely powerful Web-page–design tools. Dreamweaver enables you to modify both the appearance and the structure of your HTML tables through a combination of Property inspectors, dialog boxes, and click-and-drag mouse movements. Mastering tables is an essential skill for any modern Web designer and worth the somewhat challenging learning curve. When working with tables, here are the key points to keep in mind:

✦ An HTML table consists of a series of rows and columns presented in a gridlike arrangement. Tables can be sized absolutely, in pixels, or as a percentage, relative to the width of the browser's window.

✦ Dreamweaver inserts a table whose dimensions can be altered through the Insert bar or the Insert ➪ Table menu. After it is placed in the page, the table must be selected before any of its properties can be modified through the Table Property inspector.

✦ Table editing is greatly simplified in Dreamweaver. You can select multiple cells, columns, or rows — and modify all their contents in one fell swoop.

✦ You can assign certain properties — such as background color, border color, and alignment — for a table's columns, rows, or cells through their respective Property inspectors. The properties of a cell override those set for its column or row.

✦ Dreamweaver brings power to table-building with the Format Table and Sort Table commands, as well as a connection to the outside world with its Import Tabular Data option.

✦ Dreamweaver's Layout mode enables you to quickly prepare the basic structure of a page by drawing out layout cells and tables.

✦ Putting a table within another table — also known as *nesting tables* — is a powerful (and legal) design option in HTML. Nested tables are easily accomplished in Dreamweaver's Layout mode by inserting a layout table.

In the next chapter, you learn how to create and use forms in your Web pages.

✦   ✦   ✦

Interactive Forms

A form, in the everyday world as well as on the Web, is a type of structured communication. When you apply for a driver's license, you're not told to randomly write down personal information; you're asked to fill out a form that asks for specific information, one piece at a time, in a specific manner. Web-based forms are just as precise, if not more so.

Dreamweaver has a robust and superior implementation of HTML forms — from the dedicated Forms category in the Insert bar to various form-specific Property inspectors. In addition to their importance as communication tools connecting the browsing public to Web server applications, forms are an integral part of building some of Dreamweaver's own objects. Forms also serve as major tools for Web developers because they can be altered on-the-fly; it's possible, for example, for a selection in one drop-down list to determine the contents of another. The dynamic aspects of forms are covered in Chapter 22.

In this chapter, you learn how forms are structured and then created within Dreamweaver. Each form object is explored in detail — text fields, radio buttons, checkboxes, menus, list boxes, command buttons, hidden fields, and password fields.

How HTML Forms Work

Forms have a special function in HTML: They support interaction. Virtually all HTML elements apart from forms are concerned with layout and presentation — delivering the content to the user, if you will. Forms, on the other hand, enable the user not only to read information passively from the screen, but also to send information back. Without forms, the Web would be a one-way street.

Forms have numerous uses on the Web, such as for surveys, electronic commerce, guest books, polls, and even real-time custom graphics creation. For such feedback to be possible, forms require an additional component beyond what is seen onscreen so that each form can complete its function. Every form needs some type of connection to a Web server, whether it is through one of the Dreamweaver server models or a common gateway interface (CGI) script.

Forms, like HTML tables, are self-contained units within a Web page. All the elements of a form are contained within the form tag pair `<form>` and `</form>`. You cannot nest forms as you do tables, although there's nothing to stop you from having multiple forms on a page.

The most commonly used attributes of the `<form>` tag include the following:

✦ `method` — Tells the browser and the Web server how to present the form contents to the application that will process the form. The two possible `method` values are `get` and `post`. The `get` method passes the attached information with a URL; it is less frequently used these days because it places limitations on the amount and format of data that can be passed to the application. The `post` method enables the application program to receive the information as standard input and imposes no limits on the passed data.

✦ `action` — Determines what should be done with the form content. Most commonly, `action` is set to a URL for running a specific Web application or for sending e-mail.

Typical HTML for a `<form>` tag looks something like the following:

```
<form method="post" action="http://www.idest.com/_cgi-bin/mailcall.pl">
```

Note   The `.pl` extension in the preceding example form tag stands for *Perl* — a scripting language often used to create CGI programs. Perl can be edited in any regular text editor.

Within each form is a series of input controls — text fields, radio buttons, checkboxes, and so on. Each type handles a particular sort of input; in fact, the main tag for these elements is the `<input>` tag. With one exception, the `<textarea>` tag, all form input types are implemented by specifying the `type` attribute. The text box tag, for example, is written as follows:

```
<input type="text" name="lastname">
```

All form input tags must have a `name` attribute, which identifies the control. In the preceding example, `name` is assigned a value of `"lastname"`. Information input by the user in a control, such as a text field, is sent to the server along with the value of that control's `name` attribute. Thus, if I were to fill out a form with a text box asking for my last name, such as the one produced by the foregoing tag, part of the message sent to the server would include the following string:

```
lastname=Lowery
```

Servers send all the information from a form in one long text string to whatever program or address is specified in the `action` attribute. It's up to the program or the recipient of the form message to parse the string. For instance, if I were to fill out a small form — with my name, e-mail address, and a short comment such as "Good work!" — the server would send a text string similar to the following:

```
lastname=Lowery&address=jlowery@idest.com&comment=Good+work%21
```

As you can see, the various fields are separated by ampersands (&), and the individual words within the responses are separated by plus signs. Most non-alphanumeric characters — such as the exclamation mark in the example — are represented by their hexadecimal values. Decoding this text string is called *parsing* the response.

Tip   To ease maintenance of your code, choose a name that is descriptive, but that is not a reserved word. For example, it is better to name a text field *lastname* than just *name*.

Inserting a Form in Dreamweaver

A form is inserted just like any other object in Dreamweaver. Place the cursor where you want your form to start and then either click the Form button in the Forms category of the Insert bar (see Figure 14-1) or choose Insert ➪ Form from the menu. Dreamweaver inserts a red, dashed outline stretching across the Document window to indicate the form.

Form   Form outline

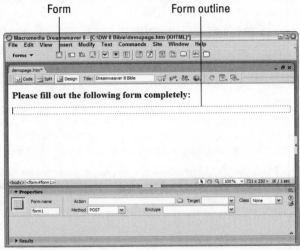

Figure 14-1: Inserting a form creates a dashed, red outline of the form and, if the Property inspector is open, displays the Form Property inspector.

Tip   If you can't see the outline of the form, choose View ➪ Visual Aids ➪ Invisible Elements. If you still can't see the form, choose Edit ➪ Preferences (Dreamweaver ➪ Preferences) and select the Form Delimiter checkbox in the Invisible Elements category. Clear the checkbox if you don't want to see the form outline.

If you have the Property inspector open, the Form Property inspector appears when you insert a form. As Figure 14-1 shows, you can specify several values regarding forms; in addition to the Action and the Method, which correspond to the attributes previously discussed, you can also specify a Form Name, Enctype value, and Target.

Because of the interactive nature of forms, Web programmers often use them to gather information from the user. To do this, programmers must specify a form name, which enables them to reference a form using JavaScript or other languages.

In the Action text box, you can directly enter a URL or mailto address, or you can select the folder icon and browse for a file.

Declaring the Encoding Type (Enctype)

The `<form>` attribute `enctype` is helpful in formatting material returned via a form. It specifies how the information is being sent, so the server software knows how to interpret the input.

By default, `enctype` is set to `application/x-www-form-urlencoded`, which is responsible for encoding the form response with ampersands between entries, equal signs linking form element names to their values, spaces as plus signs, and all non-alphanumeric characters in hexadecimal format, such as `%3F` (a question mark).

A second `enctype` value, `text/plain`, is useful for e-mail replies. Instead of one long string, your form data is transmitted in a more readable format, with each form element and its value on a separate line, as shown in the following example:

```
fname=Joseph
lname=Lowery
email=jlowery@idest.com
comment=Please send me the information on your new products!
```

Another `enctype` value, `multipart/form-data`, is used only when a file is being uploaded as part of the form. There's a further restriction: The method must be set to `post` instead of `get`.

Dreamweaver includes an Enctype list box on the Form Property inspector so you can easily specify the encoding type. You can choose a value from the drop-down list, or manually enter a value in the Enctype list box.

Note   Sending your form data via a mailto address is not without its problems. Some browsers, most notably Internet Explorer, are set to warn the user initially whenever a form button using mailto is selected. Although many users let the mail go through, they do have the option to stop it from being sent.

The method defaults to `post`, the most commonly used option. You can also choose `get` or `default`, which leaves the method up to the browser. In most cases, you should leave the method set to `post`.

Enctype stands for encoding type; this value tells the server in what format the data is being sent. For more information, refer to the sidebar titled "Declaring the Encoding Type (Enctype)" in this chapter.

Finally, the Target field tells the server which frame or window to use when displaying a response to the form. If you don't specify a target, any response displays in the current frame or window.

Forms cannot be placed inline with any other element such as text or graphics. Keep in mind the following additional considerations when it comes to mixing forms and other Web page elements:

✦ Forms expand as objects are inserted into them; you can't resize a form by dragging its boundaries.

✦ The outline of a form is invisible in a browser; there is no border to turn on or off.

✦ Forms and tables can be used together only if the form either completely encloses the table or is completely enclosed inside the table. In other words, you can't have a form spanning part of a table.

✦ Forms can be inserted within layers, and multiple forms can be in multiple layers. However, the layer must completely enclose the form. As with forms spanning tables, you can't have a form spanning two or more layers. (A workaround for this limitation is discussed in Chapter 11.)

Using Text Fields

Anytime you use a form to gather text information typed in by a user, you use a form object called a *text field*. Text fields can hold any number of alphanumeric and punctuation characters. The Web designer can decide whether the text field is displayed in one line or several. When the HTML is written, a multiple-line text field uses a `<textarea>` tag, and a single-line text field is coded with `<input type="text">`.

Inserting Text Fields

To insert a single-line text field in Dreamweaver, you can use any of the following methods:

✦ From the Forms category of the Insert bar, click the Text Field button to place a text field at your current cursor position.

✦ Choose Insert ➪ Form ➪ Text Field from the menu, which inserts a text field at the current cursor position.

✦ Drag the Text Field button from the Insert bar to any existing location in the Document window and release the mouse button to position the text field.

Note   You can use any of these methods to insert text fields in either Design view or Code view. When you insert a text field or most other form controls in Code view, the Tag Editor for the `<input>` tag opens automatically, enabling you to specify any attributes for the tag.

When you insert a text field, the Property inspector, when displayed, shows you the available attributes (see Figure 14-2). You measure the size of a text field by the number of characters it can display at one time. You can change the length of a text field by inserting a value in the Char Width text box. By default, Dreamweaver inserts a text field approximately 20 characters wide. The *approximately* is important here because the *final* size of the text field is ultimately controlled by the browser used to view the page. Unless you limit the number of possible characters by entering a value in the Max Chars text box, the user can enter as many characters as desired, but not all the characters will necessarily be visible at one time; the text scrolls horizontally in the box as the user types.

Note   The value in Char Width determines the visible width of the field; the value in Max Chars actually determines the number of characters that can be entered.

Text field

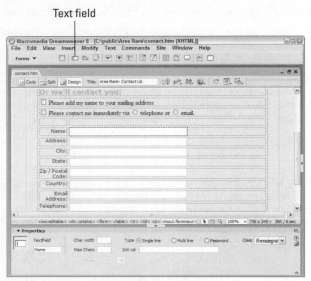

Figure 14-2: The text field of a form enables the user to type any required information.

The Init Value text box on the Text Field Property inspector is used to insert a default text string. The user can overwrite this value, if desired.

Creating Password Fields

Normally, any text entered into text fields is displayed as you expect — programmers refer to this process as *echoing*. You can turn off echoing by selecting the Password option in the Text Field Property inspector. When a text field is designated as a password field, all text entered by the user shows up as asterisks or dots.

Use the password field when you want to protect the user's input from prying eyes (just as your PIN is hidden when you enter it at an ATM, for instance). The information entered in a password field is not encrypted or scrambled in any way, and when sent to the Web application, it is received as regular text.

Only single-line text fields can be set as password fields. You cannot make a multiline `<textarea>` tag act as a password field without employing JavaScript or some other programming language.

Cross-Reference   Making sure that your user fills out the form properly is called *validating* the input. Dreamweaver includes a standard form validation behavior, covered in Chapter 12.

Inserting Multiline Text Areas

When you want to give your users a generous amount of room to write, you can expand not just the width of the text area, but also its height. Dreamweaver gives you the following options for creating a multiline text area:

✦ Insert a single-line text field on the page as previously described and convert the field to multiple lines by choosing the Multiline option in the Text Field Property inspector.

✦ Directly insert the Textarea form element using the Insert bar or Insert menu. To do this, position your cursor where you want to insert the text area and choose Insert ⇨ Form ⇨ Textarea or click the Textarea button in the Forms category of the Insert bar.

Constructing Neat Forms

Although they are especially good when you are working on a larger, complex form, I find that tables and forms are made for each other—even in this age of CSS. Besides the speed of layout, another advantage that tables offer is the capability to right-align text labels next to your text fields; it's worth noting that the align attribute for the <td> tag is still valid HTML. The top form in the following figure uses preformatted text to get different-sized form fields to line up properly, whereas the bottom form in the figure uses a table.

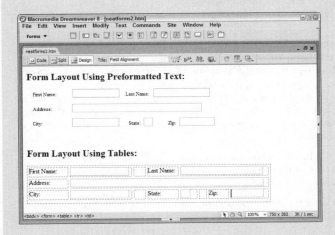

Combining different-sized text fields on a single row—for example, when you're asking for a city, state, and ZIP Code combination—can make the task of lining up your form even more difficult. Most often, you spend a fair amount of time in a trial-and-error effort to make the text fields match. Be sure to check your results in the various browsers as you build your form.

Tables are just the beginning stage in creating a clean, easy-to-read form. For greater control, be sure to read "Styling Forms with CSS" later in this chapter.

Figure 14-3 shows a typical multiline text field embedded in a form.

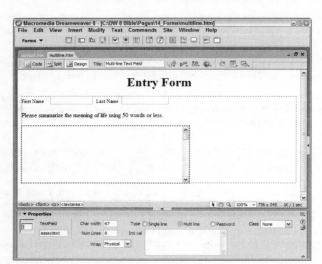

Figure 14-3: The Multiline option of the Text Field Property inspector opens up a text area for more user information.

The text area that is initially created is approximately 18 characters wide and 3 lines high, with horizontal and vertical scroll bars. You control the width of a multiline text area by entering a value in the Char Width text box of the Text Field Property inspector, just as you do for single-line text fields. The height of the text area is set equal to the value in the Num Lines text box. As with the default single-line text field, the user can enter any amount of text. Unlike the single-line text field, in which you can restrict the number of characters that can be input through the Max Chars text box, you cannot restrict the number of characters the user enters into a multiline text area.

When you place a multiline text field on a form, you can specify how text entered into that field should wrap. You indicate this using the Wrap field in the Property inspector. You can select one of the following options:

✦ **Default:** With this option selected, the browser determines the scrolling characteristics of the multiline text field. Browsers and browser versions vary in their default handling of wrapping.

✦ **Off:** With this option selected, text entered into a multiline text field does not wrap when it reaches the right edge of the text area; rather, it keeps scrolling until the user presses Enter (Return).

✦ **Virtual:** This option causes text on the screen to wrap when it reaches the right edge of the text area, but not when the response is submitted to the server; the text is sent as one long string without hard carriage returns.

✦ **Physical:** This option causes text to wrap on the screen and converts the soft returns on the screen to hard returns when the data is submitted to the server.

Caution The `wrap` attribute is not supported consistently between browsers or even between different versions of the same browser. For example, Netscape 6.0 ignores any value of the `wrap` attribute, and simply never wraps text; whereas Netscape Navigator 4.61 does respect the wrapping options.

Grouping Form Controls

In desktop applications, you may be used to seeing related controls grouped together, with a thin border around them. You can achieve a similar effect in your HTML forms by enclosing the related form elements within the `<fieldset>`...`</fieldset>` tag pair, as shown in the following code:

```
<fieldset>
  <legend>Address</legend>
    <label>Street <input type="text" name="street" ></label>
    <label>City <input type="text" name="city" ></label>
    <label>State <input type="text" name="state" ></label>
    <label>Zip <input type="text" name="zip"></label>
</fieldset>
```

In this example, the `<fieldset>` tags group the text fields, and the `<legend>` tag creates a label describing the group of controls. In the most recent browsers, the legend appears as a label above the control group, as shown in the following figure.

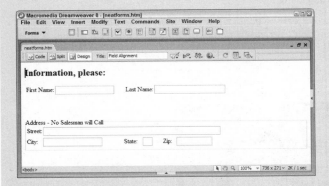

In Dreamweaver's Code view, you can add the `<fieldset>` and `<legend>` tags by selecting a set of existing controls that you'd like to group and then clicking the Fieldset button in the Forms category of the Insert bar. If you are in Design view when you click the Fieldset button, Dreamweaver automatically switches to the split view and makes Code view active. However, it is best to apply the `<fieldset>` tag in Code view so you can be sure you have correctly selected all the HTML tags to be grouped.

Note that the `<fieldset>` tag is not supported in all browsers, but Dreamweaver renders it just fine.

Another option when creating multiline text fields is to preload the text area with any default text you like. Enter this text in the Init Val text box of the Text Field Property inspector. When Dreamweaver writes the HTML code, this text is not entered as a value, as it is for the single-line text field, but rather goes in between the `<textarea>`...`</textarea>` tag pair.

Providing Checkboxes and Radio Buttons

When you want your Web page user to choose between a specific set of options in your form, you can use either checkboxes or radio buttons. Checkboxes enable you to offer a series of options from which the user can pick as many as he wants. Radio buttons, on the other hand, restrict your user to only one selection from a number of options.

Tip   You can achieve the same functionality as checkboxes and radio buttons with a different look by using drop-down lists and menu boxes. These methods for presenting options to the user are described shortly.

Checkboxes

Checkboxes are often used in a "Select All That Apply" type of section, when you want to enable the user to choose as many of the listed options as desired. You insert a checkbox in much the same way you do a text field: Select or drag the CheckBox object from the Insert bar or choose Insert ➪ Form ➪ CheckBox.

Like other form objects, checkboxes can be given a unique name in the CheckBox Property inspector (see Figure 14-4). If you don't provide a name, Dreamweaver inserts a generic one, such as checkbox4.

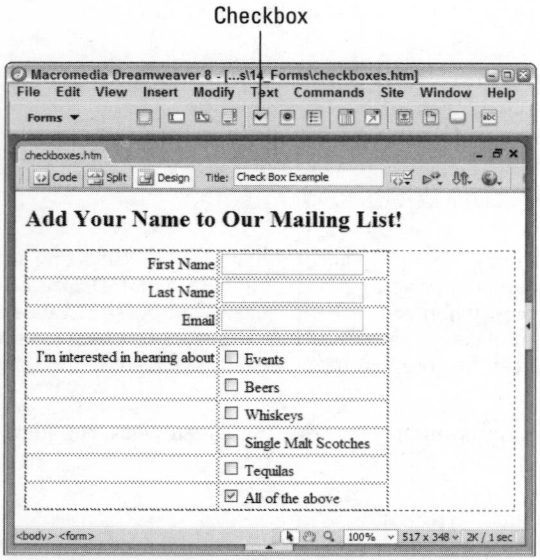

Checkbox

Figure 14-4: Checkboxes are one way of offering the Web page visitor any number of options to choose from.

In the Checked Value text box, fill in the information you want passed to a program when the user selects the checkbox. By default, a checkbox starts out unchecked, but you can change that by changing the Initial State option to Checked.

Radio Buttons

Radio buttons on a form provide a set of options from which the user can choose only one. If a user changes his or her mind after choosing one radio button, selecting another one automatically deselects the first choice. Dreamweaver gives you the following options for inserting radio buttons:

✦ To insert radio buttons one at a time, select or drag Radio Button from the Forms category of the Insert bar, or choose Insert ⇨ Form ⇨ Radio Button.

✦ To insert several related radio buttons at one time, select or drag the Radio Group button from the Forms category of the Insert bar, or choose Insert ⇨ Form ⇨ Radio Group.

Unlike checkboxes and text fields, each radio button in the set does not have a unique name — instead, each group of radio buttons has a name. If you give the entire set of radio buttons the same name, browsers can assign one value to the radio button set. That value is determined by the contents of the Checked Value text box in the Property inspector. Figure 14-5 shows two different sets of radio buttons. The figure shows the Property inspector for one of the radio buttons in the osRadio group, on the right. In this example, each button in the group is assigned the name osRadio.

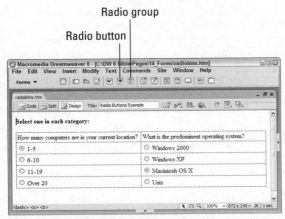

Figure 14-5: Radio buttons enable a user to make just one selection from a group of options.

To designate the default selection for each radio button group, you select the particular radio button and make the Initial State option Checked instead of Unchecked. In the form shown in Figure 14-5, the default selection for the osRadio group is Macintosh.

Tip   Because you must give all radio buttons in the same set the same name, you can speed up your work a bit by creating one button, copying it, and then pasting the others. Don't forget to change the Checked Value for each button, though.

Building a Form, Part 1

In this Technique, you create a form that eventually incorporates all of the form elements. You add the form to the page, the table to hold the form elements, and the first of the form objects: text fields and radio buttons.

Note: For this Technique, make sure the Accessibility options are disabled by opening Edit ⇨ Preferences (Dreamweaver ⇨ Preferences), selecting the Accessibility category, and de-selecting the Form Objects option.

1. In the Files panel, switch to the Dreamweaver Bible working site previously created.

2. Go to Techniques\14_Forms and open the file `forms_start.htm`.

3. Place your cursor at the end of the first paragraph under the Tell Us What You're Looking For heading and press Enter (Return) to create a new line.

4. In the Insert bar, switch to the Forms category and click the Form object.

5. With your cursor inside the red form outline, change to the Common category and choose Table.

6. When the Insert Table dialog box opens, insert a 6-row, 2-column table that is 400 pixels wide with 0 borders.

7. Select all the cells in the first column and, from the Property inspector's Style list, choose formLabel.

The formLabel CSS rule makes all the content in the designated cells align right and bold.

8. Place your cursor in the first cell, first column and enter **I want to:**.

Be sure to leave a space after the colon to add separation between the label and the form elements.

9. Switch back to the Forms category in the Insert bar and drag a Radio Button into the first row, second column.

10. With the radio button still selected, enter **buyRentRB** into the name field of the Property inspector and **buy** in the Value field.

11. Move your cursor to the right of the radio button and add the text **Buy**.

12. Repeat steps 9–11 to add a second radio button. Use the same name (**buyRentRB**), a different value (**rent**), and a corresponding label (**Rent**).

13. In the second row, first column, enter the text **I can afford up to:**.

Again, be sure to leave a space after the colon to add separation between the label and the form elements.

14. From the Insert Bar's Forms category, drag a Text Field into the adjacent cell.

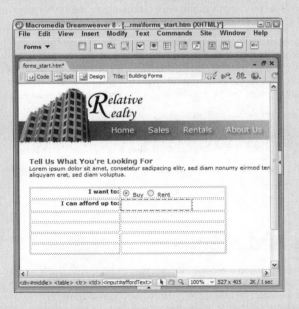

15. With the text field selected, enter **affordText** in the Property inspector's Name field.

16. Save your page.

In the next Technique, you complete the form, adding the remaining form elements.

You can create an entire set of radio buttons at one time using the Radio Group command. When you select the Radio Group button from the Forms category of the Insert bar, or choose Insert ⇨ Form ⇨ Radio Group, the Radio Group dialog box appears, as shown in Figure 14-6. This dialog box not only lets you define multiple radio buttons at once, but it automatically formats them either in a table or using line breaks, at your discretion.

Figure 14-6: Use the Radio Group dialog box to create an entire set of radio buttons at one time.

Follow these steps to set up your radio button group in the Radio Group dialog box:

1. In the Name text box, replace the default name with a meaningful name for your new set of radio buttons.

2. Each entry in the list represents a separate radio button in the group; the dialog box opens with two filler buttons as an example. Click the first entry in the Label list and replace the word Radio with the label for the first button in your group. Press Tab to move to the Value column, and replace the default with the appropriate value for your button; this is the data that is sent to the server when the radio button is selected.

   Repeat this step for the second radio button in your set.

3. If you have more than two radio buttons in your set, click the Add (+) button to add another item to the list and fill out the appropriate value, as explained in step 2.

4. Specify whether you want your radio buttons inserted on separate lines using the ⟨br⟩ tag, or automatically formatted in a table.

5. Finally, click OK.

Creating Form Lists and Menus

Another way to offer your user options, in a more compact form than radio buttons and checkboxes, is with form lists and menus. Both objects can create single-line entries in your form that expand or scroll to reveal all the available options. You can also determine how deep you want the scrolling list to be — that is, how many options you want displayed at one time.

Drop-Down Menus

A drop-down menu should be familiar to everyday users of computers: The menu is initially displayed as a single-line text box with an arrow button at the right end; when the button is clicked, the other options are revealed in a list or menu. (Whether the list pops up or drops down depends on its position on the screen at the time it is selected. Normally, the list drops down, unless it is close to the bottom of the screen.) After the user selects one of the listed options and the mouse is released, the list closes, and the selected value remains displayed in the text box.

Insert a drop-down menu in Dreamweaver as you would any other form object, with one of the following actions:

✦ From the Forms category of the Insert bar, select the List/Menu button to place a drop-down menu at the current cursor position.

✦ Choose Insert ⇨ Form ⇨ List/Menu to insert a drop-down menu at the current cursor position.

✦ Drag the List/Menu button from the Insert bar to any location in the Document window and release the mouse button to position the drop-down menu.

With the List/Menu object inserted, make sure the Menu option (not the List option) is selected in the Property inspector, as shown in Figure 14-7. You can also name the drop-down menu by typing a name in the Name text box; if you don't, Dreamweaver supplies a generic "select" name.

List/Menu

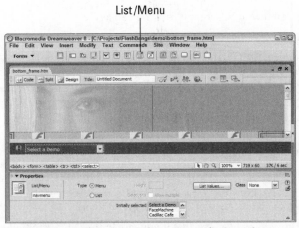

Figure 14-7: Create a drop-down menu by inserting a List/Menu object and then selecting the Menu option in the List/Menu Property inspector.

Tip To clear the selection in the Initially Selected list, hold down the Ctrl (Command) key as you click the highlighted item.

Scrolling Lists

A scrolling list differs from a drop-down menu in three respects. First, and most obviously, the scrolling list field has up and down arrow buttons, rather than an option arrow button; and the user can scroll the list, showing as little as one item at a time, instead of the entire list. Second, you can control the height of the scrolling list, enabling it to display more than one item — or all available items — simultaneously. Third, you can enable the user to select more than one item at a time, as with checkboxes.

A scrolling list is inserted in the same manner as a drop-down menu — through the Insert bar by choosing Insert ➪ Form. After the object is inserted, select the List option in the List/Menu Property inspector.

Enter items for your scrolling list just as you do for a drop-down menu, by starting with the List Values button in the Property inspector and filling in the List Values dialog box. Figure 14-9 shows a sample list box, as it appears in the Document window.

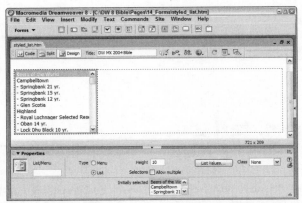

Figure 14-9: Unlike menus, scrolling lists can show more than one item on the screen at a time.

By default, the Selections checkbox for Allow Multiple is cleared in the List/Menu Property inspector. When you enable multiple selections (by selecting the Allow Multiple checkbox), the user can select more than one item in the list by using two keyboard modifiers, the Shift and Ctrl (Command) keys:

✦ To select several adjacent items in the list, the user must click the first item in the list, press the Shift key, and select the last item in the list.

✦ To select several nonadjacent items, the user must hold down the Ctrl (Command) key while selecting the items.

Other than the highlighted text, no acknowledgment (such as a checkmark) appears in the list. As with drop-down menus, the Web designer can preselect options by highlighting them in the Initially Selected menu. Use the same techniques with the Shift and Ctrl (Command) modifier keys as a user would.

Keep in mind several factors as you are working with scrolling lists:

✦ If you disable the Allow Multiple Selections box and set a Height value of 1 or clear the Height field entirely, the list appears as a drop-down menu.

✦ With Allow Multiple Selections enabled, if you do not set a Height value at all, the browser determines how many items appear onscreen. Internet Explorer, by default, shows four items at a time; Netscape Navigator displays all the items in your list. In the Dreamweaver Document window, only one item is displayed. To exercise control over your scrolling list, it is best to insert a Height value.

✦ The number of characters in the longest label determines the widths of both the scrolling list and the drop-down menu. To widen the List/Menu object, you must directly enter additional spaces ( ) in the HTML code; Dreamweaver does not recognize additional spaces entered through the List Values dialog box. For example, to expand the example Favorite Beer List/Menu object, use the Code inspector or another editor to change

```
<option value="oatmeal">Oatmeal Stout</option>
```

to the following:

```
<option value="oatmeal">Oatmeal Stout
   </option>
```

Building a Form, Part 2

Now you're ready to complete the form started earlier in this chapter.

Note: For this Technique, make sure the Accessibility options are disabled by opening Edit ➪ Preferences (Dreamweaver ➪ Preferences), selecting the Accessibility category, and de-selecting the Form Objects option.

1. In the Files panel, re-open the `forms_start.htm` file you previously worked on.

2. In the first column of the third row, enter this label: **I need these many bedrooms:**.

3. From the Insert bar's Forms category, drag a List/Menu object into the second column of the third row.

4. In the Property inspector's Name field, enter **roomList**.

5. Click List Values in the Property inspector.

6. When the List Values dialog box opens, enter the following Item Label/Value pairs:

Item Label	Value
1	1
2	2
3	3
4	4
5+	5+

Click OK when you're done to close the dialog.

7. From the Initially Selected list in the Property inspector, choose the first value, 1.

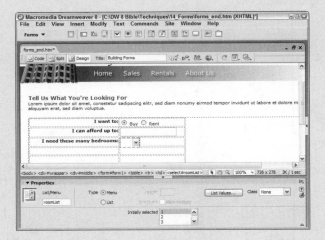

8. Place your cursor in the first column of the next row and enter the label **I need:**.

9. From the Insert bar, drag a checkbox object into the second column of the same row.

10. In the Property inspector name field, enter **laundryCB**.

11. Move to the right of the checkbox, add a space and enter the label **Laundry Room**; press Shift+Enter (Shift+Return) to create a line break.

12. Repeat steps 9–11 twice more to insert one checkbox with the name **garageCB** and labeled **Garage** and another named **viewsCB** and labeled **Views**.

To adjust the position of the associated label, you'll need to change the vertical alignment of the table cell.

Continued

Continued

13. Place your cursor next to the I need: label and, from the Property inspector's Vert list, choose Top.

14. In the second-to-last row, first cell, enter the label **My special needs are:**.

15. From the Insert bar, drag a Textarea object into the second column of the same row.

16. In the Property inspector's Name field, enter **needsArea**.

17. Drag a Submit button from the Insert bar to the second column in the last row.

18. In the Property inspector's Value field, enter **Send Info**.

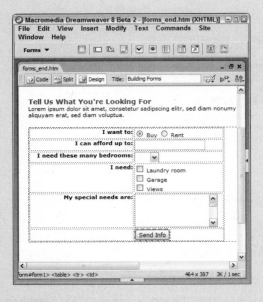

19. Save your page.

Navigating with a Jump Menu

It's not always practical to use a series of buttons as the primary navigation tool on a Web site. For sites that want to offer access to a great number of pages, a *jump menu* can be a better way to go. A jump menu uses the menu form element to list the various options; when one of the options is chosen, the browser loads — or jumps to — a new page. In addition to providing a single mechanism for navigation, a jump menu is easy to update because it doesn't require laying out the page again. Because they are JavaScript-driven, jump menus can even be updated dynamically.

Dreamweaver includes a Jump Menu object that handles all the JavaScript coding for you — all you have to provide is a list of item names and associated URLs. Dreamweaver even drops in a Go button for you, if you choose. The Jump Menu object is easily used in a frame-based layout for targeting specific frames. After the object is inserted, you can modify the Jump Menu object like any other list object, through the List/Menu Property inspector. To insert a jump menu, follow these steps:

1. Position your cursor in the current form, if one exists, where you'd like the jump menu to appear. If you haven't already inserted a form, don't worry. Dreamweaver automatically inserts one for you.

2. From the Forms category of the Insert bar, click the Jump Menu button. The Insert Jump Menu dialog box, shown in Figure 14-10, is displayed.

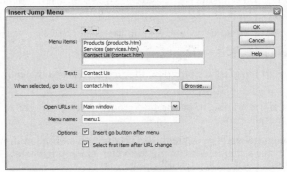

Figure 14-10: Consolidate your Web site navigation through a jump menu.

3. In the Insert Jump Menu dialog box, enter the label for the first item in the Text field. When you confirm your entry by tabbing out of the field, Dreamweaver updates the Menu Items list.

4. Enter the path and filename of the page you want opened for the current item in the When Selected, Go to URL field; alternatively, you can click the Browse button to select your file.

5. To add additional jump menu items, click the Add (+) button and repeat steps 3 and 4.

6. You can adjust the positioning of the items in the jump menu by selecting an item in the Menu Items list and using the up and down arrows to move it higher or lower.

7. From the Open URLs In list, pick the destination target for the page. Unless you're working in a frameset, you have only one option — Main Window. When a Jump Menu object is added in a frameset, Dreamweaver displays all frame names, as well as Main Window, as options.

8. If you want, enter a unique name for the jump menu in the Menu Name field.

9. To add a button that activates the jump menu choice, select the Insert Go Button After Menu option.

10. To reset the menu selection to the top item after every jump, choose the Select First Item After URL Change.

11. Click OK when you're finished.

Wrapping Graphics Around a Jump Menu

Jump menus are useful in many circumstances, but as a raw form element, they often stick out of a Web page design like a sore thumb. Some designers solve this dilemma by including their jump menu within a specially constructed graphic. The easiest way to create such a graphic is to use a program such as Fireworks, which enables a single image to be sliced into separate parts. The slices are then exported to an HTML file and reassembled in a table.

When you create your graphic, leave room for the jump menu to be inserted in Dreamweaver. Reserving space for a jump menu usually entails designating one slice as a nongraphic or text-only slice in your graphics program. After you bring the HTML into Dreamweaver, insert the Jump Menu object in the empty table cell.

Here are a few pointers for wrapping a graphic around a jump menu:

✦ Use a flat color — not a gradient — as the background for the menu.

✦ Work with Web-safe colors in the graphics program; they're far easier to match in Dreamweaver.

✦ Set the background color of the graphic to be the background color of the cell of the table holding your jump menu.

✦ Make sure you leave enough height in your graphic to accommodate the jump menu in all browsers. Netscape displays a standard list/menu form element approximately 24 pixels high on a PC; try leaving about 30 pixels in your graphic.

✦ Form elements are drawn by the user's operating system and are vastly different on each platform. Test your designs extensively.

✦ Integrate your Go button, if you're using one, right in the graphic. Be sure to set it as its own slice, so that it comes in as a separate image and can be activated with a Jump Menu Go behavior. In the following figure, a graphical Go button appears to the right of the jump menu.

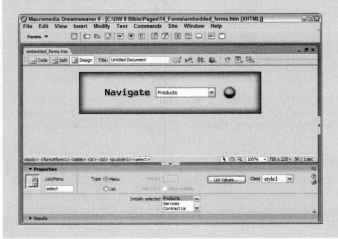

Dreamweaver inserts the new jump menu with the appropriate linking code.

On the CD-ROM

Macromedia's Jump Menu object opens the selected URL in the current page or in one of the frames in a frameset. To open a Web page in a new window, use another extension, Jump Menu Fever! by Drew McLellan. This object is located in the Additional Extensions folder on the CD-ROM. To open a new window with Jump Menu Fever!, choose _blank from the list of available targets.

Modifying a Jump Menu

After you've inserted your Jump Menu object, you can modify it in one of two ways: through the standard List/Menu Property inspector or through the Jump Menu behavior. Whereas the List Property inspector uses a List Value dialog box, editing the Jump Menu behavior opens a dialog box similar to the one used to insert the Jump Menu object.

To alter the items in an existing jump menu via the List/Menu Property inspector, select the jump menu and click the List Values button. In the List Values dialog box, the jump menu labels are on the left and the URLs are on the right. You can add, move, or delete items as you would with any other list.

Caution

One caveat for adding new URLs to the jump menu through the Property inspector: Any file-names with spaces or special characters should be URL-encoded. In other words, if one of your filenames is `about us.htm`, it should be entered using the hexadecimal equivalent for a space (%20): `about%20us.htm`. Also, if you enter a filename or URL that contains special characters in the List Values dialog box, the resulting code translates the special characters into their HTML codes, thus breaking the URL. Most notably, an ampersand (&) entered in the List Values dialog box is encoded as `&amp;`.

If you'd prefer to work in the same environment as you did when creating the Jump Menu object, go the Behaviors panel route. Select the jump menu. Then, from the Behaviors panel, double-click the Jump Menu action. The Jump Menu dialog box opens — it's identical to the Insert Jump Menu dialog box except that the Go button option is not available.

Activating Go Buttons

The Dreamweaver jump menu is activated immediately whenever a user makes a selection from the list. So why would you want a Go button? The Go button, as implemented in Dreamweaver, is useful for selecting the first item in a jump menu list. To ensure that the Go button is the sole means for activating a jump selection, you need to remove an attached behavior. Select the jump menu item, open the Behaviors panel, and delete the Jump Menu event.

Tip

Some Web designers prefer to use a non-URL option for the first item, such as Please Select A Department. When entering such a non-URL option, set the Go to URL (or the value in the List Value Properties) to `javascript:;` to create a null link.

The generic Go button is a nice convenience, but it's a little, well, generic. To switch from a standard Go button to a graphical Go button of your choosing, follow these steps:

1. Insert the image that you want to use as your new Go button next to the jump menu.

2. With the new graphic selected, open the Behaviors panel.

3. Select Jump Menu Go from the Add Event drop-down list. Dreamweaver displays a dialog box showing all available jump menus.

4. Choose the name of the current jump menu from the Jump Menu Go dialog box list and click OK when you're finished.

5. If necessary, delete the Dreamweaver-inserted Go button.

Activating Your Form with Buttons

Buttons are essential to HTML forms. You can place all the form objects you want on a page, but until your user clicks that Submit button, there's no interaction between the client and the server. HTML provides three basic types of buttons: Submit, Reset, and Command.

Submit, Reset, and Command Buttons

A Submit button sends the form to the specified action (generally the URL of a server-side program or a mailto address) using the noted method (generally `post`). A Reset button clears all the fields in the form. Submit and Reset are both reserved HTML terms used to invoke specific actions.

A Command button permits the execution of functions defined by the Web designer, as programmed in JavaScript or other languages.

To insert a button in Dreamweaver, follow these steps:

1. Position the cursor where you want the button to appear. Then either select Button in the Forms category of the Insert bar, or choose Insert ➪ Form ➪ Button from the menu. Alternatively, you can simply drag the Button control from the Insert bar and drop it into place on an existing form.

2. In the Button Property inspector, select the button Action type. In Figure 14-11, the Property inspector indicates that the Submit form button action is selected (this is the default). To make a Reset button, select the Reset form option. To make a Command button, select the None option.

3. To rename a button as you want it to appear on the Web page, enter the new name in the Label text box.

When working with Command buttons, it's not enough to just insert the button and give it a name. You have to link the button to a specific function. A common technique is to use JavaScript's `onClick` event to call a function detailed in the `<script>` section of the document:

```
<input type="BUTTON" name="submit2" value="yes"    ⤶
onClick="doFunction()">
```

Button

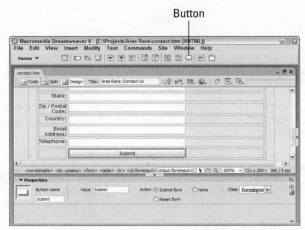

Figure 14-11: You can choose an action and a label for a button through the Button Property inspector.

Graphical Buttons

HTML doesn't limit you to the browser-style default buttons. You can also use an image as a Submit, Reset, or Command button. Dreamweaver has the capability to add an image field just like other form elements: Place the cursor in the desired position and choose Insert ➪ Form ➪ Image Field, or select the Image Field button from the Forms category of the Insert bar. You can use multiple image fields in a form to give users graphical options, as shown in Figure 14-12.

Image field

Figure 14-12: Each flag in this page is more than an image; it's an image field that also acts as a Submit button.

When the user clicks the picture that you've designated as an image field for a Submit button, the form is submitted. Any other functionality, such as resetting the fields, must be coded in JavaScript or another language and triggered by attaching an onClick event to the button. This can be handled through the Dreamweaver behaviors, covered in Chapter 12, or by hand-coding the script and adding code for the onClick event to the button.

In fact, when the user clicks a graphical button, not only does it submit your form, but it passes along the x, y coordinates of the image. The x coordinate is submitted using the name of the field with an .x attached; likewise, the y coordinate is submitted with the name of the field with a .y attached. Although this latter feature isn't often used, it's always good to know all the capabilities of your HTML tools.

Another technique is involved if you want to include more graphical buttons than a single Submit button on your form. Because only one image field can be used as a Submit button, a standard image is inserted, and JavaScript handles the programming chores required for submitting or resetting the form. An advantage to this technique is that the image can even be set up as a rollover, meaning that the image changes as the user moves the mouse over the button.

To use an image for a Submit or Reset button, follow these steps:

1. Choose Insert ⇨ Image or click the Image button in the Common category of the Insert bar.

2. In the Insert Image dialog box, enter the path to your image or select the folder icon to locate the file. The image can be in GIF, JPEG, or PNG format.

3. Give the image a name and, if you want, alternative text using the appropriate text boxes in the Property inspector.

4. In the Link field of the Property inspector, enter the following code for a graphical Submit button:

```
javascript:document.form1.submit()
```

Similarly, enter this code for a Reset button:

```
javascript:document.form1.reset()
```

Note   Be sure to change the code to reflect your specifics: the name of your form as well as the name of your images.

Using the Hidden and the File Fields

You should also be aware of two other special-purpose form fields, the *hidden field* and the *file field*, which are supported by all major browsers. The hidden field is extremely useful for passing variables to your Web application programs, and the file field enables users to attach a file to the form being submitted.

The Hidden Input Type

When passing information from a form to a CGI program, the programmer often needs to send data that should not be made visible to the user. The data could be a variable needed by the CGI program to set information on the recipient of the form, or it could be a URL to which the server program redirects the user after the form is submitted. To send this sort of information unseen by the form user, you can use a hidden form object.

The hidden field is inserted in a form much like the other form elements. Place your cursor in the desired position and choose Insert ⇨ Form ⇨ Hidden Field or click the Hidden Field button in the Forms category of the Insert bar.

The hidden object is another input type, just like the text, radio button, and checkbox types. A hidden variable looks like the following in HTML:

```
<input type="hidden" name="recipient" value="jlowery@idest.com">
```

As you would expect, this tag has no representation when it's viewed through a browser. However, Dreamweaver does display a Hidden Form Element symbol in the Document window. You can turn off the display of this symbol by deselecting the Hidden Form Field option from the Invisible Elements category of Preferences.

The File Input Type

The file input type, which enables any stored computer file to be attached to the form and sent with the other data, is rarely used. Formerly, it was used primarily to enable the easy sharing of data. The file input type has now been largely supplanted by modern e-mail methods, which enable files to be attached to messages.

The file field is inserted in a form much like the other form elements. Place your cursor in the desired position and choose Insert ⇨ Form ⇨ File Field or click the File Field button in the Forms category of the Insert bar. Dreamweaver automatically inserts what appears to be a text box with a Browse button. In a browser, the user's selection of the Browse button displays a standard Open File dialog box from which a file can be selected to go with the form.

Improving Accessibility

You can do several things to make your HTML forms more accessible to people with visual impairments, who may be using a nonvisual browser or a screen reader. Many of these options are also useful for users accessing the page visually.

Dreamweaver makes it easy for Web page authors to improve the accessibility of their Web forms by setting an option in the Accessibility category of the Preferences dialog box.

To turn on the accessibility controls for forms, choose Edit ⇨ Preferences (Dreamweaver ⇨ Preferences) and then, in the Accessibility category, select the Form Objects checkbox. With this option enabled, every time you insert a form object, the Input Tag Accessibility Attributes dialog box, shown in Figure 14-13, is displayed.

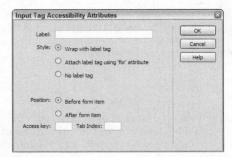

Figure 14-13: The Input Tag Accessibility Attributes dialog box is displayed only when you have enabled the Form Objects option in the Accessibility category of Preferences.

Note The Input Tag Accessibility Attributes dialog box does not appear when you insert Jump Menus or Radio Groups. However, it does appear when you insert individual radio buttons.

In the Input Tag Accessibility Attributes dialog box, the Label field associates a textual label with the form object you are inserting. It does this by inserting `<label>...</label>` tags in your form. This label is visible in the browser window. By using the `<label>` tag, you can explicitly associate the text with a particular control. You have two options for achieving this association:

✦ **Wrap with Label Tag:** This option encloses the form element within the `<label>...</label>` pair. Here's an example of its construct:

```
<label>First Name
  <input type="text" name="mytextfield">
</label>
```

✦ **Attach Label Tag Using** `for` **Attribute:** This option adds an attribute to the `<label>` tag that matches the `id` attribute of the form element. Choose this option, for example, when you use a table to align form elements, and the label and control appear in separate table cells. Here's an example that illustrates the use of the `for` attribute:

```
<label for="mytextfield">First Name</label>
  <input type="text" name="textfield2" id="mytextfield">
```

Note You can also insert a `<label>...</label>` pair by clicking the Label button in the Forms category of the Insert bar. This button is best used in Code view.

Although you may visually achieve the same effect by simply typing the text in the Document window, a nonvisual browser cannot associate plain text with any particular object. This effect is also what happens if you choose the No Label Tag option.

The final option you have when inserting a label is whether it should appear before or after the form element you are inserting.

In the AccessKey field of the Input Tag Accessibility Attributes dialog box, type a single letter that serves as a shortcut to the form element. When users press the shortcut key for a given control, focus goes to that form element. Depending on their browsers and operating systems, users may have to hold down an additional key, referred to as a modifier key, such as Ctrl, Alt, or Command, for the shortcut to work.

The final control in the Input Tag Accessibility Attributes dialog box is the Tab Index. It adds the `tabindex` attribute to the `<input>` HTML tag. In this field, type a positive number indicating the order in which the control should receive focus when the user is tabbing through the form. Lower numbers receive focus first in the tabbing order; if items have the same number, the form element that appears first in the page receives focus first. Form elements with a `tabindex` of zero or with no `tabindex` specified appear last in the tab order.

Styling Forms with CSS

In many ways, forms are the real workhorses of the Web — but that doesn't mean they have to be plain. Until CSS use became prevalent, little could be done to alter the way forms and form elements looked on the Web. Standardizing text field sizes between PC and Macintosh was a problem because the different operating systems interpreted character width differently; moreover, the field sizes may vary from browser to browser.

CSS gives the form designer much more flexibility, both to integrate and isolate the form and form elements. Text fields, for example, can take on a shade of a site's background color or adopt the same typeface used on the page. Similarly, you can draw attention to the form itself by giving it a contrasting background; this enables you to format lengthy drop-down lists for easy reading.

Cross-Reference If you're not familiar with CSS in general or, specifically, how it is applied in Dreamweaver, see Chapter 7.

Encompassing the Form

The `<form>` tag is a containing element that, like the `<div>` tag, is not rendered by default. Both tags, in fact, can be styled with CSS — you can even position a form on the page via CSS declarations. Browser support varies for some of the more esoteric CSS properties applied to the form tag, but more common attributes such as background color and border are rendered properly in most cases. Best of all, if CSS does not support certain attributes, these attributes are just ignored and the form renders plainly.

Frequently, a Web page only contains a single form. In these situations, styling the `<form>` tag itself will have the desired results. For example, this CSS rule gives the entire form a bright orange background and a blue border:

```
form {
    background: #FF9900;
    border: thin solid #0000FF;
    padding: 10px;
}
```

Padding is added to move the form elements in from the edges, as shown in Figure 14-14.

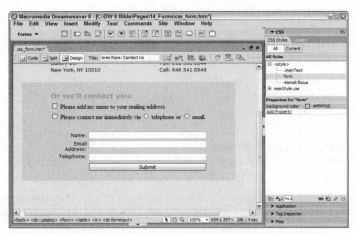

Figure 14-14: Apply CSS coloring to the form to make it stand out on the page.

Should your page contain more than one form and you want to style each one differently, create a CSS ID selector for each form. In this situation, choose the Advanced selector in the New CSS Rule dialog box and enter a unique ID—such as form#topform or form#bottomform—in the Selector field. Also set the ID of the form tag when using this method.

Altering Input Fields

One way in which the `<form>` and `<div>` tags differ in regard to CSS is in the matter of inheritance. Elements within a form do not inherit the CSS properties of the form, but elements within a `<div>` tag do inherit the div's CSS attributes. You must, therefore, take another route for styling all the text fields in a given form. The best way to affect multiple form elements all at once is to style the `<input>` tag. You may recall that the `<input>` tag is used to create text fields, radio buttons, checkboxes, and Submit buttons.

For example, this CSS rule gives all the input elements a uniform background color as well as a specific color, font, and size for the text fields:

```
input {
    background-color: #F5F5F5;
    color: #660099;
    font: 10px Verdana, Arial, Helvetica, sans-serif;
}
```

CSS styles the text fields for initial text as well as text entered by the user, as shown in Figure 14-15.

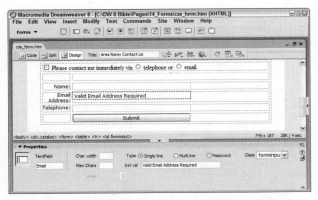

Figure 14-15: Keep the text in your text fields looking like the rest of your page through CSS styling of the input tag.

Tip   Remember that a multiline text field is really a different tag—textarea—than the single-line text field. You have to create a CSS rule for both input and textarea tags.

One of the best uses for CSS and text fields is setting the width. This method is far more flexible and responsive than using the Char Width field on the Property inspector for each individual text field. It is best to set the width on a CSS class rather than alter it directly in the CSS rule for the input tag. Why? The width setting not only affects all the single-line text fields, but it also alters checkboxes and radio buttons—which are also input tags. After the CSS rule is defined, set the class of a selected text field from the Property inspector.

Distinguishing Lists and Menus

The select list/menu object is composed of two tags: `<select>` and `<option>`. The `<select>` tag is the overall container for the list items; use `<select>` to style the width, typeface, and font size of all drop-down lists on the page uniformly. Individual list items can be styled by setting a class on the separate option tags. Although this operation must be performed by hand and is somewhat tedious, it does open the door to many possibilities.

If you have a very long drop-down list that includes a wide-range of items organized by category, with judicious CSS styling, main category headings can be in one color and subitems in another, as shown in Figure 14-16.

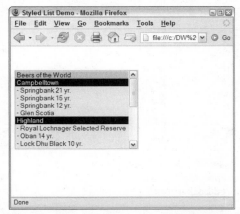

Figure 14-16: CSS classes for menu items must be applied by hand to separate `<option>` tags.

Changing Labels and Legends

A form is more than a collection of text fields and checkboxes; labels play an equally important role in form organization and usability. Form labels are often applied in one of two ways. The standard technique is to place most of the labels in a single column of a table, with the form elements in another. Designers are also increasingly using the `<label>` tag as a means of enhancing accessibility. A Dreamweaver CSS methodology is available for whichever route you take when labeling your forms.

In a situation where all the labels are arranged in a table column, it's best to create a CSS class for your labels and apply it to the `<td>` tags. The most efficient way to do this is to first select the column containing the labels and then choose the desired class from the Style list on the Property inspector. Dreamweaver applies the selected class to each of the `<td>` cells in the column.

If your layout uses `<label>` tags, CSS control is even easier. Add a specific CSS style for the `<label>` tag to create a uniform appearance for all your labels. Note that you may still need to adjust the dimensions of the label column separately because setting the width in CSS for the `<label>` tag has no effect.

Two other form-related tags — `<fieldset>` and `<legend>` — are available for CSS styling. As described earlier in this chapter in the sidebar "Grouping Form Controls," the two are used together to visually associate related form elements. Style the `<fieldset>` tag to alter the outlining border or add padding from the edge of the border. Change the `<legend>` style when you want to give it a separate background color and/or border, as shown in Figure 14-17.

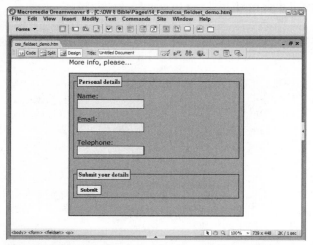

Figure 14-17: Style the `<fieldset>` and `<legend>` tags to really make them stand out from a form with a colored background.

Highlighting Focus

Want to spotlight the interactivity of a form? CSS includes a pseudo-element selector (so called because it is valid only when an element is in a particular state) that takes effect when a form element is selected. The CSS selector is `:focus` and it works with `<input>`, `<select>`, and `<textarea>` tags.

To create a `:focus` selector, follow these steps:

1. Select New CSS Rule from the CSS Styles panel.

2. In the New CSS Rule dialog box, select the Advanced selector option.

3. Enter the name of the tag you want to affect followed by `:focus` in the Selector field. For example, if you wanted to alter all the text fields, radio buttons, checkboxes, and buttons when they receive focus, enter `input:focus`.

4. Click OK to close the New CSS Rule dialog and open the CSS Rule Definition dialog.

5. Choose the desired styles from the various categories and click OK when you're finished.

Preview the page in a compatible browser such as Mozilla Firefox, Netscape 6 or better, Safari, and so on to experience the CSS changes (see Figure 14-18).

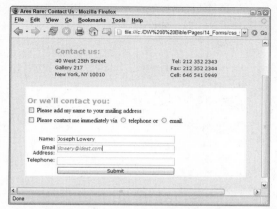

Figure 14-18: Text in a selected field is shown in bright red and bold, thanks to the :focus selector.

Caution Unfortunately, the :focus selector is not supported in any version of Internet Explorer, as of this writing. You can, however, simulate the effect by triggering JavaScript functions with the onFocus() and onBlur() events that manipulate the class attributes.

Summary

HTML forms provide a basic line of communication from Web page visitor to Web site applications. With Dreamweaver, you can enter and modify most varieties of form inputs, including text fields and checkboxes. When adding forms to your Web pages, keep these points in mind:

✦ For the most part, a complete form requires two working parts: the form object inserted in your Web page and a CGI program stored on your Web server.

✦ To avoid using a server-side script, you can use a mailto address, rather than a URL pointing to a program in a form's action attribute. However, you still have to parse the form reply to convert it to a usable format.

✦ The basic types of form input are text fields, text areas, radio buttons, checkboxes, drop-down menus, and scrolling lists.

✦ Dreamweaver includes a Jump Menu object, which uses a drop-down list as a navigational system.

✦ After a user completes a form, it has to be sent to the server-side application, usually through a Submit button on the form. Dreamweaver also supports Reset and user-definable Command buttons.

✦ You can gain a lot more control of how your form integrates into your Web page by applying CSS styles to the form elements — including the form itself.

In the next chapter, you learn how to use Dreamweaver to create bulleted and numbered lists.

✦   ✦   ✦

Creating Lists

Lists serve several different functions in all publications, including Web pages. A bulleted list can itemize a topic's points or catalog the properties of an object. A numbered list is helpful for giving step-by-step instructions. From a page designer's point of view, a list can break up the page and simultaneously draw the viewer's eye to key details.

Lists are an important alternative to the basic textual tools of paragraphs and headings. In this chapter, you study Dreamweaver's tools for designing and working with each of the three basic types of lists available in HTML:

✦ Unordered lists

✦ Ordered lists

✦ Definition lists

The various list types can also be combined to create outlines. Dreamweaver supplies a straightforward method for building these nested lists.

Creating Unordered (Bulleted) Lists

What word processing programs and layout artists refer to as *bulleted lists* are known in HTML as *unordered lists*. An unordered list is used when the sequence of the listed items is unimportant, as in a recipe's list of ingredients. Each unordered list item is set off by a leading character, and the remainder of the line is indented. By default, the leading character is the *bullet*, a small, filled-in circle; however, you can create a custom bullet through Cascading Style Sheets.

You can either create the unordered list from scratch or convert existing text into the bulleted format. To begin an unordered list from scratch, position the cursor where you want to start the list. Then click the Unordered List button, supplied conveniently on the Text Property inspector, or use the Text ⇨ List ⇨ Unordered List command. You can also click the Unordered List button in the Text category of the Insert bar. Figure 15-1 shows an unordered list and the associated Text Property inspector.

If you are changing existing text into a list, select the paragraphs first and then use the menu command or the Unordered List button on the Property inspector or Insert bar.

Dreamweaver creates one list item for every paragraph. As you can see from Figure 15-1, list items are generally rendered closer together than regular paragraphs. A list, unlike block elements such as paragraphs or headings, is not formatted with additional space above and below each line.

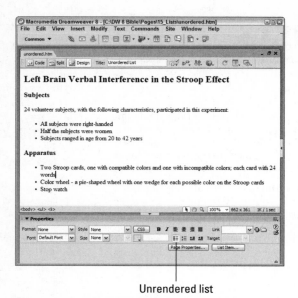

Unrendered list

Figure 15-1: An itemized list that doesn't need to be in any specific order is perfect for formatting as an unordered list.

Caution   In Dreamweaver, the word *paragraph* is used literally to mean any text designated with a paragraph tag. Certainly, you can apply a heading format to an HTML list, but you probably won't like the results: The heading format reinserts that additional space below and above each list item — the ones generally not used by the list format. If you want your list items to appear larger, change the font size through Cascading Style Sheets, the Property inspector, or with Text ⇨ Size Change.

Editing Unordered Lists

After a series of paragraphs is formatted as an unordered list, you can easily add additional bulleted items. The basic editing techniques are the same for all types of lists:

✦ To continue adding items at the end of a list, simply press Enter (Return) to create each new list item. Another bullet is inserted, as long as the preceding item is not empty.

✦ To insert an item within an unordered list, place your cursor at the end of the item above the desired position for the added item and press Enter (Return).

✦ List items can be copied or cut and pasted to a different place on the list. When selecting a list item, use the Tag Selector in the status bar to be sure you select the tags enclosing the list item, not just the list item text. Position your cursor at the start of the list item that will follow the pasted entry and choose Edit ⇨ Paste.

✦ To end a bulleted list, you can press Enter (Return) twice or deselect the Unordered List button on the Text Property inspector.

List Tags

You may occasionally need to tweak your list code by hand. Two HTML tags are used in creating an unordered list. The first is the outer tag, which defines the type of list; the second is the item delimiter. Unordered lists are designated with the `<ul>...</ul>` tag pair, and the delimiter is the `<li>...</li>` pair. The unordered list code in the Code inspector looks like the following:

```
<ul>
   <li>All subjects were right-handed</li>
   <li>Half the subjects were women</li>
   <li>Subjects ranged in age from 20 to 42 years</li>
</ul>
```

Tip   If you are working in Code view, you can click the List Item button in the Text category of the Insert bar to insert a `<li>...</li>` pair. Insert the tags `<ul>...</ul>` by clicking the Unordered List button on the Insert bar.

If a list item is too long to fit in a single line, the browser indents the text that wraps. By inserting a line break code, you can emulate this behavior even when you're working with lines that aren't long enough to need wrapping. To insert a line break, click the Line Break button in the Characters category of the Insert bar or choose Insert ➪ HTML ➪ Special Characters ➪ Line Break. Alternatively, use the key combination Shift+Enter (Shift+Return), or just type `<br>` in your code. Figure 15-2 shows examples of both approaches: inserted line breaks to force wrapping and the long paragraph that wraps naturally.

Note   If you are creating an XHTML document, you must use `<br />` instead of `<br>`. When you press Shift+Enter (Shift+Return), Dreamweaver automatically determines the correct format to use for the break tag based on the `DOCTYPE` statement, visible at the top of the document in Code view.

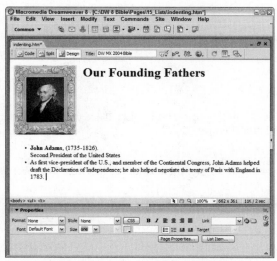

Figure 15-2: A list is indented if the text wraps around the screen or if you insert a line break.

Adding Unordered Lists

In this section, you practice adding an unordered list to a Web page.

1. In the Files panel, switch to the Dreamweaver Bible working site previously created.

2. Go to Techniques\15_Lists and open the file `lists_start.htm`.

3. Place your cursor below the paragraph following the Relative Realty Benefits heading.

4. In the Property inspector, click Unordered List.

   A bullet symbol appears, indicating the first list item.

5. Enter the following text: **Local realtor team**

6. Press Enter (Return) and enter the next bullet point: **Highly qualified personnel**

7. Press Enter (Return) and enter the next bullet point: **A-Z assistance**

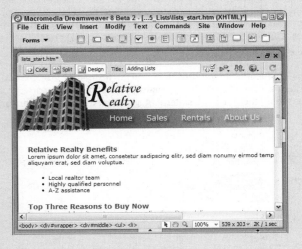

8. You can nest one unordered list inside another to create sublists. Place your cursor after the second bullet point and press Enter (Return).

9. In the Property inspector, click Text Indent.

10. You can also create a sublist by pressing Tab. Enter the text for the first item in sublist: **#1 Local Firm**

11. Press Enter (Return) and enter the next bullet point: **Top Ten state sales agents**

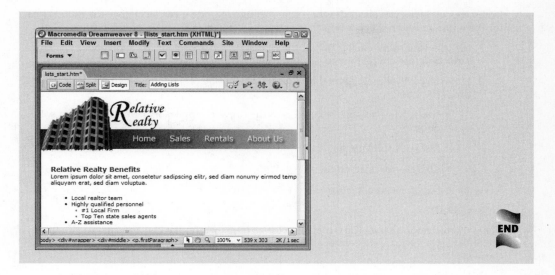

Using Other Bullet Symbols

Most browsers depict the default bullet as a small filled-in circle. In HTML, you can use any of three Dreamweaver-supported strategies to change the shape of your bullets. Your choices are to

✦ Add an attribute to the `<ul>` or `<li>` tag to specify one of several other bullet shapes.

✦ Simulate an unordered list by using an image of the bullet.

✦ Use Cascading Style Sheets to define a new bullet shape.

In HTML, the `<ul>` and `<li>` tags can include a `type` attribute that defines the shape of the bullet. Although the `type` attribute doesn't include a wide range of different bullet symbols, you have a few options. Most browsers recognize three bullet styles: bullet (the default), circle, and square. You can apply the style to the entire unordered list or to one list item at a time.

Caution

In the HTML 4.0 specification, the `type` attribute is *deprecated*. This means that although still supported by current browsers, the attribute has been replaced by a newer or more desirable method of achieving the same thing. In this case, the `type` attribute has been replaced by newer Cascading Style Sheet attributes. Because the `type` attribute is deprecated, it may not be supported at all in future versions of HTML. On a practical level, however, major browsers tend to continue supporting deprecated tags and elements so that older Web pages continue to display correctly. According to the HTML specification, if a browser stops supporting the attribute, the browser should simply ignore the attribute when encountered in a page.

Dreamweaver gives you access to the `type` attribute in Code view. To change the bullet style for the entire unordered list, follow these steps:

1. In Code view, right-click (Control+click) the `<ul>` tag for your list and choose Edit Tag `<ul>` from the context menu.

2. In the Tag Editor dialog box that appears, select one of the following from the Type drop-down list:

   • [Default] — No style is listed, and the browser applies its default, usually a solid circle

   • Disc — A solid circle

   • Circle — An open circle

   • Square — A solid square

3. Click OK.

The previous steps change the bullet style for all items within the list. You can also change the bullet style for just one item in a list, although it would be unusual to do so. Just follow these steps:

1. In Code view, right-click (Control+click) the `<li>` tag for the list item you want to change and choose Edit Tag `<li>` from the context menu.

2. In the Tag Editor dialog box that appears, make sure the Unordered List option is selected. This setting ensures that the correct list of options appears in the Type drop-down list.

3. In the Type drop-down list, select one of the bullet options (described in the preceding steps).

Note   Dreamweaver also enables you to change the `type` attribute for one list item or for an entire list by using the List Properties dialog box. To access this dialog box, click any single item in your list, and on the Properties inspector, click the List Item button. You can change the shape of the bullet for the entire list by selecting an option in the Style list; you change the bullet for just the selected item using the New Style list. Notice that only the Bullet and Square are available in the List Properties dialog box; the Circle option is not included.

A second method of changing the bullet symbol involves the time-tested solution of substituting a graphic for the bullet. Just as it does with graphical horizontal rules, the Web offers a substantial clip art collection of bullets. Using this method, you don't format your list as an unordered list at all; instead, you format your text in plain paragraphs or tables and then insert a graphic for each bullet. You can, however, have the best of both worlds by using CSS to change the bullet image, as described in the following section.

Styling Lists with CSS

The newer technique for installing bullet styles uses style sheets. Cascading Style Sheets (CSS) can switch a list or list item's bullet style to the same shapes that the `<ul>` and `<li>` `type` attribute can; but with a style sheet, you can perform one additional task. You can assign the bullet style type to a specific file — in other words, you can customize your bullet image. The minor drawback to using this technique is that the list aspect of style sheets is not supported by early browsers, such as Internet Explorer versions 3.x and earlier and Netscape versions 4.7 or earlier. Safari and other standards-compliant browsers support this feature as well.

Cross-Reference If you're totally unfamiliar with CSS, you'll be happy to know that Cascading Style Sheets are covered in depth in Chapter 7.

Here is a brief version of the steps for using a style sheet to assign a new bullet symbol:

1. Choose Window ⇨ CSS Styles or press Shift+F11.

2. In the CSS Styles panel, click the New CSS Rule button.

3. In the New CSS Rule dialog box, click the Tag radio button to redefine the HTML tag.

4. From the option list, select the ul tag.

5. Select a Define In option to determine whether the style definition is saved in the current document or in a separate style sheet file. Refer to Chapter 7 for more information about making this decision.

6. Click OK.

7. In the CCS Style Definition dialog box that appears, select List in the Category list (see Figure 15-3).

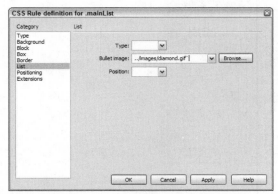

Figure 15-3: You can use Cascading Style Sheets to specify a bullet image for your Web page.

8. Find your graphics file by clicking the Browse button next to the Bullet Image text box. Click OK when you're finished.

Mastering Ordered (Numbered) Lists

Unlike a bulleted list, in which sequence is not vital, order is important in the ordered (or numbered) list. The major advantage of an ordered list is the automatic generation of list item numbers and automatic renumbering when you're editing. If you've ever had to renumber a legal document because paragraph 14.b became paragraph 2.a, you recognize the timesaving benefits of this feature.

Ordered lists offer a slightly wider variety of built-in styles than unordered lists, but you cannot customize the leading character further. For instance, you cannot surround a character with parentheses or offset it with a dash. Once again, the browser is the final arbiter of how your list is viewed.

Many of the same techniques used with unordered lists work with ordered lists. To start a new numbered list in Dreamweaver, place your cursor where you want the new list to begin. Then, in the Text Property inspector, click the Ordered List button or choose Text ➪ List ➪ Ordered List. You can also click the Ordered List button in the Text category of the Insert bar.

As with unordered lists, you can also convert existing paragraphs into a numbered list. First, select your text; then click the Ordered List button on the Property inspector or choose Text ➪ List ➪ Ordered List.

The default numbering system is Arabic numerals: 1, 2, 3, and so forth (see Figure 15-4). In a following section, you learn how to alter this default to use other numbering formats or to create an alphabetic list.

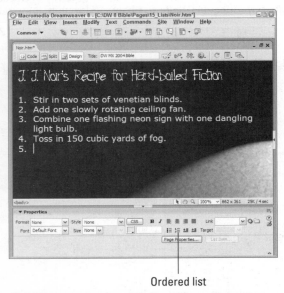

Ordered list

Figure 15-4: An ordered list is used on this page to create a numbered sequence.

Editing Ordered Lists

The HTML code for an ordered list is `<ol>`. Both `<ol>` and `<ul>` use the list item tag, `<li>`, to mark individual entries, and Dreamweaver handles the formatting identically:

```
<ol>
  <li>Stir in two sets of Venetian blinds.</li>
  <li>Add one slowly rotating ceiling fan.</li>
  <li>Combine one flashing neon sign with one dangling light bulb.</li>
  <li>Toss in 150 cubic yards of fog.</li>
  <li></li>
</ol>
```

The empty list item pair, `<li>...</li>`, is displayed on the page as the next number in sequence.

Modifications to an ordered list are handled in the same manner as those to an unordered list. The results are far more dramatic, however.

✦ To continue adding to the sequence of numbers, position your cursor at the end of what is currently the last item and press Enter (Return). The next number in sequence is generated, and any styles in use (such as font size or name) are carried over.

✦ To insert a new item within the list, put your cursor at the end of the item you want to precede the new item and press Enter (Return). Dreamweaver inserts a new number in sequence and automatically renumbers the following numbers.

✦ To rearrange a numbered list, highlight the entire list item you want to move. Using the drag-and-drop method, release the mouse when your cursor is in front of the item immediately below the new location for the item you are moving. Again, Dreamweaver automatically renumbers the list items in order.

✦ To end an item in a numbered list, press Enter (Return) twice, or press Enter (Return) and deselect the Ordered List button on the Text Property inspector.

Inserting Ordered Lists

Ordered lists are inserted in a similar fashion to unordered ones, but have the advantage of automatically being renumbered when moved.

1. In the Files panel, re-open the `lists_start.htm` file.

2. Place your cursor below the paragraph following the Top Three Reasons to Buy Now heading.

3. In the Property inspector, click Ordered List.

   The number 1 appears, indicating the first list item.

4. Enter the following text: **Lower interest rates**

5. Press Enter (Return) and enter the next item: **Best investment going**

6. Press Enter (Return) and enter the final item: **Owning your home means security**

7. You can re-order a numbered list easily. With your cursor still in the final list item, choose the `<li>` tag from the Tag Selector.

8. Drag the selected list item and drop it in front of the first list item.

   The items are automatically renumbered.

Continued

Continued

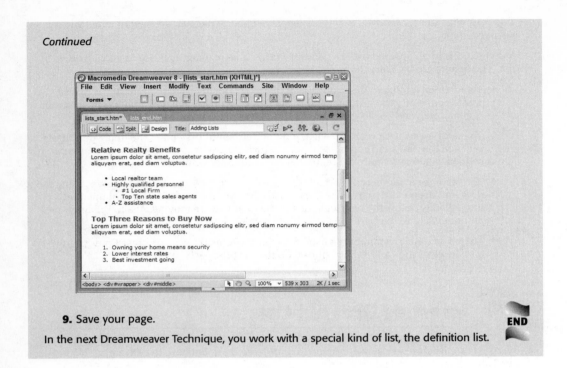

9. Save your page.

In the next Dreamweaver Technique, you work with a special kind of list, the definition list.

END

Using Other Numbering Styles

You can apply these different numbering styles to your numbered lists:

✦ Arabic Numerals — 1, 2, 3, and so forth (this is the default style)

✦ Roman Small — i, ii, iii, and so forth

✦ Roman Large — I, II, III, and so forth

✦ Alphabet Small — a, b, c, and so forth

✦ Alphabet Large — A, B, C, and so forth

You can restyle your entire list all at once, or you can just change a single list item. To change the style of the entire ordered list, follow these steps:

1. Position your cursor anywhere in an existing list.

2. If necessary, click the expander arrow on the Text Property inspector to display the additional options. Click the List Item button. The List Properties dialog box opens with Numbered List displayed as the List Type, as shown in Figure 15-5.

Figure 15-5: Use the List Properties dialog box to alter the numbering style in an ordered list.

3. Open the drop-down list of Style options and choose any of the numbering types.

4. Click OK.

Caution   If the List Item button is inactive in your Text Property inspector, make sure that you have only one list item selected. Selecting more than one list item deactivates the List Item button.

As with unordered lists, when you modify the style of one ordered list item, all the other items in the same list adopt that style. To alter the style of a single item, follow these steps:

1. Select the item you want to change.

2. In the expanded portion of the Text Property inspector, click the List Item button.

3. From the List Item section of the List Properties dialog box, open the New Style list of options.

4. Select one of the numbering options.

Although you can't automatically generate an outline with a different numbering system for each level, you can simulate this kind of outline with nested lists. See "Using Nested Lists" later in this chapter.

Creating Navigation Buttons from Lists

CSS has made many innovations possible in Web design. One of them is styled navigation buttons that look and act like sliced-bitmapped graphics with JavaScript rollover capability. CSS navigation bars, however, take up much less bandwidth, are instantly accessible, and are far easier to modify than bitmapped graphics. Although the same technique discussed in this section could be applied to a series of paragraph tags, the unordered list is a more natural fit. Of course, you don't want the bulleted list to look like a bulleted list, and CSS makes such a transformation possible with ease.

Here's an overview of the process:

1. Create background graphics for both the standard and mouse-over views.

2. Put a list of links in a `<div>` tag. Each link serves as a separate button.

3. Build the CSS file that combines the background graphics and the links.

4. Apply the appropriate CSS ID to the `<div>` tag—and let CSS do the rest.

In addition to standard rollover behavior, this technique makes it possible to style an individual list item as the current page indicator, as shown in Figure 15-6.

Figure 15-6: Turn a bulleted list into a navbar with CSS and just two low-bandwidth images.

Step 1: Preparing Background Graphics

A little bit of prep work is needed before you can begin applying CSS to your list. The first step is to use a graphics program, such as Fireworks 8, to make the button images. Two separate but similar images are needed: one for the initial button look and another for the rollover view.

Here's the process I used to create my graphic images with Fireworks:

1. In Fireworks, create a new document larger than you expect your button to be. My initial document was 300 x 200. You can, of course, create a document the same size as your button image, but Fireworks' Fit Canvas feature makes trimming the excess canvas area a one-click operation.

2. Using the Rectangle tool, draw an object slightly larger than the expected width and height of a single button; my image is 150 pixels wide by 50 pixels high. The image is to be used in the background of your navigation element and should be large enough so that it does not tile.

3. Style your rectangle however you choose. I used an orange solid fill (#FF9900) and applied a Vein texture at 80%. It's a good idea to create your graphics with the dual states in mind. I'll be able to create a darker version of my image for the rollover just by altering the texture percentage.

4. Choose Fit to Canvas to trim the excess canvas from your background image.

5. Export in either JPG or GIF format. This serves as the background for my initial button (also referred to as mouse-out), so I've named this image `listnav_out.jpg` and stored it in my Dreamweaver site.

6. Alter the graphic to represent the rollover state. I simply lowered the Vein texture setting to 60%, which darkens the image significantly. Figure 15-7 shows a comparison between the two figures.

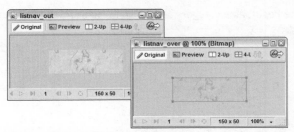

Figure 15-7: These two images were exported from the same source file; the only difference is the texture setting.

7. Export the image with an appropriate name; my second image is called `listnav_over.jpg`.

Be sure to save your source file so that you can easily make alterations as needed. With your images created, you're ready to move into Dreamweaver to create the list and encompassing `<div>` tag.

Step 2: Creating the List and Containing `<div>`

Next, create the basic HTML and text elements for the CSS navigation bar. Because one of the elements you need is an absolutely positioned `<div>` tag, you can set up your CSS file and enter the first of the CSS definitions.

Tip   It's not absolutely necessary for you to create the CSS before you insert the tags, but because Dreamweaver renders each new style as it is applied, this approach gives you a better sense of what the CSS styles are doing.

To set up the CSS file with the first of the CSS definitions, follow these steps:

1. Create a new CSS file by choosing File ➪ New and selecting CSS from the General category. I named my file `navlist.css`.

2. Open the HTML or dynamic page to which you want to add the navigation.

3. From the CSS Styles panel, select Attach Style Sheet; when the dialog opens, import your previously created style sheet. Click OK to close the dialog when you're done.

4. Now define the first of your CSS, which positions and gives the basic shape to the navigation bar. From the CSS Styles panel, select New CSS Rule.

5. In the New CSS Rule dialog box, select Advanced and enter the ID for the element to contain the list navigation. I called mine `#listnav`. You'll recall that the opening hash mark designates an ID selector in CSS.

6. Click OK to open the CSS Rule Definition dialog and switch to the Position category.

7. Set these values in the Positioning category, as shown in Figure 15-8:

Type	Absolute
Width	151 pixels
Top	50 pixels
Left	25 pixels

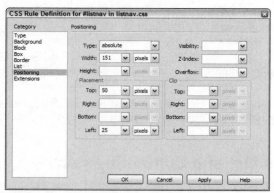

Figure 15-8: Determine where the navigation element is to appear by setting values in the Positioning category.

8. When you're finished, click OK to close the CSS Rule definition dialog. The next step combines two actions into one: inserting a `<div>` tag and assigning the CSS style you just created.

9. From the Layout category of the Insert bar, select Insert Div Tag.

10. In the dialog box, choose the just-defined CSS style from the ID list. When you click OK to close, your `<div>` is added to the page with some placeholder text. Now you're ready to add your list items.

11. Delete the placeholder text in the `<div>` and, from the Property inspector, select Unordered List.

12. Enter the text for your button labels, one button per bullet. I've got four list items:

- Home
- Products
- Services
- About

13. Be sure to avoid placing any unnecessary paragraph returns following the list. Only the list items you want to appear as buttons should be in the `<div>` tag.

14. Add a link to each list item by selecting the text and entering a filename in the Link field of the Property inspector. Alternatively, you can click the folder icon and choose a file from the Select File dialog.

At this point, you have a plain bullet list of links in an absolutely positioned `<div>` tag on your page, as shown in Figure 15-9. Now you're ready to start styling!

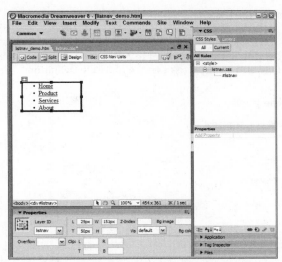

Figure 15-9: Making each list item a link is a major step toward converting them into CSS buttons.

Step 3: Building the CSS Styles

The definition of the CSS styles is at the heart of this technique. In all, six different styles are needed:

- ✦ `#listnav ul` — Defines the font face and size for all the list items, removes the standard bullet, and clears the margin and padding.

- ✦ `#listnav li` — Ensures a bottom margin is present to separate each list item.

- ✦ `#listnav a` — Extends the active area of the link to the block-level and adds a background image, width, and border.

- ✦ `#listnav a:link`, `#listnav a:visited` — Defines the look of the text when the buttons are in their standard and already-visited states, giving a specific color and removing the underline from the link.

- ✦ `#listnav a:hover` — Swaps the background image and alters the text color in the rollover state.

- ✦ `#sellistnav a:link`, `#sellistnav a:visited`, `#sellist a:hover` — Sets the look and feel of the selected button, indicating the current page in a navigation bar.

Because I've already laid the foundation with a list of links inside a `<div>` with a defined CSS ID, the changes are immediately evident in Dreamweaver.

The process is the same for defining each CSS rule. Each rule is named with the Advanced selector type chosen in the New CSS Rule dialog box, which enables the user to enter any type of selector.

To get started with #listnav ul, follow these steps:

1. From the CSS Styles panel, select New CSS Rule.

2. In the New CSS Rule dialog box, with Selector Type set to Advanced, enter #listnav ul in the Selector field and click OK to open the CSS Rule Definition dialog.

3. Set these values in the Type category:

Font	Verdana, Ariel, Helvetica, sans serif
Size	14 pixels
Weight	Bold

4. Set these values in the Box category:

Margin	0 pixels (for all)
Padding	0 pixels (for all)

5. Set these values in the Border category:

Style	Solid (for all)
Width	1 pixel (for all)
Color	#990000 (for all)

6. Set this value in the List category:

Type	None

7. When you're finished, click OK to close the CSS Rule definition dialog.

You should notice an immediate difference in Dreamweaver. The bulleted list is already starting to look much more button-like (see Figure 15-10).

The next style, #listnav li, affects each list item individually. Follow these steps:

1. From the CSS Styles panel, select New CSS Rule.

2. In the New CSS Rule dialog box, with Selector Type set to Advanced, enter #listnav li in the Selector field and click OK to open the CSS Rule Definition dialog.

3. Set this value in the Box category:

Margin-Bottom	2 pixels

   The Margin-Bottom value determines the distance between each of the navigation buttons; increase the value to make the buttons farther apart.

4. When you're finished, click OK to close the CSS Rule definition dialog.

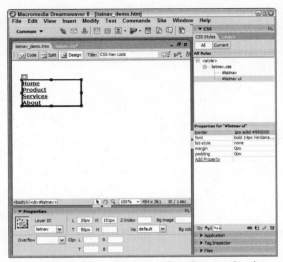

Figure 15-10: After you define the #listnav ul style, the bullets disappear from the unordered list.

Now, to build up the #listnav a style, follow these steps:

1. From the CSS Styles panel, select New CSS Rule.

2. In the New CSS Rule dialog box, with Selector Type set to Advanced, enter #listnav a in the Selector field and click OK to open the CSS Rule Definition dialog.

3. In the Background category, click Browse and choose the exported image to represent the mouse-out. For my navigation bar, the file is listnav_out.jpg.

4. Set this value in the Block category:

   Display   Block

5. Set these values in the Box category:

   Width   140 pixels

   Padding-Top   2 pixels

   Padding-Right   2 pixels

   Padding-Bottom   2 pixels

   Padding-Left   5 pixels

   These values determine the width of the block and set the position of the text within it.

6. Set these values in the Border category:

   Style   Solid (for all)

   Width   1 pixel (for all)

   Color   #CC9900 (for all)

7. When you're finished, click OK to close the CSS Rule definition dialog.

With the background image in place, the buttons are really beginning to take shape (see Figure 15-11).

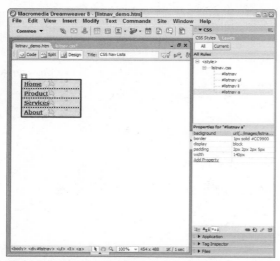

Figure 15-11: Alter the Padding-Left setting to move the text away from the left edge of the background image.

Next, to define two CSS rules — #listnav a:link and #listnav a:visited — at once, follow these steps:

1. From the CSS Styles panel, select New CSS Rule.

2. In the New CSS Rule dialog box, with Selector Type set to Advanced, enter #listnav a:link, #listnav a:visited in the Selector field and click OK to open the CSS Rule Definition dialog.

3. Set these values in the Type category:

Color	#993300
Decoration	none

   Setting Decoration to none turns off a link's underline.

4. When you're finished, click OK to close the CSS Rule definition dialog.

Next, you want to define the #listnav a:hover style. Follow these steps:

1. From the CSS Styles panel, select New CSS Rule.

2. In the New CSS Rule dialog box, with Selector Type set to Advanced, enter #listnav a:hover in the Selector field and click OK to open the CSS Rule Definition dialog.

3. Set this value in the Type category:

Color	#FFFFFF

4. In the Background category, click Browse and choose the exported image to represent the mouse-out. For my navigation bar, the file is listnav_over.jpg.

5. Set these values in the Border category:

Style	Solid (for all)
Width	1 pixel (for all)
Color	#990000 (for all)

6. When you're finished, click OK to close the CSS Rule definition dialog.

The last style won't appear to have any effect until you preview the page in a browser, as shown in Figure 15-12.

Figure 15-12: The `#listnav a:hover` style governs the rollover appearance.

The final style is applied to whatever link represents the current page. As such, it's an exact duplicate of the style just created for `#listnav a:hover`, which makes it a breeze to create. Follow these steps:

1. In the CSS Styles panel, right-click (Control+click) the `#listnav a:hover` style and choose Duplicate from the context menu.

2. In the Duplicate CSS Rule dialog box, enter `#sellistnav a:link`, `#sellistnav a:visited`, `#sellist a:hover` in the Selector field.

3. When you're finished, click OK to close the dialog.

The style you just created is really the only one that you must apply, and you take care of that last detail in the following section.

Step 4: Applying the CSS

Because of the way the CSS is written—and the fact that the containing `<div>` tag was assigned a CSS class from the beginning—almost all the styles are automatically applied. The only one left is the style that makes the current link appear selected.

To apply the selected link style, follow these steps:

1. Place your cursor in the list item that represents the current page. For demonstration purposes, I'll use Home.

2. In the Tag Selector, right-click (Control+click) the `<li>` tag for the selected item. From the menu that opens, choose Set ID ➪ sellistnav, as shown in Figure 15-13.

Figure 15-13: Changing the ID of a list item's link tag creates a down state.

That's it — your unordered list is now a fully functioning navigation bar. To modify any of the labels on the buttons, just modify the text directly. To add a new button, create a new list item by adding a paragraph return after any existing list item. Your new list item turns into a button the second you add a link to it.

Making Definition Lists

A definition list is another type of list in HTML. Unlike ordered and unordered lists, definition lists don't use leading characters such as bullets or numbers in the list items. Definition lists are commonly used in glossaries or other types of documents in which you have a list of terms followed by descriptions or explanations.

Browsers generally render a definition list with the definition term flush left and the definition data indented, as shown in Figure 15-14. As you can see, no additional styling is added. You can, however, format either the item or the definition with the Text ⇨ Style options or by using Cascading Style Sheets.

To begin your definition list in Dreamweaver, follow these steps:

1. Choose Text ⇨ List ⇨ Definition List or click the Definition List button in the Text category of the Insert bar.

2. Type the definition term and press Enter (Return) when you are finished. Dreamweaver indents the next line.

3. Type the definition data and press Enter (Return) when you are finished.

4. Repeat steps 2 and 3 until you have finished your definition list.

5. Press Enter (Return) twice to stop entering definition list items.

Tip   If you have an extended definition, you may want to format it in more than one paragraph. Because definition lists are formatted with the terms and their definition data in alternating sequence, you have to use the line break tag, `<br>` (or `<br />` for XHTML documents), to create blank space under the definition if you want to separate it into paragraphs. Press Shift+Enter (Shift+Return) or click the Line Break button on the Insert bar to enter one or two `<br>` tags to separate paragraphs with one or two blank lines.

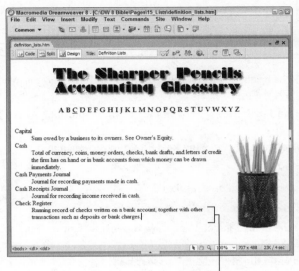

Definition data

Figure 15-14: Definition lists are ideal for glossaries or other situations in which you have a list of terms followed by their definitions.

When you insert a definition list, Dreamweaver denotes it in code using the `<dl>`...`</dl>` tag pair. Definition terms are marked with a `<dt>` tag, and definition data uses the `<dd>` tag. A complete definition list looks like the following in HTML:

```
<dl>
  <dt>Capital</dt>
  <dd>Sum owed by a business to its owners. See Owner's Equity.</dd>
  <dt>Cash</dt>
  <dd>Total of currency, coins, money orders, checks, bank
    drafts, and letters of credit the firm has on hand or in bank
    accounts from which money can be drawn immediately.</dd>
  <dt>Cash Payments Journal</dt>
  <dd>Journal for recording payments made in cash.</dd>
</dl>
```

Tip

You can vary the structure of a definition list from the standard definition term followed by the definition data format, but you have to code this variation by hand. For instance, if you want a series of consecutive terms with no definition in between, you need to insert the `<dt>`...`</dt>` pairs directly in Code view or in the Code inspector. To facilitate the insertion of these tags, you can click the Definition Term and Definition Description buttons in the Text category of the Insert bar to insert the appropriate tags in Code view.

Applying Definition Lists

Although definition lists are not used as frequently as unordered or ordered ones on the Web, they're perfect in specific circumstances.

1. In the Files panel, re-open the file `lists_start.htm` worked on in the previous Dreamweaver Technique.

2. Place your cursor below the paragraph following the Real Estate Terms heading.

3. Select Text ⇨ Lists ⇨ Definition Lists.

   Unlike the other list types, no special indicator is displayed.

4. Enter the following text for the definition term: **adjustment date**

5. Press Enter (Return) and enter the definition data: **The date the interest rate changes on an adjustable-rate mortgage.**

6. Press Enter (Return) again and enter the second term: **assessment**

7. Press Enter (Return) again and enter the second definition: **The placing of a value on property for the purpose of taxation.**

8. Press Enter (Return) again and enter the final term: **assumption**

9. Press Enter (Return) again and enter the final definition: **The term applied when a buyer assumes the seller's mortgage.**

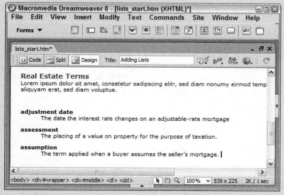

10. Save your page.

Using Nested Lists

You can combine, or nest, lists in almost any fashion. For instance, you can mix an ordered and unordered list to create a numbered list with bulleted points. You can have one numbered list inside another numbered list. You can also start with one numbering style such as Roman Large, switch to another style such as Alphabet Small, and return to Roman Large to continue the sequence (like an outline).

Dreamweaver offers an easy route for making nested lists. The Indent button in the Text Property inspector — when used within a list — automatically creates a nested list. The ordered list in Figure 15-15, for example, has a couple of bulleted points (unordered list items) inserted within it. Notice how the new items are indented one level.

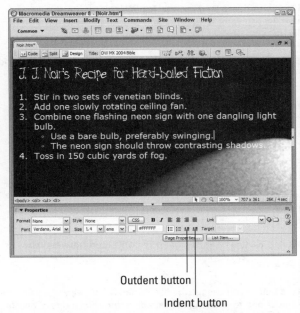

Outdent button

Indent button

Figure 15-15: Dreamweaver automatically generates the code necessary to build nested lists when you use the Indent button on the Text Property inspector.

Follow these steps to create a nested list in Dreamweaver:

1. In an existing list, select the text that you want to indent and reformat with a different style.

2. In the Text Property inspector, click the Indent button. Alternatively, you can choose the Text ⇨ Indent command. Dreamweaver indents the selected text and creates a separate list in the HTML code with the original list's properties.

Note   Nested unordered lists exhibit a cool feature in most browsers—they automatically change the list style for each level. In many browsers, the outermost level is displayed with a bullet, the second level with a circle, and the third level with a square. This feature provides automatic outlining from an unexpected source! For ordered lists, the style of indented items does not change automatically.

3. Go to the List Properties dialog box and select another list type or style, as described in preceding sections.

Caution   You can unnest your list and reverse the effects of the Indent button by clicking the Outdent button in the Text Property inspector or by choosing Text ⇨ Outdent. Be careful, however, when selecting your text for this operation. When you use the mouse to perform a click-and-drag selection, Dreamweaver tends to grab the closing list item tag above your intended selection. A better way to highlight the text in this case is to use the Tag Selector on the status bar. Place the cursor in the indented list you want to outdent and choose the innermost `<ol>` or `<ul>` tag from the Tag Selector.

To see why one list contained inside another list is considered to be *nested*, look at the code created by Dreamweaver for the following list type:

```
<ol>
   <li>Stir in two sets of Venetian blinds.</li>
   <li>Add one slowly rotating ceiling fan.</li>
   <li>Combine one flashing neon sign with one dangling light bulb.
     <ul>
        <li>Use a bare bulb, preferably swinging.</li>
        <li>The neon sign should throw contrasting shadows.</li>
     </ul>
   </li>
   <li>Toss in 150 cubic yards of fog.</li>
</ol>
```

Notice how the unordered tag pair, `<ul>...</ul>`, is completely contained between the ordered list items.

Caution   If you don't indent your list items before you change the list format, Dreamweaver breaks the current list into three separate lists: one for the original list above the selected text, another for the selected text itself, and a third list for the items following the selected text. If you don't want this arrangement, use the Tag Selector to select the entire list you want to indent, and then click the Indent button in the Text Property inspector. Dreamweaver nests the list as described previously.

Accessing Special List Types

Dreamweaver gives you access to a couple of special-use list types: menu lists and directory lists. When the tags for these lists — `<menu>` and `<dir>`, respectively — were included in the HTML 2.0 specification, they were intended to offer several ways to present lists of short items.

Unfortunately, browsers tend to render both tags as unordered lists. You can use Cascading Style Sheets to restyle these built-in tags for use in 4.0 and later browsers.

Note Both the `<menu>` and `<dir>` tags are deprecated in HTML 4.0. Because most browsers format these lists like unordered lists, you should typically just use ordered lists instead of either of these list types. Ordered lists are supported in older browsers and will continue to be supported for the foreseeable future.

Menu Lists

A menu list generally comprises single items with each item on its own individual line. To apply a menu list style, follow these steps:

1. In an existing list, select one item.

2. In the expanded Text Property inspector, click the List Item button.

3. In the List Properties dialog box, open the List Type drop-down list and choose Menu List, as shown in Figure 15-16.

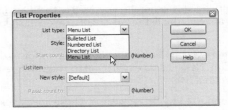

Figure 15-16: Making a menu list.

4. Click OK.

Directory Lists

The directory list was originally intended to provide Web designers with an easy way to create multiple-column lists of short items. Unfortunately, the most current browsers present the directory list's items in one long list, rather than in columns.

The directory list format is applied in the same way as the menu list, and here as well, most browsers render the format as an unordered list with bullets. To create a directory list, follow these steps:

1. In the current list, select one item.

2. In the expanded Text Property inspector, click the List Item button.

3. In the List Properties dialog box, from the List Type drop-down list (refer to Figure 15-16) choose Directory List.

4. Click OK.

Summary

Lists are extremely useful to the Web site designer from the perspectives of both content and layout. Dreamweaver offers point-and-click control over the full range of list capabilities. Keep these points about lists in mind:

✦ The primary list types in HTML are unordered, ordered, and definition lists.

✦ Use unordered lists when you want to itemize your text in no particular order. Dreamweaver can apply any of the built-in styles to unordered lists, or you can customize your own list style through Cascading Style Sheets.

✦ An ordered list is a numbered list. Items are automatically numbered when added, and the entire list is renumbered when items are rearranged or deleted. Dreamweaver gives you access to different styles of numbering — including regular Arabic, Roman numerals, and uppercase or lowercase letters.

✦ CSS styles can significantly adjust the look and feel of your lists, both unordered and ordered, even to the point of converting them into a navigation bar.

✦ Definition lists are designed to display glossaries and other documents in which terms are followed by definitions. A definition list is generally rendered without leading characters such as bullets or numbers; instead, the list terms are displayed flush left, and the definitions are indented.

✦ Dreamweaver gives you the power to nest your lists at the touch of a button — the Indent button on the Text Property inspector. Nested lists enable you to show different outline levels and to mix ordered and unordered lists.

✦ Menu and directory lists are also supported by Dreamweaver. These special lists are rendered in a similar fashion, but they can be adapted through style sheets for extensive use.

In the next chapter, you learn how to create and use image maps in Dreamweaver.

✦　　✦　　✦

Using Frames and Framesets

The first time I fully appreciated the power of frames, I was visiting a site that displayed examples of what the Webmaster considered "bad" Web pages. The site was essentially a jump-station with a series of links. The author used a frameset with three frames: one that ran all the way across the top of the page, displaying a logo and other basic information; one narrow panel on the left with a scrolling set of links to the sites themselves; and the main viewing area, which took up two-thirds of the center screen. Selecting any of the links caused the site to appear in the main viewing frame.

I was astounded when I finally realized that each frame was truly an independent Web page and that you didn't have to use only Web pages on your own site — you could link to any page on the Internet. That was when I also realized the amount of work involved in establishing a frame Web site: Every page displayed on that site used multiple HTML pages.

Be aware that the use of frames is controversial. Designers who are opposed to their use give a number of reasons. One argument is that dealing with frames often confuses users, especially as they navigate through a site. Another reason cited by designers is that search engines have difficulty indexing a frame-based site. Nonetheless, frames are valid HTML, and Dreamweaver does support their use.

Caution   Although the technology enables you to include any page on the Web within your own frameset, Internet etiquette and, in some cases, copyright law dictate that you obtain permission to display another site's pages within your own site and that you clearly credit work that is not your own.

Dreamweaver takes the head-pounding complexity out of coding and managing frames with a point-and-click interface. You get easy access to the commands for modifying the properties of the overall frame structure, as well as each individual frame. This chapter gives you an overview of frames, as well as all the specifics you need for inserting and modifying frames and framesets. Special attention is given to defining the unique look of frames through borders, scroll bars, and margins.

Frames and Framesets: The Basics

It's best to think of frames in two major parts: the frameset and the frames. The frameset is the HTML document that defines the framing structure — the number of individual frames that make up a page, their initial size, and the attributes shared among all the frames. A frameset is never displayed by itself. Frames, on the other hand, are complete HTML documents that can be viewed and edited separately or together in the organization described by the frameset.

A frameset takes the place of the `<body>` tags that contain the content of a Web page in an HTML document. Here's what the HTML for a basic frameset looks like:

```
<frameset rows="50%,50%">
  <frame src="top.html">
  <frame src="bottom.html">
</frameset>
```

Notice that the content of a `<frameset>` tag consists entirely of `<frame>` tags, each one referring to a different Web page. The only other element that can be used inside of a `<frameset>` tag is another `<frameset>` tag.

In Dreamweaver's Code view, you can directly add a `<frameset>`...`</frameset>` tag pair by clicking the Frameset button on the Frames menu of the Insert bar's HTML category. Add a `<frame>` tag in Code view by clicking the Frame button on the Insert bar. Of course, Dreamweaver gives you other ways to create framesets in Design view; see the "Creating a Frameset and Frames" section later in this chapter for more information.

Columns and Rows

Framesets, much like tables, are made up of columns and rows. The columns and rows attributes (`cols` and `rows`) are lists of comma-separated values. The number of values indicates the number of either columns or rows, and the values themselves establish the size of the columns or rows. Thus, a `<frameset>` tag that looks like this

```
<frameset cols="67,355,68">
```

denotes three columns of widths 67, 355, and 68, respectively. And this frameset tag

```
<frameset cols="270,232" rows="384,400">
```

declares that two columns exist with the specified widths (270 and 232), and two rows exist with the specified heights (384 and 400).

Sizing Frames

Column widths and row heights can be set as absolute measurements in pixels or expressed as a percentage of the entire screen. HTML frames also support an attribute that assigns the size relative to the other columns or rows. In other words, the relative attribute (designated with an asterisk) assigns the balance of the remaining available screen space to a column or row. For example, the following frameset

```
<frameset cols="80,*">
```

sets up two frames, one 80 pixels wide and the other as large as the browser window allows. This ensures that the first column is always a constant size — making it perfect for a set of navigational buttons — while the second is as wide as possible.

The relative attribute can also be used proportionally. When preceded by an integer, as in n*, this attribute specifies that the frame is allocated *n* times the space it would have received otherwise. Therefore, frameset code like this

```
<frameset rows="4*,*">
```

ensures that one row is proportionally four times the size of the other.

Creating a Frameset and Frames

Dreamweaver offers you two strategies for creating a frameset. You can explicitly create a frameset file and add content to each of the frames, or you can start with existing content and create a frameset around it. You can achieve the same results using either method. Within Dreamweaver, you can create a frameset in any of the following ways:

✦ Create a new, empty frameset using the File ⇨ New command, and then add content to the frames.

✦ Start with an existing document and use drag-and-drop to draw frames around the document.

✦ Start with an existing document and apply one of several common frameset layouts to it, using menu commands or the Insert bar.

Note　The Insert bar contains two Frames menus — each with different options. The Frames menu found in the Layout category is intended to be used in Design view, and the one in the HTML category is meant to be used in Code view.

Creating a New Frameset File

Most of the framesets employed on the Web today use two or three frames, albeit in different configurations. For example, a common setup is to have one narrow frame spanning the top of the page to hold a banner and some site navigation; below it is a left frame to hold a table of contents or additional navigation, and a large right frame to hold the content of the site (see Figure 16-1).

Dreamweaver gives you quick access to a full array of the most common setups when you create a frameset document from scratch using the File ⇨ New command. Of course, you can customize any of these initial frameset setups by resizing the frames or adding new frames, as described in the sections "Working with the Frameset Property Inspector" and "Adding More Frames," later in this chapter.

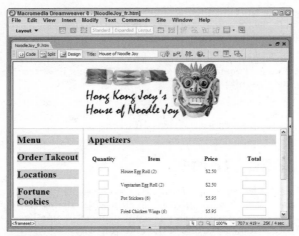

Figure 16-1: The most common designs using framesets call for only two or three frames.

To explicitly create a new frameset file, follow these steps:

1. Choose File ➪ New or press Ctrl+N (Command+N).

2. In the New Document dialog box, choose the Framesets category. A list of possible framesets appears, as shown in Figure 16-2.

3. Select the desired entry from the Framesets list. Selecting an entry displays a description of that frameset.

4. Click Create to create the frameset and display it in the Document window.

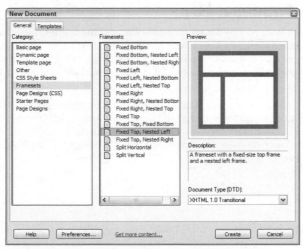

Figure 16-2: In the New Document dialog box, you can choose from many pre-formed framesets.

After you've created a new frameset, you can enter text, images, and other content in each of the frames, as you would for any other HTML document. Alternatively, you can change individual frames to contain previously created documents by clicking in a frame and then choosing the File ➪ Open in Frame command. As explained later in this chapter, you can also add more frames to the frameset, resize the frames, and change other frame properties (such as the capability to scroll).

Note For almost all the frame objects, Dreamweaver creates one or more frames with a set size. Although, by default, the set width or height is 80 pixels, you can easily resize the frame by dragging the frame border. The only framesets that do not have at least one set frame are the Split Horizontal and Split Vertical framesets (for these the two frames are divided equally). Dreamweaver also sets the Scroll option to No for frames with absolute sizes.

Hand-Coding Framesets

If you're a hand-coder, Dreamweaver provides a couple of tools to hasten frameset development. When you are in Code view, the Frames menu (found on the HTML category of the Insert bar) becomes active. Select the Frameset object from this menu to insert a set of `<frameset>` tags. Likewise, choosing the Frame object inserts the `<frame></frame>` tag pair. Code hints are available for all the frame-related attributes.

The other entries in the HTML Frames menu, Floating Frame and No Frames, are covered later in this chapter in the "Investigating Iframes" and "Handling Frameless Browsers" sections, respectively.

Creating a Frameset Visually

Another way of creating a frameset is to start with an existing document and use the mouse to drag and drop the frame borders into position. When you do this, Dreamweaver creates all the new files necessary for your frameset. To create a frameset visually, using the mouse, follow these steps:

1. If necessary, switch to Design view by clicking the Show Design View button on the Document toolbar or by choosing View ➪ Design. (You can also work in the combined Design and Code view, but these steps do not apply to Code view.)

2. Turn on the frame borders in Design view by choosing View ➪ Visual Aids ➪ Frame Borders. A 3-pixel–wide inner border appears along the edges of your Design view. These borders indicate the boundaries of your frames so that you can edit them easily; these borders do not appear when the frameset is viewed in a browser window. See "Working with the Frameset Property Inspector," later in this chapter, to learn how to make the borders visible in a browser.

3. Position the cursor over any of the frame borders. If your pointer is over any side of a frame border, it changes into a two-headed arrow; it changes into a four-headed arrow (or a drag-hand on the Mac) when it's over a corner.

4. Drag the frame border into the middle of the Document window. Figure 16-3 shows a four-frame frameset.

Dreamweaver initially assigns a temporary filename and an absolute pixel value to your HTML frameset code. Both can be modified later if you want.

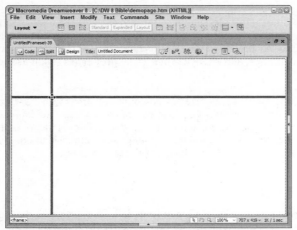

Figure 16-3: After you've enabled the frame borders, you can drag out your frameset structure with the mouse.

Tip   With the other methods of frameset creation, you can initially create a frameset with only two or three frames. Although you can further split these into additional frames, the fastest way to create a frameset with four frames is by Alt+dragging (Option+dragging) the corner of the frame border.

When the frameset is selected, Dreamweaver displays a black, dotted line along all the frame borders and within every frame. You can easily reposition any frameset border by clicking and dragging it. If you just want to move the border, make sure you don't press the Alt (Option) key while dragging the border because that action creates additional frames.

Note   Another method of creating a frameset by splitting the page into frames uses the menus. Open a document that you want to appear in one of the frames. Then choose Modify ⇨ Frameset and, from the submenu, select the direction in which you would like to split the frame: left, right, up, or down. Left or right splits the frame in half vertically; up or down splits it horizontally in half. The direction indicates where the content will go; for example, the Split Frame ⇨ Left command splits the page into "columns" and places the existing document into the left frame.

Creating Framesets Quickly with Frame Objects

Dragging out your frameset in Dreamweaver is a clear-cut method of setting up the various frames. However, despite the ease of this procedure, it can still be a bit of a chore to create even simple framesets by clicking and dragging. To hasten the development workflow, Dreamweaver uses frame objects, which can build a frameset with a single click.

As previously mentioned, most Web sites using frames follow a simple, general pattern. Dreamweaver includes frame objects for the most common frameset configurations. The frame objects are available through the Frames menu found in the Layout category of the Insert bar shown in Figure 16-4. Choose one of the basic designs, and you're ready to tweak the frame sizes and begin filling in the content. This method gives you a great combination: ease of use with design flexibility.

Frames menu

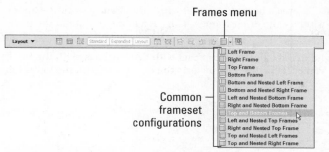

Common frameset configurations

Figure 16-4: The Frames menu of the Insert bar holds the most commonly used frameset configurations.

The frame objects are roughly organized from simplest framesets to most complex. On the Insert bar, notice that each of the icons shows a sample frameset with one blue section. The placement of the color is significant. The blue indicates in which frame the current page will appear when the frameset is constructed. For example, if you begin to construct your main content page, and then decide to turn it into a frameset with separate navigation strip frames to the left and above it, you choose the Top and Nested Left Frame button. Figure 16-5 provides a before-and-after example, first with the preframe content and then with the same content after a Top and Left Bottom Frame object has been applied.

The framesets available from the Frames menu of the Insert bar are as follows:

✦ **Left:** Inserts a blank frame to the left of the current page.

✦ **Right:** Inserts a blank frame to the right of the current page.

✦ **Top:** Inserts a blank frame above the current page.

✦ **Bottom:** Inserts a blank frame below the current page.

✦ **Bottom and Nested Left:** Makes a nested frameset with three frames; the bottom frame spans the width of the other frames. The current page is placed in the upper-right frame.

✦ **Bottom and Nested Right:** Makes a nested frameset with three frames, with the bottom frame spanning the other frames. The current page appears in the upper-left frame.

✦ **Left and Nested Bottom:** Opens a nested frameset with three frames. The left frame spans the other frames, and Dreamweaver places the current page in the upper-right frame.

✦ **Right and Nested Bottom:** Makes a nested frameset with three frames, with the right frame spanning the other frames. The current page is placed in the upper-left frame.

✦ **Top and Bottom:** Inserts a three-frame frameset, with all frames spanning the width of the entire window. Dreamweaver places the current page in the center frame.

✦ **Left and Nested Top:** Creates a nested frameset with three frames, with the left frame spanning the height of the other frames. Dreamweaver puts the current page in the lower-right frame.

✦ **Right and Nested Top:** Inserts a nested frameset with three frames, with the right frame spanning the height of the other frames. The current page is placed in the lower-left frame.

✦ **Top and Nested Left:** Creates a nested frameset with three frames, with the upper frame spanning the width of the other frames. The current page is put in the lower-right frame.

✦ **Top and Nested Right:** Inserts a nested frameset with three frames, with the top frame spanning the other frames. Dreamweaver inserts the current page in the lower-left frame.

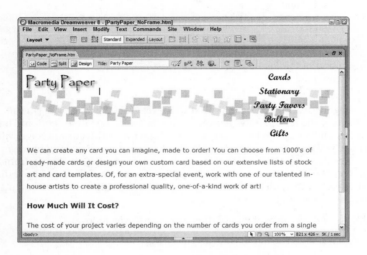

Top and nested left

Figure 16-5: *Top*: Before. *Bottom:* After. Existing content is incorporated into a new frameset when a frame object is chosen.

Using the frame object can be, quite literally, a one-click operation. Just select the desired frameset from the Frames menu of the Insert bar, and Dreamweaver automatically turns on Frame Borders, if necessary, and creates and names the required frames. For all frame objects, the existing page is moved to a frame in which the scrolling option is set at Default, and the size is relative to the rest of the frameset. In other words, the existing page can be scrolled, and it expands to fill the content.

Tip Because Dreamweaver automatically puts the existing document into an expandable frame with scroll bars, it's most efficient to apply a frame object to an existing page only if that page is intended to be the primary content frame. Otherwise, it's better to select the frame object while a blank page is open and then use the File ⇨ Open in Frame command to load any existing pages into individual frames.

Adding More Frames

Regardless of how you create your initial frameset, you're not limited to your initial frame choices. In addition to being able to move frame borders visually, you can also set the size through the Frameset Property inspector, as described in the next section. Furthermore, you can continue to split either the entire frame or each column or row as needed — using either menu commands or the mouse. When you divide a column or row into one or more frames, you are actually nesting one frameset inside another.

Tip After you've created the basic frame structure, you can choose View ⇨ Visual Aids ⇨ Frame Borders again (it's a toggle) to turn off the borders and create a more accurate preview of your page.

Using the Menus

To split an existing frame using the menus, position the cursor in the frame you want to alter and choose Modify ⇨ Frameset ⇨ Split Frame Left, Right, Up, or Down. Figure 16-6 shows a two-row frameset in which the bottom row is split into two columns and then repositioned. The Frameset Property inspector would indicate that the inner frameset (2 columns, 1 row) is selected. The direction you choose in the last part of the previous command (Left, Right, Up, or Down) indicates the frame in which the existing page will be placed. For example, selecting Split Frame Right places the current page in the right frame.

You can clearly see the nested nature of the code in the following HTML fragment describing the frameset in Figure 16-6:

```
<frameset rows="80,*">
  <frame src="ExistingTop.htm" name="topFrame">
  <frameset rows="*" cols="130,614">
    <frame src="UntitledFrame-12">
    <frame src="ExistingLower.htm" name="mainFrame">
  </frameset>
</frameset>
```

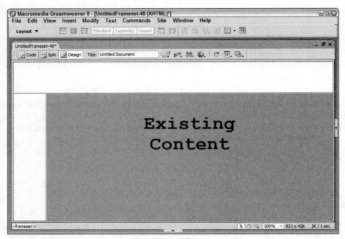

Figure 16-6: Use the Modify ⇨ Frameset menu command to split an existing frame into additional columns or rows and create a nested frameset.

Using the Mouse

When you use the menus to split a frame, only the currently selected frame is split. To create additional columns or rows that span the entire Web page, use the mouse method instead. Select the specific frameset to which you want to add or columns and then Alt+drag (Option+drag) any of the frame's borders that span the entire page, such as one of the outer borders. Figure 16-7 shows a new row added along the bottom of the previous frame structure.

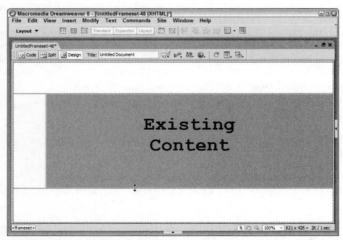

Figure 16-7: An additional frame row was added using the Alt+drag (Option+drag) method.

Selecting, Saving, and Closing Framesets

After you've initially created your frameset in Dreamweaver, you need to learn some basics before modifying the frameset or individual frames. For example, it's very easy to select framesets or individual frames if you know how. In addition, before changing your framesets, you must save your changes and close the frameset files.

Selecting Framesets and Frames

To change or view the properties of a frameset or a specific frame, you first select the frameset or frame. You can choose either the frameset itself or one of the frames within it from Design view or from the Frames panel.

The Frames panel shows an accurate representation of all the frames in your Web page. Open the Frames panel by selecting Window ➭ Frames or using the keyboard shortcut Shift+F2. As you can see on the right in Figure 16-8, the Frames panel displays the names, if assigned, of the individual frames and (no name) if none is assigned. Nested framesets are shown with a heavier border.

Click outer frame border to select frameset

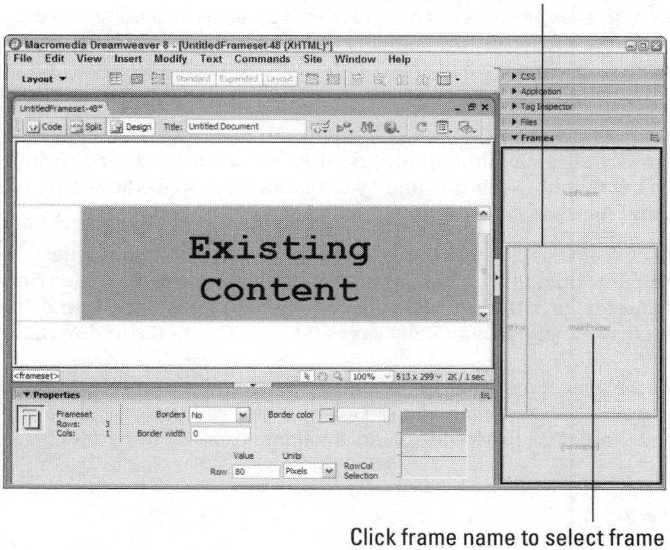

Click frame name to select frame

Figure 16-8: Use the Frames panel to visually select a frame to modify.

To select a frameset, click on an outside border of the frameset in the Frames panel. You can also select a frameset by clicking on any border of the frameset in Design view. If you can't see the frame borders, choose View ➭ Visual Aids ➭ Frame Borders.

To select a specific frame, click inside the represented image of the frame in the Frames panel. You can resize the Frames panel to get a better sense of the page layout, especially for complex pages. You can also select a frame by pressing Alt (Option+Shift) and clicking in the desired frame in the Document window.

Tip   When you are working with multiple framesets, use the Tag Selector together with the Frames panel to identify the correct nested frameset. Selecting a frameset in the Tag Selector causes it to be identified in the Frames panel with a heavy black border.

After a frame is selected, you can move from one frame to another within the same frameset by pressing Alt (Command) and then using the right and left arrow keys. You can move from a nested frameset to its parent frame by using the keyboard shortcut Alt+up arrow (Command+up arrow). Likewise, you can move from a parent frameset to its child frame by pressing Alt+down arrow (Command+down arrow).

Saving Framesets and Frames

Remember that when you're working with frames, you're working with multiple HTML files. You must be careful to save not only all the individual frames that make up your Web page, but also the frameset itself.

Dreamweaver makes it easy to save framesets and included frames by providing several special commands. To save a frameset, select the frameset as previously described and choose File ➪ Save Frameset to open the standard Save File dialog box. You can also save a copy of the current frameset by choosing File ➪ SaveFrameset As and then specifying a filename and location for the new copy.

You can save a single frame by clicking in the frame and then choosing File ➪ Save Frame. You can also make a copy of a document within a frame by choosing File ➪ Save Frame As and then entering a filename and location.

Although you can save each frame separately in the frameset, it can be a chore unless you choose File ➪ Save All. The first time this command is invoked, Dreamweaver cycles through each of the open frames and displays the Save File dialog box. Each subsequent time you choose File ➪ Save All, Dreamweaver automatically saves every updated file in the frameset.

Tip   As you are saving all the files in the frameset for the first time, you see a separate Save As dialog box for each previously unsaved file. You can tell which file you are currently saving by looking in Design view — a dotted, black line borders the frame currently being saved.

Closing Framesets

There's no real trick to closing a Dreamweaver frameset: Just choose File ➪ Close, as you would for any other file. If you have made changes to any of the frames or to the frameset itself since the last time you've saved, Dreamweaver asks if you want to save your changes before it closes the files. When you are asked to save a file, in Design view, a dotted black border appears around the frame or frameset that needs to be saved.

Establishing a Frameset

This technique uses one of the many ways in Dreamweaver to create a frameset from scratch and brings in existing content for each of the frames.

1. Within the Dreamweaver Technique site, choose File ⇨ New.

2. When the New File dialog box opens, from the General tab, choose the Framesets category.

3. Select the Fixed Top, Fixed Bottom entry from the Framesets list; click OK when you're done.

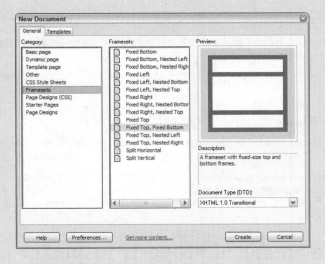

Dreamweaver creates the new frameset; each of the frames has been automatically named for you.

4. In the Title field of the Document toolbar, type **Relative Realty** and press Enter (Return).

It's best to name the frameset when it's first created because the frameset is currently selected; novices often make the mistake of applying a title to one of the frame pages rather than the frameset.

5. Choose File ⇨ Save Frameset As and, when the Save As dialog box appears, store the file in the `16_Frames` folder as `frames_start.htm`.

6. Alt+click (Option+click) in the top frame.

Continued

Continued

7. From the Property inspector, drag the Src target icon to the Files panel and point to `header_fr.htm` in the `16_Frames` folder.

Tip I find it helpful to add an `_fr` suffix to all my individual frame files to identify them as part of a frameset.

8. Click the frame border between the top and middle frames to select the frameset.

9. In the Property inspector, make sure the top frame is selected in the representation and enter **115** pixels for the Row value.

10. Alt+click (Option+click) in the middle frame and, in the Property inspector, drag the Src point-to-file icon to the Files panel and point to `home_fr.htm`.

   Depending on your screen resolution and size of your Dreamweaver window, you may see scroll bars appear.

11. Alt+click (Option+click) in the middle frame and, in the Property inspector, drag the Src point-to-file icon to the Files panel and point to `footer_fr.htm`.

12. Leave the default Row values for middle and bottom frames and choose File ⇨ Save Frameset.

If you investigate the individual frame pages, you'll see that they all connect to a different CSS file than other pages in the Dreamweaver Techniques site. For the `main_fr.css` file, the outside border attributes have been removed to work better within the frameset.

END

Working with the Frameset Property Inspector

The Frameset Property inspector manages elements, such as the borders, that are common to all the frames within a frameset. It also offers more precise sizing control over individual rows and columns than you can achieve visually by dragging the borders. If the Property inspector is not already open, choose Window ⇨ Properties to access it, and then select any of the frame borders in Design view.

Tip When a browser visits a Web page that uses frames, it displays the title found in the frameset HTML document for the entire frame. The easiest way to set that title is to select the frameset and enter the name directly in the Title field of the Document toolbar, if visible. You can also set the title by selecting the frameset and choosing Modify ⇨ Page Properties. In the Page Properties dialog box, select the General category and enter your choice of title in the Title text box, as you would for any other Web page. All the other options in the Page Properties dialog box — including background color and text color — apply to the `<noframes>` content, covered in the section "Handling Frameless Browsers" later in this chapter.

Resizing Frames in a Frameset

With HTML, when you want to specify the size of a frame, you work with the row or column in which the frame resides. Dreamweaver gives you two ways to alter a frame's size: by dragging the border or, for more precision, by specifying a value in the Property inspector.

As shown in Figure 16-9, Dreamweaver's Frameset Property inspector contains a Row/Column selector to display the structure of the selected frameset. For each frameset, click the tab along the top or left side of the Row/Column selector to choose the column or row you want to modify.

Column selector tab

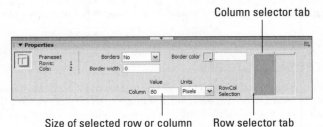

Size of selected row or column   Row selector tab

Figure 16-9: In the Frameset Property inspector, you use the Row/Column selector tabs to choose which frame you are going to resize.

Tip   The Row/Column selector shows only the rows and columns for one frameset at a time. Therefore, if your design uses nested framesets, you won't see an exact duplicate of your entire Web page in the Row/Column selector.

Whether you need to modify just a row, a column, or both a row and a column depends on the location of the frame:

✦ If the frame spans the width of an entire page, like the top or bottom row shown in Figure 16-7, select the corresponding tab on the left side of the Row/Column selector.

✦ If the frame spans the height of an entire page, select the equivalent tab along the top of the Row/Column selector.

✦ If the frame does not span either the entire height or width (refer to the middle row in Figure 16-7), select both its column and its row and modify the size of each in turn.

After you have selected the row or column, you can specify its size in several ways:

✦ To specify the size in pixels, enter a number in the Frameset Property inspector's Value text box and select Pixels as the Units option.

✦ To specify the size as a percentage of the screen, enter a number from 1 to 100 in the Value text box and select Percent as the Units option.

✦ To specify a size relative to the other columns or rows, first select Relative as the Units option. Now you have two choices:

- To set the size to occupy the remainder of the screen, delete any number that may be entered in the Value text box; optionally, you can enter **1**.

- To scale the frame relative to the other rows or columns, type the scale factor in the Value text box. For example, if you want the frame to be twice the size of another relative frame, put a **2** in the Value text box.

> **Tip** The Relative size operator is generally used to indicate that you want the current frame to take up the balance of the frameset column or row. This operator makes it easy to specify a size without having to calculate pixel widths and ensures that the frame has the largest possible size.

Manipulating Frameset Borders

By default, Dreamweaver sets up your framesets so that all the frames have borders that are invisible when viewed in a browser. You can, however, set borders to be visible, alter the border color, and change the border width. All the border controls are handled through the Frameset Property inspector.

> **Tip** Dreamweaver also provides border controls for individual frames. Just as table cell settings override options set for the entire table, the individual frame options override those determined for the entire frameset, as described in the section "Working with the Frame Property Inspector," later in this chapter. Use the frameset border controls when you want to make a global change to the borders, such as turning them all off.

If you are working with nested framesets, select the outermost frameset before you begin making any modifications to the borders. You can tell that you've selected the outermost frameset by looking at the Dreamweaver Tag Selector; it shows only one `<frameset>` in bold. If you select an inner nested frameset, you see more than one `<frameset>` in the Tag Selector.

Enabling Borders

When a frameset is first created, Dreamweaver sets borders to be invisible in all browsers. You can expressly turn the frameset borders on or off through the Property inspector.

Unfortunately, different browsers control frame borders differently. Some browsers base the presence of borders on the value in the Borders drop-down list, whereas others use the Border Width text box. To enable borders for all browsers, enter a non-zero number in the Border Width text box; and in the Borders drop-down list of options, choose Yes.

The opposite is also true; if you want borders to be invisible for all browsers, set the Borders drop-down list to No, and specify 0 for the Border Width. If you turn off the borders for your frameset, you can still work in Dreamweaver with View ➪ Visual Aids ➪ Frame Borders enabled. This option gives you quick access to modifying the frameset. The borders are not displayed, however, when your Web page is previewed in a browser.

Border Color Options

To change the frameset border color, select the Border Color text box and enter either a color name or a hexadecimal color value. You can also select the color box and choose a new border color from the color picker. If you click the small painter's palette in the upper-right corner of the color picker, the Color dialog box opens, just as with other color pickers in Dreamweaver.

Caution If you have nested framesets on your Web page, make sure that you've selected the correct frameset before you make any modifications through the Property inspector.

Modifying a Frame

What makes the whole concept of a Web page frameset work so well is the flexibility of each frame:

✦ You can design your page so that some frames are fixed in size and others are expandable.

✦ You can attach scroll bars to some frames and not others.

✦ Any frame can have its own background image, and yet all frames can appear as one seamless picture.

✦ Borders can be enabled — and colored — for one set of frames but left off for another set.

Dreamweaver uses a Frame Property inspector to specify most of a frame's attributes. Others are handled through devices already familiar to you, such as the Page Properties dialog box.

Page Properties

Each frame is its own HTML document and, as such, each frame can have independent page properties. To alter the page properties of a frame, position the cursor in the frame and choose Modify ⇨ Page Properties. You can also use the keyboard shortcut, Ctrl+J (Command+J). Alternatively, you can select Page Properties from the context menu by right-clicking (Control+clicking) any open space on the frame's page.

From the Page Properties dialog box, you can assign a title, although it is not visible to the user unless the frame is viewed as a separate page. If you plan to use the individual frames as separate pages in your <noframes> content (see "Handling Frameless Browsers" at the end of this chapter), it's good practice to title every page. You can also assign a background and the various link colors to the nonframe content by selecting the desired color box or entering a color name into the appropriate text box in the Appearance category of the Page Properties dialog box.

Cross-Reference The Page Properties dialog box respects the Dreamweaver preference for CSS or HTML when working in frames, just as it does with a standard page. For more details on setting the Page Properties, see the section "Establishing Page Properties" in Chapter 6.

Joining Background Images in Frames

One popular technique inserts background images into separate frames so that they blend into a seamless, single image. This takes careful planning and coordination between the designer of the graphic and the author of the Web page.

To accomplish this image consolidation operation, you must first *slice* the image in an image-processing program, such as Macromedia Fireworks or Adobe Photoshop. Then you save each part as a separate graphic, ensuring that no border is around these image sections — each cut-up piece becomes the background image for a particular frame. Next, set the background image of each frame to the matching graphic using a CSS rule for the body selector. Be sure to turn off the borders for the frameset and set the border width to zero.

Correctly size each piece to ensure that no gaps appear in your joined background. A good practice is to use absolute pixel measurements for images that fill the frame; and if the background images tile, set the frame spacing to Relative.

Working with the Frame Property Inspector

Using the Frame Property inspector, you can assign names to each of your frames, specify what document should display within each frame, add or remove scroll bars, specify whether the user can resize the frame, and more. To view the Property inspector for a frame, first select the frame by using the Frames panel or by holding down the Alt (Option+Shift) key as you click within the frame.

Naming Your Frames

Naming each frame is essential to getting the most power from a frame-structured Web page. The frame's name is used to make the content inserted from a hyperlink appear in that particular frame. For more information about targeting a link, see the section "Targeting Frame Content," later in this chapter.

Frame names must follow specific guidelines, as explained in the following steps:

1. Select the frame you want to name. You can use either the Frames panel or Alt+click (Option+Shift+click) inside the frame.

2. If necessary, open the Property inspector by choosing Window ⇨ Properties.

3. In the Frame Property inspector, shown in Figure 16-10, add the frame's name in the text box under the Frame Name label. Frame names have the following restrictions:

   - You must use one word, with no spaces.

   - You may not use special characters such as quotation marks, question marks, and hyphens. You may use the underscore character.

   - You may not use certain reserved frame names: _blank, _parent, _self, and _top.

Figure 16-10: The Frame Property inspector enables you to name the frame and control all the frame's attributes.

Opening a Web Page into a Frame

You don't have to build all Web pages in frames from scratch. You can load an existing Web page into any frame. If you've selected a frame and the Frame Property inspector is open, just type the link directly into the Src text box or click the folder icon to browse for your file. Alternatively, you can position your cursor in a frame (without selecting the frame) and choose File ➪ Open in Frame.

Setting Borders

You can generally set most border options adequately in the Frameset Property inspector, yet you can override some of the options, such as color, for each individual frame. These possibilities have practical limitations, however.

From the Frame Property inspector for a selected frame, you can make the borders visible by choosing Yes in the Borders drop-down list, or make them invisible by choosing No. Leaving the Borders option at Default gives control to the frameset settings. You can also change a frame's border color by choosing the Border Color swatch in a selected frame's Property inspector.

Caution

Different browser versions on different operating systems treat the border settings for individual frames differently. To complicate the situation, sometimes the settings on the overall frameset control how the individual frame border settings act. For example, if the frameset border is set to Default, and the individual frame Border is set to No, the border still appears in Internet Explorer 6.0 running on Windows — but as flat, rather than three-dimensional. If you elect to set the border property for an individual frame, be sure to test on as many browsers and platforms as possible.

Additional limitations come into play when you try to implement one of your border modifications. Because frames share common borders, it is difficult to isolate an individual frame and have the change affect only the selected frame. As an example, Figure 16-11 shows a frameset in which the borders are set to No for all frames except the one on the lower right. Notice how the left border of the lower-right frame extends to the top, including the left border of the upper-right frame. You have two possible workarounds for this problem. First, you can design your frames so that their borders do not touch, as in a multirow frameset. Second, you can create a background image for a frame that includes a border design.

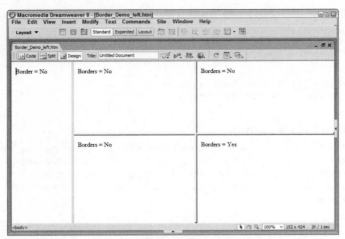

Figure 16-11: If you want to use isolated frame borders, you have to carefully plan your Web page frameset to avoid overlapping borders.

Adding Scroll Bars

One of the features that has given frames the wide use they enjoy is the capability to enable or disable scroll bars for each frame. Scroll bars are used when the browser window is too small to display all the information in the Web page frame. The browser window's size is completely controlled by the user, so the Web designer must apply the various scroll bar options on a frame-by-frame basis, depending on the look desired and the frame's content.

Four options are available from the Scroll drop-down list on the Frame Property inspector:

✦ **Default:** Leaves the use of scroll bars up to the browser.

✦ **Yes:** Forces scroll bars to appear regardless of the amount of content.

✦ **No:** Disables scroll bars.

✦ **Auto:** Turns scroll bars on if the content of the frame extends horizontally or vertically beyond what the browser window can display.

The page shown in Figure 16-12 uses automatic scroll bars in the lower-right frame; you can see one on the far right.

Resizing

Unless otherwise specified, frames are resizable by the user; that is, a visitor to your Web site can widen, narrow, lengthen, or shorten a frame by dragging the border to a new position. You can disable this resizing capability, however, on a frame-by-frame basis. In the Frame Property inspector, select the No Resize option to turn off the resizing feature.

Tip   Although it might be tempting to select No Resize for every frame, it's best to enable resizing to allow users to expand the frame if necessary except in frames that require a set size to maintain their functionality (frames containing navigational controls, for example).

Figure 16-12: The top frame of this Web page has the scroll bars turned off, and the bottom-right frame has scroll bars enabled.

When you first create a frameset using the Frames menu on the Insert bar, or by selecting an item in the Framesets category when you choose File ➪ New, the frame designated as containing the body of the page is resizable, and all other frames are fixed. Frames added by Alt+dragging (Option+dragging) the frame borders with the mouse or by choosing the Modify ➪ Frameset menu commands are resizable by default.

Setting Margins

Just as you can pad table cells with additional space to separate text and graphics, you can offset content in frames. Dreamweaver enables you to control the left/right margins and the top/bottom margins independently. If no margin values are specified, about 6 pixels of space are between the content and the left or right frame borders, and about 15 pixels of space are between the content and the top or bottom frame borders.

To alter the left and right margins, change the value in the Frame Property inspector's Margin Width text box; to change the top and bottom margins, enter a new value in the Margin Height text box. (If you don't see the Margin Width and Margin Height text boxes, select the expander arrow in the lower-right corner of the Property inspector.)

Modifying Content

You can update a frame's content in any way you see fit. Sometimes, it's necessary to keep an eye on how altering a single frame's content affects the entire frameset. Other times, it is easier — and faster — to work on each frame individually and later load them into the frameset to see the final result.

With Dreamweaver's multiple-document structure, you can have it both ways. Work on the individual frame files in one or more Document windows and the frameset in yet another. If you use File ➪ Save All to save your changes in an individual frame document, switching back to the frameset window automatically shows your changed frames.

Caution   To preview changes made to a Web page using frames, you must first save the changed files.

Deleting Frames

As you're building your Web page frameset, you inevitably try a frame design that does not work. How do you delete a frame once you've created it? Click the frame border and drag it into the border of the enclosing (or parent) frame. When no parent frame is present, drag the frame border to the edge of the page. If the frame being deleted contains any unsaved content, Dreamweaver asks if you'd like to save the file before closing it.

Tip   Because the enclosing frameset and each individual frame are all discrete HTML pages, each keeps track of its own edits and other changes. Therefore, each has its own undo memory. If you are in a particular frame and try to undo a frameset alteration, such as adding a new frame to the set, it won't work. To reverse an edit to the frameset, you have to select the frameset and choose Edit ➪ Undo, or use one of the keyboard shortcuts (Ctrl+Z or Command+Z). To reverse the creation of a frameset, you must select Undo twice.

Targeting Frame Content

One of the major uses of frames is for navigational control. One frame acts as the navigation center, offering links to various Web pages in a site. When the user selects one of the links, the Web page appears in another frame on the page; and that frame, if necessary, can scroll independently of the navigation frame. This technique keeps the navigation links always visible and accessible.

When you assign a link to appear in a particular frame of your Web page, you are said to be assigning a *target* for the link. You can target specific frames in your Web page, and you can target structural parts of a frameset. In Dreamweaver, targets for typical text or image links are assigned through the Text and Image Property inspectors. You also encounter frame target options elsewhere in the Dreamweaver interface, such as when you create a navigation bar (see Chapter 9) or when you use behaviors that create links, such as the Jump Menu behavior (see Chapter 12).

Targeting Sections of Your Frameset

In the section "Naming Your Frames," you learned that certain names are reserved. The following four special names are reserved by HTML for the parts of a frameset that are used in targeting: _blank, _parent, _self, and _top. With them, you can cause content from a link to overwrite the current frame or to appear in an entirely new browser window.

To target a link to a section of your frameset, follow these steps:

1. Select the text or image you want to use as your link.

2. In the Text (or Image) Property inspector, enter the URL and/or named anchor in the Link text box. Alternatively, you can click the folder icon to browse for the file.

3. Select the Target text box. (You may need to expand the Property inspector to see the Target text box.)

4. Select one of the following reserved target names from the drop-down list of Target options (see Figure 16-13) or type an entry into the text box:

   - `_blank` — Opens the link into a new browser window and keeps the current window available.

   - `_parent` — Opens the link into the parent frameset of the current frame, if any.

   - `_self` — Opens the link into the current frame, replacing its contents (the default).

   - `_top` — Opens the link into the outermost frameset of the current Web page, replacing all frames.

Figure 16-13: Choose your frame target from the Property inspector's Target drop-down list.

The generic nature of these reserved target names enables you to use them repeatedly on different Web pages, without having to code a particular reference each time.

Caution
A phenomenon known as *recursive frames* can be dangerous to your site setup. For example, say you have a frameset named `index_frame.html`. If you include a link to `index_frame.html` in any frame on your current page and leave the target empty or set the target as `_self`, when the user selects that link, the entire frameset loads into the current frame — including another link to `index_frame.html`. Browsers can handle about three or four iterations of this recursion before they crash. To avoid the problem, set your frameset target to `_top`.

Targeting Specific Frames in Your Frameset

Recall the importance of naming each frame in your frameset. After you have entered a name in the Name text box of the Frame Property inspector, Dreamweaver dynamically updates the Target list to include that name. This feature enables you to target specific frames in your frameset in the same manner that you target the reserved names noted previously.

Although you can always type the frame name directly in the Target text box, the drop-down list comes in handy for this task. Not only can you avoid keeping track of the various frame names in your Web page, but you prevent typing errors as well. Targets are case-sensitive, and names must match exactly or the browser won't be able to find the target.

Updating Two or More Frames at Once

Sooner or later, most Web designers using frames need to update more than one frame with a single click. The problem is, you can't group two or more URLs together in an anchor tag. Here is an easy-to-implement solution, thanks to Dreamweaver's behaviors.

Cross-Reference   If you're not familiar with Dreamweaver's JavaScript behaviors, you might want to look at Chapter 12 before continuing.

To update more than one frame target from a single link, follow these steps:

1. Select your link text or image in the frame.

2. If you selected text for your link, type **javascript:;** in the Link field of the Text Property inspector.

   The behavior cannot be attached directly to the text; instead, it must be associated with an anchor or an image. Typing javascript:; in the Link field creates the necessary anchor tag.

Tip   If one of the multiple links targets the frame that contains the hotspot, instead of typing javascript:; in the Link field, you can enter the path to the file that will load in that frame.

3. Open the Behaviors panel by choosing Window ➪ Behaviors.

4. Click the Add (+) button at the top of the Behaviors panel, and in the drop-down menu, choose Show Events For ➪ 4.0 and Later Browsers.

5. Click the Add (+) button again to display the list of available behaviors and choose Go To URL.

6. Dreamweaver displays the Go To URL dialog box (see Figure 16-14) and scans your document for all named frames. Select a target frame from the list of windows or frames.

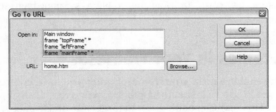

Figure 16-14: You can cause two or more frames, marked by the trailing asterisk, to update from a single link by using Dreamweaver's Go To URL behavior.

Caution   You won't be able to use this behavior until you name your frames as detailed in the section "Naming Your Frames," earlier in this chapter.

7. Enter a URL or click the Browse button to select one. Dreamweaver places an asterisk after the targeted frame to indicate that a URL has been selected for it. You can see this in Figure 16-14.

8. Repeat steps 6 and 7 for any additional frames you want to target.

9. Click OK when you're finished.

10. If onClick is not already listed in the Events column of the Behaviors panel, click the arrow button next to the event and choose (onClick) from the event list.

Now, whenever you click your one link, the browser opens the URLs in the targeted frames in the order specified.

Setting Frame Targets

In this technique you set the text navigation links to work properly with the frameset. Three links open pages within the frameset and a fourth opens a page outside the frameset.

1. Re-open the frameset previously saved, frames_start.htm.

2. In the bottom frame, select the text Home.

3. From the Property inspector, drag the Link point-to-file icon to the home_fr.htm file.

4. Select mainFrame from the Target list.

Dreamweaver automatically adds the names of frames in the current frameset to the Target list.

5. Repeat steps 2–4, with the text Sales and the file sales_fr.htm.

6. Repeat steps 2–4 again, with the text Rentals and the file rentals_fr.htm.

Make sure that you set the Target list to mainFrame for both the previous links.

7. Select the final text phrase, About Us, and drag the Link point-to-file icon to the about.htm file.

Because about.htm is a standard HTML file and not part of the frameset, you'll choose a different target.

8. From the Target list, choose _top.

9. Save your page and press F12 (Option+F12) to preview the frameset.

When you try the navigation links, you notice that the first three links open their pages within the frameset as expected whereas the fourth link, about.htm, replaces the frameset with a single page. If you click the Home link at the bottom of this page, the frameset re-opens.

Handling Frameless Browsers

Not all of today's browsers support frames. Netscape began supporting frames in Navigator version 2.0; Microsoft didn't start until IE version 3.0 — and a few of the earlier versions for both browsers are still in use, particularly among AOL users. Some less-prevalent browsers also do not support frames. HTML has a built-in mechanism for working with browsers that are not frame-enabled: the `<noframes>...</noframes>` tag pair.

A more vital reason to use the `<noframes>` tag than supporting older browsers is that most of the search-engine indexing systems (called *spiders*) don't work with frames. If your frameset is `index.html` and you want the spider to find the rest of your site, the `<noframes>` content must include descriptive text as well as navigational links to other pages in your site. Many Webmasters also include links to current versions of Communicator or Internet Explorer to encourage their nonframe-capable visitors to upgrade.

When you begin to construct any frameset, Dreamweaver automatically inserts a `<noframes>` area just below the closing `</frameset>` tag. If a browser is not frames-capable, it ignores the frameset and frame information and renders what is found in the `<noframes>` section.

> **Note**   If you are manually coding a frameset, in Code view, you can insert the `<noframes>...</noframes>` tag pair by clicking the No Frames button in the Frames menu of the HTML category of the Insert bar.

What should you put into the `<noframes>` section? To ensure the widest possible audience, Webmasters typically insert links to a nonframe version of the site. The links can be as obvious or as discreet as you care to make them and, if used, are placed on the site's home page.

Dreamweaver includes a facility for easily adding and modifying the `<noframes>` content. Choose Modify ➪ Frameset ➪ Edit NoFrames Content to open the NoFrames Content window. As you can see in Figure 16-15, this window is identical to the regular Dreamweaver Document window, with the exception of the text NoFrames Content in a label at the top of the editing area. In this window, you have access to all the same objects and panels that you normally do. When you have finished editing your `<noframes>` content, choose Modify ➪ Frameset ➪ Edit NoFrames Content again to deselect the option and return to the frameset.

Keep the following pointers in mind when working in the NoFrames Content window:

✦ The page properties of the `<noframes>` content are the same as the page properties of the frameset. You can select the frameset and then choose Modify ➪ Page Properties to open the Page Properties dialog box. While in the NoFrames Content window, you can also right-click (Control+click) in any open space to access the Page Properties command.

✦ Dreamweaver disables the File ➪ Open commands when the NoFrames Content window is onscreen. To move existing content into the `<noframes>` section, use Dreamweaver's Copy and Paste features.

✦ The `<noframes>` section is located in the frameset page, which is the primary page examined by search engine spiders. It's a good idea to enter `<meta>` tag information detailing the site in the frameset page. While you're in the NoFrames Content window, you can insert the `<meta>` tags using the Head category of the Insert bar.

Label indicates No-Frames content is displayed

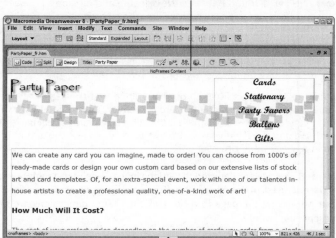

Figure 16-15: Through the Edit NoFrames Content command, Dreamweaver enables you to specify what's seen by visitors whose browsers are not frame-capable.

Investigating Iframes

The `<iframe>` tag (short for inline frames) is an HTML 4.0 specification worth noting. An Iframe is used to include one HTML document inside another—without building a frameset. What makes iframes visually arresting and extremely useful is their capability to display scroll bars automatically, as shown in Figure 16-16. Iframes are supported by Internet Explorer 4 and later, Firefox, Netscape 6 and later, and Safari.

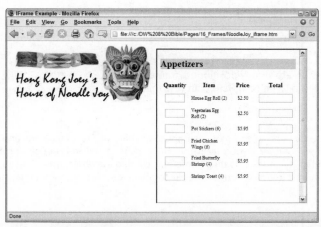

Figure 16-16: The iframe—also known as an inline frame—is a cutting-edge technique for including one HTML page within another.

The `<iframe>` tag uses the `src` attribute to specify which HTML file is to be included. Any content — text, images, or whatever — found between the opening and closing `<iframe>` tags is displayed only if the browser does *not* support iframes. In other words, it's the no-iframe content. Here's an iframe code example:

```
<iframe src="/includes/salespromo.htm" name="promoFrame"
style="position:absolute; width:200px; height:300px; top:139px;
left:530px">Iframes are not supported by this browser.</iframe>
```

If you're familiar with Cascading Style Sheet layers, you may notice that the `style` attribute is identical in iframes. This has an interesting effect in Dreamweaver: iframe code with the `style` attribute set to `position:absolute` is displayed like a layer, as shown in Figure 16-17. This makes positioning and resizing the iframe very straightforward. To see the actual iframe content, preview the page in a compatible browser.

New In Dreamweaver

Starting in Dreamweaver 8, iframes are depicted in Design view as a solid rectangle, even if absolute positioning is not used. Although you can't see the content at design-time in Dreamweaver without previewing the page in a browser, the iframe dimensions are rendered correctly to preserve the layout.

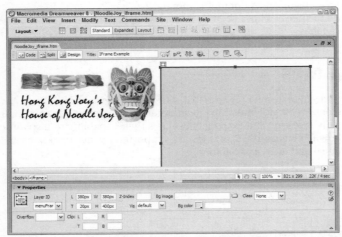

Figure 16-17: When you view an absolutely positioned iframe tag in Dreamweaver, it appears like a layer, complete with resizing handles.

Caution

Specifying `position:absolute` in the `style` attribute enables you to exactly position a floating frame on the page. However, if you specify `position:absolute` and your other content is not contained within layers, your floating frame may overlap the other content on your page. For this reason, it is best to use floating frames in combination with a CSS-based layout.

You can also specify a style of position:relative. In this case, browsers display the floating frame on the page relative to the other page content, even if that content is not contained within layers. Note, however, that Design view does not always correctly display floating frames that are positioned relatively, and sometimes the floating frame overlaps existing content, making it difficult to edit. Again, it is best to lay out your content using CSS positioning and specify position:absolute for your <iframe> if you are using floating frames.

In Dreamweaver, iframes are referred to as *floating frames*. Dreamweaver facilitates the inclusion of iframes in your documents with the Floating Frame button in the Frames menu of the HTML category of the Insert bar.

Note
Two Frames menus are available in Dreamweaver: one in the Layout category and one in the HTML category. Be sure you switch to the HTML category before attempting to insert an iframe (floating frame).

To insert a floating frame in your document, follow these steps:

1. If you are working in Design view, switch to Code view by choosing View ➪ Code.

2. Position the cursor after the <body> tag in your document.

3. Insert the <iframe> tag by clicking the Floating Frame button on the Frames menu of the Insert bar (HTML category).

Note
You cannot access the floating frame command while you are in Design view. If you are in Code and Design view, the cursor must be in the Code window for the command to be available.

4. Specify the attributes for the <iframe> tag. To do this, right-click (Ctrl+click) the tag and choose Edit Tag <iframe> from the drop-down list.

5. The Tag Editor for iframes opens. In this dialog box, specify at least the following:

   • **Source:** This is the file that will be displayed within the floating frame.

   • **Scrolling:** This attribute specifies whether scroll bars will appear in the frame.

   • **Style:** In the Style Sheet/Accessibility category, type position:absolute in the Style box. If you want to add other style options, separate them with semicolons.

   • **Alternate Content:** Select the Alternate Content category and then specify the text that will be displayed in browsers that don't support floating frames.

6. In Design view, you can size and position the floating frame as you would any layer.

Cross-Reference
Refer to Chapter 11 for more information about positioning and sizing layers.

Summary

Frames are a significant tool for Web designers. With frames and framesets, you can divide a single Web page into multiple, independent areas. Dreamweaver gives Web designers quick and easy access to frame design through its drag-and-drop interface. When you're working with frames and framesets, keep these points in mind:

✦ A framed Web page consists of a separate HTML document for each frame and one additional file that describes the frame structure, called the *frameset*.

✦ A frameset comprises columns and rows, which can be sized absolutely in pixels as a percentage of the browser window or relative to the other columns or rows.

✦ Dreamweaver enables you to reposition frame borders by dragging them to a new location. You can also add new frames by Alt+clicking (Option+clicking) as you drag any existing frame border.

✦ Framesets can be nested to create more complex column and row arrangements. Selecting the frame border displays the Frameset Property inspector.

✦ Select any individual frame through the Frames panel or by Alt+clicking (Option+Shift+clicking) within any frame. After you select the frame, you can display the Frame Property inspector.

✦ Make your links appear in a specific frame by assigning targets to the links. Dreamweaver supports both structured and named targets. You can update two or more frames with one link by using the Dreamweaver Go To URL behavior.

✦ You should include information and/or links for browsers that are not frame-capable through Dreamweaver's Edit NoFrames Content feature.

✦ Floating frames, as defined in HTML 4.0, can be implemented in Dreamweaver by initially hand-editing the `<iframe>` tag in Code view. After inserting the tag, the floating frame can be sized and positioned in Design view.

In the next chapter, you learn how to develop timelines, which enable layers and their contents to move around the Web page.

✦   ✦   ✦

Working with Timelines

Motion implies time. A static object, such as an ordinary HTML Web page, can exist either in a single moment or over a period of time. Conversely, moving objects (such as Dynamic HTML layers flying across the screen) need a few seconds to complete their path. All of Dreamweaver's Dynamic HTML animation effects use the Timeline feature to manage this conjunction of movement and time.

Timelines can do much more than move a layer across a Web page, however. A timeline can coordinate an entire presentation: starting the background music, scrolling the opening rolling credits, and cueing the voice-over narration on top of a slideshow. These actions are all possible with Dreamweaver because, in addition to controlling a layer's position, timelines can also trigger any of Dreamweaver's JavaScript behaviors on a specific frame.

This chapter explores the full and varied world of timelines. After an introductory section brings you up to speed on the underlying concepts of timelines, you learn how to insert and modify timelines to achieve cutting-edge effects. From complex multilayer animations to slideshow presentations, you can do it all with Dreamweaver timelines.

> **Note**   Because timelines are so intricately intertwined with layers and behaviors, you need to have a good grasp of these concepts. If you're not familiar with the topics of layers and behaviors, be sure to read Chapters 11 and 12.

Into the Fourth Dimension with Timelines

Dreamweaver timelines are implemented in HTML code. For the movement of one layer straight across a Web page, Dreamweaver generates about 70 lines of code devoted to initializing and playing the timeline. But just what is a timeline? A timeline is composed of a series of frames. A frame is a snapshot of what the Web page — more specifically, the objects on the timeline — looks like at a particular moment. You probably know that a movie is made up of a series of still pictures; when viewed quickly, the pictures create the illusion of movement. Each individual picture is a frame; movies show 24 frames per second (fps), and video uses about 30 fps. Web animation, on the other hand, generally displays about 15 fps. Not surprisingly, Dreamweaver's timeline is similar to the one used in Macromedia's timeline-based, multimedia authoring tool and animation package, Director.

If you have to draw each frame of a 30-second animation, even at 15 fps, you won't have time for other work. Dreamweaver uses the concept of *keyframes* to make a simple layer movement workable. Each keyframe contains a change in the timeline object's properties, such as position. For example, suppose you want your layer to start at the upper-left (represented by the coordinates 0,0) and travel to the lower-right (at 750,550). To accomplish this task, you need only specify the layer's position for the two keyframes — the start and the finish — and Dreamweaver generates all the frames in between.

Timelines have three primary roles:

✦ A timeline can alter a layer's position, dimensions, visibility, and depth.

✦ Timelines can change the source for any image on a Web page and cause another graphic of the same height and width to appear in the same location.

✦ Any of Dreamweaver's JavaScript behaviors can be triggered on any frame of a timeline.

A Few Ground Rules

Keep the following basic guidelines in mind when you're using timelines in the Web pages you create with Dreamweaver:

✦ Timelines require a 4.0 or later browser.

✦ When testing locally on Internet Explorer 6 on Windows XP operating systems with Service Pack 2 installed, the browser blocks the active content as a security measure. Designers can choose Commands ➪ Insert Mark of the Web to avoid this alert.

✦ For a timeline to animate an object, such as text, the object must be within a layer. If you try to create a timeline with an element that is not in a layer, Dreamweaver warns you and prevents you from adding the object to the timeline.

✦ Events don't have to start at the beginning of a timeline. If you want to have an action begin 5 seconds after a page has loaded, and you have a frame rate of 15 fps, for example, you can set the behavior on frame 60 of the timeline.

✦ The selected frame rate is a "best-case scenario" because the actual frame rate depends on the user's system. A slower system or one that is simultaneously running numerous other programs can easily degrade the frame rate.

✦ You can include multiple animations on one timeline. The only restriction is that you can't have two animations affecting the same layer at the same time. Dreamweaver prevents you from making this error.

✦ You can have multiple timelines that animate different layers simultaneously or the same layer at different times. Although you can set two or more timelines to animate the same layer at the same time, the results are difficult to predict and generally unintended.

Tip

If you move a timeline's JavaScript code from its file of origin into an external JS file, serious timeline execution problems can occur in some browsers. For this reason, I heartily recommend leaving all your timeline code in its original file.

Creating Animations with Timelines

Dreamweaver provides an excellent tool for managing timelines — the Timelines panel. Open it by choosing Window ⇨ Timelines or using the keyboard shortcut Alt+F9 (Option+F9).

The Timelines panel (see Figure 17-1) uses VCR-style controls combined with a playback head, which is a visual representation showing which frame is the current one. It gives you full control over any of the timeline functions.

Playback head

Behavior channels

Timeline   Frames

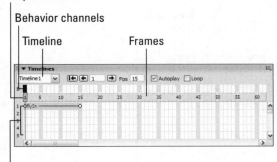

Animation channels

Figure 17-1: Dreamweaver's Timelines panel enables you to quickly and easily master animation control.

The Timelines panel has four major areas:

✦ **Timeline controls:** Includes the Timeline drop-down list for selecting the current timeline; the Rewind, Back, and Play buttons; the fps (frame rate) text box; and the Autoplay and Loop checkboxes

✦ **Behavior channel:** Shows the placement of any behaviors attached to specific frames of the timeline

✦ **Frames:** Displays the frame numbers for all timelines and the playback head showing the current frame number

✦ **Animation channels:** Represents the animations for any included layers and images

Adding Layers and Images to the Timelines Panel

As with many of Dreamweaver's functions, you can add a layer or an image to the Timelines panel in more than one way. You can insert a layer into a timeline through the menus (Modify ⇨ Timeline ⇨ Add Object to Timeline), you can drag-and-drop an object into a timeline, or you can use the keyboard shortcut, Ctrl+Alt+Shift+T (Command+Option+Shift+T). When you add an object to a timeline, Dreamweaver inserts an animation bar of 15 frames in length, labeled with the object's name. The animation bar shows the duration (the number of frames) of the timeline's effect on the object. An animation bar is initially created with two keyframes: the start and the end. To add a layer or image to the Timelines panel through the menus, follow these steps:

1. Choose Window ➪ Timelines or use the keyboard shortcut, Alt+F9 (Option+F9), to open the Timelines panel.

2. In the Document window, select the layer or image you want to add to the timeline.

   Bear in mind that you can use timelines to move a layer around the browser window, but not to move an image (unless it is contained in a layer). The only thing timelines can do with respect to an image is to change its source, causing another graphic of the same height and width to appear in the same location.

3. Choose Modify ➪ Timeline ➪ Add Object to Timeline. An animation bar appears in the first frame of the timeline, as shown in Figure 17-2.

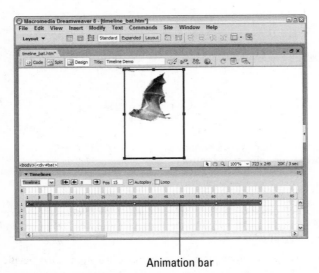

Animation bar

Figure 17-2: The default animation bar is set at 15 frames but can easily be modified.

4. To add another object, repeat steps 2 and 3. As previously noted, you can add as many objects to a timeline as you desire. Each additional animation bar is inserted beneath the preceding bar.

 Tip   The first time you add an image or layer to the Timelines panel, Dreamweaver displays an alert message that details the limitations of timelines. If you don't want to see this alert, turn it off by checking the Don't Show Me This Message Again checkbox.

You have a little more flexibility when you add an object by dragging it into the timeline. Instead of the animation bar always beginning at frame 1, you can drop the object in to begin on any frame. This approach is useful, especially if you are putting more than one object into the same animation channel. To place an object in a timeline with the drag-and-drop method, follow these steps:

1. Open the Timelines panel by choosing Window ➪ Timelines or using the keyboard shortcut Alt+F9 (Option+F9).

2. In the Document window, select the object—layer or image—that you want to add to the timeline and drag it to the Timelines panel. As soon as the object is over the Timelines panel, a 15-frame animation bar appears.

3. Holding the mouse button down, position the animation bar so that the animation begins in the desired frame. Release the mouse button to drop the object into the timeline.

Note   Your placement does not have to be exact; you can modify it later.

Placing a layer or image on a timeline is just the first step. To begin using your timeline in depth, you have to make changes to the object for the keyframes and customize the timeline.

Dreamweaver TECHNIQUE Setting Up a Slideshow

In this technique, you create a user-controlled slideshow, with the capability to play, pause, and stop. The first step is to set up the timeline and appropriate keyframes.

Caution   This Technique works only in Windows.

1. In the Files panel, switch to the Dreamweaver Bible working site previously created.

2. Go to Techniques\17_Timelines and open the file `timelines_start.htm`.

3. Choose Windows ⇨ Timelines to open the Timelines panel.

4. Drag the image above the slideshow controls down onto the timeline; be sure to position the timeline so that it starts at frame 1.

5. This particular example cycles three images through the slideshow; by design, the image will change every 10 frames, so you'll need 30 frames to complete the show.

   Drag the final keyframe to frame 30 to extend the timeline.

6. Select frame 10, right-click (Control-click), and choose Add Keyframe.

7. Repeat step 6 on frame 20.

8. Next, you set the `Src` property of the image on the timeline for each keyframe.

   Select frame 10 and, in the Property inspector, set the `Src` value to `apt_view2.jpg` in the images folder at the site root.

9. Repeat step 8 for frame 20 setting the `Src` value to `apt_view3.jpg` in the images folder at the site root.

10. Make sure that the frame 30 `Src` value is set to `apt_view1.jpg`.

11. Save your page.

The final keyframe could either be set to the last image in the series or the first. In the next Dreamweaver Technique, you set the timeline to loop as well as add player interactivity.

END

Modifying a Timeline

When you add an object — either an image or a layer — to a timeline, notice that the animation bar has an open circle at its beginning and end. An open circle marks a keyframe. As previously explained, the designer specifies a change in the state of the timeline object in a keyframe. For example, when you first insert a layer, the two generated keyframes have identical properties — the layer's position, size, visibility, and depth are unchanged. For any animation to occur, you have to change one of the layer's properties for one of the keyframes. For example, to move a layer quickly across the screen, follow these steps:

1. Create a layer. If you like, add an image or a background color so that the layer is more noticeable.

2. Open the Timelines panel.

3. Drag the layer into the Timelines panel and release the mouse button.

4. Select the ending keyframe of the layer's animation bar.

   The playback head (red rectangle) moves to the new frame.

5. In the Document window, grab the layer's selection handle and drag the layer to a new location. A thin line connects the starting position of the layer to the ending position, as shown in Figure 17-3. This line is the *animation path*.

Figure 17-3: When you move a layer on a timeline, Dreamweaver displays an animation path.

6. To preview your animation, first click the Rewind button in the Timelines panel and then click and hold down the Play button.

If you want to change the beginning position of your layer's animation path, select the starting keyframe and then move the layer in the Document window. To alter the final position of the layer's animation path, select the ending keyframe and then move the layer.

Tip   For more precise control of your layer's position in a timeline, select a keyframe and, in the layer's Property inspector, change the Left and/or Top values. You can also select the layer and use the arrow keys to move it.

Altering the Animation Bars

A Web designer can easily stretch or alter the range of frames occupied by a layer or image in an animation bar. You can make an animation longer or smoother, or have it start at an entirely different time. You can also move the layer to a different animation channel so it runs before or after another animation.

Use the mouse to drag an animation bar around the timeline. Click any part of the bar except the keyframe indicators and move it as needed. To change the length of an animation, select the first or final keyframe and drag it forward or backward to a new frame.

Use either of the following techniques to remove (delete) an animation bar:

✦ Select the animation bar by clicking anywhere on it, and choose Modify ➪ Timeline ➪ Remove Object.

✦ Right-click (Control+click) the animation bar and choose Remove Object from the context menu.

Using the Timeline Controls

As you probably noticed if you worked through the example in the preceding section, you don't have to use a browser to preview a timeline. The Timeline controls shown in Figure 17-4 enable you to fine-tune your animations before you view them through a browser.

Tip   If you're using the Timelines panel controls to play a timeline animation that moves below the visible portion of the Document window, you can press F4 to hide the Timelines panel (and all other Dreamweaver panels) to maximize screen space. To redisplay your panels, press F4 again.

At the top-left corner is the Timeline drop-down list, which is used to indicate the current timeline. By default, every new timeline is given the name Timeline*n*, where *n* indicates how many timelines have been created. You can rename the timeline by selecting it and typing in the new name. It's a good practice to give each timeline a descriptive, recognizable name; you'll appreciate it as you accumulate and use more timelines.

Caution   A timeline name must have an alphanumeric, one-word name that begins with a letter, such as FlyingBat2.

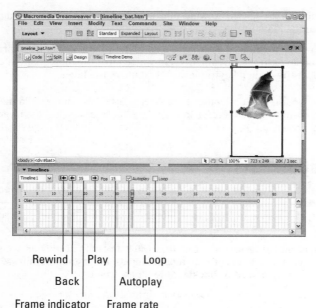

Figure 17-4: The Timeline controls enable you to move back and forth in your timeline, easily and precisely.

The next three buttons in the control bar enable you to move through the frames of a timeline. From left to right:

✦ **Rewind:** Moves the playback head to the first frame of the timeline.

✦ **Back:** Moves the playback head to the previous frame of the timeline. You can hold down the Back button to play the timeline in reverse. This behavior loops: When the first frame is reached, the playback head automatically moves to the last frame of the timeline and continues playing it.

✦ **Play:** Moves the playback head to the next frame; hold down the Play button to play the timeline normally. As with the Back button, this behavior loops: When the last frame is reached, the playback head moves to the first frame of the current timeline and continues.

The field between the Back and Play buttons is the Frame Indicator text box. To jump to any specific frame, enter the frame number in this box.

The next item in the control bar is the fps (frames per second) text box. To change the frame rate, enter a new value in the Fps text box and press Tab or Enter (Return). The frame rate you set is an ideal number that a user's browser attempts to reach. The default rate of 15 frames per second is a good balance for both Macintosh and Windows systems.

Tip   Because browsers play every frame regardless of the frame rate setting, increasing the frame rate does not necessarily make your animations smoother. A better way to create smooth animations is to drag the end keyframe farther out, which increases the number of frames used by your animation.

The next two checkboxes, Autoplay and Loop, affect how the animation is played.

Autoplay

If you enable the Autoplay option, the timeline begins playing as soon as the Web page is fully downloaded. Dreamweaver alerts you to this arrangement by telling you that the Play Timeline action is attached to an onLoad event. Autoplay is achieved by inserting code that looks similar to the following into the <body> tag:

```
<body bgcolor="#FFFFFF" onload="MM_timelinePlay('Timeline1')">
```

Caution   If you don't use the Autoplay feature, you must attach the Play Timeline action to another event and tag, such as onClick and a button graphic. Otherwise, the timeline will not play. Note that if your Show Events For option is set to 3.0 and Later Browsers, the only available event is onMouseOver. To make onClick and other events available, change the Show Events For to 4.0 and Later Browsers by choosing Add (+) from the Behaviors panel, then selecting Show Events For ⇨ 4.0 and Later Browsers.

Looping

Mark the Loop checkbox if you want an animation to repeat once it has reached the final frame. When Loop is enabled, the default causes the layer to replay itself an infinite numbers of times, although you can change this setting.

When you first enable the Loop checkbox, Dreamweaver alerts you that it is placing a Go To Timeline Frame action after the last frame of your timeline. To set the number of repetitions for a looping timeline, follow these steps:

1. In the Timelines panel, check the Loop checkbox.

2. Dreamweaver displays an alert informing you that the Go To Timeline Frame action is being added one frame past your current final frame. To disable these alerts, select the Don't Show Me This Message Again option.

3. In the Behaviors channel (the Timeline channel marked with a B, as shown in Figure 17-1), double-click the behavior you just added.

Note   When you first add a behavior to a timeline, Dreamweaver presents a dialog box reminding you how to perform this action. Select the Don't Show Me This Message Again option when you've mastered the technique.

The Behaviors panel opens, with an onFrame event in the Events column and a Go To Timeline Frame action in the Actions pane.

4. Double-click the onFrame event. The Go To Timeline Frame dialog box opens (see Figure 17-5).

Figure 17-5: Selecting the Loop option on the Timelines panel adds a Go To Timeline Frame action, which you can customize.

5. Enter a positive number in the Loop text box to set the number of times you want your timeline to repeat. To keep the animation repeating continuously, leave the Loop text box blank.

6. Click OK when you are finished.

Tip

Your animations don't have to loop back to the beginning each time. By entering a different frame number in the Go to Frame text box of the Go To Timeline Frame dialog box, you can repeat just a segment of the animation.

Adding Keyframes

Animating a timeline can go far beyond moving your layer from point A to point B. Layers (and the content within them) can dip, swirl, zigzag, and generally move in any fashion — all made possible by keyframes in which you have entered some change for the object. Dreamweaver calculates all the differences between each keyframe, whether the change is in a layer's position or size. Each timeline starts with two keyframes: the beginning and the end; you have to add other keyframes before you can insert the desired changes.

You can add a keyframe to a timeline in two different ways. The first method uses the Add Keyframe command (as practiced in the preceding Dreamweaver Technique), and the second method uses the mouse to click a keyframe into place.

Note

Do not confuse the Add Keyframe command with the Add Frame command, both of which are found in the Modify ⇨ Timeline menu. The former adds a keyframe to the timeline; the latter adds a normal frame to the timeline.

Adding Keyframes with the Add Keyframe Command

To add a keyframe with the Add Keyframe command, follow these steps:

1. In the Timelines panel, select the animation bar for the object with which you are working.

2. Select the frame in which you want to add a keyframe.

3. Add your keyframe by one of the following methods:

   • Choose Modify ⇨ Timeline ⇨ Add Keyframe.

   • Right-click (Control+click) the frame in the animation bar and, from the context menu, choose Add Keyframe.

A new keyframe is added on the selected frame, signified by the open circle in the animation bar.

While your new keyframe is selected, you can alter the layer's position, size, visibility, or depth. For example, if your animation involves moving a layer across the screen, you can drag the layer to a new position while the new keyframe is selected. The animation path is redrawn to incorporate this new position, as illustrated in Figure 17-6.

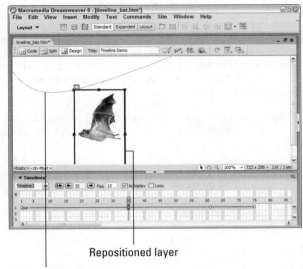

Repositioned layer

Altered animation path

Figure 17-6: Repositioning a layer while a keyframe is selected can redirect your animation path.

Adding a Keyframe with the Mouse

The second method is quicker. To add a keyframe using the mouse, simply hold down the Ctrl (Command) key and click anywhere in the animation bar. Your cursor turns into a small open circle when it is over the Timeline window to show that it is ready to add a new keyframe.

What if you want to move the keyframe? Simply click and drag the keyframe to a new frame, sliding it along the animation bar in the Timelines panel.

Tip   If, after plotting out an elaborate animation with a layer, you discover that you need to shift the entire animation — for example, 6 pixels to the right — you don't have to redo all your work. Just select the animation bar in the Timelines panel and then, in the Document window, move the layer in question. Dreamweaver shifts the entire animation to your new location.

Removing Timeline Elements

To remove an element from the Timelines panel:

1. Select the element that you want to remove.

2. Choose Modify ⇨ Timeline ⇨ Remove *Element*, where *Element* is the element you want to remove.

For example, to remove a keyframe, select the keyframe and choose Modify ⇨ Timeline ⇨ Remove Keyframe.

The context menu in the Timelines panel also contains all the removal commands. Right-click (Control+click) the Timelines panel element you want to remove and, in the context menu (see Figure 17-7), choose the desired removal command: Remove Keyframe, Remove Object, Remove Behavior, Remove Frame, or Remove Timeline. Alternatively, right-click (Control+click) the element and simply choose Delete from the context menu.

Tip   To copy or move an entire timeline to another document, select the timeline, right-click (Control+click), and use the handy Cut, Copy, and Paste commands from the Timelines panel context menu.

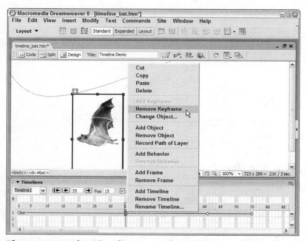

Figure 17-7: The Timelines panel context menu is extremely handy for quick editing.

Changing Animation Speed

You can alter your Dynamic HTML animation speed with two different methods that can be used separately or together:

✦ Drag out the final keyframe in the animation bar to cover additional frames, or drag it back to cover fewer frames. Any keyframes within the animation bar are kept proportional to their original settings. This method works well in conjunction with altering the speed of an individual animation bar.

✦ Change the frames per second value in the Fps text box of the Timelines panel. Increasing the number of frames per second accelerates the animation, and vice versa. Adjusting the Fps value affects every layer contained within the timeline; you cannot use this method for individual layers.

Caution Browsers play every frame of a Dynamic HTML animation, regardless of the system resources. As a result, some systems play the same animation faster or slower than others. Don't assume every system has the same timing.

Recording a Layer's Path

Plotting keyframes and repositioning your layers works well when you need to follow a pixel-precise path, but it can be extremely tedious when you're trying to move a layer more freely on the screen. Luckily, Dreamweaver provides you with an easier method for defining a layer's movement path. You can simply drag your layer around the screen to create a path, and refine the path or its timing afterward.

The Record Path of Layer command automatically creates the necessary series of keyframes, calculated from your dragging of the layer. To fine-tune your work, you can select any of these keyframes and reposition the layer or even delete it entirely. This feature is a definite time-saver for DHTML animationists.

Keep in mind that a timeline represents not only positions but also positions over time and, therefore, movement. The Record Path of Layer command is very smart when it comes to time; the slower you drag the layer, the more keyframes are plotted. You can vary the positioning of the keyframes by changing the tempo of your dragging. Moreover, the duration of the recorded timeline reflects the length of time spent dragging the layer. To record a layer's path, perform the following steps:

1. In the Document window, select the layer you are going to move.

Caution Make sure that you've selected the layer itself and not its contents. If you've correctly selected the layer, it has eight selection boxes around it.

2. Drag the layer to the location in the document where you want it to be at the start of the movement.

3. Right-click (Control+click) the selected layer and choose Record Path from the context menu. If it's not already open, the Timelines panel appears.

4. Click the layer and drag it around onscreen to define the movement. As you drag the layer, Dreamweaver draws a gray line that indicates the path it is creating (see Figure 17-8).

   Each gray dot represents a keyframe. The slower you draw, the closer the keyframes are placed; moving quickly across the Document window causes Dreamweaver to space out the keyframes.

5. Release the mouse to end the recording.

   Dreamweaver displays an alert reminding you of the capabilities of the Timelines panel. Select the Don't Show Me This Message Again option to prevent this dialog box from reappearing.

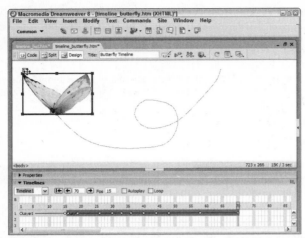

Figure 17-8: To record a layer's path, Select Modify ➪ Timeline ➪ Record Path of Layer and drag your layer in the Document window.

After you've finished recording a layer's movement, you see a new animation bar in the Timelines panel, representing the motion you just recorded. The duration of the new timeline matches the duration of your dragging of the layer. The keyframes that define your layer's movement (as described in the preceding paragraphs) are inserted in this animation bar. You can use any of the procedures previously described in this chapter to modify the timeline or its keyframes. If you select the same layer at the end of the generated timeline and perform the Record Path operation again, another animation bar is added at the end of the current timeline.

Caution   Any new paths recorded with the same layer are added after the last animation bar. You can't select a keyframe in the middle of a path and then record a path from that point; the starting keyframe of the newly recorded path corresponds to the position of the layer in the last keyframe.

Triggering Behaviors in Timelines

Adding a behavior to a timeline is similar to adding a behavior to any object on a Web page. Because timelines are written in JavaScript, they behave exactly the same as any object enhanced with JavaScript.

Use the Behaviors channel section of the Timelines panel to work with behaviors in timelines. You can attach a behavior to a timeline in four ways:

✦ Select the frame in which you want to have the behavior, then right-click (Control+click) and select Add Behavior from the context menu.

✦ Select the frame in which you want to activate the behavior and choose Modify ➪ Timeline ➪ Add Behavior to Timeline.

✦ Open the Behaviors panel and click the frame you want to modify in the Behaviors channel.

✦ Double-click the frame for which you want to add a behavior in the Behaviors channel.

When you attach a behavior to a frame, you can see in the Behaviors panel that the event inserted in the Events column is related to a frame number — for example, onFrame20. Each frame can trigger multiple actions.

Cross-Reference

For more specifics about Dreamweaver behaviors, see Chapter 12.

Behaviors are essential to timelines. Without behaviors, you cannot play or stop your timeline-based animations. Even when you select the Autoplay or Loop options in the Timelines panel, you are enabling a behavior. The three behaviors always deployed for timelines are Play Timeline, Stop Timeline, and Go to Timeline Frame.

If you are not using the Autoplay feature for your timeline, you must explicitly attach a Play Timeline behavior to an interactive or other event on your Web page. For example, a timeline is typically set to start playing once a specific picture has loaded, or once the user has entered a value in a form's text box, or — more frequently — once the user selects a Play button. You could use the Stop Timeline behavior to pause an animation temporarily.

To use the Play Timeline or Stop Timeline behavior, follow these steps:

1. In the Document window, select a tag, link, or image that you want to trigger the event.

2. Choose Window ⇨ Behaviors or click the Show Behavior button on the Launcher to open the Behaviors panel.

3. In the Behaviors panel, click the Add (+) button, and from the drop-down list, choose either of the following methods:

   • Timeline ⇨ Play Timeline to start a timeline

   • Timeline ⇨ Stop Timeline to end a timeline

4. In the Play Timeline or Stop Timeline dialog box (see Figure 17-9), choose the timeline that you want to play (or stop) from the Timeline drop-down list.

Figure 17-9: You can use the Stop Timeline behavior to stop all timelines or a specific timeline.

5. Click OK when you are finished.

6. Select an event to trigger the behavior from the drop-down list in the Events column in the Behaviors panel.

Note

As mentioned earlier, if your Show Events For option is set to 3.0 and Later Browsers, the only available event is onMouseOver. To make onClick and other events available, change the Show Events For to 4.0 and Later Browsers by choosing Add (+) from the Behaviors panel, then selecting Show Events For ⇨ 4.0 and Later Browsers.

When you select the option to loop your timeline, Dreamweaver automatically inserts a Go to Timeline Frame behavior with the first frame set as the target. You can display any frame on your timeline by inserting the Go to Timeline Frame behavior manually. To use the Go to Timeline Frame behavior, follow these steps:

1. In the Document window, select a tag, link, or image that you want to trigger the event.

2. Choose Window ➪ Behaviors or click the Show Behavior button on the Launcher to open the Behaviors panel.

3. In the Behaviors panel, click the Add (+) button and choose Timeline ➪ Go to Timeline Frame from the drop-down list.

4. In the Timeline field of the Go To Timeline Frame dialog box, choose the timeline you want to affect.

5. Enter the desired frame number in the Go to Frame text box.

6. If you'd like the timeline to loop a set number of times, enter a value in the Loop text box. Click OK when you are finished.

   Remember that if you don't enter a value, the timeline loops endlessly.

Tip   Depending on the type of effect desired, you may want to use two of the timeline behaviors together. To ensure that your timeline always starts from the same point, first attach a Go to Timeline Frame behavior to the event and then attach the Play Timeline behavior to the same event.

Dreamweaver TECHNIQUE Making the Slideshow Interactive

In this technique, you add behaviors to control the timeline, both automatically and under user operation.

Caution   This Technique works only in Windows.

1. Re-open the previously saved file, `timelines_start.htm`.

2. In the Timelines panel, select the Loop option.

3. When the dialog appears that informs you the Go to Timeline Frame action is being added to frame 31, click OK.

   The slideshow is now set to automatically repeat at the end of the timeline. Next, you add behaviors to add user control.

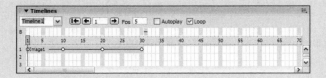

4. Select the Play image on the page.

5. From the Behaviors panel, click Add (+) and select Timelines ⇨ Play Timeline.

6. In the Play Timeline dialog box, make sure that Timeline 1 is displayed in the list and click OK.

7. Select the Pause image on the page.

8. From the Behaviors panel, click Add (+) and select Timelines ⇨ Stop Timeline.

9. In the Stop Timeline dialog box, choose Timeline 1 from the drop-down list and click OK.

10. Choose the Stop image on the page and repeat steps 8 and 9.

11. To make the stop button's effect different from that of the pause button, add a second behavior to reset the timeline.

   From the Behaviors panel, click Add (+) and select Timelines ⇨ Go to Timeline Frame.

12. In the Go to Timeline Frame dialog box, choose Timeline 1 from the drop-down list, make sure the Go to Frame value is set to 1 and that the Loop option is blank; click OK when you're done.

13. The slideshow is almost done; the last step is to slow down the speed of the timeline.

   In the Timelines panel, set the fps (Frames per Second) value to 5.

14. Save your page and preview in browser to test.

You can add as many images to your slideshow as you like by extending the timeline and including additional keyframes.

END

Summary

Timelines are effective tools for developing pages in which events need to be triggered at specific points in time.

✦ Timelines can affect particular attributes of layers and images, or they can start any Dreamweaver behavior.

✦ Use the Timelines panel to set an animation to play automatically, to have it loop indefinitely, and to change the frames-per-second display rate of the timeline.

✦ You must use one of the timeline behaviors to activate your timeline if you don't use the Autoplay feature.

In the next chapter, you begin working with dynamic content by learning the basics of establishing database connections and building recordsets.

✦　　✦　　✦

Incorporating Dynamic Data

Establishing Connections and Recordsets

Although Dreamweaver can be used to build any sort of Web application, one of its biggest strengths is its capability to present and manage dynamically accessed data. In other words, many designers use Dreamweaver to display and alter information from a database on the Web. But to handle that information, you must first establish a connection between the Web page and the desired data source and then you must define a selection of records from that data source.

Dreamweaver is adept at handling both of these pieces. You can connect to virtually any data source — databases, spreadsheets, and even standard text files — in a number of different ways. Dreamweaver offers a variety of connection types, ranging from the simplest with the highest overhead, DSN (Data Source Name), to the more complex, but most efficient, OLE DB. This chapter explains how the connections are made in Dreamweaver and why some are more robust than others.

After you have established a connection and your Web page is ready to communicate with your data source, you must create a *recordset*. You can think of a recordset as the key topic of conversation in a dialogue between a Web application and a data source. It is the result of a query made to the database based on your specifications.

For most basic recordsets, Dreamweaver provides a point-and-click interface. You can also construct more advanced recordsets that make extensive use of Structured Query Language (SQL) within Dreamweaver. Both methods are detailed in this chapter; if you are a beginner unfamiliar with database concepts, be sure to read the following section.

Data Source Basics

Data sources store information systematically. Here, the crucial word is *systematically*. Many other technologies, both low end and high end, store information — a shelf of books, a shoebox full of receipts, even a collection of Web pages. Few methods, however, store information in a way that facilitates structured and uniform retrieval. The precise nature of the structure varies from one type of database to another, but fundamentally, they are all the same.

> **Note**   The term *data source* is a more generic name for a database. In this book, the two terms are used interchangeably.

The two different types of data sources are system-based and file-based. File-based data sources store their data in physical files; Access, Excel, and dBase are all examples of file-based data sources. A system-based data source works with data stored in its own dedicated server where the database system resides. MS SQL Server, Oracle, PostgreSQL, and MySQL are system-based. Both types of data sources are structured in fundamentally the same way.

A database is made up of a series of *records*. Each record can be thought of as a snapshot of a particular set of details. The details are known as *fields*, and each field contains pertinent information or data. A single database record can be made up of any number of fields of varying types — some fields hold only numbers or only dates, whereas others are open-ended and can hold any type of information. A series of database records that have the same fields is commonly referred to as a *table* — a simple table is also known as a *flat-file database*. Like a word-processing or HTML table, a database table has rows and columns. Each column represents a field, and each row represents a record. For example, the following table called BookTitles describes a series of books.

Title	Author	Pages	Published
JavaScript Bible	Danny Goodman	1,248	2004
CSS Hacks and Filters	Joseph Lowery	266	2005
Fireworks MX Bible	Joseph Lowery and Derren Whiteman	1,016	2002

The first row in the table contains the field names: Title, Author, Pages, and Published. Each subsequent row contains a complete record. This table is in no particular order; however, one of the reasons why databases are so powerful is their sorting capability. If you were to sort the BookTitles table by page count, listing the books with the fewest pages first, it would look like the following table.

Title	Author	Pages	Published
CSS Hacks and Filters	Joseph Lowery	266	2005
Fireworks MX Bible	Joseph Lowery and Derren Whiteman	1,016	2002
JavaScript Bible	Danny Goodman	1,248	2004

To simplify data manipulation, many databases require that a table have an *index field* in which each entry is unique. In the preceding table, the Title field could serve as an index field because each title is unique. Not all tables can use a regular field as an index, however, because of duplicate titles or names. For example, you may not be able to use a CustomerName field as an index because you may have more than one John Smith in your database. If that's the case, you need to create a separate ID field using an AutoNumber type if you're working in Microsoft Access. If you're working in SQL Server, create an integer field and mark it as an Identity type. Either method guarantees a unique ID for each record by assigning an incrementing number to each entry in the database.

Index fields, also called *key fields,* become an absolute necessity when two or more tables — or flat-file databases — are combined to create a *relational database.* As the name implies, a relational database presents information that is related. For example, suppose that you create another table called BookSales to accompany the previous book database example:

Region	Sales	Title
East	10,000	*JavaScript Bible*
South	20,500	*JavaScript Bible*
West	42,000	*JavaScript Bible*
North	25,000	*JavaScript Bible*
East	15,000	*Fireworks MX Bible*
South	12,000	*Fireworks MX Bible*
West	8,000	*Fireworks MX Bible*
North	21,000	*Fireworks MX Bible*
East	8,330	*CSS Hacks and Filters*
South	6,500	*CSS Hacks and Filters*
West	8,000	*CSS Hacks and Filters*
North	7,400	*CSS Hacks and Filters*

To get a list of authors sorted according to sales figures, you have to combine the two databases. A field common to both tables is used to create the juncture, or *join*; here the common field is the index field Title. Although flat-file databases can be used in many situations, most industrial-strength applications use relational databases to access information.

In addition to changing the sort order of a table, database information can also be selectively retrieved by using a *filter.* A filter is often represented by a WHERE statement, as in "Show me the books where regional sales were at least 10,000 and less than 20,000." Applying this filter to the BookSales table results in the following table:

Region	Sales	Title
East	10,000	*JavaScript Bible*
East	15,000	*Fireworks MX Bible*
South	12,000	*Fireworks MX Bible*

The common language understood by many Web-available databases is *Structured Query Language*, or SQL. A SQL statement tells the database precisely what information you're looking for and in what form you want it. Although SQL statements can become quite complex, a relatively simple SQL statement has just four parts:

✦ SELECT — Picks the fields to display

✦ FROM — Chooses the tables from which to gather the information

✦ WHERE — Describes the filter criteria and/or the joins

✦ ORDER — Specifies the sorting criteria

A sample SQL statement translation of the "Show me the books where regional sales were more than 10,000 but less than 20,000" example looks like the following:

```
SELECT Title
FROM BookSales
WHERE (Sales > 10000) AND (Sales < 20000)
ORDER by Sales
```

Joins between two or more tables are depicted in SQL with an equals sign and are considered part of the filter in the WHERE statement. To show the sales by author's name, you could revise the SQL statement to read as follows:

```
SELECT Title, Author
FROM BookTitles, BookSales
WHERE BookTitles = BookSales AND ((Sales > 10000) AND (Sales < 20000))
ORDER by Author
```

Tip   The quick way to display all the fields in a table is to use a SQL statement with a wildcard, like this:

```
SELECT * FROM Booktitles
```

The asterisk indicates that you want to choose every field. From a server resources standpoint, however, this is an inefficient way to retrieve all records. If possible, select all your fields individually. Using the asterisk forces the database to determine what all the field names are, instead of being told exactly what to retrieve.

Understanding How Active Content Pages Work

The journey for a static Web page from user to server is straightforward, even for the most complex, graphics-laden, JavaScript-laden page. The user clicks a link that sends a signal to the server to send that page. An active content page — with full database connectivity — travels a much different route.

An active content page is a blend of traditional HTML and a database server language such as Active Server Pages (ASP) or ColdFusion Markup Language (CFML). When a user accesses an active content page, the requested page is passed through the Web and database servers where the code is processed, and a new HTML page is generated. That page is then sent on to the user. Figure 18-1 illustrates this process.

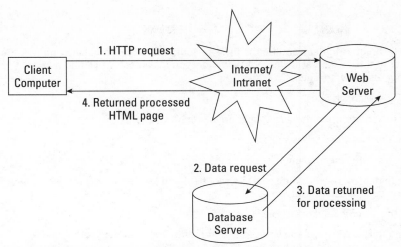

Figure 18-1: An active content page is processed by a database server prior to being sent to the user.

Active content servers can connect to more than databases. Other possibilities include the following:

✦ **Directory servers:** Directory servers control the permissions for large corporations and determine who is granted access to what group of files. With a directory server, two people — with different clearances — can see two different pages when clicking the same link.

✦ **Mail servers:** E-mail communication can be fully automated through a mail server. Responses to forms are categorized and forwarded to the proper parties. Mass mailings can go out at the click of a button. Messages can be automatically incorporated into Web pages.

✦ **File servers:** By and large, HTML by itself has no file manipulation capabilities. However, with a file server, files can be uploaded, copied, renamed, moved, deleted, and more.

The primary HTML vehicle for interfacing with a database server is the form.

Setting Up a Dynamic Site

Before you can use Dreamweaver to create dynamic pages, you have to make sure your site is defined properly. All the Dreamweaver Techniques in this chapter as well as those in the other chapters in the Incorporating Dynamic Data part of this book rely on a dynamic site.

Note: Although it is possible to use the same site previously created for the Dreamweaver Techniques, it's easier to create a second site specifically for dynamic applications.

Continued

Continued

1. Copy the Techniques folder from the CD-ROM to your Web server root. On Windows, the Web Server root is located at C:\Inetpub\wwwroot; on Macintosh you'll find it at /Users/*your_user_name*/Sites.

2. Choose Site ➪ Manage Sites.

3. Select New ➪ Site to open the Site Definition dialog box.

4. Make sure the Advanced tab is selected.

5. In the General Info category, enter `Techniques - Dynamic` in the Site name field.

6. Select the folder icon next to the Local site root field and locate the Techniques folder copied to your Web server root.

7. Switch to the Testing Server category.

8. Select the application server you want to use from the Server model list.

9. From the Access list, choose how you communicate with your application server.

   If you're using your own system for development, choose Local/Network; if you're using a remote host, most likely you'll choose FTP.

10. If you're using a local development system, click Test to verify the connection; for remote development, complete the FTP or WebDav fields before clicking Test.

11. When Dreamweaver informs you that the connection was made successfully, click OK to close the Site Definition dialog.

Any new pages you now create for your site will be configured for your server model. If, for example, you've opted for an ASP site, your new page will include ASP code at the top of the file as well as an `.asp` extension.

END

Opening a Connection to a Data Source

If you're a Star Trek fan (of any generation), you're likely to remember the phrase "Open a channel, Lieutenant." With these words, the Captain was asking to establish a communication link between the Enterprise and whatever alien vessel was hovering nearby. Not only are the technical lines of communication enabled, but any necessary translation services are also put into play. When you connect to a data source in Dreamweaver, you're opening a channel between your Web pages and a designated data source. (Notice that I'm referring to lower-case data, not Data, the android; I'll save that extended metaphor for another time.)

As noted earlier, you have numerous ways to connect to a data source. The simplest, DSN, requires some administrative setup and has a negative impact on server performance. Alternatives, such as DSN-less and OLE DB connections, require the developer to have more information on hand — such as the exact location of the data source on the server — but are less server-intensive.

Regardless of the connection method you use, Dreamweaver handles them in basically the same fashion. ColdFusion is the only language that's handled differently, either by linking to the data source directly through the DSN in the `CFQUERY` tag or through a Data Source Name Variable in the `Application.cfm` file. After you define a connection, as detailed in the following sections, a server-side include is inserted into your document above the opening `<html>` tag, like this one for ASP:

```
<!--#include file="Connections/connDBA.asp" -->
```

or this one for .NET:

```
<!--#include file ="Connections/connDBA.aspx">
```

or this one in JSP:

```
<%@ include file="Connections/connDBA.jsp" %>
```

or this one in PHP:

```
<?php require_once('Connections/connDBA.php'); ?>
```

In each case, Dreamweaver creates a folder called Connections at the site root for the server-side include files. The same file is referenced on every page that uses the defined data source connection. By using a server-side include, Dreamweaver provides a one-step method for updating all the pages using the same connection in the site. To define, edit, and manage your connections, open the Databases panel in the Application panel group, as shown in Figure 18-2.

Figure 18-2: Data source connections are managed on a site-by-site basis through the Databases panel.

The first thing you see in your Databases panel is a short checklist of what to do before you can start adding connections. Basically, you must:

1. Define a site.

2. Define a default dynamic document type for your site.

3. Set up the site's testing server.

Some server languages may have additional requirements. Each criterion contains a link that opens the appropriate dialog box for changing these settings. Once all the criteria have checkmarks next to them, you're ready to add connections. After you create your first connection, you have access to all the database information in the panel (see Figure 18-3).

Figure 18-3: Connecting to a database gives you access to all the tables, views, and stored procedures for that database.

When you've finished defining your connections, upload the files in the Connection folder so they work on your remote server. If you upload a file containing a connection and opt to include dependent files when you upload it, the connection files are uploaded automatically.

Using Data Source Names (DSN)

Data sources, like graphic files, come in different formats. Databases developed in Access are different from those developed in Oracle or FoxPro. To enable applications to access a variety of data sources, the Open Database Connectivity (ODBC) standard was developed. ODBC is a type of universal translator that enables Web (and other) applications to read from and write to databases by using a specific driver for a particular database type. Windows systems include drivers for data sources created in Microsoft Access, SQL Server, dBase, Oracle, FoxPro, Excel, and Paradox. There's even a driver for reading straight text files, which usually contain comma-separated values. Macintosh users should connect to the ODBC drivers on their testing servers.

The Data Source Name protocol was established to simplify the process of connecting via ODBC. Just as a domain name, such as `www.idest.com`, is an alias for an Internet Protocol number (for example, `64.70.242.110`), a DSN is an alias for the actual location of a data source. Locally, on Windows systems, DSNs are managed through the ODBC Data Source Administrator. Remotely, DSNs are set up by system administrators on the testing server.

Even if you ultimately decide to use a more efficient method of connecting to the data source, DSNs are very useful during the development phase. Every server model, except for PHP and .NET, supports DSNs. To set up a local DSN on a Windows system, follow these steps:

1. Windows XP and 2000 users should select Data Sources (ODBC) from the Administrative Tools folder. The ODBC Data Source Administrator opens.

Note   If you're working with a Macintosh and want to use an ODBC DSN connection — or just prefer to work with the actual data on the server — the DSN must be established on your testing server by the system administrator. All database communication is then handled online.

2. From the ODBC Data Source Administrator, select the System DSN tab. The System DSN tab lists all the DSNs previously defined for your system. If you've installed Dreamweaver, you see CafeTownsend (used in the Dreamweaver tutorial), in the list.

3. From the System DSN tab, click Add. The Create New Data Source dialog box opens.

4. Choose the appropriate driver for your data source from the list. The driver for Access databases is listed as Microsoft Access Driver (`*.mdb`); the one for Oracle databases is shown as Microsoft ODBC for Oracle. Click Finish when you're ready. A setup dialog box for the driver selected appears next. Each setup dialog box is somewhat different.

Tip   If you don't see a driver for your database listed here, get one from the manufacturer or database sponsor. If you are working with MySQL databases, you can get an ODBC driver from www.mysql.com/downloads/api-myodbc.html.

5. In the setup dialog box, enter the Data Source Name and select the data source. Following are examples of the most commonly used data sources:

   • For Access databases, click Select to locate the database (see Figure 18-4). If a username and password are required, click Advanced to enter that information.

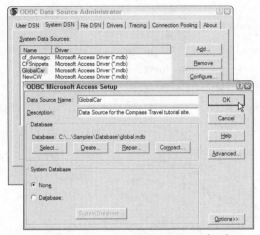

Figure 18-4: To use an existing Access database, click the Select button from the ODBC Microsoft Access Setup dialog box.

   • For Excel spreadsheets, choose Select Workbook to locate the proper file. Select Options to limit the number of rows accessed.

   • For SQL Server, select a name from the Server drop-down list. Choose (local) if your system also acts as the SQL Server. Click Finish when you are done.

   • For MySQL databases, enter the MySQL host name or IP address and the full path to the MySQL database. You can enter a username and password on the same screen. The MySQL ODBC driver also offers a wide range of options you can enable.

6. When you've closed the setup dialog box, click OK to close the ODBC Data Source Administrator.

After you've created a DSN for your data source, you're ready to create an ODBC DSN connection in Dreamweaver. Although the basic procedure is the same for all five server models, the specific steps are different enough to warrant the individual descriptions presented in the following sections.

Declaring an ODBC Data Source

A first step for ASP and ColdFusion users on Windows is to establish an ODBC data source. Although this operation is not strictly necessary for ColdFusion, it does make it setting up a connection easier.

1. In Windows, choose Start ⇨ Administrative Tools ⇨ Data Sources (ODBC).

2. From the ODBC Data Source Administrator, select the System DSN tab.

3. Click Add to open the Create New Data Source dialog box.

4. Select the Microsoft Access Driver (*.mdb) entry from the list and click Finish.

5. In the setup dialog box, enter **RelativeRealty** in the Data Source Name.

6. Next, click Select and navigate to `Relative_Realty.mdb` in the Techniques\Database\ASP_CF folder.

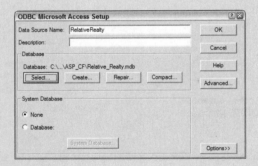

7. Click OK once to close the ODBC Microsoft Access dialog and again to close the ODBC Data Source Administrator dialog.

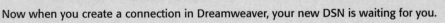

Now when you create a connection in Dreamweaver, your new DSN is waiting for you.

ASP

A DSN connection is often an ASP developer's first choice for rapid development because of its easy setup. To establish a DSN connection in Dreamweaver, follow these steps:

1. Choose Window ⇨ Databases to display the Databases panel, as shown in Figure 18-5.

2. Click the Add (+) button and select Data Source Name (DSN) from the drop-down list.

Figure 18-5: A drop-down list appears when you click the Add (+) button, enabling you to select a DSN-type connection.

3. The Data Source Name (DSN) dialog box displays. If you're creating a connection on a testing server choose the Dreamweaver Should Connect Using DSN On Testing Server option; otherwise, choose the Using Local DSN option. These options are not available on the Mac; you must always use the testing server.

4. Enter a label for your new connection in the Connection Name field. It's a good habit to identify your connections with the prefix conn; for example, you might label your connection connDBA.

5. If you're defining a local DSN connection, select an entry from the Data Source Name (DSN) drop-down list.

   If your DSN has not been previously declared, click Define to open the ODBC Data Source Administrator and, as outlined in the previous section, create a new DSN. When you're done, the new DSN appears in the list.

6. If you are defining a DSN connection on the testing server, enter the DSN name in the field.

   To select the DSN from a list of available ones on the testing server, click the DSN button. Dreamweaver attempts to connect to the testing server and retrieve a list of assigned DSNs. If your DSN is available, select it from the list.

 If your host has not set up his or her security properly, you may see DSNs other than those for your site. Alert your ISP to this security problem because it indicates that your data is accessible by others. A Tech Note on the Dreamweaver support site (www.macromedia .com/go/14961) describes steps to take to remedy this problem, which has been reported only on IIS 4.0 and 5.0 servers.

7. If necessary, enter a username and password in the appropriate fields.

8. Certain databases, such as those from Oracle, enable you to restrict the number of database items available from a connection. To limit the available tables, click Advanced and enter the desired Schema and/or Catalog.

9. To ensure that your connection is properly set up, click Test on the Data Source Name (DSN) dialog box. If the connection is established, Dreamweaver tells you the connection was successful.

10. When you're finished, click OK to close the Data Source Name (DSN) dialog box. The new connection is listed in the Databases tab of the Application panel.

Creating an ASP Connection

In this Dreamweaver Technique, you establish your connection to the DSN previously created. Work through this technique if you're using either the ASP-VBScript or ASP-JavaScript server model on a local development system.

1. In the Databases panel click the Add (+) button and select Data Source Name (DSN) from the drop-down list.

2. In the Data Source Name dialog, enter **connRelative** in the Connection field.

3. From the Data Source Name (DSN) list, choose RelativeRealty.

4. Leave both the Username and Password fields blank.

5. Make sure that the Using Local DSN option is selected and click Test.

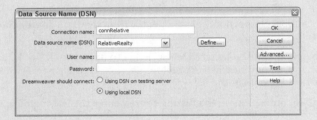

6. If Dreamweaver tells you the connection was successful, click OK to close the dialog; otherwise, double-check your settings and test again.

7. When you're finished, click OK to close the Data Source Name (DSN) dialog box. The new connection is listed in the Databases tab of the Application panel.

END

After the dialog closes, you'll see connRelative listed in the Databases panel.

ColdFusion

ColdFusion seamlessly integrates with the ODBC Data Source Administrator to use the DSNs already established on the system. Furthermore, new DSNs may be set up from within the ColdFusion Administrator. This compatibility makes establishing standard DSN connections very straightforward in Dreamweaver.

Note

In Dreamweaver, DSN connections in ColdFusion have a limitation. Dreamweaver only supports the use of stored procedures, a type of encapsulated SQL statement, for SQL Server databases with the standard DSN connection. To use stored procedures with databases other than SQL Server, you must connect via a JDBC (Java Database Connectivity) driver available through the Data Source Name — Advanced option, covered later in this section. The JDBC driver also enables Macintosh users to connect to a local database without going through ColdFusion.

You can enter new DSNs for ColdFusion either through the ODBC Data Source Administrator as detailed previously, or you can use the ColdFusion Administrator. To make a standard DSN connection for ColdFusion server models, follow these steps:

1. Choose Window ➪ Databases to display the Databases panel.

2. Click the Modify Data Sources button (see Figure 18-6) to open the ColdFusion Administrator home page.

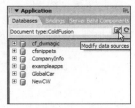

Figure 18-6: Use the Modify Data Sources button in the Databases panel to get to the ColdFusion Administrator.

3. Choose Data Sources from the Data & Services category in the left panel.

4. On the Data Sources page, select the proper driver (such as Microsoft Access) from the drop-down list, enter a Data Source Name, and click the Add button (see Figure 18-7).

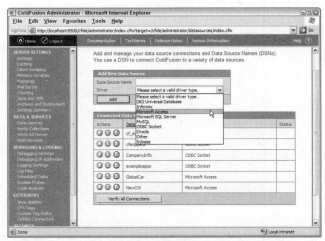

Figure 18-7: The ColdFusion Administrator includes an application for creating new DSNs.

5. On the Create ODBC Data Source page, enter the path to the database in the Database File or System Database field. Alternatively, you can click the appropriate Browser Server button to locate the file. If needed, enter a username and password.

6. When you're finished, click Submit. ColdFusion creates and verifies the DSN, displaying it in the ODBC Data Sources page.

Defining a ColdFusion Connection

Although you can define a ColdFusion connection to an Access database within Dreamweaver, it's actually easier to accomplish in the ColdFusion Administrator.

1. From the Databases panel, click Modify Data Sources to open the ColdFusion Administrator home page.

2. In the ColdFusion Administrator home page, choose Data Sources from the Data & Services category.

3. On the Data Sources page, enter **RelativeRealty** in the Data Source Name field.

4. Select the Microsoft Access entry from the Driver list.

5. Click Add. The Create ODBC Data Source page opens and displays the information established when the ODBC data source was created in the previous Technique.

6. Verify the name and the path to the database in the Database File field.

7. Click Submit.

   ColdFusion creates and verifies the ODBC data source.

8. Return to Dreamweaver and, in the Databases panel, click Refresh.

Dreamweaver does not automatically scan the ColdFusion Administrator for new connections, so a refresh is required. Feel free to expand the new entry and explore the database structure.

END

JSP

As you would expect, JavaServer Pages use the Java Database Connectivity (JDBC) standard. Dreamweaver includes six different drivers, along with an option for installing a custom driver, in its JDBC implementation. The six drivers included for the JDBC connection are as follows:

  ✦ IBM DB 2 App Driver, for use with local DB2 applications

  ✦ IBM DB 2 Net Driver

  ✦ MySQL Driver

  ✦ Sun JDBC-ODBC Driver

  ✦ I-net Driver for SQL Server

  ✦ Oracle Thin Driver

Table 18-1 presents the syntax of each of these drivers.

Table 18-1: JDBC Driver Parameters

IBM DB 2 App Driver

Supports	IBM DB2
Driver Field Parameters	COM.ibm.db2.jdbc.app.DB2Driver
URL Field Parameters	jdbc:db2:[database name]
URL Field Example	jdbc:db2:dbaEvents.mdb

IBM DB 2 Net Driver

Supports	IBM DB2
Driver Field Parameters	COM.ibm.db2.jdbc.net.DB2Driver
URL Field Parameters	jdbc:db2://[hostname]:[server port]/[database name]
URL Field Example	jdbc:db2://euripedes:1343/dbaEvents

MySQL Driver

Supports	MySQL
Driver Field Parameters	org.gjt.mm.mysql.Driver
URL Field Parameters	jdbc:mysql://[hostname]/[database name]
URL Field Example	jdbc:mysql://euripedes/dbaEvents

Sun JDBC-ODBC Bridge

Supports	Any ODBC driver, such as the one for Microsoft Access
Driver Field Parameters	sun.jdbc.odbc.JdbcOdbcDriver
URL Field Parameters	jdbc:odbc:your_DSN
URL Field Example	jdbc:odbc:dbaEvents

Continued

Table 18-1 *(continued)*

I-net JDBC Driver	
Supports	SQL Server databases
Driver Field Parameters	com.inet.tds.TdsDriver
URL Field Parameters	jdbc:inetdae:server_name: database_port?database=databasename
URL Field Example	jdbc:inetdae:euripedes:1343?database=dbaEvents.mdb

Oracle Thin JDBC Driver	
Supports	Oracle databases
Driver Field Parameters	oracle.jdbc.driver.OracleDriver
URL Field Parameters	jdbc:oracle:thin: @server_name:database_port:SID (SID is the Oracle database system identifier)
URL Field Example	jdbc:oracle:thin@euripedes:1343:dbaEvents

Many more drivers are available: You can find a list of more than 100 on the Sun Web site at java.sun.com/products/jdbc/index.html. Since the emergence of JDBC, four different types of JDBC drivers have been developed. Type 1 is the earliest prototype and the least robust; the Sun JDBC-ODBC Driver is a Type 1 driver, whereas the I-Net is Type 4. Type 4 drivers are native Java applications and offer the best connectivity. It's best to use a Type 4 driver whenever possible.

The Data Source Name is really an ODBC protocol; except for the JDBC drivers intended to interface with ODBC, other drivers do not use DSNs. However, the process is much the same — all you do is supply the proper parameters identifying the data source. To establish a connection in JSP, follow these steps:

1. Choose Window ➪ Databases to display the Databases panel.

2. Click the Add (+) button and select one of the drivers from the drop-down list. The connection dialog box for the chosen driver is displayed. Figure 18-8 shows the dialog box for the MySQL driver.

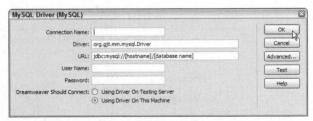

Figure 18-8: Each of the standard drivers for JSP connections uses placeholders in brackets to indicate parameters to be completed.

3. If you're creating a connection on a testing server, choose the Using Driver On Testing Server option; otherwise, choose the Using Driver On This Machine option.

4. Enter a label for your new connection in the Connection Name field.

5. Verify that the information in the Driver field is correct. If you are defining a Custom JDBC connection, enter the driver name as specified by the manufacturer.

   All standard Dreamweaver JSP drivers display the required syntax in the URL field; user-supplied parameters are surrounded with brackets.

6. If you are using a standard Dreamweaver JSP driver, replace the bracketed parameters with the information for your connection. For example, the supplied MySQL driver URL is `jdbc:mysql://[hostname]/[database name]`. If I were using a database named dbaEvents on a server named euripedes, my completed URL would be `jdbc:mysql://euripedes/dbaEvents`.

7. If you are defining a custom JDBC connection, enter the full URL as required by the driver.

8. If necessary, enter a username and password in the appropriate fields.

9. To limit the available tables, click Advanced and enter the desired Schema and/or Catalog. Not all databases support the capability to limit tables.

10. To ensure that your connection is properly set up, click Test. If the connection is established, Dreamweaver reports success.

11. When you're finished, click OK to close the dialog box. The new connection is listed in the Databases tab of the Application panel.

ASP.NET and PHP

ASP.NET and PHP don't support DSN connections. ASP.NET supports only OLE DB connections, and Dreamweaver's PHP server model supports only MySQL connections through its own ODBC drivers. See the "DSN-less Connections for ASP" section later in this chapter for more information about making connections with these two server models.

Specifying Connection Strings

Although a DSN connection may be the easiest to set up, it's not the most robust type of connection. In Dreamweaver, you can explicitly declare the details implied by a DSN connection by specifying a connection string. The connection string states the name of the driver, the path to the data source, and any additional information needed, such as username and password — all in one long string of text. Two types of connection strings are used in Dreamweaver: DSN-less connections and OLE DB connections.

DSN-less Connections for ASP

In the real world, ASP developers wanting to use the Data Source Name protocol often face a problem: They cannot get system administrators to assign DSNs. Some hosting companies limit the number of DSNs per site or charge a fee for each one. Often, it's difficult to get a hosting company to respond in a timely fashion. ASP developers can bypass all these potential headaches in Dreamweaver by using a DSN-less connection.

A DSN-less connection uses the same driver as a DSN connection, but without relying on the definition of a Data Source Name. The syntax of a DSN-less connection varies for each type of database, but basically has five parts:

✦ **Provider:** The underlying mechanism that connects the ODBC driver to the application. For ODBC drivers, the provider is MSDASQL; because the provider is always the same for ODBC, the entry is optional in a connection string and understood if omitted.

✦ **Driver:** The proper name of the driver as listed in the ODBC Data Source Administrator.

✦ **Path to data source:** Typically, this full path to a database is called the DBQ; however, with some data sources, such as Oracle and SQL Server, this parameter appears in two parts, listing both the server and the database name.

✦ **Username:** The username, if any, required for access to the data source. This element is often abbreviated UID in a connection string.

✦ **Password:** The password, if any, required for access to the data source. This element is often abbreviated PWD in a connection string.

Here's an example of a DSN-less connection string to an Access database named dbaEvents.mdb:

```
Provider=MSDASQL;Driver={Microsoft Access Driver ⤶
(*.mdb)};DBQ=c:\clients\dba\data\dbaEvents.mdb;UID=jlowery;PWD=hoosier7;
```

If the same data source were in SQL Server format (on a server named euripedes), the DSN-less connection string would look like the following:

```
Provider=MSDASQL;Driver={SQL Server};
Server=euripedes;Database=dbaEvents.mdb;
UID=jlowery;PWD=hoosier7;
```

To enter a DSN-less connection in Dreamweaver, follow these steps:

1. Choose Window ➪ Databases to display the Databases panel.

2. Click the Add (+) button and choose Custom Connection String from the drop-down list. The Custom Connection String dialog box is displayed (see Figure 18-9).

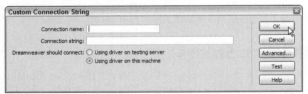

Figure 18-9: For a DSN-less connection, all your data source connectivity information — the driver, the path to the database and even the username and password — is entered in one long text string.

3. Enter a label for your new connection in the Connection Name field.

4. Enter the complete connection string in the Connection String field.

Tip   It's often easier to type your connection string into a text editor first — making sure that your syntax and parameters are correct — and then cut and paste it into the dialog box field.

5. If you're creating a connection on a testing server, choose the Using Driver On Testing Server option; otherwise, choose the Using Driver On This Machine option.

6. Certain databases, such as those from Oracle, enable you to restrict the number of database items available from a connection. To limit the available tables, click Advanced and enter the desired Schema and/or Catalog.

7. To make sure that your connection is properly set up, click the Test button in the Custom Connection String dialog box. If the connection is established, Dreamweaver reports the success.

8. Click OK to close the Custom Connection String dialog box. The new connection is now listed in the Databases panel.

Finding the Path with Server.MapPath

Right up there with the importance of getting your ASP hosting company to set up a DSN quickly is getting the company to tell you exactly where your virtual site is set up on its server. You must have this information if you're going to successfully use a DSN-less connection. Luckily, ASP includes a server-side command that you can use to find the path to your data source. The Server.MapPath() command returns the full path of the server when given the relative path to your data source.

For example, I have a site called myway.com. Within my site, I have a database, thehighway.mdb, located in the data folder off my site root. On my system, the relative path to the database is \myway\data\thehighway.mdb. When I issue the following command on my host's server:

```
Server.MapPath("/myway/data/thehighway.mdb")
```

I get back the full path, which might be something like the following:

```
E:\HTDOCS\jlowery\myway\data\thehighway.mdb
```

The Server.MapPath() function can be used in an ASP page or within the Custom Connection String dialog box to find the location of a file. Use the following code syntax for an ASP page:

```
<%@ LANGUAGE="VBSCRIPT" %>
<%
Dim ThatPath
ThatPath = Server.MapPath("\myway\data\thehighway.mdb")
Response.Write "Path to database: " & ThatPath
%>
```

After saving the ASP page and uploading it to your server, execute the page by typing in its URL. The full path to your data source appears in the browser.

Although this is adequate, your pages could break if your site is moved on the server or to another server altogether. A better method is to include the Server.MapPath() function as part of the custom connection string. Here's an example of such a string:

```
"Driver={Microsoft Access Driver (*.mdb)};DBQ=" &
Server.MapPath("/myway/data/thehighway.mdb")
```

Note the use of quotes and the ampersand before the Server.MapPath() function. Essentially, you are concatenating two text strings to make one long one.

The Server.MapPath() function can only be used when the Using Driver On Testing Server option in the Custom Connection String dialog box is selected.

OLE DB

Although DSN-less connections don't require an actual Data Source Name to be registered, they still rely on the same ODBC drivers. ODBC itself is a type of translator that relies on an OLE (Object Linking and Embedding) DB provider to make the connection. The most efficient way to connect to a data source is to use an OLE DB provider directly. Dreamweaver enables direct OLE DB connections through the Custom Connection String option.

OLE DB connection strings are similar to DSN-less connections except that only the provider parameter (not the driver parameter) is included. Here is an OLE DB connection string to an Access database:

```
Provider=Microsoft.Jet.OLE DB.4.0;
Data Source=d:\clients\dba\data\dbaEvents.mdb;
```

Different data sources require different providers. SQL Server uses SQLOLE DB whereas Oracle needs OraOLE DB. Follow these steps to create an OLE DB connection string:

1. Choose Window ➪ Databases to display the Databases panel.

2. Click the Add (+) button and select Custom Connection String from the drop-down list. The Custom Connection String dialog box is displayed.

3. Enter a label for your new connection in the Connection Name field.

4. Enter the complete connection string in the Connection String field.

5. If you're creating a connection on a testing server, choose the Using Driver On Testing Server option; otherwise, choose the Using Driver On This Machine option. This option is not available on the Mac.

6. To limit the available tables, click Advanced and enter the desired Schema and/or Catalog.

7. To ensure that your connection is properly set up, click Test in the Custom Connection String dialog box. Dreamweaver tells you if the connection was established successfully.

8. When you're finished, click OK to close the Custom Connection String dialog box. The new connection is listed in the Connections dialog box.

Tip   Create a blank .NET document and use the OLE DB Connection builders to create your DSN-less strings; then copy and paste the strings into your ASP connection dialog box.

ASP.NET and OLE DB Connections

The Dreamweaver engineers have outdone themselves when it comes to creating new connections in .NET. The connection dialog box may not be much to look at, but the Build and Template buttons on the right side make creating your connections a breeze.

To create a new OLE DB connection, follow these steps:

1. Choose Window ➪ Databases to display the Databases panel.

2. Click the Add (+) button and choose OLE DB Connection from the drop-down list. The OLE DB Connection dialog box is displayed, as shown in Figure 18-10.

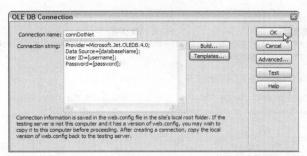

Figure 18-10: The OLE DB Connection dialog box offers a large space for you to manually type a connection string.

3. Enter a label for your new connection in the Connection Name field.

4. Enter the complete connection string in the Connection String field.

To avoid manually typing a connection, click the Build button to the right of the Connection String field (the Build button isn't available on the Mac). The Data Link Properties dialog box is displayed, as shown in Figure 18-11. Make sure that each tab is completed correctly to create your connection string.

Figure 18-11: The Data Link Properties dialog box provides a quick way to create complicated connection strings.

You can also click the Templates button in the OLE DB Connection dialog box to get a list of predefined connection string templates. Choose a template and click OK to add the connection string to the OLE DB Connection dialog box. The variables are surrounded by [and]. Just replace the brackets and variables and click OK.

5. To ensure that your connection is properly set up, click Test in the OLE DB Connection dialog box. Dreamweaver lets you know whether the test is successful.

6. When you're finished, click OK to close the OLE DB Connection dialog box. The new connection is listed in the Connections dialog box.

PHP

This release of Dreamweaver's PHP model supports MySQL connections only. To set up your MySQL connections, follow these steps:

1. Choose Window ⇨ Databases to display the Databases panel.

2. Click the Add (+) button and choose MySQL Connection from the drop-down list. The MySQL Connection dialog box is displayed, as shown in Figure 18-12.

Figure 18-12: Just complete a few form items to set up your MySQL connections in PHP.

3. Enter a label for your new connection in the Connection Name field.

4. Enter the IP or domain address of your MySQL server in the MySQL Server field.

5. Enter your database username in the User Name field.

6. Enter your database password in the Password field.

7. Enter the database name in the Database field, or click Select and choose from a list of all the databases to which you have access.

8. To ensure that your connection is properly set up, click Test in the Custom Connection String dialog box. Dreamweaver lets you know whether the test failed or succeeded.

9. When you're finished, click OK to close the Custom Connection String dialog box. The new connection is listed in the Connections dialog box.

Setting up a PHP Connection

Once your MySQL data source has been established, you can create a connection to use with PHP.

Note   You'll need to have already created and installed the Relative_Realty data source in MySQL located in the Techniques\Databases\PHP folder. See the Readme file in the folder for setup instructions.

1. In the Databases panel, click Add (+) and select MySQL Connection from the drop-down list.

2. When the MySQL Connection dialog opens, enter **RelativeRealty** in the Connection Name field.

3. Enter the IP or domain address of your MySQL server in the MySQL Server field. If you're using a local development system, enter **localhost**.

4. Enter your database username in the User Name field.

5. Enter your database password in the Password field.

6. Click Select to display the available databases and choose Relative_Realty.

7. Click Test to verify the connection.

8. If Dreamweaver indicates success, click OK to close the dialog; otherwise, re-check your entered values and test again.

You'll find your new connection listed in the Databases panel.

END

Managing Connections

In general, you create connections as needed and forget about them. All you have to do is include them in a page, and Dreamweaver handles the rest. On occasion, though, you must alter existing connections or remove outdated connections. All management of connections is handled inside the Databases panel.

To change the parameters of an existing connection, open the Databases panel, right-click (Control+click) the connection, and select Edit Connection. The type of connection determines which dialog box opens; a DSN connection, for example, opens the Data Source Name (DSN) dialog box.

Although you can alter any of the existing parameters during an editing session, you cannot switch from a DSN-type connection to a DSN-less(type connection via the Edit option. In addition, Dreamweaver does not allow you to rename an existing connection. With a bit of sleight of hand, however, you can make the conversion and keep all of your connections valid. To convert a connection from DSN to a DSN-less or OLE DB type connection, follow these steps:

1. Create a new connection of the desired type using one of the procedures described previously. This is a temporary connection that will be removed in the final step.

2. Right-click (Control+click) the old DSN connection from the Databases panel and choose Delete Connection. It's a good idea to jot down the name of the original connection before deleting it; you use the same name later in this procedure.

3. Dreamweaver warns you that this action cannot be undone. Choose OK to proceed.

4. Right-click (Control+click) the new connection and select Duplicate Connection. The appropriate dialog box is displayed depending on the type of connection being duplicated.

5. In the dialog box for the duplicated connection, enter the name of the original connection. Click OK when you're finished.

6. In the Databases panel, delete the first, temporary connection by right-clicking (Control+clicking) and choosing Delete Connection.

Although this procedure is somewhat convoluted, after you've completed it, you have effectively upgraded your connection from a DSN to an OLE DB type connection. The next time you put any of your Web pages on the remote server, be sure to include the dependent files for that page. Alternatively, you could put the file (now found in the Connections folder of the site) directly on the server.

Maintaining Design and Runtime Connection

The initial release of UltraDev enabled developers to set up two different connections—one for design time and one for runtime—with the same connection name. Dreamweaver no longer has this explicit capability, but with a little care it's possible to use a DSN connection locally and an OLE DB connection remotely.

The first step is to create the connection you'd like to use on the server and then put it on the site in the Connections folder. Next, create a local connection of a different type, named the same as the remote connection. Because Dreamweaver uses a server-side include referencing only the name of the file, your different connections are the same on both locations.

Caution   The one caveat is that when uploading your local files to your remote site, you must not use Dreamweaver's Put Dependent Files option. If you do, Dreamweaver overwrites the remote connection file with the local one.

Extracting Recordsets

Establishing a connection with a data source is not enough to begin working with that data—you must explicitly state what part of the data you want, whether it's all of it or just one record. This defined collection of data is called a recordset.

Within the code, you use a query written in SQL to define a recordset. Dreamweaver provides two methods for building recordsets:

✦ The simple Recordset dialog box, which uses a subset of SQL to enable point-and-click recordset building

✦ The advanced Recordset dialog box, which exposes the SQL format and enables you to write your SQL statement directly

After you define a recordset, Dreamweaver displays the available columns in the Bindings panel for use in Web applications, as well as a few generic data items such as first record and last record. The columns can then be placed on the page wherever needed, much like an image from the Assets panel.

Building Simple Recordsets

Many recordsets are straightforward and can be expressed in a simple sentence:

"Show me all the salesmen in the Eastern region."

"Tell me which beers are currently on tap."

"Give me a list of all the CDs in my collection by Elvis Costello."

Dreamweaver provides a point-and-click interface (see Figure 18-13) for creating simple recordsets that do not require the developer to know or write SQL. You can think of working with the simple Recordset dialog box as drilling down to the required information. You start by selecting a previously defined connection. Within that connection there may be many tables of data—in the simple Recordset dialog box, you can work with only one table.

Choose the table you want and then select the columns you need. You can use all the columns, some of them, or just one. Because servers maintain a recordset in memory during its use, it's always best to select only the data you need.

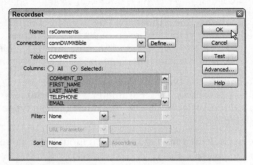

Figure 18-13: Although it is limited in power, the Recordset dialog box enables developers to construct a recordset without knowing SQL.

Next, you filter the selected columns to a particular set of data. If you leave the filter wide open, all the records are available. In the simple recordset, you may use one column as a filter; in the previous examples the filters would be something like Region = Eastern; On Tap = Yes; and Artist = Elvis Costello. Finally, after you have defined a recordset, you can sort it by one field in either an ascending or descending order.

To create a simple recordset, follow these steps:

1. From either the Bindings panel or the Server Behaviors panel, click the Add (+) button and choose Recordset (Query) from the drop-down list.

2. In the Recordset dialog box, enter an identifying label for your recordset in the Name field.

Tip   It's good practice to prefix your recordset name with *rs* — as in rsDBA. This prefix quickly identifies the recordset in the code.

3. Select a connection from the Connection drop-down list.

4. If the desired connection has not been declared, click the Define button to open the Connections dialog box. After a connection has been selected, the available tables are shown.

5. From the Tables drop-down list, select a table to work with. The chosen table's fields are displayed in the Columns list.

6. By default, all the columns are included in the recordset. To specify certain columns, choose the Selected option and then any desired field. Press Shift+click to select contiguous columns and Ctrl+click (Command+click) to select columns not next to one another.

7. All the records in the selected columns are available by default. To limit the recordset further, use the four Filter drop-down lists as follows:

   - From the first drop-down list, choose the field on which you want to base your filter. This list changes dynamically according to which table you've selected.

   - From the second drop-down list, choose the expression you want to compare with the data from the selected column in the first drop-down list. Available expressions are =, >, <, >=, <=, <>, begins with, ends with, and contains. Most of these are obvious except for <>, which means *not equal to*.

   - From the third drop-down list, choose the type of value to compare to the selected field. Available types are as follows: URL Parameter, Form Variable, Cookie, Session Variable, Application Variable, or Entered Value. (These types are explained in the following bulleted list.)

   - Enter the value to compare to the selected field in the fourth input field. Values entered are not case-sensitive.

8. To sort the data, select a column from the first drop-down list under Sort, and then select either Ascending or Descending from the second list.

9. You can see what results are returned for the recordset at any time by clicking Test.

Tip
To see how your simple recordset translates into SQL, click the Advanced button. You can return to the original dialog box by selecting Simple on the advanced Recordset dialog box.

10. Click OK when you're finished.

Perhaps the most challenging aspect to building a recordset is selecting the proper filter. Many Web applications rely on the filter mechanism of recordset queries to display the proper data. The following list describes how each of the different filter types is used:

✦ **URL Parameter:** URL parameters are arguments added onto the address of a page, typically by a form using the GET method. For example, the URL http://www.idest.com/ mail_list.asp?email=jblow@anyhoo.com indicates that the e-mail field would be set to jblow@anyhoo.com. URL parameters are encoded so that no spaces or high ASCII characters are transmitted directly.

✦ **Form Variable:** Form variables are passed by forms using the POST method. For example, a form is submitted that contains a text field named emailText. Using the Form Variable type, you can derive a recordset based on the domain of the e-mail address submitted.

✦ **Cookie:** A cookie is a small text file placed on the client's machine that may be read or written to by a Web application. Cookies are often used for authentication. After a user has been verified, the stored cookie value may be examined to permit — or deny — entrance to particular sections of the Web site.

✦ **Session Variable:** A session variable is similar to a cookie, but it is maintained on the server side. Session variables are often used to track a visitor's progress through the site.

✦ **Application Variable:** Application variables are maintained throughout the life of an application. Page counters are good examples of application variables. The life of an application lasts from the time the Web site starts (because the server was turned on or the site started) to the time the Web site stops (a server reboot or shutting down the site service).

✦ **Entered Value:** The entered value is an absolute value to which the selected field is compared. If, for example, I wanted to display only the DVDs in my database whose title started with the letter D, I would choose `begins with` as an operator and D as my entered value.

Writing Advanced SQL Statements

The simple Recordset dialog box is perfectly suited for building recordsets derived from one table and determined by one parameter. Many Web applications, however, require data to be supplied from multiple, related tables based on numerous factors. The SQL language is flexible enough to handle the most complex query — and Dreamweaver provides the advanced Recordset dialog box for this very purpose. To get a better idea of what is meant by the phrase *advanced recordset*, compare the following SQL for the plain language query "Show me all the salesmen in the Eastern region":

```
SELECT salesmen FROM employees WHERE region = "east"
```

to the SQL necessary for the query "Show me all the salesmen booking over $200,000 in sales in the Eastern and Southern regions":

```
SELECT salesmen FROM employees WHERE sales > 200000 AND ⊃
(region = "east" OR region = "south")
```

In Dreamweaver, the rule of thumb is as follows: Whenever any portion of your SQL query uses more than one element of any piece of SQL (two `ORDER BY` statements, two `WHERE` statements, or even two tables), you must use the advanced Recordset dialog box (see Figure 18-14). It is comprised of four main areas:

✦ The topmost section includes fields for entering the recordset's name and data source connection.

✦ The SQL section is comprised of a large text area, which contains the code executed to create the recordset. You can enter your SQL directly, copy and paste from a query in Access, or use the Database Items section to create your queries via point and click.

Tip

To write advanced SQL queries, you can create your queries using the Query Builder in Microsoft Access or the View Builder in Microsoft SQL. This makes it easy to create complex joins and filtering in a visual environment. You can then copy and paste the generated SQL directly into the SQL window in Dreamweaver.

✦ The third area is used for defining variables to be included in the SQL query; These variables must be entered into the SQL area manually.

✦ The area marked Database Items contains an expandable tree of all the data items available through the currently selected connection, including all tables (and their associated columns), views (also known as *queries* in Access), and stored procedures. Next to the tree is a button for three of the major clauses of a SQL statement: `SELECT`, `WHERE`, and `ORDER BY`.

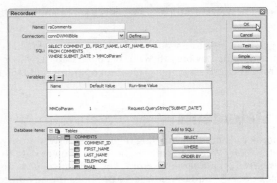

Figure 18-14: To work with more than one table or to filter against more than one field, use Dreamweaver's advanced Recordset dialog box.

To create an advanced Recordset follow these steps:

1. From either the Bindings or the Server Behaviors panel, click the Add (+) button and choose Recordset (Query) from the drop-down list.

2. If the simple Recordset dialog box displays, click Advanced. Dreamweaver remembers the last mode used to build a recordset, so the next time you create a recordset, the advanced Recordset dialog box will display.

3. In the advanced Recordset dialog box, enter an identifying label for your recordset in the Name field.

4. Select a connection from the drop-down list of that name.

5. If the desired connection has not been declared, click Define to open the Connections dialog box. Select a connection, and the available tables are shown in the Database Items tree. You can enter your SQL query by hand or by using the Database Items tree.

6. To create your SQL statement manually, enter it directly into the SQL text area.

Tip

If you're using Microsoft Access for your database, you can create your query using the Access Query Builder, switch to SQL View, copy the code, and paste the code directly into the SQL text area. This is a fast way to create complex join statements, and it can save a lot of troubleshooting time.

7. Select from the following to use the Database Items point-and-click method:

   • For the Select clause of the SQL query, expand the Tables section of the tree to pick the desired table and, under that table, the desired column. With the column selected, click the SELECT button.

   You can only add one column at a time; repeat this step to include additional columns.

- For the WHERE clause of the SQL query, choose the desired column and click the WHERE button. Complete the clause by entering an operator (such as =, <, >, or LIKE) and a comparative value. The value may be a constant or a variable defined in the Variables area.

  - For the ORDER BY clause of the SQL query, choose the desired column and click the ORDER BY button. Add the keyword ASC for an ascending sort or DESC for a descending sort.

8. To include a variable in the SQL statement, click the Add (+) button in the Variables section. Enter a name for the variable and its default and runtime values in the appropriate columns.

9. Click Test to see what results are returned by your SQL query.

10. Click OK when you're finished.

After you complete your advanced Recordset, you can click the Simple button to switch to the simple Recordset dialog box *only* if the defined recordset references one table that is filtered and ordered by one column using basic operators. In other words, the simple Recordset dialog box has to be able to build the SQL statement. If this is not the case, Dreamweaver alerts you to this and returns you to the advanced Recordset dialog box.

To give you a better idea of how the advanced Recordset dialog box is used, look at a step-by-step procedure used to create the SQL query that returns the results of a user-run search. For this example, suppose you want to search the LOCATIONS table of dbadata.mdb (an Access database). The search criteria come from a form element on another page, a text field named searchText; the search criteria are incorporated into the SQL query as a variable named varSearch. The final query reads as follows:

```
SELECT ADDRESS, CITY, STATE_COUNTRY
FROM LOCATIONS
WHERE LOCATION_NAME LIKE '%varsearch%'
ORDER BY LOCATION_NAME
```

Here's one approach to building this SQL query in the advanced Recordset dialog box:

1. Open the advanced Recordset dialog box by clicking the Add (+) button on the Bindings panel and choosing Recordset (Query) from the drop-down list.

2. Select the appropriate connection, connDBA.

3. Begin building the SQL query by expanding the Tables tree in the Database Items section, and then selecting LOCATIONS. Select LOCATION_NAME as the column under LOCATIONS.

4. With LOCATION_NAME highlighted, click SELECT.

   Dreamweaver puts the initial part of the query, SELECT LOCATION_NAME FROM LOCTIONS, in the SQL field.

5. While LOCATION_NAME is still selected, click WHERE. Dreamweaver adds the WHERE clause. The SQL query now reads as follows: SELECT TRIPNAME FROM LOCATIONS WHERE LOCATION_NAME.

6. With CITY selected, click ORDER BY.

After Dreamweaver adds the `ORDER BY` clause, the SQL query reads as follows: `SELECT LOCATION_NAME FROM LOCATIONS WHERE LOCATION_NAME ORDER BY CITY`. You've done as much as you can with the Database Items section, and it's time to add the variables and keywords.

7. In the Variables section, click the Add button and enter the following values (shown in parentheses):

   • **Name** (`varSearch`): This is the name that appears in the SQL query.

   • **Default Value** (`%`): The percent sign acts as a wildcard character for most databases. The default value is inserted into the variable if no other value is entered. With a wildcard character as a default value, if you submit the search with no criteria, all the locations in the database are returned.

   • **Runtime Value** (`Request.Form("searchText")`): The runtime value is submitted to the application server and returns with whatever was entered in the form from the input field named `searchText`.

   That does it for the variable.

8. In the SQL text field, add the phrase `LIKE '%varSearch%'` to the `WHERE LOCATION_NAME` clause, as shown in Figure 18-15. The `LIKE` operator compares two text values; and the variable is put in quotes with wildcard characters, the percent sign, on either side. This use of wildcards ensures that the entire data string is compared against the search criteria. Without them, only exact matches would return results. Click OK to add the recordset to your page.

Note Keywords in SQL, such as `SELECT`, `FROM`, and `LIKE`, are often uppercased to distinguish them from field names and other code, although you are not required to do so.

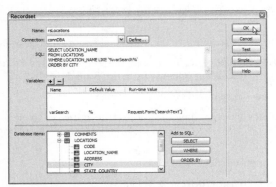

Figure 18-15: The `LIKE` operator, not available in the simple Recordset dialog box, is essential for constructing database searches.

An alternative approach to the method just described is to work out the SQL in advance and enter it directly into the SQL area without using the Database Items area at all. The only other element that you include is the variable. Which approach should you use? If you need to include complicated field names, I recommend using the point-and-click method to avoid typos. This method is also useful when you are using columns from different tables that have the same name; in this situation, Dreamweaver prepends the table name followed by a period, as follows: `LOCATIONS.LOCATION_NAME`.

Working with Recordsets

Recordsets need to be modified from time to time. To alter an existing recordset, double-click its name in the Bindings panel. The Recordset dialog box opens with the existing values. Which Recordset dialog box opens — simple or advanced — depends on two things: whether the recordset can be displayed only in the advanced dialog box and which dialog box was open last. If, for example, you are working with a simple recordset but had the advanced Recordset dialog box open last, the advanced Recordset dialog box opens.

 Caution When you're editing the recordset, be sure you're double-clicking its name rather than the plus or minus sign or the symbol in front of the name. Double-clicking the symbols only expands and collapses the recordset tree.

It's not unusual for the same recordsets to be used on different pages — and it's even more likely that similar recordsets will be needed. Dreamweaver enables you to copy a recordset from one page to another. Although this is good for those few times you use the exactly the same recordset on multiple pages, it's great for the many times when recordsets are only slightly different. To copy a recordset from one page to another, follow these steps:

1. In the Bindings panel, select the recordset you'd like to copy.

2. Right-click (Control+click) the recordset and choose Copy, as shown in Figure 18-16.

Figure 18-16: Copying a recordset from one page to another and then modifying the copy is a quick way to build similar recordsets.

3. Open the page to which you want to copy the recordset.

4. Right-click in the Bindings panel and choose Paste from the context menu. You can also choose Edit ⇨ Paste or use the keyboard shortcut, Ctrl+V (Command+V). However, you can only use the Copy command from the context menu of the Bindings panel.

Deleting a recordset from a page is very straightforward. Simply select the recordset from the Bindings panel and click the Remove (–) button.

Defining a Recordset

Once you've created a connection in one of the other Dreamweaver Techniques in this chapter, you're ready to put it to use. In this Technique, you build your first recordset and view the data chosen.

1. From the Files panel, open the recordset file for your server model in the 18_Dynamic_Connections folder. If you're working with ASP, open recordset.asp; for ColdFusion, choose recordset.cfm, and PHP users should select recordset.php.

2. Although you won't actually be placing any recordset-derived data on the page, you need to have a dynamic page open to make the Application panels accessible. From the Bindings panel, click Add (+) and select Recordset (Query) from the list.

3. When the Recordset dialog box opens, make sure you're in Simple and not Advanced mode; if necessary, click Simple.

4. In the Name field, enter **rsAgents**.

5. From the Connection list, choose RelativeRealty.

6. From the Table list, choose Agents (agents in PHP).

7. Leave the Columns option set to All.

8. From the Sort list, choose agentLastName and Ascending.

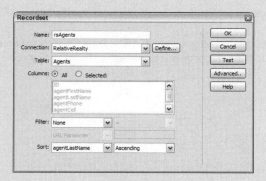

9. Click Test to view the chosen data. You should see three records, each with a several columns of data in alphabetical order by last name.

10. When you're done viewing the data, click OK once to close the Test SQL Statement dialog and again to close the Recordset dialog.

Although this Technique did not result in any dynamic data being placed on the page, recordset creation is crucial to the development of dynamic applications.

END

Summary

Although some Web applications don't use a data source, the vast majority do. Dreamweaver enables you to connect to any data source for which you have a driver through a variety of methods, ranging from the simplest to the most robust. With a connection established, setting up a recordset is the essential next step. Only after a recordset has been created can you place data on a Dreamweaver page. Mastering these two skills gives your Dreamweaver Web applications the access they require and the data they need. As you are laying the foundation for your Dreamweaver pages, keep the following points in mind:

✦ A Dreamweaver connection — after it is defined — is available site-wide. Dreamweaver uses one server-side include per page for each connection, but the connection file itself needs to be uploaded to the site only once.

✦ Although DSN connections are the most straightforward, they also carry the greatest overhead. Whenever possible, use OLE DB connections for the runtime connection.

✦ ASP developers may use the `Server.MapPath()` function to determine the physical location of their database on a remote system. Dreamweaver allows `Server.MapPath()` to be used in a custom connection string as well.

✦ Dreamweaver offers two entirely different interfaces for creating recordsets. The simple Recordset dialog box can create recordsets relying on a single table and a single criterion, whereas the advanced Recordset dialog box offers unlimited options, permitting you to write your own SQL query.

✦ Recordsets can be copied from one page to another. You can modify the copy to receive a different set of data with a minimum of effort.

In the next chapter, you learn how dynamic text is inserted, edited, and styled in Dreamweaver, as well as how to link to dynamic images and flash elements.

✦   ✦   ✦

Making Data Dynamic

By the time a visitor sees an active Web page in his or her browser, its data should blend seamlessly into the rest of the page. As with a well-crafted form letter, the reader shouldn't be able to tell where the basic structure starts and the dynamically generated data begins. Much of the work in Dreamweaver consists of properly placing and formatting data into a page layout.

You're not limited to dynamically integrating basic text into your Web applications with Dreamweaver. After text is included, you can format its look and feel on both the client and the server sides. Additionally, you can include images, form elements such as checkboxes and drop-down lists, and even multimedia elements such as Flash movies on-the-fly. Finally, Dreamweaver permits almost any HTML attribute to be dynamically altered. This chapter explores all the fundamentals necessary for integrating dynamic data into your Web page.

Working with Dynamic Text

The Bindings panel is the key tool for accessing dynamic text. With a recordset expanded, any or all of the available fields within it are ready to be placed on the page. Moreover, after a field is inserted into the page and selected, the Bindings panel reflects its current data format.

Cross-Reference

Before you begin including dynamic data, you need to establish a data source connection and recordset, so be sure you're familiar with the techniques described in Chapter 18 before proceeding.

Inserting Dynamic Text

After you have a recordset or other data source declared, adding dynamic text is as simple as dragging a field name onto the page. After the field is inserted, Dreamweaver displays it with the syntax {recordset_name.field_name}. For example, the column named CITY located in a recordset named rsLocations is displayed as {rsLocations.CITY}. If you choose View ➪ Visual Aids and enable the Invisible Elements option, the inserted data is highlighted (according to the color selected in Preferences), as shown in Figure 19-1.

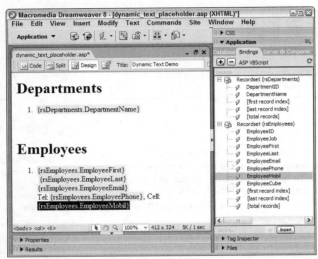

Figure 19-1: Placeholders for dynamic data are considered invisible elements in Dreamweaver and are highlighted accordingly.

Dynamic pages are a combination of standard HTML and dynamic elements. It's possible to build the page in any order. You can insert your dynamic elements first, followed by HTML objects, or you can build the HTML page before adding your data. Many designers, whether they're working by themselves or on a team, find the latter method more productive. One common technique is to use static placeholders to mark where the dynamic data should go, as shown in Figure 19-2.

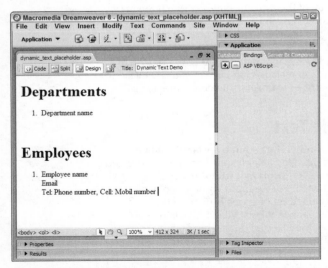

Figure 19-2: You can use plain HTML placeholders to indicate where the dynamic data should be dropped from the Bindings panel.

Perhaps the quickest way to bring dynamic data onto the page is to use the drag-and-drop capability, as detailed in the following steps:

1. In the Document window, select the static placeholder text to be replaced by the dynamic data.

2. From the Bindings panel, expand your recordset or other data source until the desired field or dynamic element is displayed.

3. Drag the dynamic data from the Bindings panel and drop it on the selected text.

   If you are not using placeholder text, you can drop the dynamic data wherever you'd like it to appear.

In some situations — when a table has many dynamic data fields, for example — the Insert method is easier than the drag-and-drop technique. For those cases, first select the placeholder text or position your cursor if no placeholders are used. Then highlight the desired dynamic data and click the Insert button on the bottom of the Bindings panel.

Tip   Occasionally, the dot notation syntax leads to extremely long names, which can make the layout process more difficult. You can switch from using the curly braces and full data name to just using the curly braces — and then switch back again — by choosing the desired option from the Show Dynamic Text As drop-down list. (This list is found under the Invisible Elements category of Preferences.)

Viewing Dynamic Data

You have three basic ways to see your page with the data extracted from the data source and fully integrated into the HTML:

✦ Upload the page to your remote testing server and view it through a Web browser.

✦ Use Dreamweaver's Preview in Browser feature to test your page on the testing server. Dreamweaver takes care of uploading the files for you.

✦ Switch to Live Data view within Dreamweaver.

The final method is, by far, the handiest to use during the design process, although the other two methods are important and should be included in a regular routine of Web application development. Live Data view has one key advantage over the other methods: You can continue to work on your page with the data in place. This facility is a major boon to application productivity.

To see your data within the page quickly, choose View ➪ Live Data. Alternatively, you can use the keyboard shortcut, Ctrl+Shift+R (Command+Shift+R); or if the Document toolbar is visible, click Show Live Data View. However you choose to enter Live Data view, you see the same actions take place. The Live Data toolbar appears in the Document window as Dreamweaver processes your page with the testing server declared in your site definition. As the page processes, notice the spinning lowercase *d* — the Dreamweaver logo — at the right end of the Live Data toolbar. If Dreamweaver is able to connect to the application server and encounters no errors, your data is displayed within the page as shown in Figure 19-3.

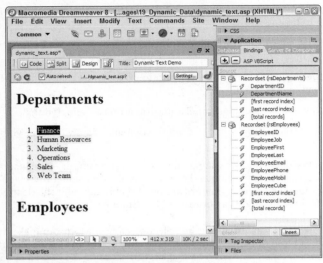

Figure 19-3: Live Data view uses your designated testing server to display actual data from your data source during design time.

Within Live Data view, you can use Dreamweaver as you would normally. If the Auto Refresh option (found on the Live Data toolbar) is enabled, any new dynamic data added to the page from the Bindings panel is automatically converted from a placeholder to the recordset data. Without any additional server behaviors — most notably Repeat Region — all data displayed is from the first record of the chosen recordset.

Cross-Reference   Live Data view has many more features than are noted here — all of which are covered in Chapter 21.

Dreamweaver TECHNIQUE   ## Adding Dynamic Data

In this Technique, you begin to familiarize yourself with binding dynamic data to the page.

1. From the Techniques - Dynamic site (established in Chapter 18), expand the 19_Dynamic_Data folder and open the `dyn_data_start` file for your server model.

2. From the Bindings panel, click Add (+) and select Recordset (Query) from the list.

3. When the Recordset dialog box opens, make sure you're in Simple and not Advanced mode; if necessary, click Simple.

4. In the Name field, enter **rsAgents**.

5. From the Connection list, choose RelativeRealty.

6. From the Table list, choose Agents (agents in PHP).

7. Leave the Columns option set to All.

8. From the Sort list, choose agentLastName and Ascending.

9. Click OK to close the dialog box.

10. Now that the recordset has been created, you can begin to bind the data to the page. You'll find it easier to work with the table if you enable Visual Aids ⇨ Table Borders and disable CSS Layout Outlines from the Document toolbar.

11. Place your cursor in the second cell from the left, in the second row under the middle of the phrase, Leading Agents.

12. In the Bindings panel, expand the rsAgents recordset.

13. Select the agentFirstName entry from the Bindings panel and click Insert.

 Note   Although you're using the Insert method here, you could have dragged the dynamic entries from the Bindings panel onto the page.

14. Move your cursor to the right of the dynamic data just inserted and add a space.

15. From the Bindings panel, choose agentLastName and click Insert.

16. Place your cursor in the cell under the Office Phone label, choose agentPhone from the Bindings panel and click Insert.

17. Place your cursor in the cell under the Cell Phone label, choose agentCell from the Bindings panel and click Insert.

18. Click Live Data View to test your operation.

19. Click Live Data View again to disable it and save your page.

In the next Technique, you add a dynamic image to the page along with some server-side-formatting.

END

Formatting Dynamic Data

After a field has been incorporated into a page, it acts just like any other text within a tag. Dynamic text can be formatted with either HTML tags — such as `<h2>`, `<strong>`, or `<span>` — or styled with Cascading Style Sheets (CSS). The easiest method is simply to replace the static placeholder text, styled as your layout demands, with the dynamic text. The tags and CSS surrounding any dynamic text can be altered at any time.

Tip   It's also possible to include HTML tags in the stored data. When the data is included in the page, the browser interprets the HTML normally. For example, you can have a memo field in an Access database (for data containing more than 255 characters) with italic tags (`<i>`) surrounding key phrases. This is perfectly acceptable to Access — which sees the tags as just text — and also perfectly acceptable to Dreamweaver.

Data Formatting

Dreamweaver not only supports client-side formatting of your dynamic data, it also offers a wide range of server-side formats, and it gives you the capability to create your own. Information is stored in databases according to a particular type. Some fields are designated as text, others are numbers, and still others fall under the date/time category. The same data type within a specific category may be formatted in numerous ways.

Dates are a good example of why data formatting is important. In the United States, dates are typically presented in a month-day-year format — such as March 31, 2002. In much of the rest of the world, however, dates are presented in a day-month-year format, as in 31 March 2002. By default, servers are generally set to display dates appropriate to their regions. The same holds true for currency: U.S. currency figures are presented with a dollar sign, for example, and UK currency is shown as euros or English pounds.

When initially inserted onto the page from the Bindings panel, dynamic data does not have a specific format applied. Data from currency and time/date use the default formats for their data types. Different formats are chosen from the Bindings panel, as outlined in the following steps:

1. Select the dynamic data that you want to format from the Document window. The corresponding field in the Bindings panel is highlighted.

2. From the Bindings panel, click the down arrow under the Format column to reveal the Format List, as shown in Figure 19-4.

Tip   The Bindings panel is usually pretty narrow. The Format column may be hidden off the right side of the screen. Use the scrollbar to move to the right and resize the Source column to make it narrower, or simply make the Bindings panel wider to get access to the right-hand columns.

3. From the Format List, select the appropriate category for your data.

4. If more than one format is available, choose a specific format from the category's submenu.

To see the newly applied format, choose View ➪ Live Data or click the Live Data button on the Document toolbar.

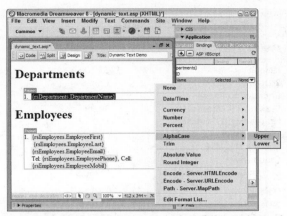

Figure 19-4: The Format List, which is different for each server model, lets you specify your data's format according to its type.

Tip   If you're already in Live Data view, enable the Auto Refresh option when applying new formats. Dreamweaver reprocesses the page and displays your new formats automatically.

Each of Dreamweaver's five server models offers slightly different data formats through the Bindings panel. A complete list of all the standard data formats, with relevant examples, is shown in Tables 19-1 (ASP), 19-2 (ColdFusion), 19-3 (JSP), 19-4 (.NET), and 19-5 (PHP).

Table 19-1: ASP Data Formats

Format	Option	Example
Date/Time	General Format	3/31/2001
	Long Format	Saturday, March 31, 2001
	Short Forma	3/31/2001t
	Weekday, Month Date, Year	Saturday, March 31, 2001
	Date Month Year	31 March 2001
	Month Date, Year	March 31, 2001
	YY-M-DD	01-3-31
	YY-MM-DD	01-03-31
	DD-MM-YYYY	31-03-2001
	M/D/YY	3/31/01
	DD/MM/YY	31/03/01
	YY/MM/DD	01/03/31
	Long Time Format	9:15:00 PM
	Short Time Format	21:15
	h:MM:SS AM/PM	9:15:00 PM
	HH:MM:SS	21:15:00
	hh:MM:SS a.m./p.m.	09:15:00 p.m
	HH:MM	21:15

Continued

Table 19-1 *(continued)*

Format	Option	Example
Currency	Default	$2,300.99
	2 Decimal Places	$23.99
	Rounded to Integer	$23.51 = $24
	Leading 0 If Fractional	$0.99
	No Leading 0 If Fractional	$.99
	( ) If Negative	($23.99)
	Minus If Negative	−$23.99
	Group Digits	$2,300.99
	Do Not Group Digits	$2300.99
Number	Default	2,300
	2 Decimal Places	23.00
	Rounded to Integer	23.51 = 24
	Leading 0 If Fractional	0.99
	No Leading 0 If Fractional	.99
	( ) If Negative	(23)
	Minus If Negative	−23
	Group Digits	2,300
	Do Not Group Digits	2300
Percent	Default	2,300%
	2 Decimal Places	23.00%
	Rounded to Integer	23.51% = 24%
	Leading 0 If Fractional	0.99%
	No Leading 0 If Fractional	.99%
	( ) If Negative	(23%)
	Minus If Negative	−23%
	Group Digits	2,300%
	Do Not Group Digits	2300%
AlphaCase	Upper	Mixed Case = MIXED CASE
	Lower	Mixed Case = mixed case
Trim	Left	" Widgets " = "Widgets "
	Right	" Widgets " = " Widgets"
	Both	" Widgets " = "Widgets"
Absolute Value	N/A	+23 or −23 = 23
Round Integer	N/A	23.51 = 24
Encode — Server. HTMLEncode	N/A	I'm <b>bold</b> = I'm &lt;b&gt;bold&lt;/b&gt;
Encode — Server. URLEncode	N/A	www.idest.com/Party Time = www.idest.com/Party%20Time
Path — Server.MapPath	N/A	Server.MapPath(/myDocs) = D:/HTDOCS/lowery/myDocs

Table 19-2: ColdFusion Data Formats

Format	Option	Example
Date/Time	General Date Format	31-Mar-01
	Weekday, Month Date, Year	Saturday, March 31, 2001
	Date Month Year	31 March 2001
	Month Date, Year	March 31, 2001
	DD-MM-YY	31-03-01
	YY-M-DD	01-3-31
	YY-MM-DD	01-03-31
	DD-MM-YYYY	31-03-2001
	M/D/YY	3/31/01
	DD/MM/YY	31/03/01
	YY/MM/DD	01/03/31
	General Time Format	9:15 PM
	h:MM:SS AM/PM	9:15:00 PM
	HH:MM:SS	21:15:00
	hh:MM:SS A/P	09:15:00 P
	HH:MM	21:15
Currency	General Format	2,300.99
	Dollar Format	$2,300.99
	Local Format	$2,300.99
	International Format	USD2,300.00
Number	Default	2,300.99
	2 Decimal Places	23.99
	Rounded to Integer	23.51 = $24
	() If Negative	(23.99)
	Minus If Negative	−23.99
	Do Not Group Digits	2300.99
AlphaCase	Upper	Mixed Case = MIXED CASE
	Lower	Mixed Case = mixed case
Trim	Left	" Widgets " = "Widgets "
	Right	" Widgets " = " Widgets"
	Both	" Widgets " = "Widgets"
	StripCR	"The End" = "The End"

Continued

Table 19-2 *(continued)*

Format	Option	Example
Math	Abs	Returns the absolute value
	Atn	Returns the arctangent
	Ceiling	Returns the next highest integer
	Cos	Returns the cosine
	DecrementValue	Lowers the number by 1
	Exp	Returns the exponent
	Fix	Rounds the number toward zero
	IncrementValue	Increases the number by 1
	Int	Returns an integer
	Log	Returns the natural logarithm
	Log10	Returns the logarithm to base 10
	Randomize	Seeds the random number generator
	Round	Rounds to the closest integer
	Sgn	Returns 1 for positive numbers, −1 for negative numbers
	Sin	Returns the sine
	Sqr	Returns the square root
	Tan	Returns the tangent
Encode — URLEncoded Format	N/A	www.idest.com/Party Time = www.idest.com/Party%20Time
Encode — PreserveSingleQuotes	N/A	'The Answer' = 'The Answer'
String — Reverse	N/A	'The Answer' = 'rewsnA ehT'

Table 19-3: JSP Data Formats

Format	Option	Example
Date/Time	General Format	31-Mar-01
	Long Format	Saturday, March 31, 2001
	Short Format	3/31/01
	Weekday, Month Date, Year	Saturday, March 31, 2001
	Date Month Year	31 March 2001
	Month Date, Year	March 31, 2001
	YY-M-DD	01-3-31
	YY-MM-DD	01-03-31
	M/D/YY	3/31/01
	DD/MM/YY	31/03/01

Format	Option	Example
Currency	Default	$2,300.99
	2 Decimal Places	$23.99
	Rounded to Integer	$23.51 = $24
	( ) If Negative	($23.99)
	Minus If Negative	−$23.99
	Group Digits	$2,300.99
	Do Not Group Digits	$2300.99
Percent	Default	2,300%
	2 Decimal Places	23.00%
	Rounded to Integer	23.51% = 24%
	( ) If Negative	(23%)
	Minus If Negative	−23%
	Group Digits	2,300%
	Do Not Group Digits	2300%
Number	Default	2,300.99
	2 Decimal Places	23.99
	Rounded to Integer	23.51 = $24
	( ) If Negative	(23.99)
	Minus If Negative	−23.99
	Group Digits	2,300.99
	Do Not Group Digits	2300.99
AlphaCase	Upper	Mixed Case = MIXED CASE
	Lower	Mixed Case = mixed case
Trim - Both	N/A	" Widgets " = "Widgets"
Math	Absolute Value (Double)	Returns a double precision number
		Returns a floating point numbe
	Absolute Value (Float)	Returns an integer
	Absolute Value (Integer)	Returns a long integer
	Absolute Value (Long)	Rounds to the nearest double
	Round Integer (Double)	precision integer
		Rounds to the nearest floating
	Round Integer (Float)	point integer
Encode — Response. EncodeURL	N/A	www.idest.com/Party Time = www.idest.com/Party%20Time
Path — GetRealPath	N/A	GetRealPath('/myDocs') = D:/HTDOCS/lowery/myDocs

Table 19-4: .NET Data Formats

Format	Option	Example
Date/Time	17-01-2001 Monday, January 17, 2001 January 17 January, 2001 2:35 PM 2:35:18 PM	17-01-2001 Monday, January 17, 2001 January 17 January, 2001 2:35 PM 2:35:18 PM
Currency	Default	$2,300.99
Percent	Default Round	2,300% 23.51% = 24%
Number	Default Round	2,300.99 23.51 = 24
AlphaCase	Upper Lower	Mixed Case = MIXED CASE Mixed Case = mixed case
Trim	Left Right Both	" Widgets " = "Widgets " " Widgets " = " Widgets" " Widgets " = "Widgets"
Encode — HTMLEncodedFormat	N/A	I'm \bold\ = I'm <b>bold</b>
Encode — URLEncodedFormat	N/A	www.idest.com/Party Time = www.idest.com/Party%20Time
Map — Server.MapPath	N/A	Server.MapPath(/myDocs) = D:/HTDOCS/lowery/myDocs

Table 19-5: PHP Data Formats

Format	Option	Example
AlphaCase	Lower Upper First Letter Upper Capitalize	My Widgets = my widgets My Widgets = MY WIDGETS My Widgets = My widgets My Widgets = My Widgets
Trim	Left Right Both	" Widgets " = "Widgets " " Widgets " = " Widgets" " Widgets " = "Widgets"

Format	Option	Example
Encode	HTML Encode	I'm bold = I'm <b>bold</b>
	URL Encode	www.idest.com/Party Time = www.idest.com/Party+Time
	Raw URL Encode	www.idest.com/Party Time = www.idest.com/Party%20Time
	URL Decode	www.idest.com/Party+Time = www.idest.com/Party Time
	Raw URL Decode	www.idest.com/Party%20Time = www.idest.com/Party Time

Editing and Creating New Data Formats

Although Dreamweaver includes a wide variety of format selections, sometimes only a custom format will do. In Dreamweaver, you can edit existing currency, number, or percent formats, or you can create your own version of any of these types from scratch. After a new format has been defined — or an old one has been altered — that format is available for any sites using the same server model under which it was created. To edit or create a new data format, follow these steps:

1. Select the inserted dynamic data in the Document window that requires the custom format. The corresponding field is highlighted in the Bindings panel.

2. In the Bindings panel, click the down arrow in the Format column and choose Edit Format List from the drop-down menu. The Edit Format List dialog, shown in Figure 19-5, is displayed.

Figure 19-5: Only currency, number, and percent format types can be edited or created through the Edit Format List dialog box.

3. To alter an existing currency, number, or percent format, select the format and click the Edit button. If you prefer to create an entirely new format, click the Add (+) button and from the pop-up list select Number, Currency, or Percent. The appropriate dialog box opens. If you attempt to edit a format other than the three types allowed, Dreamweaver notes that the format has no parameters to customize.

You can't edit any of the built-in formats or add additional formats in the .NET server model without manually editing the format configuration files in the Dreamweaver Configuration folder.

4. In the Number, Currency, or Percent dialog box, design your format by adjusting the four available drop-down lists:

- **# Digits after Decimal Point:** Choose a value from 0 to 20.
- **Leading Zero** (if Fraction): Select Yes, No, or Default for locale.
- **Negative:** Select Parentheses, Minus sign, or Default for locale.
- **Group Digits:** Select Yes, No, or Default for locale.

Although each of the dialog boxes offers different options, they work exactly the same. You can also choose Get More Formats from the drop-down list to go directly to Macromedia Exchange.

5. When you're finished, click OK to close the specific format dialog box.

6. Give the format a name to be displayed in the Format column in the Bindings panel.

7. To edit or create another format, repeat steps 3 through 6.

8. To delete a format, select it from the list and click Remove.

9. When you're finished, click OK.

Dreamweaver applies your newly created format to the selected dynamic data. Use the Live Data view to preview your new format.

Caution

A known problem exists with Windows 98 and the Edit Format List option. After applying an edited format (not a new one) to the dynamic data, Dreamweaver correctly identifies the format name in the Bindings panel. However, if you deselect the dynamic data and then reselect it, the Bindings panel Format column indicates that None is applied. Although the name is not shown, the code has not changed, and the data will render appropriately. To avoid this issue, create a new format with the desired options.

Additional Time/Date Formatting

The Edit Format List option works well for currency, number, and percent formats, but it does not permit new time and/or date formats. I recently built a site for which the client wanted the time to be shown in a particular way, for example, 9PM. The closest format in Dreamweaver displays that time as 9:00:00 PM. To show the time as desired, I needed to add some hand-coding.

This site uses an ASP server model with VBScript as its scripting language. My first task was to show only the hour portion of time. VBScript has a function that does exactly this, aptly named Hour(). When applied to my dynamic data code, it looks like this:

```
<%=Hour(rsEvents.Fields.Item("showTime").Value) %>
```

Unfortunately, the Hour() function returns values according to a 24-hour clock (also known as military time), so 9PM becomes 21. The second problem is that the Hour() function only returns a number and does not include an AM or PM designation. To solve these problems, I wrote a small ASP routine that incorporated the Dreamweaver-generated code:

```
<%
Dim myTime, myShift
myShift = "AM"
```

```
myTime = Hour(rsEvents.Fields.Item("showTime").Value)
If (myTime > 12) Then
    myTime = myTime-12
    myShift = "PM"
End If
Response.write myTime & myShift
%>
```

This routine works well for the site, but it would have to be modified to handle 12 Noon and 12 Midnight circumstances. In addition to the `Hour()` function, VBScript has similar functions to extract other time elements: `Minute()` and `Second()`. For dates, use the comparable `Month()`, `Day()`, and `Year()` functions. All these functions return number values, which you can convert to names by further use of the `MonthName()` function. The `Weekday()` and `WeekdayName()` functions are used together to display either full or abbreviated day names. For example, to get the date as Sunday, February 11, without the year imposed by Dreamweaver's standard formats, I would use code like this:

```
<%= WeekdayName(Weekday((rsEvents.Fields.Item("showDate").Value)))
& ", "
MonthName(Month((rsEvents.Fields.Item("showDate").Value)))
& " "
Day((rsEvents.Fields.Item("showDate").Value))
%>
```

There are commercial solutions to the problem of limited Date/Time formats in ASP. The DWfaq Date/Time Format Suite from `www.dwfaq.com/store/` contains more than 100 date formats and allows you to customize each one using the Edit Format steps in the previous section.

ColdFusion developers have a much easier way of manipulating times and dates with the `TimeFormat()` and `DateFormat()` functions. For example, here's the ColdFusion code for displaying a date in my example format (such as Sunday, February 11):

```
#DateFormat("#rsEvents.showDate#", "dddd, mmmm d")#
```

Making Images Dynamic

The Web is both a textual and a visual medium. You've seen how Dreamweaver replaces static text with dynamic text from a database. But how does it handle images? Dreamweaver dynamically inserts images by using the path to the image rather than the image itself. Proper database setup is critical for Dreamweaver to correctly deliver dynamic images. For example, a product database might have the following records:

SKU#	Name	Cost	Image
10101	Widget-O-Wonder	$99.99	/images/products/w_wonder.gif
10102	WidgetMatic	$49.99	/images/products/w_matic.gif
10103	Widget-Ultimo	$999.99	/images/products/w_ultimo.gif

In this example, Dreamweaver extracts the data from the Image field and plugs that data into an attribute of the `<img>` tag's `src` attribute. Because site-root-relative links are used in the data source the images can be inserted dynamically from any page in the site. If your dynamic images are located on a remote server, you must enter a full URL—with the `http://` prefix— in a text field in the data source.

Caution   Some databases, including Access, allow fields to be set up as hyperlink types. Although it may not seem logical, fields containing paths to images should be a text type, not a hyperlink type. Hyperlink type fields are used only inside Microsoft Access applications and are never used for live sites. Hyperlink type images already include the HTML code for a link. That won't work in Dreamweaver.

It is also possible to use document-relative pathnames in image fields of the database. However, you have to be careful which pages the dynamic images are inserted into; the pages must be stored in the proper location relative to the path of the images.

Perhaps the best course of action is to store just the filenames of the images themselves in the data source. When the dynamic image is inserted into Dreamweaver, additional path information can be added as needed. For example, suppose the image field contained only filenames with no path information, such as `w_wonder.gif` in a field named `images` of a recordset `rsProducts`. Here's an example of how that code would be generated by Dreamweaver for ASP:

```
<%=(rsProducts.Fields.Item("images").Value)%>
```

In Dreamweaver you can preface that code—either when it is inserted or through the Property inspector—with any necessary path information. If my document is at the site root and the images are stored in the `/images/products` folder, I adjust the code like this:

```
images/products/<%=(rsProducts.Fields.Item("images").Value)%>
```

After your data source is correctly set up for images, inserting them in Dreamweaver is very straightforward, as shown in the following steps:

1. Make sure that you define a recordset with at least one field consisting of paths to graphics.

2. Position your cursor where you want your dynamic image to appear.

3. From the Common category of the Insert bar, select Insert Image.

   Alternatively, you can drag the Insert Image button to the proper place on the page. In either case, the Select Image Source dialog box appears.

4. From the Select Image Source dialog, Windows users should choose the Select File Name From Data Sources option at the top of the page. Macintosh users should click the Data Sources button found just below the URL field.

5. If necessary, expand the data source to locate and select the desired image field, as shown in Figure 19-6. Dreamweaver places the code for inserting the dynamic image into the URL field.

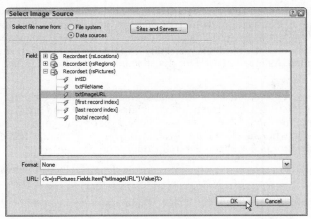

Figure 19-6: When inserting a dynamic image, you specify only the data source and field. Dreamweaver automatically inserts the image with the correct dimensions.

6. If your image data (the paths to the images) contains spaces, tildes, or other nonstandard characters, the data must be encoded properly to be read by the server. From the Format List, select Encode—Server.HTMLEncode (ASP); Encode—HTMLEncodedFormat (.NET); Encode—URLEncoded Format (ColdFusion); or Encode—Response.EncodeURL (JSP).

7. If your data is stored as filenames only, enter any required path in the URL field before the existing code. The path information may be document-relative, site-root–relative, or absolute.

8. When you're finished, click OK.

You can get a quick view of your work by choosing View ➪ Live Data or by clicking the Live Data button on the Document toolbar. The placeholder icon for the dynamic image initially appears in its default size of 32 x 32 pixels, but it expands to full size after you enable Live Data or you view the page through the testing server.

Tip If possible, store the height and width of your images in separate fields in the database. This prevents images from resizing in the browser and causing the page to jump as the browser determines each image's size. You also need the height and width for each image if you're validating against an XHTML DOCTYPE.

If you use static graphic placeholders in your design, you can use an alternative technique. From the Bindings panel, drag the field containing the image names onto the static graphic. If your data is just filenames without path information, you have to add the required path to the beginning of the src attribute in the Property inspector or Tag inspector

Some databases support storing the actual images as a Binary Large Object (BLOB). The BLOB protocol is not supported directly in Dreamweaver.

Just as you can assign a dynamic value to the `<img>` tag's `src` attribute, you can assign any data-source–derived value to any other attribute by *binding* (attaching) the field to the attribute. Attributes are generally assigned dynamic values through the Bindings panel or the Property inspector, after which the Bindings panel displays the attribute attached to each field in the Binding column. A data field used for dynamic images, for instance, shows `img.src` in its Binding column.

I recently used Dreamweaver to create a content-management system for a client. The page uses a standard template with areas for the heading, bylines, content, and images, served dynamically according to the topic. The images each have a specific alignment — some are set to the browser default, whereas others are aligned left or right. To handle this correctly, you create a separate field for image alignment in the data source.

With the database properly prepared, the attributes are set dynamically by following these steps:

1. Select the placeholder for the dynamic image, which is already inserted on the page.

2. From the Bindings panel, select the field that contains the data for the attribute you'd like to dynamically generate.

3. At the bottom of the Bindings panel, choose the desired attribute from the Bind To list, as shown in Figure 19-7, or click the down arrow in the Binding column if you've already bound an attribute to the image.

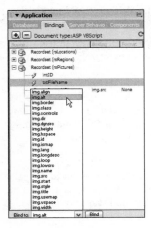

Figure 19-7: Change more than just the image dynamically by using the Bind To feature to link any tag attribute to a data source.

The Bind To list changes according to the object selected. To change the alignment on an `<img>` tag, choose `img.align` from the list.

4. Select Bind. The selected attribute is displayed in the Binding column of the chosen field.

To get an idea of what's possible, select a dynamic image and then look at the list in the Binding column. The `<img>` tag offers 23 different attributes that may be dynamically generated — everything from the heavily recommended `alt` parameter to the special case `vrml` attribute.

> To find the details on any or all of these attributes, choose Help ➪ Reference, choose O'Reilly HTML Referenced from the Book list, and then pick IMG from the list of tags.

Making Dynamic Images

The next phase in developing this dynamic page is to add thumbnail images and server-side formatting.

1. Open the `dyn_data_start` file for your server model previously worked upon.

2. Select the rsAgent.agentFirstName dynamic text on the page.

3. Press Shift+Tab to move to the previous cell.

   An alternative approach to make sure your cursor is properly placed is to enter Expanded Table mode by pressing F6.

4. From the Common category of the Insert toolbar, choose Images: Image.

5. When the Select Image Source dialog box opens, choose the Select File Name From Data Sources option.

6. Expand the rsAgents recordset and select agentPhoto.

7. In the URL field, place your cursor at the beginning of the inserted code and enter the path to the images folder: `../images/`.

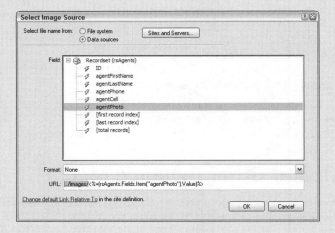

8. Click OK when you're done.

9. Test your page by clicking Live Data View.

   Formatting can be added while in Live Data View.

10. Make sure the Auto-Refresh option is selected in the Live Data toolbar.

11. From the Bindings panel, select the agentFirstName entry.

Continued

Continued

12. Select the Format list on the far right of the entry and, from the list, choose AlphaCase ➪ Upper.

You may need to scroll the Bindings panel to the left to see the drop-down arrow in the Format column. After you make the format change, the agent's first name will automatically become uppercased.

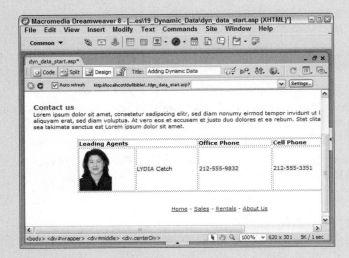

13. Click Live Data View again to leave the mode and save your page.

You'll revisit this page in the next chapter when you learn how to show additional data from a recordset on the page using a Dreamweaver server behavior.

Integrating Flash and Other Dynamic Media

Just as text and images can be inserted into documents on-the-fly, all manner of multimedia—including Flash and files requiring ActiveX controls or applets—can also be dynamically incorporated. The core technique of attaching a data source is the same for multimedia files as it is for images; when you insert a multimedia object, choose the desired data source from Dreamweaver's dialog box. The linking code is automatically written into the proper parameter for the object.

Most multimedia objects are inserted into HTML by using an `<object>` tag, an `<embed>` tag, or a combination of the two; Java applets use the `<applet>` tag. Dreamweaver handles the basic file assignments for specific programs with its own icon in the Insert bar. Examples are Flash, Director, and Generator. If you examine the code, you can see that even these objects use the `<param>` tag (short for *parameter*) to declare the source of the media file. ActiveX and applet files rely on `<param>` tags to specify needed attributes. Dreamweaver enables you to choose either static or dynamic values for any `<param>` tag.

You enter the `<param>` values through the Parameters dialog box, which is displayed when you click the Parameters button on the Property inspector. As shown in Figure 19-8, the Dreamweaver Parameters dialog box consists of two columns, one for the name of the parameter and one for the corresponding value. Entries in either column can be assigned dynamic content by clicking the lightning bolt icon. When this icon is selected, the Dynamic Data dialog box opens and an appropriate data source—from those already declared in the Bindings panel—can be assigned.

Figure 19-8: Dynamically alter parameters for any multimedia object by clicking the lightning bolt icon and picking a proper data source.

How you store the path to the movie is critical if you're dynamically switching Flash movies. As with images, perhaps the best tactic is to use only the filename in the database field and supply additional path information as needed. Here are the steps to display different Flash movies dynamically:

1. Position your cursor where you'd like your dynamic content to appear and click Insert Flash from the Common category of the Insert bar.

   Alternatively, you can drag the Insert Flash button to the proper place on the page. In either case, the Select File dialog box appears.

2. Windows users choose the Select File Name From Data Sources option at the top of the page. Macintosh users select the Data Sources button found just below the URL field.

3. Expand the data source to locate and select the desired field with the Flash movie filenames.

4. If your Flash data (the paths to the movies) contains spaces, tildes, or other nonstandard characters, the data must be encoded to be read properly by the server. From the Format List, select Encode—Server.HTMLEncode (ASP); Encode—HTMLEncodedFormat (.NET); Encode—URLEncoded Format (ColdFusion); or Encode—Response.EncodeURL (JSP).

5. If your data is stored as filenames only, enter any required path in the URL field before the existing code.

6. You can also link any Flash attributes to a dynamic source by clicking the Parameters button to open the Parameters dialog box, entering a dynamic value by clicking the lightning bolt symbol under the Name or Value column, and choosing an appropriate data source from the Dynamic Data dialog box.

7. Click OK when you're finished.

Cross-Reference   For more details on integrating Flash movies in your Web pages, see Chapter 24.

Summary

Incorporating dynamic data into your standard Web pages is a core skill for building data-driven Web applications, along with establishing a data source connection and defining a recordset. After you have these three components in place, you can begin combining HTML pages with text, images, and even multimedia data. Dreamweaver combines sophisticated connectivity with drag-and-drop simplicity for quick insertion of dynamic content. Keep the following items in mind as you begin to integrate data-driven and static content:

✦ The Bindings panel displays fields available for inserting into a Web document, much like the Assets panel, which shows available images and other elements. Like the Assets panel, data is inserted from the Bindings panel through a drag-and-drop procedure. For complex layouts, you can position your cursor precisely and click the Insert button instead of dragging and dropping the dynamic fields.

✦ Dynamic text accepts two types of formatting: client-side and server-side. Client-side formatting is another term for standard HTML and CSS formatting; dynamic text may be styled with the same tags and attributes as regular text. The final look for these tags and attributes is interpreted by the browser. Server-side formatting, on the other hand, reshapes the data from the data source before it passes it on to the browser.

✦ If you encounter trouble inserting dynamic images into your Web applications, chances are you're not doing anything wrong in Dreamweaver. The error may lie in your database setup. It's key to store the path and/or filename of the images in the data source as a text field rather than as a hyperlink.

✦ Dreamweaver does not support loading images as binary images from data sources, otherwise known as Binary Large Objects (BLOBs).

✦ Flash movies — in fact, any multimedia file — can be dynamically inserted into a Dreamweaver page. Again, storing just the filename or the filename and path in the database field is the best approach.

✦ Any attribute, whether of a multimedia object or regular image, can be dynamically derived. The Parameters dialog offers options for inputting either dynamic or static attributes and values on multimedia objects, and the Bindings panel allows you to bind dynamic data to attributes.

In the next chapter, you see how to begin managing your data in Dreamweaver.

✦   ✦   ✦

Managing Data

With the power to access the data of the world—or at least your part of it—comes great responsibility. As a Web-page designer you determine how best to present that information. Not only does this include the surrounding look-and-feel, but also how the data itself is structured. How many records should you show at once? One? Ten? All? How should the user navigate from one group of records to another? What should the user see when there are no more records to display? Obviously, there are no definitive answers to these questions; each response must take into account the intent of the page, the type of data involved, and the audience for that data. This chapter can't give you precise solutions for every Web application, but it does give you the tools to devise your own resolutions.

The Web is, almost by definition, a hotbed of constantly changing technologies. It can be frustrating when you are introduced to a technology, such as Dreamweaver's Flash buttons, and you cannot utilize its full potential. For instance, you have had no easy way to use Flash buttons to navigate recordsets—at least, not until now. The final section in this chapter describes a technique for combining the functionality of Dreamweaver's Recordset Navigation bar with the coolness of animated (and possibly sound-enabled) Flash buttons.

Displaying Data Conditionally

What makes a Web page into a Web application? Connectivity to a data source by itself does not make a Web application—after all, you're merely setting up the possibility for data integration, not actually utilizing it. Some would say that it is the power to programmatically control the display of the data that is at the heart of an application. Dreamweaver handles this conditional display of data primarily through its Server Behaviors panel. You can, for example, opt to display the data—or any other page element—only if certain conditions are met, such as an empty recordset. Before you look at the options for showing and hiding data conditionally, first examine what is perhaps the most commonly used Dreamweaver server behavior: Repeat Region.

Repeating Data

After establishing a data source connection and defining a recordset, Dreamweaver displays all the available fields in the Bindings panel. Regardless of how many records are contained in the declared recordset, you see only one record when you drag one or more fields onto your page and preview the file. To see multiple records from the same recordset on a single page, you can apply the Repeat Region server behavior.

The Repeat Region server behavior is very straightforward and extremely flexible. After selecting the dynamic data and any surrounding code you'd like to repeat, you specify the number of repetitions — you also have an option to display all the records in the recordset. The key phrase in the previous sentence is "and any surrounding code." If you select only the dynamic data itself, the data is repeated one record after another. You have to include some HTML element to enable the repeated data to appear separately, as on a different line. Some of the most commonly used separation elements and their HTML tags are as follows:

- ✦ Line break: `<br>`
- ✦ Paragraph: `<p>...</p>`
- ✦ Table row: `<tr>...</tr>`
- ✦ Table data: `<td>...</td>`
- ✦ Unordered or ordered list item: `<li>...</li>`

For the Repeat Region to work correctly, you must select both the opening and the closing tags that surround the dynamic data, as shown in Figure 20-1. The surest way to do this is to place your cursor on the dynamic data and choose the surrounding element from the tag selector.

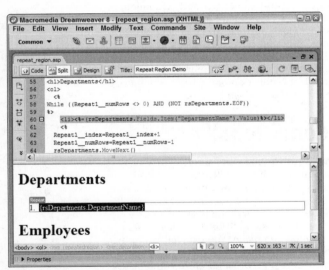

Figure 20-1: To automatically number your data, apply a Repeat Region to the `<li>` tag within an ordered (or numbered) list.

To implement a Repeat Region, follow these steps:

1. Select the dynamic data and surrounding code that you would like to repeat.

2. From the Server Behaviors panel, click Add (+) and select Repeat Region from the list. The Repeat Region dialog box, shown in Figure 20-2, appears.

Figure 20-2: With the Repeat Region server behavior, you can show some or all the records in the chosen recordset.

3. Choose the recordset you want to work with from the Recordset drop-down list.

4. If you want to present a subset of the recordset, enter the number of records you want to display in the Show: Records field.

   The default is to show 10 records at a time. You can change that value to anything you like if you select the Show: Records option.

5. If you want to display every record in the recordset, choose the Show: All Records option.

6. Click OK when you're finished.

Tip To test your implementation, make sure that the View ➪ Visual Aids ➪ Invisible Elements option is enabled. Then click the Live Data button on the Document toolbar. Dreamweaver displays each repeated selection with a highlight.

Although all the repeated elements are displayed on the screen, only the initial element within a Repeat Region can be altered. If you change the initial element's formatting, you must click the Refresh button from the Live Data toolbar to apply those changes to the other elements; this holds true even if you have Auto Refresh enabled.

Multiple Repeat Region server behaviors may coexist on the same page, extracting data from either the same recordset or a different one. However, if you use the same recordset again, you need to reset it so that Dreamweaver is extracting from the beginning. To do this, locate the second Repeat Region server behavior in the code by selecting its entry from the Server Behaviors panel and switching to Code view. Above the first line of server code, add the code appropriate to your server model (substitute the name of your recordset for `rsMine`):

```
ASP          <% rsMine.MoveFirst() %>
JSP          <% rsMine.first() %>
PHP          <? mysql_data_seek($rsMine, 0) ?>
```

Note ASP.NET and ColdFusion handle this for you. If you start a new `<asp:repeater>`, it starts from the beginning again, and the same holds true for ColdFusion `<cfoutput>` blocks based on your recordsets.

If you do not insert the resetting code, the second Repeat Region picks up where the first one left off. For example, if 10 records are displayed in the initial Repeat Region, the second Repeat Region starts with the 11th record. If you chose all records for the first Repeat Region, nothing is shown in the second Repeat Region.

Now that you know how to do this by hand, it's time to show you the quick way (I know it's cruel, but everyone has to learn the hard way first). Dreamweaver offers a fast and simple way to add a table of records with a Repeat Region in just one step. Choose Insert ➪ Application Objects ➪ Dynamic Table or click the Dynamic Table icon in the Application tag of the Insert bar. The Dynamic Table dialog box, shown in Figure 20-3, is now active.

Figure 20-3: Use the Dynamic Table Application object to add dynamic lists of tabular data quickly. You can save lots of time by skipping the tedious task of adding all your dynamic text manually.

This dialog box has just a few options:

✦ **Recordset:** Choose the recordset you want displayed in your table.

✦ **Show:** Choose whether to show a limited number of records or all records. This adds a regular Repeat Region to your field, just as you did earlier in this section.

✦ **Table attributes:** Specify your table border, cell padding, and cell spacing.

After you click OK, the table contains the field names in the first row, the data items in the second row, and a Repeat Region wrapped around the second row, as shown in Figure 20-4.

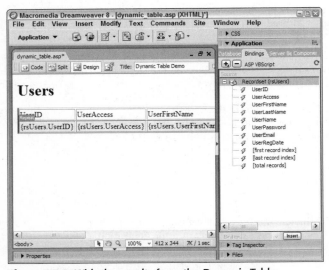

Figure 20-4: With the results from the Dynamic Table Application object, you simply change the basic table formatting and the table headings, and you're done.

Applying a Repeat Region

Repeat Region is one of the most frequently used server behaviors. In this Technique, you apply a Repeat Region server behavior to a previously created table row so multiple data records can be displayed.

1. From the Techniques - Dynamic site (established in Chapter 18), expand the 20_Managing_Data folder and open the `managing_data_start` file for your server model.

If you followed the Technique in the previous chapter, you'll recognize this page. There is, however, one small difference: an additional recordset has been added to illustrate an important concept.

2. Place your cursor in the row of dynamic data by selecting any of the inserted fields, such as rsAgents.agentPhone.

3. From the Tag Selector, choose the `<tr>` tag.

Choosing the `<tr>` tag ensures that the entire row of data will be repeated.

4. From the Server Behaviors panel, click Add (+) and select Repeat Region from the list.

5. When the Repeat Region dialog box opens, choose rsAgents from the Recordset list.

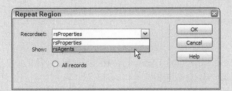

You must be sure to select the recordset you want to repeat; if you were to leave the default choice, rsProperties, no additional data would be displayed.

6. Leave the default Show 10 Records at a time option and click OK.

In Dreamweaver's Design view, a thin border appears around the row along with a tab indicating the Repeat Region.

7. Test your newly-applied server behavior by choosing View ⇨ Live Data.

Continued

Continued

Alternatively, you can click the Live Data view icon in the Document toolbar.

8. Choose View ➪ Live Data again to exit the mode.

9. Save your page.

In the next Technique, you see how to add elements to the page to indicate which records are currently displayed and to navigate through a larger recordset.

Showing and Hiding Page Elements

In the rush to push a site live, designers often pay too little attention to the user experience. When you are designing static Web pages, it's especially easy to lose sight of the importance of the user interface. However, with dynamic pages—where user interaction often determines what's on the page—an intuitive, reactive design helps to focus the audience on the content, rather than the engine driving the content. Dreamweaver provides a set of server behaviors that enable you to show or hide any area of the page dynamically: the Show Region server behaviors.

The six Show Region server behaviors are as follows:

✦ Show Region If Recordset Is Empty

✦ Show Region If Recordset Is Not Empty

✦ Show Region If First Record

✦ Show Region If Not First Record

✦ Show Region If Last Record

✦ Show Region If Not Last Record

Tip Don't let the terminology throw you: Although they are all called Show Region server behaviors, you can just as easily use them to hide an area.

Dreamweaver's capability to conditionally hide or reveal areas of the page is extremely helpful for smoothing the user experience. For example, suppose you have a Web application that shows all 23 items in a particular recordset, 5 at a time, with Next and Previous links (see Figure 20-5). The record navigation controls enable users to page through the recordset, forward and backward. When they reach the final record, the Next and Last buttons should be hidden; when they're on the first record, the Previous and First buttons should be hidden. I've used the Show Region If Not Last Record to hide the Next button and the Show Region If Not First Record to hide the Previous button.

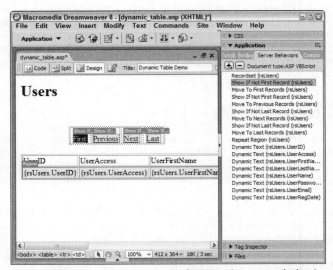

Figure 20-5: Use Dreamweaver's Show Region server behavior to display or hide navigation buttons, depending on the dynamic data shown.

To apply a Show Region server behavior, follow these steps:

1. Select the page area you would like to conditionally show.

2. From the Server Behaviors panel, click Add and select one of the server behaviors from the Show Record submenu. The dialog box for the specific Show Record server behavior you chose is displayed, like the one shown in Figure 20-6. The dialog boxes for all the Show Record server behaviors are identical.

Figure 20-6: To use a Show Record server behavior, all you do is choose a recordset.

3. From the Recordset list, select the recordset on which to base the Show Record condition.

4. Click OK when you're done.

Typically, the Show Region server behaviors are used in pairs. Apply a Show Region If Not First Record server behavior to a Previous Record link—it hides the link when the user is on the first record. Similarly, apply a Show Region If Not Last Record server behavior to the Next Record link to cause the link to disappear when the last record is called.

Only the first two Show Region server behaviors—Show Region If Recordset Is Empty and Show Region If Recordset Is Not Empty—can be applied to a page without any preconditions. The other four Show Region server behaviors require that one other type of server behavior be present on the page: the Recordset Paging server behavior. The Recordset Paging server behaviors act like VCR controls, adding a link that, when selected, displays the first, last, next, or previous set of records. The Recordset Paging server behaviors are covered in more detail in the following section.

Handling Record Navigation

So far in this chapter, you've seen how to repeat dynamic data and how to hide and display data and other page elements programmatically. Now it's time to put some real interactive controls into the hands of your Web application users. Dreamweaver includes a set of server behaviors that enable the user to page through your recordset, much as if they were flipping the pages of a catalog.

You can approach Dreamweaver's record navigation through two avenues: One is a do-it-yourself route, and the other lets Dreamweaver do most of the work for you. To better understand how record navigation works, examine the piece-by-piece approach first.

Building Record Navigation Links

As mentioned earlier, Dreamweaver includes a set of Recordset Paging server behaviors to control navigation within a recordset. Again, the application is straightforward: Select the text or image you'd like to serve as a trigger and attach the appropriate server behavior. When selected, the trigger fires the server-side code that retrieves the chosen record. If a Repeat Region is inserted on the page, the next or previous group of records is displayed.

You can find five server behaviors under the Recordset Paging submenu:

✦ Move To First Record

✦ Move To Previous Record

✦ Move To Next Record

✦ Move To Last Record

✦ Move To Specific Record

Note

Move To Specific Record is most often used in conjunction with a search routine or a master-detail application.

As noted, you can use either text or images as your controls. Navigation links, such as those shown in Figure 20-7, may include rollovers or other client-side behaviors. You can even use Flash buttons to trigger recordset navigation; see the section "Navigating Recordsets with Flash Buttons" later in this chapter for a detailed explanation of how it's done.

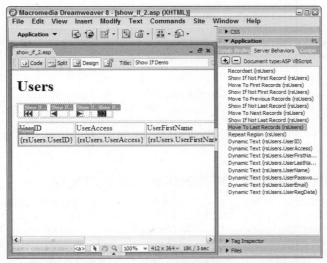

Figure 20-7: You can use images — with or without rollovers — to navigate through a recordset with Dreamweaver's Recordset Paging server behaviors.

Tip

You don't need to add an initial or placeholder link to your image or text. When the Recordset Paging server behavior is applied, the link is written for you.

To create recordset navigation links, follow these steps:

1. Select the text or image to which you'd like to attach the server behavior.

2. From the Server Behaviors panel, click Add. Choose the desired behavior from the Recordset Paging submenu. The appropriate Recordset Paging dialog box appears. If you've made a selection, it's highlighted in the Link list; otherwise, a new text link is created, as shown in Figure 20-8.

3. Make sure that the selection in the Link list is the link you want.

4. Choose the recordset you want to work with from the Recordset drop-down list.

Figure 20-8: The Recordset Paging server behaviors identify your selected target, whether it is an image or text.

5. Click OK when you're finished.

6. Repeat steps 1 through 5 to add more recordset navigation elements.

Note: Record navigation is done within a particular recordset; you can't link from one recordset to another using the Dreamweaver server behaviors or Application objects.

After you've added your navigation controls, you may want to take the next step toward a more complete user interface by adding Show Region server behaviors to ensure that the controls are displayed only when they serve a purpose. For example, if you have a navigation element that moves to the last record of a recordset, you probably want to attach a Show If Not Last Record server behavior to the trigger.

Using Application Objects for Record Navigation

Although the process for setting up a single navigation control is fairly simple, you'd have to perform that process four times (as well as attach four additional server behaviors) to accomplish what the Recordset Navigation bar does in one operation. The Recordset Navigation bar is one of Dreamweaver's Application objects — one that can take the drudgery out of a repetitive implementation. All the Application objects are accessible through either the Insert ⇨ Application Objects menu or the Application tab in the Insert bar.

The Recordset Navigation Bar Application object serves the following purposes:

✦ Adds four links to the page in a borderless, single-row table: First, Previous, Next, and Last. The links may be either text or graphics.

✦ Attaches the appropriate Recordset Paging server behavior to the four links.

✦ Inserts a Show Region server behavior to each of the links:

- Show If Not First Record is added to the First and Previous record links.

- Show If Not Last Record is added to the Next and Last record links.

✦ Centers the table on the page and sets the width to 50%.

What's even more impressive about this list of functions is that they are implemented with a single command, which, in turn, references a very simple dialog box, as shown in Figure 20-9.

Figure 20-9: The Recordset Navigation
Bar dialog box offers a choice between
text links or graphics.

Here's how it works:

1. Choose Insert ➪ Application Objects ➪ Recordset Navigation Bar or choose Insert
   Recordset Navigation Bar from the Application category of the Insert bar. The
   Recordset Navigation Bar dialog box is displayed.

2. Select the data you want to control from the Recordset list.

3. To create a series of text links, choose the Display Using Text option.

4. To use graphics to trigger the navigation, choose the Display Using Images option.

Caution

You must save the page if you select the Display Using Images option. Dreamweaver copies
images from the Shared/Dreamweaver/Images folder when you choose this option, and the
page into which they are being inserted must be saved to store the images properly in the
site. They are stored in the same folder as the page containing them.

5. Click OK.

After the Recordset Navigation bar has been inserted, you can adjust the text or images in
any way you see fit. The text may be styled or modified, and you can even swap out the
images — by changing the `src` attribute — for other graphics.

Tracking Record Status

Another Application object inserts the text and all the server behaviors necessary to identify
the records currently being viewed. By default, the syntax used by the Recordset Navigation
Status Application object is as follows:

```
Records First_Record_Shown to Last_Record_Shown of Total_Records
```

This syntax works perfectly for Web applications that use a Repeat Region server behavior to
show multiple records. When viewed through the browser, the Recordset Navigation Status
output looks like the following:

```
Records 5 to 10 of 37
```

If you're displaying one record at a time, you can adjust the Application object code inserted
so that it is similar to the following:

```
Record First_Record_Shown of Total_Records
```

Like the Recordset Navigation bar, the Recordset Navigation StatusApplication object works
with only one recordset at a time:

1. Choose Insert ➪ Application Objects ➪ Recordset Navigation or click the Recordset Navigation Status icon on the Application category of the Insert bar. The Recordset Navigation Status dialog box is displayed, as shown in Figure 20-10.

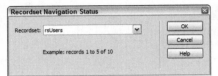

Figure 20-10: The Recordset Navigation Status Application object inserts three different server behaviors in one operation.

2. Select the data you want to control from the Recordset list.

3. Click OK when you're finished.

Establishing Recordset Navigation

In this Technique, you make sure your site visitors get a complete picture of the data you're displaying by adding two Dreamweaver Application objects: Recordset Navigation Status and Recordset Navigation Bar.

1. Open the `managing_data_start` file for your server model previously worked upon.

   The first task is to extend the table to accompany the objects.

2. Place your cursor in the first row of the table next to any of the header labels, like Leading Agent.

3. Press Ctrl+M (Command+M) to insert a new row above the current row.

4. You need to merge the second and third cells of the top table row to make room for the Application objects. Select the two cells above Office Phone and Cell Phone and, from the Property inspector, click Merge Cells.

5. To insert the first Application object, place your cursor in the first cell of the top row and, from the Application category of the Insert bar, click Recordset Navigation Status.

6. When the Recordset Navigation Status object opens, choose rsAgents from the Recordset list and click OK.

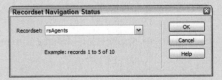

Dreamweaver inserts the dynamic code for your server model that, at runtime, will specify which records are currently being viewed.

7. Now add the capability to move through a recordset. Place your cursor in the second cell of the top row and, from the Insert bar's Application category, choose Recordset Paging: Recordset Navigation Bar.

8. In the Recordset Navigation Bar dialog box, choose rsAgent from the Recordset list, leave the default Display Using Text option and click OK.

The Recordset Navigation Bar table, along with all the necessary server behaviors, is added to the page.

9. Test your page by clicking Live Data View.

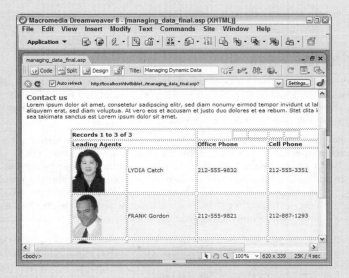

You'll see one of the results from inserting one of the objects—the Recordset Navigation Status—but not the other. Because the returned recordset contains fewer than the number of records set to be displayed by the Repeat Region server behavior, 10, the automatically applied conditional server behaviors hide the Recordset Navigation Bar. It is, however, ready to be displayed should the recordset ever expand beyond the set value.

10. When you're done, exit Live Data View by clicking its icon again and save your page.

Navigating Recordsets with Flash Buttons

Flash buttons are an excellent Dreamweaver tool for adding lively navigation aids to your Web page, but they're intended for page-to-page linking, not recordset navigation. However, with a little additional work, you can adapt standard or custom Flash buttons to control Dreamweaver's Recordset Paging server behaviors.

Flash buttons are actually Macromedia Generator Templates that, when processed by Dreamweaver, become Flash movies. As a Generator Template, the link information is compiled into the Flash movie and is not accessible for server-side processing — a necessity for moving from one record to another. Enabling Flash buttons to control recordset navigation requires four main components:

✦ Server-side code for moving from record to record

✦ A JavaScript call from the Flash button

✦ A JavaScript function in the `<head>` of the document

✦ A hidden field variable in a form

The first requirement is actually the easiest because Dreamweaver provides the necessary server-side code. The following sections lead you through the entire process.

Step 1: Prepare the Page

Before you can begin the specific steps for converting the Flash buttons for your use, some preliminary work needs to be done. First, make sure that you have added your recordset and any necessary fields. You can always add more fields from the Bindings panel later, but it's good to have one or two in the page to test the navigation buttons.

Next, add the server-side code. You can accomplish this in one of two ways: Either enter some text and attach a Recordset Paging server behavior to it, or use Dreamweaver's Recordset Navigation bar from the Insert ⇨ Application Object menu. To save time — and because you'll likely be adding multiple controls — choose the Application object route by selecting Insert ⇨ Application Object ⇨ Recordset Navigation Bar. If you follow this path, choose the Display Using Text option rather than images. Later, when you delete the links (but not the code), you'll have extraneous files in your local site if you opt for graphics now.

One final bit of prep work before you add the Flash buttons: Add a form to your page if one is not already present. If you like, give it a unique name; one convention you might try is to identify the forms on your separate pages with the name `theForm`. The form may enclose the other elements, as shown in Figure 20-11, or be separate.

Step 2: Add the Flash Buttons

Now you're ready to insert your Flash buttons. Note one small difference between the regular Flash buttons and the ones used in this section. In your version, you call a JavaScript function rather than link to another page.

Cross-Reference If you're not familiar with Flash buttons, be sure to look over Chapter 24 to understand their basic usage and learn how to use Flash MX or better to create your own custom buttons.

To insert your modified Flash button, follow these steps:

Note If you're already familiar with Flash buttons, skip to step 7.

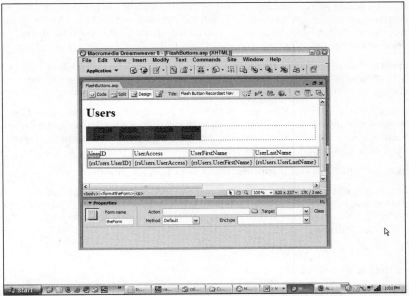

Figure 20-11: To prepare for the Flash Recordset Navigation buttons add a form and Dreamweaver's standard Recordset Navigation bar.

1. Make sure that the current document has been saved. If you're working on a new document, Dreamweaver requires that you save it before adding a Flash button.

2. Choose Insert ➪ Media ➪ Flash button. The Insert Flash Button dialog box, shown in Figure 20-12, is displayed.

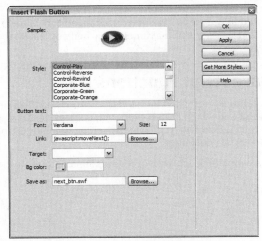

Figure 20-12: Instead of a relative URL, put a call to a JavaScript function in the Link field of your Flash button.

3. Select a button type from the Style list. The previews shown in the Sample area are live demonstrations and play as designed when moused-over or clicked. There's one exception: No sounds are played in preview; you have to preview the Flash button in the browser to get the full effect.

4. If appropriate, enter custom text in the Button Text field. The Button Text field is physically limited to 50 characters, although probably your text will be shorter. Certain symbols, such as those in the Control group, ignore the text and font settings.

5. Select a typeface from the Font drop-down list if appropriate. The fonts listed are TrueType fonts found on your system. Most of the button templates have a preselected font and text size. If you do not have the preselected font on your system, a small alert appears at the bottom of the dialog box.

6. Enter the desired font size if appropriate, in points, in the Size field.

7. Enter a JavaScript call to a function that sets the recordset navigation in the Link field. For this example, you can use the functions `moveNext()`, `movePrev()`, `moveFirst()`, and `moveLast()`. For a button that moves to the next record, the entry into the Link field reads as follows:

   ```
   javascript:moveNext();
   ```

8. Leave the Target field blank.

9. If the Flash button is to be placed on a page or in a table with a background color other than white, select the Bg Color swatch to choose an appropriate background. Alternatively, enter the hexadecimal color number or standard color name directly in the Bg Color text field.

10. Enter a path and filename for the Flash button file. If you like, you can use the suggested default name in the site root, or click the Browse button to choose a different location.

11. Click Apply to insert the button at the cursor location on the page.

12. Click OK when you're finished.

The JavaScript function names listed in the steps here may be changed to whatever you like. However, be sure to use the same names as the actual functions when you insert them in the code, as described in the next step.

Step 3: Include the JavaScript Functions

As JavaScript functions go, the functions referenced in the Flash Button Link field are as simple as they get — with just one line of code each. When executed, each of the JavaScript functions does the same thing: It sets the current URL to a value specified in a hidden form variable. You set the form variables in the next step.

Although there are four variations — one for each type of recordset navigation — the basic function looks like the following:

```
function moveNext() {
    document.location.href=document.theForm.nextHidden.value
}
```

The function name—here, moveNext()—is arbitrary, but note that it matches the function name specified in the Flash button setup. The reference to the hidden form variable is also specific to this code—again, you can name the variables whatever you like; just ensure that the names match the code in the function.

This code uses the following four functions:

```
function moveNext() {
    document.location.href=document.theForm.nextHidden.value
}

function movePrev() {
    document.location.href=document.theForm.prevHidden.value
}

function moveFirst() {
    document.location.href=document.theForm.firstHidden.value
}

function moveLast() {
    document.location.href=document.theForm.lastHidden.value
}
```

If you're totally unfamiliar with writing JavaScript, you can use Dreamweaver's Script object to insert the code. However, make sure that the code goes in the <head> section of the document. Use the following steps to accomplish that:

1. Choose View ➪ Head Content to expose the <head> region in Dreamweaver's Document window.

2. Choose Insert ➪ HTML ➪ Script Objects ➪ Script. Alternatively, you could click the Script icon in the HTML category of the Insert bar. The Script dialog box, shown in Figure 20-13, is displayed.

Figure 20-13: If you are new to JavaScript, use Dreamweaver's Script object for inserting code.

3. Select JavaScript from the Language list.

4. Enter the desired functions into the Content text area. You can enter as many of the functions as you'd like, or all of them.

5. Click OK when you're finished.

If you're more familiar with JavaScript, you can enter the functions directly through Dreamweaver's Code view. The functions can be inserted into an existing `<script>`...`</script>` tag pair, or you can create your own. Next you add the final piece of the basic puzzle: the hidden variables.

Step 4: Insert the Hidden Variables

Whenever a Recordset Paging server behavior is applied, whether manually or automatically by inserting an Application object, Dreamweaver writes a bit of server-side code in the `href` attribute of the `<a>` tag surrounding the trigger element. It is this code that you must make accessible for the Flash button to work properly as a recordset navigation tool.

The server-side code varies from server model to server model but, in essence, it's quite similar. For example, here's the code inserted when a Move To Next Record server behavior is applied:

ASP

```
<%=MM_moveNext%>
```

ColdFusion

```
<cfoutput>#CurrentPage#?PageNum_rsEmployees=#Min(IncrementValue(PageNum
_rsEmployees),TotalPages_rsEmployees)##QueryString_rsEmployees#</cfoutp
ut>
```

JSP

```
<%=MM_moveNext%>
```

.NET

```
<%# Request.ServerVariables("SCRIPT_NAME") %>?rs_currentPage=<%#
rs.CurrentPage + 1 %>
```

To keep this code accessible for server-side processing—and viable for the JavaScript function to use—it must be embedded in a hidden variable form element. After the code is transferred, the temporary recordset navigation elements previously inserted can be deleted. Here's how to accomplish this task, step by step:

1. Select the text link that matches the recordset navigation intended for your Flash button.

   You can start anywhere because you're eventually going to add Flash buttons for all your recordset navigation moves.

2. From the Property inspector, select and copy the value of the `href` attribute using the keyboard shortcut Ctrl+C (Command+C) or the context menu.

3. Position your cursor anywhere in the form and choose Insert ➪ Form ➪ Hidden Field or click the Hidden Field icon in the Forms category of the Insert bar.

It doesn't matter where the Hidden Field object is placed, as long as it's within the `<form>` tag.

4. In the Hidden Field Property inspector, change the name from the default `hiddenField` to a unique name. This name must be the same as the one used in the JavaScript function. You might want to create a name for form elements by first describing what the element relates to, followed by the type of form element. For example, the four hidden fields used in recordset navigation are called `firstHidden`, `lastHidden`, `nextHidden`, and `prevHidden`.

5. In the Value field of the Property inspector, paste the copied code as shown in Figure 20-14.

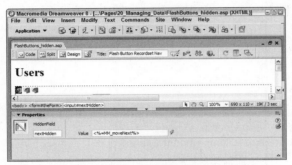

Figure 20-14: The Hidden Field form element acts a conduit to the JavaScript function, passing the processed server-side value, which, in turn, is called by the Flash button.

6. Repeat steps 1 through 5 for every Flash button recordset control intended for the page.

7. After you've added all the hidden fields needed, you're free to delete the temporary recordset navigation text links. One way to do this is to place your cursor inside of the text link, right-click (Control-click) the `<a>` tag in the Tag Selector and choose Remove Tag.

Your Flash button is now recordset-navigation ready. Test your page by using Dreamweaver's Preview in Browser feature.

Tip

Remember: If the folder for your testing server is on a different machine or in a different location from your local site root, you must transfer all the dependent files — including the SWF files used by the Flash buttons — before the Flash buttons work correctly.

To make the Flash button interface as intuitive as possible, add Show Region server behaviors to the various buttons, as detailed in the "Showing and Hiding Page Elements" section earlier in this chapter and shown in Figure 20-15.

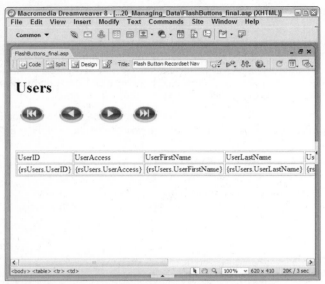

Figure 20-15: The Flash buttons appear only when they are useful, courtesy of Dreamweaver's Show Region server behaviors.

Summary

To be part of an effective Web application, dynamic data can't just be displayed; it has to be designed. Dreamweaver, through a variety of server behaviors, gives you the power to selectively repeat page elements as well as show them programmatically. Data design is an important aspect of integrating the server side with the client side. As you look for ways to manage the data in your Web applications more effectively, remember the following points:

✦ Dreamweaver's Repeat Region server behavior can help you to show as much of the data on a single page as you desire. Repeat Region server behaviors are usually applied to table rows, but they can also be used with line-breaks, paragraphs, list items, or any other HTML element.

✦ It's often necessary to show data only if a certain condition is met. Dreamweaver handles these operations through a variety of Show Region server behaviors. With these tools, you can also selectively display any element — text, graphic, or dynamic data — on the current page.

✦ After you have the capability to display a portion of your data, you must navigate the recordset. Dreamweaver's Recordset Paging server behaviors can show the next or previous record (or group of records, if the Repeat Region server behavior is used), as well as quickly navigate to the first or last record of your data.

✦ Recordset navigation can be integrated in several ways. You can add each building block (the graphics or the text, the server behaviors, and so on) by itself, or you can accomplish the same task in one operation by using a Dreamweaver Application object. Depending on the Web application, you might find it quicker to insert and modify the Recordset Navigation Bar Application object rather than build your own step-by-step.

✦ You can convert Flash buttons to act as recordset navigation aids. The step-by-step section details the necessary modifications.

In the next chapter, you learn how you can use Dreamweaver's Live Data view to enhance your workflow and test your application under a variety of circumstances.

✦   ✦   ✦

Working with Live Data

When I first started with print and design layout, I would drive all over the city to finish a job. After receiving the client's go-ahead, I had to pick my type from a phototypesetter and my images from a stat house. Then, back at my studio, I'd cut and paste — and I mean literally, with scissors and glue — the text and images into place, hoping against hope that I had specified the type and image sizes correctly. If not, it was back in the car for another trip or two around town. Ah, the good old days.

Now designers (especially those who design for the Web) have the luxury of developing their creations right in their own studio. Until Dreamweaver, however, the development of a Web application often undertook a faster, albeit parallel, course to my inner-city travels. After a basic page was designed, complete with server-side code, the document had to be uploaded to a testing server and then viewed in a browser over the Internet. If — make that *when* — changes were needed, the pages were revamped back in the studio. Because the designer was not able to lay out the page with the actual data in place, modifications were a trial-and-error process that often required many, many trips to the server and back.

Dreamweaver's Live Data view eliminates the tedium and the lengthy time required for the upload-preview-modify-upload cycle. It enables developers to work with the layout while the actual data is live on the page. If a table width needs to be adjusted because one of the records is too long, you can make the change immediately with no guesswork.

Live Data view processes the page in the chosen server model. If the page requires variables, such as search criteria, to run properly, the Live Data feature enables you to set such values as needed. Although a preliminary discussion of Live Data is was presented in Chapter 19, this chapter covers all the necessary details for using both basic and advanced Live Data capabilities.

Live Data is a terrific timesaving feature, but you can't rely on it totally for testing your Web application. You still need to preview the page in various browsers to ensure cross-browser compatibility. The final section of this chapter is dedicated to Dreamweaver's Preview in Browser feature and its relationship to your testing server.

Viewing Live Data

After your site is properly set up, entering Live Data view is just a click away. Click the Show Live Data View button on the toolbar to refresh Dreamweaver's Document window and to replace all the dynamic data placeholders with information from the declared data source. With Invisible Elements enabled (the default for Dreamweaver), the newly visible Live Data is highlighted in whatever color is specified in Preferences.

To get the most out of Live Data view — and to avoid problems — you need a firm grasp of how Dreamweaver is able to present your data, live. The following sections can help you understand this timesaving feature.

How Live Data Works

Once you've entered Live Data view, you may notice an animation of a spinning Dreamweaver logo in the right-hand corner of the Live Data toolbar before the page is refreshed. When the animation stops, Dreamweaver has all the information needed to present the completed page. Here is what's happening behind that spinning lowercase *d*:

1. The developer inserts dynamic data elements into a standard HTML page. The dynamic data is represented by placeholders that combine the recordset and field names in a set of curly braces, like `{rsEmployees.FirstName}`.

2. When the Live Data view is enabled, Dreamweaver creates a hidden, temporary copy of the current page.

3. The temporary page is stored in the folder designated in the Testing Server category of the Site Definition dialog box.

4. Dreamweaver instructs the defined testing server to execute the server-side code within the page and passes along any variables that have been specified. The URL prefix designated in the Site Definition Testing Server category is used to invoke the page.

5. When the code is executed, Dreamweaver reads the resulting HTML code.

6. Finally, Dreamweaver uses its translator capability to substitute the dynamic data placeholders shown in the original document with the data generated. The temporary document is deleted from the server.

If all goes well, a page with dynamic data placeholders (shown in Figure 21-1) is replaced with the Live Data view (shown in Figure 21-2).

If Dreamweaver encounters an error, it displays a message that explains where the process failed and suggests some possible remedies.

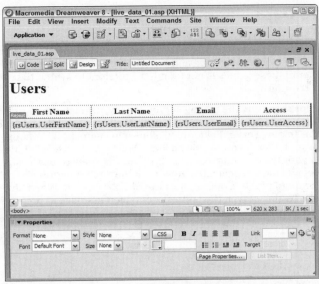

Figure 21-1: This table contains a row with four dynamic data fields, surrounded by a Repeat Region server behavior.

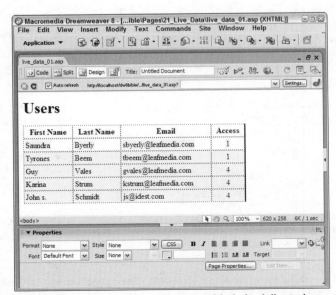

Figure 21-2: After Live Data view is enabled, the full number of records allowed by the Repeat Region is displayed and provides an accurate representation of the data.

Setting Up for Live Data

As noted in the summary of how Live Data works, several values found in the Testing Server category of the Site Definition dialog are key to this feature's operation. Live Data must know the location of the site root for the temporary page and how that location may be reached with an HTTP request. If either of these values is not found, the attempt to switch to Live Data view is aborted and an error message appears.

Two different methods exist for accessing the testing server: locally, through a network, or remotely via FTP. If the testing server is to be accessed locally, the location of the folder storing the pages is entered in the Testing Server Folder field, shown in Figure 21-3. Although it is referred to as the Testing Server folder, if you're using a local Web server such as Internet Information Services (IIS) on your local testing machine, this entry is likely to be the same as your Local Root Folder, as defined in the Local Info category of the Site Definition dialog box. The other field essential to proper Live Data operation is the URL Prefix field. When Live Data sends the HTTP request to the testing server, the address contained in this field prefaces the name of the temporary page. For example, if my temporary page is named `TMPGX123455.asp` and the URL prefix is `http://localhost/dba`, the URL used is `http://localhost/dba/TMPGX123455.asp`.

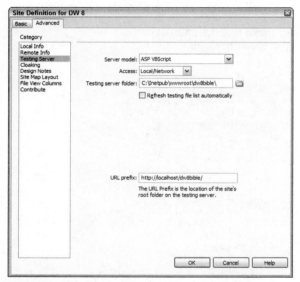

Figure 21-3: Enter the location of your local files and a locally established site in the URL Prefix field to enable Live Data view to find your application.

Tip   Localhost is common shorthand for addressing a local Web server; generally, you can also use the Internet Protocol (IP) address 127.0.0.1.

Initially, Dreamweaver inserts only the `http://localhost/` address into the URL Prefix field. This works if your local site root corresponds to the local Web server root. If your site root is in a different directory, you have to fill in the path of that directory. Most Web servers permit the creation of *virtual directories,* which are aliases recognized by the Web server. If you're using Windows 2000 or Windows XP Professional, then you may already have Internet Information Services (IIS) available, and you can set up your own virtual directories.

To create a virtual directory, follow these steps:

1. First, check to see if you have IIS by right-clicking My Computer on your desktop and choosing Manage. In the Computer Management console, expand Services and Applications. If you see Internet Information Services listed, then you've got everything you need installed and you can skip to step 2. If you don't see IIS listed, choose Start ➪ Control Panel, double-click Add/Remove Programs and choose Add/Remove Windows Components. Check Internet Information Services in the Windows Component Wizard and follow the dialogs to install IIS.

2. Right-click the Default Web Site and choose New ➪ Virtual Directory, as shown in Figure 21-4. This action opens the Virtual Directory Creation Wizard. Click Next to get started.

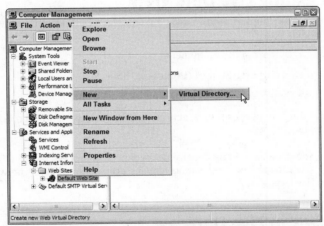

Figure 21-4: Right-click the Default Web Site in IIS and choose New ➪ Virtual Directory to open the Virtual Directory Creation Wizard. Complete the wizard to add a new virtual directory.

3. On the Virtual Directory Alias screen, enter the alias for the folder. This will be appended to the end of the `http://localhost/` address. If you name your virtual directory "dba" then the URL would be `http://localhost/dba`. Click Next to continue.

4. On the Web Site Content Directory screen, browse to the folder that contains your site and click Next.

5. Click Next on the Access Properties screen to continue, and click Finish on the next screen to add the virtual directory.

Note   ColdFusion MX developers with a local testing server need to specify the port number if ColdFusion is installed as a stand-alone server. By default, ColdFusion MX uses 8500, which results in a URL Prefix of `http://localhost:8500/`.

If you're connecting to a remote testing server, choose FTP from the Access list on the Testing Server category of the Site Definition dialog box. When FTP is selected, Dreamweaver displays the same information entered under the FTP heading in the Remote Info category. Additionally, Dreamweaver combines the entries under FTP Host and Host Directory in the URL prefix with an initial `http://`. For example, if your entry under FTP Host is `www.drinkgoodstuff.com` and Host Directory is blank, the URL prefix reads `http://www.drinkgoodstuff.com/`.

Caution   You may have to edit your URL prefix if your FTP host uses an `ftp` prefix. If my host directory were `ftp.drinkgoodstuff.com`, Dreamweaver would create the URL prefix entry `http://ftp.drinkgoodstuff.com`, an unworkable URL. Here, the `ftp` must be changed to `www`.

Entering and Exiting Live Data View

Dreamweaver provides three different methods for invoking Live Data view. Use the one that best suits your work style:

✦ Choose View ➪ Live Data from the main menu.

✦ Use the keyboard shortcut Ctrl+Shift+R (Command+Shift+R).

✦ Click the Show Live Data View button on the toolbar.

In Live Data view, executing any of these three actions returns you to Standard mode, where you see dynamic data placeholders.

Tip   If, for any reason, you need to interrupt the Live Data connection process, click the Stop button on the Live Data toolbar. The Stop button remains active only while Dreamweaver is transitioning into Live Data view.

Making Changes in Live Data

If a feature in a software program can be said to have a *raison d'etre*, then modifying the layout must surely be the *raison d'etre* of Live Data. When in Live Data view, new elements — dynamic or static — can be added and existing ones adjusted or removed entirely. Anything, including the dynamic data, can be formatted or styled using HTML or CSS.

Live Data view solves the thorny challenges of laying out a table without resorting to a time-consuming trial-and-error approach. For instance, varying lengths of data in the same column often complicate designing table layout with dynamic data. If, for example, the sample data includes a last name field that is 12 characters long and the real data contains a hyphenated name that is 25 characters long, you have a problem. When working in Live Data view, you can see the entire page as it would be generated on the server, including dynamic elements and repeating table rows (see Figure 21-5).

Stop

Refresh

Auto Refresh checkbox

Live data view

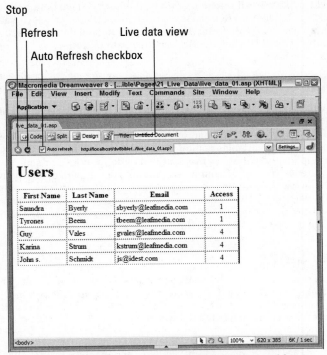

Figure 21-5: Use Live Data view to make sure your table layout works well with the actual data that appears on the page.

The Live Data toolbar includes a Refresh button that, when clicked, resends your application to the server for processing and then redisplays the page in the Document window. The Refresh option is valuable in the following circumstances:

✦ Information from the data source is reassessed. This feature enables you to make changes in the database and then see those changes incorporated into your page.

✦ Server formatting changes are applied to dynamic data. If you don't refresh after altering the current format of the inserted data, the modified element reverts to being displayed as a dynamic data placeholder.

✦ HTML formatting applied to dynamic data is also applied to Live Data displayed through a Repeat Region server behavior. Without refreshing, only the initial data is shown correctly formatted.

Cross-Reference   Repeat Region server behaviors enable multiple records from the same recordset to be incorporated into a page. For details on how to insert and manage a Repeat Region, see Chapter 20.

The Live Data toolbar provides two refresh-oriented options: the Refresh Live Data button and the Auto Refresh checkbox. When Auto Refresh is enabled, formatting changes are automatically applied. However, to display HTML formatting on Repeat Region data or to see changes made to a data source, you must click the Refresh Live Data button.

Live Data Settings

Although the capability to work with data from the current recordset is impressive, it's really only half the story of Live Data view. Many Web applications depend on variables used when the page is processed by the testing server. Users may intentionally submit these variables when they fill out a form or they may submit variables unintentionally when they navigate from a particular page. Session or application variables, from authentication routines or simple counters, may also be integrated into a page. Dreamweaver permits developers to interactively alter all such variables and preview the resulting Web page. This facility not only enables the designer to work with a wide range of real-life conditions, but it also facilitates testing of the application under a variety of circumstances. Dreamweaver offers two avenues of approach to variable handling: through the query string field and through the Settings dialog box.

Getting the Query String

Remember the first time you noticed that the link you clicked was carrying quite a bit of additional baggage? Where you might have selected a link that took you to a specific product page with a URL such as `http://www.web-shorts.com/products/widgets.htm`, the link in the Location field of your browser looked more like the following:

```
http://www.web-shorts.com/products/products.asp?prod=
widget&sessionID=2343215&login=no&visited=gadgets%20r%20us
```

The text following the question mark is called a *query string,* or the URL parameters. Query strings are a tool used by Web applications to pass information from one page to the next. Frequently, you see a query string after submitting a form. Forms using the `Get` method pass their variables by appending a question mark and the form information to the URL of the requested page. The form information is in a series of name/value pairs; and each name/value pair is linked by an equals sign, as follows:

```
Firstname=Joseph
```

Query strings may include any number of name/value pairs, separated by an ampersand. Thus, for a form that passes the data entered into a first name field and a last name field, the query string may look like the following:

```
?firstname=Joseph&lastname=Lowery
```

Neither single nor double quotes are used because they are in HTML attributes. Quotes and other characters — including spaces, apostrophes, and tildes — are represented by hexadecimal values so that they are properly understood by servers. Such strings are said to be *URL encoded*, and they are designated by an initial percent sign, followed by the ASCII value of the character in hexadecimal. Some commonly used encoding values are as follows:

Character		ASCII Value
Space		%20
Apostrophe or single quote	'	%27
Double quote	"	%22
Tilde	~	%7E
Less than	<	%3C
Greater than	>	%3E

The query string field appears in the Live Data toolbar by default, prefaced by the URL path used by Live Data plus a question mark. The URL path, question mark, and the text entered into the field comprise the complete URL submitted to the testing server when you invoke or refresh Live Data.

Note Depending on the length of the pathname, some elements, such as folders, may be represented by an ellipsis (three dots) so that Dreamweaver can display the filename and question mark.

Consider an example that uses the query string. Suppose that you've developed a page for an organization that displays employees and whether they're under contract. The contract status shown depends on the link selected by the user; the links are identical except for the query string portion. For uncontracted employees, the link reads `employees.cfm?contract=no`, whereas for contracted employees, the link reads `employees.cfm?contract=yes`. The recordset on the `employees.cfm` page uses a filter that sets the Contract field equal to the URL parameter called `contract`.

Note Although the query string field is present by default, you can disable it by switching the Method option in the Live Data Settings dialog box from `Get` to `Post`. To re-enable the query string field, choose View ➪ Live Data Settings and select `Get` as the Method option.

After entering Live Data view by any of the methods described previously, you can switch back and forth between the two sets of returned data by changing the value in the query string `name=value` pair. In this instance, the two accepted values — as defined in the data source — are `no` for employees not under contract and `yes` for employees under contract. After changing the value and pressing Enter (Return), the Live Data is refreshed, as shown in Figure 21-6.

Query String field

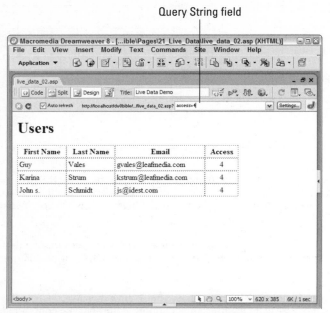

Figure 21-6: You can use the Query String field of the Live Data toolbar to test different scenarios for your Web application.

Caution   If you encounter a Live Data error indicating that the page cannot be displayed because the current record could not be found, you're probably including values in the query string that do not match any records in a recordset on the page. You have a couple of options for proceeding. Press the Esc key to dismiss the error dialog box and enter a new value in the query string field. (Don't click the Close button on the dialog box, or you'll close the Live Data view and the Live Data toolbar.) Alternatively, you can enter a name value/pair through the Live Data Settings dialog box as outlined in the following section.

Posting Responses with Live Data Settings

Although the query string is handy for changing one or two simple variables, the more complex the variables, the less convenient it becomes. Dreamweaver offers another route to controlling Live Data variables: Live Data settings. The Live Data Settings dialog box, shown in Figure 21-7, offers several important advantages over the query string:

✦ The name/value pairs are easier to enter and maintain in a straightforward two-column table.

✦ URL encoding is handled automatically by Dreamweaver; with query strings. You have to enter any necessary URL encoding manually.

✦ Variables may be sent to the application by either the Get or Post method. The query string uses only the Get method.

✦ Additional initializing code may be applied to the page. This feature enables you to test different session or environmental variables in the page, as if the server had set the values.

✦ Variable settings may be optionally stored. If you select this option, Dreamweaver uses its Design Notes facility to maintain the variables.

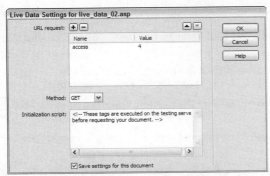

Figure 21-7: You can use the Live Data Settings dialog box to simulate forms using either the GET or POST method.

To establish variables using the Live Data Settings feature, follow these steps:

1. Choose View ➪ Live Data Settings or enter Live Data view and select Settings from the Live Data toolbar. The Live Data Settings dialog box for the current page is displayed.

2. To create a new variable, click the Add (+) button.

3. In the Name column, enter the name of the variable.

4. In the corresponding field under the Value column, enter a value for the variable.

5. Repeat steps 2 through 4 to add additional variables.

6. To delete a name/value pair, select it and then click the Remove (–) button.

7. You can adjust the sequence in which the variables are presented to the page by using the Up and Down buttons to move name/value pairs higher or lower in the list.

8. By default, Dreamweaver sends variables to a page using the GET method, which appends URL-encoded name/value pairs in a query string. To simulate a form passing variables in an encapsulated, hidden manner, choose POST from the Method list.

Tip   If you choose the GET method, enter the variables and their values without encoding them for the URL. Dreamweaver translates any necessary characters into their hexadecimal equivalents when the Live Data page is processed.

9. To establish a particular server environment, enter any necessary code in the Initialization Script text area. This code is specific to each server model and must be completely self-contained within any required tags or delimiters.

10. To store your variable settings, select the Save Settings For This Document option. Dreamweaver requires that Design Notes be enabled in order to save the Live Data settings. If Design Notes is disabled when you select this option, you get an opportunity to enable it.

Changing Live Data Settings

In this Technique, you practice working with Live Data settings, both in the dialog box and in the Live Data query string field.

1. From the Techniques - Dynamic site (established in Chapter 18), expand the 21_Live_Data folder and open the `live_data_start` file for your server model.

   Before you can use the Live Data settings to alter the preview, you need to know how the recordset is being filtered.

2. In the Bindings panel, double-click the Recordset (rsProperties) entry to re-open the associated dialog box.

3. Take note of the Filter section and you'll see that the recordset is filtered by the URL parameter `type`.

4. Click Cancel to close the recordset dialog box.

5. Now that you know what variable the recordset is filtered on, you can specify it in the Live Data settings. Choose View ➪ Live Data Settings.

6. When the Live Data Settings dialog box opens, click Add (+) and in the Name column enter **type** and press Tab.

7. In the Value column, enter **rental** and click OK.

8. Click the Live Data View icon on the Document toolbar.

   Only the rental type records are displayed. Now, switch to a different set of records.

9. In the Live Data Query String field, change the type value from **rental** to **purchase** so that the entire query string reads **type=purchase** and press Enter (Return).

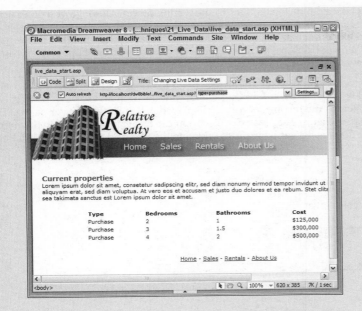

10. Click the Live Data View icon to return to standard Design view.

Although you can discover which parameters are used to filter the recordset, you can't uncover the expected values from within Dreamweaver. If they weren't provided for you as in this Technique, you'd need to examine the data source to see what values were expected and stored.

Previewing in the Browser

Live Data saves a tremendous amount of time in the early design phase, yet when it comes time to test your application in various browsers — a necessary step for virtually all Web developers — there is no substitute for previewing in the browser. Dreamweaver does a decent job of approximating a browser-eye view of your page. However, with so many variations between the major browsers — not to mention the versions within each major browser — you must test your page in as many browsers as possible. Dreamweaver's Preview in Browser feature enables you to specify up to 13 different browsers in Preferences. After this feature is defined, you can test your page by choosing File ➪ Preview in Browser ➪ *Browser Name* at any point. If the toolbar is open, you can also choose a browser under the Preview/Debug in Browser option.

To view Web applications properly, Dreamweaver must process the pages with a testing server. To use this facility, you must satisfy two requirements:

✦ Specify the route to the testing server, either via a local (or networked) folder or through FTP in the Testing Server category of the Site Definition dialog box.

✦ Transfer any dependent or related files to the testing server. Although you don't have to include dependent files such as graphics on the current page, you must transfer server-side includes, such as the connection script. Related files are other pages referenced in the Web application; Dreamweaver only uploads a copy of the current page during the Preview in Browser operation.

When the testing server is properly set up (as described in Chapter 5), you can transfer any necessary files quickly in the Site window. On the Site window toolbar, click the Testing Server button. The files on the testing server are displayed in the Testing Server pane of the Site window, as shown in Figure 21-8. Transfer files from the local site by dragging them from the local pane to the Testing Server pane or by selecting the files and then clicking the Put or Check In button.

Testing server

Remote server

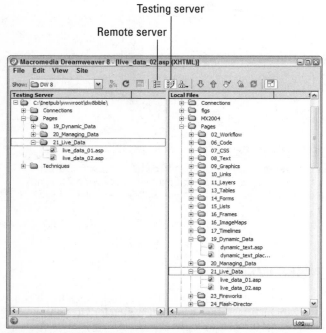

Figure 21-8: The Dreamweaver Site window enables you to connect to the testing server or the remote server.

Tip

When you begin to test a new page, let Dreamweaver transfer the dependent files for you. Simply transfer a saved copy of the current page to the testing server and okay the request to transfer the dependent files as well. To take advantage of this feature, make sure that you select the Dependent Files: Prompt on Put/Check In option found in the Site category of Preferences.

Using the Server Debug Panel with ColdFusion MX

Macromedia tightens the Dreamweaver and ColdFusion integration with every product release. Dreamweaver 8 is no exception. The Server Debug panel offers you an integrated view of all errors and server variables on your ColdFusion pages. The Server Debug view also gives you the capability to browse your site inside the Dreamweaver interface, testing values as you go. The Server Debug options are displayed for any ColdFusion page, but they work only for ColdFusion MX and ColdFusion MX 7 on Windows.

To enable debugging directly inside Dreamweaver, follow these simple steps:

1. Enable server debugging by choosing Debugging Settings in the left-hand pane of the ColdFusion MX Administrator (see Figure 21-9). The Debugging Options page opens in the right-hand pane.

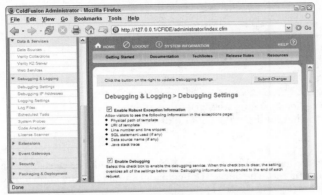

Figure 21-9: Enable the server debugging options in ColdFusion MX before using the Server Debug panel in Dreamweaver.

2. Click the Server Debug icon in the Standard toolbar, and an additional toolbar with the following buttons appears directly above your document window:

   - **Backward:** Emulates the browser Back button and takes you to the previous page in your history.

   - **Forward:** Emulates the browser Forward button and takes you to the next page in your history.

   - **Stop:** Emulates the browser Stop button and stops the current page from processing.

   - **Refresh:** Emulates the browser Refresh button and reloads the current page.

   - **Server Debug:** Toggles server debugging on and off.

   It also includes an Address Bar for passing query string values to your page and enabling you to see where you are in your site.

When you preview Live Data, you can see all the CF MX Server Debug output (see Figure 21-10), and you can browse through your pages just as you would in a regular Web browser.

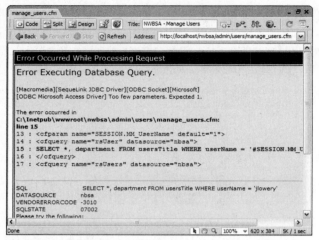

Figure 21-10: The Server Debug view gives you additional options on the toolbar for browsing your ColdFusion MX documents.

3. Open the Server Debug panel by choosing Window ⇨ Results or pressing F7 and selecting the Server Debug tab. The Server Debug panel should now be shown below the Property inspector (see Figure 21-11).

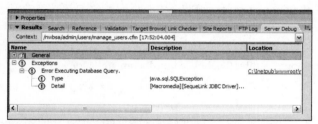

Figure 21-11: The Server Debug panel gives you a quick overview of all the returned variables from the ColdFusion MX server.

After you open the Server Debug panel, you can see all your variables, as well as any errors. Any exceptions provide a link to the page that is throwing the error. If that error was contained inside a `<CFINCLUDE>`, the URL for the page is a clickable link next to the error.

Tip If you right-click inside the Server Debug panel, you can choose Select All and copy the contents of the panel by choosing Copy from the context menu. You can then paste it inside a new document — in Dreamweaver or another text editor — for future reference or to send to another ColdFusion developer for further debugging.

Summary

Sometimes, when an unusual idea appears in a software program, it's hard to separate the merely glitzy from the truly grand. As implemented in Dreamweaver, Live Data view proves to be bottom-line functional and, thus, more than a flash in the pan—although I have to admit, it's pretty darn cool as well. To make the most of Live Data view, remember the following points:

✦ Live Data view depends on proper setup of the testing server to run smoothly. If any of the information entered into the Testing Server category of the Site Definition dialog box is incomplete or incorrect, Dreamweaver won't be able to process your Web application and display the results successfully.

✦ Select the Auto Refresh option on the Live Data toolbar to take advantage of Dreamweaver's capability to reformat dynamic data when the server formatting has changed.

✦ The query string field and the Settings button in the Live Data toolbar both offer developers a way to test their Web application with different variables. Use the query string field to emulate the passing of URL parameters, and the Settings dialog box for Post-enabled forms.

✦ To try different server environments, enter the appropriate code in the Initialization Script field of the Settings dialog box. This facility enables you to test different application variables, session variables, and other variables easily.

✦ Be sure to use Dreamweaver's Preview in Browser feature to give your Web application a real-world tryout before going live. To test your page, transfer dependent and related files using the Site window from the local site to the testing server pane.

✦ Use Dreamweaver's tight ColdFusion MX integration and the Server Debug panel to quickly debug your ColdFusion applications.

In the next chapter, you learn how to create multiple page applications.

✦   ✦   ✦

Crafting Multiple-Page Applications

In a Web site composed of static HTML pages, each page generally stands on its own and is developed individually. In a dynamic Web site, however, applications often require multiple pages to be effective. A prime example is the master-detail Web application where a search box on one page leads to a master list of results on a second page, each of which, in turn, is linked to a third dynamically generated detail page. To execute the application, variables and other information must be passed from one page to the next. The active Web site developer has a variety of tools capable of handling this task, including forms and session variables. All these methods for creating multiple-page Web applications are available in Dreamweaver and are covered in this chapter. I also show you a one-step procedure for developing a master-detail Web application.

Additionally, this chapter covers the use of form elements, such as text fields, checkboxes, and drop-down lists for dynamic data display. Form elements are extremely useful to the Web-application developer because they let the developer update objects on-the-fly. By making a choice in one drop-down list, the developer can determine which options are available in another list. Finally, this chapter describes how to put your new knowledge of form elements to work in creating a search field.

Using the URL to Pass Parameters

In a static Web site, links are used to navigate from one page to another. In a dynamic site, links can have an additional function: passing parameters to an application server so that it can determine the dynamic content on the linked page. The added parameters are known as a *query string* and follow the standard URL after a question mark, like this:

```
dvd_details.asp?movie=Bedazzled
```

Every parameter is composed of a name/value pair separated by an equals sign. If more than one parameter is sent, each pair is separated by an ampersand, as in the following example:

```
dvd_details.asp?movie=Bedazzled&genre=western
```

Unlike in HTML or other languages, quotation marks are not used to set off the values. Quotation marks and other non-alphanumeric characters including spaces, single quotes, and tildes must be translated into encoded characters so that the server interprets them correctly. Spaces, for instance, are rendered as a %20, as shown here:

```
dvd_details.asp?movie=Bedazzled&genre=western&star=Clint%20Eastwood
```

Dreamweaver provides all the tools necessary for constructing query strings within its point-and-click interface. However, if you understand the required syntax, you can quickly test your page using the URL field found on the Live Data toolbar.

Sending Parameters

With a master-detail Web application, typically only a single parameter is used. The parameter uniquely identifies the record selected on the master page and is appended to the link for the detail page. For example, suppose the detail page is `dbadetails.asp`, the identifying variable is called `tripid`, and the specific item is `Conquering K2`. The full link, with the query string, reads:

```
dbadetails.asp?tripid=Conquering%20K2
```

> **Note**   Master pages are one of two types: Either the master list is defined by the designer or by search criteria submitted by the user. The examples in this section are designer-based and rely on a specific recordset being declared. Details on how to create a search field are covered later in this chapter in the Dreamweaver Technique "Building a Search Page" section.

To create the proper code within Dreamweaver, apply a Go To Detail Page server behavior to the linking text, image, or dynamic data. Master pages also include a Repeat Region server behavior; the Go To Detail Page server behavior is attached to the text or graphic within the region, as shown in Figure 22-1.

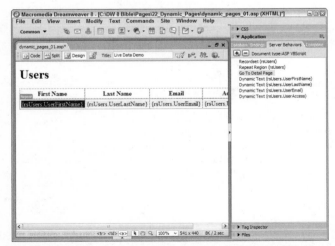

Figure 22-1: The Go To Detail Page server behavior within the Repeat Region connects the master page to the proper detail page.

To attach a Go To Detail Page server behavior, follow these steps:

1. Select the page element — text, graphic, or dynamic data — to use as the link to the detail page.

2. From the Server Behaviors panel, click Add (+) and select Go To Detail Page from the drop-down list. The Go To Detail Page dialog box, shown in Figure 22-2, is displayed. (This option is not available for ColdFusion or PHP.)

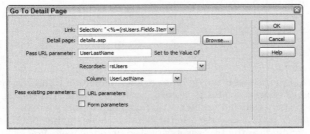

Figure 22-2: Specify the linking parameter sent from the master page in the Go To Detail Page server behavior.

3. Make sure that the page element selected is represented in the Link field. If no selection is made, Dreamweaver creates a new Detail text link.

4. Enter the path to the detail page in the Detail Page field or click Browse to locate the file in the Select File dialog box.

Tip It's a good idea to prototype all the pages in your application before you begin adding content, especially server-side code. Existing pages are easy to link to through a Select File dialog box, and doing so reduces the chance of typographical errors.

5. In the Pass URL Parameter field, enter the variable name to be sent. You can use a name of your own choosing or the name of the field in the database. Whichever name you decide upon, make a note of it somewhere because you need to reference it when the detail page itself is constructed.

6. From the Recordset list, select the recordset that contains the URL parameter.

7. From the Column list, choose the field to which the URL parameter's value is related.

8. Unless you have pre-existing URL or form parameters to send to the detail page, leave the Pass Existing Parameters options unchecked.

Caution Make sure that you leave the Pass Existing Parameters options unselected, especially if you are linking back to your master page from the detail page. Otherwise, the parameters begin to accumulate, and your linking URL will look like this nonfunctioning example:

```
detailpage.cfm?id=23&id=36
```

9. When you're finished, click OK.

Now that the link is passing parameters successfully, it's time to make sure that the detail page is set up to receive them properly.

Receiving Parameters

Dreamweaver provides two routes for your detail page to use the parameter passed to it by the master page: a filtered recordset or a Dreamweaver server behavior. In general, the first method is less processor-intensive and thus the better choice of the two. The filtered record-set technique returns a recordset of one record—the one used in the detail. If you use the server behavior technique, the entire recordset from the master page is made available, and only the specific record is displayed. You should use the entire recordset method if you want to do recordset paging from one record to the next

To learn more about recordset paging, see Chapter 20.

Regardless of which technique you use, the detail page should include whatever dynamic data is appropriate. This, of course, requires a recordset. If you're using the server behavior technique, the recordset is generally left unfiltered; in many situations, you can copy the recordset used in the master page and paste it in the detail page using the context-sensitive menus on the Bindings panel. After the recordset is pasted onto the page, you can modify it to include additional fields by double-clicking the recordset entry in the Bindings panel.

Filtering a Detail Page Recordset in Simple Mode

You can create the filtered recordset in either the simple Recordset or the advanced Recordset dialog box. To use the simple Recordset dialog, follow these steps:

See Chapter 18 for more on the simple and advanced Recordset dialog boxes.

1. From the Bindings panel, click the Add (+) button and choose Recordset from the list.

2. After you've chosen the name, connection, and table, select the fields required by your details page from the Columns list.

3. From the first Filter list, select the field that coincides with the value passed by the URL parameter, as shown in Figure 22-3. This field should contain unique values that can be used to identify each record.

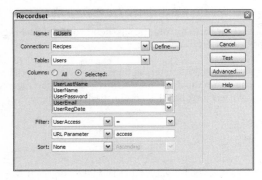

Figure 22-3: Setting a filter in the simple Recordset dialog box requires completing four fields under the Filter heading.

4. From the second Filter list, select the equals operator (=).

5. From the third Filter list, ASP, .NET, PHP, and ColdFusion users should choose the URL Parameter from the list; JSP users should select the URL/Form Variable.

6. In the fourth Filter field, enter the variable name passed by the master page in the Go To Detail Page server behavior. Avoid names with spaces or other special characters; these names must be URL-encoded and may be difficult to manage.

7. Click OK when you're finished.

You can preview the results of your detail page in Live Data view, but be sure to set up the Live Data settings option first. Choose View ➪ Live Data Settings to begin. When the Live Data Settings dialog box is open, enter the URL parameter name in the Name column and the value you'd like to test in the Value column. Make sure the Method option is set to Get and click OK. Your preview should now include the specified record, just as if the user had chosen it.

Tip   After entering Live Data view, you can test a variety of different records without reopening the Live Data Settings dialog. In the URL Parameter field found on the Live Data toolbar, change the URL parameter's current value and press Enter (Return). If you enter a value not found in the data source, Dreamweaver displays an error indicating that it cannot display the page.

To test your master-detail application, save both pages and then preview the master page in the browser. When you select the link to the detail page, you should see your chosen record.

Filtering a Detail Page Recordset in Advanced Mode

Sometimes you need to define a more complex recordset than is possible in the simple Recordset dialog box. You can effectively add the same filter-by-URL-parameter argument for such recordsets in the advanced Recordset dialog box by altering the SQL statement. Filtering in a SQL statement is handled by the WHERE clause.

To create a detail page filter, you declare a variable and add a WHERE clause referencing that variable. The runtime value portion of the variable is different for each server model. Assume you want to declare a variable called theBrand, and the field is named Brand. In the Variables section of the Advanced Recordset dialog box, click the Add (+) button and then enter the following values, according to your server model:

Server Model	Name	Default Value	Runtime Value
ASP and .NET	theBrand	%	Request.QueryString("Brand")
ColdFusion	theBrand	%	#URL.Brand#
JSP	theBrand	%	request.getParameter("Brand")
PHP	TheBrand	%	<?php echo $HTTP_GET_VARS['Brand']; ?>

In this example, the WHERE clause would read:

```
WHERE Brand = 'theBrand'
```

If you have already created a URL-parameter filtered recordset in the simple Recordset dialog box and then switch to the Advanced mode, you notice that Dreamweaver uses the variable name MMColParam. You can continue to use this variable name or change it to something more meaningful if you prefer.

Using a Server Behavior to Filter a Recordset

As noted earlier, the other method for connecting a master page with a detail page involves using a Dreamweaver server behavior. The Move To Specific Record server behavior is applied on the detail page itself and may be attached at any time. Unlike the filtered recordset approach, which uses a single record in the recordset, Move To Specific Record requires a recordset that includes all the possible records and their data. This gives you the capability to move through the recordset using the Recordset Paging Server Behaviors. The record specified by the URL parameter, as interpreted by the server behavior, is extracted from the overall recordset and its data displayed. To use the Move To Specific Record server behavior to create a detail page, follow these steps:

1. Establish a recordset that contains all the possible records that could be requested by the master page.

2. From the Server Behaviors panel, choose Move To Specific Record from the Move To Record submenu. The Move To Specific Record dialog box is displayed, as shown in Figure 22-4.

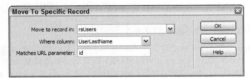

Figure 22-4: An alternative method for creating a detail page uses the Move To Specific Record server behavior.

3. Select the desired recordset from the list labeled Move To Record In.

4. Choose the field referenced in the URL parameter from the Where Column field.

5. Enter the variable in the URL parameter in the Matches URL Parameter field.

6. Click OK when you're finished.

Caution   Although Dreamweaver provides this method for creating a detail page — and I've covered it here for the sake of completeness — it's really not the recommended method. Because this technique relies on the use of a full recordset, it is far more resource-intensive than the filtered recordset method. However, this method is required if you are going to use Recordset Paging.

Automating Master-Detail Page Production

Although Dreamweaver has made crafting master detail Web applications by hand extremely accessible, it can be a tedious series of steps, especially if you have to produce a number of applications for a site. To ease the monotony — and enhance your production efforts — Dreamweaver includes the Master-Detail Page Set application object that, after a single dialog box is completed, creates all the elements for a linked master-detail Web application.

The master page elements are inserted in the current document, which must contain a recordset. The inserted elements and code, shown in Figure 22-5, are as follows:

✦ A two-row table with a column for each field

✦ A header row comprised of all the field names selected in the dialog

✦ Dynamic text for all selected fields, placed into the second row

✦ A Repeat Region server behavior surrounding the second row

✦ A Go To Detail Page server behavior linking to the newly created detail page

✦ A Recordset Navigation Bar with text links and appropriate Show Region server behaviors in place

✦ A Recordset Status Bar showing the current record count

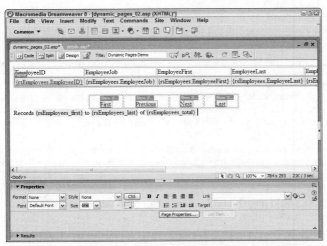

Figure 22-5: The Master-Detail Page Set application object adds all the designated fields and the required server behaviors to the current page.

The detail page is created when the Master-Detail Page Set Object is executed. As shown in Figure 22-6, the detail page is blank except for a two-column table, which contains a row for each field. The first column displays all the field names in the designated order, and the second column holds Dynamic Text elements, one for each of the fields.

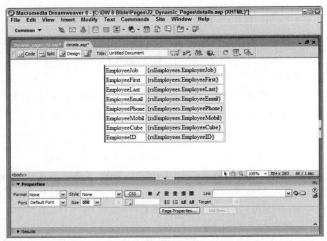

Figure 22-6: Only the fields, data, and necessary server behaviors are included in the newly created detail page.

To create a Web application using the Master-Detail Page Set application object, follow these steps:

1. Be sure that the current page, which will become the master page, includes the desired recordset and has been saved. The recordset must contain all the fields you want to display on the detail page, as well as the fields for the master page.

Tip

When creating master-detail pages, I generally create my initial recordset and choose all records. After I've created my page set, I trim down the recordset on the master page by selecting only those fields necessary for the master page.

2. Place your cursor where you'd like the table, Recordset Navigation Bar, and Recordset Navigation Status element to appear.

3. Choose Insert ⇨ Application Object ⇨ Master-Detail Page Set. You can also drag the Master-Detail Page Set icon from the Application category of the Insert bar to the desired location on the page. The Insert Master-Detail Page Set dialog box is shown in Figure 22-7.

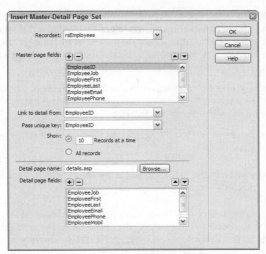

Figure 22-7: Select the fields and their relative positions to lay out the columns for both the master and detail pages.

4. Select the recordset you'd like to use from the Recordset list.

5. In the Master Page Fields area, choose any fields you do not want to appear on the master and click the Remove (–) button.

   Dreamweaver, by default, includes all the available fields in a selected recordset. If you'd like to include any fields that are not in the current recordset, you must click Cancel and modify the recordset.

6. If you change your mind after you remove a field from the list of fields to be inserted into the master page, click the Add (+) button and reinsert the field.

7. Alter the positioning of the fields in the master page table by selecting the field and using the up and down arrows above the Master Page Fields area.

   The master page table is horizontal with the topmost fields in the Master Page Fields area appearing on the left and the bottommost fields on the right. Clicking the up arrow moves a field to the left, whereas clicking the down arrow moves it to the right.

8. Choose a field from the Link To Detail From list that serves as a link to the detail page. Only the fields remaining in the Master Page Fields area are available in the Link To Detail From list.

9. From the Pass Unique Key list, select the field that identifies each record for use in the URL parameter.

Although the field in the Link To Detail From list and the one in the Pass Unique Key list could be the same, they don't have to be. You can, for example, use an employee's last name as the link and the employee ID number—not displayed in the master page fields—as the unique key. The Pass Unique Key list includes all the fields in the chosen recordset whether or not they are displayed onscreen.

10. Select the number of records you'd like displayed in the Repeat Region. Choose All to display every record in the recordset. Now that you have defined the master page portion of your application, define the elements for the detail page.

11. Enter the path to the detail page in the Detail Page Name field or click Browse to locate the file, if it exists.

Note   The master and detail pages must be in the same folder for the Master-Detail Page Set application object to function properly.

12. From the Detail Page Fields area, select any fields that you do not want to display on the detail page and click the Remove (–) button. Again, by default, Dreamweaver displays all the available fields in the recordset, and you must delete those you don't want to show.

13. To change the order in which the fields are inserted into the detail page table, select the field and use the up or down buttons above the Detail Page Fields area.

14. Click OK when you're done.

Note   After the application object has finished inserting master page elements and creating the detail page, be sure to save the master page. Dreamweaver saves the detail page automatically, but it does not save the master page as part of the creation process.

The Master-Detail Page Set application object—especially the detail page—works well with Dreamweaver templates. After the master and detail pages are created, you can apply any Dreamweaver template to integrate the results into your site. To prepare the template, just make sure that at least one editable region exists for all the visual elements inserted into the master and detail pages. I say that the Server-Object–generated detail page is especially well suited to template use because the created page contains only the table and its dynamic elements. After applying such a template, as shown in Figure 22-8, you may still need to tweak the design by altering the table properties.

Cross-Reference   To find out more about Dreamweaver templates, see Chapter 27.

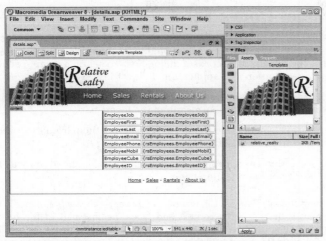

Figure 22-8: Drag a template from the Assets panel onto a detail page to quickly change the look-and-feel of a generated document.

Getting Values from a Form

Next to clicking on links, a user's prime interaction with a Web page is through the form. Forms are used in almost every Web application in one form (minor pun intended) or another. A Web page that is gathering information from a user always contains a form that uses a variety of elements, such as text fields, checkboxes, radio buttons, and drop-down lists. Although forms are important to Web applications, not every page containing a form needs to be executed by an application server. You can, however, pass information from a form to a dynamic page.

In the earlier discussions of master-detail Web applications, the master page was always generated by the developer's recordset selection without any user input. This section examines how you can develop user-driven master pages in Dreamweaver. Here are the four key elements:

✦ A static HTML page containing a form. (Although it's possible to use a dynamic page, none of what this page accomplishes requires server-side code.)

✦ One or more uniquely named form elements. (The naming of the form element is vital to getting the correct value into the application.)

✦ A link from the static page to the dynamic page inserted as a relative or an absolute URL in the action parameter of the form.

✦ A filter on the recordset of the dynamic page that reads the value passed from the form.

Passing Single Values from a Form

The recordset filter, if it relates to a single form element, can be set in the simple Recordset dialog box. More sophisticated filters, which depend on values received from multiple form elements, must be created in the advanced Recordset dialog box. To set up a form to send user selections to a master page or other Web application, follow these steps:

1. Create a static HTML page (File ⇨ New) and choose Insert ⇨ Form ⇨ Form or drag an Insert Form icon onto the page from the Forms tab of the Insert bar.

2. Add the desired input form elements into the form by selecting them from the Insert ⇨ Form Objects submenu or from the Insert bar.

3. Be sure to name each form element appropriately and uniquely. You need to recall this name when you're building your application page.

Tip

It's best to adopt a naming strategy that you can use over and over again. My preference is to name each form element with two parts: context and type. The first part of the name describes its context or how it is used on the page; the second part indicates what kind of form element is used. For example, a text field that holds the last name of a visitor is called `lastnameText`; whereas a drop-down list that lists office locations is `locationsList`. After a while, your naming convention becomes second nature to you, and you can easily remember what each form element has been named.

4. Select the `<form>` tag on the Tag Selector and, in the Action field of the Property inspector, enter the path to the dynamic page containing the application. Alternatively, you can click the folder icon to locate the file.

5. Also in the Property inspector, set the `Method` property of the form to `Post`. When you're passing variables and values via the URL query-string technique, described previously in the section "Using the URL to Pass Parameters," use the `Get` method. To pass the values of the form without exposing them in the URL, use `Post`.

Note

When you're deciding whether to use `POST` or `GET` to pass your parameters, also decide whether you want to be able to pass those variables easily to other pages. `GET` is the easier method to use when passing variables. If you're only going to use them for this single page, use `POST` to keep the query string clean.

6. Save your page.

Now you're ready to implement the receiving portion of your form-value passing application. To do so, follow these steps:

1. Create a new dynamic page for your master page application.

2. Insert a recordset by clicking the Add (+) button on the Bindings panel and selecting Recordset from the list.

3. In the simple Recordset dialog box, choose your recordset name, connection, table, and columns.

4. In the Filter area, from the first Filter list, select the field that matches the value passed by the form element. For example, if you are filtering a recordset based on the location specified in a form's drop-down list, choose the field — called location, perhaps — that contains the specified value.

5. From the second Filter list, select the equals operator (=).

6. From the third Filter list, ASP and ColdFusion users choose Form Variable from the list; JSP users select URL/Form Variable.

7. In the fourth Filter field, enter the name of the form element. In this example, the form element is named `locationList`.

8. Click OK when you're finished.

9. Apply the Master-Detail Page Application object to create the master page.

Test your application by saving the master page and previewing the initial page with the form. You can also use View ➪ Live Data Settings to try different values for your form variable; be sure to change the Method to `Post` in the Live Data Settings dialog box.

Passing Multiple Values from a Form

For more complex recordsets, you have to write the SQL statement in Dreamweaver's advanced Recordset dialog box. The same technique described earlier in the "Filtering a Detail Page Recordset in Advanced Mode" section applies here. Declare a variable that uses one of the following runtime values:

Server Model	Name	Default Value	Runtime Value
ASP and .NET	theVariable	%	Request.Form("Fieldname")
ColdFusion	theVariable	%	#Form.Fieldname#
JSP	theVariable	%	request .getParameter("Fieldname")
PHP	TheVariable	%	<?php echo $HTTP_POST_VARS['Fieldname']; ?>

The `WHERE` clause of the SQL sets the fieldname to the variable, as in this example:

```
WHERE dbadata.Location = 'theLocation'
```

Multiple form variables can also be set up in the advanced Recordset dialog box. Presume that you want your master page to display a list of employees in a particular department at a specific office. The form might include a drop-down list that displays a number of departments as well as a radio button group for the different offices. If `theDept` is the variable for the department form list value and `theLocation` is for the office radio button value, the SQL statement looks like this:

```
SELECT * FROM Employees WHERE Department = 'theDept' ⊃
AND Location = 'theLocation'
```

Passing Form and URL Values to a Related Page

Master-detail Web applications aren't the only applications that can benefit from information entered on a form. Other applications sometimes offer a link to a related page—like a special note pertinent only to a user-specified selection. To implement such pages, the application page needs the same form information passed to the master page. Dreamweaver includes a Go To Related Page server behavior that delivers the form values to the linked page; the behavior can also pass URL values by themselves or in conjunction with values from forms.

Like other server behaviors in the Go To category, Go To Related Page can be applied to text, images, or dynamic page elements. In a master page with a Repeat Region, you can attach Go To Related Page to an element within the repeating region and have it be available for every entry. To attach a Go To Related Page server behavior, follow these steps:

1. On a page that has had form or URL values passed to it, select the page element — text, image, or dynamic data — to use as the trigger for your behavior.

2. From the Server Behaviors panel, click the Add (+) button and select Go To Related Page from the list. The Go To Related Page server behavior dialog box appears, as shown in Figure 22-9.

Figure 22-9: The Go To Related Page server behavior can convey form values, URL values, or both to another dynamic page.

3. In the dialog box, verify that the text or code for the selected element displayed in the Link field is correct.

4. Enter the path to the target page in the Related Page field or click Browse to locate an existing dynamic page.

5. If you want to carry over values received from a query string, select the URL Parameters option.

6. If you want to pass values received from a form, select the Form Parameters option.

7. Click OK when you're finished.

The Go To Related Page server behavior can also be used to carry results of a form within a series of pages. In other words, if the first Go To Related Page server behavior passed the form or URL values from the master page to the first related page, you can include another Go To Related Page server behavior linked to a second related page.

Caution   You cannot use the Go To Related Page server behavior to link to a dynamic page that uses the Move To Specific Record server behavior. The Move To Specific Record server behavior overwrites the form or URL values passed by the Go To Related Page server behavior with its own. Instead of a Move To Specific Record server behavior on the target page, create a recordset filtered from the passed form/URL values.

Building a Search Page

A dynamic application that searches a database uses two pages: one to specify the search parameters and another to display the results page. In this Technique, you create the search page.

1. From the Techniques - Dynamic site (established in Chapter 18), expand the 22_Dynamic_Pages folder and open the `search_start` file for your server model.

2. Place your cursor below the opening paragraph of placeholder text.

3. From the Forms category of the Insert bar, click Form.

4. In the Property inspector, click the Action field's Browse for File folder icon and select the `results_start` file for your server model in the current folder.

5. Make sure your cursor is inside the form and, from the Insert bar's Common category, choose Table.

6. In the Table dialog box, specify these settings:

Setting	Value
Rows	2
Columns	2
Width	300 pixels
Border thickness	0 pixels

7. When you're done, click OK.

8. In the top row's first cell, enter the text **Keywords**.

9. Select the `<td>` tag from the Tag Selector and, then, from the Property inspector's Class list, choose formLabel.

10. Place your cursor in the second cell of the top row, and, from the Forms category of the Insert bar, choose Text Field.

11. With the text field still selected, enter **searchField** in the Property inspector's Name field.

12. Place your cursor in the second row, directly beneath the text field and, from the Insert bar, choose Button to add it to the page.

13. With the button selected, enter the term **Search** in the Property inspector's Value field.

Continued

Continued

14. Save your page.

In the next technique, you build the results page to accompany this search page.

Establishing Dynamic Form Elements

Forms and form elements play a much larger role in Web applications than just filtering recordsets. Forms are also necessary for inserting new records in a data source as well as for updating existing records. Dreamweaver lets you convert standard form elements into dynamic ones so that they can reflect and modify a record's data.

Although the general conversion from a static to a dynamic form element is handled in the same fashion for all elements — by applying a Dynamic Form Elements server behavior to an existing form element — almost every element has different dialog boxes with varying parameters.

Text Fields

Text fields are extremely flexible and essential for inputting freeform text into data sources. To create a dynamic text field, follow these steps:

1. Insert a text field into a form on a page with a recordset or other data source. It's a good idea to name the text field and form at this point. Although you can always change the names later, I find that naming the elements early avoids problems later.

2. Select the text field.

3. From the Server Behaviors panel, choose Dynamic Form Elements ➪ Dynamic Text Field.

4. In the Dynamic Text Field dialog box that appears (see Figure 22-10), verify that the correct form element is chosen in the Text Field list. If necessary, choose a different text field.

Figure 22-10: Use a dynamically linked text field to display data in an editable format.

5. Click the Set Value To lightning bolt icon to display the available data sources.

6. Choose a field from the Dynamic Data dialog box.

7. If you want, you can apply a server format to the data by choosing an entry in the Format list.

8. Click OK to close the Dynamic Data dialog box and, after reviewing your choices, click OK again to close the Dynamic Text Field dialog box.

The dynamic data is inserted into what is called the *initial value* of the form field. You can see the data of the current recordset by selecting View ➪ Live Data. Adjust the width of the text field to accommodate your dynamic data — and all the other standard parameters of a text field — through the Property inspector.

Tip   If Cascading Style Sheets (CSS) is an option on your Web application, it's often far better to create a custom class for the text field to control the width. Not only is the measurement standard more precise in CSS than in standard HTML, but it can be updated for all applicable text fields in one operation rather than in a tag-by-tag fashion.

After you become familiar with Dreamweaver's workings, you can use the Bindings panel to skip most of the previous steps. To use the Bindings panel, follow these steps:

1. Insert a text field into a form on a page with a recordset or other data source.

2. Select the text field.

3. Open the Bindings panel and select the dynamic data to bind to your text field.

4. Click Bind at the bottom of the Bindings panel.

Checkboxes

When you attach a checkbox to dynamic data, the checked and unchecked state reflects the true or false state of a Yes/No (also known as a Boolean) type of database field. Not only is this visual method easily understood at a glance, but checkboxes are extremely easy to update. To convert a static checkbox to a dynamic one, follow these steps:

1. Select a checkbox in a form on a page with a recordset.

2. From the Server Behaviors panel, choose Dynamic Form Elements ➪ Dynamic CheckBox. The Dynamic CheckBox dialog box appears, as shown in Figure 22-11.

Tip   Click the Dynamic button in the Property inspector to go straight to this dialog box.

Figure 22-11: Checkboxes can depict whether a particular field of a record is noted as True in the data source.

3. Verify that your selected checkbox is correctly named in the CheckBox list.

4. Click the Check If lightning bolt icon to display the available data sources.

5. Choose a field from the Dynamic Data dialog box.

6. If desired, you can apply a server format to the data by choosing an entry in the Format list. Click OK when you're finished to close the Dynamic Data dialog box.

7. Enter the value expected for a selected checkbox in the Equal To field. This value is data-source dependent. For many data sources, 1 is used to represent true; for others, a -1 is used. When working with Yes/No fields from Access databases, enter **True**; be sure to capitalize the letter *T*; lowercase *true* does not work properly.

8. Click OK when you're finished.

Tip   Although checkboxes are most typically used to show the state of Yes/No data fields, they can also be tied to text data fields and selected if the field is equal to a given value. When applying the Dynamic CheckBox server behavior, choose the text field and enter the exact text string in the Equal To field.

Radio Buttons

Radio buttons provide a good way to represent a field that has a limited number of options. Suppose your data source includes a Comment Type field, which offers three possible choices: Positive (Pos), Negative (Neg), and Other (Other). To illustrate which type of comment a user submits, your Web application might display a series of three radio buttons, one for each type. If the radio buttons are dynamically tied to the Comment Type field, they show the correct type for each comment. Like checkboxes, radio buttons are very easy to modify—one click and you're done. To link radio buttons to dynamic data, follow these steps:

1. Select a group of radio buttons on a dynamic page with an available data source.

2. From the Server Behaviors panel, choose Dynamic Form Elements ⇨ Dynamic Radio Buttons. The Dynamic Radio Buttons dialog box appears, as shown in Figure 22-12.

Figure 22-12: Radio buttons can reflect a limited number of choices within a data source field.

3. Verify that your selected form element is displayed in the Radio Button Group list.

4. In the Radio Button Values area, choose the first entry shown and, if necessary, change the Value field to reflect the expected data.

5. Repeat step 4 for every radio button in the group.

6. Click the Select Value Equal To lightning bolt icon to display the available data sources.

7. Choose a field from the Dynamic Data dialog box. Be sure to select a data source field with values parallel to those entered in the radio button group.

8. If desired, you can apply a server format to the data by choosing an entry in the Format list. Click OK when you're done to close the Dynamic Data dialog box.

9. Click OK when you're finished to close the Dynamic Radio Buttons dialog box.

List/Menus

Typographical errors are the bane of data entry. Regardless of how careful users are, whenever they must enter an exact phrase of any length, typos are inevitable. If the set of desired responses from a user is limited, the list/menu form element provides a good alternative to a text field. An e-commerce site, for instance, might use a list/menu form element (also called a drop-down list or select list) to enable the user to navigate from one product line to another. With Dreamweaver, the drop-down list may be filled (populated) with dynamic data, so that the navigation tool can keep track of the products entered in the data source.

A drop-down list is composed of two parts: the label and the value. The *label* is what the user sees when he selects the list; the *value* is what the user submits by selecting a particular list choice. In many situations, both the label and the value may be the same; in these cases, you can use the same data source field for both. Otherwise, you need data source fields available — this is how the product navigation example works. One data source field contains an entry for every product line (the label), and another field contains a URL to that product line's page on the Web site (the value). To link a drop-down list to dynamic data, follow these steps:

1. Insert a list/menu form element on a dynamic page with a recordset.

2. If you have more than one list/menu on the page, select the one you want to convert.

3. From the Server Behaviors panel, choose Dynamic Form Elements ⇨ Dynamic List/Menu. The Dynamic List/Menu dialog box (see Figure 22-13) is displayed.

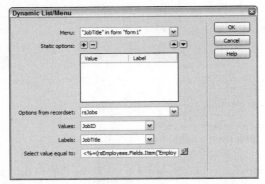

Figure 22-13: Lists give the user a distinct series of items from which to choose.

4. In the Static Options box, add any nondynamic items to the top of the list menu. This could be something as simple as a label for the list menu or as complicated as a full URL with query strings for search pages.

5. Choose the recordset you want to work with from the Options From Recordset list.

6. Verify that the desired drop-down list is displayed in the Menu list.

7. Choose the field from your data source containing the items you want submitted by the user from the Values list.

8. Choose the field from your data source containing the items you want displayed to the user from the Labels list.

9. To preselect an item, enter its value in the Select Value Equal To field, or use the lightning bolt icon to choose a value from the established data sources.

10. Click OK when you're finished.

New In Dreamweaver You should also notice the new Dynamic button on the Property inspector. Click the button to open the corresponding dialog box. This is another quick way to get to the options without going through the Server Behaviors panel.

Managing Data Sources Online

Data source connectivity is a two-way street. Not only can data be extracted and displayed over the Web, but Web applications can also manage records found in data sources. With the power to add, modify, and remove data comes a terrific opportunity. From a Web application-builder's perspective, I find that almost half of my client work is concerned with data source management.

Like the common master-detail application, Dreamweaver offers both a manual and an automatic method of performing the most common management tasks. There are Application objects for inserting and for updating records. Both methods are detailed in the following sections.

Inserting Data

To insert records into a data source, you need the following:

- ✦ An active page
- ✦ A form placed on the page
- ✦ One form element per data source field
- ✦ A Submit button
- ✦ An Insert Record server behavior

No recordset or other data source is necessary, nor are there are any special requirements for the form itself — you don't even have to specify an action or a method. The Insert Record server behavior handles most of the coding chores.

Form elements are typically arranged in a table with labels for each field, as shown in Figure 22-14. Naturally you can format the table however you like; I generally prefer a two-column table with the labels in the first column, right-aligned, and the form elements in the second column, left-aligned. It's best to name the form elements so that you can identify them easily and ensure that each element is unique. A reset button is optional — but recommended if the form has many fields.

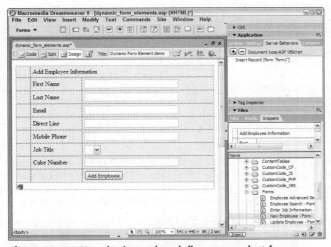

Figure 22-14: You don't need to define a recordset for an insert record page.

Tip   You can save a step in the Insert Record server behavior setup by naming your form elements the same as their relevant data source fields. Dreamweaver automatically assigns the form elements to any data fields with matching names. Unfortunately, this process could expose the field names in your database and give hackers more information about your database than you'd like them to know.

After you've constructed your table inside the form and placed the form elements, follow these steps to add the Insert Record server behavior:

1. From the Server Behaviors panel, choose Insert Record. The Insert Record dialog box appears.

2. From the Insert Record dialog box, choose a connection from the Connection drop-down list. If you need to establish a new connection, click Define.

3. Select the data table you want to use from the Insert Into Table list.

4. Enter the path to the destination page in the After Inserting, Go To field; or click the Browse button to locate the file.

   It's important that you select a confirmation or other page for users to go to after the form is submitted. If you don't, there is no feedback to the user, and no change is apparent.

5. Select the name of the form to be used from the Get Values From list. If there is only one form on the page, the form is preselected.

6. Do the following for each object listed in the Form Elements area:

   • From the Column list, select the data source field into which you want to insert the value of the form object.

   • From the Submit As list, choose the data source type for the data. The options are Text; Numeric; Date; Date MS Access; Checkbox Y, N; Checkbox 1,0; Check -1,0; and Checkbox MS Access.

7. Click OK when you're finished.

With the Record Insertion Form application object, you create a new page and apply the object. Dreamweaver creates the HTML table, includes the form elements and their labels, makes the connection to the data source, and adds the appropriate server-side code. Moreover, this application object is flexible enough to include seven different form element types — Text Field, Text Area, Menu, Hidden Field, CheckBox, Radio Group, and Password Field — as well as Text.

The Menu and Radio Group options are interesting because they enable you to enter the labels and values either manually or dynamically. To take advantage of Dreamweaver's capability to generate dynamic menus and radio buttons, you must have a recordset or other data source on the page. To insert the Record Insertion Form application object, follow these steps:

1. Place your cursor where you'd like the form to appear and choose Insert ⇨ Application Objects ⇨ Record Insertion Form. Alternatively, you can drag the Record Insertion Form object from the Application category of the Insert bar onto your page. The Insert Record dialog box appears as shown in Figure 22-15.

Figure 22-15: The Record Insertion Form application object automatically creates a label and form element for every field in the selected data table.

2. From the Insert Record dialog box, choose a connection from the Connection drop-down list. If you need to establish a new connection, click Define.

3. Select the data table from the Insert Into Table list.

4. Enter the path to the destination page in the After Inserting, Go To field or click the Browse button to locate the file. At this point, Dreamweaver has added an entry in the Form Fields area for every field in the data source.

5. Delete any unwanted fields by selecting their entries in the Form Fields area and clicking the Remove (–) button.

   It's best to remove any fields that use auto-incrementing numbers. Such fields are commonly used to generate unique identification numbers for each record and are automatically incremented when a new record is added.

6. Select the first entry in the Form Fields area.

7. If desired, modify the text in the Label field to a more descriptive term than the name of the data source column automatically supplied by Dreamweaver.

8. Choose the form element type from the Display As list. By default, Dreamweaver uses Text Field.

   If you choose either Menu or Radio Group, click the Properties button that appears to further define the form element. With text fields, text areas, and text you can set an initial value in the Default Value field. For checkboxes, select whether the element should be Checked or Unchecked.

9. Choose the data format from the Submit As list.

10. Click OK when you're done.

Updating Data

In the day-to-day operations of most Web sites, you update records more often than you insert new records. The process in Dreamweaver for creating an update records page is similar to the one for the insert records application with one important difference — you must have a recordset defined. Detail pages are good candidates to transform into update applications. They already have the features necessary for an update application; namely, they have a recordset or other method for specifying a single record, and they are often generated from master-type pages. The major difference is that an update records application also requires specific server-side code — which is supplied in Dreamweaver by the Update Record server behavior.

As with the insert record application, you can choose to either create all the components of an update record page yourself or use the application object to build them for you. To prepare the page for adding the Update Record server behavior, make sure you include a form element for every data field you want to update as well as a Submit button. Neither the action nor method attributes of the form need to be set — the Update Record server behavior handles that chore. To insert an Update Record server behavior, follow these steps:

1. From the Server Behaviors panel, choose Update Record. The Update Record dialog box appears, as shown in Figure 22-16.

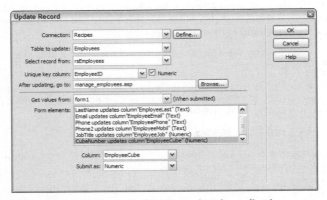

Figure 22-16: With an Update Record Web application, your data source can be modified remotely.

2. From the Update Record dialog box, choose a connection from the Connection dropdown list. If you need to establish a new connection, click Define.

3. Select the data table from the Table to Update list.

4. Choose the data source on which to base your update from the Select Record From list.

5. Select the key field from the Unique Key Column list. Dreamweaver attempts to detect whether the field is a number type and, if so, it selects the Numeric option.

6. Enter the path to the destination page in the After Updating, Go To field; or click the Browse button to locate the file.

7. Select the name of the form to be used from the Get Values From list. If there is only one form on the page, the form is preselected.

8. For each object listed in the Form Elements area

   • From the Column list, select the data source field into which you can insert the value of the form object.

   • Choose the data source type for the data from the Submit As list. The options are Text; Numeric; Date; Date MS Access; Checkbox Y, N; Checkbox 1,0; Check -1,0; and Checkbox MS Access.

9. Click OK when you're done.

If you'd prefer Dreamweaver to set up the form elements for you, use the Record Update Form application object. Before you can insert this application object, you must define a recordset or other data source from which to extract the data. The advantage of using Dreamweaver is sheer speed. Instead of manually creating the form, let Dreamweaver do the grunt work for you. To create an update record application using the application object, follow these steps:

1. Place your cursor where you'd like the form to appear and choose Insert ⇨ Application Objects ⇨ Record Update Form. Alternatively, you can drag the Insert Record Update Form object from the Application category of the Insert bar onto your page. The Insert Record Update Form dialog box is displayed.

2. From the Insert Record Update Form dialog box, choose a connection from the Connection drop-down list. To establish a new connection, click Define.

3. Select the data table to modify from the Table To Update list.

4. Choose the data source on which to base your update from the Select Record From list.

5. Select the key field from the Unique Key Column list. Dreamweaver attempts to detect whether the field is a number type and, if so, selects the Numeric option.

6. Enter the path to the destination page in the After Updating, Go To field; or click the Browse button to locate the file. At this point, Dreamweaver has added an entry in the Form Fields area for every field in the data source.

7. Delete any unwanted field by selecting its entry in the Form Fields area and clicking the Remove (–) button.

8. Select the first entry in the Form Fields area.

9. If desired, modify the text in the Label field to a more descriptive term than the name of the data source column automatically supplied by Dreamweaver.

10. Choose the desired form element type from the Display As list. By default, Dreamweaver uses Text Field.

Tip For fields that you want to display, but that you don't want users to alter — such as a unique key field — choose Text.

If you choose either Menu or Radio Group, click the Properties button that appears to further define the form element. With text fields, text areas, and text you can set an initial value in the Default Value field. For checkboxes, select whether the element should be Checked or Unchecked.

11. Choose the data format from the Submit As list.

12. Click OK when you're finished.

When these steps are completed, Dreamweaver inserts a borderless two-column table with the requested form elements and labels, similar to the one shown in Figure 22-17. As with other application objects, you can easily apply a template and include the generated elements in an editable region.

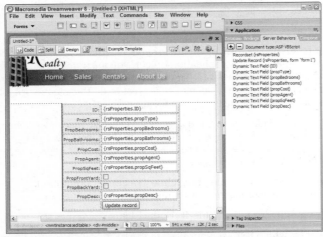

Figure 22-17: The Record Update Form application object creates all the elements and code necessary for modifying data source records online.

Deleting Data

Eliminating outdated or otherwise unneeded records is a key task in properly maintaining a data source. The Delete Record server behavior greatly simplifies the chore. All that the Delete Record server behavior requires is a recordset and a form with a Submit button.

Tip   Although it's not mandatory, it's good practice to provide enough detail — displayed in a read-only format — so that the user can be sure he is removing the correct record. A confirmation message on the Submit button (with something akin to "Are you sure you want to do this?") is nice also.

To attach a Delete Record server behavior to a form, follow these steps:

1. Make sure that a form exists on a dynamic page that includes at least one recordset.

2. From the Server Behaviors panel, choose Delete Record. The Delete Record dialog box is displayed, as shown in Figure 22-18.

Figure 22-18: Maintain an up-to-date data source with the Delete Record server behavior.

3. From the Delete Record dialog box, choose the Connection from the drop-down list. If you need to establish a new connection, click Define.

4. Select the data table to delete from the Delete From Table list.

5. Choose the data source on which to base the deletion from the Select Record From list.

6. Select the key field from the Unique Key Column list. Dreamweaver attempts to detect whether the field is a number type and, if so, selects the Numeric option.

7. Enter the path to the destination page in the After Deleting, Go To field; or click the Browse button to locate the file.

8. Choose the form that contains the delete Submit button.

The Delete Record server behavior is executed when the user clicks the Submit button in the form. It's a good idea to confirm the deletion with your user on the destination page.

Caution   There's a known problem with JSP pages that use Dreamweaver's Delete Record server behavior when they run on Apache's Jakarta Tomcat application server. The problem arises from the use of a redirect page. As a workaround, place all dynamic data on the deleted page within a Show Region If Recordset is Not Empty server behavior. By doing so, you'll allow Jakarta to link properly to the redirect page without generating an error

Inserting Variables

Variables are essential to any programming; and various variables are available depending on the server model. Although all setting of variables in Dreamweaver must be done by hand or using a custom server behavior, Dreamweaver provides a method for reading or displaying almost every kind of variable.

All variables are made available through the Add list of the Bindings panel. After a variable has been added as a data source, it can be dragged and dropped anywhere on the page or included via the Insert button. Which variables are available depends upon the server model. The vast majority of dialog boxes for variables are single entry fields, requesting the name of the specific variable, like the one shown in Figure 22-19.

Figure 22-19: After you establish a variable, it is made available for use in the Bindings panel.

Application and Session Variables

Both application and session variables are used throughout Web applications. An *application* variable is one that continues to exist as long as the application is active; in this situation, the application is the Web site itself. Application variables are available to all users of a site. A hit counter often uses an application variable to track the number of visitors to a site.

Although all users can see the results of a calculation involving application variables, *session* variables are user-specific. A session starts when a user first visits a site and ends shortly after the user leaves. Session variables are often used for user authentication and to maintain information about users as they travel through the site; shopping carts often employ session variables. Both application and session variables are available in ASP, PHP, and ColdFusion; in JSP only session variables can be inserted through the Bindings panel; .NET doesn't allow any declared variables.

Request and Other Variables

Each of the server models, with the exception of .NET, has a range of variables available aside from application and server variables. All are accessible through the Add (+) button of the Bindings panel and all, except for ASP Request variables, use a one-field dialog box for the name of the variable. In the case of the ASP Request variables, all five types of variables are available through a drop-down list on the Request Variable dialog box. After you've chosen your variable, enter its name in the Name field. Table 22-1 provides a breakdown of the available variables for each of the Dreamweaver server models.

Table 22-1: Variables for Dreamweaver Server Models

Server Model	Variables
ASP	Request, Cookie, QueryString, Form, ServerVariables, ClientCertificate, Session, Application
ColdFusion	Form, URL, Session, Client, Application, Cookie, CGI, Server Variable, Local Variable
JSP	Request Variables, Session Variable
PHP	Form, URL, Session, Cookie, Server, Environmental

Creating the Results Page

To complete the search application begun in the previous Technique, you need to create a results page. Unlike the search page, the results page contains server-side code easily inserted through Dreamweaver.

1. From the 22_Dynamic_Pages folder in the Techniques - Dynamic site, open the `results_start` file for your server model.

   To save time, a table to hold your search results has already been added to the page. The first task is to add a recordset to the page.

2. From the Bindings panel, click Add (+) and select Recordset (Query) from the list.

3. In the Recordset dialog box's Simple mode, enter **rsResults** in the Name field.

4. From the Connection list, choose RelativeRealty.

5. From the Table list, select Properties.

   To return the proper results for the search, you need to limit the recordset to records in which the database's description field contains the keyword searched for. You'll recall that text field in the search page was named searchField.

6. Set the Filter options like this:

   propDesc　　　　**contains**

   Form Variable　　**searchField**

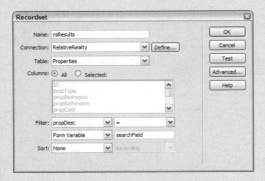

7. Leave the Sort list at its default setting and click OK.

   With the recordset defined, you're ready to begin binding data to the page.

8. In the Bindings panel, expand the Recordset (rsResults) entry.

Continued

Continued

9. Place the proper dynamic data in position:

    ✦ Drag propType to the cell under the Type label.

    ✦ Drag propDesc to the cell under the Description label.

    ✦ Drag propBedrooms to the cell under the Bedrooms label.

    ✦ Drag propBathrooms to the cell under the Bathrooms label.

    ✦ Drag propAgent to the cell under the Agent label.

10. Select any of the dynamic elements just added to the page like rsResults.propType and, from the Tag Selector, choose the `<tr>` tag.

11. From the Server Behaviors panel, click Add (+) and select Repeat Region from the list.

12. In the Repeat Region server behavior, make sure that rsResults is the chosen recordset and set the option Show All Records; click OK when you're ready.

13. Save your page.

14. In the Files panel, select both the pages of the search application — `search_start` and `results_start` — for your server model and choose Put to publish the files to the Testing server.

To test your search application, preview the previously built `search_start` page in a browser. Enter a keyword, such as "kitchen," in the text field and click Search; the results page will display any matching entries.

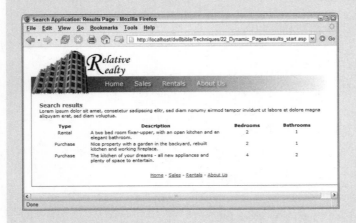

Connecting to the Customer

Fundamentally, you have two types of customers: new customers and returning customers. The goal of almost every enterprise is to turn the former into the latter. To that end, e-commerce sites try to make the customer experience as pleasant as possible. What makes for an enjoyable customer visit? Volumes have been written on that subject, so I'll concentrate here on one facet: the customer's account.

Early on in the history of Web stores, it wasn't uncommon to require returning customers to re-enter all their pertinent billing and shipping information. The e-commerce sites had no way of tracking all that data. Now, the vast majority of online stores — particularly the successful ones — offer a way for customers to open an account to store their basic information. Just as important, customers can easily identify themselves on their return, thus accessing their account information and enabling it to be applied to a new order. You may also want to restrict certain areas of your site to registered users or those who have paid for a subscription. Various levels of sophistication are possible here, but the most fundamental requirements are a way to identify returning customers and a way to add new ones.

Logging in Existing Customers

The most common way to identify returning customers is to allow them to log in. A login page can be as simple as a three-element form: two text fields — one for the username and one for the password — and a Submit button. The form connects to a data source containing a list of users and their passwords, among other information, and verifies that the submitted username corresponds with the submitted password. Dreamweaver accomplishes this task with the appropriately named Log In User server behavior.

The Log In User server behavior redirects authorized users to one page and unauthorized users to another. In addition, it creates a session variable containing the username. This session variable can then be employed on other pages as required.

To apply the Log In User server behavior, make sure your page has, at a minimum, a form with text fields for the username and password, and a Submit button. You're now ready to follow these steps:

1. From the Server Behaviors panel, click the Add (+) button and choose User Authentication ➪ Log In User. The Log In User dialog box is displayed, as shown in Figure 22-20.

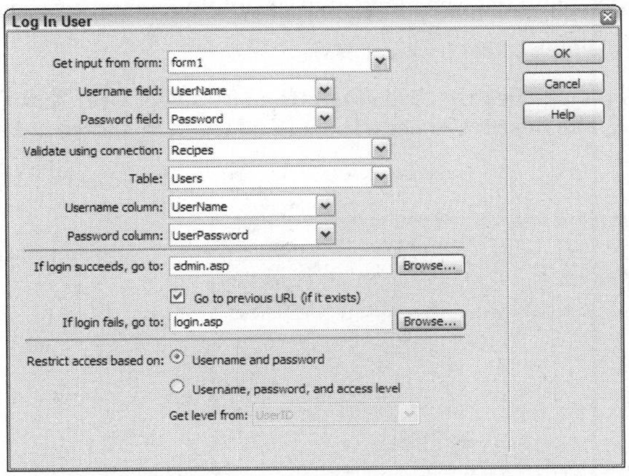

Figure 22-20: The Log In User server behavior can be used to gather information about a returning customer.

2. If there is more than one form on the page, select the form containing the username and password fields from the Get Input From Form list.

3. Select the form element used to gather the username from the Username Field list.

4. Select the form element used to gather the password from the Password Field list.

5. Choose a connection to the data source containing the table of registered users from the Validate Using Connection list.

6. Select the table of registered users from the Table list.

7. Choose the field containing the username from the Username Column list.

8. Choose the field containing the password from the Password Column list.

9. Enter the path to the page for the authorized user in the If Log In Succeeds, Go To field.

10. If you want the user to proceed to the previously selected link, rather than the page entered in step 9, select the Go To Previous URL option.

11. Enter the path to the page for the unauthorized user in the If Log In Fails, Go To field.

12. If access levels should be evaluated as part of the authentication, choose the following:

    • Restrict Access Based On Username, Password, and Access Level

    • The data source field containing the access-level data from the Get Level From list.

13. Click OK when you're finished.

Restricting Access

Now that you've got your users added and logging in, you need to protect those pages that require authorized access. These could be their user profile information or perhaps information they've paid a subscription to access. Dreamweaver provides two different types of access restriction. The first method just determines if a user is logged in or not. The second includes restriction based on access levels defined in your database.

To restrict access based on whether a user has logged in or not, follow these steps:

1. Open a dynamic page to which to restrict access.

2. In the Server Behaviors panel, click the Add (+) button and select User Authentication ➪ Restrict Access To Page. The Restrict Access To Page dialog box, shown in Figure 22-21, is displayed.

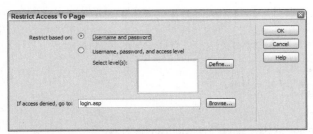

Figure 22-21: Dreamweaver's Restrict Access To Page server behaviors enable you to restrict access to sensitive parts of your site.

3. Choose the Username and Password radio button to restrict access to those users already logged in.

4. In the If Access Denied, Go To box, browse to the URL you want to send users to if they're not authorized to view the page. This page should have a sentence or two telling users why they're at this page, as well as a form for them to log in.

To restrict pages based on access level, add a login page as shown in Figure 22-21. This is handy if you want to have one login for both your administrators and your regular customers. One access level may be able to change user details, whereas another can only view those details. In step 12 of creating the login form in the previous section, choose the Restrict Access Based On Username, Password, and Access Level option. Next, choose the field from your table that contains the access levels, as shown in Figure 22-22.

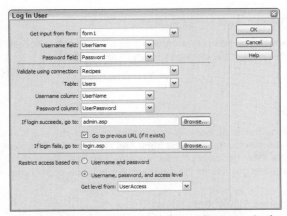

Figure 22-22: Use the Get Level From list menu in the Log In User dialog to restrict access to a page to a specific group of users. This gives you more granular control over your site.

To restrict access based on access levels, follow these steps:

1. Open a dynamic page to which you want access restricted.

2. In the Server Behaviors panel, click the Add (+) button and select User Authentication ➪ Restrict Access To Page. The Restrict Access To Page dialog box, shown in Figure 22-23, is displayed.

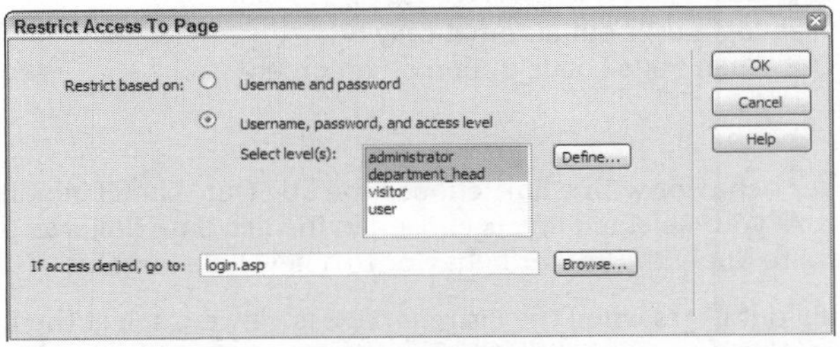

Figure 22-23: Define as many access levels as you want to restrict certain sections of your site to a subset of your members.

3. Choose the Username, Password, and Access Level radio button.

4. Choose one or more groups from the Select Level(s) area.

5. To add new groups to the Select Level(s) list:

   - Click Define to open the Define Access Levels dialog.

   - Enter the name for the access level in the Name field. The name must match a value stored in your data source in whichever column is designated for the group access levels.

   - To add additional levels, click the Add (+) button and enter another name.

   - To delete any levels, choose the level in the list area and click the Remove (–) button.

   - Click OK to close the Define Access Levels dialog box.

6. Enter the path to the file to which you redirect unauthorized users in the If Access Denied, Go To field. Alternatively, click the Browse button to locate the file.

7. Click OK when you're finished.

Helping Users Log Out

It's always a good idea to give your customer an easy way to log out of your site — a way that also destroys all the session variables associated with his login and ensures that his coworkers can't jump on his computer (right after he leaves for some coffee) and gain access to information they shouldn't have. Logging out a user in Dreamweaver is just a matter of one simple server behavior.

To use the Log Out User server behavior, follow these steps:

1. To apply the server behavior to a specific link on the page, select that link.

2. From the Server Behaviors panel, click the Add (+) button and choose User Authentication ➪ Log Out User. The Log Out User dialog box, shown in Figure 22-24, opens.

Figure 22-24: You can log a user out automatically by choosing the Log Out When Page Loads option on an order confirmation page.

3. To trigger the server behavior with a link, choose the Log Out When Link Clicked option and make sure your selected link is chosen in the list. If no link was preselected, Dreamweaver offers to apply the server behavior to a new link, Log Out.

4. To automatically log out users when the current page is viewed, select the Log Out When Page Loads option.

5. If you're using a link as a trigger, enter the path to the destination page in the When Done, Go To field. Alternatively, click the Browse button to locate the file.

Caution Do not use the When Done, Go To option if you are automatically logging out a user when the page loads. If you do, the user never sees the current page.

6. Click OK when you're finished.

Adding New Customers

An application that adds new customers is essentially the same as an insert record application, with one additional function. If you've ever tried to get a username on America Online that even remotely resembles your own name, chances are you've encountered the function I'm talking about — just ask bobsmith01234x. For a username to be useful, it must be unique; therefore, the Web application must check a submitted username for uniqueness. Dreamweaver's Check New Username server behavior does just this.

Before you can apply the Check New Username server behavior, however, you must create a page with the proper form elements for all the data necessary. Moreover, you need a Dreamweaver Insert Record server behavior (refer to Figure 22-15 earlier in this chapter). As the name implies, the Insert Record server behavior creates a new record and adds it to the specified data source.

The one difference between a standard Insert Record server behavior and the one used in this circumstance is that you leave the destination page field (After Inserting, Go To) blank. Leaving this field empty enables the Check New Username server behavior to control the redirection.

The Check New Username server behavior verifies that the requested username is not already in the data source and redirects the user if it is. To add a Check New Username server behavior to your page, follow these steps:

1. From the Server Behaviors panel, click the Add (+) button and choose User Authentication ➪ Check New Username. The Check New Username dialog box is displayed.

2. Select the form element that contains the requested username from the Username list. If a form element is called username, Dreamweaver automatically selects that entry.

3. Enter the path to the file you want a user to see if her requested name is already stored in the data source in the If Already Exists, Go To field; or click Browse to locate the file.

4. Click OK when you're finished.

Summary

Although numerous Web applications use only a single dynamic page, crafting multipage applications gives you more opportunity to build a robust user experience for your visitors. It's key for every Web developer to master the various methods for passing information from one page to another. When building your first multiple-page Web applications, keep these points in mind:

✦ Dreamweaver can send and receive parameters from one page to another by appending them in an encoded fashion to the linked URL. The additional text is known as a query string.

✦ You can send values from a form either by way of the query string or, in a hidden manner, in a separate object seen only by the server. The first technique uses the Get method and the second technique uses Post.

✦ Dreamweaver includes several application objects that reduce the building of common dynamic components — or even whole applications — to one step. Application objects can be combined with Dreamweaver templates for rapid application development.

✦ To craft applications that update records in a data source, you must know how to tie the various form elements to dynamic data. In Dreamweaver, the basic procedure is to include a standard form element and then choose the appropriate server behavior from the Dynamic Elements submenu of the Server Behaviors panel.

✦ Many Web applications are not concerned with publicly viewed sites on the Web, but rather with administrative-oriented pages designed to manage data sources remotely. Dreamweaver includes a full complement of tools for inserting new records, updating existing ones, and deleting data that is no longer required.

✦ After you've declared a variable in Dreamweaver, it is available for display through the Bindings panel. Each server model has its own set of variables.

✦ Dreamweaver enables you to create a user authentication system quickly to protect valuable customer information or paid subscription sites. You can even set different access levels for administrators and regular customers.

In the next chapter, you learn how to integrate graphics created in Fireworks into your Dreamweaver application.

✦   ✦   ✦

Including Multimedia Elements

❖ ❖ ❖ ❖

❖ ❖ ❖ ❖

Fireworks Integration

Imagine demonstrating a newly completed Web site to a client who *didn't* ask for an image to be a little bigger, the text on a button to be reworded, or the colors on the background to be revised. In the real world, Web sites — particularly the images — are constantly being tweaked and modified. This fact of Web life explains why Fireworks, Macromedia's premier Web graphics tool, is so popular. One of Fireworks' main claims to fame is that everything is editable all the time. If that were all that Fireworks did, the program would already have earned a place on every Web designer's shelf just for its sheer expediency. Fireworks has many other extraordinary graphic capabilities, however, and Dreamweaver can tap that power directly.

Macromedia's Dreamweaver 8 and Fireworks 8 are tightly integrated products. You can optimize your images — reduce the file size, crop the graphic, make colors transparent — within Dreamweaver using the Fireworks interface. Moreover, you can edit an image in any fashion in Fireworks and, with one click of the Done button, automatically export the graphic with its updated settings. Perhaps most important of all, Dreamweaver can control Fireworks — creating graphics on-the-fly — and then insert the results in Dreamweaver.

A key Fireworks feature is the capability to output HTML and JavaScript for easy creation of rollovers, sliced images, and image maps with behaviors. Starting in Fireworks 8, you can even opt to create pop-up menus with standards-compliant CSS. With Fireworks, you can specify Dreamweaver-style code so that all your Web pages are consistent. After Fireworks generates the HTML, Dreamweaver's Insert Fireworks HTML object makes code insertion effortless. Dreamweaver recognizes images — whether whole or sliced — as coming from Fireworks, and displays a special Property inspector.

Web pages and Web graphics are closely tied to each other. With the tight integration between Dreamweaver 8 and Fireworks 8, the Web designer's world is moving toward a single design environment.

Easy Graphics Modification

It's not uncommon for graphics to require some alteration before they fully integrate into a Web design. In fact, I'd say it's far more often the rule than the exception. The traditional workflow generally goes like this:

1. Create the image in one or more graphics-editing programs.

2. Place the new graphic on a Web page via your Web-authoring tool.

3. Note where the problems lie—perhaps the image is too big or too small, maybe the drop shadow doesn't blend into the background properly, or maybe the entire image needs to be flipped.

4. Reopen the graphics program, make the modifications, and save the file again.

5. Return to the Web page layout to view the results.

6. Repeat steps 3 through 5 *ad infinitum* until you get it right.

Although you're still using two different programs, the integration of Dreamweaver and Fireworks enables you to open a Fireworks window from within the Dreamweaver screen. You can make alterations with the Web page visible in the background. I've found that this small advantage cuts my trial-and-error time to a bare minimum and streamlines my workflow.

If you're not familiar with Fireworks, you're missing an extremely powerful graphics program made for the Web. Fireworks combines the best of both vector and bitmap technologies and is one of the first graphics programs to use PNG as its native format. Exceptional export capabilities are available in Fireworks with which images can be optimized for file size, color, and scale. Moreover, Fireworks is terrific at generating GIF animations, rollovers, image maps, and sliced images.

 Dreamweaver has a few graphics tricks of its own now. Even without Fireworks, you can crop, resample, and brighten images—and more. For a discussion of Dreamweaver's built-in graphics capabilities, see Chapter 9.

With Dreamweaver 8 and Fireworks 8, you have two ways to alter inserted graphics: the Optimize Image in Fireworks command and the Edit button in the Image Property inspector.

 The full integration described in this chapter requires that a current version of Fireworks be installed *after* Dreamweaver 8 or as part of Macromedia Studio 8. Certain features, such as the Optimize Image in Fireworks command, work with Fireworks 2 and later; but any other features requiring direct communication between the two programs work with Fireworks MX 2004 and up.

Optimizing an Image in Fireworks

Although you can design the most beautiful, compelling image possible in your graphics program, if it's intended for the Internet, it must be viewed in a Web page. Not only must the graphic work in the context of the entire page, but you also have to take the file size of the Web graphic into account. All these factors mean that most, if not all, images require some degree of modification after they're included in a Web page. Dreamweaver's Optimize Image in Fireworks command facilitates this modification by opening the Export module of Fireworks right from within Dreamweaver, as shown in Figure 23-1.

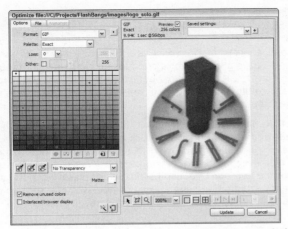

Figure 23-1: With Fireworks 8 installed, you can optimize images from within Dreamweaver.

The Export module consists of three tabbed panels: Options, File, and Animation. Although a complete description of all these features is beyond the scope of this book, here's a breakdown of the major uses of each area:

✦ **Options:** Enables you to try various export options and preview them. You can switch file formats from GIF to JPEG (or animated GIF or PNG), as well as alter the palette, color depth, loss (quality), and dithering. Transparency for GIF and PNG images is set in the Options panel. Fireworks also has an Optimize to Size wizard that enables you to target a particular file size for your graphic.

✦ **File:** Defines an image's dimensions. Images can be rescaled by a selected percentage or pixel size. Moreover, you can crop your image either numerically (by defining the export area) or visually (with the cropping tool).

✦ **Animation:** Provides frame-by-frame control for animated GIFs. Each frame's delay (how long it is onscreen) can be defined independently, and the entire animation can be set to either play once or loop a user-determined number of times.

Note   If you crop or rescale an inserted image in Fireworks, you must update its height and width in Dreamweaver. The easiest way to accomplish this is to click the Reset Size button in the Image Property inspector.

Fireworks saves its source files in an expanded PNG format to maintain full editability of the images. Graphics for the Web must be exported from Fireworks in GIF, JPEG, or standard PNG format. Dreamweaver's Optimize Image in Fireworks command can modify either the source file or the exported file. In most situations, better results are achieved by using the source file, especially when optimizing includes rescaling or resampling. Some situations, however, require that you leave the source file as is and modify only the exported files. Suppose, for example, that one source file is used to generate several different export files, each with different backgrounds (or *canvases*, as they are called in Fireworks). In that case, you are better off modifying the specific exported file, rather than the general source image.

Exploring Fireworks Source and Export Files

The separate source file is an important concept in Fireworks, and I strongly advise its use. Generally, when working in Fireworks, you have a minimum of two files for every image output to the Web: your source file and your exported Web image. Whenever you make major alterations, it's best to make them to the source file and then update the export files. Not only is it easier to work this way, but you also get a better image.

Source files are always Fireworks-style PNG files. Fireworks-style PNG files differ slightly from the regular PNG format because they include additional information, such as paths and effects used, that can be read only by Fireworks. The exported file is usually in GIF or JPEG format, although it can be in standard PNG format. Many Web designers keep their source files in a separate folder from their exported Web images so that the two don't get confused. This source-and-export file combination also prevents you from inadvertently re-editing a lossy compressed file, such as a JPEG image, and reapplying the compression (thus exacerbating the lossiness).

Dreamweaver enables you to choose which type of image you want to modify. When you first execute the Optimize Image in Fireworks or the Edit Image command, a Find Source dialog box appears (see Figure 23-2). If you want to locate and use the source file, click Use a PNG; to use the exported image that is inserted in Dreamweaver, click Use This File. If you opt for the source file — and the image was created in Fireworks — Dreamweaver reads the Design Note associated with the image to find the location of the source file and open it. If the image was created with an earlier version of Fireworks or the image has been moved, Dreamweaver asks you to locate the file with a standard Open File dialog box. By setting the Fireworks Source Files option, you can always open the same type of file: source or exported. Should you change your mind about how you like to work, open Fireworks and select Edit ➪ Preferences; then choose the desired option from the Launch and Edit panel.

Note   There's one case when Fireworks does not follow your Launch and Edit preferences: If the image chosen is a sliced image, Fireworks always optimizes the exported file rather than the source, regardless of your settings.

Tip   Because of server capacity limitations, most Web designers upload the exported GIF/JPEG image files (the files that actually appear in the Web page) to their servers, but they do not upload the source PNG image files from which these GIFs/JPEGs are derived. If you use this approach, you can take advantage of Dreamweaver's Cloaking feature to cloak your PNG files, thus automatically preventing them from being uploaded, as discussed in Chapter 5.

To use the Optimize Image in Fireworks command, follow these steps:

1. Select the image you'd like to modify in Dreamweaver.

Note   The current page must have been saved at least once before the Optimize Image in Fireworks command can be run. The current state of the page doesn't have to be previously saved, but a valid file must exist for the command to work properly. If you haven't saved the file, Dreamweaver alerts you to this fact when you call the command.

2. Choose Commands ➪ Optimize Image in Fireworks.

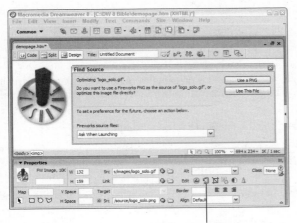

Optimize in Fireworks

Figure 23-2: Set the Find Source dialog box to use the source graphics image (PNG) or the exported image (GIF, JPEG, or PNG), or to prompt for each optimization.

Tip

You can also invoke the Optimize Image in Fireworks command from the Property inspector. With the image selected, click Optimize in Fireworks — it's the second button from the left in the Edit area and looks like a c-clamp.

3. If Fireworks Preferences are set to ask whether a source file should be used in editing, and if you have not yet specified this source file, the Find Source dialog box opens. Click Use a PNG to use the PNG format source file or Use This File to work with the exported file. The Optimize Images dialog box appears.

4. Make whatever modifications are needed from the Options, File, or Animation tabs of the Optimize Images dialog box.

5. When you're finished, click the Update button or click Cancel to return to Dreamweaver without modifying the image.

Note

If you're working with a Fireworks source file, the changes are saved to both your source file and the exported file; otherwise, only the exported file is altered.

Editing an Image in Fireworks

Optimizing an image is great when all you need to do is tweak the file size or rescale the image. Other images require more detailed modification — such as when a client requests that the wording or order of a series of navigational buttons be changed. Dreamweaver enables you to specify Fireworks as your graphics editor. If you've done so, you can take advantage of Fireworks' capability to keep every element of your graphic always editable. Believe me, this is a major advantage.

Optimizing Graphics

Dreamweaver and Fireworks' tight integration makes it possible to resize your graphics visually in Dreamweaver and use the Fireworks engine to optimize it to your chosen physical size as well as a reduced file size.

1. From the Techniques site, expand the 23_Fireworks folder and open the `fireworks_start` file.

   The top image on the page is too big and needs to be reduced both in file size and dimensions.

2. Select the image of the two-story house, `residential_home_01.jpg`, so that the sizing handles appear.

3. Begin dragging the size handle in the lower-right corner and then press and hold the Shift key to constrain the resizing.

   If you don't constrain the resizing, the width to height proportion may not be consistent with the original image.

4. Resize the picture until it's approximately 2/3 of its original size.

5. When the image size is more appropriate to the page, select Optimize in Fireworks from the Property inspector.

   The Optimize in Fireworks dialog box opens with the selected image already resized to your specifications.

6. In the Options tab of the Optimize in Fireworks dialog box, select the 2 Preview Windows option near the bottom of the dialog.

   You'll use the two preview windows to find the best balance between the visual quality of the image and file size.

7. Drag the Quality slider down around 60 until you find suitable image quality and file size.

   At 55%, the file size drops from the original size of 29K to less than 9K — a significant reduction, without a noticeable image quality change.

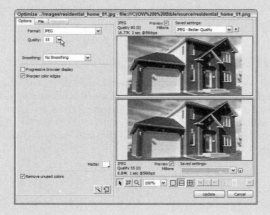

8. When you're ready, click Update.

The image is optimized and you're returned to Dreamweaver.

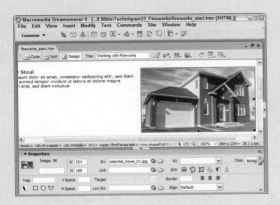

9. If the Property inspector displays the width and height dimensions in bold, click the adjacent Reset Image To Original Size icon.

10. Save your page.

The Optimize in Fireworks command is great for adjusting the dimensions or file size of an image; in the next Dreamweaver Technique, you see how to send images for more elaborate editing to Fireworks from Dreamweaver.

In Dreamweaver, external editors can be set for any file format; you can even assign more than one editor to a file type. When installing Studio 8, Fireworks is preset as the primary external editor for GIF, JPEG, and PNG files. If you install Fireworks outside the Studio setup, Dreamweaver Preferences handles the external editor assignment. To assign Fireworks to an existing file type, follow these steps:

1. Choose Edit ⇨ Preferences to open the Preferences dialog box.

2. Select the File Types / Editors category.

3. Select the file type (GIF, JPEG, or PNG) from the Extensions list, as shown in Figure 23-3.

4. Click the Add (+) button above the Editors list. The Select External Editor dialog box opens.

5. Locate the editor application and click Open when you're ready.

6. Click the Make Primary button while the editor you want is highlighted in the Editors list.

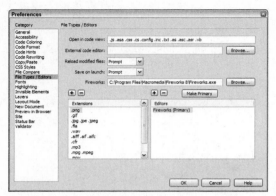

Figure 23-3: Define Fireworks as your external editor for GIF, JPEG, and PNG files to enable the back-and-forth interaction between Dreamweaver and Fireworks.

Now, whenever you want to edit a graphic, select the image and click the Edit in Fireworks button in the Property inspector. (You can also right-click [Control+click] the image and select Edit with Fireworks to start editing it.) Fireworks starts up, if it's not already open. As with the Optimize Image in Fireworks command, if the inserted image is a GIF or a JPEG and not a PNG, Fireworks asks if you'd like to work with a separate source file, if that option in Fireworks Preferences is set. If you choose to do so, Fireworks automatically loads the source file.

When the image opens in Fireworks, the document window indicates that the image is being edited from Dreamweaver in Fireworks, as shown in Figure 23-4. A Done button is also available in the Document window for completing the operation after you've made the alterations to your file in Fireworks. Alternatively, you can choose File ➪ Update or use the keyboard shortcut Ctrl+S (Command+S). If you're working with a Fireworks source file (PNG), both the source file and the exported file are updated and saved.

Figure 23-4: Fireworks graphically depicts the source of the current image being edited.

Replacing an Image Placeholder Using Fireworks

As discussed in Chapter 9, when designing a page, you can defer the task of inserting final art-work by using image placeholders instead of actual images; then, at the appropriate time, you can replace these image placeholders with the actual images. Working this way can facilitate smooth, trouble-free interaction between your Web site design and graphics departments.

To use Fireworks to replace your Dreamweaver image placeholders, follow these steps:

1. In Dreamweaver, open the page that contains the image placeholder you want to replace.

2. Select the image placeholder and click the Property inspector Create button. Or simply Ctrl+double-click (Command+double-click) the image placeholder.

   Fireworks launches and creates a new, blank PNG file whose canvas size is set to the width/height of the placeholder image, as shown in Figure 23-5.

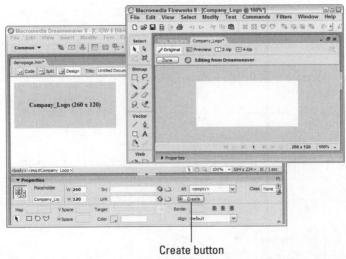

Create button

Figure 23-5: You can use Fireworks to replace your Dreamweaver image placeholders with actual images.

3. In Fireworks, create the desired image.

4. When you are finished, click the Done button.

   Fireworks first prompts you to save the image as a PNG (source) file. It then prompts you to export the file in a suitable Web format, GIF or JPEG. Dreamweaver automatically replaces the selected image placeholder with this exported image.

After you've used this procedure to replace a Dreamweaver image placeholder, you can easily edit the image in Fireworks by using the techniques described in the previous section of this chapter (the Property inspector Edit button and the Edit with Fireworks command).

Combining Images in Fireworks

In this Dreamweaver Technique, you use Dreamweaver's Edit in Fireworks capability to combine an image on the page with another.

1. Open the `fireworks_start.htm` file previously worked upon.

2. Select the bottom image on the page, `residential_home_02.jpg`.

3. From the Property inspector, click the Edit in Fireworks icon.

   Fireworks launches and displays the selected image in a special editing window.

4. Now select a second image to blend with the first by opening the Fireworks menu and choosing File ⇨ Import.

5. In the Import dialog box, navigate to the Techniques\images folder and choose `sold_sign.png`.

6. Place the angle cursor near the top left of the image and click once to place the imported graphic.

   The imported file is in standard PNG format with transparency enabled, so it can blend into the other image seamlessly.

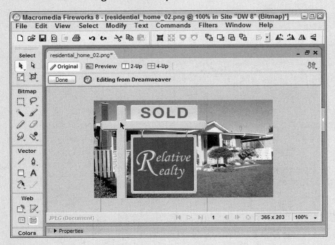

7. Reposition the imported image to your liking; when you're satisfied, click Done.

8. Fireworks closes and Dreamweaver is brought to the forefront; when your revised image appears, save your page.

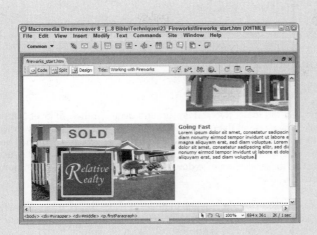

Combining images is just one of the ways you can use Dreamweaver and Fireworks together.

Inserting Rollovers

The rollover is a fairly common, but effective Web technique to indicate interactivity. Named after the user action of rolling the mouse pointer over the graphic, this technique uses from two to four different images per button. With Fireworks, you can both create the graphics and output the necessary HTML and JavaScript code from the same program. Moreover, Fireworks adds some sophisticated twists to the standard on/off rollovers to enable you to easily enhance your Web page.

Rollovers created in Fireworks can be inserted into Dreamweaver using several methods. First, you can use Fireworks to build the images, and then you just export them and attach the behaviors in Dreamweaver. This technique works well for graphics going into layers or images with other attached behaviors. The second method of integrating Fireworks-created rollovers involves transferring the actual code generated by Fireworks into Dreamweaver—a procedure that can be handled with one command: Insert Fireworks HTML.

Using Dreamweaver's Behaviors

With its full-spectrum editability, Fireworks excels at building consistent rollover graphics simply. The possible states of an image in a rollover—up, over, down, and over while down—are handled in Fireworks as separate frames. As in an animated GIF, each frame has the same dimensions, but the content is slightly altered to indicate the separate user actions. For example, Figure 23-6 shows the different frame states of a rollover button, side-by-side.

Image	 BUTTON	BUTTON	BUTTON	BUTTON
Viewer's pointer	up	over	down	over while down
Fireworks frame	1	2	3	4

Figure 23-6: A Fireworks-created rollover can be made of four separate frames.

Note   Many Web designers use just the initial two states — up and over — in their rollover buttons. The third state, down, takes place when the user clicks the button, and it is useful if you want to indicate that moment to the user. The down state also indicates which button has been clicked (which is down) when a new page appears but the same navigation bar is used, notably with frames. The fourth state, over while down, is called when the user's pointer rolls over the previously selected button.

You can attach the rollover behaviors to your images in several ways in Dreamweaver. The following technique uses Dreamweaver's Rollover object. To create a rollover by attaching Dreamweaver behaviors to Fireworks-created graphics, follow these steps:

1. Create your graphics in Fireworks, using a different frame for each rollover state.

Caution   You cannot use Fireworks' Edit ⇨ Insert ⇨ New Button command to build your button for this technique because the separate states are not stored as frames.

2. In Fireworks, choose File ⇨ Export. The Export dialog box opens (see Figure 23-7).

Figure 23-7: From Fireworks, you can export each frame as a separate file to be used in Dreamweaver rollovers.

3. If you want, type a new name in the File Name text box. In this operation, the File Name text is used as a base name by Fireworks to identify multiple images exported from a single file. When exporting frames, the default settings append _fn, where n is the number of the frame. Frame numbers 1–9 are listed with a leading zero (for example, MainButton_f01).

4. In the Save As Type list box, select Frames to Files.

5. If desired, select the Trim Images option. When Trim Images is on, Fireworks automatically crops the exported images to fit the objects on each frame. This procedure makes for smaller, more flexible image files.

Caution

I recommend that, in most situations, you opt to trim your images when exporting frames as files. But here's an exception to watch out for: If a button in one frame has a drop shadow, its trimmed size will be slightly larger than the non-drop–shadow buttons. Swapping it forces it to fit the smaller button's image space, which causes a jagged, amateurish swap display.

6. Click the Save button to store your frames as separate files.

7. From the Common category of the Insert bar, choose the Rollover Image object.

8. In the Insert Rollover Image dialog box, click the Original Image Browse button to locate the image stored with the first frame designation, _f01.

9. If you want, give your image a unique name different from the one automatically assigned in the Image Name text box.

10. Click the Rollover Image Browse button to locate the image stored with the second frame designation, _f02.

11. When you're finished, click OK.

12. If you'd like to use the down (_f03) and over while down (_f04) images, attach additional Swap Image behaviors to the image files. For help, see Chapter 12.

Many Web designers build their entire navigation bar — complete with rollovers — in Fireworks. Rather than create and export one button at a time, all the navigation buttons are created as one graphic, and slices or hotspots are used to make the different objects or areas interact differently. You learn more about slices and hotspots later in this chapter.

Using Fireworks' Code

In some ways, Fireworks is a hybrid program, capable of simultaneously outputting terrific graphics and sophisticated code. You can even select the type of code you want generated in Fireworks: Dreamweaver HTML, Dreamweaver XHTML, Dreamweaver Library, or code compatible with other programs such as GoLive and FrontPage. You can also find a more general Generic code option. All these options can be chosen during the Export procedure.

For rollovers, Fireworks generally outputs to two different sections of the HTML document, the <head> and the <body>; only the FrontPage style keeps all the code together. The <head> section contains the JavaScript code for activating the rollovers and preloading the images; <body> contains the HTML references to the images themselves, their links, and the event triggers used (onClick or onMouseOver).

The general procedure is to first create your graphics in Fireworks and then export them, simultaneously generating a page of code. Now, the just-generated Fireworks HTML page can be incorporated in Dreamweaver. Dreamweaver includes two slick methods for including your Fireworks-output code and images. The Insert Fireworks HTML object places the code — and the linked images — right at your current cursor position. You also have the option to export your Fireworks HTML directly to the clipboard and paste it, verbatim, into Dreamweaver.

Caution   If you paste the Fireworks rollover code manually into a Dreamweaver HTML document, take care to merge the existing `<head>` and `<body>` code with the Fireworks rollover code. And remember: An HTML document can have only one `<head>` and one `<body>` tag!

Just as an image requires a link to create a rollover in Dreamweaver, a Fireworks image needs to be designated as either a *slice* or a *hotspot*. The Fireworks program describes slices and hotspots as being part of the graphic's Web layer. The Web layer can be hidden or locked, but not deleted. Figure 23-8 shows the same button with both a slice and a hotspot attached.

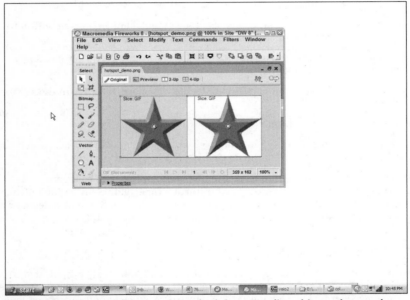

Figure 23-8: The Fireworks image on the left uses a slice object, whereas the image on the right uses a polygon hotspot.

Slices are rectangular areas that permit different parts of the same graphic to be saved as separate formats — the entire graphic is formatted as an HTML table. Each slice can also be given its own URL and have one or more behaviors attached to it.

A Fireworks *hotspot* is an area defined for an image map. Hotspots can be rectangular, elliptical, or polygonal — just like those created by Dreamweaver with the Image Map tools. Because Fireworks is an object-oriented graphics program, any selected image (or part of an image) can be automatically converted to a hotspot. Like slices, hotspots can have both URLs and behaviors assigned to them.

Note In addition to the technique outlined in the text that follows, you can also use Fireworks' Button Editor (available by choosing Insert ➪ New Button) to create your rollover images and behaviors.

To include Fireworks-generated code in your Dreamweaver document, follow these steps in Fireworks:

1. Create your graphics in Fireworks, placing the image for each interactive rollover state — up, over, down (optional), and over while down (optional) — in its own frame.

2. With the object in its first frame selected, create the hotspot(s) or slice(s).

   To do so automatically, choose Edit ➪ Insert ➪ Hotspot or Edit ➪ Insert ➪ Rectangular Slice. To do so manually, use the Hotspot or Slice tools in the Fireworks toolbox.

3. Where appropriate, use the Fireworks' Property inspector to assign URLs to hotspots or slices.

4. Click the target symbol displayed in the center of the hotspot or slice to display a menu of available behaviors.

   Alternatively, you can open Fireworks' Behavior inspector and click the Add Behavior (+) button.

5. If you are working on a slice, select the Simple Rollover or Swap Image behavior. If you are working on a hotspot, choose the Swap Image behavior (Simple Rollover is not available for hotspots).

Tip The Simple Rollover behavior is used to create single- or multiple-button rollovers in which one image is replaced by another image in the same location; only two frames are used for a Simple Rollover. Use the Swap Image behavior to create more complex rollovers, such as those in which the rollover triggers an image change in another location. A third alternative, the Nav Bar, should be used in situations where the navigation system is to be placed in a frameset. The Nav Bar behavior can display all four states (up, over, down, and over while down).

6. Export the object by choosing File ➪ Export to open the Export dialog box.

7. Enter a name in the File Name text box and make sure that the HTML and Images option is displayed in the Save As Type drop-down list.

   If you intend to use the graphics in several places on your site, choose Dreamweaver Library (.lbi) from the Save As Type drop-down list.

8. To change the type of HTML/XHTML code generated, click the Options button and make a selection from the Style drop-down list.

   Dreamweaver HTML code is the default style; other options include GoLive, FrontPage, and Generic HTML and XHTML.

9. Select the location in which to store your HTML code by navigating to the appropriate folder. Note that Dreamweaver Library code must be saved in a site's Library folder.

   If you prefer to not save your HTML, select Copy To Clipboard from the HTML drop-down list.

10. To save your graphics in a separate folder, select the Put Images In Subfolder option.

Caution Fireworks defaults to placing the graphics in a subfolder called Images, even if one does not exist. To specify a different folder, click the Browse button.

11. When you're finished, click Save.

When Fireworks completes the exporting, you have one HTML file (unless you've chosen the Copy To Clipboard option) and multiple image files — one for each slice and frame. Now you're ready to integrate these images and code into your Dreamweaver page. Which method you use depends on the HTML style you selected when the graphics were exported from Fireworks:

✦ If you chose Dreamweaver HTML, use the Insert Fireworks HTML object.

✦ If you chose Dreamweaver Library, open the Library panel in Dreamweaver and insert the corresponding Library item.

✦ If you chose Copy To Clipboard, position your cursor where you'd like the graphics to appear and choose Edit ➪ Paste or type Ctrl+V (Command+V).

Both the Library and Clipboard methods are one-step, self-explanatory techniques — and using the Insert Fireworks HTML object is only a bit more complex. To insert the Fireworks code and images into your Dreamweaver page using the Insert Fireworks HTML object, follow these steps:

1. Make sure that you've exported your graphics and HTML from Fireworks with the Dreamweaver HTML style selected.

2. Select the Fireworks HTML object from the Images menu of the Insert bar's Common category or choose Insert ➪ Image Objects ➪ Fireworks HTML. The Insert Fireworks HTML dialog box, shown in Figure 23-9, appears.

Figure 23-9: Import Fireworks code directly into Dreamweaver with the Insert Fireworks HTML object.

3. If you want to delete the Fireworks-generated HTML file after the code is inserted, select the Delete File After Insertion option. This can help keep your site folder tidy.

4. Enter the path to the Fireworks HTML file or click the Browse button to locate the file.

5. When you're finished, click OK. Dreamweaver inserts the Fireworks HTML and graphics at the current cursor location.

Note If you're a hands-on Web designer, you can also use the Code inspector to copy and paste the JavaScript and HTML code. If you do, you can find helpful comments in the Fireworks-generated HTML file such as "Begin copying here" and "Stop copying here."

All the methods for inserting Fireworks HTML work with images that have either hotspots or sliced objects (or both), whether or not behaviors are attached.

Modifying Sliced Images

Placing sliced images on your Web page couldn't be simpler, thanks to the Insert Fireworks HTML command. However, like standard non-sliced graphics, sliced images often need to be modified. One technique that many designers use is to create a framing graphic that contains HTML text; in Fireworks, a sliced area designated as a text slice can hold any HTML content. Text often has to be modified. If it is in a framing graphic, the image may need to be changed so that the table cells remain the same size as in the original design. This prevents the separate slices from becoming apparent.

In Dreamweaver, sliced images from Fireworks are recognized as a Fireworks Table and can be modified through a dedicated Property inspector, as shown in Figure 23-10. The Fireworks Table Property inspector displays the PNG source file and an Edit button for sending the entire table back to Fireworks for alterations. As with non-sliced graphics, click Done on the document title bar in Fireworks when your modifications are complete to update the source and exported files. The newly exported images are then reloaded into Dreamweaver.

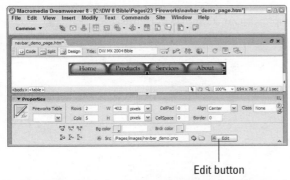

Edit button

Figure 23-10: Modify sliced graphics by first selecting the surrounding table and then clicking the Edit button in the Fireworks Table Property inspector.

Caution   Although Fireworks attempts to honor any changes you make to the HTML table in Dreamweaver, certain changes may cause Fireworks to modify your Dreamweaver table code. If, for example, you add or remove cells from the table in Dreamweaver and then go to edit the table in Fireworks, Fireworks displays an alert that it will replace the table in Dreamweaver. To avoid having your original table modified inappropriately by Fireworks, simply click Done right away when you get such an alert (before making any changes). Doing so keeps the original table as-is in Dreamweaver. At this point, make a backup of the entire current page; then go ahead and try out your Fireworks table edit.

Editing JavaScript-Based Fireworks Pop-Up Menus

As discussed in Chapter 12, you can use the Dreamweaver Show Pop-Up Menu and Hide Pop-Up Menu behaviors to create a pop-up menu that is activated by mousing over an entire image or an image hotspot/slice. You can create the same type of pop-up menu in Fireworks.

Caution   The Dreamweaver Pop-Up Menu behaviors work exclusively with the older-style JavaScript-based pop-up menus generated by Fireworks MX and MX 2004, and not with the new CSS-based versions in Fireworks 8. The older pop-up menus have many limitations, including the inability to work well with Dreamweaver templates, and are not recommended for use. Wherever possible, you're better served by outputting your pop-up menus with the CSS option enabled in Fireworks and importing the menus into Dreamweaver through the Insert Fireworks HTML command discussed in the earlier section, "Using Fireworks' Code." The following instructions are included for the sake of designers working with legacy pages who are switching to the CSS style pop-up menus.

Conveniently, if you are working in Dreamweaver and encounter a Fireworks-created pop-up menu that you need to edit, you can do so within Dreamweaver. Just follow these steps:

1. In Dreamweaver, select the image, hotspot, or slice with which the pop-up menu is associated.

2. In the Behaviors panel, double-click the Show Pop-Up Menu behavior to open the Show Pop-Up Menu dialog box.

3. Make your changes to the pop-up menu, as shown in Figure 23-11.

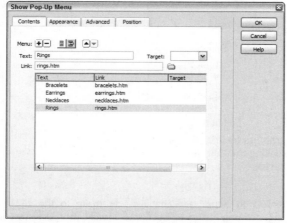

Figure 23-11: You can easily edit pop-up menus created in Dreamweaver or in Fireworks MX and Fireworks MX 2004.

4. When you are finished, click OK.

Controlling Fireworks with Dreamweaver

Dreamweaver and Fireworks integration extends deeper than just the simplified insertion of code and graphics. Dreamweaver can communicate directly with Fireworks, driving it to execute commands and return custom-generated graphics. This facility enables Web designers to build their Web-page images based on the existing content. Interprogram communication promises to streamline the work of the Webmaster like never before — and that promise is already beginning to be fulfilled with existing Dreamweaver commands.

Creating a Web Photo Album

Online catalogs and other sites often depend on imagery to sell their products. Full-scale product shots can be large and time-consuming to download, so it's not uncommon for Web designers to display a thumbnail of the images instead. If the viewer wants to see more detail, clicking the thumbnail loads the full-size image. Although it's not difficult to save a scaled-down version of an image in a graphics program and link the two in a Web layout program, creating page after page of such images is an overwhelming chore. The Dreamweaver/Fireworks interoperability offers a way to automate this tedious task.

The Dreamweaver Create Web Photo Album command examines any user-specified folder of images and then uses Fireworks to scale the graphics to a set size. When the scaling is finished, the thumbnail graphics are brought into a Dreamweaver table, complete with links to a series of pages with the full-size images. Create Web Photo Album is an excellent example of the potential that Dreamweaver and Fireworks intercommunication offers.

The Create Web Photo Album command works with a folder of images in any format that Fireworks reads: GIF, JPEG, JPEG 2000, TIFF, Photoshop, PICT, BMP, and more. The images can be scaled to fit in a range of sizes, from 36 x 36 to 200 x 200 pixels. These thumbnails are exported in one of four formats:

✦ **GIF WebSnap 128:** Uses the WebSnap Adaptive palette, limited to 128 colors or fewer.

✦ **GIF WebSnap 256:** Same as the preceding format, with as many as 256 colors available.

✦ **JPEG Better Quality:** Sets the JPEG quality setting at 80 percent, with no smoothing.

✦ **JPEG Smaller File:** Sets the JPEG quality setting at 60 percent, with a smoothing value of 2.

The images are also exported in one of the same four settings at a user-selected scale; the default scale is 100 percent.

To create a thumbnail gallery using Create Web Photo Album, follow these steps:

1. Choose Commands ➪ Create Web Photo Album. The Create Web Photo Album dialog box appears, as shown in Figure 23-12.

Figure 23-12: Use the Create Web Photo Album command to create a thumbnail gallery page, linked to full-size originals.

2. Enter the appropriate information in the Photo Album Title, Subheading Info, and Other Info text fields.

3. In the Source Images Folder field, enter the path to the folder of source images or click the Browse button to locate the folder.

4. Enter the path in the Destination Folder field or click the Browse button to locate the folder. Dreamweaver creates up to three subfolders in the Destination Folder: one for the original, optionally rescaled images; another for the thumbnail images; and a third for the HTML pages created.

5. Select the desired thumbnail size from the drop-down list with the following options: 36 x36, 72 x 72, 100 x 100, 144 x 144, and 200 x 200.

6. Select the Show Filenames option if you want the filename to appear below the image.

7. Choose the number of columns for the table.

8. Select the export settings for the thumbnail images from the Thumbnail Format option list.

9. Select the export settings for the linked large-sized images from the Photo Format option list.

10. Choose the size of the linked large-sized images in the Scale field. If you don't want to rescale the images, leave the setting at its default value of 100 percent.

11. If you want, select the Create Navigation Page For Each Photo option. Each photo's navigation page includes links to the Next and Previous images as well as the Home (main thumbnail) page, as shown in Figure 23-13.

Figure 23-13: You can add simple, clear navigation options to your Web Photo Album.

12. When you're finished, click OK.

Custom Graphic Makers: Converting Text and Bullets to Images

Excited by the potential of Dreamweaver and Fireworks communication, I built two custom extensions, originally called StyleBuilder and BulletBuilder. Macromedia took these extensions, enhanced them, and then released them as two-thirds of the InstaGraphics Extensions. StyleBuilder—now called Convert Text to Image—enables you to convert any standard text in your Dreamweaver Web page to a graphic. The command converts all text in a standard HTML tag (such as <h1> or <b>), any custom XML tag, or any selection. The graphics are based on Fireworks styles displayed in a small swatch in the Convert Text to Image dialog box (see the following figure). You can specify a font on your system as well as a text size to be used. Fireworks styles can be updated at any time, and the swatch set re-created on-the-fly in Fireworks.

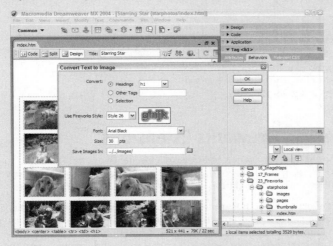

Convert Bullets to Images (nee BulletBuilder) is similar, but instead of changing text to graphics, this command converts the bullets of an unordered list to different graphic shapes. Choose from 10 different shapes including diamonds, stars, starbursts, and 4 different triangles. The chosen shape is rendered in any available Fireworks style at a user-selected size. You have the option to convert the current bulleted list or all such lists on the page.

You can find both commands online at the Dreamweaver Exchange as part of the InstaGraphics Extensions—be sure to look for the Dreamweaver 8 compatible version!

If it is not already open, Fireworks opens and begins processing the images. When all the images are created and exported, Fireworks returns control to Dreamweaver. Dreamweaver then creates a single HTML page with the title, subheading, and other information at the top, followed by a borderless table. As shown in Figure 23-14, each image is rescaled proportionately to fit within the limits set in the dialog box.

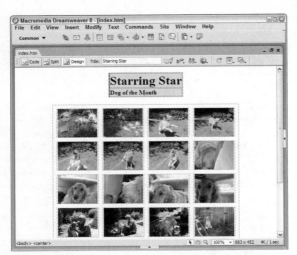

Figure 23-14: Here is the thumbnail gallery that Dreamweaver (with Fireworks' help) automatically created from the dialog box settings in Figure 23-12.

Building Dreamweaver/Fireworks Extensions

To make communication between Dreamweaver and Fireworks viable, two conditions had to be met. First, Fireworks had to be scriptable. Second, a link between the two programs had to be forged. The Dreamweaver/Fireworks combination meets both criteria — and then some.

As with Dreamweaver, almost every operation is under command control in Fireworks. This is most apparent when you are using either program's History panel. If your action appears as a repeatable item in the History panel, a corresponding JavaScript function controls it. Fireworks' wealth of JavaScript functions also exposes its control to Dreamweaver — and the first condition for interoperability is handled. To create a strong link between programs, Dreamweaver engineers expanded on the Fireworks API used in the Optimize Image in Fireworks command, where Dreamweaver actually launches a streamlined, headless version of Fireworks. This operation is controlled by a C-level extension called FWLaunch. Here's a step-by-step description of how Dreamweaver is typically used to communicate with Fireworks:

1. The user selects a command in Dreamweaver.

2. Dreamweaver opens a dialog box.

3. After the user has filled in the dialog box and clicked OK, the command begins to execute.

4. All user-supplied parameters are read and used to create a JavaScript scriptlet or function, which serves as instructions for Fireworks.

5. If used, the scriptlet is stored on the disk.

6. Fireworks is launched with a command to run the Dreamweaver-created scriptlet or function.

7. Fireworks processes the scriptlet or function while Dreamweaver tracks its progress via a cookie on the user's machine.

8. After Fireworks has finished, a positive result is returned.

   The Fireworks API includes several error codes if problems, such as a full disk, are encountered.

9. While tracking the Fireworks progress, Dreamweaver sees the positive result and integrates the graphics by rewriting the DOM of the current page.

10. The dialog box is closed, and the current page is refreshed to correctly present the finished product.

To successfully control Fireworks, you need a complete understanding of the Fireworks DOM and its extension capabilities. Macromedia provides documentation for extending Fireworks from its support site: www.macromedia.com/support/fireworks.

Tip The History panel in Fireworks is useful — especially the Copy Command to Clipboard function. To see the underlying JavaScript used to create an object in Fireworks, first make the object. Next, highlight the History panel steps and click the Copy To Clipboard button. Paste the clipboard contents in a text editor to see the exact steps Fireworks used; you can then begin to generalize the statements with variables and other functions.

On the Dreamweaver side, the FWLaunch C Library has seven useful methods, detailed in Table 23-1.

Table 23-1: FWLaunch Methods

Method	Returns	Use
bringDWToFront()	N/A	Brings the Dreamweaver window in front of any other application running
bringFWToFront()	N/A	Brings the Fireworks window in front of any other application running
execJsInFireworks (javascriptOrFileURL)	Result from running the scriptlet in Fireworks. If the operation fails, it returns an error code: 1: The argument proves invalid 2: File I/O error 3: Improper version of Dreamweaver 4: Improper version of Fireworks 5: User canceled operation	Executes the supplied JavaScript function or scriptlet
mayLaunchFireworks()	Boolean	Determines if Fireworks may be launched

Continued

Table 23-1 *(continued)*

Method	Returns	Use

`optimizeInFireworks`
`(fileURL, docURL,`
`{targetWidth},`
`{targetHeight})`
	Result from running the scriptlet in Fireworks. If the operation fails, it returns an error code:
	1: The argument proves invalid
	2: File I/O error
	3: Improper version of Dreamweaver
	4: Improper version of Fireworks
	5: User canceled operation
		Performs an Optimize in Fireworks operation, opening the Fireworks Export Preview dialog box

`validateFireworks` `(versionNumber)`	Boolean	Determines if the user has a specific version of Fireworks

Summary

Creating Web pages is almost never done with a single application: In addition to a Web layout program, you need a program capable of outputting Web graphics — and Fireworks is a world-class Web graphics generator and optimizer. Macromedia has integrated several functions with Dreamweaver and Fireworks to streamline production and simplify modification. The following are some of the key features:

✦ You can update images placed in Dreamweaver with Fireworks in two ways: optimize or edit. With the Optimize Image in Fireworks command, just the Export Preview portion of Fireworks opens; with the Edit Image command, the full version of Fireworks is run.

✦ Graphics and HTML exported from Fireworks can be incorporated into a Dreamweaver page in numerous ways: as a Library item; as an HTML file (complete with behavior code); or as an item pasted from the clipboard.

✦ New interapplication communication between Dreamweaver and Fireworks makes commands such as Create Web Photo Album possible.

✦ Dreamweaver includes a special C-level extension called FWLaunch, which provides the primary link to Fireworks.

In the next chapter, you learn how to incorporate Flash and Shockwave movies into your Dreamweaver Web pages.

✦   ✦   ✦

Inserting Flash and Shockwave Elements

Animated splash screens, sound-enabled banners, button bars with special fonts, and other exciting Web elements are often built with Macromedia's Flash. Flash combines vector graphics and streaming audio into great-looking, very low bandwidth files that can be viewed in a browser using the Flash Player plugin. Flash's vector graphics have also turned out to be just the thing for Web-based animations. Beginning with version 4, Flash gained its own scripting language, ActionScript, and added MP3 compression to its streaming audio. Over later versions, Flash morphed into a solid application platform, with player implementations in cell phones, handheld devices, and even billboards. With a huge base of installed Web-based players — as of this writing, well over 90 percent of browsers can view basic Flash content — Flash is an excellent way to liven up a Web page.

But Flash is not Macromedia's only solution for building interactive presentations for the Web. To many Web designers, Shockwave has represented the state of the art in Web interactivity since Macromedia first created the format in 1995. With Shockwave, multimedia files created in Macromedia's flagship authoring package, Director, can be compiled to run in a browser window. This functionality gives Web designers the capability to build just about anything — including interactive Web interfaces with buttons that look indented when pushed, arcade-style games, multimedia Web front-ends, and complete Web sites built entirely in Director — bringing a CD-ROM look-and-feel to the Web. Today, Shockwave continues to be an important force on the Web, as the ongoing success of Macromedia-started Shockwave.com amply demonstrates.

As you might expect, Macromedia makes it easy to incorporate Shockwave and Flash files into your Dreamweaver projects. All these formats have special objects that provide control over nearly all their parameters through the Property inspector — and each format is cross-browser compatible by default. Using Dreamweaver's Flash Button and Flash Text tools, it's delightfully easy to incorporate customized, well-crafted Flash elements in your Web page without knowing a bit of Flash.

To take full advantage of the enhanced graphics potential of Flash and the multimedia capabilities of Shockwave, you need to understand the differences between Director and Flash, as well as the various parameters available to each format. In addition to covering this material, this chapter shows you how to use independent controls — both inline and with frames — for your Shockwave and Flash movies.

New In Dreamweaver   One of the most exciting innovations in Dreamweaver 8 is the introduction of Flash video. This topic is covered in Chapter 25.

Director and Flash: What's the Difference?

Director (the program you use to make Shockwave movies) and Flash share many features — interactivity, streaming audio, support for both bitmaps and vector graphics, and shocked fonts. Both can save their movies in formats suitable for viewing on the Web. So how do you choose which program to use? Each has its own special functions, and each excels at producing particular types of effects. Director is more full-featured, with a complete programming language called Lingo that enables incredible interactivity. Director movies can also include Flash animations. Director, however, has a much steeper learning curve than does Flash. Flash is terrific for short, low-bandwidth animations with or without a synchronized audio track; however, the interactive capabilities in Flash are limited compared to Director.

Director is really a multimedia production program used for combining a variety of elements: backgrounds, foreground elements called *sprites*, and various media such as digital audio and video (see Figure 24-1). With Director's Lingo programming language, you can build extraordinarily elaborate demos and games with Internet-specific commands. When you want a high degree of interactivity, build your movie with Director.

Figure 24-1: Director works mainly with bitmaps and video and enables multimedia programming and 3D visualizations.

One of the primary differences between Director and Flash is the supported graphic formats. Director is generally better for bitmap graphics, in which each pixel is mapped to a specific color; both GIF and JPEG formats use bitmap graphics. Flash, on the other hand, uses primarily vector graphics, which are drawing elements described mathematically. Because vector graphics use a description of a drawing—a blue circle with a radius of 2.5 centimeters, for instance—rather than a bitmap, the resulting files are much smaller. A fairly complex animation produced with Flash might be only 10K or 20K, whereas a comparable digital video clip could easily be 10 times that size.

The other feature that distinguishes vector graphics from bitmap graphics is the smoothness of the line. When viewed with sufficient magnification, bitmap graphics always display telltale stair steps or *jaggies*, especially around curves. Vector graphics, on the other hand, are much smoother. In fact, Flash takes special advantage of this characteristic and enables users to zoom into any movie—an important effect that saves a lot of bandwidth when used correctly.

However, these differences were significantly blurred with the recent releases of both products, starting with Director 7, which incorporated its own native vector graphics and introduced the capability to include Flash movies within Director movies. Director MX 2004 strongly supports 3D-graphics creation. Flash 4 blurred the line the other way by incorporating streaming MP3-encoded audio and QuickTime integration, things that were traditionally the province of Director. In Flash 5, Flash's scripting capabilities were significantly beefed up with the expansion of ActionScript into a JavaScript-based programming language. Flash 8 (see Figure 24-2), the most recent incarnation, contains many exciting new features, such as support for built-in visual effects, incorporating video into Flash movies, enhanced graphic design tools, a customizable ActionScript editor, and much more.

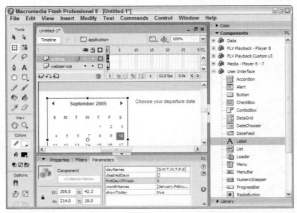

Figure 24-2: Flash is a truly multi-faceted tool capable of outputting motion graphics and application interfaces with ease.

Flash animations can be used as special effects, cartoons, and navigation bars within (or without) frames. Although Flash isn't the best choice for games and other complex interactive elements, you can use Flash to animate your navigation system—complete with sound effects for button-pushing feedback.

If Flash is a power tool, Director is a bulldozer. Director has been significantly expanded to handle a wide variety of file types — QuickTime, MP3, RealAudio, and RealVideo, for example — with advanced streaming capabilities. Supporting multimedia interactivity is Director's own programming language, Lingo, which has also been enhanced. Furthermore, Director now includes multiplayer support for network game play and chat rooms, XML parsing, embedded compressed fonts, up to 1,000 sprite channels, and a potential frame rate of 999 frames per second. Luckily, Dreamweaver enables you to pack all that power into a Web page with its Shockwave object.

Including Flash and Shockwave Movies in Dreamweaver Projects

Dreamweaver makes it easy to bring Shockwave and Flash files into your Web pages. The Insert bar provides an object for each type of movie, located in the Media menu of the Common category.

Because Shockwave and Flash objects insert both an ActiveX control and a plugin, Dreamweaver enables you to play the movie in the Document window. When not playing, Dreamweaver displays a plugin placeholder icon (see Figure 24-3).

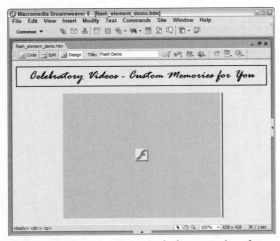

Figure 24-3: Dreamweaver includes many interface elements for working with Shockwave and Flash.

Before you can successfully include a Shockwave file, you need to know one small bit of information — the dimensions of your movie. Dreamweaver automatically reads the dimensions of your Flash file when you insert the Flash movie object. Unfortunately, if you're incorporating a Shockwave movie, you must enter the dimensions in the Shockwave Property inspector.

To find the width and height of a Shockwave movie, load it into Director and then choose Modify ➪ Movie ➪ Properties to open the Property inspector. The dimensions are located on the Movie category of the panel.

Note It is essential to know the movie's height and width before you include it in Dreamweaver-built Web pages. During the development phase of a Dreamweaver project, I often include the movie dimensions in a filename, as an instant reminder to take care of this detail. For example, if I'm working with two different Shockwave movies, I can give them names such as `navbar125x241.dcr` and `navbar400x50.dcr`. (The `.dcr` extension is automatically appended by Director when you save a movie as a Shockwave file.) Because I consistently put width before height in the filename, this trick saves me the time it takes to reopen Director, load the movie, and choose Modify ⇨ Movie to check the measurements in the Movie Properties dialog box. The alternative to keeping track of the Director movie's dimensions is to choose File ⇨ Save as Shockwave Movie in Director. Doing this creates an HTML file with all the necessary parameters (including width and height), which can be inserted into Dreamweaver. You can find a detailed description of this process later in this chapter.

To include either a Shockwave or Flash file in your Web page, follow these steps:

1. Position the cursor in the Document window where you'd like the movie to appear.

2. Insert the movie using any of the following methods:

   • Choose Insert ⇨ Media ⇨ Shockwave or Insert ⇨ Media ⇨ Flash from the main Dreamweaver menu.

   • From the Media menu of the Insert bar's Common category, click either the Shockwave or Flash Button.

   • Drag the movie object from the Assets panel to the Document window. Remember to choose the appropriate category in the Assets panel: Shockwave or Flash.

3. In the Select File dialog box, enter the path and the filename in the File Name text box or click the Browse button to locate the file. Click OK.

Note If you drag the movie from the Assets panel, this step is not applicable because Dreamweaver automatically sets the File attribute to that of your movie file.

4. If you clicked OK in the Select File dialog box, and if Media is selected in your Accessibility preferences (Edit ⇨ Preferences ⇨ Accessibility), the Object Tag Accessibility Attributes dialog box appears, as shown in Figure 24-4.

Figure 24-4: Use the Object Tag Accessibility Attributes dialog box to specify a title, access key, and tab index for your inserted media objects.

5. In the Title field, enter a title for your media object.

6. In the Access Key field, enter a one-letter access key for your object. To select the object in the browser, press Alt (Command) + access key; for example: Alt+G (Command+G).

Generating HTML within Director

In Director, you can generate a file with all the appropriate HTML code at the same time that you save your Shockwave movie with just the selection of a checkbox. When you choose File ⇨ Save as Shockwave Movie in Director, the dialog box contains a Generate HTML option. Selecting this option causes Director to save an HTML file with the same name as your Shockwave movie but with an appropriate file extension (.html for Macintosh and .htm for Windows). You can easily copy and paste this HTML code directly into Dreamweaver.

When you open the Director-generated HTML file, you see the name of your file and the Shockwave placeholder, correctly sized and ready to preview. To move this object into another Web page in progress, just select the Shockwave object and choose Edit ⇨ Copy. Then switch to your other page and choose Edit ⇨ Paste. Naturally, you can also use the keyboard shortcuts or, if both pages are accessible, just drag and drop the object from one page to another.

Note   Entering an Access Key value only places the accesskey attribute in the <object> tag; it's up to the browser to properly interpret what action, if any, should be taken when the access key combination is pressed.

7. In the Tab Index field, enter a number for the tab index of your object. By entering a number, you can specify the order in which users tab through objects and links on your page. Pressing Tab successively jumps from the object or link whose tab index is set to 1, to the object or link whose tab index is set to 2, and so on. For this to work correctly, you must specify the tabindex attribute for all the page's objects and links.

   Dreamweaver inserts a small plugin placeholder in the current cursor position, and the Property inspector displays the appropriate information for Shockwave or Flash.

   If you inserted a Shockwave movie, be sure to enter the correct width and height dimensions in the Property inspector. Dreamweaver supplies this information automatically for Flash files.

8. Preview the Flash or Shockwave movie in the Document window by clicking the Play button in the Property inspector. You can also choose View ⇨ Plugins ⇨ Play.

9. End the preview of your file by clicking the Stop button in the Property inspector or choosing View ⇨ Plugins ⇨ Stop.

Tip   If you have more than one Flash or Shockwave movie on your page, you can control them all by choosing View ⇨ Plugins ⇨ Play All, and View ⇨ Plugins ⇨ Stop All. If your files appear in different pages in a frameset, you have to repeat the Play All command for each page.

Shockwave and Flash have some different features in the Dreamweaver Property inspector. These differences are covered separately in the following sections.

Specifying Shockwave Properties

After you've inserted your Shockwave file, you're ready to begin entering the specific parameters in the Property inspector. The Property inspector takes care of all but one Shockwave attribute, the palette parameter. Some of the information, including the ActiveX Class ID, is automatically set in the Property inspector when you insert the movie.

On the CD-ROM

In the Dreamweaver 8\Configuration\Commands folder on the CD-ROM that accompanies this book, you can find a custom command called Insert Shockwave HTML that automates the process of inserting a Shockwave movie and its Director-generated HTML. If you'd prefer a version developed by Macromedia that does the same job, visit the Dreamweaver Exchange to download the Insert Shockwave extension. To access the Dreamweaver Exchange, choose Commands ➪ Get More Commands from within Dreamweaver.

To set or modify the parameters for a Shockwave file, follow these steps:

1. Click the Shockwave placeholder icon.

2. In the Shockwave Property inspector, enter the width and height values in the W and H text boxes, respectively, as shown in Figure 24-5. Alternatively, you can click and drag any of the three resizing handles on the placeholder icon.

Figure 24-5: Modify parameters for a Shockwave property through the Shockwave Property inspector.

Tip

If you press the Shift key while dragging the corner resizing handle, you maintain the current aspect ratio.

3. Set and modify other Shockwave movie attributes as needed; see Table 24-1 for a list.

Table 24-1: Property Inspector Options for Shockwave Objects

Shockwave Parameters	Description
Align	Enables you to choose an option to alter the alignment of the movie. In addition to the browser default, your options include Baseline, Top, Middle, Bottom, Texttop, Absolute Middle, Absolute Bottom, Left, and Right.
Bg	Enables you to specify a background color for the movie area. Note that this color also appears while the movie is loading and after it is done playing.
V Space	Enables you to increase the amount of space between other elements on the page and the top and bottom of the movie plugin by entering a pixel value in the V (Vertical) Space text box. Again, the default is zero.
H Space	Enables you to increase the space to the left and right of the movie by entering a value in the H (Horizontal) Space text box. The default is zero.

Continued

Table 24-1 *(continued)*

Shockwave Parameters	Description
Name	Enables you to enter a unique name in the unlabeled field on the far left of the Property inspector. The name is used by JavaScript and other languages to identify the movie.
W	Sets the width of the movie.
H	Sets the height of the movie.
Class	Applies the CSS class to the movie.

Additional Parameters for Shockwave

As with other plugins, you can pass other attributes to the Shockwave movie via the Parameters dialog box—available by clicking the Parameters button on the Property inspector. Use Tab or the Add (+) button to insert additional parameters. Enter the attributes in the left column and their respective values in the right. To remove an attribute, highlight it and click the Remove (–) button.

Automatic Settings for Shockwave Files

When you insert a Shockwave or Flash file, Dreamweaver writes a number of parameters that are constant and necessary. In the `<object>` portion of the code, Dreamweaver includes the ActiveX Class ID number as well as the `codebase` URL; the former calls the specific ActiveX control, and the latter enables users who don't have the control installed to receive it automatically. Likewise, in the `<embed>` section, Dreamweaver fills in the `pluginspage` attribute, designating the location where Navigator users can find the necessary plugin. Make sure you don't accidentally remove any of this information—however, if you should, all you have to do is delete and reinsert the object.

Only one other general attribute is usually assigned to a Shockwave file, the `palette` parameter. If you want to deploy this attribute, you have to add it by hand in Code view. There are two possible values for `palette`:

✦ `background`—The movie's color scheme does not override that of the system; this is the default.

✦ `foreground`—The colors of the selected movie are applied to the user's system, which includes the desktop and scroll bars.

`palette` is not supported by Internet Explorer.

Caution　Web designers should take care when specifying the `palette=foreground` parameter. This effect is likely to prove startling to the user; moreover, if your color scheme is sufficiently different, the change may render the user's system unusable. If you do use the `palette` parameter, be sure to include a Director command to restore the original system color scheme in the final frame of the movie.

Designating Flash Attributes

Flash movies require the same basic parameters as their Shockwave counterparts—and Flash movies have a few additional optional parameters as well. As it does for Shockwave files, Dreamweaver sets almost all the attributes for Flash movies through the Property inspector. The major difference is that several more parameters are available.

To set or modify the attributes for a Flash file, follow these steps:

1. After your Flash movie has been inserted in the Document window, make sure that it is selected. Dreamweaver automatically inserts the correct dimensions for your Flash movie.

2. Set any attributes in the Property inspector as needed for your Flash movie. (Refer to the previous descriptions of these attributes in the section "Specifying Shockwave Properties.") In addition, you can also set the parameters described in Table 24-2.

Table 24-2: Additional Property Inspector Options for Flash Objects

Flash Parameter	Possible Values	Description
Autoplay	Checked (default)	Enables the Flash movie to begin playing as soon as possible.
Loop	Checked (default)	Plays movie continuously if checked; otherwise, movie plays once.
Quality		Controls anti-aliasing during playback.
	High (default)	Anti-aliasing is turned on. This can slow the playback frame rate considerably on slower computers.
	Low	No anti-aliasing is used; this setting is best for animations that must be played quickly.
	Auto High	The animation begins in High (with anti-aliasing) and switches to Low if the host computer is too slow.
	Auto Low	Starts the animation in Low (no anti-aliasing) and then switches to High if the host machine is fast enough.
Src		Specifies the .fla Flash source file. To edit a .swf Flash movie file, you must modify the movie's .fla source file.
Scale		Determines how the movie fits into the dimensions as specified in the Width and Height text boxes.
	Show All (default)	Displays the entire movie in the given dimensions while maintaining the file's original aspect ratio. Some of the background may be visible with this setting.
	Exact Fit	Scales the movie precisely into the dimensions without regard for the aspect ratio. It is possible that the image could be distorted with this setting.
	No Border	Fits the movie into the given dimensions so that no borders are showing and maintains the original aspect ratio. Some of the movie may be cut off with this setting.

Setting the Scale in Flash Movies

To avoid unexpected results, be careful when setting the Scale parameter. If you have to size a Flash movie out of its aspect ratio, the Flash Player must know what to do with any extra room it has to fill. Figure 24-6 demonstrates the different results that the Scale attribute can provide. Only the picture on the left is at its proper dimensions.

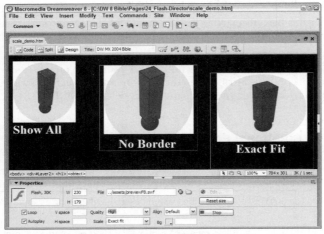

Figure 24-6: Your setting for the Scale attribute determines how your movie is viewed when resized with the plugin width and height measurements.

Tip   Dreamweaver makes it easy to rescale a Flash movie. First, in the Property inspector, make sure the original width and height of your file are displayed in the W and H text boxes. Then, while holding down the Shift key, click and drag the corner resizing handle of the Flash placeholder icon to the new size for the movie. By Shift+dragging, you retain the aspect ratio set in the Property inspector, which enables you to quickly enlarge or reduce your movie without distortion.

Additional Parameters for Flash

Flash has two additional attributes that can be entered through the Parameters dialog box (click the Parameters button on the Property inspector): `salign` and `swliveconnect`. The `salign` attribute determines how the movie aligns itself to the surrounding frame when the Scale attribute is set to Show All. In addition, `salign` determines which portion of the image is cut off when the Scale attribute is set to No Border. The alignment can be set to L (left), R (right), T (top), or B (bottom). You can also use these values in combination. For example, if you set `salign` to RB, the movie aligns with the right-bottom edge or the lower-right corner of the frame.

The `swliveconnect` attribute comes into play when you're using FSCommands or JavaScript in your Flash movies. FSCommands are interactive commands, such as Go to URL, issued from inside the Flash movie. The Netscape browser initializes Java when first called — and if your Flash movie uses FSCommands or JavaScript, it uses Java to communicate with the

Netscape Plugin interface, LiveConnect. Because not all Flash movies need the LiveConnect connection, you can prevent Java from being initialized by entering the swliveconnect attribute in the Parameters dialog box and setting its value to false. When the swliveconnect=false parameter is found by the browser, the Java is not initialized as part of the loading process — and your movie loads more quickly.

Integrating Flash Elements

Flash has evolved into a truly multifaceted tool with the capability to convey graphics, video, streaming sound, and data with equal ease. One major hurdle facing Flash use on the Web, however, is integration with HTML. As you've seen, it's fairly easy to drop a Flash movie into a page and have it play automatically. But to really integrate it into your page, you want to control more aspects of how it looks and how it acts. The traditional route to solving this dilemma is to craft each Flash movie for a particular layout — a time-consuming and often expensive task. Now, Macromedia has created an easier way to integrate Flash movies and Web pages: Flash elements.

Flash *elements* are a product of the Flash MX evolution. Starting with the first MX release, designers had the capability to create *components* in Flash; components are self-contained objects that enable designers to quickly add frequently used functionality to a Flash movie. Initial components included user interface objects, such as checkboxes, radio buttons, and drop-down menus. A key advantage of these components is that after they are inserted on a page, the designer can easily change various associated parameters, such as labels, color, font, and even content. Whereas the parameters of Flash components must be changed within Flash, the parameters of a Flash element can be altered in Dreamweaver. A Flash element is, in actuality, a compiled Flash component. Flash elements are stored in a format different from that of the standard Flash movie. You can identify a Flash element by its .swc file extension as opposed to the .swf associated with a Flash movie.

The process for working with Flash elements is a bit different from that of a Flash movie. Here's an overview of how Flash elements work:

1. Flash elements have their own category on the Insert bar — you can drag the object right onto the page where you'd like it to appear.

2. When you insert a Flash element, you're asked where you want to store the file, rather than which source file to use.

   Dreamweaver is actually placing a copy of the compiled .swc file in your site in .swf format.

3. After the file has been copied to your specified location, the Flash placeholder appears on your page. All standard Flash attributes are available in the Property inspector.

4. The Tag Inspector panel displays a Flash element tab that lists all the specific parameters for the selected object. Modify the parameters by selecting the corresponding default value; depending on the type of parameter, a new interface may appear. For example, the bgColor attribute, which sets the color for the background, displays a color picker. The titleSize attribute, on the other hand, uses a standard text field for entering new font size values for the object's title.

5. Review the Flash element in Dreamweaver by clicking Play on the Property inspector. To test it out fully, preview the page in the browser either locally or on your site, as shown in Figure 24-7.

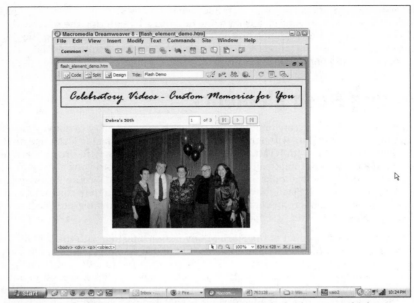

Figure 24-7: To be viewed, Flash elements require Flash Player 7 or higher.

6. Upload to your site as you would normally. The Flash file is considered a dependent file of the page and is transferred automatically by Dreamweaver.

Dreamweaver comes with one Flash element, Image Viewer. More Flash elements are available through third parties on the Macromedia Exchange and other sites. The following sections describe how to add an Image Viewer to your Web page and how to use it.

Working with the Image Viewer

The Image Viewer Flash element is, in essence, a slide-show utility. With it, you can specify any number of images to display in a contained area, complete with transitions and navigation controls. Images are loaded dynamically and automatically scaled to fit into the viewing area, which you can resize. You also have control over the background color and overall title, and you can individually caption pictures for easy identification. Preset navigation controls enable users to move from one picture to another in sequence or go directly to a particular image. Ten different transitions are available to choose from — or you can opt to use them all, randomly.

Note
Prior to the release of Flash Player 8, it was only possible to load standard JPG images on-the-fly; the latest version, however, supports GIF, PNG, and progressive JPG images as well. Before incorporating such image types, however, it's important to make sure that the Flash 8 Player has sufficient penetration in your target market by checking your Web site statistics.

Inserting the Image Viewer

Adding the Image Viewer Flash element to your page is just like inserting a Flash movie—with one little twist. To bring an Image Viewer into your Web page, follow these steps:

1. Choose Insert ⇨ Media ⇨ Image Viewer from the menu or select Image Viewer from the Flash element category of the Insert bar.

2. When the Save Flash Element dialog box is displayed, enter a name for the Flash movie to be stored in your site.

   The Image Viewer file is assigned a `.swf` file extension automatically.

3. When you're finished, click Save to close the dialog box and insert the Flash movie.

Dreamweaver inserts the placeholder for the Image Viewer, initially set to 400 pixels wide by 325 high, as shown in Figure 24-8. Like any other Flash movie, you can use the resizing handles to change the dimensions of the movie.

Image Viewer   Flash Element Tag Inspector

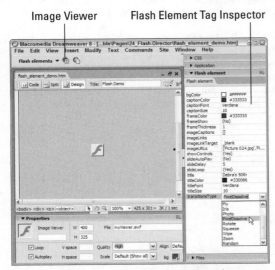

Figure 24-8: The standard Flash Property inspector appears when you select an inserted Image Viewer, but the Tag inspector reveals a host of modifiable parameters.

Modifying Parameters

Whereas changing parameters is, in many Flash movie cases, an optional operation, it's a necessity with the Image Viewer. At the very least, you must specify which images the Flash element should show. That, however, is just the tip of what's possible. In all, the Image Viewer has 19 different parameters that you can alter.

To simplify entry of a wide range of parameters, the Image Viewer offers four different types of attribute value fields.

✦ **Text field:** A typical text field for entering values directly, used in the Image Viewer to specify caption size, frame thickness, and other numeric values — as well as standard text for titles.

Caution   There is no error checking on the values entered in the text fields. Any unusable values (if you enter ten instead of 10 for captionSize, for example) are ignored.

✦ **Color picker:** Dreamweaver's standard color picker, which appears when the color swatch is selected.

✦ **Menu list:** A list of acceptable values for the associated parameter. The menu list is used for parameters that require a Yes or No (such as slideLoop), as well as for those with a much more extensive list to choose from (such as captionFont).

Note   All the drop-down lists are editable — which means that you can enter your own values to supplement the provided ones. In only one case — the imageLinkTarget attribute — is this truly useful; in all other situations, choose a value from the provided list.

✦ **Array values:** Displays a separate dialog box for entering an array of values. The Image Viewer Flash element uses array lists for the captions (the imageCaptions attribute), links (imageLinks), and source files (imageURLs). When picking links and source files, the Edit Array Values dialog box also provides a folder icon, which opens a Select File dialog (see Figure 24-9). Dynamic values cannot be assigned. Values can also be entered by hand into the field; they must be quoted with single quotes and separated by commas.

Figure 24-9: The Edit Array dialog box offers a somewhat restricted Select File dialog, limited to local files and defined servers.

Caution   Be sure to upload the images referenced in the Image Viewer to the specified location on your remote server; Dreamweaver does not see them as dependent files and does not transfer them automatically.

Table 24-3 details Image Viewer parameters. Required entries are noted with an asterisk (*).

Table 24-3: Image Viewer Parameters

Parameter	Type of Attribute	Use
bgColor	Color picker	Sets the solid color of the surrounding the image; this option does not affect the background color of the controls.
captionColor	Color picker	Sets the color of the captions displayed with each image.
captionFont	Menu list	Sets the font face used for the captions.
frameColor	Color picker	Sets the color for the border, if any, around the Image Viewer.
frameShow	Menu list	Determines whether a border around the Image Viewer should be shown.
frameThickness	Text field	Sets the size of the border.
imageCaptions	Array values	Sets the text to accompany each of the images.
imageLinks	Array values	Sets the links associated with the images; such links can be used to show a larger version of the image displayed.
imageLinkTarget	Menu list	Sets the target for the linked files; standard target values (_blank, _self, _top, and _parent) are provided and custom targets names (for example, mainFrame) can be used.
imageURLs*	Array values	Lists the URLs of the source files shown in the Image Viewer. URLs should either be document-relative or absolute; site-root–relative URLs do not work properly. (Default is http://macromedia.com/)
showControls	Menu list	Determines whether the controls are displayed. If the controls are not shown, be sure to enable the slideAutoPlay option.
slideAutoPlay	Menu list	Determines if the slide show should start automatically.
slideDelay	Text field	Sets the delay between images during a running slide show, in seconds. Default value is 5.
slideLoop	Menu list	Determines whether the slide show should continuously repeat.
title	Text field	Sets the overall title for the Image Viewer, which appears to the left of the controls.
titleColor	Color picker	Sets the color for the title.
titleFont	Menu list	Sets the font face for the title.
titleSize	Text field	Sets the font size for the title.
transitionsType	Menu list	Determines which transition (if any) to use between images. Options are None, Blinds, Fade, Fly, Iris, Photo, PixelDissolve, Rotate, Squeeze, Wipe, Zoom, and Random (default).

Adding Other Flash Elements

Although none is available at the time of this writing, Macromedia and independent developers are known to have other Flash elements in the works. The best source for Flash elements — as it is for other Dreamweaver extensions — is sure to be the Macromedia Exchange. Visit the Exchange by choosing Commands ⇨ Get More Commands and then searching for the term *Flash element*. After you find one you'd like to try, download and install it using the Extension Manager. Some extensions may vary, but chances are you'll find your new Flash elements available from that category of the Insert bar.

Building a Flash Interactive Slide Show

In this Dreamweaver Technique, you use the Flash Image Viewer to create interactive slide show, complete with transitions and captions.

1. From the Techniques site, expand the 24_Flash folder and open the `flash_start` file.

2. If necessary, select View ⇨ Visual Aids ⇨ CSS Layout Outlines and place your cursor in the div named slideshow below the placeholder paragraph.

3. From the Flash elements category of the Insert bar, click Image Viewer.

4. In the Save Flash Element dialog box, navigate to the 24_Flash folder, enter **slideshow** in the File Name field and click Save.

   The Flash placeholder is inserted and the Flash element panel opened.

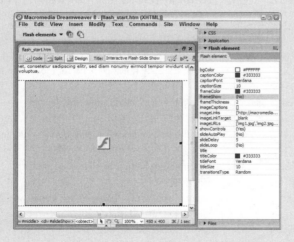

The first attributes to customize are the caption and title colors.

5. In the Flash element panel, select the color swatch next to captionColor and sample the dark brown from the left side of the Relative Realty logo; follow the same procedure to change the titleColor color swatch.

6. Select the property field next to imageCaptions and click the Edit Array Values icon that appears.

7. When the Edit 'imageCaptions' Array dialog box appears, click Add (+) and enter the phrase **Living Room**; click Add (+) two more times to add **Kitchen – East View** and **Kitchen – West View**. When you're done, click OK to close the dialog.

8. In the imageLinks property field, select and delete the entire entry: ['http://macromedia.com/','http://macromedia.com/','http://macromedia.com/'].

   Although you can include a separate link for each of your slides, this is not the desired behavior for this slide show.

9. Now you're ready to choose the images for the slide show. Select the imageURLs property field and click the Edit Array Values icon.

10. In the Edit 'imageURLs' Array dialog box, select the first entry and then click the folder icon that appears.

11. When the Select File dialog opens, browse to the images folder within the Techniques site root and choose `apt_view1.jpg`.

12. Repeat steps 10 and 11 to select `apt_view2.jpg` and `apt_view3.jpg` to replace the second and third entries, respectively; click OK when you're done.

13. Select the slideLoop property field and choose (Yes) from the drop-down list.

14. In the Title field, enter **Your Next Apartment**.

15. Select the transitionsType field and choose Wipe from the list.

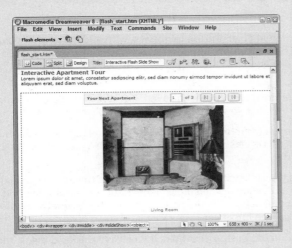

16. Save your page.

You can test your slide show right in Dreamweaver by selecting the Flash element and clicking Play on the Property inspector, or you can click F12 to preview in your browser.

Creating Flash Buttons

The original argument against using Flash was: "Not everyone has the Flash plugin, so not everyone can see Flash movies." Nowadays, this argument is more or less moot with Flash plugin market penetration at 98+ percent for Flash Players 2, 3 and 4, 97+ for Flash Player 5, 96+ for Flash Player 6 and, as of this writing, just less than 90% for Flash Player 7.

Although Flash is often used to create standalone movies, cartoons, and interactive games, it is also capable of making excellent navigation aids. One feature of traditional user interfaces — audio feedback, the sound that you hear when a button has been clicked onscreen — has been long missing on the Web because of the lack of a universally available sound engine. With navigation buttons created in Flash, sound is very easy to incorporate, as are animation effects and smooth blends. Best of all, these effects require extremely low bandwidth and often weigh less on a page than a comparable animated GIF file, even without the sound.

Dreamweaver designers can add the power and beauty of Flash objects to their Web page design palette. Designers can also create both animated Flash Buttons and static Flash Text (covered later in this chapter) directly within Dreamweaver. Flash Buttons are based on template designs created in Flash and customized in Dreamweaver. This separation of design and implementation enables Flash graphic designers to create the overall look for a navigational button or button series, and Dreamweaver layout artists can incorporate this look into the proper page design, adding the appropriate button text, links, and background color where needed. Flash Buttons, like any Flash movie, can be previewed in Dreamweaver and resized as needed.

Tip   If your appetite is whetted by Flash Buttons, but you'd like more control — as well as the possibility of adding sounds and making your buttons dynamic — check out the author's extension, FlashBang! You can find information about this extension at www.flashbang media.com.

Dreamweaver comes with 44 different Flash Button templates, with additional styles available at the Macromedia Exchange. The buttons are intended to be used primarily as links to other Web pages, although some are designed as VCR-like player controls. To insert a Flash Button, follow these steps:

1. Make sure that the current document has been saved. If you're working on a new document, Dreamweaver requires that you save it before adding a Flash Button.

2. Select the Flash Button object from the Media menu on the Insert bar's Common category or choose Insert ➪ Media ➪ Flash Button. The Insert Flash Button dialog box, shown in Figure 24-10, is displayed.

3. Select a button type from the Style list. The previews shown in the Sample area are live demonstrations and play as designed when moused-over and/or clicked. There is, however, one exception: No sound is heard in preview; you have to preview the Flash Button in the browser to get the full effect.

4. Enter the button text label in the Button Text field. If you leave this field blank, the button will have no label. The Button Text field is physically limited to 50 characters, although for most practical purposes, your text will be shorter. Certain symbols, such as those in the Control group, ignore the text and font settings.

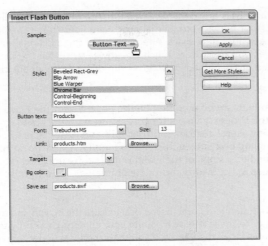

Figure 24-10: Click Apply to test typeface and text size variations when creating your Flash Button.

5. Select a typeface from the Font drop-down list. The fonts listed are TrueType fonts found on your system. Most of the button templates have a preselected font and text size. If the default font is not found on your system, a small alert appears at the bottom of the dialog box.

6. Enter the font size, in points, in the Size field.

7. If the button is to link to another page, enter the absolute or document-relative URL in the Link field. Alternatively, you can click the Browse button to locate the file.

   Flash movies don't handle site-root–relative links correctly, so your link needs to be either absolute, such as www.idest.com/dreamweaver/, or document-relative. Use document-relative links only if the Flash Button is to be stored in the same folder as the page referenced.

8. If you are working in a frame-based site or you want the link to open in another page, select an option from the Target drop-down list. The standard system targets — _blank, _self, _parent, and _top — are always available. Additional frame names appear if the Flash Button is inserted in an existing frameset.

9. If the Flash Button is to be placed on a page or in a table with a background color other than white, select the Bg Color swatch to choose an appropriate background. Alternatively, the hexadecimal color number or standard color name may be entered directly into the Bg Color text field.

10. In the Save As text box, enter a path and filename for the Flash Button file. If you like, you can use the suggested default name in the site root. You also can click the Browse button to choose a different location.

11. Click Apply to insert the button in the cursor location on the page.

12. Click OK when you're finished.

Tip   If you'd like to see what other styles are available, open the Insert Flash Button dialog box and select Get More Styles. Your primary browser launches and goes to the Dreamweaver Exchange, where you can search for new styles. After you install the additional extensions using the Extension Manager, you need to relaunch Dreamweaver to see the new styles. Note that selecting Get More Styles immediately closes the dialog box without creating a button.

After your Flash Button is inserted, it can be modified on the page. Select the Flash Button object to activate the Flash Button Property inspector that, along with the standard Flash Property inspector, offers two new useful custom controls: Edit and Reset Size. Click Edit to reopen the Insert Flash Button dialog box and enable you to modify any of the settings. Click Reset Size if you have altered the dimensions of the Flash Button — by dragging one of the sizing handles or entering new values in the Width and/or Height fields — and want to return to the original size.

Tip   If you move an existing Flash Button to a frame-based design, click the button and then click Edit in the Property inspector. To make it easy to target your content chosen by the Flash Button link, you can find names for all the frames in your new frameset under Target.

Working with Flash Text

The addition of Flash Text to Dreamweaver goes a long way toward solving one of the Web designer's most perplexing problems: how to achieve good-looking text that uses nonstandard fonts. HTML enables you to specify the use of a nonstandard font in a Web page, but the font appears in a user's browser only if the user happens to have that particular font installed on his or her system. For this reason, few designers stray outside tried-and-true options, such as Arial, Helvetica, and Times New Roman, for the majority of their content. This use of limited fonts is especially grating to print designers coming to the Web who rely on typography as a primary design tool. The advent of Dynamic HTML promised to bring a wider selection of typefaces with so-called *dynamic font technology*, but lack of built-in cross-browser support for any one system dashed those hopes.

The Flash Text feature enables the designer to use any TrueType font to create low-weight, jaggies-free headings, right from within Dreamweaver. The ubiquitous nature of the Flash Player ensures cross-browser support without resorting to GIF images, which are often not as crisp as required. Moreover, with Flash Text, you can easily declare a second color for automatically enabled rollovers — you don't even have to attach a Dreamweaver behavior.

The Flash Text feature is especially useful for creating headings in a corporate-approved typeface. Because it doesn't involve downloading a font resource, as dynamic font technologies do, there is no concern about the misuse of copyrighted fonts. The only downside to Flash Text when compared to a dynamic font technology is that Flash Text cannot be searched on a page. To overcome this limitation, Web designers can include key phrases in <meta> tags.

To use the Flash Text object, follow these steps:

1. Make sure that you have saved your page before proceeding.

2. Select Flash Text from the Media menu on the Insert bar's Common category or choose Insert ➪ Media ➪ Flash Text. The Insert Flash Text dialog box appears, as shown in Figure 24-11.

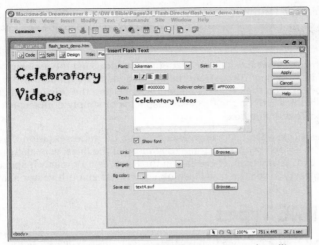

Figure 24-11: Use the Flash Text object to create headlines with a nonstandard or custom font.

3. Select the typeface from the Font drop-down list.

4. Enter the font size in the Size field.

5. Choose Bold and/or Italic styles for your text, if you want.

6. Select the alignment on the page: left, center, or right.

7. Select a basic color from the color swatch or enter a hexadecimal value or valid color name in the Color field.

8. If you want, you can choose a secondary color for the text to change to when the user moves his or her mouse over the Flash Text from the Rollover Color swatch.

9. Enter text in the Text field. Other than practical considerations, there's no real limit to the amount of text that can be entered, and line returns are acceptable.

10. If you want to see the text in the default font in the Text field — rather than your selected font — disable the Show Font option.

11. If you want, enter an absolute or document-relative URL in the Link field. As with Flash Buttons, site-relative links are not available in Flash Text objects.

12. If you're working in a frame-based site or want the link to open in a new browser window, choose the appropriate Target from the drop-down list.

13. Optionally, choose a background color from the Bg Color swatch.

14. Enter a path and filename to store the object in the Save As field. Alternatively, click the Browse button to locate a folder. If you're using document-relative links in the Flash Text object, be sure to store the object in the same folder as the current document.

15. Click Apply to preview what the button will look like in your document and click OK when you're finished.

Caution   When you are editing a Flash Text button, clicking Apply overwrites the existing button file and replaces it with your new, edited version. Alas, there is no undo for the Apply command, so think twice before clicking that button!

As with Flash Buttons, you can resize a Flash Text object by dragging the resizing handles; press the Shift key while dragging to constrain the dimensions to their initial width and height ratio. Click Reset Size on the Property inspector to restore the original dimensions. To edit a Flash Text object, click Edit on the Property inspector or simply double-click the object to open its Insert Flash Text dialog box.

When you create a Flash Text object, Dreamweaver makes a GIF representation that can be displayed during layout — you may notice some roughness in the lines, especially if you resize the object. You can, at any time, click Play on the Flash Text Property inspector (or choose Preview in Browser) to see the true Flash object with its smooth vector shape.

Configuring MIME Types

As with any plugin, your Web server has to have the correct MIME types set before Shockwave files can be properly served to your users. If your Web page plays Shockwave and Flash movies locally, but not remotely, chances are good that the correct MIME types need to be added. The system administrator generally handles configuring MIME types.

The system administrator needs to know the following information to be able to correctly configure the MIME types:

   ✦ **Shockwave:** application/x-director (`.dcr`, `.dir`, `.dxr`)

   ✦ **Flash:** application/x-shockwave-flash (`.swf`)

Both Shockwave and Flash are popular plugins, and it's likely that the Web server is already configured to recognize the appropriate file types.

Managing Links in Flash Movies with Dreamweaver

Many Web sites rely heavily on Flash movies, substituting movies for entire pages that would otherwise be created with HTML. Others take advantage of Flash's interactivity in their main navigation buttons. Adding links to buttons in Flash is easy, but embedding multiple URLs into multiple SWF files can make modifying a site's structure a nightmare, forcing you to re-create every SWF file in your site. Luckily, Dreamweaver comes to the rescue with link management features that are SWF-savvy.

Dreamweaver extends its link management capabilities to include the links contained in Flash SWF movies. Edit links within an SWF file manually in the Site Map, or move SWF files in the Site Files view and let Dreamweaver clean up behind you.

Within the Files panel, you can drag SWF files to new folders just as you would an HTML file. Unless your Update Links When Moving Files preference is set to Never, Dreamweaver either modifies the links in the SWF file accordingly or prompts you for permission to do so.

Caution

Be careful with the type of links you use—Flash (or, more accurately, browser playback of Flash) can't handle every type. Absolute URLs are very common in Flash movies because they can be used in every situation. Document-relative links may be used successfully in all cases if the Web page and the Flash file are stored in the same folder. Site-root–relative links, such as /products/widgets.htm, should not be used in Flash movies.

To modify the links in an SWF file manually, follow these steps:

1. Display the Site Map of a site by pressing F8 to open the Files panel, selecting the site from the drop-down list, clicking the Expand/Collapse button to display the expanded Files panel, and clicking the Site Map button.

2. Choose View ➪ Show Dependent Files to include dependent files such as Flash movies in the Site Map.

3. Locate the SWF file that you want to modify. If it contains any links, a plus sign is shown next to its icon. Click the plus sign to expand a branch of links from the SWF file, as shown in Figure 24-12.

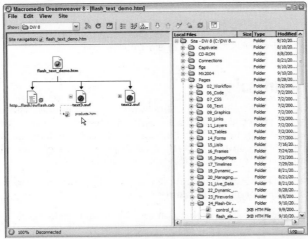

Figure 24-12: Dreamweaver's Site Map displays links contained in Flash SWF movies.

4. To change a link, select it and choose Site ➪ Change Link, press Ctrl+L (Command+L), or right-click (Control+click) the link and choose Change Link from the shortcut menu. Dreamweaver displays a Select HTML File dialog box.

5. Select a new file by navigating to an HTML file or entering a URL. Click OK when you're finished.

Note

If your preferences call for Dreamweaver to prompt you before updating links, Dreamweaver asks you to confirm that you want the link changed.

The link in your SWF file is changed.

Caution Dreamweaver changes links within SWF files, but the links in the original Flash document that you edit in Flash itself remain unchanged. Make sure you update your Flash document before exporting a revised SWF file.

Providing User Interaction with Flash and Shockwave Movies

What happens after you've installed your Shockwave or Flash files? Many movies are set to play automatically or upon some action from the user, such as a mouse click of a particular hotspot within the page. But what if you want the user to be able to start or stop a movie in one part of the page, using controls in another part? How can controls in one frame affect a movie in a different frame?

Dreamweaver includes a Control Shockwave or Flash behavior that makes inline controls — controls on the same Web page as the movie — very easy to set up. However, establishing frame-to-frame control is slightly more complex in Dreamweaver and requires a minor modification to the program-generated code.

Cross-Reference Both of the following step-by-step sections rely on Dreamweaver behaviors. If you're unfamiliar with using behaviors, review Chapter 12 before proceeding.

Creating Inline Controls

Certainly, it's perfectly acceptable to make your Shockwave or Flash movies with built-in controls for interactivity, but sometimes you want to separate the controls from the movie. Dreamweaver includes a JavaScript behavior called Control Shockwave or Flash. With this behavior, you can set up external controls to start, stop, and rewind Shockwave and Flash movies. Follow these steps to create inline Shockwave or Flash controls:

1. Insert a Shockwave or Flash object in your page by clicking either the Shockwave or Flash Button in the Media menu of the Insert bar.

2. From the Select File dialog box, enter the path to your file in the File Name text box or click the Browse button to locate your file.

3. For Shockwave, enter the width and height of your movie in the W and H text boxes, respectively, in the Property inspector. The dimensions for Flash movies are entered automatically.

4. Enter a unique name for your movie in the text box provided.

5. If you are inserting a Flash movie, deselect the Autoplay and Loop options.

6. To insert the first control, position the cursor where you'd like the control to appear on the page.

7. Type the text or insert the image that will function as your control. Select this text or image.

Tip You can also use a form button to serve as a user interface control; if you do, there's no need to add a link like the one described in step 8.

8. In the Link box of the Property inspector, enter `javascript:;` to create an empty target.

9. Open the Behaviors panel by pressing Shift+F3.

10. If necessary, change the selected browser to 4.0 and Later Browsers by clicking the Add Action (+) button and choosing Show Events For ⇨ 4.0 and Later Browsers.

11. Use the Add Action (+) button to choose the Control Shockwave or Flash action.

12. In the Control Shockwave or Flash dialog box (see Figure 24-13), select the movie you want to affect from the Movie drop-down list.

Figure 24-13: In the Control Shockwave or Flash dialog box, you assign a control action to an image button or text link.

13. Select the action for your control. Choose from the four options: Play, Stop, Rewind, and Go to Frame. If you choose the Go to Frame option, enter a frame number in the text box.

14. Click OK to close the Control Shockwave or Flash dialog box.

15. Repeat steps 6 through 14 for each movie control you'd like to add. Figure 24-14 shows a sample Web page with Play, Stop, and Rewind text controls.

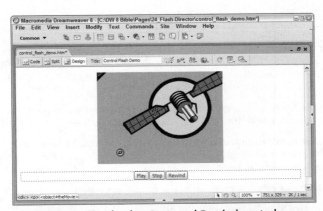

Figure 24-14: Simple Play, Stop, and Rewind controls were added to this page in just a few minutes using the Control Shockwave or Flash behavior.

Playing Movies in Frames

Framesets and frames are great for Web sites in which you want your navigation and other controls kept in one frame, and where you also want the freedom to vary the content in another frame. It's entirely possible to set up your movie's playback buttons in one frame and the Shockwave movie in another. The method and the tools used are similar to those used in the preceding Dreamweaver Technique for adding same-page controls to a Shockwave movie. For this method using frames, some HTML hand-coding is necessary, but it is relatively minor — only one additional line per control!

As you saw in the previous section, Dreamweaver's Control Shockwave or Flash behavior lists all the Shockwave and Flash movies in the page and enables you to choose the one you want to affect. Unfortunately, the behavior looks on only one page, not through an entire frameset. However, with a little sleight-of-hand and a bit of JavaScript, you can get the effect you want.

Note   Before you begin applying this method, you should construct (and save) your frameset and individual frames. Be sure to give each frame a unique name, because you have to provide the names to address the correct frames.

Follow these steps to place Shockwave controls in frames:

1. In one frame, insert the images or links that are going to act as the Shockwave controls. (For this example, the control frame is named `frControl`.)

2. In another frame, insert the Shockwave file by choosing the Shockwave object from the Media menu of the Common category of the Insert bar. (For this example, the movie frame is named `frMovie`.)

3. Be sure to modify the Shockwave Property inspector with the necessary parameters: name, width, and height.

4. Copy the Shockwave placeholder by selecting it and choosing Edit ➪ Copy.

5. Position the cursor in the `frControl` frame and paste the placeholder in a temporary position by choosing Edit ➪ Paste. At this point, the placement for the placeholder is not critical, as long as it is in the same frame as the images or links you are going to use as controls. The placeholder is deleted shortly.

   Instead of using the Copy and Paste commands, you can hold down the Ctrl (Command) key and click and drag the placeholder to its new temporary position.

6. Now select the first image or link you want to use as a control. As described in the preceding section, attach the Control Shockwave or Flash behavior to the selected object. As you learned in the preceding exercise, this entails the following actions:

   • With the image or link selected, open the Behaviors panel.

   • Add the Control Shockwave or Flash action.

   • In the Control Shockwave or Flash dialog box, specify the movie and select the required action (Play, Rewind, Stop, or Go to Frame).

7. The major work is finished now. All that's left to do is add a little HTML. Switch to Code view, open the Code inspector, or use your favorite external editor to edit the current file.

8. Locate the image or link controls in the code. Each JavaScript routine is called from within an `<a>` tag and reads something like the following, where `fMovie` is the name of the Flash movie:

```
<a href="javascript:; "
    onClick="MM_controlShockwave('document.fMovie',
'document.fMovie','Play')">
```

9. Wherever you see the JavaScript reference to document, change it to

```
parent.frameName.document
```

where `frameName` is the unique name you gave to the frame in which your movie appears. In this example, `frameName` is `frMovie`, so after the replacement is made, the tag reads as follows:

```
<a href="javascript:;"
onClick="MM_controlShockwave('parent.frMovie.document.
fMovie','parent.frMovie.document.fMovie','Play')">
```

By making this substitution, you've pointed the JavaScript function first to the parent of the current document—and the parent of a frame is the entire frameset. Now that you are looking at the entire frameset, the next word (which is the unique frame name) points the JavaScript function directly to the appropriate frame within the frameset.

Tip   If you have a number of controls, you might want to use Dreamweaver's Find and Replace features to ensure that you've updated all the code.

10. Finally, delete the temporary Shockwave movie that was inserted into the frame containing the controls.

Figure 24-15 shows Shockwave controls placed in a frame.

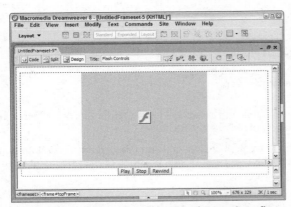

Figure 24-15: The same setup as in the previous figure, but with the controls and movie in separate frames.

Test the frameset by pressing F12 (Option+12) for your primary browser, or Shift+F12 (Command+F12) for your secondary browser. If you haven't changed the Property inspector's default Tag attribute (the default is Object and Embed), the Shockwave movie should work in both Netscape and Internet Explorer.

Triggering Behaviors from Flash Movies

Flash includes several of its own behaviors for creating interactivity, but Flash behaviors don't use JavaScript as Dreamweaver behaviors do. A Flash-heavy project might benefit from Dreamweaver's Open Browser Window or Popup Message behaviors as much as the next site. The methodology in this section shows you how to trigger Dreamweaver behaviors from buttons in a Flash movie.

What Flash Buttons do is specified in the Flash authoring environment, not in Dreamweaver. Dreamweaver can attach behaviors to HTML elements, such as anchor tags and body tags, but not to plugins. The solution lies in creating dummy buttons in Dreamweaver and copying the JavaScript code from those links into the actions attached to Flash Buttons, within Flash itself.

To trigger Dreamweaver behaviors from Flash Buttons, follow these steps:

1. Create a new Dreamweaver document or open an existing one.

2. Create a null link that represents a button in your Flash movie. If you want a Flash Button to open a new browser window, attach the Open Browser Window behavior to your null link, as shown in Figure 24-16.

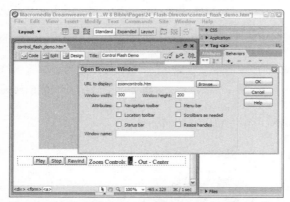

Figure 24-16: Attach a behavior you want to trigger from Flash to a null link in Dreamweaver.

3. Place your cursor within the null link and select the ⟨a⟩ tag from the Tag Selector in Dreamweaver's status bar to completely select the link.

4. Choose View ➪ Code and Design to display page code and design together. Note that the null link is selected in both the Code and Design portions of the Document window and looks something like the following:

```
<a href="javascript:;" ⟳
    onClick="MM_openBrWindow('index.htm','newWindow', ⟳
    'status=yes,scrollbars=yes,width=200,height=300')">
 Play</a>
```

5. Select everything between the "..." quotes in the `onClick` attribute — including the parentheses — and copy it to the clipboard. This is the actual JavaScript that you want the Flash Button to execute.

6. In Flash, select the button to which you want to add the Dreamweaver behavior and then open the Actions pane.

7. Click the Add Action (+) button and choose Actions ⇨ Browser/Network ⇨ getURL to add a getURL behavior to your Flash Button. In the URL text box, enter the following

   `javascript:`

   and then paste the contents of the clipboard — your JavaScript code — so that you have something that looks like the following:

   ```
   javascript:MM_openBrWindow('myBuddy.htm','','↵
   scrollbars=yes','width=250,height=200')
   ```

8. Repeat steps 2 through 7 for each additional button or behavior you'd like to use. Note that multiple function calls in a `javascript:` statement must be separated by semi-colons:

   ```
   javascript:funcCall1(arglist); funcCall2(arglist); etc.
   ```

9. Export your Flash movie as an SWF file and place it into the same page in Dreamweaver where you built your null links. Note that the `<head>` tag of this page contains JavaScript functions that match your null links and the JavaScript inside your Flash movie.

10. Delete your null links — but not the JavaScript functions in the `<head>` tag — and publish your page.

When users click the buttons in your Flash movie, `javascript:` URL sends the commands to the browser, executing the JavaScript functions in your Web page. Flash Buttons open new browser windows, pop-up messages, and so on. This works in Netscape and in Internet Explorer.

Tip   Shockwave authors can also use JavaScript URLs from Lingo to trigger Dreamweaver behaviors in a manner similar to the procedure just shown. JavaScript-savvy people can also reference their own JavaScript functions using this method.

Editing Flash Movies from within Dreamweaver

You can only modify Flash movies so much within Dreamweaver — certain changes require that the movie source be altered in Flash itself. Dreamweaver now provides a direct connection to Flash: Flash Edit. You can now edit your Flash movies from within Dreamweaver (provided, of course, that you have Flash MX or later installed on your system and the FLA source file). Dreamweaver doesn't do the actual movie editing work, of course. Here's how it works.

When you click the Flash Edit button, Dreamweaver launches Flash; you edit your movie in Flash, save your update, exit Flash, and end up back in Dreamweaver. It makes for a seamless Dreamweaver/Flash collaboration.

To edit a Flash movie from within Dreamweaver, follow these steps:

1. In Dreamweaver, open the document that contains the Flash movie.

2. Do one of the following to begin editing your movie in Flash:

   • Select the Flash movie placeholder, and in the Flash Property inspector, click the Edit button.

   • Ctrl+double-click (Command+double-click) the Flash movie placeholder.

   • Right-click (Control+click) the movie placeholder, and choose Edit With Flash from the shortcut menu.

3. Dreamweaver launches Flash and automatically opens the selected movie's source FLA file or prompts you to open it manually. (To enable Flash to open the FLA file automatically, you must assign it to the Flash object's Src field in Dreamweaver.)

4. In Flash, make changes to your movie. The Flash Document window indicates that you are editing a movie from Dreamweaver, as shown in Figure 24-17.

Figure 24-17: Using Dreamweaver's Flash Edit button, you can edit your Flash movies without having to exit/restart the Dreamweaver program.

5. When you are finished editing in Flash, click the Done button. Flash saves your changes to the source FLA file, updates the SWF file, and then whisks you back to Dreamweaver.

Summary

Together, the interactive power of Shockwave and the speedy glitz of Flash can enliven Web content like nothing else. Dreamweaver is extremely well suited for integrating and displaying Shockwave and Flash movies. Here are some key points to keep in mind:

✦ Saving your Director movies as Shockwave movies enables them to be played on the Web with the help of a plugin or ActiveX control.

✦ Flash movies are a way to enhance your Web pages with vector animations, interactivity, and streaming audio. Flash movies require the Flash Player plugin or ActiveX control.

✦ Dreamweaver has built-in objects for both Director and Flash movies. All the important parameters are accessible directly through the Property inspector.

✦ You need only three parameters to incorporate a Shockwave movie: the file's location, height, and width. Dreamweaver automatically imports a Flash movie's dimensions. You can get the exact measurements of a Shockwave movie from within Director.

✦ Aside from inserting Flash movies, Dreamweaver offers three other kinds of specialized Flash objects: Flash Buttons, Flash Text, and Flash elements. The first Flash element, called Image Viewer, is a highly configurable slide-show viewer, perfect for displaying any number of digital photographs with a range of transitions.

✦ Dreamweaver comes with a JavaScript behavior for controlling Shockwave and Flash movies. This Control Shockwave or Flash behavior can be used as-is for adding external controls to the same Web page, or — with a minor modification — for adding the controls to another frame in the same frameset.

✦ Dreamweaver behaviors can be triggered from a Shockwave or Flash movie.

✦ You can launch Flash to edit Flash movies right from within Dreamweaver.

In the next chapter, you learn how to add video to your Web pages.

✦　　✦　　✦

Adding Video to Your Web Page

In a world accustomed to being entertained by moving images 50 feet high, it's hard to understand why people are thrilled to see a grainy, jerky, quarter-screen-size video on a Web page. And in truth, it's the promise of video on the Web, not the current state of it, that has folks excited. Many of the industry's major players, including Microsoft and Apple, are spending big bucks to bring that promise a little closer to reality.

In the last number of years, video on the Web has truly come into its own. From online video's humble beginnings as a grainy, jerky, quarter-screen-size moving image to the full-screen, high-fidelity movie-like imagery of today, video is an essential element for many Web sites.

QuickTime, RealVideo, and Windows Media Player are the most popular formats on the Web, and all are cross-platform. Video can be downloaded to the user and then automatically played with a helper application, or it can be streamed to the user so that it plays while it's downloading.

This chapter describes the many different methods for incorporating video — whether you're downloading an MPEG file or streaming a movie — into your Web pages through Dreamweaver.

Video on the Web

It may be hard for folks not involved in the technology of computers and the Internet to understand why the high-tech Web doesn't always include something as low-tech as video. After all, television has been around forever, right? The difficulties arise from the fundamental difference between the two media: Television and radio signals are analog, and computers are pure digital. Sure, you can convert an analog signal to a digital one — but that's just the beginning of the solution.

The amount of information stored on a regular (analog) VHS cassette is truly remarkable. Moving that amount of information about in the ones and zeros of the digital world is a formidable task. For example, storing the digital video stream from any digital video camcorder uses up storage space at the rate of about 1GB every five minutes, and that video is already compressed. Large file sizes also translate into enormous bandwidth problems when you are transmitting video over the Web.

To resolve this issue of mega-sized files, industry professionals and manufacturers have developed various strategies, or *architectures*, for the creation, storage, and playback of digital media. Each architecture has a different file format, and thus each requires the user to have a playback system — whether a plugin, ActiveX control, or Java applet — capable of handling that particular format.

In an effort to keep file sizes as small as possible, Web videos are often presented in very small dimensions. It's not uncommon to display a video at a puny 180 x 120 pixels. Furthermore, you'll notice a major difference between conventional and Web-based video in terms of quality. Television video displays at 30 frames per second and film displays at 24 frames per second; but the best Web video rarely gets above 15 frames per second — virtually guaranteeing choppy motion in scenes with any action. Lossy compression also leads to *artifacting* — visible flaws introduced by the compression itself.

Given all the restrictions that video suffers on the Web, why use it at all? Simply because nothing else like it exists, and when you need video, you have to use video. Take heart, though. Advances are occurring at a rapid rate, both in the development of new video architectures and codecs (a *codec* is a compression algorithm) and in new, higher-speed Internet delivery systems, such as cable and DSL modems. What you learn in this chapter enables you to include video in your Dreamweaver-built Web pages today and gives you a good foundation for accommodating future enhancements.

The Flash Video Revolution

With the introduction of video in Flash MX, Macromedia planted the seeds of a revolution. Suddenly, video on the Web was easy. Although early Flash video did not have the same quality as the more established players like QuickTime, it had one major advantage: ubiquity. With a cross-platform player proliferation over 90%, Flash video's accessibility outweighed its drawbacks. Macromedia built on the intense interest generated by the early player's capabilities and improved the video output and experience with each subsequent release. Video output by the current version, Flash Professional 8, is certainly as good as video displayed by any other Web method — and, in many ways, superior.

New In Dreamweaver   Dreamweaver joined and extended the video revolution with the latest version's ability to insert Flash video in any Web page. Now, any Dreamweaver Web designer or developer has the power to easily incorporate high-quality video into any site. Ease of entry is a key factor and Dreamweaver makes it drop-in simple; designers can even gain the majority of benefits of Flash video without incurring the additional expense of a specialized server. For those clients and projects that require a higher-end experience, Flash offers a streaming alternative. As you learn later in this chapter, Dreamweaver's Insert Flash Video feature handles either option easily.

Encoding Video

To incorporate Flash video on your site, you'll need to first acquire the video, either by importing it directly from a digital camcorder or by retrieving a file in a video format, like `.avi`, `.mpg`, `.mov`, or `.wmv`. After you have a video file, you'll need to convert it to a Flash Video file (FLV) in a process called *encoding*. Encoding a video compresses it using a specific algorithm or *codec*. The Flash Player can read FLV files encoded with either Sorenson Spark or On2 VP6; FLV files encoded with Sorenson Spark can be played in Flash Player 6 and higher, whereas VP6-encoded FLV files require Flash Player 8. Many of the special features of Flash Professional 8 video, such as alpha channel transparency, are only available with VP6 encoding.

Numerous paths to encoding FLV files are available, including the following:

✦ **Flash Video Import Wizard:** A feature of Flash Professional 8, the Flash Video Import Wizard works with all popular video formats including QuickTime movies, Video for Windows (.avi), Windows Media (.wmv), and video directly retrieved from your camera (.dv or .dvi). The Flash Video Import Wizard works with one video file at a time.

✦ **Flash 8 Video Encoder:** The Flash 8 Video Encoder is a separate program included with Flash Professional 8 (see Figure 25-1). The key advantage to the Flash 8 Video Encoder is that it allows you to encode many video files (again, from all formats) to an FLV-compatible codec. Encoding a video file can be time intensive: a 35-second video took 23 minutes to encode in On2 VP6 format at medium quality.

Figure 25-1: Open the Flash 8 Video Encoder settings to choose the optimal delivery quality for your Flash video.

✦ **FLV QuickTime Export plugin:** Another utility that comes with Flash Professional 8 is the FLV QuickTime Export plugin. This plugin works with QuickTime 6.1.1 or higher to allow video editing tools to export FLV files directly. Supported video editors include Adobe After Effects, Apple Final Cut Pro, Apple QuickTime Pro, and Avid Xpress DV.

✦ **Third-party applications:** A number of third-party batch encoding tools now support the FLV format as well. For example, you can convert video to FLV format with Autodesk Cleaner, Riva VX, or Anystream Agility. As of this writing, these third-party applications are only capable of applying the older Sorenson Spark codec.

When encoding, you'll need to decide which type of video output to use: streaming or progressive. The relative pros and cons are discussed in the next section.

Tip   There is a third type of Flash video output to use: embedding. When you embed video in a Flash movie (which would then be inserted into the Web page), you're combining both video and Flash animation in a single movie. This process results in a much larger file and is only really useful for videos lasting 5 seconds or less. It is strongly recommended that your video remain an external file and not be embedded.

Progressive Download versus Streaming

One of the first questions you'll need to address when adding Flash video to your Web page is: How will the video be delivered? The two core methods available are progressive download and streaming. Both methods are alike in that they use external video files in .flv format in conjunction with a .swf file that acts as a video player.

Progressive download begins playing as soon as the first segment has been received by the site visitor and continues to download while the video is playing. Typically, the delay is relatively short, but there is often a perceived delay. There is, however, a major plus for progressive download over streaming: you can host the files on any kind of server. Because progressive download does not require a specialized server such as Flash Media Server (formerly Flash Communication Server), it is much less expensive to display.

Tip   You'll need to require at least Flash Player 7 if you use the progressive download method; streaming video can use Flash Player 6 or better.

Streaming video, however, can definitely be worth the cost. Video begins playing almost immediately and is more efficient for both the network in general and the viewer's computer specifically. Streaming video is also fully *seekable*—in other words, the video playhead can be moved anywhere to instantly view video from that point; with progressive download, you can only seek portions of the video that have already been downloaded. The truly advanced features of Web video—live feed, interactive control, video messaging, and so on—are only possible with streaming video.

Note   A couple of hosted streaming services are available for Flash video. Macromedia has partnered with a number of content delivery providers under their Flash Video Streaming Service umbrella aimed at enterprise customers; learn more by visiting www.macromedia. com/software/flashcom/fvss/. One of the content providers, VitalStream, has also spun-off a separate hosting service for small business called PlayStream (www. playstream.com/). A free extension to insert PlayStream streaming videos is available from WebAssist (www.webassist.com) and is included on this book's CD-ROM.

Inserting Flash Video

The Flash Video object makes it as easy to add video to your Web page as it is to add any other Flash movie—with even greater flexibility and control. Not only is your video added to the page, but it's accompanied by your choice of built-in controller. Flash detection code is automatically added to your page and you can even insert a custom message to site visitors if they don't have the required version.

As noted before, your choice of delivery method for your video—either progressive download or streaming—is a key one. The importance of this choice is reflected in the Insert Flash Video dialog box; depending on your choice, different options appear and the steps for including a video object vary. For this reason, instructions for including a Flash Video object of each type are presented separately.

Including Progressive Download Flash Video

To add a progressive download Flash Video object to your page, follow these steps:

1. Place your cursor where you'd like the Flash Video object to appear.

2. From the Insert bar's Common category, choose Media: Flash Video.

   The Insert Flash Video dialog box appears, as shown in Figure 25-2.

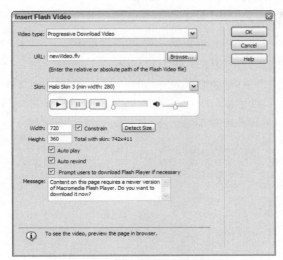

Figure 25-2: Progressive download video can be hosted on any standard Web server.

3. Make sure that Progressive Download Video is selected in the Video Type list.

4. Click Browse to locate the desired .flv video file or enter the path directly into the URL field.

Caution   If you're working on a Macintosh and your .flv file is two or more levels up from your HTML file, you'll need to use an absolute URL, like http://www.bigco.com/media/newvideo.flv.

5. Choose the type of controller you'd like from the Skin list.

   You have three basic choices (Clear Skin, Corona Skin, and Halo Skin), each in three variations. Each variation within a given style offers a different set of controls and requires a different minimum width. The preview area gives you a clear idea of what to expect and the minimum widths are listed for each entry.

6. Enter the dimensions of the movie (including controller) either by clicking Detect Size or entering the values directly into the Width and Height fields.

7. If you'd like the movie to begin as soon as possible when the page loads, select the Auto Play option.

8. If you'd like the movie to rewind to the beginning after it has played, enable the Auto Rewind option.

9. If desired, change the alert text displayed to viewers without the proper version of the Flash Player in the Message area.

10. Click OK when you're done.

You can see your video in action by previewing the page in a browser.

Adding Streaming Flash Video

To add a streaming Flash Video object to your page, follow these steps:

1. Place your cursor where you'd like the Flash Video object to appear.

2. From the Insert bar's Common category, choose Media: Flash Video.

3. In the Insert Flash Video dialog box, choose Streaming Video from the Video Type list.

   The options in the dialog box change, as shown in Figure 25-3.

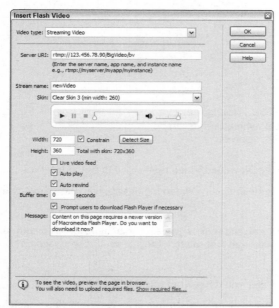

Figure 25-3: Streaming video requires a specialized Flash Video server, such as Flash Media Server.

4. Enter the path to the streaming server, application, and instance in the URI field.

   Streaming servers like the Flash Media Server use the Real Time Messaging Protocol, designated by `rtmp://`. An example of a full URI is `rtmp://123.45.678.90/bigVid/bv`.

5. Enter the name of the `.flv` file you'd like to display in the Stream Name field.

   You can leave off the `.flv` file extension if you like; it's understood by the server.

6. Choose the type of controller you'd like from the Skin list.

   You have three basic choices (Clear Skin, Corona Skin, and Halo Skin), each in three variations. Each variation within a given style offers a different set of controls and requires a different minimum width. The preview area gives you a clear idea of what to expect and the minimum widths are listed for each entry.

7. Enter the dimensions of the movie (including controller) either by clicking Detect Size or entering the values directly into the Width and Height fields.

8. If you're broadcasting live video, click the Live Video Feed option.

9. If you'd like the movie to begin as soon as possible when the page loads, select the Auto Play option.

10. If you'd like the movie to rewind to the beginning after it has played, enable the Auto Rewind option.

11. Enter the number of seconds of video you'd like to buffer before it begins playing.

    The default buffer value is 0, which means the video will be available for playing immediately after the page loads. Extend the buffer value if your video is encoded at a higher bit rate than the site visitor's connection speed or if connectivity problems persist.

12. If desired, change the alert text displayed to viewers without the proper version of the Flash Player in the Message area.

13. Click OK when you're done.

You'll need to publish your files to the server, as described in the next section, before you can view the streaming video in your Web page.

Publishing Flash Video Files

A Flash Video object actually requires three files to be viewed on the HTML page. In addition to the encoded video file with the `.flv` extension, it requires a container file either called `FLVPlayer_Progressive.swf` or `FLVPlayer_Streaming.swf`, depending on your choice of delivery method; this container file is the actual Flash movie called by the Flash Player. A file holding the video controls or skin is also used; for example, `Clear_Skin_1.swf`. Both of these support files are created for you by the Insert Flash Video object in the same folder as the HTML page the video is inserted in. Streaming video also requires that another generated file, `main.asc`, be placed in the Application folder of your Flash Media Server or Flash Communications Server.

Publishing the files to the server for either type of Flash video delivery can be accomplished in a simplified operation. If you're publishing a progressive download video, make sure Dreamweaver Preferences are set to prompt you to upload dependent files when your page is put or checked in. Both `.swf` support files and the `.flv` video file are considered dependent files by Dreamweaver and will be published to their correct locations when you click OK to upload dependent files.

Caution   If you don't rely on Dreamweaver's capability to publish dependent files, make sure you publish all the associated files or your video will not be visible to your site visitors.

A similar publishing ability is available for streaming Flash videos, but in a totally different way. When you select the inserted streaming video object, a custom Property inspector is displayed. In addition to permitting the modification of most Flash Video object attributes, the Property inspector also contains an Upload Media button. When you click Upload Media, the two created `.swf` files for the container and the skin are uploaded to the specified Web server; as noted by a Dreamweaver alert, you will be required to publish the `main.asc` and the `.flv` file to your streaming server Applications folder.

Tip   Should you choose not to take advantage of the Upload Media feature, you can select the Show Required Files link in the Property inspector to see what files need to go where for your streaming video.

Modifying Flash Video Parameters

Each of the different types of Flash Video object has its own Property inspector. Both allow easy modification of most previously set attributes; only the type of delivery, progressive video or streaming, is omitted. If you need to change a movie from one delivery type to another, you'll need to delete the inserted object and re-select Insert Flash Video to choose a different type.

With a streaming Flash Video object, you have the option of altering the dimensions, the skin, the options to Auto Play or Auto Rewind and, most importantly, the video source (see Figure 25-4). Because the `.flv` video source file is external to the video container, database-driven applications can even set the source dynamically.

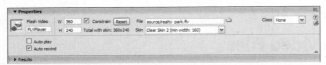

Figure 25-4: Once a progressive download video object has been inserted into the page, you can alter almost all the parameters through the custom Property inspector.

Caution   As noted earlier, the Insert Flash Video object stores the additional dependent files it creates in the same location at the current Web page. If you want to move either the skin `.swf` or the source `.flv` to a more appropriate folder, you'll have to adjust the inserted code. Although Dreamweaver will ask if you want to update the `.swf` and Web page, the `<object>` and `<embed>` tags that comprise the Flash movie are not changed. If you move the skin `.swf` file, change the Skin value in the `FlashVars param` statement of the `<object>` tag and equivalent `flashvars` attribute of the `<embed>` tag. Likewise, if you move the source `.flv` file, change the `streamName` value in both tags.

Adding Flash Video

In this Dreamweaver Technique, you insert a progressive download video into a Web page, complete with overlaid video controls.

1. From the Techniques site, expand the 25_Video folder and open the `flash_start` file.

2. Place your cursor at the start of the placeholder paragraph, below the Explore the Neighborhood headline.

3. From the Common category of the Insert bar, choose Media:Flash Video.

4. When the Insert Flash Video dialog box opens, make sure that Video Type is set to Progressive Download Video.

5. Click Browse and locate the `realty_park.flv` file in the 25_Video folder.

6. From the Skin list, choose Corona Skin 2 (min width: 141).

7. Click Detect Size to retrieve the original video dimensions.

8. Select the Auto Rewind option.

9. Leave the default Message and click OK to close the dialog box.

10. Save the file and then press F12 to preview the file in your browser.

The video controls are displayed on the initial image until you click Play. After the movie begins playing, if you move your cursor off the video, the controls disappear; they reappear whenever your mouse pointer hovers over the video.

Mainstream Streaming Media

Technologies — and the companies that create them — come and go on the Internet. Over the past few years, quite a few different streaming media solutions have presented themselves and then faded away, leaving us with the current Big Three: RealMedia, QuickTime, and Windows Media. These three technologies together represent almost the entire streaming media market — outside of the already-covered Flash video — and the vast majority of Internet users have at least one of the corresponding players; many have two or even all three.

RealMedia

RealNetworks released the first streaming media system — RealAudio — in 1995. Over the years, RealAudio has evolved into RealMedia and now supports video, images, text, Flash movies, and standard audio types such as AIFF and MP3. All these media types can be combined into a single presentation using Synchronized Multimedia Integration Language (SMIL). The three primary software components of RealMedia are as follows:

✦ **RealPlayer:** This is the newest client software for viewing RealMedia content. RealPlayer is free and offers a full set of basic RealMedia viewing features. RealPlayer Plus is an enhanced player available for around $20 or bundled with a subscription service called SuperPass that costs about $10/month. RealPlayer is available at www.real.com/. The RealPlayer interface is shown in Figure 25-5.

Figure 25-5: RealPlayer's interface enables the user to forego a Web browser completely when browsing for streaming media.

✦ **RealProducer:** This encoding software converts most types of audio and video (MPEG, QuickTime, and so forth) files to RealMedia (.rm) files. You can get Helix Producer Basic for free or the full-featured Helix Producer Plus for around $200. Read all about it at www.realnetworks.com/products/producer/.

✦ **Helix Server:** This server software serves up RealMedia over Real-Time Streaming Protocol (RTSP). Helix Server Basic, which is free, is limited to 1 Mbps throughput. For a larger throughput, move up to one of the commercial versions of the Helix Universal Server (available as Advanced, Edge, or Relay, depending on your needs). For more information, go to www.realnetworks.com/products/media_delivery.html.

Note You can still offer RealMedia to your users over the Web's regular HTTP without any special server software. HTTP streaming is, however, far more limited than RTSP streaming.

RealNetworks has led the way in cross-platform authoring and playback. Versions of RealPlayer are available for Windows, Macintosh OS X, and the full range of available mobile devices. The previous version of the player is also available for Macintosh OS 9, Unix, Linux, and even OS/2. MSN TV even plays RealAudio 3.0. By contrast, QuickTime is limited to Windows and Macintosh, and Microsoft's streaming video solution is basically Windows-only.

RealNetworks has also led the way in terms of users; for years it was the only option for large-scale streaming media sites. Even now, when it faces the stiffest competition it's ever had, its market share is very high. RealPlayer is included with major browsers, as well as with Windows and Red Hat Linux.

Tip See www.real.com for examples of RealMedia content.

QuickTime

What *QuickTime* refers to is widely misunderstood. Some people mix up the video format QuickTime Video with QuickTime itself. But QuickTime Video is just one of the things a QuickTime movie might contain. Sometimes the high-profile QuickTime Player is confused with QuickTime, but it is just one dependent application.

The best way to explain QuickTime is to say that it's a multimedia operating system, enabling applications such as CD-ROM titles to run on top of it and use the features it provides. These features include support for audio, video, images, 3D objects, MIDI music (including a software wavetable synthesizer), streaming video, Flash movies, and MP3 audio. After you have QuickTime 4+ installed on your computer, Macromedia Director can access digital video, Flash can export complete QuickTime presentations, and otherwise pedestrian applications can play synthesized music.

With the inclusion of streaming video in QuickTime, Apple dressed up the QuickTime MoviePlayer with an eye-catching brushed metal look and changed its name to QuickTime Player. QuickTime movies have a .mov filename extension.

Like RealMedia, QuickTime streaming has three main software components:

✦ **QuickTime and QuickTime Player:** All the viewing goodness of QuickTime and QuickTime Player (see Figure 25-6) is free and available for Macintosh and Windows at www.apple.com/quicktime/. QuickTime is also included with all Macintosh computers, and installed on Windows by CD-ROM titles. Just as with RealPlayer, users can spend more time in QuickTime Player and less in a browser because of the favorites storage and Flash navigation elements in many streaming presentations.

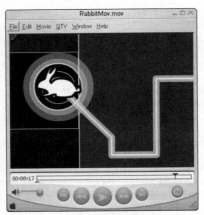

Figure 25-6: The QuickTime player offers a slick interface with retractable controls.

✦ **QuickTime Pro and QuickTime Player Pro:** For about $30, Apple sells you a key code that unlocks the content creation features of QuickTime and turns it into QuickTime Pro, enabling QuickTime-dependent applications to create a vast range of QuickTime content. QuickTime Player becomes QuickTime Player Pro: a great piece of software that provides easy content conversion and cut-and-paste video compositing, although the interface is Spartan and sometimes hides functionality. Apple has a directory of third-party QuickTime authoring resources at http://developer.apple.com/quicktime/.

✦ **QuickTime Streaming Server:** QuickTime Streaming Server delivers video over the Web using the standard RTSP, just like RealPlayer. Apple released QuickTime Streaming Server as open source software, and it is available completely free—no per stream charge, either for Mac OS X 10.4 and higher. See www.apple.com/quicktime/streamingserver/.

Note   You can find examples of QuickTime streaming content on the QuickTime home page at www.apple.com/quicktime.

Windows Media

Microsoft has released a succession of media technologies over the years in an effort to gain some sort of foothold in content creation and delivery. The history of Microsoft multimedia is an incredible story of acquisitions, rebranding, orphaned technologies, and outright copying of everybody else.

With Windows Media, however, Microsoft has gone all out, providing a solid solution with lots of partners. Still, Windows Media's greatest asset is its automatic inclusion with every Windows PC, virtually guaranteeing it a huge installed base as time goes on. Windows Media files have filename extensions of .asf or .asx. The software involved in Windows Media includes the following:

✦ **Windows Media Player:** The supercharged Windows Media Player (see Figure 25-7) received a complete face-lift when it evolved from version 6 to version 7 — and with the new changeable skins feature, it's quite the literal face-lift. Now, at version 10, it's even more powerful. In addition to Web streaming, the Windows Media Player accesses many other media types, including audio CDs, Internet radio, and portable devices. It supports many file extensions, including .asf, .asx, .avi, .mpg, .mpeg, .mp3, .qt, .aif, .mov, and .au. The Windows Media Player home page is at www.microsoft. com/windows/windowsmedia/download/default.asp. Macintosh users can find it at www.microsoft.com/mac/downloads.aspx?pid=download&location=/mac/ download/misc/winmp_osx.xml&secid=80&ssid=8&flgnosysreq=True.

Figure 25-7: The Windows Media Player offers instant access to many media types as well as switchable skins (shown here is the sexy Raptor skin).

✦ **Content creation and server software:** You can find a directory of tools for working with Windows Media at www.microsoft.com/windows/windowsmedia/. Most are from Microsoft, and all are Windows-only.

Note The Windows Media home page is located at www.windowsmedia.com and includes sample content.

Working with Video Clips

If you have short video clips you'd like to put on the Web, you may not need the industrial strength — or the hassle and expense — of a streaming media solution. Short video clips can be included in a Web page just by linking to them or embedding them.

Depending on the viewer's software setup, video clips either download completely and then start playing right away; or start playing as soon as enough of the video has arrived to make uninterrupted playback possible, as shown in Figure 25-8.

Video clips come in a few common formats, described in Table 25-1. In addition to the video format itself, what *codec* (en**co**der/**dec**oder) a particular video clip uses is also important. A codec provides video compression, and it is required for decompression at playback time. Many codecs are included with Windows and with QuickTime, so codecs are not usually a problem unless you're authoring for platforms other than Windows and Macintosh.

Figure 25-8: QuickTime Player starts playing video clips when it has downloaded enough to ensure that playback is uninterrupted.

Play position

End of presentation

Download progress indicator

Beginning of presentation

Table 25-1: Video Clip File Formats

Video Format	Typical Filename Extension	Description
MPEG	`.mpg, .mpeg, .mpe`	The MPEG video format is the work of the Motion Picture Experts Group. Windows computers usually play MPEG video clips with Windows Media Player or another, older Microsoft player. Macintosh systems play MPEG clips with QuickTime.
QuickTime	`.mov`	QuickTime movies can contain a multitude of media types and usually require QuickTime for playback.
QuickTime Video	`.mov`	A QuickTime movie that contains plain video only and can be played by almost any video player on a machine that doesn't have QuickTime installed, as long as the right codec is available.
Video for Windows (AVI)	`.avi`	The popular (but now officially unsupported) format used by Microsoft's Video for Windows (also known as ActiveMovie or NetShow). As with QuickTime Video, clips can be played in almost any player, as long as the right codec is installed.

Caution

One codec to watch for if you're making cross-platform movies is the Intel Indeo Video codec, sometimes used for Video for Windows (AVI) files. The Indeo codec for Macintosh is not included with QuickTime and must be installed manually by Macintosh users.

MPEG, QuickTime Video, or AVI clips are good candidates for linking or embedding because a wide variety of players on multiple platforms can play them. QuickTime movies are best aimed squarely at the QuickTime Player because of the multiple media types that they contain.

Linking to Video

To keep 21st-century TV/movie-addicted users interested in your site, you might want to spice things up by including a (low-bandwidth!) video or two. To add a video clip to your Dreamweaver Web page, follow these steps:

1. Select the text, image, or dynamic element that you want to serve as the link to the video file.

Tip If you use an image as a link, you might want to use a frame from the video clip in order to provide a preview.

2. In the Property inspector, enter the name of the video file in the Link text field or click the Folder icon to browse for the file. To choose a dynamic source, choose the Select File Name From Data Sources option in the Select File dialog box. Be sure your selected data source contains either relative or absolute links to a video file.

3. Because video files can be quite large, it's also good practice to note the file size next to the link name or enter it in the Alt text field, as shown in Figure 25-9.

Figure 25-9: You can insert any video file for user-download by creating a link to it, as if it were a simple Web page.

Embedding Video

You can gain more control over the way your video clip plays by embedding it in the Web page with the `<embed>` tag. Modifying the attributes of the `<embed>` tag enables you to modify how the video is presented. Video clips inserted this way play back in whatever players are available, just as linked video clips do.

The Assets panel includes a Movies category that holds QuickTime movies, MPEG videos, and Windows Media file types. As with all the other Assets panel categories, you must click the Refresh Site List button (the curved arrow at the bottom of the Assets panel) to initially populate the panel with all the movies in the current site. The preview pane includes a Play button for displaying the movies before they are inserted in the page.

To embed a simple video clip in a Web page, follow these steps:

1. Choose Insert ➪ Media ➪ Plugin. Alternatively, you can select the Plugin object from the Media menu of the Insert bar found in the Common category or drag the file from the Movie category of the Assets panel to your Web page.

2. If you inserted a Plugin object, select the video file in the Select File dialog box. Movies dragged onto the page from the Assets panel already include the source path. The Plugin placeholder is displayed as a 32 x 32 icon.

3. In the Plugin Property inspector, enter the dimensions of your video clip in the width and height boxes, marked W and H, respectively, or size the Plugin object directly by dragging one of its selection handles.

Playing Videos within Dreamweaver

Dreamweaver can access and use Netscape plugins to display video right in the Document window at design time. These plugins can be installed in Netscape's Plugins folder, in Internet Explorer's Plugins folder, or in Dreamweaver's own Plugins folder. Dreamweaver checks all three every time it starts up. Many plugins come with browser-specific installation programs. You can maintain your plugins more easily if you install the correct plugins into Netscape and enable Dreamweaver to use them from there.

Whenever a file is embedded for playback via a plugin, a green Play button appears in the Property inspector. To play a particular video in Dreamweaver's Document window, all you have to do is select the Plugin placeholder and click the Play button. The video begins playing, and the green Play button becomes a red Stop button. To stop playback, just click the Stop button.

Tip   How can playing a video during the design phase be useful? I've used this capability to sample the background color of the page from the background of a video's title or ending frame so that the video clip fits seamlessly into the page.

You can also use the menus and the corresponding keyboard shortcuts to control the digital video in the Document window: View ➪ Plugins ➪ Play or Ctrl+Alt+P (Command+Option+P), and View ➪ Plugins ➪ Stop or Ctrl+Alt+X (Command+Option+X). If you have multiple videos inserted on the page, you can play them all by choosing View ➪ Plugins ➪ Play All or by using the keyboard shortcut Ctrl+Alt+Shift+P (Command+Option+Shift+P). You can stop them with View ➪ Plugins ➪ Stop All or Ctrl+Alt+Shift+X (Command+Option+Shift+X).

Caution   Unsupported plugins are listed in the UnsupportedPlugins.txt file in Dreamweaver's Configuration/Plugins folder. As of this writing, no plugins are listed in this file. If you continue to have problems playing plugins in Dreamweaver, check the file for compatibility.

Inserting QuickTime Movies

The HTML command for incorporating a QuickTime movie (or any other medium that requires a plugin) is the <embed> tag. Because so many different types of plugins exist, Dreamweaver uses a generic Plugin inspector that enables an unlimited number of parameters to be specified. If you regularly work with QuickTime movies, try using a custom QuickTime Dreamweaver object such as the one shown in Figure 25-10 from Brendan Dawes. This object, available on the CD-ROM that comes with this book, can streamline the process. Although you must still add some parameters by hand, having easy access to the most common ones can be a real timesaver.

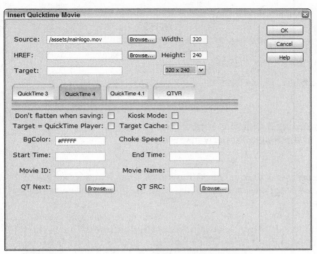

Figure 25-10: Add a third-party QuickTime object to
Dreamweaver to simplify embedding QuickTime movies.

Only three `<embed>` tag parameters are absolutely required for a QuickTime movie: the source of the file, the movie's width, and the movie's height. The QuickTime Plugin, however, also offers an amazing array of additional `<embed>` tag attributes to enable you to fine-tune the way content is presented.

Note The QuickTime Plugin is used by both Netscape and Internet Explorer on both Windows and Macintosh to enable the browser to interface with QuickTime.

To insert a QuickTime movie in your Web page, follow these steps:

1. Choose Insert ⇨ Media ⇨ Plugin. Alternatively, you can select the Plugin object from the Media group of the Insert bar found in the Common category or drag the file from the Movie category of the Assets panel to your Web page.

2. If you insert a Plugin object, select the QuickTime movie file in the Select File dialog box. If you drag the movie file from the Assets panel, the Plugin's Src attribute is automatically set to the QuickTime movie file pathname.

Tip If you're working on a Macintosh and your QuickTime movie doesn't have a filename extension, add **.mov** to the end of its name before embedding it or placing it on the Web.

3. In the Plugin Property inspector (shown in Figure 25-11), enter the dimensions of your QuickTime movie in the width (W) and height (H) fields, or size the Plugin object directly by dragging one of its selection handles.

Width field   Plugin Src text field

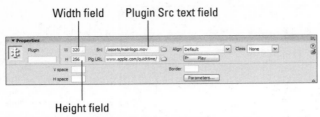

Height field

Figure 25-11: When inserting a QuickTime movie, specify the properties and values in the Plugin Property inspector.

Tip   If you don't know the dimensions of your QuickTime movie, open it in the QuickTime Player, choose Movie ⇨ Get Movie Properties, and select Size from the options list on the right of the dialog box that appears.

4. In the Plg URL text field, enter **http://www.apple.com/quicktime/**. This is the Web address to which users who don't have QuickTime are directed by their browser.

5. Click the Parameters button in the Plugin Property inspector to open the Parameters dialog box (see Figure 25-12), where you can enter additional `<embed>` tag attributes: the name in the left column and the value in the right column. Use Tab to move between the columns. Table 25-2 lists the most commonly used `<embed>` tag parameters for QuickTime movies. Use this list to add any parameters and click OK when you're done.

Note   Any of the parameters or their values can be linked to a data source by clicking the lightning-bolt icon in the value field and choosing an appropriate data field from the Dynamic Data dialog box that opens.

Figure 25-12: Use the Parameters dialog box to enter attributes for any plugin. Dynamic values can be entered by clicking the lightning-bolt icon and choosing a field from a defined recordset.

Table 25-2: QuickTime Plugin Parameters

QuickTime Plugin Parameter	Possible Values	Description
Autoplay	True or false; default set by user in QuickTime Plugin Settings	When set to false, a movie won't play until the user clicks Play in the controller. Otherwise, it starts playing as soon as enough data is downloaded to ensure uninterrupted playback.

QuickTime Plugin Parameter	Possible Values	Description
Bgcolor	RGB colors in hexadecimal, such as "#FFFFFF"; or valid HTML color names, such as "red"	Specifies the color of the space set aside by the width and height attributes but not taken up by the QuickTime movie. Add a border to a QuickTime movie by setting the appropriate bgcolor and increasing the width and height attributes by a few pixels.
Cache	True or false; default set by user in QuickTime Plugin Settings	Specifies whether the browser should store the movie in its cache for later retrieval. Doesn't work in IE.
Controller	True (default for most movies) or false (default for QuickTime VR, Flash, and image files)	Displays the controller panel attached to the bottom of the movie.
Dontflatten whensaving	(does not take a value)	When included, using the Save As QuickTime option on the QuickTime Plugin's controller menu saves the movie without resolving references (not self-contained).
endtime	30-frame SMPTE time-code — hours:minutes:seconds:frames (30ths of a second)	Indicates the point in the movie where playback should stop.
Height	A value in pixels; usually the height of the movie	Reserves a space in the page for the QuickTime movie.
Hidden	(does not take a value)	Tells the QuickTime Plugin not to show the movie. Audio is played, however.
Href	URL	A link to go to when the movie is clicked. You can supply either an absolute or a relative URL. QuickTime movies replace the current movie in-place; Web pages open in the browser.
kioskmode	True or false (default)	Eliminates the QuickTime Plugin's controller menu when set to true.
Loop	True, false (default), or palindrome	Causes the movie to loop continuously when set to true. The palindrome value causes the QuickTime Player to play alternately forward and backward.
Movieid	A number	A number identifying the movie so that another wired sprite movie can control it.
Moviename	A name	A name identifying the movie so that another wired sprite movie can control it.
Playeveryframe	True or false (default)	When set to true, forces the movie to play every frame, even if it must do so at a slower rate than real time. Disables audio and QuickTime Music tracks.
Pluginspage	www.apple.com/quicktime	Where users who don't have QuickTime should be sent to get it.

Continued

Table 25-2 *(continued)*

QuickTime Plugin Parameter	*Possible Values*	*Description*
Qtnextn	URL	Specifies a movie as being *n* in a sequence of movies. The movie specified in the src attribute is movie 0 (zero).
Qtnext	goto*n*	Tells the QuickTime Plugin to open movie *n* in an already specified sequence of movies.
Qtsrc	URL	Tells the QuickTime Plugin to open this URL instead of the one specified by the src attribute. This is a way to open files that don't have a .mov filename extension — such as MP3 files — with the QuickTime Plugin, regardless of how the user's system is set up. Use a dummy movie in the src attribute.
qtsrcchokespeed	Movie-rate, or a number in bytes per second	Downloads the movie specified in the qtsrc attribute in chunks; movie-rate indicates to use the movie's data rate.
scale	tofit, aspect, or a number (default is 1)	Resizes the QuickTime Player movie. By setting scale to fit, you can scale the movie to the dimensions of the embedded box as specified by the height and width values. Setting scale to aspect resizes the movie to either the height or the width while maintaining the proper aspect ratio of the movie. Set to a number; the size of the movie is multiplied by that number.
starttime	30-frame SMPTE time-code — hours:minutes:seconds:frames (30ths of a second)	Indicates the point in the movie where playback should start.
Target	Name of a valid frame or window (_self, _parent, _top, _blank, or an explicit frame/window name) or QuickTimePlayer	Enables the link specified in the href attribute to be targeted to a specific frame or window. The value QuickTimePlayer causes the movie specified in the href attribute to be opened in the QuickTime Player.
Targetcache	true or false (default)	Same as the cache attribute but for the movie called by a poster movie using the href attribute. (Poster movies are discussed later in this chapter in the sidebar entitled "Using a Poster Movie.")
Volume	0 to 100 (default)	Controls the volume of the audio track(s). 0 is softest; 100 is loudest.
Width	A value in pixels; usually the width of the movie	Reserves a space in the page for the QuickTime movie.

Using a Poster Movie

One of the nicest features of the QuickTime Plugin is the capability to have one movie replace itself with another. This enables you to place very lightweight (small file size), single-image *poster movies* into your Web pages instead of the full clips, so that the rest of the elements in your page load quickly. When the user clicks a poster movie, it replaces itself with your full movie, which begins downloading or streaming immediately. A poster movie can be a preview of the full movie that replaces it or a generic QuickTime image, as shown in the following figure. It's even possible to use poster movies to place a number of movies in a single page, enabling the user to choose which ones to view without downloading the rest, as shown in the following figure.

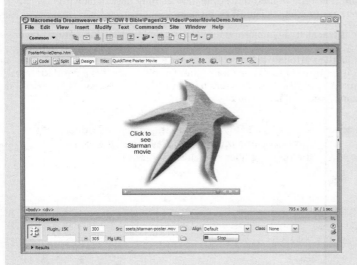

Creating a poster movie requires QuickTime Pro. Simply open your movie in QuickTime Player Pro and move to the frame you'd like to use as a preview. Choose File ➪ Export, and select Movie to Picture from the Export options list and Photo-JPEG from the Use options list. This exports the current frame as a QuickTime Image using JPEG compression. Choose File ➪ New Player to create a new untitled movie, and then select File ➪ Import to import your picture into this new movie. Save your work as a self-contained movie. A good idea for a filename might be the name of your full movie with *poster* prefixed.

Embed your poster movie in your Web page as described previously in this chapter and use the Plugin Property inspector's Parameters button to add the `href` attribute with the value set to the URL of your full movie, so that the `<embed>` tag looks like the following:

```
<embed src="my_poster_movie.mov" width="360" height="180"
      href="my_full_movie.mov">
</embed>
```

You can also make multiple-frame poster movies. As long as you keep the file size low, your pages seem to load more quickly, and you provide your users more control over the way they experience them.

Tip   Dreamweaver's Plugin Property inspector enables you to enter several additional attributes generally used with other objects, such as images. These include `Align` (alignment), `V Space` (vertical space), `H Space` (horizontal space), and `Border` (border). You can also enter a name in the Plugin text field if you plan to refer to your QuickTime movie in JavaScript or another programming language.

QuickTime Versions

Before inserting a QuickTime movie into a Web page, it's helpful to know what version of QuickTime your movie requires. Because QuickTime movies can contain a variety of track types, each containing a different type of medium, some movies may play back with QuickTime 3, whereas others require QuickTime 4 or higher.

You can identify the different tracks in a QuickTime movie by opening it in QuickTime Player and choosing Movie ⇨ Get Movie Properties. In the QuickTime dialog box that appears, the options list on the left details the various tracks, as shown in Figure 25-13. If your movie has Flash or MP3 audio tracks, it requires QuickTime 4 or higher for playback. It's a good idea to note this somewhere in your Web page and offer users a link to `http://www.apple.com/quicktime/` so that they can upgrade if necessary.

Figure 25-13: In addition to the streaming video track, this QuickTime movie has a Flash track that provides the opening titles and closing credits.

Playing QuickTime VR

QuickTime VR (QTVR) enables the user to look around in a virtual space created from a panoramic image or to rotate an object around its center point in three dimensions (object movies). The QuickTime VR author can also designate certain areas in the movie as hotspots that, when selected by the user, activate a link to another page or another movie. Although purists argue that QTVR is not really virtual reality, the technology is a low-bandwidth, quick-and-dirty virtual reality that makes sense on today's Web. QTVR is commonly used to show homes, cars, and other products to potential buyers.

When you view a QuickTime VR movie, the QuickTime Player provides Zoom buttons (– and +), as shown in Figure 25-14, and a custom mouse pointer pans the image left and right.

QuickTime VR `<embed>` tag attributes are entered in the same manner as other QuickTime Plugin attributes: Click the Parameters button in the Plugin Property inspector to open the Parameters dialog box and enter attributes and values. As with a regular QuickTime Player movie, the only required parameters for a QTVR movie are the source file, movie width, and movie height.

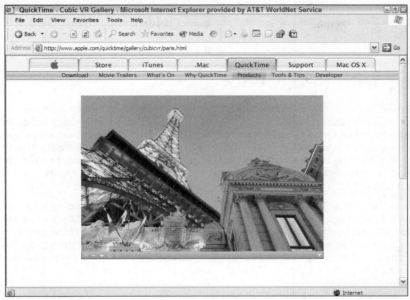

Figure 25-14: QuickTime VR's panoramic views enable the user to look around in a panoramic picture by moving the cursor right, left, up, and down.

Table 25-3 lists the QuickTime Plugin `<embed>` tag attributes that work with QuickTime VR only.

Table 25-3: Additional Parameters for QTVR Movies

QuickTime VR Parameter	Possible Values	Description
Correction	None or full (default)	Applies the correction filter.
Fov	0 (default) to 360	Specifies the initial field-of-view angle, in degrees.
Hotspotn	URL	Defines the URL for any designated hotspot. Replace *n* with the identification number given the hotspot during QTVR authoring.
Node	A number less than or equal to the number of nodes in the movie	Specifies which node of a multinode movie is opened first.
pan	0 (default) to 360	Sets the initial pan angle in degrees.
target{n}	_self, _parent, _top, _blank, a frame or window name	Targets the URL of the similarly numbered hotspot at a specific frame or window.
tilt	−42.5 to 42.5 (0 is the default)	Sets the initial tilt angle in degrees.

Caution   Some parameters, meaningful to regular QuickTime Player movies, are not appropriate for QuickTime VR movies. These include `autoplay`, `controller`, `hidden`, `href`, `loop`, `playeveryframe`, `target`, and `volume`.

Streaming with RealMedia

If you've ever downloaded a few minutes of digital video over a slow modem connection, you know the reason why streaming video was invented. In an age when immediacy rules, the wait until the complete video file is transferred and then loaded into the video player can seem to last an eternity. *Streaming*, on the other hand, enables the multimedia content to begin playing as soon as the first complete packet of information is received, and then to continue playing as more digital information arrives. Video is just one form of media to get the streaming treatment: You can also stream audio, animation, text, and other formats.

Regardless of which streaming video protocol you use, the procedure for incorporating the file on your Web page is basically the same, although the details (such as filename extensions) differ. In order to demonstrate the general technique and still offer some specific information you can use, the next section shows you how to include streaming RealMedia clips with Dreamweaver. Check with the developer of the streaming video format you plan to use to get the precise installation details. Typically, a great deal of information is available for free on the developers' Web sites.

Creating RealMedia Metafiles

When incorporating RealMedia into your Web pages, you have a variety of playback options. You can set the video so that a free-floating RealPlayer is invoked, or you can specify that the video appears inline on your Web page. You can also customize the controls that appear on your Web page so that only the ones you want — at the size you want — are included.

RealMedia uses its own specialized server software called RealServer to transmit encoded video files. Rather than call this server and the digital video file directly, RealMedia uses a system of *metafiles* to link to the RealMedia server and file. A metafile is an ordinary text file containing the appropriate URL pointing to the RealServer and video file. The metafiles are distinguished from the media files by their filename extensions:

✦ RealMedia files: `.rm`, `.ra`, `.rp`, `.rt`, `.swf`

✦ Metafile that launches the independent RealPlayer: `.ram`

✦ Metafile that launches the RealPlayer Plugin: `.rpm`

To create the metafile, open your favorite text editor and insert one or more lines pointing to your server and the video files. Instead of using the `http://` locator seen with most URLs, RealMedia files address the RealServer with an `rtsp://` (Real-Time Streaming Protocol) indicator. The contents of the file should take the following form

```
rtsp://hostname/path/file
```

where `hostname` is the domain name of the server on which the RealMedia files are stored, `path` is the path to the file, and `file` is the name of the RealMedia file. For example, to display a training video, the metafile contents might look like the following:

```
rtsp://www.trainers.com/videos/training01.rm
```

HTTP Streaming

To gain the maximum throughput of your RealVideo files, it's best to use the RealServer software. However, some Web site clients must economize and can't afford the specialized server. It is not widely known that you can use a regular World Wide Web server to stream RealVideo and other RealMedia files over HTTP.

Two prerequisites exist for HTTP streaming: Your system administrator must first correctly configure the MIME types, and you must provide multiple files to match the right user-selectable modem speeds. The proper MIME types are as follows:

+ audio/x-pn-RealAudio (for `.ra`, `.rm`, or `.ram` files)

+ audio/x-pn-RealAudio-plugin (for `.rpm` files)

+ video/x-pn-RealVideo (for `.ra`, `.rm`, or `.ram` files)

+ video/x-pn-RealVideo-plugin (for `.rpm` files)

RealServer automatically selects the right file for the user's modem connection. If you are using HTTP streaming capabilities, you should offer multiple files to accommodate the various Internet connection rates, such as 28.8K, 56K, and higher (for cable and DSL).

Besides a reduction in download speed, the other disadvantage to using HTTP streaming instead of RealServer streaming is the reduced number of simultaneous users who can be served. RealServer can handle hundreds of connections at the same time; HTTP streaming is far more limited.

You can include multiple video clips by putting each one on its own line, separated by a single return. RealMedia plays each clip in succession, and the user can skip from one clip to another.

Inserting RealMedia in Your Web Page

After you've created both the encoded RealMedia file and the metafiles, you're ready to insert them into your Web page. You have two basic techniques for including RealMedia, either as a link or using the `<embed>` tag.

Using a Link

Generally, if you want to invoke the free-floating RealPlayer, you use a link; the `href` attribute is set to an address for a metafile, as follows:

```
<a href="videos/howto01.ram">Demonstration</a>
```

When the link is selected, it calls the metafile that, in turn, calls the video file on the RealServer. As the file begins to download to the user's system, the RealPlayer program is invoked and starts to display the video as soon as possible through the independent video window. The link can be inserted in Dreamweaver through either the Text or Image Property inspector.

Using <embed>

If, on the other hand, you'd like to make the video appear inline with the Web page's text or graphics, you use Dreamweaver's Plugin object to insert an <embed> tag. Position the pointer where you want the RealMedia to be displayed, and either choose Insert ➪ Media ➪ Plugin or select the Plugin object from the Media category of the Insert bar. In the Select File dialog box that appears, select the video's metafile.

When the Plugin object representing the RealMedia clip is selected, you can enter values for the <embed> tag in the Property inspector. The only attributes required for a RealMedia clip, as with the QuickTime Player object, are the file source and the width and height of the movie. Similarly, as you can with QuickTime Player, you can control your RealMedia movie with a healthy number of attributes. Enter attributes by clicking the Parameters button on the Plugin Property inspector and entering attributes and their values in the Parameters dialog box (shown earlier in Figure 25-9). RealMedia parameters are listed in Table 25-4.

Table 25-4: Parameters for RealMedia Movies

RealMedia G2 Parameter	Possible Values	Description
Autostart	True or false (default)	Tells RealPlayer to start playing as soon as content is available.
Console	*name*, _master, _unique	Determines the console name for each control in a Web page that has multiple controls. Force controls on a page to refer to the same file by giving them all the same *name*. A value of _master links to all controls on a page, whereas _unique connects to no other instances.
Controls	All (default), controlpanel, imagewindow, infovolume panel, infopanel, playbutton, positionslider, positionfield, statuspanel, statusbar, stopbutton, statusfield, volumeslider	Enables the placement of individual control panel elements in the Web page. You can use multiple controls in one attribute or multiple <embed> tags to build a custom RealMedia interface.
nolabels	True or false (default)	Suppresses the Title, Author, and Copyright labels in the Status panel. If you set nolabels to true, the actual data is still visible.

Summary

Digital video on the Web is in its infancy. Bandwidth is still too restricted to enable full-screen, full-motion movies, no matter what the format. However, you can include download-able as well as streaming video content through Dreamweaver's Plugin object and Plugin Property inspector. If you're considering adding video to your Web pages, keep these points in mind:

✦ Even with compression, digital video has steep storage and download requirements.

✦ Flash Video is an easy-to-use, comprehensive solution now immediately available in Dreamweaver in either progressive download or streaming delivery modes.

✦ You can include a digital video movie to be downloaded in your Web page by linking to it as if it were a Web page.

✦ Use Dreamweaver's Plugin object when you want your video to be presented inline on your Web page. The Plugin Property inspector then enables you to alter the video's parameters for any video architecture.

✦ QuickTime is a cross-platform, multimedia architecture that offers much more than just video. QuickTime movies can include QuickTime VR, MIDI music, 3D objects, Flash movies, and more.

✦ To enable your visitors to view your digital video clips as soon as possible, use a streaming video technology such as RealMedia, QuickTime, or Windows Media. Streaming video files can be displayed in a separate player or embedded in the Web page.

In the next chapter, you learn how Dreamweaver helps you incorporate sound and music into your Web pages.

✦   ✦   ✦

Using Audio on Your Web Page

Web sites tend to be divided into two categories: those totally without sound, and those that use a lot of it — there's not much middle ground. Many music and entertainment sites rely heavily on both streaming audio and downloadable audio files, such as MP3.

In this chapter, you learn how to use audio in the Web pages you design with Dreamweaver. You look at traditional digital audio formats such as AIFF and WAV, and how you can turn these into files suitable for publishing on the Web, in formats such as MP3 and RealAudio. You also look at music formats, such as standard MIDI files and QuickTime Music.

Lest you forget that you're Dreamweavinghere, you also look at some Dreamweaver extensions you can use to get audio-enabled sites up and running in no time. But before you leap into those deep waters, it's a good idea to get an overview of digital audio and its place on the Web.

Cross-Reference Because the primary technologies for distributing streaming audio are also the primary technologies for streaming video, you may find it helpful to familiarize yourself with the Big Three streaming media technologies — RealMedia, QuickTime, and Windows Media — introduced in Chapter 25.

Digital Audio Fundamentals

Digital audio files are digitized representations of sound waves. Although not as heavy as digital video, digital audio files — even those that have been compressed — are still a strain for today's Web. As usual, you can provide a better experience for users of your Web site if you minimize file sizes wherever possible.

File Formats

Many different formats for digital audio files are in use today across the various computer platforms. The most common formats are described in Table 26-1 and can be identified by their unique filename extensions and/or by their icons on Macintosh systems.

Table 26-1: Web Digital Audio File Formats

Audio Format	Typical Filename Extension	Description
AU	.au, .snd	Very common on the early Unix-dominated Web. Uncompressed and no longer suitable for Web use.
AIFF	.aif, .aiff	The Audio Interchange File Format was developed by Apple. Uncompressed versions can be played in most browsers, but avoid using AIFF on the Web if possible because of its large file sizes.
Flash	.swf	Not just an animation format, Flash streams PCM- or MP3-compressed audio at various bit rates.
MP3	.mp3, .mp2	The MPEG Audio Layer 3 format features high-quality digital audio files with excellent compression. MP3 has become the standard for downloadable music. It plays in QuickTime Player 4+, RealPlayer 6+, Windows Media Player 5.2+, and a whole range of stand-alone players that work as browser helper applications.
QuickTime	.mov	A QuickTime movie with a soundtrack only.
RealAudio	.ra or .ram	The audio component of RealNetworks' RealMedia. Lots of players. Good quality at low bit rates, but not as good as MP3.
Rich Music Format	.rmf	Beatnik's hybrid audio/music format. Samples are either PCM or MP3 compressed.
Shockwave Audio	.swa	The audio component of Shockwave, they're low bit-rate MP3 files with a different file header. They stream over HTTP, and any MP3 player can play them locally.
WAV	.wav	Co-developed by Microsoft and IBM, this is the default audio format for Windows. Uncompressed versions play in browsers, but avoid using WAV files on the Web whenever possible because of their large file sizes.
Windows Media	.asf, .asx, .wma, .wmv	Microsoft's streaming media solution.

Which audio format should you choose? That depends on a combination of factors, including your target audience, available bandwidth, and the purpose of the audio content.

Although most browsers can play standard digital audio files, such as AIFF and WAV, the sheer uncompressed bulk of these files renders them unsuitable for the Internet, especially now that so many highly compressed formats exist. In the early days of the Web, with slower computers and less advanced compression technologies, these uncompressed audio files were the only game in town. But today, fast computers are capable of easily decoding MP3 and RealAudio, and free players for those formats are common.

A live Internet broadcast dictates a streaming solution such as RealAudio, QuickTime, or Windows Media. If you're offering complete songs for download, you may not have to look any further than MP3. It's not uncommon to offer a sound file in multiple formats. Although many users have more than one player, offering your audio in a few formats gives you a better chance of reaching everybody.

Converting one audio file format to another typically involves opening the source file in an audio editor that can read that format and exporting it in another format. If you lack a professional audio editor such as SoundForge or Peak, a simple alternative is to use QuickTime Pro; it reads and writes a lot of formats. You can also easily cut and paste sections of files — to remove or add a few seconds of silence, for example.

Making Audio Files Lighter

In addition to categorizing audio by file format, you can also think of audio on the Web as being in one of two categories: uncompressed and compressed. AIFF and WAV audio files come in compressed and uncompressed formats, but only the uncompressed versions play in Web browsers. If you can't compress an audio file in some way, the only way to reduce its file size is to reduce its quality in one of three ways:

✦ **Convert a stereo file into a mono file:** A stereo file has two audio channels, whereas a mono file has only one. Converting a stereo file to mono halves its file size.

✦ **Lower the bit depth:** from 16-bit to 8-bit, for example. A lower bit depth reduces the accuracy and cleanness of the stored audio waveforms.

✦ **Lower the sample rate:** from 44 kHz to 22 kHz, for example. This lowers the range of audio frequencies in the recording, chopping off the "high end" or treble frequencies.

You can make the preceding conversions by opening the audio file in an application, such as Sonic Foundry Sound Forge, and changing the parameters, as shown in Figure 26-1.

Network-ready audio file types that are specifically created for the Internet, such as MP3 and RealAudio, are compressed through encoding. Rather than arbitrarily lowering the quality of the file to make it lighter, you pick a target bit rate, as shown in Figure 26-2, and the encoding software produces the best quality file it can at that bit rate. If you've ever exported a JPEG graphic from an image editor and specified a target file size, the principle is the same.

When working with a compressed audio format, you ideally start with the best master copy that you have in an uncompressed format, such as AIFF or WAV, and then encode that audio file as MP3 or RealAudio. If you want your audio to move quickly, even over dial-up connections, choose a low bit rate such as 24 Kbps, but be aware that the sound quality will be less than ideal.

Caution   Always keep a master copy of your audio file when you're encoding. Encoding a file is often a *lossy* compression; in other words, information/quality is lost in order to create smaller files. Although you can convert an MP3 back to an AIFF, it will not be the same quality as the original AIFF from which the MP3 was made. The process is similar to converting a TIFF to a JPEG; if you try to convert back to the TIFF, the quality of the image is reduced.

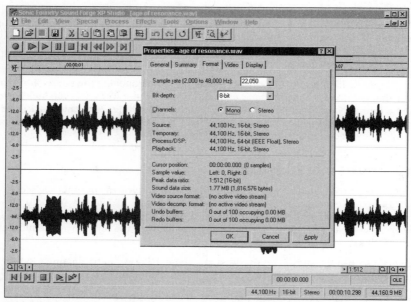

Figure 26-1: Changing a WAV file's Sample Rate, Bit-depth, and Channels settings in Sound Forge from 44,100, 16-bit, stereo to 22,050, 8-bit, mono will produce a much smaller file with significantly degraded sound quality.

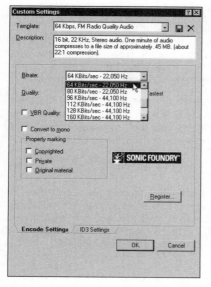

Figure 26-2: Choosing a 32K bits-per-second (32 Kbps) rate when converting a WAV file to an MP3 file in Sound Forge.

MIDI Files

In the 19th century, before the technology to electronically record audio existed, a musical performance could be "recorded" by making a series of stipples on a cylinder. The performance could then be played "live" for the listener through a music box. Later, player pianos used rolls of paper with appropriate holes punched in them to cause the piano keys to mimic the performances of far away or long-dead musicians. In the early 1980s, electronic musical instrument manufacturers created the Musical Instrument Digital Interface (MIDI) to enable the keys of one electronic keyboard to trigger the sounds in another. It wasn't long before somebody realized that the MIDI information being output by all electronic keyboards could be recorded, thus turning any electronic instrument into a modern-day music box or player piano.

The key to using MIDI files on the Web is their very small file size. A MIDI file is the ultimate in compressed sound: The musical instruments aren't even included! For example, a 3-minute, full-fidelity, 128 bps stereo MP3 file weighs in at just under 3MB. A QuickTime movie that contains only a music track can give you 10 minutes of music for 60K with similar fidelity, although you're limited to the sounds contained in the QuickTime synthesizer.

Today, MIDI files appear on the Web in one of three ways:

✦ **QuickTime Music:** MIDI information is stored as a music track within a QuickTime movie, and it is played back through the QuickTime software synthesizer (or through a hardware synthesizer such as a sound card if the user has configured QuickTime to use one). The QuickTime synthesizer sounds have often been criticized for being a little bland. Music tracks can coexist with all other kinds of QuickTime media in one movie, so they make excellent soundtracks for digital video tracks. QuickTime movies have a filename extension of `.mov`.

✦ **Rich Music Format:** Beatnik's hybrid audio/music format. MIDI information is played through the Beatnik player's software synthesizer, which contains generally excellent and often original sounds. Moreover, additional instrument sounds can be included in an RMF by adding digital audio samples with the Beatnik Editor. RMF files are unique among music file formats in that users cannot get the raw MIDI data out of them. Some content authors see this is as an advantage. RMF files have an `.rmf` filename extension.

✦ **Standard MIDI files:** This is the raw data of MIDI music files. Their biggest drawback is that the Web author cannot know what kind of synthesizer the user will employ to play back a MIDI file. If he is using older Windows machines, this synthesizer may not even include actual instrument sounds, but instead use FM synthesis to come up with very poor approximations. Standard MIDI files have a filename extension of `.mid`, `.midi`, or `.smf`.

Occasionally, you may want to render a MIDI file as a digital audio file in order to play it in a situation where a synthesizer is unavailable. Doing this the hard way involves playing the file through a synthesizer and recording the output to a digital audio file. You have an easier way, however, if you have QuickTime Player Pro. Open your QuickTime Music or import your Standard MIDI file into QuickTime Player Pro and then choose File ➪ Export and specify Music to AIFF. QuickTime Player Pro creates a digital audio file of its "performance" of the music using the QuickTime software synthesizer. You can also convert a QuickTime Music track back into a Standard MIDI file. Choose Music to Standard MIDI when you export.

Caution   RMF files are designed to disallow this conversion. Always keep the original Standard MIDI file when you create an RMF.

MP3 Mini-Primer

The MP3 audio format has quite simply taken the Web—and the world—by storm. Whereas other downloadable music formats come with caveats such as ownership by one company or built-in limitations on how users can use the files they purchase, MP3 just did the work and got the job done. MP3 software players are common. A number of manufacturers offer MP3 hardware for a variety of uses, including home, car, and personal stereos.

 Tip   MP3.com remains the one-stop place for information about MP3. Visit www.mp3.com.

Generally, the MP3 "scene" shows interest in new and/or unusual artists, offers a selection of dynamic, full-featured players (see Figure 26-3), and maintains an attitude of music appreciation. Conversely, non-MP3 downloadable music has generally featured bland players, corporate music, proprietary technologies, and an unhealthy fascination with watermarking and controlling content. It's not hard to see why the market chose MP3.

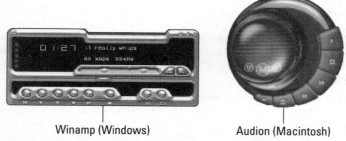

Winamp (Windows)   Audion (Macintosh)

Figure 26-3: Many stand-alone MP3 players, such as Winamp and Audion, feature sexy looks that can be changed by applying new *skins*.

Player Support

Table 26-2 lists common MP3 player software—including old friends such as RealPlayer that now handle MP3—and the URLs where they can be found. Many of these applications offer to set themselves up as browser-helper applications. You might feature some of these links at the bottom of pages with MP3 content, so users who are new to MP3 can get a leg up.

Table 26-2: Common MP3 Players

Player Software	URL
Audion (Mac only)	www.panic.com/audion/
iTunes	www.apple.com/itunes/
QuickTime Player	www.apple.com/quicktime/

Player Software	URL
RealOne Player	www.real.com/
Winamp (Windows only)	www.winamp.com/
Windows Media Player	www.microsoft.com/windows/windowsmedia/download **(Windows)** http://www.microsoft.com/mac/downloads.aspx?pid=download&location=/mac/download/misc/winmp_osx.xml&secid=80&ssid=8&flgnosysreq=True **(Mac)**

Note Providing users with a link to MP3.com (www.mp3.com) is another way to offer them a great selection of players.

Encoding MP3

The most common MP3 files are downloadable music files. These files aim for CD quality and so are recorded with a bit rate of 128 Kbps. This works out to a little less than 1MB per minute for a stereo, 44.1 kHz file, which is too heavy to move quickly on today's Web. You can encode an MP3 using a variety of bit rates, however. Lower bit rates mean lower quality, but even at 16 Kbps, speech sounds pretty good; and the 60K per minute bulk of a mono file will be music to your ears.

Caution Beware of MP3 encoders that sacrifice quality for speed. Many encoders simply eliminate the upper audio frequency range so that they can encode the rest in record time. Although this might be fine if you're encoding your CD collection into a massive jukebox on your computer, it is less than ideal for content creators who want the best-quality encoded files. One source for more information is www.mp3-converter.com/encoders/mp3_encoder_reviews.htm.

Linking to Audio Files

The simplest way to add sound to a Web page is to create a link to an audio file by specifying the filepath in the Link text box of the Text or Image Property inspector. When the user clicks that link, the sound file downloads, and whatever program has been designated to handle that type of file opens in a separate window. An exception to this is the QuickTime Plugin. Instead of opening linked audio files in the QuickTime Player, it opens them within the browser window as if they were a new Web page. To get back to your Web page, the user clicks the browser's Back button.

To create a link to an audio file in Dreamweaver, follow these steps:

1. Select the text or image that you want to serve as the link to the audio file.

2. In the Property inspector, enter the name of the audio file in the Link text box, or click the Folder icon to browse for the file. To link to a dynamic source, choose Select File Name from Data Sources and select an appropriate field from the available recordset(s).

3. Because audio files can be large, it's good practice to note the file size next to the link name, as shown in Figure 26-4, or to enter it in the Alt text box for your image.

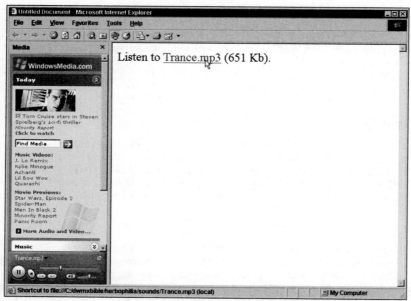

Figure 26-4: When the Trance.mp3 link is clicked, Internet Explorer 6 downloads the `Trance.mp3` file and then opens/plays it in the browser's built-in MP3 player (lower left).

When you use the link technique for incorporating sound, you have no control over the position or appearance of the player. However, you can control these factors and more by embedding your audio.

Embedding Sounds and Music

Embedding a sound file truly integrates the audio into your Web page. Embedding the sound file also gives you a much greater degree of control over the presentation of the audio player itself, including the following:

✦ The clip's play volume

✦ Which part, if any, of the player's controls is visible

✦ The starting and ending points of the music clip

As with any other embedded object, you can present the visual display inline with other text elements — aligned to the top, middle, or bottom of the text, or blocked left or right to enable text to flow around it. Dreamweaver controls all these parameters through two different objects: the Plugin object and the ActiveX object. Each type of object calls a specific type of player. Calling the Windows Media Player as an ActiveX object explicitly enables you to modify a great number of parameters for Internet Explorer — which are completely ignored by Navigator. You learn about all your embedding options, including techniques for cross-browser audio, in the next few sections.

Note
The Assets panel does not include a Sound or Audio button. To insert audio elements, you must use the Plugin button in the Media group in the Common category of the Insert bar.

As with video, Dreamweaver uses the generic Plugin object to embed audio in your Web page. The object requires only three parameters: the source of the audio file and the width and height of the object. To embed an audio file in your Web page, follow these steps in Dreamweaver:

1. Position the cursor where you want the control panel for the audio file to appear.

2. Insert the Plugin object by choosing Insert ⇨ Media ⇨ Plugin or by clicking the Plugin button from the Media menu from the Insert bar's Common category.

3. In the Select File dialog box that appears, choose your audio file.

4. Use *either* of these two techniques to size the Plugin placeholder:

   • Click the resizing handles on the Plugin placeholder and drag it out to a new size.

   • Enter the desired values in the W (Width) and the H (Height) text boxes of the Property inspector.

   For a default audio plugin, start with a width of 144 pixels and a height of 60 pixels. These dimensions are slightly larger than necessary for Internet Explorer's audio controls, but they fit Navigator's controls perfectly, as shown in Figure 26-5, and the control panel does not appear to be clipped when viewed through any browser. You may need to adjust the width and/or height after further testing.

When the Plugin object is inserted, Dreamweaver displays the generic Plugin placeholder.

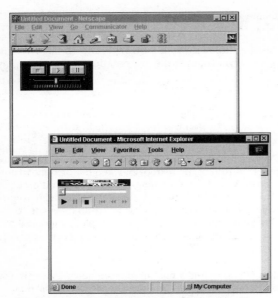

Figure 26-5: Internet Explorer's Windows Media Player needs less space than Netscape's LiveAudio player, so it fills the rest with a smaller version of its logo.

Playing Background Music

Background music, played while the user is viewing online material, is one of the Web's hidden treasures. When used tastefully, background music can enhance the overall impact of the page. Conversely, when abused, it can drive users away in droves.

Making a regular embedded sound into a background sound is as simple as adding a few parameters to the `<embed>` tag: `hidden` tells the browser not to display any controls, `autostart` tells it to start playback automatically, and `loop` tells it to play the audio continuously. Although you can add these attributes to the `<embed>` tag manually in the HTML Code window, it's easier to add them using the Property inspector. Follow these steps to embed background music in a Web page:

1. Position the cursor near the top of your Web page. Choose Insert ⇨ Media ⇨ Plugin or click the Plugin button from the Media group in the Common category of the Insert bar.

2. Choose your audio file in the Select File dialog box.

   Dreamweaver inserts a 32 x 32 pixel placeholder to indicate where the Plugin code is located. You can resize the placeholder so your layout won't be affected.

3. In the Property inspector, enter **2** in both the H (Height) and W (Width) text boxes.

Note Entering a width and height attribute is necessary for compatibility with older browsers.

4. If your Property inspector is not already expanded, expand it now (by clicking the arrow icon in the lower-right corner of the inspector). Click the Parameters button to open the Parameters dialog box.

5. In the Parameters dialog box, click the Add (+) button and enter **hidden** in the Parameter column. Click in the Parameter column and type in the first parameter. Use Tab to move to the Value column and enter **true**, as shown in Figure 26-6. Use Tab again to move to the next parameter. The following list can help you navigate and use this dialog box:

   • Use Shift+Tab if you need to move backwards through the list.

   • To delete a parameter/value pair, highlight it and click the Delete (–) button at the top of the Parameters column.

   • To add a new parameter, click the Add (+) button to move to the first blank line, and use Tab to move to the next parameter.

   • To move a parameter from one position in the list to another, highlight it and click the up or down arrow buttons at the top of the Parameters column.

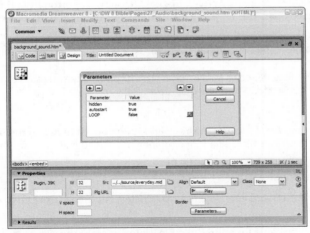

Figure 26-6: Dreamweaver inserts a 32 x 32 pixel placeholder denoting a Plugin object for playing a MIDI file as background music.

6. Enter **autostart** as the next parameter and give it the value **true**.

7. To make the audio clip repeat, enter **loop** as the next parameter; and in the Value column, enter the number of times you want the sound to repeat. To make the audio repeat indefinitely, enter **true** as the value.

8. Click OK to finish.

Targeting Specific Plugins

You can exercise a much finer degree of control over the audio in your pages by calling specific plugins. The trade-off, unfortunately, is that by designating a plugin, you reduce the size of your potential audience. Some plugins are specific to a browser or browser version. Moreover, plugins that aren't distributed with the major browsers face an uphill battle in terms of market penetration. If you use a plugin, you can always expect some users to be resistant to downloading the necessary software. Before you incorporate any plugin, you must weigh these issues against your overall design plan.

Windows Media Player Audio

The Windows Media Player is Internet Explorer's default multimedia player. You can use it to play the standard audio formats, including MP3, WAV, AIFF, AU, or MIDI files. Calling Windows Media Player directly as an ActiveX control, however, gives you far more flexibility over the player's appearance and functionality: its width, height, control panel display, loudness, number of loops, and so on.

Calling the Windows Media Player ActiveX Control

To incorporate the Windows Media Player ActiveX control, follow these steps:

1. Position the cursor where you would like the Windows Media Player control panel to appear. Choose Insert ➪ Media ➪ ActiveX or click the ActiveX button from the Media category of the Insert bar. The Property inspector displays the ActiveX object options.

2. In the ClassID text box, enter the ID for the Windows Media Player control: **CLSID:22d6f312-b0f6-11d0-94ab-0080c74c7e95**.

Tip   If you've entered this long Windows Media Player class ID previously, you can click the arrow button and choose the ID from the drop-down list.

3. Change the width and height values in the W and H text boxes to match the desired control display. The Windows Media Player display resizes to match your dimensions as closely as possible.

4. Click the Parameters button.

5. Click the Add (+) button and enter the first parameter: **FileName**. Use Tab to move to the Value column.

6. Enter the path and filename for your audio file. Unfortunately, there is no Browse button in the Parameters dialog box, so you must enter the pathname by hand. If the audio file resides in your site, be sure to specify a relative URL rather than an absolute one.

7. Continue entering the desired parameters and values for your audio file, as shown in Figure 26-7.

8. Click OK when you're finished.

The Windows Media Player ActiveX control has many parameters to choose from — 34, to be exact. Explaining all these parameters is beyond the scope of this book; but Table 26-3 describes the key parameters.

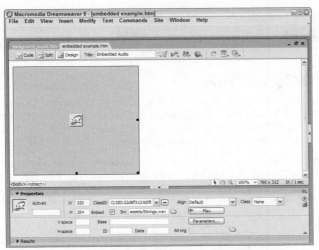

Figure 26-7: Inserting a Windows Media Player ActiveX control object into a Web page.

Note As with plugins, all the parameters and/or values of an ActiveX control may be linked to a dynamic source. From the Parameters dialog box, click the lightning-bolt icon in either the Parameter or Value column to expose the available recordset fields.

Table 26-3: Windows Media Player Parameters

WMP Parameter	Possible Values	Description
AutoStart	true (default) or false	Determines if the sound begins playing when the download is complete.
FileName	Any valid sound-file URL	Specifies the sound file to be played.
PlayCount	Any integer	Sets the number of times the file should repeat. If the value is 0, the sound loops continuously. The default is 1.
SelectionStart	Number of seconds	Determines the beginning point for the audio clip, relative to the start of the file.
SelectionEnd	Number of seconds	Determines the ending point for the audio clip, relative to the start of the file.
ShowControls	true (default) or false	Shows the control panel if set to true.
ShowDisplay	true or false (default)	Shows the display panel if set to true.
Volume	Any integer, from 0 (loudest, default) to 10,000 (softest)	Sets the loudness of the audio.

Caution   Windows Media Player's default volume setting is 0, but this is the highest setting, not the lowest setting. Specifying a higher number for the volume parameter lowers the volume of the sound.

Using Embed with ActiveX

All ActiveX controls are included in HTML's `<object>`...`</object>` tag pair. Dreamweaver codes this for you when you insert any ActiveX control. Netscape doesn't recognize the `<object>` tag, and Internet Explorer doesn't recognize the `<embed>` tag when it's within an `<object>` tag, so it's possible to target both browsers with one `<object>` and `<embed>` pair.

After you've entered the `FileName` parameter and value for the Windows Media Player ActiveX control, select the Embed checkbox in the Property inspector. The same name that you specified as the `FileName` now appears in the Embed text box. Dreamweaver takes advantage of the fact that Netscape doesn't recognize the `<object>` tag by inserting the `<embed>` tag inside the `<object>`...`</object>` tag pair. The resulting HTML looks like the following:

```
<object classid="CLSID:22d6f312-b0f6-11d0-94ab-0080c74c7e95"
 width="193" height="270">
  <param name="FileName" value="sounds/Fantasy.mid">
  <param name="PlayCount" value="0">
  <param name="ShowDisplay" value="true">
  <embed src="sounds/Fantasy.mid" width="193" height="270"
   filename="sounds/Fantasy.mid" playcount="0" showdisplay="true">
  </embed>
</object>
```

Note that Dreamweaver picks up the attributes and parameters from the ActiveX control to use in the `<embed>` tag. You often have to adjust these, especially the width and height values, which differ markedly for Internet Explorer and Netscape audio player displays.

Installing Streaming Audio

Although audio files are not nearly as large as video files, downloading them can take a long time. Audio-on-demand — or *streaming audio* — is an alternative to such lengthy downloads.

For streaming audio, you have the same Big Three choices as you do for streaming video — RealMedia, QuickTime, and Windows Media — plus Shockwave streaming audio and Flash movies.

Cross-Reference   Streaming audio files have a lot in common with streaming video files. Streaming video is discussed in Chapter 25.

Shockwave and Flash are covered in Chapter 24.

Playing Sound with Flash

Flash is a solid alternative for playing MP3 audio, whether in the background or through an in-page controller—you can even control it through JavaScript in Dreamweaver. Flash has supported sound from early on and in recent years has strengthened its MP3 playback mechanism. If you're working with a Flash designer, creating a MP3 playback movie is relatively straightforward.

One robust solution for incorporating Flash audio is provided by Hayden Porter with his FlashSound API project (http://www.flashsoundapi.com/). The FlashSound API is an open source JavaScript library, freely available. The site contains a range of tutorials and full documentation.

If you're looking for a drop-in solution, a series of low-cost commercial players are available from WimpyPlayer (http://www.wimpyplayer.com/). These Flash MP3 players support both PHP and ASP as well as XML playlists.

Working with Floating or Embedded RealAudio Players

Before including a link to a RealAudio file, you first must make a basic choice: Is the player free-floating or is it embedded in the page? It's purely a design decision, but the coding necessary for each option is completely different. To insert a RealAudio streaming audio file with a free-floating player, shown in Figure 26-8, follow these steps:

1. Select the link or image that you want to use to begin the RealAudio file.

2. In the Property inspector, enter the path to the RealAudio metafile in the Link text box or use the Browse For File button to locate the file. Make sure that the metafile has a .ram or .rpm extension.

An embedded player is best inserted using Dreamweaver's ActiveX object—the embedded player consists of multiple ActiveX objects, one for the player control (or controls) and one for the audio file itself. The separation of content and player makes it easy to link the content to a data source while maintaining the same control panel.

Note   ActiveX objects can only be displayed/played in Internet Explorer on Windows; Netscape does not support ActiveX, and it is not supported on the Macintosh.

If desired, your design may include a single control panel or a series of controls—play, stop, fast-forward, rewind, and so on—all affecting your audio. The two key RealAudio parameters are controls and console. The controls parameter sets the type of control being inserted; the console parameter indicates which embedded audio file is being played.

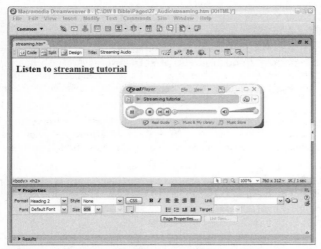

Figure 26-8: This is a free-floating RealPlayer player, opened by clicking the streaming tutorial link.

To embed a RealAudio file with separate controls, you must follow a two-phase procedure. First, embed the actual audio file or, if the source is dynamic, a link to a data source. Follow these steps:

1. Choose Insert ➪ Media ➪ ActiveX or select the ActiveX object from the Media category of the Insert bar. Dreamweaver inserts an ActiveX placeholder.

2. From the ActiveX Property inspector, set the ClassID to **RealPlayer**.

3. Change the Width and Height values in the W and H text boxes to **0** for audio-only playback.

4. If you know the `codebase` URL, enter it in the Base text box. The `codebase` property is an Internet location from which the ActiveX control can be automatically downloaded and installed if the browser does not find the control on the user's system. The codebase values are provided by the ActiveX control creator.

5. Click the Parameters button to display the Parameters dialog box.

6. Click the Add (+) button and enter the first parameter: **src**. Use Tab to move to the Value column and enter the path and filename for your file. To serve different audio files from a data source, click the lightning bolt icon in the Value column. In the Dynamic Data dialog box, select an appropriate field containing URLs of RealMedia files.

7. Enter the next parameter, **console**, in the left column.

8. In the Value column, enter a unique name for the sound file. This unique console name is used to link the controls to the audio file.

9. Click OK when you're finished.

10. In the Property inspector, select the Embed option to make the audio cross-browser compatible.

Now you're ready to add the controls that enable user interactivity. Follow these steps:

1. Again, choose Insert ➪ Media ➪ ActiveX or select the ActiveX object from the Media menu on the Insert bar's Common category.

2. From the ActiveX Property inspector, set the ClassID to **RealPlayer**.

3. Change the Width and Height values to the size desired for the type of controls selected. Some common dimensions are as follows:

    - **All:** Width: 375, Height: 100
    - **ControlPanel:** Width: 350, Height: 36
    - **PlayButton:** Width: 44, Height: 26
    - **PlayOnlyButton:** Width: 26, Height: 26 (These dimensions apply to all individual controls, such as PauseButton and FFCtrl.)

4. Select Parameters in the Property inspector.

5. In the Parameters dialog box, enter **controls** in the first column; and enter the name of the control (that is, all, controlpanel, playbutton, pausebutton, and so on) in the second column.

6. Add a second parameter, **console**. The value of console should be the same as entered for the audio file in step 8 of the previous series of steps.

7. Click OK to close the Parameters dialog box.

8. Select Embed on the Property inspector to ensure cross-browser compatibility, as shown in Figure 26-9.

Figure 26-9: An embedded RealPlayer control panel is very flexible; here the width is set to 375 pixels and the height is set to 100, showing all controls.

Repeat these steps to add additional individual controls. When you're done, test your Web page by previewing it in a browser.

Accessing RealAudio Parameters

For a streaming audio file, only the source file and the dimensions are really required, but it probably comes as no surprise to you that a great number of attributes are available. You can add any of the attributes found in Table 26-4 through the Parameters button of the selected RealAudio file's Property inspector.

Table 26-4: RealAudio Parameters

RealPlayer Attribute	Possible Values	Description
autostart	true (default) or false	Enables the RealAudio clip to start playing as soon as content is available
console	_master or _unique	Determines the console name for each control in a Web page that uses multiple controls. To force controls on a page to refer to the same file, use the same console=name attribute. The console name _master links to all controls on a page; _unique connects to no other instances.
controls	all, controlpanel, infovolumepanel, infopanel, statuspanel, statusbar, playbutton, playonlybutton, pausebutton, ffctrl, rwctrl, stopbutton, mutectrl, mutevolumectrl, volumeslider, positionslider, positionfield, or statusfield	Enables the placement of individual control panel elements in the Web page. You can use multiple controls in one attribute, or multiple <embed> tags to build a custom RealAudio interface.
nolabels	true or false (default)	Suppresses the Title, Author, and Copyright labels in the Status panel. If you set nolabels to true, the actual data is still visible.

Summary

Adding sound to a Web page brings it into the realm of multimedia. Dreamweaver gives you numerous methods to handle the various audio formats, both static and streaming. When you use custom Dreamweaver objects and actions, enhancing your Web site with audio is a snap. When adding audio to your Web pages, keep these points in mind:

✦ The common downloadable audio file formats are MP3, AIFF, WAV, AU, and RMF.

✦ The common downloadable music file formats are MIDI, QuickTime Music, and RMF.

✦ You can either link to a sound or embed it in your Web page. With standard audio, the linking technique calls an independent, free-floating player; the embedding technique incorporates the player into the design of the page. Hiding the player creates background music or sound.

✦ Third-party plugins offer far greater control over the appearance and functionality of the sound than relying on a browser's default plugin; to use a third-party plugin, however, your user must download it.

✦ Streaming audio provides almost instant access to large audio files, and RealAudio is one of the leaders in player deployment.

In the next chapter, you learn how to use Dreamweaver templates to enhance your Web-page creation skills.

✦   ✦   ✦

Enhancing Productivity and Web Site Management

◆ ◆ ◆ ◆

◆ ◆ ◆ ◆

Using Dreamweaver Templates

Let's face it: Web design is a combination of glory and grunt work. Creating the initial design for a Web site can be fun and exciting, but when you have to implement your wonderful new design on 200 or more pages, the excitement fades as you try to figure out the quickest way to finish the work. Enter templates. Using templates properly can be a tremendous timesaver. Moreover, a template ensures that your Web site has a consistent look and feel, which, in turn, generally means that it's easier for users to navigate.

In Dreamweaver, you can produce new documents from a standard design saved as a template, just as you do in a word processing program. Furthermore, you can alter a template and update all the files that were created from it earlier; this capability extends the power of the repeating element Libraries to overall page design. Templates also form the bridge to one of the hottest technologies shaping the Web — Extensible Markup Language (XML).

Dreamweaver makes it easy to access all kinds of templates — everything from your own creations to the default blank page. This chapter demonstrates the mechanism behind Dreamweaver templates and shows you strategies for getting the most out of them.

Understanding Templates

Templates exist in many forms. Furniture makers use master patterns as templates to create the same basic design repeatedly, using new wood stains or upholstery to differentiate the final product. A stencil, in which the inside of a letter, word, or design is cut out, is a type of template as well. With computers, templates form the basic document into which specific details are added to create new, distinct documents.

Dreamweaver templates, in terms of functionality, are a combination of traditional templates and updatable Library elements. After a new page is created from a template, the document remains attached to the original template unless specifically separated or detached. The new document maintains a connection to previous pages in a site. If the original template is altered, all the documents created from it can be automatically updated. This relationship is also true of Dreamweaver's repeating element Libraries. In fact, templates can include Library elements.

Cross-Reference   Library items work hand-in-hand with templates. See Chapter 28 for a detailed discussion of Library items.

When a template is first created, the entire page is locked; locked sections of a template cannot be changed in a document derived from that template. A key process in defining a template is to designate certain areas as regions that can be changed in some way in a template-derived document. Dreamweaver supports four different regions in a template:

✦ **Editable regions:** The area, such as all the code, within an editable region may be altered. Thus in a page where all the navigation code is locked, the content area can be designated as an editable region.

✦ **Editable attributes:** Within a locked tag, specific attributes can be made editable. You can, for example, unlock the border attribute for a table while keeping the cell padding and cell spacing secure.

✦ **Optional regions:** Content within an optional region may or may not be displayed, depending on certain conditions set by the template designer.

✦ **Repeating regions:** Certain areas in an otherwise locked object (typically a table), can be repeated as many times as needed in a template-derived document. Repeating regions are great for controlling the overall look and feel of a table but allowing the number of detail rows to vary.

All the various region types require template markup within the document. You can also combine certain template regions — you could, for example, make some of the content within a repeating region editable and keep some of it locked.

Naturally, templates can be altered to mark additional editable areas or to relock editable areas. Moreover, you can detach a document created from a template at any time and edit anything in the document. You cannot, however, reattach the document to the template without losing (or seriously misplacing) inserted content. On the other hand, you can give a document based on one template a completely different look (without changing the content) by applying another template with identical regions.

Let's look at an example template. The layout, background, and navigation controls are identical on every page. One basic template page (shown in Figure 27-1) is created, and all the final pages are created from the template. Notice the highlighting surrounding certain areas in the template. In a template, the specified regions are highlighted, and the locked areas are not. A tab further identifies each region to make it easier to add the right content in the right area.

Editable region   Templates menu

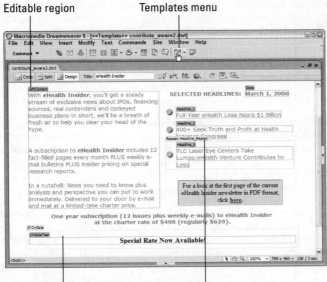

Content in an optional region   Repeating region

Figure 27-1: In a template, designated regions are clearly marked and distinguished from the rest of the page, which is locked and cannot be changed.

Creating Your Own Templates

You can use any design you like for your own template. Perhaps the best course to take is to finalize a single page that has all the elements that you want to include in your template. Then, convert that document to a template and proceed to mark all the changeable areas — whether text or image — as a type of region. Before saving your file as a template, consider the following points when designing your basic page:

    ✦ **Use placeholders where you can:** Whether it's dummy text or a temporary graphic, a placeholder gives shape to your page. Placeholders also make it easier to remember which elements to include. If you are using an image placeholder, set a temporary height and width through the Property inspector or by dragging the image placeholder's sizing handles. Of course, you can also just insert a sample graphic.

    ✦ **Finalize and incorporate as much content as possible in the template:** If you find yourself repeatedly adding the same information or objects to a page, add them to your template. The more structured elements you can include, the faster your pages can be produced.

✦ **Use sample objects on the template:** Often, you have to enter the same basic object, such as a plugin for a digital movie, on every page with only the filename changing. Enter your repeating object (with as many preset parameters as possible) on your template page. Then, you only have to select a new filename for each page.

✦ **Include your** `<meta>` **information:** Search engines rely on `<meta>` tags to get the overview of a page and then scan the balance of the page to get the details. You can enter a Keyword or Description object from the HTML category of the Insert bar so that all the Web pages in your site have the same basic information for cataloging.

You can create a template from a Web document with one command: File ➪ Save As Template. Dreamweaver stores all templates in a Templates folder created for each defined site with a special file extension (.dwt). After you've created your page and saved it as a template, notice that Dreamweaver inserts <<Template>> in the title bar to remind you of the page's status. Now you're ready to begin defining the template's editable regions.

Note   You can also create a template from an entirely blank page if you like. To do so, open the Assets panel and select the Templates category. From the Templates category, click the New Template button. You can find more information about how to use the Assets panel of the Templates category later in this chapter. Another approach to achieve the same result is to choose File ➪ New to display the New Document dialog box, select the Template Page category, and then choose the type of page — static or dynamic — that you want to create. Use this method when you want to build an XHTML-compliant template from scratch.

Using Editable Regions

As noted earlier, when you convert an existing document into a template via the Save As Template command, the entire document is initially locked. If you attempt to create a document from a template at this stage, Dreamweaver alerts you that the template doesn't have any editable regions, and you cannot change anything on the page. Editable regions are a key element in templates.

Marking Existing Content as Editable

Editable regions can either surround existing content or stand alone without any content. As noted earlier, in both cases you must give the region a unique name. Dreamweaver uses the unique name to identify the editable region when entering new content, applying the template, and exporting or importing XML.

Note   As I noted previously, each editable region must have a unique name, but the name need only be different from any other editable region on the same page. The same name could be used for objects, JavaScript functions, or editable regions on a different template.

To mark an existing area as an editable region, follow these steps:

1. Select the text, object, or area on the page that you want to convert to an editable region.

Tip

The general rule with editable regions is that you need to select a complete tag pair, such as `<table>...</table>`. This strategy has several implications. For instance, although you can mark an entire table, one or more contiguous rows, or a single cell as editable, you can't mark multiple cells, separated rows, or a column. Attempting to do so marks a multiple row region. You have to select each cell individually (`<td>...</td>`). In addition, you can select the content of a layer to be editable and keep the layer itself locked (so that its position and other properties cannot be altered). However, if you select the layer to be editable, you can't lock the content.

2. Choose Insert ⇨ Template Objects ⇨ Editable Region. You can also use the keyboard shortcut Ctrl+Alt+V (Command+Option+V), or right-click (Control+click) the selection and choose Templates ⇨ New Editable Region from the context menu. Whichever method you choose, Dreamweaver displays the New Editable Region dialog box shown in Figure 27-2.

Figure 27-2: The descriptive name you enter for a new editable region must be unique.

Now, editable template regions — as well as the other region types — are just a mouse click away. From the Common category of the Insert bar, choose the Templates group and click once on the Editable Region icon. You can also drag the icon over the selected text. Either action brings up the New Editable Region dialog box.

3. Enter a unique name for the selected area. Click OK if you're finished, or click Cancel to abort the operation.

Caution

Although you can use spaces in editable region names, some characters are not permitted. The illegal characters are the ampersand (&), double quote ("), single quote ('), and left and right angle brackets (< and >).

Dreamweaver outlines the selection with the color picked in Preferences on the Highlighting panel, shown if View ⇨ Visual Aids ⇨ Invisible Elements is enabled. The name for your newly designated region is displayed on a tab marking the area; the region is also listed in the Modify ⇨ Templates submenu. If still selected, the region name has a checkmark next to it in the Templates submenu. You can jump to any other editable region by selecting its name from this dynamic list.

Tip

Make sure that you apply any formatting to your text — either by using HTML codes or by using CSS styles — before you select it to be an editable region. Generally, you want to keep the defined look of the content, altering just the text; so make sure that only the text is within the editable region and exclude the formatting tags. It's often helpful to have both the Code and Design views open for this detailed work.

Inserting a New Editable Region

Sometimes it's helpful to create a new editable region in which no content currently exists. In these situations, the editable region name doubles as a label identifying the type of content expected, such as `CatalogPrice`. Dreamweaver always highlights the entry in the template in a small tab above the region.

To insert a new editable region, follow these steps:

1. Place your cursor anywhere on the template page without selecting any item in particular.

2. Choose Insert ➪ Template Objects ➪ Editable Region. Alternately, click the Editable Region icon on the Templates menu of the Insert bar.

3. Enter a unique name for the new region. Click OK when you're finished, or click Cancel to abort the operation.

Dreamweaver inserts the new region name in the document, marks it with a named tab, and adds the name to the dynamic region list (which you can display by choosing Modify ➪ Templates).

Two editable regions, one for the Web page's title and one for other `<head>` content, are automatically created when you save a document as a template. The title is stored in a special editable region called `doctitle`, and the `<head>` content region is named `head`. To change the title (which initially takes the same title as the template), enter the new text in the Title field of the Document toolbar. You can also use the keyboard shortcut Ctrl+J (Command+J) to open the Page Properties dialog box. Finally, you can select View ➪ Head Elements and click the Title icon — with the visible region outline — to enter the new text in the Property inspector.

The `head` editable region may not appear very useful during the template creation phase, but when you begin creating documents based on a template it really shines. New `<meta>` tags, CSS style links and rules, and behavior-added JavaScript all take advantage of the `head` editable region.

Creating Links in Templates

A common problem that designers encounter with Dreamweaver templates centers on links. People often add links to their templates and discover that these links do not work when new pages are derived from the templates. The main cause of this error is linking to a non-existent page or element by hand — that is, typing in the link, rather than using the Select File dialog box to choose it. Designers tend to set the links according to their final site structures, without taking into account how templates are stored in Dreamweaver.

For example, when creating a template, suppose you have links to three pages — `products.htm`, `services.htm`, and `about.htm` — all in the root of your site. Both `products.htm` and `services.htm` have been created, so you click the Folder icon in the Property inspector and select those files. Dreamweaver inserts those links as follows: `../products.htm` and `../services.htm`. The `../` indicates the directory above the current directory — which makes sense only when you remember that all templates are stored in a subfolder of the site root called Templates. These links are correctly resolved when a document is derived from this template to reflect the stored location of the new file.

Let's assume that the third file, `about.htm`, has not yet been created, and so you enter that link by hand. The common mistake is entering the pathname as it should appear when it's used: `about.htm`. However, because the page is saved in the Templates folder, Dreamweaver converts that link to `/Templates/about.htm` for any page derived from the template — and the link will fail. This type of error also applies to dependent files, such as graphics or other media.

The best solution is to always use the Folder or the Point-to-File icon to link to an existing file when building your templates. If the file does not exist, and if you don't want to create a placeholder page for it, link to another existing file in the same folder and modify the link manually.

There is one special circumstance in which you would not use the Folder or Point-to-File icon to do your linking for you. Let's suppose your site design calls for each page to link to a CSS file in the same folder as the file itself; a technique like this is used when you want to vary pages by departments and each department has its own folder. In this circumstance, linking in the standard template manner wouldn't work because you're effectively linking to a number of files and not just one. To accomplish this goal, you'll need to use a special syntax in your `href` attribute, like this:

```
<link href="@@('departmentStyles.css')@@" rel="stylesheet"
type="text/css" />
```

As you see later in this chapter, the double-@ signs and parentheses characters are used to designate template expressions. Here, they're used to tell Dreamweaver not to alter the `href` value. These types of links will obviously need to be coded by hand.

Locking an Editable Region

Inevitably, you'll sometimes mark as editable a region that you'd prefer to keep locked. Similarly, you may discover that every page constructed to date has required inputting the same content, so it should be entered on the template and locked. In either event, converting an editable region to a locked one is a simple operation.

To lock an editable region, follow these steps:

1. Place your cursor in the editable region you want to lock.

2. Choose Modify ⇨ Templates ⇨ Remove Template Markup. The same menu selection is available from the context menu.

Caution

If you are removing a newly inserted editable region that contains only the region name — which happens when an empty editable region is added — the content is not removed and must be deleted by hand on the template. Otherwise, it appears as part of the document created from a template and won't be accessible.

Adding Content to Template Documents

Constructing a template is only half the job — using it to create new pages is the other half. Because the basic layout is complete and you're only dropping in new images and entering new text, creating pages based on templates takes just a fraction of the time needed to create regular Web pages. Dreamweaver makes it easy to enter new content as well — you can even move from one template region to the next, much like filling out a form (which, of course, is exactly what you're doing).

To create a new document based on a template, follow these steps:

1. In the Template category of the Assets panel, select the desired template and choose the New from Template option from the panel's context menu. Alternatively, choose File ➪ New. Then from the New Document/New from Template dialog box (the title of the dialog changes according to which tab is chosen) select the Templates category and choose the site and desired template as shown in Figure 27-3.

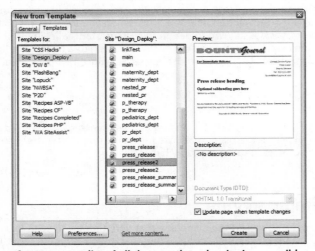

Figure 27-3: A list of all the templates by site is accessible by choosing File ➪ New.

2. If you want to maintain a connection between the template-derived document and the template, leave the Update Page When Template Changes option selected. To detach the template from the newly created document and make the entire page editable, deselect the option.

3. Click OK when you're finished.

When your new page opens, the editable regions are again highlighted, as shown in Figure 27-4; furthermore, the cursor is only active when it is over an unlocked region. If you have the Code view open, you also see that the locked region is highlighted in a different color — by default, gray. Document highlighting makes it easy to differentiate the two types of regions.

Note   A document created from a template is known as an *instance* of that template.

Locked region cursor   Editable region

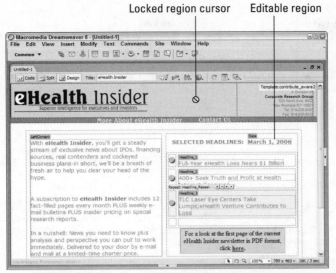

Figure 27-4: In a document based on a template, the template regions are clearly marked, as are the locked portions in the Code view.

Generally, it is easiest to select the editable region name or placeholder first and then enter the new content. Selecting the editable regions can be handled in several ways:

✦ Highlight the region name or placeholder with the mouse.

✦ Position your cursor inside any editable region and select the `<mmtinstance:editable>` tag in the Tag Selector.

✦ Choose Modify ➪ Templates and select the name of your editable region from the dynamic list.

Note   If all your editable regions are separate cells in a table, you can tab forward and Shift+Tab backward through the cells. With each press of the Tab key, all the content in the cell is selected, whether it is an editable region name or a placeholder.

Naturally, you should save your document to retain all the new content that's been added.

Tip   Behaviors can be added without any additional coding or workarounds to links within editable regions. You cannot, however, add a behavior to text or an image in a locked region.

Converting a Page to a Template

In this Dreamweaver Technique, you convert an existing page to a template and apply editable regions to several page elements.

1. From the Techniques site, expand the 25_Template folder and open the `template_start` file.

2. Choose File ➪ Save as Template.

3. In the Save As Template dialog box, enter **house_listing** in the Save As field and click Save.

4. When the Update Links dialog box appears, click Yes.

5. Dreamweaver stores the new file in the Templates folder as `house_listing.dwt`. Notice that the term <<Template>> is now visible in the Dreamweaver title bar. The next task is to begin adding editable regions to the template. Select the text A Real Steal by dragging across it with your mouse.

6. Because you want to make just the text inside the <h1> tag an editable region and not the entire tag, it's best not to use the Tag Selector. From the Insert bar's Common category, choose Templates: Editable Region.

7. In the New Editable Region dialog box, enter **Headline** in the Name field.

8. If you have Visual Aids ➪ Invisible Elements enabled, you'll see a border appear around the editable region as well as a tab naming the area. Delete the selected original text and enter the placeholder text **Short Headline**.

9. Place your cursor in the first paragraph of text and choose the `<p.firstParagraph>` tag from the Tag Selector.

10. Repeat steps 6 and 7 to create a new editable region; name the region **Description**.

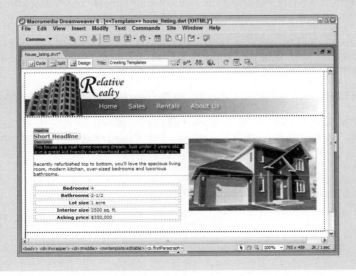

11. Press Delete to remove the selected original text. Press Enter (Return) to create a new paragraph and enter this placeholder text: **Enter lively description of property here. Use upbeat adjectives and short declarative sentences. Make sure the firstParagraph style is applied.**

12. In the Property inspector, choose firstParagraph from the Style list.

13. Select the second paragraph in the Tag Selector and click Delete to remove it.

14. Save your page; Dreamweaver notes that the Headline editable region is within a block tag. Click OK to acknowledge that this is by design.

In the next Technique, you expand on this template.

Making Attributes Editable

Now that you understand the basics of template design and implementation, you can proceed to some of the more advanced features. Editable regions can encompass any portion of the page, from a single tag up to the entire <body>. But what if you want to make just a portion of a tag — an attribute — editable and keep the rest of the tag locked? I once worked on a site where the client wanted to tie the background color of a table's header row to a graphic on the page. Every couple of weeks, I would get an e-mail asking for help to fix the page — broken while the client was trying to change the one attribute, bgcolor. It was a frustrating situation for both the client and me.

Dreamweaver gives you control over your editable areas right down to the attribute level. Not only can an attribute be made editable, but you can restrict its type and even provide default values. All the editable attributes on a page are displayed within a single dialog box, centralizing updates. The various types of attributes — text, number, URL, color, Boolean — each have a specific interface for choosing a value. A color-type attribute, for example, uses a Dreamweaver-style color picker.

To make an attribute editable, follow these steps:

1. With the template open for editing, select the tag or object that contains the attribute you want to make editable.

Note   Your selection should be outside an editable region. If you try to change the attribute of a tag within an editable region, Dreamweaver reminds you that this tag is already fully editable.

2. Choose Modify ⇨ Templates ⇨ Make Attribute Editable to display the Editable Tag Attributes dialog box as shown in Figure 27-5.

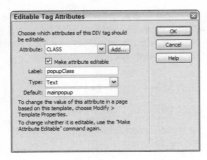

Figure 27-5: With the Editable Tag Attributes dialog box, you can extend access to any attribute — even a custom one — of any tag in a locked area.

3. Select the desired attribute from the Attribute drop-down list.

Tip   For quicker editing, make sure your selected tag already contains the attribute you'd like to make editable. The Attribute drop-down list shows all the parameters within a selected tag, whether they have values or not.

4. If the attribute you want is not available from the drop-down list, click Add and enter the attribute in the pop-up dialog box. After you've confirmed your entry in the pop-up dialog box by clicking OK, your attribute appears in the Attribute drop-down list. New entries are always uppercased in the list, but do not appear uppercased in the code if specified otherwise in the Tag Library Editor.

5. Select the Make Attribute Editable option. The Make Attribute Editable option may seem redundant in this dialog box, but it enables you to make a number of attributes editable in the same tag while leaving others locked.

6. Enter a unique name for the tag's editable attribute in the Label field. The Label is used to identify this specific editable attribute and is displayed in the Template Properties dialog box when the attribute is modified. Pick a name that identifies both the tag and the attribute, like `logoTableBgColor` for the `bgcolor` attribute of a table containing the logo.

7. Select a Type from the drop-down list. Here are the five options:

   • **Text:** Select this type for attributes requiring a text-based value, such as the `<img>` tag's `alt` attribute.

   • **URL:** Choose this type when the attribute value points to a file or requires an Internet address, such as the `href` attribute of the `<a>` tag. Designating an attribute as a URL type enables Dreamweaver to update the link if the file is moved or renamed.

   • **Color:** Use the Color type for those attributes specifying a color value, such as the `<tr>` tag's `bgcolor` attribute. The major benefit of identifying color-related attributes as such is the color picker that is made available in the Template Properties dialog box.

   • **True/False:** Select this type if the attribute is a Boolean, meaning it accepts value of true or false only — for example, the `<embed>` tag's `hidden` attribute.

   • **Number:** Choose the Number type when an attribute requires a numeric value, such as the `<img>` tag's `height` and `width` attribute.

Caution   If you need to enter a percentage, like 50%, or other value that contains both numbers and other characters, select the Text type for your editable attribute. Although you might think the Number type is more logical, Dreamweaver generates errors when the template is saved with this type entered.

8. Enter the desired initial value for the attribute in the Default field. If the attribute is already present in the selected tag, the current value is displayed in the Default field. For new attributes, the Default field is initially blank.

9. Click OK when you're finished.

Editable attributes are noted in the code by surrounding the values with double @ signs, like this:

```
<img src="@@(monthlyImageSrc)@@" width="100" height="50"
align="@@(monthlyImageAlign)@@">
```

In this example, the `<img>` tag has two editable attributes, `src` and `align`, which are set to variable values: `@@(monthlyImageSrc)@@` and `@@(monthlyImageAlign)@@`, respectively.

Tip   You can apply the same editable attribute to different tags. For example, you might want different cells of various tables on the page to share the same `bgcolor`. Although you can repeat the Make Attribute Editable command for every variable, you might find it more efficient to simply copy and paste the variable value.

When you examine the template file, note two Macromedia comments inserted in the `<head>` section:

```
<!-- TemplateParam name="monthlyImageSrc" type="URL" value="../images/admin.gif" -->
<!-- TemplateParam name="monthlyImageAlign" type="text" value="left" -->
```

These `TemplateParam` tags are used by Dreamweaver to identify the editable attributes and provide their types and default values.

Caution   The default values set in Editable attributes are not rendered when viewing the template in the Design view, only in the template-derived document. This is a known bug in Dreamweaver.

Setting Editable Attributes

After you've inserted your editable attributes in the template, Dreamweaver provides a straightforward user interface for editing them in template-derived documents. Whether you choose File ➪ New or select the template in the Assets panel to create your new document, you find a new command available under the Modify menu: Template Properties.

The Template Properties dialog box, shown in Figure 27-6, lists all the editable attributes found on a single page. Selecting each property brings up the editing options for that particular attribute type (text, number, color, URL, and true/false) and the current associated value. After modifying any or all of the template properties, Dreamweaver refreshes the page and displays the attributes with their new values.

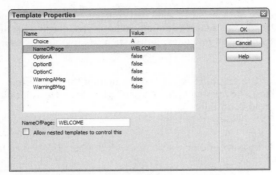

Figure 27-6: How you specify the value for an editable attribute in the Template Properties dialog box depends on the type of attribute.

With each of the Template Properties types, you have the option to allow the nested template to control the attribute. Select this option if you intend to save the current document as a template—thus creating a nested template—and if you want documents based on that nested template to set the attribute value. You can also choose this option when editing a nested template. Nested templates are covered in depth later in this chapter.

To set the editable attributes on a template-based document, follow these steps:

1. Choose Modify ➪ Template Properties. The Template Properties dialog box is displayed.

2. Select the attribute to specify its value.

3. If you want to allow the attribute to be modified in a document based on a nested template, choose the Allow Nested Templates to Control This option. If the option is selected, the phrase `pass through` in parentheses replaces the attribute value editing options.

4. Enter the new value for the attribute. Depending on the type of attribute you select, you enter the value differently:

   • For Text, Number, and URL type attributes, enter the new value in the text field next to the editable attribute name.

   • For Color type attributes, select the color picker to sample the desired color from the color palette or any area on the screen. You can also enter the hexadecimal color value or color name directly in the associated text field.

   • For True/False type attributes, select the Show Attribute Name option to set the value to true and deselect it to set the value to false.

5. To set the value of any other editable attribute on the page, choose the attribute from the list and repeat steps 3 and 4.

6. Click OK when you're finished.

Enabling Repeating Regions

Data-driven pages handle repeating regions elegantly. A single row of a table is bound to data, and the application server returns as many requested rows as are available. However, not all pages are data-driven — and not all areas of a page that repeat can be bound to a data source. Dreamweaver provides solutions for both the server-side — the Repeat Region server behavior — and the client-side — the template-based repeating region feature.

A repeating region, like an editable region, is applied to a template and may surround any *tag-complete* area (an area containing both a beginning tag and an ending tag) on a page. Typically, repeating regions wrap around the same type of areas as their server behavior cousins, such as table rows. However, unlike the Repeat Region server behavior, template repeating regions are expanded and manipulated manually in a template-based document. Keep in mind one other important aspect of repeating regions: They aren't automatically editable — you have to include an editable region within a repeating region to make it so. The capability to lock specific portions of repeating regions makes this an extremely powerful feature.

To insert a repeating region, follow these steps:

1. Select the portion of the page that you want to repeat. As noted earlier, a repeating region cannot overlap a tag pair. If you attempt to do this, Dreamweaver automatically extends the selection so that the entire tag is included.

2. Choose Insert ➪ Template Objects ➪ Repeating Region or, from the Templates group of the Insert bar, click the Repeating Region icon as seen in Figure 27-7.

Repeating region   Repeating region icon

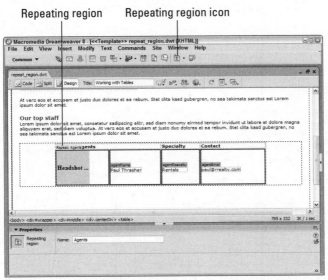

Figure 27-7: Repeating regions are marked in templates with an outline and named tab, just like editable and optional regions.

3. Enter a unique name in the New Repeating Region dialog box and click OK. Dreamweaver automatically provides a name, but as always, it's best if you supply a meaningful name.

As mentioned earlier, repeating regions are not, by default, editable. To make a repeating region editable, select the content within the repeating region — not the repeating region itself — and then create an editable region by either clicking the Editable Region icon in the Templates menu of the Insert bar or choosing Insert ➪ Template Objects ➪ Editable Region. You must give the editable region a unique name as usual.

Caution

You may notice that the repeating and editable regions tabs overlap, making it difficult to see the repeating region name. I've found it handy to use fairly long names for the repeating region, such as dataRowRepeating, and relatively short names for the editable region, such as dataRow, to enable me to see portions of both tabs. Also, although all template regions use the same color established in Preferences, the highlight for a repeating region is significantly lighter than that for editable regions. This color variation makes it much easier to identify the different types of regions.

Modifying a Repeating Region

The power of repeating regions isn't apparent until you open a template-based document containing one. With Invisible Elements enabled, you notice a series of buttons above each repeating region, as shown in Figure 27-8. With these controls, new entries — identical to the content contained within the repeating region — are added, deleted, or moved from one position to another. You can even copy and paste content within a repeating region.

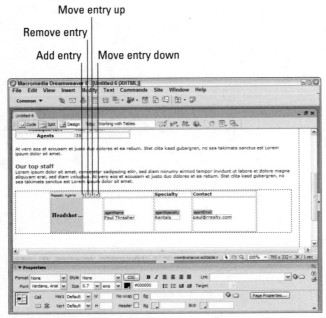

Figure 27-8: Entries cannot only be added and removed in a repeating region; they can also be re-ordered.

To modify a repeating region in a template-based document, follow these steps:

1. Make sure View ➪ Visual Aids ➪ Invisible Elements is enabled.

2. Locate the four buttons above the repeating region:

   - To add a new entry, click the Add (+) button. New entries are inserted below the current cursor selection. New entries are selected after they are created.

   - To delete an existing entry, position your cursor in the entry and click the Remove (–) button.

   - To move an entry down, place your cursor in the entry and click the Down button.

   - To move an entry up, place your cursor in the entry and click the Up button.

3. To copy and paste an entry, follow these steps:

   a. Position your cursor in the entry.

   b. Choose Edit ➪ Repeating Entries ➪ Copy Repeated Entry.

   c. Choose Edit ➪ Paste or Edit ➪ Repeating Entries ➪ Paste Repeated Entry.

If you prefer to work with Invisible Elements off, Dreamweaver provides corresponding menu options under both the main and context menus. In fact, the menu options are, in some ways, more powerful and can be immediate timesavers. Look in the main menu under Modify ➪ Templates ➪ Repeating Entries or, in the context menu under Templates, for these commands:

- ✦ New Entry Before Selection
- ✦ New Entry After Selection
- ✦ New Entry At End
- ✦ New Entry At Beginning
- ✦ Cut Repeating Entry
- ✦ Copy Repeating Entry
- ✦ Delete Repeating Entry
- ✦ Move Entry Up
- ✦ Move Entry Down
- ✦ Move Entry to Beginning
- ✦ Move Entry to End

Constructing a Repeating Table

Repeating regions are used so commonly in tables that Dreamweaver provides a tool to create both a table and a repeating region at the same time. The Repeating Table object opens the standard table dialog box with the added capability to define which rows are within a repeating region. When inserted, the repeating region is all set up — and even includes a separate editable region in each cell as shown in Figure 27-9.

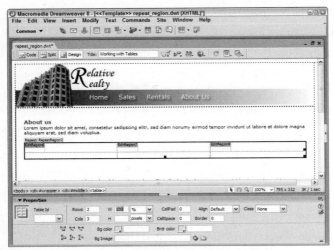

Figure 27-9: The Repeating Table object also includes editable regions for every cell in the repeating region rows.

To insert a Repeating Table, follow these steps:

1. In your template open for editing, position your cursor where you'd like the table to appear and choose Insert ➪ Template Objects ➪ Repeating Table. Alternatively, you can drag the Repeating Table icon from the Templates menu of the Insert bar. The Insert Repeating Table dialog box, shown in Figure 27-10, is displayed.

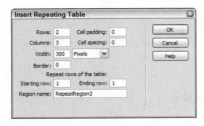

Figure 27-10: With the Repeating Table feature, you can define multiple rows to repeat.

2. Enter the values desired for the table attributes: Rows, Columns, Cell Padding, Cell Spacing, Width, and Border.

Cross-Reference   If you're not familiar with setting up a table, see Chapter 13.

3. Determine which rows of the table are to be repeated by entering the number of the first row in the Starting Row field and the number of the last row in the Ending Row field. For example, if you want only the second row of the table to repeat, your values are Starting Row: 2 and Ending Row: 2. However, if you want three rows to repeat starting with row 2, the values are Starting Row: 2 and Ending Row: 5.

4. Enter a unique name for the repeating region in the Region Name field or leave the Dreamweaver-supplied default name.

5. Click OK when you're finished.

After the table is created, notice that every cell in the designated repeating region is editable. Dreamweaver automatically inserts separate editable regions and names them incrementally EditRegion1, EditRegion2, and so on. By defining each cell as editable, rather than the entire row, Dreamweaver gives you the option to retain the editability on a cell-by-cell basis. If the cell should not be editable, position your cursor anywhere in the cell and choose Modify ➪ Templates ➪ Remove Template Markup.

Applying Additional Editable Regions

In the previous Dreamweaver Technique, you began the process of converting an existing page into a template. This Technique takes the next step and includes editable regions within a table.

1. Open the file created in the previous Dreamweaver Technique from the Templates folder, `template_start.dwt`.

2. You can apply editable regions to more than just text. Images are also good candidates, but first, it's a good idea to create a generic image placeholder. Select the image of the house in the page and delete it.

3. From the Insert bar's Common category, choose Images: Image Placeholder.

4. When the Image Placeholder dialog box opens, enter **House** in the Name field, **325** in Width, and **180** in Height; click OK when you're done.

5. Select the image placeholder and, from the Property inspector's Class list, choose imageRight.

6. With the image selected, choose Template: Editable Region.

7. In the New Editable Region dialog box, enter **House Image** in the Name field.

8. Tables are another page element that are easily made template-friendly. Select the value in the table cell next to the Bedrooms label and choose Templates: Editable Region.

9. In the New Editable Region dialog box, enter **Bedrooms** in the Name field and click OK.

10. Repeat steps 6 and 7 to create editable regions for each of the values in the second column of the table; make your selections and name your editable regions like this:

Selection	Editable Region Name
2 1/2	Bathrooms
1	Acres
2500	Square Feet
350,000	Price

Continued

Continued

11. Save your page; click OK to acknowledge that some block content is within an editable region — if desired, you can select the Don't Show Me This Message Again option to avoid this alert in the future.

Editable regions are a cornerstone of the template structure and, as you can see, have a great number of uses.

END

Establishing Optional Regions

One of my clients quite regularly wanted to feature one of his products over the others, so we developed a special logo exactly for that purpose. Whenever a product was to be highlighted, I modified the page to include the special logo rather than the standard one. Typically, this took up to a half-hour every time the change was made. Not only did I have to find the catalog page with the to-be-featured item and replace the logo — something else I had to hunt for — I also had to find the previously featured item page and revert the special logo placed there to the standard one. Not difficult work, but certainly tedious.

Dreamweaver's Optional Region feature is intended to reduce, if not eliminate, such tiresome chores. Content placed on a template within an optional region is conditionally shown or not shown on the template-derived page. In the just-described situation, this feature enables me to put both logos in the same template, each in its own optional region. By default, the main logo is shown, but if I decide not to show it, the special logo is shown in its place. Optional regions are extremely powerful.

Optional regions work somewhat like a cross between repeating region and editable attributes. Like repeating regions, optional regions can surround any portion of a page; also, they are not editable by default, although it's possible to create an editable optional region. After an optional region has been placed on the template page — as with editable attributes — the Template Properties dialog box is used to set the condition that displays or hides the content on a template-derived page.

The conditions that control an optional region range from a basic true-false or Boolean statement to more complex, evaluated expressions. Reflecting this, the New Optional Region dialog box contains two tabs, Basic and Advanced. Under the Basic tab, you simply enter the name for the optional region and indicate whether to display the region by default. The Advanced tab, shown in Figure 27-11, gives you the opportunity to set the condition dependent on another existing template parameter or enter a template expression.

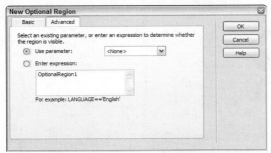

Figure 27-11: Optional regions can be controlled by the state of another parameter directly or by the evaluation of a template expression.

Note
The Basic and Advanced tabs are mutually exclusive. The tab showing when OK is selected determines which template parameter is used.

Now, look at an example to see how both the Basic and Advanced approaches work together. Take the situation, described at the beginning of this section, which requires the use of a special logo every so often. To accomplish this, I create one optional region using the Basic tab of the New Optional Region dialog box. In this region, I just enter a name, mainLogoRegion, and enable the Show By Default option. In this region, I place my standard logo. The Basic tab creates a template parameter with code like this in the <head>:

```
<!-- TemplateParam name="mainLogoRegion" type="boolean" value="true" -->
```

Next, I create a second optional region and, this time, select the Advanced tab of the New Optional Region dialog box. I want this region to be displayed only when the other region is not. To achieve this effect, I select the Enter Expression option and enter the following in the text area:

```
mainLogoRegion != true
```

With optional regions, the name is the same as the condition; so translated into English, this expression reads, "Show this region if mainLogoRegion is not shown." As shown in Figure 27-12, Dreamweaver uses the condition as the name of the optional region, and this name is represented in the tab above the optional regions.

Figure 27-12: Complex expressions can be used to show or hide optional regions.

Dreamweaver template expressions support a subset of JavaScript operators, so I could have also written this expression like this:

```
!mainLogoRegion
```

In a different situation, you might want to tie a number of noncontiguous optional regions together so that if the main region shows, the others would as well. You achieve this by setting Use Parameter to the name of the main region. You'll find a more detailed discussion of template expressions a little later in this chapter.

To insert an optional region, follow these steps:

1. Choose Insert ➪ Template Objects ➪ Optional Region or, from the Templates menu of the Insert bar, click the Optional Region icon.

2. If you want to create a template parameter, from the Basic tab, follow these steps:

    a. Enter a unique name for the optional region in the Name field.

    b. Choose the Show By Default option if you want to make the region initially viewable.

3. If you want to link this optional region to the state of another optional region, from the Advanced tab, follow these steps:

    a. Select the Use Parameter option.

    b. Choose an existing optional region from the drop-down list.

4. If you want to control the optional region display with a template parameter, from the Advanced tab, follow these steps:

    a. Select the Enter Expression option.

    b. Enter the desired expression in the text area.

5. Click OK when you're finished.

Combining Editable and Optional Regions

Similar to repeating regions, optional regions by themselves are not editable. Many uses exist for optional regions with the designed content either displayed or not displayed. However, in certain situations, the optional content needs to be editable as well. For such situations, Dreamweaver provides the Editable Optional Region object.

The procedure for adding an editable optional region is exactly the same as for inserting an optional region—Dreamweaver automatically includes an editable region within the optional region. The new editable region is also automatically named.

Tip
You can change the name of the automatically added editable region by selecting the template region tab or its tag in the Tag Selector and then changing the name in the Property inspector.

To add an editable optional region, follow these steps:

1. Choose Insert ➪ Template Objects ➪ Editable Optional Region or, from the Templates menu of the Insert bar, click the Editable Optional Region icon.

2. Follow the procedure outlined for inserting an optional region.

3. Click OK when you're finished.

Of course, if you want to add an editable region to an optional region containing locked content, you can always do so when editing the template.

Setting Optional Region Properties

Although you set up an area of the page to be optionally displayed in the template, you actually choose the display option—whether to show or hide the region—in the document created from the template. As with editable attributes, the Template Properties dialog box handles control of the optional regions. Unlike editable attributes, optional regions only use true/false values to determine whether a selected region is either shown (true) or not shown (false).

Instead of the template parameter statement found in templates, Dreamweaver inserts instance parameters into the <head> section of the template-derived document, like this one:

```
<!-- InstanceParam name="mainLogoRegion" type="boolean" value="true" -->
```

To set the parameters of an optional region in a template-based document, follow these steps:

1. Choose Modify ➪ Template Properties. The Template Properties dialog box is displayed.

2. Select the optional region you want to affect.

3. If you want to allow the optional region to be modified in a document based on a nested template, choose the Allow Nested Templates to Control This option. If the option is selected, the phrase pass through in parentheses replaces the Show Attribute Name options and appears in the list.

4. Otherwise, select the Show *Attribute Name* option to set the value to true and deselect it to set the value to false.

5. To set the value of any other optional regions on the page, choose the entry from the list and repeat steps 2 through 4.

6. Click OK when you're finished.

Evaluating Template Expressions

So far in this chapter, you've seen a little of what template expressions can do. With optional regions, template expressions are either set explicitly or evaluated to true or false. Template expressions can also be used throughout the template to great effect. Here is a short list of what's possible with template expressions:

✦ Alternate the background color of a row contained in a repeating region.

✦ Automatically number each row in a repeating region.

✦ List the total number of rows in a repeating region.

✦ Show an optional region if a certain number of rows are used, or another region if that number of rows is exceeded.

✦ Create sequential navigation links, allowing users to page to the next — or previous — document in a series.

✦ Compute values displayed in a table, displaying items such as basic cost, tax, shipping, and total.

✦ Display particular content depending on the position of the row — first, second, second-to-last, or last, for example — in the repeating region.

Two types of template expressions exist: template expression statements and inline template expressions. Template expression statements take the form of a specialized HTML comment, like this:

```
<!-- TemplateExpr expr="fileExt" -->
```

Template expression statements are coded by hand. Inline template expressions are surrounded by parentheses and double @ signs, like this:

```
@@(fileExt)@@
```

Inline template expressions can only be entered by hand, but they are very flexible. You can insert an inline template expression as an attribute into any of Dreamweaver's text field interfaces, such as the Link field of the text Property inspector or the Bg (Background Color) field of the row Property inspector. Template expressions not entered as attributes appear as Invisible Elements with a double-@ sign symbol as shown in Figure 27-13. Template expression statements appear with a script icon.

Caution   Although you can enter an inline template expression without a problem in the Code view, you cannot enter one on the page in Design view.

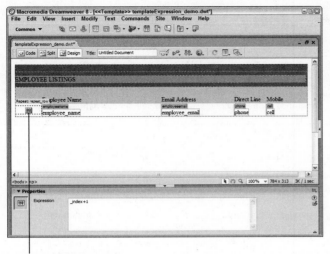

Inline template expression

Figure 27-13: Template expressions can either be entered as statements or inline code.

Template Expression Language and Object Model

Template expressions are written in their own language, which uses a subset of JavaScript operators and its own object model. The syntax of template expressions closely resembles that of JavaScript, and both use a similar dot notation to refer to the properties of a specific object. Similar to JavaScript, Dreamweaver template expressions also have their own object model, although the object model for template expressions is much more limited in scope.

The elements supported by Dreamweaver template expressions are detailed in Table 27-1.

Table 27-1: Template Expression Features and Operators

Literals	*Syntax*	*Example*
Numeric Literal	Double-quoted numbers	"123"
String Literal	Double-quoted string	"Chapter"
Boolean Literals	true/false	true
String Concatenation	string1 + string2	"Number of rows: " + _numRows
Ternary Operator		
Conditional	condition ? resultA : resultB	(_index & 1) ? #FFFFFF : #CCCCCC

Continued

Table 27-1 *(continued)*

Logical Operators	Syntax	Example
Logical NOT	!operand	!mainLogoRegion
Logical AND	operand1 && operand2	onSale && nowFeatured
Logical OR	operand1 || operand2	onSale || nowFeatured

Arithmetic Operators		
Addition	operand1 + operand2	_numRows + 1
Subtraction	operand1 – operand2	_index – 1
Multiplication	operand1 * operand2	basePrice * taxBase
Division	operand1 / operand2	numSold / quantityShown
Modulo	operand1 % operand2	_index % 2

Comparison Operators		
Less Than	operand1 < operand2	inStock < numSold
Greater Than	operand1 > operand2	numSold > numShipped
Less Than or Equal	operand1 <= operand2	_index <= _numRows
Greater Than or Equal	operand1 >=operand2	_numRows >= pageLimit
Equal	operand1 = = operand2	_index == 10
Not Equal	operand1 != operand2	_numRows != 1

Bitwise Operators		
Bitwise NOT	~operand	~4
Bitwise AND	operand1 & operand2	_index & 1
Bitwise OR	operand1 | operand2	4 | 8
Bitwise XOR	operand1 ^ operand2	2 ^ 4
Bitwise Signed Right Shift	operand1 >> n	8 >> 1
Bitwise Left Shift	operand << n	1 << 0

The template expressions document model is made up of two primary objects: _document and _repeat. The document object contains all the template variables found on the page. For example, if you create an optional region with the name altImageRegion, you can refer to it in a document expression with the following statement:

```
<!-- TemplateBeginIf cond="_document.altImageRegion" -->
```

However, the _document prefix is implicit, and the same statement can be written like this:

```
<!-- TemplateBeginIf cond="altImageRegion" -->
```

As you may suspect, the _repeat object refers to a repeating region. The _repeat object has a number of very useful properties, as shown in Table 27-2.

Table 27-2: _repeat Object Properties

Property	Description
_index	Returns the index number of the current entry. The _index property is zero-based, so for the first entry of a repeating region, _index equals zero.
_numRows	Returns the total number of entries in a repeating region.
_isFirst	Returns True if the current entry is the first entry of a repeating region, False otherwise.
_isLast	Returns True if the current entry is the last entry of a repeating region, False otherwise.
_prevRecord	Returns the _repeat object for the entry before the current entry. For example, if _index = 2, then _prevRecord._index = 1. If _prevRecord is used in the first entry, an error occurs.
_nextRecord	Returns the _repeat object for the entry after the current entry. For example, if _index = 2, then _nextRecord._index = 3.
_parent	Returns the _repeat object for a repeating region enclosing the current repeating region. For example, use _parent._numRows to find the total number of rows of the outer repeating region.

The _repeat object is also implicit, and it is not necessary to reference it specifically in a template expression.

Multiple-If Template Expressions

Certain template expressions cannot be handled by referencing a single condition — "If A is true, show B" does not cover every possible circumstance. What if you wanted to test against multiple conditions and provide multiple results? Can Dreamweaver handle something like "If A is true, show B; but if C is true, show D — and if neither of them are true, show E"? With the help of multiple-if expressions, you bet it can.

With a multiple-if template expression, you can test for any number of conditions and act accordingly. Multiple-if expressions use two different template expressions: one to close the entire expression and another one for each separate case. Here is an example:

```
<!-- TemplateBeginMultipleIf -->
<!-- checks value of template parameter SKU and shows the desired image-->
  <!-- TemplateBeginIfClause cond = "SKU == 101">
    <img src = "/images/ring101.gif" width="125" height="125">
```

```
<!-- TemplateEndIfClause-->

<!-- TemplateBeginIfClause cond = "SKU == 102">
 <img src = "/images/bracelet102.gif" width="125" height="125">
<!-- TemplateEndIfClause-->

<!-- TemplateBeginIfClause cond = "SKU == 103">
 <img src = "/images/necklace103.gif" width="125" height="125">
<!-- TemplateEndIfClause-->

//default display if none of the other conditions are met
<!-- TemplateBeginIfClause cond = "SKU != 103">
 <img src = "/images/spacer.gif" width="125" height="125">
<!-- TemplateEndIfClause-->
<!-- TemplateEndMultipleIf -->
```

In this code, if none of the conditions are met, a blank spacer image is displayed. As with other template expressions, multiple-if expressions must be coded by hand.

Template Expression Examples

Template expressions obviously have a great deal of power built-in, but how do you put it to use? Let's look at some specific examples to help you get a better understanding of template expressions in general, as well as to give you some useful tools.

Alternating Row Background Colors

If you have a data-filled table of any significant size, alternating background colors for each row greatly increases the readability of the data. Template expressions provide a technique for specifying the two background colors — and automatically applying the right color whenever a new row is added in a repeating region. The key to this technique is the conditional operator.

The conditional operator has three parts: the condition and the two results. If the condition is evaluated as true, the first result is applied; if it is not, the second is applied. In this case, the condition that is examined involves the _index property, which returns the position of the current row. By combining the _index property with the bitwise AND operator, &, like this:

```
_index & 1
```

True is returned every other row, starting with the second row. The full template expression specifies the two colors as hexadecimal values; the second value specified (here, a light yellow) is returned in the first row, the first value (white) in the following row, and so on:

```
@@((_index & 1) ? '#FFFFFF' : '#FFFF99')@@
```

This template expression is entered as the bgcolor attribute for the table row containing the data in a template's repeating region. Note the use of the single quotes around the color values; quotes are needed in the conditional operator syntax, and single quotes are used here because Dreamweaver encloses the entire attribute value with double quotes.

Here's the code for the entire table in the template document. The tag containing the alternating row background color is shown in bold:

```
<table width="100%" border="0" cellspacing="0" cellpadding="0">
  <tr>
    <th>Item</th>
    <th>SKU</th>
    <th>Price</th>
  </tr>
  <!-- TemplateBeginRepeat name="repeatRow" -->
  <tr bgcolor="@@((_index & 1) ? '#FFFFFF' : '#FFFF99')@@">
    <td><!-- TemplateBeginEditable name="itemEdit" -->itemEdit<!--
TemplateEndEditable --></td>
    <td><!-- TemplateBeginEditable name="skuEdit" -->skuEdit<!--
TemplateEndEditable --></td>
    <td><!-- TemplateBeginEditable name="priceEdit" -->priceEdit<!--
TemplateEndEditable -->
    </td>
  </tr>
  <!-- TemplateEndRepeat -->
</table>
```

You won't see any changes in the template itself — for the full effect, you have to open up a document based on the template and add a few rows. As you can see in Figure 27-14, whenever another entry is added to the repeating region in the template-based document, the alternating color is automatically applied.

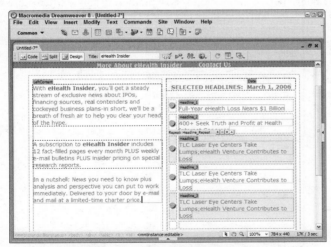

Figure 27-14: Using a conditional operator for the `bgcolor` attribute automatically generates alternating row colors in a repeating region.

Tip

As written, the code in this technique alternates color every row. To alternate the color every two rows, change the value in the condition from 1 to 2 so that the template expression reads:

```
@@((_index & 2) ? '#FFFFFF' : '#FFFF99')@@
```

Automatic Row Numbering

In a template with a repeating region, you often want the flexibility of adding as many rows as required and adding a reference number to each row. The _index property of the template object model provides an easy way to number rows automatically. The only trick to this technique is to remember that _index is a zero-based property and you add a 1 to have the correct row number displayed.

Here's the template expression by itself:

```
@@(_index + 1)@@
```

This code should be entered directly in Code view within the repeating region. You can combine this with any other text, such as a following period or color or styles. Here's an example, bolded, in a right-aligned table cell with several non-breaking spaces trailing to create a decimal-align look:

```
<td align="right">@@(_index + 1)@@     </td>
```

The right-align and non-breaking space combination keeps numbering in line when more than 10 entries are involved, as shown in Figure 27-15.

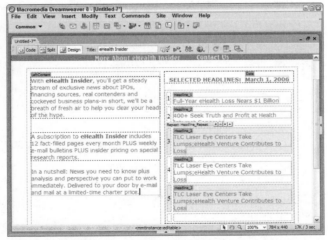

Figure 27-15: The _index property helps to automatically number rows in a repeating region.

Computing Values in a Table

After a value has been entered for a template expression variable, it can be used in calculations and can also be used as a deciding factor in a multiple-if statement. For example, each page of a template shows a catalog item and all the relevant information. Included in that relevant information is the price — an element that may fluctuate far more than the description or picture of the item. Should the client want to offer a special discount for higher quantities, template expressions can automatically calculate the new price as well as the savings.

In this example, I've set up one template parameter, `priceVar`, and given it a default value of `100`:

```
<!-- TemplateParam name="priceVar" type="number" value="100" -->
```

This code goes in the non-editable portion of the template's `<head>`. The example application, shown in Figure 27-16, uses three different template expressions. The first, `@@priceVar@@`, displays the parameter set with the Template Properties dialog box.

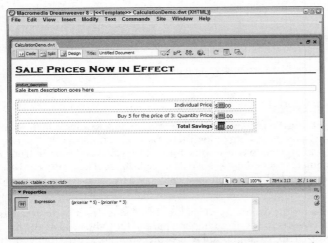

Figure 27-16: Template expressions, set in Template Properties, can be used to calculate other values in a template-based document.

The second shows the quantity price — which, here, is the base price times 3:

```
@@(priceVar * 3)@@
```

The third expression displays the savings a buyer could receive by buying in quantity. In this example formula, the price times 3 is subtracted from the price times 5:

```
@@((priceVar * 5) - (priceVar * 3))@@
```

Again, you can add whatever text or styles are necessary. Here, a dollar sign is placed in front of every expression that is followed by a decimal point and two zeros, as you can see in Listing 27-1.

Listing 27-1: Template Expressions Computing Example

```
<table width="100%" border="0" cellspacing="0" cellpadding="0">
  <tr>
    <td width="77%" align="right">Individual Price</td>
    <td width="23%" align="right">$@@(priceVar)@@.00</td>
  </tr>
  <tr>
    <td align="right">Buy 5 for the price of 3! Quantity Price</td>
    <td align="right">$@@(priceVar * 3)@@.00</td-
  </tr>
  <tr>
    <td align="right"><strong>Total Savings</strong></td>
    <td align="right"><strong>$@@((priceVar * 5) - ↲
(priceVar * 3))@@.00</strong></td>
  </tr>
</table>
```

Now the calculations on this template are ready to be used for any product in the catalog, at any price point, offering the same deal.

Sequential Navigation Links

Although much of the Web is based on the principle that you can link to any page from any other page, certain situations — such as help or instructional applications — require sequential navigation. Numerous help applications use some form of Previous and Next buttons, for example. If these files are named sequentially — such as docFile10, docFile11, docFile12, and so on — template expressions can be used to automatically code the links to the prior and subsequent pages.

Rely on template expressions for the capability to handle string concatenation to create these auto-updating links. The first task is to set up a template parameter to be used as the number of the current file in the series. If, for example, you're creating docFile5.htm from your template, the template parameter is set to 5. To accomplish this task, use Dreamweaver's editable attribute facility to create the template parameter. This example assumes that you are editing a template with Previous and Next buttons already in place. Follow these steps:

1. Select the `<a>` tag surrounding the Previous button from the Tag Selector.

2. Choose Modify ⇨ Templates ⇨ Make Attribute Editable.

3. In the Editable Tag Attributes dialog box, click Add (+) and enter a dummy attribute name such as **baseLink**. Choose an attribute name that will be ignored by browsers rather than a real attribute.

4. Make sure that Make Attribute Editable is selected.

5. Choose Number as the Type of attribute from the drop-down list.

6. Enter a default number. This number is set for every file created, so the default value is merely a placeholder.

Now you can use the template parameter set up in a template expression. Follow these steps:

1. Click the Previous button or link on the template page.

2. In the Property inspector, enter code similar to the following in the Link field:

```
@@('cFile' + (baseLink - 1) + '.htm')@@
```

In this example, the sequential files are all within the same folder and named `docFile1.htm`, `docFile2.htm`, and so on. My template parameter, defined in the previous step, is called **baseLink**.

3. Next, click the Next button to perform a similar operation.

4. In the Link field, enter code like this:

```
@@('docFile' + (baseLink + 1) + '.htm')@@
```

Here, instead of subtracting a number from the base value, as you did for the Previous button link, you add one.

After the template is saved, create a file based on the template. Now you're ready to specify the template parameter. Follow these steps:

1. Choose Modify ⇨ Template Properties and select the editable attribute established in the template.

2. Enter the number value corresponding to the filename of the current sequentially named page. For example, if the file is named `docFile5.htm`, enter **5**.

3. Click OK when you're finished.

When you preview your page, notice that the Previous and Next buttons now link the proper pages in the sequence, as shown in Figure 27-17.

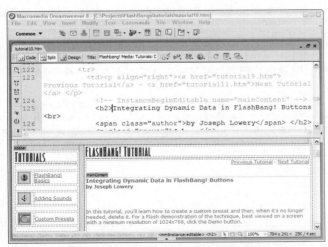

Figure 27-17: Although it looks like a standard link, this code was generated by Dreamweaver during the design-time construction of this template-based document.

Tip   You can also use optional regions to hide the Previous button when the template-based page is the first in the series and the Next button when a page is the last in the series. It's all in the power of template expressions.

Nesting Templates

The simple template with its combination of locked and editable regions truly reflects the reality of many Web pages where the overall structure is constant and the details of the content vary. Often, however, a single locked area is too rigid to really be useful in a complex site. Suppose for a moment you're working on a site for a magazine publisher with multiple brands. The client wants a general look and feel for the entire site with separate navigation and content for each magazine. One way to achieve this effect is to use multiple templates — one set for each magazine, all incorporating the parent-company style. The problem here is that to affect changes on the highest level, all the templates need to be changed. Another way — a better way — is to use nested templates.

Nested templates allow template-based documents to have numerous tiers of locked regions. With nested templates, the magazine publisher in our example could make a change to just the master template and the modifications would ripple through all the other magazine-specific templates and on down to their related pages. Best of all, there's no real limit on nesting templates: Your template-based files can be as deeply nested as you need them to be.

Here's an overview of how nested templates work:

✦ A new page based on the master template is created and saved as a template; this new document is the nested template.

✦ Within the editable areas originally setup in the master template, new editable areas are placed. All areas not designated as editable in the nested template are locked.

✦ A new document is created, based on the nested template. The only editable areas are those inserted in the nested template.

✦ When modifications are made to the nested template, the changes are reflected in the pages based on that template. When modifications are made to the master template, the changes are applied to both the nested template and to documents based on the nested template.

Dreamweaver employs a color-coding system to help you differentiate editable regions inserted in the master template from those added in the nested template. Although you can't tell it in this black-and-white screen shot, the master template editable regions are shown in orange, whereas nested template editable regions are shown in blue (see Figure 27-18).

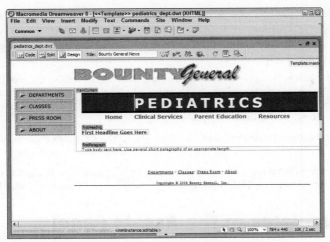

Figure 27-18: The master template editable region — the region on the left side here — is highlighted with an orange outline. The nested template editable regions, the right-side regions, are blue.

To create a nested template, follow these steps:

1. Create a master root-level template by choosing File ⇨ Save As Template for an existing page or selecting New Template from the Template category of the Assets panel for new documents. The master template contains all the elements — navigation, logos, footers, and so on — common to all template-based pages in the site.

2. Insert editable regions wherever variable content is desired in the master template and save the template when you're ready.

3. Create a new document based on the master template by following these steps:

   a. Choose File Í New to open the New Document dialog box.

   b. Select the Templates category.

   c. Make sure the current site is selected in the Templates For list.

   d. Select the desired master template from the Template list.

   e. Click Create.

4. Save the newly created document as a template. By saving a template-derived document as a template, a nested template is created.

5. In the nested template, make any changes needed within the editable regions. These changes are locked in any document based on the nested template.

6. Add any desired template regions (editable, repeating, or optional) within the existing editable regions from the master template. When the first editable region is inserted in the nested template, the editable regions from the master template turn orange to differentiate them from the new regions.

7. After you've finished adding the desired template regions to the nested template, save the file.

Now, when creating documents based on the nested template, you are still able to modify content within an editable region — but only those editable regions added in the nested template.

Working with Templates in the Assets Panel

As a site grows, so does the number of templates it employs. Overall management of your templates is conducted through the Templates category of the Assets panel. You can open the Templates category by choosing Window ➪ Assets and clicking the Template icon on the left side of the Assets panel. The Templates category, shown in Figure 27-19, displays a list of the current site's available templates in the lower pane and a preview of the selected template in the upper pane.

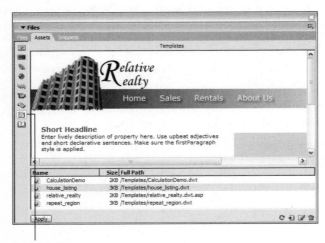

Template icon

Figure 27-19: Use the Templates category of the Assets panel to preview, delete, open, create, or apply your current site's templates.

The Templates category has these five buttons along the bottom:

✦ **Apply:** Creates a document derived from the currently selected template if the current document is blank; if the current document is based on a template, this option changes the locked regions of the document to match the selected template.

✦ **Refresh Site List:** Displays the list of all templates currently in the site.

✦ **New Template:** Creates a new blank template.

✦ **Edit:** Loads the selected template for modification.

✦ **Delete:** Removes the selected template.

The Assets panel's context menu offers all these options and more, as explained in Table 27-3.

Table 27-3: Template Category Context Menu

Command	Description
Refresh Site List	Displays the list of all templates currently in the site cache.
Recreate Site List	Reloads the template site list into the cache.
New Template	Starts a new blank template.
Edit	Opens the selected template for modifying.
Apply	Creates a document derived from the currently selected template if the current document is blank. If the current document is based on a template, this option changes the locked regions of the document to match the selected template. The same effects can also be achieved by dragging the template from the Assets panel to the current document.
Rename	Renames the selected template.
Delete	Removes the selected template.
Update Current Page	Applies any changes made in the template to the current page, if the current page is derived from a template.
Update Site	Applies any changes made in any templates to all template-based documents in the site.
Copy to Site	Copies the highlighted template, but none of the dependent files, to the selected site.
Locate in Site	Opens the Site panel and highlights the selected template.

Creating a Blank Template

Not all templates are created from existing documents. Some Web designers prefer to create their templates from scratch. To create a blank template, follow these steps:

1. Open the Templates category of the Assets panel by selecting its symbol.

2. From the Templates category, select New Template. A new, untitled template is created.

3. Enter a title for your new template and press Enter (Return).

4. While the new template is selected, click the Edit button. The blank template opens in a new Dreamweaver window.

5. Insert your page elements.

6. Mark any elements or areas as editable regions using one of the methods previously described.

7. Save your template.

Opening and Deleting Templates

You can edit a template — to change the locked or editable regions — in several ways. To use the first method, choose File ➪ Open and, in the Select File dialog box, change the Files of Type to Template Files (*.dwt) on Window systems, or select Template Files from the Show drop-down list on Macintosh systems. Then, locate the Templates folder in your defined site to select the template to open.

The second method of opening a template for modification uses the Templates category of the Assets panel. Select a template to modify and click the Edit button. You can also double-click your template to open it for editing. Finally, if you're working in the Site panel, open a template by selecting the Templates folder for your site and opening any of the files found there.

Tip

After you've made your modifications to the template, you don't have to use the Save As Template command to store the file — you can use the regular File ➪ Save command or the keyboard shortcut Ctrl+S (Command+S). Likewise, if you want to save your template under a new name, use the Save As command.

As with any set of files, there comes a time to clean house and remove files that are no longer in use. To remove a template, first open the Templates category of the Assets panel. Next, select the file you want to remove and click the Delete button.

Caution

Be forewarned: Dreamweaver does not alert you if files exist that were created from the template that you're about to delete. Deleting the template, in effect, "orphans" those documents, and they can no longer be updated via a template.

Applying Templates

Dreamweaver makes it easy to try a variety of different looks for your document while maintaining the same content. After you've created a document from a template, you can apply any other template to it. The only requirement is that the two templates have editable regions with the same names. When might this feature come in handy? In one scenario, you might develop a number of possible Web site designs for a client and create templates for each approach, which are then applied to the identical content. Or, in an ongoing site, you could completely change the look of a catalog seasonally but retain all the content.

To apply a template to a document, follow these steps:

1. Open the Templates category of the Assets panel.

2. Make sure the Web page to which you want to apply the style is the active document.

3. From the Templates category, select the template you want to use and click the Apply button.

Tip You can also drag onto the current page the template you'd like to apply or choose Modify ➪ Templates ➪ Apply Template to Page from the menus.

4. If content exists without a matching editable region, Dreamweaver displays the Choose Editable Region for Orphaned Content dialog box. To receive the content, select one of the listed editable regions from the template being applied and click OK.

The new template is applied to the document, and all the new locked areas replace all the old locked areas.

Mapping Inconsistent Template Regions

When Dreamweaver applies a template to a page, it attempts to map the regions on the two pages to one another. If there is a one-to-one correspondence between the regions on the page and on the template — for every editable region in the template, an editable region exists with the same name on the page — everything goes smoothly, and the template is applied without incident. If, however, the region names do not match — for example, the template's main content area is called `theContent`, whereas the page's main content area is called `mainContent` — Dreamweaver gives you the opportunity to place the content properly with the Inconsistent Region Names dialog box, shown in Figure 27-20.

Figure 27-20: The Inconsistent Region Names dialog box works with the full range of template regions: editable, optional, and repeating.

The Inconsistent Region Names dialog box appears automatically when Dreamweaver finds regions that do not match in a template and the document to which the template is being applied. You can map the content in the document to any region in the template or discard the content. However, you cannot ignore the unmapped content; Dreamweaver does not proceed with the template application until all inconsistently named regions are addressed in some fashion.

To handle inconsistently named regions, follow these steps:

1. When the Inconsistent Region Names dialog box appears, select the first unresolved region.

2. From the Move Content To New Region drop-down list, select the region you want to assign to the unmapped region.

3. If no region is suitable and you want to discard the content, choose Nowhere from the list.

4. To use the same choice for all regions displayed, choose the Use For All option.

5. To map another region, select its name from the list and repeat steps 2 through 4.

6. Click OK when you're finished.

You always find certain regions, such as `doctitle` and `head`, listed in the Move Content To New Region list. In general, you would not want to move any body-area content into these regions.

Tip   The region names must match precisely—including the case of the two names—or the Inconsistent Region Names dialog box appears.

Updating Templates

Anytime you save a change to an existing template—whether or not any documents have been created from it—Dreamweaver asks if you'd like to update all the documents in the local site attached to the template. You can also update the current page or the entire site at any time, just as you can update Library elements. Updating documents based on a template can save you an enormous amount of time—especially when numerous changes are involved.

Caution   The template structure changed significantly in Dreamweaver MX when compared to earlier versions of the program. When you open a template created in Dreamweaver 4, or an earlier version, in Dreamweaver 8, the structure is updated. After being updated, the template cannot be modified in any version except Dreamweaver MX or higher.

To update a single page, open the page and choose Modify ➪ Templates ➪ Update Current Page or select the same command from the context menu of the Assets panel. Either way, the update is instantly applied.

To update a series of pages or an entire site, follow these steps:

1. Choose Modify ➪ Templates ➪ Update Pages. The Update Pages dialog box, shown in Figure 27-21, appears.

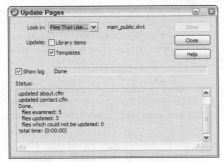

Figure 27-21: Any changes made to a template can be applied automatically to the template's associated files by using the Update Pages command.

2. To update all the documents using all the templates for an entire site, choose Entire Site from the Look In option; then select the name of the site from the accompanying drop-down list.

3. To update pages using a particular template, choose Files That Use from the Look In option and then select the name of the template.

4. To view a report of the progress of the update, make sure that the Show Log option is enabled.

5. Click Start to begin the update process.

The log window displays a list of the files examined and updated, the total number of files that could not be updated, and the elapsed time.

Removing Template Markup

Mistakes are made, clients change their minds, bosses change directions — for whatever reason, you'll find that you need to remove template markup from time to time. Luckily, Dreamweaver has made it as easy to delete the template indicators as it is to insert them. With a little know-how, you can remove template markup from an editable attribute for an entire site.

Deleting Template Markup Individually

Quite often I find I need to convert an editable region to a locked area. You can accomplish this change in one of two ways — you can delete the surrounding template tags in the code or you can use a Dreamweaver command, Remove Template Markup. Personally, I find the command approach to be much faster and more efficient. Individual template markup can only be removed from the template itself.

To remove any surrounding template code via the command, place your cursor within the template region and choose Modify ⇨ Templates ⇨ Remove Template Markup. Alternatively, right-click (Control+click) and choose Templates ⇨ Remove Template Markup.

The Remove Template Markup command works only on the template markup immediately enclosing the cursor position. If, for example, you need to remove an editable optional region and convert the content to being locked, you issue the Remove Template Markup command twice: once to remove the editable region and again to remove the optional region.

Caution   Using the Remove Template Markup command to remove an optional region does not delete the corresponding TemplateParam statement in the `<head>` tag. If no other optional region uses the same TemplateParam statement, you must remove the code manually.

Removing Template Markup from an Entire Page

Template-derived documents don't need to stay template-derived documents forever. All you need do is to detach the document from its template, and all template markup in the page is removed. To detach a document from the template choose Modify ➪ Templates ➪ Detach from Template.

Note   If, for any reason, you need to remove all the markup from a template itself, the fastest way is to create a document from that template and then issue the Detach from Template command.

Exporting a Site without Template Markup

Not all sites are template-based. Dreamweaver gives you the power to strip all the template markup from template-based documents in an entire site. This command is particularly useful when migrating previously template-based documents to a site that does not use templates. Just to hedge your bets, Dreamweaver optionally exports the data from your template-based documents into XML files so that, if necessary, the data can be applied to a new template.

The Export without Markup command handles more than just the templates, however. An entire copy of your site is copied to a new folder, sans template markup. Even the Template folder itself, with all the site's templates intact, is copied. Best of all, this is not necessarily a one-time feature. If repeated, you have the option to extract only the modified files.

To export a site without template markup, follow these steps:

1. Choose Modify ➪ Templates ➪ Export without Markup. The Export Site WithouTemplate Markup dialog box, shown in Figure 27-22, appears.

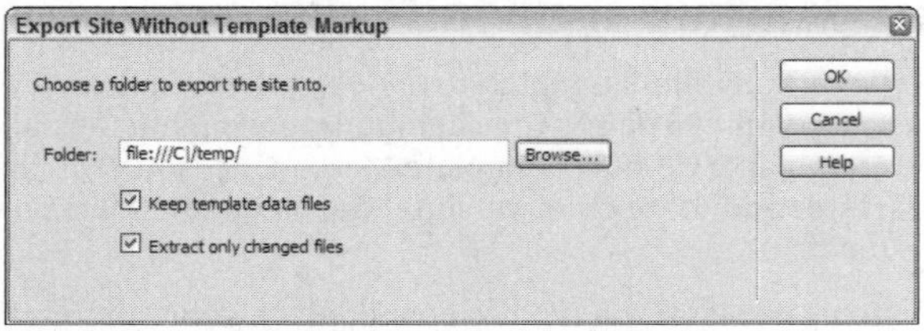

Figure 27-22: The Export without Markup command duplicates your entire site in another folder while simultaneously removing all markup from template-derived files.

2. Enter the path to the folder to hold the exported site or click the Browse button to locate the folder. Because the entire site is exported, the folder you choose may not be contained in the current site.

3. If you want to maintain the data from the template-based documents, choose the Keep Template Data Files option.

Dreamweaver stores the data in a standard XML file format. For more about Dreamweaver's XML export features, see Chapter 31.

4. If you have previously exported the site with this command and want to update your export, choose the Extract Only Changed Files option.

5. Click OK when you're finished.

After the operation is completed, you'll probably want to define a new site to manage the exported files — Dreamweaver does not do this task for you automatically.

Changing the Default Document

Each time you open a new document in Dreamweaver, a blank page is created. The code that makes up that blank page depends on which document type you choose — HTML, XML, ColdFusion, or ASP.NET, among others. The default documents on which the new pages are based are all stored in the Dreamweaver 8\Configuration\DocumentTypes\NewDocuments folder. A selected default page works in a similar fashion to the templates in that you can create new documents from it, but no editable or locked regions exist — everything in the page can always be altered. For example, the basic HTML document is a bare-bones structure with only a few properties specified — a document type and a character set:

```
<!DOCTYPE HTML PUBLIC "-//W3C//DTD HTML 4.01 Transitional//EN"
"http://www.w3.org/TR/html4/loose.dtd">
<HTML>
<HEAD>
<TITLE>Untitled Document</TITLE>
<meta http-equiv="Content-Type" content="text/html; charset=">
</HEAD>

<BODY>

</BODY>
  </HTML>
```

Naturally, you can change any of these elements — and add many, many more — after you've opened a page. But what if you want to have a `<meta>` tag with creator information in every page that comes out of your Web design company? You can do it in Dreamweaver manually, but it's a bother; and chances are good that you'll forget. Luckily, Dreamweaver provides a more efficient solution.

In keeping with its overall design philosophy of extensibility, Dreamweaver enables you to modify the default file as you would any other file. Just choose File ➪ Open and select the appropriate file from the Dreamweaver 8\Configuration\DocumentTypes\NewDocuments.

After you have made your changes, save the file as you would normally. Now, to test your modifications, choose File ➪ New and select your document type. Your modifications appear in the new document.

Summary

Much of a Web designer's responsibility is related to document production, and Dreamweaver offers a comprehensive template solution to reduce the workload. When planning your strategy for building an entire Web site, remember that templates provide these advantages:

✦ Templates can be created from any Web page.

✦ Dreamweaver templates combine locked and editable regions. Editable regions must be defined individually.

✦ After you declare a template, you can create new documents from it.

✦ With Dreamweaver's repeating regions, you can add or remove data from tables without altering the table structure.

✦ Show or hide content with each new template-derived document with Dreamweaver optional regions.

✦ Nested templates can be used to structurally organize locked and editable content.

✦ If a template is altered, pages built from that template can be automatically updated.

✦ The default template that Dreamweaver uses can be modified so that every time you choose File ➪ New and select a file type, a new version of your customized template is created.

In the next chapter, you learn how to streamline production and site maintenance by using repeating page elements from the Dreamweaver Library.

✦   ✦   ✦

Using the Repeating Elements Library

One of the challenges of designing a Web site is ensuring that buttons, copyright notices, and other cross-site features always remain consistent. Fortunately, Dreamweaver offers a useful feature called *Library items* that helps you insert repeating elements, such as a navigation bar or a company logo, into every Web page you create. With one command, you can update and maintain Library items efficiently and productively.

In this chapter, you examine the nature and the importance of repeating elements and learn how to effectively use the Dreamweaver Library feature for all your sites. In addition, you see how to use server-side includes — generally known as SSIs — to integrate code and content at both design time and runtime.

Dreamweaver Library Items

Library items within Dreamweaver are another means for you, as a designer, to maintain consistency throughout your site. Imagine that you have a navigation bar on every page that contains links to all the other pages on your site. It's highly likely that you'll eventually (probably more than once) need to make changes to the navigation bar. In a traditional Web development environment, you must modify every single page. This creates numerous opportunities for making mistakes, missing pages, and adding code in the wrong place. Moreover, the whole process is tedious — ask anyone who has had to modify the copyright notice at the bottom of every Web page for a site with more than 1,000 pages.

One traditional method of updating repeating elements is to use *server-side includes*. A server-side include causes the server to place a component, such as a copyright notice, in a specified area of a Web page when it's sent to the user. This arrangement, however, increases the strain on your already overworked Web server, and many hosting computers do not permit server-side includes for this reason. To add to the designer's frustrations, you can't lay out a Web page in a WYSIWYG (What You See Is What You Get) format and simultaneously see the server-side scripts (unless you're using Dreamweaver). Therefore, you either take the time to calculate the specific amount of space the server-side script takes up on the Web page, or you cross your fingers and guess.

Dreamweaver offers you a better way. You can use an important innovation called the *Library*. The Library is designed to make repetitive updating quick, easy, and as error-free as possible. The Library's key features include the following:

✦ Any item — whether text or graphic — that goes into the body of your Web page can be designated as a Library item.

✦ After they are created, Library items can be placed instantly in any Web page in your site, without your having to retype, reinsert, or reformat text and graphics.

✦ Library items can be altered at any time. After the editing is complete, Dreamweaver gives you the option to update the Web site immediately or postpone the update until later.

✦ If you are making a number of alterations to your Library items, you can wait until you're finished with all the updates and then make the changes across the board in one operation.

✦ You can update one page at a time, or you can update the entire site all at once.

✦ A Library item can be converted back to a regular non-Library element of a Web page at any time.

✦ Library items can be copied from one site to another.

✦ Library items can combine Dreamweaver behaviors — and their underlying JavaScript code — with onscreen elements, so you don't have to rebuild the same navigation bar every time, reapplying the behaviors repeatedly.

Using the Library Assets Panel

Dreamweaver's Library control center is located on the Assets panel in the Library category. Here you find the tools for creating, modifying, updating, and managing your Library items. Shown in Figure 28-1, the Library category is as flexible and easy to use as Dreamweaver's other primary panels, with straightforward command buttons, a listing of all available Library items, and a handy Preview area.

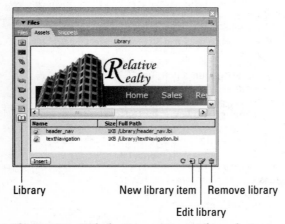

Figure 28-1: With the Dreamweaver Library feature, you can easily add and modify consistent objects on an entire Web site.

You have two ways to access the Library items:

✦ Choose Window ➪ Assets.

✦ Click the Library icon on the Assets panel.

Caution

To use Library items, you must first create a site root folder for Dreamweaver, as explained in Chapter 5; Library items cannot be modified when you are working directly with an FTP or RDS server. A separate Library folder is automatically created to hold the individual Library items and is used by Dreamweaver during the updating process.

Ideally, you save the most time by creating all your Library items before you begin constructing your Web pages, but most Web designers don't work that way. Feel free to include, modify, and update your Library items as often as necessary as your Web site evolves — that's part of the power and flexibility you gain through Dreamweaver's Library.

Adding a Library Item

Before you can insert or update a Library item, that item must be designated as a Library item within the Web page. To add an item to your site's Library, follow these steps:

1. Select any part of the Web page that you want to make into a Library item.

2. Open the Library category of the Assets panel.

3. From the Library category (refer again to Figure 28-1), click the New Library Item button.

   The selected page element is displayed in the preview area of the Library category. In the Site list — the Library item list — a new entry is highlighted with the default name *Untitled*.

Note

If the text you've selected has been styled by a CSS rule, Dreamweaver warns you that the appearance may be different because the style rule is not included in the Library item. To ensure that the appearance is the same, include the Library item only on those pages with the appropriate CSS styles.

4. Enter a unique name for your new Library item and press Enter (Return). The Library item list is re-sorted alphabetically, if necessary, and the new item is included.

When a portion of your Web page has been designated as a Library item, yellow highlighting is displayed over the entire item within the Document window. The highlighting helps you to quickly recognize a Library item. If you find the effect distracting, you can disable it. Go to Edit ➪ Preferences (Dreamweaver ➪ Preferences) and, from the Highlighting panel of the Preferences dialog box, deselect the checkbox to the right of the Library Items color selection. Alternatively, deselecting View ➪ Visual Aids ➪ Invisible Elements hides Library Item highlighting, along with any other invisible items on your page.

Caution

Dreamweaver can include Library items only in the `<body>` section of an HTML document. You cannot, for instance, create a series of `<meta>` tags for your pages that must go in the `<head>` section.

Drag-and-Drop Creation of Library Items

A second option for creating Library items is the drag-and-drop method. Simply select an object or several objects on a page and drag them to the Library category (either the preview area or the Site list pane); release the mouse button to drop them in.

You can drag any object into the Library panel: text, tables, images, Java applets, plugins, and/or ActiveX controls. Essentially, anything in the Document window that can be HTML code can be dragged to the Library. Similarly, as you might suspect, the reverse is true: Library items can be placed in your Web page by dragging them from the Library category and dropping them anywhere in the Document window.

Moving Library Items to a New Site

Although Library items are specific to each site, they can be used in more than one site. When you make your first Library item, Dreamweaver creates a folder called Library in the local root folder for the current site. To move the Library item to a new site, follow these steps:

1. Open the Library category from the Assets panel.

2. Right-click (Control+click) the Library item you want to move.

3. Put your mouse over the Copy to Site section of the context menu and then choose the site you want to copy the Library item to.

Caution   Be sure to move any dependent files or other assets, such as images and media files associated with Library items. The Copy to Site function does not move dependent files.

Inserting a Library Item in Your Web Page

When you create a Web site, you always need to incorporate certain features, including a standard set of link buttons along the top, a consistent banner on various pages, and a copyright notice along the bottom. Adding these items to a page with the Library items can be as easy as dragging and dropping them.

You must first create a Web site and then designate Library items (as explained in the preceding section). After these items exist, you can add the items to any page created within your site. To add Library items to a document, follow these steps:

1. Position the cursor where you want the Library item to appear.

2. From the Library category, select the item you want to use.

3. Click the Insert button. The highlighted Library item appears on the Web page.

Tip   As noted earlier, you can also use the drag-and-drop method to place Library items in the Document window.

When you add a Library item to a page, you notice a number of immediate changes. As mentioned, the added Library item is highlighted. If you click anywhere on the item, the entire Library item is selected.

Dreamweaver treats the entire Library item entry as an external object being linked to the current page. You cannot modify Library items directly on a page. For information about editing Library entries, see the section "Editing a Library Item," later in this chapter.

While the Library item is highlighted, notice that the Property inspector also changes. Instead of displaying the properties for the HTML object that is selected, the item is identified as a Library item, as shown in Figure 28-2.

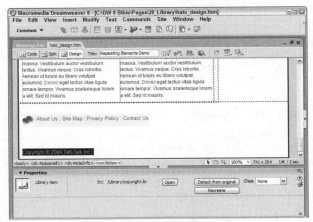

Figure 28-2: The Library Item Property inspector identifies the source file for any selected Library entry.

You can also see evidence of Library items in the HTML for the current page. Open the Code inspector, and you see that several lines of code have been added. The following code example indicates one Library item:

```
<!-- #BeginLibraryItem "/Library/Copyright.lbi" --><span ⤸
class="fineprint">Copyright &copy; 2004</span><!-- #EndLibraryItem -->
```

In this case, the Library item happens to be a phrase: Copyright (c) 2004. (The character entity © is used to represent the c-in-a-circle copyright mark in HTML.) In addition to the span wrapping the copyright, notice the text before and after the HTML code. These are commands within the comments that tell Dreamweaver it is looking at a Library item. One line marks the beginning of the Library item:

```
<!-- #BeginLibraryItem "/Library/Copyright.lbi" -->
```

and another marks the end:

```
<!-- #EndLibraryItem -->
```

Two items are of interest here. First, notice how the Library demarcation surrounds not just the text (Copyright (c) 2004) but all its formatting attributes as well. Library items can do far more than just cut and paste raw text. The second thing to note is that the Library markers are placed discretely within HTML comments. Web browsers ignore the Library markers and render the code in between them.

The value in the opening Library code, `"/Library/Copyright.lbi"`, is the source file for the Library entry. This file is located in the Library folder, inside of the current site root folder. Library source (`.lbi`) files can be opened with a text editor or in Dreamweaver; they consist of plain HTML code without the `<html>` and `<body>` tags.

The `.lbi` file for the title example contains the following:

```
<span class="fineprint">Copyright &copy; 2004</span>
```

The power of repeating elements is that they are simply HTML. You need not learn proprietary languages to customize Library items. Anything, except for information found in the header of a Web page, can be included in a Library file.

The importance of the `<!-- #BeginLibraryItem>` and `<!-- #EndLibraryItem>` tags becomes evident when you start to update Library items for a site. You examine how Dreamweaver can be used to automatically update your entire Web site in the section "Updating Your Web Sites with Libraries," later in this chapter.

Deleting an Item from the Library

Removing an entry from your site's Library is a two-step process. First, you must delete the item from the Library category. Second, if you want to keep the item on your page, you must make it editable again. Before you complete the second step, Dreamweaver maintains the Library highlighting and, more importantly, prevents you from modifying the element.

To delete an item from the Library, follow these steps:

1. Open the Web page containing the Library item you want to delete.

2. Open the Library category by choosing Window ➪ Assets.

3. Select the Library item in the Site list and click the Delete button.

4. Dreamweaver asks if you are sure you want to delete the item. Click Yes, and the entry is removed from the Library item list. (Or click No to cancel.)

5. In the Document window, select the element you are removing from the Library.

6. In the Property inspector, click Detach from Original.

7. As shown in Figure 28-3, Dreamweaver warns you that if you proceed, the item cannot be automatically updated (as a Library element). Click OK to proceed. The yellow Library highlighting vanishes, and the element can now be modified individually. Check the Don't Warn Me Again box to disable any future warnings about detaching Library items.

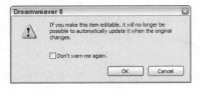

Figure 28-3: When you are making a Library item editable, Dreamweaver alerts you that, if you proceed, you won't be able to update the item automatically using the Library function.

Note Should you unintentionally delete a Library item in the Library category, you can restore it if you still have the entry included in a Web page. Select the element within the page and, in the Property inspector, click the Recreate button. Dreamweaver restores the item, with the original Library name, to the Library item list.

Renaming a Library Item

It's easy to rename a Library item, both in the Assets panel and across your site. Dreamweaver automatically updates the name for any embedded Library item. To give an existing Library entry a new name, open the Library category and click the name of the item twice, slowly — do not double-click. Alternatively, you can select Rename from the context menu of the Assets panel. The name is highlighted, and a small box appears around it. Enter the new name and press Enter (Return).

Dreamweaver then displays the Update Files dialog box with a list of files in which the renamed Library item is contained. Select Update to rename the Library item across the site. If you select Don't Update, the Library item is renamed only in the Library category. Furthermore, your embedded Library items are orphaned — that is, no master Library item is associated with them, and they are not updatable.

 ## Building a Library Item

One of the most common — and useful — applications for a Library item concerns site navigation. In this Dreamweaver Technique, you create a Library item for the bottom, text-based navigation and apply it to a number of pages.

1. From the Techniques site, expand the 28_Library_Items folder and open the `library_items_start1.htm` file.

2. In Design view, move to the bottom of the page and place your cursor in the footer area text navigation.

3. In the Tag Selector, select the `<p>` tag.

   Although you can create a Library item out of any code fragment, it's generally best to work with a complete tag.

4. From the Files panel group, click the Assets tab.

5. Choose the Library category, the last icon on the left side of the Assets panel.

6. Click New Library Item from the bottom row of the Assets panel.

7. Dreamweaver reminds you that the Library item may not look the same when inserted in other pages because of the associated CSS; click OK to acknowledge the reminder.

   Your selection is converted into a Library item and displayed in the Assets panel.

8. Replace the Untitled Library item name with **textNavigation** and press Enter (Return).

9. Dreamweaver asks if you'd like to update the links in the current `.lbi` file; click Update.

Continued

Continued

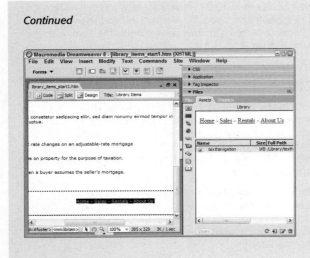

10. Save your page.

If you have Invisible Elements enabled, you might notice a light yellow highlight around the text navigation now; this indicates that it is no longer directly editable and is now a Library item.

Editing a Library Item

Rarely do you create a Library item that is perfect from the beginning and never needs to be changed. Whether because of site redesign or the addition of new sections to a site, you'll find yourself going back to Library items and modifying them, sometimes repeatedly. You can use the full power of Dreamweaver's design capabilities to alter your Library items, within the restraints of Library items in general. In other words, you can modify an image, reformat a body of text, or add new material to a boilerplate paragraph, and the resulting changes are reflected across your Web site. However, you cannot add anything not contained in the HTML `<body>` tags to a Library item.

To modify Library items, Dreamweaver uses a special editing window identifiable by the double-angle brackets surrounding the phrase Library Item in the title bar. You access this editing window through the Library category or the Property inspector. Follow these steps to modify an existing Library item:

1. In the Library category of the Assets panel, select the item you want to modify from the list of available entries.

2. Click the Open Library Item button. The Library editing window opens with the selected entry, as shown in Figure 28-4.

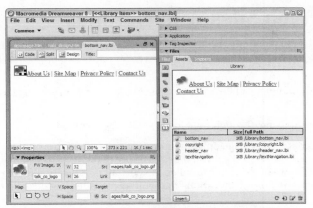

Figure 28-4: Use the Library editing window to modify existing Library items.

3. Make any necessary modifications to the Library entry.

4. When you are finished with your changes, choose File ⇨ Save or press Ctrl+S (Command+S).

5. Dreamweaver notes that your Library item has been modified and then asks if you would like to update all the Web pages in your site that contain the item. Click Yes to update all the Library items, including the one just modified, or click No to postpone the update. (See the next section, "Updating Your Web Sites with Libraries," for a more in-depth explanation of the updating process.)

6. Close the editing window by clicking the Close button or choosing File ⇨ Close.

After you've completed the editing operation and closed the editing window, you can open any Web page containing the modified Library item to view the changes.

Tip

If your Library item is styled with an external style sheet and you'd like to see how it renders while editing, use Dreamweaver's Design Time Style Sheet feature. From the CSS Styles panel Option menu, select Design Time; when the Design Time Style Sheet dialog opens, select the style sheet from the Show Only at Design Time area.

Dreamweaver now allows you to use native Dreamweaver behaviors inside Library items. That means you can place a navigation bar, a link for a pop-up window, or any other Dreamweaver behavior inside your Library item. When the Library item is added to the page, the accompanying JavaScript is also added.

Caution

You cannot use some features to the fullest extent when editing Library items. These include custom JavaScript and styles. Each of these modifications requires a function or link to be placed in the `<head>` tags of a page — a task that the Dreamweaver Library function cannot handle for styles and custom JavaScript.

Updating Your Web Sites with Libraries

The effectiveness of the Dreamweaver Library feature becomes more significant when it comes time to update an entire multipage site. Dreamweaver offers two opportunities for you to update your site:

✦ Immediately after modifying a Library item, as explained in the preceding steps for editing a Library item

✦ At a time of your choosing, through the Modify ➪ Library command

You can immediately update every page on your site when you edit a Library item. After you save the alterations, Dreamweaver asks if you'd like to apply the update to Web pages in your site. If you click Yes, Dreamweaver not only applies the current modification to all pages in the site, but it also applies any other alterations that you have made previously in this Library.

The second way to modify a Library item is by using the Modify ➪ Library command; when you use this method, you can choose to update the current page or the entire site.

To update just the current page, choose Modify ➪ Library ➪ Update Current Page. Dreamweaver quickly checks to see what Library items you are managing on the current page and then compares them to the site's Library items. If any differences exist, Dreamweaver modifies the page accordingly.

To update an entire Web site, follow these steps:

1. Choose Modify ➪ Library ➪ Update Pages. The Update Pages dialog box opens (see Figure 28-5).

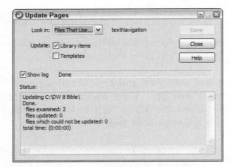

Figure 28-5: The Update Pages dialog box enables you to apply any changes to your Library items across an entire site and informs you of the progress.

2. If you want Dreamweaver to update all the Library items in all the Web pages in your site, select Entire Site from the Look In drop-down list and choose the name of your site in the drop-down list on the right. You can also have Dreamweaver update only the pages in your site that contain a specific Library item. Select the Files That Use option from the Look In drop-down list and then select the Library item that you would like to have updated across your site from the drop-down list on the right.

3. If you want to see the results from the update process, leave the Show Log checkbox selected. (Turning off the Show Log option reduces the size of the Site Update dialog box.)

4. Click the Start button. Dreamweaver processes the entire site for Library updates. Any Library items contained are modified to reflect the changes.

Note Although Dreamweaver does modify Library items on currently open pages during an Update Site operation, you have to save the pages to accept the changes.

The Update Pages log displays any errors encountered in the update operation. A log containing the notation

```
item Library\Untitled2.lbi -- not updated, library item not found
```

indicates that one Web page contains a reference to a Library item that has been removed. Although this is not a critical error, you might want to use Dreamweaver's Find and Replace feature to search your Web site for the code and remove it.

Note When updating Library items, every page is physically changed with the necessary Library item code. This means that every file containing a Library item must be uploaded to the server.

Applying and Modifying Library Items

In this Technique, you see how easy it is to add a Library item to the page and update them as necessary.

1. From the Techniques site, open the `library_items_start2.htm` file from the 28_Library_Items folder.

2. Place your cursor at the bottom of the page in the `#footer` div.

3. Select the placeholder `<p>` tag there and remove it by pressing Delete.

4. From the Assets panel, select the Library category if necessary.

5. Choose the textNavigation entry.

6. Click Insert at the bottom of the Assets panel.

   You can also drag Library items onto the page.

7. Save your page.

8. Now that you have the same Library item in a couple of locations, alter it. Double-click the textNavigation Library item.

   Dreamweaver opens the Library item file in its own window.

Continued

Continued

9. Place your cursor after the About Us link and enter the following: **- Guides**.

10. Select the word Guides and, from the Property inspector's Link field, drag the Point to File icon to the file `guides.htm` in the 28_Library_Items folder.

    It's always best to let Dreamweaver create the links for templates and Library items.

11. Choose File ⇨ Save.

12. Dreamweaver displays the Update Library Items dialog box with the pages containing the current Library item. Click Update.

13. While Dreamweaver processes the modifications, the Update Pages dialog box is displayed; click Close when it's finished.

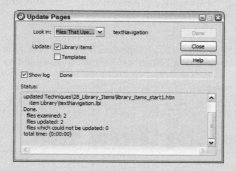

14. Close the `textNavigation.lbi` file.

    Notice that the `library_items_start2.htm` file has been modified and the new item is now available from the text navigation.

15. Choose File ⇨ Save to store `library_items_start2.htm` file.

If you like, you can open the original file, `library_items_start1.htm`, to verify it too has been updated.

END

Applying Server-Side Includes

In some ways, the server-side include (SSI) is the predecessor of the Dreamweaver Library item. The difference between them is that Dreamweaver updates the Web pages with Library items at design time; whereas, the server handles the updating with server-side includes at runtime (when the files are actually served to the user). Server-side includes can also include server variables, such as the current date and time (both local and Greenwich mean time) or the date on which the current file was last saved.

Because server-side includes are integrated in the standard HTML code, a special file extension identifies pages using them. Any page with server-side includes is most often saved with either the `.shtml` or `.shtm` extension on UNIX servers and `.asp` or `.aspx` on Windows servers. When a server encounters such a file, the file is read and processed by the server.

Caution

Not all servers support server-side includes. Some Web-hosting companies disable the function because of potential security risks and performance issues. Each .shtml page requires additional processing time, and if a site uses many SSI pages, the server can slow down significantly. Be sure to check with your Web host as to its policy before including SSIs in your Web pages.

Server-side includes are often used to insert header or footer items into the <body> of an HTML page. Typically, the server-side include itself is just a file with HTML. To insert a file, use SSI code like the following:

```
<!-- #include file="footer.html" -->
```

Note how the HTML comment structure is used to wrap around the SSI directive. This ensures that browsers ignore the code, but servers do not. The file attribute defines the pathname of the file to be included, relative to the current page. To include a file relative to the current site root, use the virtual attribute, as follows:

```
<!-- #include virtual= "/main/images/spaceman.jpg" -->
```

As evident in this example, you can use SSIs to include more than just HTML files — you can also include graphics.

With Dreamweaver's translator mechanism, server-side includes are visible in the Document window during the design process. In Dreamweaver, server-side–include translation is now automatic as long as the Show Contents of Included File option, found in the Invisible Elements category of Preferences, remains enabled.

One of the major benefits of SSIs is that information can be inserted from the server itself, such as the current file size or time. One tag, <!-- #echo -->, is used to define a custom variable that is returned when the SSI is called, as well as numerous environmental variables. An *environmental variable* is information available to the server, such as the date a file was last modified or its URL.

Table 28-1 details the possible server tags and their attributes.

Table 28-1: Server-Side Include Variables

Tag	Attribute	Description
<!-- #config -->	errmsg, sizefmt, or timefmt	Used to customize error messages, file size, or time and date displays
<!-- #echo -->	var or environmental variables such as last_modified, document_name, document_url, date_local, or date_gmt	Returns the specified variable
<!-- #exec -->	cmd or cgi	Executes a system command or CGI program
<!-- #flastmod -->	file or virtual	Displays the last modified date of a file other than the current one
<!-- #fsize -->	file or virtual	Displays the size of a file other than the current one
<!-- #include -->	file or virtual	Inserts the contents of the specified file into the current one

Adding Server-Side Includes

Dreamweaver has made inserting a server-side include in your Web page very straightforward. You can use a Dreamweaver object to easily select and bring in the files to be included. Any other type of SSI, such as declaring a variable, must be entered by hand, but you can use the Comment object to do so without opening the Code view.

To use server-side includes to incorporate a file, follow these steps:

1. In the Document window, place your cursor at the location where you would like to add the server-side include.

2. Choose Insert ➪ Server-Side Include or choose Script:SSI from the Insert bar's HTML category. The standard Select File dialog box appears.

3. In the Select File dialog box, type the URL of the HTML page you would like to include in the File Name text box or use the Browse button to locate the file. Click OK when you're finished.

Note   Through the Select File dialog box, you can also select a data source for a dynamically inserted SSI or link to an SSI already published on a server through the Sites and Servers interface. However, SSIs inserted in this manner can be previewed in Dreamweaver only in the Live Data view.

Dreamweaver displays the contents of the HTML file at the desired location in your page. Should the Property inspector be available, the SSI Property inspector is displayed (see Figure 28-6).

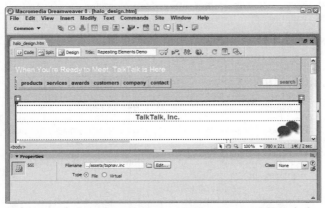

Figure 28-6: The selected text is actually a server-side include automatically translated by Dreamweaver, as evident from the SSI Property inspector.

4. In the Property inspector, if the server-side include calls a file-relative document path, select the Type File option. Alternatively, if the SSI calls a site-root–relative file, choose the Type Virtual option.

Editing Server-Side Includes

As is the case with Library items, you cannot directly edit files that have been inserted into a Web page using server-side includes. In fact, should you try, the entire text block highlights as one. The text for a server-side–included file is not editable through Dreamweaver's Code view, although the SSI code is.

To edit the contents of the server-side–included file, follow these steps:

1. Select the server-side include in the Document window.

2. Click the Edit button in the SSI Property inspector. The file opens in a new Dreamweaver window for editing.

3. When you've finished altering the file, choose File ➪ Save or use the keyboard shortcut, Ctrl+S (Command+S).

4. Close the file editing window by choosing File ➪ Close.

Dreamweaver automatically reflects the changes in your currently open document.

Unlike when you are editing Library items, Dreamweaver does not ask if any other linked files should be updated because all blending of regular HTML and SSIs happens at runtime or when the file is open in Dreamweaver and the SSI translator is engaged.

Summary

In this chapter, you learned how you can easily and effectively create Library items that can be repeated throughout an entire site to help maintain consistency. When you work with Library items, keep these points in mind:

✦ Library items can consist of any text, object, or HTML code contained in the `<body>` of a Web page.

✦ The quickest method to create a Library item is to drag the code from the Dreamweaver Document window into the Library category's list area.

✦ Editing Library items is also easy: Just click the Edit button in the Assets panel or choose Open from the Property inspector, and you can swiftly make all your changes in a separate Dreamweaver Library Item window.

✦ The Modify ➪ Library ➪ Update Pages command enables easy maintenance of your Web site.

✦ Server-side includes enable the server to insert files into the final HTML at runtime. Dreamweaver's translation feature enables you to preview these effects.

In the next chapter, you learn how to ensure cross-browser compatibility with Dreamweaver.

✦   ✦   ✦

Maximizing Browser Targeting

Each new release of a browser is a double-edged sword. On the one hand, an exciting array of new features becomes possible. On the other, Web designers have to cope with yet another browser-compatibility issue. In today's market, you find all the following in use:

♦ A fair number of current browsers that, although fairly standards-compliant, are still different from one another in implementation.

♦ A decreasing number of 4.x browsers, which are limited in some basic functionality. The exception here is Netscape 4.x, which maintains a small but significant cadre of loyal users.

♦ A miniscule contingent of 3.x browsers in the machines of determined users who have never (and may never) upgrade.

♦ A diverse assortment of browsers outside the mainstream, including MSN TV (formerly known as WebTV), and Navigator for Linux.

♦ Various versions of America Online browsers, which range from being completely proprietary to being a blend of current and special technologies. (As a specific example, AOL 9.0 is not the same as Internet Explorer 6.0, although it is based on it.)

Browser compatibility is one of a Web designer's primary concerns (not to mention the source of major headaches); and many strategies are evolving to deal with this matter. Dreamweaver is in the forefront of cross-browser Web page design, both in terms of the type of code it routinely outputs and in its specialty functions. This chapter examines the browser-targeting techniques available in Dreamweaver. From multibrowser code to browser-validation capabilities, Dreamweaver helps you get your Web pages out with the most features to the widest audience.

Converting Pages in Dreamweaver

Web sites are constantly upgraded and modified. You'll eventually need to enhance a more traditional site with new features, such as layers. Some of the older sites used elaborately nested tables on their pages to create a semblance of absolute positioning; normally, upgrading these Web pages takes hours and hours of tedious cutting and pasting. Dreamweaver can bring these older pages up to speed with the Convert Tables to Layers command, which you reach via Modify ➪ Convert ➪ Tables to Layers. Dreamweaver also includes a command to convert tables to layers, preserving their location but enabling greater design flexibility and dynamic control. A Webmaster's life just got a tad easier.

The Convert Tables to Layers command can also be used to convert a page created by another Web authoring program (NetObjects Fusion, for example) that uses nested tables for positioning. After tables have been transformed into layers, the layout of the entire page is much easier to modify. It's even possible to make the switch from 3.0 to 4.0 capabilities, modify your page, and then, with the Convert Layers to Tables command, re-create your 3.0-compliant page.

The name of the Convert Tables to Layers command is a little misleading. After you issue this command, *every* HTML element in the new page — not just the tables — is placed in a layer. Moreover, every cell with content in every table is converted into its own layer. In other words, if you are working with a 3 x 3 table in which one cell is left empty, Dreamweaver creates eight different layers for just the table.

Note   If you want to convert a 3.0-compatible page to a page with layers, but the page has no tables, Dreamweaver places all the content in one layer, as if the `<body>` tag were one big single-cell table.

To convert a 3.0-browser–compatible Web page with (or without) tables to a 4.0-browser–compatible Web page with layers, follow these steps:

1. Choose Modify ➪ Convert ➪ Tables to Layers.

2. Select the desired options from the Convert Tables to Layers dialog box that opens (see Figure 29-1):

   • **Prevent Layer Overlaps** — Isolates each layer from one another. Layers need to remain separate if the opposite process (Convert Layers to Tables) is invoked.

   • **Show Layers Panel** — Displays the Layers panel for easy selection and renaming of the newly created layers.

   • **Show Grid** — Reveals the standard grid, useful for aligning layers.

   • **Snap to Grid** — Every new layer created is positioned to the closed grid point. Exercise caution when choosing this option, because your table layout is likely to be highly revised.

Figure 29-1: The Convert Tables to Layers dialog box.

3. When you're done, click OK to close the dialog.

Dreamweaver converts the page immediately. If you need to return to a table-based layout, choose File ➪ Convert ➪ Layers to Tables.

To learn how to use Dreamweaver's Layers to Tables roundtrip features, see Chapter 11.

Ensuring Browser Compatibility

As more browsers and browser versions become available, a Web designer has two basic options to stay on the road to compatibility: internal and external.

✦ The *internal* method uses scripts on the same Web page; the scripts deliver the proper code depending on the browser detected. Many of Dreamweaver's own behavior functions manage the browser issue internally.

✦ The *external* approach examines each visitor's browser right off the bat and reroutes the user to the most appropriate Web page.

Both methods have their pluses and minuses, and each is better suited to particular situations. For example, it is impractical to use the external method of creating multiple versions of the same Web pages when you are working with a large site. Suddenly, you've gone from managing 300 pages of information to 900 or 1,200. Of course, you don't have to duplicate every page—but because of the open nature of the Web, where any page can be bookmarked and entered directly, you have to plan carefully and provide routing routines at the key locations. Conversely, sometimes you have no choice but to use multiple versions, especially if a page employs many browser-specific features.

The internal and external strategies are not mutually exclusive. Several sites today are routing 4.0 browsers to one page and using internal coding methods to differentiate between the various 5.x and above browser versions on another page. This section examines techniques for implementing browser compatibility from both the internal and external perspective.

Internal Coding for Cross-Browser Compatibility

Imagine the shouts of joy when the Web development community learned that the 4.0 versions of Navigator and Internet Explorer both support Cascading Style Sheet layers! Now imagine the grumbling when it became apparent that each browser used a different JavaScript syntax for calling them. You get the picture: It all boils down to differences in each browser's Document Object Model (DOM).

Navigator 8.0 incorporates the W3C standard for layers, which is also largely supported by Internet Explorer 4.0 and later. Although this standard will eventually simplify compatibility issues for Web designers, Navigator 4.x browsers remain in use, primarily at universities and corporations where new product adoption is always delayed, and whether or not to have Dreamweaver insert the code for handling layers in those browsers should be taken into consideration.

Calling Layers

When referring to a layer, Navigator 4.*x* uses the following syntax:

```
document.layers["layerName"]
```

whereas Internet Explorer uses this syntax:

```
document.all["layerName"]
```

The trick to internal code-switching is to assign the variations — the `document.layers` from Navigator and the `document.all` from Internet Explorer — to the same variable, depending on which browser is being used. Here's a sample function that does just that:

```
function init() {
  if (navigator.appName == "Netscape") {
    var layerRef = "document.layers";
  }
  else {
    var layerRef = "document.all";
  }
}
```

In this function, if the visitor is using a Netscape 4.x browser, the variable `layerRef` is assigned the value `document.layers`; otherwise, `layerRef` is set to `document.all`.

Calling Properties

If you're trying to assign or read a layer property, one variable is only half the battle. Another difference exists in the way properties are called. With Navigator, the property is called like this:

```
document.layers["layerName"].top
```

With Internet Explorer, the property is called a little differently:

```
document.all["layerName"].style.top
```

Internet Explorer inserts an extra hierarchical division, `style`, which Navigator doesn't use. The solution is another variable, `styleRef`, which for Internet Explorer is set as follows:

```
var styleRef = "style";
```

The Navigator `styleRef` is actually set to a *null string*, or nothing. You can combine the two variables into one initialization function, which is best called from an `onLoad` event in the `<body>` tag:

```
function init() {
  if (navigator.appName == "Netscape") {
    var layerRef = "document.layers";
    var styleRef = "";
  }
  else {
    var layerRef = "document.all";
    var styleRef = "style";
  }
}
```

After these differences are accommodated, the variables are ready to be used in a script. To do this, you can use JavaScript's built-in `eval()` function to combine the variables and the object references. Here's an example that sets a new variable, `varLeft`, to the `left` value of the layer named `myLayer`:

```
varLeft = eval(layerRef + '["myLayer"]' + styleRef + '.left');
```

Luckily, the variations between the Navigator and Internet Explorer DOM are consistent enough that a JavaScript function can assign the proper values with a minimum of effort.

Calling Objects within Layers

The two DOMs also diverge in another major area. When you are attempting to address almost any entity inside a layer, Navigator uses an additional hierarchical layer to reference the object. Thus, a named image in a named layer in Navigator is referenced as follows:

```
document.layers["layerName"].document.imageName
```

whereas the same object in Internet Explorer is called like this:

```
document.imageName
```

Macromedia gets around this problem by using the `dwscripts.findDOMObject()` function, which you can examine in the dwscripts.js file, found in Dreamweaver 8\Configuration\ Shared\Common\Scripts.

Designing Web Pages for Backward Compatibility

The previous section describes a technique for handling the differences between 4.0 and later browsers, but how do you handle the much larger gap between third- and fourth-generation browsers? When this gap becomes a canyon, with DHTML-intensive pages on one side and incompatible browsers on the other, the ultimate solution is to use *redirection* to send a particular browser to an appropriate page. However, browsers can coexist in plenty of cases — with a little planning and a little help from Dreamweaver.

When you are designing backwardly compatible Web pages, browsers generally offer you one major advantage: ignorance. If a browser doesn't recognize a tag or attribute, it just ignores it and renders the rest of the page. Because many of the newer features are built on new tags, or on tags such as `<div>` that previously were infrequently used, your Web pages can gracefully devolve from 4.0 to 3.0 behavior, without causing errors or grossly misrendering the page.

Take layers, for instance. One advantage offered by this DHTML feature is the capability to make something interactively appear and disappear. Although that's not possible in 3.0 browsers (without extensive image-swapping), it is possible to display the same material and even enable some degree of navigation. The key is proper placement of the layer code — not the layer itself. Browsers basically read and render the code for a Web page from top to bottom. You can, for example, make several layers appear one after another in a 3.0 browser, even if they are stacked on top of one another in a 4.0 browser. All you have to do is make sure that the HTML code of the layers appears in the document sequentially. You can see this effect in Figure 29-2. The three layers are overlapped, but their HTML code is sequential:

```
<div id="Layer1" style="position:absolute; left:150px; top:110; ⤵
width:200; height:170; z-index:3">
   Layer1 code ...
</div>
```

```
<div id="Layer2" style="position:absolute; left:150px; top:80;
width:200; height:200; z-index:2">
   Layer2 code ...
</div>
<div id="Layer3" style="position:absolute; left:150px; top:50px;
width:200; height:230; z-index:1">
   Layer3 code ...
</div>
```

The navigational links in the upper-left have two roles: They are linked to the named anchor next to the layer's code and, through the Behaviors panel, are set to show and hide the appropriate layers when selected (using the onClick event).

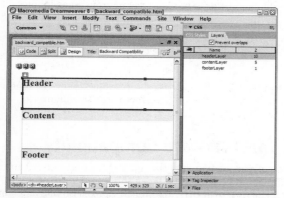

Figure 29-2: Careful placement of the code for layers can be an effective tool for backward compatibility.

Because the HTML code for the three layers is situated sequentially, browsers that do not understand the style attribute in the <div> tags — which create the layers — simply render the information contained within all three tags, one after the other.

Note   Although it may seem obvious, don't forget to preview your pages in a 3.0 browser, if available, to see the results of these positioning techniques.

Validating Your Code

Most browsers are very forgiving. They can take a document riddled with HTML infractions and, through "intelligent" interpretation, manage to display the page beautifully, with no indication that anything is awry with the underlying code. As a responsible Web author, however, you should never rely on the kindness of your users' browsers! It's far safer to take the extra time to validate the correctness of your code's syntax rather than risk having a browser be less forgiving than you had hoped.

Fortunately, Dreamweaver can help. You can use its built-in Validator to check a document's code for tag or syntax errors. The Validator supports a wide range of tag-based languages, including HTML (several versions), XHTML, XML, JSP (JavaServer Pages), CFML (ColdFusion Markup Language), and WML (Wireless Markup Language). And you can customize how the Validator works, as discussed in the next section, "Setting Validator Preferences."

To validate your code, follow these steps:

1. Open the document you want to validate.

2. If it is an XML or XHTML file, choose File ➪ Check Page ➪ Validate as XML. For all other files, choose File ➪ Check Page ➪ Validate Markup or press Shift+F6. After the Validator runs, the results are listed in the Validation panel: filenames, line numbers, and error descriptions, as shown in Figure 29-3.

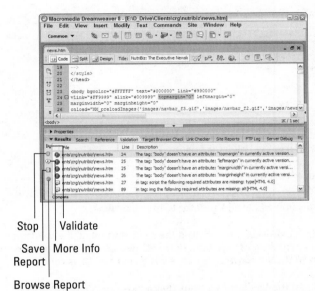

Stop | Validate

Save | More Info
Report

Browse Report

Figure 29-3: It's up to you to decide how to handle errors flagged by Dreamweaver's Validator.

3. Double-click an error in the list to display the offending code in the document.

4. To display the error report in your primary browser, click the Browse Report button. To keep a record of the report, print the browser page or click the Save Report button to generate an XML report file.

Tip   Right-click (Control+click) in the Validation panel to bring up a context menu that lets you browse the error report, save the report, and more.

Setting Validator Preferences

You can customize how the Validator works by changing its preferences. For example, you can specify which languages the Validator should check against and which types of errors the Validator should hunt down. To set your Validator preferences:

1. Choose Edit ⇨ Preferences (Dreamweaver ⇨ Preferences) to open the Preferences dialog box and then click the Validator category to display the Validator options (see Figure 29-4).

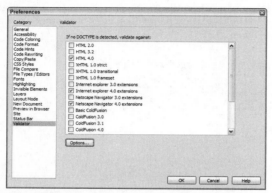

Figure 29-4: You can use the Validator options in the Preferences dialog box to customize the workings of your Dreamweaver Validator.

2. Select the languages you want the Validator to check against.

Caution

If you validate CFML (ColdFusion) and HTML in the same document, the Validator won't be able to assess the number sign (#) correctly. Why not? Because, in CFML, # is an error and ## is correct, but in HTML, the converse is true: ## is an error and # is correct.

3. Click Options to open the Validator Options dialog box (see Figure 29-5).

4. Under Display, select the error types you want the Validator report to display. Under Check For, select the items you want the Validator to look for.

5. Click OK to close the Validator Options dialog box; then click OK to close the Preferences dialog box.

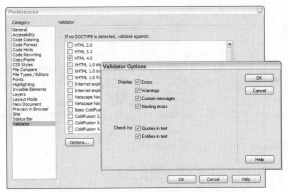

Figure 29-5: Use the Validator Options dialog box to exercise further control over your Validator's range.

 Validating and Correcting a Web Page

In this Technique, you validate a Web page and then correct the noted errors. Once you pass validation, you prepare to print out the report.

1. From the Techniques site, expand the 29_Browser_Targeting folder and open the `validation_start` file.

   Note that the page appears normal in Design view.

2. From the Document toolbar, choose Validate Markup: Validate Current Document.

   The Validation panel opens and, after the validation is complete, displays the found errors.

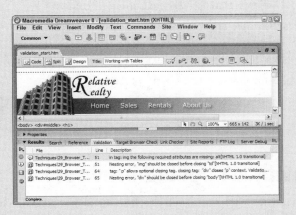

Continued

Continued

3. Double-click the first error.

   Dreamweaver enters Split view with the offending line of code highlighted; you may need to adjust the border to see both Code and Design view equally well.

4. The first error indicates that the `alt` tag is missing in the highlighted tag; expand the Property inspector, if necessary, and in the Alt field, enter **Frank Gordon**; press Tab when you're done.

5. Double-click the second error in the Validation panel.

   This error is described as a Nesting error and the tag following the problematic `img` tag is highlighted. Because this page is validated under XHTML rules, all tags must be closed, and this particular `img` tag is missing a closing slash.

6. Place your cursor before the closing bracket of the `img` tag and enter a forward slash: **/**.

7. Double-click the third error in the Validation panel.

   Although this error is listed as optional, it's best to always use a closing paragraph tag. Again, the tag following the detected error — the `</div>` tag — is highlighted.

8. In Code view, move your cursor in front of the selected `</div>` tag and enter a closing paragraph tag: `</p>`.

   With Dreamweaver's tag completion feature, you only have to type the first two characters, `</`.

9. Double-click the final error in the Validation panel.

   Another nesting error is indicated. Here, the closing `</div>` tag for the footer `div` is missing and you need to add it in front of the selected `</body>` tag.

10. Move your cursor in front of the `</body>` tag and insert the `</div>`. Again, if tag completion is enabled, all you need to enter is the first two characters, `</`.

11. Now that you've addressed all the errors, it's best to make sure the page validates. From the Document toolbar, choose Validate Markup: Validate Current Document.

    The Validation panel indicates that there are no errors. To maintain a record of this accomplishment, you can output a report.

12. From the Validation panel toolbar, click Save Report.

    Dreamweaver displays the Validator results in your primary browser.

With the report displayed in the browser, you can print out a copy, save it, or send it via email.

Testing Your Page with a Targeted Browser

Testing is an absolute must when you're building a Web site. It's critical that you view your pages on as many browsers/versions and platforms as possible. Variations in color, gamma, page offset, and capabilities must be observed before they can be adjusted.

A more basic, preliminary type of testing can also be done right from within Dreamweaver: code testing. Browsers usually ignore tags and attributes they do not understand. However, sometimes these tags can produce unexpected and undesirable results, such as exposing code to the viewer.

Dreamweaver's Browser Targeting feature (File ➪ Check Page ➪ Check Target Browsers) enables you to check a Web page — or an entire Web site — against any number of browser profiles. Currently, Dreamweaver comes with profiles for the following browsers:

- ✦ Firefox 1.0
- ✦ Internet Explorer 3.0
- ✦ Internet Explorer 4.0
- ✦ Internet Explorer 5.0
- ✦ Internet Explorer 5.2, Macintosh
- ✦ Internet Explorer 5.5
- ✦ Internet Explorer 6.0
- ✦ Mozilla 1.0
- ✦ Navigator 3.0
- ✦ Navigator 4.0
- ✦ Navigator 6.0
- ✦ Navigator 7.0

- ✦ Navigator 8.0
- ✦ Opera 2.1
- ✦ Opera 3.0
- ✦ Opera 3.5
- ✦ Opera 4.0
- ✦ Opera 5.0
- ✦ Opera 6.0
- ✦ Opera 7.0
- ✦ Opera 8.0
- ✦ Safari 1.0
- ✦ Safari 2.0

You can choose to check your page or site against a single browser profile, all of them, or anything in between. Though not a substitute for real-world testing, Browser Targeting gives you an overview of potential errors and problematic code.

Automatically Checking Your Pages

Given the vast array of browsers — and their widely varying capabilities — many designers find that keeping a page problem-free is a significant challenge. Dreamweaver can help you stay on your chosen path, alerting you to errors when a page is first opened.

Reflecting the importance designers have placed on checking their code against specific browsers, Dreamweaver automatically checks pages on opening — and designates errors it finds by placing a highly visible icon in the Document toolbar. Mouse-over the Browser Check icon to see the number of errors or warnings found at a glance. The Browser Check menu allows you to see a list of all the problems so you can take further action or adjust your settings as needed. Switch to Code view and you see the code causing the errors underlined in red.

Not only does Dreamweaver check the code in your page, it checks external style sheets as well.

Choosing the Browsers to Target

The Auto Check On Opening option, found under the Document toolbar's Browser Check menu, is selected by default. With this option enabled, Dreamweaver tests the page when it is opened against the browsers selected in the Target Browsers dialog box, as shown in Figure 29-6.

Figure 29-6: Use the Target Browsers dialog box to choose the minimum browser versions that you want to work correctly with your pages.

To modify the current settings, follow these steps:

1. Choose Settings from the Browser Check menu or from the Target Browser Check panel Options menu.

2. In the displayed Target Browsers dialog box, select the browsers you want to verify your pages against.

3. For each selected browser, choose the minimum version for testing from the drop-down list.

4. When you're finished, click OK.

Excluding Page Elements from Error Checking

Dreamweaver includes built-in syntax rules for each browser, which, generally, are applied to each file checked. However, you have the option to exclude specific tags, attributes, or attribute values from the testing process. This feature is extremely useful when your designs must include an element unsupported by one or more browsers and you don't want to be reminded of the issue each time the page is checked. The list of excluded elements is contained in the Exceptions.xml file maintained in the Configuration/BrowserProfiles folder. Dreamweaver gives you quick access to modifying this file when you open the Browser Check menu and choose Edit Ignored Error List.

To modify the Execeptions.xml file, follow these steps:

1. From an HTML file, open the Browser Check menu from the Document toolbar and choose Edit Ignored Error List.

Tip   This command is not available from XML files.

Dreamweaver opens the Exceptions.xml file.

2. Enter any desired exceptions in the XML file between the <exceptions>...</exceptions> tag pair. As noted in the file comments, the following five types of exceptions are allowed:

Element	Example
Tag	`<tag tag="applet"/>`
Attribute	`<attribute tag="acronym" attribute="onMouseWheel"/>`
Attribute Value	`<attributeValue tag="div" attribute="language"/>`
CSS Property	`<cssProperty property="font-weight"/>`
CSS Value	`<cssValue property="font-weight"/>`

3. Add the desired exception in the proper format. Make sure that your code is outside the commented section but inside the `<exceptions>`...`</exceptions>` tag pair.

4. When you're finished, save the file.

Viewing and Correcting Errors

If Dreamweaver finds any errors on your page, they are listed in the Target Browser Check panel. You can display this listing by opening the Browser Check menu and choosing Show All Errors. Double-click any error listing to view the offending code highlighted in a wavy red underline. To see the errors one at a time in Code view, choose Next Error or Previous Error. After you've corrected the problem, the red underline is removed. You can verify your change has eliminated the error by using any of the methods described in the following steps:

1. Open the Browser Check menu and choose Check Browser Support or choose File ⇨ Check Page ⇨ Check Target Browsers. Dreamweaver checks the page and lists the results in the Target Browser Check panel, as shown in Figure 29-7. This is a very handy debugging tool. For each error found, the filename, line number, and a short description are listed. Double-clicking an item in the list displays the offending code in Code view, highlighted and ready to be debugged. Dreamweaver displays the results temporarily and deletes them when you check another page or close the program.

2. To display a report of these results in your primary browser (see Figure 29-8), click the Browse Report button.

3. To keep a hard copy record, print the Target Browser Check page from your browser. To keep a digital record, click the Save Report button in the Target Browser Check panel to generate an XML report file.

The Dreamweaver Target Browser Check report offers both a summary and a detail section. The summary lists the browser(s) being tested and any errors or warnings. Totals for each category are listed beneath the columns.

The detail section of the browser check report, shown in Figure 29-9, lists the following:

✦ Each offending tag or attribute

✦ The browsers that do not support the tag or attribute

✦ An example HTML line

✦ Additional line numbers indicating where the error occurred

Browser check menu

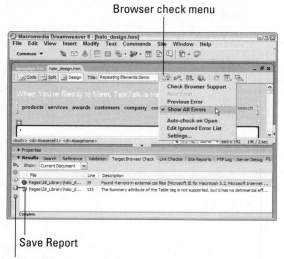

Save Report

Browser Report

Figure 29-7: The Target Browser Check panel displays a summary of all the errors it finds for the current file.

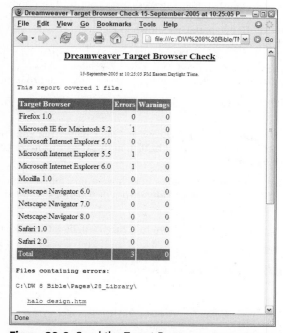

Figure 29-8: Send the Target Browser error report to your browser for printing or easy viewing.

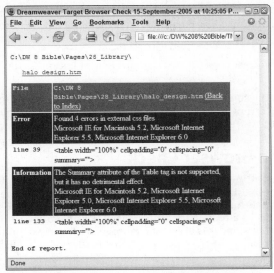

Figure 29-9: You can find detailed information on the lower half of the Dreamweaver Target Browser Check report.

Testing Browser Compatibility for an Entire Site

With Dreamweaver, you can check browser compatibility for an entire Web site as easily as you can check a single page. Dreamweaver checks all the HTML files in a given folder, whether or not they are actually used in the site. To check the current site against specific browser targets, follow these steps:

1. Open the Results panel by choosing Window ⇨ Results or pressing F7.

2. Select the Target Browser Check category of the Results panel.

3. Click the Check Target Browser button (the green triangle) and select Check Target Browsers for Entire Site from the drop-down list, as shown in Figure 29-10.

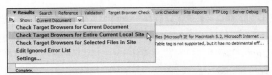

Figure 29-10: Before you go live, check your entire site against all your targeted browsers to catch any remaining errors.

As Dreamweaver checks the pages, the results are listed in the Target Browser Check panel. Click the Browse Report button to display these results in your primary browser.

Tip   You can flip between displaying errors for the current page and the entire site by choosing Current Document or Site Report from the Show drop-down list of the Target Browser Check panel.

4. To save the results, print the browser page or click the Save Report button (in the Target Browser Check panel).

When you're checking multiple files, the summary section of the Target Browser Check report gives you a list of the files containing errors as well as an error count. For clarity, each file's errors are grouped together in the report.

Using the Results of the Browser Check

How you handle the flagged errors in Dreamweaver's Target Browser Check report is entirely dependent on the design goals you have established for your site. If your mission is to be totally accessible to every browser on the market, you need to look at your page and/or site with the earliest browsers and pay special attention to those areas of possible trouble noted by the report. On the other hand, if your standards are a little more relaxed, you can probably ignore the 3.0 browser warnings and concentrate on those appearing in the NS4.x and IE 5 and higher categories.

Note   Many code items flagged as errors aren't, *per se*, incorrect — they're just not supported in the targeted browser. For example, checking a page with rollovers against Internet Explorer 3 displays an error stating "The onMouseOut attribute of the Hyperlink Anchor tag is not supported." If you load this page in Internet Explorer 3, the rollover won't work, but Explorer fails gracefully, without displaying an error message box.

Customizing a Browser Profile

For Dreamweaver's Browser Targeting feature to be effective, you must have access to profiles for all the browsers you are checking. You can create custom browser profiles to cover any new browser versions or browsers as they become available. The browser profile file is a text file and can be created or altered in any text editor.

This section describes the required structure and format for a browser profile file and the steps for building one based on an existing file.

Understanding the Browser Profile Structure

In order for Dreamweaver to properly process an HTML file using any browser profile, the profile must follow a precise format. Here's an excerpt from the Internet Explorer 6.0 browser profile:

```
<!ELEMENT Fieldset >
<!ATTLIST Fieldset
    Align ( left | center | right )    !Warning !msg="The reference of ⊃
Internet
Explorer 4.0 lists the <ALIGN> attribute as valid. However, it only appears to
```

```
have some effect on the FIELDSET itself, not on the contents of the ⊃
FIELDSET as
documented."
     Class
     Dir
     ID
     Lang
     Language
[...]
>
```

As you can see, the HTML tag is listed in a very specific syntax. Here's how the syntax is formed:

```
<!ELEMENT htmlTag >
<!ATTLIST htmlTag
unsupportedAttribute1 !Error !msg="The unsupportedAttribute1 of the ⊃
htmlTag is not supported. Try using thisAttribute for a similar effect."
supportedAttribute1
supportedAttribute2 ( validValue1 | validValue2 | validValue3 )
unsupportedAttribute2 !Error !htmlmsg="<b>Don't ever use this ⊃
unsupportedAttribute2 of the  htmlTag !!</b>"
>
```

The variables in the syntax are as follows:

✦ `htmlTag` — The tag as it appears in an HTML document; in this example this is the `fieldset` tag.

✦ `unsupportedAttribute` — Indicates invalid attributes so that a custom error message can be offered. Otherwise, all attributes not specifically listed are assumed to be unsupported. In this example, use of the `Align` attribute triggers a warning.

✦ `supportedAttribute` — A valid attribute; all valid attributes must be listed. Only attributes listed without an `!Error` designation are supported. `Class`, `Dir`, `ID` and `Lang` are all supported attributes in this example.

✦ `validValue` — A value, like `left`, `right`, and `center`, supported by the attribute.

Several other not-so-obvious rules must be followed in order for Dreamweaver to correctly read the profile:

✦ The name of the profile must appear as the first line of the file, followed by a single carriage return. This is the profile name that appears in the Check Target Browser(s) dialog box and in the report.

✦ The key phrase `PROFILE_TYPE=BROWSER_PROFILE` must appear as the second line.

✦ In every `<!ELEMENT` line, a single blank space must appear before the closing angle bracket (>).

✦ In the attribute sections, a blank space must appear after every opening parenthesis (( ), before every closing parenthesis ( )), and before *and* after each pipe character (|) .

✦ An exclamation point (!) must appear, without an intervening space, before every instance of the words ELEMENT, ATTLIST, Error, msg, and htmlmsg, as follows:

```
!ELEMENT, !ATTLIST, !Error, !msg, !htmlmsg.
```

✦ You can only use plain text in !msg messages, but an !htmlmsg message can use any valid HTML, including links.

✦ Don't use HTML comment tags, <!-- -->, because they interfere with the regular Dreamweaver processing of the file.

Creating a Browser Profile

As you can see, Dreamweaver browser profiles have a specific structure. Consequently, it's far easier to modify an existing profile than to write one from scratch. To create a browser profile, follow these steps:

1. Find an existing profile that is similar to the one you are creating in the Dreamweaver 8\ Configuration\BrowserProfiles folder. Open this profile in a text editor. Rename the profile file, if necessary, so that you don't accidentally overwrite the existing profile.

2. Add any tags and attributes that are supported in the target browser but not in the existing profile.

3. Remove any tags or attributes not supported by your target browser. Alternatively, you can add an !Error message after any attribute to flag it for Dreamweaver's Target Browser Check operation.

For example, the code fragment illustrated in Listing 29-1 contains a portion of the browser profile I created for WebTV (before Microsoft bought WebTV and renamed it MSN TV). Note the custom error messages after the <applet> tag and the rel attribute of the <a> tag.

Listing 29-1: **Excerpt from Browser Profile File for MSN TV**

```
MSNTV 1.0
PROFILE_TYPE=BROWSER_PROFILE

<!ELEMENT A Name="Hyperlink Anchor" >
<!ATTLIST A
        Class           !Error
        HREF
        ID
        Name
        OnClick
        OnMouseOut
        OnMouseOver
        Rel             !Warning !msg "The rel attribute has been ⏎
modified by WebTV."
        Style           !Error
        Selected        !Error
        Target          !Error
>

<!ELEMENT Address >
```

```
<!ATTLIST Address
        Class           !Error
        ID              !Error
        Style           !Error
>

<!ELEMENT APPLET Name="Java Applet" > !Error !msg "WebTV does not ⤸
support Java Applets."
<!ATTLIST APPLET
        Align ( top | middle | bottom | left | right | absmiddle | ⤸
absbottom | baseline | texttop )
        Alt
        Archive         !Error
        Code
        Codebase
        Height
        HSpace
        Name
        VSpace
        Width
        Class
        ID
        Style
>

<!ELEMENT AREA Name= "Client-side image map area" >
<!ATTLIST AREA
        Alt             !Error
        Class           !Error
        Coords
        HREF
        ID
        Name
        NoHREF
        NoTab
        OnMouseOut
        OnMouseOver
        Shape
        Style           !Error
        Target
>

<!ELEMENT AUDIOSCOPE Name="Audioscope" >
<!ATTLIST AUDIOSCOPE
        Align
        Border
        Gain
        Height
        LeftColor
        LeftOffset
```

Continued

Listing 29-1 *(continued)*

```
        MaxLevel
        RightColor
        RightOffset
        Width
>

<!ELEMENT B Name="Bold" >
<!ATTLIST B
        Class           !Error
        ID              !Error
        Style           !Error
>

<!ELEMENT Base >
<!ATTLIST Base
        HREF
        Target
>

<!ELEMENT BaseFont >
<!ATTLIST BaseFont
        Size
>
<!ELEMENT BGSOUND Name="Background sound" >
<!ATTLIST BGSOUND
        Loop
        Src
>

<!ELEMENT Big >
<!ATTLIST Big
        Class
        ID
        Style
>

<!ELEMENT Blackface >

<!ELEMENT Blink !Error >

<!ELEMENT Blockquote >

<!ELEMENT Body >
<!ATTLIST Body
        ALink                   !Error
        Background
        BGColor
        BGProperties
```

```
        Credits
        LeftMargin
        Link
        Logo
        OnBlur            !Error
        OnFocus           !Error
        OnLoad
        OnUnload
        Style             !Error
        Text
        VLink
>

<!ELEMENT BQ Name="Block Quote" >

<!ELEMENT BR Name="Line break" >
<!ATTLIST BR
        Clear ( left | right | all )
>
```

Summary

Unless you're building a Web site for a strictly controlled intranet (for which everyone is using the same browser), it's critical that you address the browser-compatibility issues that your Web site is certain to face. Whether it's cross-browser or backward compatibility you're trying to achieve, Dreamweaver has features and techniques in place to help you get your Web pages viewed by the maximum number of users. When addressing browser-compatibility issues, keep these points in mind:

✦ Dreamweaver can take a Web page created with layers and create another Web page that uses tables instead. Tools in Dreamweaver, such as Convert Layers to Tables, make it quick and straightforward.

✦ You can use JavaScript within a Web page to handle cross-browser compatibility problems with 4.0 and later browsers.

✦ Careful placement of your DHTML objects can help with backward compatibility.

✦ You can use Dreamweaver's built-in, customizable Validator to check your code for tag or syntax errors.

✦ Dreamweaver enables you to check your Web page, selected pages, or an entire Web site against a browser profile to look for tags and attributes that do not work in a particular browser version.

✦ Browser profiles can be customized or copied and modified for a new browser or browser version.

In the next chapter, you learn how to use Dreamweaver for building Web sites in a team environment.

✦   ✦   ✦

Building Accessible Web Sites with a Team

Major Web sites that are designed, developed, and maintained by one person are increasingly rare. After a site has reached a certain complexity and size, it's far more timely and cost-effective to divide responsibility for different areas among different people. For all its positive aspects, team development has an equal number of shortcomings — as anyone who has had his or her work overwritten by another developer working on the same page will attest.

Dreamweaver includes a number of features that make it easy for teams to work together. In addition to the existing Check In/Check Out facility, version control and collaborative authoring have been enabled in Dreamweaver through the connectivity to Microsoft's Visual SourceSafe and the WebDAV (Web Distributed Authoring and Versioning) standard.

An important addition to the Macromedia Studio family, Contribute, is tightly integrated with Dreamweaver. Contribute-enabled sites can be administered directly from within Dreamweaver with full access to the latest version of Contribute administrative controls.

In addition to providing links to industry-standard protocols used in team development, Dreamweaver also includes a more accessible Design Notes feature. When custom file columns (which rely on Design Notes to store their information) are set up, a project's status is just a glance away. For more detailed feedback, Dreamweaver's Reports command provides an interactive method for uncovering problems and offers a direct link to fixing them. As with many Dreamweaver features, the Reports mechanism is extensible, which means JavaScript-savvy developers can create their own custom reports to further assist their team. This chapter examines the various Dreamweaver tools — both old and new — for developing Web sites with a team.

Following Check In/Check Out Procedures

Site development can be subdivided in as many different ways as there are site development teams. In one group, all the graphics may be handled by one person or department, whereas layout is handled by another, and JavaScript coding by yet another. Or, one team may be given total responsibility over one section of a Web site — the products section, for example — whereas another team handles the services division. No matter how the responsibilities are shared, the danger of overlap always exists. Two or more team members might unknowingly work on the same page, graphic, or other Web element — and one person's work might replace the other's when the work is transferred to the remote site. Suddenly, the oh-so-efficient division of labor becomes a logistical nightmare.

Dreamweaver's core protection for team Web site development is its Check In/Check Out system. When properly established and adhered to, the Check In/Check Out system stops files from being overwritten improperly. It also lets everyone on the team know who is working on what file, and it provides a direct method of contacting team members, right from within Dreamweaver.

As with any team effort, to get the most out of the Check In/Check Out system everybody must follow the rules:

✦ **Rule Number 1:** All team members must have Check In/Check Out set up for their Dreamweaver-defined sites.

✦ **Rule Number 2:** All team members must have Design Notes enabled in their site definition (in order to share Design Notes information).

And, arguably the most important rule:

✦ **Rule Number 3:** All team members must use Dreamweaver to transfer files to and from the remote server.

If the Check In/Check Out system fails and a file is accidentally overwritten, it is invariably because Rule Number 3 was broken: Someone uploaded or downloaded a file to or from the Web server using a tool other than Dreamweaver.

Check In/Check Out Overview

Before I discuss the Check In/Check Out setup procedure, examine how the process actually works with two fictional team members, Eric and Bella:

1. Eric gets an email with a note to update the content on the About Our Company page with news of a merger that has just occurred.

2. Bella receives a similar note — except Bella is the graphic artist and needs to change the logo to reflect the new organization.

3. Eric connects to the remote site, selects the `about.htm` file, and clicks the Check Out button on Dreamweaver's Files panel toolbar. If Eric had clicked Get instead of Check Out, he would have received a read-only file on his system.

4. Dreamweaver asks Eric if he would like to include dependent files in the transfer. Because he doesn't know that Bella needs to work on the site also, he clicks OK. The file on the remote system is downloaded to Eric's machine and a small green checkmark appears next to the name of each file transferred in both the Remote Site and Local Files views, as shown in Figure 30-1.

5. Bella connects to the remote site in Dreamweaver and sees a red check next to the file she needs to work on, `about.htm`. Next to the file is the name of the person who currently has the file, Eric, as well as his email address.

6. Bella selects the link to Eric's email address and drops him a note asking him to let her know when he's done.

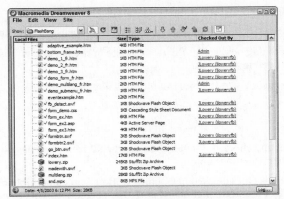

Figure 30-1: For a checked-out file, a checkmark is placed next to the filename on both the local and remote sites. The checkmark is green if you checked it out, and red if someone else checked it out.

7. Eric finishes adding the content to the page and clicks the Check In button to transfer the files back to the remote server. The checkmarks are removed from both the Remote and Local views and the local version of about.htm is marked as read-only by Dreamweaver, indicated with a closed padlock symbol. This feature prevents Eric from working on the file without first checking it out.

8. Bella receives Eric's "I'm done!" email and retrieves the file by clicking the Check Out button in the Files panel toolbar. Now, on Bella's machine, the transferred files have a green checkmark and her name, whereas on Eric's screen, the checkmarks are displayed in red.

9. After she's finished working on the graphics side of the page, ensuring that Eric's new content wraps properly around her new logo, Bella selects the HTML file and then clicks Check In. By opting to transfer the dependent files as well, all her new graphics are properly transferred. Again, the checkmarks are removed, and the local files are set to read-only.

10. The work is completed without anyone stepping on anyone else's toes—or files.

Caution Dreamweaver places a small text file with a .lck (lock) extension on both the server and local site for each checked-out document. The .lck file stores the Check Out name of the person transferring the files and, if available, his or her email address. These files must not be deleted from the server because their existence signals to Dreamweaver that a file has been checked out. After the file is checked back in, the .lck file is deleted from the server.

Enabling Check In/Check Out

Dreamweaver's Check In/Check Out system is activated through the Site Definition dialog box. The Check In/Check Out settings must be input individually for each site; no global option exists for all sites. Although it's generally best to set it up when the site is initially defined, you can enable Check In/Check Out at any time.

To establish the Check In/Check Out feature, follow these steps:

1. Choose Site ➪ Manage Sites or select Manage Sites from the Site list in the Files panel.

2. From the Manage Sites dialog box, select the desired site in the list and choose Edit or click the New button to define a new site.

3. Select the Remote Info category in the Site Definition dialog box.

4. From the Access list, choose either FTP or Local/Network.

5. Choose the Enable File Check In And Check Out option.

6. If you want to automatically check out a file when opening it from the Files panel, select the Check Out Files When Opening option.

   When you select the Check Out Files When Opening option, you can double-click a file in the Files panel or select it and then choose File ➪ Open Selection. This transfers the corresponding remote file to the local system and designates the file as being checked out. Choosing File ➪ Open does not automatically check out a file.

7. Enter the name you displayed under the Checked Out By column in the Check Out Name field. It's a good idea to use a name that not only identifies yourself, but also the system on which you're working. Thus, jlowery-laptop or jlowery-iMac is a better choice than just jlowery.

8. To enable team members to send you a message from within Dreamweaver, enter your full email address in the E-mail Address field.

   Entering an email address converts the Checked Out By name to an active link. If you select the link, you prompt the default email program to display a new message form. (The To field contains the supplied email address, and the Subject field contains the site name and filename, as shown in Figure 30-2.)

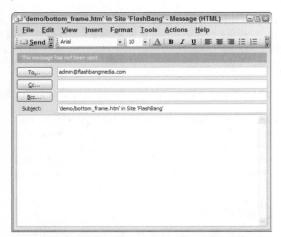

Figure 30-2: Dreamweaver lets you contact the team member working on a file with the email address feature. The subject line is automatically added to reference a particular file and site.

9. Make sure that any other information necessary for establishing an FTP or network connection is entered.

10. By default, Dreamweaver hides the Checked Out By file view column for performance reasons. If you want to display the link to the person who has checked out the file in the Files panel, switch to the File View Column category, select the Checked Out By entry, and select the Show option.

11. Click OK to close the Site Definition dialog box.

12. From the Manage Sites dialog box, click Done.

Note   The preceding procedure works for both FTP and network-connected remote sites. If you are working within a Visual SourceSafe or WebDAV environment, see the sections later in this chapter that discuss enabling Check In and Check Out protocols for those environments.

Checking Files In and Out

After the Check In/Check Out feature is enabled, additional buttons and commands become available. The Files panel toolbar shows both a Check Out File(s) button and a Check In button, as shown in Figure 30-3, and the Site ➪ Check Out and Site ➪ Check In commands become active. The redundancy of these commands makes it feasible to check files in and out from wherever you happen to be working in the Dreamweaver environment.

Check In

Check Out

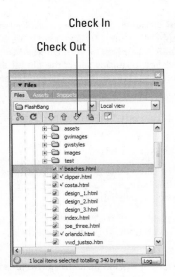

Figure 30-3: The Check In and Check Out buttons do not appear unless Enable Check In/Check Out has been selected in the Site Definition dialog box.

To check out a file or series of files from the Files panel, follow these steps:

1. Choose Window ➪ Files to open the Files panel. If you prefer to use keyboard shortcuts, press F8.

2. If necessary, select the desired site — where Check In/Check Out has been enabled — from the Site drop-down list.

3. Click the Connect button in the Files panel toolbar. If you've chosen Local/Network as your remote access method, you're connected automatically.

4. Choose the HTML or other Web documents you want to check out from the Files panel (it doesn't matter whether you're using Local view or Remote view). It's not necessary to select the dependent files; Dreamweaver transfers those for you automatically.

5. Click Check Out File(s) in the Files panel toolbar or select Site ⇨ Check Out. If you *get* the files instead of checking them out, either by clicking the Get button or by dragging the files from the Remote Site listing to the Local Files listing, the local file becomes read-only, but the remote files are not marked as checked out.

6. If the Prompt On Get/Check Out option is selected in Preferences, Dreamweaver asks if you'd like to transfer the dependent files. Click Yes to do so or No to transfer only the selected files. When Dreamweaver has completed the transfer, green checkmarks appear next to each primary file (HTML, ASP, ColdFusion, and so on) in both the Remote Site and Local Files views; dependent files are made read-only locally, designated by a padlock symbol.

I recommend checking out all the files that you need in a work session right at the start. Although you can check out an open document — by choosing Site ⇨ Check Out or by selecting Check Out from the File Management button on the toolbar — Dreamweaver transfers the remote file to your local system, possibly overwriting any changes you've made. Dreamweaver does ask you if you want to replace the local version with the remote file; to abort the procedure, click No.

Tip   To edit a graphic or other dependent file that has been locked as part of the checkout process, you can unlock the file from the Files panel. Right-click (Control+click) the file in the Files panel and, from the context menu, choose Turn Off Read Only. (The Turn Off Read Only option is called Unlock on the Macintosh.) One related tip: To quickly select the file for an image, choose the image in the Assets panel; and from the context menu, choose Locate In Site.

After you've completed your work on a particular file, you're ready to check it back in. To check in the current file, follow these steps:

1. Choose Site ⇨ Check In or click Check In on the Files panel toolbar.

2. If you haven't saved your file, but you've enabled the Save Files Before Putting option from the Site category in Preferences, your file is automatically saved; otherwise, Dreamweaver asks if you want to store the file before transferring it.

3. If Prompt On Put/Check In is enabled, Dreamweaver asks if you want to transfer the dependent files as well. If any changes have been made to the dependent files, click Yes.

   After the files are transferred, Dreamweaver removes the checkmarks from the files and makes the local files read-only.

Note   Ever start working on a file only to realize you're working on the wrong one? If you make this or any other mistake that makes you wish you could go back to the original version when working with a checked-out file, don't worry. Even if you've saved your changes locally, you can choose Site ⇨ Undo Check Out (or select Undo Check Out from the Site button on the Files panel toolbar) to retransfer the posted file from the remote site. The local file is made read-only, and the file is no longer checked out under your name.

Keeping Track with Design Notes

When several people are working are on a site, they can't just rely on the Web pages to speak for themselves. In any team collaboration, a great deal of organizational information needs to be communicated behind the scenes: who's working on what areas, the status of any given file, when the project is due, what modifications are needed, and so on. Dreamweaver includes a feature called Design Notes that is designed to facilitate team communication in a very flexible manner.

Dreamweaver Design Notes are small files that, in a sense, attach themselves to the Web pages or objects they concern. A Design Note can be attached to any HTML page, graphic, or media file inserted into a page. Design Notes follow their corresponding file whenever that file is moved or renamed using the Dreamweaver Files panel; moreover, a Design Note is deleted if the file to which it is related is deleted. Design Notes have the same base name as the file to which they are attached — including that file's extension — but are designated with an .mno extension. For example, the Design Note for the file index.htm would be called index.htm.mno; Design Notes are stored in the _notes subfolder, which is not displayed in the Dreamweaver Files panel.

Design Notes can be entered and viewed through the Design Notes dialog box, shown in Figure 30-4. This dialog box may optionally be set to appear when a file is opened, thus passing instructions from one team member to another automatically. In addition to the Design Notes dialog box, you can configure File view columns to display Design Note information right in the Files panel; the File view columns feature is covered in the "Browsing File View Columns" section.

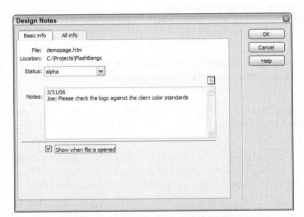

Figure 30-4: You can configure a Design Note to pop up whenever a file is opened to alert a fellow team member of work to be done.

Setting Up for Design Notes

Design Notes are enabled by default, but they can be turned off on a site-by-site basis. To disable Design Notes, follow these steps:

1. Choose Site ➪ Manage Sites or select Manage Sites from the Site listing to open the Manage Sites dialog box.

2. In the Manage Sites dialog box, select the site you want to alter and choose Edit.

3. In the Site Definition dialog box, select the Design Notes category (see Figure 30-5).

Figure 30-5: Design Notes play an important role in cross-product integration when working with Fireworks, Flash, and Contribute.

4. Deselect the Maintain Design Notes option to completely stop Dreamweaver from creating Design Notes. Dreamweaver alerts you to the consequences of disabling Design Notes. Click OK to continue.

5. If you want to work with Design Notes locally, but don't want to automatically transfer them to the remote site, leave Maintain Design Notes checked and uncheck Upload Design Notes For Sharing.

6. To remove Design Notes that no longer have an associated file — which can happen if a file is deleted or renamed by a program other than Dreamweaver — click the Clean Up button. Dreamweaver gives you an opportunity to confirm the delete operation.

7. Click OK to close the Site Definition dialog box, and then click Done to close the Manage Sites dialog box.

Design Notes serve two different purposes. From a team perspective, they're invaluable for tracking a project's progress and passing information among team members. However, Design Notes are also used by Dreamweaver and other Macromedia products, including Fireworks, to pass data between programs and program commands. For example, Fireworks uses Design Notes to store the location of a Fireworks source file that is displayed in the Image Property inspector when you select the exported graphic in Dreamweaver.

Keep in mind the dual nature of Design Notes. I strongly recommend—whether you work with a large team or you're a team of one—that you keep Design Notes enabled and fully functioning.

Setting the Status with Design Notes

What is the one thing a Web site project manager always wants to know? The status of every page under development: What's still in the planning stages, what has been drafted, what has made it to beta, and what's ready to go live? The manager who has an awareness of each page's status can prioritize appropriately and add additional resources to the development of a page if necessary. Individual team members who are working on a page should also know how far along that page is.

Design Notes put the Status category front and center for all files. It's the one standard field that is always available, and it offers eight different values and one custom value. Entries may be date-stamped in the Notes area to show a history of revisions, as shown in Figure 30-6. Optionally, you can elect to display the Design Note the next time the file is opened by anyone.

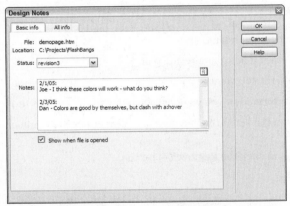

Figure 30-6: Design Notes can maintain a history of revisions for any Web page.

To enter the status of a file, follow these steps:

1. Choose File ⇨ Design Notes to open the Design Notes dialog box. To insert a Design Note for an object embedded on a Web page, such as a graphic, Flash movie, or other multimedia element, right-click (Control+click) the object and choose Design Notes from the context menu.

2. On the Basic Info tab of the Design Notes dialog box, choose one of the following standard options from the Status drop-down list: draft, revision1, revision2, revision3, alpha, beta, final, or needs attention.

3. To add the current date (in m/d/yy format, such as 3/7/01) to the Notes field, click the Calendar icon.

4. Enter any desired text into the Notes field. The same Notes text is displayed regardless of which Status option you choose.

5. If you'd like the Design Notes dialog box with the current information to appear the next time the page is loaded, select the Show When File Is Opened option. The Show When File Is Opened option is only available for Design Notes attached to pages, not for Design Notes attached to page elements such as images.

6. Click OK when you're finished.

Creating Custom Design Notes

Aside from monitoring the status of a project, you can use a Design Note to describe any single item. The All Info tab of the Design Notes dialog box enables you to enter any number of name/value pairs, which can be viewed in the Design Note itself or — more effectively — in the File view columns. This mechanism might be used to indicate which graphic artist in your department has primary responsibility for the page, or how many billable hours the page has accrued. You can also use the All Info tab to set a custom value for the Status list on the Basic Info tab.

To enter a new name/value pair, follow these steps:

1. Choose File ⇨ Design Notes to open the Design Notes dialog box.

2. Select the All Info tab. If a Status and/or Notes entry has been made on the Basic Info tab, you'll see these values listed in the Info area.

3. Click the Add (+) button to enter a new name/value pair.

4. In the Name field, enter the term you want to use.

5. In the Value field, enter the information you want associated with the current term.

6. To edit an entry, select it from the list in the Info area and alter either the Name or Value field.

7. To delete an entry, select it and click the Remove (–) button.

8. Click OK when you're finished.

As noted earlier, you can create a custom Status list option in the All Info tab. To do so, just enter **status** in the Name field of a new name/value pair and enter the desired listing in the Value field. If you switch to the Basic Info tab, you find your new status entry listed as the last item. You can only add one custom status entry; if you add another, it replaces the previous one.

Viewing Design Notes

To fully view a Design Note, you have several options. You can choose File ⇨ Design Notes to open the dialog box; in Windows, this option is available from either the Document window or the Files panel. A second method is to right-click (Control+click) the file in either the File or the Site Map view of the Files panel and select the Design Notes option from the context menu. Finally, if a Design Note is attached to a file, you'll see an icon in the Notes column of the File view, as shown in Figure 30-7. Double-clicking the Notes icon opens the Design Note associated with that file.

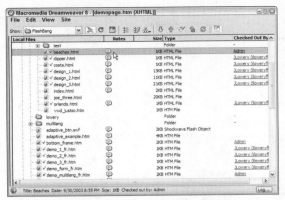

Figure 30-7: Get immediate access to previously created Design Notes by double-clicking the icon in the Notes column.

Browsing File View Columns

Although Design Notes can hold a lot of information about a Web page or element, the details are kept out of sight. With an eye toward heightening the visibility of Design Notes data — thus making them more useful — the Dreamweaver engineers have tied the columns of the Files panel's File view directly to Design Notes. In the previous section, you saw how the Notes column indicated that a Design Note existed for a particular file; now you learn how to create custom File view columns to display any value stored in a Design Note.

With custom columns in the File view, a quick glance at the Files panel can reveal which files are completed, which are in revision, and which need attention. Moreover, custom columns can be sorted, just as regular columns. You can, for instance, easily group together all the files with the same due date, or those coded by the same programmer. File view columns — even the built-in ones such as Type and Modified — can be realigned, re-ordered, or hidden. Only the Name column cannot be altered or moved. With this level of customization possible, virtually the entire File view can be reshaped, like the one in Figure 30-8.

The six standard columns — Local Files (which shows the filename), Notes, Size, Type, Modified, and Checked Out By — can be supplemented by any number of custom columns. Modification of the column setup is handled in the File View Columns category of the Site Definition dialog box. File views are managed on a per-site basis; when defining the file views, you can determine if the views are to be seen by anyone accessing the development site. Likewise, any custom column can optionally be shared among team members.

To create a custom File view, follow these steps:

1. Open the File View Columns category with one of these methods:

   - Select Manage Sites and open the Site Definition for the desired site. Then select the File View Column option from the category list.

   - Choose View ➪ File View Columns from the Files panel on Windows systems or choose Site ➪ Site Files View ➪ File View Columns on the Macintosh.

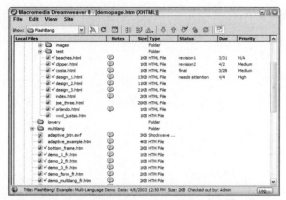

Figure 30-8: File view columns can be substantially reorganized to reflect the concerns of your team on a project-by-project basis.

2. If you'd like team members to see the custom columns you're developing, select Enable Column Sharing. You also need to choose the Share With All Users Of This Site option for each custom column you want to share.

3. To add a custom column, click the Add (+) button. A new entry at the end of the list is created.

4. Enter a unique name for the column in the Column Name field. If you enter an existing name, Dreamweaver warns you and requests a new name before proceeding.

5. Pick a Design Note field to link to the new column from the Associate With Design Note list. You can choose one of the suggested Design Note fields (assigned, due, priority, or status) or you can enter your own. Design Note fields can be uppercase, lowercase, or mixed-case; multiple words are also allowed.

6. Select an Alignment option from the list: Left, Center, or Right. Columns that hold numeric or date values should be aligned to the right.

7. Make sure the Show option is selected.

8. To share this column with fellow team members, choose the Share With All Users Of This Site option. Selecting this option causes Dreamweaver to create a file called `dwSiteColumnsAll.xml` within the _notes folder on the remote site. When another member of your team connects to the site, Dreamweaver reads this file and incorporates it into that person's site definition. This enables any other user to see the same column set up on his or her system.

9. Use the up and down arrows to reposition the column.

10. To add additional columns, repeat steps 3 through 9.

11. Click OK when you're finished.

How might a team benefit from custom File view columns? Some of the possibilities for custom columns include the following:

✦ Project Manager

✦ Lead Designer

✦ Lead Programmer

✦ Date Due

✦ Date Created

✦ Template Used

✦ Percentage Complete

✦ Client Contact

Caution   File view columns are sorted alphabetically even if the values are numeric. For example, if you have three files with the numeric values 100%, 50%, and 10%, an ascending sort displays 10%, 100%, 50%. As a workaround, use decimal values (.10, .50, and 1.00) to represent percentages, and the files will sort correctly. If your columns require date values, use leading zeros in dates, such as 01/03, to ensure that the columns are properly sorted.

Although having the Design Notes information visible in File view columns is extremely helpful for maintaining an overview of a Web site, Dreamweaver takes the feature a step further. After a custom file column is established, you can handle additions and modifications to the Design Note from the Files panel. Click in the custom column of the file; the existing information, if any, is highlighted and can be altered. If there is no data in the column, the column becomes editable.

Note   Although the Design Note is actually a separate file, you cannot change File view columns for a locked file. One solution is to temporarily turn off the read-only feature and then add the File view info and relock if necessary.

To turn off the read-only feature, right-click (Control+click) the file in the Files panel and, from the context menu, choose Turn Off Read Only. (The Turn Off Read Only option is called Unlock on the Macintosh.)

Generating Reports

Although custom File view columns can present a tremendous degree of detail, the data is only viewable from the Files panel. Often, managers and team members need to extract certain bits of information about a site in order to know where they stand and fix problems in an organized, timely fashion. Some Webmasters use third-party utilities to comb their sites and generate lists of errors, which can then be assigned for resolution. These utilities can also be used to establish workflow patterns as they gather information, such as which pages are currently incomplete, or who is currently working on what site elements.

Dreamweaver reports give the Webmaster and team members a new tool for efficiently building Web sites. The information from a Dreamweaver report can be instantly used — double-clicking any report detail opens the referenced file — or stored as an XML file for later output. Dreamweaver includes seven standard reports that may be generated individually or combined into one. As with many Dreamweaver features, the Reports command is extensible, enabling users to build custom reports.

How do Dreamweaver reports work? The user must first choose from a variety of scopes: the current document, selected files in the site, all the files in a particular folder, or the entire site. After the scope has been selected, the report elements — what the report actually covers —

are selected. The report is then run, and Dreamweaver outputs the results into a floating panel, as shown in Figure 30-9. Each entry in the Results panel is capable of opening the listed file; in the case of reports querying the underlying HTML, the entries lead directly to the referenced code.

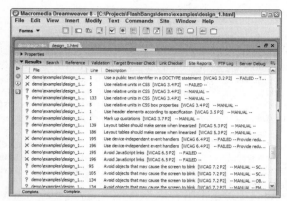

Figure 30-9: Dreamweaver reports return interactive results — just double-click any listed entry to open the related file.

Generated reports can also be saved for later use. The reports are saved in an XML file format that can be imported into a Web page, database, or spreadsheet program. Although this information can be extracted by hand, the structured format of the XML file makes it a perfect candidate for an automated process handled by an extension or other utility.

Two different types of Dreamweaver reports are available: those concerned with the code in the pages themselves and those accessing workflow details.

To access a Dreamweaver report, follow these steps:

1. Choose Site ➪ Reports or click the Play icon in the Site Reports panel. Windows users can choose the command from either the Document window or the Files panel menus.

2. Select which reports you'd like to include from either the Workflow or HTML Reports categories.

3. If you choose an option from the Workflow category or the Accessibility option in HTML Reports, the Report Settings button activates. Click it to define the report search for Workflow reports (see Figure 30-10), or the accessibility options (see Figure 30-11) for the Accessibility HTML Report.

Note   Section 508 is the United States government statue concerning accessibility on the Internet and in software development. To learn more about Section 508 standards, see www.section508.gov.

Dreamweaver remembers the Report On setting each time you run this command. The Report Settings options are covered in detail later, in the section "Using Workflow Reports."

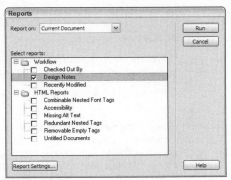

Figure 30-10: Only certain reports, like Design Notes, offer additional Report Settings.

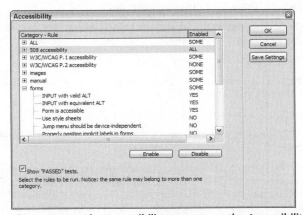

Figure 30-11: The Accessibility report uses the Accessibility options to determine which pieces of your pages to test against Section 508 standards.

4. Click the Run button. The Site Reports panel appears if it isn't already active. As the report is processed, results are listed in the upper window.

5. From the Site Reports panel, you can click the Stop icon to halt the report.

6. To open any referenced file, double-click the entry or right-click (Control-click) the entry and select Open File from the context menu.

7. To store the report as an XML file, select Save Report and enter a file and path in the Save File dialog box.

Entries in the Site Reports panel are initially sorted by filename in an ascending order; however, selecting any column heading (File, Line, or Description) re-sorts the list accordingly. If many result listings are returned, the Site Reports panel can be resized to display more of them.

Outputting HTML Reports

Dreamweaver includes six options under the HTML Reports category:

✦ **Combinable Nested Font Tags:** This query looks for code in which the font tag has been applied to the same text at different times, as shown in the following example:

```
<font color="#000000"><font size=+1>Monday, December 15th
@7pm</font></font>
```

✦ **Accessibility:** A very powerful report that examines your site for compatibility under either the Section 508 guidelines or the W3C guidelines; you can check all the guidelines or select certain ones to verify or ignore. In addition to showing which aspects need attention, this report will optionally note guidelines that were successfully implemented.

✦ **Missing Alt Text:** This report searches for <img> tags in which the alt attribute is empty or missing entirely. To comply with accessibility guidelines established by the W3C, all images should have alt attributes that describe the graphic.

✦ **Redundant Nested Tags:** This report identifies tags nested within themselves, as shown in the following example:

```
<b><b>On Sale!</b></b>
```

✦ **Removable Empty Tags:** This search finds non-empty tags (that is, tags with both an opening and closing element) with no content, as in this code:

```
<div align="center"> </div>
```

✦ **Untitled Documents:** This report looks for pages that have no title or use the default Untitled Document text.

You can run any or all the HTML reports at once — just select the desired report(s) from the Reports dialog box. The Site Reports panel lists the name of the file, the line number where the search condition was found, and an error message for each entry. Selecting a file displays the error message with additional detail, if available, in the Detailed Description area. Select Open File from the context menu or double-click an entry to load the file if it's available. If the file is currently locked, Dreamweaver asks if you'd like to view the read-only file or unlock it. All HTML report files are displayed in the split-screen Code and Design view.

Using Workflow Reports

Workflow reports, unlike HTML reports, don't examine the code of Web pages. They look at the metadata — the information about the information — of a site. Three standard reports are available under the Workflow heading:

✦ **Checked Out By:** This report displays any file checked out by a particular person as designated in the Report Settings dialog box. If nothing is entered in the Report Settings dialog box, a list of all files in the selected scope that have been checked out by anyone is returned.

Caution   To run this report, you must be able to connect to your remote site.

✦ **Recently Modified:** Returns a list of pages modified in a user-definable period along with their modification date; you can, optionally, search for pages modified by a specific user, if the site is being administered by Contribute.

In addition to the Results panel listing, this report also automatically opens a print-ready version in your primary browser with links to each page listed, as shown in Figure 30-12. The pages can either be viewed locally — best for static pages — or through the testing server, which is necessary for dynamic pages.

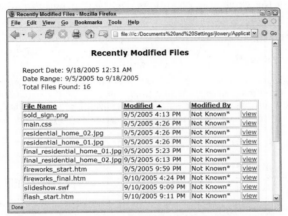

Figure 30-12: Get a complete printable report on files changed in a given time frame by running the Recently Modified report.

✦ **Design Notes:** This report examines the designated files according to search criteria set up in the Report Settings dialog box. Searches can be conducted on a maximum of three criteria. If no criterion is entered, a list of all files with Design Notes in the selected scope is returned.

The Report Settings dialog box for the Design Notes reports is relatively flexible, because it enables *and*-type searches. To use the Design Notes Report Settings dialog box, follow these steps:

1. In the Reports dialog box, select the Design Notes option under the Workflow category. The Report Settings button is made available.

2. Click Report Settings. The Report Settings dialog box opens; the previous Design Notes Settings are restored.

3. In the Report Settings dialog box, enter the name of the Design Notes field in the first column. The name of the Design Notes field is case-sensitive, so entering Status in the Report Settings dialog box will not match status in the Design Note.

4. Choose a criteria type from the middle column drop-down list. The options are as follows: contains, does not contain, is, is not, and matches regex.

5. In the third column, enter the value of the Design Notes field being sought. As with the Design Notes field, the value search is also case-sensitive.

6. To add a second or third condition to the query, repeat steps 3 through 5 in the second and third line of the Report Settings dialog box. Additional conditionals are applied in an *and*-type search. For example, a setting where the first line reads

```
status is revision3
```

and the second line reads

```
done is 1.00
```

returns all Design Notes for which both conditions are true. Currently, there is no way to perform an *or*-type search.

7. Click OK when you're finished.

8. Click Run to execute the search.

Of all the criteria options — *is, is not, contains*, and so on — available in the Report Settings dialog box for Design Notes, the most powerful is matches regex. Regular Expressions are pattern-matching mechanisms and, as such, are extremely flexible. The syntax, however, is unique and requires a bit of use before it becomes second nature. Here are some examples you might find useful:

Regular Expression	Matches
.*	Any text
[^.]	An empty string
\d	Any single number
[0-5]	Any digit from 0 to 5
graphics|code	Either the word graphics or the word code

Administering Macromedia Contribute Sites

One of a Web designer's greatest challenges is the ongoing maintenance of a site. In many situations, Web sites thrive on current information and, without continual updates, lose their effectiveness. Site maintenance is a prickly thorn bush for all involved: Web developers find it time-consuming and a distraction from their primary business, design. Web site owners want editorial control and immediate access — without the technical administrative headaches.

Macromedia Contribute was introduced to solve the thorny problem of Web site upkeep. Contribute makes it easy for non-technical users to modify and add content to their Web sites; if your users are familiar with a word processor and a browser, they'll be able to master Contribute with little effort. After a content contributor has an established connection to a site — a process Contribute greatly simplifies — all he does is browse to a page, make his edits, and publish it back to the Web. The Contribute interface, shown in Figure 30-13, is designed with the non-technical user in mind.

If you're a designer working with content contributors using Contribute, you can easily set up your site to be compatible. Contribute compatibility relies on key team-oriented features discussed elsewhere in this chapter: Check In/Check Out and Design Notes.

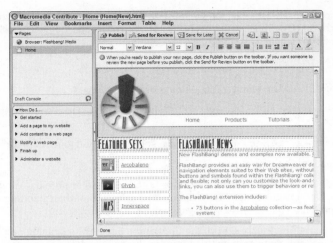

Figure 30-13: Contribute packs a lot of power in a simplified interface, allowing the non-technically savvy to modify Web pages with ease.

For medium-to-large sites, Macromedia recommends its Web Publishing System. The Web Publishing System combines Studio 8 for design purposes, a number of Contribute 3 licenses for content entry, and an administrative application, Contribute Publishing Services. Contribute Publishing Services (CPS) is a server-side application designed to act as an administrative center; CPS is primarily used to track user access and publishing activities on the Web site. You'll find a brief description for implementing CPS later in this chapter.

The key to Contribute is controlled access. Although the program makes it easy for anyone to modify pages on the Web, it also restricts what changes can be made. Some of the restrictions are inherent in the type of pages that make up the site — Dreamweaver templates, for example, are ideally suited for allowing only designated sections of a document to be edited. However, many basic limitations, such as which pages can be edited, are established by the Contribute administrator. Although Contribute sites can be administered from within Contribute itself, its tight integration with Dreamweaver provides another path: The same administrative options are available within Dreamweaver.

Note   To administer Contribute from within Dreamweaver 8, Contribute 2.0 or better must be installed on the same machine as Dreamweaver; greater functionality comes from working with Contribute 3.1 or higher.

Setting Up Contribute Compatibility

Like other sitewide settings, Contribute compatibility is managed through the Site Definition dialog box. As noted earlier, Contribute utilizes several optional Dreamweaver features — Design Notes and Check In/Check Out — controlled through the same interface. For your convenience, if you opt to establish Contribute administration, Dreamweaver enables all the necessary options with one click, if you have not previously done so.

Note　To make Contribute compatibility available, the site must be configured with the proper form of remote access, such as FTP or SFTP. Neither WebDAV nor SourceSafe are compatible with Contribute. RDS-based sites require custom settings for Contribute compatibility.

To set up Contribute compatibility for your current site, follow these steps:

1. Choose Site ⇨ Manage Sites. The Manage Sites dialog box is displayed.

2. With the current site selected in the Manage Sites dialog, click Edit. The Site Definition dialog appears.

3. From the Advanced view of the Site Definition dialog, select the Contribute category.

4. Select the Enable Contribute Compatibility option.

5. If you have not previously enabled Design Notes (for both local and remote use) and Check In/Check Out, Dreamweaver displays a dialog informing you of their necessity and offers to automatically enable these settings; click OK to continue.

6. If Check In/Check was not previously set up, the Contribute Site Settings dialog box is displayed. Enter a checkout name and email address in the appropriate fields and click OK. Dreamweaver displays the Site Root URL for the current site, as shown in Figure 30-14, gathered from the information entered in the Remote Site category.

Figure 30-14: After you've enabled Contribute compatibility, be sure to test the connection.

7. To verify the Site Root URL, click Test.

8. Click OK when you're finished to close the Site Definition dialog box.

The Contribute category in Preferences updates to reflect the newly set-up Contribute administration. In addition to the URL to the site, you'll also see indicators concerning the status of rollback (the ability to reinstate previous versions) and CPS (Contribute Publishing Services).

Entering Sitewide Administrator Settings

Each Contribute site has a single administrator. The administrator is responsible for controlling overall access to the site as well as establishing editing parameters. Among other options, the administrator can allow pages edited by Contribute users to be rolled back to previous versions. When you enable Contribute compatibility, you're establishing yourself as the site administrator.

Note   Before you can set up yourself as an administrator, Contribute compatibility must be enabled as described in the previous section, and you must have a network connection.

To begin modifying Contribute settings, click Administer Site In Contribute in the Contribute category of the Site Definitions dialog box. The primary administrative interface, shown in Figure 30-15, opens after a connection is established.

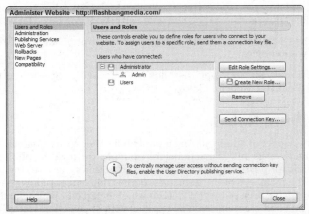

Figure 30-15: The Administer Website dialog available through Dreamweaver is the same as the one found in Contribute.

To modify the settings that control administration, follow these steps:

1. From the Administer Website dialog box, select Administration. The Administration dialog box is displayed, as shown in Figure 30-16.

2. To change the administrator's email address, enter a valid email address in the Contact E-mail Address field.

Tip   For administrative duties, it's a good idea to use a special email address that is different from your check out address, such as administrator@idest.com. Use your email client to sort the incoming administrative queries into a special folder.

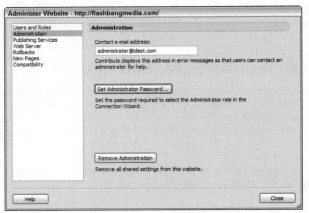

Figure 30-16: Modify primary administrative settings through the Administration category.

3. To alter the current administrator password, click Set Administrator Password and enter the old password and new password where indicated in the Set Administrator Password dialog box; click OK to return to the Sitewide Settings dialog box.

4. To stop administering the Contribute site, click Remove Administration and click Yes when asked to confirm your choice.

After you've chosen all the necessary sitewide options, click OK to close the Sitewide Settings dialog box and return to the Administer Website dialog.

Establishing Contribute Roles

The proper use of roles is a key aspect of administering a Contribute site. A *Contribute role* is a collection of users with common tasks and restrictions; for example, those in the public relations department responsible for posting press releases — and nothing else — to the Web might be in one role, whereas the members of the human resources department might be in another. Each role can have a specific area of the Web site in which it can edit pages; furthermore, different options for editing and creating, such as working with specific templates, may be available for each role. All these options, as well as the basic creation and removal of roles is handled by the Contribute administrator from the Edit Role Settings section of the Administer Website dialog box.

Managing Roles

Two roles are created by default when Contribute administration is declared: administrator and users. The primary difference between these two roles, initially, is that administrators can delete the files they are able to edit whereas users cannot. However, these preliminary settings are only starting points and can easily be altered by the administrator.

Basic role management — creating, removing, duplicating, and editing — is handled directly in the Edit Role Settings section of the Administer Website dialog box, as shown previously in Figure 30-15. The following list explains how to do these tasks:

✦ To define a role, click Create New Role; when the New Role dialog opens, select the role you want to copy and enter a name in the provided field.

✦ To remove an existing role, select the role to be deleted and click Remove. You'll be asked to confirm the removal.

✦ To modify the settings of any role, select the role from the list and click Edit Role Settings. Another dialog box with several categories, discussed in the following section, is displayed.

If your Contribute site does not have CPS enabled, you can assign users to specific roles by creating a Connection Key; CPS-enabled sites manage users independently. Both approaches are described later in this chapter.

Any changes made concerning role management are written to the server after the Administer Website dialog is dismissed by clicking OK.

Modifying Role Settings

As administrator, you have extensive control over what each defined role can do in Contribute. If you want, you can define members of particular roles to modify the text only in specific areas of existing pages. You may grant other roles a broader responsibility to create new pages based on specific templates, and you can give them full rein on those pages. All the settings are applied by selecting the role and clicking Edit Role Settings in the Administer Website dialog box.

Eight categories are available when setting role options:

✦ **General:** Sets the role description and home page.

✦ **Folder/File Access:** Determines which folders (and all the files and what they contain) are available for editing. It also determines if the role may delete files.

✦ **Editing:** Governs user actions on non-template pages and various editing options including paragraph spacing and accessibility options.

✦ **Styles and Fonts:** Controls whether users are allowed to apply HTML or CSS styles or both.

✦ **New Pages:** Sets the type of new pages, if any, that the user can create.

✦ **File Placement**: Determines where dependent files are stored on the site.

✦ **Shared Assets**: Defines images, Flash movies, or Dreamweaver Library items to be available by all users within a particular role.

✦ **New Images:** Limits the size of the uploadable images.

Contribute stores these settings on the site's remote server in a hidden folder called _mm.

General

The opening category of the Edit Role Settings dialog box offers three basic options: the ability to publish files, the Role Description, and the Role Home Page. Users are either able to publish their Contribute-modified page directly to the site or not; if the Allow Users To Publish Files option is disabled, the user must submit the page for review to another user, typically one in a managerial capacity. The reviewer has the option of sending it back to the user with comments, publishing it, or submitting it to another user for review.

Users see the Role Description when they initially connect. It is, generally, used to explain who comprises the role and what restrictions are applied; this information is entered directly into the Role Description field as shown in Figure 30-17.

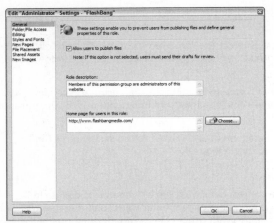

Figure 30-17: For most roles, the right to publish files directly — set in the General category of the Edit Role Settings dialog — is a key defining element.

The third option, Home Page For Users in this Role, sets the starting point for the current role. Enter the absolute URL for the desired folder in the field or click Choose to locate the folder in the site.

Tip It's a good idea to be as specific as possible when setting the home page for a given role because it makes it easier for members of the role to navigate more quickly to their pages. Note, however, that without setting further restrictions in the Folder/File Access category, the users can still edit pages on other parts of the site.

Folder/File Access

The Folder/File Access category (see Figure 30-18) is used to limit the current role's editing to the files in specific folders as well as their options for deleting files. Initially, users are allowed to modify files in any folder within the site. Whenever possible, it's advisable to limit roles to folders specific to their needs; this reduces user error and keeps users targeted to their tasks.

To specify one or more folders for a role, follow these steps:

1. From the Folder/File Access category of the Edit Role Settings dialog box, choose the Only Allow Editing Within These Folders option.

2. Click Add Folder to open the Choose Folder dialog box.

3. Navigate to the desired folder and click Select; when you're finished, click OK.

4. Repeat steps 2 and 3 to add more folders.

After a folder has been added, you can modify your choice by selecting the folder and clicking Edit to select a different folder or Remove to keep the files in the folder from being edited.

Users may also be given the power to delete the files they can edit. In the File Deletion area of the Folder/File Access category, choose the Allow Users To Delete Files They Have Permission To Edit option. After this option is enabled, you may also decide to allow such a deletion to remove the files stored as rollback versions.

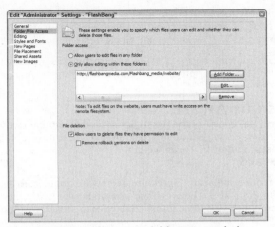

Figure 30-18: Add as many folders as needed
for any given role.

Editing

The Editing category of the Edit Role Settings dialog governs much of the hands-on experience of the Contribute user. Here, the administrator sets the overall access granted for modifying pages as well as for enabling special options that make the process more familiar to
non-technical users. The three main areas in this category are General Editing Restrictions,
Paragraph Spacing, and Other Editing Options, as shown in Figure 30-19.

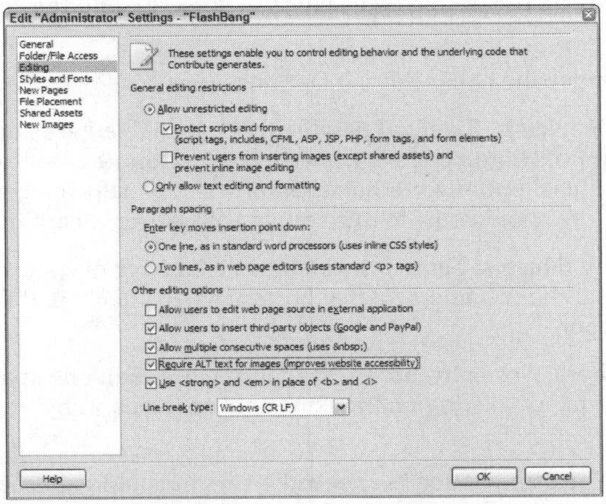

Figure 30-19: Enhance the Contribute experience
by enabling Word-like options from the Editing category.

The General Editing Restrictions area of the Editing category applies to pages not constructed
from Dreamweaver templates. Here, two key options exist: you can either allow unrestricted
modifications to the pages or limit the user to just editing and formatting text. If you choose
the Allow Unrestricted Editing option — which also allows users to add images and Flash

movies among other elements — it is highly recommended that the Protect Scripts And Forms option remain enabled. If this option is deselected, server-side code as well as forms can be deleted or changed. User-supplied images as well as image editing can also be put off-limits.

The two paragraph spacing options control what happens when a Contribute user presses the Enter (Return) key. If you choose the One Line option, a single line separates headings and paragraphs, like this:

BigCo, Inc. Wins Major Award

BigCo, Inc. is proud to announce the receipt of the prestigious Giant Company award. The Giant Company award is presented semi-annually to companies that have obtained a particular size without collapsing under their own weight.

BigCo CEO to Accept Award

The single-line format probably feels more familiar to Contribute users who come from a word-processing background; to create more space between paragraphs, users just press Enter (Return) again. However, to accomplish this look, inline CSS styles are used, resulting in code that can be harder to maintain.

Selecting the Two Lines option results in content looking like this:

BigCo, Inc. Wins Major Award

BigCo, Inc. is proud to announce the receipt of the prestigious Giant Company award. The Giant Company award is presented semi-annually to companies that have obtained a particular size without collapsing under their own weight.

BigCo CEO to Accept Award

Code entered when the Two Lines option is selected uses standard heading and paragraph tags. Which option you choose depends on the design constraints of your site and the sophistication of its users.

Six miscellaneous options are found under the Other Editing Options areas:

✦ **Allow Users To Edit Web Page Source In External Applications:** If enabled, this option allows users to open the current Contribute page in Dreamweaver or another editor. Though this is an extremely beneficial option for administrators, it is equally dangerous for most other roles; administrators should enable this setting with extreme caution.

✦ **Allow Users to Enter Third-Party Objects:** Contribute includes a number of special functions that insert a Google search form and a PayPal button; when checked, this option allows users to add the code.

✦ **Allow Multiple Consecutive Spaces:** Normally, browsers ignore more than one space in a row; select this option to allow users to add non-breaking spaces ( ) by pressing the spacebar.

✦ **Require ALT Text for Images:** When this option is checked, users must add alternative text for every inserted image. Moreover, Contribute warns users that when Flash content is added, users with disabilities may not be able to access it.

✦ **Use <strong> And <em> In Place Of <b> And <i>:** This option ensures that `<strong>` and `<em>` tags are used instead of the deprecated `<b>` and `<i>` tags when users elect to bold or italicize their text. Almost all browsers render the text as expected with the `<strong>` and `<em>` tags.

✦ **Line Break Type:** Choose an option from this list to set the characters used to end lines in the Contribute code. The choices — Windows (CR LF), Macintosh (CR), and Unix (LF) — refer to the Web site host machine and not the Contribute users system.

Styles and Fonts

Much of the specific look of a page — and the underlying code that generates that look — is controlled by the Styles and Fonts category of the Edit Role Settings dialog (see Figure 30-20). Overall, the administrator can allow or disallow users to apply new styles and/or new fonts and text sizes to text. If these options are disabled, the user can only work with styles in existing paragraphs. If the options are enabled, the administrator has the further choice of preferring CSS over HTML.

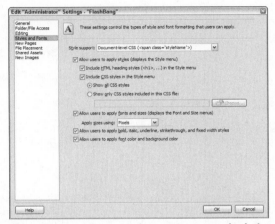

Figure 30-20: Determine how users can style their Contribute pages through the Styles and Fonts category of the Edit Role Settings dialog.

Keep the Allow Users To Apply Styles option enabled if you want Contribute to display the Style drop-down list when editing pages; if this option is disabled, new paragraphs inherit the style of the previous paragraph. Choose the Include HTML Heading Styles In The Style Menu to display Heading 1 through Heading 6 and Paragraph styles in the drop-down list. If the Include CSS Styles In The Style Menu option is checked, Contribute automatically lists all the available styles. Which styles are available is determined by two further options: Show All CSS Styles and Show Only Styles Included In This CSS File. If the latter option is selected, the administrator should select a relevant CSS file that includes CSS classes to be made available to the Contribute user.

Tip   You don't have to actually use a fully defined CSS file to filter your CSS classes for Contribute users; all you need is the class selector names and opening and closing curly braces, like this: `.firstparagraph, .memberContent, .copyrightInfo, .legalNotice {}`.

If your pages do not use CSS — or you want to offer your users more control over their pages — enable the Allow Users To Apply Fonts And Sizes option; when this option is disabled, neither the Font nor Size drop-down lists are shown in Contribute. If you've allowed the option, choose between using HTML Tags or Inline CSS Styles by selecting the appropriate radio button. When you select Inline CSS Styles, an additional option is enabled that determines how sizes are set: by points, pixels, or ems. Administrators can also restrict the use of applied styles such as bold, italic, underline, strikethrough, and fixed-width styles and/or font and background color.

New Pages

Although many Contribute users begin by modifying the content on existing pages, some, if not all, eventually create new pages within the site. The New Pages category of the Permissions Role dialog box, shown in Figure 30-21, offers a full range of options for this important task. As administrator, you can limit users to creating new files based on specific Dreamweaver templates or enable them to start from scratch; alternatively, you can completely disable the option and restrict their access to existing pages.

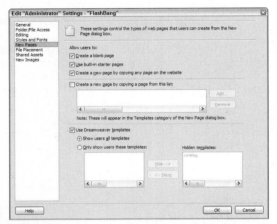

Figure 30-21: How — and if — Contribute users create new pages for the site is set in the New Pages category.

This category has five primary options, which can be enabled or disabled in any combination:

✦ **Create A Blank Page:** Allows users to start with a totally empty page, just as in Dreamweaver.

   Contribute doesn't have all the editing power that Dreamweaver includes, and letting users start with a blank page causes more problems than it solves. I generally recommend that this option not be checked.

✦ **Use Built-In Starter Pages:** Contribute includes a nice range of simple style pages, including calendars and photo-album layouts; selecting this option allows users to create pages based on the sample layouts.

✦ **Create A New Page By Copying Any Page On The Website:** Many users adhere to the adage that imitation is the sincerest form of flattery — and it's also an easy way to create a new page. Select this option when you want to make it possible for users to base their pages on any existing page found on the site.

✦ **Create A New Page By Copying A Page From This List:** This option is a refinement of the previous one. Rather than allowing users to use a copy of any page from the site as a starting point, if you enable this option you specify which pages may be copied. After the option is enabled, the Add and Remove buttons become active so you can choose files to copy and remove those choices later.

✦ **Use Dreamweaver Templates:** Dreamweaver templates are ideal for working with Contribute because they maintain the overall look and feel of a page while focusing contributors on working within editable areas. If you enable this option, you can choose between allowing members of a given role to copy any template or just specific ones in the site. Templates can be hidden from a role and later revealed or vice versa.

Initially, I find it helpful to limit the options for creating new pages, such as copying specific standard pages, working with certain templates, or both. Keep in mind that, if necessary, role options can be altered at any time.

File Placement

The File Placement category allows the administrator to specify where dependent files, added by Contribute users, are stored in the site. This category is tremendously useful for organizing file clutter by standardized rules. Initially, three document types are predefined, as shown in Figure 30-22; the administrator can modify these settings and declare any others necessary.

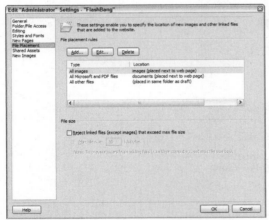

Figure 30-22: Organize your Contribute-dependent files automatically by defining rules in the File Placement category.

Dependent files, such as images, Word files, PDFs, or SWFs, can be placed in three types of places:

✦ **Same Folder As Draft:** Places files in the same folder as the current page.

✦ **Folder Next To Each Draft:** Stores files in a subfolder within the same folder as the current page. Administrators define the name of the subfolder and it will be automatically created on first use.

✦ **Specific Folder On Your Website:** Puts files of a given type in a single specified folder; administrators can browse for the file to identify its path. If this option is selected, an option to write site-root relative links is provided.

Although it takes a degree of upfront planning, it is highly recommended that you attempt to set rules for all the various types of dependent files on your site as early as possible. Although rules such as this take effect immediately when defined, they're not retrospective and you could save yourself a great deal of clean-up with thoughtful application of the File Placement category.

Shared Assets

One of the challenges of managing a Contribute-powered site is maintaining design control. At a certain level, if you give users the opportunity to insert any type of image or Flash movie, they will respond with often undesirable choices. The Shared Assets feature of Contribute makes it possible to specify images, Flash movies, or Library items (see Figure 30-23).

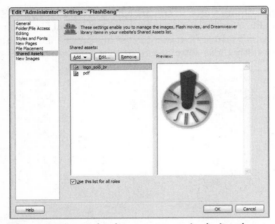

Figure 30-23: Help shape your user's choices by declaring images, Flash movies, and Library items as Shared Assets.

The ability to include Library items is particularly powerful. This option makes it possible to define blocks of content that can be quickly and easily integrated into a Web page. Not only can one or more paragraphs of text be defined, but also fully designed tables, mixtures of graphics and text, or any other page elements. You can integrate Dreamweaver behaviors in your Library items, and Contribute will automatically include the necessary JavaScript code when the shared Library item is inserted into the page.

New Images

With the ease of digital photography, inserting images on the Web becomes a double-edged sword. On one hand, it's now incredibly easy to add graphics to a page—however, unless optimized for the Web, digital images can slow page loading to a crawl. In the New Images category of the Edit Role Settings dialog (see Figure 30-24), the dimensions of images—and even the JPEG quality—are restricted. You can even reject images over a certain file size.

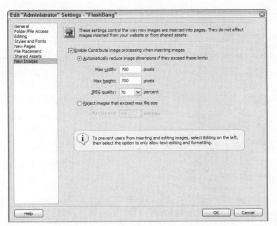

Figure 30-24: Before you grant your Contribute users the capability to upload images of any size, think about the impact such a decision has on page-load size.

The default is to allow users to alter images using Contribute's image editing tools (crop, rescale, flip, and lighten/darken) and to restrict those images to a particular set of dimensions. Administrators can optionally choose to set an upper limit on file size.

Tip   Although no hard and fast rules exist about what limit, if any, to set, use your own guidelines as a starting point. If you typically design sites where images are 50k or smaller, you might consider entering 50 into the kilobyte field. However, if you keep in mind that Contribute users are probably not as adept as designers at optimizing images, you might want to relax this restriction a bit and set a value between 60 and 80k.

Connecting Users

For a site of any size, managing the Contribute users can be as challenging as establishing the roles. Contribute gives you two paths to follow for user management: Connection Keys or CPS. Connection Keys are ideal for Contribute sites with a limited number of users, whereas the user management options provided by CPS are suitable for medium to large organizations.

Working with Connection Keys

One of the most successful innovations introduced with Contribute is the concept of the Connection Key. A Connection Key is an encrypted file that contains all the information users need to publish to a given Web site — including complex and potentially dangerous info like FTP addresses and passwords — geared to a specific role. Because the file is encrypted, it can be safely transmitted or posted in a network location. All the user does upon receipt is to open the file and supply the administrator-chosen password, and Contribute does the rest. You can even send the Connection Key right from Dreamweaver via email.

To create a Connection Key, follow these steps:

1. From the Administer Website dialog box, choose Send Connection Key. The first screen of the Connection Key Wizard appears, as shown in Figure 30-25.

Figure 30-25: Use the Connection Key Wizard
to create and send or store Contribute Connection Keys.

2. Choose whether you want the user to receive the current connection settings or a customized set:

   • If you want to send your connection settings, select Yes; if the remote site is connected through FTP, select the Include My FTP Login And Password option unless the user has his own FTP login and password.

   • To specify a different connection, choose No.

   When you're finished, click Next.

3. If you opted to set up custom settings, the next screen of the Connection Key Wizard enables you to choose the type of connection (FTP, Secure FTP, or Local/Network) and to provide the relevant information (such as FTP server name and login). Click Next when you're finished.

4. From the Role Information screen of the Connection Key Wizard, select the role the connection key is intended for. All the currently established roles are listed. Click Next when you're ready.

5. On the Connection Key Information screen (see Figure 30-26), first decide what you want to do with the Connection Key when it is created: send by email or store on the local machine.

Tip   Even though the Connection Key is encrypted, many organizations are not comfortable with sending sensitive information over the Web. As an alternative, consider storing the Connection Key in a password-protected area of the network and send the user the details for retrieving the file.

6. Enter the password needed to unlock the Connection Key in both fields of the current screen. The password can be either a single combination of words and letters or a phrase. Whichever you use, you must communicate this to the user in some way. When you've entered the password or phrase twice, click Next.

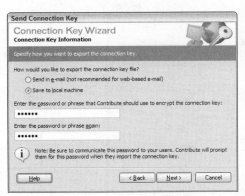

Figure 30-26: Connection Keys can be sent over a company intranet by email or stored in a secure location on a network.

7. After verifying your choices on the Summary screen of the Connection Key Wizard, click Done. To change any settings, click Back.

8. If you've elected to send the Connection Key through email, an email message opens with the Connection Key attached, and a preliminary subject and message are supplied. Supply the email address, customize the message as you see fit, and send.

To apply the Connection Key, your users need only have Contribute installed on their systems and online access to their sites. When they open the Connection Key file, Contribute launches, if necessary, and displays the dialogs to get them started.

Adding Users through Contribute Publishing Services

Much of the power of the Contribute Publishing Services application comes from its ability to manage users centrally. Rather than working with a disparate set of Connection Keys, user access and role assignment is handled through a single interface. Users can be entered singly or automatically through CPS's integration with existing user directory services such as Lightweight Directory Access Protocol (LDAP) or Microsoft's Active Directory. Once a user is available to the system, he or she can be assigned to any defined role and reassigned or removed as needed.

To add a new user using CPS's manual entry option, follow these steps:

1. Open the CPS Administrator in your browser by visiting https://[servername]:8900/contribute/admin/server.cfm where [servername] is the network name of your server.

2. Enter your password in the provided field and click Log In.

3. From the main Contribute Publishing Services screen, choose User Directory.

4. Make sure that the Directory Type list is set to File-based.

5. Click Add to view the Add User dialog box as shown in Figure 30-27.

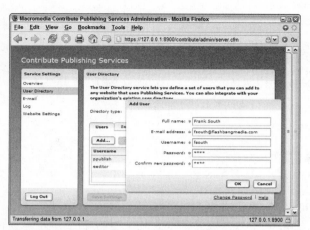

Figure 30-27: Enter new users one at a time through CPS's User Directory File-based interface.

6. Enter the user's name, email address, username, and password in the provided fields and click OK when you're done.

All entries are listed in the User area and can easily be edited or removed. The next time you open the Administer Site dialog box of the CPS-enabled site, you'll see the users available for assignment.

Rolling Back a Contribute Page in Dreamweaver

If you've enabled Contribute compatibility in Dreamweaver and the administrator has enabled rollbacks, you can revert to a previous version of a modified page. This feature can be a life-saver, especially when you're dealing with less-accomplished Contribute users who may just be finding their way. The rollback feature even enables you to see a preview of the page to make sure you're bringing back the correct version.

Caution Whether rollbacks are allowed — and how many previous versions to make available — is a significant decision. Enabling this option means that all users can store previous versions of all their edited pages and that all users can roll back any page they can access, whether they or someone else made the edits. You also should make sure that adequate server space is available to store the number of files maintained by the rollback option.

Before you can roll back a page in Dreamweaver, however, the ability to do so must be enabled through Contribute administration, as described in the following steps:

1. From the Contribute category in the Site Definition dialog, select Administer Site.

   Dreamweaver indicates that rollbacks are not enabled.

2. Enter the administrator's password in the provided dialog box.

3. When the Administer Website dialog box appears, select the Rollbacks category.

4. Click the check box so that the Enable Rollbacks option is selected.

5. Specify the number of versions to be kept by entering a number in the pop-up list; by default, Contribute maintains the previous three versions of every page in a folder on the server called _baks — you can opt to store up to 99 versions.

6. Click Close to verify the changes to the Administer Website dialog.

   Dreamweaver now shows that rollbacks are enabled.

7. Click OK to dismiss the Site Definition dialog.

To roll back a page in Dreamweaver, follow these steps:

1. In the Files panel, right-click (Control+click) the page you want to revert and choose Roll Back Page from the contextual menu. The Roll Back Page dialog is displayed, listing each of the previous versions and when they were published and by whom.

2. To view a page version, select it from the list and choose Show Preview. The Roll Back Page dialog box expands to display a preview as shown in Figure 30-28. While the preview is open, you can choose another version from the list to view.

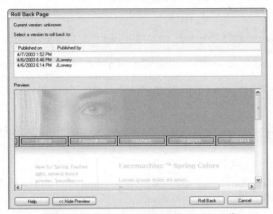

Figure 30-28: Roll back any page in a Contribute-enabled site right from within Dreamweaver.

3. When you've found the version you want to use, click Roll Back. Dreamweaver switches the current version of the page with the selected version on the server, and the Roll Back Page dialog closes.

What happens to the page replaced during a rollback operation? It also becomes a rollback version and, if necessary, can be brought back through the same process.

Integrating Dreamweaver with Visual SourceSafe

Microsoft's Visual SourceSafe (VSS) is an industrial-strength, version-control tool. With VSS, team members can check files in and out just as they can with Dreamweaver. In addition, other valuable features are also available, including the capability to get a history of changes, to compare two or more versions to one another to see the differences, and to restore a previous version. Visual SourceSafe is generally used in larger corporations where many different departments are involved in a Web development project. VSS is bundled with the Enterprise edition of Visual InterDev, as well as being sold separately.

Dreamweaver integrates its own Check In/Check Out system with that of Visual SourceSafe. When a Dreamweaver site is connected to a VSS database, checking out a file in Dreamweaver checks out a file from the VSS project. Likewise, when a file is checked back in Dreamweaver, it is noted as being checked-in in the VSS database. This integration enables Dreamweaver to be smoothly integrated into a large-scale Web development project in which both Dreamweaver users and non-users may be working together, accessing the same files.

Visual SourceSafe is currently only available on the Windows platforms. Dreamweaver requires that the Visual SourceSafe version 6 client be installed on the local machine.

After it is set up, the Dreamweaver/VSS integration is virtually seamless. Files are checked in and out, just as they would be if VSS were not involved. Dreamweaver performs what SourceSafe sees as an Exclusive file checkout. To enable a Multiple Check Out — which enables several people to check out the same file — you must go through VSS. Other VSS administrative features, such as Show History and Differences, must be handled from within SourceSafe by a user with administrator privileges.

> **Note** Two Dreamweaver site commands are not accessible with a SourceSafe connection: Synchronize and Select Newer. In order to use these commands, Dreamweaver must know how the local system and remote server relate time-wise — are they in the same time zone or is one behind the other? It's not feasible in the current implementation to get time stamp information from a VSS database; consequently, the features that depend on this information are not available.

As noted earlier, the Visual SourceSafe connection is managed through the Site Definition dialog box. To set up VSS connectivity, follow these steps:

1. Choose Site ⇨ Manage Sites.

2. From the Manage Sites dialog box, choose the site to be connected to the VSS database from the list and click Edit.

3. Select the Remote Info category.

4. From the Access drop-down list, choose SourceSafe Database.

5. Click the Settings button. All the connection information is entered through the displayed Open SourceSafe Database dialog box, shown in Figure 30-29.

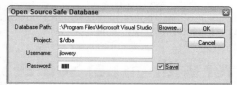

Figure 30-29: Visual SourceSafe projects require a username and password for access.

6. Enter the path and filename of the SourceSafe database in the Database Path field. Alternatively, click Browse to locate the file.

7. Enter the VSS project name in the Project field. The name of every VSS project begins with a $/ prefix—for example, $/bigco—and Dreamweaver supplies this prefix in the Project field.

8. Enter your VSS login name in the Username field.

9. Enter your VSS password in the Password field.

10. To circumvent automatic logon to the VSS database when connecting in Dreamweaver—which causes Dreamweaver to prompt you for a password every time—deselect the Save option.

11. Click OK when you're finished to close the Open SourceSafe Database dialog box.

12. If you want to automatically check out a file when opening it from the Files panel, select the Check Out Files When Opening option. When this option is enabled, double-clicking a file in the Files panel (or selecting it and then choosing File ⇨ Open Selection) automatically performs the checkout procedure.

13. Click OK to close the Site Definition dialog box.

14. Click Done to close the Manage Sites dialog box.

As mentioned earlier, the procedures for checking out and checking in files are almost identical to those described in the "Checking Files In and Out" section. Simply select the files you want in the Files panel and click the Check Out button or use the menu command, Site ⇨ Check Out.

Note   When Multiple Check Out is enabled, the file view column, Checked Out By, displays a list of names separated by commas.

Similarly, you can check a file back in by clicking the Check In button. There is one difference, however: Dreamweaver gives you an opportunity to attach a comment (which is written into the VSS database) to a file when it is checked in. To view the comments in Visual SourceSafe, select the file and click the Show History button; in the History dialog box, select Details and check the Comments field of the History Details dialog box.

Communicating with WebDAV

Web Distributed Authoring and Versioning (WebDAV) is an Internet protocol that enables Web developers to collaborate over the Web itself. Just as Visual SourceSafe enables teams to work together over a network, WebDAV enables developers to log in over the Web to work on a common set of files. Normally, the HTTP protocol, the basis for most Internet communication, only permits files to be read. With the WebDAV set of extensions installed, you can also write files to the server. More importantly, you can lock files to prevent multiple, simultaneous edits; in other words, files may be checked out for modification and checked in when the update is complete.

Dreamweaver supports the WebDAV protocol, enabling developers and designers around the world to work together on a single site. The WebDAV setup is, like VSS, handled through the Remote Info category of the Site Definition dialog box. After it is established, the Dreamweaver/WebDAV connection is transparent, and the Check In/Check Out features work as they do on a standard FTP or network connection.

Dreamweaver's implementation of WebDAV connectivity is geared toward Microsoft IIS and Apache servers. Both have been fully tested and are supported. WebDAV implementations on other servers may interact erratically, or not at all, with Dreamweaver. For more in-depth information on WebDAV, including a list of publicly available servers, visit www.webdav.org.

To establish a WebDAV connection, follow these steps:

1. Choose Site ➪ Manage Sites.

2. From the Manage Sites dialog box, choose the site to be connected to the WebDAV server from the list and click Edit.

3. Select the Remote Info category.

4. From the Access drop-down list, choose WebDAV.

5. Click the Settings button. All the connection information is entered through the displayed WebDAV Connection dialog box, shown in Figure 30-30.

Figure 30-30: After WebDAV is enabled, team members can collaborate over the Web itself to develop Web sites.

6. Enter the absolute URL to the WebDAV server in the URL field.

7. Enter your WebDAV login name in the Username field.

8. Enter your WebDAV password in the Password field.

9. Enter your email address in the Email field. The username and email address are displayed for checked-out files.

10. To circumvent automatic logon to the VSS database when connecting in Dreamweaver — and cause Dreamweaver to prompt you for a password every time — deselect the Save option.

11. Click OK when you're finished to close the WebDAV Connection dialog box.

12. If you want to automatically check out a file when opening it from the Files panel, select the Check Out Files When Opening option. When this option is enabled, double-clicking a file in the Local Files view (or selecting it and then choosing File ➪ Open Selection) automatically performs the checkout procedure.

13. Click OK to close the Site Definition dialog box.

14. Click Done to close the Manage Sites dialog box.

To use the WebDAV server, click the Connect button on the Files panel toolbar or choose Site ➪ Connect.

Note WebDAV is a technology that should definitely remain on every Web developer's radar screen, whether you are currently involved in a WebDAV project or not. WebDAV technology is the underpinnings for Microsoft's Web Folder feature found in Internet Explorer 5 and later and in Office 2000 products.

Summary

The expression "many hands make light work" certainly applies to Web site production and maintenance—but without some type of authoring management, the many hands may soon create a disaster. Dreamweaver offers both built-in and industry-standard authoring management solutions to aid in the development of Web sites. In addition to the precautions against overwriting files, Dreamweaver includes several other key features to help with team communication and to keep those many hands working together. For your team to get the most out of Dreamweaver, keep the following points in mind:

✦ In order for Dreamweaver's standard Check In/Check Out feature to be effective, everybody on the team must have the system engaged and in use for all file transfers.

✦ Metadata—information about information—about a project can be tied to any Web page or Web object through Dreamweaver's Design Notes feature. Again, to get the most out of this feature, it is essential that all team members use Dreamweaver's Files panel to manage their files.

✦ Dreamweaver includes interactive report capabilities that enable team members to quickly check the status of various HTML and workflow conditions, which can, if necessary, enable them to open a file directly for repair.

✦ Dreamweaver can tie into existing development projects through the Visual SourceSafe integration or the WebDAV standard support.

In the next chapter, you learn about working with XML in Dreamweaver.

✦   ✦   ✦

Integrating with XML and XSLT

XML, short for Extensible Markup Language, has quickly become a powerful force on the Web and an important technology for Web designers to master. XML enables designers to define the parts of any document — from Web page to invoice — in terms of how those parts are used. When a document is defined by its structure, rather than its appearance, as it is with HTML, the same document can be read by a wide variety of systems and put to use far more efficiently.

Dreamweaver includes *Roundtrip XML* as a complement to its Roundtrip HTML core philosophy. Roundtrip HTML ensures that the defined tags of HTML remain just as you've written them. With XML, no one defined set of tags exists — XML tags can be written for an industry, a company, or just a Web site. Roundtrip XML permits Web designers to export and import XML pages based on their own structures.

You can find XML all throughout Dreamweaver, just under the hood. The Design Notes feature is based on XML, as is the completely customizable menu system and even the HTML Styles feature. The Third-party Tags file is pure XML and can describe any kind of tag. In fact, you can use XML to describe most anything, even HTML. This chapter explores the basics of XML, as well as the implementation of Roundtrip XML in Dreamweaver. You'll also find techniques for presenting XML data in a Web page using Extensible Style Sheet Transformation (XSLT) technology; this exciting feature of Dreamweaver allows the easy display of such XML data as RSS feeds from blogs and other Web services.

Understanding XML

XML is to structure what Cascading Style Sheets (CSS) are to format. Whereas Cascading Style Sheets control the look of a particular document on the Web, XML makes the document's intent paramount. Because there are almost as many ways to describe the parts of a document as there are types of documents, a set language — such as HTML — could never provide enough specification to be truly useful. With XML, you create your own custom tags to describe the page, which makes XML a truly extensible language.

XML became a W3C Recommendation in February 1998, after a relatively brief two-year study. The speed with which the recommendation was approved speaks to the need for the technology. XML has been described as a more accessible version of SGML (Standard Generalized Markup Language), the widely used text-processing standard. In fact, the XML Working Group that drafted the W3C Recommendation started out as the SGML Working Group.

What can XML do that HTML can't? Suppose you have a shipping order that you want to distribute. With HTML, each part of the document — such as the billing address, the shipping address, or the order details — is enclosed in tags that describe its appearance, like this:

```
<h2 align="center"><strong>Invoice</strong></h2>
<p align="left">Ship to:</p>
<p>J. Lowery<br>
101 101st Avenue, Ste. 101<br>
New York, NY 10000</p>
```

With XML, each section of the page is given its own set of tags, according to its meaning, as follows:

```
<documentType>Invoice</documentType>
<noTax/>
<ship-toHeader>Ship to:</ship-toHeader>
<customer>J. Lowery<br></customer>
<ship-toAddress>101 101st Avenue, Ste. 101<br>
New York, NY 10000</ship-toAddress>
```

Like HTML, XML is a combination of content and markup tags. Markup tags can be used in pairs, such as `<customer>`...`</customer>`, or they can be singular. A single tag is called an *empty tag* because no content is included. Single tags in XML must include an ending slash — as in `<noTax/>`, for example — and are used to mark where something occurs. Here, `<noTax/>` indicates that no sales tax is to be applied to this invoice.

Also like HTML, XML tags can include attributes and values. As with HTML, XML attributes further describe the tag, much like an adjective describes a noun. For example, another way to write the `<ship-toHeader>` tag is as follows:

```
<header type="Ship To">
```

With a more generalized tag such as this one, you can easily change values, as in `<header type="Bill To">`, rather than include another new tag.

In all, XML recognizes six kinds of markup:

✦ **Elements:** Elements are more commonly known as *tags* and, as in HTML, are delimited by a set of angle brackets `<>`. As noted previously, elements can also have attributes set to particular values.

Caution

Although surrounding values with quotes is optional in HTML — such as in `color=white` — quotes are mandatory in XML.

✦ **Entity references:** Certain characters in XML, such as the delimiting angle brackets, are reserved in order to permit markup to be recognized. These characters are represented by entities in XML. As in HTML, character entities begin with an ampersand and end with a semicolon. For example `&lt;Content&gt;` is XML code to represent `<Content>`.

✦ **Comments:** XML comments are identical to HTML comments; they both begin with `<!--` and end with `-->`.

✦ **Processing instructions:** XML processing instructions are similar to server-side includes in that the XML processor (like the server) passes them on to the application (like the browser).

✦ **Marked sections:** XML can pass blocks of code or other data without parsing the markup and content. These blocks of character data are marked with `<![CDATA[` at the beginning and `]]>` at the end:

```
<![CDATA[If age < 19 and age > 6, then the kids are in ⮍
school]]>
```

Communication between XML and HTML is greatly eased because large blocks of data can be passed in this fashion.

✦ **Document type declarations:** Because every XML document is capable of containing its own set of custom tags, a method for defining these tags must exist. Although a discussion of the formats of such document type declarations is beyond the scope of this book, it's helpful to know that such declarations can be made for elements, attributes, character entities, and notations. Notations refer to external binary data, such as GIFs, that are passed through the XML parser to the application.

XML documents may begin with an XML declaration that specifies the version of XML being used. The XML declaration for a document compliant with the 1.0 specification looks like the following:

```
<?xml version="1.0" encoding="utf-8"?>
```

A much more detailed document type declaration (DTD), in which each tag and attribute is described in SGML, is also possible. XML documents including these types of DTDs are labeled *valid XML documents*. Other documents that respect the rules of XML regarding nesting of tags and other matters, but don't include DTDs for the elements, are known as *well-formed XML*. Dreamweaver exports well-formed XML documents, but can import either well-formed or valid XML.

Exporting XML

How do you make an XML page? You can choose File ➪ New and select XML from the Basic category, or you can convert an existing document into XML format with one command. Currently, Dreamweaver creates its XML pages based on a template's editable regions. With this approach, the true content of a page — what distinguishes it from all other pages of the same type — can be separated and applied independently of the original Web page. In other words, after the XML information is gathered from a Web page, it can be imported into any other application to be displayed, read, spoken, translated, or acted upon.

Cross-Reference To get a better idea of how to use XML, you need to understand Dreamweaver templates, which are discussed in Chapter 27.

Dreamweaver templates are composed of *locked* and *editable* regions; the locked regions are repeated for each page created from the template, whereas the content in the editable regions is added per page. The connection between XML and templates is similar to the relationship between a database form and its data. In a database, each field has a unique name, such as LastName, FirstName, and so on. When you create a database form to present the data, the placeholders for the data use the same field names. Then, when data from one record flows into the form, the information from the field goes into the areas with the corresponding field names. Likewise, each editable region has a unique name — in essence, a field name. The content within the editable region is the field's data. When the template data is exported as an XML file, the name of the editable region is converted to an XML tag that surrounds its data.

For example, Figure 31-1 shows a Dreamweaver template for a purchase order. On the left are the headings (To, Company, Address, and so on) for the information in a locked area, whereas the specific shipping data (on the right) resides in a series of editable regions, each with its own name.

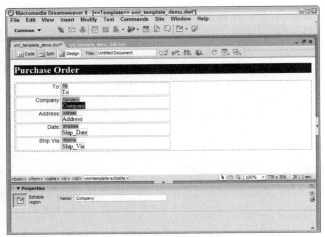

Figure 31-1: Dreamweaver creates XML pages based on templates and editable regions. This template is now ready to be exported as an XML file.

When exported as XML by Dreamweaver, the resulting XML file looks like the following:

```
<?xml version="1.0" encoding="utf-8"?>
<po template="/Templates/po.dwt" codeOutsideHTMLIsLocked="false">
    <ShipDate><![CDATA[10 Oct 2002]]></ShipDate>
    <doctitle><![CDATA[
<title>Purchase Order</title>
]]></doctitle>
    <head></head>
    <Address><![CDATA[1234 AnyStreet<br>
        Anytown, USA]]></Address>
    <ShipVia><![CDATA[UPS]]></ShipVia>
    <Company><![CDATA[John's Does]]></Company>
    <To><![CDATA[John Doe]]></To>
</po>
```

Note several important items about the XML file. First, notice the use of self-evident labels for each of the tags, such as `<Company>` and `<ShipVia>`; such names make it easy to understand an XML file. Even the one tag not based on a user-defined name, `<doctitle>`, is straightforward. Second, all the data included in the XML tags is marked as a `CDATA` area; this ensures that the information is conveyed intact, just as it was entered. Finally, if you look at the `<Address>` tag data, you see that even HTML tags (here, a `<br>` tag) are included in the `CDATA` blocks. This practice enables you to carry over basic formatting from one page to the next. You can avoid this by designating just the inner content — without any of the formatting tags — as an editable region.

Dreamweaver can create one of two different types of XML tags during its export operation. The first is referred to as *Dreamweaver Standard XML* and uses an `<item>` tag with a name attribute set to the editable region's name. For example, if the editable region is named `ShipVia`, the Dreamweaver Standard tag is

```
<item name="ShipVia">Content</item>
```

The Dreamweaver Standard XML file has one other distinguishing characteristic. The XML file is saved with a reference to the defining Dreamweaver template, like this:

```
<templateItems template="/Templates/PO.dwt">
```

When importing a Dreamweaver Standard XML file, if the specified template cannot be found, a dialog box appears asking that you select another template.

The other option is to use what Dreamweaver refers to as *Editable Region Name tags*. This method uses the editable region names themselves as tags. In the case of the editable region name `ShipVia`, the tag pair under this method is `<ShipVia>...</ShipVia>`.

To create an XML file from within Dreamweaver, follow these steps:

1. Open a Dreamweaver document based on a template that has at least one editable region.

2. Choose File ➪ Export ➪ Export Editable Regions As XML. The Export Template Data as XML dialog box opens, as shown in Figure 31-2.

Figure 31-2: You can convert any template-based page to an XML document by using the Export Template Data as XML dialog box.

3. Choose the format for the XML tags by selecting one of the Notation options:

   • **Use Standard Dreamweaver XML Tags:** Select this option to produce `<item>` tags with `name` attributes set to the names of the editable regions.

   • **Use Editable Region Names As XML Tags:** Select this option to produce XML tags that use the editable region names directly.

Selecting either option displays sample tags in the Sample area of the dialog box.

   4. Click OK when you're finished. An Export Editable Regions as XML Save File dialog box appears.

   5. Enter the path and name of the XML file you want to save in the File Name text box. Click Save when you're finished.

Importing XML

As part of Roundtrip XML, Dreamweaver includes an Import XML command. Like the Export XML command, Import XML works with Dreamweaver templates. The content information in the XML document fills out the editable regions in the template, much as data fills out a form in a database.

With this import capability, you can independently create and store content in an XML file and then, if you want to publish the page to the Web, simply import it into the Dreamweaver template.

To be imported, XML files must follow one of the two structures used when exporting a template to XML: Standard Dreamweaver XML or Editable Region Names used as XML tags. Although it's a matter of personal preference, I find the Editable Region Names format to be easier to read and, in general, simpler to work with.

Note   When you're importing XML files, make sure that the XML files that you're importing have the necessary template declarations in order for Dreamweaver to find the appropriate template to format the incoming data.

How do you create a file from the XML? Naturally, you could open a template for your XML document and fill in the data by hand—but that, in a sense, defeats the purpose of automating your workflow via XML. A more efficient scenario is to use a database to accept and store content; the database entry form is easily accessible over a network or over the Internet. A report, generated by the database application, blends the content data and the XML structure, resulting in an XML file to be imported into Dreamweaver.

To import an XML file into a Dreamweaver template, follow these steps:

   1. If desired, open a file based on a Dreamweaver template.

   2. Choose File ➪ Import XML into Template. The Import XML dialog box opens.

Caution   Any existing information in the Dreamweaver document in the editable regions is replaced by the information in the corresponding tags of the XML document.

   3. Select an XML file from the Import XML dialog box.

   4. Select Open when you're finished.

The XML file is imported into Dreamweaver, and the editable region placeholder names are replaced with the data in the XML document.

Building Your Own XML Files

Dreamweaver now supports editing XML files directly in the Dreamweaver interface. No Design view is available, but Dreamweaver code coloring and syntax checking can make writing your own XML files much easier than writing them in a standard text editor.

In order to take full advantage of Dreamweaver's code-editing features, you use tag libraries to set up all the tags you need to create your XML files. If you use the previously discussed template file as an example, you can define a set of XML tags for describing your purchase order details.

Cross-Reference To find out how to define your own tag libraries, see the section on the Tag Library Editor in Chapter 32.

Figure 31-3 shows the XML tags defined for the Purchase Order XML files. You can even specify attributes for each of the tags. Now if you type `<address` in Code view, you bring up the attributes you've defined; adding the trailing `>` supplies the closing `</address>` tag.

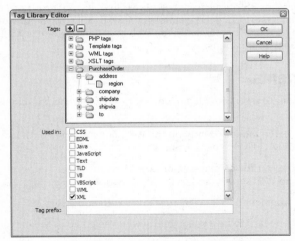

Figure 31-3: With Dreamweaver's Tag Library Editor, you can completely customize the crafting of new XML files.

Styling with XSL

Whereas HTML code has some degree of built-in styling — browsers render content enclosed with `<p>` tags much differently from what's within an `<img>` tag — XML has none: it's all just data. The Extensible Stylesheet Language (XSL) specification developed the W3C is intended to give designers the power to shape XML data. In fact, XSL has the potential to go beyond styling to actual transformation; functions within XSL can, for example, sort the XML data it is passed.

New In Dreamweaver Dreamweaver 8 embraces XSL in a major way. Dreamweaver now has the power to create XSL documents to fit a variety of situations, including both server-side and client-side options. This facility opens a whole new world of possibilities for Dreamweaver users. For example, designers can now include information from RSS (Really Simple Syndication) feeds right in their Web pages—styled to fit into the look-and-feel of their site—through a very straightforward process. For intranet developers, XML reports, like those generated by Dreamweaver's own Reports system, can now be presented in a suitable fashion.

XSL is actually a family of W3C specifications. In addition to the XSL standard, a separate specification covers *XSLT*, short for XSL Transformations. Many of the Dreamweaver XSL features involve XSLT functions that convert XML to HTML and CSS. Another key component under the XSL umbrella is the XML Path Language or *XPath*. XPath is an expression language that allows the XML data to be selectively presented; XPath powers Dreamweaver features like the XSL Repeat Region.

Dreamweaver creates two different types of XSL content: a full XSLT page that displays HTML and transformed XML data together, or an XSLT fragment that only contains the transformed XML data. An XSLT fragment is embedded in a standard Web page much like a server-side include; a feed from the Yahoo! Weather RSS service (`http://weather.yahoo.com/rss/`) embedded in the home page of a ski resort is a good example of how an XSLT fragment would be used. XSLT fragments are used far more frequently on the Web in general, whereas XSLT pages are more often seen in intranet applications.

Including XSLT Fragments

The comparison of an XSLT fragment to a server-side include (SSI) is a good one, for a number of reasons:

✦ Neither type of file can be viewed independently on the Web, because they both lack necessary HTML tags including `<html>`, `<head>`, and `<body>`.

✦ Both require an application server for display in a browser. Dreamweaver supports ASP, ASP.NET, ColdFusion, and PHP server models for XSLT fragments.

✦ You can edit either an XSLT fragment or SSI in Dreamweaver with equal ease.

✦ Each XSLT fragment and SSI appears to be a single entity when selected in the embedded page at design time.

Unlike SSIs, XSLT fragments have a page type all their own and can be created directly from the New Document dialog box. To create an XSLT fragment, follow these steps:

1. Choose File ➪ New.

2. From the New Document dialog box's General category, select the Basic page category and the XSLT (Fragment) entry; click Create when you're ready.

   Dreamweaver then asks which data source you'd like to use for your new XSLT fragment, as shown in Figure 31-4.

3. In the Locate XML Source dialog box, select the Attach A Local File On My Computer Or Local Area Network option if you want to incorporate data from a static XML file available on your system; use the Browse button to open the Select File dialog box or enter the path to the file by hand in the provided field.

Figure 31-4: Read the latest for any RSS feed by using the remote XML data option.

4. If you're displaying XML data from a file on the Web, choose the Attach A Remote File On The Internet option and enter the full Internet address in the available field.

5. Click OK when you're done.

6. Save the newly created document with an `.xsl` filename extension, that is, `rssfeed.xsl`.

Binding XSL Data to the Page

Once the fragment page is created, you're ready to create the HTML structure to hold the data and bind the data. You can use any standard HTML objects, like tables and `<p>` or `<br/>` tags to hold your data. The data itself is displayed in the Bindings panel, as shown in Figure 31-5.

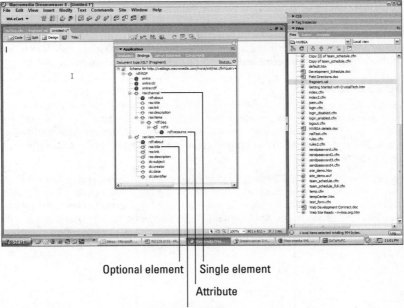

Optional element   Single element

Attribute

Repeating element

Figure 31-5: Once connected to an external XML source like an RSS feed, the Bindings panel displays the available data structure.

Dreamweaver provides the following visual indicators when displaying XML data:

◇	Child elements that occur once within a parent are identified with a double-angle bracket.
◇+	Child elements that occur one or more times are identified with a double-angle bracket followed by a plus sign.
◇?	Optional child elements are identified with a double-angle bracket followed by a question mark.
@	Attributes of a parent are identified with an at-sign, @.

Bind data to a page by dragging an element from the Bindings panel and dropping it in the desired place or by positioning your cursor on the page and double-clicking the selected data element in the Bindings panel.

Tip

In addition to displaying XML data as text, you can also use it in a link. Select the text, data, or image you want to use as a link and then, from the Property inspector's Link field, click the Browse for File icon. When the Select File dialog box opens, select Data Sources; the XML data tree appears just like in the Bindings panel. Choose the data field you want to use as the `href` value, typically labeled link or rss:link, and then click OK twice to close the open dialog boxes. The XML data appears in the Link field wrapped in braces, like this {rss:link}.

The basic code inserted by Dreamweaver for XSL data looks like this:

```
<xsl:value-of select="rdf:RDF/rss:channel/rss:title"/>
```

where the value of the `select` attribute is the XPath description of where the data is located in the XML file. Forward slashes represent parent nodes, much like folders in a URL.

Repeating XSL Data

A common use of XSLT fragments is to incorporate results from an RSS feed onto the page. Generally, you would include a few heading elements, such as the main feed title and author, followed by a series of titles, short descriptions, and links, each concerning a particular item in the RSS feed. The layout for such a fragment often involves a table to contain the repeating data as shown in Figure 31-6.

To display repeated data, an XSLT Repeat Region object is used. Similar to a Repeat Region server behavior, the XSLT Repeat Region object wraps the necessary code around a selection, typically one or more rows of a table. Just as you'd identify which recordset to use with a Repeat Region server behavior, the XSLT Repeat Region object requires that you identify which element in the XML schema repeats. You'll remember that Dreamweaver identifies such items in the Bindings panel with a double-angle bracket and plus sign combination.

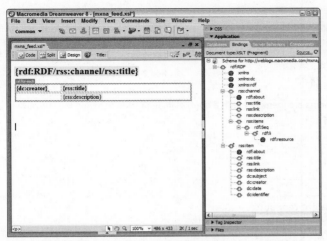

Figure 31-6: Use basic HTML tools like headings and tables to structure the data in an XSLT fragment.

The XSL code for repeating elements is `<xsl:for-each>` and, when applied to a table row, looks like this example:

```
<xsl:for-each select="rdf:RDF/rss:item">
  <tr>
    <td>...</td>
  </tr>
</xsl:for-each>
```

The `select` attribute in the `<xsl:for-each>` tag refers to the repeating element in the XML data. Dreamweaver inserts this code after you've identified the repeating item in the XPath Expression Builder (Repeat Region) dialog box.

To set an XSLT fragment area to repeat in Dreamweaver, follow these steps:

1. Select the HTML and XSL data you want to repeat.

   It's best to select the containing tag pair around the XSL data, like the `<tr>` or `<p>`.

2. From the Insert bar's XSLT category, choose Repeat Region.

   Alternatively, you can select Insert ⇨ XSLT Objects ⇨ Repeat Region; either approach opens the XPath Expression Builder (Repeat Region) dialog box.

3. In the XPath Expression Builder (Repeat Region) dialog box, select the element you want to repeat (see Figure 31-7).

   Repeatable elements are identified with the double-angle brackets and plus sign, +. Be sure to choose the parent repeating element of any item you want to display.

4. Click OK when you're done.

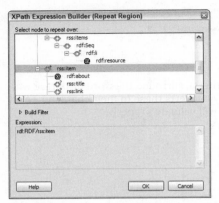

Figure 31-7: Choose the parent repeating element with the plus sign (disclosure triangle on the Macintosh).

In Design view with Invisible Elements enabled, Dreamweaver displays a border around the repeated area with the label `xsl:for-each`.

Filtering XSL Data

While XPath Expression Builder (Repeat Region) dialog box makes setting up a repeat region a simple point-and-click operation, it also permits you to establish filters for the data. You could, for example, use this feature to limit the items from the Macromedia XML News Aggregator to those concerned with Dreamweaver. Filters can be applied at the same as the XSLT Repeat Region or afterward.

To apply a filter to an existing XSLT Repeat Region, follow these steps:

1. Select any of the XML data within the repeat region.

2. From the Tag Selector, choose `<xsl:for-each>`.

3. In the Property inspector, click the lightning bolt next to the Select field.

4. When the XPath Expression Builder (Repeat Region) dialog box re-opens, select Build Filter.

   The dialog box expands to display the filter controls.

5. Click Add (+) to start a new filter criteria.

   The initial filter criteria is set up to use the previously selected repeating data element in the Filter By column; your focus will be on choosing values for the Where, Operator, and Value columns.

6. Select the data element you want to filter by from the Where list.

   For example, if you wanted to filter by the subject field of the Macromedia XML News Aggregator feed, you'd choose `dc:subject`.

7. Choose the operation you want to use in your filter from the Operator list.

   For string comparisons, you would select the equals sign, = or !=. Other operators include <, <=, >, >=, and <>.

8. Enter the desired filter keyword or other value in the Value column (see Figure 31-8).

   If you're using a text value in your filter criteria, surround the word or phrase with single quotes. Dreamweaver automatically converts these to their character entity equivalents — ' — so that the code will validate properly.

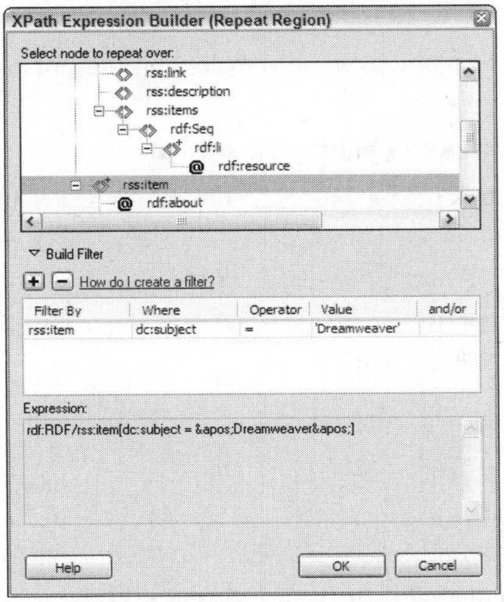

Figure 31-8: Choose the parent repeating element with the plus sign.

9. To add additional conditions, select either and or or from the And/Or column and repeat steps 5–8.

10. Click OK when you're done.

Test your XSLT fragment by previewing in the browser, and Dreamweaver will create the necessary code to display the page.

Showing XSL Data Conditionally

Another tool for shaping your XML data through XSL are the conditional XSLT objects in Dreamweaver. Both the XSLT Conditional Region and Multiple Conditional Region objects are used to display XML data or even standard HTML if your custom conditions are met. Unlike the filtering mechanism of the XSLT Repeat Region object, the conditional objects work with data that has already been made available to the page. You could, for example, display the optional description element from an RSS feed along with the Description label, but only if the description value exists.

The XSLT Conditional Region, when applied by itself, tests for a single condition and renders the enclosed content if the condition is met, very much like an If-Then clause in programming. In fact, the code uses a the `<xsl:if>` tag. For example, if you wanted to display text indicating the final item from an RSS feed, you'd use code like this:

```
<xsl:if test="position()=last()">
   <p>Last item:</p>
</xsl:if>
```

The `test` attribute checks to see if the `position()` function—which refers to the current item—is the same as the one the `last()` function returns and, if so, displays the text. To apply the XSLT Conditional Region object, follow these steps:

1. Select the text, image, page object, or code you want to make conditional in either Design or Code view.

2. From the Insert bar's XSLT category, choose Conditional Region.

3. When the Conditional Region dialog box opens, enter the condition to evaluate in the Test field (see Figure 31-9).

Figure 31-9: Display or hide anything in an XSL fragment through the XSLT Conditional Region object.

4. Click OK.

While the XSLT Conditional Region object displays or doesn't display some code based on a single condition, the Multiple Conditional Region is much more flexible. Although the Multiple Conditional Region object initially tests a single condition, it provides alternative output leading to an either/or code output. For example, say again you wanted to test for the final item and note it as such when it appears, but you also wanted to display other text, that is, `Next item:`, until it appears. In this situation, your XSL code would look like this:

```
<xsl:choose>
   <xsl:when test="position()=last()">
      <p>Last item:</p>
   </xsl:when>
   <xsl:otherwise>
      <p>Next item:</p>
   </xsl:otherwise>
</xsl:choose>
```

You can add additional condition testing by including more `<xsl:when>` tags prior to the `<xsl:otherwise>` tag. In Dreamweaver, this is accomplished by applying the XSLT Conditional Region object prior to the `<xsl:otherwise>` tag. By using the two conditional objects in conjunction with one another, you can test for as many conditions as you'd like and retain a default result.

To create multiple XSLT conditional regions, follow these steps:

1. Select the text, image, page object, or code you want to render if the first condition is true.

2. From the Insert bar's XSLT category, choose Multiple Conditional Region.

3. When the Multiple Conditional Region dialog box opens, enter the condition to evaluate in the Test field; click OK when you're done.

   Dreamweaver displays three different tabs: the `<xsl:choose>` area surrounds the `<xsl:when>` — which holds your previously selected content — and the `<xsl:otherwise>` area, which displays the placeholder text Content goes here, as shown in Figure 31-10.

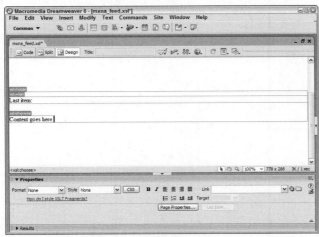

Figure 31-10: Dreamweaver displays the content for both outcomes in a Multiple Conditional Region.

If you just want to insert a single condition with a default result, you can stop here.

4. To add additional conditions and results, place your cursor in the placeholder content in the `<xsl:otherwise>` area and choose the `<xsl:otherwise>` tag in the Tag Selector.

5. Press the left-arrow key to move the cursor in front of the `<xsl:otherwise>` tag.

6. From the Insert bar's XSLT category, choose Conditional Region.

7. When the Conditional Region dialog box opens, enter the next condition you want to evaluate in the Test field; click OK when you're ready.

   Dreamweaver adds an `<xsl:when>` tag with placeholder content.

8. Repeat steps 4–7 to add more conditional regions.

After you've created all the conditions desired, replace the placeholder text with the actual page elements or code you want rendered if the condition is true.

Styling XSLT Fragments

Although you can use CSS to style your XSLT fragments, you shouldn't link to an external style sheet or embed styles within the fragment page. If you do, the CSS links and embedded styles will appear in the body of your document, along with the XSLT fragment. What's the solution? Design time style sheets.

Cross-Reference   To refresh your memory on how to implement a design time style sheet, visit Chapter 7.

Typically, the page intended as the receptacle for the XSLT fragment is built prior to the fragment itself, along with the CSS style sheet. To view your XSLT fragment with the desired styles, attach the same style used by the host page as a design time style sheet. Once the designtime style sheet is in place, you can assign CSS styles to the XML data and surrounding structures, as shown in Figure 31-11.

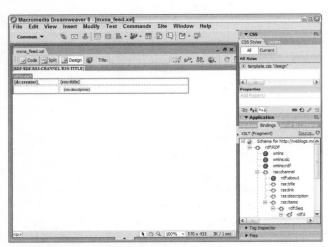

Figure 31-11: Style XSLT fragments through Dreamweaver's design time style sheet feature.

Adding XSLT Fragments to Web Pages

Once your XSLT fragment has been completed, it's very straightforward to include it in your server model page. The actual code insertion is handled by a server behavior, XSL Transformation. To include an XSLT fragment, follow these steps:

1. Place your cursor where you'd like the XSLT fragment to appear.

2. From the Server Behaviors panel, click Add (+) and select XSL Transformation from the list.

3. In the XSL Transformation dialog box, click Browse next the XSLT File field.

4. When the Select File dialog box appears, locate the .xsl file that contains your fragment and click OK.

Dreamweaver automatically populates the XML URI field with the address of the XML data as shown in Figure 31-12.

Figure 31-12: The XSLT Transformation server behavior is used to select the XSLT fragment for inserting.

5. If you need to add any parameters to affect the XSLT fragment, click Add (+) in the XSLT Parameters area and enter the name and value of the parameter.

6. Click OK when you're done.

Dreamweaver displays the XSLT fragment in the page; when selected, it appears as a solid, uneditable block. Unlike with server-side includes, a custom Property inspector is not available for inserted XSLT fragments. You can preview the page in the browser to see the data within the document.

The XSLT Parameters option found in the XSL Transformation dialog boxes allows you to set up parameters to pass to the XSLT fragment. You could, for example, create an XSLT parameter named ItemLimit with a value of 5 if you wanted to restrict the number of XML items shown to 5 or less. To ensure that the XSLT fragment works properly with this parameter, you'd need to set a filter criteria, as described in the "Filtering XSL Data" section, where the position() function is less than or equal to the variable $ItemLimit.

Building Full XSLT Pages

As noted earlier, Dreamweaver gives you the option to create either an XSLT fragment or XSLT page. Although XSLT fragments are more typically used, the full XSLT page has advantages including the ability to transform XML data on the client side without an application server such as ASP, ColdFusion, or PHP.

Much of the information covered in the previous XSL fragment discussion applies to full XSLT pages. XML data appears in the Bindings panel and is bound to the page in the same manner. All the objects in the Insert bar's XSLT category — including the Repeat Region and Conditional Region objects — can and should be used when crafting the XML data in an XSLT page.

Client-Side Pages

Dreamweaver's client-side XSL feature set is quite remarkable. With it, you can post XML data to be transformed by an XSLT page and viewed in a modern browser, without the use of server-side code. There are, however, a number of limitations:

✦ Only full XSLT pages, and not XSLT fragments, can be used.

✦ The XML file must be stored locally; you can't link to a remote XML feed.

✦ Both the XML and the XSLT page must be published to the same folder on the Web server.

✦ Only a limited number of browsers can be used to view the completed page.

It's important to understand how XSLT pages interact with XML files to present the completed HTML page for the browser. Although XSL stands for Extensible Stylesheet Language, it's not an exact parallel to Cascading Style Sheets. The primary difference is that an XSLT page contains HTML as well as XSLT code, unlike an external CSS file, which does not incorporate any HTML. Another key point is that both the XML and XSL files refer to one another, whereas with HTML and CSS, the only connection is the link or import code in the HTML page. The final concept to grasp is that you're actually displaying the XML file, although it is transformed by the XSLT page. All links from other pages to show the data must be to the XML file.

Here's a general overview of the workflow for applying an XSLT page to an XML file:

1. Create an XSLT page.

2. Attach the XML data to the XSLT page.

3. Bind the XML data to the XSLT page.

4. From the XML page, link to the XSLT page.

5. Publish both files to the Web.

6. View the XML page.

Creating XSLT Pages

Dreamweaver provides two paths to approach the initial step, creating an XSLT page. You can build a page from scratch by choosing File ➪ New Document and then selecting the Basic page category and choosing XSLT (Full page). Or, if you have an existing HTML page you want to use to incorporate XML data, you can convert your HTML page into XSLT format.

To convert an HTML page to an XSLT page, follow these steps:

1. Open the page you want to convert in Dreamweaver.

2. Choose File ➪ Convert ➪ XSLT 1.0.

Dreamweaver automatically saves the converted file under its original name with a new `.xsl` extension. For example, `rss_feed.html` becomes `rss_feed.xsl`.

Caution   Neither templates nor template-derived pages can be converted to an XSLT document. You'll need to detach the template-derived page from the template before converting.

Attaching XML Data to an XSLT Page

Attaching XML data to an XSLT page is just as straightforward as converting the page:

1. From the Bindings panel, click the XML link in the displayed step: Please Attach XML Source Document (see Figure 31-13).

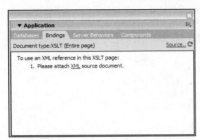

Figure 31-13: Attach an XML file to an XSLT page through the Bindings panel.

2. When the Locate XML Source dialog box opens, make sure that the Attach A Local File On My Computer Or Local Area Network option is selected.

3. Click Browse to open the Select File dialog box and locate the XML file; click OK when you've found it.

4. Click OK in the Locate XML Source dialog box to confirm your choice.

Dreamweaver parses the XML file and displays the structure in the Bindings panel.

Binding the XML Data

Binding the data in an XSLT page is handled in exactly the same way as with an XSLT fragment. Data is dragged from the Bindings panel onto the page or double-clicked to be inserted at the cursor position. Likewise, repeat and conditional regions are applied in the same manner as described in the previous sections, "Repeating XSL Data," "Filtering XSL Data," and "Showing XSL Data Conditionally."

Unlike with XSLT fragments, it's not necessary to use design time style sheets because the XSL page contains the HTML — as well as the link to the CSS external style sheets. Style can be applied to XML data just like any other page element.

Linking from an XML File

All of the work so far has been centered around the XSLT page. Now it's time to shift focus to the XML document. The first action is to link the XSLT page from the XML file. Recall that the browser actually loads the XML file, which in turn calls the XSLT page to transform the data into HTML.

Tip   Client-side XSL transformations only work with local XML files. To use the data from an RSS feed, you'll need to save the data page from your browser and publish it to your own Web server.

To link an XML to an XSLT page, follow these steps:

1. Open the XML file attached in the XSLT document.

2. Choose Commands ➪ Attach an XSLT Stylesheet.

3. When the Attach an XSLT Stylesheet dialog box opens (see Figure 31-14), click Browse to locate the XSLT file you've been working with.

Figure 31-14: Link your XML file to the appropriate XSLT Stylesheet.

Caution   Remember that both the XML and XSLT files must be in the same folder. If the XSLT file is in a separate folder, all the dependent files (including images, CSS, and includes) will not be found.

Publishing and Viewing XML and XSLT Files

XML files can be published to the server like any other document in Dreamweaver. Best of all, Dreamweaver is smart enough to automatically publish your XSLT files — and any files referenced in that document — if you opt to put dependent files.

It's vital to remember that you must view the XML file in your browser and not the XSLT document. Given that the XSLT page has all the visual elements, this approach might feel a bit unnatural, but it's the way it works.

Only modern browsers are capable of viewing an XML file and processing the XSLT correctly on the client-side. Among capable browsers are:

✦ Internet Explorer 6 and higher

✦ Netscape 8 and higher

✦ Mozilla 1.8 and higher

✦ Firefox 1.0.2 and higher

✦ Opera 8 and higher

✦ Safari 1.3 and higher

Server-Side Pages

Though most designers and developers working with application servers will prefer to work with XSLT fragments, they do have the option of working with full XSLT pages. One advantage to taking the full page approach is that it allows for complete separation between the server-side code and the presentation code; organizations that deploy strictly divided Web teams may find this useful.

Adding Data to an XSL Page

In this Technique, you convert an existing HTML page to XSLT format and then integrate data from an XML file into it.

1. From the Techniques site, expand the 31_XML folder and open the `xml_start.htm` file.

2. Choose File ➪ Convert ➪ XSLT 1.0.

Dreamweaver converts the file and saves it as `xml_start.xsl`.

3. From the Bindings panel, select the XML link in step 1.

4. When the Locate XML Source dialog box appears, click Browse.

5. In the Locate Source XML for XSL Template dialog box, locate the `properties.xml` file in the 31_XML folder and click OK; click OK again to confirm your choice in the Locate Source XML dialog box.

The Bindings panel is populated with the XML data schema.

6. From the Bindings panel, drag proptype to the cell under the Type label, desc under Description, bed under Bedrooms, and bath under Bathrooms.

The next step is to apply a repeat region so that all the XML data will be displayed.

7. Select the proptype XML data placed on the page.

8. From the Tag Selector, choose the `<tr>` tag.

9. Choose Insert ➪ XSLT Objects ➪ Repeat Region.

Continued

10. When the XPath Expression Builder (Repeat Region) dialog box opens, choose property and click OK.

11. Save your page.

The final step is to make the connection from the XML file to the XSLT page.

12. From the Files panel, open the `properties.xml` file in the 31_XML folder.

13. Choose Commands ⇨ Attach an XSLT Stylesheet.

14. When the dialog box opens, click Browse and locate `xml_start.xsl`; click OK when you're ready.

15. Save your XML page.

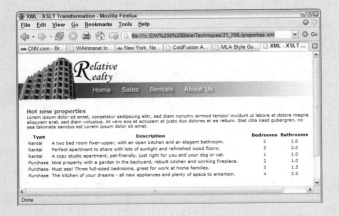

Preview the page by pressing F12 (Option+F12). If you're using a recent browser version, you'll see the XML data embedded in the page.

Server-side XSL transformations suffer almost none of the drawbacks seen with client-side transformation:

✦ Both full XSLT pages and XSLT fragments can be used.

✦ The XML file can be stored locally or remotely.

✦ Because the transformation occurs on the server-side, any browser can be used to view the transformed page.

The only similar restriction for both client-side and server-side transformations is that if a local XML file is used for the data, both must be contained in the same folder.

In Dreamweaver, server-side XSL transformations have been developed for most of the supported server models: ASP, ASP.NET, ColdFusion, and PHP. Only JSP is not supported.

The workflow for creating a server-side XSLT transformation is similar to that of a client-side transformation, with a number of key differences:

1. Create an XSLT page.

2. Attach the XML data to the XSLT page.

3. Bind the XML data to the XSLT page.

4. Remove all HTML from your application page.

5. From the dynamic page, link to the XSLT page.

6. Publish both files to the Web.

7. View the dynamic page.

The primary differences pertain, as you might expect, to the server-oriented nature of the page. As noted in the fourth step, you'll need to remove all HTML from your application page. This is a necessary action because the full XSLT page already contains the HTML framework — `<html>`, `<head>`, and `<body>` tags — and to leave it in the application page would cause errors.

Another difference is the manner in which the XSLT page is connected to the data. Rather than link to the XSLT page from the XML file, you apply a Dreamweaver server behavior in the dynamic page to create a connection to the XSLT file and its related XML data.

To link to the full XSLT page from the dynamic page, follow these steps:

1. With the dynamic page open, choose Window ➪ Server Behaviors.

2. In the Server Behaviors panel, click Add (+) and select XSL Transformation from the list.

   You may find the XSL Transformation box familiar; the same functionality is used when you create an XSLT fragment.

3. In the XSL Transformation dialog box, select the Attach A Local File On My Computer Or Local Area Network option if you want to incorporate data from a static XML file available on your system; use the Browse button to open the Select File dialog box or enter the path to the file by hand in the provided field.

4. If you're displaying XML data from a file on the Web, click the Attach A Remote File On The Internet option and enter the full Internet address in the available field.

5. Click OK when you're done.

Before viewing on your Web server, you'll need to publish your dynamic and XSLT page to your Web server. Unlike with the client-side transformation, Dreamweaver will not automatically include the XSLT file as a dependent file. When the files have been posted, view the dynamic page to see the page with the XML data and XSLT transformations.

Summary

XML is a vital future technology that is knocking on the door of virtually every Web designer. As the development tools become more common, the Roundtrip XML capability within Dreamweaver makes interfacing with this new method of communication straightforward and effortless. When you work with XML, keep the following points in mind:

✦ XML (Extensible Markup Language) enables content to be separated from the style of a Web page, creating information that can be more easily used in various situations with different kinds of media.

✦ Tags in XML reflect the nature of the content, rather than its appearance.

✦ Dreamweaver includes a Roundtrip XML facility that makes it possible to export and import XML files through Dreamweaver templates.

✦ Use tag libraries to create custom XML tags and take advantage of Dreamweaver's Code Hints and Code Completion.

✦ XML data can be presented on the Internet with all the style of a standard Web page through the use of Extensible Style Sheet Transformation (XSLT). Dreamweaver includes functionality for creating either client-side or server-side XSLT pages.

In the next chapter, you learn about customizing Dreamweaver, including how to use tag libraries.

✦　　✦　　✦

Extending Dreamweaver

Customizing Dreamweaver

The Web is a dynamic environment, with new technologies continually emerging. Until recently, HTML standards were changing every year or so; even now, products are routinely introduced that use the Web as a jumping-off place for new methods and tools. Keeping pace with the constantly shifting work environment of the Web has been beyond the capabilities of any suite of Web authoring tools, much less a single one—until Dreamweaver debuted, of course.

The initial version of Dreamweaver had a high degree of extensibility built right in, with its customizable HTML objects and JavaScript behaviors. Macromedia continues to enhance this flexibility with each release. With the implementation of the W3C Document Object Model and a tremendous number of new API functions, objects, and behaviors, Dreamweaver features have been beefed up so that they are much more powerful than ever. In addition, Dreamweaver presents a host of ways to extend its power. Here are just some of the options:

- **Menus:** The entire Dreamweaver menu system is completely customizable. You can add context menu items, rearrange the main menu, and even add completely new menus, all by modifying a single XML file.

- **Keyboard shortcuts:** Macromedia makes it easy to use the same keyboard shortcuts across its product line—even extending that ease to other products—with the Keyboard Shortcut editor. In addition to adopting the most comfortable set of key combinations, shortcuts for individual commands can be personalized.

- **Commands:** Commands are JavaScript and HTML code that manipulate the Web page during the design phase, much as behaviors are triggered at runtime.

- **Custom tags:** The rapid rise of XML makes custom-tag support essential in a professional Web authoring tool. Dreamweaver gives you the power to create any custom tag and control how it displays in the Document window.

✦ **Property inspectors:** Custom Property inspectors go hand-in-hand with custom tags, enabling the straightforward entry of attributes and values in a manner consistent with the Dreamweaver user interface.

✦ **Custom panels:** Dreamweaver enables you to create custom panels that supplement its variety of built-in panels.

✦ **Translators:** Translators enable server-side and other content to be viewed in the Document window at design time, as well as in the browser at runtime.

✦ **C-level extensions:** Some special uses require a root-level addition to Dreamweaver's capabilities. Macromedia's engineers have "popped the hood" on Dreamweaver and made it possible for a C or C++ language library to interface with it through C-level extensions.

✦ **Custom toolbars and objects:** The Insert bar and all other toolbars are now fully extensible, enabling quick and easy access to your most frequently used Dreamweaver objects and commands.

✦ **Tag libraries:** Dreamweaver enables you to create, edit, and delete tag libraries.

Although a few of these extension features require programming skills beyond those of the typical Web designer, most are well within the reach of an HTML- and JavaScript-savvy coder. Moreover, the Keyboard Shortcut editor employs a graphical user interface, making it accessible to all. As with behaviors and objects, the source code for all but the C-level extensions is readily available and serves as an excellent training ground. This chapter, combined with these standard scripts, provides all the tools you need to begin carving out your own personalized version of Dreamweaver.

Adding New Commands

By their very nature, objects and behaviors are single-purpose engines. A custom object inserts a single block of HTML into the `<body>` of a Web page, whereas custom behaviors add JavaScript functions to the `<head>` and attributes of one tag. Commands, on the other hand, are multifaceted, multipurpose, go-anywhere, and do-anything mechanisms. Commands can do everything objects and behaviors can do—and more. In fact, commands can even masquerade as objects.

For all their power, commands are one of the most accessible of the Dreamweaver extensions. This section describes the basic structure of commands, as well as how to use the standard commands that ship with Dreamweaver. You can also find information about how to create your own commands and control their integration into Dreamweaver.

Understanding Dreamweaver Commands

When I first encountered commands, I thought, "Great! Dreamweaver now has a macro language." I envisioned instantly automating simple Web design tasks. Before long, I realized that commands are even more powerful—and a bit trickier—than a macro recorder. Dreamweaver's adoption of the W3C Document Object Model (DOM) is one of the factors that make commands feasible. The DOM in Dreamweaver *exposes*, or makes available, every part of the HTML page—every tag, every attribute, every bit of content—which can then be read, modified, deleted, or added to. Moreover, Dreamweaver commands can open, read, and modify other files on local systems.

A command can have a parameter form or not, depending on how the command is written. Generally, commands are listed in the Commands menu, but by altering the menus.xml file (as discussed in the "Adjusting the menus.xml File" section later in this chapter), you can cause any command to appear as part of any other menu — or to not appear at all. Because one command can call another, such hidden commands are more easily modified.

My original vision of a macro recorder came true with the commands Start Recording and Play Recorded Command. Now, any onscreen action can be instantly logged and replayed — and through the History panel, even converted into a permanent, repeatable command.

So how, specifically, are commands being used? The following list describes some of the commands that have been built by Web designers outside Macromedia:

✦ **Tag Stripper:** Removes all instances of any tag from a Web page. By Massimo Foti.

✦ **Breadcrumbs:** Automatically adds navigation elements on a page. By Paul Davis.

✦ **Borderless Frames:** Sets all frames in a frameset to no borders. By Massimo Foti.

✦ **Add Old Browser Message:** Inserts a message that can be seen only by browsers that do not support the W3C DOM. By Rachel Andrews.

✦ **Replicator:** Duplicates any selected element any number of times. By this book's author, Joseph Lowery.

As is obvious from this list, commands come close to being limited only by the author's imagination.

For further evidence of just how useful commands can be, the following sections look at a few of Dreamweaver's standard commands.

Cross-Reference   Dreamweaver comes with a number of standard commands that, in addition to adding some extra functionality, give you a taste of just how powerful commands can be. You can find a full description of them in Chapter 3.

The Apply Source Formatting and Apply Source Formatting to Selection Commands

All the code created by Dreamweaver is structured according to the current Tag Library settings. The Tag Library identifies which codes are indented and which are on their own lines, as well as numerous other specifications regarding HTML writing. Occasionally, a Web designer must work with Web pages created earlier, by other designers using other programs, or even by hand. The Apply Source Formatting and Apply Source Formatting to Selection commands can rewrite the original code — of an entire Web page or a selected part of the page, respectively — so that it is structured according to the current Tag Library settings. The more accustomed your eye is to following Dreamweaver-style HTML, the more you value this command.

Note   You learn more about the Tag Library feature later in this chapter.

The Apply Source Formatting and Apply Source Formatting to Selection commands are examples of Dreamweaver commands that don't display dialog boxes to gather the user's selected parameters — because there are no parameters to set. To invoke the commands, choose Commands ⇨ Apply Source Formatting or Commands ⇨ Apply Source Formatting to Selection. The commands are applied immediately, with no confirmation or feedback indicating that they are complete. To verify their execution, you have to sneak a peek at your source code.

The Clean Up HTML and Clean Up XHTML Commands

Dreamweaver tends to produce compact, uncluttered HTML/XHTML code, which is not always the case with other HTML/XHTML editors and hand-coded efforts. One of the most common problems is redundant `<font>` tags, which can result when you select some text, change the font, change the font size, and, finally, change the font color. The resulting code is likely to resemble the following:

```
<font face="Arial"><font size="4"><font color="green">
Bonanza!</font></font></font>
```

The Clean Up HTML and Clean Up XHTML commands are custom made to consolidate redundant tags and to remove some of the code clutter that can accumulate during a page's design. In all, you have seven different cleaning operations from which to choose. Note that the Clean Up HTML and Clean Up XHTML commands are applicable only to the current page and cannot be applied sitewide.

XHTML syntax is much less forgiving than HTML; your XHTML code must be nearly perfect to work correctly. The Clean Up XHTML command fixes XHTML code syntax errors, lowercases all tag attributes, and adds (or reports) missing required tag attributes.

To use the Clean Up HTML or Clean Up XHTML commands, follow these steps:

1. Load the desired HTML or XHTML document into your Dreamweaver workspace.

2. Choose Commands ➪ Clean Up HTML (for an HTML document) or Commands ➪ Clean Up XHTML (for an XHTML document). The Clean Up HTML/XHTML dialog box appears, as shown in Figure 32-1.

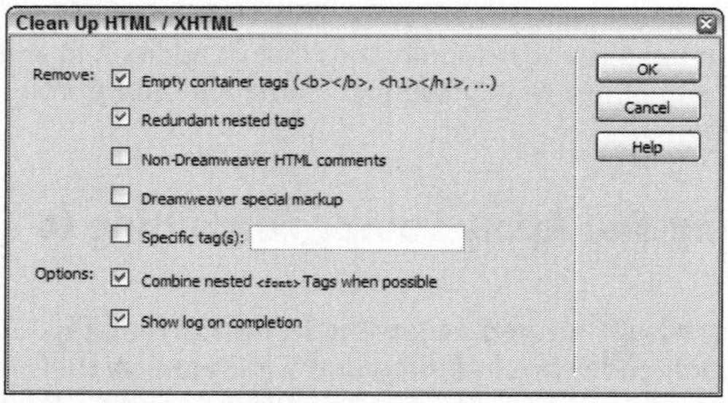

Figure 32-1: Reduce your page's file size and make your HTML more readable with the Clean Up HTML/XHTML command.

3. Choose from these options in the dialog box:

   • **Remove: Empty Container Tags** — Deletes empty tag pairs with no code between them (such as `<b></b>`).

   • **Remove: Redundant Nested Tags** — Eliminates superfluous tags that repeat the same code as the tags surrounding them, as shown in the following example:

```
<font color="white">And the <font color=
"white">truth</font>
is plain to see.</font>
```

- **Remove: Non-Dreamweaver HTML Comments** — Deletes any HTML comments that were not created by Dreamweaver to mark a Library or template item.

- **Remove: Dreamweaver Special Markup** — Clears all Dreamweaver-specific comments, such as

```
<!— #BeginEditable "openingPara" —>
```

- **Remove: Specific Tag(s)** — Erases any specific tag and all its attributes. Select this option and then type the tag name or names in the text box.

 Note Enter tag names without angle brackets; separate multiple tags with a comma. For example: font, blink.

- **Combine Nested** <font> **Tags When Possible** — Consolidates <font> tags.

- **Show Log On Completion** — Lets you view a report of the changes applied to your document.

4. Click OK when you're finished.

Dreamweaver performs the actions requested on the current document. If you select the Show Log option, an alert displays the changes made, if any.

Recording and Replaying Commands

I'm a big fan of any kind of work-related automation, and I consider myself a power user of word-processing macros, so you can imagine my delight when a similar capability was added to Dreamweaver. You save a tremendous amount of work with the capability to record onscreen actions and then replay them instantly — with the option of saving them as a command or simply pasting them into another document. Nearly every onscreen action can be replicated.

How could you use such a macro-like capability in Dreamweaver? Suppose you have a series of 10 images on a page, and you want to give each image a vertical space of 10, a horizontal space of 8, and a 2-pixel border. You could perform each of these actions one at a time, entering in the same border value and selecting the center alignment button, but it would get rather tedious after the third or fourth image. With Dreamweaver, you can easily automate the procedure by following these steps:

1. Select the first image.

2. Choose Commands ⇨ Start Recording or use the keyboard shortcut, Ctrl+Shift+X (Command+Shift+X). The cursor changes to a recording tape symbol, indicating you're in recording mode.

3. Enter the new values in the Property inspector.

4. Choose Commands ⇨ Stop or the same keyboard command again: Ctrl+Shift+X (Command+Shift+X). The cursor changes back to its normal state.

5. Select another image.

6. Choose Commands ⇨ Play Recorded Command.

7. Repeat steps 5 and 6 for every image you want to change.

Most of the commands and onscreen moves can be replicated in this manner, but not all. The major exception is the use of the mouse. Dreamweaver cannot repeat mouse moves and selections. You cannot, for example, begin to create a drop-cap by recording the drag selection of the first letter in each paragraph. You can, however, use the arrow keys and any keyboard-related combination.

For example, suppose that you have this standard list of names in your document:

```
Joseph Lowery
Andrew Wooldridge
Al Sparber
Simon White
Derren Whiteman
```

You want to change these names to a *Lastname, Firstname* format. To make this change with command recording, follow these steps:

1. Position your cursor at the beginning of the first name.

2. Choose Commands ➪ Start Recording.

3. Press Ctrl+Shift+right arrow (Command+Shift+right arrow) to select the first word. Dreamweaver highlights the first word and the following space.

4. Press Ctrl+X (Command+X) to cut the selected word.

5. Press End to move to the end of the line.

6. Type a comma and a space.

7. Press Ctrl+V (Command+V) to paste the previously cut word.

8. Press the backspace key to remove the trailing space.

9. The first line is complete, but to position the cursor to perform the recorded command again, press the right arrow to move to the start of the next line. (Because the cursor was left at the end of the last line, the right-arrow key moves it to the front of the following line.)

10. Choose Commands ➪ Stop Recording.

11. Choose Commands ➪ Play Recorded Command for each name in the list, as shown in Figure 32-2.

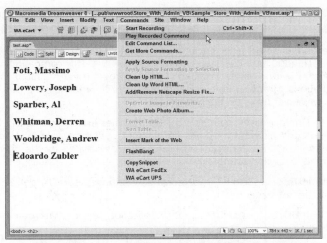

Figure 32-2: After the steps for formatting the first image are recorded, formatting the other images is a one-step process with Dreamweaver's command recorder.

If you try to include a mouse move or selection when recording a command or playing back a recorded command, Dreamweaver issues a warning and asks if you'd like to stop recording. If you choose to continue, Dreamweaver ignores the attempted mouse move and resets the pointer in its previous position.

> **Tip** If you try to record your navigations around a table, Dreamweaver does not record the Tab or Shift+Tab keys. However, you can still record your table moves by using Home and End in combination with the arrow keys; note that this works in Standard mode only, not in Layout mode. To move from cell to cell, from left to right, press End and then the right arrow. To move right to left, press Home and then the left arrow. You can also move up and down columns by pressing Home or End and then either the up or the down arrow.

Recorded actions are maintained in memory, and when you issue the Start Recording command again, the previously recorded steps are replaced. You can, however, use the History panel to convert recorded steps into a command that you can use repeatedly in any document or site.

To convert recorded steps into a command, follow these steps:

1. Record a series of actions as described in the preceding set of steps.

2. Play the recorded actions at least once by choosing Commands ➪ Play Recorded Command.

3. On the History panel, the collective recorded actions are displayed as a single step, Run Command. Select the Run Command item listed last.

4. Click the Save Selected Steps as a Command button at the bottom of the History panel.

5. In the Save as Command dialog box, enter an appropriate name for your command and click OK.

New commands saved in this manner are dynamically added to the Commands menu.

Multiuser System Customization

Starting with the MX version, Dreamweaver became compatible with multiuser operating systems including Windows NT, 2000, and XP, as well as Macintosh OS X. This compatibility means that multiple users can work with a single installation of the program yet maintain their own preferences and configurations. Moreover, network administrators can maintain a group of common settings for all Dreamweaver users on the network.

To achieve such flexibility, Dreamweaver maintains customized files in a special folder for each user. These folders are stored in different locations on different operating systems. Under multiuser systems, the folders are within the specified user folder, designated by the user's ID or login name as shown in the following examples:

✦ **Windows 2000 and Windows XP:** C:\Documents and Settings*User ID*\Application Data\Macromedia\Dreamweaver 8\

✦ **Mac OS X:** Macintosh HD/Users/*User ID*/Library/Application Support/Macromedia/ Dreamweaver 8/

Note   Windows systems are shown using drive C, whereas Macintosh users use the Macintosh HD drive; naturally, the drive letter or name may be different if another system drive is used.

All custom extensions installed by Dreamweaver—either by the features in the program itself (such as the History panel's Save Selected Steps as a Command feature) or by the Extension Manager—are automatically inserted in the proper multiuser folder. Folders are created on an as-needed basis; you won't see an Inspectors folder in your multiuser Configuration folder unless an inspector extension is installed.

In fact, you may need to take one additional step before any user folders are visible. Certain folders—particularly those dealing with system administration—are hidden by default in Windows operating systems. To gain access to such files, open Windows Explorer and set the Folder Options to show hidden files and folders.

Scripting Commands

Commands, like most behaviors, are a combination of JavaScript functions and HTML forms; the HTML provides the user interface for any parameters that must be set, and JavaScript carries out the particular command. Although you can combine both languages in a single HTML file, many programmers, including those from Macromedia, keep the JavaScript in a separate .js file that is incorporated in the HTML file with a <script> tag, as shown in the following example:

```
<script language="javascript" src="Clean Up HTML.js">
```

This separation enables easy modification of the user interface and the underlying code, and the sharing of the JavaScript functions.

Commands are very open-ended. In fact, only two Dreamweaver functions are specific to commands-canAcceptCommand() and commandButtons()—and neither function is required. Two other command—oriented functions, receiveArguments() and windowDimensions(), are also used elsewhere; but again, neither is required.

The `canAcceptCommand()` function controls when the command is active in the menus and when it is dimmed. If `canAcceptCommand()` is not defined, the command is always available. This function returns `true` or `false`; if `false` is returned, the command is dimmed in the menus.

You can see `canAcceptCommand()` in action in both the Sort Table and Format Table commands. For either of these commands to be effective, a table must be indicated. Rather than require that a table be selected, the `canAcceptCommand()` function calls a subroutine, `findTable()`, which returns `true` if the user's cursor is positioned inside a table:

```
function canAcceptCommand(){
  if (dw.getDocumentDOM() == null)
    return false;
  else if (dw.getDocumentDOM().getShowLayoutView())
    return false;
  else if (findTable())
    return true;
  else
    return false;
}

function findTable(){
  var tableObj="";
  var selObj = dw.getDocumentDOM().getSelectedNode();

  while (tableObj=="" && selObj.parentNode){
    if (selObj.nodeType == Node.ELEMENT_NODE && selObj.tagName=="TABLE")
    tableObj=selObj;
  else
    selObj = selObj.parentNode;
  }
  return tableObj;
}
```

Macromedia recommends that the `canAcceptCommand()` function not be defined unless at least one case exists in which the command should not be available. Otherwise, the function is asked to run for no purpose, which degrades performance.

The `commandButtons()` function defines the buttons that appear on the parameter form to the right. This expanded functionality is extremely useful when developing commands. Some commands require that an operation be enabled to run repeatedly and not just the one time an OK button is selected. As noted earlier, you don't have to declare the function at all, in which case the form expands to fill the dialog box entirely. If you do not use this standard Dreamweaver method for creating your command buttons, in most cases, you need to define them yourself.

Each button that is declared has a function associated with it, which is executed when the user selects that particular button. All the buttons for a command are listed in an array, returned by `commandButtons()`. The following example declares three buttons: OK, Cancel, and Help:

```
function commandButtons() {
    return new Array("OK","goCommand()","Cancel",
                     "window.close()","Help","displayHelp()")
}
```

Notice that two of the buttons, OK and Help, call user-defined functions; but the Cancel button simply calls a built-in JavaScript function to close the window. Although no limitations exist on the number of buttons a parameter form can hold, you should always strive to keep your parameter forms as simple and uncluttered as possible.

The receiveArguments() function is used in conjunction with runCommand(). Whenever runCommand() calls a specific command — from a behavior, object, or other command — it can pass arguments. If receiveArguments() is set up, that is the function executed, and the arguments are read into receiveArguments(). This function enables the same command to be called from different sources and have different effects, depending on the arguments passed. The receiveArguments() function is used extensively in menu commands and is explained more fully later in this chapter in the section "Building Menu Commands."

You can use the windowDimensions() function, like behaviors and objects, with commands to set a specific size for the associated dialog box. If windowDimensions() is not defined, the size of the dialog box is set automatically. Macromedia recommends that windowDimensions() not be used unless your parameter form exceeds 640 x 480.

The remainder of the user interface for a command — the parameter form — is constructed in the same manner with the same tools that are used for objects and behaviors. A command parameter form or dialog box uses an HTML <form> in the <body> of the file. If no <form> is declared, the command executes without displaying a dialog box. All the form elements used in objects — text boxes, radio buttons, checkboxes, and lists — are available in commands.

Useful Command Routines

When programming a command, I often get stuck on one small point. "If only I knew how to _____, I'd be home free," is my usual refrain. The following routines and explanations will help you "fill in the blank" as you begin to construct your own custom commands.

Getting a User's Selection

Although many commands work with the entire HTML document, some require just a portion of text or an object that has been selected by the user. Although it seems a simple task, some quirks in the API make getting a selection a little tricky.

Selecting Text

The usual method for determining — and acting on — what the user has selected requires the getSelection() function. getSelection() returns 2-byte offsets that mark the beginning and end of the user's selection. The difficulty appears when you try to extract the character data that corresponds to those byte offsets. The offsetsToNode() function, which is used to make this translation, expands the offsets to the nearest tag — the innerHTML, in other words. For example, the following function attempts to get the user's selection and report it in an alert:

```
function testCase() {
  var theDom = dreamweaver.getDocumentDOM("document");
  var offsets = dreamweaver.getSelection();
  var theNode =
      dreamweaver.offsetsToNode(offsets[0],offsets[1]);
  var nodeText = theNode.data;
  alert(nodeText);
}
```

If a user selects the word *gray* in the line "The old gray mare just ain't what she used to be," the function returns the entire line. To get just what is selected, you need to use the `nodeToOffsets()` function in combination with `offsetsToNode()` and the JavaScript `substring()` function.

The sample code in Listing 32-1 demonstrates the proper substring technique; it is taken from the Change Case command included on the CD-ROM that accompanies this book.

Listing 32-1: **Getting Selected Text**

```
function lowerCase(){
  var theDom = dreamweaver.getDocumentDOM("document");
  var offsets = dreamweaver.getSelection();
  var theNode =
      dreamweaver.offsetsToNode(offsets[0],offsets[1]);
  if (theNode.nodeType == Node.TEXT_NODE) {
    var nodeOffsets = dreamweaver.nodeToOffsets(theNode);
    offsets[0] = offsets[0] - nodeOffsets[0];
    offsets[1] = offsets[1] - nodeOffsets[0];
    var nodeText = theNode.data;
    theNode.data = nodeText.substring(0,offsets[0]) +
      nodeText.substring(offsets[0],offsets[1]).toLowerCase()
      + nodeText.substring(offsets[1], nodeText.length);
    window.close();
  }
  else { //it's not a TEXT_NODE
    var nodeOffsets = dreamweaver.nodeToOffsets(theNode);
    offsets[0] = offsets[0] - nodeOffsets[0];
    offsets[1] = offsets[1] - nodeOffsets[0];
    var nodeText = theNode.innerHTML;
    theNode.innerHTML = nodeText.toLowerCase();
    window.close();
  }
}
```

Notice two branches in the example `lowerCase()` function — either the selected string is text (a `TEXT_NODE`), or it's not. If the node is something other than a `TEXT_NODE`, the `data` property is not available, and you must use `innerHTML` instead. This situation occurs when a user selects an entire paragraph. In fact, all the user has to select is the last character before the closing tag — such as a period at the end of a paragraph — and the node type switches to `ELEMENT_NODE`.

Selecting Objects

By comparison, you have far fewer hoops to jump through to reference a selected object: You only have to get its `outerHTML` property, as shown in Listing 32-2.

Listing 32-2: Getting a Selected Object

```
function replicate() {
  var theDom = dreamweaver.getDocumentDOM("document");
  var offsets = dreamweaver.getSelection();
  var selObj =
      dreamweaver.offsetsToNode(offsets[0],offsets[1]);
  if (selObj.nodeType == Node.TEXT_NODE) {
    helpMe2();
    window.close();
    return;
  }
  var theCode = selObj.outerHTML;
}
```

Listing 32-2 also includes a small error routine that checks whether the user's selection is text (selObj.nodeType == Node.TEXT_NODE) and, if so, uses helpMe2() (a custom function that must be defined elsewhere in the script) to put up an advisory and then closes the window to enable the user to reselect.

Using a Command as an Object

Commands offer a tremendous range of power and can perform actions not available to behaviors or objects. To take advantage of this power with a point-and-click interface, it's best to disguise the command as an object. As an object, the command appears in both the Insert bar and the Insert menu.

A Dreamweaver object usually consists of two files: an HTML file for the code and a GIF image for the button, all in the Dreamweaver 8\Configuration\Objects*Category* folder. (The value of *Category* is the name of the folder that corresponds to the Insert bar category in which the object resides.) When using a command as an object, however, you can have as many as five files split between the Dreamweaver 8\Configuration\Objects*Category* and Dreamweaver 8\Configuration\Commands folders. The standard Rollover object is a good example: three associated rollover files are in the Dreamweaver 8\Configuration\Objects\Common folder, and two are in the Commands folder. (The Dreamweaver 8\Configuration\Objects\Common subfolder alerts you to the fact that the Rollover object resides in the Common category of the Insert bar.) Here is how these rollover files are used:

✦ **Dreamweaver 8\Configuration\Objects\Common\Rollover.gif:** The image for the Rollover button that appears in the Common category of the Insert bar.

✦ **Dreamweaver 8\Configuration\Objects\Common\Rollover.htm:** A shell file (called by the Rollover button) that reads Objects\Common\Rollover.js.

✦ **Dreamweaver 8\Configuration\Objects\Common\Rollover.js:** Contains the objectTag() function, which references the Commands\Rollover.htm file.

✦ **Dreamweaver 8\Configuration\Commands\Rollover.htm:** Builds the user interface for the object and reads all external JavaScript files, including Commands\Rollover.js.

✦ **Dreamweaver 8\Configuration\Commands\Rollover.js:** Contains the actual code for the function that performs the required operations, which returns its value to the Objects\Common\Rollover.htm file by way of the Objects\Common\Rollover.js file.

The key to understanding how to use a command as an object is the code linking the two types of extensions. In the Dreamweaver 8\Configuration\Objects\Common\Rollover.js file is the `objectTag()`, which is used to write an object into an existing Web page with its return value. In this case, the function first gets the Document Object Model of the relevant command file (Dreamweaver 8\Configuration\Commands\Rollover.htm); this procedure enables the current function to reference any variable set in the other file. Then the `popupCommand` is executed, which runs Dreamweaver 8\Configuration\Commands\Rollover.htm-which, in turn, launches the dialog box and gets the user parameters. Finally, a result from that command is set to the return value of `objectTag()` and written into the HTML page. Here's the `objectTag()` function in its entirety from Dreamweaver 8\Configuration\Objects\Common\Rollover.js:

```
function objectTag() {
  var rolloverTag = callCommand("Rollover.htm");
  if (rolloverTag) { //if inserting call, update behavior funcs as needed
  updateBehaviorFns("MM_findObj","MM_swapImgRestore",
                    "MM_preloadImages","MM_swapImage");
  }
  else {
    rolloverTag = '';
  }
  return(rolloverTag);
}
```

Some custom commands disguised as objects make the DOM connection in the command file, rather than the object file. All `iCat` objects (written to integrate a shopping cart into Dreamweaver), for example, establish the link in the primary functions of their command JavaScript files, in the following manner:

```
var dom = dreamweaver.getDocumentDOM("../Objects/iCat/Add To Cart.htm");
dom.parentWindow.icatTagStr = icatTagStr;
```

Then, the corresponding `objectTag()` function simply returns the `icatTagStr` variable.

Placing Code in the <head> Section

It's relatively straightforward to insert text wherever the cursor has been set in the document — you just set a text string equal to the [`innerHTML | data`] property of the DOM at that point. But how do you insert code in the <head> section of a Web page, where you don't generally find the cursor? Certain code, such as <script> tags that hold extensive JavaScript functions, must be inserted in the <head>. By design, behaviors return code specifically intended for the <script> tag — except you can't easily use a behavior to include a line such as the following:

```
<script language="Javascript" src="extend.js"></script>
```

You can insert such a line with commands, however. This technique, developed by Dreamweaver extensions author Massimo Foti, shows the way.

Unfortunately, no equivalent to the `body` property exists in the Dreamweaver DOM for the <head> section. The way around this minor limitation is to first locate the sole <head> tag in the document. You can accomplish this task in two lines of JavaScript code:

```
theDom = dreamweaver.getDocumentDOM("document");
theHeadNode = theDom.getElementsByTagName("HEAD");
```

Now the script variable needs to be set. Whenever Dreamweaver encounters a closing `</script>` tag in a JavaScript function, the tag is flagged because it seems to be missing a mate. To avoid this problem, split the tag into two concatenated strings, as follows:

```
theScript = '<script language="Javascript" src="extend.js"><' + '/script>';
```

Finally, find the first item in the `<head>` section and append the script to its `innerHTML` property:

```
theHeadNode.item(0).innerHTML = theHeadNode.item(0).innerHTML + theScript;
```

The full function looks like the following:

```
function insertScript() {
  var theDom, theHeadNode, theScript;
  theDom = dreamweaver.getDocumentDOM("document");
  theHeadNode = theDom.getElementsByTagName("HEAD");
  theScript = '<script language="Javascript" src="extend.js">< ' + 'script>';
}
```

On the CD-ROM

You can find numerous examples of Massimo Foti's commands and other extensions on the CD-ROM that accompanies this book. Just look in the Additional Extensions folder under his name.

Using Commands to Call Other Commands

As you've seen, the `runCommand()` function plays a key role in scripting commands. It's worth emphasizing that this same function is used when you want one command to invoke another command. The proper syntax is:

```
var doNew = dw.runCommand("commandFileName");
```

where `commandFileName` is the name of an HTML file in the Dreamweaver 8\Configuration\Commands folder. No value is returned with `runCommand()`; the function executes whatever command is called, passing any optional arguments. The function takes the following format:

```
dreamweaver.runCommand("myCommand.htm","argument01","argument02");
```

The called command's dialog box is presented and must be completed or canceled before the originating command can continue.

Tip

Many commands—especially those disguised as objects—are not intended to be directly accessed by the user. However, Dreamweaver lists any valid command found in the Commands folder on the menu—unless you add a comment as the first line of your HTML file in the following format:

```
<!- MENU-LOCATION=NONE ->
```

This code line inhibits the command name from being automatically displayed in the Commands menu list.

Creating a Blank Document

Commands aren't limited to working on the current document—you can use a command to read, modify, and even create new files. Any new file created using `createDocument()` or `createXHTMLDocument()` is an HTML or XHTML page based on the `Default.html` or `Default.xhtml` file found in the Dreamweaver 8\Configuration\DocumentTypes\ NewDocuments folder.

Occasionally, however, a command must make a new non-HTML/XHTML document, such as an XML or SMIL file or other file type that doesn't use the `<html> ... </html>` structure. To accomplish this task, you first create an HTML file and then replace its entire contents with your own data—or nothing at all. The following custom function, developed by Andrew Wooldridge, makes and saves a new, blank text file:

```
function doNew() {
  var newDOM = dreamweaver.createDocument();
  var theDoc = newDOM.documentElement;
  theDoc.outerHTML = ".";
  theDoc.innerHTML = " ";
  dreamweaver.saveDocument(newDOM, '../../empty.txt');
}
```

Remember that all the Dreamweaver document functions—such as `saveDocument()`—use addresses relative to the file calling them. For example, if the `doNew()` function is included in a command and, therefore, stored in the Commands folder, the `empty.txt` document is saved two folders above the Commands folder in the Dreamweaver root directory, because the full path to it is Dreamweaver 8\Configuration\Commands.

Managing Menus and Keyboard Shortcuts

Dreamweaver offers numerous ways to perform almost every task: through the Property inspector, context menus, keyboard shortcuts, and even entering code directly. However, in the search for ever-faster, more efficient ways of working, you may often find it desirable to take control of the menus and other command methods and make them work the way you and your team prefer them to work. If, for example, you insert a great number of layers and always define your links via the Property inspector, you are probably better off redefining Ctrl+L (Command+L) to Insert Layer, rather than its default, Make Link.

Dreamweaver places all menus and keyboard shortcuts under your control. Not only can you add new items, but you can also rename menu items, change their keyboard shortcuts, determine when a menu item is active or dimmed—and even add entirely new menu strips. Moreover, all this functionality is available with the context menus as well.

One file—`menus.xml`, found in the Dreamweaver 8\Configuration\Menus folder—is responsible for menu and keyboard shortcut set-up. Although you have to edit the XML file by hand to reconfigure the menus, Dreamweaver includes a Keyboard Shortcut editor for modifying the keystroke commands. Details are in the "Using the Keyboard Shortcut Editor" section later in the chapter.

Menu customization brings a whole new level of functionality to Dreamweaver. It's entirely possible for a company to create custom subsets of a program for certain departments. For example, each of several departments in a large firm might be responsible for its own section of the Web site. A customized version of Dreamweaver could include a predefined site and disable the Define Site commands in the Site menu. It could also offer a specialized menu for calling up Help screens, tied to the standard F1 keyboard shortcut for Help.

In addition to the fully open architecture of the menus.xml file, command menu items created by the History panel can be managed right in the Document window. Before you delve into the relatively complex structure of menus.xml, take a look at the Edit Command List feature.

Handling History Panel Commands

Whenever you save a series of History panel steps as a command, that command is instantly added to the bottom of the Commands menu list. Dreamweaver enables you to manage these custom added items — renaming them or deleting them — through the Edit Command List feature.

To manage History panel recorded commands, follow these steps:

1. Choose Commands ⇨ Edit Command List. The Edit Command List dialog box appears, as shown in Figure 32-3.

Figure 32-3: Manage your recorded commands through the Edit Command List dialog box.

2. To remove a command, select it and click Delete.

3. To rename a command, select it and enter the new name or alter the existing one.

Using the Keyboard Shortcut Editor

Whenever I'm learning a new program, one of the tasks I set for myself is to memorize the half-dozen or so essential keyboard shortcuts of the software. Keyboard shortcuts are terrific for boosting productivity — so terrific, in fact, that almost every program uses them. Although this is a good thing from a single-program user's perspective, in reality no Web designer uses just one program, and having to remember the keyboard shortcuts for every program can be an absolute nightmare.

To put the brakes on keyboard shortcut overload, Macromedia has implemented a standard Keyboard Shortcut editor for its key Web products — Flash, Fireworks, and Dreamweaver. Where possible, common features share the same shortcut across the product line. For example, opening the Behaviors panel is accomplished with the same keyboard shortcut in Dreamweaver and Fireworks: Shift+F3. Dreamweaver also includes a set of shortcuts matching those from HomeSite and BBEdit to smooth your transition from those text-based editors. Best of all, you can personalize any existing set of shortcuts to work with the way you truly work best.

To access the Keyboard Shortcut editor, shown in Figure 32-4, choose Edit ➪ Keyboard Shortcuts.

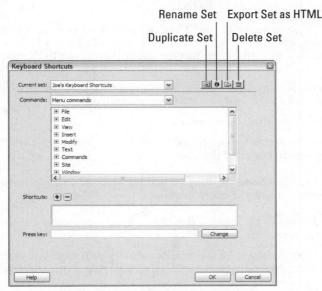

Figure 32-4: Use the Keyboard Shortcut editor to establish the easiest-to-remember mnemonics for your keyboard shortcuts.

The standard Keyboard Shortcut editor includes four standard sets of shortcuts:

✦ **BBEdit:** Keyboard shortcut set matching those found in BBEdit.

✦ **Dreamweaver MX2004:** This set uses the standard shortcuts found in Dreamweaver MX 2004. These additional shortcuts are not necessarily the same as those in the Macromedia Standard set because keystrokes may be added or modified for new features in the latest version.

✦ **HomeSite:** Keyboard shortcut set matching those found in HomeSite.

✦ **Macromedia Standard:** The default set of shortcuts incorporating common keyboard combinations in Dreamweaver, Fireworks, and Flash.

To change from one set to another, open the Keyboard Shortcut editor and choose the desired set from the Current Set drop-down list. The changes take effect immediately upon closing the dialog box; you don't have to relaunch Dreamweaver.

The standard sets are locked and cannot be altered — you can only customize a copy of one of the standard sets. Dreamweaver provides all the controls to accomplish this on top of the Keyboard Shortcut editor. The four buttons are as follows:

✦ **Duplicate Set:** Copies the current set (standard or custom) and appends the word *copy*. The duplicate set can be fully customized.

✦ **Rename Set:** Renames the current shortcut set.

✦ **Export Set as HTML:** Saves a list of the current set of keyboard shortcuts in an HTML format that can be viewed or printed in a browser.

✦ **Delete Set:** Removes a keyboard shortcut set. When Delete Set is chosen, a list of all custom sets is displayed, and any set except the active one may be removed. To remove a sole custom set, select any of the standard shortcut sets prior to choosing Delete Set.

Each command has up to two shortcuts assigned to it. This facility makes it possible to retain the originally assigned keyboard shortcut and to add a more personal one.

To create a custom keyboard shortcut set, follow these steps:

1. Choose Edit ➪ Keyboard Shortcuts to open the editor. The editor might take a few moments to load your current keyboard shortcuts.

Note   From the Department of Pointless Nonsense, Irony Division: the Keyboard Shortcuts feature is one of the few commands without a keyboard shortcut.

2. From the Current Set drop-down list, select a standard keyboard shortcut set upon which to base your custom set.

3. Click the Duplicate Set button, type in an appropriate name for your custom shortcut set, and click OK. When the duplication is finished, select your new shortcut set from the Current Set list.

4. Choose the type of commands you want to modify from the Commands drop-down list. Dreamweaver has five different command types in Windows — Menu commands, Site panel, Code editing, Document editing, and Site window — and three under the Macintosh system — Menu commands, Code editing, and Document editing.

5. Select the specific command whose keyboard shortcut you want to modify. If you've chosen Menu or Site panel from the Commands list (Windows only), click the plus (+) sign next to the menu heading containing the command. The listing expands to show the first level of menu items. If the command you want to alter is contained within a submenu, click the plus (+) sign next to the submenu. Click the minus (-) sign to collapse an expanded listing.

6. With the desired command selected, click the Add (+) button in the Shortcuts section. The cursor moves into the Press Key field.

7. Press the keyboard combination you want to assign to the command. If Dreamweaver detects a conflict with an existing keyboard shortcut, an alert is displayed beneath the Press Key field telling you the command to which that shortcut is currently assigned.

8. Select Change to confirm your choice.

If the shortcut you selected is already in use, you can reassign it to your new choice. When you click Change under these circumstances, Dreamweaver brings up an alert dialog box warning you that the shortcut is currently assigned. It also tells you which command is using it, and asks if you want to reassign it to the command you are editing. To reassign the keystroke, click OK. To choose a new keyboard shortcut, click Cancel.

If a command already has two shortcuts assigned to it, you select the one you want to change.

9. Click OK when you're finished to save your keyboard shortcut set.

Tip   The personalized keyboard shortcut files are stored in the Dreamweaver 8\Configuration\ Menus\Custom Sets folder as XML files. To make a keyboard shortcut set available on another system, copy the appropriate XML file to the corresponding folder in the user's Dreamweaver 8\Configuration\Menus\Custom Sets folder. For more details on the location of the user's folders, see the "Multiuser System Customization" sidebar earlier in this chapter.

Adjusting the menus.xml File

When Dreamweaver is launched, the program reads the menus.xml file and builds the menu system. You can even customize menus.xml and reload the file from within Dreamweaver to instantly update your menu and shortcuts. The key, of course, is editing the XML file.

Caution   Be aware of two points when tackling the menus.xml file. First, you have to make sure you're editing the correct version of the file. If you are using a multiuser operating system (Windows NT, Windows 2000, Windows XP, or Mac OS X), the file is in your user Configuration folder. System administrators and users of Windows 98 should use the menus.xml file found in the program's Configuration folder. Second, the syntax for menus.xml is quite complex. Dreamweaver ignores any syntactically incorrect entries and disables their corresponding menu items. So take great care when you edit menus.xml to use proper syntax, and make sure you create a backup of the file *before* you begin editing.

The typical procedure for changing an existing menu item or shortcut is to open the file in a text editor (after backing up the original) and make the necessary changes. When adding menus or menu items, follow the file's syntax exactly, as described in the following sections.

Generic Shortcuts

Although Dreamweaver now provides a user interface for editing the keyboard shortcuts, sometimes power-users must go to the source for major modifications — and the source for shortcuts is menus.xml. The menus.xml file is divided into two main sections: <shortcutlist> and <menubar>. The <shortcutlist> divisions are, as you might suspect, a list of keyboard shortcuts. The <menubar> areas are concerned with the various menu bars — in the main Document window, in the Site panel (Windows only), and in the numerous context menus. <shortcutlist> and <menubar> share several characteristics. They both follow the same basic structure:

```
<shortcutlist id="shortcutListID" [platform="win|mac"]>
  <shortcut attributeName="value" attributeName="value" ... />
```

```
<shortcut attributeName="value" attributeName="value" ... />
other shortcut items...
</shortcutlist>

<menubar name="menubarname" id="menubarID" [platform="win|mac"]>
  <menu name="menuname" id="menuID">
    <menuitem attributeName="value" attributeName="value" ... />
    <menuitem attributeName="value" attributeName="value" ... />
    other menuitem items...
  </menu>
  other menu items...
</menubar>
```

Shortcuts for menu items are primarily defined within the `<menubar>` code; the
`<shortcutlist>` is mainly concerned with those shortcuts that do not have a menu item
associated with them, such as moving from one word to another. By default, Dreamweaver
defines six `<shortcutlist>` sections: `DWMainWindow` for the Document window menu,
`DWMainSite` for the Site panel menu (Windows only), `DWHTMLContext` for the Code inspec-
tor/Code view context menu, `DWServerBehaviorContext` for the Server Behaviors panel
context menu, `DWDataBindingContext` for the Bindings panel context menu, and
`DWServerComponentContext` for the Components panel context menu.

> **Note**   The key difference between the `<shortcutlist>` and the `<menubar>` sections is that
> although you can define new menu items or change existing ones in the `<menubar>` por-
> tion of the code, you can only alter existing shortcuts—you cannot add new shortcuts.

Each `<shortcutlist>` tag has one required attribute, the ID. The ID refers to a specific window or panel and must be unique within the `<shortcutlist>` section. The same ID is
repeated in the `<menubar>` section to refer to the same window or panel. For example, the
Document window ID is `DWMainWindow`, whereas the one for the context menu of the Server
Behaviors panel is `DWServerBehaviorContext`. The `<shortcutlist>` tag takes one optional
attribute, `platform`, which must be set to either `win` or `mac`, for Windows and Macintosh systems, respectively. (Note that in syntax statements, optional attributes are enclosed in brackets.) If no platform attribute is listed, the `<shortcutlist>` described applies to both
platforms. Here, for example, is the beginning of the `<shortcutlist>` definition for the Files
panel, which only appears in the Windows version of the software:

```
<shortcutlist id="DWMainSite" platform="win">
```

A separate `<shortcut>` tag exists for every keystroke defined in the `<shortcutlist>`. The
`<shortcut>` tag defines the key used, the tag's ID, the command or file to be executed when
the keyboard shortcut is pressed, and the applicable platform, if any. Shortcuts can be
defined for single special keys or key combinations using modifiers. The special keys are as
follows:

✦ F1 through F12

✦ PgDn, PgUp, Home, End

✦ Ins, Del, BkSp, Space

✦ Esc and Tab

Modifiers can be used in combination with standard keys, special keys, or by themselves. A combination keyboard shortcut is indicated with a plus sign between keys. Available modifiers include those described in Table 32-1.

Table 32-1: Dreamweaver Shortcut Modifier Keys

Key	Example	Use
Alt or Opt	Alt+V; Option+V	Indicates the Alt (Windows) or Option (Macintosh) key modifier
Cmd	Command+S	Indicates the Command (Macintosh) key modifier
Ctrl	Ctrl+U	Indicates the Ctrl (Windows) key modifier
Shift	Shift+F1	Indicates the Shift key on both platforms

You can also combine multiple modifiers, as in this example:

Command+Shift+Z

The format of the `<shortcut>` tag is identical to that of the `<menuitem>` tag, as described in the following section.

Menubar Definitions

Each `<menubar>` section of the `menus.xml` file describes a different menu strip, either on a window or on the context menu associated with a panel. Nested within the `<menubar>` tag is a series of `<menu>` tags, each detailing a drop-down menu. The individual menu items are defined in the `<menuitem>` tags contained within each set of `<menu>` ... `</menu>` tags. Here, for example, is the context menu for the HTML Styles panel (I've abbreviated the complete `<menuitem>` tag for clarity):

```
<menubar name="" id="DWHtmlStyleContext">
  <menu name="HTML Style Popup" id="DWContext_HTMLStyle">
    <menuitem name="Edit..." />
    <menuitem name="Duplicate..." />
    <menuitem name="Delete" />
    <menuitem name="Apply" />
    <separator />
    <menuitem name="New..." />
  </menu>
</menubar>
```

The `<menubar>` and `<menu>` tags are alike in that they both require a name — which is what appears in the menu system — and an ID. The ID must be unique within the `<menubar>` structure to avoid conflicts. If a conflict is found (that is, if one item has the same ID as another), the first item in the XML file is recognized, and the second item is ignored.

Note   You can put a dividing line between your menu items by including a `<separator id="idname"/>` tag between any two `<menuitem>` tags. (`idname` is any legal, unique XML name string.)

Numerous other attributes exist for the ⟨menuitem⟩ tag. The required attributes are name, id, and either file or command, as marked with an asterisk in Table 32-2.

Table 32-2: Menuitem Tag Attributes

Attribute	Possible Value	Description
name*	Any menu name	The name of the menu item as it appears on the menu. An underscore character causes the following letter to be underlined for Windows' shortcuts-for example, _Frames becomes Frames.
id*	Any unique name	The identifying term for the menu item.
key	Any special key or keyboard key plus modifier(s)	The keyboard shortcut used to execute the command.
platform	win or mac	The operating system valid for the current menu item. If the platform parameter is omitted, the menu item is applicable for both systems.
enabled	JavaScript function	If present, governs whether a menu item is active (the function returns true) or dimmed (the function returns false). Including enabled=true ensures that the function is always available.
command* (required if file is not used)	JavaScript function	Executed when the menu item is selected. This inline JavaScript function capability is used for simple functions.
file* (required if command is not used)	Path to a JavaScript file	The JavaScript file is executed when the menu item is selected; the path is relative to the Configuration folder.
checked	JavaScript function	Displays a checkmark next to the menu item if the function returns true.
dynamic	N/A	Specifies that the menu item is set dynamically by the getDynamicContent() function, which resides in the Menu Commands file specified by the file attribute.

Tip   The menus.xml file is quite extensive. You can find the main menu for Dreamweaver — the one you most likely want to modify — by searching for the second instance of its ID, DWMainWindow. The first instance is used by the corresponding ⟨shortcutlist⟩ tag.

You can create submenus by nesting one set of `<menu>` tags within another. The following example is a simplified look at the File ➭ Import commands, as structured in `menus.xml`:

```
<menu name="_File" id="DWMenu_File">
  other menu items...
  <menu name="_Import" id="DWMenu_File_Import">
     <menuitem name="_XML into Template..." />
     <menuitem name="_Word HTML..." />
     <menuitem name="_Tabular Data..." />
  </menu>
  other menu items...
</menu>
```

Note how the `<menu>` tag defining the Import submenu is nested within the `<menu>` tag that defines the File menu.

Building Menu Commands

When examining the `menus.xml` file, notice that many menu items have JavaScript functions written right into the `<menuitem>` tag, such as this one for File ➭ New:

```
<menuitem name="New _Window" key="Cmd+N" enabled="true"
       command="dw.newDocument()" id="DWMenu_MainSite_File_New" />
```

When the user selects File ➭ New, Dreamweaver executes the API function `dw.newDocument()` in what is referred to as a *menu command*. Menu commands are used to specify the action of every menu item; what makes them unique is that you can use them to create and activate dynamic menus. Dynamic menus update according to user selections; the Preview in Browser list is a dynamic menu.

A menu command, like most of the other Dreamweaver extensions, is a combination of HTML and JavaScript. If the menu command is extensive and cannot be referenced as one or two functions directly in the `menus.xml` file, it is contained in an HTML file, stored in the Dreamweaver 8\Configuration\Menus folder. Menu commands can even use a dialog box, such as standard commands for accepting user input.

Tip   You can find many examples of menu commands, written by the Dreamweaver engineers, in the Dreamweaver 8\Configuration\Menus\Mm folder.

Menu commands have access to all the Dreamweaver API functions and a few of their own. None of the seven menu command API functions, listed in Table 32-3, is required, and three are automatically called when the menu command is executed.

Table 32-3: Command Menu API Functions

Function	Returns	Description
canAcceptCommand()	Boolean (true or false)	Determines whether the menu item is active or dimmed
commandButtons()	An array of labels and functions, separated by commas	Sets the name and effect of buttons on the dialog box
getDynamicContent()	An array of menu item names and unique IDs, separated by a semicolon	Sets the current listing for a menu
isCommandChecked()	Boolean	Adds a checkmark next to the item if true is returned
receiveArguments()	Nothing	Handles any arguments passed by the <menuitem> tag
setMenuText()	A text string	Sets the name of the menu item according to the given function; not to be used in conjunction with getDynamicContent()
windowDimensions()	Width,Height (in pixels)	Determines the dimensions of the Parameters dialog box, like windowDimensions(300,500)

Working with Custom Tags

With the advent of XML — in which no standard tags exist — the capability to handle custom tags is essential in a Web authoring tool. Dreamweaver incorporates this capability through its third-party tag feature. After you've defined a third-party tag, Dreamweaver displays it in the Document window by highlighting its content, inserting a user-defined icon, or doing neither depending on the Preferences selected and the attributes assigned. Third-party tags are easily selected through the Tag Selector below the Document window; therefore, they are easy to cut, copy and paste, or otherwise manipulate. Perhaps most important, after a third-party tag is defined, you can apply a custom Property inspector that enables tag attributes to be entered in a standardized user interface.

Third-party tags can be defined directly within Dreamweaver. Just as object files use HTML to structure HTML code for easy insertion, Dreamweaver uses XML to make an XML definition for the custom tag. A custom tag declaration consists solely of one tag, <tagspec>, with up to seven attributes. The following list describes all of the tag's legal attributes:

✦ tag_name — Defines the name of the tag as used in the markup. Any valid name — no spaces or special characters are allowed — is possible. A tag with the attribute tag_name="invoice" is entered in the document as <invoice>.

✦ tag_type — Determines whether the tag has a closing tag (nonempty) and is thus capable of enclosing content or if the tag describes the content itself (empty). For example, the <invoice> tag could have a tag_type="nonempty" because all the content is between <invoice> and </invoice>.

✦ `render_contents`—Sets whether the content of a non-empty type tag is displayed. The `render_contents` attribute value is either `true` or `false`; if `false`, the tag's icon is displayed instead of the contents.

✦ `content_model`—Establishes valid placement and content for the tag in the document. The possible options are as follows:

- `block_model`—Tags defined with `content_model="block_model"` appear only in the `<body>` section of a document and contain block-level HTML tags, such as `<p>`, `<div>`, `<blockquote>`, and `<pre>`.

- `head_model`—Defines a tag that appears in the `<head>` section and can contain text, for example: `content_model="head_model"`.

- `marker_model`—You can place tags with the attribute `content_model=marker_model` anywhere in the document with no restrictions on content. The `marker_model` value is most often used for inline tags that are placed within a paragraph or division.

- `script_model`—Like the `marker_model` tag, `script_model` tags can be placed in either the `<head>` or `<body>` section. All content within a `script_model` tag is ignored by Dreamweaver. This feature enables server-specific scripts to be included without alteration.

✦ `start_string`—The initial delimiter for a custom string-delimited tag; `start_string` and `end_string` must both be defined if one is declared. Lasso tags, for example, use a `start_string` of a left bracket, (`[`).

✦ `end_string`—The closing delimiter for a custom string-delimited tag. The `end_string` for a Lasso tag is the right bracket, (`]`).

✦ `detect_in_attribute`—A Boolean value that determines whether Dreamweaver should ignore string-delimited tags used as attributes in other tags. The default is `false`, but for most string-delimited functions, the `detect_in_attribute` value should be set to `true`.

✦ `parse_attributes`—A Boolean value that determines whether Dreamweaver should inspect and parse the attributes within string-delimited tags. By default, Dreamweaver parses all attributes; set `parse_attribute` to `false` to force Dreamweaver to ignore the attributes.

✦ `icon`—Empty tags or non-empty custom tags with `render_content` disabled require a GIF file to act as an icon in the Document window. The icon attribute should be set to any valid URL, relative or absolute (as in `icon="images/invoice.gif"`).

✦ `icon_width`—Sets the width, in pixels, of the icon used to represent the tag. The value can be any positive integer.

✦ `icon_height`—Sets the height, in pixels, of the icon used to represent the tag. The value can be any positive integer.

✦ `is_visual`—Sets whether the tag is rendered in the Design view; either a `true` or `false` value is acceptable.

Here's the complete code for a sample custom tag, the Template Expressions tag (which, although created by Macromedia, is technically a third-party tag):

```
<tagspec tag_name="dwtemplate" start_string="@@(" end_string=")@@"
detect_in_attribute="true" icon="TemplateExpr.gif" icon_width="18"
icon_height="18"></tagspec>
```

Figure 32-5 shows an example of the Template Expressions custom tags; the page is set up so that the items on the menu can be altered with template expressions.

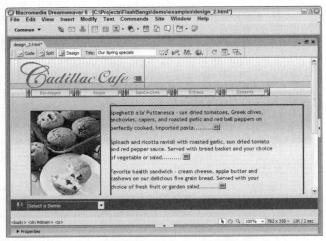

Figure 32-5: Third-party tags, such as these representing template expressions, can be displayed — and manipulated — in Design view.

Tip   If the content is to be rendered for a custom tag, you can easily view it in the Document window by enabling the Third-Party Tags Highlighting option in the Highlighting panel of the Preferences dialog box. Make sure that View ➪ Visual Aids ➪ Invisible Elements is enabled.

After a custom tag is defined, the definition is saved in an XML file in the ThirdPartyTags folder, in Dreamweaver's Configuration folder. If you are establishing a number of custom tags, you can place all the definitions in the same file. Macromedia refers to this as the Tag DB or Database.

Customizing Property Inspectors

Property inspectors are used throughout Dreamweaver to display the current attributes of many different types of tags: text, images, layers, plugins, and so on. Not only do Property inspectors make it easy to see the particulars for an object, they make it a snap to modify those parameters. With the inclusion of custom tags in Dreamweaver, the capability to add custom Property inspectors is a natural parallel. Moreover, you can create custom Property inspectors for existing tags, and the custom Property inspectors are displayed in place of the built-in Property inspectors.

Like objects, commands, and behaviors, custom Property inspectors are composed of HTML and JavaScript; the Property inspector HTML file itself is stored in the Dreamweaver 8\ Configuration\Inspectors folder. However, the layout of the Property inspector is far more restrictive than that of the other Dreamweaver extensions. The dialog box for an object, command, or behavior can be any size or shape desired — any custom Property inspector must fit the standard Property inspector dimensions and design. Because of the precise positioning necessary to insert parameter form items such as text boxes and drop-down menu lists, layers are used extensively to create the layout.

Very elaborate Property inspectors are possible. The FlashBang! Property inspector, created by Joseph Lowery and Edoardo Zubler, is shown in Figure 32-6. Property inspectors, like other extension types, can also incorporate CSS styles, Flash movies, and Shockwave files.

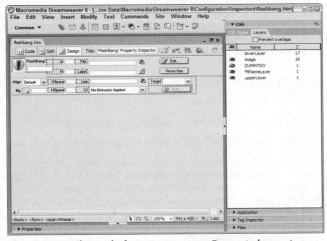

Figure 32-6: The code for some custom Property inspectors, such as this one from FlashBang!, takes advantage of Dreamweaver's layer and CSS styles support.

Coding a Property Inspector

Like many of the other standard extension files, most of the Property inspector files that ship with Dreamweaver are composed of an HTML file that calls a separate JavaScript file. It is entirely possible, however, to combine HTML and JavaScript into a single file. No matter how it's structured, a custom Property inspector HTML file requires the following four key elements:

✦ An initial DTD (Document Type Definition) line for custom Property inspectors:

```
<!DOCTYPE HTML SYSTEM "-//Macromedia//DWExtension ↵
layout-engine 6.0//pi">
```

✦ An HTML comment line immediately preceding the opening `<html>` tag that identifies which tag the Property inspector is for; here's the HTML comment line for a META tag Property inspector:

```
<!- tag:META,priority:5,selection:within,vline,hline ->
<html>
```

✦ The function `canInspectSelection()`, which determines whether the Property inspector should be displayed according to the current selection.

✦ A second function, `inspectSelection()`, which updates the tag's HTML when new values are entered in the Property inspector.

If any of these elements is missing or incorrectly declared, Dreamweaver ignores the file and does not display the Property inspector.

Cross-Reference

In addition to the mandatory functions and definitions, custom Property inspectors are capable of using any of the other Dreamweaver JavaScript functions, with the exception of the `getBehaviorTag()` and `getBehaviorElement()` functions. If you include the `displayHelp()` function, a small question mark in a circle appears in the upper-right corner of your custom Property inspector, which, when selected by the user, executes whatever routines your Help function has declared.

The Property Inspector Definition

Two main items define a custom Property inspector:

✦ The custom Property inspector DTD, which must be the first line in the file

✦ An HTML comment line, which must immediately precede the opening `<html>` tag

More than one Property inspector can be defined for a particular tag, making it possible for separate inspectors to be used if different attributes are specified. Therefore, each Property inspector is assigned a priority that determines the one to be displayed. Property inspectors are further defined by whether the current selection is within the tag indicated or if it contains the entire tag; this feature enables two different Property inspectors to be defined, as with the `<table>` tag. Finally, optional graphic elements are definable: a horizontal line to delineate the upper and lower portions of the Property inspector, and a vertical line to separate the object's name from the other parts of the Property inspector.

Here is the custom Property inspector DTD:

```
<!DOCTYPE HTML SYSTEM "-//Macromedia//DWExtension ⊃
layout-engine 6.0//pi">
```

The HTML comment line uses the following syntax:

```
<!- tag:ID,priority:1-10, ⊃
selection:exact|within,hline,vline,serverModel ->
```

(The last three values of the selection attribute—`hline`, `vline`, and `serverModel`—are all optional.) For example, the Property inspector for the `<link>` tag (a `<head>` element) is defined as follows:

```
<!- tag:LINK,priority:5,selection:within,vline,hline ->
```

The individual sections of the definition are as follows:

✦ `tag`—The name of the tag for which the Property inspector is intended. Although it's not mandatory, the tag name is customarily uppercased. The tag ID can also be one of three keywords: `*COMMENT*`, when a comment class tag is indicated; `*LOCKED*`, when a locked region is to be inspected; or `*ASP*`, for all ASP elements.

Note The asterisks on either side of the `tag` keywords are mandatory.

✦ `priority` — The `priority` of a Property inspector is provided as a number from 1 to 10. The highest priority, 10, means that this Property inspector takes precedence over any other possible Property inspectors. The lowest priority, 1, marks the Property inspector as the one to use when no other Property inspector is available.

Note You can find an example of how `priority` is used in the `<meta>` tag and the `Description` and `Keywords` objects. The Property inspectors for `Description` and `Keywords` have a higher priority (6) than the one for the basic `<meta>` tag (5), which enables those inspectors to be shown initially if the proper criteria are met; if the criteria are *not* met, the Property inspector for the `<meta>` tag is displayed.

✦ `selection` — Depending on the current selection, the cursor is either within a particular tag or exactly enclosing it. The selection attribute is set to `within` or `exact`, according to the condition under which the Property inspector should be displayed.

✦ `hline` — Inserts a 1-pixel horizontal gray line (see Figure 32-7) dividing the upper and lower halves of the expanded Property inspector.

✦ `vline` — Places a 1-pixel vertical gray line (see Figure 32-7) between the tag's name field and the other properties on the upper half of the Property inspector.

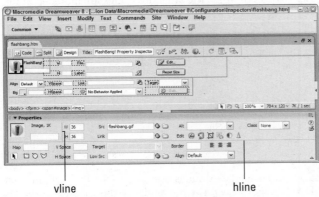

vline   hline

Figure 32-7: The Property inspector for the `<img>` tag uses both the `hline` and `vline` attributes.

The canInspectSelection() Function

To control the circumstances under which your custom Property inspector is displayed, use the `canInspectSelection()` function. Like `canAcceptBehavior()` and `canAcceptCommand()` for behaviors and commands, respectively, if `canInspectSelection()` returns `true`, the custom Property inspector is shown; if it returns `false`, the Property inspector is not shown.

As noted earlier, the `canInspectSelection()` function is mandatory. If no conditions exist under which the Property inspector should not be displayed, use the following code:

```
function canInspectSelection() {
  return true;
}
```

Access to several of the standard Dreamweaver `<head>` elements' Property inspector files is restricted by the `canInspectSelection()` function to specific tags. In the following example, from the `<meta>` Description object, the current selection is examined to see if a `<meta>` tag is selected, and the `name` attribute is set to `description`:

```
function canInspectSelection() {
  var dom = dw.getDocumentDOM();
  var metaObj = dom.getSelectedNode();
  if (!metaObj || !metaObj.getAttribute) return false;
  return (metaObj.tagName && metaObj.tagName == "META" &&
    metaObj.getTranslatedAttribute("name") &&
    metaObj.getTranslatedAttribute("name").toLowerCase()=="description");
}
```

The inspectSelection() Function

The `inspectSelection()` function is the workhorse of the custom Property inspector code and is responsible for pulling the information from the selected tag for display in the various Property inspector fields. Depending on the code design, the `inspectSelection()` function can also be used to update the HTML code when the attribute values are modified in the Property inspector.

Here's an excerpt of the `inspectSelection()` function from the Link Property inspector file:

```
function inspectSelection() {
  TEXT_HREF = findObject("Href");
  ...
  if (linkObj.getAttribute("href"))
    TEXT_HREF.value = linkObj.getAttribute("href");
  else
    TEXT_HREF.value = "";
  ...
}
```

In this example, if an attribute (`href`) exists, its value is assigned to the Property inspector's appropriate text box value (`TEXT_HREF.value`). The remainder of the `inspectSelection()` function for the `<link>` tag consists of a series of statements such as those shown in the sample code.

Tip   You can design a Property inspector that displays a different interface depending on whether or not it is expanded, as the Keywords Property inspector does. If an inspector is not expanded, the `argument(0)` property is set to the value `min`; when it is expanded, `argument(0)` is equal to the value `max`.

Many Property inspectors update their HTML tags when a change occurs in one of the input boxes. No real standard method exists to accomplish this, due to the many possible variations with Property inspectors. However, one of the most commonly used events is onBlur(), as in the following example, taken from the Keywords Property inspector file:

```
var minText = '<textarea name="Keywords" onBlur="setMetaTag()" '
  + 'style="width:350;height:32" rows="2" wrap="virtual"></textarea>'
```

The setMetaTag() function that is called is a local one that assigns whatever is currently in the textarea of the Property inspector to the content attribute.

Designing a Property Inspector

All the attributes for a Property inspector must fit into a tightly designed space. Although it's helpful to look at examples found in the Inspectors folder, many of the standard Property inspectors are built in to the core functionality of the program and are not immediately accessible on the design level. The following specifications and tips should make it easier to design your own custom Property inspectors:

✦ An expanded Property inspector is 100 pixels high: 50 pixels for the top portion and 49 pixels for the bottom portion (the dividing line between the two is 1-pixel high).

✦ If the hline attribute is specified in the Property inspector definition, a 1-pixel-high line is drawn the entire width of the inspector, 51 pixels down from the top (reducing the bottom portion's height to 49 pixels).

✦ If the vline attribute is specified, a single-pixel line is drawn across the top half of the Property inspector, 118 pixels from the left.

✦ The image placed on the upper-left corner of the Property inspector is generally sized at 36 pixels square and placed 3 pixels from the top and 2 pixels from the left. Although you are not required to keep this size image — or its placement — following these guidelines helps make your custom Property inspectors resemble the standard Dreamweaver ones.

✦ It's a good idea to lay out your Property inspector with the View ➪ Visual Aids ➪ Invisible Elements option disabled. The small icons that indicate layers can alter the perceived spacing.

✦ Keep the Layers panel visible. Many custom Property inspectors use multiple layers to position the elements exactly and the Layers panel makes selecting individual layers for adjustment a snap.

✦ Use nested layers to position and group associated items in the Property inspector. Almost all the form objects for user input in Property inspectors, such as text boxes and drop-down lists, are identified by labels. Placing both the label and text boxes in their own layers, while grouping them under one parent layer, provides maximum flexibility and ease of placement.

✦ Apply CSS styles within the Property inspector to easily manage font sizes and design your Property inspector in a WYSIWYG environment.

Making Custom Floating Panels

Property inspectors are an excellent way to manage the attributes of most elements in a single, consistent user interface. The Property inspector user interface, however, is not the best solution for all situations. Recognizing this, the Macromedia engineers have added another extension type for Dreamweaver: floating panels.

A *floating panel* is a cross between a Property inspector and a command. Like Property inspectors, floating panels can stay on the screen while you work on the Web page; like commands, floating panels are not restricted to a set size and shape. Custom floating panels have the same basic interface as standard Dreamweaver panels. Any floating panel can be resized or grouped with other floating panels, standard or custom. After it is grouped, a custom floating panel also has a tab that, when selected, brings the floating-panel interface to the front. A couple of noteworthy differences exist between built-in and custom floating panels:

✦ Built-in floating panel tabs can display names and icons; custom floating panel tabs can only display names.

✦ Built-in floating panels can be assigned a minimum size; custom floating panels cannot (that is, the user can shrink them down to about 100 x 100 pixels).

Floating panels, like most other extensions, are a combination of HTML and JavaScript. HTML is the main file that is called; it provides the user interface via an HTML form. JavaScript provides the functionality from the `<head>` of the HTML page.

Note   Like Property inspectors, floating panels have their own DTD that you must include as the first line in your custom floating panel files: `<!DOCTYPE HTML SYSTEM "-//Macromedia//DWExtension layout-engine5.0//floater">`.

Floating panels are stored in the Dreamweaver 8\Configuration\Floaters folder. However, unlike commands or objects, you can't just save your custom floating panel in a particular folder to make it accessible. You must call a function that displays the floating panel, either `dw.setFloaterVisibility(floaterName,true)` or `dw.toggleFloater(floaterName)`. Most often, these functions are called from a `<menuitem>` tag in the menus.xml file, like the following custom floating panel:

```
<menuitem name="HelpBuilder" enabled="true"
command="dw.toggleFloater('helpBuilder')"
checked="dw.getFloaterVisibility('helpBuilder')" />
```

The checked attribute ensures that a checkmark is displayed next to the menu item if the floating panel is visible.

Caution   When naming a custom floating panel, be sure to avoid names reserved for Dreamweaver's built-in elements: assets, behaviors, codesnippet, CSS styles, dataSource, documenttype, frames, helpbook, HTML, insertbar, layers, library, objects, or history properties, reference, samplecontent, serverBehavior, serverFormat, serverModel, site, taglibrary, site files, site map, templates, timelines, timelines, or toolbar.

As indicated in the preceding paragraphs, floating panels have their own API functions, and several methods of the Dreamweaver object are applicable. The floating panel API functions, none of which is required, are described in Table 32-4.

Table 32-4: Floating Panel API Functions

Function	Returns	Use
displayHelp()	Nothing	Specifies whether a Help button should appear beneath the OK and Cancel buttons
documentEdited()	Nothing	Executes after the current document has been edited
getDockingSide()	A string containing left, right, top, and/or bottom	For Dreamweaver 8 (Windows only) Specifies where a floating panel can dock
initialPosition(platform)	A string in the format left,top	Sets the position of the floating panel onscreen when it is first called; if left onscreen when Dreamweaver quits, it reopens in the last location
initialTabs()	A string in the format floating Panel1, floating Panel2,. . .	Indicates what other floating panels are grouped with the current floating panel when it first appears
isATarget()	Boolean	For Dreamweaver 8 (Windows only) Specifies if other panels can dock to this panel
IsAvailableInCodeView()	Boolean	Determines if the floating panel is enabled when Code view is active
isResizable	Boolean	Specifies whether the floating panel can be resized by the user
selectionChanged()	Nothing	Executes after the current selection has been altered

Caution   Macromedia strongly cautions programmers against using documentEdited() and selectionChanged() unless these functions are absolutely necessary. Because they constantly monitor the document, both functions can have an adverse effect on performance if implemented. Macromedia suggests that programmers incorporate the setTimeout() method to temporarily pause these functions so that the user can continue to interact with the program.

Within the Dreamweaver API are two pairs of methods and a single function that relate to floating panels as follows:

✦ getHideAllFloaters() — Reads the state of the Show/Hide Floating Panel menu option to determine if all floating panels should be hidden (true) or shown (false)

✦ setHideAllFloaters() — Sets the Show/Hide Floating panel to a particular state, to Hide (true) or Show (false)

✦ getFloaterVisibility(floaterName) — Reads whether the given floating panel is currently displayed and frontmost (true) or hidden (false)

✦ setFloaterVisibility(floaterName,isVisible) — Brings the named floating panel forward if the isVisible argument is true

✦ toggleFloater(floaterName) — Toggles the visibility state of the given floating panel between hiding and bringing to the front

Floating panels have a great deal of potential with their flexible interface and constant onscreen presence. The example shown in Figure 32-8, and built by WebAssist, manages the global settings for a shopping cart on three different tabs.

Figure 32-8: The custom floater, built by WebAssist, controls global settings as well as merchandising rules for a shopping cart extension, WA eCart.

Developing Translators

For any markup tag to be depicted in the Document window — whether it's <b> for bold or a custom third-party tag such as Tango's <@cols> — it must be translated. Dreamweaver's built-in rendering system translates all the standard HTML code, along with a few special custom tags such as those for ASP and ColdFusion. However, to display any other custom tags, or those that perform special functions such as server-side includes, the tag developer must build a custom translator.

As part of its expansion efforts, Dreamweaver supports *custom translators*. This enhancement enables programs that output nonstandard HTML to be displayed onscreen integrated with the regular code. One of Dreamweaver's main claims to fame is its capability to accept code without rewriting it. With Dreamweaver translators, you can visually insert, show, and edit your custom code.

Here's a brief overview of how translators work:

1. When Dreamweaver starts, all the properly coded translators in the Dreamweaver 8\ Configuration\Translators folder are initialized.

2. If a document is loaded with nonstandard HTML, the code is checked against the installed translators.

3. The translators are enabled.

Note   With the exception of the SSI translator, all translators are automatically active all the time — no preference setting determines their availability.

4. The code is processed with the translator and temporarily converted to a format acceptable to Dreamweaver.

5. Dreamweaver renders the code onscreen.

6. If a change is made to the page, Dreamweaver retranslates the document and refreshes the screen.

7. When the page is saved, the temporary translation is discarded, and the original code, with any modifications, is stored.

Developers continue to break new ground with the use of translators. Some translators that have been developed so far include those for the following:

✦ **Server-side includes:** Standard with Dreamweaver, the SSI translator effortlessly inserts, at design time, files that you normally don't see until delivered by the Web server. (To learn more about SSI, see Chapter 28.)

✦ **XSSI:** The Extended Server-Side Include (XSSI) extension, developed by Webmonkey authors Alx Ladygo, Nadav Savio, and Taylor for Macromedia, includes a translator that brings the Apache-served code right into the Document window.

✦ **Tango:** Developed by Pervasive Software, the Tango translator compensates for differences between database-oriented code and standard HTML. Additionally, Tango includes a manually controlled Sample Data translator that enables the Web designer to view the page complete with an example database.

Translator Functions

Like other Dreamweaver extensions, such as behaviors and commands, translators are HTML files with JavaScript. Translators have no user interface. Other than deciding when to invoke it, you have no parameters to set or options from which to choose. All the pertinent code is in a script located in the `<head>` of the translator, which, along with any necessary support routines, includes two essential JavaScript functions: `getTranslatorInfo()` and `translateMarkup()`. Any other Dreamweaver JavaScript API functions not specific to behaviors can be used in a translator as well.

Note　Because of the limitations of JavaScript, much of the heart of custom translation is handled by specially written C-level extensions. These compiled code libraries enhance Dreamweaver's capabilities so that new data types can be integrated. C-level extensions are covered in the "Extending C-Level Libraries" section later in this chapter.

The getTranslatorInfo() Function

The `getTranslatorInfo()` function simply sets up and returns an array of text strings that are read by Dreamweaver during initialization.

The structure of the array is relatively rigid. The number of array elements is specified when the `Array` variable is declared, and a particular text string must correspond to the proper array element. The array order is as follows:

✦ **translatorClass:** The translator's unique name used in JavaScript functions. The name has to begin with a letter and can contain alphanumeric characters as well as hyphens or underscores.

✦ **title:** The title listed in the menu and the Translation category. This text string can be no longer than 40 characters.

✦ **nExtensions:** The number of file extensions, such as .cfml, to follow. This declaration tells Dreamweaver how to read the next portion of the array. If this value is set to 0, all files are acceptable.

✦ **extension:** The actual file extension without the leading period.

✦ **nRegExps:** The number of regular expressions to be declared. Should this value be equal to 0, the array is closed.

✦ **RegExps:** The regular expression to be searched for by Dreamweaver.

✦ **runDefault:** Specifies when the translator executes (always, never, or conditionally).

The number of array elements — and thus, the detail of the function — depends entirely on the translator. Here, for example, is the code for getTranslatorInfo() from Live Picture's translator, where a file must have a particular <meta> tag to be translated:

```
function getTranslatorInfo(){
  returnArray = new Array( 5 );
  returnArray[0] = "FPX";       // translatorClass
  returnArray[1] = "Flashpix Image Translator";     // title
  returnArray[2] = "0";         // number of extensions
  returnArray[3] = "1";         // number of expressions
  returnArray[4] = "<meta http-equiv=\"refresh\" content=\"0;url=http://";
  return returnArray;
}
```

By comparison, the standard SSI translator's getTranslatorInfo() function has 10 array elements, and Webmonkey's XSSI has 17.

The translateMarkup() Function

Although the getTranslatorInfo() function initializes the translator, the translateMarkup() function actually does the work. As noted earlier, most translators rely on a custom C-level extension to handle the inner workings of the function, but translateMarkup() provides the JavaScript shell.

The translateMarkup() function takes three arguments, which must be declared, but whose actual values are provided by Dreamweaver:

✦ docName — The file URL for the file to be translated.

✦ siteRoot — The site root of the file to be translated. Should the file be outside the current site, the value would be empty.

✦ docContent — A text string with the code for the page to be translated.

Typically, the docContent text string is parsed using either JavaScript or a C-level extension within the translateMarkup() function that returns the translated document. Dreamweaver then displays this translated document.

Here's an excerpt of the translateMarkup() function from the ColdFusion translator:

```
function translateMarkup(docNameStr, siteRootStr, inStr) {
  var outStr = "";
  ...
  // translate
```

```
if (inStr.indexOf("<cf") != -1 || inStr.indexOf("<CF") != -1) {
  var TM =
    new TranslationManager(TRANSLATOR_CLASS, SERVER_MODEL_FOLDER, "");
  TM.serverModelAlwaysCheckTag = myAlwaysCheckTag;
  TM.serverModelAlwaysCheckAttribute = myAlwaysCheckAttribute;

  var split = TranslationManager.splitBody(inStr);
  outStr = TM.translate(split.inStr);
  if (outStr != "")
    outStr = split.preInStr + outStr + split.postInStr;
}
...
return outStr;
}
```

In this example, notice that the translated document in the form of `outStr` is built by creating a `TranslationManager` object named `TM` and then calling this object's `translate()` method: `TM.translate(split.inStr)`.

Locking Code

Translations are generally intended for onscreen presentation only. Although there's no rule prohibiting translated content from being written out to disk, most applications need the original content to run. To protect the original content, Dreamweaver includes a special locking tag. This XML tag pair, `<MM:BeginLock>`...`<MM:EndLock>`, stops the enclosed content (the translation) from being edited, while simultaneously storing a copy of the original content in a special format.

The `<MM:BeginLock>` tag has several attributes:

- ✦ `translatorClass` — The identifying name of the translator as specified in `getTranslatorInfo()`.

- ✦ `type` — The type or tag name for the markup to be translated.

- ✦ `depFiles` — A comma-separated list of any files on which the locked content depends. If any of these dependent files are altered, the page is retranslated.

- ✦ `orig` — A text string with the original markup before translation. The text string is encoded to include four standard HTML characters:

  `<` becomes `%3C;`

  `>` becomes `%3E;`

  `"` becomes `%22;`

  `%` becomes `%25;`

To see how the special locking tag works, look at an example taken from the Tango Sample Data translator. Tango uses what are called meta tags, which begin with an @ sign, such as the `<@TOTALROWS>` tag. The Tango Sample Data translator replaces a result drawn from a database with a specified sample value. The original code is

```
<@TOTALROWS samptotalrows=23>
```

After the code is translated, Dreamweaver refreshes the screen with the following code:

```
<MM:BeginLock translatorClass="TANGO_SAMPLEDATA" type ="@TOTALROWS"
    orig="%3C@TOTALROWS samptotalrows=23%3E">23<MM:EndLock>
```

The 23 in bold is the actual translated content that appears in Dreamweaver's Document window.

Note　You don't actually see the locking code, even if you open the Code inspector when a page is translated. To view the code, select the translated item, copy it, and then paste it in another text application, or use the Paste As HTML feature to see the results in Dreamweaver.

Extending C-Level Libraries

All programs have their limits. Most limitations are intentional and serve to focus the tool for a particular use. Some limitations are accepted because of programming budgets — for both money and time — with the hope that the boundaries can be exceeded in the next version. With Dreamweaver, one small section of those high, sharply defined walls has been replaced with a doorway: C-level extensions. With the proper programming acumen, you can customize Dreamweaver to add the capabilities you need.

As with most modern computer programs, the core of Dreamweaver is coded in C and C++, both low-level languages that execute much faster than any noncompiled language, such as JavaScript. Because C is a compiled language, you can't just drop in a function with a few lines of code and expect it to work — it has to be integrated into the program. The only possible way to add significant functionality is through another compiled component called a *library*. With the C-level extensions capability, Dreamweaver enables the incorporation of these libraries, known as DLLs (Dynamic Link Libraries) on Windows systems and as CFMs (Code Fragment Managers) on Macintosh systems.

One excellent example of the extended library is DWfile. This C-level extension is used by several Dreamweaver partners, including RealNetworks and iCat, to perform tasks outside the capabilities of JavaScript — namely, reading and writing external text files. By adding that one library, Dreamweaver can now work with the support files necessary to power a wide range of associated programs. DWfile is described in detail in the following section.

C-level extensions are also used in combination with Dreamweaver's translator feature. As discussed earlier in this chapter, translators handle the chore of temporarily converting non-standard code to HTML that Dreamweaver can present onscreen — while maintaining the original code in the file. Much of this functionality isn't impossible for JavaScript; the conversion would be too slow to be effective. C-level extensions are definitely the way to go when looking for a powerful solution.

Note　A discussion of programming in C or C++, as required by C-level extensions, is beyond the scope of this book. Developers are encouraged to scour the Dreamweaver Support Center for relevant information: www.macromedia.com/support/dreamweaver/.

Calling C-level Extensions

C-level extensions, properly stored in the Dreamweaver 8\Configuration\JSExtensions folder, are read into Dreamweaver during initialization when the program first starts. The routines contained within the custom libraries are accessed through JavaScript functions in commands, behaviors, objects, translators, and other Dreamweaver extensions.

Take a look at how Macromedia's C-level extension DWfile is used. DWfile has 14 main functions:

✦ copy()—Copies a file from one file URL (the first argument) to another (the second argument). DWfile.copy() can be used to copy any type of file, not just text files.

✦ createFolder()—Creates a folder, given a file URL.

✦ listFolder()—Lists the contents of a specified folder in an array. This function takes two arguments: the file URL of the desired folder (required) and a keyword, either "files" (which returns just filenames) or "directories" (which returns just directory names). If the keyword argument is not used, you get both files and directories.

✦ exists()—Checks to see if a specified filename exists. This function takes one argument, the filename.

✦ getAttributes()—Returns the attributes of a specified file or folder. Possible attributes are R (read-only), D (directory), H (hidden), and S (system file or folder).

✦ setAttributes()—Sets the attributes of a specified file.

✦ getCreationDate()—Returns the date when the file was initially created.

✦ getCreationDateObj()—Returns the JavaScript object that represents the date when the file was initially created.

✦ getModificationDate()—Returns the date a specified file or folder was last modified.

✦ getModificationDateObj()—Returns the JavaScript object that represents the date a specified file or folder was last modified.

✦ getSize()—Gets the size of a specified file.

✦ read()—Reads a text file into a string for examination. This function also takes one argument, the filename.

✦ write()—Outputs a string to a text file. This function has three arguments; the first two—the name of the file to be created and the string to be written—are required. The third, the mode, must be the word append. This argument, if used, causes the string to be added to the end of the existing text file; otherwise, the file is overwritten.

✦ remove()—Places the referenced file in the Recycling Bin (Windows) or Trash (Macintosh) without requesting confirmation.

The following JavaScript function, which could be included in any Dreamweaver extension, uses DWfile to determine whether theFile, named in a passed argument, exists. If it does, the contents are read and presented in an alert box; if theFile doesn't exist, the function creates it and outputs a brief message.

```
function fileWork(theFile) {
```

```
var isFile = DWfile.exists(theFile);   // does theFile exist?
if (isFile) {
  alert(DWfile.read(theFile));          // yes: display it in an alert box
}
else {                                  // no: create it and display msg
  DWfile.write(theFile,"File Created by DWfile");
  }
}
```

Note how the C-level extension name, DWfile, is used to call the library and its internal functions. After the library has been initialized, it can be addressed as any other internal function, and its routines are simply called as methods of the function using JavaScript dot notation, such as DWfile.exists(theFile).

Building C-Level Extensions

You must follow strict guidelines to enable Dreamweaver to recognize a C-level extension. Specifically, you must include two files in the library, and you must declare each function for correct interpretation by Dreamweaver's JavaScript interpreter.

Macromedia engineers have developed a C-Level Extension API in the form of a C header, mm_jsapi.h, that contains definitions for more than 20 data types and functions. To insert mm_jsapi.h in your custom library, add the following statement:

```
#include "mm_jsapi.h"
```

Tip   You can find the latest version of mm_jsapi.h on the Dreamweaver Exchange, which you can get to by choosing Help ➪ Dreamweaver Exchange in Dreamweaver or by loading the URL www.macrromedial.com/exchange/dreamweaver in your browser.

After you've included the JavaScript API header, you declare a specific macro, MM_STATE. This macro, contained within the mm_jsapi.h header, holds definitions necessary for the integration of the C-level extension into Dreamweaver's JavaScript API. You must define MM_STATE only once.

Each library can be composed of numerous functions available to be called from within Dreamweaver. For Dreamweaver's JavaScript interpreter to recognize the functions, each one must be declared in a special function, JS_DefineFunction(), defined in the library. All the JS_DefineFunction() functions are contained in the MM_Init() function. The syntax for JS_DefineFunction() is as follows:

```
JS_DefineFunction(jsName, call, nArgs)
```

where *jsName* is the JavaScript name for the function, *call* is a pointer to a C-level function, and *nArgs* is the number of arguments that the function can expect. For example, the MM_Init() function for DWfile might appear as follows:

```
void
MM_Init() {
  JS_DefineFunction("exist", exist, 1);
  JS_DefineFunction("read", exist, 1);
  JS_DefineFunction("write", exist, 2);
  }
```

Because `MM_Init()` depends on definitions included in the C header `mm_jsapi.h`, it must be called after the header is included.

Tip If you're building cross-platform C-level extensions, consider using Metrowerks CodeWarrior integrated development environment. CodeWarrior can edit, compile, and debug C, C++, and even Java or Pascal for both Windows and Macintosh operating systems. Perhaps most important, Macromedia engineers used CodeWarrior to test C-level extensions.

Customizing Your Tag Libraries

Previous versions of Dreamweaver required you to manually edit the `sourceformat.txt` file to change code formatting, including tag case, attributes, indentation, and line wrapping. Dreamweaver gives you a well-designed dialog box called the Tag Library Editor to make all those changes for you. You can use that editor to customize every single tag you place in Dreamweaver, and you can even add additional tags if you're using a proprietary server or design XML files with commonly used tag sets.

All tag-related attributes and color code settings are stored in a tag database (the Tag Library), which is manipulated through the Tag Library Editor. Click the Tag Library Editor link in Preferences or choose Edit ⇨ Tag Libraries.

Editing Tag Libraries, Tags, and Attributes

To edit the properties for a tag library, follow these steps:

1. Choose Edit ⇨ Tag Libraries to open the Tag Library Editor dialog box, and select the tag library whose properties you want to set, as shown in Figure 32-9.

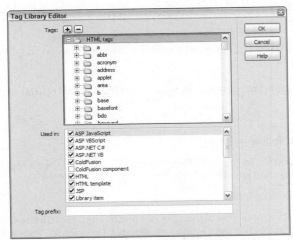

Figure 32-9: You use the Tag Library Editor to customize Dreamweaver's tag libraries.

2. In the Used In list box, choose every type of document that should use the selected tag library. Note that the tags in the selected library are available only in the document types you've chosen.

3. If the tags in the selected tag library require a prefix, enter this prefix in the Tag Prefix field. The Tag Prefix box enables you to add a prefix to the beginning of every tag in that particular library. For example, if you developed a tag library for XSL documents, you add xsl: as the tag prefix to add the prefix to the beginning of every tag.

4. When you are finished, click OK to close the Tag Library Editor dialog box.

To edit a tag in a tag library, follow these steps:

1. Choose Edit ⇨ Tag Libraries. In the Tag Library Editor dialog box, open a tag library and select the tag you want to edit.

2. Set your desired Tag Format options:

   - **Line Breaks:** Changing the line breaks option changes where Dreamweaver places line breaks in your code. Choose between four options: No Line Breaks; Before and After Tag; Before, Inside, After; and After Tag Only. This option is great for preventing line breaks after `<td>` tags and before `</td>` tags to ensure that no unwanted whitespace shows up in your code.

   - **Contents:** This setting affects how the content inside your tags is formatted. The indentation settings are based on your code format preferences. Choose between Not Formatted, Formatted but Not Indented, and Formatted and Indented.

   - **Case:** The case settings affect how the tag and its attributes are capitalized. XHTML for example requires that everything be lowercase. Options are Default, Lowercase, Uppercase, and Mixed Case. Choosing Mixed Case gives you a prompt to type in exactly how you want the tag to appear. Clicking Set Default enables you to set the default for all tags, which is the same as changing your tag case preferences in Edit ⇨ Preferences ⇨ Code Format (Dreamweaver ⇨ Preferences ⇨ Code Format).

The Preview area below the Tag Format options enables you to see exactly how your tag will be written to the page.

Tip I recommend setting your default case to lowercase to comply with XML/XHTML standards.

To edit an attribute for a tag, follow these steps:

1. Choose Edit ⇨ Tag Libraries. In the Tag Library Editor dialog box, open a tag library and select the attribute you want to edit.

2. Set your desired attribute options:

   - **Attribute Case:** This option sets the case of your attribute. Attribute Case is completely independent of the tag. Options are Default, Lowercase, Uppercase, or Mixed Case. Choosing Mixed Case enables you to enter exactly how you want the attribute formatted. Clicking Set Default alerts you to return to the Code Format category of Preferences.

- **Attribute Type:** There are 10 different attribute types for your tag: Text, Enumerated, Color, Directory, File Name, File Path, Flag, Font, Relative Path, and Style. Setting the type affects how Dreamweaver asks for information when using Code Hints in Code view or the Quick Tag Editor. Choosing color for an attribute causes a color palette to appear if you add the attribute in Code view. Setting the Type to Relative Path gives you a Select File dialog box.

- **Values:** The Values field is used only for the enumerated attribute type and gives you a list of valid values for a particular attribute.

3. Click OK.

Creating and Deleting Tag Libraries, Tags, and Attributes

The following sets of steps show you how to create a new tag library, add a tag to an existing library, or add an attribute to an existing tag.

To add a new tag library, follow these steps:

1. Choose Edit ⇨ Tag Libraries.

2. Click the Add (+) button and choose New Tag Library.

3. Enter a name for your new tag library and click OK.

4. Your new tag library is now shown at the bottom of the list. You're ready to start adding new tags.

To add new tags to one of your tag libraries, follow these steps:

1. Choose Edit ⇨ Tag Libraries.

2. Click the Add (+) button and choose New Tags.

3. Choose the Tag Library to add to in the list menu.

4. Enter one or more tags to add. To add a several tags at one time, simply enter a comma-separated list of tags into the dialog. This method enables you to add a large number of tags very quickly.

5. Choose whether your tag requires matching end tags. Choosing matching end tags gives you tags like <a>text</a>. Choosing not to have matching end tags gives you tags like <br> and <img>.

To add a new attribute to an existing tag, follow these steps:

1. Choose Edit ⇨ Tag Libraries.

2. Click the Add (+) button and choose New Attributes.

3. Choose the Tag Library that contains the tag you want to add attributes to from the first list menu.

4. Choose the tag you want to add attributes to from the second list menu.

5. Enter one or more attributes to add. If you want to add several attributes at one time, simply enter a comma-separated list of attributes into the dialog. This enables you to add a large number of attributes very quickly.

To delete a tag library, tag, or attribute, follow these steps:

1. Choose Edit ➪ Tag Libraries.

2. In the Tag Library Editor dialog box, select the tag library, tag, or attribute you want to delete.

3. Click the Remove (-) button. If you are asked to confirm the deletion, do so.

4. To make your deletions permanent, click OK. To discard your deletions, click Cancel.

Caution

After you click that OK button, your deletions are permanent. You cannot undo them, so ponder deeply before clicking that mouse or you could be forced to reinstall!

Importing a DTD or Schema to Create a New Tag Library

Dreamweaver enables you to create a new tag library by importing tags from an existing XML Document Type Definition (DTD) file or schema. In many instances, you may want to add a new tag library. If you're working on a proprietary server or a language that's not supported by Dreamweaver, you can add all the necessary tags into a new tag library.

To create a new tag library by importing a DTD file or schema, follow these steps:

1. Choose Edit ➪ Tag Libraries.

2. In the Tag Library Editor dialog box, click the Add (+) button and choose DTDSchema ➪ Import XML DTD or Schema File.

3. In the File or Remote URL field, enter the file or URL of the DTD or schema file.

4. In the Tag Prefix field, enter the prefix to be used with the tags you're importing, to identify the tags as part of this tag library.

5. When you're finished, click OK to create your new tag library.

Summary

Dreamweaver's commitment to professional Web site authoring is most evident when you examine the program's customization capabilities. Virtually every Web site production house can benefit from some degree of personalization — and some clients absolutely require it. As you examine the ways in which you can make your productive life easier by extending Dreamweaver, keep the following points in mind:

✦ Dreamweaver includes a full range of customizable features: objects, behaviors, commands, third-party tags, Property inspectors, and translators. You can even extend the program's core feature set with the C-Level Extensibility option.

✦ You can use commands to affect any part of your HTML page and automate repetitive tasks.

✦ In addition to accessing custom commands through the Commands menu, you can configure them as objects for inclusion in the Insert bar. You can also make a command appear in any other standard Dreamweaver menu by altering the menus.xml file.

✦ To make it easy to work with XML and other non-HTML tags, Dreamweaver enables you to create custom tags complete with individual icons or highlighted content.

✦ Attributes for third-party tags are viewable — and modifiable — by creating a custom Property inspector.

✦ Dreamweaver's C-Level Extensibility feature enables C and C++ programmers to add new core functionality to a program.

✦ Tags from server-side applications can be viewed in the Document window, just as they can be when browsed online, when a custom translator is used. A custom translator often requires a C-level extension.

✦ You can use the Tag Library Editor to customize your Dreamweaver tag libraries.

In the next chapter, you learn how to create and use Dreamweaver 8 objects.

✦   ✦   ✦

Handling Server Behaviors

Server behaviors are the heart of Dreamweaver, the essential
engine that puts the *dynamic* in dynamic Web applications.
Server behaviors insert server-model–specific code that handles
everything from displaying dynamic data to authenticating users.
Even the basic data source connection and the establishment of a
recordset are, in reality, server behaviors. Without server behaviors,
no dynamic capabilities would be possible in Dreamweaver.

Server behaviors are valuable for novices and veteran coders alike.
They enable designers who have never heard of an ASP Request collection to gather information from a form — a procedure that utilizes
the ASP Request collection — with point-and-click ease. Even serious
code jockeys can appreciate the productivity potential of server
behaviors, especially the capability to create their own. With the
Server Behavior Builder, programmers can build a library of their
custom functions, complete with fully functional dialog boxes for
maximum flexibility. After these functions are crafted, you can drop
any of the custom server behaviors directly onto the page — and, if
need be, easily alter the parameters.

This chapter includes an overview of server behaviors as well
as basic information about their use and management. For your
reference, you also find a detailed description of each of the
standard Dreamweaver server behaviors. Finally, you look at ways
to extend Dreamweaver's core functionality with the Server Behavior
Builder.

Understanding Server Behaviors

In contrast to Dreamweaver's JavaScript behaviors — with their
numerous required functions and many more optional ones — a
server behavior may be as simple as one line of code. The difference,
and it's a key one, is that the code is intended to be executed by the
application server, not the browser.

Another difference between server behaviors and JavaScript behaviors is that server behavior code may exist outside the bounds of the
HTML page. Any page with a recordset has a section of code before
the opening `<html>` tag, and a smaller block of code after the closing
`</html>` tag. Dreamweaver automatically places the code in the

proper place—and code placement is very important on the server side—when any of its standard server behaviors are used. Dreamweaver includes more than 25 standard server behaviors; the exact number varies for each server model. Figure 33-1 displays the available server behaviors for ASP.

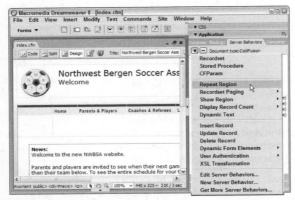

Figure 33-1: Apply any server behavior from the Server Behaviors panel.

The Server Behaviors panel is the focal point for inserting, removing, and managing server behaviors. Unlike the Behaviors panel, which only displays the JavaScript behaviors attached to the selected tag, the Server Behaviors panel displays all the server behaviors included in the current page, in the order in which they were applied. Selecting a specific server behavior listed in the Server Behaviors panel highlights the attached page element, if visible in the Document window. Some server behaviors, such as Recordset, have their own Property inspector, whereas others display dynamic code as an attribute in a text or other Property inspector.

Although the simplest server behaviors can insert code without any additional user input, each built-in server behavior has a dialog box for specifying parameters. These vary in complexity from a single drop-down list to multiple-section dialog boxes with every type of input element available. As you learn in the next section, after you have inserted a server behavior, you can easily modify its parameters.

Applying and Managing Server Behaviors

If you have ever completed any Web applications in Dreamweaver, you've likely already discovered how to apply and update a server behavior. The Server Behaviors panel is the primary tool for inserting, modifying, and removing server behaviors. You can display the Server Behaviors panel in several ways:

✦ Choose Window ➪ Server Behaviors.

✦ Select the Server Behaviors tab from the Application panel.

✦ Use the keyboard shortcut, Ctrl+F9 (Command+F9).

The Server Behaviors panel remains available regardless of whether you are in Design view, Code view, or the split-screen Code and Design view.

Inserting and Removing Server Behaviors

To add a particular server behavior to your page, click the Add (+) button in the Server Behaviors panel and select the desired behavior from the list. Many of the server behaviors have prerequisites that must be in place — such as a recordset, form, or selected element — before they can be installed, but these requirements vary from server behavior to server behavior. If you attempt to insert a server behavior and some precondition has not been met, Dreamweaver alerts you to the missing element; you are prevented from inserting the server behavior until all the required pieces are in place.

After you select the server behavior from the Add drop-down list, a dialog box appears to enable you to select or enter the needed parameters. Each dialog box is specific to the chosen server behavior, and they vary widely in terms of parameters offered and complexity. For information about a specific server behavior, see the corresponding section for that server behavior later in this chapter. Each section provides step-by-step explanations about completing the pertinent dialog box.

Removing an existing server behavior is simple. Select the entry for the server behavior in the Server Behaviors panel and click the Remove (–) button. Dreamweaver immediately removes all the associated code without requesting confirmation.

Caution   With JavaScript behaviors, if you delete a page element that has a client-side behavior attached, you automatically delete that behavior. This is not always the case with server behaviors, and it's best to always use the Server Behaviors panel's Remove (–) button before deleting any associated text, graphics, or form elements.

Editing the Parameters

To modify the attributes or parameters of an inserted server behavior, double-click its entry in the Server Behaviors panel. You can differentiate between multiple applications of the same server behavior in two ways. First, the entry for each server behavior lists one or two of its key attributes in parentheses. For example, a Dynamic Text server behavior applied to the LastName column in the rsMaillist recordset is displayed as follows:

```
Dynamic Text(rsMaillist.LastName)
```

Second, you can tell which server behavior is associated with which page element by selecting the server behavior — the associated text, graphic, or other page element is also selected in Design or Code view.

When the dialog box for a server behavior reopens, you can alter any of the parameters that remain active. In some situations, as with the Go To Detail Page server behavior shown in Figure 33-2, one or more fields may be disabled and so rendered unable to be changed. If you need to alter a disabled parameter, delete the server behavior and reapply it.

Figure 33-2: When modifying certain server behaviors, some fields, such as the Link field in this Go To Detail Page dialog box, are disabled and cannot be changed.

Standard Server Behaviors

Dreamweaver ships with more than 25 server behaviors, and it offers the option to add many more. The default server behaviors are geared toward handling basic Web application tasks such as repeating an area and inserting records in a data source.

In the following sections, each server behavior is briefly described, along with any prerequisites. Step-by-step instructions for including the server behavior are provided; for more contextual information on using the particular server behavior, see the cross-referenced chapter.

Recordset (Query)

To create a simple recordset, follow these steps:

1. From the Server Behaviors panel, click the Add (+) button and choose Recordset (Query) from the drop-down list. The Recordset dialog box, shown in Figure 33-3, is displayed.

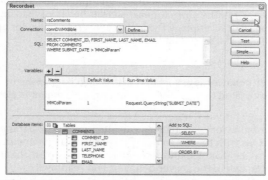

Figure 33-3: You can add recordsets from either the Server Behaviors panel or the Bindings panel through two different dialogs; the Advanced Recordset dialog shown here enables you to enter SQL statements directly.

2. In the Recordset dialog box, enter an identifying label for your recordset in the Name field. It's considered good practice to prefix your recordset name with rs — as in rsDBA. This prefix quickly identifies the recordset in the code.

3. Select a connection from the drop-down list of that name.

4. If the desired connection has not been declared, choose Define to open the Connections dialog box. After a connection has been selected, the available tables are shown.

5. Select a table to work with from the Tables drop-down list. The chosen table's fields are displayed in the Columns list.

6. By default, all the columns are included in the recordset. To specify certain columns, choose the Selected option and select any desired field. Shift+click to select contiguous columns, and Ctrl+click (Command+click) to select noncontiguous columns.

7. By default, all the records in the selected columns are available. To limit the recordset further, use the four Filter drop-down lists as follows:

   • Choose the field on which you want to base your filter from the first drop-down list. This list changes dynamically according to which table you've selected.

   • From the second drop-down list, select the expression with which to compare the data from the selected column in the first drop-down list. Available expressions are =, >, <, >=, <=, <>, begins with, ends with, and contains.

   • Choose the type of value to compare to the selected field from the third drop-down list. Available types are URL Parameter, Form Variable, Cookie, Session Variable, Application Variable, and Entered Value.

   • In the fourth input field, enter the value to compare to the selected field. Values entered are not case-sensitive.

8. To sort the data, select a column from the first drop-down list under Sort and choose either Ascending or Descending from the second list.

9. At any time, you can see what results will be returned for the recordset by clicking Test.

Tip   To see how your simple recordset translates into SQL, click the Advanced button. You can return to the original dialog box by clicking Simple on the advanced Recordset dialog box.

10. Click OK when you're finished.

Cross-Reference   For more information on defining recordsets, see Chapter 18.

Repeat Region

The Repeat Region server behavior replicates a selected page area as many times as specified. If the Repeat Region surrounds dynamic data, the record pointer advances for each repetition. A tab and highlight note the boundaries of the Repeat Region when Invisible Elements is enabled.

Requirements: One or more selected page elements, such as a table row or a line ending in a line break tag (<br>).

To implement a Repeat Region, follow these steps:

1. Select the dynamic data and the surrounding code you'd like to repeat.

2. From the Server Behaviors panel, click the Add (+) button and select Repeat Region from the list.

   The Repeat Region dialog box, shown in Figure 33-4, appears.

Figure 33-4: With the Repeat Region server behavior, you can show some or all of the records in the chosen recordset.

3. From the Repeat Region dialog box, choose the recordset you want to work with from the Recordset list.

4. If you want to display a subset of the recordset, enter the number of records you'd like to display in the Show Records field.

5. If you want every record in the recordset to be displayed, choose the Show All Records option.

6. Click OK when you're done.

Cross-Reference For more information on the Repeat Region server behavior, see Chapter 20.

Recordset Paging

The Recordset Paging server behaviors move the record pointer to the indicated data record in a given recordset. They are frequently used in combination to navigate through a recordset. In all, five Recordset Paging server behaviors exist; however, you insert the following four in an identical fashion:

✦ Move To First Record

✦ Move To Previous Record

✦ Move To Next Record

✦ Move To Last Record

The fifth server behavior in this category, Move To Specific Record, uses a different procedure, which is covered in the following section.

Requirements: A selected page element and at least one recordset with more than one returned row.

To use any of the four basic Recordset Paging server behaviors, follow these steps:

1. Select the text or image to which you'd like to attach the server behavior.

2. From the Server Behaviors panel, click the Add (+) button and choose the desired behavior from the Recordset Paging submenu. The appropriate Recordset Paging dialog box appears. Your selection is highlighted in the Link list, as shown in Figure 33-5.

Figure 33-5: The Recordset Paging server behaviors (such as Move To Last Record) identify your selected target, which may be an image or text.

3. Make sure that the link selected is one of those showing in the Link list.

4. Choose the recordset you want to work with from the Recordset drop-down list.

5. Click OK when you're finished.

 For more information on these Recordset Paging server behaviors, see Chapter 20.

Move To Specific Record

The Move To Specific Record server behavior is used after a recordset has been created to navigate through the records. To use the Move To Specific Record server behavior (not available in ColdFusion or PHP), follow these steps:

1. Select the text or image to which you'd like to attach the server behavior.

2. From the Server Behaviors panel, choose Move To Specific Record from the Recordset Paging submenu. The Move To Specific Record dialog box is displayed, as shown in Figure 33-6.

Figure 33-6: An alternative method for creating a detail page uses the Move To Specific Record server behavior.

3. Select the desired recordset from the list labeled Move To Record In.

4. Choose the field referenced in the URL parameter from the Where Column field.

5. Enter the variable in the URL parameter in the Matches URL Parameter field.

6. Click OK when you're finished.

 Cross-Reference For more information on the Move To Specific Record server behavior, see Chapter 22.

Show Region

The Show Region server behavior displays an area of the screen if a particular condition is true. These are often called conditional regions. A different set of server behaviors applies for each server model.

ColdFusion and PHP:

✦ Show If Recordset Is Empty

✦ Show If Recordset Is Not Empty

✦ Show If First Page

✦ Show If Not First Page

✦ Show If Last Page

✦ Show If Not Last Page

ASP.Net C# and ASP.Net VB:

✦ Show If DataSet Is Empty

✦ Show If DataSet Is Not Empty

✦ Show If First Page

✦ Show If Not First Page

✦ Show If Last Page

✦ Show If Not Last Page

JSP, ASP JavaScript, and ASP VBscript:

✦ Show Region If Recordset Is Empty

✦ Show Region If Recordset Is Not Empty

✦ Show Region If First Record

✦ Show Region If Not First Record

✦ Show Region If Last Record

✦ Show Region If Not Last Record

Requirements: One or more selected page elements and at least one recordset.

Applying a Show Region server behavior is straightforward. Just follow these steps:

1. Select the page area you'd like to show conditionally.

2. From the Server Behaviors panel, click the Add (+) button and select one of the server behaviors from the Show Region submenu. The dialog box for the specific Show Region server behavior you chose is displayed, like the one shown in Figure 33-7. The dialog boxes for all the Show Region server behaviors are identical.

Figure 33-7: To use a Show Region server behavior, just choose a recordset.

3. Select the recordset on which to base the Show Record condition from the Recordset list.

4. Click OK when you're finished.

 Cross-Reference For more information on the Show Region server behavior, see Chapter 20.

Go To Detail Page

The Go To Detail Page server behavior is used in master-detail Web applications to navigate from a chosen link on the master page to a designated detail page. This server behavior passes a unique record ID via the URL query string method. The Go To Detail Page server behavior isn't available in ColdFusion, .NET, or PHP.

 Cross-Reference For more on master-detail Web applications, see Chapter 22.

Requirements: A selected page element and at least one recordset.

To attach a Go To Detail Page server behavior, follow these steps:

1. Select the page element — text, graphic, or dynamic data — you'd like to use as the link to the detail page.

2. From the Server Behaviors panel, click the Add (+) button and select Go To Detail Page from the drop-down list. The Go To Detail Page dialog box, shown in Figure 33-8, is displayed.

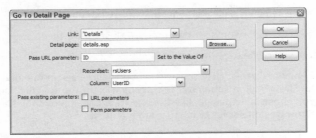

Figure 33-8: Specify the linking parameter sent from the master page in the Go To Detail Page server behavior.

3. Make sure that the page element selected is represented in the Link field. If no selection was made, Dreamweaver creates a new Detail text link.

4. Enter the path to the detail page in the Detail Page field or click Browse to locate the file in the Select File dialog box.

5. Enter the variable name you'd like to be sent in the Pass URL Parameter field. You can use a name of your own choosing or the name of the field in the database. Whichever name you decide upon, make a note of it somewhere because you need to reference it when the detail page itself is constructed.

6. Select the recordset of the URL parameter from the Recordset list.

7. From the Column list, choose the field to which the URL parameter's value is related.

8. Unless you have preexisting URL or Form parameters to send to the detail page, leave the Pass Existing Parameters options unchecked.

9. Click OK when you're finished.

Cross-Reference   For more information on the Go To Detail Page server behavior, see Chapter 22.

Go To Related Page

The Go To Related Page server behavior links to a new page that conveys the form and/or URL variables previously passed to the current page.

Requirements: A selected page element and at least one recordset. The page on which the server behavior is inserted must have had form or URL values passed to it.

To attach a Go To Related Page server behavior, follow these steps:

1. Select the page element—text, image, or dynamic data—you'd like to use as the trigger for your behavior.

2. From the Server Behaviors panel, click the Add (+) button and select Go To Related Page from the list. The Go To Related Page server behavior dialog box appears, as shown in Figure 33-9.

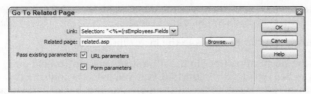

Figure 33-9: The Go To Related Page server behavior can convey form values, URL values, or both to another dynamic page.

3. In the dialog box, verify that the text or code for the selected element displayed in the Link field is correct.

4. Enter the path to the target page in the Related Page field or click Browse to locate an existing dynamic page.

5. If you want to carry over values received from a query string, select the URL Parameters option.

6. If you want to pass values received from a form, select the Form Parameters option.

7. Click OK when you're finished.

Cross-Reference   For more information on the Go To Related Page server behavior, see Chapter 22.

Insert Record

The Insert Record server behavior adds a new record to a chosen table in a data source.

Requirements: A form with form elements and a Submit button.

To add the Insert Record server behavior, follow these steps:

1. From the Server Behaviors panel, click the Add (+) button and select Insert Record. The Insert Record dialog box appears, as shown in Figure 33-10.

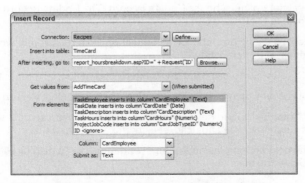

Figure 33-10: Users may add new data directly to a connected data source.

2. From the Insert Record dialog box, choose the connection from the drop-down list. If you need to establish a new connection, click Define.

3. Select the data table you want to use from the Insert Into Table list.

4. Enter the path to the destination page in the After Inserting, Go To field, or click the Browse button to locate the file. It's important that you select a confirmation or other page to go to after the form is submitted. If you don't, no feedback is provided to the user, and no change is apparent.

5. Select the name of the form to be used from the Get Values From list. If there is only one form on the page, the form is preselected.

6. For each object listed in the Form Elements area:

   • Select the data source field into which the form object's value is to be inserted from the Column list.

   • Choose the data source type for the data from the Submit As list. The options are Text; Numeric; Date; Date MS Access; Checkbox Y, N; Checkbox 1,0; Check -1,0; and Checkbox MS Access.

Note   Be sure to give your form fields meaningful names so you can easily choose which form field goes into each database column.

7. Click OK when you're finished.

Cross-Reference   For more information on the Insert Record server behavior, see Chapter 22.

Update Record

Use the Update Record server behavior to modify existing records in a data source.

Requirements: A recordset, a form with form elements linked to the dynamic data, and a Submit button.

To insert an Update Record server behavior, follow these steps:

1. From the Server Behaviors panel, choose Update Record. The Update Record dialog box appears, as shown in Figure 33-11.

2. From the Update Record dialog box, choose a connection from the drop-down list. To establish a new connection, click Define.

3. Select the data table you want to use from the Table to Update list.

4. Choose the data source on which to base your update from the Select Record From list.

5. Select the key field from the Unique Key Column list. Dreamweaver attempts to detect whether the field is a number type and, if so, selects the Numeric option.

6. Enter the path to the destination page in the After Updating, Go To field or click the Browse button to locate the file.

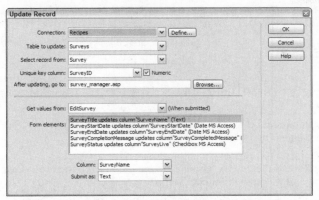

Figure 33-11: With an Update Record server behavior, you can modify your data source remotely.

7. Select the name of the form to be used from the Get Values From list. If there is only one form on the page, the form is preselected.

8. For each object listed in the Form Elements area:

   • Select the data source field into which the form object's value is to be inserted from the Column list.

   • Choose the data source type for the data from the Submit As list. The options are Text; Numeric; Date; Date MS Access; Checkbox Y, N; Checkbox 1,0; Check -1,0; and Checkbox MS Access.

9. Click OK when you're finished.

Cross-Reference

For more information on the Update Record server behavior, see Chapter 22.

Delete Record

The Delete Record server behavior is used to remove existing records from a data source.

Requirements: A recordset, a form, and a Submit button.

To attach a Delete Record server behavior to a form, follow these steps:

1. Make sure that a form exists on a dynamic page that includes at least one recordset.

2. From the Server Behaviors panel, choose Delete Record. The Delete Record dialog box is displayed, as shown in Figure 33-12.

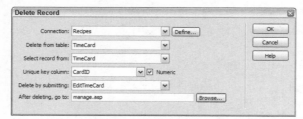

Figure 33-12: Maintain an up-to-date data source with the Delete Record server behavior.

3. From the Delete Record dialog box, choose a connection from the drop-down list. If you need to establish a new connection, click Define.

4. Select the data table you want to modify from the Delete From Table list.

5. Choose the data source on which to base your update from the Select Record From list.

6. Select the key field from the Unique Key Column list. Dreamweaver attempts to detect whether the field is a number type and, if it is, selects the Numeric option.

7. Enter the path to the destination page in the After Deleting, Go To field or click the Browse button to locate the file.

8. Choose the form that contains the Delete button.

9. Click OK when you're finished.

Cross-Reference For more information on the Delete Record server behavior, see Chapter 22.

User Authentication

The World Wide Web is all about accessing information from anywhere in the world. Sometimes, however, you need to restrict access to certain areas of your site to authorized users. Dreamweaver supplies a full complement of server behaviors to support authenticating the user against a specified data source. The user authentication server behaviors are not available for .NET.

Log In User

The Log In User server behavior redirects authorized users to one page and unauthorized users to another and creates a session variable for the username.

Requirements: A recordset, a form, appropriate form elements for a username and a password, and a Submit button.

1. From the Server Behaviors panel, click the Add (+) button and choose User Authentication ➪ Log In User. The Log In User dialog box is displayed, as shown in Figure 33-13.

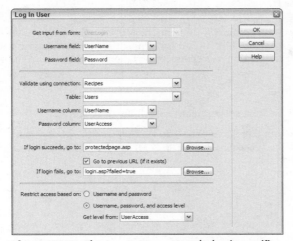

Figure 33-13: The Log In User server behavior verifies that the user may be granted access.

2. If there is more than one form on the page, select the form containing the username and password fields from the Get Input From Form list.

3. Select the form element used to gather the username from the Username Field list.

4. Select the form element used to gather the password from the Password Field list.

5. Choose a connection to the data source containing the table of registered users from the Validate Using Connection list.

6. Select the table of registered users from the Table list.

7. Choose the field containing the username from the Username Column list.

8. Choose the field containing the password from the Password Column list.

9. Enter the path to the page for the authorized user in the If Log In Succeeds, Go To field.

10. If you want the user to proceed to the previously selected link, rather than the page entered in step 9, select the Go To Previous URL option.

11. Enter the path to the page for the unauthorized user in the If Log In Fails, Go To field.

12. If access levels should be evaluated as part of the authentication:

   • Select the Restrict Access Based On Username, Password, and Access Level option.

   • Choose the data source field containing the access level data from the Get Level From list.

13. Click OK when you're finished.

Cross-Reference

For more information on the Log In User server behavior, see Chapter 22.

Restrict Access To Page

The Restrict Access To Page server behavior prevents unauthorized users from viewing specific pages by checking a session variable. After it is defined, the server behavior can be copied and pasted onto another page by using the context menu commands from the Server Behaviors panel.

Requirements: A dynamic page.

To apply the Restrict Access To Page server behavior, follow these steps.

1. From the Server Behaviors panel, click the Add (+) button and choose User Authentication ⇨ Restrict Access To Page. The Restrict Access To Page dialog box, shown in Figure 33-14, is displayed.

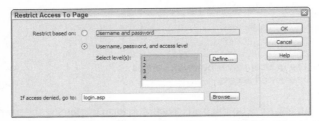

Figure 33-14: Any dynamic page can be protected against unauthorized viewing with the Restrict Access To Page server behavior.

2. If you don't want to restrict admission by access levels, be sure that the Restrict Based On Username and Password option is selected.

3. To set group permissions for the page:

   • Choose the Restrict Based On Username, Password, and Access Level option.

   • Choose one or more groups from the Select Level(s) area.

4. To add new groups to the Select Level(s) list:

   • Click Define. The Define Access Levels dialog box opens.

   • Enter the name for the access level in the Name field. The name must match a value stored in your data source in whichever column is designated for the group access levels.

   • To add additional levels, click the Add (+) button and enter another name.

   • To delete any levels, choose the level in the list area and click the Remove (–) button.

   • Click OK to close the Define Access Levels dialog box.

5. Enter the path to the file to which you want to redirect unauthorized users in the If Access Denied, Go To field. Alternatively, click the Browse button to locate the file.

6. Click OK when you're finished.

For more information on the Restrict Access To Page server behavior, see Chapter 22.

Log Out User

The Log Out User server behavior clears the username session variable established by the Log In User server behavior and redirects the user to an exit page. You can set up the Log Out User server behavior so that a user selects a link to log out or is automatically logged out when a particular page, such as one confirming the completion of an order, is viewed.

Requirements: A Log In User server behavior on another page.

To use the Log Out User server behavior, follow these steps:

1. To apply the server behavior to a specific link on the page, select that link.

2. From the Server Behaviors panel, click the Add (+) button and choose User Authentication ⇨ Log Out User. The Log Out User dialog box is displayed, as shown in Figure 33-15.

Figure 33-15: You can log a user out automatically by choosing the Log Out When Page Loads option on an order confirmation page.

3. To trigger the server behavior with a link, choose the Log Out When Link Clicked option and make sure your selected link is chosen in the list. If no link was preselected, Dreamweaver offers to apply the server behavior to a new link, Log Out.

4. To automatically log out users when the current page is viewed, select the Log Out When Page Loads option.

5. If you're using a link as a trigger, enter the path to the destination page in the When Done, Go To field. Alternatively, click the Browse button to locate the file.

Caution Do not use the When Done, Go To option if you are automatically logging out a user when the page loads. If you do, the user never sees the current page.

6. Click OK when you're finished.

For more information on the Log Out User server behavior, see Chapter 22.

Check New Username

The Check New Username server behavior verifies that the requested username is not already in the data source, redirecting the user if it is.

Requirements: An Insert Record server behavior, a form, and appropriate form elements.

1. From the Server Behaviors panel, click the Add (+) button and choose User Authentication ⇨ Check New Username. The Check New Username dialog box is displayed, as shown in Figure 33-16.

Figure 33-16: Make sure a requested username is not already taken by using the Check New Username server behavior.

2. Select the form element that contains the requested username from the Username Field list. If a form element is called USERNAME, Dreamweaver automatically selects that entry.

3. In the If Already Exists, Go To field, enter the path to the file you want a user to see if the name the user requests is already stored in the data source. You can also click Browse to locate the file.

4. Click OK when you're finished.

Cross-Reference

For more information on the Check New Username server behavior, see Chapter 22.

Dynamic Elements

With one exception, dynamic elements in Dreamweaver refer to form elements, linked to a data source field. Data-connected form elements are typically used in Web applications that update records. The single exception is Dynamic Text, which is described in the following section. Dynamic Form Elements (which aren't available in .NET) are covered later.

Dynamic Text

Inserting a Dynamic Text server behavior is the same as dragging a field from a recordset on the Bindings panel onto the page. It's a matter of individual preference which technique you use; personally, I find dragging-and-dropping from the Bindings panel much faster and more intuitive than using the Dynamic Text server behavior.

Requirements: A dynamic page.

To use the Dynamic Text server behavior, follow these steps:

1. Place your cursor on the page where you'd like the dynamic text to appear.

2. From the Server Behaviors panel, choose Dynamic Elements ⇨ Dynamic Text. The Dynamic Text dialog box is displayed, as shown in Figure 33-17.

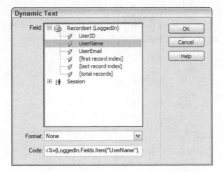

Figure 33-17: You can insert dynamic text through either the Server Behaviors panel or the Bindings panel.

3. If necessary, expand the recordset or other data source to select the desired dynamic data.

4. Choose any necessary server format from the Format list.

5. Enter any required adjustments to the dynamic data in the Code field. In most situations, no changes are necessary.

6. Click OK when you're finished.

Cross-Reference For more information on adding dynamic text, see Chapter 22.

Dynamic List/Menu

The Dynamic List/Menu server behavior binds data to one or more aspects of a drop-down list. Dynamic data from a recordset is typically bound to both the values and labels of a list or menu element; static values and labels may also be combined with the dynamic data. In addition, you have the option to dynamically set the selected value, a feature often used when updating a record.

Requirements: A list/menu form element and a recordset.

To link a drop-down list to dynamic data, follow these steps:

1. Insert a list/menu form element on a dynamic page with a recordset.

2. If you have more than one list/menu on the page, select the one you want to convert.

3. From the Server Behaviors panel, choose Dynamic Form Elements ⇨ Dynamic List/Menu. The Dynamic List/Menu dialog box, shown in Figure 33-18, is displayed.

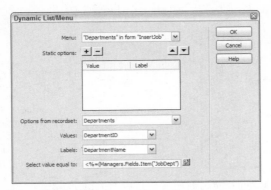

Figure 33-18: Lists give the user a distinct series of items from which to choose.

4. Verify that the desired drop-down list is displayed in the Menu list.

5. In the Static Options box, add any nondynamic items you want to the top of the list menu. This could be something as simple as a label for the list menu, or as complicated as a full URL with query strings for search pages.

6. Choose the recordset you want to work with from the Options From Recordset list.

7. Choose the field from your data source containing the items that you want displayed to the user from the Labels list.

8. Choose the field from your data source containing the items you want submitted by the user from the Values list.

9. To preselect an item, enter its value in the Select Value Equal To field or use the light-ning bolt icon to choose a value from the established data sources.

10. Click OK when you're finished.

For more information on the Dynamic List/Menu server behavior, see Chapter 22.

Dynamic Text Field

Unlike the Dynamic Text server behavior, the Dynamic Text Field server behavior is not just for show. The Dynamic Text Field server behavior is often used for applications that update records and may be applied to either a text field or text area form element. According to the server model used, the data in the text field can be formatted server-side in a number of ways, such as upper- or lowercase.

Requirements: A text field or text area form element and a recordset.

To link a text field or text area to dynamic data, follow these steps:

1. Insert a text field into a form on a page with a recordset or other data source. It's a good idea to name the text field and form at this point. Although you can always change the names later, naming the elements early on avoids problems later.

2. Select the text field.

3. From the Server Behaviors panel, choose Dynamic Form Elements ➪ Dynamic Text Field.

Caution

Be sure to choose Dynamic Text Field and not Dynamic Text from the Dynamic Elements sub-menu. If you select Dynamic Text while your text field is highlighted, the form element is replaced.

4. In the Dynamic Text Field dialog box that appears (see Figure 33-19), verify that the correct form element was chosen in the Text Field list. If necessary, choose a different text field.

Figure 33-19: You can make a data field editable by connecting it to a Dynamic Text Field.

5. Click the Set Value To lightning bolt icon to display the available data sources.

6. Choose a field from the Dynamic Data dialog box.

7. If desired, you can apply a server format to the data by choosing an entry in the Format list.

8. Click OK to close the Dynamic Data dialog box and, after reviewing your choices, click OK again to close the Dynamic Text Field dialog box.

Cross-Reference

For more information on the Dynamic Text Field server behavior, see Chapter 22.

Dynamic CheckBox

Checkboxes provide users with a method of selecting one or more options in a group; a Dynamic CheckBox server behavior marks any affiliated checkbox as selected if the desired criteria are met. This server behavior is often used in conjunction with a Boolean data field, also known as a True/False or Yes/No data field.

Requirements: A checkbox form element and a recordset.

To convert a static checkbox to a dynamic one, follow these steps:

1. Select a checkbox in a form on a page with a recordset.

2. From the Server Behaviors panel, choose Dynamic Form Elements ➪ Dynamic CheckBox. The Dynamic CheckBox dialog box appears, as shown in Figure 33-20.

Figure 33-20: Checkboxes can depict whether a particular field of a recordset is True or False.

3. Verify that your selected checkbox is correctly named in the CheckBox list.

4. Click the Check If lightning bolt icon to display the available data sources.

5. Choose a field from the Dynamic Data dialog box.

6. If desired, you can apply a server format to the data by choosing an entry in the Format list. Click OK when you're finished to close the Dynamic Data dialog box.

7. Enter the value expected for a selected checkbox in the Equal To field. This value is data source–dependent. For many data sources, 1 is used to represent True; for others, a –1 is used. When working with Yes/No fields from Access databases, enter **True**; be sure to capitalize the word, because lowercase does not work properly.

8. Click OK when you're finished.

Cross-Reference   For more information on the Dynamic CheckBox server behavior, see Chapter 22.

Dynamic Radio Buttons

Radio buttons are employed in a form when the designer wants the user to make an exclusive choice among a set number of options. As with the Dynamic CheckBox server behavior, the Dynamic Radio Buttons server behavior is used to mark a particular element as selected when the defined criteria are met.

Requirements: Two or more radio button form elements and a recordset.

To link radio buttons to dynamic data, follow these steps:

1. Select a group of radio buttons on a dynamic page with an available data source.

2. From the Server Behaviors panel, choose Dynamic Form Elements ➪ Dynamic Radio Buttons. The Dynamic Radio Buttons dialog box appears, as shown in Figure 33-21.

Figure 33-21: Radio buttons can reflect a limited number of choices within a data source field.

3. Verify that your selected form element is displayed in the Radio Button Group list.

4. In the Radio Button Values area, choose the first entry shown and, if necessary, change the Value field to reflect the expected data.

5. Repeat step 4 for every radio button in the group.

6. Click the Select Value Equal To lightning-bolt icon to display the available data sources.

7. Choose a field from the Dynamic Data dialog box. Be sure to select a data source field with values parallel to those entered in the radio button group.

8. If desired, you can apply a server format to the data by choosing an entry in the Format list. Click OK to close the Dynamic Data dialog box.

9. When you're finished, click OK to close the Dynamic Radio Buttons dialog box.

Cross-Reference

For more information on the Dynamic Radio Buttons server behavior, see Chapter 22.

Stored Procedure/Command/Callable

Many advanced Web applications use a stored procedure application object. Stored procedures are known under a variety of names: ASP users call them *commands,* whereas JSP developers know them as *callables;* only ColdFusion users refer to them solely as stored procedures. Stored procedures are complete SQL queries that may return recordsets or other data. Stored procedures are often used for complex data source management such as inserting new tables on the fly.

Stored procedures are created and compiled in the data source itself, such as Microsoft's SQL Server. Because they are precompiled, they execute faster than similar SQL statements entered directly into the Web application. Stored procedures, like recordsets, can be defined as a data source through either the Bindings panel or the Server Behaviors panel.

To define a stored procedure as a data source through the Server Behaviors panel, follow these steps:

1. From the Server Behaviors panel, click the Add (+) button and, depending on your server model: for ASP, choose Command (Stored Procedure); for ColdFusion, choose Stored Procedure; and for JSP, choose Callable (Stored Procedure). The stored procedure dialog box for the appropriate server model is displayed; for example, Figure 33-22 shows the Command dialog box seen by JSP users.

Note

Stored procedures and the variables necessary to use them are database- and server model–dependent. A stored procedure on SQL server is completely different from a ColdFusion stored procedure or another SQL-type database. The Stored Procedure/Command/Callable dialog box may change based on the type of database to which you're connecting, as well as the server model.

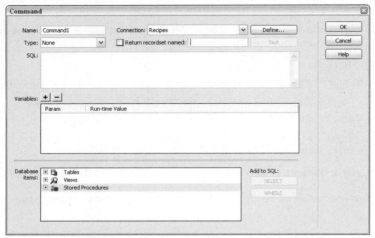

Figure 33-22: Stored procedures must be included in the data source before they can be added as a data source in Dreamweaver.

2. In the Command/Callable/Stored Procedure field, enter a unique name.

3. From the Connection list, choose the connection in which this stored procedure may be found.

4. ASP users should choose Stored Procedure from the Type list.

Note   The ASP Command (Stored Procedure) server behavior includes additional types: Insert, Update, and Delete. These work identically to the Prepared (Insert/Update/Delete) server behavior described in the following section on JSP server behaviors.

5. If the stored procedure returns a recordset, choose the Return Recordset option and enter a name in the Returned Recordset Named field.

6. From the Database Items area, expand the Stored Procedure list and choose the desired stored procedure. It's a good idea to click Test to be sure your connection is working properly at this point.

7. To modify the stored procedure, select any other element in the Database Items area and click the Column or Where button.

8. Enter any necessary variables by clicking the Add (+) button in the Variables area and entering the values under each column: Name, Type, Direction, Size, Default Value, and Runtime Value.

9. Click OK when you're finished.

Special JSP Server Behaviors

A number of server behaviors are only available for sites based on the JSP server model. An important feature of JavaServer Pages is the capability to use *JavaBeans*. JavaBeans are Java components or classes that process events and transmit results to the calling program and other JavaBeans. Dreamweaver offers two JavaBean-related server behaviors: JavaBean and JavaBean Collection.

Prepared (Insert/Update/Delete)

JSP users may employ what's referred to as a Prepared command to insert, update, or delete data sources.

To use a Prepared command, follow these steps:

1. From the Server Behaviors panel, click the Add (+) button and choose Prepared (Insert/Update/Delete) from the list. The Prepared (Insert/Update/Delete) dialog box, shown in Figure 33-23, is displayed.

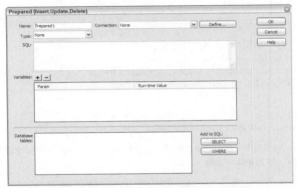

Figure 33-23: You can include three different types of Prepared statements — Insert, Update, or Delete — as JSP data sources.

2. In the Name field, enter a unique name that will appear in the Server Behaviors panel.

3. From the Connection list, choose the connection in which your stored procedure may be found.

4. Select the prepared statement you want to insert from the Type list: Insert, Update, or Delete. Dreamweaver inserts appropriate code into the SQL area for each selection.

5. Complete the SQL code manually by entering columns and values in the SQL area.

6. As an alternative to manually entering the column names in the SQL statement, you can select any other element in the Database Items area and click the Select or Where button to insert them.

7. Enter any necessary variables by clicking the Add (+) button in the Variables area and entering the values under each column: Param and Runtime Value.

8. Click OK when you're finished.

JavaBean

To insert a JavaBean as a data source, follow these steps:

1. From the Server Behaviors panel, click the Add (+) button and select JavaBean from the list. The Java Bean dialog box, shown in Figure 33-24, is displayed.

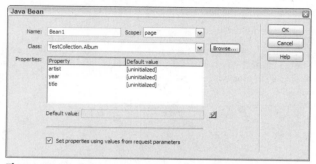

Figure 33-24: Dreamweaver supports JavaBean classes in an individual CLASS (.class) file or compressed in a ZIP or JAR archive.

2. If desired, enter a unique name in the Name field.

3. Set how the JavaBean variables may be accessed. Methods include selecting a Scope: page, request, session, or application.

4. Select a JavaBean class from the Class field or click the Browse button to locate the file. JavaBeans may be in CLASS (.class), ZIP (.zip), or JAR (.jar) files.

5. To set the default value of any of the bean's properties, select the item from the Properties area and enter a new value in the Default Value field. To set the default value to dynamic value, click the lightning-bolt icon.

6. Click OK when you're finished.

JavaBean Collection

To insert a JavaBean Collection as a data source, follow these steps:

1. From the Server Behaviors panel, click the Add (+) button and choose JavaBean Collection from the list. The JavaBean Collection dialog box, shown in Figure 33-25, is displayed.

Figure 33-25: Dreamweaver automatically reads the indexed property for a selected JavaBean Collection data source.

2. Select a JavaBean class from the Class field or click the Browse button to locate the file.

3. Select an Indexed Property to use from the list.

4. Make sure the Item Class entered by Dreamweaver is correct, modifying it if necessary.

5. Set how the JavaBean variables may be accessed by choosing a Scope: page, request, session, or application.

6. Click OK when you're finished.

ASP.NET Server Behaviors

Two special server behaviors make displaying dynamic data quick and easy: DataGrid and DataList.

DataGrid

The DataGrid server behavior enables you to rapidly add an editable DataGrid to your page. The DataGrid can also include Insert, Update, and Delete buttons.

Requirements: One DataSet on the current page.

To add a DataGrid, follow these steps:

1. From the Server Behaviors panel, click the Add (+) button and select DataGrid from the list. The DataGrid dialog box, shown in Figure 33-26, is displayed.

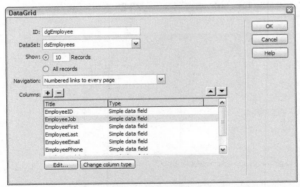

Figure 33-26: DataGrids cover all the necessary functions of inserting, updating, and deleting records.

2. In the ID field, enter a unique name that will appear in the Server Behaviors panel.

3. From the DataSet list, select the DataSet you want to display.

4. Enter the number of records to display in the Show box.

5. Choose the type of navigation from the Navigation list: Links to Previous and Next pages, or Numbered Links to Every Page.

6. In the Columns area, use the Add (+) and Remove (–) buttons to change the columns displayed in the DataGrid. You can add five different types of fields:

- Simple Data Field
- Free Form
- Hyperlink
- Edit, Update, Cancel Buttons
- Delete Button

7. Click Edit to change the way a specific column is submitted to the database and displayed in the grid.

8. Click Change Column Type to change the type of a column already in the Columns list.

9. Click OK when you're finished.

DataList

Using the .NET DataList provides a quick way to add columnar or repeating data to your page.

Requirements: One DataSet on the current page.

To add a DataList, follow these steps:

1. From the Server Behaviors panel, click the Add (+) button and choose DataList from the list. The DataList dialog box, shown in Figure 33-27, is displayed.

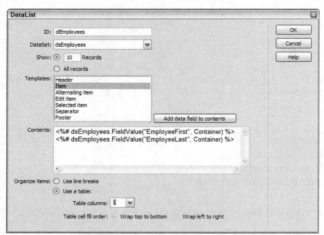

Figure 33-27: DataLists enable you to display repeating data in easy-to-define template regions.

2. In the ID field, enter a unique name that will appear in the Server Behaviors panel.

3. From the DataSet list, select the DataSet you want to display.

4. Enter the number of records to display in the Show box.

5. The Templates box contains the seven template regions of the DataList. Select each region and enter the content to be displayed in the Contents box. Click the Add Data Field to Contents button to add data from your DataSet. The seven template regions are as follows:

   - **Header:** The style for the header at the beginning of the list (if any)

   - **Item:** The style for individual items

   - **Alternating Item:** The style for every other item (alternating item)

   - **Edit Item:** The style for the item being edited

   - **Selected Item:** The style for the selected item

   - **Separator:** The style for the separator between each item

   - **Footer:** The style for the footer at the end of the list (if any)

6. Use the Organize Items radio buttons to specify how to organize the list, either using line breaks or a table. Choosing Use a Table enables the table controls at the bottom of the dialog box.

7. If you've chosen Use a Table, specify a number of table columns and how to wrap the cell contents.

8. Click OK when you're finished.

Installing Additional Server Behaviors

Although Dreamweaver's standard server behaviors perform many important functions, they're just the tip of the iceberg in terms of what's possible. You can add additional server behaviors — whether created by Macromedia, yourself, or a third party — at any time. Although you can transfer files to the appropriate places in the Dreamweaver Configuration folder, most custom server behaviors rely on the Extension Manager for installation.

The Extension Manager is an auxiliary program that installs files compressed in the Macromedia Extension Program format; such files carry an `.mxp` file extension. To access the Extension Manager, choose Commands ➪ Manage Extensions or Help ➪ Manage Extensions. The Extension Manager displays all the extensions — including server behaviors — installed in your system. It also includes information about each extension, such as its type and creator.

The Web offers numerous sources for MXP files, but perhaps the best known is the Dreamweaver Exchange, located on the Macromedia site. After you've downloaded the file, you can install it by following these steps:

1. From Dreamweaver, choose Commands ➪ Manage Extensions to open the Extensions Manager.

Tip

Dreamweaver need not be open for you to install an extension — just double-click the MXP file to invoke the Extension Manager and begin the installation process. However, if you have multiple Macromedia products on your system, it's better to open the Extension Manager before beginning the installation.

2. From the Extension Manager, choose File ➪ Install Extension or use the keyboard short-cut, Ctrl+I (Command+O). You can also click the Install New Extension button (Windows) or Install (Mac) on the Extension Manager's toolbar.

3. Use the Select Extension to Install dialog box to locate the desired MXP file.

4. When you've located the file, click Install (Open). As part of the installation process, Dreamweaver displays the Macromedia Extensions disclaimer.

5. Click Accept in the Macromedia Extensions Disclaimer dialog box to continue. Dreamweaver continues to install the extension, and alerts you if a problem is encountered or if the procedure was successful.

6. Dreamweaver notifies you if the installed extension requires you to restart Dreamweaver before it can be used.

After the server behavior has been properly installed, it appears in the standard list found under the Add (+) button of the Server Behaviors panel, and it can be applied like other server behaviors. Any special requirements or directions are noted in the bottom pane of the Extension Manager.

Creating Custom Server Behaviors

Editing Existing Server Behaviors

One of the wonders of Dreamweaver is the capability to extend every piece of the program. This includes making new server behaviors and editing existing ones. Out of the box, Dreamweaver allows you to edit only those server behaviors you've personally created. Editing is controlled by an XML attribute in the .edml file for each individual server behavior. You can gain access to these server behaviors by changing that XML attribute.

Before you continue, please understand that many of the Dreamweaver server behaviors are extremely complex and may not work correctly if edited using the Server Behavior Builder. Instead of editing, I suggest you create a new server behavior, and copy an existing server behavior to make sure you don't break anything beyond repair.

In order to show a server behavior in the Server Behavior Builder, follow these steps:

1. Locate the necessary server behavior .edml file. These are located in your Configuration directory. On a PC the default location is Dreamweaver 8\Configuration\{Datasources or Server Behaviors}\{server model}\{server behavior name}.edml. For this example, open the Datasources\ASP_Vbs\Request Variable.edml file.

2. The first line of the .edml file should look like this:

```
<group serverBehavior="Dynamic Data.htm" hideFromBuilder="true">
```

3. Change hideFromBuilder="true" to hideFromBuilder="false".

4. Restart Dreamweaver.

The Request Variable server behavior is now available in the edit list of the Server Behavior Builder.

Dreamweaver provides a very sophisticated tool for creating custom server behaviors, the Server Behavior Builder. With the Server Behavior Builder, you can modify an existing server behavior you've created or create a new one from scratch. You can use the Server Behavior Builder in any server model configuration supported by Dreamweaver.

Tip   By default, you're not allowed to edit or copy the default Dreamweaver server behaviors. See the sidebar "Editing Existing Server Behaviors" to learn how to access all the built-in server behaviors.

The Server Behavior Builder breaks up any server behavior into discrete segments called *code blocks*. Each code block is surrounded by the delimiters for the particular server model: `<%. . .%>` for ASP, .NET and JSP; `<cftag>. . .</cftag>` for ColdFusion; and `<?. . .?>` for PHP. Each code block may contain one or more user-supplied parameters. The user enters the parameters in a dialog box; the Server Behavior Builder even creates the dialog box for you.

The Server Behavior Builder can also control the positioning of any individual code block. On the server side, code is executed from the top of the page to the bottom, and it is often critical that a particular code segment follows another in order to be processed properly.

You have the option of modifying an existing server behavior, modifying a copy of an existing server behavior, or creating an entirely new server behavior. The process is about the same for all three methods:

✦ Choose your server behavior. If it already exists, select it from the list; if it's new, give it a name.

✦ Work in the Server Behavior Builder to modify and create code blocks and parameters. The Server Behavior Builder is also used for code block positioning.

✦ Set up the dialog box for any parameters. The Generate Server Behavior Dialog Box command enables you to determine the type and order of any parameter elements.

To modify an existing server behavior, follow these steps:

1. From the Server Behaviors panel, click the Add (+) button and select Edit Server Behaviors from the list. The Edit Server Behaviors dialog box, shown in Figure 33-28, appears.

Figure 33-28: You can create server behaviors for different server models, regardless of the server model of the current site.

If you want to create a new server behavior, select New Server Behavior instead of Edit Server Behaviors and skip to step 4.

2. From the Server Model list, select the type of code you want to modify.

3. From the Server Behaviors list, select the specific server behavior you want to adapt. Dreamweaver posts a warning that if you are modifying a server behavior, the Server Behaviors panel may not be able to identify any instances of it already inserted into the

current page. In this situation, it is strongly recommended that you choose New Server Behavior (see Figure 33-29) instead and create a different server behavior based on an existing server behavior.

Figure 33-29: When creating a new server behavior, you can either model it on an existing one or start fresh.

After selecting the desired server behavior, the Server Behavior Builder opens, as shown in Figure 33-30.

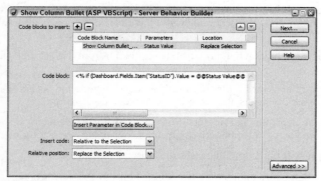

Figure 33-30: Dreamweaver's Server Behavior Builder offers tremendous flexibility in positioning code blocks.

4. Highlight the code block you want to change.

5. Modify the code as desired in the Code Block area.

6. To insert a new parameter, place your cursor in the Code Block area where you want to place variable and click Insert Parameter in Code Block.

Tip   To replace a value with a variable, select the value in the Code Block before clicking Insert Parameter in Code Block.

7. Enter a unique name for the variable in the Parameter Name field of the Insert Parameter in Code Block dialog box. Click OK when you're finished. The new parameter is inserted in the following format: @@parametername@@.

8. Determine the positioning of the code by first choosing an option from the Insert Code list: Above the `<html>` tag, Below the `</html>` tag, Relative to a Specific Tag, or Relative to the Selection.

9. If you've chosen Insert Code: Relative to a Specific Tag, select the tag name from the Tag list that appears.

10. From the Relative Position list, select the option best suited for the code block.

11. If you've chosen Relative Position: Custom Position, enter a numeric value in the Custom Position field.

Caution

Positioning of code blocks is very important. In particular, make sure you don't insert code that depends upon a recordset above the code that creates that recordset.

12. Repeat steps 4 through 11 for every code block you need to modify.

13. Click the Advanced button, and choose how you want the server behavior to be displayed in the Server Behaviors panel. You can add or remove parameters to customize the display. If you don't want it to show in the Server Behaviors panel at all, uncheck the Identifier checkbox.

14. In the Code Block area, choose which code block you want Dreamweaver to select when it chooses from the Server Behaviors panel.

15. Click Next to proceed. If there are parameters in your server behavior, the Generate Behavior Dialog Box dialog box appears.

16. Set the position of your parameters by selecting an item in the list and using the up and down arrows.

17. Set the type of control for the parameter by choosing the down arrow next to the Display As column.

    Dreamweaver offers 17 controls to choose from:

    - Recordset Menu
    - Recordset Field Menu
    - Editable Recordset Menu
    - Editable Recordset Field Menu
    - CF DataSource Menu
    - Connection Menu
    - Connection Table Menu
    - Connection Column Menu
    - Text Field
    - Dynamic Text Field
    - URL Text Field

- Numeric Text Field

- Recordset Fields Ordered List

- Text Field Comma Separated List

- List Menu

Note   If you choose List Menu, you must manually open the created server behavior file to populate the list menu.

- Checkbox

- Radio Group

The Text Field control is the default.

18. Click OK when you're finished.

Dreamweaver builds the new or modified server behavior and includes it in the Server Behaviors panel.

Summary

Server behaviors are, quite literally, essential to building dynamic pages in Dreamweaver. Without the server-side code that they insert, Web pages would just be static HTML. As you begin to investigate all that server behaviors can do for you, keep the following points in mind:

✦ Although Dreamweaver provides many of the same server behaviors for ASP, ColdFusion, JSP, ASP.NET, and PHP, each server behavior outputs code specific to the site's chosen server model.

✦ The Server Behaviors panel is the primary conduit for applying, removing, and modifying server behaviors.

✦ After a server behavior has been inserted, you can modify the user parameters at any time by double-clicking the item in the Server Behaviors panel.

✦ Server behaviors often have requirements — such as forms or other server behaviors — that must be in place on the page before they can be inserted.

✦ Dreamweaver enables you to modify standard server behaviors. You can also create new ones based on the standard server behaviors or build them from the ground up with the Server Behavior Builder.

What's on the CD?

The CD-ROM that accompanies the *Dreamweaver 8 Bible* contains the following:

✦ Fully functioning trial versions of several Macromedia products, including Dreamweaver 8 and Flash 8 Professional.

✦ Code examples used in the book.

✦ Interactive simulations of each Dreamweaver Technique found in the book, created with Macromedia Captivate.

✦ A vast array of Dreamweaver extensions from the leaders in the Dreamweaver community, designed to make your work more productive. The types of extensions include behaviors, server behaviors, objects, commands, inspectors, and floaters.

Using the Accompanying CD-ROM

The CD-ROM included with this book is a *hybrid CD-ROM*, which means it contains files that run on more than one computer platform — in this case, both Windows and Macintosh computers.

Several files, primarily the Macromedia trial programs and the other external programs, are compressed. Double-click these files to begin the installation procedure. Most other files on the CD-ROM are uncompressed, and you can simply copy them to your system by using your file manager. A few of the Dreamweaver extensions with files that must be placed in different folders are also compressed.

In the Configuration folder, the file structure replicates the structure that Dreamweaver sets up when it is installed. For example, objects found in the Dreamweaver\Configuration\Objects folder should be in that location for both the CD-ROM and the installed program. One slight variation: In the Additional Extensions folder, you'll find the various behaviors, objects, and so on, filed under the author's name.

System Requirements

Be sure that your computer meets the minimum system requirements listed in this section. If your computer doesn't match up to most of these requirements, you may have a problem using the contents of the CD.

Macintosh

Macromedia recommends the following minimum requirements for running Dreamweaver on a Macintosh:

- ✦ 600 MHz G3 or higher
- ✦ Mac OS 10.3, 10.4
- ✦ 256MB of available RAM
- ✦ 300MB of available disk space
- ✦ Thousands of colors display capable of 1024 x 768 resolution
- ✦ CD-ROM drive

Windows

Macromedia recommends the following minimum requirements for running Dreamweaver on a Windows system:

- ✦ Intel Pentium III processor, 800 MHz or equivalent
- ✦ Windows 2000, XP
- ✦ 256MB of available RAM
- ✦ 650MB of available disk space
- ✦ Thousands of colors display capable of 1024 x 768 resolution
- ✦ CD-ROM drive

Files and Programs on the CD-ROM

Dreamweaver 8 Bible contains a host of programs and auxiliary files to assist your exploration of Dreamweaver, as well as your Web page design work in general. The following sections provide a description of the files and programs on the CD-ROM that accompanies this book.

Macromedia Demos

If you haven't had a chance to work with Dreamweaver (or Fireworks or Flash), the CD-ROM offers fully functioning trial versions of key Macromedia programs for both Macintosh and Windows systems. Each of the demos will run for 30 days; they cannot be reinstalled in order to gain additional time. The following trial programs are included on the CD:

- ✦ Dreamweaver 8
- ✦ Fireworks 8
- ✦ Flash 8
- ✦ Contribute 3.1
- ✦ JRun Server
- ✦ ColdFusion MX 7 Server

To install any of these programs, just double-click the program icon in the main folder of the CD-ROM where the programs are located and follow the installation instructions on your screen.

Caution The trial versions of Macromedia programs are very sensitive to system date changes. If you alter your computer's date, the programs will time-out and no longer function. It is a good idea to check your system's date and time before installing them. Moreover, if you've previously run the trial version of the same program from another source (such as downloading it from the Internet), you won't be able to run the trial version again.

Dreamweaver Extensions

Dreamweaver is extremely extensible, and the Dreamweaver community has built some amazing extensions. In the Additional Extensions folders of the CD-ROM, you'll find hundreds of behaviors, server behaviors, objects, commands, inspectors, and more. The extensions are grouped according to author, and within each author's folder, they are organized by function.

Where available, extensions are packaged in an .mxp file, which can easily be installed using the Extension Manager. To run the Extension Manager from Dreamweaver, choose Commands ⇨ Manage Extensions. Then choose File ⇨ Install Extension and browse to the location of the extension's .mxp file.

Note A small number of extensions were written prior to the availability of the Extension Manager and do not require that program for installation. Extensions that contain files that must be placed in different folders, such as the Commands and Inspectors directories, are compressed in a WinZip format. In those instances, a ReadMe file explains where the files must be placed.

You'll find a ReadMe.htm file in each author's folder, with links to the author's Web site and more information about his or her creations.

Dreamweaver Techniques Simulations and Files

One special feature of the *Dreamweaver 8 Bible* is the Dreamweaver Techniques found in most of the chapters in the book. Each technique contains all the requisite sample HTML files and graphics files, each within its own folder. For most techniques, there is a starting file and a completed file; open the start file to work through the technique and the final file to see how the finished file should look. To start, copy all the files in the Techniques folder of the CD-ROM to your system and establish a Dreamweaver site with that folder as the local site root; the Dreamweaver Technique "Setting Up Your Site" in Chapter 5 describes the steps to accomplish this task.

Accompanying each of the Dreamweaver Techniques is a simulation that guides you interactively through each of the Techniques. These simulations, created by Mark Fletcher with Macromedia Captivate, can be viewed through any browser equipped with the Flash Player.

Dreamweaver 8 Bible Code Examples

The Code folder on the CD provides sample code used in the book. You can easily view the files through Dreamweaver or your browser without transferring the files to your system. If you do wish to transfer the files, copy the entire folder over to your system.

To incorporate the external style sheets in your Web sites, copy files with .css extensions into your local site's root folder. Then follow the instructions in the "Attaching an External Style Sheet" section found in Chapter 7.

Web Resource Directory

The World Wide Web is a vital resource for any Web designer, whether a seasoned professional or a beginner. The CD-ROM contains an HTML page with a series of links to resources on the Web. These are links to general resources as well as to Dreamweaver-specific references.

Troubleshooting

If you have difficulty installing or using any of the materials on the companion CD, try the following solutions:

✦ Turn off any anti-virus software that you may have running. Installers sometimes mimic virus activity and can make your computer incorrectly believe that it is being infected by a virus. (Be sure to turn the anti-virus software back on later.)

✦ Close all running programs. The more programs you're running, the less memory is available to other programs. Installers also typically update files and programs; if you keep other programs running, installation may not work properly.

✦ Reference the ReadMe.txt: Please refer to the ReadMe file located at the root of the CD-ROM for the latest product information at the time of publication.

If you still have trouble with the CD, please call the Wiley Product Technical Support phone number: (800) 762-2974. Outside the United States, call 1 (317) 572-3994. You can also contact www.wiley.com/techsupport. Wiley Publishing, Inc. provides technical support only for installation and other general quality control items; for technical support on the applications themselves, consult the program's vendor or author. To place additional orders or request information about other Wiley products, please call (800) 225-5945 or visit www.wiley.com.

✦　　✦　　✦

Index

Continued

Continued

Continued

Continued

Continued

Wiley Publishing, Inc.
End-User License Agreement

READ THIS. You should carefully read these terms and conditions before opening the software packet(s) included with this book "Book". This is a license agreement "Agreement" between you and Wiley Publishing, Inc. "WPI". By opening the accompanying software packet(s), you acknowledge that you have read and accept the following terms and conditions. If you do not agree and do not want to be bound by such terms and conditions, promptly return the Book and the unopened software packet(s) to the place you obtained them for a full refund.

1. **License Grant.** WPI grants to you (either an individual or entity) a nonexclusive license to use one copy of the enclosed software program(s) (collectively, the "Software") solely for your own personal or business purposes on a single computer (whether a standard computer or a workstation component of a multi-user network). The Software is in use on a computer when it is loaded into temporary memory (RAM) or installed into permanent memory (hard disk, CD-ROM, or other storage device). WPI reserves all rights not expressly granted herein.

2. **Ownership.** WPI is the owner of all right, title, and interest, including copyright, in and to the compilation of the Software recorded on the disk(s) or CD-ROM "Software Media". Copyright to the individual programs recorded on the Software Media is owned by the author or other authorized copyright owner of each program. Ownership of the Software and all proprietary rights relating thereto remain with WPI and its licensers.

3. **Restrictions on Use and Transfer.**

   (a) You may only (i) make one copy of the Software for backup or archival purposes, or (ii) transfer the Software to a single hard disk, provided that you keep the original for backup or archival purposes. You may not (i) rent or lease the Software, (ii) copy or reproduce the Software through a LAN or other network system or through any computer subscriber system or bulletin-board system, or (iii) modify, adapt, or create derivative works based on the Software.

   (b) You may not reverse engineer, decompile, or disassemble the Software. You may transfer the Software and user documentation on a permanent basis, provided that the transferee agrees to accept the terms and conditions of this Agreement and you retain no copies. If the Software is an update or has been updated, any transfer must include the most recent update and all prior versions.

4. **Restrictions on Use of Individual Programs.** You must follow the individual requirements and restrictions detailed for each individual program in the About the CD-ROM appendix of this Book. These limitations are also contained in the individual license agreements recorded on the Software Media. These limitations may include a requirement that after using the program for a specified period of time, the user must pay a registration fee or discontinue use. By opening the Software packet(s), you will be agreeing to abide by the licenses and restrictions for these individual programs that are detailed in the About the CD-ROM appendix and on the Software Media. None of the material on this Software Media or listed in this Book may ever be redistributed, in original or modified form, for commercial purposes.

5. Limited Warranty.

(a) WPI warrants that the Software and Software Media are free from defects in materials and workmanship under normal use for a period of sixty (60) days from the date of purchase of this Book. If WPI receives notification within the warranty period of defects in materials or workmanship, WPI will replace the defective Software Media.

(b) **WPI AND THE AUTHOR(S) OF THE BOOK DISCLAIM ALL OTHER WARRANTIES, EXPRESS OR IMPLIED, INCLUDING WITHOUT LIMITATION IMPLIED WARRANTIES OF MERCHANTABILITY AND FITNESS FOR A PARTICULAR PURPOSE, WITH RESPECT TO THE SOFTWARE, THE PROGRAMS, THE SOURCE CODE CONTAINED THEREIN, AND/OR THE TECHNIQUES DESCRIBED IN THIS BOOK. WPI DOES NOT WARRANT THAT THE FUNCTIONS CONTAINED IN THE SOFTWARE WILL MEET YOUR REQUIREMENTS OR THAT THE OPERATION OF THE SOFTWARE WILL BE ERROR FREE.**

(c) This limited warranty gives you specific legal rights, and you may have other rights that vary from jurisdiction to jurisdiction.

6. Remedies.

(a) WPI's entire liability and your exclusive remedy for defects in materials and workmanship shall be limited to replacement of the Software Media, which may be returned to WPI with a copy of your receipt at the following address: Software Media Fulfillment Department, Attn.: *Dreamweaver 8 Bible* Wiley Publishing, Inc., 10475 Crosspoint Blvd., Indianapolis, IN 46256, or call 1-800-762-2974. Please allow four to six weeks for delivery. This Limited Warranty is void if failure of the Software Media has resulted from accident, abuse, or misapplication. Any replacement Software Media will be warranted for the remainder of the original warranty period or thirty (30) days, whichever is longer.

(b) In no event shall WPI or the author be liable for any damages whatsoever (including without limitation damages for loss of business profits, business interruption, loss of business information, or any other pecuniary loss) arising from the use of or inability to use the Book or the Software, even if WPI has been advised of the possibility of such damages.

(c) Because some jurisdictions do not allow the exclusion or limitation of liability for consequential or incidental damages, the above limitation or exclusion may not apply to you.

7. U.S. Government Restricted Rights.
Use, duplication, or disclosure of the Software for or on behalf of the United States of America, its agencies and/or instrumentalities "U.S. Government" is subject to restrictions as stated in paragraph (c)(1)(ii) of the Rights in Technical Data and Computer Software clause of DFARS 252.227-7013, or subparagraphs (c) (1) and (2) of the Commercial Computer Software - Restricted Rights clause at FAR 52.227-19, and in similar clauses in the NASA FAR supplement, as applicable.

8. General.
This Agreement constitutes the entire understanding of the parties and revokes and supersedes all prior agreements, oral or written, between them and may not be modified or amended except in a writing signed by both parties hereto that specifically refers to this Agreement. This Agreement shall take precedence over any other documents that may be in conflict herewith. If any one or more provisions contained in this Agreement are held by any court or tribunal to be invalid, illegal, or otherwise unenforceable, each and every other provision shall remain in full force and effect.